TABLE OF CONTENTS

FOREWORD

Carroll Quigley, historian and teacher at Georgetown University, died January 5, 1977, leaving unfinished a manuscript on <u>Weapons Systems and Political Stability: A History</u> upon which he had been working for the preceding twelve years. His colleagues and friends, upon reviewing the manuscript, decided to press forward with its publication. Although the manuscript is frustratingly incomplete in time sequence--it ends its narrative in the 15th century--it carries further toward completion the uniquely anthropological holistic analysis of history which is the theme of his earlier works, <u>Tragedy and Hope</u>, and <u>Evolution of Civilizations</u>.

Quigley's observations on the uses of war are penetrating. In his introductory chapter, he suggests themes which are developed throughout the manuscript. Reference to a few of them might indicate their intriguing nature. They include such as: "The real goal of military operations is agreement" (p. 28). Therefore, the statements of military leaders that "the battle is the pay-off" or the demand for an unconditional surrender betray an insensitivity to the primary necessity of accomplishing a durable peace.

Similarly, Quigley notes that "We assumed, as late as 1941, that a rich state would win a war. This has never been true. . . .Rich states throughout history have been able to defend their positions only if they saw the relationship between wealth and power and kept prepared (for war). . ." (p. 29).

Of special interest is Quigley's observation that "the peasants. . .were, throughout history down to the 19th century, not only the most numerous class but were also. . .the economic support of the power structure. . . Their power has always been insignificant, except in the few, relatively brief periods when they have been of military importance. . ." (p. 37).

Throughout history, society's decisions regarding its weapons systems have been decisive in shaping human social, economic and political decisions. Of special interest today is Quigley's division of Western weapons systems over the last thousand years into five successive stages, each associated with a different political system:

Dates	Weapons	Politics
970-1200	knight and castle	feudalism
1200-1520	mercenary men-at-arms and bowmen	feudal monarchy
1520-1800	mercenary muskets, pikes, artillery	dynastic monarchy
1800-1935	mass army of citizen soldiers	democracy
1935-	army of specialists	managerial bureaucracy

In Quigley's social analysis the dominance of democracy in the 20th century is attributable to the acceptance in the 19th century of a weapons system that favored democracy, the hand gun and rifle. In the consequent tilt toward an atomistic society, loyalties to the once strong social structures of family, church and workplace break down. With the immediate availability of weapons to alienated individuals, violence then becomes endemic. Yet weaponry such as the nuclear bomb, which a technologic society produces, is both irrelevant to the domestic need for order and threatening, in its requirements for corporate decision-making, to individual self-interest democracy.

The temptation to explore further Quigley's speculations on the themes of history is difficult to resist. But the reader must undertake that responsibility and, in so doing, will join Quigley's friends in realizing their loss.

In acceptance of the fact that the manuscript is incomplete, a substantial portion of a relatively recent article by Quigley is placed at the conclusion of the text. It is entitled "Structure of Revolutions with Application to the French Revolution." It is an immediate analysis by Quigley of the uses of force in our modern age of social disintegration. The article is followed by an excerpt from the third Oscar Iden Lecture, delivered by Quigley in late 1976 in his last public appearance at the School of Foreign Service, Georgetown University. That excerpt sets forth valuable concise observations on the role of weapons systems in international conflict in our present-day society.

Quigley left no maps, no illustrations, and no visual aids of any description for any of these writings. After careful consideration, it was decided that selection and introduction of such visual aids would require textual accommodation. The effort, no matter how supportive, would dilute the personal uniqueness of Quigley's work. We decided to accept the incompleteness of the presentation.

After careful consideration, the decision was also made against any substantial editing effort. It is certain that Quigley would have undertaken that editing effort in his own preparation of the manuscript. But after his death, it seemed better to preserve Quigley's work as uniquely his. That decision had the further advantage in that his highly personal style, which would be sacrificed in any tightly disciplined present revision, has value in itself. It is a style expressly his own, and in preserving it, his presence almost continues among those who knew him or had read his earlier works.

Quigley is incredibly successful in abstracting essence from reality—in analyzing mankind's experience in socializing. He describes weaponry as not an end in itself. It is part of a whole in which by far the greater part of persuasion and cooperation is accomplished by institutionalization of ideologies.

This book is one of those human efforts which shapes the mind.

Harry J. Hogan
Washington, D.C.
1982

CARROLL QUIGLEY: SOME ASPECTS OF HIS LAST
TWELVE YEARS
Recollections from Personal Correspondence
by
Carmen Brissette-Grayson
School of Foreign Service, 1962

In the last 12 years of his life, from 1965 to
1977, Carroll Quigley taught, observed the American
scene, and reflected on his basic values in life. He
was simultaneously pessimistic and radically optimistic.

Teaching was the core of Quigley's professional
life and neither his craving to write nor his discouragement with student reaction of the early seventies diminished his commitment to the classroom. "I am sure that
you will enjoy teaching increasingly, as I do," he had
written in 1965:

> it is the one way we can do a little good in
> the world. The task is so important, the
> challenge so great, and the possibilities for
> improvement and for variation as infinite that
> it is the most demanding and most difficult of
> human activities. Even a virtuoso violinist
> can be made to order easier than a good teacher.[1]

Six years later, in his 30th year of teaching at
Georgetown, he was less hopeful. "I find teaching harder
every year, as the students are less and less receptive.
. . ."[2] The turmoil of the Vietnam years spilled into
the lecture hall and, on at least one occasion, students
disrupted a class. He worried about the dilution of
academic standards and feared the increasing bureau-
cratization of education. Such problems, he lamented,
"will give you a glimmering of what teaching has become
in the tail end of a civilization. . . ."[3]

Despite these pessimistic readings of student
responsiveness, the School of Foreign Service senior
classes of 1973 and 1974 both honored him as the outstanding professor of the year. Quigley himself continued throughout this period to address a variety of
audiences--bureaucrats, scientists, an Irish-American
club, even a Catholic high school religion class. "A
rather daring experiment in religious enlightenment,"
he concluded in describing that encounter with Catholic
adolescents.[4] "I accept. . .outside lectures (and also

. . .I give courses I never gave before in my final
year of teaching) because," he explained, "it makes
me clarify my own thoughts about what is really important. I often say things in my lectures that I
never realized before."[5]

Quigley revised his lectures to the end of his
teaching days even in classes which he had taught for
over a decade. "I am never satisfied with my courses,
so keep working on them."[6] In his final weeks at Georgetown he broke off just before Thanksgiving and told his
students in "The World Since 1914" class that there was
little point in discussing the Third World when they
knew so little about how their own society works:

> So I told them about the USA--really very-
> hair-raising when it is all laid out in se-
> quence:. . . .1. cosmic hierarchy; 2.
> energy; 3. agriculture; 4. food; 5.
> health and medical services; 6. education;
> 7. income flows and the worship of GROWTH;
> 8. inflation. . .showing how we are violat-
> ing every aspect of life by turning everything
> into a ripoff because we. . .have adopted the
> view that insatiable individualistic greed
> must run the world.[7]

He feared "that the students will come to feel that all
is hopeless, so I must. . .show them how solutions can
be found by holistic methods seeking diversity, decentralization, communities. . .etc."[8] Pleased with
the class response, he later recalled:

> The students were very excited and my last
> lecture in which I put the whole picture
> together was about the best lecture I ever
> gave. That was 10 Dec. [1975], my last
> full day of teaching after 41 years.[9]

Unlike his underlying faith in the efficacy of
teaching, Quigley found little basis for optimism
about the future of American society. A journal asked
him in 1975 to write an upbeat article on the country's
prospects. "I told the editor that would be difficult,
but I would try. I wrote it and they refused to pub-
lish it because it was not optimistic enough. . ."[10]
In 1976 he wrote congratulating my husband for his decision to give up any idea of leaving state politics

for the federal arena. "It is futile," Quigley concluded, "because it is all so corrupt and the honest
ones are so incompetent. I should not say this, as
students said it to me for years and I argued with
them."11

It was more than the institutionalization of the
American political system which concerned him: "We
are living in a very dangerous age in which insatiably
greedy men are prepared to sacrifice anybody's health
and tranquility to satisfy their own insatiable greed
for money and power."12 He feared that these values
had virtually destroyed the roots of the Western outlook and had made the creation of a satisfying life
in contemporary America a hazardous undertaking. "I
am aghast at what. . .selfishness, and the drive for
power have done to our society. . . .I worry. . .as
I find the world so increasingly horrible that I do
not see how anything as wonderful as. . .your life
can escape."13 Less than six months before he died
he advised: "The best thing you can do is. . .to
keep some enclaves of satisfying decent life."14 Yet
pessimism about American society did not weaken a
radical optimism rooted in his essential values:
nature, people, and God.

The greatest source of pleasure for Quigley, outside of his scholarly pursuits and his personal life,
came from his profound love of nature. In 1968 he
bought an 82-acre farm near the small town of Glengary,
West Virginia:

> in the case of the permanent residents they
> are the same individuals (or their offspring)
> that we have known for years. We are chiefly
> impressed with their distinctive personalities,
> and intelligence. . .marvelous, so steady, hard-
> working. . .and unafraid. . .[others] were
> really neurotic, afraid of everything. . .15

This sounds like unremarkable country gossip until one
realizes that the "permanent residents" to which he
refers were several generations of bluebirds which he
had been studying.

I once made the mistake of writing to him about
my war of attrition with racoons who were foraging in

our trash. Quigley rushed back a reply to prevent me
from making any further intrusions in the cosmic
hierarchy:

> If the racoons make your trash disposal a prob-
> lem, why not cooperate with nature instead of
> resisting it? The big solution to our pollution
> problems is to increase the speed of biodegrada-
> tion, and what is more natural than for animals
> to eat? Here I feed a fox every night if our
> local skunk does not get to it first (I buy
> chicken backs and necks for 19 cents a pound,
> but am afraid to give these too frequently for
> fear they may have injurious hormones injected
> into the live chickens). . .My fox never leaves
> a crumb or a mark on the concrete platform where
> he eats. . . .
> Last summer when he had a mate and young ones,
> we gave him more food and he always took the
> best. . .away to his family. We used to time
> him: it took 4 minutes before he was back for
> something for himself. . .We have found that
> wild things are so wonderful.[16]

He concluded with a revealing description of what to
him was a particularly satisfying weekend--writing,
observing birds, and on Saturday night "Beethoven's
birthday, we sat. . .reading near the fire, while the
radio played all nine of HIS symphonies."[17]

Thus, discouragement about the course of American
life existed simultaneously with happiness derived from
those aspects of life he knew to be lasting. "I am fed
up with. . .everything but God and nature. . .and human
beings (whom I love and pity, as I always did)."[18]
His loyalty was to a religious-intellectual outlook:
"I feel glad I am a Christian," he wrote, "glad I am
. . .without allegiance to any bloc, party, or groups,
except to our Judeo-Christian tradition (modified by
science and common sense)."[19] Over the years he usually
closed such letters with what could serve as a characteristic valedictory: "God keep you all. . .and help you
to grow."[20]

x

REFERENCES--from personal correspondence between Carroll
Quigley and Carmen Grayson, 1965-1976.

1. April 1, 1965. On Quigley's writing and the evolution of this manuscript see Foreword by Harry Hogan.

2. October 6, 1971.

3. Ibid.

4. January 5, 1972.

5. April 13, 1975.

6. January 2, 1975.

7. January 2, 1976;   December 4, 1975.

8. December 4, 1975.

9. January 2, 1976.

10. October 8, 1975.

11. June 28, 1976.

12. May 4, 1976.

13. November 29, 1973;   May 20, 1974.

14. November 8, 1973.

15. May 24, 1975.

16. January 10, 1973;   December 17, 1972.

17. December 17, 1972.

18. November 8, 1973.

19. November 29, 1973.

20. November 7, 1974.

A Tribute to Carroll Quigley by Dean Peter Krogh

For forty years, Professor Carroll Quigley's teaching quickened and disciplined the minds of students of the School of Foreign Service of Georgetown University. His inspired lectures in the "Development of Civilization" and the "World Since 1914" delivered over four decades and to as many thousands of students, literally defined the School and its brand of education.

Professor Quigley's pedagogy was synonymous with discipline and with holistic methods of analysis and interpretation. He imparted to students analytical paradigms that enabled them to integrate their multidisciplinary knowledge and to draw meaning from subsequent intellectual and practical experiences. His teaching transcended contingent information to give students a permanent and independent basis for understanding the constantly changing world around them.

Professor Quigley was known -- even renowned -- for his determination to make students think. The impact of this determination was not always immediately or fully appreciated, but no teacher of the School was more respected by the alumni who daily, in their working lives, progressively discovered the value of a Quigley education.

Professor Quigley was an arch enemy of grade inflation as his students quickly and painfully discovered. His stinginess with letters at the top of the alphabet was noted on a sign in the School's lobby. Affixed to a sign reading "Jesus Loves You" was written the following plaint from a student: "If that is true, why did Professor Quigley give me a F." Alumni who recall Dr. Quigley's lectures on the providential deity understand that there is no logical inconsistency between Jesus's love and a low grade from Professor Quigley.

Professor Quigley became an institution indistinguishable from the School of Foreign Service. His death at age 65 in no way diminished this fact. On the contrary, Dr. Quigley's latest manuscript, published posthumously between these covers, stands as continuing, living testimony to the power of his intellect, the breadth and depth of his knowledge and the total uniqueness of his mind. These three dimensions of the man informed and drove the School of Foreign Service in its formative years and continue to be the standard against which the School's ongoing work is measured.

Peter F. Krogh
Dean,
School of Foreign Service
Georgetown University

"The interpretation of the events of one age in the light of the assumptions and prejudices of another can never produce satisfactory history."

--Bernard Smail, Crusading Warfare (Cambridge University Press, 1956), page 15.

"It is never possible to consider war on its own, as an activity closed in on itself, but, on the contrary, one must, in order to study it, link it up with other human activities. Briefly, it has to be placed in context among the entire mass of actions and chain reactions. Everything is involved: politics, economy, society, evolution of civilizations, technical progress, the human spirit. A worthwhile 'military history' requires this. It must overflow broadly into other fields of history."

--Piero Pieri, "Sur les dimensions di l'histoire militaire," Annales/E.S.C. XVII (1963), page 625.

ACKNOWLEDGMENTS

This publication is the final work of Carroll Quigley, a man whose impact upon his special area of study, the history of civilization, upon his chosen college, the School of Foreign Service of Georgetown University, and upon his associates and friends, was extraordinary. Of the wide range of those who felt themselves affected by this man's presence, it is proper to recognize particularly those whose help made this publication possible. Many of them are officials of the University or former colleagues of Quigley. All of them were his friends. Among them are Dean Peter Krogh of the School of Foreign Service and Dr. Dorothy Brown, Chairman of the History Department at the time publication decisions were made. Both of them made the sensitively crucial support decisions necessary for preparation of the manuscript for publication. In that support, Constance Holden, Administrative Officer of the Departmental staff and friend of Quigley, was especially helpful. Joseph Jeffs, Librarian of Georgetown University, made the basic documents easily available and, with the Library reference staff, provided invaluable help in regard to the bibliography. Michael Foley and Jules David, colleagues of Quigley in the Georgetown History Department, served as members of a special board with Carmen Brissette-Grayson, former student of Quigley and presently a member of the History Department of Hampton Institute. The special board addressed the problems of decision-making in regard to all of Quigley's manuscripts and devoted many hours of work in respectful memory of a beloved colleague. In that effort the assistance of Quigley's graduate assistant, Helen Veit, was especially important. Jo Ann Moran and Tom Ricks of the History Department were also helpful in reviewing the manuscript. Invaluable also was the work of a volunteer research assistant, William Longo, whom Quigley never knew but who, like many others, admired his work. In stepping forward to help, he expressed the interest of many of Quigley's readers who, upon his death, suffered a felt loss. In special fashion, acknowledgment must be made of the support given Quigley all his professional life by Lillian Quigley, his wife since his days as a graduate assistant at Princeton University. Lastly, as his lifelong friend, I should add my personal gratification that I have had this opportunity to perform a role in preparation for publication of his last great work.

Harry J. Hogan

1. The Human Condition and Security

The earliest moments of my day are divided about
equally between the morning newspaper and the cat.
At six A.M., as I cautiously open the front door to
get the paper from the porch, my mind is concerned
with achieving my purpose as unobtrusively as possible. I am not yet prepared to be seen by my neighbors, and, accordingly, I open the door hardly more
than a foot. But that is enough for the cat, who has
been patiently waiting my appearance. It slips
silently through the opening, moves swiftly to the
center of the living room and pauses there to emit
a peremptory "miow." The cry tells, as plainly as
words, of its need for food, so I must put my paper
down to follow its jaunty waving tail to the kitchen
to get its morning meal of cod fillet from the
refrigerator.

While the cat daintily mouths its fish in the
kitchen, I return to my paper in the living room,
but have hardly grasped the world news on the front
page before the cat is back, rubbing its arched back
against my leg and purring noisily in the early morning quiet. By the time I have turned to page two,
the cat, still purring, has jumped lightly to the
sofa and is settling down to its daylong nap. Within
minutes, it is sprawled in complete relaxation, while
my own nervous system, spurred up by the violence and
sordid chaos of the news, is tensing to the day's
activities.

The contrast between the simple pattern, based
on simple needs, of the cat's life and the activities
of men as reflected in the daily press, makes me, for
brief moments, almost despair of man's future. The
cat's needs are few and simple. They hardly extend
beyond a minimal need for physical exercise, which
includes a need for food, some expression of the
reproductive urge, a need for some degree of physical
shelter and comfort in which to rest. We could list
these needs under the three headings of food, sex,
and shelter.

No such enumeration of man's needs could be made, even after long study. Man has the basic needs we have listed for the cat, but in quite different degrees and complexity. In addition, man has other, and frequently contradictory, needs. For example, man has the need for novelty and escape from boredom, but, at the same time, he has a much more dominant and more pervasive need for the security of established relationships. Only from such established patterns of relationships covering at least a portion of his needs, can man successfully strike out on paths of novelty to create new relationships able to satisfy other needs, including the need for novelty. Surely man has social needs for relationships with other humans, relationships which will provide him with emotional expression, with companionship or love. No man can function as a cat operates in its narrower sphere of activities unless he feels that he is needed, is admired, is loved, or, at least, is noticed by other humans.

Even less tangible than these emotional needs of man's social relationships are needs which man has for some kind of picture of his relationship with the universe as a whole. He has to have explanations of what happens. These need not be correct or true explanations; they need only to be satisfying, at least temporarily, to man's need for answers to his questions of "how?" and "why?" the universe acts the way it seems to act. This search for "how" and especially for "why" is particularly urgent with reference to his own experiences and future fate. Why does he fail in so many of his efforts? Why are his needs for companionship and love so frequently frustrated? Why does he grow older and less capable? Why does he sicken and die?

As a biological organism functioning in a complex universe which he does not understand, man may be regarded as a bundle of innumerable needs of very different qualities and of a great variety of degrees of urgency. It would be quite impossible to organize these needs into three or even four categories, as we did with the cat, but we could, perhaps, in a rough fashion, divide them into a half dozen or more groups or classes of needs. If we do this, we shall find that they include: (1) man's basic material needs usually listed as food, clothing, and shelter; (2)

2

the whole group of needs associated with sex, reproduction, and bringing up the young; (3) the immense
variety of relationships which seek to satisfy man's
need for companionship and emotional relationships
with his fellow men; and (4) the need for explanation
which will satisfy his questions about "how?" and "why?"

Yet certainly these four do not exhaust the range
of man's needs, for none of these can be enjoyed unless man can find intervals in which he is not struggling to preserve his personal safety. Food, sex,
companionship, and explanation must all wait when
man's personal existence is in jeopardy and must be
satisfied in those intervals when he has security
from such jeopardy. Thus the need for security is
the most fundamental and most necessary of human needs,
even if it is not the most important.

That last statement is more acceptable to a reader
today than it would have been fifty years ago, because,
in the happier political situation of that now remote
period, security was not considered of primary significance and was not regarded as comparable with
men's economic or personal needs. That blindness,
for such it was, arose from the peculiar fact that
America a generation ago had had political security
for so long a time that this most essential of needs
had come to be taken for granted and was hardly recognized as a need at all, certainly not as an important
one. Today the tide of opinion has changed so drastically that many persons regard security as the most
important of all questions. This is hardly less
mistaken, for security is never important: it is
only necessary.

The inability of most of us to distinguish between what is necessary and what is important is another example of the way in which one's immediate
personal experience, and especially the narrow and
limited character of most personal experience, distorts one's vision of reality. For necessary things
are only important when they are lacking, and are
quickly forgotten when they are in adequate supply.
Certainly the most basic of human needs are those required for man's continued physical survival and, of
those, the most constantly needed is oxygen. Yet we
almost never think of this, simply because it is al-

3

most never lacking. Yet cut off our supply of oxygen,
even for a few seconds, and oxygen becomes the most
important thing in the world. The same is true of
the other parameters of our physical survival such
as space and time. They are always necessary, but
they become important only when we do not have them.
This is true, for example, of food and water. It is
equally true of security, for security is almost as
closely related to mere physical survival as oxygen,
food, or water.

The less concrete human needs, such as those for
explanation or companionship are, on the other hand,
less necessary (at least for mere survival) but are
always important, whether we have them or lack them.
In fact, the scale of human needs as we have hinted
a moment ago, forms a hierarchy seven or eight levels
high, ranging from the more concrete to the less concrete (and thus more abstract) aspects of reality.
We cannot easily force the multi-dimensional complexities of reality and human experience into a
single one-dimensional scale, but, if we are willing
to excuse the inevitable distortion arising from an
effort to do this, we might range human needs from
the bottom to the top, on the levels of (1) physical
survival; (2) security; (3) economic needs; (4) sex
and reproduction; (5) gregarious needs for companionship and love; (6) the need for meaning and purpose;
and (7) the need for explanation of the functioning
of the universe. This hierarchy undoubtedly reflects
the fact that man's nature itself is a hierarchy,
corresponding to his hierarchy of needs, although we
usually conceal the hierarchical nature of man by
polarizing it into some kind of dualistic system,
such as mind and body, or, perhaps, by dividing it
into the three levels of body, emotions, and intellect.

In general terms, we might say that the hierarchy
of human needs, reflecting the hierarchy of human nature, is also a hierarchy ranging from necessary needs
to important needs. The same range seems to reflect
the evolutionary development of man, from a merely
animal origin, through a gregarious ape-like creature,
to the more rational and autonomous creature of human
history. In his range of needs, reflecting thus both
his past evolution and his complex nature, are a bundle
of survivals from that evolutionary process. The same

4

range is also a kind of hierarchy from necessary things (associated more closely with his original animal nature) to important things (associated more closely with his more human nature). In this range the need for security, which is the one that concerns us now, is one of the more fundamental and is, thus, closer to the necessity end of the scale. This means that it is a constant need but is important only when we do not have it (or believe we do not have it). That is why the United States, in the 1920s and 1930s, could have such mistaken ideas about the relative significance of security and prosperity. Because we had had the former, with little or no effort or expense to ourselves, from about 1817 to at least 1917, we continued to regard this almost essential feature of human life as of less significance than prosperity and rising standards of living from 1920 till late in the 1930s or even to 1941. Accordingly, we ignored the problem of security and concentrated on the pursuit of wealth and other things we did not have. This was a perfectly legitimate attitude toward life, for ourselves, but it did not entitle us to insist that other countries, so much closer to the dangers of normal human life than we were, must accept our erroneous belief that economics was more fundamental than politics and security.

Many years ago, when I talked of this matter to my students, all in uniform and preparing to go off to fight Hitler, one of them, who already had a doctorate degree in economics, challenged my view that politics is more fundamental than economics. The problem arose from a discussion of the Nazi slogan "Guns or butter?" I asked him, "If you and I were together in a locked room with a sub-machine gun on one side and a million dollars on the other side, and you were given first choice, which of these objects would you choose?" He answered, "I would take the million dollars." When I asked, "Why?," he replied, "Because anyone would sell the gun for a lot less than a million dollars." "You don't know me," I retorted, "because if I got the gun, I'd leave the room with the money as well!"

This rather silly interchange is of some significance because the student's attitude about buying the gun with some fraction of the money assumes

a structure of law and order under which commercial
agreements are peaceful, final, and binding. He is
like the man who never thinks of oxygen until it is
cut off; he never thinks of security because he has
always had it. At the time I thought it was a very
naive frame of mind with which to go to war with the
Nazis, who chose guns over butter because they knew
that the possession of guns would allow them to take
butter from their neighbors, like Denmark, who had it.

In recent years there has been a fair amount of
unproductive controversy about the real nature of
man and what may be his real human needs. In most
cases, these discussions have not got very far because the participants have generally been talking
in groups which are already largely in agreement,
and they have not been carrying on any real dialogue
across lines of basic disagreement. Accordingly, each
group has simply rejected the views most antithetical
to its own assumptions, with little effort to resolve
areas of acute contradiction. There are, however,
some points on which there could hardly be much disagreement. These include two basic facts about human
life as we see it being lived everywhere. These are:
(1) Each individual is an independent person with a
will of his own and capable of making his own decisions;
(2) Most human needs can be satisfied only by cooperation with other persons. The interaction of these two
fundamental facts forms the basis for most social problems.

If each individual has his own autonomous will
making its own decisions, there will inevitably be
numerous clashes of conflicting wills. There would
be no need to reconcile these clashes, if individuals
were able to satisfy their needs as independent individuals. But there are almost no needs, beyond those
for space, time, oxygen, and physiological elimination,
which can be satisfied by man in isolation. The great
mass of human needs, especially those important ones
which make men distinctively human, can be satisfied
only through cooperative relationships with other
humans. As a consequence, it is imperative that men
work out patterns of relationships on a cooperative
basis which will minimize the conflicts of individual
wills and allow their cooperative needs to be satisfied. From these customary cooperative relationships
emerge the organizational features of the communities

of men which are the fundamental units of social living.

Any community of persons consists of the land on which they are, the people who make it up, the artifacts which they have made to help them in satisfying their needs, and, above all, the patterns of actions, feelings, and thoughts which exist among them in relationships among persons and between persons and artifacts. These patterns may be regarded as the organization of the people and the artifacts on the terrain. The organization, with the artifacts but without the people as physical beings, is often called the "culture" of the community. Thus we might express it in this way:

1. Community = people + artifacts + patterns of thoughts, feelings and actions

2. Community = people + culture

3. Community = people + artifacts + organization.

The significance of these relationships will appear later, but one very important one closely related to the major purpose of this book may be mentioned here.

When two communities are in conflict, each trying to impose its will on the other, this can be achieved if the organization of one can be destroyed so that it is no longer able to resist the will of the other. That means that the purpose of their conflict will be to destroy the organization but leave the people and artifacts remaining, except to the degree that these are destroyed incidentally in the process of disrupting their organization in order to reduce their capacity to resist. In European history, with its in-dustrialized cities, complex division of labor, and dense population, the efforts to disrupt organization have led to weapons systems of mass destruction of people and artifacts, which could, in fact, so dis-rupt European industrial society, that the will to resist is eventually destroyed. But these same weapons, applied to a different geographical and social context, such as the jungles of southeast Asia, may not disrupt their patterns sufficiently to lower their wills to resist to the point where the people are willing to submit their wills to those of Western communities; rather they may be

7

forced to abandon forms of organization which are susceptible to disruption by Western weapons for quite different and dispersed forms of organization on which Western weapons are relatively ineffective. This is what seems to have happened in Vietnam, where the Viet Cong organizational patterns were so unfamiliar to American experience that we had great difficulty in recognizing their effectiveness or even their existence, except as the resistance of individual people. As a result, we killed these people as individuals, without disrupting their Viet Cong organization, which we ignored because it was not similar to what we recognized as an organization of political life in Western eyes, and, for years, we deceived ourselves that we were defeating the Viet Cong organization because we were killing people and increasing our count of dead bodies (the majority of whom certainly formed no part of the Viet Cong organization which was resisting our will).

The importance of organization in satisfying the human need for security is obvious. No individual can be secure alone, simply from the fact that a man must sleep, and a single man asleep in the jungle is not secure. While some men sleep, others must watch. In the days of the cave men, some slept while others kept up the fire which guarded the mouth of the cave. Such an arrangement for sleeping in turns is a basic pattern of organization in group life, by which a number of men cooperate to increase their joint security. But such an organization also requires that each must, to some degree, subordinate his will as an individual to the common advantage of the group. This means that there must be some way in which conflicts of wills within the group may be resolved without disrupting the ability of their common organization to provide security against any threat from outside.

These two things--the settlement of disputes involving clashes of wills within the group and the defense of the group against outside threats--are the essential parts of the provision of security through group life. They form the opposite sides of all political life and provide the most fundamental areas in which power operates in any group or community. Both are concerned with clashes of

8

wills, the one with such clashes between individuals or lesser groups within the community and the other with clashes between the wills of different communities regarded as entities. Thus clashes of wills are the chief problems of political life, and the methods by which these clashes are resolved depend on power, which is the very substance of political action.

All of this is very elementary, but contemporary life is now so complicated and each individual is now so deeply involved in his own special activities that the elementary facts of life are frequently lost, even by those who are assumed to be most expert in that topic. This particular elementary fact may be stated thus: politics is concerned with the resolution of conflicts of wills, both within and between communities, a process which takes place by the exercise of power.

This simple sentence covers some of the most complex of human relationships, and some of the most misunderstood. Any adequate explanation of it would require many volumes of words and, what is even more important, several lifetimes of varied experience. The experience would have to be diverse because the way in which power operates is so different from one community to another that it is often impossible for an individual in one community and familiar with his own community's processes for the exercise of power to understand, or even to see, the processes which are operating in another community. Much of the most fundamental differences are in the minds and neurological systems of the persons themselves, including their value systems which they acquired as they grew up in their own communities. Such a value system establishes priorities of needs and limits of acceptance which are often quite inexplicable to members of a different community brought up in a different tradition. Since human beings can be brought up to believe almost anything or to put up with almost anything, the possible ways in which the political life of any community can be organized are almost limitless.

In our own tradition, the power which resolves conflicts of wills is generally made up of three

elements. These are force, wealth, and ideology.
In a sense, we might say that we resolve conflicts
of wills by threatening or using physical force to
destroy capacity to resist; or we use wealth to
buy or bribe consent; or we persuade an opponent
to yield by arguments based on beliefs. We are so
convinced that these three make up power that we
use them even in situations where different communities with quite different traditions of the
nature of power are resisting. And as a result,
we often mistake what is going on in such a clash
of communities with quite different traditions of
power. For example, in recent centuries, our Western culture has had numerous clashes with communities of Asiatic or African traditions whose understanding of power is quite different from our own,
since it is based on religious and social considerations rather than on military, economic, or ideological, as ours is.

The social element in political power rests on
the human need to be a member of a group and on the
individual's readiness to make sacrifices of his own
desires in order to remain a member of such a group.
It is largely a matter of reciprocity, that individuals mutually restrain their individual wills in
order to remain members of a group, which is necessary to satisfy man's gregarious needs. It is similar to the fact that individuals accept the rules
of a game in order to participate in the game itself.
This was always the most important aspect of power
in Chinese and other societies, especially in Africa,
but it has been relatively weak in others, such as
our Western society or in Arabic culture of the Near
East. The religious element was once very important
in our own culture, but has become less so over the
past five centuries until today it is of little influence in political power, although it is still very
important in forming the framework of power in other
areas, most notably in traditional Tibet, and in
many cultures of Asia and Africa.

The inability of persons from one culture to
see what is happening in another culture, even when
it occurs before their eyes, is most frequent in
matters of this kind, concerned with power. Early
English visitors to Africa found it quite impossible
to understand an African war, even when they were

10

present at a "battle." In such an encounter, two tribes lined up in two opposing lines, each warrior attired in a fantastic display of fur, feathers, and paint. The two armies danced, sang, shouted, exchanged insults, and gradually worked themselves up into a state in which they began to hurl their spears at each other. A few individuals were hit and fell to the ground, at which point one side broke and ran away, to the great disgust of the observing English. The latter, who hardly can get themselves to a fighting pitch until after they have suffered casualties or lost a battle or two, considered the natives to be cowardly when they left the field in flight after a few casualties. What they did not realize was that the event which they saw was not really a battle in the sense of a clash of force at all, but was rather an opportunity for a symbolic determination of how the spiritual forces of the world viewed the dispute and indicated their disfavor by allowing casualties on the side upholding the wrong view. The whole incident was much more like a European medieval judicial trial by ordeal, which also permitted the deity to signify which side of a dispute was wrong, than it was to a modern European battle.

In the most general terms we might say that men live in communities in order to seek to satisfy their needs by cooperation. These needs are so varied, from the wide range of human needs based on man's long evolutionary heritage, that human communities are bound to be complex. Such a community exists in a matrix of five dimensions, of which three dimensions are in space, the fourth is the dimension of time, and the fifth, which I shall call the dimension of abstraction, covers the range of human needs as developed over the long experience of past evolution. This dimension of abstraction for purposes of discussion will be divided into six or more aspects or levels of human experience and needs. These six are military, political, economic, social, religious, and intellectual. If we want a more concise view of the patterns of any community, we might reduce these six to only three, which I shall call: the patterns of power; the patterns of wealth; and the patterns of outlook. On the other hand, it may sometimes be helpful to examine some part of human activities in

more detail by subdividing any one of these levels
into sub-levels of narrower aspects to whatever
degree of specific detail is most helpful.

In such a matrix, it is evident that the patterns of power may be made up of activities on any
level or any combination of sub-levels. Today, in
our Western culture we can deal with power adequately
in terms of force, wealth, and ideology, but in earlier history or in other societies, it will be necessary to think of power in quite different terms, especially social and religious, which are no longer
very significant in our own culture. The great
divide, which shunted our culture off in directions
so different from those which dominate the cultures
of much of Asia and Africa down to the present,
occurred about the sixth century B.C., so if we
go back into our own historical background before
that, we shall have to deal with patterns closer
to modern Asia or Africa than to our own contemporary
culture.

2.   Security and Power

Just as our ideas on the nature of security
are falsified by our limited experience as Americans,
so our ideas are falsified by the fact that we have
experienced security in the form of public authority
and the modern state. We do not easily see that the
state, especially in its modern sovereign form, is a
rather recent innovation in the experience of Western
civilization, not over a few centuries old. But men
have experienced security and insecurity throughout
all human history. In all that long period, security
has been associated with power relationships and is
today associated with the state only because this is
the dominant form which power relationships happen to
take in recent times. But even today, power relationships exist quite outside of the sphere of the state,
and, as we go farther into the past, such non-state
(and ultimately, non-public) power relationships become more dominant in human life. For thousands of
years, every person has been a nexus of emotional
relationships, and, at the same time, he has been
a nexus of economic relationships. In fact, these
may be the same relationships which we look at from
different points of view and regard them in the one

12

case as emotional and in another case as economic. These same relationships, or other ones, form about each person a nexus of power relationships.

In the remote past, when all relationships through which a person expressed his life's energies and obtained satisfaction of his human needs were much simpler than today, they were all private, personal, and fairly specific relationships. Now that some of these relationships, from the power point of view, have been rearranged and have become, to a great extent, public, impersonal, and abstract, we must not allow these changes to mislead us about their true nature or about the all-pervasive character of power in human affairs, especially in its ability to satisfy each person's need for security.

The two problems which we face in this section are: what is the nature of power? and, what is the relationship between power and security? Other questions, such as how power operates or how power structures change in human societies, will require our attention later.

Power is simply the ability to obtain the acquiescence of another person's will. Sometimes this is worded to read that power is the ability to obtain obedience, but this is a much higher level of power relationship. Such relationships may operate on many levels, but we could divide these into three. On the highest level is the ability to obtain full cooperation. On a somewhat lower level is obedience to specific orders, while, still lower, is simple acquiescence, which is hardly more than tacit permission to act without interference. All of these are power relationships which differ simply in the degree and kind of power needed to obtain them.

The power to which we refer here is itself complex and can be analyzed, in our society, into three aspects: (1) force; (2) wealth; and (3) persuasion. The first of these is the most fundamental (and becoming more so) in our society, and will be discussed at length later. The second is quite obvious, since it involves no more than the purchase or bribery of another's acquiescence, but the third is usually misunderstood in our day.

13

The economic factor enters into the power nexus when a person's will yields to some kind of economic consideration, even if this is merely one of reciprocity. When primitive tribes tacitly hunt in restricted areas which do not overlap, there is a power relationship on the lowest level of economic reciprocity. Such a relationship may exist even among animals. Two bears who approach a laden blueberry bush will eat berries from opposite sides of the bush without interfering with each other, in tacit understanding that, if either tried to dispossess the other, the effort would give rise to a turmoil of conflicting force which would make enjoyment of the berries by either impossible. This is a power relationship based on economic reciprocity and will break down into conflict unless there is tacit mutual understanding as to where the dividing lines between their respective areas of operation lie. This significant subjective factor will be discussed later.

The ideological factor in power relationships, which I have called persuasion, operates through a process which is frequently misunderstood. It does not consist of an effort to get someone else to adopt our point of view or to believe something they had not previously believed, but rather consists of showing them that their existing beliefs require that they should do what we want. This is a point which has been consistently missed by the propaganda agencies of the United States government and is why such agencies have been so woefully unsuccessful despite expenditures of billions of dollars. Of course it requires arguing from the opponent's point of view, something Americans can rarely get themselves to do because they will rarely bother to discover what the opponent's point of view is. The active use of such persuasion is called propaganda and, as practiced, is often futile because of a failure to see that the task has nothing to do directly with changing their ideas, but is concerned with getting them to recognize the compatibility between their ideas and our actions. Propaganda also has another function, which will be mentioned later and which helps to explain how the confusion just mentioned arose.

On its highest level the ideological element in power becomes a question of morale. This is of the greatest importance in any power situation. It means that the actor himself is convinced of the correctness and inevitability of his actions to the degree that his conviction serves both to help him to act more successfully and to persuade the opposition that his (the actor's) actions are in accordance with the way things should be. Strangely enough, this factor of morale, which we might like to reserve for men because of its spiritual or subjective quality, also operates among animals. A small bird will often be observed in summer successfully driving a crow or even a hawk away from its nest, and a dog who would not ordinarily fight at all will attack, often successfully, a much larger beast who intrudes onto his front steps or yard. This element of subjective conviction which we call morale is the most significant aspect of the ideological element in power relationships and shows the intimate relationship between the various elements of power from the way in which it strengthens both force and persuasion.

It also shows something else which contemporary thinkers are very reluctant to accept. That is the operation of natural law. For the fact that animals recognize the prescriptive rights to property, as shown in the fact that a much stronger beast will yield to a much weaker one on the latter's home area, or that a hawk will allow a flycatcher to chase it from the area of the flycatcher's nest, shows a recognition of property rights which implies a system of law among beasts. In fact, the singing of a bird (which is not for the edification of man or to attract a mate, but is a proclamation of a residence area to other birds of the same habits) is another example of the recognition of rights and thus of law among non-human life.

Of course, in any power situation the most obvious element to people of our culture is force. This refers to the simple fact of physical compulsion, but it is made more complicated by the two facts that man has, throughout history, modified and increased his physical ability to compel, both by the use of tools (weapons) and by organization of numerous men to increase their physical impact. It is also confused, for many people, by the fact that such physical compulsion is usually aimed at

15

a subjective target: the will of another person. This last point, like the role of morale already mentioned, shows again the basic unity of power and of power relationships, in spite of the fact that writers like myself may, for convenience of exposition, divide it into elements, like this division into force, wealth, and persuasion.

Assuming that power relationships have the basic unity to which I have just referred, what is the relationship between such power and the security which I listed as one of the basic human needs? The link between these two has already been mentioned in my reference to the fact that most power relationships (but not all) have a subjective target: they are aimed at the will of the opposition.

Before we consider this relationship, we must confess that there are power relationships which are purely objective in their aims and seek nothing more than the physical destruction of the opponent. If an intruder suddenly appears in one's bedroom at night, or if a hostile tribe suddenly invades another tribe's territory with the aim of taking it over, the immediate aim of the offended party may go no further than the complete physical destruction of the intruder, and this, surely, will have no subjective goal involving submission or surrender. The reason for this is that there already exists a subjective relationship covering the situation. This is the recognition by both parties that the interloper is an intruder entering an area he has no right to enter. In most such situations the defender would prefer to force the intruder to withdraw rather than to have to destroy him with incidental risks to the defender as well. Such withdrawal would be a symbol of the subjective acquiescence or obedience to which I have referred. In the rare cases where the defender's sole aim is the destruction of the intruder, this abandonment of the more frequent, and more complicated, situation is usually based on fear.

Leaving such unusual cases aside, the normal goal of power relationships or the application of power by one party against another is for the pur-

16

pose of establishing a subjective change in the mind of the opponent: to subject his will to your power, as a common and rather inaccurate version of the situation sometimes expresses it. The reason for this aim lies in the very significant fact that all power situations have two aspects, an objective aspect and a subjective, psychological, aspect. In practice, we sometimes call the objective relationship "power" and the subjective aspect "law." But the two are ordinarily inseparable, and security rests in the relationship between the two.

In any ordinary relationship between two persons, or two groups, there is usually the relationship itself as an objective entity and there is also their subjective idea of that relationship. Put in its simplest form, there is security only when both parties have a roughly similar subjective idea of the objective relationship, and such security will be stable only when their relatively similar picture of that situation is fairly close to the real factual relationship.

This probably sounds complicated, but it is really fairly simple. When two boys first come together, they have no idea of their relative power. Eventually, they will disagree about something, and this disagreement will be resolved in some fashion. They may fight each other, or they may simply square off to fight and one will yield, or one may simply intimidate the other by superior courage and moral force. In any case, if there is no outside interference, some kind of resolution will demonstrate to both what is their power relationship, that is, who is stronger. From that moment, their power relationship has the double aspect (1) the fact that one is stronger than the other, and (2) that each knows who is the stronger. From that day on, they may be good friends and live together without conflict, each knowing that, when an acute disagreement arises and the stronger insists, the weaker will yield. Within and around this double relationship, each has freedom to act as he wishes. It is this freedom of action within a framework of <u>power relationships which are clear to all concerned</u> that is security. The opinion which they share of their mutual power relationship is <u>law</u>, as the objective relationship which they recognize is <u>fact</u>. Law, in

17

this sense, is a <u>consensus</u> on the factual situation
as held by the persons concerned with it.

This relatively simple situation has become
fearfully complicated in modern times in regard to
the relationships between states, but basically
the situation is the same. There is an objective
power situation, made more significant by the fact
that the modern state is an organization of power,
and there is a consensus of a subjective kind as
to what this objective power relationship is.
This consensus is the picture they have of their
legal "rights" in relationship to each other. It
is subjective, although it may be written down on
paper in verbal symbols such as in a treaty. In
that case, we have three parallel entities, of which
the first (the real situation) and the third (the
treaty) are objective, but the vital one, the second,
the consensus, is subjective. Peace and stability
are secure only so long as all three are similar,
by the second and the third reflecting, as closely
as possible, the first.

From this situation two rules might be established:

1. Conflict arises when there is no longer a
consensus regarding the real power situation, and
the two parties, by acting on different subjective
pictures of the objective situation, come into
collision.

2. The purpose of such a conflict, arising from
different pictures of the facts, is to demonstrate
to both parties what the real power relationship is
in order to reestablish a consensus on it.

The chief cause of conflict is that the real
power relationship between two parties is always in
process of change, while the consensus, or the treaty
based on it, remains unchanged. All objective facts,
including power, are constantly dynamic, changing
year by year, or even moment by moment to some degree,
while the subjective, legal, consensus changes only
rarely and usually by abrupt and discontinuous stages,
quite different from the continuous changes of power
itself. Conflict arises when men act in the objective world, because they act upon the basis of their

subjective pictures, or even upon their symbolic verbalizations of those pictures. In the objective world where men act, they are bound to act more or less in accord with their real power, and their pictures of their power relationships are bound to diverge as their power and their actions based upon it diverge. This leads to conflict unless their consensus can be reestablished. But it is very difficult to reestablish a common subjective picture until there has been an objective demonstration of what their real power relationship is in some mutually convincing fashion. This is what conflict does. In fact, conflict is a method of measuring power to achieve such a mutually convincing demonstration and thus to reestablish consensus and stability.

So long as men, or nations, have the same picture of the power relationships among them, their acts will not lead to conflict because any act which might do so will lead to a warning (like the growling of a bear at a blueberry bush) which will recall both parties to look again at their consensus and bring their action into accord with it, but, when the factual power situation changes (as it inevitably does), the realization of the changes will penetrate the minds of the parties to different degrees (and even in different directions) so that their subjective pictures will diverge from the previous consensus, and their resulting actions, based on such different pictures, will lead to collision and conflict. It is, of course, perfectly possible for the subjective pictures in the minds of either or both to change without reference to the objective power relation at all. This is much more likely in the present period when most persons' ideas of power and of these relationships are increasingly unrealistic, because of the ordinary man's limited actual experience of power today.

This whole situation is clearly applicable to the two boys I have mentioned. Suppose these boys, whose relative power, say at age eleven, was clear to both, with A stronger than B, were to meet only infrequently over the next four years. During that interval, B, formerly the weaker, might, by exercise

19

and more rapid growth, become the stronger. When these two come together again at age fifteen, with B in fact stronger than A and with A still retaining, as his subjective picture of their relative strength, the now erroneous idea that he is stronger than B, a situation of potential conflict exists. In such a case, B, formerly weaker but now stronger, has no clear picture of their relative strengths, because, while he knows he is stronger, he has no way of knowing what increase of strength has been achieved by A. Once they are together, some difference of opinion may give rise to conflict, commencing, perhaps, with a simple effort of one to push the other from a doorway or pull him from a chair. As this test of strength develops and B discovers, perhaps to his surprise, his new ability to stand up to A, the latter, resenting this refusal of A to accept the older picture of their relationship, strikes out, and conflict begins. When it ends, it has demonstrated to both the true facts of their relative power (that is why it ends) and, by making this clear to both, has created a new consensus which becomes the basis of peaceful life together in the future.

Unfortunately this kind of fighting between young boys now occurs much more rarely than it did before (say a century ago) with the result that boys of today grow up to manhood and go off to fight, or to run the State Department, without any conception of the real nature of power and its relationships. This lack is, at the same time, one of the causes of juvenile delinquency and of adults' mistaken belief that the role of war is the total destruction, or the unconditional surrender, of one's opponent, instead of being what war really is, a method of measuring relative power so that they can live together in peace.

The role of any conflict, including war, is to measure a power relationship so that a consensus, that is a legal relationship, may be established. War cannot be abolished either by renouncing it or by disarming, unless some other method of measuring power relationships in a fashion convincing to all concerned is set up. And this surely cannot be done by putting more than a hundred factually unequal states into a world assembly where they are legally equal. This kind of nonsense could be accepted only by people who have been personally so remote from real power situations all their pampered, well-protected lives that they do not even recognize the existence of the power structures in which they have lived and which, by protecting them, have prevented them from being exposed to conflict sufficiently to come to know the nature of real power.

To this point we have discussed power relationships in a simplified way, as relationships between two actors, and have introduced only briefly complications which can arise from three other influences: (1) the triple basis of power in our culture; (2) the dual nature (objective and subjective) of power situations; and (3) the changes which time may make to either side of power's dual nature. Now we must turn to two other sources of complication in power relationships: (4) the changes which space may make in power relationships; and (5) the fact that most power relationships are multilateral and not simply dual.

The influence which distance has upon power is perfectly obvious and may be stated as a simple law that distance decreases the effectiveness of the application of power. While no rule exists regarding the rate of such a decrease, it must be understood that the decrease is out of all proportion to the increase in distance and might be judged, in a rough fashion, to operate, like gravity, light, or magnetic attraction, inversely as the square of the distance. Thus, if the distance between two centers of power is doubled, their effective ability to apply their power against one another is reduced to one-quarter.

This example, which is given simply as an illustration and not as a rule or law, is made somewhat unrealistic by the fact that it assumes that the increased distance between two centers of power is of a homogeneous nature without discontinuities or intrusive obstacles. But of course all distances in the real world are full of discontinuities and obstacles. A simple wall between two power groups may reduce the effectiveness of the application of their power to near zero. The two boys whom we have

21

mentioned as coming together after an absence (which is distance in space as well as time) of four years find their previous consensus about their power relationship is now unreal because their remoteness from one another in space over that interval made it impossible for them to observe each other's changes in power. If, when they come together and begin to clash, some adult steps between them to suspend the conflict, or one of them slips into a house and slams the door, the intrusive adult or door becomes an obstacle to the application of their power and thus prevents the measurement of their power relationship. In fact, the two possibilities I have given are not the same. The door presents a case of the reduction of power by a discontinuity in space, while the interfering adult is an example of the introduction into a dual power relationship of a third power entity (which is factor 5 above rather than factor 4).

Space with all its discontinuities is, of course, one of the chief elements in any power situation and is blatantly obvious in relationships between states. The English Channel, as a discontinuity in the space between Hitler's power and England's power in 1940, became one of the chief elements in the whole history of German power in the twentieth century. Anyone who examines this situation carefully can hardly fail to conclude that Hitler's attack on the Soviet Union on June 22, 1941 was a consequence of the existence of the English Channel which made it impossible for him to apply his power to England directly. The decision to attack Russia was based on Hitler's judgment that, for his power, the distance to London was shorter by way of Moscow than it was by way of the Channel. Napoleon had made the same decision in 1812.

The usual discontinuities in space which reduce the application of power drastically are usually accidents of terrain (such as mountains, deserts, swamps, or forests) or the discontinuity of water. However, simple distance, as found in the Soviet Union or China, or as seen in the two oceans which shield the United States, reduce the ability to apply power rapidly. Nor should we minimize the role which a simple wall may play in reducing the application of power. Hannibal wandered freely over Italy for fifteen years after the battle of Cannae (216 B.C.) but

22

could not defeat Rome because he found the walls of
the city of Rome impenetrable. And the period of
European history after 1000 A.D. was dominated, on
the power side, by the role of the castle wall, which
fragmented power in Europe into numerous small areas
and decentralized it so completely that it became almost purely local and private.

We should be equally aware of the fact that the
damping role which space and its discontinuities have
on power may be reduced by human actions in improving
communications and transportation. These elements
will be considered in the next section.

The role which distance plays in security rests
on the two problems of the amount by which power is
reduced by distance and by human judgments in respect
to this amount. For example, if, in 1941, the power
of the United States in Omaha was 100, and the power
of Japan in Tokyo was 60, and the techniques of both
for dealing with distance were the same, there was a
point, or line, between them where their ability to
apply power was equal. Since we have assumed that
their rates of decrease of power over distance were
the same, the line of equal power would have been
much closer to Japan than to the United States. Let
us say that it would have been somewhere along the
165th meridian. If their power was equal along that
line, Japanese power would have been greater west of
it and American power would have been greater east
of it. We are speaking here of the facts of power,
that is of the ability of each to mobilize more power
than the other on its side of the line. If both
governments were aware of that situation, there should
have been peace and security for both, since Japan
would not have insisted on the United States doing
anything east of the line, and the United States
should not have insisted on Japan doing anything
west of the line.

This was, indeed, the situation between these
two countries from about the end of 1922 until about
1940, because the Washington Conference of 1922 had
fixed the relationship between the two in terms of
capital ships, aircraft carriers, and naval bases so
that the power of each fleet in its home waters was
superior to the other. This situation was modified

23

in the late 1930s by changes in naval technology, especially the development of fleet tankers, refueling at sea, and the range of both vessels and aircraft, but it was still true in 1941 that each was superior to the other in its own area. The American demand that the Japanese break off their attack on China, the American protectorate over the Philippines, the Japanese decision to take over Malaya and the Dutch Indies, and the Japanese sneak attack on Hawaii, were probably all in violation of the existing power relationship between these two countries in 1941, with the situation made more uncertain by the fact that British, French, and Dutch contributions to the stability of the Far East had been neutralized by the Nazi conquest of Europe in 1940. From the change and uncertainty came the conflict of 1941-1945 in which the power of Japan and the United States was measured to determine which would prevail and to make possible the reestablishment of a new subjective consensus and a new stable political relationship based upon that.

The last major influence which complicates power relationships arises from the fact that such relationships rarely exist in isolation between two powers but are usually multilateral. The complication rests on the fact that in such relationships among three or more powers, one of them may change the existing power situation by shifting its power from one side to the other. Of course such shifts rarely occur suddenly because the application of power in international affairs is rarely based on mere whim; and, insofar as it is based on more long-term motivations, changes can be observed and anticipated. Moreover, a system involving only three states is itself unusual, and any shift by one power in a three-power balance will usually call forth counter-balancing changes by fourth or other powers tending to restore the balance.

Such multilateral systems explain the continued existence of smaller states whose existence could never be explained in any dual system in which they would seem to be included entirely in the power area of an adjacent great power. The independence of the Low Countries cannot be explained in terms of any dual relationship, as, for example, between Belgium and Germany, since Belgium alone would not have the power to justify its continued existence within the

24

German power sphere. But, of course, Belgium never had to defend its existence in any dual struggle with any one of its three great neighbors. It could always count on the support of at least one of them, and probably two, against any threat to its independence from the third. That means that any threat to the independence of Belgium would bring into existence a power coalition sufficient to preserve its freedom. And that is why the Netherlands, which had become part of the Spanish Habsburg territory by inheritance early in the sixteenth century, obtained its independence late in that same century and has preserved it since, against attacks from Spain, Louis XIV, Napoleon, Kaiser Wilhelm, and Hitler.

These same considerations apply to the independence of Switzerland, balanced between German, French, Austrian, and Italian power, but with the added consideration that Swiss terrain serves to reduce the effective power of any potential attacker, so that Swiss power itself may play a significant role in maintaining Swiss independence, without constant challenges. The Scandinavian countries are in a situation like that of Switzerland, with Britain, Germany, Russia, France and others balancing to create an interstice in a power nexus where they may survive. The obstacles of terrain, plus great power influence, also serve to balance the Scandinavian countries among each other within the other, larger, power system.

Of course if the three or more balancing great powers which preserve the independence of lesser states by their interactions were to reach an agreement on the division of these lesser states, the latter would pass out of existence, probably without conflict. We can see clear examples of this in the history of Poland, where tripartite agreements of 1772, 1792, and 1795 among Prussia, Russia, and Austria ended the independence of Poland. Poland was restored in 1918 because of the unlikely arrival of a situation in which Germany and Russia, fighting each other with power much greater than Poland's, over Polish territory, were both defeated, and more remote states (France, Britain, the United States, Belgium, and others), whose powers contributed to this defeat of both Poland's neighbors, used their temporary superiority in Eastern Europe

25

to recreate Poland, without any consideration for the future real power situation in that area. As a result, the new state continued for only twenty years in a precarious and unstable balance in which continued support from the Western powers which had recreated Poland was so remote and thus weak that Poland continued to survive only from the temporary weakness of Germany and the Soviet Union and their enmity, which applied their power in opposite directions, thus creating a power interstice in which Poland could continue to exist only so long as these two did not reach any agreement to destroy it. Once they reached such an agreement, as they did in August 1939, Poland was doomed, since the events of 1938 had shown that French and British power in Eastern Europe was also neutralized to a point where they were unable to preserve Poland in the face of any Soviet-German agreement to destroy it. And Poland could be restored, as a satellite rather than an independent state, only when the Soviet-German agreement in Eastern Europe broke down into open conflict again.

In any actual power situation, all the factors I have mentioned play roles in producing the events of history. We can see an excellent example of this in the history of Turkish power in Eastern Europe. That history can be divided into four periods over a total duration of six or seven centuries. The first and third of these periods, covering roughly about 1325-1600 and 1770-1922, were periods of war and political instability, because in both Turkish power was different in law from what it was in fact. In the second and fourth periods, covering about 1600-1770 and since 1922, there was relative stability because Turkish power was about as extensive as the area recognized as Turkish territory in the international consensus and legal documents. In the first period of instability, Turkish power was greater and wider than was recognized by legal provisions, and the Turks were struggling to obtain such wider recognition. This explains the constant wars in which the Turks sought to demonstrate that their version of their power was correct. As soon as the Turks were able to show (and obtain recognition that they had shown) that their power was greater than any other, not only in the lower Balkans, but also in the upper Balkans and even in

26

Hungary, although they were not able to hold Austria or to capture Vienna, it was possible to reach a rough agreement to this effect, and the second period, one of relative peace and stability, began. But Turkish power began to decay even more rapidly than it had risen, and, from 1770 onward the Turks had legal claims to areas where, in fact, they no longer could exercise their will. As a result, once again there was a disparity between their real power and their legal rights, although now in the opposite direction, with their legal position wider than their actual power. From this came the third period of their history, one of great instability and war, as the powers concerned tried to discover what was the real power situation in southeastern Europe. This became almost the most acute problem in European international affairs, known as "the Eastern Question." It was the chief cause of Europe's wars, including such events as the Greek Revolution of the 1820s, the Crimean War of 1854-1856, the Russo-Turkish War of 1877, the Tripoli War of 1911, the Balkan Wars of 1912-1913, and the First World War of 1914. It also gave rise to innumerable diplomatic crises, such as that of 1840 over Egypt, the Congress of Berlin of 1878, the Bulgarian crisis of 1885, the Bosnian crisis of 1908, and many episodes involving the question of which powers would replace the nominal suzerainty of the Sultan in North Africa.

The fourth period of Turkish history, since 1922, has been one in which Turkey has been a force of peace and stability in its area, because, once again, its area of legal power has coincided with its area of real power. This would not have been true if the Treaty of Sevres, imposed on the Sultan at the end of World War I, had been permitted to stand, because that treaty reduced the area of Turkish legal power to more restricted limits than the real Turkish ability to rule. If it had not been replaced by the more lenient Treaty of Lausanne in 1922, Turkish instability would have continued. Fortunately, the Turkish nationalists challenged the Treaty of Sevres and were able to prove that their power was wider than the area conceded to them by that earlier document.

27

A similar analysis could be made of the international position of the Habsburg Empire in the nineteenth century. In fact, the whole history of European international relations in that century could be written around three sharp divergences between power and law. These would center on the Ottoman and Habsburg Empires and on the rise of Prussia to become the German Empire. In the first two the area of legal power was wider than the area of factual power, while in the third the opposite was true.

In all such crises of political instability, we can see the operations of the factors I have enumerated. These are (1) the dichotomy between the objective facts and subjective ideas of power situations; (2) the nature of objective power as a synthesis of force, wealth, and ideology in our cultural tradition; and (3) the complication of these operations as a consequence of changes resulting from time, from distance, and from a multiplicity of power centers.

3.   The Elements of Power

As we have said, war is a method of measuring power, and it is continued until the adversaries agree as to what their power relationship is in a particular situation. War is the application of force against the organizational patterns of the opponent to reduce his ability to resist, until agreement can be reached. Since the real goal of military operations is agreement, all such operations are aimed, in the final analysis, at the opponent's mind, or rather at his will, and not at his material resources or even at his life. This has long been recognized by military men, although it is a truth which has not spread very widely among the civilian population. Even among military men, the recent growth of elaborate mechanical instruments for applying power, and especially the growing influence of the advocates of air power in military thinking, has made war more impersonal and thus concealed the real aim of military operations, but to military theorists it has long been a maxim that "the goal of strategy is. . .to break the will of the enemy by military means." The airplane crew or missile operators who concentrate on enemy installations as targets easily lose sight of the real target, the

28

enemy's will, behind those installations, but thousands of years of human history show the truth of the older maxim about the goal of strategy.

Parallel with our recent confusions about strategy have been equally unfortunate confusions about the relationship between wealth and force. The relationship between these two is essentially the relationship between potential and actual. Wealth is not power, although, given time enough, it may be possible to turn it into power. Economic power can determine the relationships between states only by operating within a framework of military power and, if necessary, by being transformed into military power itself. That is, potential power has to become actual power in order to determine the factual relationship between power units such as states. Thus this relationship is not determined by manpower, but by trained men; it is not established by steel output, but by weapons; it is not settled by energy production, but by explosives; not by scientists, but by technicians.

When economics was called "political economy" up to about 1840, it was recognized that the rules of economic life had to operate within a framework of a power structure. This was indicated at the time by the emphasis on the need for "domestic tranquility" and for international security as essentials of economic life. But when these political conditions became established and came to be taken for granted, political economy changed its name to "economics," and everyone, in areas where these things were established, became confused about the true relationships. Only now, when disorder in our cities and threats from external foes are once again making life precarious, as it was before the 1830s, do we once again recognize national security and domestic tranquility as essential factors in economic life.

In the past century we have tended to assume that the richest states would be the most powerful ones, but it would be nearer the truth to say that the most secure and most powerful states will become the rich ones. We assumed, as late as 1941, that a rich state would win a war. This has never been true. Wealth as potential power becomes effective in power relationships, such as war, only to the degree that it becomes actual power, that is, military force. Merely as economic power it helps to win a war only potentially and actually hampers progress toward victory. We could almost say that wealth makes one less able to fight and more likely to be attacked. Throughout history poor nations have beaten rich ones again and again. Poor Assyria beat rich Babylonia; poor Rome beat rich Carthage; poor Macedonia beat rich Greece, after poor Sparta had beaten rich Athens; poor Prussia beat richer Austria and then beat richer France several times. Rich states throughout history have been able to defend their positions only if they saw the relationship between wealth and power and kept prepared or, if they were able when attacked to drag out the war so that they had time to turn their wealth into actual military power. That is what happened in the two World Wars. In each case the victims of German aggression were able to win in the long run only because there was a long run. If the Germans had been able to overcome the English Channel, their victims would not have had time to build up their military power.

Thus we see that wealth in itself is not of great importance in international affairs. It must be turned into military power to be effective, but then it ceases to be wealth. Wealth turned into guns no longer is wealth. But guns can protect wealth.

Another aspect of this error is to be found in the belief that the factual relationship between states is something which can be bought. All through the period after 1919 this illusion played a major role in foreign policies. During World War II we believed that the support and cooperation of neutrals like Turkey, Spain, or even Vichy France could be bought. We have sent such states goods, bought their goods at high prices, and given them loans. All of this meant only so much as our actual power at the time could make it mean. These acts could win nations over to cooperate with us only to the degree that it is clear that we have the real power to enforce our desires. The subsidy which Great Britain gave to Romania in 1939 did not prevent that country from cooperating with Germany, for the simple reason

30

that Germany had the power in that area to enforce
Romanian cooperation and Britain did not.

Another example of this same error can be seen
in the efforts of the League of Nations or the satisfied powers to compel obedience to their desires by
economic sanctions without military sanctions, as
against Italy in 1935. Many persons, even today, are
eager to use economic warfare, but shrink from using
military methods, without seeing that the former will
be effective only to the degree that they are backed
up by military power. Since 1945 the United States
has given billions of dollars in such economic bribes
to scores of states throughout the world without increasing our power or obtaining our desires or even
winning good will, if that was what we wanted, to any
significant degree. In fact, the old, and cynical,
adage "If you want to lose a friend, give him money"
seems to operate in international relations as well
as in personal ones.

Confusions such as these, and even worse confusion which mistook verbal legalisms, such as CENTO,
SEATO, and even NATO, for power, could have arisen
only in a period of remarkably untypical human experience. The nineteenth century from about 1830
to about 1940 was such a period. The failure to
see the relationship between economics and power,
like the confusions between law and power, could
arise when people had security for so long that they
came to accept security as part of the natural order
like oxygen. The confusion is seen in laissez-faire
in domestic life as well. In the feudal period or
in the long mercantilistic period which followed,
conditions of insecurity were close enough for all
to see what the real nature of power was. But in
the century before 1939, security, at least for the
English-speaking peoples, became accepted, and the
separation of political from economic life became
possible because security was present. But at that
time, as always, prosperity was based on resources
and security, and both of these depended on power
to get and to hold. In Western Europe, where laissez-
faire was established <u>for this reason</u>, these truths
could be ignored because the Western nations, especially the English-speakers, were expanding over
such a wide area of far weaker peoples and there

31

were, at first, so few of these expanding states, that they could continue to expand in relative peace with little interference with each other and with only minor conflicts. In fact, their conflicts with their African and Asiatic victims were hardly regarded as wars at all. But this expansion was firmly based on military superiority. The wars which did arise, such as the Opium War on China, the destruction of the American Indian (even when the weapon of destruction was whiskey or measles virus), the Sepoy Rebellion, the Zulu or Ashanti Wars, and such, were firmly based on the fundamental foundation of military superiority. In many cases this military superiority was so great that it did not have to be applied in battle. The native rulers yielded and allowed their own communities to be de-stroyed by the non-military weapons of Europe, such as its disease, commercial practices, and legal rules. From this arose the curious result that the English-speaking peoples were able to persuade themselves that they had not needed their military power at all. They spoke of "peaceful economic pene-tration of colonial areas" even when natives were dy-ing by millions, as in China, from the innovations they had brought in. By "peaceful" they came to mean, not that weapons had not been used because European military power was so overwhelming, but that weapons had had nothing to do with it. The perfect example of this is the opening of Japan to Western commerce by Perry over a century ago. Only to Americans did this appear as peaceful economic action; the Japanese knew then, as we know now, that it was a conflict of power even if that did not become overt.

That pleasant situation in which economics con-quered the world for the West did not last long, but long enough to mislead the West into the belief that economics could prevail in world politics independent of military power. By 1890 that period was passing: politics and economics began to come together again, in what the West called "imperialism." This happened partly because some of the non-Europeans like the Japanese began to use political methods against European exploiters and their fellow exploited alike, but chiefly because the available colonial areas of the world became fewer, just as the numbers of the

32

European exploiting states became more numerous, with Germany, Italy, and the United States being added to Britain, France, the Netherlands, and other earlier colonists. As a result, economics came increasingly to rely on armed force in the international scene, especially when the late arrivals, like Germany, openly took to armed force in order to compensate for the head start enjoyed by Britain and France. These latter, by that time quite befuddled about how they actually had taken over so much of the world, tried to compete with the new imperialists by economics alone. They even insisted that economic methods of expansion were the only morally acceptable methods, and that Germany and Italy were immoral for attempting to use the weapons which the earlier imperialists had either not had to use or had forgotten that they had used. It was hard for the Germans to believe that the British, who had won Hong Kong in 1842 by using the crudest of forceable methods, were not being hypocrites in 1911, when they were horrified at Germany sending a gunboat to Agadir to protect German commercial interests in Morocco. An event such as Agadir convinced many Germans that all British were hypocrites as it convinced many English that all Germans were aggressors.

In the same way in which misconceptions about the relationship of politics and economics came into international politics, similar misconceptions came into domestic life about the idea of laissez-faire. These underestimated the need for tranquility at home and the need for political power, including force, as a framework for business in the same way that a political basis for economic action was needed in the international field. These domestic errors included two beliefs: (1) the belief that there are eternal economic laws to which political activity must be subordinated; and (2) the belief that economic methods and especially economic inequality could function without regard to the power situation in the community. As one consequence of this, when Germany about 1937 was violating our economic "laws," we felt that the Nazi regime would soon go bankrupt. I can recall Salvemini in 1936 tracing a graph of the Italian gold reserves as a steadily falling line from about the early 1930s until the date in 1935 when these figures ceased to be published and then, by extrapolation into

33

the future, finding the date when Italy would have no more gold and the Mussolini regime would fall from power. As if any nation with power and resources needs an economic convention like gold to operate, even in a world which accepts such conventions.

In this confusion of misconceptions and errors arising from the nineteenth century, Americans led the world, because Americans had been shielded from the realities of human life for generations. In the nineteenth century we were not only shielded from other powers by distance, but that distance consisted of the world's two greatest oceans, with only backward states lacking navies on the farther shore of the Pacific and with the British fleet patrolling the waters of the Atlantic. And, to complete the picture of paradisical unreality, the good conduct of the British fleet was guaranteed by the fact that we held Canada as a hostage for such good behavior because of the long, undefended Canadian border. Thus we had security without any real effort or expense of our own and without even recognizing that it depended upon the power of other states. Even today, the past role of the British fleet and of the Canadian hostage in our nineteenth century security is largely unrecognized and will even be denied as a historical fact when I mention it. But in that pleasant fool's paradise, Americans developed their dangerously un-realistic ideas of the nature of human life and politics. Since security is necessary rather than important, it was, like air, taken for granted by Americans who put other things, especially eco-nomics, higher on their list of priorities. Thus Americans were naive in their relations to power, a quality which is carried over into their personal lives by their overprotected childhoods.

The events of 1941 gave a rude jolt to American naivete, but the effects of such jolts are such as to demonstrate the importance of power rather than to teach its nature. We now do recognize its impor-tance, but are still widely uninformed about its nature and modes of operation, a condition of igno-rance which seems to be as deep among our recent Secretaries of State as among more humble citizens. For the achievement of a higher degree of wisdom on this subject there are few topics more enlightening

34

than the history of weapons systems and tactics, with special reference to the influence that these have had on political life and the stability of political arrangements. Experience may be the best teacher, but its tuition is expensive, and, when life is too short, as it always is, to learn from the experience of one's own life, we can learn best from the experiences of earlier generations. All such experiences, whether our own or those of our predecessors, yield their full lessons only after analysis, meditation, and discussion.

One thing we learn from experience with power is that force is effective in subjecting the will of one person or group to that of another person or group only in a specific situation. There can be no general subordination of wills, because, as situations change, the wills of both parties may change. A man who will continue to pay a share of his crops to a political superior may refuse to permit the rape of his daughter by that superior.

In any specific situation the ability of one party to impose its will on another is a function of five factors making up the element of force. These are (1) weapons; (2) the organization of the use of such weapons; (3) morale; (4) communications; and (5) transportation or logistics. The last two indicate the importance of distance, already mentioned, since no one can be made to obey or yield to force, unless orders can be conveyed to him, his subsequent behavior can be observed, and force can be applied through the distance involved to modify his behavior. This seems more obvious to us than it has been in history, because our recent experience has been with such efficient communications and transportation that we tend to forget that, for much of human history, it was almost impossible to know what was happening, even a few miles away, and was even more difficult to influence such happenings when they were known. As recently as two generations ago, events and even acute crises in Africa were usually settled one way or another before the home governments in Europe knew they had occurred.

I shall frequently use the terms "power sphere"

or "power area" to refer to the territory over which
a power system can operate or prevail as a consequence of the five factors mentioned. It is obvious
that power spheres are limited by the existence of
other power spheres, as well as by the limitations
arising from the five factors. It is equally evident that technological improvements in the five
factors, especially, perhaps, improvements in communications and transportation, will serve to widen
areas of power and that in any given geographic confine, such as Europe, such improvements will, by making it possible to compel assent over wider areas,
make the areas larger and reduce the number of power
units in such a geographic confine. Since the ability to command assent has increased in some periods
and decreased in other periods, the number and sizes
of political units in any fixed confine such as Europe
have changed. Such changes have generally not been
explained by historians, but they should be, as will
be done in this book. Periods in which the ability
to obtain assent over wider and wider areas is increasing are periods in which offensive power is
dominant. On the other hand, periods in which defensive power is dominant are periods in which there
is a tendency for power units to grow smaller and
more numerous. In time, if such defensive power
continues to prevail for a long time, power will
be so reduced that the state will gradually disappear, and eventually public authority will also
vanish, and all authority will be private authority.
This may seem impossible to us, but it has happened
several times in European history, notably at both
ends of the duration of classical civilization,
about 1000 B.C. and again, two thousand years
later, about A.D. 1000.

It must be recognized that fluctuations of
power areas are influenced by other factors in addition to those I have mentioned, but these additional factors are relatively less significant and
are often of a contingent character, in the sense
that their influence is dependent, to a large degree, on the five basic factors. Of these contingent factors the most important is the ideological
one. It must be clear that any structure of power
over a power area must have some basis in ideology
on which to make an appeal to the allegiance of at

36

least some of the inhabitants of that area. The basis for such an appeal will usually have to be modified as the power area expands or contracts, and this change will frequently have to be a change in social extension as well as in a real extension, in the sense that it may have to appeal to different social groups or to new levels of social classes even in the original area.

In this connection it is revealing that the ideological appeal for allegiance in the last two thousand years of Europe's history (and, indeed, in most of mankind's earlier history) made almost no effort to reach or to attract the peasants, who were, throughout history down to the nineteenth century, not only the most numerous class in society but were also, of course, the economic support of the power structure. This failure to make ideological appeal to the most numerous and most necessary group in the community was a consequence of the facts of power which are being discussed in this book. Whatever the number of the tillers of the soil or the indispensable nature of their contribution to the community, their power has always been insignificant, except in the few, relatively brief periods when they have been of military importance to the community. Except for the period before about 4000 B.C., and for a few centuries in Roman history and an even briefer period in some areas of Greek history, the peasantry has played almost no role in military life and, accordingly, almost no role in political life of the communities which have made history. This military and political incapacity of the tillers of the soil, so glaringly evident under feudalism or during the Thirty Years' War, was a function of the distribution of weapons and of military organization, and is a remarkable example of the weakness of economic necessity in contrast with the role of force in any society. As we shall see, the rise in political significance of peasants and farmers in the nineteenth century, a rise which never took them to a dominant position, was a consequence of changes of weapons, a fact almost unmentioned by historians of the modern period. A similar neglect of peasants has existed in most of history, but on a gigantic scale, in Asia and in Africa, and, above all, in China, as we shall see.

37

Of the five factors we have mentioned as determining fluctuations in the size of power areas, the first two (weapons and organization) have operated together and have been more significant than the last two (communications and transportation), which have also operated together. In the influence of the first pair, which taken together could be referred to as a weapons system, the most important consequences have arisen from the relative balance between defensive and offensive power.

We might define the superiority of a defensive weapons system in terms of the ability it gives to those who have it to say "No" to orders and to sustain that "No." This statement indicates the greater importance of the first pair of factors over the last pair, because it shows ability to refuse obedience even when an order can be communicated and its consequence observed. Thus the ability of a messenger to arrive with an order will have little meaning if the defensive power of the recipient of the message is much greater than the offensive power of the sender.

Weapons systems not only influence the size of power areas; they also influence the quality of life within that area. The most significant factor here is concerned with whether a weapons system is "amateur" in character or is "specialist." By "amateur" I mean weapons which are cheap to obtain and easy to use, while by "specialist" weapons I mean those which are expensive to obtain and difficult to use. Both of these criteria can be defined more narrowly. A weapons system is "cheap" if it can be obtained by the savings of an ordinary man in the community over no more than a year. A weapons system is "easy to use" if such an ordinary man can become adept in its use in a training period measured in weeks or months. By these criteria the period about 1880 was the golden age of amateur weapons, for at that time the best weapons available in the world were probably the Winchester rifle and the Colt revolver. Both could be bought by the ordinary man for not much more than a hundred dollars, and, in the United States at least, most men could obtain a hundred dollars in the course of a year. Moreover, any man could learn how to use these two weapons in a period of days or weeks. Thus about 1880 the ordinary citizen of the United States could obtain the best weapons available at that time, and no government could obtain any better weapons. In such a situation, in which most or many men can get the best weapons, men are relatively equal in power and no minority can easily force a majority to yield to its rule. Thus there is a tendency, in such a period, for the appearance of political equality and majority rule (or at least for rule by the large group which can obtain weapons). Such amateur weapons have been dominant only rarely in history, most notably in Athens in the fifth century B.C. and in Rome shortly after that time. At those two periods also, there was a tendency toward political democracy.

On the other hand, on many occasions in the past, the best available weapons have been so expensive that only a few persons in the society have been able to obtain them, and usually, at such times, the weapons available have been difficult to use so that long periods of training were necessary to use them effectively. About A.D. 1100 in Europe, there were two "supreme" weapons, the medieval knight and the medieval castle. Both of these, especially the castle, were so expensive that not one man in a hundred could afford them, and they could be used effectively only with years of training. The same thing was true about 1200 B.C., when horse-drawn chariots and stone castles, as at Homeric Troy, were the dominant weapons. And now a similar situation has been developing over the last few decades, so that today the most effective weapons, such as jet planes, armored vehicles, mobile artillery, and even nuclear weapons are so expensive that only governments rather than individuals can afford them, and some of them cannot be afforded by many governments. The training periods required for the effective use of such weapons is measured in years rather than in months, although in the United States, as a survival from 1880 we still try to man an army equipped with such weapons by drafting men for two years. This is just another example of the failure of the twentieth century to recognize the passing of the nineteenth century and of our persistence in retaining patterns which grew up in the previous period into the present where they are largely not applicable.

In any such period of specialist weapons, which can be obtained and used by a small minority of the population, there is a tendency for the government which can command such forces to become increasingly authoritarian.

As we shall see in the next and subsequent sections, these two relationships concerned with offensive-defensive and with amateur-specialist weapons have a great deal to do with the nature of political power and its changes in history. In fact, much of history is the record of the consequences of changes in patterns of men's living resulting from changes in these relationships of weapons systems.

4.   A General Pattern of Weapons History

If we look at the great panorama of military history and power relations in the past, our first impression is one of chaotic confusion and complexity in which even the greatest events seem to be the result of personal and accidental influences. For want of a nail, the horse, the battle, and the kingdom were lost. That was Tolstoy's conclusion in regard to Napoleon's defeat in Russia, but, since a similar fate also occurred to other invaders of Russia, like the Teutonic Knights in 1242, the Swedes in 1709, or Hitler in 1941, it seems likely that there may be something more than simple accident determining what happens.

A longer examination of these confused events, a study in which we constantly shift our attention from the individual detail to the overall picture and back again to the individual episode, will gradually reveal to us that there is, to some degree, an underlying pattern or patterns to the flow of events. Such an examination seems to indicate a number of major oscillations or cycles in this flow of history, or at least in Western history.

The first such pattern is concerned with the obvious fact that there have been, in the history of weapons, shifts of emphasis between shock weapons and missile weapons. Shock weapons are those in which the combatants hurl themselves onto each other in physical collision. They include fists,

hand weapons (such as daggers, clubs, or swords),
spears, sabers, bayonets, and so forth. Fighting
cavemen, Sumerian spearmen, Greek hoplites, Macedonian phalanxes, Roman legions, medieval knights,
and the bayonet charges of the period from about
1800 through World War I, are examples of the use
of shock weapons. On the other hand, javelins,
slings, bows and arrows, catapults, crossbows, firearms, grenades, and our contemporary bombs and rock-
ets are examples of missile weapons. With these
the combatants hold back from each other, at least
temporarily, and hurl their weapons at their
opponents.

The relationship between shock weapons and missile weapons has often been misunderstood by historians of military affairs, especially by academic
military historians, who often write as if peoples
of the past had a free choice as to whether they
would use a shock weapon or a missile, and often
made that choice on an exclusive basis, that is,
they adopted one to the exclusion of the other.
Thus we may read in history books that the European
Middle Ages were "dominated" by the shock weapons of
the medieval knight or that the Scythians or other
grassland cavalry used only missile weapons. This
gives a quite misleading impression of what was going
on, since missiles and shock are not alternatives but
are complementary, at least to the point that they
perform different functions and play different roles
in the use of applied force in human relations.
Missiles are generally weapons of destruction, while
shock weapons are generally weapons of duress. The
former can kill men, but the latter can force men to
obey. This is why a distinction is made in police
science between "deadly weapons" and "police weapons." The distinction rests upon the fact that
"police" (that is "shock") weapons can be used to
varying degrees of violence, as a policeman's baton
can be used for a slight tap or for a knockout blow
or a bayonet can be used against a prisoner for a
persuasive dig or a deadly thrust. Because of this
wide range of violence which is possible with shock
weapons, such weapons can be used against individuals
to force them to obey an order, such as to get into
a vehicle.

Missile weapons are quite different because

they lack any intermediate degrees between being fired and not fired; they cannot be half used or half fired, except by the user tossing them away. The reason for this is that the user of a missile weapon loses control of it the moment he has fired it or hurled it at his opponent, and, at that same moment he has become disarmed (unless his missile weapon has some kind of repeating mechanism). Thus the user of such a missile has little choice except to try to kill, since, once he has released his weapon, he is disarmed in the presence of a live opponent (unless, of course, he has some other weapon, such as a shock weapon). Obviously, a non-repeating missile weapon like a hand grenade, or even a repeating missile weapon like an automatic rifle, cannot be used to make a prisoner do what one wants, such as to get into a vehicle; these can, of course, be used to kill the prisoner, or to threaten to kill him, but this does not make him get into the vehicle if he flatly refuses to do so. Thus obedience obtained from individuals by duress requires shock weapons, which can be controlled at all stages and degrees of use. For this reason, any defense system dominated by missile weapons must also have shock weapons, although it is not so necessary for a defense system dominated by shock weapons to have a complementary missile component (however any exclusively shock defense system will often find situations in which the users cannot do things which they desperately would like to do).

There is another important aspect of this distinction between these two kinds of weapons. Missile weapons, being deadly, are often more effective against formations of fighters, while shock weapons are more effective against individuals. Since battles begin as conflicts between formations, but continue as applied force against individuals, battles, as we know them, usually use missile weapons in the first stage and follow this up with shock weapons in the second stage, the first seeking to shatter or disrupt the enemy formations, the second seeking to force the enemy as individuals or small groups to do what the victors wish, such as to surrender for ransom, slavery, or exchange. Such application of shock weapons in the later stage of a battle usually involves a pursuit of fleeing enemy forces, not only to force individual obedience, but also to prevent the enemy from reforming his formations. Thus a typical model of a battle in our tradition can be viewed as consisting of three stages: missile attack, shock assault, and pursuit (with emphasis on shock weapons). Thus I have usually called this sequence, a M-S-P battle. In the nineteenth and early twentieth centuries this sequence used artillery barrage (increasingly supplemented by musket or rifle fire), then bayonet assault, and finally ended with cavalry pursuit. This sequence of artillery, bayonet, and cavalry, my students called "an A-B-C battle."

Although this sequence of weapons and aims has often appeared in battles throughout history, the point at which the combatants shift from one stage to another has not usually been determined by exclusively tactical considerations, but has been influenced by personal tastes, mistaken ideas, and traditions, often to the detriment of the combatant's military advantage, so that decisive victories (and defeats) have often resulted from making the shift from one stage to another too early or too late. The Indo-European tradition of individual combat and emphasis on shock weaponry has given Europe a persistent tendency to shift as soon as possible from stage I to stage II in a battle to such a degree that the missile opening of a battle became almost insignificant. This has been true of European fighting since the Indo-Europeans arrived there about 2000 B.C. and replaced the preceding missile tradition based on archery (the so-called "Bell Beaker" tradition) by the shock tradition which we see in the Homeric and classical battles. Among the latter, the Greeks and Romans were so eager to get to grips with the enemy with their spears and swords that the opening missile stage of the battle was often reduced to little more than each infantryman hurling a javelin or two as he advanced on the enemy with his shock weapon. But the fact remains that this opening missile stage was present, however briefly, in all battles of the classical period and was usually much more significant than the accounts either of contemporary observers or of modern historians might indicate. Thus the role of "light" infantry, such as peltasts among the Greeks after about 400 B.C.

or of velites in the Roman forces until about 100 B.C. (when they were replaced by foreign auxiliaries) was always more significant than most writings on the subject might lead us to believe.

The failure to pick the correct moment in a battle to shift from the missile stage to the shock stage can also occur in making the shift from the shock stage to the pursuit stage. Antiochus the Great lost two important battles in 217 and 190 B.C., the first against Ptolemaic Egypt and the second, the decisive battle of Magnesia, against the Romans, by going in pursuit of the fleeing left wing of the enemy, leaving the main enemy formation still intact.

As we shall see, the European devotion to shock weapons after 2000 B.C. was matched by a growing Asiatic devotion to missile weapons after that same date. While Asiatic archers always had shock weapons to follow up their original missile attack on an enemy formation, they were usually reluctant to make the shift from missiles to their daggers, swords or spears, and sometimes lost the victory from such delay. One of the weaknesses of any missile attack is that the assailants may run out of ammunition before the enemy formation is broken or the defenders may have such defensive armor that they cannot be broken with the attackers' supply of missiles. Since this was generally true in the Asiatic missile tradition from before 2000 B.C. until after the advent of firearms, the Asiatic missile tradition consistently tried to trick their opponents into breaking their own formation by the famous Asiatic grasslands tactic of the feigned retreat, by which cavalry archers would suddenly break off their tempestuous missile assault and make a rapid retreat, hoping to draw the enemy into a premature pursuit and thus to get them to break their formation, so that the fleeing archers could whirl about and resume their attack against a now scattered enemy.

As we shall see later, these two traditions after about 2000 B.C. were not just a matter of taste and training but had sound ecological reasons rooted in the fact that shock tactics were better adapted to the peasant economies of forested Europe, while missile tactics were better adapted to the

44

nomadic, and commercialized economies of Asia's grasslands, but both practices were carried to extremes from the force of traditions and training.

The historical sequence of emphasis on missile and shock weaponry is distorted by this long-term persistence of shock weapons in Europe and missile weapons in grasslands Asia over the period of more than 3500 years from about 2000 B.C. to after A.D. 1500. Another distortion, if we may call it that, has rested on the fact that civilized urban societies, with their higher standards of living, have been able to afford more complex defense arrangements and often have a variety of weapons systems, including missiles, shock, infantry, artillery, fortified castles and towns, cavalry, and naval forces. If we keep these two exceptional influences at the back of our minds, we can see a rough historical sequence or cycle in the alternation of missile and shock tactics.

We cannot speak of battles or war in the Stone Age, because the use of violence in that period was not associated with any formations or specialized functions. Even when one group attacked another group, the conflict was simply disorganized individual combat. Weapons were all shock, except for throwing of stones. Although spears were thrown in hunting, and the atlatl or spear-thrower was known in the late Paleolithic period in Europe, it is unlikely that spears were thrown in conflict, since a missed aim would leave the thrower unarmed, unless he was carrying more than one spear. The atlatl, which greatly increased the effectiveness of the thrown spear in hunting by almost doubling its range, would not generally be used in fighting, since increased range would be of little advantage and would be more than over-balanced by increased uncertainty of aim. The sling was also known in Europe in the Upper Paleolithic period, and is more likely to have been used in fighting than the atlatl or even the thrown spear, since a slinger would have a sufficient number of stones for missiles. On the whole, however, any fighting in the Paleolithic would probably have been with the spear or thrown rocks. And it seems very likely that fights in that period were rare and between individuals rather than groups or tribes.

Missile weapons began to take over with the invention of the bow and arrow in the Mesolithic period, probably in south Asia and before 20,000 B.C., at a time when Europe was still in the glacial Paleolithic. The blow-gun with poisoned darts was invented in the same cultural context, that is, a tropical or semi-tropical thickly forested river bank where peoples lived a rather sedentary life on fish, shellfish, root crops, and small animals, with considerable use of wicker-work for fish traps, baskets, and shelters and of cords for fish lines, nets, snares, but the use of poison for fighting was not feasible since it acted too slowly.

The use of the bow spread widely, reaching much of the Old World, including the oceanic islands which could be reached by boats, also a Mesolithic invention, and coming into the New World with the ancestors of the American Indians. In its progress, the bow spread to the peoples who were still in the earlier hunting stage as well as to the later stage of Neolithic gardening cultures. By 4000 B.C. the simple self-bow, made of a homogeneous shaft of wood, was known over most of the earth, although some peoples who knew it did not make much use of it, while others, who used it for hunting, did not use it for fighting. As we shall see, numerous improvements could be made in the bow and were developed over the period down to about the time of Christ, most of these in central Asia, as a consequence of interactions between peoples of the Asiatic grasslands and those of the forests which fringed these grasslands on the north. On the western end of these grasslands in what we regard as part of Europe, north of the Black Sea, the Indo-European peoples developed and became numerous in the period of Atlantic climate, which was rather warm and wet, from before 6000 B.C. to after 3000 B.C. When the climate became drier after 3000 B.C., these Indo-European peoples moved westward into Europe (as well as southward and southeast, into regions of more civilized cultures), enserfing the agricultural peoples and the Beaker peoples whom they found there, and replacing the bow as the prevalent weapon of central and eastern Europe by the battle-axe, the dagger, and the spear, all shock weapons (after 2000 B.C.).

46

This period of shock weapon predominance in Europe gradually covered most of Europe, ignoring the bow, although it was known, and missing some of the chief improvements in the design of the composite bow, regarding the bow as a weapon for backward and inferior people, such as their own peasants. The period of shock weapons in Europe lasted from after 2000 B.C. to after A.D. 1400, when increased use of the bow, the crossbow, and firearms inaugurated a long period of missile weapons dominance in which we are still today. In fact, this fourth period in the cycles of this aspect of weapons history reached its peak only in the twentieth century with the eclipse of the bayonet in the generation 1914-1941. The process took about a thousand years from the last peak of the previous shock weapon period, as seen in the medieval knight about A.D. 1000, with the decisive crossover in the slow shift from pikes to muskets in the sixteenth to eighteenth centuries. It is of considerable significance that this period of shock weapons dominance from about 1900 B.C. to after A.D. 1500 was also a period in which the horse was a very significant part of military life, and that the horse and the last significant shock weapon (bayonet) left the scene almost simultaneously after 1914. The decline of shock weaponry required centuries because of the persistent tradition of the heroic Indo-European warrior class, which was as devoted to shock and individualistic tactics as it was to horses. Much of European military history over the period of about six centuries after A.D. 1350 revolved about the efforts to judge, usually unsuccessfully, the degree of the shift from impact weapons to missiles and, at the same time, to judge the shift of fighters from horsemen to infantry. The persistence of the European shock tradition despite the steady increase in missile firepower culminated in 1916 in the dismal spectacle of more than two and a half million casualties in the battles of Verdun and the Somme without any military decision to show for them.

The Asiatic grasslands were just as persistent in clinging to their missile tradition as Europe was to its shock tradition. As a result, the two areas responded quite differently to technological innovations and did so for reasons which were cultural and ecological rather than tactical, as we shall see. When the wagon and chariot spread after 2400 B.C., Europe combined the chariot and spear in what we regard as "Homeric warfare," while Egypt, western Asia, and Shang China combined the chariot with archery. The chief difference was that a spearman had to dismount from his chariot to fight, while the bowman could fight from his vehicle; both needed a driver to handle the vehicle, in spite of the literary and pictorial misrepresentations which pretend that the hero was alone in his glory. The two traditions, embedded in social training and individual neurological patterns, persisted through ages of weapons changes, often imposing grave restraints on the effective use of new weapons. Such restraints can be seen in the shift from chariots to cavalry in the first millennium B.C., when Asia shifted to mounted bowmen while Europe shifted to mounted spearmen. All the subsequent improvements in horse-riding, including the improved bit, the firm saddle, body armor, stirrups, and horseshoes, are only significant details on these two distinct traditions.

The area of contact between these two traditions has been in the Near East and across the steppe frontier of eastern Europe. The victories of Rameses III's bowmen over the Peoples of the Sea about 1190 B.C., the victory of Greek spears over Persian bowmen at Marathon in 490 B.C., the victory of Parthian horse archers over Roman legions at Carrhae in 53 B.C., the victory of European shock over Seljuk mounted bowmen at Dorylaeum in the First Crusade (1097), the victories of Mongol archers over Polish and Hungarian knights at Liegnity and Muhi in 1241, and the victory of Russian archers over the Teutonic Knights on Lake Peipus in 1242; these are familiar examples of the collisions of these two traditions. Even the victory of David over Goliath should be included in such a list.

The persistence of the Western shock tradition in the face of tactical drawbacks and long after better methods were known can be seen in naval history. As we shall see, naval history began in the Mediterranean with oared galleys which fought by

48

ramming about 900 B.C. This shock tactic of ramming
or boarding hampered the exercise of seapower in the
Mediterranean and the Atlantic for more than 2500
years. The shift from such shock tactics to missiles
was not so much a consequence of the arrival of guns
in the sixteenth century as it was that the locale
of decisive naval battles shifted from the Mediterranean Sea to the Atlantic in the west and to the
Indian Ocean in the east, areas where vessels could
no longer be propelled by rowing and therefore
areas where the use of ramming was no longer feasible.
We could date the shift over at the date between the
battle of Lepanto of 1571, in which the Habsburgs
defeated the Turks in the Mediterranean, and the
British victory over the Spanish Armada in the English Channel in 1588. The former was a victory by
ramming, while the latter was a victory for guns and
seamanship. Yet the shock tradition continued to be
strong in many navies. As late as the era of Nelson
(killed at Trafalgar in 1805), when the British navy
was fully devoted to battle by gunfire, the new
American navy was cluttered with grappling irons,
boarding pikes, and boarding nets, and rowed galleys were still being used in the Mediterranean.
Thus the shock tradition was so strong in naval
tactics that the complete shift to missile tactics
required 250 years after the shift of naval power
from the Mediterranean to the Atlantic had made
rowed naval vessels obsolete. The interesting point
is that there was an earlier missile and sailing
tradition in the Mediterranean before ramming was
adopted, for the victory of Rameses III over the
Peoples of the Sea in 1190 was a victory for marine
bowmen. If the Ptolemies, who took over Egypt in
323 B.C., had continued the naval tradition of Rameses, instead of importing the Western tradition of
ramming, the history of the Mediterranean might
have been quite different; with small maneuverable
vessels filled with eastern archers, instead of her
unwieldy galleys, Cleopatra might have defeated
Augustus at Actium!

The Western, especially American, shock tradition, which is still evident in many ways, such as
the great emphasis on "contact" sports like football,
also influences history which has emphasized battles
and shock tactics to a degree which has seriously

distorted the whole of military history. We have been given ancient military history in terms of Greek hoplites and Roman legions and medieval history in terms of knights charging across grassy fields. As a result the history of missile weapons, of siege tactics, of logistics, and of the vital role of weapons in controlling flows of incomes from land and trade have been neglected, leaving our view of the past not only incomplete but mistaken.

To sum up this first cycle in military history: we can see, in the West at least, four phases giving two completed cycles: a prehistoric phase of shock dominance lasting hundreds of thousands of years; a second phase of rising emphasis on missiles in the archaic period from the Mesolithic to the early Bronze Age (in Europe until about 2000 B.C.); a third phase of shock dominance in the West from the spread of the Bronze Age warrior peoples to the spread of the crossbow, the longbow, and firearms (that would be from about 1900 B.C. to after A.D. 1300-1600); and finally a fourth phase of growing emphasis on missile weapons from the longbow to the Vietnam War of 1965-1972, which had no place for shock weapons at all.

A second pattern in military history is that between offensive dominance and defensive dominance already mentioned. The prevalence of either dominance is not entirely a matter of weapons, since organization and morale may be equally important. In this second pattern also we seem to have a sequence of eight phases giving four full cycles. This oscillation seems to show that defensive power was very strong in the prehistoric period before 4000 B.C., reached a second phase of great defensive dominance just after the Iron Age invasions in Europe (say, about 1000 B.C.), reached a third similar dominance in Europe about A.D. 1000, and finally reached a lesser and brief episode of defensive dominance in Europe about 1916. These four phases of defensive dominance were balanced by five periods of offensive superiority. There may have been a first such period associated with the spread of the bow and arrow and the appearance of the state as a religious organization in the fourth millennium B.C. A second offensive phase is associated with the spread of bronze weapons and the rise of the great Bronze Age empires of the middle of the second millennium B.C., say about 1700-1300. The third offensive phase is associated with iron weapons, the rise of cavalry, and the growth of the Iron Age empires of the last five centuries before Christ. The fourth phase was a wavering advance of offensive power associated with the spread of firearms and great improvements of military logistics until the late nineteenth century. A fifth such phase may be seen in the great increase in offensive power which seems to have culminated about 1950.

Each of these periods of growing offensive power is associated with a growth in size and intensity of political organization, as follows: (1) the growth of the earliest states, replacing kinship groupings, based on the archaic religions, after 4000 B.C.; (2) the growth of the Bronze Age empires about 1700-1200, including Babylon, the New Kingdom and Empire in Egypt, the Hittite Empire, Harappa in India, and the Shang Empire of China; (3) the growth of the classical empires (the Assyro-Persian, the Macedonian-Roman, Maurya in India, and Han in China), all in the millennium after 700 B.C.; (4) the growth of the European dynastic and national states culminating about 1870; and (5) the growth of "continental blocs" about the middle of the twentieth century.

Any effort such as this to arrange historical changes on a wide geographic basis runs into certain difficulties such as problems of geographical lag. Moreover, in dealing with the recent period, there is a many-pronged problem associated with any observer's tendency to overemphasize the foreground of the most recent period, making a tendency to mistake minor oscillations for long-term trends. This is intensified by the well-recognized difficulties of studying contemporary history, and the problem, to which I have made such frequent reference, for the post-nineteenth century to be unrealistic about its political arrangements.

This last problem appears as a persistent and

perverse proclivity to ignore, or even to counteract, the influence of force in political organizations. For example, the political arrangements of the peace treaties of 1919-1923, which disrupted the Habsburg, Ottoman, and Romanov Empires by creating a number of new states on "nationality" lines, represented the defensive stalemate of 1916 rather than the growing power of the offensive in 1917-1950 and was one of the reasons for the surprisingly easy liquidation of so many of these states in the 1938-1942 period when this offensive superiority asserted itself. The appearance of scores of new states, or rather pseudo-states, since 1945 reflects a similar misconception of the real nature of political organization. Many states admitted to the United Nations since 1945 are so remote from the realities of the world power structure that they do not represent any power structure at all. In the seventeenth century, when the modern states system came into existence and the basis was laid for the modern system of international law, it became understood that the state was a structure of power on a territorial basis and that the existence of such a structure could be recognized by its ability to defend its frontiers against external aggressors and to maintain law and order for its peoples within those frontiers. This system of international law, often associated with the name Grotius (1583-1645), was not based on whim or theories but on observation of the activities of the power structures in the new European states system. The unrealistic experiences of the nineteenth century, which largely destroyed European, and especially English-speakers', ability to observe political facts because of a growing obsession with myths and verbalisms, led to the actions of the twentieth century in which men made such unrealistic political decisions that untold millions were hurled into death and misery for the sake of untested theories remote from facts. Today, states which have not the slightest ability to defend their frontiers or to exercise simple police powers over their own citizens are recognized as states for no other reason than that they are admitted to the United Nations.

The correlation I have made between offensive superiority and the growth of size of political units, with its contrary correlation of defensive power with the stabilization or contraction of the size of power areas, is distorted by a number of lesser influences.

There are four of these lesser influences. The first is simple lag in time, so that changes of size may be a generation or a century later than the establishment of the dominant weapons system. The length of such a lag has been reduced in the course of history. Some of this is due to our perspective, which makes closer time intervals look longer than more remote time intervals which were actually longer. But the change also rests on the speeding up of communications and transportation throughout history, so that, with the exception of some aberrant periods, news and the recognition of conditions have spread more rapidly in recent periods.

The second distorting influence arises from the role played by logistics in weapons systems. For example, in the period 1815-1865, increase in fire-power through the rapid introduction of paper cartridges, percussion-cap ignition, breech-loading, rifling, and the use of brass cartridges greatly increased the obsolescence of shock weapons such as bayonets and cavalry sabers and also increased the strength of the defense over the offense. These two influences would have stabilized the size of power areas as they were about 1850 with much of Europe remaining in small kingdoms and principalities, such as Bavaria, Hanover, Modena, the Two Sicilies, and such. This increasing power of the defensive was recognized even by a poet in the Crimean War ("Some one had blundered"). It was also evident in the American Civil War from the failure of Pickett's charge, through the mounting casualties of Grant's advance on Richmond and his failure to capture that city from the stalemate before Petersburg. This last engagement, with its withering defensive fire-power, its use of trenches and counter-mining, and its use of balloons for artillery-spotting, was a foretaste of 1915 (by which time the defense had been further strengthened by barbed wire and machine guns). This steady growth of defensive weapons power was countered

in the opposite direction by the application to military affairs of the advancing techniques of improved
communications and transportation, notably by the
post, telegraph, and the railroad, to give the
shattering offensive triumphs of the German victories of 1866 and 1870. A repetition of these
successes was avoided only by a narrow margin in
1914 at the Marne, leading to the defensive stalemate of the next three and a half years. This was
based on the increase in defensive fire-power in the
interval 1870-1916.

A third distorting influence in our simple correlation of the offensive-defensive balance with the
size of power areas rises from the fact that the advances of technology in historical time, however
intermittent, have required scarce resources, highly
trained personnel, and great accumulations of capital
that fewer and fewer political units could provide.
It is clear that almost any group could provide itself with stone weapons; fewer groups could provide themselves with iron weapons and even fewer
with steel ones; only a few could make jet airplanes, while very few could make nuclear weapons.
This growing concentration in the production of
weapons, combined with improved transportation and
communications which more advanced states could obtain made it possible for such advanced political
units to extend their rule over wider and wider
areas which were unable to obtain these advantages.
This resulted in the increased size of political
units from small bands and later tribes to the continental blocs of today through the fluctuations of
defensive and offensive weapons systems. As we
shall see later, it is conceivable that this long
secular trend may now be reversing itself, as it
did on some occasions in the past.

The fourth distorting influence in this correlation of weapons and power areas is concerned
with the oscillations between amateur and specialist weapons already mentioned. One aspect of this
relationship, sufficiently distinct to deserve mention as an independent cycle, is the shift in military history between walking to war and riding to war.

This third cycle could be expressed as the old

54

distinction between infantry and cavalry, but it is
a difference much wider than that since fighting
men have traveled in other ways than on the backs
of animals, and the cycle must be seen in terms of
all conveyances, rather than in terms of any single
one of them. Before men rode horses to war, they
rode in chariots, and, after they gave up horses
completely, they traveled in trucks, tanks, and
planes. Interspersed between these modes of riding
to war, there were periods of walking to war, so
that the whole sequence presents three complete
cycles, thus:

1. infantry, before 2500 B.C.
2. chariots and cavalry (in some areas),
   2500-600 B.C.
3. infantry (in Europe), 600 B.C.-A.D. 500
4. return to cavalry dominance, 500-1450
5. infantry as "the Queen of battles,"
   1450-1917
6. mechanized conveyances, 1917-

This table is somewhat less reliable than our
other cycles because this particular oscillation is
more subject to geographic variation, chiefly from
the fact that areas with sufficient supply of fodder
for animals retained animal conveyances longer, while
areas with inadequate fodder, such as the Mediterranean,
found it difficult to make much use of horses. Similarly, in the post-equine period, areas which were
industrialized could use mechanical conveyances
while non-industrialized areas were largely excluded,
or much hampered, in the use of such vehicles. In
general, the above chronology is that for areas of
greater political significance in the West, as the
Mediterranean basin was in the classical period and
as Western Europe has been since about 1100. The
shift of European political power from south of
the mountains to north of the Alps in the Dark Ages
arose because Christian civilization at that time
was threatened by mounted invaders from the Eurasian
grasslands, and the northwest, with rainfall in all
four seasons of the year, had more adequate supplies
of fodder and could defend itself against mounted
invaders by mounted defenders.

This pattern of change between riding and walking is of considerable importance, not because one method is intrinsically superior to the other, but because when men fought on foot, a larger part of the community was involved in the fighting and was expected to fight. As a result, periods of infantry dominance have been periods in which political power has been more widely dispersed within the community and democracy has had a better chance to prevail. On the other hand, periods in which men have fought from mounts have generally been periods in which only a minority have been expected to fight and this minority could hold political control over the majority and compel this majority to work to support such an expensive military system.

In general, in applying this last cycle, we must remember that most of history has been in transitional phases rather than at the peak of any cycle, and, on the whole, infantry has lasted longer in areas which were economically poorer, while cavalry lasted longer in areas which were richer. This almost to say that infantry was retained in areas of mountain and forest, while cavalry flourished better in grasslands and valleys, a simple reflection of the fact that better agricultural areas were generally richer in most of history. However, areas which have been rich for any reasons, even outside agriculture, have often been able to afford cavalry. Thus, for almost 500 years before the fall of Troy (say, 1700 to 1200 B.C.), Greece was rich from trade crossing it from the Aegean Sea to central Europe and could afford chariots for warriors, but when this commerce ended, in the Iron Age invasions of the twelfth century, the poor agricultural resources of Greece could not afford castles, chariots, or even much cavalry, so that Greece turned to infantry for defense, while farther east, in Mesopotamia and Persia, mounted fighters remained important long after they had become insignificant in Greece.

The fourth cycle in military history is that between amateur and specialist weapons as already defined. This cycle has passed through three complete oscillations, with a possible fourth in the prehistoric era. The early Stone Age was a period in which an ordinary man could obtain weapons about as good as his neighbor merely by making them. Accordingly, men were roughly equal in power, the differences in this respect being not much greater than their natural physical endowments. The advent of metals and later the beginnings of cavalry made these elements of warfare so expensive that only a minority could engage in war, reaching a peak with bronze weapons, stone castles, and chariots in Mycenaean Greece and late Bronze Age western Asia about 1400 B.C. Iron was potentially cheaper and more democratic than bronze because it is one of the most common elements, but the processes of manufacture were skilled and expensive until after 600 B.C., so that weapons and politics remained concerns of an authoritarian minority of men after the destruction of Mycenaean society about 1200 B.C. and the slow beginnings of a new society after 1000 B.C. based on iron. But by 600 the cost of iron slowly fell and standards of living among the Greeks also rose, so that a substantial part of the men in most Greek areas could afford the weapons of the Greek hoplite fighter. This led to the domination of the new classical Mediterranean society by its citizen-soldiers from about 600 to about 400 B.C. in the Greek world, somewhat later (about 300 to 50 B.C.) in the western Mediterranean. As areas of political power became larger after 400 in the east and after 200 in the west, equipment became more expensive, tactics more complex, supplies more important, and campaigns extended for years, so that citizen-soldiers, who could not be away from their livelihoods for such long periods were gradually replaced by mercenary professional soldiers. This growing cost of wars and fighting eventually bankrupt classical civilization, and the state found it impossible to defend the whole area. After A.D. 400, the state retracted its forces to the east, leaving the west to invaders who were increasingly devoted to shock mounted combat; this was so expensive in an impoverished society that more than a hundred peasants were needed to support each mounted fighter, a condition which continued in northwest Europe for much of the period until about 1400. Accordingly, society was divided into two chief classes, the small minority who were expected to fight and the larger majority who were expected to support the fighters.

The introduction of gunpowder after 1350 did not change this situation because guns, for over four hundred years, were expensive to obtain and difficult to use, although this new weapon did help to shift tactical superiority from cavalry to infantry and made the private castle obsolete by 1580. Only with the arrival of a cheap and convenient hand gun in the nineteenth century and the economic revolution to mass production did men (and women) become equal in power, a change which was reflected in politics by the arrival of new slogans: "one man, one vote," "majority rule," "the voice of the people is the voice of God," and even "votes for women." The threat to authority from amateur weapons began to appear in the period 1775-1815, at first in America in such events as Braddock's defeat, Concord and Saratoga, and the victories of French citizens over professional forces at Valmy and under Napoleon in 1799-1813. Equality of men and majority rule became established in England, western Europe, and America in the period 1830-1870. This did not appear in southern Europe or the east because the economic changes spread so slowly and standards of living rose so gradually that the peoples of those areas could not afford guns before the introduction of more expensive, specialist weapons, beginning with machine guns and rapid firing artillery. These newer weapons and their successors, such as tanks and airplanes, began once again to increase the power of the minority and led to a shift away from democracy in political life. The process is parallel to the changes in weapons and politics in classical antiquity in the period 450 to 50 B.C. Like all historical parallels, this one is not exact because the recent shift was not only from amateur to specialist, but was also a change from foot soldiers to those who moved in conveyances, while in antiquity infantry remained supreme for many centuries. As a consequence, the shift which took place in antiquity in two steps over several centuries took place recently in little more than a single generation.

If we combine the four cycles we have mentioned, we can make a chronology of the history of weapons and political forms in the West from the archaic period to the present. This table, of nine stages, has weaknesses. It is more concerned with weapons

than it is with the organizations in which those
tools were used or with the outlooks and morale
which determined how effectively they were used.
Moreover, the table concentrates on the northwest
quadrant (from the Himalayas to the Atlantic) or
even more narrowly. This geographical limitation
is in no way justified by the greater importance
or more frequent innovations of the West, at
least in the earlier period. It is rather justified by the fact that it covers the areas with
which readers of this book will be more familiar.
As we shall see, other areas not covered by this
chronology were at least as important as this one,
at least up to A.D. 1500. The most significant
omission from this outline is that of the great
empires of the mobile missile warriors of central
Asia, which will be considered in detail in their
proper place. This table may serve as an outline
for the West until more adequate detail can be
arranged around it as this book progresses.

Relationship of Weapons and Politics

Periods	Weapons	Politics
Stone Age	Amateur (to 3000 B.C.)	Democratic (to 2500 B.C.)
Bronze Age Early Iron Age	Specialist (3000-600 Specialist B.C.)	Authoritarian (2500-500 B.C.) (Archaic empires)
Early classical period	Amateur (600 B.C.-400 B.C.)	Democratic (500-350 B.C.)
Late classical Medieval Early modern	Specialist (infantry) Specialist (cavalry) Specialist (infantry) (400 B.C.-A.D. 1780)	Authoritarian (350 B.C.- A.D. 1830) (Classical empires; feudal; dynastic states)
Late modern	Amateur (infantry) (1780-1917)	Democratic (1830-1934) (National states)
Contemporary	Specialist (mechanized) (1917-)	Authoritarian (1934- (Continents; blocs)

(blank page 60, intentionally omitted)

CHAPTER II
THE PREHISTORIC PERIOD, TO 4000 B.C.

In recent years a small number of influential writers have been trying to persuade us that man is by nature a violent and murderous creature. Their arguments have not been based on any careful observations of human behavior. Indeed, on the whole, the careful observers of human behavior on a comparative basis, the anthropologists, do not adopt these arguments, but generally reject them.

Those writers who seek to portray human nature as essentially that of a bloodthirsty killer base their arguments generally on two kinds of inferences, both of which are more typical of late-Victorian methods of writing and argument than of the more scientific methods of our own day. These two are: (1) by inference from the behavior of animals other than men; and (2) by inferences about the life and nature of our earliest human ancestors. Fair representatives of these two types would be Konrad Lorenz, whose On Aggression (1966) was largely based on inference from animal behavior, and Robert Ardrey, whose African Genesis (1961) was based on a very selective examination of the evidence on human origins. Somewhat apart from these two groups are a number of novelists who revel in violence and whose fictional works need no evidence at all, but carry conviction to some readers simply from their ability to tell a story. The most influential example of this might be William Golding's Lord of the Flies (1955).

There is nothing new in such writings, either in the point of view or in the kind of evidence used, although it must be admitted that the quantity of evidence piled up, especially by writers like Ardrey, was not available to most earlier writers. The idea that man originated as a solitary, violent killer goes back to classical antiquity and has appeared and reappeared, periodically, through the last two thousand years of the Western tradition. Its origins in the West can be traced back to Zoroaster and the Pythagorean rationalists (including Plato), who assumed that man, insofar as he was a physical body

61

living in the material world, was basically evil, because matter, the world, and the flesh were evil.
This view was contrasted with the opposing idea, derived from Egyptian, Mesopotamian, and Hebrew outlooks, that the world, the flesh, and nature were
good. In some cases, this more optimistic view of
the world, nature, and the flesh was supported by
the argument that all of these were the creations
of a good and omnipotent deity and could not, in
view of this origin, be evil in any essential way.

The more optimistic view is somewhat older, although neither view could have been formulated until
the period of the great transformation (1500-500 B.C.),
when men's ideas about the nature of deity were emerging from the ambiguities of the earlier archaic period.
Among the new attributes of deity, goodness, omnipotence, and oneness seem to have appeared slightly
earlier than the idea that deity must be transcendental, at least in the Near East; the first three of
these attributes contributed to the more optimistic
view of man and the world, while the last two of
these four attributes contributed to the pessimistic
view, especially among Indo-European peoples, especially the Persians and among those Hebrews who
were influenced by the Persians after 600 B.C. The
Zoroastrian, Pythagorean, Platonic view, by making
deity transcendental tended to make matter and the
flesh ungodly, and often came to embrace the view
that these ungodly elements of human experience,
being evil, must have been created by Satan, since,
as Plato wrote (The Republic, II, 379-380), "God, if
he be good, is not the author of all things, as many
assert, but he is the cause of a few things only,
and not of most things that occur to men. For few
are the goods of human life, and many are the evils,
and the good is to be attributed to God alone; of
the evils the causes are to be sought elsewhere, and
not in Him." As we shall see later, the appearance
of this intellectual problem, in the sixth century
B.C., was closely related to the simultaneous Indo-
European invention of two-valued logic.

These two points of view about the nature of
man, already in head-on collision more than two thousand years ago, eventually sorted out into two basic,
and usually unexamined (or even unconscious) assump-

tions about the nature of evil. In one of these, represented in Western civilization by what might be called the mainline of Christianity, evil became a negative quality, simply the absence of good. In this assumption, evil is in no sense a positive quality or entity. It is simply a low level of goodness, which in its most extreme manifestation, might be a total absence of goodness, measurable simply as a zero-quantity of good, but not by any positive amount or quantity of evil. In this view, everything is on the same side of the baseline, extending from zero goodness up to the total and infinite goodness of God.

The other point of view, explicitly found in Zoroaster and Plato, provides what might be called the dissident or heretical minority of the Western tradition. In this view the forces of evil are a real, positive quality, opposed to goodness, just as real, capable of existing independently of goodness, and capable of being quantified by a positive amount on the opposite side of any zero baseline which divides good from evil.

In the history of the West, these two points of view have been represented by the clash between the successors of the dualist tradition (the Paulicans, Bogomils, Cathars, Manichaeans, and Jansenists, including some kinds of Puritans), and the hierarchical point of view of the established church in the West (in England as well as on the continent). In political theory this contrast can be seen between men like Thomas Hobbes(1588-1679), who believed that nature is essentially violent and that man is basically evil, and more traditional thinkers, like Richard Hooker (Laws of Ecclesiastical Polity, 1954), who felt that man and nature were good, or, at least, were potential and could be trained in any direction. In the eighteenth century, the same contrast can be seen between the upholders of one of the chief religious antagonists of the day, Jansenists and the thinkers of the Enlightenment.

If these names and terms are not readily recalled by the reader, their significance may be pointed out by indicating the contrasting attitudes of the two groups in regard to their ideas on "nature" and on "human nature." The one side, represented by Hobbes, saw nature as a jungle of murderous conflict and violence, "red in tooth and claw," while the other group saw nature as good, peaceful, and beneficient, a view often attributed to Rousseau, but represented more clearly in that period by the French priest Bernardin de Saint-Pierre (<u>Paul et Virginie</u>, 1787).

Parallel to their disagreement about nature was a similar dispute about the nature of man, the "hard liners" viewing man as descended from a solitary, violent, probably cannibalistic, killer, while the "soft liners" saw man, at least originally, as a good, loving, gregarious, cooperative, onmivorous creature.

In the nineteenth century, the two opposing outlooks were represented, on the one side, by the apologists for individualistic, competitive, industrial capitalism, such as Herbert Spencer and the social Darwinists, and the supporters of aggressive nationalism, like Heinrich von Treitschke, while the opposite point of view found its spokesmen in figures like Prince Kropotkin and the humanitarian reformers such as Robert Owen or John Ruskin. Once again, the "hard liners" insisted on the inevitable role that must be played in human life by selfishness, individualism, competition, and conflict, while the other group, widely ignored at the time, emphasized the importance of cooperation, community, love, and mutuality. The great success of Karl Marx as a thinker at the end of the century rested, to some extent, on his ability to synthesize the two points of view, a process which is necessary for any thinker's work to have permanent value within the Western tradition, which itself contains the two points of view as major and minor themes and achieves greatness only in those periods when the two have some synthetic reconciliation in the prevalent outlook of the period.

In this connection, and very relevant to our main purpose here, is the fact that the general preponderance of the "hard line" in the 1880s was accompanied by the belief that human personality is a consequence of genetic and hereditary factors, so that we could, if we wished, breed men for personality types we regard as desirable, just as we can breed

racehorses for speed. It is no accident that the metaphor about breeding men as we breed horses is to be
found as a subordinate theme in the history of the
"hard line" tradition from Plato to Hitler and was
very prevalent in the biological thinking of the
last century, while the opposite point of view,
from Christ to the majority of present-day anthropologists and behavioral workers, has been the dominant theme in the Western idea of human nature. In
fact, the chief efforts of the last generation, in
such controversial matters as racial desegregation,
criminal and penological reform, mental health, and
educational reform (especially in such controversial
matters as "tracking" or "channeling" for ability,
intelligence testing, and earlier starting ages
for schooling) rest on efforts by the great mass
of workers in the social sciences to change our
current institutional and procedural arrangements
which were set up in the 1860-1910 period on the
then accepted "hard line" assumptions about the
hereditary nature of individual abilities.

This recapitulation of the history of these two
outlooks would have no place in a book on weapons
and political stability were it not for the fact
that the two outlooks are still with us and are
still debated, except that today there is very little
discussion of the general assumptions of the two but
simply vigorous, inconclusive, and uncompromising
arguments on the special issues, such as on American
foreign and domestic policies or human origins. In
the foreign policy debate the issue between the "hard
liners" and the "soft liners" is drawn between "hawks"
and "doves," and, in general, between those who emphasize the dominant role of force and weapons in
international relations and those who would, on the
contrary, emphasize the role of cooperation, reciprocity, mutuality, and conciliation in these matters.
The same contrast may be seen in the controversies
over crime and urban violence in American domestic
problems, the "hawks" in both cases urging the increased use of force and severe punishments, while
the "doves" are more concerned with finding the
causes of these evils, so that understanding and
humanitarian action may result in social reform to
prevent the causes and achieve the rehabilitation
rather than the punishment of the culprits.

As in most controversies, the two extreme positions are both untenable, and the truth lies in a
more inclusive position which covers them both.
That is to say, human nature, like nature itself,
is neither good nor evil, but is potential and thus
capable of developing in either direction. Man is
born with the capacity to be either aggressive or
submissive, or any degree between the two. He acquires as personality traits those behavioral patterns which have been effective in satisfying his
desires over his whole past experience. His personality may include traits which seem incompatible,
but which exist in him for use in different situations. Thus he may be submissive with superiors
and aggressive with inferiors. The process by
which any individual acquires the traits which
make up his personality is called "socialization";
it begins at birth or even at conception. It is a
process by which his inherited potential characteristics are developed, eliminated, or distorted to
become the traits which are subsequently observable
in his personality. The inherited characteristics
are much broader and much more numerous than the
fewer and more specific traits which develop in
the socialization process. The latter can be observed, but the former, because they are potential
and not actual, cannot be observed, but can only be
inferred later when they have become observable
traits. These characteristics of human nature or of
the nature of any individual are, of course, derived
from the genetic endowment which he has inherited
from his ancestors, just as the potential capacity
of any group, tribe, or nation consists of the gene
pool which has been handed down through biological
inheritance from that group's ancestors. Such a
genetic endowment is often called a "gene pool,"
but it would be better to regard it as a "genetic
river," in respect to either the individual or the
group, since it pours downward from generation to
generation over millions of years of selection, or
elimination, and of gene damage. In the case of man,
this genetic river should be regarded as a torrent
which gets wider and wider, in the kinds and diversity of genetic materials flowing along (this from
the growing hybridization of the human population,
especially over the last few millenniums) and it
also carries along an increasing mass of wreckage

66

made up of damaged and injurious genes (this from
the advance of medical science, which increasingly
permits the survival and reproduction of persons
with such damaged genes, including those which produce diabetes, hemophilia, cystic fibrosis, and
other genetic disabilities). Since the genetic
endowment of any individual or group cannot be observed but must be inferred from the small fraction
of its potentialities which ever become observable
traits, scientific method requires that we assume
that the genetic endowment of any individual or
group is the same as any other individual or group,
and that the observable differences of personality
traits should be attributed to the environmental
factors by which what was potential becomes actual
traits. Thus we must assume that any individual or
group is potentially capable of doing what any other
individual or group is able to do, unless we can obtain such an identical environmental experience and
context that factors of this kind can be disregarded.
Since this last proviso is almost impossible to obtain, scientific method requires, through the so-
called "Rule of Simplicity" or "Rule of Economy" in
scientific hypothesis, that we assume that human
nature and its characteristics are the same for all.

This may sound complex, but it can be made very
simple if we contrast the genotype, which is inherited, with the phenotype, which is acquired, and
be consistent in the different words we use in reference to each. Thus:

Genotype	Phenotype
nature	personality
characteristics	traits
potential	actual
inferred	observable
inherited	acquired
assumed to be the same	seen to be different
general	specific
broad boundary limitations	narrower learned behavior
needs	desires

The significance of this distinction lies in the
fact that the subject of this book is human behavior,
not human nature, for the simple fact that all men
who have made history have been socialized. Thus

67

they respond to desires and not to needs. In fact, it is very doubtful if men have any innate recognition of their needs, except as they have been socialized in a particular social context to respond to drives (which are innate) by desires (which are socialized responses). Thus, when an individual experiences a hunger drive, he needs food, but he does not desire food; he desires whatever his upbringing and past experience have trained him to regard as food: steak or fried locusts or even whale blubber. In fact, men throughout history have starved when they were surrounded by "food" in terms of their needs, but which they had been trained not to consider as food, and thus to desire. Almost anywhere in the world where men are living, or have lived, there are insects and plants (or on the sea, plankton and other living creatures) which are digestible to man, but which most men would regard as inedible.

This distinction between needs and desires is of some significance to the subject of this book, as we shall see, since the basic need for security may lead to desires which are either irrelevant to security or even destructive to it. Men have no more innate appreciation of what makes security or even when they are secure, than they have of what objects are edible or poisonous. The desires which a society or a tradition may associate with security are not only often self-defeating, but they are usually unconscious, so that a people may know that they feel secure or insecure, but they often do not know what it is in a situation which engenders such feelings or what security is made up of in their own traditions and experience.

The distinction which I have made between genotypes and phenotypes is, like everything else, the result of the whole evolutionary process which created the universe in which human experience takes place. In studying the early history of man to see the forms that this distinction took in the evolution and early history of man, we must not be misled by the controversies between "hawks" and "doves," but rather we must try to see how a living creature whose behavior was originally almost completely regulated by innate patterns came to be almost completely regulated by learned patterns.

Man is descended from the primates, insect-eating and fruit-eating arboreal creatures who developed visual acuity and stereoscopic vision from the need for accuracy in judging distances in reaching for fruit and in moving about in the trees. Their food was more plentiful in open forest and parkland, rather than in deep jungle forest or on open grasslands, and man, as a descendant of primates who originally flourished under these conditions, has flourished best under similar conditions ever since.

Life in the trees, with its associated diet of fruit, nuts, insects, perhaps supplemented by eggs and nestling birds, developed other features of primate evolution, including a grasping hand, with nails but not claws, an upright body from sitting on a branch and reaching upward or outward for another branch or for edibles upon it. The coordination of hand and eye, to replace a projecting snout or teeth for grasping, along with growing emphasis on sight and decreasing emphasis on smell, led to the development of a straight face, while the accustomed diet, with reduction in use of the mouth for grasping, increased the use of rotary chewing processes, avoiding the development of fangs (projecting canine teeth), which would have prevented such chewing. This left this primate with dental equipment of a relatively human kind, well adapted to ingestion of food but almost valueless for defense, for grasping, or for biting food from large objects, either animal or vegetable.

Those primates who left the trees earlier or spent more time on the ground developed fangs for protection, but our human ancestors sought protection in other ways, including retreat to the trees.

By fifteen million years ago, when some primates were adapting to an increased degree of terrestrial living, man's ancestors were still largely, although not completely, arboreal, and, in consequence, had found security, not in any natural de-

69

velopment of physical organs of defense but in evading and avoiding danger. The result was a small ape-like creature, probably widespread in the open forest areas of Africa, Asia, and even Europe, similar to the fossil ape known as Ramapithecus.

By fifteen million years ago, however, increasing dryness was beginning to reduce the areas of such open forest, replacing it with expanding stretches of grassland and savannah. The remaining areas of open forest became increasingly dependent on subterranean groundwaters and less dependent on local rainfall, with the result that open forest began to break up into discontinuous forest separated by widening barriers of savannah.

For ten million years, from about thirteen million to about three million years ago, this process of increasingly erratic rainfall and increasingly diverse vegetation, with dwindling forest, greatly reduced the primates of Africa and pushed the survivors in four different directions: (1) those who became or remained arboreal; (2) those who remained in the forest, although largely terrestrial--the African apes; (3) those who were already adapted to ground life on the grasslands--the ancestors of the baboons; and (4) those who were pushed suddenly--too suddenly to deal with the problem by physical responses--from dwindling groves of trees onto the grasslands--the hominids.

The great contrast here is not between the hominid ancestors of man and their closest relatives among the apes, such as the ancestors of the chimpanzees, but between the baboons and the hominids, because of the different ways in which these two groups responded to the same challenge of how to live on the ground among scanty arboreal refuges. The baboons met that problem largely by physical adaptation, longer fangs, a projecting snout, quadrupedal locomotion, use of the mouth as well as the forelimbs for picking up food, infants who retained their ability to cling to their mothers' fur from their earliest days, and, of course, mothers who retained their fur, and, above all, by the elaboration of militant interdependent social life and group solidarity. It is interesting that when the

70

savannah-dwelling pair, baboon or man, feel endangered, they seek safety in the trees, but when the forest-dwelling pair, chimpanzee or gorilla, seek safety, they fall from the trees to the ground and run away. The four should be paired and compared in this way. When this is done, the contrast of man with baboon is fundamental. The hominids, who remained in the arboreal environment longer and had no time to get the kind of physical changes which allowed the baboons to adapt to life on the grasslands, had to respond to the sudden decrease of open forest by social and behavioral responses rather than by physical ones.

Few hominids were able to deal successfully with this problem of how to live on savannah without the physical equipment for defense and food procurement. There can be no doubt that most failed to meet the challenge and perished. Any observer of the hominids over the last million years of the Pliocene might have seen little hope for hominid survival. Yet some did survive.

How they succeeded must be made clear. It was not by physical changes, such as the growth of fangs or claws, or the development of armor, speed, or great size, or even by the acquisition of some special weapon of a natural kind such as we find in the skunk. Nor did they survive by the making of artifacts, that is tools or weapons. This crisis was faced at least a million years before men learned to make tools or other artifacts such as fire, which might have protected them against predators or have helped to obtain food. We do not, of course, know when men began to use stones or sticks, casually found, to dig up roots for food. But such implements would have been little help for protection against danger from predators. Rather, it is clear that man survived this most critical period in his long history, as he has survived lesser crises since, mostly by changes of behavior. Man was saved by new patterns of action, feelings, and thought, not by new bodily organs or by artifacts of material kinds.

The new behavioral patterns which allowed the hominids to survive the crisis from before 4.5 mil-

71

lion years ago to after one million years ago involved two kinds of behavioral innovations: (1)
increasing cooperation and mutual dependence, including improved communication among members of a
group; and (2) increasing freedom from inherited
patterns of behavior and increasing dependence on
learned behavior, with growing freedom of choice
and decreasing predictability of behavior. Man
survived by cooperation, group communication, and
freedom to use variable and non-predictable behavior, not by physical changes, use of tools or
weapons, nor by rigidity of either organization or
behavior. It is necessary to emphasize this because, ever since and most frequently today, we
find persons who believe that security and survival
can be obtained by weapons, organizational structures, and rigidity of behavior and of loyalties.
What Professor Sherwood Washburn said of baboons,
"The troop is the survival mechanism. To not be
a social animal is to be a dead animal," is even
truer of early man, or of any man (although today
the arrival of death to a non-social man is slower
and perhaps less violent) than it is to baboons.
The reason is that human security in the period
of human origins, or since, is placed more totally
on socialization than on either physical organs
or artifacts.

There were, of course, some genetic changes
in man during that crisis three million years ago.
It might even be argued that all the changes which
took place were possible because of genetic changes.
The point is that we usually think of genetic
changes producing deterministic traits, but in
man the most important genetic changes led to non-
deterministic results, as we shall see. Moreover,
some of the more important deterministic genetic
changes in human evolution did not influence his
obvious external characteristics, such as could
have been observed at the time and might even have
left evidence in the archaeological record, like
head size or body height, but modified less obvious but more fundamental changes in endocrine
secretions and metabolic cycles.

To this point I have discussed human evolution
without using names that have been given to different

72

types of creatures which flourished at different stages in the process. I have simply referred to them all as hominids and have also refrained from giving any firm dates as to when any particular type may have been alive. This has been deliberate and rests on the fact that our knowledge of this subject and our theories about it have been changing so rapidly that any explicit statement made today would be out of date in a few years. Moreover, human evolution occurred as a sequence of roughly six hundred thousand generations of living creatures from the period in the very late Miocene, about 15 million years ago, to the present time. Each generation in that sequence from Ramapithecus to the present differed from its parent and from its offspring by no greater differences than any child differs from its parents today. There were no breaks, and, so far as we know, there were no sudden mutation jumps. Accordingly, we are giving a false impression of distinct differences and of the nature of both our knowledge and theories, when we divide those 600,000 generations up into four or five or six types of creatures, whose names, in the usual binomial form of biological nomenclature, indicate genus and species. Today we know that all types of men form a single species, because we know that individuals from very different types, such as negro and pygmy or pygmy and Chinese, are mutually fertile and can produce fertile offspring (the accepted criterion for species distinction; thus horses and donkeys are regarded as different species, because, while they can produce mules, almost all mules are infertile). But we have no way of knowing if Ramapithecus and modern man, or even Ramapithecus and the Australopithecines could have been mutually fertile or not. Thus the names given by scientists to the subdivisions they may choose to make in the endless chain of human ancestry are quite different from the names that are given by biologists to types of animals alive today. We need such designations in order to talk about the process and to indicate how far along it we are speaking of in any sentence we may write. This is particularly true since our knowledge of the changes which took place is better than our certainty of the dates at which these changes may have happened. But when scientists dispute over how many species of

73

Australopithecines there were, or whether we should admit a type Homo habilis as an intermediary between any Australopithecine species and Homo erectus, they are talking nonsense, especially as we cannot be certain that any one of these is directly descended from any other, nor that any of them is directly ancestral to modern man.

It must be made clear that we can be certain of very little beyond the general trend of what happened, especially as the evidence which has survived in the archaeological record gives us information about the less important changes, such as changes in bones and tools, but provides almost no evidence about the more important matters such as when men began to talk or when men began to provide food for their own children. Even in those matters in which evidence has survived, we cannot be sure when our ancestors first began to use tools or what the surviving tools were used for.

The types which are usually put in the sequence of human evolution are (1) Ramapithecus, an ape; (2) various types of Australopithecines, as links between apes and men; (3) Homo habilis, who may have been the earliest tool-maker; (4) Homo erectus, formerly known as Pithecanthropus; and (5) Homo sapiens, which now includes the former Neanderthal types. The dates of these are still tentative, with Ramapithecus placed about 15 million years ago at the end of the Miocene; the earliest evidence of Australopithecus is almost ten million years later, about 5.5 million years ago, in the Pliocene period near Lake Rudolf. Since varieties of Australopithecus continued to exist until well into the Pleistocene, as late as 1.2 million years ago, there was a period of overlap with Homo habilis, whose earliest evidence may be two million years old. Thus tool-making could be two million years old, while tool-using is probably much older, since it is found among all the apes, although much more commonly among the hominids. The dividing line between the apes and man is not to be found in tool-using or perhaps even in tool-making of a simple kind. There is even increasing evidence that much of the behavior of the African apes is learned rather than instinctive. The primatologists A. Kortlandt and M. Kooij studied this matter and concluded that the behavior of the apes was largely learned; they wrote, "This applies to locomotion, nest building, food choice, sexual behavior, social intercourse, etc., and, to some extent, even to maternal care." The great gap between man and other primates came with the development of language and the growth of conceptualization and abstract thought which followed. This has left little evidence in the archaeological record and thus cannot be dated, but it certainly goes back to Homo erectus, the type of hominid which prevailed for most of the Pleistocene, that is the last two million years at least. Modern man, whom we call Homo sapiens, is very recent, probably less than 100,000 years old.

There were three chief areas of activity in which human evolution took place: survival, food procurement, and sex. Although our concern is with security and thus with survival, the three cannot be separated, for individual survival was of little significance unless it was joined to eating and reproduction. Both of these latter in turn influenced individual survival on a reciprocal basis. For a very long time, man was an omnivorous gatherer, wandering about, either erratically or on regular routes, eating whatever turned up. He was not a hunter on a systematic basis until relatively late, say after 700,000 B.C. As a gatherer, he was a semi-scavenger, and thus in a certain degree of competition with other scavengers. In this, perhaps relatively less significant, aspect of food procurement, increased size could be a benefit, and the evidence shows a fairly steady increase in size of men for much of human history, until the later Pleistocene period. In sexual changes, little is revealed by archaeology, but the greatest event in this area was the loss of any connection between the estrus cycle and the ovulation cycle in the female, or perhaps this should be worded as the disappearance of the first of these and the increased frequency of the second. In the earlier arrangements human females must have been like other primates, willing to accept sexual activities from a male only when in estrus, with production of the ovum for fertilization at that same period. In the course of human evolution, probably in the Homo erectus stage, the estrus cycle was replaced by constant sexual interest and activities, and the frequency of ovulation (the menstrual period) increased from yearly or seasonally to monthly. This became the basis of the human family, since it tied male and female to each other on a more permanent basis, developing through food-sharing to love and joint care of offspring. These activities of food-sharing and child-caring became more necessary, as men had to range more and more widely to find food, carrying their infants with them. This wide-ranging character of human life is of great importance since it required that the hands be free to carry food or children, and thus made man a bipedal walker. This meant that man, for much of his history, was relatively few in numbers but of very wide geographical distribution, moving constantly, so that, being few, he never became a target of predation, and, moving constantly, he remained a single species over most of the whole world. All three of these human activities are interrelated and cannot be discussed separately.

The chief subject of confusion is the question of predation, which is so closely linked to human survival and has been totally misunderstood by those who would portray early men as violent, carnivorous hunters. This misunderstanding is pervasive in our society and includes both the nature of "wild" nature and the nature of predation. The whole history of man, and especially Western man, has been a series of steps by which he has become more alienated from nature. These steps have included the beginnings of language and conceptualized thinking; the development of culture, especially artifacts, as a buffer area between man and nature; the development of agriculture, including domestic animals, as part of culture; and the appearance of transcendental deity outside of nature as a religious belief. These and other steps in the same direction have made it very difficult for Western man to see what nature is really like.

We have seen nature as "wilderness," as something wild, dangerous, and unfriendly, even as a precinct outside the area of godliness and decency and as an area of violence and bestiality. That last word itself reveals our misconceptions, for bestial behavior is not found among beasts but among men.

It is quite untrue that organic nature is casually and persistently violent and destructive. On the contrary, violence and destruction in living nature is, except in rare cases, restrained within narrow and limited boundaries to such an extent that it is almost ritualized. One of the weaknesses of our Western outlook is our failure to see how nature is covered with a network of behavioral restraints and how, in consequence, much natural behavior, including food getting, mating, defense, aggression, rearing of the young, and inter-individual behavior is ritualized.

This ritualization of behavior is particularly significant among the carnivores (with the exception of man), who form a late and relatively specialized group in nature. These do not casually kill, although they are fully capable of doing so, but kill under sharply defined restrictions of time, place, necessity, species of victims, and methods of operation.

As it happened, the period in which the primates (with numerous other families and even orders) were in decline and man was developing, was also the period in which a number of other biological groups were proliferating. These include the birds, the ungulates, the rodents, and the carnivores. The last of these developed their specialized methods of food procurement (with specialized teeth to go with these) in terms of the other groups which were increasing with them, especially with the ungulates and the rodents. Of these two, the history of the ungulates is more immediately important for the history of man because the expansion of this group, like that of man himself, was a consequence of the expansion of the savannah grasslands on the earth's surface. It was this expansion of the ungulates, and, to a lesser extent, of the rodents, which made possible the accompanying expansion of the carnivores during the late Tertiary and early Quaternary.

In this expansion, man occupied one angle of a triangular relationship, in which the carnivores and the ungulates occupied the other two angles. There was, however, in this triangle, an early and

77

established relationship between the ungulates and
the carnivores, while there was no established relationship between man and either of the others.
In fact, man was the neglected angle of this triangle, since he was of no importance to the carnivores and, for a long time, was not capable of killing the ungulates himself. Both of these facts
made human survival easier.

There is a well established relationship between any carnivore and its prey species, namely
that the prey is always very much more numerous
than the predator, both forming part of the biological pyramid of living things in which grass is
more plentiful than grass-eaters and such herbivores are more plentiful than the carnivores who
prey on them. Man, until quite recently, was always a relatively rare animal. On the African grasslands, where man developed, the ungulates were numerous, tasty, easily found, and acted in predictable
ways, especially when attacked, while man was rare,
not particularly meaty or (apparently) edible,
difficult to kill, and acted in unpredictable ways,
especially when attacked. As a consequence, the
African carnivores developed patterns for hunting
the ungulates and did not develop patterns for
hunting men. And, for complex reasons we cannot
go into here, man was in even less danger from carnivores in Asia, Europe, and ultimately in America.

Thus man was never in any danger as a species
from carnivore predators, and even as individuals
men have always been extremely safe from their at-
tentions. Population numbers of human groups have
probably never been influenced by carnivores, even
in places like India and parts of Africa where unarmed native gardeners have lived close to the
greatest carnivores like tigers or lions. In
Africa the only real danger to men has been from
crocodiles, as in India it has been from poisonous
snakes, both dangers arising from the customs of
the natives and not from the nature of the danger
itself. It is true that "man-eating" tigers or
lions have rarely appeared. In both cases these
are aberrations, the tigers being old or crippled
and thus unable to hunt, the lions, apparently
turning to eat humans only in the case of unsexualized

young males who turned to human flesh as a response to their emotional problems and may have become addicted to human cadavers.

This view of African predators may seem strange to many readers, because until recently we have been indoctrinated by sensational journalists and other writers and by the cinema with the perils of the African wilderness. We have been filled with lies about the Dark Continent, the intrepid explorers who opened it up, and the courageous sportsmen who followed them. The only dangers encountered by the explorers came, not from wild animals, but from fever and other humans. Except for these two, it has always been perfectly safe to walk alone from Cape to Cairo, and numerous persons have done this. By "perfectly safe" here, I mean safer than a solitary walk in almost any American city today. Carl E. Akeley, who collected the animals for the Roosevelt African Hall at the American Museum of Natural History in New York and some of the animals in the Field Museum in Chicago, as well as for other places, devoted his life and many of his writings, including his book, In Brightest Africa (1923), to changing the mistaken popular picture of Africa and its animals. Others have followed in his footsteps, but, in cases like this, the work of many scientific students can be overturned in a brief period by a single unscientific sensationalist like Robert Ardrey.

What is true of Africa is also true of other places where early men spread and increased in numbers. In the temperate zone, the wolf has been given a totally undeserved reputation as a deadly danger to humans. This is untrue. The greatest contemporary authorities on the wolf in America have been unable to find a single case in history of a man being killed or even attacked by a wolf. In Europe, where the record is more complex, all cases of attacks by wolves on humans seem to have occurred because the animals were rabid. Certainly, in all of history it would seem that more persons have been killed by domestic dogs than by wild wolves. The most dangerous predator on man would seem to have been the bear (in America, the grizzly).

Predation is universally misunderstood by all

79

except a few experts. It is never a threat to a prey species and is usually beneficial to it, strengthening it by eliminating the old, the weak or sick, the careless and erratic, and the young, but not the mature and healthy breeding population. A lifelong student of the subject, the American, Paul Errington, concluded just before his death that any persistent predator is beneficial because it performs a necessary culling operation.

This seems to be true in Africa. Of course, we do not know much about the behavior of the African predators in the days when man was first beginning, but from what we know about their physical remains and from what we know about predation in general and about today's African predators, it would seem that early men were in greater danger of going hungry themselves than of being eaten by someone else. Today, each African carnivore has developed its own pattern for obtaining food: the leopard, like the tiger of Asia, a solitary hunter in the forest or on its edges; lions cooperative hunters on the grasslands and open forest; wild dogs pack killers at night on the savannah. All of these can be avoided by man, and, as I have said, early man's chief method for dealing with danger was to avoid it. One way in which this was done was by venturing on the grassland in the heat of the day, as in a restricted sense the baboon does. Man is one of the few animals who has developed an effective bodily mechanism for dissipating metabolic heat, by eliminating hair, replacing this with an elaborate development of sweat glands in a darkened skin (I do not mean by "darkened skin" the specialized and relatively recent development of negro skin). Dogs, for example, have a very poor mechanism for this purpose and thus have to lie under cover in the heat of the day in Africa.

Another way, and probably the chief one, by which early men avoided predators was by cooperative action, including study of the existing predators. Not only did men cooperate in seeking safety and food, they also communicated with each other and thus were able to build up a shared social tradition and steadily accumulating body of knowledge on these vital matters. What this could mean in terms of security can be seen by taking the lion as an example.

The lion's method of attack is known as "stalk and pounce." One or several lions, or more likely lionesses, creep up on a potential victim, using every available bit of cover and moving only when the prey is not looking, until the distance between has been reduced to forty yards or less. Then, when the target is not looking, the lion makes a rush at high speed, leaping at the animal's neck and closing its jaws on the neck or base of the head, putting its nearest paw over the neck or back and its off paw under the neck or head to pull these toward it. The victim hears the sound of the rush and panics, darting forward. The success of the strike depends on how soon the victim hears the lion and begins to move, because, if it hears soon enough, it will move so far forward before the lion hits that he will land too far back to deliver a killing blow. Such a blow generally requires that his jaws close on a vulnerable part of the head or neck, killing either by bleeding or suffocation, but in most kills the cause of death is a broken neck, suffered when the lion hits just as the prey darts forward and the lion immediately pulls the head and neck toward himself with his off paw which went under the neck; in this case the combined impetus of the victim's panic and the lion's charge, with the pulled neck and head, throws the animal to the ground with the lion on top of its neck, the jaws locked in a fatal grip. If the neck breaks, the victim dies at once; otherwise, the lion simply lies there until the victim dies from the bite. In those cases where the prey heard the charge sooner, the lion generally hits the target too far back either to get a fatal bite or to throw its victim to the ground. In such a case, the lion lets go almost at once and allows the prey to escape, usually to the care of the hyenas that night. Since the lion must not only kill with its jaws but hold the victim with these also, failure to get a fatal bite at the first hit makes it difficult to shift to a more effective bite without releasing it, which often allows it to get away, if it has not been thrown to the ground. If it has been thrown down, it frequently goes into shock and is helpless. The point is that the lion's charge is a missile from short range, and if it misses a fatal hit, little effort is made to pursue the game. A lion rarely hits from the front because it will not charge a victim which is looking at it; if it does, it tries for a strangulation bite on the throat. With a zebra or a large antelope, this could be dangerous, as the lion could be trampled by the prey's front hooves.

Safety against a lion rests on the fact that he will not charge more than about forty yards and will not attack a victim who is looking at him. As George Schaller said, "A seen lion is a safe lion." Thus a group of humans who know this can be safe, if some members of the group always keep any lions in view and do not allow any to get too close. Such knowledge requires group experience and some method of intra-group communication to pass such knowledge along from person to person and from gen- eration to generation. It was knowledge and communi- cations such as this, which builds up to group tradi- tions and individual learning, which provided secur- ity for man in the early stages of his development from an ape in trees to a man on the ground.

The same kind of traditions also provided food for early man. If the threat to early man from predators was less than is usually believed, the difficulties of the food quest were probably much greater. The savannah may have been covered with grass-eating ungulates as well as meat-eating car- nivores, but neither was a major factor in the lives of the incipient humans. On the grasslands, the supply of fruit, nuts, insects, nests with young birds or eggs, was less than it had been in the ex- tensive forests which were now dwindling. But the reduced forest areas were forcing the hominids out of the forest onto the grasslands, at the same time that they were being forced out of nature and into culture by being compelled to replace innate be- havior with learned behavior. This ejection was compelled by the food quest, and this had little to do with the needs of security. In fact, the two were working in opposite directions. Security alone would have retained man in the trees, no matter how small the grove of trees became, and he undoubtedly did return to the trees at night for safety and continued to do so for generations, as the baboons still do. But food, as the baboons have discovered, could not be provided by a grove of trees, or even by a small tract of forest. In order to remain in forest, man required very extensive tracts large enough to contain such a great variety of food-producing trees that some kind would be ripening or available in all weeks of the year. Man was already omnivorous, but even with a diet of fruit, nuts, insects, and casually found eggs, nestlings, reptiles, rodents, tortoises, and injured or young animals, he would have to range over very extensive forests with a great variety of trees.

Failure of the forests forced man out onto the grasslands, where he found additional kinds of food, especially roots and tubers, as well as more accessible nests and animal young "frozen" in their forms in the grass. The search for these not only required knowledge, which could only be acquired by socially transferred knowledge and traditions, but also required that man cover large areas of ground and do so, for safety, with his head above grass-level. These requirements gave man the nearest thing he has to a physical specialization: he became the world's greatest walker, and a bipedal walker at that.

This specialty as one of the world's greatest walkers kept man moving in small bands over the earth's surface, in a search for food. These bands, as I have said, moved so constantly that they covered a major portion of the earth's surface, in constant encounters with other similar bands, so that constant interbreeding over huge areas kept man a single species for most or even all of his history. Such encounters were almost certainly friendly for hundreds of thousands of years, with individuals shifting bands as they wished, especially for sexual purposes. In time such breeding out of the group may have been institutionalized by incest taboos and established exogamy. Recent studies of children brought up in a kibbutz show that they almost never marry each other, apparently because their childhood intimacy prevents them from experiencing sexual attraction after puberty. Thus the practice of exogamy as an early social rule in human history probably required no rule but was a normal consequence of permissiveness within the group. This was more likely

83

because there was at that time little economic division
of labor and, without hunting, women were probably
even more productive of food than men, as seems to
be the case among gathering economies today.

Cooperation, mutuality, sharing, and intra-group
communication remained the keynotes of all three of
the activities so necessary to human survival in
that early period (food gathering, defense, and
child-rearing), as they still are today among the
bushmen and pygmies. Bushmen, for example, are incapable of eating alone and share food no matter how
little it is. When questioned about this and asked
what would happen, in a time of hunger, if a member
of the group found food and hid it to reserve it for
himself, they could not imagine such a thing and
roared with laughter at the suggestion; when the
questioner pressed the point, they refused to believe that it could happen and said that any person
who would think of doing such a thing was not a human
being (that is, a bushman) but an animal.

Some such way must have operated among early
men, although it must be recognized that these two
kinds of gatherers (bushmen and pygmies) are far in
advance of early men, since they have been forced
by pressures from more advanced humans into deserts
and jungle and have been able to cope with these conditions because they have advanced tools and artifacts, such as bows and arrows, arrow poisons, fire,
and very sophisticated knowledge of the resources of
the local environment, all of which early men lacked.

These things came to early men in time, especially
the most important, familiarity with local botany, especially knowledge of what grassland products were
edible and how they could be obtained. It is worth
noting that a surprisingly large part of the diet of
baboons and of bushmen comes from roots, tubers, and
rhizomes which cannot be found without special knowledge of the local botany and a capacity for classification of plants, at least into edible and inedible.
In some cases, the roots of such plants, often a
large nutritious object far beneath a wisp-like and
unpromising-looking plant, cannot be obtained without
arduous digging. Neither baboons nor men have any
adequate natural equipment for such digging. After

lengthy observation of baboon behavior in the field, S.L. Washburn and Irven De Vore concluded that a very large increase in food procurement would result if baboons adopted very slight behavior changes such as systematic search for eggs or nestlings or the young of animals hiding in the grass, or even by the most casual use of sticks for digging roots. It is very likely that these are just what our early ancestors did to obtain food.

Tool using, especially for digging, probably went on for well over a million years before rudimentary tool making began, probably before 3 million B.C. These earliest shaped tools, usually called pebble tools, were probably used for sharpening digging sticks, but may have been used also for digging or even for smashing bones or separating meat obtained from scavenging. In any case, these stone objects are tools and not weapons and were not capable of contributing anything to defense or to hunting.

In this way several million years passed (say from about 3.5 million to about 700,000 B.C.), during which the hominids changed from Australopithecine to Homo erectus, moved farther along the road from innate to learned behavior, increased their skills in communication with each other, and greatly improved their knowledge of their natural environment. The most important change of the period, however, was one that left no traces in the archaeological record and has obtained little attention from the students of human evolution, although the four successive editions of Theodosius Dobzhansky's Genetics and the Origin of Species (1937-1971; the fourth edition is called Genetics of the Evolutionary Process) have shown increasing emphasis on this process as an element in human evolution.

I refer to the growing indeterminism of the human genetic endowment. Most people today are aware of the process of selection by which biological evolution works: the line of each individual as well as that of each partially segregated human group has a pool of genes, each capable of establishing some trait in a deterministic way, if the occasion for the emergence of that trait arises. In each generation, and indeed in each individual's

85

life, there is a selective process which establishes
what offspring will be produced and survive to reproduce. This process of selection is usually conceived in terms of long survival or early death,
although, of course, the real issue is not how long
an individual lives but how many children he has
and whether they reproduce. In any case, it is
assumed that the genes in question, whether they
pass on or not, are deterministic of specific traits
to be indeterminant, that is that a gene may not be
determinant of a specific trait but could be indeterminant for a broad spectrum of traits. To be
specific, there could be selection of a gene carrying the possibility that the phenotype would be in
a range of tallness from five feet two inches to
five feet ten inches and rejection (and loss from
the pool of genes) of a gene with a much narrower
range, say from 64 to 66 inches only. This selection
for broader indeterminism of the phenotype is the
most essential feature of human evolution and is the
reason why man moved almost completely from a creature with largely innate behavior to a creature with
almost completely learned behavior.

The distinction between genotype and phenotype
is, of course, evident in all living creatures, both
plants and animals. We all recognize this in our
assumption that the size, weight, activity, longev-
ity and other traits depend to a great extent on the
experience of the individual as he grows, especially
his diet and physical environment. We also recognize the element of learned behavior in all animals,
although few people realize what a large part of the
behavior of even the lowest form of life is learned.
We may be familiar with the fact that pet turtles or
goldfish will come for food if they are trained to
respond to a certain signal, such as striking the
edge of their tank with the food package, but it is
a surprise to most people to learn that some bird
songs are learned, or that a chimpanzee does not
know how to perform sexual intercourse, how to hold
its newborn young, or how to nurse it, unless it has
seen these things done by other chimpanzees, since
these actions are, apparently, not "instinctive,"
although the drive to do them may be innate but
undirected.

In man's case the selective evolutionary process moved in an increasingly indeterministic direction in respect to the relationship between the phenotype and its genotype, much more so in respect to behavior than to physical appearance, and in physical traits much more so in respect to the non-visible than to the visible features. At the same time, the gene pool in any individual or group became increasingly varied and diverse.

There were four reasons for these changes. One was that man spread so widely over the world that he was subject to a great variety of terrain, climate, food, and general environment. A second was that he continued to move, thus continually exchanging genes and mixing gene pools. A third was that growing mutual dependence and need for others led to altruistic conduct and mutual care which allowed divergent, aberrant, injured, and even incompetent types to live, and even to breed. This last process has, of course, continued to the present and is now one of the chief consequences of contemporary medical science and social welfare policy. As a result the cliche theories of nineteenth century evolutionary theory were quite inapplicable to man from his beginnings, without, apparently, the dire consequences which those theorists expected. This means that the culling operation which is performed in nature by predation not only was not performed in culture, but that the nature of human culture worked in the opposite direction by protecting and preserving the culls.

The fourth and last of the causes of this process was the fact that the Pleistocene period, covering the last two or three million years, was an age of drastic and often rapid changes, especially in climate and thus in man's biological environment, both botanical and zoological. These changes led to great migratory movements of men, seeking to follow their accustomed environment as it moved about the earth, especially by changes in latitude, or in some cases remaining in a locality as its conditions changed in an effort to cope with the changes by cultural adaptation. Thus the Pleistocene was a period of surging migrations and drastic modifications of men, plants, and animals, and of increasing cultural diversity.

87

The basis of these great climate changes of the Pleistocene was that there were four great glacial ages in it, each with major and minor advances and retreats of the ice, separated by interglacial periods in which the climate of our "temperate zones" was often much warmer than today. The glacial ice as it advanced and retreated came down the altitudes of high mountains, even on the equator, as well as down the latitudes from the polar ice cap. In doing so, it brought the polar high pressure zone southward, pushing the temperate zone westerly rain belt southward to the sub-tropical latitudes, so that these experienced pluvial periods during the glacial ages and long dry spells during the interglacial ages. These pluvials served to build up grasses, animals, and men in sub-tropical areas, like the Sahara and Arabia, later killing them off or driving them out in the inter-pluvials, just as Europe and continental Asia did in the interglacial and glacial periods. Thus human populations were built up, partly destroyed, and pushed around the Old World landmass, as well as forced to adapt to changing conditions, while being cut off in segregated gene pools in the glacial periods and subsequently mixed together again in the interglacial periods. This last condition arose from the fact that the glaciers came down altitudes as well as latitudes, closing mountain passes during the glaciers so that, for example, areas like the Far East, central Asia, the European plain, and the Mediterranean were sometimes cut off from each other at the heights of the glacial ages. On the other hand, open corridors through the ice, such as that across the European plain from west to east or that from north China to Alaska and south to the American Great Plains east of the Canadian Rockies, became important migration routes for glacial and tundra herbivores and for the men who hunted them, especially in the fourth glacial age.

Absolute dating of these subdivisions of the Pleistocene period is now very tentative, more so than forty years ago when we believed that the whole Pleistocene lasted only about a million years. Now that that period has been extended to more than 2.5 million years, we are much less sure of its subdivisions. The four glacial ages still seem to be con-

88

centrated in the last half of it, with the second
and third glaciers much more intense and the first
glacier by far the least cold. All four had fluctuations which complicate the problem, but the
fourth lasted more than 75,000 years, with two
or three peaks, and ended in Europe about 12,000
B.C. The second and third glaciers may have lasted
about twice as long as the fourth, were separated
from it by the third interglacial period, which
could have been as much as 100,000 or more years
and were separated from each other by the second
or Great Interglacial period, which could have been
up to 300,000 years long. Of the first glacier and
the following first interglacial period we can say
very little, but the glacier could have been no more
than 50,000 years and, indeed, traces of it cannot
be found in many places, while the ensuing first interglacial might have been no more than 100,000 years.
The short period since the fourth European glacier
retreated to Scandinavia and to the heights of the
Alps and the Caucasus is known as the Holocene,
but might be a fourth interglacial period; it has
lasted only about 13,000 years so far.

    These figures add up to less than a total of a
million years since the advent of the first glacier
and are certainly too brief, but they will give the
reader some idea of the divisions of time and the
climate conditions in which his Homo erectus ancestry was creating human culture. The Homo sapiens
type of man, in which we classify all men living today, probably originated in the Sahara area in its
fourth pluvial period, during the fourth European
glacial age. We must not make too much of the advent of Homo sapiens, as his differences from late
Homo erectus are not that significant. Moreover,
the evolution of man and his culture in the pre-
sapiens period was certainly much more important
than anything which has happened since, although
it is difficult for our egocentric minds to admit
this. If we do admit it, it may signify no more
than the fact that changes which covered several
million years are likely to be greater than those
covering less than 80,000 years.

    If we look at all the changes of human history,
it is clear that there never was a time in which

change was not taking place. Nevertheless, we may
if we wish speak of three revolutionary periods in
human history in which drastic shifts of direction
took place. The first of these I have spoken of as
the great crisis of about three million years ago,
in which ape became man, was driven from the forest
to the savannah, and was forced out of nature into
culture. The second of these great revolutionary
periods occurred less than a million years ago and
is marked by the fact that man moved from the gathering stage to what I call "the Heroic Hunting" stage.
The third great revolutionary stage has been going
on since man became an agriculturalist about 10,000
years ago, and its chief event was the discovery of
civilization as an organizational form (with writing,
city life, and the state) about 4000 years ago.

We have discussed the first of these revolutions
in an incomplete and cursory fashion, from which the
reader might gather that it has nothing significant
to contribute to the subject of weapons and political
stability, since there were no weapons and there was
really no political life. On the contrary, however,
this early and lengthy period has a good deal to
contribute to our subject, firstly by establishing
that man is not by nature violent, but rather the
contrary, and, secondly, that human social needs
for other people, so much neglected today, can be
used to replace what we regard as political life
and do so by persuading people to subject their individual wills to the group for the sake of internalized social and emotional rewards, rather than
from the pressures of an external power structure,
as we consider normal today. As this book progresses, we shall see that on most occasions in
human life such internalized controls supplement
externalized political controls, at least for large
portions of the population and that on numerous occasions such internalized controls take over more
or less completely, when external systems of force
and power break down.

Before we turn to the second great revolution
in human history, we might point out that we live,
without much thinking about it, with many survivals
of this early period of human history. For example,
the human digestive system is largely a creation of

90

this period, with the major exceptions of the mechanisms for digesting protein, fat, and milk, which largely developed later. The relatively great length of the human digestive tract reflects man's complex dietary history, but is that of a herbivore rather than of a carnivore, since the latter is usually rather short and less complex. Moreover, unlike most herbivores, the digestive system of man is adapted to starch consumption rather than herbage in general. Interestingly enough, the history of human diet can be dimly traced along his digestive tract. His teeth derive from his omnivorous diet while yet an ape living largely on fruit, insects, and nuts, to which his teeth are still well adapted. The hominid shift to the grasslands added many starchy roots to his diet, a change which is reflected in the presence of the enzyme ptyalin in human saliva to split starches into sugar, a notably non-carnivore feature. The mechanisms for digesting protein, milk, and fats are found much lower in the digestive system, the last two mostly in the intestines; and the facility for digestion of milk is still missing from many humans, since this item, for adult consumption, was added very late in man's dietary history, after about 4000 B.C. and only in certain areas (not, for example, in China). It is likely that human protein and fat digestion was improved and extended as part of the evolution of the Heroic Hunting cultures, which we are about to discuss. In the Neolithic stage (after about 8000 B.C.) starch once again became the chief element in the human diet, but the digestive system was already prepared for it. Milk became available in the Neolithic, but did not become a major or chief element in the diet until certain peoples adopted a largely pastoral way of life after 4000 B.C.

The advent of heroic hunting as a way of life may be attributed to the Homo erectus type of man, almost certainly on a grassy or very open forest terrain, and in the period from the second glacial, through the Great Interglacial, and into the third glacial period. Since the change probably occurred in Africa, we should perhaps say "pluvial" instead of "glacial." The changes involved in this revolution did not occur all at once, or even in a brief period, but extended over about half a million

91

years (say, 700,000 to about 200,000 B.C.) and over
an area from Africa to the Far East. It may have
begun with the "invention" of the spear, which we
can neither date nor place and may have culminated
with the controlled use of fire, which we can date
in China during the second glacial age (about
350,000 B.C.). The use of fire allowed men for the
first time to live in caves by denying access to
cave bears, but it did not reach Europe until late
in the Great Interglacial, came into use in the Near
East only in the fourth glacial (about 100,000), and
did not spread to Africa until after about 80,000 B.C.

The spear cannot be dated or placed because it
is an obvious invention like the wooden club which
went with it, was made of wood which is perishable
except under very unusual conditions which are found
in Europe, but are quite unusual in Africa or south
Asia, and is not so important in itself as an invention but rather in the discovery of how to use
it for hunting big game. It is this latter discovery,
rather than the spear itself, which we call "Heroic
Hunting." The oldest evidence we have of such a
hunt is so elaborate that we cannot consider it an
early example. It was at an extensive ancient elephant butchering ground at Torralba, Spain, where
an elephant migration trail passed close enough to
a morass for a large number of hunters to drive the
herd into the soft ground where the beasts could be
killed more easily while they were hampered by the
poor footing. With the bones, dating from the last
stage of the second glacial period, were 28 pieces
of wood which seemed to be broken parts of wooden
spears. Considerably later are two positive spears,
both made of yew wood. Of these, the earlier is a
piece over 15 inches long, found at Clacton, Essex,
England, and dated to the Great Interglacial; the
other, dated from the third interglacial, was found
with the remains of a dismembered Elephas antiquus,
near Lehringen, Lower Saxony. This example was 96
inches long, with flutings at the lower end running
to the fire-hardened point, and had been driven between the ribs of the dead elephant. The number of
stone implements of Levalloisian IV type lying
about the elephant's head showed that many persons
participated in the hunt, although clearly not the
great number which were engaged in the earlier
great hunt at Torralba, Spain.

The significant point here, as elsewhere, is not
the spear, which must have been invented long before,
but the fact that a large number of men cooperated
on such an elaborate hunt and the fact that the
elaborateness of the hunt was possible from the
fact that the site was a very valuable possession
because of the fact that the migration route of
the elephants passed close to a morass into which
the animals could be driven for slaughter. The
whole situation implies good communication within
the group and careful planning. The latter requires the use of verbal symbols so that elephants
could be talked about when not present and men
could discuss what they were going to do beforehand. All of this indicates that man had, by about
450,000 years ago, reached a point where his mind
was totally different from any animal mind we know.
Such a mind implies a very long background of verbal symbolizing and conceptual thinking, and an even
longer background of increasingly elaborate social
organization.

We do not have any direct evidence of the social organization and anything to say about that
will be largely inferential, but we do have evidence
of the growing complexity of the human mind and that
the direction of that complexity was toward verbal
symbolization and conceptual thinking. This evidence is to be found in the growing size of the
human skull.

The growing size of the human skull over a period of several million years must imply growing
size and probably complexity of the brain within
that skull. Phillip V. Tobias' recent careful
study of this subject (1971: The Brain in Hominid
Evolution) shows that the mean cranial capacity of
the available samples increased from 494 cubic
centimeters for the Australopithecus africanus to
656 cubic centimeters for Homo habilis; to 859
cubic centimeters for Homo erectus erectus; to
1043 cubic centimeters for Homo erectus pekinensis;
to 1350 cubic centimeters for Homo sapiens. Not
only did the size of the skull and presumably of
the brain increase over the whole span of several
million years, but the range of size for each successive type increased, and there was an accelera-

93

tion of the rate of increase with the appearance and development of Homo erectus from the latter part of the Lower Pleistocene onward. This development continued into the early stage of Homo sapiens in the Upper Pleistocene, but has ceased and even dropped somewhat since about 60,000 years ago, when human mean brain size seems to have reached its peak. Tobias believes that the tendency was most strong with Homo erectus and attributes it to "factors such as the rise of systematic stone tool-making, organized and systematic hunting, and symbolic behavior including symbolic speech" (p. 99). This could be worded in a number of different ways, one of which would be that the increasing trend toward learned behavior required more mental activity because it required more decision-making.

The shift in economic activity from gathering to hunting had many other consequences. It shifted the diet toward increased protein consumption and, because of its strenuous character, reduced the role of women in food getting and made them economically more dependent on men. This was much more of a change than might appear at first glance, because the earlier technique of food gathering was an activity at which women were at least as good as men, and were, in fact, probably somewhat superior. This was replaced by a situation of very substantial inferiority, in spite of the fact that food gathering by females continued to play a considerable role in total food procurement for the community, if we can judge from the study of modern hunting peoples. One reason for the drastic shift in the social position of the sexes in regard to each other was the increased size of the human skull. Like so many drastic changes in evolutionary processes, several apparently independent changes were mutually reinforcing. The increase in the size of the head made childbirth more difficult and gave a selective advantage to any woman who did not carry her unborn infant to full term, as it also gave an advantage to any infant whose cranial sutures closed belatedly. The net result was that infants were born somewhat more prematurely and the period of gestation was probably somewhat shortened. This meant that the infant was more helpless than previously, was more dependent on the mother and for a longer period.

94

Thus from this cause also both mother and child became more dependent on the male hunter.

Clearly this process could not have succeeded unless the establishment of relations between male and female in a family bound together by economic need, emotional dependence, sexual commitment, and personal affection had occurred. This certainly began much earlier, but the exogamous, nuclear family was undoubtedly solidified as the primary social grouping by these fundamental changes over half a million years ago. However, some larger organizational system than the nuclear family was needed to get together the larger number of men needed for heroic hunting of large herd animals. Although we have no direct evidence, it seems clear, from the study of recent hunting peoples, that that larger grouping must have been based on kinship. We have suggested that exogamy probably was established relatively quite early in human evolution, at a time when the sexes were socially equal and when the cooperative group and the nuclear family were probably the only forms of social organization. As female dependence increased with the growth of heroic hunting, virilocal mating, in which the female comes to reside with the male, became established. Some recent students such as Elman R. Service have suggested that exogamous marriage and virilocal residence together could lead to larger and more permanent social groups by customary exchange of women between moieties, the latter forming parts of a larger, relatively permanent social organization which might include hundreds of persons and thus could provide dozens, or possibly a few scores, of men for more elaborate heroic hunting activities. The pressures to form such larger organizations would soon have become more than simple economic convenience because of the introduction of a new element in human life: weapons and warfare. Before we look at this, we must take a closer look at the economic activities which called it forth.

To hunters who have the spear and the club but still lack the bow or arrow poisons, it is inefficient to hunt small animals such as rabbits or squirrels, or any animals which can easily escape into woods or rocks for concealment or refuge. The most efficient

95

use of a spear in hunting is against large grass-eating herd animals of open forest or savannah. Such hunting requires large numbers of men because the animals have the option to move in any direction on the grassland; they must be pinned down, distracted, surrounded. It is true that men are such efficient walkers and have such a good metabolism that a few men can "walk down" grazing animals simply by concentrating on one animal and following it persistently so that it does not have time to graze and eventually runs out of fuel. But this technique is not one which can be used for a regular supply of human food, especially as the hunter may catch up with his victim, a large and heavy beast, many miles from his hungry dependents. Thus heroic hunting as a way of life required large groups of men. Such groups could get vast amounts of meat in group drives of animals into narrow defiles, over cliffs, into swampy or very soft ground, as at Torralba, or, in the later Pleistocene, in fire-drives.

This new hunting technique reduced the need for relatively aimless wandering over vast areas and permitted more systematic hunting over more limited areas. As such hunting techniques improved, fear arose that the game might be reduced, move away, or just disappear, leading to anxiety about the reproduction of game animals and a whole nexus of ideas about luck, taboos, animal spirits, and the role of the male in reproduction. The same fear resulted in growing efforts to exclude those who were not members of the local hunting group from its hunting grounds. Thus territoriality appeared and with it the beginnings of warfare over territory. This was especially likely when such hunting grounds included spots such as have been mentioned where animals congregated or had to pass in their migrations between feeding grounds.

The beginnings of the possibility of warfare increased the need for a larger group with more males and gave an advantage to any group which could find some principle of loyalty or allegiance wider than the simple social cooperation and conjugal attachment which had been sufficient for the earlier gatherers. This principle of allegiance, found in a wider conception of kinship, gave solidarity to the in-group at the same time that it excluded the outsiders. It was a belief which could be accepted by both as justification for group solidarity and mutual animosity regardless of the truth of the whole situation.

Thus began one of the most pervasive influences in subsequent human history, the triumph of subjective ideas, especially human systems of categorization, over objective actuality and the competition between groups based on these as the chief element in the need and achievement of security. The convergence on kinship as the key to this effort gave rise to elaborate and complicated methods of dividing people of any group into relationships, reflected chiefly in the names which various peoples devised to talk or merely to think about such relationships. The study of such relationships and terms forms a major part of the anthropological examination of the cultures of primitive peoples. We do not have to go into this complex and disputed subject, except to say that, once virilocal residence was established, patrilineal descent relationships could be used to recognize wider loyalty groupings on a kinship basis, at first perhaps on the basis of the male descendants of a living ancestor and later, forming a much larger group, of the male descendants of the most remote remembered ancestor. In any case, any loyalty grouping based on kinship has limits and, as we shall see, can be exceeded in size and thus in power by loyalty groupings based on some other principle such as common religious belief.

The establishment of such loyalty groupings, by establishing divisions among peoples and restricting social contacts across loyalty barriers, fostered linguistic diversity, so that separate dialects and eventually separate languages developed. But crossbreeding remained sufficient to maintain man in a single species, although as the Pleistocene went on into the Holocene very different physical types, on a regional but not on a tribal or kinship basis, appeared. In places where game was scarcer or more difficult to obtain, and population was accordingly more widely scattered, rivalries between kinship, linguistic, or tribal groupings were sometimes suspended at certain seasons of the year to allow courting and marriage across the barriers of group loyalties, thus avoiding too close inbreeding and adding some variety of women within the territorial or tribal group. In a few cases marriage by capture may have occurred, but this certainly was never a general rule.

The struggles between hunting tribes over hunting grounds were usually symbolic or ritualistic in nature rather than fights to the death. Such struggles frequently began as an intrusion by an alien group, a challenge and confrontation by the local group, perhaps a clash in which someone was hurt or some blood was spilled, followed by withdrawal by the intruders. Certainly, for most of the prehistoric period, hunting territories and game were not so scarce nor men so numerous that there was ever any rational reason for extended warfare or for fights to the death between tribal groups. In most periods of human history, exploitation of natural resources to satisfy human needs could be achieved with less expenditure of energy and with less danger, even in less desirable territories. In other words, war has never been a rational solution for obtaining resources to satisfy man's material needs. That is why even the most undesirable areas of the globe, such as the Arctic, the Australian and Kalihari deserts, and jungles like the Matto Grosso have been inhabited and used.

But of course, men have never been rational. They are fully capable of believing anything and of adopting any kind of social organization or social goals, so that warfare became at least a minor part of life in most societies where hunting large game animals was a significant portion of economic activities. To justify such warfare, many different theories and customs arose, including tribal initiations for the young, head-hunting, ritual cannibalism of enemy corpses, and other strange activities. On the whole, these were rarely, if ever, a significant part of the processes by which real human needs were satisfied.

While patrilineal, patriarchal, warlike, hunting groups spread on grasslands and in open forest, over the last half million years, other groups which did not adopt the heroic hunting way of life continued to follow some variant of the earlier pattern of cooperative, more egalitarian bands of collectors and gatherers. Being relatively peaceful, these were forced out of the grasslands, savannah, and even the open forests, into the deeper forest, seashores, swamps, hills, semi-deserts, or forested river banks, where they gradually evolved a quite different, and ultimately more productive, way of life which we call Mesolithic. This may have happened long ago, but we have little sure evidence of its existence until about 40,000 B.C.

The heroic hunting way of life was so successful that the population of the globe increased greatly for long periods, but it was also precarious, being dependent on adequate rainfall to support the necessary grasses to provide the grazing animals on which carnivore men must live. And the Pleistocene was an era of changing weather conditions, as we have seen. In the periods of prosperity, the hunting peoples had the weapons, the combative spirit, and the group solidarity to protect their hunting grounds, so that their growing populations had to move toward more remote or less desirable territory, pushing the gatherers before them. Thus men, while remaining relatively small in total numbers and a single species on a worldwide basis, spread to all parts of the globe, including the oceanic islands when boats became available about 40,000 years ago.

During this process, as we have indicated, the world was undergoing climate convulsions based on the movement of the polar high-pressure zones downward to the middle latitudes, bringing ice and cold, while pushing the temperate rainfall tracks toward the equator so that rain fell more frequently on subtropical areas which previously had received rain only in winter (as the Mediterranean or South Africa) or even to more remote areas (like the Sahara or the Kalihari) which had previously been a desert. Thus, as I have said, the Sahara was subjected to pluvial ages, and became relatively habitable, in the periods when Europe was subjected to glaciers and became relatively uninhabitable. In these periods the immense sloping surface of the Sahara became an area of great grasslands with flowing streams, lakes, and abundant wildlife, the kind of place where heroic hunters could flourish and increase in numbers to the carrying capacity of the conditions. But in the interpluvial periods, the Sahara became much as we know it in today's interglacial period, an arid area of scanty vegetation, greatly reduced wildlife, and few men. Both animals and humans, in such a period, had to get out or perish. Most of them perished, but enough were able to leave the Sahara, either to go to the savannah which still existed south of the growing desert or across the Levant to Asia or Europe, where climate conditions were steadily improving.

As a result of these changes over the last half of the Pleistocene, men were sucked out of Africa into western Asia and Europe by way of the Levant, only to have the process reversed scores of thousands of years later. In using the expression "sucked" in this sentence, I am regarding the glaciers as a piston which pushed men out of Europe in its advance and sucked them back again as it retreated. It would be much truer, of course, to see this process as one in which men followed the pluvial belt (which we know as the prevailing westerly winds which bring rain over Europe in all four seasons) northward as the glacier retreated and southward to Africa as the glacier advanced again. A similar advance and retreat may have been going on in the Far East (and possibly also in India) with men moving backward and forward between north China and Java as the glacier, by its advance and retreat, not only made north China alternately a hardship area and a desirable place to live but also, by its extraction of water from the seas to pile it up as ice on land, alternately opened and then, by melting, resubmerged the land bridges connecting Asia and much of Malaysia and Indonesia into a single continuous land area.

The big difference between glacial conditions in Europe and in the Far East arose from the fact that most European precipitation comes from the westerly winds coming from the Atlantic Ocean, but much of the rain of the Far East is of seasonal monsoon origin in the interglacial periods. As a result, much of the land surface of the Far East in the glacial ages was ice-free tundra. Perhaps for this reason, the human inhabitants of the Far East worked out ways of living under very cold conditions much sooner than the inhabitants of Europe obtained such techniques, probably by diffusion from the Far East. As I have suggested, the greatest of these new techniques was the discovery of how to make and control fire, which was obtained in China in the second glacial age, but reached Europe more than 100,000 years later. Other techniques for coping with the problems of living on glacial tundra were also of Asiatic origin, although we do not have the details of places and dates. They probably occurred over a long period of time. Fire made it possible to live in caves because it allowed its possessors to displace the cave bears and to keep them out by cooperative fire maintenance and shared guard obligations. Later came skin clothing, use of sunken dwellings with skin roofs, improved stone weapons, including compound tools in which blades and handles were separate pieces, and other advances. There were also physical responses to the extreme cold conditions by the Asiatics who first remained in the north in the glacial ages, resulting in more compact bodies, rounder heads with shorter necks and limbs, possibly with more hirsute bodies and flatter faces. Some of these characteristics were simply those of Homo erectus intensified by the cold, but toward the end of the Pleistocene, the pluvial age of the Sahara developed a sharply contrasting type of man, Homo sapiens sapiens. This human variety was thin, long-limbed, long-headed, dark skinned. Both of these types were of the same species, and both had a number of varieties, with considerable numbers of groups intermediate between them, but, in general the two we have mentioned, sometimes called Neanderthal and Sapiens men, were recognizably different in appearance, probably spoke quite different kinds of languages, and lived quite different lives, though both were hunters. To our eyes Neanderthal men would have seemed heavily built, relatively hairy, and relatively short-legged, while the Sapiens type would have seemed slim, long-legged, tall, hairless, and dark skinned.

Since variations on these two types continued to exist and these two met and hybridized on the western fringe of Asia during the final peak of the last glacier, from 40,000 to about 10,000 B.C., there is little need to emphasize the difference between

them, except to say that no question of superiority
or inferiority is involved, and it would be a mistake to believe that later types were potentially
any better in any genetic way than earlier ones.
What can be pointed out, however, is that the hy-
brid of the two in western Asia became what we call
Alpine man, while the Sapiens type was more directly
the ancestor of what we call Nilotic, Mediterranean,
and, much later, Nordic man. The language sequence
is more complex and less clearly known. Alpine man
and Asiatic or earlier African man apparently spoke
the kind of language known as agglutinative in
which meaningful syllables were "glued" together
to give long complex words, such as we still find
in the Ural-Altaic languages, while the later
Sapiens type of man spoke somewhat later kinds
of languages which we call "inflected," including
the Hamitic, Semitic, and Indo-European languages.
The predecessors of these inflected languages seem
to have developed with the Sapiens type of man in
the Sahara in the final pluvial age, at which time
most of Eurasia was speaking agglutinative languages,
but the expulsion of the inflective Sapiens out of
the Sahara by the retreat of the last glacier spread
both this physical type and this language outward
into the Near East and Arabia, and later northward
across the Eurasian Highland Zone into the Northern
Flatlands of the Pontic and Kirgiz steppes. This
created a series of alternative belts of both physical and language groupings, running diagonally
from northwest to southeast across Eurasia, with
agglutinative Alpines in the northeast (Finno-Ugrian),
with developing Indo-European Nordics next to these
to the southwest, followed by agglutinative Alpines
in the Highland Zone from the Pyrenees to the Caucasus (or even to the Pamirs, where they joined to
the Asiatic-Ugric speakers), then, still moving
south and west, the next belt of the Mediterranean
Hamito-Semites, while beyond these were, in ancient
times, a very mixed situation, where taller Sapiens
negroes had been pushed south and west across the
persisting savannah into increasingly forested areas
of equatorial rainfall inhabited by surviving stock-
ier agglutinative speakers, from which, in recent
times, emerged the Bantu-speaking negroes. These
successive belts were finished off at either extreme,
in the Far East and on the extreme western and southern

102

fringes of Africa by the survivors of earlier stock-
ier, short-legged, hairier, yellowish-skinned peoples
whose former agglutinative languages showed a tendency
to lose their agglutinative characteristic to form
languages whose words were becoming isolated monosyllables distinguished by tones or other distinctive
sounds such as clicks, made necessary by the fact
that any language of isolated monosyllables must
distinguish between numerous homonyms (like rain,
rein, and reign).

These racial-linguistic belts were perhaps most
clearly evident about 3000 B.C., just before they began to be mixed up from the migrations arising from
the drier sub-Boreal climate of 3000-1000 B.C. In
these later movements the descendants of the Sapiens-
inflected speakers emerged from the northern and
southern grasslands of Eurasia as warlike, pastoral
Indo-Europeans and Semites to overrun the more stocky
and more peaceful agglutinatives of the Highland Zone
between, obliterating their languages and frequently
enslaving their bodies as far as the Atlas Mountains
of northwestern Africa and the Pyrenees Mountains of
southwestern Europe, with the Germans and Slavs ultimately spreading northward and northeast to overrun
the Baltic and Finnish peoples, while in Africa the
Arabic-speaking Mediterraneans pushed southward and
southwest to harass the Bantu-speaking negroids.
These more recent events bring us down to the last
few centuries, since the Slavs still press eastward
across Asia against Ural-Altaic-speaking peoples,
and Arabic influence is still moving southward across
Africa through Bantu-speakers.

As we shall see, these triumphs of the Indo-Europeans and Semites are not due to their technological
and cultural innovations, but, on the contrary, are
due to their concentration on warlike and aggressive
actions rooted in their hunting and later pastoral
heritage. The technological and cultural innovations
of history have come rather from the more peaceful,
earth-loving peoples, whose traditions were rather
those of the gatherers and planters, and whose physical types and languages were closer to the Alpine-
agglutinative line of development. In the Far East
the Chinese of this line were the creative peoples,
while in Africa south of the Sahara Bantu gardeners

were the chief creative peoples. But before either
of these, in pre-historic antiquity, the most creative peoples of all were the original Alpine agglutinatives of Highland west Asia. These latter gave
us the third great revolutionary change of direction
in man's development which I have mentioned. This
gave us, in the period from 10,000 to 1,000 B.C.,
agriculture, metallurgy, writing, the wheel, and
much else, including the first civilizations.

As we go on through history, we must remember
the pattern of racial-linguistic-cultural belts which
we have mentioned to see how they were formed and
gradually destroyed. They centered in the Near East,
along the axis of the Levant especially just north of
it, not only because this was the crossroads of peoples moving between Africa, Asia, and Europe, but
also because it was the meeting area between grasslands, both north and south, with the highlands of
open forest between, but it was also the crossroad
between the Mediterranean waterways to the west and
the Indian Ocean waterways to the east (through the
Persian Gulf and the Red Sea), and it was also one
of the western termini of the caravan routes leading
eastward to northwest India and to China. But we
must not forget that the contributions of this Near
East did not arise from any racial causes, but from
the fact that it was an area of mixture. The role
of languages in this process could also be significant, but here the key might lie in mixture of agglutinative practicality and inflective conceptuality.

We have no need to narrate the history of mankind
on the landmass of Eurasia in the period of the final
glacial retreat from about 40,000 B.C. to about
11,000 B.C. Suffice it to say that at the beginning
of that period the most successful way of life was
that of the heroic hunters, equipped with stone tools,
organized on a kinship basis, who lived off large
grazing and browsing animals in open terrain under
varied climate conditions from cold tundra, through
temperate grasslands, to sub-tropical savannah, although in many backward enclaves an older way of life
based on gathering and collecting was still to be
found. Sometime after 40,000 and again after 11,000
B.C., two new ways of living were discovered, the
Mesolithic and the Neolithic.

The Mesolithic way of life was developed by peoples with a gathering culture, living under forest conditions, possibly on the banks of some river flowing into the Indian Ocean drainage basin. This river may have been in southeast Asia, perhaps the Irawaddy. At any rate, these people developed a new way of life based on root crops, fishing, and a detailed familiarity with their botanical environment. This included vegetal reproduction of root crops such as yams; possibly the cultivation of large seeded utility crops such as gourds (for containers) and maybe, ultimately, the planting of smaller seeded crops for raw materials and narcotics, such as opium poppy, hemp, or strychnos vine; the use of poisons for capturing fish in quiet waters; extensive use of wicker and woven reeds for baskets, fish weirs, and animal traps; extensive use of plant fibers for snares, woven bags used as containers, bow strings, fishing lines and fishnets; the early use of dugout boats and paddles; very extensive use of fish and shellfish as protein supplements to a diet whose carbohydrate content came from roots and seeds of largely non-cultivated plants.

From this Mesolithic complex came a new tool, the bow and arrow, which for tens of thousands of years was adapted, improved, and changed to play a variable role, originally in hunting, but later in warfare. The invention was probably made by people who wished to hunt small animals or large birds in heavy forest, the kind of game and hunting for which the spear of the grassland hunters was almost useless.

The bow and arrow diffused so that it was reaching into many corners of the world by 6000 B.C. It reached the Americas, most of Eurasia and Africa, and many islands such as Japan, but not Australia. Evidence of its spread may be found in the appearance of small stone points, often called "microliths," in the archaeological remains of early men. At an early stage in its development it used a head which killed by poison, rather than by impact or bleeding. This is inferred from the fact that the most remote gatherers of the Old World such as the bushmen and pygmies of Africa, and the negritos of southeast Asia or the Philippines, used arrows with poisoned heads and are very familiar with other uses of poisons, such as fish poisons or on the darts of blowguns. Such poisoned

arrows are effective in obtaining food, but are almost useless for protection against predators or in
warfare, because the poison acts too slowly. Thus
archery originally was part of a peaceful rather
than a warlike culture, associated with gatherers
rather than with heroic hunters, and used in a
heavily forested terrain for small game rather
than on grasslands for big game. When archery
later spread to peoples with heroic hunting traditions, as it did in Europe in the Aurignacian period,
it was often adopted as a hunting weapon only, with
the spear retained for warfare, either by religious
taboo or by personal taste and tribal traditions.
This can be seen on a large scale among the European
Indo-Europeans after 2000 B.C. or, on a small scale,
among the Jivaro head hunters and head shrinkers of
South America. By 4000 B.C. archery was about to embark on several thousand years of spectacular improvements as a weapon, a development which we shall
examine later.

Shortly after 10,000 B.C., possibly as an offshoot of south Asian Mesolithic planting, another
new way of living was developed in west Asia. This
was Neolithic agriculture, the most revolutionary
and, in some ways, the most unusual innovation that
men have ever achieved. It appeared in the hilly
parklands of western Asia, somewhere between Armenia,
Anatolia, Syria, and Iran, about 9000 B.C. and formed
the first agricultural society to cultivate the grain
crops (barley and wheat) and care for the domestic
animals (sheep, goats, and cattle, but not horses)
we still have today. This culture was unusual from
its organization and outlook rather than from its
artifacts, including stone hoes and pottery, because
it was centered on female activities. Women tilled
the crops, while men continued to engage in desultory
hunting and cared for the animals. In time women became the center of the economic system, the social
system, and the intellectual system, for men's two
chief desires, the production of crops and the production of children, were both regarded as under
female control. This power was personified in the
Neolithic religious system which centered about the
worship of an Earth Mother goddess, with complete
identification of food production, production of
children, and the rebirth of dead individuals in

106

eternity, all three achieved, it was felt, by the burial of the dead seed or of the dead person in the body of the mother, either in fact or in symbol, since the earth was the mother and there was complete identification of womb and tomb.

This culture was peaceful and had few weapons and no use for warfare. Derived from Mesolithic gatherers (themselves often women) rather than from Paleolithic hunters, it lacked the tradition of masculine violence and the need for war of the heroic hunters. It neither made weapons nor war, but instead spread peacefully across the loess and parklands of the upland hills of Eurasia and North Africa. This diffusion was relatively rapid, since lack of knowledge of how to replenish the fertility of the soil made it necessary to practice shifting cultivation, sometimes in the form called "slash-and-burn" in which trees were girdled, their branches cut and burned, and the seed planted in the warm ashes, replanted in the same place for a few years, when the village moved on to a new site, where the operation was repeated. This culture could not operate very well in the deepest forest or jungle and could not go out on the grasslands, whose deep sod was impenetrable to hoe cultivation. Thus the Neolithic garden cultures avoided direct contact with the heroic hunting peoples. By 2300 B.C., when these hunters, by that time converted to pastoral activities as well as hunting, began to move in the earliest warrior peoples migrations, the Neolithic peoples had reached Britain in the west, China and Japan in the Far East, the Baltic in the north, and the Sudan and edge of the Sahara in the south.

By that date, as the third pre-Christian millennium and the early Bronze Age were about to end in an interval of explosive and long-sustained turmoil, the state as a form of political organization was already more than a thousand years old. This, the greatest political invention of human history, replaced kinship as an organizational principle and provided a new form for organizing power and security. This will be examined in the next chapter. Before we turn to that we must emphasize that this new invention came into a world in which there were at least four types of earlier systems existing, each

107

associated with a different way of life in the broad-
est sense. These were: (1) the collector-gatherers,
equipped with an ingenious array of technical inventions and specialized knowledge, organized in small
bands on a cooperative basis, with basic equality of
the sexes, wandering over increasingly limited territories; (2) the heroic hunting cultures who lived
by social hunting of large herd animals on grasslands
or savannah, using the spear, or later the bow and
arrow; these were organized in tribal groups based
on kinship, had male dominance, hunted over relatively sharply defined territories which they were
prepared to defend by warfare, and, in the temperate
zone at least, had regular patterns of annual movements over those territories, following the movements
of monsoon or cyclonic rainbelts; (3) the Mesolithic
peoples, who lived a sedentary life in small groups,
close to forested water courses, with considerable
sexual equality, supplementing their collecting activities with some vegetal planting, chiefly of root
crops or a few large seed utility plants, supplemented
by protein from fish and shellfish, with some snaring,
trapping, and shooting of small forest animals or
birds, and with great emphasis on their knowledge
of their botanical environment, especially its phar-
macopeia, on wicker work and on cords from vegetable
fibers; (4) the Neolithic garden peoples, whose cultures have just been described, semi-sedentary, peaceful, female-dominated, organized in villàges rather
than in tribes or kinship groupings, and with an extraordinary outlook which confused in a typically
archaic fashion cultivation, sex, immortality, and,
as we shall see, power.

Of these four cultures only the heroic hunters
obtained security by a power system based on force.
They had weapons, the spear and later the bow, a
power structure of organized force on a territorial
basis, seeking security through warfare in terms
which would be familiar to us.

The other three cultures found security by
avoidance of danger, as their earliest human ancestors had done, and generally lacked weapons
for using organized force to achieve security. Of
these four ways of life, distorted versions of each
have survived until recent times, but it must be

emphasized that these recently surviving versions are distorted by many millennia of interactions among each other, but, above all, by the pressure of structures of wealth and power achieved by civilized communities, utilizing technologies and organizational structures not conceivable among the peoples of these four earlier ways of life. As we shall see, these later richer and more powerful systems of human living arose from the peaceful Neolithic cultures but reached their greatest might only after conquest by those who had been trained in heroic hunting traditions.

The Neolithic gardeners and the heroic hunters, however, are not the direct parents of the world of today. There are at least two or more different ways of life intervening between them and us. The two were both substantially modified in the archaic period, 4000-500 B.C. and in the subsequent classical period, 1000 B.C.-500 A.D., to say nothing of the changes brought about in the medieval period, A.D. 500-1500, and the startling events of the modern era, since A.D. 1500. The changes of the archaic period transformed the grassland heroic hunters into warlike, sky-worshipping, pastoral peoples, many of whom were devoted to missile weapons, while the Neolithic garden cultures were changed, in the Old World alluvial river valleys, into the first civilizations, whose ruins and debris still clutter the fringes of Asia.

The four ways of life which existed before 4000 B.C. contributed little to the history of weaponry, but that little was essential. The spear of the heroic hunters and the archery of the Mesolithic had obvious limitations. The spear remained a wooden implement without an attached head for hundreds of thousands of years. Eventually stone heads, shaped by blows, were used, but these could be attached only by lashing with rawhide or vegetable fibers and were rarely very secure. Later, from the Mesolithic and Neolithic tradition, came points shaped by grinding (called in Europe "polished" stone points), but these suffered the same weakness, although they were widely used for arrowheads and later as spearheads. We need say nothing of the elaborate developments of stone tools used for purposes other than weapons, such as hand axes, scrapers, burins, and others, used for working bone, wood, skins, and for cutting flesh.

109

An effective spearhead came only with the discovery of how to cast metals, copper after 4000 B.C., bronze about 3000 B.C., and iron much later (in the Far East about 1000 B.C., but in Europe not until almost 500 B.C.). Because the high temperatures needed for casting iron were so difficult to obtain and because cast iron is so brittle, spearheads and arrowheads continued to be cast of bronze until well into the first millennium B.C., although wrought iron spearheads, made with flanges which could be rolled around the shaft could be made in some areas of the West before 1400 B.C.; but these were expensive and remained rare.

The bow and arrow spread relatively rapidly and reached Europe while that area was still in the Paleolithic age (Aurignacian). Its passage can be marked by microliths and, more confidently, by rock carvings or paintings, across the Near East, through the Horn of Africa into the Dark Continent, across North Africa, the Sudan, and parts of the Sahara, to the Maghreb and to Spain, in what are sometimes referred to as Capsian and Azilian cultures. It is possible that the bow had already developed to what we call the reflex type by the date at which we end this chapter. This is a bow, still made entirely of wood, but permanently bent by heat so that, in strung but not drawn condition, the grip curved backward toward the archer, almost touching the string. This allowed an archer of fixed arm length to make a longer draw and thus to use a longer and more powerful bow. This development seems to have been made somewhere in the West, either in North Africa or even in southwest Europe. It probably may have had some influence on the beginning of the use of archery in warfare, possibly in Egypt. This marks a major break in human life, for until about 4000 B.C. war was not a significant element in human life. Until the advent of civilizations and pastoralism most human societies were not warlike, nor organized for war, and most weapons were for hunting game and not for killing men. These innovations are subsequent to 4000 B.C. and we must now turn to that period. One of its outstanding features was that man discovered a new principle for organizing human societies, religion rather than kinship. This not only allowed the formation of much more numerous groupings, but it allowed much more elaborately organized societies with division of labor in specialized activities, including warfare.

110

CHAPTER III
THE ARCHAIC PERIOD, 4000-1000 B.C.

1.   Introduction

The period 4000-500 B.C. was the fourth great period of transition in human history, following the extrusion of the hominids from nature into culture before 3 million B.C., the establishment of the heroic hunting cultures about 700,000 B.C., and the discovery of agriculture about 9000 B.C. In this archaic period there were two·great changes: (1) the establishment of the first civilizations, derived from the Neolithic garden cultures in the alluvial river valleys of Afro-Asia, and (2) the creation of semi-nomadic pastoralism about 2000 B.C. when the heroic hunters of the grasslands of south Russia and Arabia obtained the technique of domestication of animals and the use of metals from the Highland Zone agriculturalists between them. Our lives to this day are permeated by the contributions of these two cultures to our ways of life and especially by the consequences of the relations between these two, arising from the conquest of the archaic civilizations by the grassland pastoralists. Both of these cultures are now so remote from us and so alien in their ways of looking at life that it is almost impossible for us to grasp how they operated.

The key point to remember about these cultures is that they were "archaic," that is that power rested on religious and social factors and not directly on military, economic, political, or even ideological factors, as with us today. This archaic basis of power in human society continued to exist in most of Asia and in much of Africa, as well as in the civilized areas of the New World, long after 500 B.C. in all cultures which were above the hunting-gathering level. In Asia this situation in which political systems rested on archaic foundations continued to exist until the mid-nineteenth or even into the twentieth century, but generally the archaic cultures and civilizations were destroyed by the Iron Age civilizations and empires following 500 B.C.

111

These archaic power systems, based on religion and social relations, began to be eclipsed in the sixth century B.C. by the invention of new, more secular, power structures rooted in quite different foundations, in which the chief ideological elements were transcendental ethical monotheism and two-valued logic. Both of these were products of grassland and pastoral cultures, with emphasis on male, celestial deities, the one from the Semites of the southern grasslands of Arabia, the other from the Indo-Europeans of the northern flatlands of the Eurasian steppes. The earliest Iron Age civilizations, like classical antiquity, Hindu civilization in the Middle East, and Sinic civilization in the Far East, never became monotheistic societies but continued to be a battleground between archaic fertility or virility beliefs and more monotheistic celestial ideas. And of course, two-valued logic, as an Indo-European invention, did not become significant in the Far East and, although very influential in the Hindu civilization, it never became an explicit and accepted system of logic there, as it did farther west where Persian and Greek influence was stronger. Only in the next, third generation of civilizations, after A.D. 500, did transcendental monotheism become a dominant influence in the form we know as providential empires (that is, in Islamic, Western, and Russian civilizations, but not really in either Chinese or Japanese civilizations). The victories of these later forms of organization reflect the greater organizing power of the state and the idea of citizenship over the earlier archaic idea of a divine king served by worshipful subjects.

This change after 500 B.C. should not blind us to the political power of the archaic idea, which was as superior to the earlier idea based on kinship as structures based on sovereignty and omnipotent monotheism have been to the archaic principle.

Today power is embodied for us in the impersonal power of a sovereign state, a system which distinguishes citizens from aliens or compatriots from foreigners. The primitive system before 4000 B.C. was organized in terms of a personal system of authority based on kinship, which divided mankind into kindred and non-kindred. The intervening archaic system was a transitional one in which members were sub-

112

jects of a living deity (or deities) in a totalitarian system and mankind was divided into believers and non-believers. Each system was superior to the previous system because it permitted the organization of larger numbers of men or held their loyalties more tightly to a single allegiance, just as the earliest of the three, the kinship group, was superior to the earliest form of human organization, the cooperative hunting band.

Unfortunately, these different systems for organizing life's activities, and especially for organizing power to provide security, are so different that it is very difficult for a person in one to understand the functioning of any of the others. Thus a tribal African today has difficulty understanding the nature of the impersonal sovereign state (since both "impersonality" and "sovereignty" are outside his fundamental experience). And, in the opposite sense, it is difficult for us today to really grasp the nature of any of the earlier systems, just as it was difficult for Herodotus (about 484-425 B.C., at the very beginning of the post-archaic period) to grasp the nature of the archaic political systems of the East.

In fact, understanding of the nature of one of these systems by people who live under a different one is so difficult that each of these systems, as it developed and worked out its potentialities, came to include within its members large groups of persons who continued to function, mentally, in an earlier system. Thus, for example, the cultural area which I have called the "Pakistani-Peruvian axis," stretching across the Near East, the Mediterranean, and Latin America, has remained today to a considerable degree in the mental confines of the kinship system, with the consequence that its peoples are generally not capable of operating a system based on impersonal sovereign public authority, and their efforts to do so seem to us, who are mentally tuned to the sovereign state system, to be largely filled with what we call "corruption," but what seems to them to be nothing more than loyalty to a narrower and more personal social pattern.

2. The Alluvial Valley Cultures

The alluvial valley civilizations arose in the

period 6000 B.C. to 2000 B.C. when the Neolithic garden cultures moved into the alluvial river valleys and worked out organizational techniques which permitted them to build up sedentary city life with elaborate division of labor and of social functions in a proto-bureaucratic society. The survival of such an elaborate society in an alluvial valley depended on water control and a calendar, neither of which was available in the preceding Neolithic culture. The advantages of life in an alluvial valley were very great and included the following: (1) the land could be worked every year because the annual flood which had built up the soil restored its fertility and moisture content every year; (2) this meant that permanent settlements could be established, since neither shifting cultivation nor fallow rotation was needed to ensure that seed be put in sufficiently fertile soil; and (3) working of the soil was easier since it contained neither large stones nor trees as obstacles to cultivation.

But there were also two great obstacles to the use of these valleys as centers of civilization: (1) the flood's arrival was originally unexpected, devastating, and dangerous; and (2) since the annual flooding came from monsoon climate conditions, the growing season often ended with a long rainless period in which irrigation was needed to bring the crops to maturity. These two problems were handled by flood control and irrigation structures which required large scale mobilization of food and labor and also required the invention of a calendar which would show the length of the year and the date of the annual flood. This required a long period of astronomical study. Both of these cultural innovations--the calendar and water control--were lacking in the Neolithic garden cultures, but were obtained by the alluvial valley civilizations, for the simple reason that these civilizations could not have existed without them. It is noteworthy that these two attributes remained essential characteristics of these civilizations throughout their histories, and are regarded as normal features of governmental activity even today.

The beginnings of calendar study began in the late Paleolithic cultures which observed that the

114

year was about as long as twelve cycles of the moon. Later the Neolithic peoples seem to have had a system of counting based on twelve and may have carried their celestial observations far enough to have divided the annual path of the sun through the sphere of fixed stars into twelve zones, which we call the zodiac. There seems also to have been a common recognition that the annual withdrawal and return of the sun centered in what we consider the third week of December and that the return of the sun to the north reached its extreme position in what we consider the third week of June. This recognition of the winter and summer solstices was also shared by all the alluvial valley civilizations, but each one, apparently, had to discover the length of the year independently, as well as the number of days between the two solstices, and the date of the arrival of the annual flood in terms of these two turning points.

There were at least four, and possibly more than six, of these alluvial valley civilizations, including that in Mesopotamia (founded about 5500 B.C.), one on the Nile (about 5000 B.C.), a third in the Indus Valley (about 3500 B.C.), and the fourth in the valley of the Yellow River of China (about 2000 B.C.). Others, of which we know little or nothing at present, may have grown up on the Ganges and in the chief river valleys of southeast Asia.

The organizational device which made civilized life possible in these alluvial river valleys was not, as Wittfogel believed, the political power provided by water control, since water control and irrigation, being the consequence (and not the cause) of control of great masses of labor, required the power to mobilize human labor to build these projects and could not possibly be regarded as a consequence of the control of such projects.

The power behind the alluvial valley civilizations was the same for all of them and continued in a number of later civilizations which were not in alluvial valleys. It was the power of an idea, a religious idea, usually known as "archaic kingship" or "sacral kingship." This idea made it possible to organize men in a larger unit than was possible on the basis of kinship such as had been used previously for tribal organizations.

Tribal organization, as we have seen, was found
chiefly among the heroic hunting people. It could
be used to unite thousands of persons if they could
be made to believe that they were descended from a
common ancestor and, for that reason, should cooperate together. The limited ability of a hunting economy to support large numbers of persons, in frequent
enough contact to maintain linguistic intelligibility,
did not allow mobilization of loyalty sufficiently
wide nor sufficiently intense to build elaborate water
control projects in river valleys. Moreover, the Neolithic garden cultures had only very weak kinship
feelings, since these had already been eclipsed among
agricultural peoples by a religious idea, devotion to
the fertility of the Earth Mother.

To understand the idea of the Earth Mother and
of the fertility religion among early agricultural
peoples, we must look at two fundamental things quite
differently from the way we see them today. Things
which to us appear quite distinct and separate, such
as birth of children, or production of crops, or salvation in the hereafter, seemed to them to be but
different manifestations of a single underlying reality. Moreover, they felt much more insecure about
the operations of the natural world than we do, because we believe in natural laws which continue to
function regardless of what we do. To those early
people the functioning of the world was the consequence of the constant interventions of powers behind
the obvious manifestations of the natural world, and
these manifestations, such as the sun rising or the
crops growing, would not occur unless the mysterious
power behind things did this. And that mysterious
power would function only if man, by symbolic acts
and ritual, continually urged it on and showed it
what to do. The archaic peoples felt that the cosmos
would fall apart and cease to operate unless human
beings, by ritual and symbols, gave the underlying
power behind all things the necessary encouragement
and urging to move. In the Neolithic period that
power was fertility; in the archaic religions, it
was virility; and in the high civilizations it was
the union of these two.

The fertility religions associated with the
Earth Mother goddess sought three things about

116

which humans felt very uncertain and insecure. All
were regarded as different aspects of one thing, fertility. These three were that the earth produce crops;
that women produce children; and that the dead be born
again. The power which achieved the Summum Bonum which
had these three aspects was fertility, that is the
power of the female, as manifested in the Earth Mother
or in any woman. It was manifest in the monthly cycle
of the moon and the menses, but also was manifest in
many other phenomena which functioned in an endless
cycle of four stages: death, burial, gestation, rebirth. A man (or seed) died; was buried in the Earth
(or a woman); lay there for months; and was reborn
in glory. Planting the seed; sexual intercourse; or
burial of the dead were not merely analogous; they
were identical. Any one of them could stand for the
others and could produce the others. Similarly,
sprouting of the crop; birth of a child; or spiritual rebirth in the Herafter were identical. Thus
sexual intercourse in the autumn could make the crops
come up in the spring, just as such intercourse at a
funeral or wake could make the dead person achieve
rebirth (salvation) in the future life. All of these,
in the eyes of the Neolithic peoples, were simply re-
flections of the mysterious fertility powers of the
Earth Mother and were triggered by a myriad of symbolic signs and acts associated with the female and
the general idea of fertility.

This point of view could easily lead, as it
sometimes did, to ritual acts which seem very horrible to us. For example, the cycle begins with
death, symbolized by the cutting down of the grain
and eating it, before burial of the next year's seed
in the ground. This could be ritualized by selection
of a choice male, who after ritual sexual intercourse
with the goddess (represented by a priestess) would
be buried in the ground, to rise in triumph with the
sprouting crops in the spring. In some cases, parts
of this human sacrifice were eaten, as part of the
seed was eaten, before the rest was put in the ground.
From actions such as these came human sacrifice,
ritual cannibalism, and temple prostitution as we
saw them in degraded form thousands of years later
in the historic period, after 3000 B.C.

The changes made in this Neolithic religious out-

look and its rituals in the subsequent alluvial valley civilizations were chiefly associated with the
substitution of the male for the female, of virility
for fertility, and the elaboration of the whole outlook into a political system. This included a shift
from the moon to the sun, as a focus of worship, with
increased emphasis on the year (rather than the
month), as signified in the annual withdrawal and
return of the sun from June to the following June.

The reasons for this shift of emphasis were at
least twofold. In the alluvial valleys, the vital
importance of the annual flood and of calendar study
as the chief step in water control focused attention
on the sun, which became a male symbol, represented
by a disk or circle (with rays), in contrast to fertility represented by the crescent moon, or its
various equivalents such as the ship, or horned
gateway to a tomb. A second reason was that in
such alluvial valleys men once again became the
center of the economic system with the invention
of the plow, drawn by draft animals, to replace
the Neolithic hoe or digging stick used by women
in the earlier gardening cultures.

At the same time, as these vital changes in
outlook and behavior were taking place, the older
tripartite Summum Bonum of the Neolithic garden
cultures was expanded to take on a fourth aspect,
the power and stability of the political system as
a manifestation of the structure of the universe
itself. In this way the virility of the king not
only kept security, order, and peace in political
and social life, but it also made the year turn,
the sun withdraw and return, the annual flood come,
the crops sprout and flourish, and the domestic
animals produce their young. This whole process
would function only so long as the virility (that
is the maleness) of the king was convincingly practiced and demonstrated by satisfying the sexual desires of his harem and by smiting with mighty blows
all enemies of this system of power, prosperity,
order, and permanence. The enemies of this Summum
Bonum were all those persons who were not members
of the system and most obviously all those who were
not part of the alluvial valley productive enterprise.

In these archaic civilizations, smiting all disturbers of the order of the system (the solar universe) with a mace (a phallic symbol, represented today by a scepter) was as much a part of the king's duties as was his obligation to keep the system going as a productive enterprise by exercise of his sexual virility. His life was filled with both activities, both actually and in an endless sequence of symbolic and ritual acts. In performing these acts the king was, simultaneously, god, the symbol of god, and the chief intermediary of men to god.

This system of life and government is difficult for us to grasp because historic memory goes back only to the later, and often decadent, stages of it, and the religious, cognitive, and political changes which ended it in western Asia after 600 B.C. have covered it with deep layers of slander, distortion, and falsehood, and have cut us off so completely from the ritual and symbolic system which was its very foundation that we are almost incapable of understanding it today and usually fail to recognize its symbols and residues, although these still surround us on all sides.

It should be recognized, however, that this system of archaic kingship with its accompanying archaic religion was the most powerful, most persistent, and most successful (in terms of duration and intensity) social organization that ever existed. It lasted for at least three thousand years (in the Near East from 4000 B.C. to about 1000 B.C.), without any real challenge, over an area from Egypt to Japan, and continued to persist, in some form or other, through most of the nineteenth century to the destruction of the last archaic empires in the twentieth century. Remnants and fragments of its beliefs and practices still are visible across that whole vast terrain, and, until recently, continued to function as sacral kingship in black Africa.

Obviously, a system such as this over such vast extensions of time and space, and with such extraordinary intensity of power, had a complicated influence on security and weapons systems. Such a complex story can be treated here only in brief form.

119

We have said that there were four of these alluvial valley civilizations. Of these we know very
little about that in the Indus Valley (the Harappa
civilization), and it is clear that it contributed
very little to the mainstream of history. We know
more about the Sinic civilization which arose in the
Yellow River basin of north China and eventually
covered much of east Asia. This early portion of
Chinese history was also derivative rather than con-
tributory to the mainstream of history. Its basic
artifacts were derived from western Asia and its
organizational features were those of a cosmic sacral
kingship. Its chief distinguishing character came
from its role as an eastern buffer against the pastoral peoples of the Asiatic grasslands, but, until
after its replacement by a new Chinese civilization
after the time of Christ, it contributed little to
the mainstream of history.

This mainstream was in the Near East, in the
zone from the Adriatic Sea eastward to Baluchistan
and bounded on the north and south by the grasslands
of south Russia and of Arabia and the Sudan. In that
area the central axis was the Levant, the block of
land from Sinai to the Gulf of Alexandretta, with
the Mediterranean Sea on the west and the deserts
of Arabia and Syria on the east. The Levant was
originally a passageway, north and south, although
by 2000 B.C. it had its own distinctive Canaanite
civilization. Until that time, or shortly before,
it could be pictured as a capital letter F with the
upright line going south toward Egypt and the horizontal line at the top going eastward over the Syrian
Saddle to the Euphrates River and Mesopotamia. The
cross bar led eastward from the main north-south road
by way of Jerusalem and the Dead Sea to Jericho and
the desert.

After 3000 B.C. this F changed to a cross, as
it has remained ever since, the cross bar connecting
a great civilization on the island of Crete, and the
Mediterranean Sea in general, with the great civilization of Mesopotamia to the east, and beyond it the
Persian Gulf, the Indian Ocean, and the southern seas
of wealth and mystery. The upright on this cross

continued to link Syria with Egypt to the south but, after 2500 B.C., extended northward as well, toward the metalliferous mountains of Armenia and Anatolia and the great civilization of the Hittites in the valley of the Halys River of central Asia Minor. This crossing in Syria, based on the Syrian Saddle which links the Euphrates and the east with the Syrian coast and the Mediterranean west has been one of the most strategic spots on the globe. Until the end of the Bronze Age, about 1000 B.C., it was the most strategic spot and the commercial center of the civilized world as well, the crossroads between Egypt and Hittite on a north-south axis and between Mesopotamia and the Mediterranean on an east-west axis. Until about 2500 B.C. there were only two of these arms, but after the centuries of turmoil associated with the years 2000-1800 or later, there were always four directions leading outward from Syria.

These years of turmoil about 2000-1800 B.C. and the next great period of turmoil about 1200-900 B.C. mark the natural breaks in the general history of the Near East as well as in the special subject of weapons systems and security. Accordingly, we shall deal with our subject as two distinct periods, divided by the period of turmoil after 2000 and ended by the dark age about 1000 B.C.

It must be obvious from what has been said that political power and security in the archaic period was not organized on the basis of military force, economic production, and ideology as it has been in the West in recent times, but was organized by religious and social functions. The archaic kingship itself, even in its most elaborate development, with a bureaucratic structure extending over great areas, never impinged immediately and directly on the vast majority of the population, the peasants, in any individual, personal way. Instead, its power impinged at the lowest level on either villages or families (or both) rather than on individuals, the latter being totally absorbed in either the village or the kinship group (or some combination of these) in which social pressures bound the individual in such a close nexus that there was no real alternative to consent and acquiescence.

121

In such an archaic culture, as it continued to exist in much of Asia until well into the nineteenth century, these social units at the bottom were joined to the archaic imperial system at the top by long chains of bureaucratic and economic intermediaries which directed flows of men, labor, and goods upward from the villages and kinship groups to the archaic imperial system at the top, with little or no economic return to the peasants, since, unlike our culture, where the incomes of cities and governments are compensated by flows of reciprocal goods and services downward, in the archaic and classical empires obligations to contribute were based on power and legal claims and not upon exchange of goods and services, such as we expect.

Although we speak of these early civilizations collectively as "archaic civilizations" because of their similar organizational structures and outlooks, their experiences as historical entities were very different. Egypt, for example, had a history quite different from Mesopotamia, because the geographic conditions were different.

Egypt was isolated, not only by natural features, such as barren desert and seas, but its neighbors were at a much lower level of culture and could threaten it with invasion or attack only under most unusual circumstances. Mesopotamia, on the other hand, was open to invasion from the grasslands within the Fertile Crescent as well as from the Highland Zone peoples outside that Crescent. Moreover, the Highland Zone peoples north of Mesopotamia were the inventors of the artifacts and techniques on which all the archaic civilizations were based, including some items, such as the use of metals, which were of primary significance to military life. Accordingly, Mesopotamia's neighbors were only slightly less advanced than the civilization itself and were often superior in some military matters.

There was also a significant difference between the two civilizations in terms of the alluvial riverine systems and annual floods on which their continued survival depended. The Nile was a great line of water, with no significant tributaries, flowing through largely desert country, and with fairly regular and predictable behavior as far as its annual flood was concerned. The Tigris-Euphrates system was much more irregular, had numerous significant tributaries and was right in the middle of all the turmoil and bustle associated with the invention and evolution of civilized living.

From these basic differences between Egyptian and Mesopotamian conditions flowed another difference of such fundamental character that it might be regarded as primary. That was that Egypt was a unified state from the period of the pre-historic and semi-legendary Menes, about 3400 B.C., and fell into disunity only partly and rarely, from internal decay rather than from any external political or military challenges. Mesopotamia, on the other hand, achieved unity and maintained it only as a consequence of almost superhuman efforts by men of very superior ability who were partly successful only under unusually favorable conditions. In a word, unity was natural to Egypt, but was unnatural to Mesopotamia, and, as a consequence, war within the system was very rare in Egypt but was practically the customary way of life for Mesopotamia.

This difference was largely a reflection of the geographic differences. In Egypt the only way of communication was the River Nile, admirably adapted to unify the country even under a rudimentary technology, since the current flowed northward and the prevailing winds blew southward. This means that men and materials could float downstream, and any sail capable of filling on a following breeze could carry the vessel back upstream. Moreover, because of the desert, agricultural production was possible only on land within easy reach of the stream and controllable from it. Thus the land of Egypt could be held under unified control by any power which controlled the river, and the degree of power necessary to do that, in an area with no alternative sources of wealth and power and with no significant external enemies, was relatively small.

In Mesopotamia, on the other hand, everything was pluralistic, changeable, and unpredictable. The Tigris-Euphrates had numerous tributaries and separate flood and drainage basins which could be-

123

come independent bases of power simply by the establishment of archaic political organizations on these independent economic bases. Travel on the two rivers was complex and difficult, especially going upstream which was essential to any effort to control separate power units in different drainage basins. In fact, the expense, in terms of manpower, of using the river for upstream movement of men and goods, was so great that it was cheaper to go overland, since the flat land surface and the Mesopotamian possession of the wheel (2000 years before it was known in Egypt) made overland transportation relatively cheaper. But since political unity in Mesopotamia meant upstream movement of power onto divergent tributaries, it led to dispersal rather than concentration of forces, encouraging disruptive counterattacks. Moreover, any upstream movement of power in Mesopotamia led to dispersal of power because of the constant danger of flank attacks from the surrounding hillsides and the need to defend against these. Such attacks were not only frequent but were likely to be successful, at least temporarily, because the hill peoples were outstanding fighters, the rewards to their aggressions were very attractive in view of the disparity of wealth between the civilized valley and the rugged hillsides, and the attacking hillsmen could easily cut the dispersed political-military system of the valley, loot its substance, and escape reprisal by flight into the hills again.

Finally, any effort to establish political unity in Mesopotamia by an upstream extension of a power system was almost doomed to failure from the fact that there was no natural boundary or defendable limit moving upstream in Mesopotamia, such as was provided by the gorges at the Second Cataract of the Nile. Movement upstream in Mesopotamia led to the upper Euphrates which brought one to the Syrian Saddle, which was the very antithesis of a defendable boundary. It was, on the contrary, a flat open road across grasslands leading westward to the Mediterranean. And even when the Mediterranean was reached, it was far from being a defensible terminus, since it was open as we have indicated, to attack from north or south, from Anatolia or from the Levant, along coastal passages which were a constant threat to the east-west crossing on the Syrian Saddle. Thus any effort seeking political unity in Mesopotamia led to increasingly difficult problems, leading eventually to a bottomless pit for devouring men, resources, and power at the western end of the Syrian Saddle, an area which could be supplied from a civilized base in Mesopotamia only by a constantly lengthening, upstream, supply line. This is one of the reasons that the successive efforts to unify Mesopotamia by the Sumerians about 2380 B.C., followed by the Akkadians about 2316 B.C., then the Babylonians about 1750 B.C., the Assyrians (about 660 B.C.), and finally the Persians (about 500 B.C.), in each case centered farther upstream and operated from power bases more closely associated with the hills and the Highland Zone itself.

Both in Egypt and Mesopotamia it was not sufficient to control the alluvial valley itself but was necessary to push outside into surrounding areas. This need arose from the fact that such valleys, although astounding producers of food, lacked both ores and lumber. As the need for these absent commodities increased, especially the need for metals for weapons, both civilizations had to push outward. The Egyptians largely did without metal weapons until after 2000 B.C. but a thousand years earlier had been seeking lumber in the hills of Lebanon. The peoples of Mesopotamia sought metals on the shores of the Persian Gulf as far south as Oman, but their chief supply had to come from the Highland Zone to the north, even as far as Anatolia and the Caucasus, and eventually came by sea from Bohemia, Spain, and even Cornwall to the Syrian ports which led to the Syrian Saddle. These needs drove both civilizations toward Syria and made it necessary for them to subdue the less civilized peoples who could threaten the way there. Egypt thus found itself in constant conflict with the Semitic peoples of Sinai and the Levant, while any Mesopotamian power was at enmity with neighbors on both sides of its route from the Persian Gulf to Syria. These neighbors included Semites on the left side of the route, and the formidable Elamites, Lullabi, Guti, Assyrians, and Hurrians along the right side of the route.

It is obvious that the problems of weapons and security were much more complex and advanced much more rapidly in Mesopotamia than in Egypt. For that

125

reason we shall discuss first the simpler case of Egypt,
despite the fact that civilization was earlier in
Mesopotamia. Before we do either, however, we should
have before our eyes a brief outline of the history
of both civilizations:

Egypt (Dynasty numbers in Roman numerals)

Prehistoric: before 3200
Early Dynastic (I-II): 3200-2780
Old Kingdom (III-VI): 2780-2280
First Intermediate Period (VII-X): 2280-2060
Middle Kingdom (XI-XII): 2060-1780
Second Intermediate ["Hyksos"] Period (XIII-XVII):
    1780-1570
New Kingdom ["Egyptian Empire"] (XVIII-XX): 1570-1085
Decline 1085-525
Persian Conquest (525); Macedonian Conquest (332);
    Roman Conquest (30 B.C.)

Mesopotamia

Prehistoric: before 3300
Uruk and Proto-Literate: 3300-2800
Early Dynastic (Sumerian): 2800-2400
Akkadian: 2400-2230
Neo-Sumerian: 2230-2000
Old Babylonian: 2000-1595
Kassite: 1595-1168
Early Assyrian: 1365-738
Assyrian Empire: 738-612
Neo-Babylonian (Chaldean): 612-539
Persian Empire: 539-331
Seleucid: 312-248
Parthian: 248 B.C.-A.D.226

4.   Egypt

Egypt was shielded on the west and east by barren deserts, the latter backed up by the Red Sea.
Only one real threat ever came from either direction.
On the south, Egypt was protected by the narrow gorges
of the upper Nile, by the deserts surrounding those
gorges, and by the primitive culture of the barbarian
peoples of that area. Danger from that direction was
likely only when Egypt itself fell into decay. On the
north, the area was protected by the Mediterranean Sea,

126

from which a real threat came only once (the Peoples of the Sea, about 1230-1190 B.C.). The only opening in the defense perimeter of Egypt was in the extreme northeast on the Sinai frontier which was very narrow and easily defensible, but which gave out onto the most dangerous and tumultuous area of the world, the Levant, battleground of the earliest civilizations.

Egyptian weapons were of the simplest kind--the spear, the mace, a cutting ax, the bow, and a long dagger. These were sufficient to allow the Pharaoh to maintain his power within the country and to defend its borders against uncivilized outsiders. The prestige of the sacral kingship, the extraordinary and almost uninterrupted prosperity of alluvial agriculture, and the logistic advantages of the Nile itself, permitted the ruler to fulfill all his duties of security and defense with a relatively simple military organization and with a low level of tactical understanding. He alone could equip and maintain large bodies of men with the existing weapons because no other authority could obtain sufficient wealth to make the weapons or could maintain the manpower to establish any counter force to his position. When conflict occurred, almost invariably on the frontiers, the opposition consisted largely of naked savages who could be overcome relatively easily by the quantity of Egyptian forces without regard either to quality of weapons or elaborate tactics. Only beyond Sinai was there any real challenge, and it should be recognized that there was no real political power in the southern Levant (Palestine) until at least the Canaanite period, after 2000 B.C. Encounters of the Egyptians with the Semites of the Levant before the Canaanites were on the whole inconclusive, since the higher quality of Asiatic weaponry there was cancelled out by the size and quantity of Egyptian military efforts arising from the superior Egyptian economic and political organization.

So far as we can judge, Egyptian tactics were as simple as their weapons, and did not extend much beyond the fact that the order in which weapons were engaged in combat was in accord with the range of the various weapons. That is, as enemies advanced on each other, bowmen, if present, went into action while still at a distance; at closer range, javelins or spears were thrown; at short range, the mace and cutting ax, or, as weapon of last resort, the dagger might be used. The battle itself consisted of a melee of hand-to-hand fighting at this last stage, in which the superior numbers of the Egyptians made the outcome inevitable in most cases.

Although Egyptian weapons were of good quality, they were obsolescent in terms of Asiatic weapons long before the pyramid age (about 2650-2500 B.C.). The sword was ineffective and could be used only for stabbing and not for slashing before the advent of bronze swords about 1400 B.C. Accordingly, these existed only as daggers in the earlier period. Asia had bronze for this purpose by 3000, but Egypt did not get bronze in any significant amount until over 1200 years later. The bow was not effective until the composite bow, which was an Asiatic invention, unknown in Egypt before the Hyksos period (about 1700-1580 B.C.).

The mace and the cutting ax were used in Egypt long after they had been replaced by the piercing ax in Asia, because Egypt's chief enemies down to 2000 B.C. lacked helmets.

Despite the intrinsic weaknesses of the Egyptian military system, the country was defended successfully from the combination of strong natural defenses and no major enemy close at hand. The collapse of the Old Kingdom was political rather than military and arose from the fact that central control over local resources and over local agents lacked organizational techniques and mechanisms so that central control depended to a dangerous degree upon ideological rather than organizational forces. For example, the absence of any system of money meant that all supply activities were carried on in kind, not by shifting actual goods but by shifting claims on such goods with minimal movement of the goods themselves. This means that local produce, although owned by the ruler, was left close to its source of origin until granted by the ruler to some local agent as remuneration for his services to the ruler. In the same way, men recruited locally were trained, armed, and stationed under local control. In time, land and peasants were granted to royal agents to provide remuneration for services, with only nominal attributions of goods, power, and loyalty to the Pharaoh. In 3000, when only the Pharaoh was immortal and divine and all other men were simply temporary aggregates of dust, loyalty to the Pharaoh was sufficient to overbalance all kinds of organizational weaknesses, but by 2000, when eternal life had come to be attainable by any man able to pay for the embalmment which might keep his corpse intact after death, religious loyalty had weakened so that it was unable to overbalance the growing local control of all real entities, such as land, labor, food, weapons, and water. The elaborate bookkeeping arrangements which had grown up to keep track of the claims and rights of the central government were quite unable to counterbalance the simple fact that all the real elements on which the central power depended were in local control.

As a consequence of this development, central power reached its peak, in real terms, about 2600 B.C., a condition represented by the enormous mobilization of centralized resources required to build the great pyramid of Cheops, but, from that point on, central power steadily dispersed into local hands. This process is recognized by historians as the rise and decline of the Old Kingdom (from about 2780 to about 2260 B.C.). As the local agents of the central power became hereditary local lords (called "nomachs"), the Old Kingdom disintegrated into a chaos of these struggling "nomachs."

This process is an excellent illustration of the differences between an archaic state and a modern state. Under modern conditions (since 500 B.C.) shifts from centralized to local power and the reverse constitute a process in which the chief elements are likely to be material ones, either weapons systems, an administrative organization, or technology. But the disintegration of the centralized power of the Old Kingdom seems to have been much more a consequence of ideological and religious changes, notably the growing disbelief that the Pharaoh was a living god and the extension of immortality (previously a divine quality) from a royal monopoly to an aim achievable by many men. Certainly

129

the change had little or nothing to do with changes
in weapons systems, for there was none.

Even more puzzling is the slow restoration of
centralized authority by the extension of the power
of the nomachs of Thebes to create a new Middle Kingdom. It seems possible that these leaders from the
far south, in what was, at that time, a frontier
zone, found sufficient psychological support from
the widespread reaction against disorder, insecurity, and localism, to extend their rule gradually
over an increasingly large part of Egypt.

The nature of the disorder of the First Intermediate period, with its implication of social upheaval, may be gathered from an old papyrus which
says, "The offices of officials were stormed, and
the records destroyed. Serfs became lords. The
land was revolving like a potter's wheel. The high-
born were starving, and the fat lords had to work
in place of the serfs. Their children were hurled
against the walls. High honors went to female
serfs, who wore precious ornaments, while former
great ladies went around in rags begging for food.
Weeds were eaten and water was drunk; food had
to be taken from the pigs. The learned man had
only one wish: !May the people perish and no more
be born.' Those who had been poor suddenly became
rich. Upstarts now rule, and the former officials
are now their servants."

The Middle Kingdom, which soon shifted its
capital north to Memphis, lasted only briefly,
through two dynasties (XI and XII, 1991-1786 B.C.).
It was a period of relative peace, great prosperity,
and commercial expansion into the Levant. Local
officials were kept under central control by taking from them all military powers and centralizing
these into a new organization under the direct control of the Pharaoh, and supported by an autonomous
endowment of property. This meant, in effect, that
the hard-working peasantry and the black soil of
Egypt had to support three separate establishments:
a civil bureaucracy which included the governors
and local lords; the military system headed by
the Pharaoh; and a new establishment of priests
and temples to replace that of the Old Kingdom,

130

whose immediate wealth had been largely dispersed during the First Intermediate period. The armed forces were kept busy trying to extend the ruler's power up the Nile beyond the cataracts.

The Middle Kingdom was ended by a revolutionary event: the invasion of Egypt from the Levant and Sinai by intruders known as Hyksos. These Hyksos were largely Semites (Canaanites) with a mixture of Hurrians (speaking Asiatic languages) and a few Indo-Europeans as leaders. This invasion was part of the general movement of peoples which arose from the drying up of the grasslands in the centuries after 2500 B.C. The Indo-Europeans whom we call Mitanni and Hittites came over the Caucasus about 2000 B.C. and drove a great wave of the stocky High-land Zone Hurrians southward before them. The Mitanni stopped on the Syrian Saddle about 1800, while the Hurrians continued southward into the Levant (which at that time was being occupied by immigrants from the southern grasslands of the Fertile Crescent, the semi-pastoral Semites we know as Canaanites). The Canaanites, with new weapons derived from the Mitanni and Hurrians, pushed down into Egypt as conquering invaders. They set up a capital at Avaris in the Sinai area and ruled over the Nile delta, acting as a tribute-collecting upper class from about 1720 to about 1580. Eventually, they were expelled from Egypt by Amose, ruler of Thebes, who founded the XVIIIth Dynasty.

The impact of the Hyksos on Egypt, and of the Mitanni on the whole Levant, was revolutionary, since they brought the first large scale use of bronze to Egypt, the composite bow, the horse, and the war chariot. These techniques, added to the psychological jolt of the invasion itself, profoundly changed Egypt's weapons and politics. Their introduction brought Egypt into the western Asiatic imperial struggles which continued for the five centuries of the New Kingdom (1580-1085), until the way of life associated with these techniques and with the imperial systems they supported were wiped away in the new migrations of peoples called the "Iron Age invasions" (1200-1000 B.C.) and the subsequent dark ages.

131

5.   Mesopotamia, 4000-2000 B.C.

While this relatively simple process was going on in Egypt, much more complicated developments were going on in western Asia, centered in Mesopotamia but closely interlinked with developments in the two grasslands and the intervening Highland Zone.

In Mesopotamia, by 2800 B.C., military weapons and tactics had already developed far beyond those which Egypt knew at the time of the Hyksos invasion, a thousand years later. In the Proto-Literate period, under Sumerian leadership, infantry were organized in massed phalanxes, each man armed with a spear, a metal helmet, and a studded cape for body protection. The last two defensive items led to development of a piercing ax of copper or bronze with a socket for attachment to a handle. At the same early date, war vehicles of four-wheel and two-wheel types, drawn by asses or onagers, were available.

Battle tactics in Mesopotamia in the Sumerian period (before 2400 B.C.) seem to have consisted of a charge by four-wheeled wagons, each with a driver and a fighting man, against the enemy's massed infantry in an effort to disrupt its formation, followed by a charge of the infantry phalanx.

The vehicles were drawn by four beasts harnessed by a yoke arrangement to a central pole. The two-wheel vehicle seems to have been used for carrying commands and messages on the field, while the four-wheel vehicle and its two passengers were used for direct assault on the enemy in an effort to spread panic among his forces. The fighter from his moving platform used javelin and spear, but not the bow, against the enemy. Only later did the bow, a long range weapon, become the chief weapon associated with chariot warfare. The earlier, bowless, chariot had solid wheels made of three pieces of wood, with stud nails along the wheel rims to dig into the earth.

By 2500 B.C. the mace and cutting ax were largely eliminated from Mesopotamian armaments because of the increasing strength of metal helmets. They were replaced by piercing axes and the first appearance of the sickle sword, a heavy curved sword with a short handle used for slashing at the enemy, and accordingly having its cutting edge on the outside of the curved blade rather than on the inside of the curve as in an agricultural sickle. There was also some use of the throwing stick and the sling in western Asia in the early period, although both of these seem to have been weapons more familiar to hunters and shepherds than to military men and more useful in the Levant than in Mesopotamia itself.

With these weapons, especially with the spear-armed infantry led by the four-wheeled chariots, the Sumerians dominated all of Mesopotamia and briefly reached the western edge of the Syrian Saddle, if not the Mediterranean itself, about 2500. But superiority shifted from one city to another, and by 2400 the Sumerians were being replaced by the quite different Akkadians whose center of influence lay just north of Sumer in the Mesopotamian valley.

The shift from Sumerians to Akkadians was a change of great significance, for the round-headed, stocky, clean-shaven Sumerians, dressed in skirts and speaking agglutinative languages represented the old Asiatic peoples of the Highland Zone who had first established the Neolithic garden cultures about 9000 B.C. and the city civilization in the alluvial valley in the sixth millennium B.C.

The Akkadians, on the other hand, were related to the Assyrians, both being long-headed, heavily bearded Semitic peoples who came into the Fertile Crescent from the drying grasslands of the Syrian desert and northern Arabia before 3000 B.C. By 2400 these Akkadians were exerting their supremacy in Mesopotamia. Their success, under Sargon the Great and his grandson, Naram-Sin, about 2350, may have been the result of superior weapons, for they had the formidable composite bow, capable of penetrating defensive armor, and a much improved sickle sword.

These weapon improvements, especially the composite bow, were expensive and required greatly increased training and professionalization of military personnel. This, plus the steady increase in warfare, had a double consequence in Mesopotamian society:

133

earlier elements of democracy were weakened and replaced by authoritarian and militarized influences;
and the original priesthood who had built up the system was gradually eclipsed and almost totally replaced by military rulers. The shift from Sumerian
to Semite dominance in the second half of the third
millennium B.C. marked a notable step in this change.
At the same time, many other aspects of life were
modified very drastically: the older matriarchal
elements in society and religious belief were over-
laid by patriarchal elements, the peaceful and earth-
worshipping aspects derived from the society's Neolithic heritage were almost totally replaced by warlike, violent forces, strongly associated with the
worship of sky deities and storm gods. Steadily
intensified efforts to achieve and retain political
unity in the whole Mesopotamian valley from the Persian Gulf to the Mediterranean Sea greatly accelerated
this whole process.

In Mesopotamia, as in Egypt, the Sumero-Akkadian
empire broke down at the end of the third millennium
from organizational weakness, especially from inability of any central authority to retain control
over local agents. Inadequate communications and
transportation, and especially lack of administrative
techniques, made this impossible. Thus disintegration
of the Akkadian empire, leading to a temporary resurgence of Sumerian influence and a great intensification of local warfare, weakened defense of the
valley just as new waves of Semitic pastoral peoples
began to pour out of the deserts into the whole Fertile Crescent about 2200 B.C.

6.   Grasslands Pastoralism, 3000-1000 B.C.

We have already indicated the importance of
the advent of pastoralism as a way of life subsequent
to the invention of urban civilization itself, in the
period 4000-2000 B.C. We have now reached a stage
in our story where pastoralism played a major role
in civilized history for the first time. Accordingly,
we must get a better idea of its nature.

Like most terms used in history "nomadic" and
"pastoralism" are ambiguous. The former has a narrower meaning than the latter and is historically much

later. "Pastoralism" means little more than that people live by herding animals, but it does not imply that they live from this activity exclusively. "Nomadic," on the other hand, comes close to implying exclusive reliance on domestic animals, since "nomadic" implies movement, with herds and flocks, over considerable distances on a regular periodic basis. This might mean, in fully developed "nomadic pastoralism," that its practitioners live exclusively from their animals and are almost constantly on the move, without permanent homes or permanent agricultural fields of any kind. This fully developed nomadic life is, however, a late development, associated with riding on the backs of animals (horses or camels); since such riding is not established as a regular activity until after 1000 B.C., it is not a concern of this chapter.

On the other hand, pastoralism as an adjunct to settled agricultural life is much older, going back to at least 3000 B.C. It may be, as Owen Lattimore suggested, a consequence of a climate of increasing dryness and decreasingly available grass, which forced the herders of agricultural villages to go farther and farther afield in search of forage for their animals. Eventually such pastoralists would be away from their homes and fields for longer and longer periods and would obtain increasing portions of their needs from their domestic animals with less reliance on supplies from arable sources. The final stage in this transition from a partial to a fully nomadic life would come when the animal keepers periodically returned to the soil tillers to exchange products of the two different activities. This final stage was reached when men became riders on animals' backs after 1000 B.C.

This long period of transition from incipient pastoralism to full nomadism probably covered close to 2500 years, from before 3000 to after 500 B.C. Its implications for our subject can be traced in terms of two quite separate developments concerned with the animals and with wheeled vehicles.

The use of animals for logistic rather than nutritional purposes over this 2500 years has three parts: (1) as pack animals; (2) as draft animals;

135

and (3) as riding animals. The first of these may go back before 4000 B.C., when the donkey and the onager were domesticated on the southern flatlands. The history of the horse as a pack animal is at least a thousand years later, after 3000, and in the northern flatlands of western Asia, as we shall see.

Use of draft animals also was earlier south of the mountains, probably in Mesopotamia, where the wheeled cart may have been invented and probably goes back before 3500 (although the wheel could be a millennium older). The draft animals of Mesopotamia were still the onager and, more rarely, the ass.

Use of draft animals on the northern flatlands was considerably later, perhaps not before 2500, and the draft animal used at first was the ox. The horse as a draft animal is not earlier than 2500, even north of the mountains where the horse originated. The outburst of these northern warrior peoples as invaders southward across the mountains to Anatolia, the Aegean, the Levant, and Mesopotamia in the period from just before 2000 to about 1700 spread this use of horse-drawn vehicles and, at the same time, made them a significant element in warfare by the introduction of spoked wheels, and the light two-wheeled chariot, to go along with the horse.

The development of the wheel and its use on a vehicle is really a separate story, whose early history has been handled in a most unsatisfactory way by historians.

The wheel as an artifact goes back to at least 4500 B.C. when it was invented, not as a transport device but as a religious and ritual object, representing the sun. Just as the lunar crescent and the ship stood for the female principle, so the disk or wheel stood for the masculine principle. This explains the appearance of a spoked wheel on pottery as early as 4700 B.C. and the appearance of wheels and ships together on mortuary pottery down to at least 700 B.C. (Greek geometric pottery). These early solar disks, along with lunar crescents and other devices, were placed on the walls of early temples and were also erected on poles before the temple doors. On critical festivals (often in the

third week of our month of December) these disks
were rolled in solemn ritual from the temple to
water (a female element) and returned, in order to
make the sun, which had been retreating southward
for six months, return northward. The difficulty
of rolling a ceremonial wheel, like a hoop, for
any distance without some sacrilegious accident,
led to the stabilization of the wheel, with other
similar wheels, on an axle and later on a cart.
The body of this cart was originally a sledge, in
use since at least 5000 B.C. Such a cart, dragged
from the temple to some distant rendezvous with the
female goddess of the earth (symbolized as water or
a ship or some other symbol such as a cave, a tomb,
or the temple nave itself), became a mortuary vehicle (what V. Gordon Childe calls "a hearse").
This use of an animal-drawn wheeled vehicle as a
funeral carriage became a prevalent form of mortuary ritual on a very wide geographic basis from
at least 3000 B.C. down to the recent past. It involved a complex group of religious beliefs associated with the archaic religion, including the
idea that the deceased would return, after crossing
water and interment in the womb (or tomb) of the
earth, as the sun returns annually from its winter
visit. This complex idea has remained with us in
such discrepant examples as the Juggernaut car of
pagan India or the funeral caisson of President Ken-
nedy crossing the river to Arlington Cemetery.

Before 3000 this use of wheeled vehicles for
funerary ritual had been supplemented by their use
in warfare. A third usage, in economic activities
as farm vehicles, is largely unrecorded in history
but may also precede the year 3000. With farm
usage we are not concerned here, but it must be
recognized that we have great difficulty in distinguishing, in the historical evidence, those vehicles which have a symbolic, ritual, mortuary role
from those which have a military role, except when
the context makes it clear that we are concerned
with warfare and battles. On the whole, it seems
fairly clear that military vehicles until about
2000 were equipped with solid wheels and were
drawn by onagers. This weapon was of vital significance in extending the area of Sumerian power
up the Mesopotamian valley to Syria about 2500,

almost a full millennium after the device first appeared, probably as a funerary vehicle, in Erech.

This war machine of the Sumerians was so successful that it was soon copied, reaching the Asian steppes and the Indus valley by 2500, south Russia, Crete, and Anatolia about 2000. The subsequent diffusion to a wider area, reaching China by 1300 (where it became one of the chief supports of Shang power), the Balkans about 1600, Sweden and all northern and central Europe before 1000, was of spoked wheels on a two-wheel, horse-drawn, vehicle.

The spoked wheel was so expensive that it could be used only for military purposes and was invented in this context, probably in northern Mesopotamia, shortly after 2000. But despite its expense, it was so superior in a military sense, especially when drawn by horses instead of onagers and with a light body on two spoked wheels, instead of the earlier and heavier four-wheeled war wagon, that it was copied everywhere that horses could be sustained or skilled workmen could be obtained to build the vehicle. The question of expense was of little importance when the economic burden was borne by people who were not consulted on the matter. In fact, all of these changes in the period 2100-1700 were linked together, including the drastic increase in the component of force and the parallel decrease in the religious component in the power structure of all areas, including Egypt. In those places from northwestern Europe to India and beyond, where warlike fighters conquered more peaceful peasants, the fighters in their chariots hardly gave a second thought to the expense which was borne by the peasants.

The consequences of all this were summed up by Childe in two passages which read, "The replacement of onagers by horses, and the substitution of spoked for solid wheels, evidently revolutionized warfare in the Near East. The results were catastrophic. By the eighteenth century B.C., the new weapon of offense had provoked new means of defense that reacted on town planning; in Palestine, for instance, huge glacis at Jericho and other cities replaced the nearly vertical ramparts that had provided adequate security for over 2000 years. . . . Chariotry was

138

the decisive factor in the great wars of empire
that ravaged Hither Asia in the sixteenth and following centuries B.C., and it was the rapid communications maintainable by horse-drawn chariots
that enabled the Egyptians, the Hittites, and the
Assyrians to organize and administer empires vastly
larger and more durable than the domains conquered
by the Kings of Agade and Ur less than a millennium
earlier. The establishment of the first Celestial
Empire by the Shangs, in the valley of the Hoang-Ho,
may be attributed to a like cause."

The chief event which bound all these diverse
factors together was the explosion of the warrior
peoples, or Bronze Age invaders, out of the south
Russian steppes in the millennium centered on 2000
B.C. The site and sequence of this event was roughly as follows.

When the Neolithic garden culture was already
spreading across the hills and parklands of the
Highland Zone, the heroic hunting cultures continued to survive on the grasslands both north and
south of the Highland Zone. North of that zone,
in the great area from the Kirgiz steppes and Alma
Ata in the east to the Carpathian Mountains in the
west runs the Steppe Corridor through the grassy
passage between the southern end of the Ural Mountains and the northern edge of the Caspian Sea.
This Steppe Corridor has played a role as an east-
west passage north of the Highland Zone parallel
to that played by the Syrian Saddle south of the
Highland Zone, both serving as passages for Asiatic
influences to move westward toward Europe.

But long before the Steppe Corridor played any
significant role as an east-west passage, it was an
area of heroic hunting cultures, broken up into
hunting territories organized on a north-south basis
rather than as an east-west passage. These hunting
peoples were, as might be expected, patriarchal,
warlike, wanderers who never were exposed directly
to any of the softening influences of the Highland
Zone Neolithic garden cultures and who retained,
and intensified, their violent characteristics when
they became pastoral peoples after 3000 B.C. This
change occurred by selective adoption from the High-

139

land Zone and the city civilizations farther south of certain cultural elements, notably domestication of animals and use of metal weapons. These could be adopted into the heroic hunting outlook and patterns of behavior without destroying it but, on the contrary, served to intensify it. In a somewhat similar fashion, the hunting Indian tribes of the American plains adopted the horse from the Spaniards after 1543, as an intensifying rather than a disruptive influence.

The heroic hunters of the Asiatic grasslands north of the Highland Zone applied the new technique of domestication after 3000 B.C. to the animals they had been hunting, the horses of the steppe and the cattle of their southern boundary areas. The peoples who did this spoke the basic Indo-European languages, and we shall identify them by this name from here on. East of these Indo-European-speakers and somewhat later, a similar change from hunting to domestication was undergone by speakers of Ural-Altaic languages.

In a similar way, south of the Highland Zone and the city civilizations of Mesopotamia, in the Arabian grasslands, the Semite peoples, speaking inflected languages remotely related to Indo-European, also received domestication and metal weapons from the more civilized Highland Zone agglutinative speakers (especially the Sumerians) north of them. These Semites were hunters and after 3500 were pastoral herders (chiefly of sheep and donkeys) in the grassy areas, now largely desert, which were enclosed by the Fertile Crescent and the water boundaries consisting of the Red Sea, Arabian Sea, and Persian Gulf. The Fertile Crescent, like a horseshoe opening southward, consisted of two halves: the Levant and Mesopotamia joined together on the north by the Syrian Saddle.

Both of these language groups, the Semites and the Indo-Europeans, benefited by the long period of moist Atlantic climate from 6000 to after 3000 B.C. This provided a plentiful supply of grass and of grass-eating herd animals in their respective areas. But the shift to a drier, sub-Boreal climate about 3000 B.C. (a little earlier in the south; somewhat later in the north) greatly reduced the supply of grass and forced these pastoral warriors to move out of their grasslands toward the Highland Zone and the city civilizations from which all material blessings seemed to flow regardless of climatic variations.

The Semite pressure from the Syrian and Arabian grasslands was fairly steady from about 3500 to 1000 B.C. and resumed again in another period of increasing dryness after A.D. 200. However, there were four major peaks of Semite pastoral pressures on the town and urban areas of the Near East: (1) the Giblite-Akkadian-Assyrian migrations before 3000 B.C.; (2) the Canaanite-Amorite migrations just before 2000 B.C.; (3) the Aramean-Chaldean migrations just before 1000 B.C.; and (4) as a quite distinct event, the Arab migrations after A.D. 600.

The Indo-European migrations from the steppes were much more explosive and devastating than those of the Semites further south, and were largely concentrated in three terrific outbursts of warlike pastoral sky-worshippers. These were: (1) the Bronze Age migrations around 2000 B.C.; (2) the Iron Age migrations just before 1000 B.C. (say from 1400 B.C. in central Europe to about 1100 in the Near East); and (3) the Germanic migrations, pushed by Ural-Altaic peoples like the Huns and Avars, after A.D. 200. To complete this listing of steppe pastoral population extrusions we might add: (4) the final outburst of Ural-Altaic pastoralists, the Mongols and Turks, in the period A.D. 800-1600; and (5) the outburst of Bedouin Arabs from the Red Sea area across north Africa in the 11th century.

The impact of these nine migrations of grassland pastoralists into areas of agricultural peasants and urban civilizations makes up much of the structure of Old World history, from Ireland to the Far East. The history of these events is not our concern here, but it is obvious that the significance of these events on weapons systems and security was very great. To assess that significance we must have a much clearer view of the nature of Indo-European grassland pastoralism, and assume that other pastoralisms were simply more confused, ambiguous, or diluted versions of this way of life.

The chief contribution of Indo-European grasslands pastoralism to history, even to military history, was ideological. This ideological contribution remains of major importance even today, and
eclipses any contributions which these people have
made to weapons or to organizational patterns in
the use of weapons. Before we concentrate on this
ideological contribution, however, we should have
a rough idea of the total way of life of Indo-European grasslands pastoralism.

In the third millennium B.C. the Indo-Europeans,
with cattle, horses, and probably sheep, followed
the grass as it became available, northward in the
spring and summer, then southward, toward the hills
and wooded valleys of the Highland Zone in the autumn and winter. They carried their goods, along
with the young, the old, and their personal possessions, in high-sided, two-wheel, ox-drawn carts.
These carts were often used for living quarters in
bad weather and were drawn into a defensive circle
around the camp fires at each stop. Residence otherwise was in tents, sod houses, and even log houses
at various stages of the annual migration, which
often moved hundreds of miles, north and south,
from the wooded hills of the Highland Zone to the
edges of the deciduous forests of the northern
flatlands. These routes, although hundreds of
miles north and south, were probably no more than
forty or fifty miles wide, with enemy, or at least
rival, tribes moving on parallel routes on either
side. Tents and clothing were made of horsehide,
horsehair, furs, and wool felt. Food consisted of
beef, cheese and other milk products, berries,
game animals and some agricultural products. Drink
was beer or mare's milk fermented in leather bags.
Social life was extremely patriarchal, competitive,
violent, and convivial. It seems likely that young
men established their right to marry and assume a
role in the tribe by proving their merit and obtaining an economic base for family life by cattle
raiding and horse stealing from the neighboring
tribes on either side.

The most important contribution of these people to history and to us is in outlook and ideology,
although their influence on our culture is significant in all aspects of life. Today, as a result of
this influence, we carry, as our family name, that

142

of our father rather than of our mother; when we
think of God we think of a masculine rather than
a feminine Being and raise our eyes to heaven rather than lowering them to the earth; we readily
turn to violence when we are crossed; we are simultaneously competitively individualistic and solidly
tribalistic in our social attitudes rather than cooperative or communal, like many Asiatics; we speak
Indo-European languages and accept all the cognitive
assumptions associated with the structure of such
languages; we celebrate all social occasions and
almost any social gathering by drinking alcohol;
these traits and many others are parts of our social heritage from our Indo-European pastoral social ancestry.

The chief contribution of that social ancestry,
however, especially to weapons systems and security,
is ideological, and, strangely enough, it is the
aspect of this heritage which is least well understood, or even recognized. Although it involves a
total attitude toward life and human experience, it
can be described in two basic parts: (1) dualistic
rationalism, such as we previously associated with
Zoroaster and Pythagorean rationalism; and (2) fanatical extremism. I shall say no more about the
former, but the latter is fundamental to our subject.

We have seen that grassland hunters, from their
very mode of life, are likely to be patriarchal and
warlike. Among the Indo-Europeans, however, these
attributes were much intensified and distorted by
their religious history which interacted with the
harsh and extreme environment of their northern
continental grasslands to create an almost psychopathic outlook. Climatic conditions on the grasslands were violent, extremist, and very changeable.
Bitterly cold winters with winds and blizzards were
contrasted with hot summers under a relentless beat-
ing sun. All life was dominated and enclosed by
the sky, constantly changing, sometimes incredibly
beautiful but often incredibly frightening with
surging clouds, sudden winds, even tornados, and
often violent thunder and lightning able to kill
men, horses, and cattle with a single instantaneous
bolt. To those Indo-Europeans the sky became deity:
violent, fickle, changeable, overpowering, and daz-

143

zling both in serenity and in anger. Their name for
deity was a word which has come down to us, vari-
ously, as dyess, deus, zeus, or, with the attached
word for "father," as zu-piter, zu-pater, or jupiter.
The basic meaning of this name was, apparently,
"dazzling sky."

The nature of this deity as extremist, changeable, violent, and annihilatingly powerful became,
to some extent, the ideal model of human masculine
behavior for the Indo-Europeans, a trend which was
solidified by the appearance of a new religious idea
concerned with personal salvation or "immortality"
among the Indo-European tribesmen about that same time.

This new idea of personal salvation, probably
instigated by vague reports about the ideas of such
salvation among more civilized peoples, is well-
represented by the ambiguities of the word "immortality."

This word, to us, has two quite distinct meanings: (1) personal salvation in the Hereafter; and
(2) being remembered after death by people still
alive. To the Indo-European warrior peoples these
two meanings were really one: an individual won
salvation by being remembered among the living;
so long as a man was remembered and talked about,
his deeds narrated, admired, and emulated, he was
not truly dead but still survived.

This belief is the basis for the heroic and
epic tradition found among all Indo-European peoples, from the Aryan invaders of India to the Vikings of Scandinavia and Ireland, and is well represented by the heroic, bardic ideas of the Greeks,
Slavs, Latins, and others in between. How did a
man obtain immortality? By being remembered?
And how could he insure that he would be remembered?
By being so "god-like" (in the Indo-European sense)
in his violence, extremism, and power that he could
not be forgotten, and poets would sing of his deeds
forever. Such deeds were generally destructive,
simply because excessive and memorable destruction
is so much easier to achieve than memorable con-
structiveness. This included killing, burning,
raping, and drinking. For any of these, in exces-

sive degree, men would be remembered. In peacetime a man could be remembered by the prodigious quantities of alcohol he could consume, the great quantities of game he could kill (under the most dangerous circumstances), and the way he could excel other men in games and physical prowess. But the real mark of a memorable man could be found in war, above all by dying gloriously in a totally destructive Gotterdammerung in which hordes of the enemy, in nameless ignominy, were taken to death with him.

These ideas are still with us, explicitly so up to 1916, in every barracks, war memorial, fraternity, gun club, athletic event, hunting safari, dueling code, or roll of honor. We of the English-speaking and Teutonic tradition, at least until World War I, regarded these values as so universal and unquestioned that we were hardly aware that we had them. We regarded the majority of the world's peoples who lacked them, or any individuals in our own society who questioned them, as spiritually inferior, de-masculinized, gutless persons made to be bullied and ruled over by the dauntless Indo-European, or Anglo-American-Teutonic minority, who still embraced these views. The power of such views, in classical civilization, and, after 1500 years of Christianity, in Western and Russian civilization, is a notable example of their power and persistence. Chaudhuri has recently pointed out their persistence in Hindu culture in his book, The Continent of Circe (1966).

Even today many readers of these words will be irritated at my efforts to provide an objective picture of these ideas, and will regard my efforts to do so as somewhat subversive. They will be especially annoyed by my suggestion that these beliefs could be carried to neurotic and psychotic degrees. For that reason, the implications of this suggestion must be stated.

The Indo-Europeans early recognized that all superhuman or heroic achievement required an extremism which required a man to escape from the restrictions of his own identity and his own everyday life. The use of the words "superhuman" and "heroic" in that last sentence is significant, since to the Indo-European both terms carried implications of deity.

145

In fact, the gods were the "Immortals," as they were among the Greeks, that is, beings whose only non-human quality was that they never died. An ordinary "mortal" (that is, specifically "one who died") could become "immortal" by escaping from his mortality and personal identity by a psychosomatic experience which carried him outside the normal boundaries of ordinary human experience into the supernatural. This could be obtained or stimulated by excess: excess of fear, hatred, rage, alcohol, speed, violence, narcotics, or self-hypnosis. The condition was recognized in all Indo-European cultures, was considered to be capable of self-induction, and was considered to make an individual who achieved it impervious to pain, fear, personal consideration, or weariness. It gave rise to attitudes and personality types which Nietsche has called "Dionysian." It was admired by the early Indo-Europeans and considered to reach its highest level in a kind of self-induced frenzy which became, in their tradition, part of the preparation for battle. It was, however, like all divinity, so rare, that one who achieved it was often allowed to fight in battle alone, or at least in a preliminary engagement, as champion of his side. The condition to which I refer was often mentioned in Indo-European heroic and bardic literature, but, as such literature became the study of Christian scholars and pedantic classicists in our own society, the meaning has been generally lost and the words have been translated as "frenzy," "divine inspiration" or something like that.

The two waves of Indo-European migrations before 1000 B.C. are known as the Bronze Age invasions (roughly 2000 B.C.) and the Iron Age invasions (roughly 1200 B.C.). The first burst out of the south Russian grasslands and penetrated into all areas from central Europe to India and Mongolia. Unfortunately the migrants have been given a different name in each area, such as warrior peoples in central Europe, Achaeans in the Balkans, Minyans and Hittites in Anatolia, Mitanni in the Levant, Iranians and Aryans in Persia and India. In most areas they became an upper class, with horses, sky gods, bronze weapons, and patriarchal violence, ruling over earth-worshipping, more peaceful, peasant peoples.

146

This combination gave a certain discipline, power, and capital accumulation to those areas, such as the Balkans, Anatolia, and Iran, which were yet uncivilized, and by direct or indirect influence moved the civilized areas toward the great Bronze Age empires, whose clashes make up so much of the period 1700-1000 B.C. in the Near East.

The subsequent Iron Age invasions of the Indo-Europeans exploded, with even greater violence, out of the northern Balkans after 1200. This movement, starting from a more western area, had catastrophic consequences in central Europe, the Balkans, and Anatolia, where the Bronze Age cultures were destroyed, but had only incidental impact on the Levant, Egypt, or Mesopotamia, and little influence in Iran, India, or Mongolia. As a result, most of western Asia and the Near East was pushed into a dark age by 1000 B.C. The area west of Anatolia came out of it, into a more civilized mode of life, called classical after 900 B.C.

In understanding this process, we must remember that the two Indo-European pastoral intrusions were fitted in with the three (somewhat less pastoral and somewhat earlier) Semitic intrusions which were associated, at intervals of about a thousand years, with the Assyrio-Akkadians, the Canaanite-Amorites, and the Aramean-Chaldeans, over the same 3200-1000 B.C. period. Fortunately for our cluttered memory, these Semites, in emerging from the Syrian and Arabian grasslands as they dried up, went into only three areas: west to the Levant, east to Mesopotamia, and southwest to Africa and Ethiopia.

7. Bronze Age Rivalries, 2000-1000 B.C.

Although the second millennium was dominated on the international scene by the exploits of the great empires, Egypt, Babylonia, and the Hittites, the background against which these states performed was made up of the mass movements of great numbers of lesser peoples. The platform on which these all performed was the Fertile Crescent, a horseshoe of adequately watered land which stood like a rounded arch on the two bases of the Persian Gulf in the east and the Sinai peninsula in the west. This

147

Crescent, beginning in the marshes at the mouths of the Tigris and Euphrates Rivers, curved up the two-river valley to the northwest, with deserts on the left and the Highland Zone on the right, crossed the Syrian Saddle to the Mediterranean Sea and then ran south toward Egypt, with the deserts still on the left (eastern side) but the Mediterranean Sea on the right (west). In the period 2300-1800 the population of the Fertile Crescent was largely re-placed with two very different peoples, the stocky, round-headed, agglutinative speaking (Asiatic) Hur-rians and Kassites coming in from the Highland Zone, while the taller, more long-headed, inflective lan-guage speakers (Semites), the Amurru, came in from the deserts inside the Crescent. The Amurru, gen-erally called the Canaanites in the Levant or the Amorites in Mesopotamia, were the forefathers of the Hebrews, Phoenicians, Hyksos, and Babylonians. By 1700, when the imperial conflicts were building up, the whole Fertile Crescent was a mixture of Amurru principalities and wandering tribal groups interspersed with innumerable Hurrian-Kassite vil-lages and towns. The battles and struggles of the great monarchies such as Egypt, Hittite, Mitanni, Elam, and Assyria took place above this complex tapestry of lesser peoples, supported by their economic activities, but conducted in different languages and with different purposes. The reasons for this are simple enough: the monarchies had weapons and organization totally separated from the activities of the great mass of Amurri-Hurrians, a situation clearly reflected in the Biblical ac-counts of the Hebrew relations with the Pharaoh of Egypt.

The everyday activities of this mass of peoples were carried on almost totally separated from the activities of the governmental structure which reared above them, as remote as heaven itself! The government assumed no responsibility for the welfare, peace, safety, or education of the peo-ple as individuals. These things, if obtained at all, were available from the social, cooperative, and above all family activities of the people them-selves. Law and order, including settlement of dis-putes (except a few involving property rights) were handled locally. The essence of the situation was

148

that the enormous mass of the people were excluded
from the system, except as contributors of economic
goods and manpower, a situation reflected in the
fact that they were subjects, not citizens. This
situation, slightly alleviated, continued in the
Western world until the eighteenth century and in
eastern Europe until the nineteenth.

The period between the two Indo-European invasions is also complicated by an economic factor
of which we know very little. This was the appearance on the international scene of civilizations
which were not based on alluvial valley agriculture,
but which were able to produce enough to provide
manpower and weapons to sustain great power status.
The first of these was the sea kingdom centered on
the island of Crete, which appeared before 2500,
became the dominant power in control of the sea
after 2000, but never was a significant land power
until the Mycenaean period after 1400 B.C.

The second of these new non-alluvial powers
was the Hittite monarchy and empire of central Anatolia, which became one of the chief contenders for
control of the Syrian Saddle after 1600, along with
Egypt and the Mitanni.

The third of these non-alluvial civilizations
was that of the Canaanites which arose in the Levant
after 2000, was largely destroyed there by the contending Iron Age great powers after 700 but continued to exist as a sea power in the western Mediterranean until 146 B.C. as the Punic state of Carthage.

We do not know how these non-alluvial valley
civilizations produced sufficient food (and thus
manpower) to provide large forces armed with metal
weapons and other expensive equipment, but they
did so from before 2000 B.C.

In this connection, it is interesting to note
that control of metal ore mines never became a
chief source of political power in the ancient
world. This was probably because the processing
of such ores into metals and weapons required such
specialized knowledge and skills and was concentrated in such inaccessible areas (Armenia, the

149

Caucasus, Bohemia, Nubia, etc.) that it could be obtained only by concessions rather than by duress. But, on the other hand, the mobilization of troops to use such weapons was so expensive that only areas with outstanding production, especially of food, could support large forces of armed men. To this must be added, of course, that wealth and weapons of themselves were not sufficient to provide any people with political power, since organization and morale (ideology) were equally significant, so that those areas, like Egypt after 1200, which had wealth but lacked or had lost organization and morale soon found that other peoples, like the Greeks, who lacked wealth but had the other two factors, took over Egypt's wealth for themselves.

This may explain why the areas of great mineral resources (Armenia, Cyprus, Spain, Bohemia, even Anatolia) never became centers of great political power, except briefly (in Bohemia about 1450 B.C. and in Anatolia under the Hittite empire about 1650-1250).

Another development of significance in this millennium was a great increase in offensive power of political units from about 2000 to about 1300 followed by a very rapid and almost total decrease of such power in the period 1300 to after 1000 B.C. By "offensive power" here, as elsewhere, I mean the ability to impose one's political will over increasing distances and with growing intensity over individuals (two very different qualities).

There can be little doubt that the growth of offensive power in the first half of the second millennium B.C. was associated with improved weapons of a more expensive type and above all by increased facility of both transportation and communications. In this process the central fact was the advent, throughout the Near East, of the light horse-drawn war chariot, and the diffusion of the composite bow and of bronze weapons (both offensive and defensive) of better quality and in far greater quantities.

The horse and the new speedy chariot with four-spoke wheels were both spread by the Indo-Europeans, chiefly the Mitanni, who settled on the Syrian Saddle,

150

imposed tolls on passing merchants, and raised horses which they sold to all who could afford to pay. Within about a century, 1700-1600, the war chariot had spread to Mesopotamia, to Egypt, to the Hittites of Anatolia, and to the Canaanite-Hurrian mixture of the Levant. These chariots usually carried a driver and a fighting man armed with a composite bow (the Hittites had two such fighters, usually armed with spears). Some peoples fought by shooting arrows from the vehicle; others dismounted and fought on foot, usually with a spear; many did both.

Infantry continued to fight in solid phalanx, usually with the spear, but with much better equipment including helmets and protective coats (usually leather).

Supply, intelligence, and communications were greatly improved, using chariots for the last and four-wheel wagons, usually drawn by oxen, for the first. These wagons replaced the previously prevalent mode of transport by pack asses. Horse-drawn wagons remained exceptional, except for very light loads. Although the anatomical structure of a horse's neck is quite different from that of an ox, horses were harnessed, for more than two thousand years, in an ox-like fashion so that it was impossible for them to pull effectively. This situation was not ended completely until the invention of the horse collar and modern harnessing with traces and shafts in the Asiatic grasslands before A.D. 500, which reached Europe in the Dark Ages about A.D. 900.

Down into the classical period, horses were yoked in pairs on either side of a pole which was attached to the yoke and to the vehicle. In this system, as in the variant of it used in classical antiquity, the horse could not put his weight into the traction, as can be done with modern harnessing, was subjected to considerable chafing, and, lacking horseshoes, suffered considerable hoof wear on the rocky lands of the Near East and Mediterranean. In consequence, horses were subject to very light loads in ancient times, and heavy loads had to be moved by oxen, who travel at less than two miles per hour.

The terrain we are discussing was, with the exception of the grasslands and deserts, not only rocky, but it was also hilly and broken. Roads were thus a necessity, but almost none existed before the sixth century B.C.

Until the late second millennium B.C., the only roads were processional or ceremonial, connecting the city or its palace with a nearby temple. According to R.J. Forbes, "Even the much used great coastal road from Egypt to Gaza, Syria, and Mesopotamia was little more than a track, impassable for wheeled traffic." The solutions to this problem were of a triple character: (1) short stretches of road or bridges were built where they were most needed, as across defiles or water courses; (2) the minimizing of transportation by storage of produce and other supplies locally in depots along possible lines of operation; and (3) the construction of light vehicles designed to be disassembled at different points on the way.

The third of these was used by all powers, as it is intrinsic in the problem, but was organized in an elaborate fashion by Tiglath-Pileser I of Assyria (c.1115-1102), who put great emphasis on all transport problems. All vehicles were made as light as possible, with the bodies made of wicker (or interlaced leather in the case of chariots). When they reached a difficult point, they were disassembled, with the wheels, body, and load carried by soldiers over the obstacle. In crossing streams of water these burdens were floated across, pushed by swimming soldiers, on inflated skins.

This method could not be used, however, for the heavy beams and weights which formed part of a siege train, also organized in a serious way by Tiglath-Pileser, so that the development of this military arm in the late Bronze Age made road construction a necessity. Accordingly, this became a serious concern of the Assyrian empire (to 612 B.C.) but was established in an effective way only by their successors, the Persians, in the late sixth and early fifth centuries.

The second solution to the problem of supply,

the gathering of agricultural produce into hundreds
of towns and citadels scattered all over the Near
East, was a double-edged instrument. It meant that
any army could obtain the major portion of its food
and fodder en route, facilitating movement and extending the range of military operations. But at
the same time these depots were accessible to an
invading enemy or to local agents who revolted
against higher powers.

This last point, of course, intensified another
problem, the strengthening of fortifications and the
counter-emphasis on siege operations. As a result,
this subject was more highly developed than any
other aspect of military life in the pre-classical
period, most of it in the Levant.

The practice of fortifications in this critical
area goes back to the elaborate and puzzling citadel
at Jericho whose date seems to be earlier than 6000
B.C. Surrounded by a wall of stone 5-7 meters high,
inside a ditch 3 meters deep and 9 meters wide cut
into the rock, an area of about ten acres may have
held over two thousand inhabitants. Within the wall,
a circular tower, 10 meters tall and 13 meters in
diameter at its base, enclosed a staircase which
gave access to the top of the tower, possibly for
an observation post. Why this elaborate structure
was built, how the food and manpower were mobilized
for its construction, or even how it could have been
made with the primitive stone tools of eight or nine
thousand years ago, remains inexplicable.

In these terms, this early citadel of Jericho
has little bearing on our subject except to establish
the priority of the Levant in the science of fortification. Such knowledge became indispensable with
the accumulation of population and wealth in the
temple cities of the whole Near East in the fourth
millennium B.C.

By 3000 the whole Fertile Crescent, including
Egypt, was familiar with the basic principles of
fortification: high walls of brick or stone, a
dozen or more feet thick and thus wide enough to
provide a passage along the top; square bastions
at intervals from which attackers could be assailed

when they approached the walls; fortified gates
with narrow and twisting entrance passages which
exposed the sides or backs of those who forced the
passage to counterattacks. In the course of the
third millennium, bastions became circular, and
the walls were constructed with overhanging bal-
conies at the top to attack besiegers trying to
undermine the walls or to scale them. Scaling
ladders became increasingly elaborate, some
mounted on wheels so they could be brought to the
walls more easily (Egypt, VIth Dynasty), and movable roofs were often provided to protect those
seeking to undermine the walls. These improved
measures of attack led to improved counter-meas-
ures of defense: higher walls and a moat to
keep the attackers away from the walls. By 2000
B.C. these elaborations of defense, including use
of several walls with a moat between them, gave
rise to counter-developments of the offense, notably the development of increasingly elaborate
battering rams, including some which were mounted
on wheels, protected from counterattack from
above by a roof, and with a ram which operated
like a pendulum suspended from the roof. This
soon gave rise to the use of a defensive glacis,
a steep upward slope from some distance away to
the foot of the walls. Attacks on fortified
areas through such increasingly elaborate defenses
were weakened by raining arrows down on the attackers from the top of the city's walls and towers.
To counter this, the attackers tried to clear the
defenders from the walls by even heavier flights
of arrows, and, in the third millennium, constructed
siege towers to help attacking archers do this.

By 1800, or even earlier, defensive fortifications (as at Buhen, Nubia, 1900-1700 B.C.) were
about as elaborate as those of the European High
Middle Ages (about A.D. 1200), but the evidence
seems to indicate that the offensive was slowly
forging ahead. Certainly the archaeological and
written evidence shows that even the strongest
fortifications were attacked successfully by starvation or treachery, or by breaching the walls and
overwhelming the defenders.

Another element in the growing power of the

offensive in the first half of the second millennium B.C. was the growing ability to cross water. This included the use of sea transportation to supplement supply of armies in distant combat areas as well as ability to take chariots and supplies across local streams. The Egyptians, for example, seem to have shipped chariots and siege towers to Levantine ports to supplement their overland invasion of Syria. Infantry forces crossed streams by wading or swimming, but chariots, wagons, and supplies were carried on rafts or on frameworks sustained on inflated bullock skins. Individuals with limited swimming ability also used such skins as life preservers.

The gradual growth of offensive military power in the second millennium B.C. was an essential foundation for the development of the imperial political systems which dominated the Near East in the centuries after 1500 B.C. This offensive ability rested on improved and more plentiful bronze weapons, on greatly increased mobility (both in tactics and in logistics) from the advent of the horse, the chariot, and improved (meaning lighter) wagons, from substantial advances in siegecraft, and especially by great advances in combined weaponry, which is always the chief military advantage of civilized societies. In this case, the combination of archery with chariots, of infantry archers with the older spear phalanx, and the coordination of these together with better intelligence, communications, and supply made it possible for the greatest states to mount offensive attacks hundreds of miles from their bases and to control large forces in the vicinity of the enemy sufficiently to engage in elementary tactical movements such as flank attacks and the coordination of more than one column.

The political history of this millennium is so complicated that it would be a relief to avoid it entirely, but a rapid survey is necessary since many of the techniques of international relations which we regard as modern inventions were carried on at that time, more than four thousand years ago. Among these are balance of power, dynastic marriages, the use of satellite, tributary, and buffer states, and the introduction of economic motivations into warfare.

155

The key to the period was the intersection of two political conditions: (1) that archaic monarchy in the Bronze Age had structural weaknesses that made the king's position precarious unless he was physically present; and (2) that the two great powers of the period, Egypt and the Hittites, were so far from the objective of their imperialist wars, Syria, that it was at the very edge of their power ranges. Thus neither Egypt nor the Hittites could defeat the other and bring Syria securely within its power sphere, and the power of each was so attenuated at that distance that other, much lesser, states, such as the Mitanni or the Hurrian-Canaanite princes of the Levant, could preserve their autonomy in the area, and could even control it when the two great powers were absent. Usually one, and often both, were absent, since their kings had to return to their own lands frequently to put down revolts or attempted <u>coups d'etat</u>, instigated by their own close relatives or by the great nobles of their courts.

In this view, the Pharaoah of Egypt and the King of the Hittites could be regarded as centers of power capable of shifting from their own lands outward to Syria where, if they met each other, they were too evenly matched to win a decisive victory, but where, if one were absent, the other was able to establish his rule over the local people (often with little or no resistance).

Furthermore, each of the great powers felt insecure on that edge of its power sphere farthest away from Syria: the Pharaoh on the upper Nile and in Nubia, where he was threatened by tribal peoples like the Beja, and the Hittite king in southwest Asia Minor or along the Black Sea coast, both areas where Hittite power was never securely established. For example, the Hittites had almost constant trouble with the King of Arzawa in western Asia Minor, while their own King Mursilis II made campaigns northward toward the Black Sea in ten different years of his 28-year reign (1334-1306).

The structural weakness of the archaic empires rested on two facts: that the constitutional principle of succession was based on designation and not on inheritance; and that all political action, including conquest, was regarded as service to the god of the state and the extension of the obligation of such service to the conquered. The latter meant that war and conquest was a religious process of more or less forced conversion, leaving the conquered peoples eager to throw off the political bondage in order to resume worship and service to their old gods. The former meant that the ruler (in theory the god acting through the ruler) picked his successor, usually from members of his own family, and no fixed principle of inheritance, such as primogeniture, became established. This not only made the succession uncertain, but it opened the way to questions why one son was chosen rather than another, and thus weakened the legitimacy of any succession so that challenges were endemic in the system. The fact that the rulers' plural wives and many concubines provided numerous sons to dispute succession to the throne further weakened the system, just as it weakened the influence of diplomatic marriages. This failure to establish a hereditary system in a monarchical or imperial government is a source of very great weakness, as it has been throughout history in the Roman empire, the Byzantine and Ottoman empires, and the Russian empire. Strangely enough, this vital source of constitutional weakness is often not recognized by historians of these systems, especially the last named, where it continues today as the greatest weakness of the Soviet constitutional system.

In the period of the archaic empires with which we are concerned, no really satisfactory solution of these two weaknesses was achieved until the Persians. The north-south oscillation of Hittite-Egyptian rivalry in the Levant in their struggles to control the Syrian Saddle was complicated, as we have said, by the existence of other, secondary powers and by even more fundamental basic economic and social realities.

The secondary powers were the following: (1) Crete to the west; almost entirely a commercial and naval power, until taken over about 1400 by the Mycenaeans, who exercised considerable influence on the Syrian coast in the 1400-1200 period; (2) the Mitanni on the eastern part of the Syrian Saddle,

157

with sufficient local power to hold the Assyrians
just northeast of them as a tributary state from
about 1500 to 1360. They arose after the collapse
of Hammurabi's empire about 1700, were allied to the
Egyptians in 1410-1340, and were finally destroyed
by the Assyrians in 1340. (3) In Babylonia the Kassites ruled relatively peacefully from 1595 to 1162.
They gained control at the earlier date when a Hittite raid sacked Babylon and ended the old Babylonian
empire, and they were wiped from history themselves
by the Elamites in 1162. (4) On the eastern border
of Mesopotamia were the Elamites and other Asiatic
peoples who intervened, often at the most critical
moments, in the history of the area. (5) On the
upper Tigris, growing intermittently in power from
1365 to their great triumph in 911 were the Assyrians.
(6) Northeast of the Elamites, Assyrians, and other
hillside neighbors of Mesopotamia were the Indo-European Medes and Persians, whose final triumph was
delayed until 539.

In some ways this situation in the Near East
has strange analogies to the Cold War between the
United States and the Soviet Union in recent years.
It was a two-power world in which neither superpower
could defeat the other without destroying itself,
but in which both interfered at and beyond the limits
of their power spheres in the area of secondary powers
between them, doing so for personal advantages which
could probably have been achieved with less cost
either by cooperation or by mutual withdrawal of
military effort and political intervention to allow economic and diplomatic influences to operate.
The secondary powers, then as now, found independence
only in the mutual stalemating of the superpowers,
while these, neglecting their real problems at home
and the rise of other threats (like Assyria, or the
Iron Age invaders) outside the balance, jeopardized
the future of both.

The first power to emerge from the confusions
of the Bronze Age invasions of the Near East in the
period about 2100-1700 were the Amorite invaders of
Mesopotamia, followed about 1700 by the Hittites and,
somewhat later (about 1580) by the Egyptian rebound
from the Hyksos domination. The Amorite period of
power (1894-1595) culminated in Hammurabi of Babylon,

in the eighteenth century B.C., but by 1700 the dynasty of Hammurabi was in decay.

This period of decay ended with a shattering event, a Hittite raid, from central Anatolia across the Taurus Mountains into Syria, then across the Syrian Saddle to the twin rivers and down the valley of Mesopotamia to the city of Babylon, which they captured and sacked (1595 B.C.). The Hittite king, Mursilis I (1620-1590) had to withdraw to his homeland almost immediately because of the political instability of his Anatolian base and was murdered within five years, but his destruction of Babylon ended Mesopotamia as a significant political power for almost a thousand years. It is possible that this extended eclipse of Mesopotamian power was a consequence of socioeconomic factors of which we know relatively little, such as increased salinity of the soil from extended irrigation or disruption of the irrigation works themselves, leading to reduction of food output and inability to support (that is to feed and equip) a large army. Whatever the reasons, Mesopotamia underwent, from 1595 until about 750 B.C., a period of political eclipse in which the area was ruled by Kassite princes from about 1550 until about 1162. These Kassites were largely Highland Zone Asiatic peoples (with a few Indo-European leaders) who provided moderate political stability but no political glory over their period of rule.

Kassite independence in Mesopotamia was insured by the balance of forces around the Syrian Saddle, where from about 1530 to 1340 a somewhat similar mixed people, the Hurri-Mitanni, maintained a moderately powerful state of a semi-pastoral character in the grasslands between the upper Euphrates and the upper Tigris at the eastern end of the Syrian Saddle. For much of this period (specifically 1530-1360) the Mitanni held the Assyrians beyond the Tigris as vassals, and, at times, they were able to extend their control westward across the Syrian Saddle to the Mediterranean Sea. But for most of this millennium, the Levant (Syria-Palestine) was made up of independent tribes and city-states of Hurrians and Canaanites.

From about 1780 to about 1580, the Egyptians were dominated by the Hyksos, a similar mixed group of Canaanites and Hurrians, with a few Indo-European leaders. These Hyksos controlled the Sinai peninsula and the Egyptian delta until after 1580, when a new resurgent Egypt, led by Pharaohs of the XVIIIth Dynasty (1575-1308) rejected these "shepherd kings" and invaded the Levant from the south.

This Egyptian invasion began with Thutmose I who raided up the Levant from Sinai to the Euphrates as early as 1520, but the real drive began under Thutmose III (1490-1436) about 1480 and culminated in the battle of Megiddo in 1466. Nine years later, Thutmose defeated the Mitanni (1457), who soon allied with Egypt against this rising threat from Assyria on their northeastern side.

Another threat appeared about 1455, when the Hittites again emerged from Anatolia and captured Aleppo, but as usual, instability at home made the Hittite threat to the Levant an intermittent one, and they withdrew again for almost a century. Then about 1370, they reappeared in great force, under their greatest king, Suppiluliumas (1372-1335). This marked the end of the Mitanni empire, although they remained as a local power east of the Euphrates River for another generation. Appeals to the Pharaoh for aid led to no immediate response, for the family intrigues and religious innovations of Amenophis IV (also called Ikhnaton, 1367-1347) and the extreme youth of his successor, Tutankhamen (1347-1339), made any Egyptian intervention in Syria impossible. In the same period, three brothers fought for control of the Mitanni throne, and dynastic murders were the chief political events of that country in the mid-fourteenth century B.C. As a result, Assyria, shielded from Hittite power by the chaos of Mitanni and from Mesopotamia by the stasis of the Kassites, was able to free itself from Mitanni vassalage and finally overthrow that power completely by 1340. Thus, when Suppiluliumas died in 1334 B.C., the greatest power in the Near East was still Hittite, but Assyria was rising rapidly and beginning a struggle with the Elamites for control of Babylon.

At that point, in the late fourteenth century,

the advent of a new dynasty in Egypt (the XIXth, 1308-1184), renewed the energies of that power and brought it back into the Levantine imbroglio with both feet. The great Ramesses II (1290-1224) invaded Syria from the south and in 1285 came into full collision with the Hittites at the battle of Kadesh.

This, the most famous battle of the Bronze Age, was indecisive and, while the two imperial contenders for control of Syria hung in balance, the rising power of Assyria to the east suddenly began to alarm them both. Shalmaneser I (1274-1245), greatest warrior of the early Assyrian monarchs, conquered the Guti and Armenians to the east and north and then turned on the scattered Hurrian principalities to the southwest, destroying nine fortresses and capturing 180 cities. Shortly afterwards, his successor Tukulti-Ninurta (1244-1208), captured Babylon to the southeast.

This new threat may have brought some recognition of the realities of power in the area to the Egyptians and Hittites, for in 1269, sixteen years after their indecisive battle at Kadesh, they signed a treaty (drawn up both in Akkadian and in hieroglyphics) and Ramesses took a Hittite princess as a wife.

The terms of this famous treaty of 1269 are of no significance, for they came too late to free the great empires from their meaningless foreign struggles in order to turn their time and energies to the internal decay which was sapping the strength of all archaic political systems; this failure to reform left such systems without the power to resist the new technological and ideological forces which were beginning the shift from the Bronze Age archaic monarchies to the Iron Age classical states, which took control after 850 B.C. The interval from about 1050 to about 850 B.C. constituted a dark age (similar in organizational patterns to the more famous Dark Ages of A.D. 850-1000 which marked the transition to the new Western civilization of the period since A.D. 1000).

The key to the dark age of 1100-850 B.C. was

a decline in the offensive power of weapons systems
in the sense that rulers could no longer enforce
obedience at any considerable distance. At the same
time that defensive dominance increased, weapons became relatively more expensive, from a widespread
decrease in prosperity, so that fewer persons could
possess weapons and some types (such as siege trains)
could no longer be used. This meant that local people who had weapons could enforce obedience in local
areas without inferference from distant rulers. Thus
power became increasingly local, defensive, and
private.

This change, while reflected in weapons, was
largely caused by other factors: (1) changes in outlook destroyed the ability of archaic rulers to retain the allegiance of their subjects; and (2) the
lowering of economic prosperity, marked by shortening
chains of circulation of incomes from production to
consumption (thus eliminating both specialized craftsmen and merchants), reduced the size of armies and
the diversity and mixture of weapons systems. Eventually such dwindling prosperity reduced military
activities to a few simple weapons and made it impossible (and unnecessary) to maintain elaborate
fortifications, leading to a decline of city life
with its specialized activities and its stores of
goods, and to the almost total disappearance of
cities west of the Jordan River.

This may be regarded as an example of the five
steps by which civilized life in literate urban
centers rises and falls: (1) increasing political
security leads to (2) growing commerce (at first
distant trade in luxury items, and later local
trade in more essential commodities), with a resulting growth of specialized economic activities;
(3) the appearance of new social classes, merchants
and artisans, who become city residents with a social position as a middle class, between the ruling
elite and the peasantry; (4) the growth of a town,
usually around a ritual center or citadel; and (5)
growing literacy and the appearance of vernacular
literature. The same five steps mark a civilization's decline, with the steps in the same sequence
but each step in the reverse direction: decreasing
political and personal security leading to a decline

in distant trade and in luxuries but later, also, in local trade in necessities; followed by erosion of the urban and middle classes, who follow the food supply back to its source in rural areas, the growing ruralization accompanied by growing militarization of life, as the society moves toward a two-class society of warriors and peasants, with declining literacy.

The decrease in political security, in this case, began as far back as 1400 B.C. and was rather the consequence of ideological and organizational changes than of changes in weapons or their use. We have mentioned the weaknesses of a political structure based on sacral kingship once it embarks on imperialism: conquered peoples who might have accepted political subjection were restive under religious subjection which betrays their most profound convictions. Moreover, the burden on an archaic monarch to prove his virility by satisfying a harem, with its polygamous marriages and concubinage, and its numerous children, greatly increased dynastic rivalries, while weakening the effectiveness of alliances based on dynastic marriage. The elective or cooptative element in archaic kingship intensified these dynastic weaknesses, while the personal nature of the kingship made it difficult to establish any stable idea of a royal office as distinct from a transitory king and thus weakened the royal influence as soon as he moved any distance away.

This weakening of the royal authority at a distance from his person was greatly intensified by two other influences: on the one hand, the archaic mind associated with archaic modes of action was concrete and existential, rather than abstract and general, so that the concept of royal authority as an abstract impersonal matter regardless of the particular place, health, or condition of the king as a person was largely lacking; on the other hand, no real bureaucratic structure for carrying on the royal authority could be built up so long as the remuneration of royal agents had to take the form of income-yielding properties (usually land or slaves). For this the invention of money, which could be kept more immediately under royal control and separated from actual economic goods, was needed, but this did

163

not come until about the eighth century.

Four other factors, two of them already mentioned, also contributed to the weakening of centralized political power in the period 1400-1000
B.C. These were: (1) the constant warfare which,
by destroying fortifications again and again,
gradually impoverished the whole Near East to the
point that, after 1400, each subsequent rebuilding
of such fortifications left them less substantial;
(2) the decline of Minoan sea power in the eastern
Mediterranean after 1400, which reduced seaborne
trade from the west and northwest and eventually
opened up the Levant to the seaborne raiders from
the Aegean area; (3) the introduction of iron,
and especially of the long, straight, slashing
sword; and (4) the movements of waves of Indo-European and Semitic invaders into the Near East after
1250, the former armed with the new iron weapons.

CHAPTER IV
THE GREAT TRANSFORMATION AND
THE RISE OF SEA POWER, 1500-500 B.C.

1. Introduction

History does not move forward in one direction, or even at a steady rate. It often flounders
for extended periods, churning about in almost the
same position, going in circles, while generations
of nameless persons are born, grow up, reproduce,
and die. Then, in some mysterious way, some society
in one area finds an organizational structure and a
particular cognitive system which gives it a pattern
in which people's energies can be applied in a more
or less common purpose and direction. On that basis,
for many generations, that society moves in a single
direction, exploiting the possibilities of that organizational structure and its cognitive system.
Eventually, the possibilities of those cultural
patterns become exhausted, and their essential nature becomes corrupted or lost, the society slows
down, wavers in its course, and begins to weaken
both in its ability to satisfy the basic needs of
its members and even to defend them as a group
against outside threats. That society may perish
or it may persist in weakness and corruption for
many generations before some outside society comes
upon it with sufficient strength to destroy it;
but, in either case, until it disappears, its history, once again, takes the form of endless churning about in aimless circles without purpose or
large-scale group satisfactions.

When a society finds a fruitful organization
and outlook, other societies may copy its organization (although not its outlook), either in emulation or in self-defense against such a superior
organization of human efforts represented by that
superior system. When this occurs, numerous distinct societies over a wide area and over an extended period of time may seem to be moving, almost simultaneously, in meaningful and purposeful
directions. Such periods of reciprocal copying
and resistance to other societies can be observed

165

if we look at human history from a broad enough point of view. Such a transformation is familiar to us in the worldwide repercussions following the application of steampower and modern technology to production in the eighteenth century.

A panoramic view of the history of earlier times will show at least five similar periods of transformation. One would be the process, over the period from about three million B.C. to about half a million B.C., in which a creature whose behavior was largely determined by genetic and inherited factors was transformed into a creature whose actions were largely directed by learned behavior (including the use of tools and the appearance of alternative possibilities of human organizational arrangements).

The second great transformation, from about half a million years ago to some 50,000 years ago, but continuing, in some areas down to recent times, was based on the exploitation of the possibilities of using kinship patterns of organization to mobilize larger numbers of men into larger and more centralized and more flexible structures. This innovation, applied first to the use of spears and group hunting of large grass-eating herd animals on the Old World grasslands (the so-called "Heroic Hunting cultures"), continued to be applied to new and more advanced technological bases to form the great tribal societies of history, such as the early Mongols or even the Zulus of South Africa in the mid-nineteenth century.

A third great transformation was associated with the so-called "Neolithic Revolution" which began about 9000 B.C. with the discovery and expansion of agriculture (including both the planting of crops and the domestication of animals, either together or separately). This technique became the basis for two additional advances in special areas, in the establishment of permanent agricultural settlements in Old World alluvial river valleys and in the establishment of nomadic or semi-nomadic pastoralism on the Old World grasslands. These two consequences of the discovery of agriculture developed in the four millenia following 5000 B.C.

The fourth great transformation was associated with the use of religion (rather than blood relationships) as the basis for organizing large numbers of men for common purposes in a single society. These religious ideas with their accompanying rituals are what we usually call the "archaic outlook" and became the cement which bound together in common purpose what we have been calling the "archaic cultures" which culminated in the archaic Bronze Age empires we have just discussed.

These archaic societies began to appear in certain areas as early as 5000 B.C. and were able to mobilize both men and the productive capacity of agriculture to an unprecedented degree, especially in the alluvial river valleys. They culminated in the Bronze Age empires which were so conspicuous about 1500 B.C. and which were so ignominiously destroyed by the following fifth transformation with which this chapter is concerned.

The fifth great period of transformation covered the millennium, or slightly less, following 1400 B.C. It continued until about 500 B.C. and centered in the dark ages of the period from about 1050 to 850 B.C., although the new cognitive system which formed the basis for the new classical cultures did not appear, after almost a millennium of struggle, until the sixth century. This new cognitive system is listed below as the "sixth century revolution." While it provided part of the psychological basis for classical Mediterranean civilization, the organizational basis of that civilization was established earlier in the dark ages of the period 1050-850 B.C.

This great transformation of the near-millennium 1400-500 is so complex that it cannot be described in simple terms, and it is very difficult for us, with our different modern outlook, to envision it. The archaic cultures, both in outlook and in organization, were so different from anything that modern men have experienced, especially in the ways in which members of either looked at human experience and in the value they placed on such experiences, that they are almost incomprehensible to us unless we make a deliberate

167

and intensive effort to escape from our own modern outlook. The subsequent classical cultures, on the other hand, are much more familiar, although in my opinion, we falsify much of these by trying to reduce them to our terms of understanding and experience. We might express the problem this way: the classical cultures were sufficiently like our modern cultures so that we can get a dim picture of their nature by examining them through modern eyes, but the archaic cultures were so different that their natures cannot be seen through modern eyes; they can be seen only if we train our eyes to observe in totally different ways, and they can be discussed only if we use a quite different vocabulary.

Fortunately, these great differences of the three cultural types concerned (archaic, classical, and modern), were most different in their cognitive systems, that is in their categories of thought and their value systems; we can, accordingly, see with greater success the other aspects of their cultures, that is, their artifacts and their organizational structures.

In these terms, the great transformation of 1400-500 involved the following points:

1. A great increase in violence and political instability among many of the peoples, both civilized and barbaric, in western Asia and the eastern Mediterranean from the 15th century B.C.

2. The appearance of iron weapons, probably in southern Armenia, in the 15th century, although the use of iron weapons spread most rapidly in the 12th century B.C. and continued to do so until modern times.

3. The first appearance of sea power, arising from the first sharp distinction between merchant ships and war vessels. This occurred in the Mediterranean about 1300.

4. The culmination of the sub-Boreal dry climate phase of 2500-1000 in the mass migrations of peoples, especially of Indo-European Iron Age

invaders from the northern Balkans, in the 12th century.

5. The great increase in the dominance of defensive over offensive weapons about 1000, a development which was reversed with increasing rapidity in the period following 800 B.C. In this process of growing defensive power, we can discern at least two sub-stages: the first associated with the castle, the chariot, and the shift from bronze to iron weapons, from about 1400 to after 1100; and the second sub-stage associated with the eclipse of the castle, the replacement of the chariot by cavalry, and a widening distribution of iron weapons, related to a reduction in size of power units to self-sufficient agricultural and sedentary pastoral units, often organized as clans or extended families with their retainers and domestic slaves. Through both of these sub-stages there was an increasing decentralization of power, leading to the disappearance of the state and eventually, by 1000 B.C., to the ending of all public authority, with the result that all power and authority came to be private power and private authority. In this continuing process, over several centuries, power in civilized areas west of the Euphrates became so dispersed among so many hands that it was no longer possible to mobilize sufficient manpower to construct stone castles or even to keep such castles in repair, adequately manned to defend their walls, or adequately supplied to withstand any extended siege. Accordingly, castles ceased to be used, and power became dispersed among those families which, for various reasons, could afford horses and iron weapons. These manors or plantations were locally dominant units of power, consisting of those men armed with iron swords which each such unit could mobilize. This dispersal of power reached its extremity somewhat after 1000 B.C.

6. Offensive power began to rise again after 1000, at first very slowly, but after 750 with increasing speed. This process was based on a gradual decrease in political disorder and violence, the replacement of chariots by cavalry, and the

169

growth of new organizational patterns reflected
in the joint emergence of a nobility and of religious controls and rituals which were largely in
the hands of this new nobility. The military position of that nobility, which was the real basis of
their power, was their possession of iron weapons
and cavalry horses.

7. This first appearance of cavalry does
not imply that men fought while mounted on their
horses; usually they did not, at least at first,
but such men had a mobility which gave them a
vastly superior military power, eventually replacing the earlier chariot.

8. This whole process culminated in the
sixth century revolution, a worldwide intellectual
phenomenon, which had two distinct but interrelated
parts: the advent of two-valued logic among the
Indo-Europeans and the advent of transcendental
ethical monotheism among the Semites. These two,
both separately and together, created a cognitive
framework which released the West from the ancient archaic outlook, opened the way to a dynamic
future for the West, but, eventually, imprisoned
the Western mind in a framework of assumptions
(which were largely unconscious) and excluded
from Western awareness much of human experience,
including any real understanding of the still
archaic, or semi-archaic, East.

2.   Commerce and the Threat of Violence

This whole great transformation began with a
rise in violence, disorder, and political instability, which reached its destructive peak in the
twelfth century when the semi-pastoral Indo-European peoples of the northern flatlands, with recently acquired iron weapons, began to raid southward into civilized areas of western Asia and the
Mediterranean. This instability began as early as
1400 B.C. along the northwestern edge of the civilized portion of western Asia. This edge formed a
great arc from Crete, through Mycenaean Greece,
the Troad of northwestern Anatolia, the Hittite-
Armenian boundary in eastern Anatolia, and the
Mitanni-Assyrian boundary across Kurdistan. All

of these areas had been conquered earlier by the Indo-European Bronze Age invaders of the early second millennium B.C. in a process by which these warlike intruders became a ruling upper class over the more peaceful, frequently earth-worshipping, and often more matriarchal, peasant peoples of these areas. The conquerors used their superior war-making abilities to extract food and other tribute from their peasant subjects, using these surpluses to construct a warlike, barbaric, heroic culture which sponsored trade to distant places, vigorous decorative arts, fortified residences, and often heroic epic poetry to celebrate their violent exploits. Examples of these exploitative relationships existed about 1400 in the great central European Bronze Age, in the Mycenaean culture of the Aegean, in Bronze Age Troy, in the Hittite civilization of Anatolia, in the Mitanni and Kassite cultures of the Syrian Saddle and Mesopotamia, and in the Aryan principalities of northern India.

In many of these areas, the presence of these pastoral conquerors can be discerned by the barbaric burials of their chieftains with their bronze weapons (often axes), their horses and dogs, and, in some cases, with their sacrificed wives and retainers. In many areas they have left fortresses, often of stone, built by the enslaved labor of their subjects. Of these fortresses the best known are those of Mycenae, Troy, and the Hittites. Similar fortresses were constructed in the Fertile Crescent by the Semite peoples, especially in the Levant during the second millennium B.C., but these structures, from the hands of various Canaanite and Amorite peoples, were simply added to the fortified structures of the Near East previously reared by those who had been controlling the two great alluvial valley civilizations of Mesopotamia and Egypt.

These Bronze Age invaders of the sub-Boreal period exploited, without seriously modifying, the peasant agricultural activities of the areas they occupied and also the patterns of trade.

These patterns of trade obtained their main outlines in the third millennium B.C., when the

irrigation civilizations of Mesopotamia and the
Nile created two areas of great wealth that became powerful magnetic attractions for the kind
of luxury goods of remote origin which always
form the basis for any beginning commercial process. The chief elements in those trading patterns
were the movement of metals to the alluvial valleys, which were, inevitably, great producers of
consumer goods but were totally lacking in metals
and were largely lacking in heavy construction
materials such as lumber and stone. The movements
of lumber and stone were early organized in terms
of the river systems of the alluvial valleys and
rarely extended outside these except for the great
attraction of the logs from the Levant known to
history as "the cedars of Lebanon." But goods of
mineral origin, both metals and jewels, were followed by the incense gums of southern Arabia. These
three kinds of goods dominated long-distance trade
after 3000 B.C. and did not allow great distances
to hamper their activities.

The commercial activities which arose from the
irrigation civilizations' demands for metals and
precious or semi-precious materials must not be
viewed as a movement outward by the residents of
the alluvial valleys in search of the objects they
desired. The trade and trade routes undoubtedly
began in this fashion, but, from a very early period, at least for Mesopotamia, the news of demand
for these goods spread faster and farther than the
valley residents themselves ventured to go and,
accordingly, more remote and barbaric peoples began to send or to carry these goods toward the
valleys. The alluvial civilizations, under the
attraction of the purchasing power of their great
productive capacity, drew metals and other valued
goods from the remote extremities of the Old World
landmass, the goods moving from hand to hand,
along routes leading to the civilized centers as
if attracted by a vacuum or by a great magnet.
This attraction concentrated at first at the
extremities of the valleys concerned: at the
southern end of the Nile, in the Sudan; at the
northern end of the Nile reaching toward Sinai
and the Levant; eventually, to some extent, from
the middle Nile to the Red Sea and down that sea

toward Somaliland and the southern ocean; from southern Mesopotamia, the Persian Gulf and the Arabian Sea to Bahrain, Oman, and Sind. But by far the greatest trade route of the early civilized era was that drawing goods toward the upper valley of Mesopotamia. This was based on two factors: the position of the earliest metal producing area of the world, north of Lake Van, where northern Kurdistan and southern Armenia reach toward each other, and the geographical significance of the Syrian Saddle, already mentioned.

From the upper Euphrates River, over the Syrian Saddle, the way was open, north and northwest to Lake Van, Cappodocia, and Anatolia; westward to the Mediterranean; and southwest to the Levant, Sinai, and Egypt. By the twentieth century B.C., Assyrian traders were in fortified posts in Cappodocia, where they left written records of their activities. It is very likely that similar, unrecorded trading activities were going on in that same area of southern Anatolia a millennium earlier. By 2000 and in much of the following millennium, that area was extending its trading tentacles across Anatolia toward Troy in the extreme northwest.

In quite a different fashion, in the third millennium, as we have seen, both Egypt and Mesopotamia were trying to control the trade passing north and south through the Levant in the hands of the local Semites.

But far more significant than these northern and southern offshoots of the Syrian Saddle trade were the seaways extending westward along the Mediterranean. Before 3000 the Semites of Syria, speaking in all probability a dialect related to Akkadian and Assyrian, were pushing westward by sea into totally uncivilized and unknown areas. In Cyprus, as the name indicates, they found copper ores, while in the Cyclades and on Crete they established trading relations with the Anatolian peasant farmers already on those islands. By 3000 they were pushing farther westward and, within four or five centuries had reached southwestern Spain (near Almeria) by way of Malta,

173

Sicily, and Sardinia. In many of these areas, they stirred up local activities and local migrations, not only by their demands for metals but also by their missionary activities, spreading a megalithic, solar religion whose original focus, before 4000 B.C., had been in the Red Sea area. From southern Spain, local peoples carrying the double message of metal-seeking and megalithic religious ideas, both much distorted by a variety of local influences, spread northward across Catalonia, the Pyrenees, and southern France to Switzerland, the Rhine, and northwestern Europe. A similar movement, by the middle of the third millennium, with a more generous mixture of the original eastern Mediterranean influence, was spreading by sea out onto the Atlantic and onward to Portugal, southern Brittany, Cornwall, Ireland, and even, by way of the English Channel, to the north (Denmark and elsewhere).

Somewhat more slowly and somewhat later (after 1900 B.C.), similar eastern Mediterranean and western Asiatic influences were drawing northwestern European treasures across Europe to the Aegean, by way of the north European rivers, to Bohemia, the Danube, and the Aegean.

Much of this trade operated like a bucket brigade, with valuables passing from hand to hand both ways, each link in the chain carrying goods over the length of a single link, say from Ireland to Brittany, from Brittany to Portugal, from Portugal to Spain, or from Sicily to Crete, from Crete to Syria (on the trans-Mediterranean route) or from Crete to Argos (on the trans-European route). Overland the links were probably even shorter than by sea, with even greater variety and diversity of influences along the way.

Until after 2500, the main lines of this trade from Syria to the West were on the trans-Mediterranean route, including the dangerous Atlantic voyage to gold-producing Ireland, tin-producing Cornwall (the Cassiterides), or even to the amber-producing Baltic coast around Denmark. This was because the wet Atlantic climate of 6000-2500 had made the forests of central Europe

174

so thick as to hamper trans-European traffic, even by way of the rivers.

The shift to the drier sub-Boreal climate about 2500, by opening the forests of Europe, gave a great impetus to the transcontinental trade routes crossing Bohemia along a northwestern-southeastern axis, and made all of Europe southwest of a line from Brittany to Malta fall into a commercial and cultural backwater into which few stimulating new influences entered for over a thousand years (say from about 2000 to the arrival of the Villanovans and Etruscans in Italy more than thirty generations later).

During this same thirty generations, many new influences led to exciting innovations east of this imaginary line connecting Brittany with Malta. These innovations were focused in central Europe, the Aegean and Crete. In central Europe and the Aegean, the Bronze Age Indo-European invaders established flourishing barbaric cultures based, as we have indicated, on the parallel domination and exploitation of the more peaceful peasant peoples (who supplied them with food and manpower) and the more peaceful trading peoples (and itinerant bronze-workers) who supplied them with luxury goods and metal products as tribute for allowing free passage. In Crete, where the Indo-European invaders did not arrive until after 1450, the earlier Semitic-Anatolian amalgam took advantage of the disruption of productive activities by the Bronze Age invasions in the Aegean, Anatolia, the Levant, and even Egypt (the Hyksos) to shift its own economic activities from its earlier simple role of a commercial middleman between the Near East and Europe to a greater emphasis on craft production for export (bronze weapons, worked gold and silver, pottery which often contained oil or wine). In general, raw materials like Irish gold, Cornish tin, Danish amber, Spanish (and later Bohemian) copper and tin, Balkan silver, and Cypriot copper, moved south and eastward, while manufactured goods, especially bronze weapons, decorative metals, glass or faience, ceramics, and dyed textiles moved west and north. By the sixteenth century, when this prosperous age was approaching its peak, metal workers of bronze in Bohemia, Troy, and central Anatolia (Hittites) or of silver in Greece, or of ivory, faience, cloth, and ceramics from Syria and Egypt, were all contributing to a vigorous network of trade along the lines we have indicated.

The intrusion of the sub-Boreal invaders of the Bronze Age (down to about 1400) did not destroy these lines of trade. The Indo-European Bronze Age invaders generally established themselves at critical control points along these lines of trade, in the parallel exploitation of peasants and traders which we have described. Thus the Minyans became established at Troy, the Achaeans at Mycenae, Tiryns, Pylos, and ultimately at Knossos in Crete, the Mitanni became established at the eastern edge of the Syrian Saddle whence they supplied horses and chariots to much of the Near East. At all these places, these Indo-Europeans kept elements of their earlier pastoral, patriarchal, warlike, violent, and heroic culture derived from the northern grasslands and were able to afford this by the food they extracted from their peasant serfs and from the tribute they imposed on the commercial travelers passing through the key points under their control. A somewhat similar situation grew up in northwestern India where Aryan princes set themselves up over the native Dravidian peasants shortly after 1500 B.C. But in Iran the peasant peoples of Asiatic languages were more scattered and less affluent, while traders were much rarer. Accordingly, in Iran the Indo-European Medes and Persians retained much of the pastoral tradition that their ancestors had developed long before in the south Russian grasslands farther north.

I have said that the Bronze Age invasions made no fundamental changes in the trade patterns of the northwest quadrant. That refers to the short run, say from the date of the invasions in the 2300-1700 period. But eventually, and clearly by the thirteenth century, the system was breaking up. This was because the Indo-Europeans retained their "heroic tradition."

The meaning of the expression "heroic tradition" has been much confused. I use it to refer to the essential core of the Indo-European outlook on life, especially their system of values. The key to this system was the Indo-European idea of immortality: that a person achieves spiritual survival only by being remembered by his fellow men and those who live after him. From this idea flowed much of the rest of the Indo-European outlook, notably its extremism: a man achieved remembrance by being exceptional, in the same way that the sky-god of the northern grasslands was exceptional, by being extremist, unstable, violent, unpredictable, and fickle, so that such a man could neither be ignored nor forgotten; he was a hero who was remembered "forever" because his deeds were sung by bards and poets.

With ideals such as these, whose influence is still very strong among peoples of Indo-European culture, it was not easy for the Indo-European princes of the Bronze Age to be satisfied with supervision of the agricultural activities of peasant serfs or extracting a mere ten per cent toll from passing traders. Instead, horse riding, horse stealing, horse racing, sports, hunting, and physical competition, drinking alcohol, the use of narcotics (hemp and the opium poppy), fighting, and war: these were the characteristics of real living and the only way in which immortality could be won. Accordingly, by 1400, having built their fortresses, the Indo-European conquerors turned to raiding and fighting, to horse stealing and wife stealing, and in general to competitive violence, not against the peasants and traders on whom their prosperity and power was based, for those two groups saw little value in competitive violence, but against each other. In a short time, the best claim to immortality and thus to semi-divinity was to have earned the title, "Sacker-of-cities."

This Bronze Age Indo-European self-indulgence in destructiveness could not fail to have adverse effects on political stability, commercial prosperity, cultural achievement, and even on agricultural production. Above all, it eroded the ability of this barbaric Bronze Age Indo-European culture to defend itself against any new intrusion from the northern grasslands. And such an intrusion was building up in the thirteenth century B.C. This rising threat from the north, resulting from the growing population of the grassland pastoralists and the increasing dessication of those grasslands, and perhaps from the spread of iron weapons among the pastoralists of Moldavia, Bulgaria, the Ukraine, and the Pontic steppes, was ignored by the Bronze Age princes ruling in Knossos, Pylos, Mycenae, Troy, and central Anatolia. They continued to seek immortality by competitive violence and sacking of cities.

A somewhat similar development was going on in the southern grasslands which surrounded the civilized regions of Egypt, Mesopotamia, the Levant, and central or eastern Anatolia. These civilized areas also were engaged in chronic warfare, not to achieve individual immortality but for other reasons, but the consequences were similar. In the more civilized areas of the south and east, surrounding the Levant, the threat from the southern grassland pastoralists was not nearly so great, since these Semites and Hamites did not have either horses or iron weapons as their numbers increased and the grasses dried up in the period 1300-1100 B.C. On the other hand, the more civilized areas of the Near East were much more sensitive to any decrease in security on the seas, since much of their commerce was waterborne and their seashores were not prepared for defense, for they had long been regarded as barriers to danger rather than as avenues for its approach.

On the other hand, the pastoral peoples of the Near Eastern grasslands, both the Semites of western Asia and the Hamites of northern Africa, had not been standing at rest but had been increasing in both numbers and in technical skills during the middle and late Bronze Age (second millennium B.C.). This was particularly true of the Semites of the Syrian desert and of the northern areas of the Arabian desert. Many of these Semites had taken to metallurgy, as they moved about seeking new grass for their herds of asses, sheep, and goats. By 1500 they had discovered how to make

bellows from goatskins and sticks. This diffused
north to the Caucasus area and contributed substantially to the growth of ironworking in that
area. Moreover, many of these Semite wanderers
had become mercenary fighters as a way of making
a living in a region torn by imperialist wars
among richer and more civilized peoples. Finally,
about 1200, just before the hurricane struck, the
peoples of the Near East began to acquire a new
pastoral animal, the camel, although the great increase in nomadic warfare which became possible
from this innovation did not have its full impact
until after the time of Christ.

3.   Maritime Commerce, Piracy, and the Rise of
     Sea Power

     The history of water transportation begins in
the Mesolithic period, more than ten thousand years
ago, as is evident from the first human settlement
of oceanic islands such as Japan, Crete, the Canar-
ies, and Ireland. Naturally, no direct evidence
of the type of boats used at that time has survived, although at Mesolithic sites in the north,
like Starr Carr in England (7500 B.C.), fragments
of paddles have been found, and we have a dugout
from Holland dated about 6300 B.C.

     There have been numerous traditions for con-
struction of water craft, but only one, the vertebrate structure based on a keel, originally derived from a dugout canoe, is of significance.
Other traditions numbered at least seven. These
included: (1) the use of boats and canoes formed
by fastening together bundles of reeds, as was
done in the southern flatlands of Africa and in
parts of South America; (2) the use of log rafts,
which can be both steered and sailed, as Heyerdahl
has reminded us, on a worldwide basis, especially
in Africa and western South America; (3) the use
of hide-covered wicker boats, widespread over the
northern flatlands from Mongolia to Ireland; (4)
the use of inflated skins, as buoys, in the rivers
flowing from the Highland Zone of western Asia;
(5) the worldwide use of bark canoes in the northern
circumpolar forest zone; (6) the junk-type construction of the Far East based on the principle

179

of a watertight box; and (7) the ancient Egyptian
ship, constructed as an inverted arch, whose balance
of forces among outside pressures was an engineering
miracle but far too delicate for the stresses of
sea voyaging. The last two of these are worthy of
much more attention than we can give them here,
but they played little role in the history of sea
power, so we must pass them by. Both permitted
large vessels, but the Egyptian type, although useful on a calm river, was not fit for a seaway, while
the junk type, although fitted to ocean travel and
capable of large size, was nonetheless inferior to
the keel-constructed vessel and very vulnerable to
injury from grounding or ramming.

The advantages of keel-construction are numerous: it provides strength in general, because of
the keel backbone, and especially for mounting a
mast, a steering mechanism, or a mooring point along
its longitudinal axis; it can be made in any size;
the keel allows it to be grounded, beached, or even
moved across land on rollers, with minimal damage,
and also permits repairs to be made so long as
damage is not to the keel itself.

Such keel-construction represents a long tradition which goes back to the use of dugout canoes in
a tropical, Mesolithic cultural context at least
twelve to fifteen thousand years old (and possibly
up to twice that long). From various evidence
(including diffusion of seashells of Indian Ocean
origin to places as distant as England), it seems
likely that one of the original sources of this
Mesolithic cultural context was in southeastern
Asia, possibly along one of its major rivers, such
as the Irrawaddy. In that context, large logs were
dug out to form canoes which were often stabilized
by attaching a second, smaller hull, soon reduced
to an outrigger. Such an outrigger canoe could be
paddled or sailed, and its sides could be raised to
provide more freeboard by attaching strakes of
wooden planking. These strakes were attached by
vines or vegetable cordage, similar to that which
the same peoples used for fishing lines, nets,
animal snares, or bow strings. In time, skill
in making "sewn boats" reached such a level that
the strakes could be attached, edge to edge, with-

out the sewing cord being externally visible. The method for doing this can be seen on primitive watercraft or in archaeological evidence as far apart as the Far East and northwestern Europe, providing strong grounds for the belief that the technique was established at some central point, probably in the Indian Ocean, before it diffused to the two extremes. The date for such a diffusion, like the other cultural techniques of this Mesolithic way of life, was before there was any civilized way of life, or even any Neolithic revolution, in the Near East. In fact, the rapid advance of cultural development in the Near East after 6000 B.C., especially the use of metals, created a gap in the diffusion area, so that the sewn boat continued to be found in western Europe, the Indian Ocean, East Africa, and the Far East long after the Near East had iron-nailed boats (about 900 B.C.). In many areas, there were intermediate stages between sewing and nailing strakes of which the chief was the use of wooden pegs (trunnels or treenails) to fasten sideplanking to the vessel's ribs. This intermediate stage continued in many areas for a very long time: King Solomon was building nailed ships at Ezion-Geber on the Gulf of Aqaba, using Phoenician shipwrights, before 900 B.C., but use of wooden treenails continued in some areas down to recent times. The Achaeans in Homer (Iliad, II, 135) had sewn ships, and Aeschylus in his Supplices speaks of a ship "sewn with flax," but when Odysseus made a boat (Odyssey, V, 243-248) he fastened it with wooden dowels.

As might be expected of a method of transportation, shipbuilding techniques diffused widely, but at the same time left earlier techniques still persisting in backward areas. In most significant developments the Near East seems to have been a chief center, although there seems to have been an earlier wide diffusion of a hide-covered boat with an animal head stem, steered from the port quarter, which spread as far as India and Ireland by passing farther north across the Pontic area.

The improved keel-built vessel spread much more widely and became the basis for most future

181

ships. In its earlier form, going back before
3000 B.C., it had: (1) a keel which often projected in front of the upright stem; (2) adz-cut
strakes (the longitudinal sideplanks) which were
sewn together; (3) ribs which were installed,
after the strakes were sewn, by inserting them
through cleats on the inner sides of the strakes,
from the gunwale down into the keel; these
cleats were integral parts of the strakes, which
required adz construction; (4) a high stern (generally higher than the stem) with steering from
the starboard quarter.

    All actual remains of early north European
wooden watercraft, including two from the Scandinavian Bronze Age, one from the German Iron Age,
and several from the Iron Age in England have
integral cleats and sewn strakes. In one case
(North Ferriby, East Yorkshire) the sewing holes
were concealed within a dovetail seam, in a fashion
used in modern times on the Gujarat coast of India.
According to J. Hornell and H. Lollemand, this
method was used in dynastic Egypt. Furthermore,
the use of cleats on strakes to hold inserted ribs
has been found in recent times in the Moluccas,
the Solomon Islands, and at Botel Tobago, near
Formosa. While we know nothing about the use of
cleats or of inserted ribs on ancient Egyptian
craft, Hornell has offered some rather inconclusive
arguments for believing that they were used. Even
if we rejected those inferences, the known distribution of cleat construction and of sewn hulls would
seem to indicate that these methods originated at
some more central point and must have been distributed across that central zone (the Near East) before the plank-cutting saw or iron nails came into
use in this central zone. Before these innovations,
the only alternative method for fastening a hull
would be by treenails, as a merchant ship wrecked
off Cape Gelidonya about 1200 was constructed.
The plank-cutting saw is very old, used by the
Egyptians in ship construction as early as the
Fifth Dynasty (c. 2500 B.C.). This could have
been justified, in view of the unusual way in
which large Egyptian ships were constructed and
the fact that Egypt had such a lack of large trees
of hardwood. But elsewhere, adz construction, al-

though arduous and expensive, had great advantages over sawn planks so long as integral cleats were used. The only alternative was the much cheaper, but much weaker, use of wooden pegs for fastening planks on ribs. The introduction of iron nails sometime after 1000 B.C. made ships both cheaper and stronger by allowing the use of sawn planks. This seems to have been a necessary prerequisite for the introduction of ramming as a naval tactic, perhaps sometime about 800 B.C.

The introduction of ramming not only established a naval tactic which continued to be used in the Mediterranean for about 2400 years (until about A.D. 1600) but it also completed a process which began about 1300 B.C. in which naval vessels became distinctly different from merchant vessels.

Until the great transformation in sea power began about 1300, ships in a form we would recognize, consisting of a keel, stem and stern posts at either end with ribs between, the whole sheathed in planking, had been navigating the Mediterranean for at least three thousand years. This shipping largely originated in Syria and was in the hands of Semites, speaking Akkadian dialects until about 1500 B.C. and Canaanite dialects thereafter, but with growing competition from Etruscan and above all Indo-European dialects after 1100 B.C. until largely replaced by Greek-speakers after 600 B.C.

These ships were rowed or sailed or both. In general terms, smaller vessels would be rowed and larger ones would be sailed, but since all merchant ships were neither small (below 20 feet in length) nor large (over 50 feet in length), most such vessels were built to be rowed or sailed as the occasion warranted. However, from the construction point of view, there was a fundamental antithesis between these two methods of propulsion. This was based on the fact that carrying capacity and stability (especially under sail) required high sides and broad beam, while rowing effectiveness required narrow beam and low freeboard. The recognition of this fact in a practical way, that is by building two types of vessels, the one nar-

row and low, for rowing and fighting, and the other
higher and rounder, for sailing and cargo carrying,
is what I mean by "the beginning of sea power."
Of course, this does not mean that cargo ships were
never rowed nor that fighting ships were never
sailed, but simply means that the distinction between the two was recognized and accepted by constructing two different kinds of ships, each
capable of doing one function more effectively
and the other function much less effectively.
The dating of this change in construction design
is a very risky business, but may be placed, as a
rather slow process, in the period 1400-1100,
although it could have occurred earlier.

Until this change, it would seem that most
vessels were trading ships which had a length about
four times their beam, the latter being about 9
feet amidships while the former was about 38 feet.
These dimensions apply to vessels of Syrian make
in the eastern Mediterranean of which we have
some evidence, either from pictorial or verbal
remains or from wrecks, notably the wreck of the
ship sunk off Cape Gelidonya, the western promon-
tory of the Gulf of Adalia in southern Anatolia,
about 1200.

We know, however, that ships were sailing the
Mediterranean much earlier, perhaps as far back as
4000 B.C. and that there was some commercial intercourse, not necessarily direct and certainly not
by continuous voyage, between the eastern Mediterranean and southeastern Spain sometime between
3000 and 2500 B.C. But of these ships we know
little.

The only ships of which we know much in the
period before about 1500 are the ones used in
spectacular voyages sponsored by various Pharaohs
of Egypt, but these were not regular or ordinary
maritime enterprises. Rather they were state-
sponsored exploration expeditions, early maritime
versions of our own Lewis and Clark expedition.

Before 2500 Pharaoh Snefru brought forty
ships filled with cedar logs from Lebanon to
Egypt. By 2000 Egyptian ships were sailing the

Red Sea southward to "Punt" to get incense, obtainable only in southern Arabia (the Hadrawmat) and Somaliland, near Cape Guardafui. Over this same period, the evidence of grave objects in both Crete and Egypt shows commercial interchange between these two.

The ships which brought lumber to Egypt from Lebanon may have been Egyptian in the earliest days, but the trade was soon taken over by the much smaller but more efficient Levantine ships, so that an Egyptian scribe, writing about 2200, complained that "no ships go north to Byblus anymore." The vessels going on the Red Sea to Punt were unquestionably Egyptian, but such voyages were intermittent and unusual; most incense came to Egypt by caravan across Arabia and was carried across the Red Sea directly by smaller boats, probably manned by local Semite peoples. Of the boats which traded between Egypt and Crete, we know nothing, but we are safe in inferring that they were not Egyptian, from the known unseaworthiness of Egyptian vessels and the Pharaoh's inability to retain control of the much more important trade with Lebanon.

These Egyptian expeditions to Punt were resumed in a spectacular way by Queen Hatshepsut in the early fifteenth century, but this again was a stunt, not an example of normal trade.

During this same period, the rulers of Mesopotamia were sending similar expeditions down the Persian Gulf, into the Arabian Sea, and perhaps as far away as the Indus valley, but of these vessels we know nothing, since we lack both text and pictures such as provide us with information about Egyptian maritime activities. It seems likely, however, that these southern maritime expeditions from Mesopotamia were as unusual as the Pharaoh's voyages to Punt from Egypt. It is likely that maritime activity on the southern seas (the Red Sea, the Persian Gulf, the Arabian Sea, and the Indian Ocean) remained a relatively backward affair in the hands of local Arabic fishermen whose voyages were largely coastal trips in sewn boats, until King Solomon tried to establish regular shipping in the Red Sea in full Iron Age (tenth century B.C.).

In the Mediterranean, however, matters were quite different, with regular shipping carrying goods from before 3000. It seems likely that no single people and surely no single state monopolized this Mediterranean shipping enterprise. But there can be little doubt that the dominant role throughout was played by the Semite peoples. At various times, perhaps at all times, before 1400 B.C. other peoples participated in this Mediterranean maritime activity, with little obvious conflict, not only because the activity was so dangerous in itself but also because it was so mutually beneficial to all concerned that cooperation was preferable to competition and surely far preferable to violent competition, and, perhaps most notably, because fighting between merchant ships was ineffective.

This kind of a commercial system outside any structure of power or law is so unusual that it is worth emphasizing here. Its parallel on land was the "silent trade" which Herodotus describes and which we know from other evidence was also practiced in other places at other times. According to Herodotus, the early Phoenician traders of the Mediterranean had no trading posts but instead landed on some customary beach, placed a display of their goods on the beach, then retired to their ships while the natives came down to the beach, examined the goods on display, deposited near them goods for barter which they judged of equal value, and withdrew from the beach again; the Phoenicians then landed, examined the offered barter goods and, if satisfied with their value, took them away to the ships, at which the natives returned to the beach and took away the Phoenician goods, thus completing the transaction. But if the Phoenicians were not satisfied with the value of the proffered goods, they left both supplies of goods on the beach and returned to their ships again, so that the natives could return to the beach, see that the Phoenician traders were not willing to do business at the offered value and could add to the barter goods until the amount of these was large enough to persuade the Phoenicians

186

to take them, concluding the deal. If, on the contrary, at any point in the process either side wished to break off the negotiation, they could take away their own goods, leaving the other goods, thus indicating that no deal was possible.

A "silent trade" similar to this took place in the savannah grasslands of West Africa in the medieval period when trans-Sahara caravans of Berbers exchanged salt for gold without any personal contact.

Such "silent trade" can function as exchange outside any structure of law and power only when the trade is recognized as mutually beneficial to both sides so that it is to the interest of both to trust each other in order to maintain the trade. Such mutuality is, of course, the chief basis for any law and order. It seems very likely that most maritime trade on the Mediterranean before about 1400 B.C. was of this type, not, to be sure, "silent trade" in the strict sense, but trade which all concerned wished to maintain as mutually beneficial, so that it could function without any rule of law or power on the sea. This is but another way of saying that there was, accurately speaking, no "sea power" and no "rule of the sea" before 1400. But any situation such as this is always precarious and will continue only so long as all concerned recognize their own future interest in maintaining the relationship by taking a small benefit at each transaction rather than to break off the relationship without future by grabbing all that can be grabbed in one swoop.

In saying this, I am saying that the maritime commerce of the Mediterranean as it existed for more than a thousand years previous to 1400 could continue so long as no personalities like the Indo-European extremists got in on it. For the very nature of the Indo-European attitudes and, if you wish, of "the heroic tradition," was to sacrifice routine daily functioning of life for the sake of the one big grab. It reflected a personality which gambled and risked all on one excessive moment, which killed the goose which laid golden eggs, and which saw nothing wrong (but, on the contrary,

187

everything admirable), in cashing in a capital
gain rather than holding on for an annual return.
It was, in a word, a method of operation which
could not be continued long if a "sacker of cities"
appeared on the scene. Many such "sackers of
cities" appeared on many scenes in the second half
of the second millennium B.C., and they have been
with us, more or less, ever since.

It seems very likely that the Minoans of Crete
were the dominant maritime peoples from about 1800
to about 1400. Professor Cyrus A. Gordon has
identified their writing, known as Linear A, as a
dialect of northwestern Semite related to Akkadian.
This fits well into the rest of the evidence which
links early maritime activity in the eastern Mediterranean with the first Semitic inhabitants of the
Levant, the Giblites, called by the Egyptians
"Fenkhu," who were but a local variant of the
Akkadians and Assyrians who made up that first
wave elsewhere in the Fertile Crescent. In Crete
these Fenkhu or Akkadians found Anatolian peasant
peoples whom they organized, with additional Egyptian influences, into the Minoan civilization. The
majority of Cretans were still Anatolian, but the
seafaring cities, palaces, and writing were outside
elements associated with the ruling groups.

These ruling groups, the Minoan Semites,
were the chief power on the Mediterranean, at
least as far west as Sardinia, and also exercised
great influence northward along their trade routes
across Greece to the Danube and on to Bohemia.
By a system of mutual adaptation, the Indo-European
Bronze Age invaders of Greece, the Achaeans, were
gradually Cretanized and thus civilized into what
we call Mycenaean and what, later somewhat modified, after the Iron Age Dorian invasions, became
Ionians.

These Cretanized Achaeans profited, both economically and culturally, from Cretan trade and
influence and probably served the Minoans as mercenary soldiers and marines. They may have migrated peacefully into the Cretan capital at Knossos so that the city became, to some extent, a
Greek-speaking city, just as New York or Miami
have in recent years become cities with large Span-

ish-speaking districts.

This Minoan dominance on the Mediterranean for four centuries previous to 1400 was economic rather than political, as we have indicated. It is unlikely that the Cretans had any naval vessels or engaged in naval battles on the sea, but they did enforce order on the sea by retaliatory raids on the land bases of those who interfered with Minoan trade, property, or persons. In fact, we are told by Herodotus (VII, 169-171) that Minos, on one such retaliatory raid, was killed in Sicily. Thus, strangely enough, amphibious operations in which fighting men were transported by sea to wage battles on distant shores may be older than naval battles between ships.

Crete was not the only state to engage in amphibious warfare. The Pharaoh Sahure about 2550 B.C. transported an army from the Nile to some Asiatic shore and the long-lived Pharaoh Pepi II did the same thing a century and a half later. Almost a millennium later, in the fifteenth century, the Egyptian empire over much of the Levant was established and closely controlled by Thutmose III's seaborne troops and supply lines. But within another century, after 1400, the whole eastern Mediterranean was the prey of sea rovers, raiders, and pirates.

This disappearance of law and order on the sea after 1400 was the consequence of a number of events already mentioned. The Mycenaeans and other early Indo-European groups turned to competitive violence and sacking of cities. Above all, they replaced the Minoans in control of Knossos, although not the rest of the island of Crete. This seizure of Knossos was not achieved, as some experts like Lionel Casson believe, by an unrecorded naval victory of the Mycenaeans over the Minoans, and may not have been accompanied by any immediate destruction of Knossos itself. More likely, the Mycenaean population of Knossos which had migrated in peaceably as workers and perhaps mercenary fighters and marines simply rose up and took over the city by coup, possibly, as some accounts have it, on receiving news of Minos' defeat and death

189

in Sicily. The Palace of Minos was destroyed several
times in less than two centuries after this, but at
least one of these destructions seems to have been
by fire, resulting from an earthquake or a vol-
canic explosion on the island of Thera. It is
possible that the Mycenaean coup took place after
this natural disaster rather than after the defeat
of Minos in Sicily.

In other words, the exact sequence of events
is hazy, but what is quite clear is that Mycenaeans
obtained control of Knossos and did so, almost certainly, not by defeating the Minoan fleet and conquering the island by force. But the long range
consequences were the same: Minoan influence on
the sea was ended and was not replaced by any
single political power, least of all by the Mycenaeans (who were not themselves a single political power). The numerous Indo-European principalities not only in Greece and Crete but in the
Aegean, Anatolia and Asia began to establish con-
fiscatory tolls on peaceful traders and to fight
among themselves for trade and glory. The trading
peoples, including the Semites of the Levant, began to turn to piracy and raiding, as did the
Indo-Europeans also.

As peaceful commerce declined and piracy rose,
it became profitable for those who inclined to the
latter to construct ships better adapted to piracy
than to trade. At this point, still in the fourteenth century, or even earlier, the contrast between merchant vessels and sea rovers' ships appeared. The merchant vessels remained small, high
sided, almost oval in shape (with beam as much as
one-third the length), largely propelled by sail,
slow and capacious. The naval vessel became longer,
with much lower freeboard, often undecked or only
partly decked, slim and swift (with beam as little
as one-fifth the length), and propelled by oars,
at least while functioning as a raider. These
raiders' ships were as different from the merchant
vessels of the day as the Viking ships 2500 years
later were from the Santa Maria. Of course the sea
raiders' ships of 1300 B.C., although similar to
Viking ships in general appearance and use, were
far inferior as ships just as those who sailed them

190

were far inferior to the Vikings as sailors: there was more iron in both Viking ships and Viking sailors. The raiders of 1300 B.C. stayed close to shore, on which they landed every night for food and rest, and they had not as yet any really effective way of fighting other ships. When this was necessary they overtook their victim, assailed him with missile weapons such as slings, arrows, and spears, and finished the struggle by boarding and engaging in hand-to-hand fighting on deck.

This method of fighting between vessels was so difficult and so precarious that it was not engaged in unless the outcome seemed certain and likely to be unusually rewarding. That would only occur when the merchant vessel as victim seemed unusually rich and the attacking pirate vessels were numerous.

In preference to this precarious attack on other vessels at sea, most of the sea rovers' attacks were raids on land: a fleet of raiding vessels or even a single vessel attacking an unsuspecting and undefended shore would suddenly land, pillage and burn, and quickly escape back to sea with captives to sell as slaves. By 1100 such activities had become part of trading, so that raiding and trading were hardly distinguishable, a vessel landing to trade and sell slaves where attack seemed likely to be unsuccessful or in a friendly port, the goods and the slaves being, in many cases, the booty of raids made a few days earlier somewhere else.

The Semites of Syria (by this time speaking a Canaanite dialect we call Phoenician) were the chief participants in this trading-raiding activity for the whole period from the end of dominant Minoan activity about 1400 until the rapid rise of Greek sea trading, under Phoenician example, after 800 B.C. But others engaged in this trading-raiding during this whole period. The key to the six hundred years 1400-800 B.C. was that the proportions between trading and raiding changed with the trading element decreasing from 1400 to 1000, and then increasing again from 1000 onward.

The Mycenaean and other Bronze Age Indo-Europeans also engaged in these activities but not as
successfully as the Semites and were soon joined
by increasing numbers of new Iron Age Indo-European
invaders, who were encouraged to surge southward
from their northern homes to Crete and southern
Anatolia by the increasing political disorder and
growing defensive weakness of the whole Mediterranean basin. These Indo-Europeans, whether descendants of earlier Bronze Age invaders or more
recent Iron Age invaders (known as Dorians, Phyrgians, Lydians, and other names) or mixed groups
(including mixtures with Semites or even Asiatic
speakers from parts of Anatolia) were not as skilled
sailors as the Canaanites, but were, on the other
hand, far superior in mounting amphibious assaults
and permanent conquests of foreign shores.

Of such assaults by Indo-European or mixed
groups the most famous were the attacks on Egypt
and the southern Levant in the late thirteenth
and twelfth centuries. The earliest of these
raids, by Lydians from southern Asia Minor, came
as early as the reign of the Pharaoh Ikhnaton
(1380-1362), a religious reformer rather than a
military leader, who lost most of the Levant and
all of its seaways to raiders. Two subsequent
raids in 1221 and in 1194, in which "Libyans"
joined in the assault, were repulsed, but the
greatest attack, far more than a raid, was in
1190. By that time, the raiders were in control
of, or allied with, many of the Syrian ports,
and had assembled a great force of various peoples, some of them from as far away as Anatolia.
These proceeded to the attack on Egypt both by
land, southward across the Levant, and by sea, in
an amphibious assault on the Nile delta. Ramesses
mobilized all his forces to resist them. The land
invasion was really a migration, a great caravan
of heavy two-wheeled oxcarts protected by the fighting forces who surrounded it. This land force was
completely destroyed by Ramesses, probably in the
southern Levant. The Pharaoh then hurried back
to Egypt to face the amphibious assault with his
own naval forces, backed up by his land army.
The counterattack was made after the invaders
had entered "the harbor" (probably a branch of

the Nile) where the enemy ships could be attacked by archers from the land as well as from the Egyptian galleys. The invaders were at a disadvantage, sails furled, without oars, and armed with swords and spears, while the Egyptians, being rowed, were more agile and could attack with arrows while still at a distance. Both sides had vessels of about the same size and design, both with curved hulls and relatively straight stems and stern posts, each with a single short and heavy mast, amidships, for carrying the single square sail which had propelled watercraft since the beginning of sailing, but the invaders' masts, topped by crows nests, contained a lookout. The invaders can be distinguished by their weapons and head gear as well as by the difference in their ships.

This, the first naval battle of which we have a picture, was a melee, apparently without distinctive tactics except that the Egyptian archers against barbarian spearmen, along with the superior Egyptian mobility from the use of oars, made the invaders' situation almost hopeless. Vessels crashed into each other and capsized, but there was no deliberate ramming, and no vessel had a ram, a device which was not invented for several centuries.

This great amphibious assault on Egypt in the early twelfth century was not an isolated event, but part of that ultimate chaos which ended the archaic world in the Mediterranean area. The great movement of peoples was, by 1190, in full process, and the earlier occupants of that area were still so busy fighting each other that they had little time to concentrate on the influx of nomadic and semi-pastoral peoples. While Ramesses was defending Egypt in the far south, the siege of Troy had already commenced, and that city fell, if we accept the traditional date, six years later in 1184. This event, however, may have been as much as 150 years earlier.

It is worthy of note that Troy fell by deception, not by assault, an indication of the strength of such defensive castles, but the ability of any society to maintain an economic and administrative basis able to support such structures was being steadily eroded long before 1180 and was totally destroyed in the course of that century.

What that economic and administrative basis entailed is recorded in the Linear B tablets, especially those at Pylos, much better than in Homer, for the poet was concerned with being a bard in the heroic tradition and not with recording the economic and administrative basis which was being torn apart by that tradition.

The most astonishing feature of the Linear B records is how different the picture they offer is from that provided by Homer. To be sure, part of that difference arises from the different forms of concern we have just mentioned, but it is equally true that the evidence describes two different situations. In the Linear B records everything revolves about the devotion to the goddess Potnia, and those actions are about as unheroic as could be: they are routine, bureaucratic, quantitative, planned, disciplined. Supplies and men are gathered, prepared, counted, instructed, trained, and all tied together by a centralized system of communications, based on written orders but also based on bureaucratic authority and arranged signals. The most significant elements in the system were (1) reverence and service to Potnia; (2) the centralized, bureaucratic structure of authority dependent from that reverence; and (3) fear of the sea.

Of these three the most interesting for us is the third: coast watchers covered the shores with a network of sentinels; signal fires were ready on every headland and mounted messengers were ready in every bay to call out the population for defense when sea raiders appeared. It is obvious from the destruction of Pylos, Mycenae, and other political centers of the late Bronze Age that the enemy, in the long run, were successful, although it is not so clear that the destroyers came from the sea (except in Crete and other islands) since much of the latest destruction came from overland invaders like the Dorians or even from fellow Achaeans.

The threat from the sea which began about 1400 had a great influence on the situation of the cities of the Mediterranean. To avoid danger from pirates, most of these cities, even those which were great trading centers in the classical period, were not on the coast but were several miles from the seaport which served them. In many cases, such as Athens, the city was not originally established to be a commercial center, but was simply a defensive stockade and shrine on a hilltop to which the farming people of the area could go for safety when any threat arose. When a city later developed around such a citadel and sea trade became one of its activities, a port had to be developed on the shore some distance away. Thus Piraeus developed as the port of Athens, although eventually, after many centuries, the whole space between them was filled with people and buildings to make one continuous urban center from the Acropolis to the harbor.

Long before Athens and, indeed, long before this transitional period which we are calling "the great transformation," with its great increase in piracy and threats from the sea, the sea had appeared as a threat to many, and the growth of towns and cities had begun around a citadel which stood back from the sea. The word "city" like the word "citadel" (and the parallel terms in the Teutonic languages: "berg," "buhr," "bourg," or borough) meant fortress and referred to a stockaded enclosure on a hill to provide a refuge for peasants in time of danger. Thus, even Knossos was not on the coast, but had its port at Amnisos, several miles away; the great cities of Argos, like Mycenae and Tiryns, were not on the sea, but had a port at Asine.

The significant exceptions to this rule were the Phoenician cities; these were usually seaports, sometimes (as at Tyre) on small islands just off the coast. The significance of this was that the Semites of that Levantine coast of north Syria were at home on the sea: to them danger came from the land, and, when danger came to other peoples from the sea, it came, as likely as not, from the Phoenicians. As part of this uniqueness, it should be pointed out that the

195

Phoenicians were the only people of the ancient
world who did not worry about control of agricultural lands; they purchased their food from
their landbound neighbors. To ensure this they
generally maintained friendly relations with neighboring peoples, solidified by their sound business
relationships with them. As an example of this,
it might be mentioned that Carthage, founded on
rented land in 814, was still paying rent to the
local natives centuries later.

Sea power in the sense it is used here, to
mean a state with a navy of specialized fighting
vessels for maintaining political influence on the
sea, was a product of the Greek dark ages. Technically it involved three items: (1) specialized
ships; (2) the ram; and (3) methods of oarage
which culminated in the trireme about 500 B.C.
We do not know what people invented these techniques, although Thucydides attributes the origin
of the trireme to the Corinthians. On the whole,
whatever the merits of this claim, it seems likely
that the Phoenicians played a major role in all
three items.

These three, of course, are linked together.
The ram could not be used so long as ships were
built by sewing or pegging together strakes to
form a hull or wooden skin, then later inserting
the ribs and frame. The sewn or pegged ship of
the period before 1000 B.C. would shatter itself
by ramming an enemy vessel; a galley for ramming
needs a ship made in the later fashion, of sawn
planks fastened by iron nails to the framework of
keel, ribs, and thwarts constructed first. We know
that ships of nailed planks were being built at
Ezion-Geber by Phoenician shipwrights in the employ
of King Solomon before 900 B.C. If these Canaanite peoples invented the sawn plank, iron-nailed
ship, it is possible that they also invented the
ram which appeared about the same time and may
have contributed to the process by which the
Phoenicians took control of the sea after 1000
B.C. from the diverse, largely Indo-European
Peoples of the Sea who had dominated it about
1200-1100 B.C.

Phoenician control of the sea was relatively brief, although it was not destroyed completely until Alexander the Great captured Tyre in 332 and Rome won the Second Punic War of 218-201. The Phoenicians were concerned with the sea for commercial rather than military reasons, and their primacy on the water in the period 1000-500 B.C. was due as much to lack of competition as to any technological initiatives or aggressive tactics on their own part. Their "control" of the sea replaced that of Indo-Europeans, chiefly the Mycenaeans, after 1000, and they were replaced in turn by other Indo-Europeans, the Greeks, in the century 550-450 B.C. This century was also the period in which the penteconter with 50 rowers was replaced as the dominant naval vessel by the trireme with 170 rowers. It is possible that the shift in naval power from Canaanite to Greek was related to the rise of the trireme. The Phoenicians had triremes and may even have invented the trireme and the ram, but the Greeks, followed later by the Macedonians and the Romans, had the aggressive spirit which was needed in any naval conflict based on ramming with triremes.

The traditional date for this shift in naval power is 480 B.C., the date when the Greeks in the eastern Mediterranean defeated the Phoenician naval forces of Persia at Salamis, while on the same day, we are told, the Greeks of Syracuse, Sicily, in the west were destroying a Carthaginian fleet at Himera. In fact, Carthaginian power in the west, both on land and on sea, continued to expand (although not in Sicily) until after 300 B.C.

Before 1000 B.C. the only naval weapon beyond the open rowed galley itself was the grappling iron used in the second stage of a naval battle for boarding an enemy vessel which had been shaken in the first stage by missile weapons. As we might expect from the Asiatic partiality for missile weapons and the European favor for shock weapons, there was a tendency for the peoples of North Africa and the Levant to extend the missile stage of any battle to the neglect of the second stage, while the peoples of Europe and the Aegean got through the missile stage as soon as possible to

197

reach the more decisive stage of hand-to-hand combat. This is part of the Indo-European aggressive
spirit and may well be offered as an argument that
we should consider the ram a Greek, or at least a
European, invention, even in the period of Asiatic
(Phoenician) naval primacy.

Once Mediterranean navies became committed to
ramming, as they did by 800 B.C., the boundaries
within which naval technological innovation could
occur became relatively narrow. The chief problems which were faced became little more than how
the ship, especially its bow, could be strengthened
to withstand the shock of the ram; how the speed
and maneuverability of the vessel could be increased;
and how missiles could be excluded from the battle
as much as possible. Other matters, such as how
naval vessels could be kept at sea for extended
periods or in less favorable weather, were
largely ignored.

The need to increase the speed and power of the
ship in the period covered by this chapter widened
the difference between naval vessels and merchant
ships, since the former became lower and narrower
in its hull, while the cargo vessel's hull became
wider and rounder. As a result, the original ratio
of length to width in both changed from about 5:1
towards 3:1 for the merchant ship, while naval hulls
moved from about 5:1 to more than 9:1. Length,
however, could not be increased too far in the naval
galley, so long as the keel was made of a single
log and the vessel was beached every night if possible. This constant return to shore was necessary,
not only to rest and feed the men, but also to dry
out the hull so that combat speed would not be lost
by the wood and the bilge taking in water.

The combat vessels of 850-750 B.C. were generally triaconters about 75 feet long with 30 oars
and penteconters about 125 feet long and 13 feet
wide with 50 oars. To protect the rowers from missiles and to provide space for fighting men above
the rowers, the latter were lowered into the hull,
rowing through ports below the gunwale, while a
raised deck along the centerline above the oarsmen
provided a fighting platform for marines. The

search for more speed and power by putting more rowers in the same length of hull drove the naval designers upward in an effort to get more rowers in the "room" of forty inches or slightly less required by each oarsman. In this effort a second level of rowers were seated above and somewhat forward and outside of the original line of oarsmen rowing in the hull. The opening between the outer edge of the fighting deck and the gunwale was soon closed (originally with leather curtains, according to Lionel Casson) to protect the rowers from missiles.

As a result of these changes, the older open galley (aphract) of Homer became an enclosed vessel (cataphract), and the penteconter of fifty rowers on the same level could become much shorter with fifty rowers divided between two banks. Such vessels are shown in the Assyrian reliefs of Sennacherib (705-681 B.C.).

The idea of going upward to find space for more rowers undoubtedly suggested to many minds the possibility of a third level of oarsmen above the existing two levels, but the problem was not simple, since the vessel could get top-heavy and the oars could get too long for one man to handle them. As a result the trireme was introduced slowly, mostly in the period 650-550, although the two-level ramming galley came into use as early as 700 B.C. and the three-level version was probably known in the seventh century. The Penteconters were replaced by triremes as ships of the line only in the navies of the more affluent states and not until 550-480 B.C. By 480 the trireme was the key to naval power, a position it held for a century and a half. By 330 B.C., when the Athenian navy had 492 triremes ("threes"), Athens already had 18 "fours"; six years later in 324, it still had its triremes, but had increased its "fours" to 43 and had added 7 "fives": a new era of naval competition had begun, as we shall see.

The third level of rowers for the trireme were added above, slightly forward, and outward of the second level. In the Phoenician fleet

199

this was done by working the oars and rowers, 85
on each side, with three banks of 27 rowers, plus
four additional rowers on the top level astern;
the latter four had no rowers beneath them since
the vessel was less long below. If we ignore
these four at the top stern, we can see the others
in 27 "rooms" on each side of the hull, each "room"
(called metron in Greek, interscalium in Latin) a
space about 40 inches fore and aft, and about 5.5
feet high, but leaning forward and outward, since
each rower in a "room" was a little higher, forward, and farther out than the rower below him in
the same "room." In the Athenian trireme, the
lowest oars were rowed in ports only 18 inches
above the waterline, while the top oars were
worked on an outrigger which extended about two
feet outside the hull. The oars were almost 14
feet long, while the vessel was about 118 feet
long, 12 feet wide across the gunwales, but 16
feet wide including the outriggers, with a flat
bottom about 10 feet wide, a freeboard of only
4.5 feet, and an overall height above the water
of only 8.5 feet.

Such a trireme had 120 more rowers in slightly
less length than the penteconter had two centuries
earlier, but the "threes" were much less seaworthy
from increased height, greater weight topside,
and 54 rowing ports only a foot and a half above
the water. These ports had to be closed with a
leather collar in any seaway, so that the trireme
was not usable except in summer and in calm weather. Since they were hauled out of the water each
night (one reason they were flatbottomed), they
were not put in the water if the next day was
rough; this was quite alright, since no enemy
trireme could go out that day either. The war
at sea was suspended until the weather improved.

It is obvious that triremes were very expensive
to build and operate, many times the cost of penteconters. This increase in cost, which did not stop
in 500 B.C. but continued to accelerate in naval
construction for another five centuries, gradually
reduced the number of states which could afford
to be naval powers. Just as occurred in European
history in A.D. 1500-1900, the costs of naval com-

petition gradually reduced the number of competitors to a few and eventually to one.

4.   The Competition of Weapons

The period of the great transformation, like somewhat similar periods in A.D. 250-850 and A.D. 1300-1600, was a period of confused competition among weapons. In all three cases, people had a variety of weapons available but were not able to settle on any established relationships among them or reach any consensus on their relative merits or on the ways in which they could be used together. This failure, of course, rested on the double fact that the outcome of battles offered such conflicting evidence that it was not clear what conditions were best suited to which weapons and on the additional fact that, even when evidence is tolerably clear, peoples' minds are too set in other directions to analyze it and to agree on its meaning.

The most tenacious example of such a "set mind" in the history of weaponry has already been mentioned, the fact that Europe was shifted about 1900 B.C. from its earlier emphasis on missile weaponry (as in the Bell Beaker archery tradition) to a shock tradition based on axes, daggers, and spears. This European tradition persisted through many modifications of weapons and tactics to the suicidal bayonet charges of World War I. Since Asia, with one notable exception (the Iranian cataphract) to be discussed later, continued in the missile tradition until it was overpowered by European guns in the nineteenth century, there was, for about 3500 years, a sharp contrast between the Asiatic missile tradition and the European shock tradition.

The archery tradition in Asia can be traced from the wooden stave bow, through the reflex bow and various kinds of compound and composite bows, to its culmination in the so-called "Hunnish" or "Turkish" bow of horn and sinew. The value of archery as a weapon depends on its range, penetration power, and accuracy, and perhaps to a lesser extent on the ease with which it can be used. These

201

characteristics depend on a large number of factors which cover the quality and length of the bow itself, the way in which the arrow and string are held in the draw, the weight of the arrow, and several other factors. Early efforts before 4000 B.C. discovered that the length of the bow was limited by the length of the archer's draw, which was limited by the length of his arms. In an ordinary stave bow the string is farthest from the stave at the grip, near the center of the stave. This distance could be added to the length of the draw and thus to the power of the bow if the stave was permanently curved backward toward the archer and the ends of the stave were curved forward away from the archer so that the stave was close to the string at the center. This reflex bow would be made into this shape by heat, as was done in many areas in the prehistoric period. Its stave could be a single piece of wood (called a "self bow").

In a composite bow the stave is made of different materials, a back which resists stretching and a "belly" which resists compression, so that the draw pulls the former around the latter. The two materials had to be glued together to form a single piece. Many materials could be used, as, for example, the Lapps in the eighteenth century used composite bows made of a birch rod which resists compression with a more elastic pine back glued on. In some cases, a bow with composite qualities could be made of a single piece of wood cut from a log so that the belly of the stave was heartwood while the back was more elastic sapwood. However, from an early date, before 5000 B.C. it was discovered in central Asia, probably by hunters from the forests north of the grasslands, in contacts with Neolithic farmers on the oases south of the grasslands, that sinew and horn (keratin) made the best combination for the back and belly of a bow. Gad Rausing places and dates this invention by inference from the known distribution of such bows (including their diffusion with Indian migrants to the North American plains) and the fact that woodland hunters could not boil the necessary glue until they had obtained pottery from the central Asiatic Neolithic peoples near Anau.

There have been many variants of both bows and arrows, a fact which is of historical importance, since an invading tribe which appeared suddenly with a superior innovation could destroy or enslave a tribe which tried to defend its traditional territory. Even a small improvement could make a substantial difference. For example, Sir Ralph Payne-Gallwey, the outstanding English authority on the Turkish bow, tells us that by fledging their arrows with parchment rather than with feathers, the Turks extended their range thirty yards. Since the invention of the composite bow occurred in Asia on the edge of the grasslands and most of the subsequent improvements appeared in the same ecologic context, but increasingly farther east, in the same areas where pastoralism and full pastoral nomadism appeared and where the sub-Boreal and post-classical drier climate periods had their greatest effects, we can see how these three factors combined to force devastating warrior invasions outward into the crescent of more civilized areas of the Far East, south Asia, the Near East, and even Europe in the period 2500 to 1100 B.C. and again in the period A.D. 350 to 1600. As Frank E. Brown, who helped work out some of these relationships put it, each improvement was "adopted by a wave of nomads and thus transmitted to the civilizations of the marginal crescent."

It is not necessary in this book to explain all the detailed changes of these or any other weapons, but it must be recognized that such advances in weapons technology played a considerable role in establishing or disturbing political stability throughout history. In this book the main lines of these changes will be given, without details in how they worked themselves out, especially as we are not yet sure of many of the technological changes. Technically the composite bow reached a peak in the Turkish bow as late as 1800. This was an exquisite triumph of engineering skill, superior to the contemporary European military musket or even to the Rhenish rifle of that day, in rate of fire and accuracy, if not in range, but it required such skill in its construction, stringing, and use that it could be used as a weapon only by a small number of persons who could devote time

203

to the long training needed to acquire and keep
the strength and muscular coordination needed to
string it and to shoot it. As a result, even the
Turks used it only on special occasions and equipped
their regular troops with muskets as soon as these
were available. The difficulty in stringing and
drawing the Turkish bow rested on the fact that it
was little more than three feet long and very
fragile, yet had a pull well over a hundred pounds.
Only constant practice and use of a special stance
provided the coordinated effort of leg and body
muscles which could string such a bow without
shattering it.

Unstrung such a bow lies almost in a circle,
coiled like a rattlesnake, with the horn on the
outside and the sinew inside, but when strung, the
horn is on the inside belly of the bow and the
sinew is on the outside or back. The two materials
are attached on a thin strip of wood, usually in
pieces, with glue, and the combination is usually
covered with bark, lacquer, or some other kind of
protection against worms, insects, humidity, and
heat, all of which are very damaging to a composite
bow. When not in use, the bow is immediately unstrung and placed in a case for further protection.
In fact, the bow is so delicate that Odysseus did
not take his great bow to war, but left it at home
where the suitors tried in vain to string it, and
on his return ten years later, its owner examined
it carefully for worm damage before stringing it.

The fact that Odysseus did not take his composite bow to war, but apparently used it only for
hunting, may be a reflection of the European shock
tradition in warfare, while many people of the missile tradition used their composite bows only for
war and used self bows or reflex bows, along with
spears, in hunting.

For the reasons we have given, the composite
bow was often not used by people who knew of it,
or was given up by people who used it in earlier,
more prosperous times, but abandoned it when less
affluent conditions arrived. It was very much an
elitist weapon, from its expense (which was very
great, since it sometimes took years to make) as

well as the long and constant training required for its regular use. For this reason, it was often found only in the upper class of a society or tribe, while the lower classes either used no archery or were restricted to use of a simple or reflex bow. In European history there were three occasions in which archery went into eclipse and was replaced by shock weapons; in each of these cases an invasion was followed by an attempt to establish a wide-ranging upper class rule which collapsed and was followed by a period of depressed prosperity based on shock weapons. Of these three occasions, the first, about 1900 B.C., probably did not have the composite bow, but the bow prevalent before the Indo-European invasion was replaced as the dominant weapon by the invaders' shock weapons, and the bow probably was left to the lower, subjected peasants as a hunting weapon. In the other two cases, both of which resulted in real dark ages about 950 B.C. and again about A.D. 950, the composite bow disappeared completely, leaving the upper class with shock weapons and the subjected peasants with no weapons except a few simple bows. In the earlier case, the composite bow used by Odysseus disappeared completely from mainland Greece, and when bowmen were desired later, in the sixth century B.C., Scythian archers with composite bows were hired from the Pontic grasslands. In the later case, the double convex composite bow, which the Franks had adopted from the Roman cavalry in the Merovingian period, vanished in the ninth century, leaving shock weapons to the upper classes and the simple bow to the lower classes. As we shall see, in the fourteenth century, this lower class weapon, in the form of the English longbow, emerged from obscurity to destroy upper class shock chivalry.

The earlier case, which is the concern of this chapter, was similar to this last case. The Greek experience was not unique but was shared by barbarian Europe in the period 1500-500 B.C. As central and northern Europe moved toward the prosperity of the great central European Bronze Age which slowly arose from the post-invasion depression of 1900 B.C., the composite bow, which may not have been known previously in northern and central Europe, came in as a hunting weapon from the east European grass-

lands, as it did to Mycenaean Greece and to Odysseus.
Spears and axes remained the chief weapons of war
for all the Teutonic peoples until after 500 B.C.
The next wave of invaders, in the period 1250-1000,
with its subsequent European dark age, wiped away
the use, and possibly even the knowledge, of the
composite bow among the Scandinavians and other
Teutonic peoples. The Scandinavians and Celts
continued to use the simple bow, mostly in the
longbow form, but the use of archery among the
Germans became rare, and these latter were largely
reduced to spears, javelins, and axes. Thus the
Celtic peoples but not the Germans had bows, but
not composite bows, when the Romans attacked them,
and the Scandinavians used self bows freely, even
in Viking sea battles, when they entered the stage
of history after A.D. 600. Otherwise in Europe,
the composite bow came back in the first millennium
A.D. only in a few places, chiefly to the Gauls
from the Romans and possibly in some places from
the Huns who wandered over much of Europe in the
period A.D. 375-460. The composite bow seems to
be known in Beowulf and the Nibelungenlied from
the use of the word Hornbogi (in the latter case
as a personal name), but these are only passing
traces of the Huns, wiped away in the later Dark Ages.

The composite bow had equal difficulty establishing itself in the south, possibly from lack of
the needed materials and because of the rapid deterioration of such a bow from climate and insects
in that area. Thus the composite bow did not
reach Egypt until at least a millennium after it
was being used in Mesopotamia, and it is doubtful
if it was ever made there, as most of the few surviving examples seem to be made of wood like white
birch and ash which do not grow in Egypt. There
are over thirty such surviving bows from Egypt,
one of the Seventeenth Dynasty, the rest later,
but mostly dated 1600-1000 B.C. Of these the
first one collected and the oldest one known are
in museums in Brooklyn and New York. So far as
we can see, the composite bow was not known in
the rest of Africa and in Arabia until after the
Islamic conquests which began in A.D. 632.

The missile tradition of Asia is reflected in

other weapons than the bow, including the persistent use of slings in stony areas and the Chinese invention of the crossbow, which is a composite bow attached to a grooved stock so that it can be drawn by mechanical power, can be held at the draw by a trigger until the target is exposed, and shoots bolts much shorter than the distance of the draw.

These two traditions, embedded in social training and individual neurological patterns, persisted through ages of weapons changes, often imposing grave restraints on the effective use of new weapons. Such restraints can be seen in the period with which we are concerned in the shift to chariots about 1900 B.C. and the shift to horse riding a thousand years later. In each of these shifts, the Europeans changed the method of mobility while retaining the spear, while Asiatics made the same change in mobility while retaining archery. This persistence resulted in a long history of collisions between the two traditions in western Asia and across the steppe frontier between the two. The history of those collisions is of some importance in the long story of shifting political power.

When this history began, about 4000 B.C., the grasslands of both central and western Asia were abodes of the white race, speaking Indo-European languages, with speakers of Ural-Altaic and Asiatic all about them, in the hills and mountains to the south, in the woods to the west, north, and northeast, and even on the grasslands to the east of them. These Indo-European whites were probably the inventors of equine mobility, both chariot and horseback (or at least, they exploited it more intensively and more successfully than others), and they may have been the inventors of both pastoralism about 2500 B.C. and of full nomadism two thousand years later, at least north of the mountains, but their devotion to the shock tradition and the fact that the composite bow and most of its improvements were originated among Altaic speakers (at first white in race, but later farther east among peoples of the yellow race), plus the fact that the grassland dessication was earlier and more extensive in the east than in the west, all these factors tended to push both the Indo-European speakers and the shock weapons tradition westward out of Asia. This had numerous consequences.

Among these consequences were the following. The lines of contact between missile and shock, between Indo-European and Altaic languages, and between the yellows and whites in grassland Eurasia were pushed westward so that they ceased to be in east central Asia, where they had been about 4000 B.C., and moved west past the Carpathians and the Ukraine, where they were to be found about A.D. 1500. The eastern archery-using Indo-Europeans, such as the Hittites, Mitanni, Medes, Persians, Aryans of India, and Parthians and Sassanians of Iran, were all eliminated by missile-using non-Indo-European speakers, generally by Turkish-Mongolian speakers in the hilly plateau areas and by Semitic-speakers, chiefly Arabs, in the lower, more southern, and more desert areas. Thus the shock weapon tradition became largely a European tradition, and the Indo-European languages became restricted chiefly to the two areas indicated by that name (that is to Europe and India, by being eliminated from central and western Asia, except for some scattered mountain areas).

These changes had, of course, even more profound influences in Europe, not only shifting it from its archery tradition to the shock tradition, but also shifting it linguistically from Asiatic-type languages of proto-Finnish character to Indo-European languages which became the ancestor tongues of the Romance, Celtic, Teutonic, and Slavic languages. This process, which moved the Celtic-speakers from central Asia to the westernmost fringes of Europe is continuing today as Slavic languages, especially Russian, continue to push Finnish and Samoyed and similar speeches backward in the forests of Eurasia, while Spanish continues to intrude on Basque in the mountains of northern Iberia. This Indo-European movement into Europe from the east came in along the grasslands corridor into Hungary and then pushed westward through mountains and forests like a wedge dividing the missile-using, non-European speakers into the two groups whose remnants remain today in southwest and northeast Europe. For a considerable period in the pre-Christian era, parts of Europe such as Iberian Spain and the Finnish occupied forests, as well as isolated valleys of the Caucasus, remained in the missile, bow and arrow tradition until they were subjugated by the battle-axes, spears, and swords of the Indo-Europeans. The importance of the Hungarian plain as the gate to Europe from the east for grassland marauders can be seen from the fact that it bears the name and today speaks the language of two later Altaic intruders, who followed the original Indo-European speakers in over an interval of thousands of years (the Huns about A.D. 350-450 and the Magyars about 850-950).

These remarks about the two weapons traditions apply more clearly to barbarian areas than to civilized ones, for civilizations will have a greater variety of weapons, may use specialized units of both kinds, will have greater flexibility in their use, and will have more elaborate, more disciplined, and other supplementary arms (such as siege trains and a navy). In all these respects uncivilized or "barbarian" peoples operate on a lower level and are, simultaneously, less complexly organized, with less discipline, if more spirit, and with more, and hampering, persistence in retaining their established weapons traditions. When less civilized peoples conquer more civilized peoples, it usually is due to higher morale and more spirit and only rarely to better organizations or better weapons.

In thinking about these matters, we must not be misled by the fact that barbarian weaponry, because it is simpler, is easier to perceive and to think about than is civilized weaponry. Much military history has been distorted by this danger. We must remember (1) the multiple use of weapons; and (2) the complementary relationship between missile and shock weapons, especially in complex societies.

As we have indicated, weapons have at least two distinct functions: (1) to defend the society against its external enemies; and (2) to maintain "domestic tranquility" within the society. The first of these is simple enough and is the use

which springs to mind as soon as we mention weapons.
But the second use is equally significant and far
more complex in its operations. Let us look at
this second use more closely.

   Every society, and especially every complex
society, above all every civilization, has as its
most distinctive feature the flows of incomes within it. These flows, which depend in the final
analysis on inequitable distribution of the economic product of the society, determine the character of the society, what it does with its wealth,
its successes and failures. If each productive
unit in a society consumed what it produced, that
society would be operating on the lowest level,
which we call the "subsistence level." In fact,
such a society, lacking any exchange of goods
and services, would not be regarded as a society
at all, since each production unit would be so
independent that no substantial organization of
such units into a larger society would be very
stable and thus no aggregation of such units would
form a proper society. A society exists as a durable organization only when its social product cir-
culates within the society in a roundabout fashion,
with various members of the society providing a
variety of satisfactions for each other, exchanging these in accordance with flows of incomes and
other exchanges within the society. The number
of links in such internal flows of incomes helps
to determine the complexity and the basic nature
of the society.

   As we have seen, the original civilizations
possessed roundabout flows of income for religious
reasons, because the primary producers, the peasants, wanted the crops to grow, the irrigation waters
to flow, their wives and livestock to bear young
ones, and the seasons and heavenly bodies to continue to move in their usual courses. They were
willing to yield up part of their produce to the
god, or to the god's representatives on earth, to
obtain these things which they were sure they could
not obtain by their own actions. The social product
of the society was thus diverted away from immediate
consumption into the hands of priests and temples,
who might divert some of it to soldiers for protec-

tion, to specialists for studies of nature, for technological innovations, for art or literature, or to craftsmen for artifacts, or to traders for exotic goods from remote places. These recipients of peasant-created wealth through priests, in turn, diverted parts of their incomes to diverse purposes.

Such complicated roundabout flows of incomes within a society determine the chief obvious characteristics of the society and are, of course, essential for the existence of any civilization or even of what scholars like Stuart Piggott call "high barbarism."

The establishment and maintenance of such roundabout flows of incomes within a society depend upon a variety of factors: religious and ideological convictions; established customs; control of weapons; social reciprocities; recognition that such a system may provide a higher standard of living and a more varied life in the future. These factors, however, can be reduced ultimately to two kinds: inward, subjective convictions and external, objective, duress. In the same way, as we have seen, the basic diversion of social product from original producers, either peasants or traders, is achieved either by religious or by military means, that is, by belief or by force--the one internal and the other external. In the internal case, the role played by weapons in maintaining the diversion of flows of incomes is remote and indirect, but it is there; in the external case, the role played by weapons in maintaining the diversions of wealth is both immediate and direct. As we shall see in the course of this book, there have been major shifts in emphasis from one of these kinds of maintenance powers to the other, both in general history and in the historical process of individual civilizations.

The second factor we must keep in mind is the fundamental distinction in usage of missile and shock weapons, especially in complex societies: missile weapons are more "deadly" than shock weapons. This distinction between "control" weapons and "deadly" weapons is increasingly used today in

211

police science and indicates the fact that shock weapons are more capable of achieving degrees of duress in usage, while missile weapons have no intermediate stages between being fired and not being fired. If a policeman or soldier is trying to make a recalcitrant individual get up off the ground, move along a street, or get into a vehicle, this can be done more successfully with a spear, a bayonet, a billy-club, or even a cattle-prod, than it can be done with a bow and arrow, a hand grenade, or a gun. Missile weapons are "deadly" because, if they are used, they may kill the target even if the officer has no desire to kill but is merely seeking obedience. Simply stated, the use of a deadly weapon to obtain obedience may put the target into a condition in which he is incapable of obeying an order because he is gravely injured or dead. This distinction between the two kinds of weapons is quite clear to police officials, but is not so clear to citizens or historians. It is the reason why police and riot squads are usually armed with batons, guns with bayonets but without bullets, or even with firehoses or water-cannon when they are called upon to quell civil disturbances.

When a society suffers a lowering of its standards of living, as when it enters a dark age, it may not be able to afford a variety of weapons, even when it knows of them, but may be forced by poverty to make a choice between shock weapons and deadly weapons. In such a case, one element in its decision may be whether the decision-makers judge their more urgent need to be external defense or internal income diversion from primary producers. If their choice is for defense, they are more likely to opt for deadly weapons, while if their decision is for income diversion they are more likely to choose shock weapons. It is significant to note that on the two occasions on which Europe made such a choice, in the dark age after the fall of Mycenaean society about 1000 B.C. and in the similar dark age after the fall of Rome and of the Carolingian empire about A.D. 900, it opted for income diversion and shock weapons, the Homeric chariot and the medieval knight. In both cases, trade was reduced to a very low level, and income diversion had to operate on local and isolated peasantry in heavily wooded ter-

212

rain. In Asia such total dark ages did not occur, trade continued, and the terrain remained open, with long-range visibility, especially on the prevalent grasslands. Even in periods of low prosperity and severe political disturbances, Asiatic mounted archers could hope to create wide areas of relative peace across which traders could establish commercial routes on which income diversion through tolls could be maintained by such mounted archers. As we shall see, creation of such trading areas subject to tolls remained a chief aim of Asiatic warriors for the whole historic period. This may have been one of the reasons why Asiatic warriors clung to their missile tradition so long.

A civilized and prosperous society is freer from such restraints on choice and is thus in a much better position for achieving both security and capital accumulation. That is why civilized societies are generally victorious over barbarian peoples, unless internal discords and disloyalty are at such a high level that the defense forces are disorganized. Of course to survive, any society must be able to achieve a minimum degree of both security and income diversion.

Even in achieving security, both kinds of weapons are needed because they usually play different roles in conflicts between societies. In any battle, there is a double process: first to disrupt the enemy organization and then to subdue the individuals within that organization. These two stages in a battle may require different weapons. Thus the enemy military formations may be disrupted in the early stage of the battle by missiles, but the victor may then have to shift to shock weapons if he wishes to subdue the enemy as individuals, because he wants to enslave them, to hold them for ransom, to sacrifice them to the gods as the Aztecs did, or to annex their territory as a functioning entity. An enemy force may be disrupted by missile weapons, but its members can be subdued only by shock weapons. The point at which an army shifts from one weapon to the other may depend upon variable factors, including traditions. Armies may use up their supply of missiles, but shock weapons do not run out, because they are

213

made not to break and are not used by being thrown
from the user.

The point in a battle at which an army shifts
from disruptive weapons to subduing weapons is
usually based on tradition rather than on military
realities. Most horse archers in history, such as
Scythians, Huns, Parthians, Mongols, or American
Indians operated their attack with arrows and then
charged the enemy with swords, spears, war clubs,
or tomahawks. The shift was made before they ran
out of arrows. Often the defending formations were
not shattered or even much weakened before the shift
was made. The Greeks and Romans, on the other hand,
made the shift to shock much earlier in the battle,
opening with skirmishing by peltasts or by flights
of javelins, but immediately charging with spear
and sword while the enemy formations were still
intact. In European battles from Napoleon to Luden-
dorf, the bayonet charge came increasingly early in
the conflict, before the enemy formations were seriously disrupted by artillery fire, and the final
cavalry pursuit with drawn sabers was steadily reduced from an anticlimax at battles like Wagram
(1809) to nothing at all in the Somme (1916). Recently, the American missile assault on Vietnam
could shatter any organizational structure they
had, but it could not make any enemy individual
obey any order we gave. This last case shows the
total demise of the Indo-European tradition of
shock weaponry which spread over Europe about 2000
B.C. and created the conflict between a European
shock tradition and the Asiatic missile tradition.

Before 2000 B.C. most of Eurasia and North
Africa was in a missile tradition in the sense
that any conflict was settled in the missile phase
of the encounter, although other weapons were known
and daggers or clubs were also used. The archery
tradition was strong across Africa from Egypt to
Morocco and across the Iberian peninsula into Europe.
In the late third millennium that archery tradition
was strengthening from Spain to central Europe and
to northeastern Europe by the spread of the Bell-
Beaker influence which had originated in Iberia
and was extending outward as far as Bohemia and
the Baltic. The Beaker peoples were skilled

metal workers as well as skilled archers and were welcomed for both reasons. Their chief weapons were the bow and the bronze dagger.

These Bell Beaker influences had hardly reached the middle Danube and the upper Vistula Rivers and begun to organize the mineral resources of the Bohemian area when the first wave of the Indo-Europeans, armed with spears, axes, daggers, and horse-drawn vehicles began to move into the same areas, coming from the steppes between the lower Danube and the Caucasus. This Bronze Age invasion of Indo-European warrior peoples moved north and west to the North Sea and the Baltic and was followed, over the next two millennia, by similar waves of pastoral, horse-loving, warlike, patriarchal, sky-worshipping peoples, who in each case became an exploitative upper class over the lower groups of peasants, traders, and metal workers.

In the period from 1700 to 1200 B.C., this structure of high barbarism gave Europe its first great period of prosperity and material progress, as the Indo-Europeans, organized in local principalities, diverted incomes by military force from peasants and traders to command higher agricultural production, increased trade in metals and luxury goods, increased metal production, and the building of fortified residences and citadels of logs and even of stone. A similar process, as we have seen, was going on in these same centuries in the Balkans, Anatolia, the Levant, and Sinai under Achaean, Trojan, Hittite, Mitanni, Hurrian, Canaanite, and Hyksos princes. There was a constant interchange of goods, men, technological skills, and ideas among all of these, so that it is not possible to say with any assurance where new techniques and weapons began. On the whole, interchange was sufficient to maintain a certain general uniformity of weapons and social structure.

As part of this process, increased skills in metalworking slowly changed the dagger to a long slashing sword by 1400. In the stone age the stone dagger had been strengthened by developing a midrib, and this feature was carried over into copper and bronze in the third millennium. In the follow-

215

millennium, with more skilled metalworking, the
dagger continued, but dirks appeared, followed,
by 1600, by rapiers, some of which were more than
three feet long. These longer weapons retained
the mid-rib or were triangular or even oval in
cross section. The chief weakness was in how a
handle could be attached. At first this was
riveted on, but such a joint was too weak to
allow any stroke except a direct thrust. Many
such weapons broke in use from a sidewise blow.
By 1500 the blade was being made with an integral
flat tang at the top or with a T-shaped tang to
which other materials could be riveted to provide
a handle. By 1400 the tang was being made with
flanged edges on both sides so that two pieces of
bone, wood, or other material could be riveted to
provide a stout handle. As the handle was strengthened, the blade was flattened, making it possible
to shift from the older thrusting stroke to a
slashing attack. According to H.H. Coghlan this
change transferred the limitation on the power of
the blow from the strength of the blade to the
strength of the human arm which held it.

Other weapons also benefited from more skill-
ful metallurgy in the second millennium B.C. In
the Near East socketed axes with wooden handles
appeared in Mesopotamia in copper before 3000 B.C.
to cope with metal helmets which, with spears,
were the chief arms of the massed phalanxes of
the Sumerians. But the spears themselves remained
with weak hafting long after metal heads appeared
in the third millennium. About 2000, in the Near
East, the heads were made with pointed tangs,
which were bent at right angle near the end which
was inserted in a cleft in the end of the wooden
shaft and bound round with twine. Only in the
18th century were spear heads made with an integral
socket in the Near East; within a century or so
socketed spear heads two feet long appeared in the
Mycenaean shaft graves, and continued on through
the Palace period (1450-1350). With their shafts
of wood, these provided a weapon at least ten feet
long and may have been better suited to hunting
wild boars or lions than for use in battle. Similar smaller spear heads are also found in Crete
and the mainland in this period (1600-1350). In

most cases the socket on these blades was made by rolling a flat tang around a mandrel, and thus represent a lower level of skill than the cast bronze sockets of the Near East. This is probably because, as Hilda Lorimer has suggested, the slashing sword was the favorite weapon of the Mycenaean Greeks. The implications of this suggestion are important: the spear, by remaining a thrusting weapon, continued to be the preferred weapon of infantry troops organized in masses, as in the Sumerian phalanx of 2500 B.C. or the Macedonian phalanx of 350 B.C., but the slashing sword was better adapted to the highly individualistic combat of the Indo-European invaders, whose slashing tactics with long swords was not suitable for mass formations. Only in the last stage of the Mycenaean world did these Greeks turn to mass formations of spearmen, a tactic which reappeared among the classical Greeks as the hoplite "revolution" about 700 B.C. Such severe disciplining of the individual fighter to a formation of mass infantry, which is a symbol of the strength of classical civilization in both Greece and Rome, never spread north to barbarian Europe, either among the Celtic peoples or, even less, to the Germans, in either ancient or medieval times.

In this same mid-second millennium of Europe, growing metallurgical skills also provided the first examples in that continent of metal helmets and of body armor. As a rule, as in the Near East, helmets are developed as a defense against shock weapons and body armor as a defense against missile weapons. The sequence is particularly clear in the Near East where the mace and cutting axe led to the metal helmet in Asia and this, in turn, gave rise to the piercing axe and sickle sword. In Europe the advent of the slashing sword led to both helmet and corselet of bronze, while greaves, if we can believe the poet Alcaeus (c. 600 B.C., Frag. 54), were protection against missiles. These pieces of armor could be made in Europe after 1500 when the new knowledge of tempering and hammering provided sheet metal. A bronze helmet found at Beitzsch in Brandenburg and a similar one found in a grave at Knossos on Crete are both earlier than 1400 B.C., while a grave at Dendra near Mycenae has revealed both greaves

217

and a complete suit of plate bronze torso armor of eleven pieces, dated about 1425. A two-piece bronze corselet found at Czaka in Slovakia may be late 13th century. Thus the complete equipment of the classical Greek hoplite, except the shield which gave him his name, was known in Greece at least six hundred years before the hoplite appeared in historic Greece. The use of this equipment, but not the phalanx formation, spread to the Levant with the Philistines in the 12th century and was worn by Goliath in his fatal meeting with David in the early 10th century. The Biblical account (I Samuel 17:4-7) mentions Goliath's coat of mail, greaves of bronze, and "shaft of his spear like a weaver's beam." The conflict was another collision between European shock and Asiatic missile, in this case the Levantine sling. The use of a duel by a champion from each army to replace the battle was part of the grassland pastoral tradition found among Semites, Indo-European, and Ural-Altaic peoples so long as they retained their grassland traditions from at least the second millennium B.C. to the second millennium A.D. among the Mongols, Turks, and European knights. An early example of such a duel was the challenge of the Egyptian, Sinuhe, by a Semite in Syria in the 20th century B.C. In this case, both fighters had bows, but Sinuhe killed his opponent after evading his arrows.

In this second millennium B.C., while metallurgical skills were increasing, thus aiding shock weapons, the composite bow was spreading with much less influence on weaponry, because the bow, unlike shock weapons, required even greater skill in its use than it did in its manufacture. At the same time, mobility in warfare was undergoing a two-stage revolution, from the advent of chariots about 1900 B.C. and the arrival of horseback riding about a thousand years later. The use of the word "revolution" in this connection, or indeed even the suggestion of two separate events for driving and riding, is misleading, for man's use and control of the horse was an erratic and yet continuous development for more than 3500 years, from before 2500 B.C. to after A.D. 1000. The steppe horses before 2500 B.C. were small, short-legged, short-necked, heavy-headed beasts. North of the mountains, where rain was available in all seasons and the horse was a native animal, domesticated horses could be sustained on the available grasses and could be used as a food or pack animal. To use it as a draft animal required a proper harness with its accessories, and this was not achieved successfully until about A.D. 500 in east Asia and about four hundred years later in Europe.

The horse was used as a draft animal only after 2500 B.C., although it had been domesticated about 500 years earlier. The wheel was invented south of the mountains, probably near Mesopotamia before 4000 B.C., as a religious symbol representing the sun. It developed into a vehicle as a ritual object, and this was used for other purposes only gradually, at first with four wheels and later with two wheels, but it still retained its ceremonial and ritual character. In the south about 3000 B.C. it became a working and military vehicle, drawn by the onager, the only equine available in Mesopotamia which could be used as a draft animal. The Semites copied this technique on the southern flatlands during the third millennium B.C., using donkeys and asses. But these required a smaller and lighter vehicle and were generally used only as pack animals in the second millennium, although ridden increasingly in the first millennium B.C.

About the same time that the Indo-Europeans domesticated the horse, they adopted the wheeled vehicle from the south, but generally used it on wagons drawn by oxen. Only about a millennium later, after 2000, did the Indo-Europeans copy this arrangement to get horse-drawn chariots. But in doing so, they applied the oxen yoke to the horse, for which it was not adapted. This meant that two horses were yoked side by side on either side of a central pole attached to the vehicle. This was probably better fitted to the early steppe horse than it was to the larger, long-legged and long-necked horse which developed in the early first millennium B.C. With modern harnessing, the horse pulls the vehicle by leaning his weight against a rigid and padded horse-collar which is attached to the vehicle by traces

219

or long strips of leather. In this superior system, the horse's ability to pull a wagon does not depend on his strength but on his weight, so that large horses can pull heavy loads by leaning their weight on the collar and thus forcing it to move forward, the vehicle following because it is attached to the collar. In the last millennium B.C., with larger horses than those of the Bronze Age, no real advantage could be taken of the increased size and weight of the animal, as a draft animal, although the increase in size and strength was almost essential to its use as a riding animal. For this reason, the use of the horse in the pre-classical and classical periods (that is, in the period 700 B.C. to A.D. 900) as a draft animal decreased just as his use as a riding animal was increasing. In that period, changes in harnessing which were not really improvements took place, so that the animal was attached to the vehicle between two shafts by bands of cloth and cords around his neck and chest and fastened to the shafts. Thus the shafts were used for drawing the vehicle in the classical period and not merely for turning it, as in modern harnessing. With the modern horsecollar the animal can lower his head and throw his full weight against the collar, but in classical harnessing the animal was pulling with his throat and found that his head was pulled upward and backward and his windpipe cut off unless the total weight of load and vehicle was kept below 1100 pounds. Even below this weight, the horse was easily winded and had to be frequently rested. For steady work under this arrangement it was necessary to have substitute horses and change those who were working rather frequently. For this reason, oxen continued to be the preferred draft animal for work, although they were very slow (about two miles an hour) and could not be used more than about five hours a day, while horses could be used about seven hours a day, were more than twice as fast, and thus delivered more work in a day despite the smaller load they drew. The real reason for the superiority of oxen over horses in the classical period was not the amount of work they did but the fact that horses competed directly with human slaves for food.

This competition between slave labor and equine labor in the classical Mediterranean world rested on

the fact that this southern area had winter rains
and summer drought and thus was not an area where
either the horse or fodder for horses was natural.
The grasses of the rocky Mediterranean basin were
both scanty and lacking in nourishment. This meant
that horses could be worked hard or even survive in
workable condition only when their natural forage
was supplemented with grain. This put the horse
into direct competition with slaves for food. The
initial investment was less for a slave than for a
horse, especially in periods of successful warfare
which provided captives for the slave marts; the
slave could be driven harder and made to do more
work and he could be fed on the grain which would
have been used as supplementary feed for a horse.
Moreover, a slave could be used every day while a
horse could not.

The hooves of an unshod horse wear steadily
as he works and wear very rapidly in a dry or rocky
soil such as that of the Mediterranean. The rocky
character of this southern region is, of course,
one of the reasons that the sling persisted as a
weapon there or why criminals or victims of persecution were "stoned to death" there. In that area
horses' hooves wore down at least three times as
fast as they would on the steppe grasslands. To
recover from such wear, horses in the south had
to be rested on soft ground or even in marshes for
their hooves to regrow. This meant that a person
who expected to have a horse for use every day
could achieve this by owning three or four horses
in the north, but needed at least five in the
south. This problem continued to be a limit on
the use of the horse until horseshoes came in,
rather slowly, about the same time as modern harnessing after the end of the classical period
(after 550 A.D.).

All these factors (lack of fodder, of horseshoes, and of modern harnessing) which made it impossible for the horse to do heavy work and put
him in direct competition with slaves for food
meant that in all situations where heavy work
had to be done or where economic costs were a
consideration, slaves would be used rather than
horses in the Mediterranean area. Only the pres-

221

tige value of using horses and their greater speed with light loads kept them in use in those conditions, such as in the public service, where costs were not a primary consideration. Even so, travel remained very slow, about 25 miles a day in 50 B.C., until after A.D. 1750, when turnpikes and coaches with modern harnessing and other equipment became available for private persons. The use of four-wheeled vehicles was under great restraints because of the difficulty of turning corners before the introduction of the front pivoted axle with smaller wheels able to turn under the floor of the wagon. This was known in the fifteenth century in Europe but did not come into general use until late in the seventeenth century, so that travelers were restricted either to horse riding or two-wheeled vehicles in the country or to walking or to sedan chairs in the towns. Ordinary people walked in both areas until about 1690.

These restrictions on the use of the horse in work or in ordinary travel seem very great to us, but, of course, it did not appear this way when the horse was first coming into use, and most of these restraints did not apply to the horse in warfare until very recent times. Above all, the restraints were much less in regard to riding horses than in using them as draft animals, and even as draft animals they were a very welcome asset for several thousand years.

Even in riding there were technological obstacles which had to be overcome before the horse could be used to its full effectiveness. We do not usually think of these, and when we do, we think chiefly of those which still remained in the classical period, such as lack of stirrups, shoes, and a firm saddle. But in the second millennium B.C., when horse riding was developing, there were other obstacles, notably the small size of the steppe horse in comparison with size and weight of a man, especially when he was wearing armor. Also it was necessary to devise a bit which could control an unruly horse, especially if stallions were to be used. And with a weapon like the bow, which requires both hands, or a spear or saber, which uses shock tactics and thus needs a firm seat, some kind of a suitable saddle is needed. Moreover, with either of these weapons, especially the bow using both hands, some kind of protection is needed against missile weapons. A mounted spearman may have a shield in one hand, if he holds his lance in the other, but if he has a heavy pike which requires both hands, he is as unprotected as the mounted archer who has no way to use a shield. The answer which seems obvious to us is to wear armor, but this required two technological innovations which were not available when men first rode horses: sheet metal and horses strong enough to carry a man loaded with plate armor. We have seen that such body armor came into use in Europe after 1500 B.C. It could be made in the Near East even earlier by hammering out copper or bronze, but that area was never very enthusiastic about plate armor because it was too hot for it in most times of the year, especially in the campaign season, which was after the crops were in, about April or May.

Riding of horses occurred in early times and is depicted in art even before 2000 B.C. But it was about a thousand years later before horses began to be ridden as a combat arm in warfare, and it was only in the ninth and eighth centuries B.C. that we find organized cavalry of mounted spearmen and archers, among the Assyrians, depicted in the civilized areas of the globe. Individual riders, probably acting as scouts, had been used by both sides in the Egyptian wars in Syria, as far back as the battle of Kadesh (1285 B.C.) and probably earlier. These early riders seem to be on mares, and it may well be that stallions could not be controlled well enough for regular use as mounts in war.

The growing use of cavalry is a result of the interaction of several factors in the period from about 1200 to about 700, in the area from the upper Tigris-Euphrates to the Caucasic steppes. These were a shift from mare riding to the use of gelded male horses; the development of metal bits for more adequate control of a spirited animal; and the development of a better and larger animal from a combination of selective breeding, better feeding, and gelding. Horses of a better type than the

223

steppe breed, with longer legs and neck, the latter arched and supporting a smaller head, with high and narrow withers, are shown on Assyrian bas-reliefs as early as 800 B.C., and the Pazyryk burial mounds of the Altai Mountains, dated in the fifth century B.C., show similar horses. Eugen Darko placed the original home of mounted archers in the steppes of Turan, north of Iran, the same area in which Hancar believed that this better breed of horse was developed. But V.O. Vitt, the Russian authority on the sixty-nine horses found in the Altai tombs of the fifth century B.C., found all degrees of intermediate gradations between the steppe horse and the better kind and believes that the distinction is to be attributed less to a distinct breed than to different treatment such as diet, age of gelding, and age of first riding. These horses ranged in height from 128 to 150 centimeters (that is 13 to 15 hands).

In the first half of the first millennium B.C., the new technique of cavalry riding spread westward into central Europe and thence into Spain, Gaul, and Britain and eastward to Turkic-speaking peoples and to peoples of Mongoloid blood such as those which began to threaten China from the steppes after 500 B.C. These riding peoples created a new way of life associated with distinctive cultural traits such as wearing trousers, the use of felt, a new art form (the "Scytho-Siberian animal style") of grotesque and contorted animals in conflict, represented in applique textiles on felt, and in very skilled metalwork. The origins of this culture, or rather of this combination of cultural traits, seems to be in the western steppes rather than in the east, among peoples of the white race and of Iranian languages. Sulimirsky, an outstanding authority on the prehistory of the south Russian steppes, has been arguing that the origins of many of these traits can be found in Transcaucasia, that is in the well-watered valleys and hills south of the mountains and east of the Black Sea. This is very close to the areas where the significant advances in iron metallurgy were being developed in this same period (1200-500 B.C.) and, as we shall see in a moment, the new iron weapons are closely associated with the new skills in cavalry warfare.

The advent of iron weapons was a significant but hardly a crucial element in these changes. Iron is not necessarily better than bronze for weapons; it is both better and cheaper in the long run, but to reach that superior stage requires control of higher temperatures and much more complex techniques of metallurgy than those used in the production of bronze weapons. Cheapness lies in the fact that iron is one of the common elements, while copper is fairly rare and tin is very rare, so that bronze weapons were intrinsically expensive, while iron weapons were potentially cheap. This cheapness required that the costs of manufacture be reduced and that was achieved in the West only in civilized areas and in two steps, about 600 B.C. and after A.D. 1400. It never occurred in Asia.

Because the process of making iron fit for weapons is so complex, the history of how this was discovered is also complex and is not fully known. One thing which is certain is that we cannot attribute the "discovery" to any one place, time, person, or people, because it was worked out by largely illiterate metal workers over thousands of years and over the whole Old World.

The reason for the complexity of the problem is that iron is not fit for weapons; only steel is, but the problem of making iron and then transforming at least some of it to some degree into steel is very complicated. Iron is both rigid and tough only within a narrow range of carbon content (the range from 0.3 per cent to 2.0 per cent, which we call "steel"), and these qualities change so rapidly within that narrow range, and in opposite directions, that very great skill is needed to reach an acceptable compromise between rigidity and toughness for weapon quality. "Pure" iron (with less than 0.3 per cent carbon) is too soft for weapon use because it will bend and turn its edge more easily than copper. Cast iron (with a carbon content over two per cent) is too brittle to be used, as it will shatter. These two extremes lie on either side of steel and are associated with different temperature ranges, as increased carbon lowers the melting point of the metal, from about 1530 degrees Centigrade for wrought iron to about

1170 degrees Centigrade for cast iron, the melting point falling as the content of carbon or other "impurities" increases. This range of temperatures, which, of course, includes the range in which steel will melt, was just beyond the range which men could reach in the early Bronze Age. An open fire can reach about 600-700 degrees, just below the range needed to reduce copper from its ores of oxides and carbonates (700-800° C.). Pottery kilns, however, could reach a high enough temperature to process copper, especially with forced draught which provides a temperature up to 1100° C., just beyond the melting point of copper (1085° C.), but still considerably below that of wrought iron (1530° C.). The goatskin bellows, which made it possible to raise temperatures by forced draught, were invented in the Near East, possibly by Semite copper workers like the Kenites, about 1600 B.C., but were not capable of raising working temperatures to allow melting of relatively pure iron. Thus cast iron could not be made in the West until such high temperatures were attainable after A.D. 1300. But in China, where a much higher skill in bronze working was reached in the first half of the first millennium B.C., they had, apparently, a much clearer idea of the problem and concentrated on methods of reaching higher temperatures, including continuous forced draught, enclosing the furnace to retain heat, and more skilled use of fire clays and molds for handling the metal. Thus, when the Chinese began to work iron about 500 B.C., they could melt and thus cast iron almost at once, especially by using ores containing phosphorus and other "impurities" which lowered the melting point of cast iron about 200 degrees Centigrade. Within a couple of centuries, the Chinese had developed a double-acting piston bellows which provided continuous draught, especially when worked by water-power as it soon was (1st century A.D.).

In the West, working with lower temperatures, iron had to be extracted from its ores and worked by forging (that is by heating, hammering, and sudden cooling by quenching), and not by melting. Certain kinds of ores were heated to expel many of the impurities, thus raising the melting point of what remained, a mass of porous wrought iron full of slag and gas holes. This mass, known as a bloom, was then heated and hammered to expel the slag and gases, a process which required frequent reheating and violent pounding. Gradually the mass was reduced to iron up to 98-99 per cent pure. If this was allowed to cool gradually it became rather soft wrought iron, but if it was heated in a bed of charcoal or other source of carbon, so that it took in this element, at least on its surface, and was then cooled rapidly by being plunged into cold water, the carbon was trapped in it in a crystallized form known as cementite. These crystals formed an iron-carbon alloy within the range we call steel. Of course, an implement made of such a mixture would be effective only if the purer wrought iron was inside the object and the steeled portion was at the points where strains might develop, especially along its cutting edges.

Thus we see that the only really useful forms of iron implements, especially those used for weapons, had to be of steel and could not be of soft wrought iron or of brittle cast iron. Thus also the name "Iron Age" is a misnomer, for as far as weapons were concerned, the whole problem everywhere was how to get steel at least to the degree and at the points where both rigidity and toughness were necessary. This aim was achieved in China and the West from opposite directions, since the Chinese had to reach steel by eliminating the excess carbon found in cast iron, while the West had to reach steel by adding carbon to wrought iron. Since the earliest implements in China were made by casting, they were brittle and accordingly could be used for farming tools, where blows and strains can be controlled to some degree, but in the West, where the earliest implements were made by forging, it was essential to obtain steel to some degree if iron was to be used at all, since farm tools which bend when they are used are not very helpful. For this reason, the Chinese began to get iron tools as early as 400 B.C., but generally continued to use bronze weapons for centuries, while in the West the earliest iron implements were weapons, beginning with daggers and stabbing swords, as early as the Early Dynastic period in Mesopotamia (3000-2700), but found in scattered and isolated

objects with increasing frequency after 2000 B.C.
The earliest of these iron objects, used as jewelry
for small pieces but for daggers when larger pieces
were obtained, were made from the nickel iron of
meteorites, but by 1500 the metal workers of Armenia and the Kurdistan highlands were approaching
the secret of how to forge wrought iron and to car-
burize it.

We are now in a position to see the extraordinary complexity of this problem. Since both the
quality of the alloy and its melting point depended
on the kind and amount of the impurities in the
iron, these could hardly be understood or controlled
(especially within the limited temperature range
available in the West), when the workers did not
even recognize or know the elements which were present, from the various ores or the fuels used, the
temperatures obtained, or the processes used. The
fact that carbon was not only the most significant
alloy for establishing the nature of the finished
product and was also the fuel used in making that
product (as wood, charcoal, or coal) meant that
the carbon content could be observed and controlled
only with the greatest difficulty and on the basis
of long experience. Moreover, in processing iron
to get steel, what happened to the metal was influenced by the range of the temperature almost as
much as by the range of carbon content so that the
result varied not only from one batch to another,
but from one point to another in any single batch
of metal and within any implement or small piece
of metal from the batch.

We have seen that the West had "iron" weapons
almost a millennium before China had iron implements (say from 1400 to 450 B.C.), while the
Chinese had cast iron at least 1700 years before
the West, since the West, or at least Europe, did
not get high enough temperatures until almost 1400
A.D. In both areas, however, the effort to reach
weapon steel moved toward what we call damascene
steel, that is the achievement of weapons in which
there were alternative layers of over-carbonized
and under-carbonized metal very thin and very close
together, the layers being observable as a pattern
of wavy layers similar to water markings in other

materials. This aim and the techniques to achieve it were probably discovered independently in the Far East and the West, although the word used to designate it in the West, "damascene," is derived from Damascus in the Levant, because the swords of this character found in the West in the medieval period sometimes came from Damascus, although the steel from which these swords were made was a product of Hyderabad province and its environs in south central India.

In this very complicated history, in which local advances in techniques were interrupted by localized losses of skills, we can give only the barest outline.

In China the excess carbon of cast iron was reduced by pumping air through the mixture, thus in effect burning off the carbon. About a thousand years later (6th century A.D.), China obtained a "co-fusion" method, as Joseph Needham calls it, by which chips or blocks of both wrought iron and cast iron were heated together, the cast iron melting and bathing the pieces of wrought iron so that its surface took in carbon from the surrounding liquid cast iron. In the West a somewhat similar result was reached by heating a piece of wrought iron in a bed of hot charcoal at a relatively low temperature, so that incompletely burned carbon from the charcoal was absorbed into the wrought iron to give it a skin of steel. Both of these give only a coat of steel, called "case hardening," and are rather expensive in terms of fuel consumption. Thus a wrought iron billet left in a bed of charcoal at 950° C. for five hours is carburized only one-sixteenth of an inch deep. For this reason, such processing and also the original smelting generally took place in areas of mountain or hilly terrain with thick forests for fuel. Because of the high costs of transportation, it was uneconomical to carry the ores very far, so generally the smelting was done very near the mines, and the wrought iron was sold in small pieces to forges over wide areas, to be made into implements as desired. Such forging also became specialized in forested hilly regions.

Although we must emphasize that many peoples in many places contributed to the knowledge of steelmaking, in the West the greatest contributions came from Armenia and from Noricum (Carinthia) in central Europe. We have already said that the origin of agriculture and of metal working are to be sought in the hilly zone where Anatolia is attached to Asia along the line from Alexandretta Gulf north to the Black Sea near the Caucasus Mountains. The beginnings of our kind of agriculture may lie near the southern end of this line, south of Lake Van; the early history of copper and bronze seems to lie on the same line but probably north of Lake Van, while the vital steps in the western use of iron seem to have happened even farther north, in Armenia itself. There, it would seem, the smelting of iron from its ores goes back to about 2000 B.C., and the carburizing of the resulting wrought iron was advancing by 1500 B.C. At that time the nearest civilized society was the Hittite, and it may be that the Hittite government tried to keep the developing innovation secret for some centuries. This would not be so difficult as we might imagine, for not only was the technique a difficult one that only an experienced metallurgist could understand, but the metal workers of this region had been very secretive about their earlier skills in copper metallurgy so that they could obtain high pay for the use of their skills, selling their products but not allowing their methods to be known. In fact, the early history of metallurgy is full of wandering groups or guilds of such workers who moved about, filling orders as they obtained them, and then moving on, with the tools of their trade on pack animals and the secrets of their skills kept locked in their heads, to be passed on only to their sons or apprentices.

The case hardening of wrought iron soon led to two other innovations: (1) the "fagotting" of iron by welding together a pile of thin pieces of case hardened iron; and (2) the tempering of iron by reheating and hammering, which hardens it. This latter seems to have been discovered about 1100 B.C., although it may be much older. Quenching, by suddenly cooling hot iron in water or oil, also hardens it by locking in the crystals of cementite. Tempering was much more economical of fuel than fagotting, but the great popularity of damascene blades kept the former methods in use and, indeed, led to imitation damascene blades by etching a blade's surface with acid without regard for its internal quality. A fagotted blade from Luristan in Iran of seventh century date has as its basis a pile of eight case hardened strips, hot forged but air-cooled, without quenching. This last technique may be no older than the sixth century B.C.

The technical skills which had been reached by 1200 B.C. were not widespread enough and certainly were not sufficiently reliable to support an Iron Age weapons system. But these skills in the West, such as they were, were scattered widely by the Iron Age invasions of the period 1150-900 B.C. and the destruction of the Hittite empire which had tried to keep these methods secret.

The period after the destruction of the Mycenaean and Hittite empires and the subsequent outpouring of Indo-European peoples from the northern Balkans and the Pontic steppes, as well as the movements of the Semites whom we call the Arameans and Chaldeans from the Arabian and Syrian grasslands into the Levant and the valley of Mesopotamia, is a fairly typical dark age. That is, it was a period of impoverishment and of innovation. It was a period of innovation chiefly because new techniques such as iron working and horseback riding were now scattered over wide areas; it was a period of impoverishment not only from the destruction of looting invaders and the consequent reduction of production in many places, but also from the liquidation of accumulations of capital and the disruption of methods of capital accumulation for investment in new methods of production. This resulted in a drastic curtailment of what economists used to call roundabout income flows, so that not only were incomes reduced in many areas but the incomes which remained went more directly to consumption and not along circuitous ways from producers to landlords, temples, or rulers, and from them to traders and artisans, and from these to local merchants and other craftsmen, and then from these

231

latter to other primary producers for food and raw
materials. Such a reduction of the number of links
in the circulation of incomes from several steps to
only one or a few, or even to none at all (when a
peasant reduces his production to what he consumes
in his own household) is a mark of any dark age.
It may go so far as to reduce the population of
any area to only two classes, peasants and warriors,
or even to peasants alone. In such a case, civilization disappears, as it did about 1100 B.C. in the
Aegean area and in Anatolia, but even in civilized
areas it may move civilization down to a lower level
in which literacy, commerce, and governmental activities are greatly reduced, or largely vanish
entirely.

In central Europe, northern Italy, the Balkans,
and Anatolia, the central European Bronze Age cultures and their far-flung trading enterprises were
destroyed by new Indo-European invaders pushed westward by the Cimmerians and others from the Pontic
steppes. In Greece and western Anatolia, where the
Achaean Greeks were in the process of destroying
each other and sacking their great citadels at Mycenae, Troy, Pylos, and Knossos, the new intruders
whom we call Dorians, Phyrgians, or Lydians came in
and destroyed the established Bronze Age culture,
tearing it down to a low level of poverty, insecurity,
illiteracy, and self-sufficiency.

In the Levant, the Philistines, probably from
the Aegean area or from western Anatolia, were repulsed from Egypt with other "Peoples of the Sea"
and moved into Palestine, pushing inward with iron
weapons against the Canaanite principalities of
that area (and thus changing the name of the area
from Canaan to Palestine). Farther north and in
the interior of the Levant, the Canaanites broke
up into distinctive linguistic and social groupings
which we call Phoenician in western Syria, Hebrew
in the Negev and Jordan, while semi-nomadic barbarian
Arameans moved about them in confused struggles.
In Mesopotamia, close relatives of the Arameans,
the Chaldeans, flowed among the Kassites and Hurrians. Even Egypt did not escape, as Libyans,
Nubians, and other African pastoralists who were
already shifting from their earlier ass-pastoral-

ism to the newer camel-pastoralism moved toward
the Nile.

Despite the intrusions of new peoples, it was
the older peoples whose ancestors had come in during
the earlier Bronze Age invasions of the 1900-1700
period who led the way into the new Iron Age cultures of the classical period in the first millennium B.C. These included the Greeks, Etruscans,
Celts, and Persians of the non-civilized areas,
and the Hebrews, Phoenicians, and Assyrians of the
civilized areas. As we shall see, the chief contributions to the cognitive systems and non-material
cultures of the new millennium came from the Persians, Greeks, and Hebrews. In weaponry, as we
have indicated, the chief innovations, iron and
cavalry, had both been known before 1200. In both
of these weapons innovations, the most significant
developments took place in reciprocal interrelationships between civilized and uncivilized areas, especially around the Caucasus.

In that region the closest civilized area,
after the destruction of the Hittite empire about
1150 B.C., was Assyria on the northwest fringe of
Mesopotamian civilization. The nearest steppe peoples were the Cimmerians on the Pontic grasslands
north of the Caucasus Mountains and the Black Sea.
We do not know enough about the Cimmerians to
evaluate their contribution to cavalry warfare,
but it would seem that Assyrians were the chief
contributors to the new developments in warfare
by combining the new advances in cavalry taken
from their Cimmerian neighbors in the north with
the new advances in iron weaponry taken from their
Anatolian neighbors to the west and north.

It would be foolish to attempt to establish
which peoples in this frontier region contributed
which elements to the new weapons mixture which
emerged there in the period from 1100 to 800 B.C.
What is clear is that the Cimmerians were expelled
from the Pontic steppes, where they had been for
several centuries (going back to 1850 B.C., according to Tadeusz Sulimirski), by close relatives,
the horse-riding Scythians, who came from beyond
the Volga and chased the Cimmerians off the Pontic

steppes, eventually following them across the Caucasus Mountains into Iran and Anatolia (ninth and eighth centuries). Later some of the Cimmerians, mixed with Thracians, were chased westward from the steppes into Europe where their advent marks the beginning of the central European Iron Age, generally known to archaeologists as the Hallstatt period (in Danube area about 800 B.C., reaching Gaul about 725). It seems likely that the superiority of the Scythians over the Cimmerians on the steppes rested on the superiority of horse riders over chariot drivers. Both sides had the bow and the spear, but the Cimmerians may have relied more on the spear, at least those who finally arrived in Danubian Europe did so. It also seems possible that the Scythians may have been the first steppe horsemen who used a saddle, which was unknown to the Assyrians and remained unknown to the Greeks and Romans throughout the classical period. And finally, we know that the Scythians gelded their horses, as did all subsequent steppe horsemen. Thus the Scythians could have had larger, stronger, and more tractable horses, and thus could use both hands on the bow, which would give them a great superiority over the Cimmerians and all other peoples of that Asian-European borderland at that time. At any rate, the Scythians are the earliest peoples we know who made full use of the famous steppe tactics of shooting arrows both forward and backwards while riding at full gallop.

According to Sulimirsky, this replacement of the Cimmerians by the Scythians, by the latter's drive from the Volga to the Don River and beyond, may have begun as early as the thirteenth century B.C. and was completed by the tenth century, although the Scythians continued to expand into Anatolia and the West until after 600 B.C.

Over these centuries, the Scythians may have developed full pastoral nomadism, so that they could live from the milk and meat of their animals without any dependence on agricultural activities. Homer and Hesiod, both before 700 B.C., speak of the Scythians as mare milkers and milk drinkers. In the same centuries, these peoples acquired many cultural traits, including improved iron

234

weapons, from the peoples south of the Caucasus Mountains. The new iron weapons were acquired relatively late, in the eighth and seventh centuries. These better weapons included a straight dagger-sword, double edged, known as <u>akinake</u>, an iron battle-axe, and, most significant, a small, cast bronze socketed three-edged pyramidal arrowhead, which had great penetration power.

It seems likely thus, that the Scythians, in the first half of the last millennium of the pre-Christian era, developed most of the characteristics which we regard as typical of the subsequent steppe nomads of the northern grasslands from Hungary to the Chinese border, and that they did so by adapting various cultural traits from the transmontane hill and mountain peoples, as well as from some of the northern woodland cultures, mixing these in the east Pontic steppelands.

This new combination of traits gave the Scythians such formidable power for a few centuries that they became not only masters of the steppes of western Eurasia, but were also able, for a brief time, to extend their power south of the grasslands. They harassed the Armenians, Assyrians, and Iranians in this period. Their king Bartatua married a daughter of Esarhaddon of Assyria in 674 and they held parts of northwestern Iran at various times until finally expelled from Asia into Europe about 600 B.C. It may be that they cooperated with the Medes in the overthrow of the Assyrian empire in 612 B.C.

In Asia south of the grasslands, the Scythian influence could not result in permanent rule as they were too prone to plunder and oppression. There, and in Europe west of the steppes, they helped to establish that two-class society of peasants and warriors, which, like the heroic tradition, seems to accompany any Indo-European peoples who invade agricultural areas. Their barbaric graves, complete with slaughtered horses, wife, and servants, show this tradition, which spread as far west as France and as far east as the Chinese border.

A second, even more significant consequence of
the Scythian oppression in civilized areas, in the
period from the ninth century to the fourth, was
the partial adoption of Scythian weapons, tactics,
clothing, and other traits. An early example of
this adaptation is to be seen in Assyria as early
as 900 B.C. and in China as late as 300 B.C., as
both of these states tried to cope with nomadic
weapons and tactics by adopting and adapting them.
In both these cases the chief change was a shift
from chariots to riding and increased use of the
steppe bow in its changing forms. After 600 B.C.,
the adoption of riding included the use of the so-
called "two holed snaffle bit" and the early soft
steppe saddle. Both of these improved the facility
with which mounted archers could shoot their arrows.

Another contribution of the Scythian steppe
warriors was more beneficial and remained a model
for most subsequent steppe conquerors. This was
the establishment of the Pax Scythica.

We have seen that the Scythian attacks in Asia
led to reactions which led to their expulsion from
Asia back into Europe about 600 B.C. This, of
course, increased their pressures on Europe and
on the peasant peoples and fisher folks on the
borders of the Black Sea and of the European forest areas. It was just at this time that the Greeks
appeared on the Black Sea, as a result of the Greek
expansion and possibly also of the first acquisition
by the Greeks of a ship able to overcome the rapid
out-flowing currents of the Straits from the Black
Sea to the Aegean Sea. This ship could use sails
and the western breezes to move eastward into the
Black Sea area. There the Greeks sought grain,
fish, and residential sites for their excessive
population. The Scythians welcomed them, eager
to exchange the surplus grain and salt fish they
could extort from their subject peoples and willing
to extend the areas from which they acquired grain,
and later metal ores, if the Greeks would provide
them with luxury articles, finished metal products
in Scythian styles, and such new luxuries as wine
and olive oil.

By this process the expansion of the Greeks

into Euxine was assisted, the expansion of Greek culture was spread outward to barbarian peoples, and the Scythian peoples were softened by the inflow of Greek luxury. Especially the Scythian chiefs discovered that they could get more out of their subject peoples if they extorted a smaller tribute on the basis of steady harvesting and that the profits of trade over larger areas was greater and more reliable than the extortion of great amounts on any intermittent basis. This became the basis of the Scythian culture as we know it from the historical records and of most subsequent nomadic imperial systems which spread over wide areas of steppe in the next two thousand years, culminating in the Pax Mongolica which Marco Polo so admired in the thirteenth century of the Christian era. In this latter case, traders and travelers could move safely over thousands of miles of grassland trade routes from the Far East to the eastern edges of Europe in the Mongol peace. The Scythian peace of the fifth to third centuries B.C. was the first of many such wide-flung peaceful trading areas.

The idea of such a Pax Nomadica on the Eurasian steppes became a chief motivation to the shifting power relationships of that area until after 1500 A.D. We cannot work out the details of these changes, but the main outlines are clear enough. By 500 B.C., the whole steppe zone from Hungary to the Far East was held by nomad tribes who largely operated on north-south movements between the edge of the forest to the north and the mountains and deserts to the south. There was little stability in this situation on the steppes. Each tribal group moved on its basic north-south migrations following the grasses in its annual cycle; there was a constant temptation for cattle raiding, horse stealing, and abducting women across tribal boundaries; efforts to create a Pax Nomadica were always precarious and generally had to be established and maintained by force, because the rational argument that a steady moderate income from tolls was to be preferred to an immediate total plundering of trade required foresight and willingness to follow cooperative rather than egotistic lines, both of which were weak arguments to warriors brought up on the heroic tradition; moreover, any extended

237

period of peace resulted in increased population which, sooner or later, depending on rainfall and condition of the grass, led to outbursts of migrations and plundering. Other complications made the stability of political life on the steppes even more precarious. Innovations in weapons systems, either in technology or in organizational patterns, anywhere along the line of the steppe from Manchuria to Hungary, could give rise to a major upheaval, as the innovators discovered that this gave them a power advantage over their neighbors and they began to make use of that advantage by pushing outward into the territory and grazing areas of other tribes. The chief innovation in organization, which was rediscovered many times, was that the limitations on numbers of fighters in one's following based on a kinship system of organization could be overcome by an organization based on clientage.

This last point is so important and has been so often misunderstood by scholars that it must be considered here at greater length. Its true nature has been recognized by very few historians, notably by Owen Lattimore in Asiatic history and by E.A. Thompson in European history. There are two points which must be recognized about the use of a method of organization based on clientage: (1) that it is fundamentally anti-tribal and anti-kinship in its operations, although it works best when it is used in a tribal context; and (2) that it provides a sudden great increase in power when it is first adopted, but that it is self-destructive in the long run and usually disappears with extraordinary rapidity.

The real strength of any tribal organization rests on the belief that families and individuals have an obligation to be loyal to their kinfolk. If a political system is based on this loyalty, it can grow in manpower only slowly with severe limitations in size, and thus in power, over time. Even if a man has numerous sons who also have numerous sons, the fighting manpower available is limited, not only by numbers and the impossibility of replacing casualties, but by the fact that each individual's span of fighting years is

238

limited to about thirty (say from about 16 to 46) at the most. Thus the maximum number of warriors which could be mobilized on this basis while the patriarchal founder of the line is still living could be counted in scores but not in hundreds, and could be defeated by superior numbers alone if a different method of obtaining loyalty is devised. The most obvious way to do this is to consider as kin all the descendants of a _remembered_ ancestor rather than as all descendants of a _living_ ancestor.

If an ancestor can be remembered for numerous generations, say up to ten or a dozen, it would be possible, under the best conditions, to mobilize tribal warriors in the hundreds or even in the low thousands. But such a mobilization would have intrinsic weaknesses, not only because each warrior must be able to justify his loyalty by his ability to recite his own distinctive genealogical descent from the original tribal founder but he must continue to regard this loyalty as paramount over many other more immediate and less remote appeals to his interests. Thus such tribal organizations of loyalty and of military efforts are both limited in size and often very limited in strength.

If kinship loyalty can, however, be supplemented by clientage relationships, it can be increased in both size and strength. This is done when a leader can show other persons, especially other lesser leaders, that they can obtain greater security and greater satisfaction of their more immediate interests by accepting a position of subordinated personal loyalty to the greater leader, so that each client becomes a sworn follower of a patron who is equally bound, if not sworn, to further his follower's specified interests; thus a new organizational structure of power can arise suddenly and in greater size. Such a new power system can defeat its tribal neighbors and, on defeating each of them, can force it, through its leader, to become a client of the victorious leader. In this way, such an organization can mobilize warriors in tens and scores of thousands under the best conditions.

239

Such a system of combined clientage and kinship loyalties can emerge quickly, can establish wide areas of commercial peace and thus accumulate great wealth to reward its clients and their kin. Such wealth, however, cannot rise to a high level if it remains mobile wealth such as any nomadic people can take along in their annual movements following the grass, since mobile wealth is inevitably limited by the need for mobility. Even if it remains in the form of livestock, concubines, and what can be carried in wagons, the wealth of any individual is severely limited in a system which remains nomadic. The inevitable consequence is that the leaders gradually give up their nomadism, establish permanent residences, fill these with luxury goods from more civilized peoples on whose trade they have been imposing tribute, such as furniture, vases, textiles, exotic foods, and such. As these leaders lose their mobility, they lose contact with the lesser leaders and the subordinate individuals in the system, since these, if they remain nomadic, will be far away from leaders' residences much of the year. The client leaders themselves often have their residences far apart, and the personal loyalty on which their relationship is based becomes weaker, simply from the fact that it is not exercised in daily contact as it was originally. To bring greater strength to the whole system as its growing weakness is recognized, increased efforts are made to extend the enjoyment of luxuries to lesser leaders and even to individuals by allowing these to share in looting of defeated armies, which means increased use of war to maintain the system, with resulting injury to the nomadic peace and to the yields of tribute from commercial tolls. As trade and tolls decrease, the need to increase booty to maintain the system becomes greater. The fact that personal loyalty plays such a vital role in the system makes it very vulnerable; the death in battle of one or only a few of the chief leaders may disrupt it into fragments, especially as there is no provision, in most cases, for any rules of legal succession in such very personal relationships based on individual loyalty. Even a single death, such as that of the top leader or of one of his chief lieutenants, may disrupt the system overnight, so that it vanishes almost as rapidly as it rose.

We do not know to what degree this element of clientage operated in the early nomadic empires of the steppes, such as those of the Scythian and Sarmatian groups, but something of this kind obviously did exist from the fact that both of these early systems had superior and inferior tribes capped by "Royal Scythians" and "Royal Sarmatians" and also had client tribes, as well as subject trading and agricultural peoples. In the later Hunnish, Mongolian, and Turkish empires we can see the process operating more clearly since we have written evidence. The Hunnish empire of Attila, for example, was clearly based on client lieutenants, some of them not Huns, on joint exploitation of both traders and agricultural subjects, and on client tribes, some of which were not Huns, such as the Visigoths and the Alans. This empire extended from the Danube River to the Baltic Sea about A.D. 440, yet was totally disintegrated within seven years of Attila's death in 453. The latest of these nomadic empires, that of the Mongols, lasted longer because its constituent sections either remained nomadic, like the Golden Horde of south Russia, or became an alien dynasty and people ruling over a civilized society, as the Yuan dynasty in China (A.D. 1260-1368).

The first civilized state to feel the double impact of the metallurgical advances of the Caucasus region and the mobile warfare of the steppes was Assyria. This state, rising in the remote northern portion of Mesopotamian civilization from a Semitic people who had been there since they emerged from the Syrian grasslands, along with the Akkadians, before 3000 B.C., took advantage of the collapse of other states as early as 1100 B.C. They had a variety of weapons, adequate manpower, and a driving impulse to conquer even before the influence of iron and cavalry came to help their conquests. About 900 they were still using the chariot with six-spoke wheels pulled by two horses, although a third horse, attached as a spare outrider, is often shown in Assyrian art of the early period. These artistic representations of weapons and warfare are much more realistic than most art of the period and, accordingly, allow us to see some of the difficulties of using horses in warfare. The

241

chariots are relatively heavy and usually carry
three men, an archer, a driver, and a shield
bearer to protect the other two. This concern
for their archers is also shown with those on foot
who often have with them a shield bearer to protect the archer from enemy missiles. In a few
cases, there are four men in a chariot, both
archer and driver being covered by individual
shield bearers. Even with a crew of three, these
chariots must have been awkward and very hard on
the horses. The ability of a chariot to turn at
speed requires that the axle be placed as far back
on the body as possible, but this, of course, increases the weight to be borne by the horses,
since it makes the shaft bear down on them. With
three men in the vehicle, the horses must have required frequent rests. That is probably why the
extra horse was taken along on early Assyrian
chariots, but this practice seems to have been
given up, as it would certainly have to be against
any foe with missile weapons, since an extra
horse increased the target area for an enemy
archer who could turn the whole arrangement into
chaos by wounding any of the three horses. The
horses, of course, were not protected, although
many of the archers, both on foot or mobile, had
coats of mail. Horse armor did not appear, as we
shall see, until the Sarmatians about 200 B.C.

From such a hampered chariot, the Assyrians
quickly shifted to riding as soon as they were
threatened by the steppe cavalry. The decorations
of the palace of Assurnasirpal II (883-859) at
Nimrud show unarmored mounted warriors of Assyria,
using bows, arrows, and spears. They have no
stirrups nor any saddles, are often barefooted,
and obviously have a problem handling a horse
while both hands are occupied with their archery.
In several cases, this problem is taken care of to
some extent by having the archers work in pairs,
one rider using a bow while the other rider holds
the reins of both horses. In some cases, as with
infantry archers, the attendant tries to protect
the archer with a shield. This rather lavish use
of shield bearers indicates that the Assyrians must
have had a plentiful supply of manpower, as well as
a greater regard for the safety of their own soldiers than we might expect from such bloodthirsty
warriors.

The whole Assyrian army shows a similar lavish expenditure for equipment from the beginnings until Assyria's final defeat by the Medes in 612. This is particularly evident in siege warfare in which the Assyrians were highly skilled. They used all methods known at that time for capturing cities and used them very well, which explains their success in annexing territory. This included assault with scaling ladders, trying to burn the gates, clearing the walls with missiles, mining the walls, and breaking them down with several different kinds of battering rams and digging machines, mounted on four or even six wheels, armored with wicker shields all over the sides, and even with domed tops of unknown material. Some of these siege machines look in profile like children's drawings of military tanks of World War II, with a long battering ram protruding from the front like a cannon beneath a domed turret. The Assyrians had no siege techniques or weapons which had not existed in the Near East a thousand years before in 1900 B.C., but they used what they had in elaborate profusion, at least as we see the process in their pictures. They did not, of course, have siege artillery for smashing walls with rocks and bolts hurled by mechanical power; these did not appear until 399 B.C. in the Greek-speaking world.

Our references to the value of Assyrian art for information on their weapons requires us to make a few remarks about this subject in general. It has already been mentioned that Egyptian art is often very erroneous in regard to military realities because of the need to present the Pharaoh and the Egyptian state in terms of the archaic religious traditions, with the ruler larger than life, alone in his triumph, and with nothing obscuring his view from the world. Nothing obvious of this archaic tradition appears in Assyrian art, except that the king is always shown as a heroic and total victor, either in war or in hunting. Accordingly, the representations of weapons in Assyrian art are a valuable source of information on weapons and tactics.

This cannot be said of the art of the Greeks and Romans, especially in the early period, con-

243

temporary with the Assyrians. Greek geometric art was never an effort to show anything as it operated in the world of everyday affairs. Especially in the early period, and above all in the geometric period, pictures have been taken with naive and unsophisticated faith by students of the classics, but these cannot be regarded as realistic, especially on funerary objects which are the chief source of such pictures. Such objects had as their chief aim to assist the immortality of the dead person, not so much in the heroic Indo-European sense as in the archaic sense in which immortality was to be obtained, along with food, children, security and political power, by joining male and female principles either actually or through ritual and symbols. Thus, Greek funerary vases of the geometric period showing a ship on one side and a chariot on the other side must be taken with caution as depicting either a real ship or a real chariot of the period, since the ship is really a lunar symbol of the earth goddess and the chariot (or even a single wheel) is really a solar symbol of the sky-god, with no effort by the craftsman who produced the pot to give a close representation of either ship or chariot, if he knew these. Similar symbols are found in pre-dynastic Egypt, in much of very early highland west Asia and among the earliest settlers of much of the Old World landmass. As religious and ritual symbols, these pictures cannot be used uncritically for technological history, any more than similar modern survivals, which sometimes show a ship of good hope on a modern grave stone, can be accepted as pictures of a ship of today or of any day.

The collapse of the great Bronze Age political systems, such as the Egyptian, Hittite, and Mycenaean empires, as well as the lesser Kassite, Mitanni, and Canaanite principalities in the dark age following 1200, allowed new peoples to rise to local power in the interstices between the decaying older power systems. Among these were the Assyrians, whom we have mentioned, in northern Mesopotamia, the Phoenicians in western Syria, the Hebrews in Palestine, and various local princes in western Anatolia and the so-called neo-Hittite states which rose in southeastern Anatolia running eastward across the

244

Syrian Saddle to the Euphrates River. These intermediate states between the great Bronze Age power
systems and the full Iron Age power systems, such
as Persia, Macedonia, and even the Greeks and
Romans, had rather brief, but often very important,
periods of glory between the approach of the dark
age about 1150 B.C. and the full Iron Age about
500 B.C.

There is no need for us to pay much attention
to these transitory states in Anatolia, such as
Lydia and Phyrgia, but we should say a few words
about the situation in the Levant, where the Hebrews and Phoenicians had a brief period of independence from about 1000 B.C. until they were
destroyed or overrun by the Assyrians by 640 B.C.
The Assyrians, who were one of these transitory
states, were themselves destroyed by the full Iron
Age Medes and Persians, who conquered the whole
Near East as far as the Indus River by 520 B.C.

The Hebrews were a Canaanite people who won
a distinct identity in the course of a complex
and varied history by adopting a monotheistic
creed in the midst of the very complicated polytheism of the other Canaanites. This history
covered about a thousand years from Abraham just
before 1900 B.C. to Solomon before 900 B.C. The
Hebrews were able to take Palestine away from the
Canaanites and the Philistines because they increased in numbers in the eastern hills of Palestine in the period from about 1400 B.C. and were
able to combine fanatical determination with
good organization in a joint Philistine-Hebrew
assault on the Canaanites followed by a Hebrew
assault on the Philistines to obtain control of
the chief routes of Palestine, and then to conquer the other inhabitants of the country piecemeal. These victories, mostly under Saul and
David (1028-973), were consolidated by Solomon
(973-933) to form a united kingdom, but this
split into the two kingdoms of Israel and Judah
after Solomon's death in 933.

The united kingdom of Solomon was sustained
by an original organization of the available
local resources of the area, sufficient to domi-

nate the southern Levant in this chronological gap between the days of greater power systems. Advantage was taken of Israel's geographic position to form a link between the Indian Ocean trading area by way of the Gulf of Aqaba and the Mediterranean Sea trading area by way of the Phoenician cities, notably Tyre. Solomon built a seaport at Ezion-Geber on the Gulf of Aqaba, where he founded an ultra-modern shipbuilding center. This was ultra-modern because it intruded into an area where ships were sewn together and made of adz-cut planks with integral cleats through which ribs were inserted after the side strakes were sewn together. This older method of shipbuilding remained for many centuries in the Red and Arabian Seas and continued, at least in part, for millennia in the peripheries of the Old World landmass. The new method of Iron Age ship construction was not invented by the Hebrews (in fact, it is not clear where it was invented), but Solomon's shipyard on the Gulf of Aqaba is not only one of the earliest examples of the new method of construction, it is the most advanced.

The advanced character of Hebrew shipbuilding before 900 B.C. may be seen from the fact that vessels were built on great keels with sawn plank strakes nailed with heavy iron nails onto ribs already adfixed to the keel. The evidence for these advances in ship construction, including six-inch iron nails and ropes several inches through, was found by Nelson Glueck when he excavated the site of Ezion-Geber. In the same area he also found the remains of advanced iron smelteries, using the prevailing winds funneled through the fires, to provide higher temperatures. It is clear that the Hebrew kingdom added iron to the trade goods which came into the country from the southern seas, selling both kinds to customers anywhere in the Near East, and transshipping much of these overland to the Phoenicians, especially to Tyre, who were in process of taking over much of the maritime commerce of the Mediterranean in succession to the Mycenaean-Minoan traders of the Bronze Age. It is interesting to note that the destruction of the Hebrew kingdom by the Assyrians destroyed this important link in the In-

246

dian Ocean-Mediterranean Sea route, and the shipping and ship construction methods of the Red Sea area fell back to the earlier sewn or, at most, wooden treenail methods of construction which survived until the end of the nineteenth century.

The Hebrew power system of the period from about 950 to about 600 B.C. had other elements. For example, as the Mitanni collapsed under Assyrian pressures, Solomon and his successors replaced these as the chief supplier of horses and of chariots to the Levant area. We have, for example, remains of a stud farm or chariot supply depot at Megiddo in northern Israel near the grassland passage. This had stalls for 450 horses which seems to indicate a base for 150 two-horse chariots, with a spare animal for each. It was in operation about 900 B.C.

This archaeological evidence helps to explain the rather ambiguous verbal evidence provided in the Old Testament about the Hebrew political situation, such as the alliance with Hiram of Tyre, the references to the number of chariots available to various leaders and the shift from a semi-monopoly of iron, from which the Hebrews were excluded, in the earlier period, to the plentiful supply of both chariots and iron evident in the tenth and ninth centuries. The Hebrew control of commerce on the Red Sea also explains the visit of the Queen of Sheba, from southwest Arabia, to make certain that the commerce in incense gum from the Hadrawmat of southern Arabia was not interrupted on its way to the temples of Egypt and the urbanized Near East.

The Hebrew state was worn down and disintegrated from its internal weaknesses under pressures from the new power systems which I have called full Iron Age. These new states, including the Medes, Persians, Greeks, Macedonians, and Romans, are actors in a new historical era which we know as the classical period. As we shall see, that new era was dominated by Indo-European peoples and largely by shock weapon tactics, but above all, it was dominated by new cognitive and ideological fashions in looking at human experience. We shall examine this new era in the next chapter, but before we do

so, we must say a few more things about the meaning of full Iron Age and about the new outlooks
which dominated it.

The inability of the West to cast iron made
it difficult for it to use one of its favorite
weapons, the slashing sword, which had been
achieved in bronze about the middle of the second
millennium B.C. It was almost a full millennium
before a similar sword could be made in iron. The
successful method for hafting either sword was by
an integral tang with flanged edges to hold a
handle of non-metallic material. This was achieved
in iron only in the sixth century B.C., although
various substitute methods were used as alternatives,
not only before the date of success but often for
centuries afterwards. One of the chief alternative
methods was to make the sword of both bronze and
iron, with the hilt using bronze which could be
cast and the blade of steeled iron, with a variety
of methods of uniting the two with a firm joint.
By 500 B.C. it was possible to make full iron
slashing swords.

A somewhat parallel experience occurred with
metal arrowheads. We have seen that the Scythians
had learned from the Transcaucasus metal workers
how to make superior cast bronze arrowheads which
were three-sided and less than an inch long but
had superior penetrating ability. It must be con-
fessed that such bronze arrowheads were probably
not superior but rather inferior to good stone
arrowheads, but they could be made on a mass basis,
which could not be done with stone points, especially when the best stone material was found only
in certain localities. For this reason, bronze
replaced stone most places in the second millennium. The advent of iron did not replace bronze
for arrowheads, however, even when iron had replaced bronze for almost all other purposes.
Other methods were used to make iron arrow points
by hammering, and it was only after 500 B.C. that
socketed iron points were available. A similar
process, as we have seen, took place in regard to
socketed spear heads of iron.

These changes in weapons and military tactics
which were part of the great transformation from

1500 to after 700 B.C. did not provide the civilized areas of the Old World with better weapons than the uncivilized areas. In fact, weapon for weapon, we could argue that the civilized areas of Iron Age societies had more inferior weapons than their non-civilized neighbors. These non-civilized areas consisted of the grasslands thinning off into deserts and the forested areas of mountains and hills and the more remote temperate forests to the north and the equatorial forests to the south. The civilized areas continued through the classical period to be on the sub-tropical and sub-temperate fringes of the great continents, on the shores of the Mediterranean Sea, in and around the alluvial valleys draining the Highland Zone of Eurasia, and in the Indian sub-continent.

These areas remained civilized, or became civilized in the classical period as, for example, the western Mediterranean did, for reasons we should recapitulate here.

In the first place, civilized areas had modes of organization superior to the kinship or kinship-with-clientage methods which were the best that non-civilized people could attain. These civilized methods of social organization included religious and political methods which permitted them to establish state structures of various kinds which were capable of rousing the loyalties and allegiances of men to higher levels of discipline, self-discipline, and self-sacrifice than most non-civilized people could achieve. Closely related to this, as we shall see in a moment, is the fact that civilized societies can achieve cognitive patterns and levels of sophistication in thinking which are impossible for non-civilized peoples, partly because the use of writing by civilized communities provides more accurate and more complete social memory, but also because the greater productivity and more complex division of activities allows members of civilized societies to get more opportunities to acquire knowledge and to think about such knowledge.

As a third advantage, civilized societies

249

have, almost by definition, superior productivity
per man-year of labor and also have what is perhaps even more important, great accumulation of
capital for non-subsistence activities of all kinds.
What these two advantages mean in respect to weaponry
is that civilized societies, before they go into
their stage of decay, can afford a greater variety
of weaponry. The significance of this is obvious:
a combination of a variety of different kinds of
weapons (defensive as well as offensive; mobile
as well as static; shock as well as missile; sieging and besieging as well as field forces) is far
superior to any simple arithmetical sum of the addition of such different kinds, from the fact that
the mere possession of a different weapon or weapons
system increases the effectiveness of a quite different weapon or system merely by its existence, if
its possession is properly coordinated with the
other weapon or weapons.

In the classical period which we are now approaching in this study, barbarian weapons were,
on occasions, superior to civilized weapons, but
the civilized peoples had, in addition to the normal
advantages just mentioned, the additional advantage
that the climate in the classical period, which we
call "sub-Atlantic" climate, was favorable to the
grasslands and was thus, from more adequate rainfall, more favorable to grasses, to animal raising,
and thus to the general prosperity of the pastoral
and nomadic peoples of those grasslands. It is of
some historic significance that the grasslands peoples, who had been pastoral for more than two thousand years in the mid-first millennium B.C. began
to move toward full nomadism at this later date
and had achieved such full nomadism in some areas
just after the civilized areas reached what I have
called "full Iron Age" in the sixth century B.C.
Thus the grasslands about 500 B.C. had a double
reason to retain their people in the sub-Atlantic
climate period, instead of shooting them off into
other areas as the preceding drier and hotter sub-
Boreal climate period (3000-1000 B.C.) had done.
With better rainfall, cooler climate, lusher grasses, and a better technique of using such grasses
in fully nomadic ways, the need to emigrate from
the grasslands toward surrounding forested or civi-

lized areas was reduced until the full benefits of
these changed conditions and techniques were lost
by gradual population increase to the limits of
the carrying capacity of the grasslands under these
new conditions. This point of new population pressures on the northern grasslands seems to have arrived just about the same time that the sub-Atlantic
climate period had run its course, that is about
A.D. 200. Thus the outward migration of these
nomadic peoples began just when classical civilization and Sinic civilization in the Far East were
moving toward their stage of decline, if not decay,
creating military pressures in the A.D. 200-600 period which neither the Roman empire nor the Han empire could handle.

5.   The Ideological Transformation

The great transformation which created the
technological and organizational conditions which
made the classical civilizations possible included,
in the West, cognitive and ideological changes
which, like the other aspects of the great transformation, had been in process for almost a full millennium in 500 B.C. Modern historians have often
called this ideological aspect "the sixth century
revolution," without, in most cases, fully recognizing either its long preparation of its mani-
fold characteristics. Accordingly, they have not
seen the basic unity of the whole period 1400-500
B.C. or that it centered on the so-called dark ages
from about 1100 to about 850, during which three
civilizations (the Cretan, Hittite, and Indus valley cultures) vanished and four others (Mesopotamian, Egyptian, Canaanite, and the Sinic in north
China) were severely damaged.

The sixth century intellectual revolution had
two parts to it, both coming into the eastern Mediterranean and western Asia from the grassland pastoralists, from the Indo-Europeans of the northern grasslands and from the Semites of the southern grasslands. From the north there came two-valued logic
and some elements of transcendental ethical monotheism, while from the Hebrew Canaanites, with
some assistance from the Egyptians, came a full
dose of transcendental, ethical monotheism. To-

gether, these two drove the earlier archaic outlook from the conscious awareness of the civilized regions of the West, so that today we have some difficulty in grasping the nature of the preceding archaic outlook.

The archaic outlook did not see the world or human experience in terms of fixed categories, and it lacked, almost completely, any elements of a two-valued logic as we know it. The archaic mind saw the universe as a chaos of flux and constant change in which the material and spiritual were not distinct phenomena, but were confused interminglings of changing forms and appearances in which the essential element was a confusion of spiritual powers and deities. These spiritual aspects of material objects by their interrelationships determined everything which happened. There was no conception of unchanging rules, laws, or deity above this welter of intermingling powers, and, accordingly, all archaic thinking operated on a low level of abstraction, in a descriptive rather than in an analytical or conceptual way. Two-valued logic changed all this in a most drastic fashion, by what was later identified (by Aristotle) as two laws or principles: (1) the principle of identity and (2) the principle of contradiction.

The first of these "principles" established that any entity or individual was itself and not something else and remained itself throughout the discussion. This means that any object or individual may change but does not lose its identity or become something else while we are talking or thinking about it. Its identity is fixed.

The second of these "principles" assumed that all such individuals could be classified in categories and that no individual could both be and not be in such a category in the same way at the same time.

The first of these rules establishes that Socrates is Socrates and remains Socrates throughout his lifetime and whenever we subsequently think about him or discuss him he does not, no matter what happens to him (in his lifetime or since) become someone else.

The second of these principles establishes that Socrates is a man and not something else (not animal nor a god, two classification categories below and above human status).

Two-valued logic served to create a world of strict abstract categories outside of the universe of dynamic, existential experience and made it impossible to accept the constant confusions and interminglings of the archaic outlook, which was quite willing to accept that the Pharaoh was, simultaneously, both god and man, was both alive and dead, and was able to make plants grow, the seasons change, animals become pregnant, to insure peace and stability on earth, to keep the stars in their courses, to grant eternal life to favored individuals—and to do all these things by an act of virility symbolized by his mace or scepter. The key point here was that to the archaic mind deity was in the world, immanent in everything, almost indiscriminately. If this is difficult for us to grasp, that is simply because we are living and our mental processes are formed on this side of the sixth century revolution. We are post-Aristotle.

The arrival of transcendental, ethical monotheism in the sixth century was even more revolutionary. It was the culmination of almost a millennium of religious thinking (going back before Ikhnaton and before Moses); its influence was felt all across the Eurasian landmass from Confucius in China, Buddha in India, Zoroaster in Persia, Pythagoras in Greece, and the great desert prophets of the exilic and post-exilic periods in Israel. As a consequence of this millennium of thought and discussion, the idea of deity came to include much more than that of powers greater than man and added, in rough order, the beliefs that god must be: (1) creator; (2) anthropomorphic; (3) immortal; (4) omnipotent and omniscient; (5) monotheistic; (6) just; (7) merciful; (8) transcendental; (9) good. The archaic deities in general possessed none of these qualities, although some of them may have had one or more of

them to some degree. Even the Greek gods had
only one of these qualities (immortality), the
very one which archaic gods were least likely
to have. By 500 B.C., however, the Hebrew prophets had reached the point where their idea of
deity included all of these. Such a god was irreconcilably incompatible with any archaic deity,
because he was transcendental, he was One, and
he was good. This means that deity was outside
this universe of space and time, that his monopoly
of power excludes any other possessors of absolute
power, and, above all, that there are fixed rules
regarding right and wrong (ethics) to which everything, even god, is subject. It was quite impossible to reconcile a deity such as this with any
archaic ideas of god or with ritual which included
a dying god, human sacrifice, temple prostitution,
or any connections between sex, the seasons, political sovereignty, the growing crops, and spiritual salvation.

Although these two innovations were distinct
in origin, there was considerable intermingling of
the two, especially in a figure like Zoroaster.
In general, however, while the Greeks had the full
dose of two-valued logic and the Hebrews had the
full dose of transcendental ethical monotheism,
it was not until the Roman empire was in decline
that these two began to flow together to create
the new Western civilization which would accept
both. But long before that, by 500 B.C., these
two, either singly or together, had made it very
difficult for many people west of the Syrian Saddle to accept the archaic outlook anymore.

This weakening of the appeal to archaic deity
involved not only a change in religious ideas.
It also involved changes in the total structure
of any civilized society, since all civilized
societies until 1000 B.C. had rested on belief
in and service to an archaic deity.

This fact must be stated as emphatically as
possible: in the archaic period all successful
political and organizational systems (and indi-
dentally all economic prosperity and social stability as well) rested on the idea of service to a

deity. This deity may have been Amon as in Egypt, or Marduk as in Babylon, or Potnia as in Pylos, or Rhea as in Crete, or even Assur as in Assyria, but the key to the whole archaic system was service to "the god" and to his earthly equivalents and agents, whether priests or rulers. We moderns, who do not share these ideas, tend to ignore the references to them in the documents, but the basic fact is clear: without these ideas there would have been no early civilizations. All civilizations, as highly organized structures involving large numbers of men, must have some principle of organization. That principle to the end of the Bronze Age in the West (and to recent times in the East) was service to the deity.

At a time when technology did not permit the successful mobilization of non-human sources of energy (that is no windpower, waterpower, or even effective animal power), no complex organizational structure could function very long unless it could mobilize the allegiance of men. Until after 1000 B.C., this mobilization of allegiance in civilized societies was based almost entirely on service to the gods. The key event, perhaps, of the great transformation was to have found an alternative basis for allegiance, that is loyalty to the state for patriotic reasons. But it must be noted that human service, in the archaic period, was voluntary, in the sense that allegiance was obtained before service was required: that is, men worked for the system because they believed. To us, the laboring multitudes working to build the Pharaoh's tomb may seem to be slaves. But they were not slaves in the sense of "involuntary servitude" based on force. Force was used, but it was accepted, even before it was used, as a legitimate exercise of divine power.

The great transformation, especially the influence of the Indo-Europeans (and most especially the influence of the Iron Age Indo-European invaders, who did not have time to be "archaized," or, in the Aegean, "cretanized"), destroyed this archaic system.

From this destruction of the archaic system

255

in the West emerged a whole series of revolutionary consequences of which two are not obvious.

In the first place, the destruction of the archaic system in the West meant that no civilization (that is, no highly organized and complicated structure of human endeavor involving coordinated division of labor and ability to achieve internal order and external security) would be possible in the Mediterranean area until some alternative method of organization, replacing the archaic method, could evolve. This was the task of the dark age from 1000 down to 800 B.C. It met its great challenge in withstanding the Persian attack on Greece shortly after 500 B.C., and it continued to work out the implications of its own principles and environmental conditions for a thousand years after that. That is the classical system.

But in the second place, it is clear that the classical system made no significant technological advances over the archaic system and certainly achieved very little in the direction of mobilizing non-human labor, such as wind, water, or animal power. That means that some alternative method of organizing large numbers of men had to be devised so that the energies of such men could be coordinated and directed and so that they could be deprived of much of what they produced in order to accumulate capital to be used for the creation of non-subsistence enterprises (from art and literature to war and monuments). The method which the classical civilization eventually worked out was based on a precarious version of the heroic tradition in which men won immortality by being remembered for their service to the state, but, as might be expected from its Indo-European background, any power system based on this would have a much greater element of force in its power arrangements and a much smaller element of persuasion, than, for example, under the archaic system. Moreover, mobilization of human energies under such a heroic tradition would be much less persuasive or appealing to those whose energies were being mobilized on a mass basis, especially when force rather than persuasion was dominant. Accordingly, the significant method for mobilizing manpower in the

256

classical world, at least from the point of view of capital accumulation even if not in terms of the absolute numbers involved, was by slavery. In a sense, slavery, as a significant element in social organization, was an invention of the classical world and outlived it. The classical world, at least in terms of the persisting reputation of the Roman empire, organized involuntary servitude with such apparent success that it continued to be used until the technological advances of the next dark ages (say A.D. 850-1000) made it possible to utilize horsepower effectively. Even at that, with the addition of waterpower and windpower in the medieval period, slavery continued in many areas until the nineteenth century despite its inefficiency in comparison with other, post-Roman, technologies.

(blank page 258, intentionally omitted)

CHAPTER V
CLASSICAL CIVILIZATION: GROWING OFFENSIVE POWER AND WIDENING PARTICIPATION, 1000 TO 323 B.C.

1. The Nature of Classical Mediterranean Society

Few subjects have been studied as much as the history of classical Mediterranean society, but even today the basic fundamentals on which it rested are generally ignored. The chief reason for this is that the study of ancient history has concentrated largely, in many cases exclusively, on written evidence. Written evidence in any culture will contain only that information of which the people concerned are aware and which they try to communicate, and, in any culture, the people who make it up will not talk or write about many things, including very important ones, and may be unaware themselves of many of the more significant aspects of their society. But in classical culture this situation was made worse from the fact that a kind of social censorship served to prevent or to eliminate evidence on many things which were known and even written down.

This censorship arose from the fact that for the first time in Western history there was publication, that is materials were written to circulate and to be read by persons whom the writer did not know. But this process was expensive, so that generally it was available only to well-to-do persons, to those who could afford to keep or hire slaves as scribes. Thus it was generally available, until classical civilization was approaching its end, only to those who were favored by the system and who favored it. In this way, all the writings of Plato survived, while none of Anaxagoras' did.

Part of this voluntary censorship about classical civilization arose from the fact that it rested on slavery and on force more than any earlier society. This does not appear clearly from the surviving writings of classical antiquity, and it is, moreover, a matter which the literary-inclined students of classical culture prefer to ignore.

259

As we have said, the early civilizations, with their archaic pattern of organization, utilized manpower through religious appeal and on a "voluntary basis" (as already defined). Thus archaic cultures, and much of Asia down to recent times, operated in systems of power which were religious and social. Classical civilization and its four descendants (Byzantine, Islamic, Western, and Russian) have operated in systems of power whose chief elements were military and political. So also did Sinic civilization in China (1800 B.C.-A.D. 300) and much of Hindu civilization (since 1500 B.C.).

Classical civilization could be defined in an operational way as the civilization on the shores of the Mediterranean Sea in the period 1000 B.C. to A.D. 700. Both the place and the period have great significance.

Classical civilization was on the shores of the Mediterranean and penetrated into the hinterland of those shores to a surprisingly short distance. The central Balkans, central Anatolia, most of Spain, even most of the spine of Italy, and, for that matter, a major portion of the Po valley (the most fertile land in the whole Mediterranean area outside of the Nile valley) were never fully part of classical civilization. Indeed, as a consequence, many of these areas remained remote and semi-civilized (like Albania) even at the end of the nineteenth century A.D.

This littoral aspect of classical culture rested on the greater efficiency of water transportation over land transportation and, as a corollary, on the influence which these relative efficiencies had on military logistics.

Until horses could be effectively harnessed (that meant, in Europe, until after A.D. 900), inland districts could not be linked, culturally, economically, or politically, with a system whose central core consisted of the waterways of the Mediterranean Sea. For the whole period covered by this chapter the Po valley was farther from Rome than the Nile valley was, just as in an earlier period Arcadia or central Thessaly were more

260

remote from Athens than Sicily or Syria.

Thus sea power was the central fact of the whole system of classical Mediterranean civilization. But it was a very peculiar kind of sea power, since it was based on ships and tactics which could not keep at sea for any extended period. In fact, the naval vessels of the whole classical period were so limited in range of operations and in ability to stay at sea (not over about 24 hours) that they generally were expected to haul out on a beach each night or at least anchor so close to shore that their crews could eat and sleep on land.

What this meant in practice was that navies of the classical period could not operate effectively off a hostile shore and, in effect, that it was almost impossible to blockade an enemy seaport from the sea.

This situation meant that no state's power on the sea could extend very much beyond the area over which it could exercise power on land. Ultimately, this meant that Rome built up an empire whose central feature was control of the waterways of the Mediterranean Sea, but that the ultimate basis of its domination of those waterways rested on the ability of its legions to control the shores of the sea.

The key to this situation was the nature of sea power in the period from about 850 B.C. (when the ram was invented as part of a rowed war galley) to about A.D. 1500 (when the Portuguese and others began to exercise power on the broad reaches of the Atlantic and Indian Oceans, where the rowed galley could not function).

Some authorities (such as J.S. Morrison of Cambridge University) believe that the ram was used on oared galleys in the Bronze Age, or even earlier, because they see a projecting keel, which they regard as a ram, beneath the bow of vessels shown in paintings, clay models, and petroglyphs, going back long before 1000 B.C. Even where these vessels are war craft (in the period after 1400) the projecting keel was not a ram and the method

261

of combat at sea was by boarding and not by ramming. The projecting keel was used in pulling the vessel up on the beach, as was done frequently, and in the case of war galleys, almost every night.

Until the advent of iron nails in the tenth century B.C., planks on all vessels were fastened by sewing or by wooden pegs (both mentioned in Homer). In neither case were the fastenings strong enough to justify ramming as a method of naval combat. L. Cohen, whose work (1938) has been ignored by the chief English authorities (such as Morrison's Greek Oared Ships, 900-322 B.C., published in 1968, or T.C. Lethbridge's many works, including his chapter in volume II of Charles Singer, et al., A History of Technology in 1954) has argued convincingly that the ram and ramming as a deliberate tactic of naval conflict appeared about the ninth century. This is now accepted by Lionel Casson (1971).

From that time on, for all of classical antiquity, the war galley was a fighting machine in about the same way that the eight-oared shell is a racing machine: both are so specialized in function, and thus in construction, that neither provided any facilities for eating, resting, or transporting supplies. Moreover, in both, the rowing in action was so exhausting that it set narrow limitations on the range within which the vessel could be used. Men in galleys could row not much more than about three miles an hour and for not much more than six to eight hours a day, a total distance of no more than 18-24 miles per day, which could take the vessel, if it depended on rowing, no more than a dozen miles from land. Of course the galley was not dependent on rowing when it was not in action, but even under sail, it never could get far from land, where its crew must return to get the food or rest they needed. When the time came for combat, the sails had to be removed, the mast taken down, and, if possible, removed from the vessel, in order for all the oarsmen to have space to row. In action the work was so exhausting that it could not be sustained for more than an hour, and any extensive rowing to get to the scene or maneuvering before the combat began greatly jeopardized the chances for victory because of the weakness of the oarsmen.

The consequences of all these restrictions were complex. Classical civilization was tied together into a single cultural and economic entity by the superiority of sea transportation over land transport on its shores, but this superiority applied only to merchant shipping. Naval vessels, on the contrary, were tied to the shore so closely that they could sustain any state's power on the sea only if that state's land forces could control the shores. Under such conditions, there was no such thing as sea power in antiquity, in any accurate meaning of that term. Ancient sea power was like Napoleon's idea of sea power: a belief that the sea could be controlled if one could control all the shores and ports around it, and England could be blockaded without any real control of the sea if Napoleon controlled all the ports with which England might trade.

This idea of sea power which, of course, was a complete failure for Napoleon, nevertheless did work for the Romans, but only because Rome's legions could control all the readily available shores and ports, while Napoleon's could not.

This brings us, by way of the Roman legion, to another part of our basic framework of classical civilization, its chronology. It is recognized by all that the legion was supreme on the Mediterranean shores for many centuries, from at least 200 B.C. to after A.D. 200. It is also well known that the legion was the culmination of a long development of land warfare in that area from Homeric chariots, through Greek noble cavalry, to Greek hoplites, and the Macedonian phalanx, before the Roman legion became supreme.

What is not generally recognized is that this whole process took place in a relatively small and relatively isolated locale. The key to that isolation is to be found not only in the role of water transport on the Mediterranean in holding classical civilization relatively close to its shores for the major part of that civilization's lifetime, but also in the fact that the sub-Atlantic climate of the period 1000 B.C.-A.D. 200 made the grasslands so lush that there was relatively little

263

pressure on pastoral peoples of the grasslands to invade the Mediterranean basin and threaten the security of the classical peoples. There were, of course, isolated raids of pastoral and non-Mediterranean peoples into the classical living space, but these were impelled only by normal pressures of population growth and not by the need for large tribal groups to migrate in search for new lands, as did occur after the climate became warmer and drier about A.D. 200. As we shall see, the threat after A.D. 200 was made much worse by other factors, notably that the Roman empire was greatly overextended by 200 and was faced by weakening allegiance and loyalty as well.

This does not mean that classical civilization was powerful in a military sense in its earlier life. On the contrary, in that earlier period, in which loyalty and self-sacrifice for the public good was much higher than later, its weaponry and military sophistication was relatively low. This was true of the early Greeks and the early Romans, but was not true of the later Greeks (including the Macedonians) and the Romans of the period after about 200 B.C. The reason for this improvement in military skills was that both Greeks and Romans were exposed to different weapons systems away from the Mediterranean shores only gradually and on a voluntary basis, and were able to adjust to these challenges without risking destruction, while learning to adopt what was valuable in them. In fact, as a result of this favorable situation in military education, the Greeks were familiar with Asia and the Mediterranean hinterland long before Alexander the Great (fourth century B.C.), and the Romans were in a similar favorable position by the end of the second century B.C. long before Caesar ventured into Gaul or Lucullus and Pompey invaded Asia (all in the last century B.C.).

In these favorable conditions and on this relatively isolated stage, from about 1000 B.C. until about 600 A.D., classical civilization worked out its possibilities. There were two other sides to this stage, both almost equally neglected by classicists. We have already touched on both of these. One is concerned with the tech-

264

nology of the classical world and the other with its ideology and outlook.

On the whole, the technology of the Greeks and Romans was inferior to that of the Near East except in a few limited areas concerned with mining and construction, especially in stone. For this reason, they were no more able to use non-human energy in getting work done than the Mesopotamians and Egyptians had been. This meant that they were equally dependent on human labor, but were, as a consequence of a different outlook and ideology, less able to mobilize human labor on a voluntary basis. Where scores and hundreds of thousands had labored without need for excessive physical duress for the benefits of archaic Near Eastern deities (and for their priests, servants, and administrators), the classical peoples had a different outlook, both more secular and more ready to use force. These two qualities had to go together, for the key to the success of any civilization is its ability to organize energy. On a technological level in which energy can be organized successfully only in terms of human efforts, no advance whatever would be represented by the shift from archaic to classical societies if there was not at least an equivalent ability to organize human energy. Classical civilization with its much lower level of religious appeal and its consequent reduction in ideological ability to mobilize human efforts would have experienced a reduction in ability to organize energy in absolute terms unless some compensation, such as increased duress, appeared to make up for the loss in religious or ideological appeal. The concrete form which this increased duress took in classical society was the increase in human slavery but the increase in cost was very great.

Many classicists would argue that I am over-emphasizing the role of slavery in classical society, and would seek to refute me by statistical evidence seeking to show that slaves constituted only a minority of the population in any classical state.

Such figures are contentious and irrelevant.

265

The level of any civilization is marked by the quantity of social surplus available in it and the purposes for which that social surplus is used. Of the three most frequent sources of such social surplus (private savings, government accumulation, and diversion of income flows by organizational arrangements) only the third played a very significant role in classical society, at least during the Greek period. Under the Romans this third method was greatly increased, but so also was socialistic accumulation by governmental action (chiefly taxation). Under that third method for the accumulation of social surplus (organizational diversion of income flows) the only significant organization used in classical antiquity was by slavery. Production and trade for private profit was present, but not of great significance, while methods used by us, like savings banks, flotation of securities, and creation of credit were not used.

Thus, regardless of the number of slaves in classical antiquity in either absolute or relative figures, slavery was probably the most significant method for the accumulation of social surplus in the society (at least before the state became more bureaucratic and more socialistic after A.D. 200).

Slavery as a method of accumulating a social surplus has some drastic drawbacks. One of these is the very obvious decrease in ease of personal relationships and in domestic security when one person is not only subjected to involuntary service to another but when he is physically owned by another. This is a matter on which both the ancient sources and modern classicists have been reticent, but there can be no doubt that this gave elements of fear and tension to classical society, especially in Rome after 200 B.C., when fear of slave revolts or of individual slave attacks was increasingly present.

Even greater social cost came from the problem of finding a supply of slaves. Originally, slaves came from three sources: biological reproduction of slaves; judicial condemnation to slavery (as for debts or criminal acts); and from war captives.

266

Judicial condemnation may have been a significant source of slaves in the early years (say down to 500 B.C.), but it was abolished in most states (as by Solon in Athens in 594 B.C.) and ceased to be important. Biological reproduction has never been sufficient to keep any system of slavery supplied with the numbers needed, as we know from the history of slavery in the United States and other places. Its inadequacy has been made worse whenever a society has a widespread practice of manumissions, or freeing of slaves, as the Romans did. Such a practice may be a credit to the humane instincts cf owners who free their slaves but, from the point of view of the society as a whole, it is a problem, since it reduces the society's ability to accumulate the social surplus needed to fill its investment needs. In any case, even without manumission, a slave society is not self-sustaining in slaves, and the practice of manu-mission makes the problem more acute.

This leaves war captives as the chief source of slaves in any society which does not have extensive enslavement by judicial condemnation. The slaves who came to the United States were war captives, the consequence, generally, of in-tertribal warfare in Africa. The warfare and en-slavement did not become a part of the regular customs of the United States itself, and the individuals who participated in the slave trade were a small minority and were held in low esteem.

In classical society it was quite otherwise. Since the society depended on slaves and the sup-ply of slaves depended on war, the society became necessarily involved in war making and in the plundering of human beings to keep the system going. Few persons, either then or since, have been explicit on this issue, but the fact remains that the states of classical society increasingly became war-making machines, one of whose chief motivations was the acquisition of slaves. Until about 300 B.C. this was not obvious, but as men became increasingly reluctant to make war for patriotism, they had to be offered other incentives. The chief of such incentives, in an age of mercenary fighters, was economic gain, including shares in the

267

plunder and looting whose major part was made up
of the value of enslaved war captives.

In the earlier period, down to about 200 B.C.,
such wars were easily engendered by the fact that
there were many states, mostly under belligerent
leaders, within classical society. As Rome's conquests reduced the number of states within the system, the supply of slaves was kept up by tacitly
allowing piracy to run rampant in much of the
Mediterranean, with pirate captives purchased
as slaves. When public opinion finally forced
Rome to take steps to suppress piracy about 67
B.C. and the conclusion of the civil wars (another good source of slaves) left only one state
in the Mediterranean, it became necessary for the
system to find more war captives to serve as slaves
by waging wars farther and farther from the Mediterranean. Efforts to extend the Roman empire across
the Sahara, across the Arabian desert, into Parthia
(or even from the Euphrates to the Tigris), across
the Danube (except for Dacia), across the Rhine
into Germany, and into the Celtic lands of Great
Britain, all failed. The result was the establishment of the permanent frontiers of the empire (limes)
by A.D. 50. But without anyone being explicitly
aware of it, this meant that the slave system was
doomed simply because the offensive power of Rome's
armies was no longer adequate to supply Rome with
the slaves necessary to keep the system going.

All of this shows that the character of classical society changed constantly in the course of its
history and that its ability to continue to function
rested on a complex interplay of numerous and subtle factors.

One of these factors to which I have not given
sufficient attention is ideology. I have said that
the ability of the classical system to mobilize human
energy rested on a power system in which the component
of duress was greater and the component of religious
belief was less than in earlier archaic societies.
This increased component of duress came quite

readily from the Indo-European contribution to the classical synthesis because resort to force and violence came so easily to Indo-Europeans.

There was, however, another element in the Indo-European outlook which contributed substantially to the functioning of the classical system, especially in its earlier stages (say down to 200 B.C.). This was what we sometimes refer to as the "aristocratic" element in classical culture. This aristocratic element was a temporary, but very valuable, modification of the Indo-European emphasis on immortality. Where the early adherents to this outlook had sought immortality from extremism, especially in competitive violence, the later ones, especially upper class Greeks of the period from 600 on, sought to win renown and a permanent place in the memories of their fellow citizens by public service to the state and to its citizens, by erecting public buildings or monuments, by financing public water supply equipment, public colonnades, a fighting ship, or production of a drama. This valuable element in the classical outlook was almost essential for the successful functioning of the classical system, yet it was crushed out long before the Roman supremacy in the Mediterranean was established (in 146 B.C.) between the pressures of other elements in the classical outlook, such as materialism, an anthropocentric universe, and a growing emphasis on existential violence. By 100 B.C. the Mediterranean was being engulfed, as a consequence of this process, in a power struggle of crude force.

Within this larger framework the subject with which we are concerned, that is the relationships between weapons systems and political stability, both internal and external, followed a relatively simple pattern which had fundamental lessons to us today. The only additional complicating factor which we should keep in mind is based on an additional geographic feature of the Mediterranean basin.

This feature, that the Mediterranean really consists of two basins, an eastern and a western, divided at the sea passages on either side of Sicily and Malta, means that there was a tendency

for each basin to follow the chronological evolution
of classical civilization at a different pace, with
the eastern basin about 200 years in advance simply
because civilized conditions, including writing,
coinage, technology, democracy, cosmopolitan imperialism, and rapid growth in the size of political units, all came from the east and moved
westward generations later.

As it happened, these two basins of the Mediterranean throughout classical civilization and long
afterwards remained somewhat different in culture
from the fact that the eastern portion was basically
Greek in language, while the western portion became
basically Latin. This distinction was of great importance following the loss of political unity after
the fall of Rome, leading to the division of Christianity into Orthodox and Latin churches following
the division into Eastern and Western empires after
A.D. 335.

2.   The Chronology of Classical Mediterranean Society

Because of this chronological distinction between east and west in the Mediterranean, I shall
give this analysis of the interrelations of weapons
and political stability in terms of the Greek-speaking world, with the understanding that the western
Mediterranean followed along about 200 years later.

Two dynamic changes which have already been
mentioned are the two characteristic features of
weapons systems: (1) either defensively dominant
or offensively dominant; and (2) either specialist
weaponry or amateur weaponry. In terms of these
two, the history of classical civilization is simple,
for each of these passed through a single cycle during the whole of classical antiquity, the chief difference being that the change back to the original
pattern took place much more rapidly in the specialist-amateur cycle than it did in the defensive-of-
fensive cycle. Put in different terms, this means
that the offensive was growing in classical society
for a very long time, from about 800 B.C. to about
A.D. 100, reaching its peak about 50 B.C., while
the growth of amateur weaponry was relatively
brief, say from 800 B.C. to about 400 B.C. in

the Greek world, reaching its peak about 450
(this peak would be about 150 B.C. in the western
Mediterranean). Since political forms follow the
cycle specialist-amateur with a delay of at
least a generation, the period of democracy in
the Greek world reached its peak about 430 (in
Rome, about 140 B.C.), being preceded and followed
by periods of more authoritarian government, sustained by more specialist weaponry.

The more important cycle was that flowing
from the relationship between defensive and offensive dominance, since this gave rise to much
more complex and more persistent political consequences.

From this point of view, the period 1200-900
B.C. was one of decreasing offensive power so that
it became steadily less possible for any political
power to enforce its will at any distance from its
own center of power. That means that communications
and transportation were breaking down at the same
time that ability to sustain applied force at a
distance was decreasing. At the same time, the
shift from castles and chariots to cavalry and
the beginnings of the shift from bronze to iron
weapons, marked a cheapening of the available
weapons systems, so that these could become available to a somewhat larger number of persons (the
nobles, rather than only the kings). As a result,
weapons and power were dispersed to a larger number of persons, but on a geographically smaller
and more limited basis, so that scores of power
centers among the Greeks about 1300 became hundreds by 900. Power dissipated so widely ceased
to be public and became private, and the state
disappeared. This whole process was, of course,
speeded up by the intrusion of invaders whose experiences had been private, social, and tribal,
rather than public, political, and statist. The
kings were wiped away or were reduced in power
to largely religious or ceremonial functions
(sometimes associated with judicial activities),
and the society as a whole came to be organized
in terms of tribal units (or clans) centered about
the manor house or plantation of the local noble.

271

The social changes, like the ideological ones, which accompanied the military and political changes, are of great significance but much less clearly known to us. They seem to be related to economic processes rather than to political ones and are associated with the question of how easily a man could get his daily bread rather than with the admittedly more basic question of how he could achieve political security and sleep safely at night.

In general, however, the social changes seem to show a process which runs parallel to the military and political changes. This means that kinship groupings (such as the clan or family) and localized groupings (such as the village, town, or city) moved through stages in a single cycle, parallel to the cycles we have already indicated. The social groupings got smaller (and the territorial groupings got larger) until about the time of Christ (say A.D. 100) and then began to grow larger again. Thus at the beginning, about 900 B.C., the basic social grouping in society seems to have been a tribe or large clan, the descendants of some known ancestor. This phyle or genos began to break up, at first into the extended family (the male descendants, with their wives and children, of their oldest living ancestor), but later into the nuclear family (of husband with wife and children), and still later to atomistic individualism in which family relations are not very significant nor binding.

These kinship groupings were originally units of religious cult, property control, and social responsibility. In the early period they probably included the dead ancestors and the unborn descendants, and this may have been the basis for the very early inalienability of property (since the consent of these could not be obtained). Society was made up of these groupings and not of individuals, so that other, outside groupings impinged on these groups and not on the individual members. This meant that the religious, criminal, property, and military obligations of the group were met by the group as a whole and were regulated within the group against individual members without outside interference.

272

The breakup of these kinship groupings to smaller and smaller units (that is, in Greece, especially in Athens, from phylae to phratriai, to gene to anchisteis and ultimately to individuals) was accompanied by the growth in the size, power, and jurisdiction of the state, which developed, we might say, by accumulating the powers which were dropped aside at each subdivision of the functions of the kinship groups to smaller ones. There was, of course, more to the process than this, for at least two other processes were serving to increase the powers of the state. On the one hand, powers were being transferred from kinship groupings to territorial or local groupings; and, on the other hand, the accelerating speed of social change, by disrupting customary patterns of action, gave rise to an increasing need for decision-making and rules on matters which had been regulated by customary patterns previously. These innovative decision-making and rule-making activities tended to go to territorial public authorities rather than to the decreasingly effective kinship groupings.

The net result of all this was that about 900 B.C. the individual had almost no rights, being absorbed in a totalitarian kinship group, in a system of such groups with no state and no real idea of public authority. By A.D. 100 the individual was an atomistic and almost defenseless entity who again had no rights, being absorbed in a totalitarian state which hardly recognized any rights for kinship groups or individuals, even in the most personal or most subjective matters (such as religious beliefs). In between, say about 350 B.C. in the Greek world or about 100 B.C. in the Roman world (when the state, the kinship group, the individual, and various voluntary associations shared rights and responsibilities in a pluralistic system), the rights, liberties, and responsibilities of individuals were at their maximum extent.

The framework within which these complex and changeable interactions took place was that triangular area of human experience bounded by ideology and outlook on one side, by organizational

patterns of action on the second side, and by the
objective physical world of technology artifacts,
and geographic environment on the third side.
Weapons systems, consisting of both artifacts
and organizational patterns, cross two of these
sides and are but one of the elements which allowed the state to extend its power, with greater
intensity and over wider areas, in the period 900
B.C. to about A.D. 100.

The historian can follow these processes,
such as the disintegration of kinship groupings
and the patriarchal family, in terms of the laws
of property (especially real property) and the
rules of family discipline, such as the responsibility of such kinship groups for the crimes or
other actions of its members. In this whole development the old Indo-European pastoral patriarchal system broke down, as relatives, children,
and ultimately wives became legally capable of
owning and alienating property and became increasingly free from patriarchal power and able
to enter or leave the kin through divorce,
adoption, or individual marriage choice. Finally,
members of kinship groups became increasingly
responsible, as isolated individuals, for their
own actions.

By A.D. 100, however, the tide was beginning
to turn, in the area of social change as in so
many others. Individuals began to cling more
closely together, in emotional and religious associations, leading to increased economic cooperation and joint social responsibility. Slowly,
the family regained its legal significance, a process greatly increased by the growing political insecurity, the growing example of barbarian (largely
Germanic) invaders, and the increased ruralization
of society.

One aspect of this whole process of social
change is to be seen in the shift from an almost
totally rural way of life west of the Levant about
1000 B.C. to a largely urban way of life for a
large proportion of people about A.D. 100, but
to a largely rural society again about A.D. 1000.
The return was not quite to the same place, how-

ever, because, where the dominant social unit of
1000 B.C. had been based on blood (the kinship
group), the dominant social unit of A.D. 1000
was based on contiguous residence in a village
or parish.

3.   Fighters by Birth: the Age of the Nobles,
     900-650 B.C.

It is easy for us to put the history of any
people or society into a tabular form showing few
or many stages.   But anyone who uses such an outline must remain fully aware that changes go on
constantly, so that the divisions we make are
nothing more than a convenience for our processes
of thought and communication.

This is true of the age of the nobles, regardless of how we date it.   It was a period in which
power was becoming increasingly dispersed into
the hands of local magnates.   This means that the
kings were disappearing or being reduced to purely
religious or largely ceremonial functions.   Thus
there was a tendency for public authority to decrease, leaving only private power in kinship systems.   But all of these processes took place over
such an extended period, from before 1000 to after
600 B.C., that they were still in process when contrary currents appeared, leading ultimately to the
shift of power from kinship to local groupings and
to the reappearance of public authority in these
new territorial terms.

In this process the Dorian states took the
lead, especially in Crete and in the Peloponnesus.
The chief apparent reason for this was that the
Dorian tribes had enserfed so many conquered peoples that it was necessary for the invading Dorians
to abandon their divisive kinship rivalries and
establish a united front against their serfs over
the whole of the conquered territory.   In the Ionian
areas, on the other hand, the earlier Mycenaean
idea of public authority over a large territory
persisted much longer.   However, the technological
conditions of weapons, communications, and transportation made it impossible to implement this idea,
with the result that Ionian areas continued to break

up into autonomous villages at a time when the Dorians, who had no real traditions of a state, were already in process of re-inventing it.

An additional reason for this Dorian precocity in the rediscovery of public authority was that the geographic position of the Dorian districts, in the south, across the Peloponnesus and Crete, and eastward to Rhodes and southwestern Anatolia, put them right in the path of the reopening of Mediterranean trade by the Phoenicians. Moreover, the great trans-Hellas trade route from east to west, along the Saronic Gulf, across the Isthmus of Corinth, and along the Gulf of Corinth to the Adriatic Sea, was in control of Dorian states like Corinth, Sicyon, and Megara.

This process of the revival of public authority will be discussed in a moment, but first we must complete our discussion of the two earlier portions of this period in which the kings were eclipsed and the nobles dominated society.

The "nobles" of 800 B.C. were simply those who had weapons and horses, with experience of how to use these. With these things they were able to make lesser people obey and to insure possession (and ultimately legal ownership) of lands and other forms of wealth in their own families. They took to themselves the right to settle the disputes of lesser peoples and control of the religious rituals, except for those which they left to the descendants of the earlier kings. These kings remained significant only to the degree that they retained some power by possession of arms, horses, and families themselves.

It should be pointed out that "king" was not an archaic and not an Indo-European idea or title. That is why the usual Greek names for king such as Wanax, basileus, or tyrannos were not Indo-European words. The essential point about "king," even in modern times, is that it is a religious title. In modern history a king is a ruler who has been consecrated with holy oils in an archepiscopal cathedral; coronation has always been a religious ceremony. The Roman aversion to the

276

name "rex" was based on this religious aspect rather than, as is usually explained, because of their hateful memories of the Etruscans.

Although the warrior invaders had little knowledge of the idea or name of king, the Bronze Age invaders such as the Achaeans or Hittites soon picked it up, as is very evident from the Linear B documents if not from Homer. Moreover, the later Iron Age invaders had at least heard of the institution. By 500 B.C. the Celts, and later the Germans, had some idea of the name and function of king except that the pastoral peoples, such as the Indo-Europeans, and to a lesser extent the Semites, always saw the king more as a war leader than as a religious figure.

In early Indo-European times, leaders were more likely to be seen as biologically distinguished persons (perhaps as the chief descendant of an outstanding ancestor) and as a war leader. These two were not necessarily joined in the same person, at least in the historic period. Even when the Indo-Europeans absorbed the idea of king in the archaic sense, this usually remained an office, quite separate from the prestige of noble birth or the function of war leader.

For these reasons the kings who were forced to share or give up their powers after 900 were in a confused and changeable situation. Usually their functions as war leaders were taken away more completely or earlier; their functions as magistrates or settlers of disputes were taken away less completely and later; and their functions as ritual leaders or priests were taken away last, less completely, or not at all. In some cases, as at Corinth, the kings were killed and the office abolished. In Sparta there were two kings, probably descendants of leaders of two conquering Dorian families. They remained as hereditary war leaders down to the Roman period, but were constantly hemmed in by the five ephors, who probably represented originally the five villages of Sparta as well as the fact that the Spartan army had been shifted from the basis of three hereditary tribes (phylae) to five regi-

ments (lochoi) based on local residence, as early
as the 8th century. The parallel change in Athens,
from four regiments based on four hereditary tribes
to ten based on local residence, did not occur until
Cleisthenes' reforms about 508 B.C.

When the royal powers were divided or assumed
by others, these others were in fact those who had
the forces to compel such a change. These were
later regarded as persons of superior blood: that
is, "nobles." Generally, the earlier this was done,
the smaller that group was. In Sparta it was the
Gerousia, a body of 30 men (including the two kings)
elected for life after the age of 60; in Corinth
it was a single clan, the Bacchiadae. In some
cases, where these processes occurred very late,
this group may have included persons from families
which were not regarded as noble.

Another factor in this process was that the
magistrates who took over "royal" powers were
chosen by a narrower suffrage, from a smaller
reservoir of potential candidates, and for longer
terms of office (even for life) depending on how
early the change took place. In some cases it took
place in more than one step, a narrower early
change being succeeded, generations later, by a
wider and more liberal system.

The rate of historical change was so slow in
the early years from 1000 B.C. to about 700 B.C.
that the same families often retained their integrity, weapons, and animals, passing them on
from generation to generation. Inevitably they
retained their power, but this possession of power
was not justified (if it ever had to be) by the
families' possession of weapons and horses but by
their blood descent from the earliest ancestor
they could remember. When this was accepted (as
it more or less had to be) by lesser persons, the
greater families became "noble" in the correct
usage of that term--a family or individual whose
superior social position is based on birth and
blood (even when, in fact, it is based on weapons).

This distinction between the theory (noble
blood) and the facts (possession of weapons) is

of increasing significance when the facts are changing, as they continued to do in the centuries following 800 B.C. For as the facts changed, the theory of noble blood and of its rights and privileges came under severe challenges.

The changing facts of 900-600 B.C. were these: (1) peace, order, and political security increased over what they had been before 900; (2) iron weapons and even horses became cheaper and more readily available; (3) the general level of economic prosperity rose; (4) population increased, but inequitably among families, so that some were reduced while others proliferated; (5) the larger blood groupings began to disintegrate, moving from clans toward extended families and even, in some cases, from extended families to nuclear families; (6) there was a general economic shift from emphasis on pastoralism and animals (such as sheep) toward increasing emphasis on crop growing (and possibly a shift of emphasis within planting from grain to olives and grapes); (7) the Phoenicians began to restore order on the seas, to reestablish long-distance commerce, from Syria to beyond Gibraltar, and to introduce knowledge of luxury goods, writing, measurements, and the use of the sea; (8) noble families in many districts began to cooperate together to establish religious confederations, to build joint defensive centers, and ultimately to ship some surplus populations overseas to new colonies, at first in the Aegean, but later in the Black Sea, and in the central, and even western, Mediterranean (Sicily, southern Italy, and southern Gaul); and (9) the use of silver coinage was introduced from Anatolia possibly from Lydia, at first to Aegina about 650.

Three of these (spread of iron weapons, increased population, and the spread of private ownership of land, with the right to mortgage or to sell) combined to create a situation of revolutionary instability in the seventh century B.C. We should look at these three factors.

As iron weapons became somewhat cheaper and certain families became somewhat richer, the group of persons who had weapons became larger than it had been and, most significantly, became larger than the group of nobles. If the nobles were, for example, five per cent of the families and as much as ten per cent of families were equipped with the best available weapons, the attribution of legal power to the nobles might still be maintained. But if the weapons holders became twenty, or even thirty or forty, per cent, the ability of the nobility to retain their political privileges and attributed rights to power, land, and slaves could, in fact, be challenged. Such a dichotomy between law and the facts of power is essentially an unstable and irresponsible government (in the sense that "responsibility" means a situation where the law and theories reflect the facts relatively closely). At any time, in such an unstable situation, the facts may simply explode and force a sudden and drastic change in the theories (law). This is the essence of revolution.

4.   Fighters by Wealth: the Age of Tyrants, 650-500 B.C.

As revolutionary pressures built up, even in states which sought to alleviate such pressures by reform, the forces of change, especially the spread of iron weapons to wider groups of persons, became almost overwhelming in the course of the seventh century. The triggering event was a drastic change in military tactics about 700 B.C. from a more individualistic and more "noble" type of fighting to that of fighting in a close formation of heavily armed hoplites which dominated Greek battlefields from the seventh century to the fourth, when it was replaced by the phalanx.

In the preceding two centuries (900-700 or so) fighting had been reserved to the small percentage of the population who arrived on the field on horseback, dismounted in most cases, and fought by hurling a spear or two, then closed on an opponent to settle the conflict with swords. In this pre-hoplite period, body armor was scanty and the shield had a hand grip at the center and a strap slung round the neck. It could hang from the strap, leaving both hands free, and in retreat could be slung round to protect the owner's back.

The hoplite style was entirely different from
the fact that it had required close cooperation in
tight infantry formation. The shield was smaller
with two handles, one at the center and the other
at the outer edge. The left arm was thrust through
the handle at the center, up to the elbow, and the
outer handle was grasped by the left hand. This
shield, with no neck strap, was useless in retreat,
to protect the back, and was so small and so firmly
fastened to the left forearm that it protected only
the left two-thirds of the body, leaving the right
side to be protected by the shield of the next man
standing to the right. This required a tight formation and made it essential that the men stand and
move closely together as a group rather than as
individuals. This tactic made individual brilliance
a handicap rather than an asset and was quite incompatible with the traditions of the nobility. Defensive armor also included a breastplate of metal
and often greaves on the front of the legs. The
spear was heavier and was not thrown but held in
formation with the other troopers. The sword was
hardly more than a dirk, perhaps thirty inches
long or even less.

The vital point about this shift to hoplite
tactics in the seventh century was that victory,
and even individual safety, no longer rested on
brilliance, individual courage, or excess of any
kind, but on steadfast discipline and on holding
the line fast while putting maximum pressure as a
bloc on the enemy formation in order to disrupt it,
by forcing it backward onto less level or broken
terrain or by outflanking it to roll up the line,
something which could be done most easily from
its right side. This latter danger led to a consistent tendency for each man and the line as a
whole to yield to the right, toward each person's
less protected side, to avoid being outflanked
on that side.

Such a formation, so long as it remained firm,
with all its spears extending outward in a continuous line, could resist a frontal cavalry charge,
especially as the horseman of that day had no stirrups and no adequate saddle, but simply sat on a
pad holding a lance or sword too short to reach

281

through the line of hoplite spears in formation.
But such a formation was very vulnerable to cavalry
attack from the flank or rear.

These hoplite tactics were so successful in
the circumstances in which they arose (they would
have been very ineffective against any force, especially horsemen, armed with composite bows, the
chief Assyrian weapon of that time) that a considerable demand arose for Greek mercenary hoplites,
especially from Asia Minor and Egypt, but later
also from Persia.

Within Greece this extension of ownership of
weapons would have been no threat to the nobles
from the great mass of the population who remained
too poor to obtain weapons. It did threaten the
nobility, however, from the acquisition of weapons
by non-nobles who were as wealthy as the nobles
yet were excluded from political life simply because
they were not noble. The much larger group of poorer
persons who were economically exploited yet could do
little to remedy their situation from lack of weapons, nonetheless presented a substantial threat to
public order, because, however potent hoplites may
have been in battle formation, as individuals scattered in the community they were as vulnerable to
violent attack with rocks, clubs, or daggers as
any unarmed peasant.

In many states, the movement toward reform was
triggered when some discontented noble joined these
two dissatisfied groups (the armed non-noble rich
excluded from political life and the unarmed, economically exploited poor) to make a tripartite attack on the legal privileges of the nobles. In
many cases, the leader of this coalition was able
to obtain power by a coup d'etat or even by an invasion from foreign soil with the support of mercenary fighting men hired by his own resources or
from the contributions of foreign states. In some
cases, most notably Solon of Athens (594 B.C.), the
dissident nobles who led this movement were as interested in heading off a revolution of the economically exploited peasants as they were with secur-
ing an extension of political privileges to the non-
noble rich. In general it must be clear that the

282

situation and the motives of those involved were
very complex and varied greatly from state to
state, but the essential fact in the situation
was the ability to mobilize forces to change legal
arrangements which no longer reflected the facts
of power.

The great groundswell of economic discontent
which made it possible to float these reforms came
from the interaction of two factors: that some
families were becoming poorer and falling into debt
and that the monopoly of judicial process by the
nobility was raising increasingly violent dis-
satisfactions.

The growing poverty and indebtedness of some
peasant landowners was a consequence of unequal
fertility among families and the growing right
to alienate land. As ownership of land began to
pass from large kinship groups to smaller ones,
the right to alienate such lands by sale, bequest,
or mortgage began to appear. This process was
much slower to develop among the nobility, where
inalienability of land (a kind of entail) continued
in some areas down into the historic period.

Those families who had many sons, in contrast
with those who had only one or two heirs, became
impoverished when the growing right to alienate
land was used to divide it among sons. In time,
the descendants had plots too small to support
their dependents except in years of unusually good
crops. In poorer years, when they were faced with
the prospect of lacking sufficient food to get
to the next harvest, they borrowed grain from their
more affluent neighbors at interest rates of forty
or fifty per cent, a suicidal arrangement when
their lands would hardly support their families
in the average year. For collateral on such a
loan, they could mortgage either themselves or
their land (if alienable); the former often seemed
preferable since it would, in case of default, at
least leave the land to their dependents. But in
either case, the situation was almost hopeless.
If the man was foreclosed before the land, he became a slave, and it was only a question of time
before his owner would foreclose on the land also,

bringing him, at times, to a situation in which he worked as a slave on land which he had formerly owned. In cases where the harassed head of a family was able to mortgage the land rather than his own body, he soon lost the land and was either evicted from it or remained as a sharecropper when the right to the crop passed to his creditor. In such cases, the debtor's situation was still hopeless since he could not support a family on part of the crop, when the whole had previously been insufficient.

In many cases of this kind there were bitter disputes over the legal details of these arrangements: the percentage of interest, the date the payment was due, the fields, persons, or share of the crop covered by the mortgages. In such disputes the cases went before the magistrates, who were invariably nobles in the earlier period and who naturally tended to make decisions favorable to themselves and their fellow nobles, or at least to favor creditors over debtors. The debtors were outraged, not only at biased judgments, but also at the noble judges' versions of the laws themselves. For the laws were unwritten and were simply local customs as remembered by these noble judges. In cases of such critical importance, it is only to be expected that the debtor would challenge the judge's memory of the law as well as his partiality in the judgment of the case under that law.

This led to demands that the laws be written down, a requirement which became more urgent when it was evident that some of the older laws were no longer fitted to the changed conditions. As an example, we might point out that homicide, in early Greek as in early Roman law, had no distinctions (as between deliberate murder or the most innocent accidental manslaughter) and was a matter of religious importance (pollution requiring expiation) and was a family's responsibility (requiring retaliation or compensation) but was not a concern of the growing public authority.

When the demands for written laws were met (as in Draco's code of about 621 in Athens or the Law of the Twelve Tables of about 450 B.C. in Rome) they usually retained archaic elements in such mat-

284

ters as severity of punishments or the rights of
nobles over plebeians, but they often contained
advanced elements in regard to the growing authority of the state and the parallel development of
the rights of the individual, both expanding at
the expense of the larger blood groupings like
the tribe or the clan.

The provision of written laws, still interpreted and applied by nobles, like the export of
dissatisfied men to found colonies in distant
places, may have lowered the revolutionary pressures a little, but did nothing to solve the problems of the day or to satisfy the discontents of
major segments of the community. Demands for redistribution of land ownership and demands that
political and judicial activities be opened more
fully to non-nobles continued to rise. Eventually
these discontents had to be met, especially when a
few dissident nobles appeared willing to lead the
revolutionary agitations and, above all, when the
extension of weapons and the growing border clashes
with neighboring communities made it necessary to
open military service to the non-nobles who could
afford weapons.

The border clashes with neighboring communities
arose from the tendency, already explained, for any
social system in crisis to seek solution to its
problems by extensive rather than by intensive activities. Intensive solutions required a reform
of the system so that, with better organizational
methods, there could be greater output from the
same or lesser resources. But as always, those
who feared that their interests might be injured
by reform, and the majority of persons who did not
analyze the situation at all, felt that the problems of the community could be solved most simply
and directly by extending the community's existing
organizational patterns to wider resources. In
many cases, this solution seemed obvious: if there
was a lack of land, why not take land from a neighboring community?

That seems simple enough. But what if the
neighbor thus threatened with loss of land by aggression seeks to strengthen its ability to resist

by admitting the more well-to-do non-nobles to its armed forces, including the cavalry, if men can afford this? In that case the aggressor must move toward a similar reform. But such a sharing with the non-nobles of the right to participate in defense will mentally entail a similar sharing in decision-making regarding defense and other policies, as well as judicial actions.

The demands of the non-landowning noble for reformist changes in this direction could be presented more forcibly and earlier if these demands were associated with a possible alliance of the non-noble well-to-do with the discontented land-hungry poor.

In this fashion the forces for progressive change tended to ally together and to compel "progressive" reforms, unless a drastic counterrevolutionary effort was able to bring together a mobilization of weapons control and ideological solidarity sufficient to stop the progressive development of the community as a whole. This is what occurred in Sparta and, much later, in Rome, but in both cases the success of the counterrevolutionary movement changed the very nature of the community and destroyed the old traditional Spartan (or Roman) system based on the superiority of a hereditary nobility and created in its place a much cruder and narrower system. In both cases, the effort to preserve a regime of privilege by the restriction of freedom led to a system in which force was dominant. From this it should be clear that the system of privilege based on blood was doomed anyway, whether the community turned to reform or to reaction.

The movement to reform, in the Greek revolutionary crisis of the seventh century, required much more than writing the laws down, the sharing of political activity, and some redistribution of land ownership. It required that the older largely rural and largely agrarian economy with its emphasis on self-sufficiency and with a social organization made up largely of two classes must be changed to a much more complex society of numerous social groupings, in several classes, with specialized activities and intensified exchange of goods and services both within the community and abroad.

This new organizational pattern of specialization and exchange in a pluralistic society was the one remedy for the revolutionary crisis of seventh century Greece which would not involve undue use of force, either for internal oppression or for aggressive external war. It was the direction taken by Athens, Corinth, various cities of Ionia, Syracuse and others. These found artisan, commercial, and service activities for their displaced peasants.

In Athens this direction for finding a solution to the revolutionary crisis of the seventh century was pointed out by the reformist work of Solon. For this reason, and also because of the intrinsic interest of the man and his work, we should take a little time to examine the subject more fully.

Solon is one of the greatest political figures in history, showing a most extraordinary ability in his analysis of political forces and in his decision, not so much to change the situation by legislation or edict, but rather to set up conditions which would allow the situation to be changed in time by the operation of natural processes of social change. He did not take powers or lands or rights from one group to give them to another group, but rather he defined rights and powers in terms of something which could be changed, namely annual incomes. This meant that the right to participate in political action ceased to be based on blood and did not become based on ownership of weapons, but instead was placed on an external and acquirable criterion (annual income in terms of measures of grain or wine). This removed the conflict over political rights from the area of birth or of weapons into the area of economic competition. Then he made economic life more hopeful by a series of economic and legal reforms which sought to open up new opportunities in crafts or trade, and in the cities.

Solon's political skill may be seen in his

desire to make changes in laws self-enforcing, if possible. For example, it is often said that he made a law requiring every father to teach his son a trade. What he did was establish in law that the existing requirement that a son was responsible for the father's support in the latter's old age was not enforceable in law if the son could show that his father had not taught him a trade. Under this version enforcement required no action by the state; it was self-enforcing.

Solon divided Athenian citizens into four income groups:

1. Pentacosiomedimnoi: those with income over 500 measures of grain or wine a year.
2. Hippeis: those with 300-500 measures.
3. Zeugitai: those with 200-300 measures.
4. Thetes: those with less than 200 measures.

Of these the Pentacosiomedimnoi and Hippeis were required to serve in the cavalry; the Zeugitai served in the hoplite infantry; the Thetes served as auxiliary and light armed skirmishers (eventually they became the chief source of the oarsmen in the navy).

Political activities were based on the same four income classes. All four could be members of the assembly of all free citizens (Ecclesia), but only the top three classes could be members of the executive committee in charge of the assembly's agenda (Boule). Only the top two classes could be elected to the chief magistracy (the archonships), but the first three classes were eligible to lower offices. In all cases election was by the assembly.

The judicial problem was reformed by a new code of law more lenient than Draco's. The council of nobles (areopagus) had many of its powers taken away, but continued to function as a constitutional court and as an administrative body with supervisory powers over retiring magistrates. It was now made up of all ex-archons (a decreasingly noble group). The judicial powers of the magistrates continued, but now their decisions could be appealed to large popular juries made up of all classes of citizens (Heliaea). In time, so many cases were appealed to juries that the trial magistrates became in effect indicting magistrates.

On the economic side, Solon forbade any more mortgaging of the bodies of citizens or enslavement for debt. Those who had been enslaved were freed, with the state buying back those who had been sold abroad; debts on land were cancelled; the drachma was devalued slightly (a benefit to exporters), while weights and measures were increased in size (a benefit to creditors); the export of all agricultural products was forbidden (a benefit to consumers) except olive oil (a benefit to large landowners who produced it); immigration of foreign craftsmen was encouraged, as was training of Athenian youths in such crafts.

Solon's program was neither democratic nor revolutionary, although it opened the way to growth toward more democratic processes and revolutionary economic and social changes. It ruined no one, although it did injure many creditors, as it also saved many debtors from ruin. The chief thing about it is that it set up a new situation in which law was closer to fact and the future was open for more hopeful developments for those who wished to work toward them.

The essential feature of Solon's reform was that political activity was shifted from blood to possession of weapons but only indirectly by being based on income which could buy weapons, without any effort to move directly from the basis of blood (nobility) to the basis of numbers (democracy). This was a transitional stage in many communities of the classical world and was an effective measurement of power so long as individuals were expected to provide their own weapons. So long as weapons were expensive enough to exclude any considerable group from owning them by reason of poverty, this meant that the poorest citizens were excluded from the armed forces, at least from the branches which required weapons of substantial cost. This meant, with one very significant exception, that the poorest citizens were able to serve only in auxiliary arms such as supply, constructing fortifications, light skirmishing with javelins or slings, and such. The one exception was a major one: the onerous task of rowing the galleys of the navy was open to the poor. For this reason, in all sea powers which had a military system based on incomes the navy became the chief defender of a democratic constitution. Thus, in Athens, when the oligarchy tried to overthrow democracy in the years following the great Athenian defeat in Sicily in 413, the navy, on several occasions, suppressed the oligarchs and restored the democratic system.

In early Rome there was a system which superficially looks like the Athenian class system, and which appears even more closely related to military service because the units often voted in military formation, in ranks of centuries. But the system was set up, as usual in the Roman constitution, without any close relationship to the real power situation. There were five classes totaling 170 centuries, plus 18 centuries of cavalry above the classes and 5 centuries of the poor (organized as work forces) below the classes. Since voting was by centuries, beginning with the richest and working downward, with the voting being stopped as soon as a majority was indicated, the centuries of the poor rarely had any chance to vote: there were 18 votes in the noble cavalry, and 80 votes in Class I (also cavalry), but the total number of votes was only 193. Thus those who served in the cavalry had 98 of 193 votes, a clear majority. This fraudulent system, with no relationship to real power distribution, was typical of the Roman system and the Roman constitution. It inevitably led to an unrealistic legal situation and to political instability because the number of centuries (and thus votes) allotted to each class had no relationship to the real power of that class and did not change as real power changed.

Solon's constitution remained the basis of Athenian political life for generations. The chief change, the growth of the number in each class as people became richer and moved upward from class to class, resulted in a wider participation in political activity without any further legislation. As a result, the income qualification for class membership ceased to be so significant and was, by the late fifth century, simply ignored without ever being abolished. Thus the archonship was opened to the Zeugitai in 457; it was never opened to the Thetes, but they were soon allowed to hold the office without the question of class being raised.

From the time of Solon to the next great internal crisis in Greek history about 450 B.C., the Athenian version of Greek life progressed steadily. The other states of Greece were strung out along the road behind Athens, with a few like Corinth or Syracuse almost as advanced, and some like Thebes or Sparta so far behind that they seemed to be going in the opposite direction, toward narrow provincialism and isolation rather than toward cosmopolitanism and internationalism, moving toward rigidity and personal enslavement rather than toward freedom, toward rigid uniformity rather than to flexibility, variety, pluralism, and inclusive diversity. In 480 when the great challenge to the Greeks came from Persia, Athens and Sparta were still close enough together in their courses to achieve a joint victory of the Greeks over the forces of Asia, but within fifty years, these two leading Greek states had diverged so far apart in their developments that their mutual fear of each other's alien ways of life brought them into the suicidal conflict of the Peloponnesian War (431-404 B.C.).

The outlines of this process which brought Hellas from progress to self-destruction and the role which weapons systems played in it can be seen by following the history of Athens, since this state not only led the vanguard but was most responsible for the tragic outcome.

A generation after Solon, another Athenian, the "tyrant" Pisistratus (561-527), moved the city farther along the road Solon had opened, by economic, social, and intellectual changes. The constitutional and political system was left as Solon had set it up, although Pisistratus undoubtedly saw to it that the constitutional processes brought his supporters to public office and not those of his opponents. The original basis of Pisistratus' power was force, the use of a paid bodyguard authorized by vote of the assembly. Once in power, other methods were used to win wider support, but the ultimate basis of his position was his paid armed retainers, including a force of Scythian archers which protected his residence on the Acropolis. His most vigorous opponents were exiled. State lands were distributed to the poor. Sharecroppers were made landowners. Public credit was advanced to smaller landowners to finance their planting of olive trees, which do not bear fruit to provide an economic return for years. The commercial groups of the coastal area were encouraged to export olive oil and wine and to import grain from the northern Aegean and Black Sea coasts. To protect this route, an Athenian base was established at Sigeum at the entrance to the Hellespont. The power exercised by the nobles through their hereditary priesthoods was reduced by the encouragement of the popular rural cult of Dionysus. A Pan-Ionian movement was encouraged by sponsorship of festivals, games, and religious cults, including the purification of the Ionian religious center on the island of Delos. Scholarship and literary criticism was sponsored by the collection and editorial review of earlier literary works, chiefly Homer's. City dwellers were encouraged to develop craft skills to export products of ceramics or metals, and were given jobs on public works projects, new temples, public buildings, and an assured water supply through an aqueduct from the distant hills. The poor residents of those hills, shepherds, charcoal burners, miners, and subsistence farmers, who had formed the core of Pisistratus' original support, were encouraged to send their products to the city and to enter into the economic and cultural life of the community. He provided rural judges who circuited the country so that these rural poor could defend their interests at law without the need to journey to Athens.

Pisistratus was a success because he based his policies on diversity superimposed on a narrow but dependable foundation of mercenary fighting men. At the same time, while doing something to appease

292

all groups, he kept the agricultural interests
(called "the Plain") and the commercial interests
(known as "the Shore") sufficiently opposed to
each other to allow his own group (the "Hill")
to wield a balance of power. After his death,
this system became unworkable because the opposition of the three groups became disruptive, and
rising prosperity had so increased the number of
weapon holders that continued reliance on a mercenary bodyguard by any tyrant became unfeasible,
and political modification of the Solon constitution in a more democratic direction became necessary.

These new political reforms were the work of
Cleisthenes (508 B.C.), who abolished the political
and military functions of the four old tribes (each
of which provided a regiment to the army), replacing them with 10 new wards based on residence rather than blood. Each of the new wards (still called
"phylai") consisted of a number of precincts (or
demes) which were scattered so that each ward had
demes in all three sections of Attica. This mingling of the interests of the three sections greatly
increased the unity of Athens, especially in the
military and political systems. A similar change
was made in the Heliaea which consisted of 6000
volunteers, 600 from each ward, from which the
individual juries (of 201, 501, or even 1001) were
drawn by lot. A few years later (501 B.C.) each
of the ten regiments was put in command of a "general" (strategos) elected from each new ward.

About this time, Athens began serious efforts
to build a navy to protect its commercial interests
in the Aegean, especially its export of wine, oil,
and metal products to the north in exchange for
grain and also to protect its cultural and other
relations with the Ionians of the Aegean and Asia
Minor (most of whom had been conquered by Persia
and crushed in an unsuccessful revolt in 499-494 B.C.).

The unsuccessful Ionian revolt marked a critical turning point in Greek history since it led to
the confrontation of Asia and Europe, through two
quite different political and cultural systems,
and a test between land power and sea power which
had major future consequences.

Before we examine this confrontation, we must conclude the story of the growth of Athenian democracy.

Athenian democracy did not reach its full growth until the Age of Pericles (461-429), some years after the Greek victory over Persia (480-479). About 488 the practice of ostracism was established to prevent any future tyranny such as that of Pisistratus. Each year the assembly voted to ostracize any citizen regarded as dangerous. Anyone whose name appeared on at least 6000 ballots was sent into exile for ten years, without confiscation of property, but with the death penalty for illegal return to the city. This law gave great power to the assembly. The following year (487) election by lot was established for the archons and later extended to most offices, but never to the strategoi. This was done to give all citizens a chance to serve in office, but one of its results was to make most office holders, except the generals, largely unknown people, leaving leadership in the state to the generals, who remained well-known persons. The first strategos, as commander-in-chief, was elected annually by the whole assembly and became in effect head of the government although his non-military influence rested very largely on his ability to persuade the assembly to accept his policies.

As part of this process, Pericles in 461, when many of the well-to-do hoplites were away in Sparta, supported a law which reduced the powers of the Council of the Areopagus. Later, in 451, he was able to establish payment for service in public office, including the juries. In time almost 20,000 persons, about a tenth of the citizenship, were on the payroll, a financial burden on the state which could be borne only from the spoils of victorious wars. Since the families most favorable to such payment were the same families who served in the navy, the three forces of imperialism, navalism, and democracy became allied in support of aggressive wars which led to the ruin of the Greek world.

The conflict with Persia was not a part of this Greek movement to imperialism but rather a defensive response to Persian pressure. The latter by 500 represented the final phase of the political develop-

294

ment of the archaic civilizations of the Near East.
It was no longer fully archaic since the Persian
state which ruled it, from the Black Sea to the Indian Ocean and from the Mediterranean and Aegean
Seas eastward to India, was a somewhat modernized
superstructure administering an enormous conglomera-
tion of archaic cultures and peoples. The Persians
themselves were a ruling minority which was in full
Iron Age and had been greatly modified by elements
of the sixth century revolution (of ethical monotheism and two-valued logic), and other forces,
including vigorous new Indo-European groups. Over
their motley diversity of subjected peoples the Persians had imposed a much more efficient continental
administrative structure, organized in provinces
(satrapies), tied together by an admirable network
of military roads, and defended by a varied and
complex assortment of Asiatic and northeast African
fighting contingents, the whole completely subordinated to the Persian king and his Persian military supporters, especially his Persian cavalry.

This system was continental. The Persians
had no real interest in the sea nor knowledge of
sea power and were prevented by their customs from
acting on it themselves. As a result, they had to
use their subject peoples, especially the Phoenicians.
But this put limitations on their ability to carry
their expansion across the sea. When, after the
Persian conquest of the Levant in 538 B.C., they
made plans to pursue the Canaanites westward by
attacking Carthage, the Phoenician sailors, on whom
the Persians were dependent to do this, refused to
move. The project had to be cancelled.

By the fifth century, the Athenians were probably the world's best naval fighters. Combat with
the ram on the sea required spirit, skill, and onerous training somewhat similar to that required by
massed hoplites on land. As I have said, the trireme was so unseaworthy that it could not be fought,
and could hardly be kept afloat even with the lowest
level rowing ports closed, in any real seaway. The
exertion of rowing was so great that no crew could
make more than two ramming attacks in any battle.
As we have seen, the effort to make these attacks
effective led to ingenious designs for getting more

295

rowers into the space of 38-40 inches needed for pulling an oar. This ingenuity took two different directions.

The first method for solving this problem was to go upward, as we have seen, but this method reached its limit in the trireme since it was not possible to go up more than three levels without making the upper oars too long to be worked by a single rower. This problem suggested the next step, to have more than one rower pulling on each oar. This second method opened a new era of naval rivalry after 400 B.C.

In a ramming attack, the galley itself was used as a missile. If it hit an enemy ship too hard, it might be buried in its victim's hull and either be pulled down with it or keep it afloat; in either case the attacking vessel would be out of action and might be overwhelmed by its rival's marines swarming aboard to capture the apparently victorious galley or might be captured or sunk by any other enemy ship which happened by. Thus attack by ramming required that the attack be strong enough to shatter the enemy hull at the waterline but not so powerful as to bury its ram in the enemy hull. To prevent this latter, the ram on Athenian galleys were made with two and later three diverging points after 400 B.C. Other Greek navies preferred to avoid the problem by keeping the single-pointed ram and ramming head-on with simultaneous boarding, but this required carrying more marines, a direction in which naval development did go after 400, even to the point of finding space for more marines by curtailing the space for rowers.

The maneuvers in such naval battles became quite complicated and required very great training and skill, whose details need not detain us here. The essence of the problem was to prevent the enemy from getting a shot with the ram at one's own broadside, while obtaining such an opportunity oneself. Since gallays were most vulnerable from the side, it was risky to engage a more numerous fleet whose surplus ships could get into a flanking position. This effort to have more galleys than one's enemy led to races in naval construction in the fifth

century, with efforts to maintain fleets of hundreds
of galleys. This continued through the Hellenistic
period (323-146 B.C.). It was very expensive.

The Athenian effort in the fifth century to
keep its fleet at 200 galleys required a force of
34,000 men and a steady building rate of 20 ships
a year as replacements. So long as men served for
patriotism and glory, the expense could be borne
by numerous states. But in the fourth century,
fighting men were increasingly mercenaries who
fought for anyone who paid. Since service on land
was less onerous and provided chances for looting
and plunder, including shares from shares of war
captives sold into slavery, mercenaries preferred
to serve on land. This made it increasingly difficult to man navies without offering higher pay and
a share in the plunder (which opened the way to
piracy). Another alternative, tried by some states,
was to buy slaves as rowers and promise them freedom if their efforts resulted in victory.

The second method for obtaining more manpower
per "room" or rowing compartment was devised by
Syracuse under the tyrant Dionysus about 400 B.C.
This method involved putting more than one man on
each oar and had the additional advantage that unskilled rowers and skilled ones could be combined
on the same oar, while there was great danger from
any oar in the hands of an unskilled rower working
alone. At first the additional man in each compartment (giving four) was added to the top oar of
the three, since that was farthest from the water
and most difficult to pull. This was called a
quadrireme ("four"). Later men were added to other
oars to give "fives" (quinqueremes), "sixes,"
"sevens."

At this point, during the fourth century a
number of factors acted on each other to revolu-
tionize naval warfare. One of these was the invention, also at Syracuse, and about the same date
(399 B.C.), of what was essentially a crossbow,
followed about sixty years later, in Macedonia
under Philip II, of catapults. Both of these
were invented (or adopted) as accessories to siege
operations, for clearing the walls of a besieged

city so that the attackers could get up to the walls with battering rams or mining equipment or even to drive the defenders from the tops of the walls so they could be stormed. The crossbow was called gastraphetes or "belly bow" because it had to be cocked by placing the stock on the ground and pushing the bow slide downward to the trigger point by leaning on it with one's stomach. It was mentioned by Heron of Alexandria and is believed by E.W. Marsden, the chief authority on the artillery of classical antiquity, to have been powered by a composite bow. In the course of the fourth century, this gastraphetes developed into a weapon able to shoot bolts six feet long and 4.5 inches in circumference, using a bow nine feet long and 3.5 inches thick. Such bolt-shooting artillery was used by Dionysus against the Carthaginians at the siege of Motya in 397 B.C. It had to be fired from a base, which eventually was attached by a universal joint.

The catapult was quite different, powered by the torsion of twisted ropes of hair. Heron says it used "sinew rope," but references to the stores in the arsenal at Athens as early as 350 B.C. speak of hair springs. This innovation soon eclipsed the non-torsion gastraphetes, and after centuries of changes and improvements, culminated in the arrow shooters and stone throwers described in Vitruvius (25 B.C.). Philip of Macedon had arrow shooters at Perinthus in 340 B.C., and his son Alexander the Great had stone throwers at Halicarnassus in 334. Two years later, at the famous siege of Tyre, Alexander had stone throwers strong enough to shake the walls of the city, if we are to believe Diodorus Siculus.

Most mentions of such artillery in ancient writers are in connection with sieges, and there can be no doubt that they were invented and chiefly used in that role. They did, however, have a considerable influence in the development of sea power, by bringing missiles back into naval warfare, and by helping to move the design of vessels toward broader and more stable hulls as sites for catapults. These developments also tended to reduce the great emphasis on speed and maneuverability

298

which had prevailed up to 400 B.C. Once the oars were
given more than one rower each, experiments in multiple
rowers showed that the maximum that could be used on
a single oar was eight, according to Lionel Casson.
But this required such long sweeps that the hulls had
to be widened, thus providing a wider fighting deck
for more marines and soon also for catapults. The
increase in power from multiple rowers on fewer oars
also made it possible to eliminate the lowest level
of rowers and thus get rid of the dangerous open ports
so close to the water. This permitted ships to stay
at sea in somewhat heavier weather.

While these changes were becoming possible,
there were also disputes about naval tactics, with
three different emphases: ramming; boarding; missiles. Probably few participants in this debate, of
which we know very little, embraced one of the three
tactics exclusively, so the debate was probably over
what combination of the three would give victory.
In general, emphasis on naval warfare with missiles
was later and weak, probably because the artillery
used torsion propellants which were so variable under
changing humidity that they were of unpredictable
range and were, for this reason, much less useful
on ships than on land. Moreover, as the projectiles
increased in size, the recoil tended to weaken the
ship and the weight of the catapults topside made
the vessel top-heavy.

In any case, the chief debate down to 323 B.C.
was between rammers and boarders, with a tendency for
supporters of democracy to be favorable to ramming
and supporters of oligarchy favorable to boarding.
The reason for this tendency lies in the fact that
oligarchs put emphasis on the army and regarded the
navy as simply an extension of the army, so that a
naval battle should be reduced, if possible, to a
battle of soldiers on ships, with the rowers there
simply to get the two sides together. The supporters
of democracy, on the other hand, saw the navy as the
chief supporter of democracy and as a service with a
mission of its own, as the chief defender of the
state against both external and internal enemies.
In this view the rowers were citizens and fighters,
not just power units for moving soldiers by water.

299

We can see the influence of this difference of opinion in Athens in the fifth century, when Themistocles, the democrat, made the navy the chief arm of the state's defense, while Kimon (in power from 478 to 461, with a pro-Spartan policy) favored boarding over ramming. When Pericles overthrew Kimon in 461, he turned Athenian policy back from Kimon's pro-army, pro-Spartan, and pro-boarding position to the more democratic, pro-naval, anti-Spartan, and pro-ramming policies which led to the final disaster of 404 B.C. The gradual triumph of oligarchy in the Mediterranean after the Athenian defeat of 404, culminating in the final victory of Rome, had a significant influence on navies and navy tactics. The period between the Athenian defeat and the Roman triumph, including the Hellenistic period from the death of Alexander in 323 to the final defeat of the Greeks by Rome in 146 B.C., was a period of naval extremism and aberration. Although it runs into the chronological limits of the next chapter, we should complete the story of navy history at this point.

The "fours," "fives," and "sixes" which were developed from 399 to 315 B.C. generally put one more rower on each oar, beginning with the top oar and moving downward; thus the "six" was a trireme with two men on each oar. By 315 the great empire of Alexander the Great had been divided among three of Alexander's generals, Antigonus in Europe, Seleucus in Iraq and the east, and Ptolemy in Egypt. These three, and a few lesser generals with smaller areas, fought to re-conquer all of Alexander's empire. The chief areas of struggle were Anatolia and the Syrian Saddle and, above all, Syria itself with the whole Levant. A considerable part of this struggle took place on the sea, since control of the Aegean and of the eastern Mediterranean was an important factor in extending power over the whole Near East, which was the real issue. The Athenian fleet was wiped out forever after its defeat by the Macedonians at Amorgos in 322 B.C., leaving control of the sea in the east to the three great kingdoms, while Syracuse, Carthage, Rome and others fought in the west. Here we are concerned only with the struggle in the east.

From 315 to 288 ships increased in size and

power, going from "sixes" to a "sixteen"; from about
280 to the death of Ptolemy IV in 203, the rivalry
on the sea produced "twenties," "thirties," and even
a "forty," although this last was for display only.
In this period, as I have indicated, ramming was replaced by boarding and increased use of catapults,
with speed sacrificed to size, height above the water
(to prevent boarding), and deck space for marines.
The oarage of these superships has been much disputed, but now seems to have been settled, in general
terms if not in specific cases for any single ship.
It was not feasible to go higher than three banks of
oars or to put more than eight men on a single oar
or sweep; in fact there were drawbacks to using the
lowest level of three banks or using more than about
six men on an oar. Even with six men, the rowers
could not remain seated, but had to rise from the
bench to push their oar forward, then pull it by
falling backward on the bench for the power stroke.

Under these conditions, the largest ship could
be, in theory, no larger than a "twenty-four" (that
is 8 men on each of three oars in a "room"), but in
fact it is doubtful if this method ever went higher
than a "sixteen," on either two or three oars (probably the former with two 8-man oars). Casson offers
good arguments that anything larger than a "sixteen"
was probably a double-hull vessel, really two ships
fastened together at a sufficient distance so that
rowers could work on both sides of both hulls,
parallel to each other, with the space between
covered over to be a wide fighting deck for marines
and catapults. The specific information we have
about Ptolemy IV's "forty" seems to allow no other
explanation since this giant had four steering oars
45 feet long, had 57-foot oars on its upper (third)
level, with a total of 4000 rowers, 2850 marines,
and 400 other deck personnel. The information is
from Athenaeus and tells us that it was double-
prowed and double-sterned, and had seven rams; it
was 420 feet long, with beam of 57 feet, its bow
72 feet above the waterline, but drawing only 6
feet. It seems likely that each "room" had 20 rowers on three oars, probably arranged with eight on
the top, seven on the middle, and five on the lowest
oar, with fifty such rooms holding a total of 1000
rowers on each of the four sides.

As I have indicated, this monster was never used
in combat and was built only for display. These
large ships were used for no more than a century,
from the beginning of the naval building race in 315
to the late years of Ptolemy IV, who died in 203.
In 306 Demetrius the Besieger, son of Antigonus I,
defeated Ptolemy I in a battle off Salamis on Cyprus; the victorious fleet had 10 "sixes" and 7
"sevens," while the Egyptian king had nothing larger than "fives." The fortunes of battle were reversed in 280, when the Ptolemaic navy, led by a
new type of "eight" (probably a double-hull vessel
with 1600 rowers and 1200 marines, the former distributed with two banks of 4-man oars in each of
50 "rooms" on each of the four sides of two hulls)
destroyed the fleet of Antigonus II, in spite of the
fact that the latter had a "fifteen" and a "sixteen."
The results of the encounter of 280 were reversed
once again, off Cos in 258, when Antigonus, with a
new fleet, totally defeated Ptolemy II. But it
was not possible for the Antigonids, with the
limited resources of the Aegean area, to outbuild
the possessors of the endless wealth of alluvial
Egypt. Before his death in 246, Ptolemy II had
in his fleet 23 ships larger than "tens" including a "twenty" and 2 "thirties." But the futility
of such giant vessels was already becoming evident
before Ptolemy IV built his "forty" toward the end
of the third century. By the end of that century
two weaknesses of the giant galleys had appeared.

The first of these weaknesses was that even
the most decisive victory on the sea had little
meaning unless it could be followed up by an invasion by land forces. This proved to be impossible, since every time it was attempted, these
land forces were defeated by the defender's army
despite the latter's earlier defeat on the sea.
The fact was that neither naval nor maritime
shipping at that time could sustain an amphibious
operation from the sea, since it could not transport or supply a sufficiently large military force
to retain control of a distant kingdom, especially
when activity on the sea was interrupted from mid-
October to mid-April. Even as late as A.D. 380,
the Theodosian Code provided a closed season for
navigation between those dates.

A second reason for the abandonment of the super-galleys was that they could not control small vessels, as the pirates discovered in this same century. Pirate vessels, built for speed and, unlike the earlier triremes, prepared to sacrifice some rowing space for more adequate sail handling, could not be caught by the large galleys, either by sailing or rowing, and did not stay around to be overwhelmed by the great galley's superior armaments. Such pirate craft operated with relative impunity out of the coves and islands of Dalmatia and southern Anatolia in the Hellenistic period until Rhodes, more concerned with commerce than with politics, adopted a semi-trireme, with three levels of rowers on only part of the hull, the rest of the space being used for marines and sail handling. Like the pirates, these vessels used both oars and sails to overtake a slower vessel, attacked with missiles, and then ran alongside for boarding. About 190, Rhodes added to its missile arms firepots, the earliest forerunner of Greek fire which became the chief naval weapon of Byzantium in the Islamic period.

Most pirate vessels of the third century were rowed with from sixteen to fifty oars on one or two levels. By the end of that century, various states led by Macedonia began to add naval versions of these vessels, called lemboi. These provided valuable support even to a navy which had a battle line of heavy galleys, performing a role on the sea similar to that which the light-armed infantry or peltasts performed for the heavy-armed hoplites in land fighting. As Casson says, "The combat lembos would dart in among the enemy's heavier units to break up their formations, interrupt their tactics, even do damage to their oars." As the super-galleys disappeared after 200 B.C., the role of these light vessels as support for the battle line of "sixes" or "tens" was assured.

As we shall see when we come to the rise of Rome in the western Mediterranean, similar developments took place in that area without ever going into the extravagances of the eastern experience with the super-galleys. The Romans defeated Carthage on the sea in the Punic Wars (264-241; 218-201) with quinqueremes, many of them on only one

level, with 27 five-man oars on each side, 270 rowers
in all. These were eventually supplemented by a
modified type of _lembos_ known as a liburnian, a two-
banked craft copied from a pirate vessel of Dalmatia.

The Romans were always landlubbers. Their merchant marine very quickly fell into the hands of
Greeks, Syrians, and other easterners. The fighting navy was similar, with marine vocabulary largely
Greek and all except the top commands held by non-
Latins and even non-Italians. Roman commanders had
little conception of naval strategy or of control of
the sea; they destroyed all the little navies, such
as that of Rhodes, and put almost nothing in their
place. This was done by imposing treaties on various defeated states, restricting them to a few ships
of designated size, and even forbidding them to have
any naval vessels, as was done to Rhodes in 42 B.C.
This policy allowed piracy to flourish in the republican period, a condition which was tacitly encouraged by the landed oligarchy of Rome because it became a chief source of slaves and kept the price of
slaves down by keeping the supply up. Only in 68
B.C., when the pirates were raiding at Ostia, the
port of Rome, and had intercepted the grain ships
coming from Egypt, did the Assembly take the problem from the hands of the Senate and grant Pompey
semi-dictatorial powers over the coasts of the
Mediterranean with a fleet of 270 ships to sweep
the seas. In this, as in all its activities on the
sea, Romans continued to believe that the sea could
only be controlled by controlling the shores and
the seaports. In view of the nature of marine technology at the time, there was of course considerable
truth in this view.

As Rome conquered all the shores of the Middle
Sea, from the Punic Wars to the final victory of
Augustus over Mark Antony and Cleopatra at Actium
in 31 B.C., it continued the practice of using a
battle line of relatively small galleys, mostly
"fives," supplemented by a large number of liburnians,
used like modern navies have used destroyers. At
Actium, which was not really a naval battle at all,
but an attempt by Antony and Cleopatra to escape
from the harbor of Actium, where they were blockaded
by Augustus and Agrippa, an attempt which was only partly

successful. Antony's support simply disintegrated. Mark Antony's flagship was a "ten," which rose only ten feet above the water and probably had a single bank of oars with ten rowers on each sweep. Augustus' fleet, which considerably outnumbered the rival force, had nothing larger than a "six," and this remained the largest vessel in the fleet for the whole subsequent imperial period, usually with only one ship of that size, the flagship at the naval base of Misenum near Naples; most of the fleet were triremes.

The shifts in naval warfare which we have traced here, followed on a parallel path the shifts in land warfare, especially in the period covered by this chapter. That path shows a sequence from a small group of professionals to a larger group of citizen fighters, followed by a return to specialists who served as mercenaries. In a similar way in which the naval forces moved to specialized heavy galleys, ground forces also concentrated for a brief period on heavy, armored infantry, the hoplites, but later, with the adoption of new supplementary arms and tactics including missiles, became more flexible with much greater use of specialized units. The period of the dominance of citizen soldiers on land and of citizen rowers on the sea was no more than 150 years, from before the Persian Wars of 492-479 to the death of Alexander in 323 in the east, with a comparable period in the west from about 300 to 100 B.C. We must now return to examine this period in the Greek world.

5.   Citizen Soldiers: the Age of Democracy, 500-323 B.C.

The period of the citizen soldier and the citizen rower among the Greeks began with the victory over Persia in the wars which followed the Persian suppression of the revolt of the Ionian Greeks in 499-494 B.C. The history of this conflict and the tactical details of the battles need not detain us.

The chief significance of the Persian defeat was that the frontier line between the last and greatest of the archaic empires of western Asia and the newly rising classical civilization was

305

established clearly for all to see, although largely
unnoticed was the continued existence of a third
cultural entity, Canaanite civilization, bridging
that frontier across the southern Mediterranean
from Phoenicia to Carthage and onward to Spain and
Morocco. The Persian efforts to extend their power
to Europe were in vain, a fact already clearly
shown by the defeat inflicted on Darius by the
Scythians north of the Danube in 513 B.C. The
three subsequent expeditions to conquer the Greeks,
in 492, 490, and 480 B.C., also failed in a series
of land battles and Greek naval victories. These
engagements showed that, in quality of men, equipment, and tactical skills, Greek soldiers and sailors were outstanding. In both cases it was clear
that the chief danger came from larger forces which
could envelop their formations to strike at their
flanks and rear, where they were relatively vulnerable. To prevent this and overcome the Greek weakness of limited numbers, both services made use of
natural obstacles, armies buttressing their flanks
on hills, water courses, or other obstacles, while
naval leaders did the same to their fleets by placing their lines of ships, in frontal formation, between islands or headlands.

On land the need to avoid attack on the flanks
or rear meant that the battle had to be restricted
to level ground, a requirement which was even more
true with the phalanx in the following century.
Moreover, this need was even greater in defense
against cavalry. The Greeks won at Marathon in
490 when the Persian cavalry was unaccountably absent from the field. Miltiades stretched his line
as wide as the Persian front and greatly weakened
his center in order to reinforce his wings. The
Persian arrows were reduced in effectiveness by
the speed of the Greek charge. When the Persians
broke the Greek center and began to pour through
that opening, the two heavy Greek wings came down
on the Persian rear. The Greek armor and longer
spear were far superior to the Persian equipment
of bow, shorter spear, wicker shield, and quilted
body tunic.

At Thermopylae in 480 the Greeks once again
eliminated the Persian cavalry by the narrowness

306

of the passageway in which only a small number of
the Persian host could get at the Greek line. There
the superior weapons and spirit of the Greeks held
up the Persian advance for two days until a Greek
traitor revealed an alternative route which allowed
the enemy to get around to attack the Greeks from
the rear.

The naval victory at Salamis was won by Themistocles' skill in forcing the great Persian fleet to
fight in the narrow coves between the island of
Salamis and the mainland (480 B.C.). And at Plataea
the following summer, the Greeks, without cavalry,
defeated the pick of the Persian forces in a confused battle after the Persian commander had been
slain.

The citizen soldiers' characteristic of high
quality but limited numbers was accompanied by limited range, partly from inadequate supply services but
chiefly from the fact that citizens were expected to
return to their normal occupations after relatively
brief campaigns. This limitation on range was really
a limitation on time, something which could be reme-
died easily by mercenary soldiers who had no other
livelihood but to campaign. This is the chief reason for the briefness of the periods in which citizen
soldiers have been dominant in history, and thus, indirectly, is also the reason why democracy, which is
so closely associated with citizen soldiers but wilts
so quickly in the presence of mercenary forces, has
had such brief periods in the historical record.

The range over which citizen soldiers could
operate in the Greek world of 450 B.C. may have been
limited, but it was far wider than the areas over
which the jurisdictions of Greek city-states were
exercised. This is one of the chief reasons for
the chronic political instability and constant warfare among the Greek states: at a time when an army
of hoplites could range over hundreds of miles and
win battles, the political units of Greece were
still only dozens or scores of miles across. The
critical problem of the crisis of the fifth century
in Greece was how the Greeks could get political
units more comparable in size to the areas over
which each unit could apply organized force. This

307

problem was never solved by the Greeks, as it has not been solved by the European states in modern times, with the consequence that the Greek city-state became obsolete as a form of political organization and was eclipsed (and conquered) by autocratic kingdoms and ultimately by Rome.

This political problem, which became acute by about 450, was accompanied by a number of other problems, the whole bundle making up "the fifth century crisis."

Of these other problems, two must be mentioned, although we have no time to discuss them. One was that the Greek socioeconomic pattern of organization, based on slavery, was as obsolete as the military-political pattern based on the city-state. The slave system, as we have said, fulfilled a needed role in capital accumulation in the early centuries of classical civilization, but it was increasingly ineffective in technological innovation and was in-efficient, from any point of view, in terms of out-put of goods in respect to input of energy. It con-tinued to work in terms of extensive exploitation of resources (such as area of land under cultivation) and was of value, in some cases, in craft output of luxury items for a small market (such as copying Plato's "Dialogues" or Homer's epics for leisured slaveowners), but it was increasingly deficient in any intensive utilization of resources (such as in-creased agricultural output per acre) as can be seen from the drastic falling off in the effectiveness of land usage in places like Sicily and Tunis under the Romans in comparison with what they had been under the native peoples before 200 B.C. Most notably, of course, the slave system by 450 B.C. was obsolete in terms of its ability to maintain the supply of slaves. By that date among the Greeks, the supply of slaves, like the pressing need for increased land under con-ditions of extensive exploitation, meant that more and more free men had to be diverted from any produc-tive economic activities to warfare, not only to keep up the supply of slaves but to lower the population of free men in a vain effort to increase the supply of land, and also because of the equally vain effort to find political security under the obsolescent city-state system.

As a consequence of this socioeconomic crisis, every war between states, after 450, tended to take on elements of a class struggle within the contending states. In this struggle, the supporters of oligarchy wanted largely self-sufficient agricultural economies, resting on an army of well-to-do hoplites, with political activity restricted to the propertied groups, and the whole welded together by traditional ideas and social customs. Generally Sparta (or even Persia) and later Rome were the models of this point of view. On the other side were those who supported a more open, more diverse, and more democratic society, based on an economy containing large elements of urban manufacturing, commercial interchange, and cosmopolitan outlook defended by a navy, with the propertyless citizen a full participant in the defense of the city and in its political and community life. Generally Athens was the model of this point of view.

The Peloponnesian Wars between Athens and Sparta were a direct collision between these two systems of values and two ways of life and were not simply conflicts between two alliances of similar states. In these terms it was a civil war as fully as it was an international conflict, with group against group and class against class within each belligerent state. When Sparta conquered a city, the latter's government and social life were remodeled in an oligarchic direction; when Athens took over a defeated state its way of life was changed in a more democratic direction. In most cases opposition groups were murdered wholesale or driven into exile. By 410 B.C. most political decisions were based on this class struggle at least as much as on considerations of military strategy. The oligarchic supporters in Athens were fully prepared to betray the city to Sparta, and to liquidate their own lower classes in order to retain control of the city's policies. The lower classes, in turn, were prepared to expel or expropriate the propertied groups if they were not allowed to direct the city's policies in directions advantageous to themselves.

We have no space to illustrate the violence and horrors of these domestic civil conflicts, which form a significant element in the whole situation from 450

B.C. on. Those who are interested may read Thucydides'
vivid account of such a struggle in Corcyra in 427.
In Sparta this conflict took the form of systematic
chronic murder of outstanding helots and the episodic
slaughter of many thousands of them. Although this
element in the situation has been played down by
classicists and by most historians, it was a major
factor in the historical development of the period.

The intellectual crisis is equally important
and even more complex, but despite its importance,
will be mentioned only briefly.

We have already indicated the great contribution
to intellectual history made by the Greco-Iranian invention of two-valued logic in the sixth century
revolution. As we have said, one of the chief elements in that invention was the use of categories
as fixed elements in the thinking process. Such
categories are indicated by collective terms as
"Man," "Greek," "Slave," "Dog." In the fifth century, violent controversy arose over the question
whether these categories (or universals) were "real"
or not. That is, did these categories really exist
in the objective world, or were they simply conveniences of human thought and communication; existing
only as subjective classifications or only as words
which we apply to quite distinct individual cases?

By the end of the fifth century, this intellectual discussion had become a violent controversy
between the "philosophic realists" (who said that
universals were real entities), such as the Pythagorean rationalists, and the "philosophic nominalists"
(who said that universals were simply names conventionally applied, often arbitrarily, to real and
changeable individual cases), such as the Sophists.

These debates may seem very abstruse and of
no consequence to us today, but in fact they were
intimately related to the other two aspects of the
crisis of the fifth century. According to the
philosophic realists, a "noble" or a "slave" was
not simply a person who was conventionally regarded
or called "noble" or "slave" by those who knew him;
in each case he was a person who had a real quality
of "nobility" or of "slavishness" in him so that he

310

was different <u>in fact</u> (not just in theory) from other men who were not nobles or slaves. This means that such terms refer to real biologically inheritable differences between men. If this is so, it is futile to make laws saying that other men should be equal to nobles or that slaves should be freed because they are really the same as other men.

From this point of view, a philosophic realist like Plato not only regarded the democratic reforms which took away the privileges of the nobility as misguided and evil, but he would look with disfavor on a noble's marriage below his social class and would reject with horror any suggestion that slaves or ordinary working men were just as good as the finest patricians in Greece.

Not many persons were suggesting in Plato's day or even later that slavery should be abolished, but many Sophists and other philosophic nominalists insisted that such social classifications were merely conventional and not natural. In fact, the big intellectual dispute of the late fifth century was based on the distinction between nature and convention, debating which social conditions fell under each of these headings. The defenders of inequality, whether they favored the declining nobility or the rising oligarchy, favored the philosophic realist position which belittled democracy by regarding social distinctions as real and natural, while the democrats and, in later generations, those who wished to extend democracy to include equalization of economic advantages as well, supported these beliefs by Sophist arguments that men were, by nature, equal, and that social and economic inequalities were conventional (and thus unnatural) and thus quite capable of being changed by legislation in the assembly.

The intellectual crisis and the social-economic crisis interlinked with the political crisis, but we must now turn our attention back to the last of these.

Essentially this political problem was: how could the city-states be replaced by a larger political structure more in harmony with the structure of power as it existed in the late fifth century.

At that time, the ability to apply power more intensively and over larger areas had been increasing for
about five centuries. Over that period, either by
consent or by force, the narrow and less intensive
power units of 900 B.C. had been replaced by the
larger and more intense ones of 500 B.C. The process was still going on, but not nearly fast enough
to alleviate the political crisis arising from the
obsolescence of the city-state. We have already
spoken of some early examples, perhaps some of them
voluntary, as in the case of Sparta where five villages came together to form one state. As late as
471, numerous small communities in Elis coalesced
to form a centralized state with a democratic form
of government. Cases of fusion based on force were
even more frequent and continued, as the history of
Rome shows. But the real problem was how to achieve
such fusion by consent rather than by force.

After the Persian Wars, when this problem became increasingly acute, most efforts at fusion
were motivated by the needs of defense and resulted
in leagues of various kinds. Of these leagues or
alliances the most famous were those formed by Sparta
or by Athens, but there were numerous others. The
communities of Phocis in central Greece formed a
league with a federal army and its own federal coinage in the sixth century as protection against Thessaly to the north and to Boeotia to the east. Boeotia itself was a similar federal league organized
about Thebes; it issued its own coinage before 550
B.C. The Greek alliance against Persia in 481 B.C.
was such an alliance: each state had one vote with
decisions based on majority rule; it met at Corinth
to agree on strategy, to appoint commanders on land
and sea, to fix contributions in men and money, and
to try and punish traitors. This council gave the
supreme command, both on land and sea, to Sparta.
The Spartan general gave orders to each state's contingent which was under a single commander (with
suspension of such usual features as multiple commands or periodic rotation of commanders). The
Spartan leader met with his contingent commanders
in council of war, but he alone gave orders.

Organizations similar to this were established
on numerous occasions among the Greeks, so that the

military history of Greece from 481 onward was really
the history of clashing leagues until the final reorganization of Greece into a Roman province after
146 B.C.

Such leagues contributed nothing to the solution
of the Greek political problem. In fact they did not
even contribute in any substantial way to defense, so
that small states which abstained from joining leagues
(like Megara in much of the fourth century) did about
as well in obtaining security as those which did join.
Even members of victorious leagues found their security endangered as the leading state of the league invariably became tyrannical to the other members.

It has often been said that the Greeks failed
to get larger political units, and especially a single
unit for most Greeks, because they failed to invent
the technique of political representation which would
have made it possible to make a union which could
have avoided exploitation of weaker members by the
strongest. This argument seems to be in error on
both accounts. The Greeks did know and often used
political representation, most notably in the council of the Greeks set up by Philip of Macedon after
his victory at Charonaea in 338. This federal union,
called "The Greeks," included all mainland states
south of Olympus, except Sparta. It had all the elements necessary to establish the foundation for a
unified state of the Greeks, except the most vital
one: a common loyalty. Its members agreed to observe a general peace; to use military sanctions
in collective security against any violator of the
peace; to respect the freedom and autonomy of each
member state under its existing constitution, which
could be changed only by constitutional process;
to suppress brigandage and piracy; to stop the practice of execution of domestic political rivals, the
political redistribution of landed property, and
other violent manifestations of class antagonism.
The governing body "The Council of the Greeks" was
made up of delegates from each member state in proportion to its military and naval strength.

This organizational form was far from perfect,
and it came too late by far, after Greek independence
had been lost by the Macedonian conquest. In many

ways its provisions sound like Geneva under the
League of Nations in 1927: well-intentioned, unrealistic, too little and too late, and above all,
not supported by any widespread, sustained political allegiance.

This last point is the key to the problem:
peoples' minds were not prepared to give their
allegiance to a political unit larger than the
polis. As a result, all such larger units were
temporary and fluctuating entities, utilized to
meet a temporary problem of security but not a
permanent vehicle of security because they were
not a permanent vehicle of allegiance. As a result,
such allegiance could be obtained only under the
duress of force sustained long enough to make it
clear that there was no alternative vehicle of
security available or likely to be.

Here again we find a situation where the experts, in this case the classicists and political
scientists, have not been helpful. The entity to
which the Greeks gave their allegiance in succession to kinship groups was called the polis. This
is an untranslatable term which is usually translated "city-state." But "city-state" sounds like
a political entity. The polis was far more than
this; it was, like the kinship group it replaced,
a social entity which was capable of absorbing and
expressing most of a man's social actions and social needs. It was, for example, a religious entity
at least as much as it was a political one. It was
an economic and an educational entity as well, even
if to a somewhat lesser degree. It was regarded,
at least to the time of the Sophists, as a natural
entity, and later, when the distinction between
natural and conventional became established, many
thinkers continued to believe that the polis was
natural to the Greeks, as lesser entities like
tribes were natural to barbarians. By "natural"
here we mean a biologically inherited proclivity.

The key to this situation lies in the fact
that we, as a consequence of the historical experience of the later Dark Ages of A.D. 900, in which
there was no longer any state in western Europe,
make a distinction between "state" and "society."

To us a "society" is necessary to the development of those qualities, such as speech and rationality, which we regard as human, while a "state" is simply a convenient form of organization which we adopt for certain specific political purposes, notably security. In writing of society some thinkers speak of "the cake of custom." If we accept this metaphor, we might regard the state as frosting or icing on the "cake of custom." As such, that frosting can be made as wide or deep as seems necessary for the political purposes at hand. Or it may be omitted entirely as occurred in western Europe about A.D. 900 (or in the Greek world about 900 B.C.). In any case, the state to us is never an entity in which man finds satisfaction of the total of his human needs. Even those who in recent times are explicitly upholding the doctrine of a "totalitarian state" hardly go that far.

But in Greece, even a century after the polis was clearly obsolete and no longer capable of satisfying the need for security, it continued to be defended, by the greatest thinkers, as the all-inclusive and essential social unit, not as a political form for specifically political ends. To Aristotle, about 350 B.C., the polis was a koinonia, a community. It was not only social and almost total; it was also natural and it was organic, in the same sense that a living body is organic. That is why Aristotle says that no man can live outside the polis; if he does, he is not a man but must be either an animal or a god. And that is why Aristotle says that a man cut off from the polis is no longer a man, just as a thumb cut off from a hand is no longer a thumb; it just looks like a thumb. If we repeat these statements using the word "state" in place of polis, they seem to us repugnant or even nonsensical, but if we repeat them using the word "society" for the word "polis" they seem to have some merit.

These ideas were not just Aristotle's personal opinions. They may have been out of date in 340 B.C., but at an earlier date they were assumed by all dwellers in the polis to be so obvious as to require no proof. The idea that society is an organism is certainly untrue, and the idea that the state is an organism is one of the most pernicious doctrines

315

ever embraced by large numbers of men (as it has been embraced, at various times, most notably by fascist and proto-fascist thinkers of the past eighty years). But to the readers of Plato's Republic it required no defense or explanation when Socrates assumed, without discussion, that the polis was an organism and, accordingly, that he could find the nature of justice in a man more easily by looking at the polis where the same quality appeared in the same way, merely written in larger letters (Republic, Book II). In fact, one of the chief points of Plato's Republic was to advocate the merits of a closed polis by assuming that it was an organic body whose members have the same relationship to each other and to the whole as the parts of any organism do. That relationship includes (1) non-interchangeability of parts and (2) subordination of the parts to the whole. This combination, according to Plato, was justice and was justifiable on the philosophic realist assumption that all apparent differences are real differences and that all real differences among men are inheritable. These beliefs explain why Plato was the first explicit eugenicist.

In Socrates' day (469-399) these ideas were assumed, and probably discussed, by ordinary citizens of the polis gathered in the agora, which was the school of the polis. At Aristotle's death, a century later (384-322), these erroneous ideas had been partly dispelled by the Sophists' nominalist approach to current problems. But the writings of the Sophists were soon largely eclipsed by the reactionary theories of Plato, Xenophon, and Aristotle. By 323 B.C. the ordinary citizen of the polis may not have been discussing these general theories about human society, but his everyday experience showed him that the interpersonal relationships, both emotional and intellectual, which made life as a human being possible came to him inside the boundaries of the polis. From his daily experience of action, talk, love, fears, and the satisfaction of basic needs, he drew the same conclusion which the greatest thinkers derived from their theories: that the polis is made up of the intimate interpersonal relationships of those who meet each other face to face. This is why Plato and Aristotle agreed that the polis cannot contain more than a few thousand people.

To be sure, ordinary Greeks, and the great thinkers as well, saw other possible allegiances: to their
own families, as personified in the familial deities
and the personal religion of Demeter and Dionysus,
on a lower level; and to all the Greeks, as personified in the Olympian deities and honored at the Hel-
lenic and Olympic games and at the great oracles.
By 323 an even higher allegiance was beginning to
appear as a consequence of the sixth century revolution and the practical teachings of Alexander the
Great. This was the idea of the brotherhood of all
men, personified in the concept of a single, high
god above all lesser spirits.

These levels of allegiance and piety existed,
in varying degrees of intensity, for all Greeks,
but neither the brotherhood of mankind nor the community of all Greeks was sufficiently close to everyday experience to justify a political community to
embody it. Such a larger political community could
come only when people became able, emotionally as
well as intellectually, to separate social life
from political action and carry on the everyday
concrete experience of the former in a local community whose security was assured by the existence
of a higher, more remote and more impersonal community, the territorial state. It was so difficult
to make this adjustment of outlook and feelings that
it could not be done in classical civilization except
after centuries of bloody conflict and generations of
enforced living under such a larger political entity
to make people recognize, in spite of themselves,
that security was obtainable, without face-to-face
contact and apart from all social experience, in
such a situation. It was never completely successful, in classical times, partly because most of the
intellectuals, and all of the authorities, could
not bring themselves to accept such a dualistic
situation, with its divorce of public life and private life, but chiefly because the ordinary man
could not adjust in this direction. Classical civilization really never found a solution to this problem and, after A.D. 200 began to collapse in a chaos
in which the state was seeking a more total and more
personal allegiance by requiring that all citizens
sacrifice to the Emperor and, at the same time,
increasing numbers of persons were finding religious

317

solace and community social satisfactions in joint
devotions to non-classical deities (including Mithra,
Isis, Epicurus, and Christ), leaving little surplus
allegiance for the state. And to complete the collapse of the classical system, at that very moment,
after A.D. 200, the political and military system of
Rome revealed its inability to provide either security
or slaves by winning battles. The mid-fifth century
B.C. was the turning point in this process because
of its three-part failure to find any acceptable solutions to its socioeconomic, intellectual, or politico-
military problems.

The solution which it did find was intensification of internecine warfare ameliorated by imperialism. In these struggles the basic principles of
balance of power were worked out, as I have described
them:

1. Adjacent political units are potential
   enemies;

2. Always have an ally on the rear or flank
   of any potential enemy;

3. No one power supreme in Hellas.

The chaos resulting from the application of
these principles was increased at that time when
(a) political units tended to be alliances, associations, and leagues; and (b) offensive power,
tending toward larger entities, was increasing.

These political rivalries became so violent in
the Greek world and the compensating feeling for the
unity of Hellas became so weak that many political
entities made common cause against their fellow
Greeks with outside, non-Hellenic powers such as
Persia, Carthage, and Rome. Thebans, Locrians,
and others fought alongside the Persians at Plataea
in 479. The Spartan alliance was victorious over
the Athenian empire in the Peloponnesian War in
404 largely by naval victories in which a major
portion of the costs were borne by Persia. This
was assured by the Spartan-Persian alliance of 411.
At that time, according to N.G.L. Hammond (1967:402),
"Athens and Sparta now realized that whoever dis-

posed of Persian money and the Phoenician fleet would win the war." The price of this alliance was that Sparta gave Persia a free hand over the Greek states of Asia Minor. This kind of betrayal of the very persons who must join together to form a political structure larger than the polis or the ineffective federal league continued as a major factor in political existence down to the Roman conquest. In fact the Roman conquest, in Greece as elsewhere in the Mediterranean, was made possible by this situation.

Two other symptoms of this deficiency of solidarity of feeling on a territorial, linguistic, or religious basis are evident. One, which we can only mention, is the constant stream of Greeks who were either traitors to their own states or who left them to take service, or at least residence, in other, often non-Greek communities. The list of these would include a major portion of the great names of Greek history.

A second symptom of this deficiency of solidarity, or even of any conception of political allegiance as we understand this quality, can be seen in the efforts of Alexander, supported by the Greeks, to create a universal, world state; in the efforts of Alexander's successors to create kingdoms as wide as possible over diverse peoples without regard to personal allegiance of the great mass of their subjects; and, indeed, in the methods and achievement of Rome. In all these cases, personal allegiance and loyalty were neglected (except in purely formalistic and symbolic religious ritual), and these political structures were reared on a combination of submission to superior force and material self-interest of the subjects. This combination of "the stick and the carrot" may work in moving a donkey, but it is not an effective method of government despite the fact that it functioned for centuries in the Mediterranean basin.

The period of Greek history following the victory of Sparta and her allies over Athens and her allies, down to the final Roman conquest in 146 B.C., may be divided into four parts: (1) the period of Spartan dominance from 404 B.C. to the Theban victory at Leuctra in 371; (2) the period of Theban

319

dominance from 371 to the Macedonian victory at
Charonaea in 338; (3) the rise and world conquests
of Philip II and Alexander the Great from 359 to
323; and (4) the Hellenistic period of internecine
warfare from the death of Alexander in 323 to the
Roman sack of Corinth in 146 B.C.

The first two of these periods, 404-338, show
the almost total political bankruptcy of the Greeks.
In 404 and again in 371 military victory went to
the two states in which this quality of political
bankruptcy was most assured. Sparta in 404 hardly
knew what to do with its victory. It wanted an
oligarchic system rather than a democratic one,
not on economic and social grounds but simply because it regarded a democratic system, probably
correctly, as more aggressive and unpredictable.
But it had no real idea of how to ensure this and
was not even prepared to use its army of occupation
to sustain the oligarchic groups in Athens against
their more powerful democratic enemies. Accordingly,
the Spartan attitude was indecisive, giving their
commanders on the spot no real guidance, with the
consequence that the Spartan support of the oligarchs was intermittent and eventually dwindled
away.

Even the peace treaty of 404 was indecisive.
Sparta's allies, led by Corinth and Thebes, wanted
andrapodismos, that is massacre of all Athenian
adult males and enslavement of the women and children. This was an established Greek political technique, but Sparta vetoed it, partly from respect for
Athens' past contributions to the Greeks, notably in
the war with Persia, but also because more slaves
was one thing Sparta did not need (the Spartiate
hoplites decreased from about 8000 in 479 to about
1000 in 371 while the helots and perioeci both increased to a total of over 300,000). Instead,
Sparta imposed payment of her war debts to Persia
on Athens and Eleusis, forced Athens to give up all
her empire (whose Aegean states became tribute-pay-
ers to Sparta, but not to Sparta's allies), took
the whole Athenian navy except twelve vessels, destroyed the Long Walls and the fortifications of
the Piraeus (which together had made it possible
for Athens to withstand any siege so long as its

fleet could protect its grain route to the Hellespont),
forced Athens to recall all exiles and to promise obedience to Sparta in matters of foreign policy.

The two notable things about this peace of 404
were that it contributed nothing to the solution of
the political problems of Greece and that its specific terms gave everything to Sparta and nothing
to Sparta's allies who had made substantial contributions to the final victory.

The Spartan generals stood by (or in Lysander's
case cooperated) while the oligarchs in the defeated
cities massacred their democratic opponents by the
thousands (6000 at Miletus, 1500 at Athens) and drove
even larger numbers into exile, but within a few
years they allowed the democrats to recapture control, or at least regain substantial influence, in
the defeated states.

As early as 403, Thebes, Corinth, and Megara
were voting against Sparta's policies in the council
of the Spartan alliance, but Sparta went ahead with
its projects. It attacked Elis in 399 for refusal
to obey its orders and in the same year was at war
with Persia over the Ionian cities, where Sparta
had given Persia a free hand in the alliance of 411.
In the early Sparta-Persian naval actions of this
new war, the Persian fleet consisted largely of Greek
mercenary rowers and was commanded by Conon, the
chief Athenian admiral of 407-404. Ten years after
the Spartan victory of 404, Conon, with this Persian
fleet, annihilated the Spartan fleet off Cnidos
(394). Conon then returned in triumph to Athens,
used his Greek and non-Greek seamen to rebuild the
Long Walls, and launched Athens anew on an independent foreign policy (391). Even earlier in 395 Athens
made a defensive alliance "for all time" with the
Boeotian League (Thebes) and with Locris, and was
cooperating with Corinth, Argos, and others on an
anti-Spartan policy. The two armies came face to
face at Coronea in August 394, where the Spartan
king, who knew of the defeat of the Spartan fleet
at Cnidos but did not tell his associates, conclu-
sively defeated the opposing allies.

Struggles of this kind continued with no final

solution or even any attempt by anyone to deal with the problems facing the Greeks. In many cases, the civil wars between states marched along with the inter-state conflicts. In the struggle just mentioned, Corinth was split completely in two, with the oligarchs supporting Sparta and the democrats opposing. When the latter suspected the former of treasonable relations with Sparta in 392, they murdered 120 of them during a sacred festival and then merged with Argos through establishment of isopolity (dual citizenship). The oligarchs then reacted by betraying the Corinthian Long Walls to Sparta, fled from the city, and fought with the Spartans elsewhere. Argos then annexed Corinth, and this great state ceased to exist for six years.

The real victor in all this fratricidal warfare was Persia, whose policy was to prevent any single Greek state from establishing hegemony over the Greeks, in order to insure Persian control of Ionia and the rest of Asia Minor. In 390 Persia was subsidizing an Argive-Corinthian navy in the Gulf of Corinth, which faced Spartan vessels operating out of Algina, while in the Aegean Persian money sustained the Athenian fleet in its conflicts with the Spartans. When Athenian victories began to restore Athenian control of the northern Aegean and the grain route to the Black Sea, and the Athenians, in alliance with Egypt, began to conquer Cyprus, Persia once again shifted sides and began to support Sparta (388).

Throughout these struggles, for more than a century Persia was one of the keys to the situation, and this influence became greater as the constant wars drove the Greeks toward bankruptcy and made Persian subsidies more essential. The role of such subsidies grew, not only from the decreasing financial resources of the Greeks, but equally from the general movement away from citizen soldiers and citizen rowers to mercenary hoplites and oarsmen after 400. During this period Persia played a role in the Mediterranean, with financial resources and land power, such as Great Britain played in Europe, with financial resources and sea power in the period A.D. 1700-1900; in each case the external power used its wealth and manpower to insure that no single state or solid coalition of states would secure hegemony in the area and justified this policy by its desire to protect the autonomy of the smaller states.

In such a situation Sparta was more valuable to Persia than Athens in that Sparta, like Persia, was basically a land power and, if restricted to that role, could neither threaten Persian control of the Greek peoples of Asia Minor nor threaten the independence of most of the states of Greece itself. Moreover, autonomy and independence of the various Greek states and opposition to any solid or effective leagues or federations of states were appealing policies to both Sparta and Persia. And in the third place, both were non-democratic powers.

The significance of Persian subsidies and the great influence which went to any individual Greek who could become a conduit for such subsidies can be seen in the role of Alcibiades in 412-407, of Lysander in 407-403, of Conon in 395-392, and of the Spartan, Antalcidas, in 392-386.

The "King's Peace" imposed on the Greeks by Persia with Spartan support in 386 was of great symbolic importance: all states in Asia, including Cyprus, to be subject to Persia; all states in Greece to be autonomous, except that the islands of Lemnos, Imbros, and Scyros were to belong to Athens. By implication, and by the understanding of those involved, these terms eliminated all leagues and federal states. When Thebes asked to sign for the Boeotian League, Sparta refused and began to mobilize the Spartan alliance. Thebes yielded, and all Greek states, including Corinth and each state in Boeotia separately, signed the King's Peace. Corinth received back her exiled oligarchs and rejoined the Spartan alliance.

The Persian-Spartan veto of Greek leagues in 386 is a clear indication that the Greek need for larger political units closer to the scope of its power areas would get little help from Sparta. The consequence was the rise of Thebes, not because Thebes offered more hope for dealing with Greece's essential military-political problems but because Sparta so clearly was a failure, except in the most narrow, military sense and even in this respect Sparta was going downhill even before 400.

323

The anti-Spartan developments after 404 were concentrated on the east-west line along the Saronic and Corinthian Gulfs. North of that line, Thebes was insulated from Spartan power to some degree by the anti-Spartan policies of Argos, Corinth, Athens, and Megara. These maintained a council at Corinth and soon mobilized support from the Acarnanian, Chalcidian, and Euboean confederations. Within this alignment, Thebes built up its power for a direct military challenge to Sparta.

This Theban challenge had to be military, and solely military, simply because Boeotia had nothing else to offer the Greeks, no imagination, little culture, no political innovation, and most emphatically no effort to deal with the real problems facing the Greeks.

We might think that a people as full of energy and curiosity as some of the Greeks, notably the Ionians, who engaged in warfare so intensely generation after generation, would come up with numerous tactical innovations. On the contrary, over many centuries, less than a handful of Greeks showed, if not tactical innovation, at least tactical imagination. These included Dionysus I, Alexander the Great and, to a lesser degree, his father Philip II. As a consequence of this lack, tactical change was purely evolutionary, that is slow, non-personal change resulting from changes in other fields than tactics itself, such as transportation or weapons supply.

Even changes in weapons were slow, because of the persistent emphasis on the spear, the dirk (although called a sword, this Greek weapon was only about thirty inches long and often had a cutting edge on one side only), shield, helmet, and body armor. Archery or cavalry were ignored or misused. This combination of weapons was used, with only minor changes, from about 700 to after 400 B.C. in tactics which involved little more than a frontal assault of massed men in an effort to push the enemy off the field and break up his formation in doing so. Before 700 most fighting was on an individual hand-to-hand basis, probably on foot, although the warriors usually rode to the battlefield. As nobles, they may have used their spears from horseback to encour-

324

age the peasants to yield to their will or way, but in battle with each other there was little cooperative offensive action and even less maneuvering, since each noble sought honor in an individual heroic action. It was this shift from individualism to cooperative solidarity which made the shift from noble warfare to hoplite tactics so difficult for the Greek nobles to accept as the new mass tactics provided such limited opportunities for individual glory.

Professor J.K. Anderson, an outstanding expert on the tactics of Greek warfare in the hoplite period, believes that this mass fighting arose from the fact that peasant villages tried to defeat each other by trampling each other's fields when the grain was in head, a tactic which could, if successful, bring the enemy to terms at a time when no peasant community had the reserve supplies to get through a cropless year and transportation was too primitive to bring enough grain from a distant site where some surplus might be available. A village could defend its field and crops by standing massed with its weapons on the flat edge of the field, and no enemy would dare to scatter to destroy the crop or even to march in mass formation across the field to trample the crop unless the defending mass had been pushed from the level ground and thus disrupted and dispersed. This theory had some difficulties itself, especially in showing how a mass formation at the edge of a field could kill or drive away dispersed enemy who are ravaging a crop without itself becoming disrupted in pursuit of scattered enemy or without trampling its own crops in the effort. In any case, it is clear that hoplite battles gradually became mass pushing struggles with spears on level ground and that any formation which was forced onto broken ground could be disrupted and its members killed because the disruption of the formation exposed the unshielded portions of their bodies to enemy weapons. During the centuries of hoplite supremacy, there were numerous occasions on which despised "light armed auxiliaries" or "peltasts" defeated massed heavy infantry, refusing to form a solid mass themselves, keeping, where possible, to broken ground, engaging the hoplite phalanx on its march or while out of formation, and relying on missile weapons and their own agile mobility to harass the hoplite forces to

desperation. These episodes were generally ignored
until after 400 B.C. Iphicrates (c. 415-353) made
a specialty of them and, while making a name for
himself, forced changes in the established phalanx
tactics.

The reasons for the persistence of the hoplite
tactics, once they were established in the eighth
century, are complex. There was, through all classical antiquity, a strong, if unconscious, tradition
that differences between states should be settled
on the field of battle where both sides would show
up to settle which was superior. Such a battle had
some of the overtones of a football game, resulting
from a mutual, if tacit, agreement to meet and settle the issue. This, like the traditional emphasis
on shock tactics with which it was related, had its
roots in the Homeric and Indo-European idea that
political disputes could be settled through conflict
of champions, in which the time and place were agreed
on. The chariot was so limited in the terrain on
which it could be used that this tradition continued;
although no time and place were usually set in advance, the fact was that no chariot battle could be
engaged unless there was mutual agreement to fight.
In the hoplite period, this tradition, although
weakened, still persisted, for the phalanx was so
inflexible that the battle had to take place on
level terrain where both sides could draw up in
formation. The necessity for the hoplites to protect their flanks by natural obstacles unless one
had very superior numbers was a further restriction.
The peltasts, with a small round shield whence they
derived their name (just as hoplites obtained their
name from their larger and heavier shield, the hop-
lon) were, of course, a much cheaper weapons system
than the hoplites, since they lacked the heavier
armor; their chief weakness was that they could
not stand off cavalry, as hoplites could, and they
could not generally stand up to hoplites in an
open field.

One reason for the delayed appreciation of the
peltasts was social snobbery based on the fact that
richer, better known, and socially established persons were hoplites. This was always a factor for
much of weapons history in the West, whenever estab-

lished shock weapons were challenged by cheaper missile weapons, as occurred, for example, in the Hundred Years' War when noble French cavalry were defeated by lower class English archers.

In the sixth century a tendency toward lighter
hoplite arms began to appear, allowing a gradual increase in the mobility of the phalanx. This first
appeared in substitution of corselets of leather or
linen in place of the plate cuirasses of the earlier
fighters. In the course of that sixth century, arm
guards and thigh pieces also were slowly eliminated,
although greaves continued into the fourth century.
In the fifth century, the heavy Corinthian helmet
which covered most of the head and hampered sight
and especially hearing, was also replaced by lighter
protection or no protection at all in the form of
the pilos, a pointed cap, sometimes of metal but increasingly consisting of the felt lining of such a
cap alone. The metal pilos is mentioned in 411 B.C.
in the drama Lysistrata, being used as a porridge
bowl, so it is not absolutely clear if the metal
pilos preceded or followed the felt cap, since the
name pilos means felt. In either case the movement
toward lighter armaments for the sake of mobility is
evident. Since lighter armaments were cheaper and
soldiers generally supplied their own arms, the movement toward lighter equipment was also a movement
toward greater participation in warfare by less affluent citizens and also toward larger forces as
well as more mobile ones.

These changes were justified by an increasingly
rigid use of hoplite tactics. Body armor was not impenetrable to a well-directed spear blow, although it
was very helpful against all kinds of missile weapons.
As the bow and arrow was eliminated from the classical
Greek armory, along with concussion weapons like picks,
clubs, battle axes, and such, the heavy helmet became
an unnecessary encumbrance along with most body armor,
and the chief defensive weapon became the shield, not
only one's own but that of the fighter on one's right.

This lightening of armaments after the sixth century permitted greater mobility of the hoplite phalanx.
We are told that the first time that such a formation
charged at the enemy on the run was in the battle of

Marathon in 490 B.C., when the Greeks wished to close the range in order to avoid the Persian missile weapons. But otherwise, there was little advance in tactics of Greek warfare in the fifth century. The solid mass of hoplites, arranged in close formation and in equal ranks, making every effort to keep its front straight and unbroken and to prevent itself from being rolled up from its weaker right side, continued. No regular use was made of unbalanced formations, of refusal of part of the front, of attack on the oblique or in echelon, or of retention of a reserve; all such elementary considerations in infantry tactics were unknown, or at least are unreported. Indeed, hoplite tactics were so rigid that there was no role for the commander once the order to attack was given, so he did not remain outside the battle to observe its progress or to take advantage of any weakness among the enemy. Instead he fought in the thick of the combat with the others, giving an example of his courage and persistence, and, since these things could be displayed best at the most dangerous position, he fought in the front line during much of the hoplite period.

All military activities, and probably all human activities, are wrapped in myths and unexamined assumptions which guide what is attempted and establish the boundaries within which the action takes place and the point at which the action stops. Classical antiquity is no exception to this rule. Divine law for at least five hundred years (900-400 B.C.) required that the dead could not be left on the field but must be buried or, in the early period, cremated, so that legal recognition that one side had possession of the field and thus was victor in the battle came to be symbolized by a request for a truce to reclaim and dispose of one's dead lying on the field. A force which did not ask for such a truce did not recognize that its opponent held the field and, accordingly, the battle was not yet over. Thus if the defeated force could recover its dead without a truce, its opponent was not victorious since its possession of the field and thus of its victory was not recognized. On the other hand, if the factual victory was recognized by the defeated opponent, as shown by the request for a truce, it would become a legal victory and accepted as such by any outside third parties. In such a case, the actual victor, thus recognized as legal victor, could symbolize his victory by erecting a trophy, that is by attaching arms captured from the defeated to a tree trunk or upright post to make a rough representation of a man, the whole structure dedicated to a god in thanks for the victory. To disturb or destroy such a trophy was an act of impiety which could call down the vengeance of the god on the violator. If such a trophy was set up and the defeated party had not asked for a truce to dispose of his dead, he could refuse to admit that the victor was master of the field when he raised the trophy, and might tear that trophy down secure in his own mind that there was no danger of vengeance from the god who would know that the claim of a victory, and thus of the right to raise a trophy, was fraudulent. Thucydides records the Milesians doing this to an Athenian trophy in 412 B.C.

Such conventional restraints on military action are still effective today, although we do not attribute their existence to religion because we are no longer a religious people in public matters. Throughout history the exercise of organized force has been subject to conventions, and in most cases those who live under them fail to recognize much of their influence, being satisfied to say that this is the way reality is without recognizing that their experience of reality is largely controlled by subjective and conventional arrangements. This is why an enemy can often inflict a crucial defeat upon a people, as the Germans defeated the French in 1940, by changes of outlook and of conventions with little or no superiority of weapons or of weapons systems.

The Greek case is of great interest because it reflects the interaction of at least four factors. The whole emphasis on the need to ask for a truce and the right to set up a trophy shows the fundamental human distinction between fact and law, as well as the need for law (which is a subjective consensus) to be symbolized by some objective symbol which can stand for the unobservable subjective agreement (like forcing one's opponent to say "uncle" or "enough" or allowing the victor in a sporting game to retain the ball). A second factor is the stage of religious development in which the classical peoples were for much of the classical period. The belief that the gods could influence the outcome of a battle gave rise to the erection of a trophy in thanksgiving, quite apart from its role as a legal symbol, and also gave rise to an effort to discover what was the general attitude of the gods to the battle before the issue was joined, by some method of taking the auspices. These actions show that the whole psychological context of a battle was different in the classical period, and especially in the early part of that period, from what it has been in modern times. This was because the archaic view of the universe as a chaotic melange of innumerable objects and powers continued even after the sixth century intellectual revolution had submerged out of consciousness the chief core of that archaic outlook centered on the fertility-virility relationship. As we shall see, a somewhat similar or parallel outlook appeared with the establishment in religious thought of the idea of a single omnipotent deity during the late classical and early post-classical period, so that the effort to take the auspices before a battle, to seek aid from the deity during the battle, and to offer thanksgiving to that Supreme Will after the battle continued, in some cases into the twentieth century.

The third and fourth factors in the context of a Greek battle are less intangible. They cover the socioeconomic and the military-political aspects of the battle. The inadequacies of transportation and the fact that all weapons and provisions had to be supplied and carried by the fighters themselves meant that these could not be away from their homes and their own fields very long. This not only restricted the area over which any power unit could operate, but it was also the chief incentive for a pitched battle to settle the dispute as quickly as possible. These restraints also served to inhibit any desire to annex territory, since there was no way in which it could be administered or through which control of a distant spot could be maintained once the main body of fighters returned to their own private activities at their own homes. For this reason wars were waged for limited goals, not to annex the defeated territory (which could not be

330

ruled from a distance by a demobilized force), not
to destroy the defeated state (since it might be
needed later as an ally against some other enemy),
but for prestige, or for some religious dispute, or
to take a few prisoners back as slaves.

The lack of a standing army, the danger or at
least inconvenience of any extended absence from
home, and the presence of other states, as potential
enemies or potential allies, all around any two
combatant states thus restricted war aims. For
reasons which we have given (no standing army and
the need to defend one's own fields), there was
little incentive to defend a state's frontiers or
its territories other than its fields, its port
(if it had one), and its stronghold. The same reasons made any stronghold or fortified position relatively immune from attack: siege tactics were primitive, transportation restraints as well as the brev-
ity of the campaign season made any sustained siege
impossible, and there was no real purpose to capturing an acropolis; the defenders would not retire
into a stronghold and allow their crops to be destroyed, but would engage in battle, after which,
whether they won or lost, no siege was needed. This
is probably the basic reason the classical Mediterranean society neglected siege tactics and the establishment of siege trains so long (until after 400
B.C.). Strongholds were valuable only after the
crops were in.

The victory of Sparta in the Peloponnesian War
of 404 B.C. was an encouragement to conservatism in
tactics, as well as in regard to social and economic
arrangements. The Spartans had not advanced further
than the original hoplite idea to bring the enemy to
battle as quickly as possible by ravaging his fields,
then to fight the battle by a pushing contest with
thrusting weapons until the enemy formation was
broken. Their only tactical innovation was to take
advantage of the fact that any phalanx front tended
to move to the right as each man tried to find cover
under the shield of the man to his right. This
meant that the right end of each front came to outflank the opposition's left and could, if it wished,
try to swing around to attack it from that side.
Of course, if both sides tried this, there would

be a tendency for the whole battle front to rotate
slowly in a counter-clockwise direction. Things
never went quite that far, but Sparta, with its
highly disciplined soldiers, discovered, almost
accidentally, at the first battle of Mantinea (418),
that a battle could be won by deliberately sliding
to the right far enough to free that wing from
enemy contact sufficiently to swing it around onto
the enemy's left flank, then drive across the field
through the enemy lines, from his left to his right,
parallel to the original front. This proved so effective for Sparta's forces that it always insisted
on taking the "place of honor" on the right of the
battle line and ignored its allies or even its own
forces on the left of its line, secure that it could
win on the right in time to overcome any defeat to
its side on the left. The tactic proved effective
until 371, when Thebes made its left wing very heavy,
with ranks fifty hoplites deep, fully capable of
putting such pressure on the Spartan front that it
could not slide to its right and, when it attempted
to do so, before contact was established, brought
down on the turning Spartan wing, with shattering
force, the Theban Sacred Band of picked homosexual
infantrymen, from where they had been stationed on
the Theban left rear for this very purpose.

     The Spartans cared little for cavalry or light
infantry. They saw no value in siege operations,
which in Greece proper, until the Macedonian period,
consisted of very expensive sieges lasting for
months or years or getting someone inside the walls
to betray the city. Neither of these could be used
by the Spartans. They had no desire for more slaves
or to extend their territories and hesitated to stay
too long away from their unstable social system in
Lacedaemon lest it explode. This social conservatism
with its accompanying rigidity of imagination and of
ideas grew stronger in Greece itself as a consequence
of the fact that military victories went to areas
like Sparta, Thebes, and Macedonia, which were shaped
in this conservative mold. As we shall see in a
moment, Greeks in other places, especially in the
West, in Sicily, were not so conservative and took
advantage of the growth in wealth, commerce, and
craft skills to advance military tactics and weapons in new directions which led to increased ability

to capture fortifications and to rule conquered territory, thus setting the patterns which Rome would follow on its road to universal empire.

In Hellas proper, the failure of Sparta in its period of supremacy, 404-371 B.C., opened the way to a brief period of Theban hegemony. The Theban triumph was purely military, since this state was even less imaginative and intelligent than Sparta. The military rise of Thebes rested on its development of the rudiments of tactics which I have mentioned: use of deeper ranks in one part of the battle line than elsewhere; attack by one part of the front while holding back the other side, in a wheeling motion; willingness to hold part of the force as a reserve, a change which involved withholding the commander away from the thick of the conflict so that he could observe the battle and take advantage of its development.

The rise of Thebes at the beginnings of these more complex tactics was largely due to the leadership of Epaminondas. The first step was to make the hoplite formation as heavy as possible, by adding additional ranks, at least at the point of its impact on the enemy line. This implied a number of other changes, including willingness to attack on the oblique, with one wing while holding back the advance of the other, lighter, wing. It also required a lengthening of the spears, and ultimately spears of greater length for the rear ranks, so that these latter could reach the enemy with their weapons and not be restricted to the push of their bodies' weight. Moreover, Epaminondas reversed the old tradition that the best troops should be put in "the place of honor" on the right wing. Both at Leuctra (371) and at Mantinea (362), he put his best troops, fifty deep, on the left wing, instructed the right to advance more slowly in a defensive posture, and placed peltasts in a detached position on the right to protect his weaker right wing from a flank attack.

These two victories for Thebes established its military superiority in Greece and also gave a number of ideas to the future king of Macedon, Philip, who was held as a hostage by the Thebans in 367-365 B.C.

While these relatively minor tactical changes were going on in Greece proper, much more significant ones were developing in the western Mediterranean, among the conflicting Carthaginian, western Greek, Etruscan, and local tribal peoples led by the Romans.

The Phoenicians reopened the Mediterranean to commerce after the turmoil of the Greek dark age, bringing back many elements of the much higher culture of the Levant including law and order on the sea, honest commercial interchange, writing, city life, and a taste for luxury goods. These new traits were even more significant in the West than in the eastern basin of the Mediterranean where they were, nonetheless, the chief impetus to the beginning of classical civilization. In the western basin of the Middle Sea, these influences continued longer because no new local autonomous civilization arose to resist the continued influence of the Levant. One consequence of this continued influence is that the far more advanced weaponry and tactics of western Asia continued to flow westward long after the more primitive Greek version of European shock tactics was well established in the Balkans. In fact, the relationship between these two different tactics is very significant because they were so different that they were not directly comparable, being complementary in the sense that each could do things which the other could not do and that each thus needed the other to have a better rounded and more effective military system capable of conquering territories and ruling them. Western Asiatic tactics were effective enough for ruling a non-military population accustomed to many generations of alien rulers who asked from their peoples little more than taxes and manpower. The tactics of Asia thus were very good at breaking up enemy formations, especially with use of missile weapons, and were particularly good at besieging the fortresses and walled cities of enemy rulers, but they lacked solidity of formations or of purpose, since mercenary or drafted troopers are unlikely to display tenacity of resistance or impetuosity of attack. On the other hand, as we have just seen, the Greeks were woefully deficient in siege tactics, missile weapons, and ability to hold and rule conquered peoples and territories.

The weapons and tactics of western Asia moved westward to Tunis, Sicily, and southern Italy from the Assyrians, to the Phoenician-Carthaginians, and finally to the Greeks of Sicily.

This Levantine influence on military tactics in Sicily appeared in three chief aspects: increased influence of missile weapons; a much higher level of besieging techniques; and a far better coordination of sea power and land forces. These three met together in a revolutionary innovation: the invention of artillery. Unlike most revolutionary innovations, this one can be pinpointed in both time and place. According to E.W. Marsden, the outstanding English-speaking expert on this subject, artillery was invented in the Syracuse of Dionysus in 399 B.C. We shall consider later the significant role which Dionysus played in adapting Greek tyranny to a wider political framework and his revolutionary influence on sea power. His role in the history of siegecraft and artillery is no less important.

The earliest form of artillery invented in 399 was a kind of crossbow, the belly bow (gastraphetes), consisting of a bow, probably composite, attached to a stock with a fitted sliding top which projected far in front of the bow when it was slack; at the rear of the stock was a concave opening into which the bowman put his stomach to lean forward and downward against the front of the sliding top which was resting against the ground. Pushing in this way forced the slide and the attached bowstring backward along a ratchet. When the string was fully drawn, the slide was fully back and could be attached to the ratchet, while the string was transferred from the slide to the trigger. An arrow or bolt placed in front of the string, on top of the attached slide, would be fired when the trigger was pulled.

Such a gastraphetes could use a bow considerably more powerful than an ordinary composite bow and could fire its missile at least fifty to a hundred yards farther (up to more than 250 yards compared to no more than 200 yards). Such a weapon was used against persons, not against fortifications.

Our information on artillery is very fragmentary
and not clearly dated, but it would appear that the
chief value of such a weapon would be defensive: it
would keep possible attackers farther from the walls.
According to Biton, who wrote in Pergamum under At-
talus I about 240 B.C., the gastraphetes was soon
improved and increased in size, being mounted on a
base through a universal joint and drawn by a winch,
so that an iron bolt six feet long and 4.5 inches
thick could be shot using a bow nine feet long.
Similar bows were adapted to shoot stones weighing
several pounds for distances up to 300 yards.

From the time of Biton in the late third century B.C., we have no mention of non-torsion artillery again until the fourth century A.D., when Vegetius speaks of small non-torsion arrow throwers as
arcuballistae. This does not mean that this type
of artillery was lost and rediscovered centuries
later, but is due to the fact that another kind of
artillery was invented which eclipsed the earlier
type because it could be made in much more powerful sizes.

This second type of heavy missile thrower is
known as the "torsion" type, because its power came
from twisted sinew or hair. It was invented shortly
after the invention of the gastraphetes, probably in
the same fourth century B.C., but we cannot say with
any assurance when or where. The earliest mention
of the new torsion artillery is in two inscriptions
of about 350 B.C. which list stores in Athenian ar-
senals and include catapults with springs of hair
in two sizes ("2-cubit" and "3-cubit"). Although
both these references are Athenian, Marsden does
not believe that this innovation began in Athens,
but believes that the torsion type has a Macedonian
background and was invented under Philip II, the
father of Alexander the Great. Wherever it may have
been invented, it seems likely that it was inspired
by the diffusion of the non-torsion type from Syracuse. About 354 Philip suffered a small but severe
defeat, when Onomachus the Phocian led the Macedonians into a trap by retreating into a valley where
he had set up non-torsion engines hidden on the surrounding hills. Many Macedonians were killed by the
missiles (bolts). Philip himself had arrow shooters

at Perinthus in 340 B.C., but there do not seem to have been any Macedonian stone throwers until Alexander's siege of Halicarnassus in 334. In Tyre in 332, Alexander had stone throwers powerful enough to shake the walls of the city; these were clearly torsion engines.

The Athenians may have contributed little to the development of these machines, but their arrival in Hellas can be followed largely in Athenian sources. The non-torsion type reached Greece from Sicily about 370 B.C.; about 345 a gravestone was set up at the port of Athens for an individual designated as an artilleryman; in 330-329, as we have seen, catapults with hair springs were listed in storehouses; in 321 a similar record shows 1800 catapult bolts in storage; and at the end of the century a decree honored Euxenides for supplying sinew for catapult springs in the four years' war of 307-304.

The sinew-rope catapults demanded great skill in manufacture, maintenance, and use, so that many states could not provide them from their own population and used mercenaries operating imported engines. This situation did not change for the better by any cheapening or simplification of the designs of such artillery. As a consequence, the extension of their use did not become more democratic but rather the contrary, although Athens made drill in their use part of the required training of young citizens shortly after the defeat of Athens by Philip at Charonaea in 338 B.C.

The use of artillery for offensive operations against fortifications required stone missiles heavy enough to make an impact on strong walls. Such weapons seem to have begun to appear in the course of the fourth century B.C. At the same time, the older western Asiatic methods of attacking fortified cities came into the Balkans from Syracuse and the West. As a consequence, when Alexander made his attack on Asia through the Persian empire in 334-323, he possessed the siege train to conquer the rather weak Persian defenses.

We do not know much about stone-throwing ar-

tillery in this period, but there can be little doubt
that this arm of warfare improved steadily in the
four centuries between Philip of Macedon and the
Roman attacks on the Levant which culminated in the
siege of Jerusalem in A.D. 69. During this period
the size of missiles increased as artillery became
more powerful, moving upward from about five pounds
before Alexander to over fifty pounds at the time of
Caesar. By the time of Philon of Byzantium (about
200 B.C.) the weight of such shot had reached a
point where its impact on a fortification was making
it necessary to modify the plans of such strongholds
to compensate for this new threat. Since such stone
throwers had to shoot at a relatively flat trajectory
to be effective, they had to be fired from not much
more than 150 yards away. Accordingly, Philon advised that there be three ditches in front of any
fortification, with the most remote edge of the
outer one at least 178 yards from the nearest wall.
About the same time, the walls themselves were
strengthened to at least 15 feet thick and 30 feet
high, with rounded towers and angles toward the direction of attack to avoid the most damaging right-
angled impact of any missile. Battlements acquired
similar angles, and the ground before the walls had
to be ditched and mined to prevent heavy machines
from getting close to the walls.

During the Roman republic, artillery was always
underemphasized and was used largely against personnel, both offensively and defensively, during sieges.
One reason for this was that there was, apparently,
no centralized supply of artillery, so its use depended very largely on the individual commander himself. Under the empire, there seems to have been
more uniformity, so that some writers believe that
each legion had its regular quota of artillery.
This view is based on the unreliable statements
of Vegetius (late fourth century A.D.), but even
if we reject this, it seems well established that
artillery was used more frequently against walls,
and was also used with field forces in battle with
greater emphasis after A.D. 50, especially by generals like Corbulo (about A.D. 60) and Arrian (about
A.D. 134) who had considerable success against the
Parthians and the Alans. At some time after this
date, probably as late as the third century A.D.,

the names used for the two kinds of artillery were
reversed, so that ever since it has not been possible
to be sure of the meaning of the words. In the earlier period, until after A.D. 100 (the time of Tacitus), arrow or bolt shooting machines were called
catapults, and stone throwers (at that time all with
two propulsion arms) were known as ballistas. By
the fourth century the two-armed stone thrower had
been replaced by a one-armed machine, familiarly
known as an onager or as a scorpion, and the older
use of the terms catapult and ballista were reversed,
with the former used for stone shooters, and ballista and its varied derivatives used for arrow and
bolt shooters. The degree of confusion in the fourth
century can be seen in the fact that Ammianus Marcellinus (about 350) says, "catapults. . .arque bal-
listis." In the same passage, he speaks of stone
throwers as "scorpions which are nowadays called
onagers."

These changes in weaponry and tactics were, of
course, accompanied by changes in economic, social,
and political life in the period covered by this
chapter, but Hellas itself, after having led these
developments in the period from about 750 to about
450, became frozen in its rigid and rather narrow
structures of the early fifth century. These structures included the polis itself as a state-community
of such small size that most of the inhabitants knew
each other, if not by sight at least by reputation,
and all political activities, including the making
of public decisions and the settlement of public
and judicial disputes, were made in public assemblies on a face-to-face basis. They also included
an economy based on slavery and the energies of
human bodies, with limited opportunities for capital investment, restricted to agriculture and to
rather primitive commercial interchange, and even
more restricted organization of handiwork and crafts.
The only significant area of continued development
after 450 B.C. was in the area of intellectual and
artistic development, in sculpture, architecture,
literature, religion, and philosophy, but in the
purely intellectual developments progress was divided and largely destroyed by increasing controversy, as the newer ideas became threats to the
vested interests of the established landholding,

slaveowning, and politically dominant class, which
began to be swallowed up and eclipsed in power by
the democratic masses and looked forward with dread
to a future in which the masses of the poor might
use their political power within the polis to change
the social and economic pattern in a more egalitarian direction. This did not happen, at least
in this period and in the more prominent states,
since the democratic masses turned to imperialist
warfare, rather than to political, economic, or
social reform.

The three great problems facing the progressive
states like Athens or Corinth about 450 were (1) how
could the greater offensive ability of new weapons
systems, including improved transportation and logistics, which permitted wider areas to be ruled
from a single center, be transformed into new political organizations and forms to provide a few, or
even one, governments among the Greeks; (2) how
could the obsolescent slave system be replaced by
a better social and economic organization which
would permit growth in more intensive, rather than
more extensive, directions, that is toward more effective technology and more motivated human energies,
to bring into the economy other sources of energies,
including animal power, windpower, waterpower, and
possibly even steampower, as well as better agricultural techniques, such as better tools and the
introduction of leguminous crops; and (3) how
could the outlook of the Greeks be freed from increasing intellectual controversy to allow full
use of recent developments in science and medicine
to provide a consensus in ideas and philosophy
along more democratic and progressive lines without
falling into the morass of what we today call "mass
culture."

All of these questions are relevant to the
problem of the relationships between weapons systems and political stability, but this relationship is most direct and immediate in regard to the
first of them. The military changes, especially in
tactics, which slowly developed in the course of the
fourth century, whether they were the result of innovations in Greece itself or slowly infiltrated into Greece from outside, chiefly from their fellow

340

Greeks in the western Mediterranean, contributed
little to any solution of any of the chief problems
facing the Greeks after 450 B.C. On the contrary,
the slow increase in offensive military power, by
allowing power systems to apply their power over
wider areas, made the crisis of political organization more acute by making the polis more obsolete.
But, at the same time, the hold which the polis had
on the emotions of the Greeks did not weaken, but
may well have increased (except to radical thinkers
like Epicurus, who was prepared to abandon most of
the remnants of the heroic outlook which still
gripped most established Greeks in its influence),
especially as other social groupings like the family
were becoming less satisfying, both emotionally and
socially, to the average Greek because the family
was ceasing to be the focus of religion, property-
holding, decision-making, and personal security.
As a result, the immediate problems of the ordinary
Greek, the problems of class animosities, intellectual controversy, of war, and of hunger (especially
land hunger) continued to grow. While no one saw
any solution to these problems or even examined
them in any scientific or even rational way, many
began to turn toward some solution on extensive
lines (to apply the existing Greek way of life to
wider resources) rather than to seek a solution
along intensive lines (that is to devise a better
way of life to be applied to the existing resources
of Greece itself). The greater resources needed
for an extensive solution seemed to many Greeks
to lie close at hand: the wealth and weakness of
Persia. To seek a solution of the problems of
Greece in that direction had the additional virtue
that it would end the bickerings and quarrels of
the Greeks among themselves by joining them together
in a common project, the conquest of the wealth,
lands, and manpower of Persia.

Once this idea began to form in people's minds,
the chief obstacle seemed to be political rather
than military. There seemed to be no question that
the Greeks could defeat Persia; the vital question
was how the Greek states could be united on this
task so that no major state would be left in the
Balkans to plunder other Greek states while those
who invaded Asia were busy plundering Persia.

341

The many battles between Greeks and Persians on land and sea over more than a century had given most Greeks full confidence that they could defeat Persia in battle. The clearest evidence of that was the exploits of the ten thousand mercenaries hired in 401 by Cyrus to overthrow his brother, the king of Persia. Although the ten thousand won their battle easily, Cyrus was killed, removing the motive for the invasion. By treachery, the Greek leaders were captured by the Persians. Nevertheless, the ten thousand, under elected leaders, marched from near Babylon to the Syrian Saddle, then north across Armenia, through hostile country to the Black Sea to safety (401-400). This exploit gave the average Greek hoplite a feeling close to contempt for the military qualities of Persia's fighting forces. And the hoplites' glimpse of the wealth of Asia, thus feebly defended, gave them a motivation which Xenophon, who was one of them, expressed to his fellow Greeks after the Persian seizure of their leaders: "We must first try to get back to Hellas and to our own people and show the Hellenes that they are poor only because they are willing to be, for they could bring their paupers over here and see them become rich."

This solution of Greece's problems became the lifelong advocacy of Isocrates of Athens (436-338), who had freed himself from the limited perspective of the city-state but felt that the only way to obtain peace and unity among the Greeks was to join them together in a common cause which could teach them to view themselves as a nation. The cause he advocated for the last half century of his very long life was war on Persia.

This aim was achieved by Macedon under Philip II and Alexander. This country consisted of a coastal zone of Greek colonial city-states and a barbaric, largely Illyrian, hinterland. The political system was a tribal monarchy of a type not uncommon on the northern grasslands: the throne was not hereditary but elective within a royal family; the king's power was not absolute but subject to the restraints of a council of fighting chiefs; the royal family was polygamous; political allegiance consisted of personal loyalty

342

to the king by the nobles, while the common people
were expected to be equally loyal to these noble
leaders, whose chief activities were fighting,
heavy drinking, and violent hunting. Each man
of a noble family wore a cord around his wrist
until he had killed a man; and he could not sit
at table with other men until he had killed a
wild boar.

This rather primitive system was changing
rapidly in the fourth century B.C., and Philip,
who usurped the throne from his three-year-old
nephew in 361, was just the man to speed up the
process. As regent and as king, he disposed of
five rival claimants to the throne, encouraged
the continued growth of littoral cities and commerce, reorganized his relations to the nobles,
crushed various revolts by lesser tribal peoples,
and intrigued in his own country and among the
struggling Greeks.

Philip, who as king owned most of the land of
Macedon, built an economic base for his military
ambitions by encouraging the growth of Greek cities
and Greek commercial relations. He formed a monetary union of the northern Balkans using his gold
coins as a base and exploited the Pangaeum mines,
which yielded him about a thousand talents a year.
With this he built up a well-trained cavalry arm,
"the Companions," recruited from noble families,
and a hoplite infantry, called "the Foot Companions,"
from the more affluent peasants and urban classes.
The lesser peoples, Macedonian, Illyrian, Greek,
and others, formed units of auxiliaries, and there
was money enough to hire mercenary soldiers and
sailors, to bribe opposition leaders, and to hire
key figures to betray besieged cities.

This military force is often called a "national
army" to distinguish it from the usual armies of the
citizens of city-states at that time. It surely was
not in any way similar to the Greek forces of citizen soldiers and still less to the increasing numbers of mercenary fighters, but it was not a national
army for the simple reason that there was no "nation"
at that time, certainly not in Macedon. There was
Philip the king, and the army was loyal to him. Our

343

ideas of a "nation" or of a "territorial state" were
alien to both the Greek and to the Macedonian situations. The Greeks recognized Hellenes but had no
Hellas; the subjects of Philip had neither; they
had a king.

This political system: personal, semi-elec-
tive, military, and polygamous had many acute weaknesses similar to those which history has revealed
in other monarchies (including the Huns, the Mongols,
the Turks, the Russians, and the Byzantine empire).
These weaknesses would have become critical if
either Philip or Alexander had lived long enough
to undertake the great effort of organizing a stable
political system. Neither was really called upon to
do so, for both were cut off by death almost before
the preliminary military stage of the state-building
effort was finished. They might have succeeded in
the second, political stage of their efforts, and
there is no doubt that each was aware of the need
for such a second stage. Moreover, each was of
such supreme ability that it is possible that either
might have been successful.

This supreme ability was not restricted to military matters, although both men were of top level in
that respect. But Philip was, if anything, a greater
diplomat and politician than he was a soldier, while
Alexander had political imagination to match his
superb military abilities. Neither had time to use
these less tangible capacities to supplement and
consolidate his military victories, for Philip died
of an assassin's knife at age 46, while his son was
killed by a fever at age 33.

In military matters both Philip and Alexander
showed a tactical imagination which allowed them to
free their minds from enslavement to the dominance
of the heavy infantry line. Philip used his cavalry,
more heavily armed and attacking in a wedge, as Alexander sometimes did, as the impact weapon for shattering formations of massed infantry, while his infantry, in a deeper but looser formation, were armed
with pikes 13 to 18 feet long (the sarissa) compared to the usual six-foot Greek spears. Moreover,
Philip had much greater tactical control over his
units and used this control more imaginatively. He

used large numbers of peltasts to cover his flanks, and had the money to hire numerous regular hoplites. At Charonaea (338) he defeated the Greek allies, numbering some 35,000 infantry, with his Macedonian forces of 30,000 foot and 2,000 cavalry. He led the "king's own" infantry on the right, opposite the Athenians, while Alexander, eighteen years old, led the cavalry on the extreme left, opposite the Thebans. As the troops engaged, Philip began to withdraw his right, drawing the Athenians out of line in pursuit. The other Greeks trying to keep their front continuous, followed to their left until a gap appeared between the hoplite infantry and the Theban "sacred band" on the extreme right. Alexander's cavalry drove into this gap and began to roll up the hoplite line just as Philip's right wing reversed its direction and charged forward against the now disorganized Athenians.

Philip's peace terms were harsh on Thebes and lenient for Athens. The Boeotian League was broken up into its constituent city-states, the exiled oligarchs were restored and a government of 300 of them set up under protection of a Macedonian army of occupation in the Theban citadel (the oligarchs at once executed or exiled all the democratic leaders); three Boeotian city-states destroyed by Thebes (Plataea, Thespiae, and Orchomenus) were reestablished. No Macedonian troops or ships were sent into Attica, but the Athenian League was dissolved, leaving Athens with five Aegean islands as colonies; Athens became an ally of Philip, and all Athenian prisoners and dead were returned to their city without ransom.

The following year all Greek states of the mainland south of Olympus except Sparta (which now had only 1000 Spartiates left) and many islands were joined in "the Greek League" at Corinth. They agreed on terms already mentioned. Each state elected members, proportionate to its military and naval strength, to a "council of the Greeks." The decisions of this body, reached by majority vote, were binding on all members and covered all aspects of political life. At each meeting the council elected five "presidents" to supervise executive activities.

At its first regular meeting in 337, the council

of the Greeks made an offensive and defensive alliance, for all time, with Philip and his descendants, declared war on Persia to avenge Xerxes' sacrilegious treatment of the temples of the Greek gods in 480, and unanimously elected Philip commander in chief (<u>hegemon</u>) of all the Greek forces.

Philip was prevented from carrying out this project by his assassination at his daughter's wedding in 336, possibly by an agent of Persia. Alexander succeeded to the throne without difficulty, but in 335, at a false report of his death, Thebes revolted, attacked the Macedonian garrison in the citadel, and accepted part of 300 talents that Persia sent through the perpetually misguided Athenian orator, Demosthenes. Alexander reached Thebes in 14 days from the extreme northwest, waited outside the walls for three days for an offer to negotiate, then, failing this, stormed the city and captured it in the first attack. Six thousand Thebans were killed and over 30,000 captured. But worse was to come. Alexander submitted the case to the Greek League whose council voted to destroy the city, sell all its inhabitants into slavery, and give all Theban lands to other states. The sentence was carried out by Alexander, who razed all buildings, except the temples and the house of the poet Pindar.

Alexander invaded Asia in 334 leaving half his Macedonian infantry under Antipater at home. He had about 30,000 infantry (of which about 12,000 were Macedonian) and about 5000 horse of which 3300 were heavy cavalry, about 1700 being Companions. He had about 5000 Greek mercenary hoplites plus 7000 hoplites and 160 triremes from the Greek League.

Over the next eleven years Alexander marched 22,000 miles, won dozens of major battles, and conquered all Asia and Egypt as far as the Jaxartes River in central Asia and the Hyphasis River (an eastern branch of the Indus). Only the refusal of his soldiers to go farther put a stop to his conquest of India (326), so he returned to Babylon by way of the Indian Ocean, the desert of Gedrosia, and the Persian Gulf.

346

The battles of Alexander show his imaginative versatility, for he was able to cope, almost instantly, with any situation which arose, even those which he had never anticipated. This included river crossings, by day and by night; regular battles in narrow passages and on open plains; assaults on walled cities and up steep mountains; battles in deep snow and against mounted archers of the central Asiatic grasslands; a successful 7-month siege on the island of Tyre, which the Assyrians had besieged in vain for 13 years, and a successful response to an attack by military elephants in India. The first three years of this campaign obtained control of the sea by the Napoleonic method of capturing all seaports and naval bases by attack from the landward side. The next seven years were devoted to the conquest of the interior of western Asia (331-324). The last year or more was devoted to reform of his government of this vast area.

In general, Alexander changed the governments of the areas he conquered relatively little. He did not have time to do much, but it seems clear that he intended to set up a personal governmental machinery over slightly modified existing governments, with fusion of blood, religion, and administrative techniques as seemed most likely to retain his personal control. He identified himself with the archaic sacral kings of Asia, by calling himself son of Ammon in Egypt and similar titles elsewhere, but, at the same time, sought to appeal to the support of all men, as fellow humans, under a rather remote high god. Self-interest was used to strengthen allegiance by using local or native personnel, even as governors, where this could be done safely, but military control was generally kept in European hands and the vital core of the armed forces was kept Macedonian. There was no social segregation, and Alexander himself, 80 of his officers, and 10,000 of his soldiers married native women. This was quite contrary to the advice of his tutor Aristotle, who on this issue of biological superiority, as in his political emphasis on the polis, clung to obsolete theories. According to Plutarch, Aristotle "advised Alexander to treat the Greeks as if he was their leader and other peoples as if he was their master; to have regard for the Greeks as for friends and kindred,

347

but to treat other peoples as though they were plants and animals."

This policy of fusion was not acceptable to most Greeks and to the Macedonians, who set aside Alexander's child by his Persian wife on the grounds that it was "half barbarian." Tens of thousands of Greeks moved eastward into Persia and Egypt, settling in the 70 military colonies that Alexander had founded or in the dozens of new cities he had established as commercial centers. Of these latter Alexandria became the greatest, set up to replace Phoenician Tyre which had been destroyed with 8000 killed and 30,000 sold into slavery after Alexander's successful siege. Alexandria could not replace Tyre (it was too far from the Syrian Saddle), but it became a great Greek city. However, it was kept almost entirely isolated from any contact with the Egyptians by the new Macedonian rulers, the Ptolemies, who monopolized all trade with the Egyptian peasants in their own hands.

It was impossible to maintain the unity of Alexander's empire, not only because his generals began to plot, beginning with Ptolemy, to seize parts of it for themselves, but because it was physically impossible to maintain unity of knowledge, command, allegiance, and control over an area so wide and so diverse as that left by Alexander. Improvements in transportation and communication (much of it by the last Persian kings) and the steady growth of mercenary soldiers and seamen, as well as the growing skill and expense in maintaining a navy and a siege train continued to extend the areas over which some kind of unified rule could be established, but this area (which varied with geographic and social conditions) was nothing like so large as Alexander's empire.

Although wheeled transport could be used in Asia over the Persian roads, and on the Macedonian roads of the northeastern Balkans, pack animals still had to be used in most of the Mediterranean. Alexander had a supply service for an army of about 40,000, but he could live off the country, and his only real transportation problem was his siege train (now more elaborate than ever). He left

348

Europe with only a month's supplies, but found he needed no more and traveled more rapidly than anyone expected. A century and a half earlier, Xerxes, with a much larger but far weaker striking force, had sent supply dumps in advance and had made considerable use of Phoenician sea transport. From Pella, the Macedonian capital, to Sestus on the Hellespont, which took Xerxes over three months to cover, took Alexander's force only twenty days.

Alexander's only significant weakness lay in his failure to see any value in sea power or in sea transport. He disbanded his naval force as soon as he reached Asia (at Miletus), saying he could defeat the Persian fleet of 400 ships by capturing its bases. After he destroyed Phoenician sea power by his sack of Tyre, two years later, he made no effort to replace it. The error in this view was shown by the increase in piracy and in the great role which sea power played subsequently, in the final destruction of the Athenian fleet at Amorgos in 322 and in the naval struggles of the successor states from 315 to the final victory of Rome at Actium in 31 B.C.

The long struggles of these successor states showed clearly that the day of the single city was passed, for Alexander's empire did not break up into cities but into large chunks, generally organized as kingdoms. The cities could participate in the power struggles of these larger (and much richer) units only by becoming members of leagues, so that the history of Greece from 323 onward was concerned with the actions of leagues.

(blank page 350, intentionally omitted)

CHAPTER VI
CLASSICAL CIVILIZATION: GROWING OFFENSIVE POWER AND DECREASING POLITICAL PARTICIPATION, 323 B.C.-A.D. 69

1. Introduction

The period of about four centuries following the death of Alexander was a period of mercenary professional soldiers and sailors, although, as always, some states experienced this stage somewhat earlier and some, notably Rome, experienced it somewhat later. In the case of Rome, this stage was not reached until Marius changed the regulations in 107 B.C., although, in fact, the process was developing rapidly a century earlier. In this, Rome's experience was somewhat like that of the United States, in which the casual impression may be that the American armed services were made up of draftees, when, in fact, they were already moving toward an army of volunteers who regarded it as a way of making a living, at least temporarily.

But if Rome's development was slow, that of some other states was rapid and early. Among these precocious cases, the outstanding example was that of Syracuse under the tyrants Gelon (485-478) and Dionysus I (405-367 B.C.). Before we look at this latter's substantial contributions to weapons development, we should identify this period in general terms a little more clearly.

This was a period of accelerating growth in offensive power and of continued growth in size of political units, culminating in the establishment of Rome's domination of the whole Mediterranean basin with the sack of Carthage and Corinth in 146 B.C. It was also a period in which the quality of internal political life continued to move from democracy to oligarchy and, simultaneously, the power of the state to impinge on the private lives of individuals grew fairly steadily. This last point could be worded, as we have already indicated, as a continued, simultaneous, weakening of social controls over individuals and the strengthening of political controls so that by A.D. 69, "the Year of the Three Emperors," the situation

351

in Rome was very close to what had become the Roman ideal: an all-powerful, totalitarian state face to face with a socially naked, atomized, individual. By 69 this situation was beginning to reverse, as individuals began to seek more satisfying personal lives in religious and emotional intimacy, on a personal basis, within their own, non-legal, voluntary groups and to ignore, if possible, the monstrous Leviathan state which Rome had become. The roots of this new development are to be found in the spread of various new "religious" associations of which the most significant, and probably one of the earliest, was Epicureanism, based on the teachings, example, and worship of Epicurus (341-270 B.C.).

This period of oligarchy and offensive military power ended about A.D. 100, with the clear recognition that the Roman empire could no longer extend its frontiers by military action and should, indeed, in view of its increasing inability to enforce its will within the existing frontiers, look forward to retracting these to more easily defendable limits. At the same time, the supremacy of the oligarchy (that is, the minority of wealthy persons) began to be curtailed by the power of military despots, a tendency which was clearly established during the century of civil war (133-31 B.C.), but was subsequently concealed behind a facade of pseudo-traditionalism, hiding naked military force under the so-called "principate" of Augustus Caesar (27 B.C.-A.D. 14). The facade was ripped off completely, fifty-five years after the death of Augustus, when three military despots became emperor of the state in the single year A.D. 69.

2. The Struggle to Dominate the Western Mediterranean

The rise of Rome to dominate the whole Mediterranean basin took almost five hundred years, from about 500 B.C. to the time of Christ, although as early as 146 B.C. it was quite clear that the Roman drive to supremacy could not be stopped. On the other hand, in 500 B.C. Rome's chances of achieving this supremacy could not have seemed good even to the most clear-sighted observer.

About 500 B.C. the western Mediterranean consisted of a trio of advanced states, all three intruders from the eastern Mediterranean or western
Asia. These three were: (1) the Carthaginian or
Punic peoples, centered in what is now Tunis, who
were Canaanite traders from Phoenicia originally;
(2) the Etruscans, who seem to have been an Asiatic
people, probably from Anatolia in the early last
millennium B.C.; and (3) the Greek colonial cities
of Sicily and southern Italy, who came from the
east in the period of Greek colonial expansion
after 750 B.C.

All three of these intruding peoples were of
advanced cultures, with the state form of political
organization and an economy fully familiar with
division of labor, specialization and exchange,
coinage, writing, and urban life. In the west they
found themselves intruders in wide areas of tribal
and semi-tribal peoples who were largely ignorant
of these new political and economic forms and still
existed, on the whole, in tribal societies, with
subsistent agrarian or semi-pastoral economies organized in rural districts (pagi), without city life
or much familiarity with writing. By 500 B.C. some
of these local peoples, led by the Romans, were already becoming familiar with these more advanced
techniques of social organization, either from the
Etruscans or from the Greeks. The Greek colonies
in the western Mediterranean by 500 B.C. were
strong and prosperous. They were also, like their
founders in the eastern Mediterranean, violently
aggressive. Thus, in the sixth century, Syracuse
destroyed its daughter colony, Camarina; a coalition led by Croton and Sybaris destroyed Siris;
Croton was then defeated by Locri and Rhegium but,
within the same generation, Croton destroyed Sybaris,
the richest state in the west, whose population may
have been half a million. These destructive acts
were accompanied by class struggles and the establishment and eviction of tyrants, with little regard for the fact that non-Greek enemies were closing in from Carthage, Etruria, the Oscan peoples,
and ultimately Rome. Moreover, the rise of these
non-Hellenic threats to the Greek cities of the west
was made more menacing from the fact that the native
peoples of the west, like the Oscans, were becoming

353

more dangerous, either by the adoption of more advanced military techniques from the civilized peoples or by serving as mercenary fighters for the four civilized peoples.

These non-civilized peoples of the west were of two kinds, both regarded by us as "uncivilized" because they were still in tribal, or semi-tribal, conditions and had not yet been urbanized. These two kinds were the earlier inhabitants of the west, like the Osco-Umbrians in Italy, or the Sicelots in Sicily, or the Iberians in Spain, and the more recent intruders from the flatlands, both north and south, such as the Gauls and the Numidians. All of these peoples were uncivilized in the sense that they were tribal and not urbanized in their political organization, although the earlier kind, in its economic organization, was completely rural and agricultural and the later kind, like the Gauls and Numidians, were somewhat more pastoral.

We might view this situation in the west in terms of three strata, or chronological layers, as in geology. The oldest layer were the peasant peoples; on these had intruded the four great civilized forces of urbanized cultures, three of them from outside (Etruscans, Carthaginians, and Greeks) and one (Romans) of local origin; while the third and latest layer was that of the recent tribalists like the Gauls, who continued to intrude sporadically into the Mediterranean basin throughout the classical period.

We might view the history of the western Mediterranean simply as the conquest of the socially more primitive tribal way of life, by the socially more advanced city-state way of life. Or we might view it, more narrowly, as a question of which of four city-state peoples (the Etruscans, Carthaginians, Greeks, or Romans) would perform this task. In either case, one element in the final decision would be ability to mobilize force as a factor; this in turn would rest, to some extent, on ability to organize men and ability to win their allegiance. Moreover, these two abilities were so clearly superior in an urbanized structure in comparison with the alternative tribal structure that the final victory

would go to one of the four urbanized contenders
and not to any of the tribalized contenders. But
this meant that the tribalized contenders would
enter into the situation as the allies, tools, or
instruments of the successful urbanized contender
more completely than as allies or supporters of the
three unsuccessful urbanized contenders.

In the historic period in the western Mediterranean, the struggle between tribal and city-state
ways of life could be viewed in geographic terms as
a struggle between the hills and the lowlands or as
a struggle between the interior hinterland and the
coastal fringes. This is because about 500 B.C.
the urbanized peoples were in control of the more
fertile lowlands and the coastal fringes, while the
tribal peoples controlled the hills and the interior
hinterlands.

This distinction arose because the urban cultures had forced the tribal cultures out of the
fertile lowlands and into the hills because of the
superior ability of the urban cultures to mobilize.
power and to apply it on more level terrain and
across seas. It is in these terms, and in terms
of other factors, such as the superior capacity of
urban cultures to sustain greater concentrations of
population (and thus of manpower) that we feel entitled to speak of "higher" and "lower" cultures.
The urban cultures were "higher" because they could
organize manpower for security, for economic production, and for satisfaction of man's non-material
needs better than tribal cultures could do this.
Thus they could organize and utilize the manpower
of the tribal cultures more effectively than these
cultures could utilize it themselves. On the other
hand, the tribal cultures could produce numbers of
population at least as well, and probably much better, than the urban cultures could. I mean by this
simply that the population reproductive rate was
higher in the lower level cultures, something with
which we are quite familiar today.

But, if urban cultures could mobilize and organize manpower better and tribal cultures could
produce population better, in any competitive struggle
among these peoples, the victory would go to the sys-

355

tem which could combine these two together.

Such a process of combination of organizational and demographic elements could be by slavery, that is by a system with superior organizational capacity using force to apply its own organization to peoples who were not yet parts of it. Hitler's Germany did this, in the twentieth century, in a still higher organizational context, just as the Greeks and Romans were attempting to do it in the period we are considering here.

The chief problem with this method of combining organization and manpower is that the use of applied force to make such a combination easily leads to a situation in which the organization of applied force becomes an institution rather than an instrument, and, instead of using its force to obtain manpower as a resource to satisfy human needs (for security, for economic goods, and for non-material satisfactions), it begins to use its force to obtain manpower, economic resources, and non-material resources for the aggrandizement and self-perpetuation of itself as an organizational structure. In brief, a military organization created to serve a community can become a military despotism acting to exploit the community in order to serve itself.

The chief alternative to enslavement by the use of applied force would be some voluntary method for joining an organizational system to surplus manpower. This is what happens when geographic areas producing surplus population become sources of voluntary emigration to other areas of superior organizational forms. Thus people may move into a city from the surrounding rural areas, as southern negroes in the United States in the 1920s moved from the rural South to the automobile factories of Detroit. Or, like the Irish in the 1850s, they may migrate to another country where labor as a resource is in short supply, while other resources, such as land or knowhow, as well as the organizational structure itself, are more than adequate to absorb extra labor.

Such voluntary movements of manpower, while raising acute social and other problems, nonetheless solve problems of population surplus in the areas of emigration and do not raise insoluble problems in the areas of immigration. In classical antiquity, unfortunately, such voluntary movements were often precluded, for reasons we must clearly recognize.

So long as the economic system of classical antiquity was based on slavery, in the sense that slavery was the chief source of capital accumulation and the master-slave relationship was the most widely recognized relationship between entrepreneurial decision and laboring manpower, there was little economic opportunity for immigrant workers in the city-state system. In fact, as we can see clearly in Athens under Pericles or in Rome under the late republic, the economic system of classical antiquity could not provide work for its own free urban poor because it could not obtain, outside the slave system, the necessary capital for tools, plant, raw materials, and supervisory personnel, except in terms of public works projects, often of dubious economic utility or aimed at warlike ends (such as armaments or shipbuilding).

In conditions such as these, not only was an ancient state going to look with regret on any influx of free labor seeking work, but the immigrants, however impoverished, were not going to accept the obvious alternative of exchanging poverty in personal freedom at home for economic security in slavery by migrating into a polis to offer themselves as slaves.

In addition to this economic obstacle to immigration there was also a political obstacles, resting in the very nature of the ancient city. The polis may have been on a higher organizational level than the tribe, but it continued to have some tribe-like attributes. Two of these are significant: it was an organization in which membership was obtained by birth, and it was totalitarian. Of these the second is the lesser obstacle, for a voluntary immigrant might have been willing to adopt the total way of life of the polis including its religion, but he could not become a citizen so long as the only way to do this was by birth. When Pericles restricted citizenship in Athens in 451 by requiring that both parents must be citizens, he made this obstacle

357

even greater because it was no longer possible for
a non-citizen to obtain citizenship for his future
children by marrying a citizen. As a consequence,
Athens, like other ancient cities, had a large class
of resident aliens (or metics) among its inhabitants,
and these were not necessarily recent arrivals in
the city, but might well have been born there of
parents and grandparents who had also been born there.

With voluntary methods of joining additional
manpower to the city-state system excluded by the
very nature of that system, the competition of these
city-states with each other in war had to lead to
competition in non-voluntary methods. Thus the ancient city-state system became a competition in enslavement, and therefore in aggressive warfare.
This began in the western Mediterranean about as
early as in the eastern Mediterranean, say in the
fifth century B.C.

From the point of view of the tribal units of
social organization, there was another aspect of
this problem. We must not see the situation as one
in which peaceful tribal peoples were being victim-
ized by aggressive city-state peoples. On the contrary, by the fifth century the tribal peoples of
the Mediterranean basin were about as aggressive as
the city-state units, but their aggressions were on
a different evolutionary stage.

We must see this situation as one of successive
evolutionary stages or levels, some more intensive
than others in the sense that a more intensive one
produces more of any desired end (economic goods,
security, psychological satisfactions and other
non-material needs) with no greater use of resources,
or by the use of resources previously unusable. On
this basis we have termed the archaic kingship higher
than the tribal system.

Just as the superior organizational system of
the city-state became aggressive because it sought
to apply its superior organizational form to additional resources, notably manpower, by aggressive
warfare, so also, at about the same time, the inferior organizational system of the tribal communities sought to apply its organizational form (gener-

358

ally more pastoral and more self-sufficient) to additional resources, notably land, by aggression. Not only were these two both aggressive, but the tribal aggressive policy was, if anything, earlier in adopting aggressive tactics in the fifth century crisis, in the western Mediterranean.

What was happening in the west in the fifth century was that the tribal units were experiencing the crisis which the eastern Greeks had experienced in the seventh century. As we have seen, the eastern Greeks in the seventh and sixth centuries had responded to a crisis of the system in two ways: (1) by extensive expansion outward to colonize larger areas, including those in the west; and (2) by intensive expansion by reorganizing their system to a higher organizational level to provide more from the same resources of land and labor. The former of these two not only brought the Greeks to the west but made the tribal peoples already living there on a low level their victims, not only by enslaving many of them but by driving them back from the sea and the more fertile lowlands into the hills.

The tribal communities' crisis in the fifth century in the west was the historical equivalent to the city-states' crisis of the seventh century in the east and they responded to it in the same two ways, but extensively rather than intensively, by trying to move down from the hills to the more fertile lowlands. Since these lowlands were already held by the intruders, the Greeks, Carthaginians, and Etruscans, this led to war. Such wars against adversaries on a higher level of culture, while not hopeless, were very difficult, with the consequence that many tribal aggressors were forced backward and sought lines of less resistance by attacking their fellow tribal peoples in different political units or by attacking those tribal units which were in process of trying to solve their crises by working upward to a higher organizational level by shifting themselves from tribal ways of life to city-state ways of life.

One of the local units which started on this more intensive road from tribal ways to city-state ways was Rome. Another was Capua. It is significant

359

that one of the critical steps in the early expansion
of Rome began in 340 B.C. when Capua, an Oscan but
urbanized community, appealed to urbanized Latin Rome
for help against the Oscan tribal Samnites. This
shows how the appeal of the city-state form could
overcome the appeal of common language or even blood
kinship.

On the other hand, the fratricidal warfare of
the Greeks was not restrained by shared organizational
forms, language, religion, or anything else. As a
result, their situation in the west deteriorated,
although not as rapidly as did the power of the Carthaginians and the Etruscans. The oldest Greek colony
in Italy was Cumae, 757 B.C.; in 421 it was destroyed
by Oscan tribesmen. In the next century and a half,
the other Greek colonies which had rimmed southern
Italy were almost destroyed in a similar way, until,
in 280 B.C., when Rome began to intervene to stop
the process, only a few small enclaves remained.

On the whole, historians of the ancient western
Mediterranean have neglected the roles played by these
tribalized peoples, except in a piecemeal fashion.
It seems, however, that these tribesmen played a vital
role in the final outcome of the struggle among the
four civilized peoples because they, on the whole,
were more willing to cooperate with, or at least
yield to, Rome than they were to the other three.
The reasons for this relatively weaker anti-Roman
attitude are complex, and rest as much on the somewhat greater deficiencies of the non-Roman trio than
they do on any positive assets on the part of Rome.
This complex situation might be summed up in the
fact that the tribal peoples had an inclination,
to some extent, to regard the city-state way of
life as higher, more advanced, or more desirable
than the tribal way of life. Rome's advantage over
the trio was that it was more willing to extend this
newer way of life to the tribal peoples than her
three rivals were.

In this competition the Greeks were handicapped
from the fact that they were often, or more generally,
racially intolerant toward non-Greeks. They regarded
non-Greeks as "barbarian" and thus as inferior on a
hereditary biological basis. We have mentioned this

360

in terms of the triumphs of Pythagorean rationalism,
such as Platonism, and in the difficulties which
Alexander encountered from the Greeks and Macedonians
in trying to build an ecumenical empire rather than a
Hellenistic exploitative empire.

Such an exploitative racial empire was an impossible remedy for the problems of classical civilization, at least in Greek terms, from the fact
that Greeks could not even agree among themselves.
Racial intolerance and fratricidal behavior were
handicaps to success separately; together they were
guarantees of failure. In the case of the Greeks,
they insured political failure despite the really
extraordinary personal ability of so many individual
Greeks.

The failures of the Greeks in politics can be
seen clearly among the western Greeks, who continued
to murder each other and to despise barbarians,
while they were being threatened with extinction
not only by the other three civilized rivals but
by the barbarians as well. The only restraint on
this Greek taste for fratricidal warfare appeared
when class animosities within Greek states rose to
such a fever pitch that it seemed that the possessing
classes might be liquidated by the nonpossessing
poor. At that point, the former were often willing
to give up their fratricidal warfare and even their
independence to a state like Rome which seemed willing to use its power to suppress civil war and social revolution. Thus, just as the barbarians accepted Rome because it seemed progressive to them,
so many Greeks accepted Rome because it seemed reactionary to them. This was, indeed, one of Rome's
assets, that it seemed backward in terms of Greek
development but advanced in terms of Italian development.

The chances of either the Etruscans or Carthaginians emerging triumphant in the struggle for control
of the west were relatively slight. The Etruscans
were about a dozen city-states, very alien and very
advanced when they dominated central Italy in the
period down to about 500. In the sixth century they
extended across the Appenines to the Po valley and
the Adriatic from their bases in Etruria north of the

361

Tiber, but in the following century they were in ebb, losing most of their colonies in the Po valley to the Gauls and their city of Capua, west of the mountains, to the Oscans about 423. They were ejected from Rome, at one time an Etruscan bridgehead at the first ford across the Tiber above its mouth. The date of Rome's overthrow of its Etruscan rulers is traditionally put at 509 B.C. but may have been later. The Roman capture of the fortified Etruscan city of Veii, nine miles north of Rome, after a long siege, about 400, marked the beginnings of the final collapse of the Etruscans.

This decline was largely due to internal decay, especially to the Etruscans' growing obsession with death and with their increasingly rigid and formalized religion which sought to ensure spiritual survival after death. But in the earlier period, from about 700 to about 500, the Etruscans played a very significant role in the western Mediterranean, especially in their cooperation with the Carthaginians to restrict the Greek colonial expansion in that area.

Although the Etruscan cities did not fight each other, neither did they unite together or even cooperate very closely in any political arrangements. They had a league of twelve Etruscan cities, but it was for religious cooperation, not military or political. Their early expansion probably rested on the fact that they possessed the city-state and superior weapons, including body armor and the chariot, before the native peoples of their area. They gave a great deal to the Romans, especially the alphabet, the city-state organization, relatively advanced weapons derived from Etruscan control of the iron industry of Tuscany and Elba, and various religious rites, including political symbols and forms.

The Carthaginians were also handicapped in the struggle for the west. They were Phoenician colonies, established as trading posts, not as agricultural colonies like the Greek settlements, and were generally on small islands separated from the shore by narrow channels of shallow water or on peninsulas of small area with narrow necks. As a result, these centers had limited areas, small populations, and no agricultural resources. Their early arrival in the west gave them a commercial monopoly, trading with the native peoples, which they tried to maintain by secrecy, without warlike activities.

The arrival of the Greeks forced the Carthaginians to change their tactics, seek agricultural lands on the mainland, and try to preserve their commercial monopoly by force. As a result, they allied with the Etruscans and began to annex the shores of the west, especially along the African coast to Morocco and in southern Spain (where they met strong opposition from the native peoples).

The Greek pressure grew steadily as they moved outward toward Carthaginian areas from their own areas in eastern Sicily, southern Italy, and southern Gaul (from Massilia near the mouth of the Rhone). While Massilia disputed eastern Spain both with the Carthaginians and the native peoples, other Greeks settled in the Carthaginian zone of western Sicily, tried to settle near Tripoli in North Africa, moved northward against the Etruscans in the area around Naples, and began to settle in Corsica at Alalia.

The Alalia colony was a threat to the Carthage-Etruria trade route and to the Etruscan iron producing areas at Elba. Accordingly, a joint Etruscan-Carthaginian naval force attacked Alalia and forced the Greeks to evacuate the site. The Etruscans took Corsica and the Carthaginians took Sardinia as a result (535).

These two allies continued their efforts to push the Greeks back, Carthage working in Spain and Sicily and the Etruscans in northern Italy. The Carthaginians were relatively successful in Spain, but in Sicily and south Italy the Greeks held their own, although greatly hampered by their wars with each other. In 524 Cumae defeated an Etruscan land attack, only to succumb to the Oscans three years later. The Carthaginians occupied southwestern Spain and tried to drive the Greeks from western Sicily in 480, in an attack which may have been coordinated with the attack of their Phoenician relatives on Greece in Persia's service. At Himera, in northwestern Sicily, the Greeks led by Gelon, tyrant of Syracuse, totally defeated the Carthaginian attack on the same day, we are told, as the Greek victory in the east at the battle of Salamis (480). Six years later, Syracuse and Cumae joined forces to inflict a great naval defeat on the Etruscans off Naples.

Despite these victories in the west over Carthage and the Etruscans, the Greeks could not consolidate their control of the area or notably advance their holdings there. On the contrary, they continued to fight each other, in civil conflicts as well as inter-state wars, while individual Greek cities fell to the Oscans or to the Romans and their allies.

The Carthaginian invasion of Sicily in 480, which ended so disastrously at Himera, was triggered by invitations from two Greek leaders, Terillus the exiled tyrant of Himera and his son-in-law Anaxilas tyrant of Rhegium (Reggio) at the toe of Italy. These two feared the growing power of Gelon and his family, who controlled Syracuse on the east coast, Acragas (Agrigentum) on the south coast, Gela on the southeast coast, and Himera, whence they had expelled Terillus, on the northwest coast.

Gelon's victory at Himera destroyed a Punic force estimated at close to 100,000 men and brought him many slaves and an indemnity of 2000 talents. He made Syracuse the most populous city of the Greek world, protected by almost impregnable fortifications, served by large forces of mercenary fighters and with a navy of about 200 ships. It was this navy which defeated the Etruscans near Naples in 474.

Gelon's family controlled Syracuse from 485 to 466, when they were overthrown by a democratic revolt. They established the pattern which Dionysus I extended a century later and which became the Roman pattern under the empire. Gelon and Dionysus came to power as anti-tyrants, that is non-democratic supporters of the upper classes, but soon were using war as a method of increasing their own personal power. These wars were fought increasingly with mercenary forces paid by money raised from the sale of enslaved prisoners of war, from the loot, ransoms, and indemnities of war and, to some extent, from taxes imposed on their own subjects. Once the system got into full operation, taxes or even citizens were hardly needed, for it became a self-financing system. In fact, Gelon, who did not have time to raise taxes, got his start by using his mercenary soldiers to enslave large numbers of his own lower classes, selling them off to distant areas. This was regarded with approval by the upper classes who felt, for awhile, that Gelon was working for them rather than for himself. To obtain manpower which would be more docile than the lower classes of free citizens, Gelon and Dionysus moved populations about from city to city on a wholesale basis, enfranchised mercenaries by the tens of thousands, and freed slaves to make them citizens. As a result, the forces of social nexus, of traditional outlook, and of personal allegiance to the community were greatly reduced, and almost wiped out, replaced by force, materialist self-interest, and personal loyalty to the chief of state solely in his role as paymaster.

It took centuries of slow historical development for this last point to be reached in Rome and, indeed, it was not found there until after A.D. 69 and thus later than the period we are now discussing, but it was in full operation in the Syracuse of Dionysus in the fourth century B.C. and was well established among the ruling class of Rome at least a century before A.D. 69.

The elimination of Gelon and other tyrants and anti-tyrants from Sicily about the middle of the fifth century led to an age of democracy, which often patterned itself on Athens, with Sicilian versions of ostracism, election by lot, multiple annually elected generals, and growing imperialism. The Syracusan victory over the invading Athenian forces in 413 gave that state a dominant position on the island. This position was used to carry on a policy of democratic imperialism which had few advantages over the earlier non-democratic imperialism. By 410 the enemies and prospective victims of Syracuse were calling upon Carthage for help. With support from various Greek and Sicel allies, Carthaginian mercenary forces captured Selinus and

Himera, executing thousands of prisoners (408).
In 405 they captured Acragas, butchered the inhabitants, razed the city, then marched on Gela.

At this moment, a demagogue, Dionysus, used a
wave of panic in Syracuse to seize the government
and have himself appointed dictator (strategos
autokrator) with unlimited powers. For thirty-
eight years (405-367), he dominated the city with
his mercenary forces, which guarded him in a citadel within a locked naval basin on the island of
Ortygia in Syracuse harbor. He paid higher wages
to mercenaries and was much more liberal in the
distribution of booty than his rival leaders, but
this munificence could be financed only with a sequence of military victories. This made war a way
of life, as it later became in Rome.

Dionysus placed great emphasis on specialized
forces, including cavalry, hoplites, peltasts, engineers, and naval technicians. His armorers produced a number of missile weapons, including the
gastraphetes, a gigantic crossbow which hurled arrows or other projectiles. Although he made no new
techniques in fortifications or siegecraft, he exploited those already available more than any of
his contemporaries. His most significant innovation was the introduction of the quinquereme, a
war galley in which more than one man pulled on
each oar and he greatly increased the role of sea
power in military success.

Dionysus fought the Carthaginians in Sicily,
attacked the Greeks of southern Italy, allied with
the Gauls against the Romans and Etruscans of central Italy, hired tribal peoples, including the
Celts, Sicels, and Iberians, as mercenaries, and
acted as a pirate on the seas. He raided cities,
trade routes, and temples, seizing treasures and
prisoners, to finance his campaigns. At one time,
he controlled two-thirds of Sicily and the toe of
Italy, had a capital city, fully fortified, of almost half a million population, and controlled the
Sicilian Sea with over 300 warships. Yet little of
permanent significance was achieved, unless we try
to argue, as some do, that he saved Sicily from being taken over completely by Carthage. In 405,

again in 378, and again after his death in 367, treaties between Syracuse and Carthage fixed the Punic-Greek boundary in Sicily at the Halycus River, west of Acragus. Clearly neither side could control the whole island, in the then-existing basis of power arrangements. One of the factors in this situation was that the native peoples of the island, led by the Sicels, usually shifted sides against the power system which was threatening to dominate the whole island.

The most significant contribution made by Dionysus to our story was on the sea, through the invention of the quinquereme. As we saw in the last chapter, this vessel, and others similar to it from the quadrireme upward to Ptolemy IV's extravagant "forty," sought to get greater power and tactical maneuverability on the sea by placing multiple rowers on each oar. This effort assumes that ramming is the established method in a naval engagement, for, if the earlier tactic of boarding enemy vessels was used, the carrying capacity of the vessel would be better used for marines than for rowers. In general, states with plenty of fighting men or with limited experience on the sea preferred to use boarding rather than ramming, as Rome did. The Greeks used ramming, but in the western Mediterranean boarding continued till very late. As late as 397, the Carthaginians used boarding tactics to defeat Dionysus off Catana, destroying more than a hundred Greek ships and 20,000 seamen. Later Carthage adopted ramming as her regular tactic in naval warfare, but was defeated on the sea by the landlubberly Romans who used boarding tactics in the Punic Wars of the third century (267-241, 218-201).

The expense of building and operating these larger warships, combined with the limited utility of sea power when naval vessels had such a short operational range, and the difficulty of getting seamen who were both willing and skilled had a double consequence. The influence of sea power in determining the size and shape of power areas was reduced, and the number of states which could engage in naval competition was greatly reduced. Moreover, the largest vessels ceased to be useful, because no one was prepared to engage them in battle. Thus they developed somewhat as battleships and aircraft carriers did in the twentieth century. As these "capital ships" became more expensive to build and to operate, so that fewer states could maintain them, they became decreasingly effective in operation and achieved their control of the sea by prestige and reputation rather than by ability to control what individuals or smaller states were doing on the sea. It was this motive of prestige which led Ptolemy IV to maintain his "forty" which required over 4000 rowers. The same situation opened the door to piracy, by permitting evasive hit and run tactics by smaller vessels.

But this situation of expensive and ineffectual naval vessels made it possible for smaller states to emerge in the interstices of power among the great states, both on land and on the sea, in the Hellenistic period. These smaller states played a vital role, in the second and third centuries B.C., by inviting Rome to intervene in the eastern Mediterranean and western Asia as a counterbalance to the three great kingdoms which arose there following the death of Alexander the Great in 323 B.C.

Of these lesser states, the chief role on the sea was played by the island of Rhodes which became a major commercial and banking center, with a large merchant marine, a very efficient navy, and a policy of suppressing piracy and maintaining freedom of the seas. Rhodes could do this because, as an island, it was beyond the reach of the land forces of the great Hellentistic kingdoms. These kingdoms, like the Persian empire earlier and the Roman empire, to a lesser degree later, tended to ignore sea power because of their absorption in bureaucratic, continental, administrative systems based on land forces, which they inherited or copied from the older archaic empires. Moreover, Rhodes (and others) could retain independence longer than justified by its own power by balancing the great Hellenistic kingdoms against each other, always offering naval, commercial, and financial cooperation to what appeared to be the weaker kingdoms against the dominance of the strongest. Thus, about 300 B.C., Rhodes supported the Antigonids of Macedonia against the dominant Ptolemies of Egypt in their growing

naval race. About 221 B.C. Rhodes headed a coalition of commercial and naval interests to prevent
Byzantium from raising the tolls on goods passing
through the Bosporus. But in 201 B.C., when the
Egyptian navy was rotting in its docks and Macedonia was still building ships steadily, Rhodes sent
a galley to Italy to ask Rome to intervene against
Macedonia to restore the balance of power. In the
resulting struggle, Rhodes played a vital role in
Rome's naval successes in the east, but by doing
so it was contributing to the ultimate elimination
of all states independent of Rome in that whole area.

The reasons why the Romans succeeded, while
their rivals failed, in the struggle to dominate
Italy and the west are complex. Geographically,
the site of Rome was of great significance: the
most important crossing on the largest river of
peninsular Italy, a vital communications center at
the intersection of important routes leading north-
west-southeast along the line of the peninsula and
southwest-northeast across the peninsula from sea
to sea; close to some of the larger areas of better
agricultural soil west of the mountains, in Latium
and Campania; a meeting ground of very diverse peoples including the Latins themselves, the Etruscans,
the Sabines, and the Samnites. Moreover, among
these peoples, the Romans obtained from their contacts with the Etruscans an earlier and more successful transition from a tribal structure to a city-
state structure.

It cannot, in honesty, be said that the success
of the Romans was attributable to their outstanding
military abilities, for they were defeated, and disastrously defeated, again and again. Rather, the
apparent military successes of the Romans seem to
be the consequences of three other factors: (1)
they never recognized or admitted that they were
beaten, no matter how often nor how overwhelmingly
they were defeated, but continued to fight and to
return to the fray again and again until the tides
of war shifted in their favor; (2) they were never
beaten by a really ruthless enemy who was interested
in destroying Rome, as the Greeks might have been or
as Hannibal would have been. Rome was defeated and
even sacked several times in its early days but never

369

had its population totally massacred and enslaved,
as it did to some of its victims; and (3) the average
Roman was unimaginative and uncritical, rather dull,
unlikely to see that there was any way to deal with
problems other than by war and violence, ready to
obey his leaders and accept their justifications of
their policies with few questions, and prepared to
go on accepting and believing all kinds of contradictory, obsolete, and nonsensical ideas, customs,
and institutions. This third point helps to explain
the first point, while the second helps to explain
how the Roman survived with the other two.

However, even when these points are recognized,
the fact remains that the Romans had certain real
military assets. One of these was the tenacity and
discipline of the ordinary Roman soldier. The Greco-
Roman method of fighting put great emphasis on these
qualities, and the Romans had them even more than
the Greeks. Both of these peoples stood in their
phalanxes or legions and pushed and slashed until
they were killed or cut to pieces. The barbarous
peoples they fought, especially the tribal peoples
that Rome conquered in the west, were brilliant,
violent, uncoordinated, undisciplined. Most of them
were still deeply involved in the Indo-European
heroic tradition in which each fighter tried to
outdo his own fellows by the violent individualism
of his warlike exploits. As the Frenchman said,
"C'etait magnifique, mais ce n'etait pas la guerre."
And it usually did not win battles against people
like the Romans. If the Gauls or Germans did not
sweep the Romans aside in their first impetuous on-
slaught, they were most unlikely to win, for at that
point their formation broke up into individuals,
each fighting for himself. Such people were vola-
tile and unstable, swept by emotions from undue
heights of optimism to equally undue depths of despair, and sometimes back again, in a few moments
with little solid reference to what was going on.
A setback in one corner of the battlefield might
spread panic to all other areas of the conflict
just at the moment that that setback had encouraged
the enemy to take some step which should well have
doomed his forces, but the Gauls or Germans, and
equally some of the other tribal enemies of Rome,
would lose the battle because of their panic at

this minor, peripheral, and opportunistic setback. In such circumstances the Roman soldier fought on steadily and methodically, following orders from officers who, as likely as not, would be experienced enough and imaginative enough to see the changes in the situation and take advantage of them.

The reasons for these differences seem clear enough. To the Romans war was a business, their specialty. To most of their enemies, it was an adventure. And the cold-blooded businesslike approach to war paid off in victories for the Roman fighting man, until that day, after the third century A.D., when there was no longer any home front or even any society to back him up in his efforts.

Closely related to these advantages in the Roman experience of war is another equally important: the quality and above all the quantity of Roman military equipment was superior to most of the people they fought against. The parallel here with the Greek victory over the Persian hosts in 490-478 B.C. is strong. Just as the Greeks with metal helmets, metal shields, and metal cuirasses were victorious over Persians with leather helmets, wicker shields, and quilted tunics, so the Romans, except when they were fighting Greeks, constantly came up against opponents whose armaments were inferior to their own by a wide margin. The oft-repeated story that the early Germans fought their battles completely naked is probably untrue, but in terms of relative armaments the Germans, the Gauls, and others were relatively naked in a defensive sense against Roman weaponry. For example, the Gauls who were destroyed at Telemon in 225 B.C. had swords with no point and only one edge which was so soft that the edge of the sword itself was bent by a single blow and had to be restored to shape by stepping on it against the ground.

The Germans, who gave the Romans as much trouble as any of their non-civilized enemies, had neither helmets nor breastplates, their shields were of wicker and thin boards, not over a quarter-inch thick at the edges, and their spears generally lacked metal points. These Germans, in the first century B.C., were about the stage the Greeks had been in 800 B.C., which the Romans had reached about 500 B.C., and which the Gauls and other Celts were about 400 B.C. They were of course still tribal, without the city-state, were semi-pastoral, and were just in process of moving from an age of kings to an age of nobles about 60 B.C. What Caesar calls their towns (oppida) were not towns at all, since no one lived in them a large part of the time; they were simply citadels like the Acropolis in Athens had been in origin.

The greatest military advantage which the Romans had was somewhat like the military advantage which the United States has shown over the past century: they were unequaled from a quantitative point of view in regard to weapons and equipment, especially in terms of the most expensive items such as their siege train, and closely associated with this was their superiority in all aspects of supply and military engineering. The Romans were the first great digging army: they built a fortified camp every night, even when they were marching with half a dozen legions (that is up to 40,000 men). They built bridges, ditches, palisades and field obstacles faster than any army they ever fought against. And when their opponents came up with similar efforts, Roman soldiers, even when they were inferior in numbers, could bury the opposition in engineering works of all kinds.

This was particularly true of siege activities. In five centuries of military conquest the Romans rarely came up against a city or fortress that they could not capture sooner or later. We must add to this that the Romans in all their wars, even against tribal peoples like the Gauls and Germans, always had important help from numerous traitors and spies among their enemies. One reason for this is that few of these enemies had the Roman assets for bribery and for rewarding services, at least after the first crucial century of Roman expansion, from about 450 to 338.

Closely related to this question of wealth is the question of numbers of men and available supplies. In spite of the figures which have been traditionally accepted, as a result of Roman propagandists, both ancient and modern, the Romans generally

372

outnumbered the enemy in battle, and they almost invariably had greater supplies. The French historian Ferdinant Lot has shown that the figures given by Caesar for the numbers of his opponents and the size of his victories are obviously gigantic falsehoods: for example, in June of 55 B.C. Caesar destroyed completely a force of 430,100 invading Germans in a battle at the confluence of the Meuse and the Rhine, yet the Romans did not suffer a single casualty! Three years later, at the siege of Avaricum (present-day Bourges), Caesar stormed the Gaulist citadel (oppidum), killing 40,000 of the enemy. In modern times, when the same area was much more heavily populated and more adequately supplied, the area occupied by the Gauls' citadel held only about 3000 people, and all of Bourges, in an area much larger than the Gauls' fortress, did not have 40,000 persons until the present century. In his first campaign in Gaul (in 58 B.C.) Caesar tells us that an invading force of 368,000 persons was defeated by him so decisively that only 110,000 escaped back into Switzerland. This represents a loss of 258,000 persons inflicted by Caesar's six legions of about 30,000 men with 4000 cavalry. Napoleon III calculated that it would require 8500 wagons with 34,000 horses to move a crowd this large, but Napoleon, as Lot points out, would have required four times as much wagonage as he estimated, a totally impossible situation. Lot doubts that Caesar ever was outnumbered by the enemy in battle. This was generally true of other Roman leaders and, in view of the qualitative inferiority of most of Rome's enemies, at least in the west, there was no reason why Rome should not have won most of the time.

In addition to their military advantages the Romans were successful because their military skills were outstanding. This may have been because their sense of power was paramount. In fact, the rise of Rome is worthy of detailed study because of the lessons it affords on the proper relationship between power and diplomacy in terms of broad strategy.

The Romans had a positive genius for seeing the sequence in which problems of power and strategy should be handled. They constantly were able to identify the greatest threat, the most powerful opponent in a situation, the weakest link in a coali-

tion. When faced by a stronger opponent, they were
able to mobilize an alliance against him and, as
soon as he was disposed of, split the alliance to
direct its members against the next strongest power,
continuing this process until the remaining powers
could be taken care of by Rome itself.

This sense of power and their personal obsession with the prestige which goes with power had
two other consequences. The Romans were prepared
to use any methods or means available to ensure the
continued aggrandizement of the power of their state
and of themselves as individuals, as families, as
clans, and as social classes, within this state.
They were not distracted by pleasures, or by wealth,
or women, or self-indulgence, or theories, or logic,
at the early stages at least. Yet they were fully
aware of the influence of these things on others,
and they were fully prepared to offer these things
to their opponents if they could obtain, in return,
the power they craved.

This craving for power was even more notable
within the Roman state than in its relations with
other states, especially among the ruling groups
which always remained a small minority, so that access to power would be restricted to a small number
of contenders. In fact, from this point of view,
the ruling groups treated their own subject majority
similar to the way in which they defeated their foreign enemies: fully prepared to give them what they
might want so long as this did not increase their
power enough to threaten the prerogatives of the
ruling groups.

These Roman ruling groups were not hampered by
theories or ideologies, although quick with rationalizations. They never found logical obstacles to
action, because they cared nothing for logic. In
fact, they had no long-range idea of what they were
doing--ever. It has often been said that the Romans
had no plans of world conquest and that they became
rulers of the world in fits of absent-mindedness,
like England acquired its empire. This may be correct, but it means nothing. The Romans had no long-
range plans for world conquest because they had no
long-range ideas on anything. But a state and a

ruling group that obsessively judges every situation and every act in terms of aggrandizement of power will end up ruling the world or will be destroyed in the process. The Romans achieved both of these.

That last statement must be modified at once, because it is not true that the Romans were obsessively concerned with power. They were not, for they were obsessively concerned with something else, with honors, or most accurately with what they themselves called "dignitas." The impression that they were obsessed with power arises from the fact that the chief methods of acquiring dignitas required the use of power. But we must see the relationship clearly, which is not easy because we must see it through Roman eyes, which were quite different from our own. Indeed, we cannot even accept this last sentence as stated because dignitas, the real motivating element in the Roman system, was not a concern of the average Roman and may have been almost as incomprehensible to such an average Roman as it is, say, to the average modern classicist. The fact is that the average Roman, or even the overwhelming majority of Romans, had almost nothing to do with the decision-making processes within the Roman system and were about as remote from the thirst for dignitas as they were from any thirst for power. In fact, excluded from both dignitas and power, the average Roman concerned himself with quite other things, including a thirst for land, or for money, or for sensual pleasures or for numerous other things. But these motivations of ordinary Romans, found, perhaps, among the majority of persons then, now, and at most times in history, were not the motivations which made history, least of all among the Romans. The vital decisions which made history in the Roman system were based, more often than not, on the thirst for dignitas possessed by that small and exclusive group who controlled the Roman system and made up the Roman establishment.

The Roman success in war, in politics, and in the use of power rested on a number of things, one of which was this obsession with dignitas. For this meant that the Roman decision makers were not emotionally involved with power, or war, or politics or popularity except as a means and not as an end.

375

That is why they approached war in such a cold-blooded way and that is also why they acquired an empire "in a fit of absent-mindedness." Both war and empire were incidental (and thus objective) concerns of their real aim. This real aim, _dignitas_, was obsessive, irrational, and possibly largely unrecognized, by them as it is by so many students of the Romans today. Since the problem of stability in the Roman system is closely concerned with this obsessive concern of the Roman ruling groups with _dignitas_, both in domestic and in foreign affairs, we must examine these two separately.

3.   The Roman System

Domestic political stability within the Roman system was destroyed by the changes in Roman weapons systems even earlier and much more dramatically than was its international political stability. The former depends to an even greater degree than does the latter on keeping a close relationship between theory and fact, between law and actual conditions. And in Rome the discrepancy between these two was wider and at an earlier date in domestic than in foreign politics, simply because the ruling groups in Rome had an interest in making matters look different from what they actually were, a feat of deception and self-deception which historians and classical scholars have done much to maintain ever since.

It must be evident already that the domestic political history of Rome followed the historical stages we have identified in the Mediterranean area only in a distorted way and, of course, at least two centuries later than they occurred among the Greeks. The age of the kings ended about 500 B.C. The age of the nobles did not end but, instead, slowly changed into an age of oligarchy, which also changed slowly into an age of warlordism. The last of these was reached by Marius about 100 B.C., but the struggle between oligarchy and warlordism continued for centuries.

This aberration in the normal (that is Greek) sequence arose from the failure of an age of tyrants to lead, as in Greece, to an age of democracy. In Rome potential tyrants and potential democrats were either bought off or were eliminated by murder. They were bought off by permission to share in the plunder of aggressive war, the potential tyrants being admitted to the oligarchic system and the potential democrats enticed to acquiescence by grants of land taken from conquered peoples but usually so remote from Rome that those who accepted such grants could not exercise their legal rights as citizens in Rome and usually found great difficulty in making an economic success of such lands because of the competition from the politically favored richer landowners near Rome.

There were a few potential tyrants in Roman history, of which the latest and most obvious were the Gracchi brothers. Other earlier potential tyrants generally sold out, although in some cases, they left a few legislative enactments of a democratic character before they sold out. Those who did not sell out were exiled, outlawed, or murdered. The failure of the Gracchi brothers and the murder of thousands of their supporters (133-123 B.C.) marked the end of any possibility of a workable democratic system in Rome and opened a century of civil wars (133-31 B.C.) to determine who would control the oligarchic system. The answer given to that question, and clearly indicated by the military "reforms" of Marius (107 B.C.), was "a military despot."

Rome began as a monarchy with a sharp distinction between nobles (patricians) and common people (plebs). The heads of the greatest patrician families (gentes) were in the Senate as an advisory body to the elective kingship, while the whole population was divided into three tribes, consisting of the patrician families with their client plebeian families. The latter included all non-noble members of the Roman system, such as the original enserfed natives and any outsiders who could gain admission to the system by being admitted to a tribe. Such admission, apparently, could be won only by gaining the patronage of one of the patrician families, possibly because naturalization was achieved by vote of the Senate and consisted essentially of admission to a tribe.

377

The three tribes were, like Greek tribes, religious, social, and military organizations. Each had a head, called a praetor, and was divided into ten curiae. Originally these thirty curiae were the basis for military service and formed a tribal assembly, the comitia curiata. The three tribes in fighting formation, called the legion, was originally an armed horde, of which some proceeded to battle on horseback and some on foot, but all fought individually on foot, in the old Indo-European tradition, determined to display memorable valor. Since those who rode arrived first, fought in fresher condition, and were better armed, being richer, they won greater prestige and sometimes even disposed of the enemy before the infantry arrived.

In time, this armed force became more formalized into three types: horsemen, full infantrymen, and auxiliaries; the full infantrymen were the backbone of the force and became increasingly dominant. This backbone probably was set at 6000 men, but at an early date, it was divided into two parts, each still called "a legion," with half the cavalry and 1200 auxiliaries. The praetor in command of each legion came to be called consul, while the third praetor retained civil functions, chiefly judicial.

This gave a legion of 4200 infantry plus 300 cavalry. To determine how many of the three types of fighting men were available, a census was held periodically to see what weapons each citizen possessed. At some date before 450 B.C. this census was classifying citizens into five classes on the basis of their incomes, with the three richer classes providing cavalry and heavy infantry, the two poorer classes providing the lighter armed auxiliaries. About the same time, but possibly earlier, the three tribes based on blood were replaced by four tribes based on locality within the city. This was similar to Cleisthenes' reform in Athens in 508 B.C.

As the city spread its rule outward, non-urban ("rustic") tribes were added. By 387 B.C. there were 17 rustic tribes; 8 more were added in 358-299, and a final two in 241. At that point, with a total of thirty-five tribes, this process ceased,

and no more tribes were established: additional
population and newly annexed areas were deprived
of citizenship or added into the existing thirty-
five. In this way the tribes came to consist of
scattered peoples, with the original four urban
tribes regarded as socially inferior and used for
poor and other undesirable persons such as ex-slaves.

Long before this, about 360 B.C., when there
were still 21 tribes, the number of legions increased to four, with each tribe contributing 200
men to each legion (4200 in all). The internal
structure of the legion had also changed, in this
period before 300.

The first great tactical change, shortly after
450, was the adoption of full hoplite tactics, with
the legion organized in a solid phalanx, probably
in three lines, with spears in front, swords and
javelins behind. Internally the legion was divided
into 60 centuries, each under a centurion and consisting of 70 men, in three ranks.

This hoplite phalanx marked a new day in Rome's
military fortunes (about 444 B.C.) and was associated,
it would seem, with the establishment of the class
system and the creation of the census and the censors in 443. It was effective until sometime in the
wars with the Samnites when it became evident that
its solid mass could not retain its solidity on
broken terrain. Accordingly, the hoplite solid
formation was replaced by the more open and flexible maniple formation. Each maniple consisted of
two centuries with ten maniples in each line, arranged so that the first two lines now had 1200
men each, while the third had only 600, the 1200
velites acting as skirmishers. Each maniple had
two centurions who had the responsibility to move
the maniples forward or obliquely to fill gaps
which appeared in the front, either from the uneven terrain or from enemy action. The flexibility
provided by the maniples was a considerable advantage to the Romans in their combats with other hoplite formations and was probably copied from the
Samnites.

Just as the earlier curiae formation had possessed a political assembly known as the comitia curiata, so the new local tribal military organization began to function as a political assembly, this one called the comitia centuriata since its basic units were centuries, both those of active service soldiers (age 17-45) and the centuries of retired veterans (over 45) subject only to reserve calls. In this assembly the voting was by classes as well as by centuries with decisions based on the count of centuries, not on the sum of the individual votes within the centuries. Moreover, the numbers of men in the centuries were not equal, partly because the centuries of reserve veterans were smaller but also for other reasons we do not fully understand. In this system 40 centuries, that is 40 votes, were allotted to the active forces of Class I and an equal number to the reserve centuries of the same class; but there were only 10 centuries for each half of Classes II, III, IV, and V. Somewhat later Class V was given 30 centuries, instead of 20, and 5 centuries of non-combatant forces were formed at the bottom, while 18 centuries of cavalry, drawn from the Class I census level, were placed at the top. This meant that Class I, the richest group, had 98 out of a total of 193 centuries and votes. The top three classes were soldiers of the line, and Classes IV and V were the velites.

When the hoplite legion was formed about 450 or so, it included 300 cavalry, 100 from each of the three blood tribes. The number of cavalry was doubled before the so-called "Servian reform" which established the class system, and these 6 centuries of cavalry remained for generations the top units in terms of social prestige, reserved for patricians and with other privileges. When the class system based on wealth was set up, 12 additional centuries of cavalry soon followed, with membership achieved by recruitment from Class I (which could, in theory, include affluent plebeians). These 18 centuries of cavalry voted first, followed by the 80 votes of Class I, with only rare need to continue voting down into the lower classes to obtain the necessary 97 votes for a majority.

In Rome as in Greece, the property (and later

income) qualifications for the military service
classes were steadily reduced. There is no certainty about either the nominal or real value of
these distinctions, but the earliest we know, in
monetary terms, is from 100,000 asses for Class I
down to 12,500 asses for Class V. The latter was
reduced, first to 11,000, then to 4,000, and finally
was done away with by Marius in 107 B.C. The original figures of Classes II and III were 75,000 and
50,000 asses, so the latter may be taken as the income needed to provide suitable weapons for service in the line of the legion. As early as 396
B.C., payment for service was established when the
siege of Veii, the Etruscan city, only nine miles
north of Rome, required the legions to remain on
active service through the winter. The state increasingly provided equipment as well as supplies,
until in 123 B.C. all self-equipment ended, although the costs continued to be withheld from pay.
These changes gave more uniform equipment and made
it possible to raise far greater numbers of soldiers, but its most important aspects were social
and political, rather than military. So long as
only the well-to-do could serve, they controlled
the arms of the community as well as its military
and political life at the cost of being willing to
serve. The well-to-do saw this and were very reluctant, at first, to share the obligation of military service with outsiders or with the lower classes. So long as they controlled the legions, they
could expect to control the state. The sacrifices
of controlling the legions were so great, however,
especially after the terrible losses of the Second
Punic War (218-201 B.C.) and the need, following
that war, to garrison overseas provinces, that the
lower classes had to be allowed to share the burden.

They were not, however, simultaneously allowed
to share the government. This dichotomy led to increasing political instability since real power,
increasingly concentrated in the legions, was increasingly remote from the theoretical or legal arrangements for access to power. This is the root
of the great instability we call the "century of
revolution," 133-31 B.C.

The cavalry, drawn from Class I, had the same

property qualification as Class I, but both the horse and its upkeep were provided by the government, from an early date. The payments, probably 10,000 asses to buy a horse plus an annual allowance to provide its fodder, were raised by a special tax on widows and orphans of richer families, whose lack of a head made it impossible for the family to fulfill its military obligation by personal service. Only those persons who had this allowance (called equus publicus) could serve in the cavalry, until the poor quality and inadequate numbers of the cavalry (only 1800) in the Second Punic War made it necessary to accept volunteer cavalry who would provide their own horses. Many of Class I were willing to do this, because cavalry service had a much higher social prestige, was far easier, was politically more influential in the voting in the comitia, and required service for only ten years compared to the infantryman's requirement of sixteen years between the ages of 17 and 46. Moreover, when payment for cavalry service was established about 380 B.C., it was three times the pay of the legion infantryman. The infantry mutinied against this in 339 B.C., demanding that the annual fodder payment made to the cavalry be ended and the cost of this item be charged to the cavalryman's pay. This was done, but the social prestige and political advantages associated with cavalry service continued down to after 100 B.C. As a consequence, those who held the equum publicum tried to retain it long after their days of active service were over, and, by the second century, members of the senate held almost all the available places, while the actual obligation to serve was left largely to the volunteer cavalry who provided their own horses. A plebiscite of 129 B.C. made membership in the senate incompatible with service in the cavalry centuries, probably a political ploy by the anti-senate forces of that day seeking advantage for the well-to-do middle class groups who were not in senatorial families.

Thus we see a sequence of stages in the obligation of military service, associated in turn with (1) noble blood; (2) possession of weapons; (3) income classes; and (4) willingness to serve for pay. From the end of stage 1, no legal distinction was made on the basis of blood, so that the distinction between patrician and plebeian became increasingly meaningless in terms of military service. But in contrast to this, the patricians tried increasingly, from 500 B.C. onward, to make ever sharper distinctions in terms of political, social, and religious differences. Within the assemblies, in the magistracies, in the priesthoods, and in other ways, the status and activities of the plebeians were restricted. The plebeians fought back and could do so successfully in the long run because their military contribution was essential to the continued existence of the state. This struggle is generally known as "the conflict of the orders." In this struggle the plebs had two chief weapons--to threaten to withdraw from the state to create their own community (called "secessio") and try to create their own assembly and magistrates to implement this threat.

This conflict of the orders was really a double struggle, one between patricians and plebes (a question of blood) and the other between rich and poor (a question of money). The former reached its peak about 450 when intermarriage between the two orders was forbidden (probably for the first time). The leaders of the plebs, almost certainly the richer ones, cared little about intermarriage and cared even less for democracy. They wanted access to the magistracies and assemblies (especially the senate) for themselves and were prepared to accept any compromise which shifted such access from blood to wealth. On the other hand, they could get nothing without the backing of the plebs as a whole, so they had to associate themselves with the demands of the poor.

The demands of the poor were very much what they had been in Greece in the seventh century: relief from debts, written laws, a fair judicial system, and land. Of these the Roman plebs did get written laws and promises of land, but they got very little real relief from their debts and never got a fair, or even rational, judicial system. But as part of the struggle, they got a state of their own within the Roman state: an assembly (the concilium plebis), magistrates (24 tribuni militum, 10 tribuni plebis, and 2 aediles), religious functions, and their own records office (in the temples of Diana and Ceres). After two centuries of conflict, ending perhaps with the Lex Hortensia (c. 287), the plebs had established inviolability of the persons of its officers by its collective undertaking to protect them, had won for its tribunes the right to veto acts of other magistrates and assemblies, and had established that its legislative enactments, the plebiscites, were binding on all Romans.

These successes, won by strikes, withdrawal from the city, violence, and threats of violence, did not lead toward any real democracy in government because the plebs generally supported Rome's aggressive wars, either from patriotism or from the hope of winning land and sharing in the booty. The richer plebs were bought off by being admitted to the magistracies and the senate and by obtaining a preferred position in sharing the plunder of aggressive wars.

Arnold Toynbee puts the situation very well in his Hannibal's Legacy: "the gulf between a politically privileged and a politically unprivileged class, which had been virtually closed as between the patriciate and the plebs, had concurrently been reopened, within the bosom of the plebs itself, between those plebeians who were, and those who were not, in an economic position that would enable them to exercise their de jure political rights de facto. This split within the plebs' own ranks had reduced a majority of the plebeians to political impotence again, and this in the very hour of the plebs' apparent victory, by depriving them of their former leaders. Worse still, their lost leaders had gone over to their patrician opponents' side. . . . The support of the masses, which had enabled the plebeian nobles to invade the citadel of patrician privilege, had not served the plebeian nobles' turn; and, now that they had won their share in the government of the state, they put at the state's disposal the political machinery of the counter-state that the support of the masses had enabled them to build up as an engine designed ostensibly for producing improvements in the masses' economic position. Within the ranks of the new composite nobility the traditional conflict between plebeians and patricians had now become a game of shadow-boxing, carried on to hoax the plebeian masses into believing that the plebeian nobility was still on the masses' side. The tribunate of the plebs, which was no more accessible, de facto, to ordinary plebeian citizens than the consulate or the censorship was, had now, for the time being, ceased in effect to be an instrument for political and social reform and had become a camouflaged and therefore potent instrument for preserving the vested interests of the 'Establishment'. . . . All Roman domestic political contests now took place inside the circle of the new nobility. The opposition to the clique of individual nobles, or of noble families, that was in power at any given moment was always another clique of nobles."

In this way the conflict of the orders abated and the distinction between patrician and plebeian was confused. But in Rome nothing ever was done completely, rationally, and logically, so that even after 100 B.C. when the number of patrician families (gentes) was reduced to 14 from the total of about 50 that had existed before 450, they still had exclusive right to some posts, especially religious ones.

The superior position of the patricians was replaced by another system of privilege which is called by various writers the "senatorial nobility" or "senatorial aristocracy." It was neither a nobility nor an aristocracy, although the former term is somewhat more accurate. It consisted of the descendants of those who had held the highest magistracies in the state. This "nobility" amounted to no more than a few score families of which only about a score were patricians. Most of the constitutional regulations were modified to retain political authority in the hands of this "nobility," and these were reinforced by political regulations, social conventions, and religious and ideological restrictions. Most family relationships, including marriage, divorce, adoption, and inheritance were regulated to build up cliques and political factions. At the same time, the competition within the "nobility" in the struggle for office and honors was so great that many nobles were forced to seek other means of achieving their desires. Those who were, at any given moment, apparently successful within the complicated rules of

385

of the "system" formed an "establishment" and were
known as "optimates" ("the best men"). Those who
were not successful within "the establishment" were
forced to seek the same desired goals of offices,
honors, power, and prestige outside "the establishment" but still within "the system" came to be
called "the populares." Both optimates and populares were of the "nobility," and both worked within
"the system," the difference being that the former
were within "the establishment." But because the
system was not based on power but on legal rules
and conventions, there was a third alternative,
namely that either optimate or populare might be
forced outside of the system itself, and seek power,
honors, and prestige in the world of money, number
of supporters, or weapons control.

Thus the Roman community, always dynamic and
changeable, might be regarded as consisting of three
concentric circles of which the largest is the community of Rome (the state), the second is "the system" of government, and the innermost circle, within
the system, is "the establishment."

The rules of the establishment were slightly
more self-consistent and rational (in the sense that
they were understandable) than those of either the
system or of the larger entity which I am calling
the community. The rules of the system outside the
establishment were full of contradictions and irrationalities, while the community, outside of the
system, was much more real in the sense that it included the elements of force, wealth, and manpower.

One of the chief purposes of the rules of the
establishment was to exclude these three real elements of power (force, wealth, and numbers) from the
system. These rules were set up like those of a
game. The game was played according to the rules
of families (rather than individuals) and the goal
of the game was to maximize the "honors" possessed
by each family. These "honors" were very concrete
objects and were on display in the atrium of every
successful establishment family. Such an atrium
was like the trophy room of a yacht club or of the
gymnasium of a great university, placed so that all
visitors to the building must pass by the display
and recognize the prestigious record of those who

own it.   Professor L.R. Taylor points out that this is what Virgil's Aeneid or Livy's histories or Cicero's life work is all about, and adds, "There was a splendid tradition of sternness, discipline, courage, and patriotism, and every noble strove to keep it alive both by recalling constantly the distinctions of his ancestors, and by striving himself to reach an equal eminence.   The atrium of the city house was adorned with the wax images of the noble's ancestors, accompanied by emblems and inscriptions recording the consulships and censorships, the priesthoods and the triumphs they had held.   In the magnificent pageantry of the public funerals of members of these great houses, these images were taken with the dead to the Rostra and were placed on descendants who were thought to resemble their ancestors.   And in the funeral orations the achievements of these ancestors were lauded along with the deeds of the man who had died."

Every great family of the senatorial nobility had a hereditary clientage of supporters and dependents.   These had the obligation to report every morning to their patron, the head of their noble family. As they came in, they paid their respects to the honors displayed in the atrium.   When their patron died, they formed part of the funeral procession, the culminating event of a noble Roman's life.   In that display the death masks, robes of highest office, and insigniae of honors were worn by relatives or other persons led by the representative of his most remote ancestor (who had made the family noble by first holding a curiale magistracy), each ancestor's representative walking in file, ending with the one who acted for the dead man himself, wearing his mask and robes, and walking just before the coffin.   Here on display was what the Roman establishment was all about, the motivation of the Roman nobility, and the key to all the strange anomalies of the Roman political and social system.

The sum total of the honors of a family (or an individual who represented a family) was his "dignitas."   As F.E. Adcock put it, "The claim of dignitas is, indeed, the most constant ingredient in the active political history of the Republic."   This was simply the Roman version of the old Indo-European pastoralist's thirst for immortality, a slightly more civilized version of the Homeric "Sacker of Cities" or of the Kwaitkiutl potlatch. It was on the same level of irrationality as the potlatch, a fact which may be difficult for us to recognize because we must see through more than two thousand years of propaganda which sought to portray the Romans and the Roman system as noble, efficient, self-sacrificing, patriotic, law-abiding and all the other virtues. It was none of these, although, as it became increasingly aware of Greek and other eastern ideas of ethics and idealism, it verbalized these and became increasingly hypocritical. This process reached one of its peaks in Cicero, although as an operational method it culminated in Augustus and in his "principate" (31 B.C.-A.D.14).

In theory the young noble, always in competition with other nobles of his own generation and always supported by the wealth, prestige, influence, and clientage of his own family, could work his way up to the honors of the establishment. His education was based on personal contact with Roman political life, the law courts, and war, while his training concentrated on public speaking, physical exercises, and military duty. About ten years of military service, not as a regular soldier but as a kind of warrant officer, was expected before he engaged in active political life, but by 150 B.C. this was being curtailed, or replaced by service with some family friend in provincial administration or possibly in study with some famous teacher in the Greek east. A year's service as an elected military tribune might be followed by a year or two in those parts of Italy where his family had estates or political influence. At age 30, he could be elected to the lowest level of the cursus honorum, the quaestorship, which also obtained admission to the senate. Nine years later, after further experience with war and provisional clientage and after seeking publicity by a lawsuit or two, either as prosecutor of some family enemy or personal rival or perhaps only as a witness, he could seek the praetorship, followed by a period as a pro-praetor in charge of a less important province. Three years after that, at age 43, he could try for the consulship, to be followed by a year as pro-consul in charge of a major province.

Until 150 B.C. the consulship could be sought again after a ten-year interval, but a law of about that date restricted an individual to a single term as consul. But Scipio Aemilianus was consul in 147 and 134 B.C. while Marius was chosen for five successive years in 104-100 B.C. The censorship completed the cursus honorum.

This sequence was, of course, often violated, although it was enacted into law in approximately these terms in 180 B.C. War or various emergencies or simply personal ambition could vary it, especially after 133 B.C., but its chief purposes, to win honors and incidentally recoup wealth for the family, remained. Wealth came from the booty and other rewards of military life and from the opportunities provided by the almost unrestrained powers of a Roman administrator in a province. In fact the whole system was financed from the booty of wars and the plundering of provinces by corrupt administrators.

Although the nobles competed with each other in this race for honors, they generally formed a united front to prevent any outsiders from getting into the system or to prevent the rules from being changed adverse to their own interests. Any outsider who broke in by winning a higher magistracy was called a "new man" (novus homo) and was not socially acceptable as an equal, although his descendants were regarded as noble.

In the hundred years before 133 B.C., the year the revolution began, 99 consuls came from only ten families. Over that period there were 92 patrician and 108 plebeian consuls; of the 92 patricians, 85 came from 10 families and 48 came from 4 of them; of the 108 plebeian consuls 74 came from 11 families and 27 from 3 of them. Thus about 20 families dominated the power of the Roman state about 200 B.C. In the following 55 years, with 110 consuls, only four were novi homines. A century later, in the 31 years from 94 to 63, only one of 62 consuls was a new man.

The Roman constitution was not rational, self-consistent, nor responsible. It was not rational because there was no sensible or orderly relationship between the functions of government and the resources to make such functions operate and the assemblies and magistrates of the Roman system. There were five chief assemblies, and at least seven civil magistracies. There was no sensible division of functions among these. In the assemblies, generally, action could be prevented rather than facilitated, from the fact that only magistrates could introduce projects and the speakers could say nothing until called upon by the presiding officers who generally called up speakers in descending rank of prestige, and there was rarely time for a major part of the members to be reached. The magistrates were "collegial" and each could prevent his fellows from acting and, in some cases, could prevent magistrates of different rank from acting. Only outside of Rome, on mission, especially in the provinces, did magistrates have autonomous power. To remedy these weaknesses there were provisions for emergency magistrates, such as dictator, inter-rex, and others who had wider powers but for very limited periods.

The system of justice was chaotic, in spite of the general impression that most Romans were legal geniuses. Actions, even criminal, were brought by private persons, or by magistrates, and were tried by the political assemblies or by commissions drawn from them, always made up of well-to-do or well-established persons. Cases could be retried or shifted from one assembly to another, and the rules were changed frequently. By the time of Cicero, bribery was, by far, the chief factor in settling any judicial case. Even without bribery, the decisions we know of often had no relationship to the merits of the evidence. One reason for this may be that the greater part of the cases we know about were politically inspired and politically decided.

Technically speaking, Rome had no constitution, since it had no rules of government which were of superior force nor enacted by a different procedure from ordinary laws. The Roman "constitution" was made up of conventions and ordinary statutes. Not only was this body of rules constantly changing; it was lacking in consistency, was violated with impunity, and was not supported by any consensus regarding its meaning or weight. It could be violated

390

without anything being done. P. Scipio Africanus
(c. 236-184) was elected aedile when he was not yet
the required age (213 B.C.) and three years later
was made pro-consul in Spain without any of the
constitutional qualifications. Pompey the Great
(106-48 B.C.) had two triumphs and was pro-consul
in Spain (77 B.C.) before he illegally forced the
senate in 71 B.C. to make him consul.

The provisions of the constitution themselves
allowed alternative actions which make it totally
impossible to analyze it in our terms of a sovereign state under established rules. Magistrates
could overrule and veto each others' actions, and,
in many cases, could also force the assemblies or
even the courts to stop their activities in mid-
flight. In view of the fact that there were 10
tribunes of the plebs and any one of them could
veto almost any action in the city of Rome itself,
it was almost always possible to find one who
would veto a political action.

A similar irresponsible power existed in the
priesthoods and in the censorship. There were two
censors, elected for 18 months, every five years.
Their chief task was to make the census, a list
of the citizens by tribes in the five census classes. But they soon obtained much wider rights including the authority to strike a name from a class
or tribe and shift it to some other grouping, for a
wide variety of reasons including "moral reputation."
Since they also obtained the right to list the members of the senate, they could, either together or
separately, remove someone from that body. Since
they supervised all leases of government property
and bids for government contracts, they also had
great economic power, especially as the chief motive
force of economic action increasingly was government spending.

A couple of cases will illustrate the arbitrary
way in which these matters functioned. Cato, as
censor in 184, made contracts on such favorable terms
for the government that some of the contractors appealed to the senate, which threw out the new contracts and ordered Cato to renegotiate them; he
did so but this time excluded those who had appealed

391

to the senate from the previous bidding.

When the contracts of 174 B.C. were badly carried out, the censors excluded the publicans who
had obtained them from the next bidding in 169.
The disqualified publicans appealed to the senate
which this time refused to intervene. They then
went to a tribune of the plebs who had a personal
grudge against the censors. The tribune tried to
annul the newly-awarded contracts, and, when the
censors refused to obey him, prosecuted both censors for treason. The case was tried in the comitia,
and the voting had gone through the high-income centuries adverse to the censor, when influential members of the senate intervened and persuaded enough
of the remaining centuries to vote for the censor
to obtain an acquittal. The censors then removed
the tribune's name from the equestrian roll and also
removed him from his tribe, in effect making him a
political non-person.

Somewhat similar to the interference of tribunes, censors, and corrupt or biased courts in the
constitutional system was the interference of the
priesthoods and the whole system of Roman political
religion. In effect, nothing could be done in Rome
without the approval of the priests; these were
controlled by the patricians, or the nobles or at
least by the wealthy. The situation has been summed
up very well by Arnold Toynbee, "Since there could
be no imperium without auspicia, the augurs had a
veto on the transaction of public business. The observation of a meteorological portent, or even the
formal announcement, by a public officer, that he
was scanning the sky on the chance that a meteorological portent might catch his eye, was enough to
place an embargo on all political activities."

Few of the ruling groups after about 150 B.C.
had any sincere belief in the state's gods and
rituals, but these continued to be used as a method
of influencing the common people. We do not know
what the common people believed, and, in themselves,
they clearly offered no threat to the ruling groups,
but the ruling groups continued to use religion as
a method of influencing the common people. This influence was steadily weakened by the divisions of poli-

392

tical support which appeared within the priesthoods after 100 B.C., so that priests of the same "college" were to be found opposing each other on a single issue, but above all by the clear indications that the ruling groups, especially those who claimed to be seeking popular support, frequently ignored or defied the priesthoods. For example, about 60-50 B.C. Crassus, Pompey, and Julius Caesar openly defied the augurs.

It would seem that religion in Rome was manipulated for political purposes from the earliest days. For example, the priests ruled out voting on the days in which any large numbers of country people might be in the city, including all market days and the seven periods of public games each year. When reform bills were about to be taken up in the tribal assembly, the priesthoods frequently were able to delay or prevent action by inserting a period of religious activities, by ordering a repetition of various religious festivals already performed, or by finding that the day, persons, or places involved were displeasing to the gods. In fact, the priesthoods, of which there were four, had many of the attributes of a supreme constitutional court except that their grounds for preventing or overruling action were always put on religious, not on legal, grounds.

Cicero, himself a member of the college of augurs and a non-believer, says that the augurs are "the highest and most responsible authority in the state."

By means such as these the priests, who were, of course, the optimates themselves in different robes, often intervened in politics, sometimes successfully. T.S. Gracchus, father of the Gracchi brothers, the censor of 169 who was tried for treason by a tribune, was consul in 177 and again in 163. In the latter case he conducted the elections which named his successors, but when he later disagreed with the policies of these successors, he wrote to the college of augurs that he had forgotten to take the auspices on his way to the assembly which elected them. The augurs declared the election invalid, and the two consuls resigned. In 122 the tribune M.L. Drusus, who had vetoed the great reform bill of his fellow tribune C. Gracchus, brought in an even broader reform bill of his own, but it was overruled by one of the consuls of the year, who was an augur, on religious grounds. Twenty-two years later, a law, passed over senate objections, to distribute lands to Marius' veterans was declared invalid by the augurs. More than a generation later, looking back on all this, Cicero wrote that the great estates (latifundia) would not have been broken up and distributed among the people if it had not been for the augurs.

In a constitutional system as chaotic and contradictory as this, the optimates played the game in their determination to run up their scores of honors and offices. In view of the limited number of such offices the most urgent of their efforts was to reduce the number of persons who were eligible. These efforts constantly tended to move the whole system toward a caste structure (that is a social system based on hereditary classes), but in each such effort it was never possible to close the caste and prevent the intrusion of new men. The reason for this failure was that these efforts were always put on a non-power basis so that power by being excluded was always left available to outsiders to be used to break in on the privileged group. In this way the patricians failed to exclude the plebs, the fusion of these two into a nobility then failed to exclude the so-called equestrian order of the wealthy, and this last, not yet firmly in power on the basis of wealth, were pushed aside, in the last century B.C., by naked military force.

Just as important, in the Roman system, as this futile effort to turn those eligible to play the game for honors into a hereditary caste, was the equally strong determination to prevent any single family from monopolizing honors by changing the system into a monarchy. This, and not hatred of the Etruscan kings, is the reason for the persistent Roman fear of monarchy. This fear was not based, as is often stated, on the Roman "love of liberty" any more than it was based on some mythical Roman "hatred of the name of king." It was simply based on the determination of those eligible to play in the game

that no single person or family should get in a
position to change the rules of the game to exclude
others who were already in.

Closely related to this last point were two aspects of the Roman system which have rarely been
sufficiently emphasized. One is the Roman emphasis
on collegiality of magistrates; the other is the
Roman insistence on a government of limited powers.
The supreme governing power (imperium) was regarded
with great suspicion by the optimates since it could
be used to change the rules of the game and especially the rules of eligibility to play in the game.
It included command in war and execution of laws,
including the power of life and death. It was thus
essential to a state and especially to a warlike
state such as Rome necessarily had to be (since the
chief honors were won in war), but it was a constant
danger to the game itself. Accordingly, all kinds
of restrictions were placed upon it, such as the requirement that it had to be granted by vote of the
oldest assembly, the comitia curiata (even to the
end of the republic when the 30 tribes were simply
represented by 30 lictors), was held collegially,
and was under other restrictions, such as limited
term and often in a limited area (outside the city
and in a specified province). In respect to collegiality, multiple magistrates not only provided
more honors to be won in the game but provided some
insurance that the imperium could not be used, as
it eventually was, to change the rules of the game.

To keep the game going as a game, it was necessary to exclude the real elements of power from the
game at the same time that the use of these was essential to winning the honors that were the goal of
the game. The game went on within the city, yet
force, without which military victories could not
be won, was permitted only outside of Rome. The
efforts to maintain this distinction led to numerous rules and laws of which the best known perhaps
was the exclusion of imperium from the city itself,
except with special permission of the senate, such
as on the day of a victorious general's triumph.
The triumph itself, all set about with strict regulations and conventions, was one of the chief ways
in which a Roman scored points for his atrium. It

is significant that points were scored by the assumption of imperium in a lex curiata which granted it and also by the ending of the same imperium in a triumph. Both scores were made matters of official record in the fasti, chronological lists of these events. Part of this same situation is the regulation violated by Caesar in January 49 B.C. when he crossed the Rubicon River which divided Italy from Cisalpine Gaul. This rule, which made it a treasonable act to cross the Rubicon with armed forces, was for the purpose of excluding force from the game of politics in Italy. It was a successor to the early rule which forbade arms within the boundary of the city (pomerium) on religious grounds.

This concern of the Roman establishment with maintaining a limited area within which a limited number of persons could play the game of cursus honorum had another significant result which can be very misleading when looked at through modern eyes. We have said that the arena in which the game was played was the city of Rome and that the need to exclude force, wealth, and numbers from the game made it necessary to exclude these from the city, while retaining their influence outside the city where the achievements of the players were performed by the use of these, for which points were awarded within the city. From this basic assumption came the idea that the city was "home" and "peace" (domi et pac), while outside the city was conflict and war (militiae et bellum). The former was sacred, while the latter was profane and outside the rules. This is why the comitia centuriata, which assembled as an army to elect the magistrates, had to meet outside the city on the Campus Martius.

The Roman insistence on retaining its organizational structure as a polis was not based, as most commentators seem to believe, on any irrational infatuation with the city-state as an organizational form but was simply an incidental consequence of the establishment's desire to keep the arena and the eligible players limited. This desire, of course, was doomed in the long run by the consequences of the use of the real elements of power outside the city. Nevertheless, the establishment, in spite of the impossibility of success in what they were trying to do, were able to postpone the inevitable consequences for centuries. Roman history, as we know it, is largely made up of the distortions which arose from this effort.

Among these distortions was another great paradox, that this most powerful of cities never really obtained, in the period covered by this chapter, a fully sovereign state. Some writers have recognized this failure and have attributed it to the fact that the Romans were some kind of early nineteenth century liberals who believed that "that government is best which governs least." Others have attributed this feature of Roman life to the great Roman respect for private property. Both of these reasons are absurd, because the Romans lacked, almost totally, either the respect for individual rights implied in the one or the respect for property rights implied in the other.

As evidence of this failure to establish a sovereign state we might point out that there was no final authority in the Roman political system for settling disputes between the various organs of government, beyond a rather vague idea that a veto or injunction was superior to a mandate or positive order. Even in this, as in all other conflicts of authorities, there was no sovereign power able to resolve such conflicts. There was no real administrative system, no real civil service, and no financial system involving any kind of budget and accounts (according to A.H.M. Jones, Rome "for the first time" obtained "a budget in the modern sense" by the reforms of Diocletian about A.D. 300), no real system of taxation, and no control over the countryside or the provinces.

As one incidental example of this whole process, we might point out that the city of Rome itself, with a population of about a million persons in 50 B.C., had no police force and no fire department.

This general attitude explains why there was no real fiscal system nor even a theory of taxation to meet government expenditures during the republic. There were a few indirect taxes, chiefly customs duties (less than 5 per cent), in harbors and a 5 per cent tax on manumission of slaves. The only direct tax was the _tributum_ which was abolished in 167 B.C. and not applied in Italy again until Diocletian's reform about A.D. 300. This _tributum_ was a one per mille tax on the property valuation established by the census. It was imposed only for war and was regarded as a compulsory loan rather than a tax, with the implication that it would be paid back out of war booty. This was done from the loot brought from Asia in 187 B.C. During the Second Punic War, when the state was struggling for its very existence in the conflict with Hannibal, the state had no means, and apparently no conception, of how to raise money from the private persons who were making fortunes out of the war. As a result, it raised the _tributum_ from 1 per mille to 2 per mille in the second year of the war, went technically bankrupt in 215, set up a specially graduated tax on the census assessments in 214 to provide wages for the rowers in the fleet, and bought war supplies on credit from 215 B.C. on. The war contractors were able to supply the war effort on credit for more than a decade, because they had so much money while the state had none. The debts were paid off by the state before the war ended in 201, in two installments of one-third each in 204 and 202, and the final third in 200 by giving the businessmen the very valuable public lands within fifty miles of the city of Rome. Having paid off its creditors in this handsome fashion, the government then repaid the taxpayers 25.5 levies of the 34 levies of _tributum_ which had been imposed during the whole war (218-201). As Toynbee says, "A Roman's life was at Rome's disposal, but his money, if he had any, was his own, and it was sacrosanct."

This policy was not, as it might appear to us, a reflection of the establishment's respect for wealth or of the influence of the wealthy as a lobbying force on the establishment. Quite the contrary. It was a reflection of the establishment's disrespect for wealth and for the wealthy, in regard to wealth, and their desire to exclude it as a factor from the system, a point well documented by H. Hill's study of _The Roman Middle Class in the Republican Period_ (Blackwell, Oxford, 1952).

On a wider view, this same attitude appears in the refusal of the establishment to engage in economic planning or, indeed, in any real consideration of the economic aspects of public authority and power. This was based, about equally, on the exclusion of wealth from the basic value system of the establishment and their refusal to permit any real system of public administration (including the intrusion of expertise of any kind into the system). At a time when the eastern monarchies, especially that of the Ptolemies in Egypt, were equipped with an elaborate civil service administration using experts and keeping track of economic resources by a system of public accounts on rational fiscal principles, Rome was still governed by a handful of amateurs who completely disregarded basic economic realities and resisted with vehemence any suggestion that they should establish a civil service, a rational system of taxes, or any explicit way of keeping track of financial or economic resources. As a result, these sides of public authority were almost totally lacking until the days of Augustus Caesar, and it was necessary to leave all these activities to private groups without any way to keep track of their behavior or even to guarantee performance of contracts.

These failures were simply part of the much wider determination to exclude wealth from the game, just as the regulations already mentioned sought to exclude either force or the number of supporters from the process. But, to the degree that these three elements are aspects of power in a community which recognizes them as such, this means that the Roman state, at its very core where it was occupied with playing the game, was not a state at all.

Wealth was excluded as an element in the system by specific legislation. Of this the chief example was the Lex Claudia of 218 B.C. which forbade senators or their sons from ownership of ships over 225 bushels capacity. This permitted them to transport agricultural produce to the city from their estates for their own use, but not to engage in commerce. Other regulations and conventions, some of which may have been included in this same Lex Claudia, prohibited senators or their families

from bidding on public contracts, from lending money
at interest, and possibly from other commercial
activities.

These regulations had a double consequence:
(1) they restricted senators to earning wealth in
agricultural activities and politics, especially as
conquering generals or as governors of provinces;
and (2) they gave rise to a new social group of the
wealthy, the so-called equestrian order who were
permitted to make money in doing these things. As
a consequence of this double process, not only was
all large-scale financial, fiscal, and economic
activity excluded from the functions of the state,
and instead became attributes of the equites outside
of the state, but the whole economic development of
Rome became uncontrolled, disastrous, and almost
unnoticed, until the nefarious consequences of this
neglect could no longer be ignored.

The equestrian order came to be those whose
census assessment entitled them to serve in the
cavalry (although very few did) but who were not
members of the senatorial establishment because
they were not descendants of curial magistrates.
In time these became a recognized hereditary class
in the community, based on free (non-slave) birth,
the equestrian census of 400,000 sesterces, and en-
rollment on the roll of the equites.

In these terms the equites were in existence
from an early period, became very influential, became very wealthy, outside the establishment from
the middle of the third century onward, but became
an order only with the legislation of Gaius Gracchus
in 122. Their fortunes were made in war contracts,
in loans at high rates of interest, and in the financial plundering of the provinces. The laws of 122
not only defined the order but set up three laws
which made it the rival of the senate. These were:
(1) senators were excluded from service as cavalry;
(2) membership on the juries which tried cases of
corruption and extortion in the provinces was taken
from senators and given to the equites; and (3) the
auctioning of public contracts to collect the taxes
of the new province of Asia was shifted from Asia
to Rome, where the new equestrian order could conveniently bid on them.

400

The affluence thus offered to the members of this new order, and the legal protection afforded to their depredations abroad by the fact that charges against them would be tried by members of their own group made a way of life and system of values, distinct from the game of cursus honorum. With ample money and no political ambitions, a successful eques, like Cicero's good friend Atticus, could live a life of luxury and culture or could engage in the hurly-burly of amassing even greater wealth as he wished. The chief problem for the equites became the problem of survival with the pressures of the senatorial establishment on one side, the urban masses on another side, and the rising tide of force and militarism on the third side. All three of these needed, or at least wanted, wealth. When this could not be obtained by plunder, looting, and corruption from enemies abroad or from provincials nominally under the Roman imperium, it could always be obtained by confiscation from the equites.

Within this same quadrangular parameter of the establishment, the equestrian order, militarism, and the nameless masses of the common people, occurred, almost unnoticed and totally undirected, the economic decline of Italy, and ultimately of the whole Mediterranean basin. In this subject, as in so many others, the turning point took place during the Second Punic War of 218-201 (just as the similar turning point in Athens, and the Greek world generally, took place about 450 B.C.). But the impetus for expansion (or if you wish, imperialism) in the Roman system was well established long before the Second Punic War. To see how this happened, how the Roman system obtained the army which made such expansion possible, and how the combination of the motivation provided by the system and the means provided by the Roman army combined to create the Roman empire, we must go back again to the beginning.

4. Roman Expansion

The expansion of Roman territory from a few hundred square miles about 500 B.C. to the whole Mediterranean basin with much of western Europe a

half millennium later was fundamentally a reflection
of the growing offensive ability of the Roman power
system. In this growth the major, but by no means
the only, factor was the increasing offensive power
of weapons systems.

We have already indicated some of the reasons
for the Roman success in the western Mediterranean
and have mentioned three important factors which may
be repeated here: (1) the Romans were lucky in the
fact that they came along at a time when the tribal
peoples of the west were looking for a way to shift
from tribal life to city-state life and the city-
state peoples, both east and west, were growing weary
of interminable wars and interminable class struggles;
(2) the Romans satisfied some of the tribal peoples
because they offered them access to urban organizational patterns and amenities on a non-racial (if
also non-power) basis; and (3) the Romans satisfied
the desires of many oligarchic peoples and the possessing classes of the older states for an ending to
both war and civil disturbances. In these latter
cases the Romans were prepared to give both tribal
groups and oligarchic urban groups the things they
wanted if these could give up their liberty and
their essential power to the Romans.

To the tribal peoples the Romans gave non-poli-
tical urbanized benefits. They gave political rights
only in stages, making it quite clear that such
rights were available on the basis of "good" behavior, not birth, but granting political participation
in stages, in theory rather than in practice, and
in form rather than in substance.

To the urbanized people the Romans gave protection from invasion, from fratricidal wars, and
from bloodthirsty class struggles by freezing the
economic and social status quo, offering benefits
within that system to those who cooperated with
Rome and annihilation to those who refused to cooperate.

In both cases, Rome took over, at first, little more than control of foreign affairs and defense,
asking, in return, little more than moderate and defined contributions of troops and tribute to pay for
the maintenance of such troops. Local government was

left to these "allies" or "colonies" or "subjects," with the existing social and economic arrangements insured. In this system most states found, at first, that they obtained political security at a cheaper price in material costs or expenditures of manpower than they had done previously as independent units and were better off so long as no price was put upon autonomy or liberty.

In political matters, the Romans extended their benefits piecemeal. First, local government, including administration of their military and financial obligations to Rome, were left in local hands (those, generally, of the already-established possessing class). Secondly, Roman civil rights, and even political rights except suffrage, were extended to these new additions to the Roman system. Thirdly, political rights, including suffrage, were extended to them, but in such a form that they could be exercised only at great cost and inconvenience and thus generally only by the wealthy.

Voting was by centuries or tribes; the former were weighed, as we have seen, in favor of the rich; the latter were gerrymandered to a similar end. All political activities had to take place through direct personal participation in Rome, which effectively disqualified any poor person who lived more than fifty miles from the city. All the poor of the city, freedmen, and other socially inferior persons were put into the four urban tribes, leaving the 31 rustic tribes under the influence of the well-to-do. The poor who wished to take up public lands as farms were often forced to give up their Roman citizenship and take Latin citizenship which (until 88 B.C.) deprived them of suffrage. While nobles used their personal connections of "friendship" or clientage to create patronage-dominated political machines, democratic methods of campaigning for office such as soliciting of votes by canvassing were outlawed. In addition to these and other legal restrictions on political activity by ordinary men, there were other restrictions of religious, economic, social and conventional nature. Even when the legal and economic restrictions were weakened, the social, practical, and conventional restrictions became more rigid. In this way, as Rome extended its boundaries outward

403

and its population increased to many millions, control of policy remained in the hands of a minority or, more accurately, in the hands of minorities. From an early date, as we have seen, these minorities were in conflict with each other, a condition which culminated in the century of civil wars, before Augustus merged control of the state with control of the armed forces.

By the time of Augustus, when the domestic political struggles reached this practical solution, the territorial expansion of the Roman state was also reaching its end from the simple fact that the state had reached the limits of the extension of its offensive power. We will make no effort here to trace the history of this expansion, but will simply outline its stages for chronological purposes.

There were four parts to the expansion of Rome, thus: (A) the conquest of Italy; (B) the conquest of the central Mediterranean; (C) the conquest of the whole Mediterranean; and (D) the conquest of the east and the north. Each of these parts falls into a number of shorter sub-stages. The dates of these latter, with some additional information, can be seen from the following outline.

A. Conquest of Italy (450-225 B.C.)
   1. Latium, 450-338 (Trifanum)
   2. Central Italy, 327-295 (Sentinium)
   3. Peninsula Italy, 292-272 (Tarentum)
   4. Continental Italy, 241-225 (Telamon)

B. Conquest of the central Mediterranean (264-201 B.C.)
   Two Punic Wars, 264-241 and 218-201, won Sicily, Sardinia, Illyria, and part of Spain.

C. Conquest of the whole Mediterranean (215-146 B.C.)
   1. Four Macedonian Wars won the Balkans
   2. The west was won (201-121).
      a. Coast of Spain, 201-197 (two provinces).
      b. Cisalpine Gaul, 191 (a province).
      c. Third Punic War, 149-146 (the province of Africa).

404

        d.   Interior of Spain, 139.
        e.   Southern Gaul, 121 (province of Narbonne).

    D. Conquest of the east and the north (88-31 B.C.)
        a.   Three Mithridatic Wars, 88-62, won much of
             Anatolia and the Levant, creating four
             provinces (Bithynia, Asia, Cilicia, and
             Syria), with five client kingdoms.
        b.   Gaul and invasion of Britain, 58-51, led
             to new provinces.
        c.   Egypt annexed, 31 B.C.

In theory this expansion of Roman territory could
have been achieved without creating any significant
political instability if three factors in the situation had been achieved. Of these factors the most
important for maintaining political stability was
that no great discrepancy should rise between the
area of Rome's actual power and the area of Roman
legal power. This means that Rome must not, at any
time, have an area over which it had the legal right
to rule which was notably larger or notably smaller
than the area she actually could control. Since on
the whole, over these five centuries, Roman power in
fact was increasing in area faster than her legal
rights were being extended, there was a considerable
discrepancy between these two. These discrepancies
were rectified by wars and battles which made it possible to change the legal situation by demonstrating
to all concerned what was the factual situation. But
a legal situation, created by force, must be sustained
by power rather than by force, since men cannot be
conducting public demonstrations of force by battles
every day. This means that two other factors must
function successfully if political stability is to
be sustained.

    These other two factors were, on the whole, de-
ficient in the Roman system. They were (1) that an
organizational structure be provided for the area of
Roman power so that political processes of rulemak-
ing, settlement of disputes, and mobilization of resources could be carried on without any need to resort to force; and (2) that, within the same area
of Roman power, the allegiance of the inhabitants be
won successfully.

    In both of these secondary factors Roman exper-
ience was less than adequate, with the consequence

that political instability was almost chronic from
the failure of these two. This brings up the double
problem of how Rome did organize political action
and appeal to allegiance within the area which was
conquered by Roman arms.

Since the Romans were a practical and empirical
people, the ways in which they organized the political action and allegiance of the areas they conquered varied somewhat from case to case and from
area to area. In general terms, there were three
cases: (1) the areas could become part of the Roman state itself so that the inhabitants had all the
rights of Roman citizens, including the right to
vote and the right to run for office (ius suffragii
et ius honorum); or (2) the areas might be given
an inferior status in which the inhabitants had no
public rights (sine suffragio) but did have all private rights including the right to marry and trade
with Roman citizens (connubium et commercium). In
the third case (3) the new territories were known
as allies (socii), since their relationship to Rome
was established by a treaty of alliance. In most
cases such a treaty established that the two parties
would have the same friends and enemies and provided that the ally state should provide each year
a specified number of troops and the funds (tributum)
to support these, operating generally under their own
officers, but under Roman general command.

In all these arrangements Rome assumed that it
was dealing with states like itself, that is city-
states (civitates), and in all three cases the local
government was left autonomous with self-government
on a municipal basis. In annexed areas where tribes
lived in districts (pagi), they were organized as
urban units (municipia) without full citizenship
rights (and thus "sine suffragio"). All annexed
territories were considered to be the property of
the Roman people (ager publicus), and the inhabitants left on them were there by revocable privilege and not by right. For defensive purposes,
military colonies were established at strategic
points on this ager publicus. These were either
"Roman" or "Latin" depending on what rights the
colonists had. If "Roman," they had full rights
of citizens and usually consisted of about 300 Ro-

man citizens of a superior property class with full
self-government as well as full political rights in
Rome itself. If "Latin," they had only private
rights and not public rights (sine suffragio), and
their relationship to Rome was fixed by a perpetual
treaty agreement. Only Roman citizens wherever
they lived were enrolled in the 35 tribes; these
served their military obligations in the legions;
others (Latin citizens or socii) had their military
activities in the auxiliaries (including the navy),
and their political life in their local municipia.
Wherever the Romans organized municipia they followed the Roman pattern: the population divided
legally into different classes on the basis of
wealth; an assembly with little powers; a senate
with considerable powers, consisting of decuriones
appointed for life by the magistrates of each fifth
year (acting as the censors did in Rome); and magistrates on the Roman pattern, that is holding office
on a collegial and annual basis; these magistrates
came to be known as duoviri even when there were
more than two. The decuriones (later known as curiales because they were members of the local senate
or curia) were, as in Rome itself, a hereditary
class of ex-magistrates or at least persons of the
magistrates' income class. They controlled their
city and bore the burden of providing its offices,
public buildings, festivals, religious ceremonies,
and entertainment, either by law or by convention.
In the republican period there were many who were
eager to assume these privileges and responsibilities, but in the imperial period, after A.D. 200,
this became a dwindling and reluctant group, especially when the burden of providing all the taxes
of the city was imposed on the decuriones as a corporate group. This burden became unbearable when
most of the local taxes were taken by the central
government. As a result, the curiales became a
hereditary caste of tax collectors, responsible
for the full payment by their own wealth. From
the third century A.D. onward, individual curiales
tried to avoid the rank, the honor, and the burden,
but the central government made any evasion of the
rank illegal while continuing to pile burdens upon it.

The extension of Roman citizenship to some of
these cities, very slowly in the period down to 90
B.C., then to all of Italy south of the Rubicon in
88 B.C., followed by the extension to Italy north

of the Rubicon to include Cisalpine Gaul in the
next forty years, did not improve the situation
very much, because the rights of citizenship thus
acquired could be exercised only in Rome by personal actions in that city half a dozen times a
year. This was something which richer citizens
of distant places could do if they had the wealth
to make it possible to get to Rome and to stay
there. But the ordinary peasant, even if he had
full Roman citizenship, could not get to Rome to
exercise his political rights unless he lived so
close that he could get there and back in a single
day, or possibly with a single night's stay in the
city. That means that the vast majority of citizens
living forty miles or so from Rome were disenfranchised
in fact even when they had full citizenship in law.
The regulations regarding exercise of these rights
were manipulated to make it even more difficult.
The peasant had to vote in his tribe; there the
poor peasant who did get to the tribal polling place
in Rome found himself vastly outnumbered by the
wealthy landed group who had no difficulty in getting to the city and staying as long as needed because these wealthy had houses of their own, or
houses of clients and "friends," in which to stay.
Moreover, the polling for the various magistrates
was scattered over days and even weeks so that no
peasant could stay for all of them. When he did
vote, he had to vote in his century as well as in
his tribe, another opportunity for the humble to
be outvoted by the rich.

These restrictions on political actions by the
ordinary man adversely affected political stability
both in terms of foreign policy and the territorial
expansion of Rome (our concern in this section) as
well as in terms of domestic stability (which will
be our concern in the following section).

If, as Rome expanded, it did not extend the
rights of full Roman citizenship to the newly annexed peoples, it suffered a double danger. On one
hand, since membership in the legions was reserved
to full citizens, it had to protect larger areas
and population with a proportionately smaller number
of citizen soldiers; and, on the other hand, it was,
in that case, faced by larger and larger numbers of

disgruntled part citizens (with less than full Roman rights) who sometimes saw no reason why they should contribute blood and money to political purposes they had no part in formulating. This is something which occurred constantly in Roman history, especially under the republic, although once again it is a matter which historians relatively neglect. By this I mean that Roman allies and Latin colonists revolted or mutinied whenever they felt there was any reasonable hope of success, which in effect meant whenever Rome suffered a military reverse in foreign policy. On the other hand, these subjects without full citizenship were in such diverse conditions, and were subject to such varied local treatment and rights, and were segregated so greatly in terms of their knowledge of the military and political conditions of Rome itself, that these revolts were usually local, sporadic, and spontaneous rather than general, widespread, or carefully planned. Only in 90 B.C. did these latter conditions prevail; the social war of that year almost destroyed Rome and was suppressed only by extending Roman political rights to most men in all of peninsular Italy.

There are historians who dispute this last point by the argument that the rebels of 90 B.C. were not seeking freedom from Rome but were, on the contrary, asking for closer union with Rome by demanding full Roman rights. This is not quite correct, for, while the rebels did stop their rebellion and accept full Roman rights, these latter were not what they were demanding: they were, it is true, seeking to maintain a unified political system, an Italian confederation, but one from which Rome would be excluded. Toynbee quite correctly calls this struggle "the Second War of Secession from Rome," reserving the designation of "First War of Secession" to the somewhat similar struggle of 340-338 between Rome and her allies. He points to the significant fact that the coinage issued by the rebel states of 90 B.C. display the Italian bull goring the Roman wolf.

The political instability which arose from the Roman territorial expansion and which arose from the growing Roman offensive power in weaponry was thus a chronic condition although it reached the explosive

stage only sporadically, most notably in 90 B.C.
But it was chronic and arose from the fact that
the legal reflection of organized political action
in Rome's territories was not an accurate reflection
of the factual power of men and weapons within
those territories.

From the point of view of the ordinary peasant
in Roman territories, the whole Roman imperial system was based on credit, that is on promises of hypo-
thetical future payments for present donations of
blood, money and anguish. The motives which led
the inhabitants of these territories to support Rome's
expansionism were varied, especially on a class basis.
Most notably, as we shall see in the next section of
this chapter, the motives of the upper classes and
especially of the Romans who were closest to the for-
mulation of political policies were alien to the
ordinary peasants (as they are alien to our ideas
on such matters today).

The motivations of the ordinary peasant were,
of course, mixed, but from the earliest days, when
Rome was still only a small town on the Tiber, land
hunger had been one of the strongest elements in
these motivations. Just as the tribal peoples of
the Italian uplands, before 400 B.C., were pushing
downward into the coastal lowlands seeking to wrest
these lowlands from those who held them, so many of
the urbanized peoples in these lowlands, in places
like Rome and the Greek colonial cities further
south, were seeking to take from their neighbors
additional lands for their agricultural activities.
It is worthy of note that these agricultural activities, as usually happens in aggressively imperial-
istic societies, were inefficient in terms of the
technological knowledge of their day. They were
seeking, in terms of the equation previously mentioned, to get more goods by extending their current organization of technology to additional resources, rather than trying the more rewarding but
far less obvious alternative of setting up a better technological organization on the resources
they already possessed. Rome's technological organization was always backward and inefficient,
which is one of the reasons why Rome's impulse to
imperialism was always so urgent. Until 200 B.C.,
at which late date Rome was already committed to a

career of damaging, if glorious, imperialism, the
Roman agricultural system was still closer to subsistence and semi-pastoral patterns than to more
productive (but perfectly possible) specialized,
commercial, planting patterns.

The events of the Second Punic War (218-201)
made this situation worse and made all elements of
crisis in the situation more acute and made all
elements of hope more remote. The reasons for this
must be examined.

Until about 200 B.C. Rome had been a system
of peasant citizen soldiers who worked family farms,
assisted occasionally by slaves but hardly dependent on slaves for their agricultural activities.
As the consequences of the Punic Wars worked themselves out, much of Rome's area, especially in central Italy, became large estates worked by gangs of
slaves under the direction of freedmen stewards,
the owners being absent (in Rome, in the provinces,
or in the war zones), looking after the political
ends of their private special interests.

The ravages of Hannibal, and the equally ravaging Roman scorched-earth defensive policies, had
destroyed much of the peasant agricultural enterprise of central and southern Italy. The land was
still there, but the animals, buildings, tools,
olive trees, grapevines, and people were gone.
When the seventeen years of war were over, the
returning veterans had neither the inclination nor
the capital to attempt to begin the years of work
needed to bring their peasant farms back into production. They sold out to war profiteers who acquired numerous peasant holdings and turned them
together into large estates to be worked by slaves.

The war and the states' favorable treatment
of war profiteers had created a great number of
these, especially when the state, which had run
the war largely on credit after 215, tried to pay
off all debts by 200. This was done in three payments after 206 of which the third, for lack of
money, could be taken by the creditors in blocks
of the desirable public lands within fifty miles
of Rome. There were at that time no banks, se-

curities, or bonds in which the wealthy, including the numerous nouveaux-riches businessmen, could invest their monies. On the other hand, because both law and custom excluded the senatorial nobility from commerce and financial dealings, land ownership and landed estates had become a matter of high social prestige because of its association with the nobility. Thus the nouveaux-riches, at a time of available lands, low prices for slaves (from the many war captives), and increased personal incomes could aspire to increased social prestige with implications of pseudo-nobility if they became proprietors of large estates. Since, in many cases, they knew little about agricultural management and had little time to devote to such management, they often put these estates, with their new bands of slave workers, in charge of some agriculturally experienced slave who was freed by the owner to qualify for his new task of steward.

These estates were inefficiently worked from the beginning, but their new owners often neither knew nor cared. Any efficiently operated agricultural enterprise will have annual fluctuations of output depending upon yearly changes of climate conditions. Since both the owner and the steward wanted real output to remain roughly the same in all years, this could be done only if the output in each year approached the output levels of the poorer years (since there was no way of making output in all years approach the levels of the best years). In this way, with a constant predictable outlook, year after year, the owner knew what to anticipate and the steward remained in his place, escaping both blame or praise. The self-interest of the steward, the lack of enterprise of the slaves, and the ignorance and absenteeism of the owners all converged to provide inefficient management despite the numerous handbooks on estate management which appeared from men like Cato (c. 160 B.C.), Varro (c. 37 B.C.), and Columella (c. A.D. 60).

Three other influences also contributed to this process. The victory over Carthage gave Rome, for the first time, control of overseas territories which had to be ruled and garrisoned. While the nobles and businessmen quarreled over which would

rule these new possessions, there was no doubt
about who would garrison them: the former peasant
farmers of Italy. Thus the Italians were shipped
overseas to serve in armies of occupation in foreign lands, while the former inhabitants of those
lands were shipped back to Italy as slaves to work
the lands of the peninsula whence their conquering
garrisons had been drawn. This meant, of course,
that the governing of Italy was left to the upper
classes of Rome with less need to consult with autonomous free Roman peasants and that there was a
tendency, in fact by 200 B.C. and in law in 107
B.C., for the Roman soldier himself to change from
a one-year draftee into a long-term professional
soldier. In the long run, over a period of about
six centuries, the population of Italy was largely
replaced by persons of different blood as the
Italians went overseas as soldiers to enslave foreigners who were brought back to work in Italy.

A another factor in this process was that the
Romans, in the overseas conquests of the Punic Wars
and associated conflicts, took over areas of large
slave gang estates, especially in Sicily and Africa.
The Romans admired and copied these systems and
eagerly read the writings of the Carthaginian agro-
nomist, Mago. At the same time, the grain produced
in these alien lands came back into Italy, as tribute or commercial exchange, so cheaply that Italy's
peasant producers could not compete. The new Italian
estate owners made little effort to compete in grain
production but turned their large properties to the
production of olive oil, wool, and wine. This led
to specialized cash crop farming and transhumance
pastoralism on large estates, in products which required large holdings which the oppressed Italian
peasant farmer could not copy. Accordingly, the
oppressed peasant tended to sell out to the large
operator and move to the city where he found awaiting him the famous Roman trilogy of idleness, bread,
and circuses.

A final factor in this process was that the
superiority (or cheapness) of water transportation
over land transportation meant that grain (especially tribute grain) could be brought more cheaply
by sea to Rome from Sicily, North Africa, and ul-

timately Egypt than any Italian peasant could transport his grain by land from a farm in Italy outside the immediate vicinity of Rome.

The influence of all this on weapons and military organization was very great. Not only did the Roman soldier become a professional on long term enlistment, but two other influences also appeared. In the first, his allegiance and devotion were slowly shifted from home, family, patriotism, and the gods of Rome to his esprit de corps and his personal loyalty to his general. This general not only recruited him, but led him personally in battle, looked out for his welfare between battles but also, and most importantly, promised to look out for his welfare as a retired veteran when active service was over. Closely linked to this was the second influence: the Roman soldier after 150 B.C. or so, no longer was fighting for land, or for the security of his family and property, in the immediate future but began, instead, to look on his actions as a struggle which would win him land and a family after he had retired from fighting. This result rested on the two facts that the serving Roman soldier was forbidden to marry while on active service (even when this continued for twenty years) and his general assumed the obligation to obtain for him a grant of land from the state when that day of retirement, including marriage and land ownership, became possible. But, as the system worked, the Roman state felt no obligation to reward veterans with grants of land and could be forced to do so only if subjected to the threat of force by the general and his soldiers (past and present).

In this way, after 100 B.C. the last link fell into place and the circle was completed. The Roman establishment by taking control of the government of Rome and the lands of Italy was able to plunder the provinces and exploit Italy as well, deporting the Italians as soldiers to enslave aliens who could be brought back to Italy as slaves to work the lands of that peninsula for the benefit of the establishment. But in such a system, organized force is superior to any organized system of law or economic or political rights, so the victorious general and his loyal soldiers could march back into Italy and, by confisca-

414

tion and mass murder, take the lands, brush aside
the slaves, and kill anyone, noble, businessman,
slave, or soldier of another general who stood in
the way.

This horrible system, growing rapidly after
200 B.C., was forseen by many by 150 B.C., but all
who attempted to divert, reform, or arrest the process were murdered by the establishment. This is
what the so-called "century of revolution" of 133-
31 B.C. was about. In that war the establishment
won, but at a price which made the ultimate ruin
of Rome inevitable.

There is another aspect to this situation.
Rome remained an archaic city, that is a political,
military, religious, and administrative center,
but never became a significant commercial, manufacturing, or economic center. This means that
the consumers' goods, including food and money,
which flowed to Rome were not paid for by goods
and services flowing outward from Rome in approximately equal value. These imports came to Rome in
fulfillment of political and legal obligations,
that is, in the final analysis, they came because
Rome was more powerful, not because Rome offered
anything significant in economic or social return.

This relationship did not appear obvious simply
because, for bookkeeping purposes, many of Rome's
imports were paid for with gold and silver, but,
since there were no gold and silver mines in the
city of Rome, these precious metals were accumulated there by the violence and extortions of Roman
generals and political figures, directed against
the inhabitants of Roman provinces or enemies along
the Roman frontiers. The plundering of the provinces
by political and legal extortions and the wars on
the frontiers were Rome's two largest businesses
and formed essential parts of the Roman balance of
payments, just as the enslavement of war captives
formed an essential element in the resources of
the Roman economic system.

Both of these necessities, precious metals and
similar items on the credit side of the Roman balance
of payments account and the steady supply of slaves

415

to keep the economy running, were based on Rome's
continued success in violence and war. But such
continued success depended on the continued offensive power of the Roman military system. The
ending of Rome's offensive power shortly after the
time of Augustus Caesar doomed these two necessities and thus doomed the whole system, although
the full impact did not fall until almost three
more centuries had passed.

The ending of this offensive power became evident not only from the inability of Roman armies to
continue Rome's territorial expansion, but also
from the Roman shift to a defensive military posture along fixed frontiers marked by increasingly
elaborate walls and barriers.

These walls and barriers were established,
in the period following Augustus, along the boundary between northern England and Scotland ("Hadrian's
Wall"), along the Rhine and the Danube Rivers, with
a precarious link across Raetia between them, then
down the Danube, across the Black Sea to Pontus,
then down a very disputed frontier in western Armenia to Syria (also disputed with the neo-Persian
empire), the Levant, the Red Sea, and Egypt, then
westward to Morocco along the northern edge of the
Sahara Desert.

These frontiers were fairly well established
at the death of Augustus in A.D. 14, except for
England (made a province in A.D. 43) and Dacia
(Romania; made a province in A.D. 106). Efforts
to expand beyond these boundaries were generally
not successful or at least were only briefly successful. The full implications of this for the
Roman political system will be described in the
next chapter, but the implications for the Roman
social and economic system are clear enough: without a constant supply of slaves and an equally constant but less visible inward flow of monetary exchange, both dependent on military victories along
constantly expanding frontiers, the Roman system
could not survive. The system had become impossible except on the basis of successful, imperialist war. This necessity was locked into the Roman community from the consequences of the Second
Punic War of 218-201 B.C. and could have been over-

come only by basic reforms within that community.
The struggle, not to obtain but to avoid such reforms,
began less than a century after the Second Punic War
and in the same generation as the Third Punic War
(149-146 B.C.).

5.   The Roman Revolution, 133 B.C.-A.D. 69

The Second Punic War made it impossible, in the
long run, for the Roman system to survive, because
it made it impossible for the establishment to continue to exclude force, wealth, and the power of
mere numbers of men from the system. The system,
of course, could have been reformed to allow these
three excluded forces to operate within its processes in accordance with a new system of constitutional and customary regulations, but when this was
not done but, on the contrary, resisted, these three
forces began to operate to destroy the system. This
gave rise to the century of civil war, 133-31 B.C.
and the century of the principate, 31 B.C.-A.D. 69.

The Punic Wars made it impossible for the system to continue into the future much longer because
it greatly increased, as mutually exclusive groupings, the three excluded elements of power (military
force, wealth, and numbers of people). The gradual
growth and increased segregation of these made it
increasingly difficult, and eventually impossible,
to preserve political stability by continuing to exclude these very real elements of power from the
operations of the system.

The ways in which these three were intensified
and mutually segregated into opposing groups rested
on the consequences of the Second Punic War: (1)
the shift of the Roman army from a force of peasant
soldiers called up for a brief defensive emergency
into a force of professional mercenary fighters engaged in offensive and police operations outside
Italy; (2) the shift of the agrarian system from
one of family farms worked by citizen peasants, possibly helped by slaves, to large estates owned by
absentee landlords and worked by gangs of slaves
under orders of freedmen stewards; (3) the shift
of land use in Italy from providing agricultural
necessities, especially food, to land used as a sym-

417

bol of social prestige in which much land was left untilled, or utilized in inefficient and unprofitable ways, while increasingly burdened by debts; (4) the creation of a class of money-grabbing war profiteers in commercial and provincial administrative activities quite apart from the senatorial upper class of nobility; and (5) the rapid growth of a large group of urban poor, gathered in Rome without ways of earning a living or of finding any meaning or purpose in their lives. From these grew the new system in which citizens went overseas to fight, while war captives were shipped back to Italy to work as slaves in the fields; Rome became overcrowded, while rural Italy became largely depopulated, and the whole system could continue to function only so long as slaves and booty flowed back to Italy from Rome's successful military aggressions along the frontiers and from the ruthless plundering of the provinces behind those frontiers.

The continuance of this new system became impossible in the century before Christ when inability to continue the military expansion of the frontiers cut off the flow of both slaves and booty back to Italy, and the looting of the provinces became the object of a struggle between the optimates and the equites. While these were in conflict, a third group appeared, the populares, often led by dissident nobility excluded from the benefits of the establishment so closely controlled by the optimates. The populares, despite this name, had no particular concern with the plight of the urban poor citizens except to the degree that these could be organized in mob violence during election campaigns in the city or could be enlisted in the legions as soldiers willing to support their commanders in any military adventure.

But when the populares organized city mobs and mercenary soldiers, and the equites tried to use the power of money to influence political decisions, the optimates found their game of cursus honorum threatened by the three factors of power which they had excluded by the rules of that game. They had to organize city mobs and mercenary soldiers of their own. Thus in 133 and 121 B.C. mobs organized by the optimates killed the founder of the populares group, Tiberius Gracchus, and his brother, the agrarian reformer, Gaius. Within a generation, the establish-

418

ment of mercenary armies by Marius and their use for political purposes in Rome led to the creation of opposing senatorial armies under Sulla. Each side murdered its opponents, confiscated their lands to reward its own supporters, and changed the rules regarding administrative and judicial procedures to ensure continued control of the levers of power by its own side. Even the revolt of Rome's Italian allies, demanding greater political rights in an Italian confederation, and a series of foreign wars in Africa and against Mithridates in Asia did not stop this civil conflict, but, on the contrary, made it clear that the one way to get the needed military forces and personal prestige to wage successful civil war in Rome was to be successful as a leader in foreign wars. Such a successful general not only could return to Rome with increased prestige, funds, and military forces: he had to do this, in order to reward the loyal support of his troops with pensions and lands, something which could be obtained only from the confiscations, sequestrations, and extortions wrung from his political rivals at home.

The total victory of the senate's champion, in the dictatorship of Sulla in 82-79, provided no end to this process, for the optimates he represented had no interest in solving the real problems of the day but simply wanted to suppress the influence of military force, wealth, and the city masses so that they could go on with their game of cursus honorum. Accordingly, other populares arose: Lepidus, Crassus, Pompey, Catiline, Caesar. And the optimates found supporters willing to oppose these: Cato the Younger, Milo, Cicero, and finally Pompey. As these civil struggles reached their peak in the period 59-45 B.C., urban mobs led by Clodius and Milo rioted within the city, and eventually, in 49-45, open civil war broke out between Caesar and Pompey. The victory of Caesar in 45 B.C. was undone with his assassination by the optimates, at the foot of Pompey's statue in the senate chamber, so the civil war continued until the final victory of Caesar's adopted son, Octavius (later Augustus), over Marc Antony and Cleopatra at Actium in 31 B.C.

The system set up by Augustus Caesar following his victory at Actium is called the principate. It

419

lasted exactly a century (31 B.C.-A.D. 69) following the period of civil war which also lasted for
a century (or rather 102 years, 133-31 B.C.). The
two periods together were an age of revolution in
the exact meaning of that term: an age in which the
facts of life burst through a facade of legal forms
to destroy the illusion in men's minds and to re-
assert the fundamental realities of the society in
question.

The situation of 133 B.C. was acutely unstable
because the constitutional procedures and the illusions in men's minds, as reflected in legal forms
and expressed in the ready cliches and slogans of
verbalized ideology, did not reflect the realities
of power in the Roman society of that period. The
legal forms and verbal illusions, as symbolized by
the formula senatus populusque Romanus, had no relationship to the facts of power as reflected in the
quadripartite foundation of power in organized force,
wealth, "the people," and the assumed, unconscious
Roman outlook and value system. By 31 B.C. these
realities, which the optimates had sought to exclude
for centuries so that they could go on with their
game of "cursus honorum," had burst through and
destroyed the legal forms, the verbal cliches, and
the ideological illusions within which the old game
had operated.

In this process, weapons systems played a more
significant role than any other factor, as is clear
from the way in which all political decisions, over
that 102 years, had been settled by force, by murder, suicide, and victory on the battlefield. A
list of the famous names of Roman political life over
the century 133-31 B.C., 32 names in all, has only
four who died natural deaths; the other 28 died from
murder or suicide. And of those favored four, two
(Marius and Sulla) were the greatest killers of the
period. A third, Lucullus, retired from public life
in time and devoted the rest of his life to sumptu-
ous eating. A few on this list, notably Crassus,
found death in a foreign battle, but most, including
the Gracchi, Cinna, Sertorius, Cataline, Caesar,
Clodius, Cicero, Cassius, Brutus, Pompey, Marc Antony, and others, died in civil conflict. The fourth
survivor, Lepidus, supported Octavius in the final

420

stages of the struggle and was forced into retirement by this ultimate victor.

Few parallels can be found in history to political carnage such as this. Perhaps England in the fifteenth century might come to mind. But the most apt parallel is not political at all; it is the world of Chicago gangsters in the days of Capone.

The principate was a complete reversal of the system as it had existed before 133 B.C. In that system political decisions had been made, behind the scenes, in the process of the game of cursus honorum, and military force had been excluded, so far as possible, from the decision-making process. Under the principate this situation was completely reversed: military force became the only significant factor, behind the scenes, in political decision-making, while the game of cursus honorum was brought out into the open and presented as a facade of elections, assemblies, honors, and ceremonial acts to conceal the way in which military dictatorship was running the show. In A.D. 69 this facade was torn aside, and the reality of a political system operating in terms of naked military force was revealed.

The principate was a completely hypocritical political system, not that hypocrisy may not be found in all political systems but, in this case, it was present to a degree which put the situation in a class by itself.

The real basis of Augustus' power was his position as commander-in-chief of the legions. It rested on his victories in the civil war over all contenders, ending with Actium. Over this reality Augustus set up a facade of legal, verbal, religious and organizational forms of a pseudo-traditional character which pretended that the political system was operating in terms of law, order, and general consensus. This fraudulent system worked during the principate of Augustus and the first few years of Tiberius (say from 27 B.C. to about A.D. 25), but, from about 16 to 69, it continued to be sustained only by the kind of bloodthirsty terrorism on the part of the government which we tend to associate with a secret police state like Hitler's or Stalin's.

The principate worked for about 45 years because of the political skills of Augustus and because Roman citizens of all classes were worn out
by more than a generation of civil war, violence,
and bloodshed, and like the Spaniards after Franco's
victory in March 1939, were prepared to accept as
ruler anyone who would put a stop to the violence.
In the case of Augustus the situation was made
easier by his willingness to allow the forms, dignities, magistrates, and assemblies, including the
cursus honorum, to continue so long as he had real
power and could obtain his political wishes. The
legal forms of his power rested on his possession
of numerous offices and magistracies himself, plus
special enactments which allowed him to do all kinds
of detailed political actions, outside of any office or magistracy. But no enumeration and summing
up of the emperor's legal powers would ever give a
total of legal power which would in any way explain
what his power really was. His power was much
greater than any such sum of diverse specific authorities. Partly this came from the fact that he
held his various offices for years and partly that
he held various different offices simultaneously.
But the real bases of his power were military and
political, not legal or constitutional. Only this
will explain the fact that when he held the office
of consul or of censor, his fellow consul or the
other censor, invariably agreed with him and allowed the emperor's will to prevail.

The legal basis for Augustus' power changed,
but was established in the form we call the principate from 27 B.C. on. Its chief elements were
the proconsular imperium, the consulship, the censorship powers, the tribunary powers (without the
office of censor or tribune), the pontifex maximus,
plus numerous special powers and privileges conferred by special laws and the intangible authority,
prestige, respect, and power associated with special titles and his own personality.

The proconsular imperium, which Augustus first
obtained in 43 B.C., was conferred for ten years in
27 B.C. It gave him command of all armies in the
provinces, but gave no control of Italy or Rome.
By giving him control of all the frontiers, it gave
him in fact control over foreign policy and questions

422

of war and peace. Its possession was signified by the title "Imperator" which should be understood to mean "Commander-in-Chief" and not "Emperor."

Augustus was selected consul for eleven consecutive years from 33 to 23 B.C., plus two later terms before his death in A.D. 14. This office gave him power in Rome and Italy.

Augustus as a patrician could not be elected tribune and had no desire to be one of the ten tribunes, but he obtained the powers of a tribune, at first piecemeal and later in totality but without the office. The first law (36 B.C.) gave him the sacrosanctity attached to the office and the last (23 B.C.) gave him the full tribunicia potestas. This gave him authority in Rome and Italy and was considered to be so important that he dated the years of his reign by the annual terms of this authority. It gave him the right to introduce legislation into the senate and to veto the acts of any other authority (except priests).

In the religious area Augustus had vague, but very real, authority and powers. His title "Augustus" conferred in 27 B.C. was religious in implication since it had previously been applied only to gods and meant "superhuman" or "more than human," in the Graeco-Roman (and ultimately Indo-European) idea of divinity. It is somewhat like our title "Reverend," if that is taken in a religious rather than social sense.

In the social sense, Augustus was "princeps," which conveys an idea which is quite clear today, and still used in modern government, especially in foreign relations. It refers to social precedence in public protocol and as a title in Roman public law meant "First" or "First Citizen" in the sense that no one else could have precedence over its holder in any public occasion. In the plural (with small case rather than a capital letter, in modern orthography), it meant the group of persons who had (or should have) precedence in public protocol: thus the "best people."

Augustus, by rebuilding the temples, endowing the performance of religious functions, and by in-

fluencing the selection of incumbents in religious
offices, and by supporting in every public way the
old Roman virtues, ethics, and religious idea and
activities, had strong religious support. He accepted some religious offices and functions himself and was named "Pontifex Maximus" for life in
12 B.C. He emphasized that, as the son of the deified Julius Caesar, he was the son of a god (divi
filius). He gradually permitted worship of himself
as a god, at first only in the east and by non-Ro-
mans, but by his death in A.D. 14, he was allowing
worship of his genius, but not of himself, in the
west as well.

Augustus also had a large number of rights and
authorities obtained by special laws. He may have
obtained the imperium maius, which gave him authority
over all other holders of imperium and thus entitled
him to interfere in senatorial provinces where there
were no troops under his regular imperium. He was
given the right to issue edicts as a magistrate, to
propose the first motion at meetings of the senate,
to propose candidates for elections to magistracies,
to exclude candidates (by his veto) from elections,
to have the dignities of a consul, including the
twelve fasces, apart from the office. He had his
own treasury, known as the fiscus, apart from the
public treasury and had his own incomes flowing into it, including the immense funds coming from Egypt
where he had all kinds of income-yielding rights
including the status of ultimate landowner of all
the lands of Egypt in succession to the Ptolemies.
He had great authority to interfere in justice,
including the right to veto and transfer cases,
to influence judges, and to hear cases on appeal
himself. The senate became the regular high court,
but Augustus could intervene in any case and established an advisory board to guide him in this. With
the censor's powers, by special legislation, Augustus
could control the membership of the senate, change
any person's status in the cursus honorum, and by
doing this could grant membership in the senate.
He revised the roll of the senate as censor in 28
B.C., again in 8 B.C., and finally in A.D. 14, reducing the number of senators from 900 to 600 on
the first occasion and fixing the necessary property
qualification for membership at a million sesterces.

424

In Rome Augustus took over control of the grain supply (much of it from Egypt which he owned) and the water supply. He organized urban police and fire fighters which he controlled because they were part of the armed forces and were originally (like the water workers) slaves owned by him or his supporters (23 B.C.). In A.D. 6 this service was reformed and consisted of 7000 freedmen, called vigiles, clients of Augustus and commanded by a prefect named by the emperor. He also named an urban prefect, with consular powers, in the city and stationed his praetorian bodyguard under a praetorian prefect around the city. This force, originally (27 B.C.) at 4500 picked soldiers, later grew in size. Its commander became a kind of chief-of-staff and second in command to the imperator, and his force became, in time, the chief force in the murdering and replacing of emperors, until eventually the frontier field armies discovered that they, too, could participate in this exciting and profitable sport (in A.D. 69).

As we have said, much of the reality of this imperial power was hidden, at least partly, by the continuation of senatorial life and the pursuit of the cursus honorum. Many offices, rights, honors, and privileges were left available to the senatorial families, and these nobles were allowed to continue their pursuit of the cursus, but now without allowing that pursuit to endanger the stability of the political system. This was insured, at first, by the fact that senatorial families were largely excluded from military activities and from the command of active troops and won their honors by access to offices. These offices were parts of the regular cursus, including the consulship, the administration of the senatorial provinces, including the governorships, and such other positions in the army or in the imperial bureaucracy and the imperial provinces as Augustus would allow. The emperor was fully prepared to allow members of senatorial families to serve in any positions which would not curtail his own power. In the administration of activities which concerned this essential area, he used equites, slaves, or freedmen, or even hired free Romans. All of these were dependent on his favor and could be depended on to carry out their tasks with greater loyalty and greater efficiency than nobles.

425

To keep up the supply of senators with consular honors, Augustus ceased to hold the office himself after 23 B.C. His holding it cut in half the number of ex-consuls (since there was only place available each year for senatorial families). But in matters of this kind, when the office becomes an honor rather than a job, there are always ways out of any difficulty, and Augustus soon found one: in A.D. 2 the term of office was cut to six months, so that there were four consuls a year rather than two; in later years, the term was gradually reduced to two months so that there were twelve places available each year for those who were avid for the honor of being an ex-consul and thus available for other high positions, such as governor (as proconsuls) of senatorial provinces.

Augustus also reformed other aspects of Roman life, including religion and morality so that his government was totalitarian at least in theory, although there were many matters on which he provided no legislation or administration. But the extent to which he was willing to go on those matters which he considered important may be seen from some of his family legislation.

Augustus was convinced that much of the weakness of Rome was due to the immorality of family life and the relations between the sexes which led, he believed, to a reluctance by men to marry and a failure of married persons to have children. Accordingly, he tried to legislate a return to the older virtues of Rome when the sexes had been socially segregated and met chiefly within the house for the purpose of having offspring. He forbade women to attend athletic games and public spectacles and allowed them to attend the theater only in seats which were separated from the men. Divorce was more strictly regulated and penalties were imposed on the unmarried or on married who had few or no children. On the other hand, rewards were provided for those who had over two children, including tax exemptions and preference in public offices. Immoral behavior which had hitherto been subject only to private legal actions was made a matter of state prosecutions.

The defense forces and the frontier defenses

426

were reorganized. The legions which amounted to
about sixty in 31 B.C. were reduced to 25 by A.D.
14. Service in them was made a career for Roman
citizens, with adequate pay (225 denari a year),
other irregular grants of money, many services provided, and a pension after twenty years' service
(later twenty-five years was required). But there
were obvious liabilities in the job, since soldiers
were subject to many limitations on their rights as
citizens and were largely segregated from normal
Roman life. Being citizens, they were largely recruited in Italy, but were stationed permanently
on the frontiers, often at a great distance from
their homes, to which they often did not return
during all their years of service, since leave from
duty was very limited, public transportation was almost non-existent, and most of the frontier posts
were very distant from home. Moreover, soldiers were
forbidden to marry during their twenty or more years
of service although their illegitimate children
could be legitimized after retirement.

The 25-30 legions, with about 160,000 men,
were supplemented by a similar number of auxiliaries,
providing a total of over 300,000 fighting men. The
legions, with about 5000 men each, consisted of citizens, largely from Italy, on twenty-year enlistments
and paid 225 denari a year; they were heavy infantry.
The auxiliaries, who served either as cavalry or
light infantry, were non-citizens, on twenty-five
year enlistments, paid 70 denari a year, and serving
in units of either 500 or 1000. On active duty they
served with the legions, either on their flanks or
even between their ranks, and were used for both the
opening and the closing of a battle. They opened as
infantry skirmishers before the impact of the legion
occurred and they closed, hopefully, in cavalry pursuit of the remnants of the enemy's formations after
the legion assault had shattered these.

As we shall see in the next chapter, Augustus
put the Roman armed forces into a defensive posture
by placing them on the frontier and digging them
into permanent or semi-permanent fortifications.
To be sure, he adopted the tactical offensive in
numerous places along the frontier, but this was
usually for the purpose of reaching a shorter de-

fensive line or for "straightening a salient," as they used to say in World War I. Some of these tactical offensives were quite elaborate, as we shall see, both under Augustus and under his successors, but on the whole, from the time of Christ onward, Roman strategy moved to the defensive, in spite of the very great pressures on the government to continue an offensive strategy. These pressures were especially powerful in those areas, such as Germany, the Near East, and later Britain, where a more secure frontier seemed available at some more advanced position (as on the Elbe in Germany, on the Tigris in the Near East, or on the Scottish seas in Britain). Such pressures came from the fact that successful aggressive wars had become a way of life with the Romans, landlords seeking cheaper slaves, equites seeking economic advantages, the soldiers themselves seeking booty. For centuries "the hawks" of ancient Rome insisted on continuing a forward policy which Rome could not afford and refused to liquidate any area, even one which was a clear liability.

The "hawks'" attitude was most persuasive at the one place on Rome's long frontier that met a powerful civilized state, in western Asia along the western frontier of the neo-Persian empire. It was impossible for Persia, even under the Sassanians (when Persia was at its strongest), to defeat Rome or for Rome to defeat Persia, yet both parties were unwilling to establish a defensive frontier and hold it, or to allow a neutral buffer state to exist between them. Thus for about seven hundred years the two states fought over Armenia, Kurdistan, Mesopotamia, and Syria, constantly interfering in Armenia because of their refusal to accept a neutral buffer Armenia and equally constantly (and with equal futility) seeking to conquer each other across Mesopotamia and Syria.

Augustus' two basic changes in the Roman situation, the reorganization of the principate itself and the indecisive movement toward a defensive posture along the Roman frontiers, led to great problems and dire misfortunes in the centuries after A.D. 14. The frontier problem will be examined in the following chapter, but the more immediately dangerous problem of the principate should be examined here.

The reform of the government by Augustus left it just as irresponsible (in the technical meaning of that term), but in the opposite sense, as it had been in 133 B.C. A responsible government is one in which the real disposition of power in the structure is the same as it is in people's minds or as it is in law (which is an objectification of how it is subjectively in people's minds). In such a case, when people act on the basis of the picture they have of the situation, they will be acting on the basis of the real distribution of power because the two are about the same. Thus, there can be no sudden rude awakening from the fact that the situation is, in fact, different from what it is reputed to be. But in 133-31 B.C., the situation was both irresponsible and unstable because the theory of power and the legal and constitutional conventions of the Roman state did not reflect the facts of power. They were not the same because neither in theory nor law was force, nor bribery, nor masses of people in the city supposed to determine who was consul, what decisions were made, or how disputes were settled.

As a result of the events of 133 B.C.-A.D. 14, the situation was changed in fact in the sense that the constitutional forms, as well as the influence of wealth and number of one's supporters, were pushed aside, and military force came to the center of the political situation. But under the principate, neither the law nor the theory explicitly provided for this role of force in such an unambiguous way that there could be no doubt in anyone's mind as to how political questions were settled, or how decisions were made, or whose will would prevail in a clash of wills. This lack of clarity and this total lack of agreement or consensus on these matters of supreme political significance is seen most clearly in the total lack of any rule of succession in Augustus' principate. Until the first imperator drew his last breath in A.D. 14, it was not clear that he would not try to change the succession with that last breath. In fact, real power at Augustus' death was in the hands of Tiberius. But this de facto power was not in his hands legally until the senate voted the _Lex de Imperio_ which gave him the authority of the principate for ten years. At the end of the decade, this authority was formally renewed.

This would have been perfectly fine so long as everyone recognized that the voting of the _Lex de Imperio_ was not an act granting power to the Princeps, but was simply a formal recognition by the senate that he had that power. But the inclusion of the term of ten years shows that the vote was not regarded as an act of recognition but was regarded as a grant of power. And such a legal grant of something which the senate itself did not have and could not mobilize nor obtain was an irresponsible act, an act of falsehood and hypocrisy as the whole principate was by its very nature and as all Augustus' life was by his very nature.

This episode shows that power in theory and in law still did not rest where it rested in fact. Authority and power were not in the same hands. That means that the conflict between fact and law could appear once again, just as it had during the century of civil wars. The fact that the conflict did not break out in Rome until fifty-five years after Augustus' death is no indication that the situation was either responsible or stable. It simply indicates that the circumstances did not arise to reveal the irresponsibility and instability which were there all the time.

All during that 55 years, circumstances could have revealed the unstable situation. It might have occurred as early as the principate of Tiberius (A.D. 14-37), if Germanicus had been of a different personality or had not died, at the age of 34, in A.D. 19.

When the circumstances did arise to reveal the unstable nature of the principate system, what it revealed was that the military power which controlled the empire was too decentralized to make it possible to devise a legal system, reflecting that power, which would permit selection of a new emperor at some central point for the whole empire.

430

The essential feature of a stable and responsible constitutional system for a political structure in which all real power is concentrated in the army would be to create a legal mechanism for choosing a ruler which would reflect the choice of the army. But by A.D. 69 the use of the word "army" in the singular would be a distortion in itself, for the Roman defense forces were increasingly pluralistic--armies with local recruitment, local economic bases, and local pride and esprit de corps. It is quite true that this growing pluralism and localism had, by A.D. 69 (and for many generations in the future), not yet proceeded to a point where the whole area of the empire could no longer be conquered by a single military commander. But it had developed to the point where each local commander had every right to think that he could conquer the whole empire in a civil war about as well as some other local commander in a different place could do so. Thus local commanders and troops were not willing to accept as their ruler a commander who had been proclaimed emperor by troops in some distant place. The only legal system which would reflect such a situation would be one in which the local commanders would agree to abjure civil war and reach agreement on whom they would accept as emperor. This would have involved some kind of a nominating convention or, perhaps, complex private communications to reach agreement on the new emperor among the chief local commanders.

This decentralization and growing pluralism of the Roman military system was closely associated with the adoption of a defensive strategy by Augustus and with his efforts to place these defense forces in permanent stations along the frontiers. At the beginning of this policy, the unified nature of the military system was retained from the fact that the economic base which supported the army was still that of the financial system of the whole empire; the men in the units were drawn from all parts of the empire, all were serving at considerable distances from their own homes, and the units were shifted about at intervals within the empire so that they did not get too deeply involved in the local life of the areas in which they were stationed.

All of these things changed under the empire.
The legions became increasingly associated, for
longer periods, with one camp. They were increasingly recruited from that area and, as generations
passed, they tended to be the sons and grandsons of
soldiers, often in the same camps. On this basis,
as time passed, loyalties to their own units and to
their own commanders became dominant over loyalty
to the empire as a whole or to Rome. This last
condition was already evident in A.D. 69. Finally,
as the imperial economy became more decentralized,
as commercial transactions involving money (which
has general, wide appeal and usage) were increasingly
replaced by payments in kind, especially in grain,
this localism became much greater for it meant that
the local legions began to have an autonomous local
economic basis. Two other developments increased
this tendency. The steady inflation in prices during the empire meant that the value of money decreased and the value of goods increased so that
the armed forces, among other groups, insisted that
its pay and other emoluments be granted in kind
rather than in money (or, at an earlier stage, in
gold rather than in coinage). Moreover, the involvement of the soldiers themselves in farming and manufacturing necessities on a local basis tended to
make the local military command area increasingly
self-sufficient in an economic sense. This greatly
increased localism of the armed forces.

All of this meant that organized military
force in the empire was becoming increasingly dispersed and diffused over the whole empire, with
notable concentration on the frontiers. This meant
not only that the local frontier forces would have
different choices for emperor (in a system in which
the armed forces determine who is emperor), but that
these differences could only be resolved by civil
war in which the military units which engaged in
such civil war must necessarily abandon the frontiers and leave them undefended against any outside enemy.

As it happened there was only one portion of
the frontier on which Rome faced an organized state,
rather than barbarian tribal groups. This was in
the Near East, where the neo-Persian empire faced

432

Rome, either directly or through client kingdoms, from the Caucasus Mountains south to the Syrian Desert. Although war along this "civilized" frontier was chronic for almost 700 years, the neo-Persians (either the Parthians or Sassanians) were not much better organized than the Romans, and neither had sufficient offensive power to conquer the other.

Elsewhere on the frontiers, no real challenge arose until the fourth century, when the Germans began to break in. These peoples were also quite weak, by any absolute military standards. Yet they were able to break in, and their relatively weak military challenge could be met only by abandoning large portions of the empire and reaching a decision to save only part of it.

Although this final threat did not have to be faced until the fourth and fifth centuries, the symptoms of the growing situation which gave rise to it were seen in A.D. 68-69, "the year of the four emperors."

During the fifty-four years from the death of Augustus in A.D. 14 to the suicide of Nero in A.D. 68, the vital military force was that of the praetorian guards of Rome, not the fighting legions on the frontiers. The man who controlled the praetorians controlled the principate. But this is a relationship in which real power rested with the troops, not with the commander. Thus the praetorians could unmake an emperor as well as make him. They had a weakness for members of the Julio-Claudian family, but within that family it did not much matter whom they had as ruler.

To the historian the partiality of the armed forces for the Julio-Claudians seems very misdirected. The rivalries within that family, the distorted characters and perversions of its members, have left a reputation of a succession of monsters. Some of this bad repute may reflect the anti-imperial sentiments of the senatorial nobility and the historical writers of the period but, even if we discount this evidence as unfairly adverse, the facts seem clear.

At the death of Augustus in A.D. 14, his position could not be inherited, since it was not an office but a motley collection of offices and diverse powers which ceased at his death. Tiberius became the second Princeps more or less by default. The family arrangements of Augustus were complicated by the fact that he had three wives, of which only the second bore him a child, his daughter Julia, a nymphomaniac. Augustus divorced Julia's mother to marry a divorcee, Livia, who had two sons. Octavia, the sister of Augustus, had a son and four daughters from two husbands. Thus Augustus had a daughter, two stepsons, a nephew, and four nieces. He juggled their lives with arranged marriages and preemptory divorces (beginning with the marriage of his nephew Marcellus to his daughter Julia), as he tried to provide for a successor to his principate but found his plans disarranged by the early deaths of his puppet descendants. In these arrangements and rearrangements, Tiberius was never Augustus' first choice as a successor but emerged as the obvious choice simply from the fact that he survived, while others with higher priorities died. Augustus' nephew and son-in-law, Marcellus, died in 23 B.C. Agrippa, Julia's next husband, died in 12 B.C. Drusus, the brother of Tiberius, whom Augustus much preferred, died in 9 B.C. The emperor's two grandsons, Lucius and Gaius, died in A.D. 2 and A.D. 4. A third grandson, Agrippa Postumus, was mentally incapable. Tiberius, who was in voluntary exile in the east for ten years (6 B.C.-A.D. 4), had to be recalled as the only possible successor in the imperial family, but even then he had to adopt Drusus' son, Germanicus (15 B.C.-A.D. 19), whom Augustus preferred. In A.D. 13 Tiberius was given the proconsular imperium and the tribunicia potestas without time limit. With this authority Tiberius was able to take control of the government when Augustus died the following year, on 19 August, but it was only after "an embarrassing and unprecedented debate" (Tacitus: Annuals, I, 19-13) that the senate proclaimed him imperator on 17 September. Mutinies of the frontier legions in Pannonia and on the Rhine broke out, and Agrippa Postumus, who had been in exile since A.D. 7, was murdered. In A.D. 16 a pretended Agrippa Posthumus appeared and was suppressed with difficulty. Until

434

A.D. 19, Tiberius' position was in danger from supporters of his nephew and adopted son, the popular
Germanicus (15 B.C.-A.D. 19).

In A.D. 15 Tiberius revived the laws on treason
(maiestas laesa) which provided the death penalty
for acts, words, or thoughts and inaugurated a system of blind and brutal political persecutions in
which any individual who brought a successful judicial action for treason profited by obtaining one-
quarter of his victim's property. Such charges were
often supported by agents provocateurs, and involved
enticement and all kinds of superstitious charges of
"black magic," astrology, and witchcraft. Casting
the emperor's horoscope, which had been made a capital offense by Augustus, was typical of the nature
of some of these "crimes." A reign of terror prevailed in Rome, especially after the death of Drusus,
the son of Tiberius, in A.D. 23. This event was commonly attributed to poison administered by the prefect of the praetorian guard, Sejanus, the emperor's
favorite. Tiberius himself, living in morbid fear
of assassination, fled from Rome to Capri in A.D. 26
and did not return to the capital during the last
eleven years of his reign (26-37). In 31 he secretly
denounced his favorite, Sejanus, to the senate. The
praetorian prefect was hurriedly executed and his
body thrown to the mob to be torn to pieces, while
all his supporters and reputed supporters were
liquidated.

The next emperor, Gaius (known as "Caligula,"
37-41), was far worse than Tiberius. In his first
year he squandered 2,700,000 sesterces left by
Tiberius, and his personal cruelty was soon notorious. He was murdered by the praetorians in less
than four years, along with his fourth wife and his
only child.

Claudius, younger brother of Germanicus, who
had been excluded from public life in the belief
that he was mentally incompetent, was found, after
Caligula's murder, hiding behind a curtain in the
palace. He was dragged out and proclaimed emperor
by the praetorian guard, while the senate was debating how to restore the republic.

435

In the early part of his reign, Claudius showed
a fair amount of moderation and common sense, but he
made two innovations which had very evil consequences.
The day after he was found behind the curtain, when it
became clear that the soldiers had wanted to make him
emperor rather than to kill him (as he had expected),
Claudius declared a "donative." That is, each soldier of the forces which saluted him as emperor was
given a gift of 15,000 sesterces from public funds.
Such donatives, once established, became an incentive
to the praetorians to overthrow an emperor in order
to get a donative from his successor. And any new
emperor, like Galba in A.D. 69, who refused to grant
a donative became an uninsurable risk.

A second innovation by Claudius took a major
step toward a new kind of government, the bureaucratic providential despotism which dominated the
next thousand years or so. This was the establishment of an imperial bureaucracy of social outcasts
whose inferior social position made them unlikely to
have any aspirations to the throne and thus made them
relatively safe associates for the occupant of such
a throne.

Rome had long had a bureaucracy of clerks, messengers, record keepers, and office maintenance
workers. But these were associated with the established magistracies and the senate and were not attached to the powers of the imperium, the princeps,
or the tribunician potestas which were the chief
elements of imperial rule. Thus the emperor had
no bureaucracy. Claudius established one, probably
to compensate for his own inexperience and lack of
personal prestige. For the same reasons he filled
it with his clients, slaves, and freedmen. The
whole system was headed by three rival freedmen,
who soon became rich and powerful from their positions. Their mutual jealousies and their intrigues
with the women around Claudius soon gave rise to a
fetid palace atmosphere which looked forward to the
systems of government which later prevailed in
Byzantium, in the late Baghdad Caliphate, or in
the harems of the Ottoman Turks.

In this way the rather hopeful beginnings of
the reign of Claudius were soon lost as he fell in-

creasingly under the influence of his wives and freedmen. His third wife, Messalina, mother of his son,
Brittanicus, was put to death as a consequence of
the freedman, Narcissus. Claudius then married his
niece, Agrippina, who was daughter of Germanicus,
sister of Caligula, and mother of Nero by an earlier
husband. She married Claudius in A.D. 49, persuaded him to adopt the 12-year-old Nero in 50,
married Nero to Claudius' daughter in 53, and had
her husband poisoned in 54. Thus her son, Nero, became emperor (54-68). The new emperor, however, refused to allow his mother to rule through himself
and instead fell under the spell of his mistress,
Poppaea. After the murder of Claudius' son, Brittanicus, by poison, Poppaea persuaded Nero to have
his wife (daughter of Claudius) and his mother murdered. While disasters piled up on the empire, including the burning of much of Rome in 64, a few
weak conspiracies tried to overthrow Nero, who kept
busy murdering scores of citizens, either with or
without trial, sometimes on the grounds that their
"virtue" was a crime because it showed up the emperor's lack of this quality. Finally in A.D. 68
the legate in Gaul revolted, Nero was betrayed by
his praetorian commanders and died by forced suicide.

The year of the four emperors (68-69) was in
the middle of the revolt of the Jews (66-70) which
culminated in the sack of Jerusalem and the destruction of the Temple by Titus.

The civil wars of 68-69 began when Vindex,
legate in Gaul revolted against Nero in the name
of the "senate and liberty." When the soldiers in
Spain saluted their governor, Galba, as emperor,
Vindex accepted him, but Rufus, commanding the
Rhine armies, invaded Gaul and destroyed Vindex.
While other leaders were wavering, following the
death of Nero, Galba reached Rome, but found the
treasury empty. His ineptness soon alienated many,
and his refusal to give the praetorians a donative
was a major tactical error. His selection of Cal-
purnius Piso as co-emperor brought Galba no additional strength and alienated Marcus Salvius Otho,
husband of Poppaea, who had been exiled to Spain
as governor of Lusitania for ten years while Nero
lived with his wife. In January 69, Otho roused

the praetorians to kill Galba and Piso and proclaim
him emperor.

The armies of Germany refused to accept Otho,
although the armies of the east were apparently
willing to do so. Unfortunately, the armies of
Germany were closer to Rome, while those in the
east were involved in the Jewish war. After pro-
claiming Vitellius, commander in Germany as emperor,
his legates invaded Italy and defeated Otho in a
series of battles around Cremona. Otho committed
suicide.

Otho, as he marched north to the Po, and Vitellius, in his triumphal march from Germany to Rome,
were unable, or unwilling, to control their troops
which plundered friend and foe alike. Vitellius as
emperor for a few months is notable only for his
prodigious gluttony on which, we are told, he spent
900,000,000 asses for food without being able to
satisfy his appetite.

While Vitellius ate in Rome, Vespasian, in
command (with his son, Titus) before Jerusalem,
cut off Rome's grain supply by seizing Egypt and
sent his surplus forces overland to attack Vitellius. The Danubian armies, very jealous of the
Rhine armies with Vitellius in Rome, anticipated
this move and, without the approval of the governors
of the three Danubian provinces, invaded Italy and
defeated the Vitellian forces before Cremona,
seized the city, and sacked it as if it were the
capital city of some traditional enemy. Most of
Vitellius' leaders deserted him, but the urban cohorts fought desperately on the Capitol Hill,
where the great Temple of Jupiter was destroyed by
fire in the conflict. Vitellius was captured and
murdered.

Vespasian as emperor (69-79) began a dynasty
of three emperors, himself and his two sons, Titus
(79-81) and Domitian (81-96). This family, known
as the Flavians, ended the fiction of the principate
(a diarchy of Princeps and senate) and established a
military monarchy which continued until the reforms
of Diocletian (284-305) and Constantine (311-337).
The Flavians and the next "dynasty," the Antonines,

learned from the errors of the Claudians to curb
the troops in Rome and to keep in touch with (and
in the favor of) the frontier armies. They retained Augustus' scheme of legions permanently
stationed on the frontier, but they ceased to use
locally recruited auxiliaries, raising these more
mobile forces on one frontier but using them on a
different remote frontier. In this way a divergence
between the legions and their auxiliaries, along
with the emperor's own cultivation of good relations
with both, reduced the dangers of the troops intervening in the imperial succession. But the price
was a growing militarization of the monarchy itself
and a reduction in the military efficiency of the
legions as defense forces.

With the soldiers excluded from politics and
the succession determined by adoption, a period of
political stability intervened between the assassination of Domitian in 96 and the assassination of Commodus in 192. The emperors between are known as
"the five good emperors" (Nerva, Trajan, Hadrian,
Antoninus Pius, and Marcus Aurelius, covering 96-
180). Each was chosen by his predecessor to be
successor, but the fifth, the "philosopher-emperor"
Marcus Aurelius, was so misguided as to choose his
son, Commodus, to be his successor. The murder of
this brutal incompetent after a twelve-year rule
in 192 opened the political crisis of the third
century (192-284).

This chapter ends in the first century after
Christ, which marks the end of a millennium of classical civilization. In that thousand years weapons
systems in the Mediterranean basin passed through
the double cycle of amateur-specialist and defensive-
offensive which I have mentioned. About 900 B.C.,
the dominant weapons had been defensive and specialist, in the form of "noble cavalry," which had succeeded to the royal castles and chariots of 1250
B.C., in the final stage of the preceding Cretan
civilization. These noble cavalry were, in 900,
probably neither noble nor really cavalry, but
probably mounted infantry, since they may have
dismounted to fight as the earlier riders in chariots had done. By 800, however, these fighters
were both noble and cavalry, rulers by birth and

increasingly fighting from the backs of their horses.

By 700 B.C. in the Greek world these noble riders were being challenged successfully, not only by rich, but non-noble, horsemen, and by infantry spearmen, the hoplites, who had discovered that if they maintained a disciplined solid mass, equipped with helmet, armor, shield, and spear, they could defeat mounted spearmen who lacked either a firm saddle or stirrups (although such cavalry remained very effective against dispersed foot soldiers and even against each other, as Paul Vigneron has shown us).

By 525 B.C., the disciplined and heavily armed hoplite, equipped at his own expense, was at the peak of his influence and was fully able to demonstrate his prowess in the Greek world, by defeating the Persian invaders of Europe in the next generation (492-479 B.C.). But, already in 479, the hoplite was beginning to change by abandoning some of his heavy armor (the helmet, the shoulder pieces and torso plates, and eventually the greaves) for the sake of rapid movement and field maneuvers. The infantry spearmen in hoplite formation remained the core of the Greek defense forces until the Roman conquest of 146 but, beginning in the fifth century and, above all, in the fourth century, the hoplite forces (themselves much lighter and more mobile than in the sixth century) were being supplemented by other forces; the peltasts, who were lightly armed skirmishing infantry, often armed with javelins, and frequently superior to the hoplites on rough or wooded terrain); sea power; missile weapons; siege trains and artillery; organized supply trains; and specialized cavalry with heavier spears and later archery. The addition of such auxiliary weaponry was very rapid in the fourth century and culminated in the army of Alexander the Great, which used all of these, except sea power, and was able to concentrate its attack through any one of these or any combination of them.

I want to emphasize this growing mixture of arms and specialized forces, since such mixture is the mark of a highly civilized society, just as increasingly elaborate roundabout circulation of in-

comes within the society is a similar mark. Such a
growing mixture also seems to be associated with an
increase in offensive power. It is quite mistaken
to believe, as is often done, that military superiority in classical antiquity rested upon infantry,
especially heavy infantry, and to explain the history of this superiority by reciting the familiar
litany of Greek hoplite, Macedonian phalanx, and
Roman legion. These terms are themselves ambiguous;
they were constantly changing, and their use ignores
the fact that the real military superiority of any
civilization lies in its "weapons mix" and in the
skill with which that mix is changed to fit the unique circumstances of each campaign or battle. Even
an elaborate "mix" such as the Romans had in the
first century A.D. is not capable of dealing with
all the military and ecological conditions which it
may encounter, as we shall see.

In this whole history the position of the Macedonian armed forces under Alexander the Great is
critical. Alexander had a mixture of arms which
he used with incredible skill, mingling arms even
within units, and adapting his tactics to the varied
terrain and conditions with a freedom and success
which no other military leader in western history
has ever displayed. To give two early examples, both
taken from Arrian's account of the campaigns, Alexander, in the northern Balkans in 335 B.C., was able
to cross a river during a battle with the rebel Clitus
by using field artillery (catapults) and heavy fire
from infantry archers wading in the water; this was
probably the first use of the catapult on a battlefield. In the second case, once again attacking
across a river, the Granicus, Alexander won his first
battle in the invasion of Persia when he himself led
a mass of cavalry armed with spears and operating
like a hoplite phalanx, pushing as a solid mass of
horses and men, across the river against the cavalry
on the left wing of the enemy forces (Arrian's Ana-
basis I.6 and 15). After Alexander's death, the
Macedonian army lost much of the flexibility, mobility,
and diversity it had had under Philip and Alexander
and fell back in a more rigid fashion on the heavy
phalanx which the Romans tore to shreds at Cynos-
cephalea (197 B.C.) and Pydna (168 B.C.). The Romans
could do this because their maniples could penetrate

441

with their swords between the long and awkward pikes of the Macedonians.

The development of Roman arms and tactics was similar to that of Greek arms and tactics but was some two centuries later, the shifts from noble cavalry to infantry phalanx, from service by birth to service by wealth, the replacement of heroic individualism by a disciplined mass, and of citizen service by mercenary professionals--all of these occurred in Rome at least two centuries after they took place in Greece. We might even regard Caesar as a rather pale imitation of Alexander, with a somewhat similar skill in flexible use of diverse weapons but cut off by assassination before he could "conquer the world."

It was this increased diversity of weapons and tactics which continued the growth of offensive power from the fourth century B.C. to the first century A.D. The Romans followed the changes which the Greeks had made but with some significant differences. The Romans established payment for service, and the state provided uniform arms for its fighters at a much earlier stage in the development than was done among the Greeks. They also provided a diversity of arms and functions for the three ranks of the infantry phalanx at an earlier stage. This movement toward diversity and flexibility, which began earlier, took a decisive step forward when the legion was subdivided into maniples able to operate as units within the legion and spaced so that they could move to the more threatened parts of the legion's front. The maniple, which the Romans may have adopted from the Samnites about 300 B.C., was associated with other changes, such as the shift from the spear (hasta) to the javelin (pilum) and, above all, the introduction of centurions as leaders of the two halves of the maniple and of the operations of the maniple within the legion formation in the thick of combat. H.M.D. Parker, who believes that the introduction of the maniple was made necessary by the shift to the pilum, also feels that the spear may have been retained by the third rank of the legion. The introduction of a larger shield (scutum) about the same time reduced the tendency which was so influential in the Greek phalanx

for the soldier to seek protection behind the shield
of the man on his right and thus for the whole
phalanx front line to have a tendency to move to the
right in combat. The legionary soldier was readier
to move or to strike in any direction as the centurion commanded. These changes also allowed the
legion to handle inequalities and unevenness in the
terrain without exposing an opening for penetration
by the enemy as the Greek phalanx did.

Among the chief obstacles to Roman conquest,
once they had defeated Pyrrhus and Hannibal, were
ecological. Macedonia's phalanx by 200 B.C. was so
inferior that there was no difficulty there. The
Macedonian pike was so long, up to eighteen feet,
that the points of up to five pikes protruded in
front of the front rank and the men were only half
as far apart as the Roman files of soldiers with
their swords. Thus each Roman came against ten pikes.
But the phalanx was so rigid that the pikes prevented
the Macedonians from turning to defend themselves
from the rear or the sides. All they had to do was
to retreat, or even to advance, to uneven ground as
they did at Pydna, and the phalanx broke itself,
the pikes parted, and the Romans darted among the
shafts to kill the enemy wholesale.

On the other hand, the barbarian peoples like
the Gauls, the Iberians, the Numidians, and others
offered very different problems, partly because they
did not operate in the same universe of assumptions
and tactics, or even of strategy, but also from their
combination of social and geographic conditions which
provided no organizational center which could be
smashed to demonstrate that they had to yield to
the Roman state.

In most cases, these peoples, like the Germans
later, generally had no, or little, system of arms
nor of tactical maneuvers, but placed almost all
their reliance on one wild overwhelming rush. If
this could be resisted, they tended to break up and
disperse, but this did not mean that they submitted,
for by dispersing, they could not be compelled to
yield collectively but had to be compelled to yield
in bits and pieces, by catching up with them as scattered entities, villages, bands, clans, or hill forts.

443

This created a very difficult problem, chiefly because it made it difficult for the Romans to maintain the necessary balance between concentration and dispersal of their own forces. Supply became a major problem among barbarian peoples who had few concentrated stores of food, with poor transport, often in rugged and wooded terrain, with few or no roads, with the supplies which did exist hidden in remote spots or locked up in small, isolated fortresses. If the Romans dispersed to live off the country, they could be ambushed piecemeal; if they concentrated for safety, as Lucullus did in Spain, they were soon hungry. This was less true in Gaul or in North Africa, but was very true in Spain, the northern Balkans, parts of Anatolia, northern Britain, and Germany. In Scotland and Spain, this was still true even in Napoleon's day, which is why we derive the expression "guerrilla warfare" from that period. But the necessity for the Romans to face such problems, mostly in the western Mediterranean, over two hundred years (250-50 B.C.) gave them the variety of weapons and flexibility in their use which allowed them to conquer the more civilized east when that opportunity arose.

The weapons and tactical problems were different with each barbarian people and even with each tribe. We have mentioned the Gallic sword of Telemon, which lasted but a single stroke, which bent it out of shape; that may have been sufficient for a people who made only one mad rush and a single downward slash at the enemy. But in that same generation and the next, the Celts of Iberia had swords better than the Romans ever obtained in numbers, of such excellent steel that they could easily cut off arms, legs, or heads with one blow, a sword with a point for thrusting and a double edge for slashing. This also was used with a wild rush, not on an individual basis as the early Gauls or the Germans, but in an organized wedge (cuneus) which cut right through the Roman maniples. The Romans responded to this by adopting the cohort formation (of three-maniple strength, 480 men) and by adopting the Spanish design for their swords, although, according to Polybius, they could never match the quality of Spanish steel.

In a similar way, when the Romans came up against the Greek and Macedonian cavalry, they soon recognized that their own cavalry lances were useless (so thin that they sometimes broke simply from the motion of the horse and lacking a spike on the butt for a second blow with that end) and their bull hide shields were so flexible that they could not turn an enemy spear and rotted in wet weather. So the Romans after 190 B.C. adopted the Greek cavalry spear, which was used with good effect in Spain by Rutilius Rufus about 134.

When the Spaniards abandoned the cuneus and guerrilla tactics were adopted by Viriathus, using horses and horsemanship which, Appian tells us, was superior to that of the Romans, the latter had to use treachery, treaty violations, and finally private assassination to overcome Viriathus. In these operations, the Iberians made much use of missile infantry forces interspersed with cavalry; Scipio responded with archers and slingers brought in, with elephants, from Numidia. Frontinus tells us that Scipio in Spain used more archers and slingers distributed "not only among his cohorts, but even among all his centuries." Thus the Romans learned from varied enemies under varied conditions. Their original army came from the Etruscans, the manipular system probably from the Samnites, its navy from Carthage, much of its siege methods from the Sicilian Greeks and from Carthage, its artillery probably from Pyrrhus and Macedonia, its famous double-edged sword (gladius) from the Spaniards. It is significant that Rome fought almost constantly from 229 to 168 B.C., in Italy, in Spain, in Africa, in the Balkans, in Anatolia, and on the sea, learning from each and applying what it learned to the others. For example, in 190 B.C., the Romans invaded Anatolia from Greece and defeated Antiochus III, who had 3000 cataphracts, that is heavily armored cavalry with long spears. As a result, the Roman cavalry were re-equipped with heavier lances and superior Greek-style shields. Polybius stresses the point by saying, "When the Romans learned these facts about Greek arms, they were not long in copying them; for no nation has ever surpassed them in readiness to adopt new fashions from other people, and to imitate what they see is better in others than themselves." As a result of such experience and adaptability, the Romans by 168, at Pydna, had weapons and tactics which had not been equaled since Alexander conquered Persia in 334-323 B.C. The only significant inadequacy in weapons which Rome had in the second century B.C. was its lack of suitable archery for both infantry and cavalry. These were obtained just about the date that this chapter ends, in the latter half of the first century A.D., probably as a consequence of the massacre of seven legions under Crassus, at Carrhae in Mesopotamia in 53 B.C., by a Parthian army of horse archers and cataphracts. Gad Rausing, our greatest authority on the history of the bow, says that the Romans adopted both the Parthian great bow (better called Median crescent bow) and the Yrzi bow in the first century B.C. Both of these were composite bows made of sinew and horn, but the latter has bone stiffening on the ears (ends), which gives a whiplash effect so that it could be made somewhat shorter and thus better fitted to use on horseback. We have archaeological evidence of the Yrzi bow in Roman campsites as far west as Scotland in the time of Antonius Pius (138-161), before the great crisis of the empire or any serious threat of barbarian invasions.

Three significant changes took place in the Roman army about 100 B.C. These were: (1) the legion was reorganized from 30 maniples to 10 cohorts to provide a larger subdivision capable of independent tactical operations; (2) the class system of service was replaced piecemeal by a system of mercenary soldiers of any social class recruited by the general himself and increasingly loyal to him and identifying with his interests; and (3) the velites, who had been drawn from the poorest draftees, along with other supplementary forces such as cavalry, slingers, and archers were all replaced by auxiliary formations of hired non-citizens. This included both the Roman cavalry and the navy, which had previously been citizen activities in theory, if not in practice. As a result, there was greatly increased use of auxiliary forces of cavalry and of missile fighters. After the time of Marius and Rutilius Rufus (107-105 B.C.) the size of forces, balance of weapons, and tactics used depended almost completely on the tastes of the general and his available resources. In spite of

446

this personal element, the legions became permanent entities with fixed numbers after about 50 B.C. Augustus insured this by establishing a permanent army, financed by an established fund, with 28 legions by 16 B.C. After two centuries of vicissitudes, there were 30 in A.D. 180, at which time the "legion" ceased to exist as a tactical operational unit by becoming an administrative headquarters for its cohorts, which could be detached for use anywhere, while the legion remained, often with only one cohort, as an administrative center at a permanent "camp" on the frontier. This last change apparently arose from the acute needs of the Marcomanni War of A.D. 167-182. In 193, when the great crisis broke out, the 30 legions were all in the same camps they had occupied in 138, except for one legion and the addition of two new ones.

From this we can see that the weaponry, organization, and tactics of the Roman armed forces were approaching their peak and stabilized form at the date this chapter ends, in the middle of the Jewish war of A.D. 66-70. We have a good description of the army at that time and of its adaptability to diverse kinds of fighting from the pen of the historian of that war, Josephus. From this evidence, the Roman army of 69 had every asset it needed for any external enemy, but was having its internal foundations eroded by domestic problems it could not cope with, but which it was fully prepared to intervene in.

(blank page 448, intentionally omitted)

CHAPTER VII

GROWING DEFENSIVE POWER, PROVIDENTIAL EMPIRE, AND THE
GRASSLANDS OFFENSIVES, 31 B.C.-A.D. 1200

1.   Introduction

The period from the establishment of the principate by Augustus Caesar after 31 B.C. to the beginnings of the expansion of western civilization
approximately two-thirds of the way through the
tenth century is almost exactly a thousand years.
Both dates are arbitrary and are of greater significance to the societies of the west with which we are
familiar than they are for the world as a whole.

On that larger stage the significant dates
could be placed more accurately somewhat later,
extending from about A.D. 200 to 1300. These dates
would mark a period of drier climate in both the
northern and southern grasslands and a widening of
the areas of desert in the Sahara, Arabia, and the
dry areas of central Asia. These changes seem to
have been caused by a retreat of the polar ice cap
and a retraction of the polar high pressure area.
This allowed the zone of cyclonic storms, which
tracks from west to east (or from southwest to northeast) in mid-latitudes, carrying rains in all seasons across France and central Europe, to move farther northward so that the Baltic, Scandinavia, and
the taiga zone of Russia were deluged with rain. At
the same time, the Mediterranean area of winter rains
had reduced precipitation, especially on its southern
edge across North Africa. And the somewhat reduced
rainfall in middle latitudes led to increased dryness and reduced grasslands across the steppe areas
of Asia from the Black and Caspian Seas to the Altai
Mountains. As one consequence of these changes the
Greenland glacier which about 500 B.C. and again
about 1850 extended to the southern end of that island had, by A.D. 1000, withdrawn northward leaving
an extensive area of vegetation and habitable terrain at that southern end.

As a consequence of this climate change in A.D.
200-1300, there were numerous migrations of peoples.

Three of these are of major historic importance.
These were: (1) the migrations of Ural-Altaic or
Mongoloid peoples outward from the grasslands of
east central Asia; (2) the movements of the Arabs
or Saracens and other bedouin peoples from the
grassland fringes of the Arabian Desert and the
edges of the Sahara; and (3) the movements of the
Teutonic peoples of Europe, in two quite separate
episodes, the Germanic peoples in the period 60 B.C.
to A.D. 500 and the Viking or Scandinavian peoples
from about 700 to after 1100.

The first two of these movements were by grassland pastoral peoples, attacking as horse-riding warriors armed with bows. The third was a much more
complex series of events, as neither the Germans nor
the Vikings were pastoralists and the Vikings, although quite familiar with the horse and cavalry
warfare, were essentially sea raiders. The key to
the successes of the Ural-Altaic, Saracen, and Viking warriors was their mobility, a startling innovation in offensive power at a time when the civilized
areas of the world, especially Rome (and later Byzantium) in the west and China in the east were putting
primary emphasis on static defenses and elaborate
fortified lines. The German relationship to all of
this is anomalous and much more complex, since their
military tactics were neither uniform nor very dangerous to others in any absolute sense.

To understand this millennium of history, we
must view the situation of the Old World landmass
as a whole, with the old civilized areas along the
fringes of Asia, extending from classical Mediterranean civilization in the west to Japan and China
in the east. In between were the successor states
in Asia to the conquests of Alexander, the Indian
sub-continent, and the civilized and semi-civilized
areas of southeast Asia and Malaysia. These in-
between areas, from the Persian Gulf to the South
China Sea, were relatively protected from outside
enemy intruders, on the north by the greatest mountain barriers on our globe from Iran, through the
Hindu Kush and Himalayas to Yunnan and on the south
by the Arabian Sea, Indian Ocean, and China Seas.
This stretch of the highland zone from Persia to
Yunnan could be regarded as an almost impenetrable

450

football defensive line from tackle to tackle facing north toward the deserts and grasslands of central Asia. Any threat from those grasslands would find its offensive choices narrowly restricted to either end of that line, to off-tackle plays into China across the grasslands of Mongolia or into the Near East across Iran, or end-runs either eastward into Manchuria or westward into central Europe.

This grasslands offensive, which had existed earlier in the period of sub-Boreal dryness (2500-1000 B.C.), had been suspended in the period of classical sub-Atlantic climate (1000 B.C.-A.D. 200) and was now resumed in the period of post-classical dryness (A.D. 200-1300). But it could not have been successful against the improved defenses of the Iron Age empires without the new technology of cavalry warfare devised in the period 400 B.C.-A.D. 400.

This new technology of cavalry warfare was invented in the northern grasslands, the earliest stages by the Indo-European peoples of the western steppes and the decisive later stages by the Ural-Altaic (chiefly Turkic) peoples of the east central steppes of Mongolia. It was, in its full development, associated with other inventions, notably a new economic system of full nomadic pastoralism and a new supra-tribal political organization based on personal loyalty to an elected khan. Both of these latter came into existence in a period centered on the late third century B.C., almost simultaneous with a revolutionary reorganization of China from a "feudal" system based on personal loyalty and personal service to a bureaucratic centralized Chinese empire.

The interaction of this new pastoral nomad system and the bureaucratic Chinese empire had repercussions all across Asia north of the highland zone, especially on the Indo-European peoples in western Asia and Europe and became one of the chief factors in driving the Germanic peoples into the Roman empire after A.D. 350.

In this later period, after A.D. 350, much of the central Asiatic cavalry technology spread to

451

the southern grasslands, especially to the Arabs, but the organizational part of the central Asiatic grasslands offensive did not spread to the south, being replaced by the organizational system associated with the spread of Islam. This combination permitted a southern grasslands offensive against the older civilized areas of the Old World.

It is worth pointing out that the offensives we are discussing required at least three (and probably four) parts: (1) a technology; (2) an economic base; (3) an organizational system; and, probably, (4) an outlook or ideology--the combination functioning within a geophysical environment which permitted, limited, or inhibited the activities of the total system. In this connection we might note that the activities of the peoples of the southern grasslands (the Arabic, Hamitic, and Berber peoples, and even the negroes of the southern savannah) were delayed, in a historical sense, more by organizational and ideological deficiencies than by technological backwardness. The partial removal of these deficiencies after A.D. 600 led to the Islamic offensive from the southern grasslands almost contemporary (but only remotely linked to) the Viking offensive from the northern forests. The period of these two later offensives against the civilized areas of the Old World also saw a continuation of the northern grasslands offensive of the Ural-Altaic peoples. In fact, this latter continued until about A.D. 1600, although the last stage of this latter offensive, from about 1300 to about 1600, was of quite a different character from the earlier northern grasslands offensive of 200 B.C.-A.D. 1300, since it rested in the hands of a different people with a different technology, a different economic base, and a different organizational structure (that is Turkish rather than Mongol or Hunnish peoples, using a bureaucratic imperial structure based on peasant agriculture rather than pastoral nomadism supporting a tenuous organization of personal loyalties and with early firearms supplementing the earlier cavalry archers). For this reason, the last stages of the northern grasslands offensive, led by the Turks, is not within the scope of this chapter which ends about 1300 (on a world basis) or 970 (on a European basis).

Within this general framework of geographic and chronological relationships we must look in sequence at five situations: (1) China and the eastern grasslands offensive; (2) the Roman west and the Germanic migrations; (3) the transformation of the Roman east into the Byzantine state; (4) Islam and the southern grasslands offensive; and (5) the Viking expansion.

2.   China and the Middle Grasslands Offensive

China was one of the original alluvial valley civilizations which were constructed on the original Neolithic base, like Mesopotamia, Egypt, and the Indus civilization. There seem to have been two successive civilizations in the same approximate geographic area. The first or Sinic civilization goes back almost to 2000 B.C., culminated in the Han empire of 220 B.C.-A.D. 220, but declined and was destroyed by barbarian invaders in the period A.D. 220-600; the second or Chinese civilization was organized in this same period of confusion, had a great age of expansion under T'ang, Sung, and Ming (618-1644), and culminated in the Manchu empire (1644-1912) which succumbed to internal decay and external invaders in the period 1790-1945. In this section we are concerned only with the Sinic civilization, the ways by which it was transformed from its archaic base to the Han centralized bureaucratic empire in the period 500-100 B.C., and the subsequent grasslands invasion.

The Sinic civilization followed a process of evolution parallel to the other archaic civilizations, in which an archaic kingship gradually lost power to specialized military leaders with bronze weapons and a striking force of chariots sustaining a fighting nobility. This system was fully developed in the Shang period before 1122 but gradually became dispersed into a more feudalized system in the early Chou period (1120-770 B.C.). Under Chou, however, Chinese culture spread steadily to wider geographic areas, from the original Sinic core area in the loess lands of the middle Yellow River valley.

This Chinese culture included such obvious features as the spread of the Chinese monosyllabic

453

tonal language and the Chinese ideographic system of writing, an economic basis in a labor-intensive agricultural system, a feudalized political system, and an ideological system rooted in the archaic "summum bonum" of combined fertility-virility ideas and symbols.

This culture was a great success in the sense that it provided power, wealth, and satisfaction of human needs for a constantly increasing population over a widening geographic area. One of the key features of this system was the economic base which I have described as "labor-intensive." This means that increasing output of produce was sought not by extensive expansion to new lands, nor by application of superior or more elaborate tools ("capital-intensive"), or by the increased use of animal power, nor even by additional use of fertilizers on the land, but by adding more and more hand labor on each unit of land. This meant that the whole system required cheap labor and an increased supply of labor and fitted in well with the archaic desire for more children and an increasing population. But, at the same time, this emphasis on land and labor tended to eliminate farm animals and to resist any improvements or additional complexity of tools. On the other hand, the application of vast amounts of labor to land could be done most productively through improvements in water controls, including drainage, irrigation, and canal transportation. All of these influences together gave a heavily populated countryside, elimination of most animals for food or power, a very late introduction of the plow (4th century B.C.), restriction of proteins to the pig and fowl (both scavenger rather than grazing animals), supplemented by fish, almost total elimination of milk and milk products from the Chinese diet, a scarcity of leather goods, and eventual use of human excrement as the chief fertilizer (which brought the most productive soils up to the city walls).

The need for water control and for mobilization of mass labor may have contributed to an authoritarian trend in political life, as Karl A. Wittfogel has claimed, but an examination of the evolution of Sinic civilization as a whole seems to show that there were

strong trends toward authoritarian political forms
long before there was any extensive use of irrigation and flood control and that these could better
be regarded as consequences of the existence of
political authority than as causes of it, originally
at least. These early authoritarian trends were
rooted in the Chinese family and ancestor worship.

Unfortunately, the history of China in the
Sinic period is still obscure, despite much written
evidence, and it is not safe to be dogmatic about
the forms it took. We do not know enough about the
Neolithic period (before 3000 B.C. to after 2000
B.C.) to be certain that it had either the archaic
outlook or archaic kingship, except from its use of
some archaic symbols and later records of archaic
folklore and linguistic archaeology. Our knowledge
of the first millennium of the Bronze Age (c. 1800-
800) is almost equally obscure, in spite of the appearance of written evidence, on "oracle bones,"
under the Shang dynasty (capital at Anyang in Honan
from 1384 to 1122).

In general, weapons and weapons systems played
a considerable role in the history of Sinic civilization culminating in the creation of a unified China
by the Ch'in dynasty (249-206 B.C.). But the role
of weapons was restrained, in dwindling degree, by
religious influence in the period from 1200 to about
500 B.C. and was again restrained, in increasing
degree, by ethical and social influences after 200
B.C. As a consequence of this last trend, the subsequent Chinese civilization (after A.D. 300) took
forms which were very different from our western
civilization despite the fact that the earlier Sinic
civilization had many surprising parallels to our
predecessor, classical civilization.

This parallelism between the classical and
Sinic civilizations, like the parallelisms between
the Roman and Han empires, can be helpful to our
understanding if not carried too far. In the problem we are studying, the parallel seems closer in
regard to changes in political structures than in
changes in weaponry.

In our study of the political evolution of the
Greeks, we saw a series of stages from kings to nobles, to tyrants, to democracy, to oligarchy, to

455

military despotism, and finally (very late, under Roman rule) to a bureaucratic empire. At the same time, we saw a sequence from a few despotic Mycenaean kings to totally dispersed and local private power in the Greek dark ages, and then a new reassemblage of power into a multiplicity of states which were gradually reduced by war and conquest to a single empire. And finally, we saw a sequence of five steps in the organization of power, from kinship to religion to a secular state to military despotism and, ultimately, to a bureaucratic empire.

All three of these sequences are evident in the history of Sinic civilization over the period of about two millennia from about 1800 B.C. to after A.D. 200, but the similarity of forms and stages helps to conceal very great differences of substance and content. The series of stages was the same in moving from kingship to nobles but the stage of political democracy was omitted and, as a consequence, its two adjacent stages of tyranny and oligarchy were abbreviated and confused. The stage of military despotism, although intense, was also of limited duration, and Sinic civilization reached the stage of bureaucratic universal empire much earlier, shortly after the creation of the empire itself, and not, as in Rome, with three centuries of confused principate and military despotism before the bureaucratic empire was achieved (hardly before Constantine). In Rome the bureaucratic empire was fully achieved only after the barbarian invasions which destroyed classical civilization and the empire in the west, so that the bureaucratic empire was the vehicle of the subsequent Byzantine civilization rather than of the earlier classical civilization. In China the bureaucratic empire appeared under Han and thus was part of Sinic civilization so that, when the barbarian invasions destroyed the Han empire and the Sinic civilization itself after A.D. 250, the empire perished while the ideology and social organization of the bureaucratic structure survived to become the principal vehicle of the subsequent Chinese civilization.

Thus in Sinic civilization we might discern the following structural sequence:

1. Age of Royalty (Shang and early Chou, c. 1400-840).
2. Age of Nobles (c. 850-c. 600).
3. Confused period of tyrants and oligarchs, with incipient democratic influences (c. 600-400).
4. Growing military despotism (400-200 B.C.).
5. The bureaucratic empire (after 200 B.C.).

On this structural sequence, we must superimpose two other sequences, one political, the other ideological. The political sequence is the simple fact that Sinic civilization moved from a single organizational structure, the Shang dynasty, through the Chou feudal dynasty (both marked by a failure to distinguish public from private power) to a growing state system based on public authority in a multiplicity of states and then, by war and conquest (after 770 B.C.) returned from that multitude of states to a single empire under Ch'in and Han, 221 B.C.-A.D. 220.

The ideological changes which accompanied this sequence were: (1) a powerful religious and ritualistic orientation before 900 B.C., which declined in influence drastically after 600 B.C., replaced by: (2) a positivist and empirical point of view, which was increasingly prevalent after 500 B.C. but gradually took on: (3) an increasingly ethical and bureaucratic outlook which became dominant in the Han empire after 200 B.C.

From every angle, the middle five centuries of the first millennium B.C. (from about 750 to 250, or a little later) was a period of accelerating change from a relatively static and stable form of political life under Shang and early Chou (say 1350-800 B.C.) to a totally different kind of society which was also relatively stable under the Han empire (206 B.C.-A.D. 220, with most stable conditions about A.D. 25-180). At both of these points of relative stability the role of weapons systems as a factor in human experience was restricted, in the earlier case, apparently, by religious belief and ritual, and in the later case by ideology and bureaucratic structure. But, in the long transitional period between these two extremes,

457

the role of weapons systems in political stability was not only large but became increasingly large, reaching a dominant position in the third century B.C. under the Ch'in dynasty (249-207 B.C.).

It is unfortunate that we do not have a clearer picture of the evolution of Sinic civilization because what we do know seems to be of considerable significance in revealing general rules about the relationships between weapons systems and political stability. Unfortunately, however, our knowledge is most obscured on just this aspect of Chinese history, its weapons development. One reason for this is that archaeological investigation in the Chinese area is still very spotty and incomplete (as well as inadequately reported). Another even more significant reason for our ignorance is that Chinese written evidence consistently comes, not only from persons who have little interest in weapons and warfare but from persons who often have a deep anti-military and even anti-power bias. The Chinese method of writing, requiring knowledge of thousands of ideographic characters, was not something which could be acquired by those who had much practical knowledge of weapons and warfare. On the contrary, its difficulty and the need for long training made it such a skilled and specialized activity that those who acquired the skill could use it to become a distinct social group with autonomous power in the community. This role of the scribes as a specialized group with their own distinctive interests and ambitions turned their eyes, thoughts, and writings away from weapons and warfare, except when these seemed likely to become threatening rivals to the scribes and scholars in the Sinic and subsequent Chinese power systems.

What we know of the history of Chinese weaponry seems to indicate that its technology changed only slowly and that its organizational context was confused (or simply seems confused to us because it is so obscure). Under Shang and early Chou down to the end of the Ch'un Ch'iu period (about 480 B.C.), the prevalent weapons were: the composite bow; the horse-drawn chariot; the lance; and the "dagger-axe," or halbert. Defensive weapons, from the Shang period, were bronze and leather helmets and pounded

458

earth ramparts, with little evidence of body armor or shields, which were probably of perishable materials, such as wood. Iron was introduced without much revolutionary impact and very late (about 500 B.C.), quite different from the situation in western Asia and Europe.

The Shang period has many similarities to the Mycenaean period of Greece. Both ruling groups were of "noble blood," led by royal families, and armed with bronze weapons and horse-drawn chariots. In China there was one dominant royal family, the Shang. The ability of this Chinese family to control its rather limited terrain in north central China rested less clearly on weapon control than among the Greeks and may have rested to a greater degree on its religious role. This religious role of the Shang monarchy was similar to that of the early pharaohs, since the Shang were not only descended from the gods but also served as the necessary intermediary to the deified forces of nature. The difference here between the Greeks and Chinese may be a consequence of the nature of our sources, for the Linear B tablets of Mycenaean Pylos seem to be as concerned with service to Potnia and her associated archaic deities as the Shang oracle bones are concerned with the powers of the Shang deities of ancestry and of nature.

H.G. Creel is skeptical of the role of chariots and doubts that they played as great a part in warfare in the Shang period as they did later under the Chou dynasty. He is even doubtful of their military effectiveness, except as a command vehicle, on the grounds that the chief Chinese weapon, the compound bow, could be fired more accurately from the ground and that a chariot attack could be frustrated in battle by a simple ditch.

Some evidence for this may be found in a peace treaty of 598 which Chin imposed on Ch'i in which the former required that all furrows in the latter's agricultural fields run east and west to facilitate invasion by Chin's chariots, coming from the east, in future wars.

This relative weakness of the chariot, a weapon

459

of the nobility, was compensated by the fact that
Shang warriors of the noble class tended to have a
monopoly control over bronze weapons, especially
helmets, and could approach an enemy so rapidly by
chariot that there would be little time to dig anti-
chariot ditches. In any case, most Shang warfare
seems to have been waged against barbarous and semi-
barbarous neighbors, apparently as slave raiding
rather than as warfare, and the Shang were not called
upon to fight against any organized system comparable
to their own until their barbarous western neighbors,
led by the Chou, had acquired from the Shang themselves the military equipment and methods with which
to overcome them.

On the other hand, Shang weaponry was fully able
to dominate their own peasantry, who had little access to bronze weapons of any kind since the manufacture of bronze seems to have been restricted to the
royal compound, along with most other craft activities. Farm tools in this period were mostly of wood,
with the chief implement a double-pointed wooden spade.

If this was so, the total ownership of land by
the Shang ruler and his complete domination of the
life of the peasantry, as described by Henry Maspero,
could be explained adequately in terms of weapon
control with little emphasis on the religious prestige and power which the Shang also possessed.

Chinese culture began in the loess lands of the
north Chinese plateau and soon expanded into the alluvial soils of the middle Yellow River. Both of
these terrains lacked stone and substantial lumber
for building, so that pounded earth (terre pise) became the chief material for walls and ramparts, especially around the royal compound which was a ritual
and military center as well as a residence for the
king and his associates and contained the chief metalworkers and traders, both of which were entirely under royal control. The Shang ruler also "owned" the
land and completely dominated the peasants who were
subject to forced labor in both agriculture and construction and may have had military duties as well.

Among the chief activities of the Shang and
early Chou, covering almost a thousand years (from

the 18th century B.C. to the 8th century), were
great mass hunts, similar to those of Jenghis Khan's
Mongols 2500 years later, and slave raiding against
the western "barbarians." All of life was saturated
with ritual and superstitions, and no significant
acts could be done without asking advice of the ancestral spirits. Since these spirits could not understand oral communications but could read, questions
were addressed to them by writing on bones and tor-
toise shells which were then exposed to the fire.
The cracks resulting from the heat gave answers from
the spirits in simple "yes" and "no" terms.

Even at this remote beginning of Chinese civilization, we can discern the earliest origins of the
subsequent domination of political life by the scribes,
for this method of divination of the spirits made it
necessary for the warrior kings to rely on the scribes
who knew the 3000 characters used in writing these
oracle bones. Moreover, according to Creel, the
diviners could predetermine the answer by how they
applied the fire to the bones to obtain the crack-
ing they wanted.

In this way, the personal power of the thirty
successive Shang kings was restricted by their superstitions. This included their weaponry. As Jacques
Gernet put it, "Each military expedition was quite
as much a deployment of magico-religious forces as
of positive physical force."

The influence of weapons and of physical force
was also restrained by the social network within
which each individual lived. In fact, there were
no individuals, since society was made up of clans
and families in which the ancestors were much more
important than living individuals. "The descendants
were to receive the blessings of heaven as long as
they walked in the steps of their forefathers." As
in classical Mediterranean civilization, so in Sinic
civilization, the rigid system of status based on
birth in a clan was gradually broken down toward
nuclear families and a condition in which status
was based on individual decisions and agreements,
but in China this development, which reached its
limit about 200 B.C., never reached complete atomized
individualism but began once again to turn backward

toward a status system based on the family and on
voluntary groupings founded on achievement, social
class status, and shared beliefs.

There is a great disagreement about the nature
of the Chou conquest of Shang in 1122 B.C. (or 1111,
according to some). Some authorities, like W. Eber-
hard, believe that the conquest was by a federation
of diverse tribes, some of which were non-Chinese
(that is Tibetan or even Turkish) with recent pastoral traditions; but other experts, such as Creel,
believe that these conquerors were simply illiterate
Chinese barbarian agriculturalists from Shensi, 300
miles southwest of the Shang capital at Anyang in
Honan.

The Chou conquest about 1100 B.C. eventually
extended over an area much greater than that controlled
by the Shang dynastry; eventually it spread from the
Wei valley in Shensi to the lower Yellow River near
Shantung. Royal control over this larger area was
much less direct than under the Shang and soon gave
rise to a feudal system in which local areas were
granted to royal princes (supported by Chou military
colonies among the native peasant peoples) in return
for personal and family loyalty as well as military
aid to the king in his own district around modern
Sian in the Wei basin. Within a few centuries, this
system began to break up into separate areas of private power, as there was no way in which the king
could force the feudal princes to submit to his rule
or to fulfill the military obligations they had assumed toward him. As soon as the princes ceased to
be aliens in their districts and were accepted by
the local people, the distinction between Chou military colonies and local peasants became blurred and
the local prince found that he had ready at hand
the wealth, manpower, and bronze workers to construct
a local power base fully able to resist any orders
from the king.

In this early or "western" Chou period (1111-
771 B.C.), chariots became much more numerous but
were no longer under a single control system. Where
the Shang records refer to armed forces as numbers
of "men," the Chou documents speak of numbers of
chariots. These vehicles consisted of a railed platform on spoked wheels, drawn by two horses, but often

462

(in the Chou period) with two additional "outside" horses (called in Chinese two "third horses") attached by traces to the vehicle, but not harnessed to the shaft. Each vehicle carried a noble bowman on the left, with a driver in the center and a defensive spearman on the right. In addition, each chariot was accompanied by a fixed number of infantry (from ten to twenty-five). The whole group, or possibly three such groups totaling up to 85 men, seems to have formed a tactical unit in combat, with the nobles and some of the infantry forces armed with reflex bows, but most of the infantry, in the Ch'un Ch'iu period (down to 481), armed with pole weapons (chiefly the dagger-axe or halberts and spears). Most combatants had bronze daggers and throwing lances, but the sword and the crossbow, both prevalent after 400, were absent in the earlier period.

We know nothing about the tactics or strategy used with this equipment, but it is quite clear that power centers from 1100 onward, for several centuries, were becoming more numerous, more limited in area, and more disintegrated from their social, economic, and ideological contexts. The Chou monarch in his western capital became a Merovingian ruler with nominal powers and rights, no longer supported by actual power. In 771 he was driven by barbarian invaders from his capital in Shenshi and fled eastward to a new capital near Loyang in Honan. By 700 he had been defeated in battle by one of his own vassals, and, from that date onward, he was simply one of numerous princes (many called "kings") across the north China plains.

This dispersal of power was accompanied by dispersal of economic rights, of social power and prestige, and of political rights. The ruling group, who participated in war, government, and religious sacrifices, became more numerous and tended to divide into three levels, as social classes began to replace kinship groupings in the social system. These three were (1) the princes, all nobles; (2) the ministers and "great officials," originally all of princely families but increasingly made up of scribes recruited from younger sons, lesser nobility, and from obscure families; and (3) the shih (knights or gentry).

The latter, whose economic level was often no higher than that of an adequately supported peasant, were regarded as nobles from their participation in warrior and ritual activities. They became a powerful force for innovative change as their economic inferiority motivated them to action, while their noble background made them emphasize their moral code of loyalty and honor. This code became the background for the later gentry ("scholar officials") and the teachings of Confucius who may have been from this shih class.

Below the nobles were the non-noble masses, mostly peasants but with a minority of "dependent" peoples, such as slaves, personal servants, artisans, and such. In the early Chou period, as previously under the Shang, the peasants owned nothing but their labor, working on the king's lands in return for maintenance. But throughout Chinese history, law has tended to be a body of specific customs rather than a system of general and abstract rules. Accordingly, property rights in China, including landed property, have always put more emphasis on possession than on titles to ownership, so that the peasants and others who actually possessed the land came to be regarded as its owners. In a similar way, the legitimacy of political office followed actual possession of functions without lingering for very long on the rights of inactive "legitimists." Transfer of power in fact became a transfer of authority which carried legitimacy along with it. In this way, both power and land ownership were dispersed downward from royal hands to lesser people in the period from 1100 to 600, but while land ownership moved downward, in many areas, into the hands of the peasants themselves, political power did not follow to such a degree of dispersal. Thus China did not reach the stage of political democracy. Instead, power moved downward from the hands of the kings and princes in 1100-800, to the hands of the ministers and nobles in 800-550, with the shih rising rapidly from 550 onward. The shih as a social class did not push the ministerial nobility into eclipse as these ministerialists had eclipsed the princely nobility previously because this social development was disrupted and the whole social system itself was destroyed by the rise of military despotism after 400 B.C.

464

This means that an evolutionary situation was replaced by a revolutionary one. As a consequence, the class structure which had replaced the earlier kinship structure was destroyed; the movement of power downward to the shih class within that structure was arrested; and the movement of power outward to an increased number of persons and thus toward democracy was reversed, being replaced by a flow of power backward toward concentration in fewer and fewer hands. Since this reduced number of hands on the levers of power after the fourth century B.C. were the hands of military despots, it seems clear that weapons, or at least weapons systems, must have played a considerable role in this revolutionary reversal of the earlier evolutionary dispersal of power.

We do not know enough about the history of Chinese weapons and we are even more ignorant of the organizational context in which weapons were used. But it seems clear that weapons, weapons systems, and probably tactics did not develop to the amateur type of weaponry but remained closer to the specialist condition, moving from feudal professional weaponry to mercenary professional weaponry (that is from the Greek condition of weaponry about 650 B.C. to the Greek condition about 300 B.C. without developing to the condition of citizen soldier hoplites as existed in Greece about 450 B.C.). It will be noted that the Chinese developmental process not only omitted a stage which the Greeks had experienced, but the whole chronology of the process in China was somewhat later than it was in Greece and thus was more nearly contemporary with the stages in Rome, passing, so to speak, from the Greek pattern to the Roman pattern somewhere about the fifth century B.C. but then speeding up so that by 200 B.C. the Chinese sequence was already several centuries ahead of Roman developments. In this sense, in the speed of changing conditions, the Chinese experience was much more revolutionary than the experience of Rome or even of Mediterranean civilization as a whole (but not more revolutionary than the Ionian Greek experience of 600-400 B.C.).

The point at which this reversal of the process in China appeared can be identified, even it it can-

465

not be precisely dated. It was the point at which
the shih class began to appeal to the peasants for
support in a coup d'etat to replace the ministerial
nobility in high office, and then discovered almost
immediately that military despots could do this
even better than the shih could. In Greece this
shift can be dated almost exactly in the personal
shift of Dionysus I of Syracuse from playing the
role of a "tyrant" to playing the role of a military
despot (about 400 B.C.).

It seems clear that chariots became less important and infantry more important fairly steadily
from at least the eighth century B.C., although we
do not hear of an all-infantry army until 570.
From the mid-seventh century onward the number of
states and the frequency of wars increased, although
the duration of such wars remained brief, often no
more than a few weeks marked by a single battle.
But the need for more fighting men and probably also
for a larger supply of bronze weapons spread the making of such weapons more widely (that is outside of
nobles' residential compounds), increased the number
of infantry to the point where increased numbers of
peasants became involved and moved both soldiers and
officers (increasingly of the shih class rather
than any higher level of nobility) toward the condition of mercenary fighters. This means that fighting continued as a professional activity but passed
from the dominance of unpaid fighters living off
their estates (that is, feudal fighters) to fighters
living from government supply. Since the shih often
allied with the infantry of peasant origin against
the upper class nobles who controlled the state
structure (similar to the Greek tyrants) the economic position of the peasants, especially in respect
to land ownership, improved, but the extension of
parallel political rights toward democracy was probably held back by the fact that infantry forces became mercenary professionals rather than becoming
peasant soldiers motivated by patriotism to a state.
Moreover, manufacture and control of weapons never
became widely dispersed.

The state continued to develop in a growing
distinction between private or personal rights or
activities and public, etatist, activities. Thus

466

by 500, the ruler arrived at a position where he controlled a growing body of public state power, supported by state-supported shih and peasant soldiers and prepared to act against the older forces of noble feudal power.

In this process two antithetical behavior patterns began to appear. One was a movement toward more chivalric warfare among shih groups in the core of Sinic civilization; the other was a movement toward more brutal and more positivist warfare among the more peripheral states on the edges of the expanding area of Sinic civilization. Both of these were evident in the early portion of the Chan Kuo period (after 480 B.C.).

The movement toward chivalry in warfare was a noble attitude, probably intensified by the shih class just because of the inferiority of their own nobility. A similar aristocratic tendency was evident in their idealization of the past, increasingly the remote past, as a golden age. As Hsu says, "For these aristocrats, a war was also a game. . .; it was a duel of moral values, a trial of honor."

Such moral restraints on violence appeared within a context of growing international law and diplomacy very much like that in Europe in the 1400-1750 period. Even as the conflicts between states intensified, rules began to be formulated regarding the ways in which inter-state relationships should be governed: the rights of ambassadors, the need to ask permission to enter a state's territory, the use of formal treaties, the use of hostages, bonds, and dynastic marriages to guarantee performance of agreements, acceptance of the legal equality of states, even a tendency toward rules that a state should not be attacked in any year in which it had suffered a popular revolt or in which its ruler had died.

This movement toward a rule of international law in inter-state relations and of chivalry in the conduct of warfare came in the same brief period in which the movement toward citizen soldiers and political democracy seemed to be developing (650-500 B.C.), but all four of these tendencies were reversed

467

after 500 B.C., chiefly under the influence of the growing intensity and brutality of warfare, especially from the more peripheral states.

As Chinese culture moved outward from its original home in the north Chinese plain, the more material elements diffused much more rapidly than the less material ones. As a result, the states of core China "found themselves faced by the outlying kingdoms who lacked their respect for ritual and moderation." One of the first of these more violent states was Ch'u on the middle Yangtze River: "Since it ignored the rules of courtly warfare and was not subject to the same religious scruples, it did not hesitate to wipe out its enemies and destroy their forms of worship." Among other things Ch'u was one of the first to establish universal conscription. But by 500 B.C. Ch'u was beginning to be threatened by more remote states, farther to the south and east like Wu and Yueh.

As the wars between states became more violent, the practitioners of unrestrained violence did not win an unqualified victory. On the contrary, the advocates of moral restraint such as the shih in contrast with the military despots, the smaller states in distinction to the greater powers, and the scribes and scholars in distinction to the warriors and rulers, by retiring from the area of violent conflict to the area of ideology and administrative expertise were able to establish non-violent restraints on violence which became a permanent part of Chinese culture. But these tendencies were relatively futile for most of the period 700-200 B.C.

The political disintegration into an increased number of states seems to have continued down to about 700. We are told that the Chou conquerors of the 12th century B.C. had distributed their conquered territory into more than 1700 holdings, in five levels of nobility with distinctive titles which are usually translated as duke, marquis, earl, viscount, and baron. These holdings must be regarded as estates rather than as states, but by 700 B.C., when they had been consolidated into about 170 power units, they were clearly states well on the road to sovereign power in the European sense. 110 of these

468

states, we are told, ceased to exist in the period 722-463 B.C., leaving only 22. Much of this consolidation was the result of military conquest. This reduced number, with greater resources, commanded larger forces, and waged wars of greater duration.

It is possible that the advent of iron about 500 B.C. may have contributed to this consolidation of size, especially as it came in a form which did not help the spread of democracy, as happened in the Mediterranean. In the latter area, iron was known at first in the form of wrought iron which was hammered out on local forges. Such wrought iron had a low carbon content and was rather soft, capable of being processed at low temperatures but unable to retain a sharp edge or point. While the Chinese knew of such wrought iron, they shifted almost at once to the manufacture of cast iron since, unlike the Europeans, they could achieve the requisite high temperatures in large furnaces. Such cast iron had a very high carbon content, was available in large quantities, but was too brittle to make sharp points or edges on weapons. Accordingly, in China iron was used for farming tools with great benefits to agricultural production, especially as the plow also arrived in China during these same centuries of the "period of the warring states" (453-221 B.C.). Weapons, however, for much of this period, continued to be of bronze, while the Chinese ironworkers slowly learned to transform cast iron into steel of variable quality by decreasing the carbon content of their cast iron by puddling it with wrought iron and melding the two together. This process, much improved by the Japanese, passed westward across India to the Arabs and Merovingian Franks after A.D. 500 to produce "damascene" steel.

Such steel, but of poorer quality, brought swords into the Chinese armament in the Han period (after 200 B.C.) and had a gradual influence on many aspects of life without the revolutionary impact that the advent of wrought iron had had in Greece in the period 1200-500 B.C. The early Chinese development of cast iron, about 1800 years before iron in this form became generally available in Europe (about A.D. 1380), may have contributed to the increasing size of political units in China from the fact that the casting method required a mobilization of skills and resources which could be obtained only in state enterprises or with large-scale government contractors.

This tendency for metal manufacture and for metal weapons to be controlled by the ruling system was general throughout all Chinese history, in sharp contrast with the opposite tendency in both classical antiquity and western civilization where both metal manufacture and weapons ownership tended to move into private hands. Among the Greeks and during much of the Roman republican period, fighting men were expected to provide their own weapons. The same thing was true for the early part of western civilization and, when this ceased to be true in the more recent period, manufacture and trade in armaments continued in private hands. This tendency has led to restraints of various kinds on the growth of state power and especially on any movement toward a totalitarian public authority.

In China such restraints on public power, derived from private manufacture, trade, and ownership of weapons, have been weak or absent. Under the Shang and early Chou, highly skilled bronze workers were originally confined to the rulers' walled compounds. Later, when metalworking spread outside these confined areas, the rulers and the growing state power retained control, as far as possible, over mines, ore-handling, manufacture of metals, and stores of weapons. Even when armies consisted largely of peasants, weapons were supplied by the government. In effect the peasants of China, in sharp contrast with those of Athens or Rome, were kept disarmed. When iron came to China, its more advanced technology there made it a much more expensive technique than iron forging in Europe or western Asia, especially the need for a continuous blast of air provided by a remarkable Chinese invention, the double-acting piston bellows, which was operated by water power as early as the Han empire. Long before this, beginning in Ch'i under Duke Huan (686-643), metal manufacture was made a government monopoly. This was copied by other states and remained a more or less permanent feature of Chinese government thereafter (however erratically enforced). In 120 B.C. under the former Han, "all iron production was carried on in fortynine factories scattered throughout the empire." This ceased to be true under the later Han.

On the whole, the influence of the advent of iron (and steel) on military and political life in China was indirect and slow. Its influence was not direct but was exercised through administrative regulations and organizational structures rather than by weapons in themselves. This can be seen very clearly in the failure of the creation of mass armies of peasant infantry to carry political organizations very far along the road to political democracy.

The significant changes in administrative organization began in the seventh century B.C., especially in Ch'i under Duke Huan and his advisor Kuan Chung, known as Kuan-tzu. These reforms included reorganization of the territory into functional subdivisions of which there were 15 regional districts for controlling the peasants and 6 additional functional groupings for controlling the artisans, merchants, and scribes. The 15 administrative districts were grouped into three provinces of five districts each, with lesser subdivisions. A chain of authority was established downward from the duke through each level to the lowest subdivision, with the chief on each level appointing his subordinates on the next lower level, largely on the basis of ability and merit without much regard to noble blood or social status. Economic controls were set up based on uniform weights and measures, centralized price controls, and the monopoly of salt and metals. The activities of lower levels were controlled through required periodic reports and a system of itinerant inspectors from the central government. The army was organized as a peasant militia, with each family required to provide a soldier to serve with others from the same territorial unit. Thus the whole armed force consisted of three armies, each with units from five districts.

This system was so successful that Duke Huan became a kind of Carolingian mayor of the palace to

471

the Merovingian king of Chou, with the new title of "protector." The system made Ch'i such a power among the contending states of China that it was copied in variation by other Chinese states.

The use of peasant militia gave rise, as we have said, to democratic tendencies, which never developed into a democratic political system. Evidence of these tendencies can be seen in such matters as growing recognition by princes and administrators of their need for popular support, the appeals by disgruntled members of the gentry to peasant discontent to support their own ambitions, and by sporadic popular revolts in the earliest stages of this development (as in Chin in 620 and in 613 in the small state of Chu).

The historical sources show the recognition by rulers of their need for support from popular armies. In 576 B.C. a minister in Cheng was estimating the strength of the enemy state of Ch'u and took comfort in the fact that the ruler of Ch'u had alienated his people. The minister said, "Let the king go on aggravating his offenses until the people revolt against him. Without people, who will fight for him?" Thirty years later in 546, when a minister of Sung invited all states to a conference to discuss disarmament, most leaders were convinced of the futility of the effort, but most of them feared to reject the effort outright for fear of an adverse reaction from their own people. In Ch'i a statesman "dared not refuse, since if word got around that he had refused to sanction the stoppage of wars, the people of Ch'i might be disaffected." About the same time, Yen-tzu, famous advisor to three rulers of Ch'i, constantly advocated seeking support from the people, saying, "The people first, then yourself." A half century later, in 502, the ruler of Wei called his people into an assembly to ask their approval for a war against Chin. They approved and promised to continue to fight "even if invaded five times."

This attention to public opinion did not move onward to general consultation and consent to government policies because of developments in weapons systems as much as anything else. Continued and probably growing government control over the supply of weapons moved the power balance in favor of

472

the government and adverse to the people. At the same time, the peasant militia never became an army of citizen soldiers but instead became a force of mercenary fighters because the conscription system, which in theory made all liable for service, in fact fell on only a small minority because of the need for agricultural production which fell on the large majority. The minority who were conscripted went away to fight and usually made a career of it, equipped with government arms and supported by government funds. In consequence their solidarity with their peasant origins was weakened and their loyalty flowed toward the government which paid them.

The growth of armies such as this along with the steady spread of a money economy, of merchants, of specialized craftsmen, and of an administrative system based on merit made it possible for the expanding states of China to carry on offensive wars which increased the territorial areas of states while, at the same time, reducing the number of states, just as happened in Europe over much of its history from 950 to 1950.

This extension of state power appeared as an increased ability to mobilize human resources over larger areas and thus to increase the extent of irrigation, flood control, and transportation canal projects. This also made it possible to build huge protective walls to increase the defensive strength of countries under attack from their neighbors. Such walls intensified the movement toward the use of infantry forces and made it necessary to increase greatly the number of such soldiers, not only to man these walls in defense but to storm them in offense. The water control projects along with the advent of the plow allowed an increase in food production and in population which allowed the defensive walls to be extended, often for hundreds of miles, while the increased capital investment in the agricultural enterprise made it more urgent to protect such investment by more expensive walls. The whole combination greatly increased state power and rulers' authority. All of this contributed to that period of over 300 years known as the period of warring states, traditionally dated 453-221 B.C.

The arrival of masses of infantry forces and of great walls resulted in some changes of weapons and less clearly perceived changes in tactics. The new infantry forces at first shifted slowly from the bow to the spear as their chief weapon. This seems to reflect the growth of more closely packed formations. The chariot continued to exist as did the halbert, but both of these seem to have become ceremonial weapons, rather than weapons of battle, in the period of the warring states. Bows must have continued to be used for defending walls, but the crossbow which appeared in the fifth century simultaneously with the proliferation of walls was probably used by large infantry forces in their attacks on such ramparts.

The crossbow, apparently a Chinese invention of the first half of the first millennium B.C., was used in hunting for a considerable period before it was adapted to warfare. Its chief advantages were that it could be drawn and held cocked a considerable time before it was fired and it could be fired without the user exposing himself so openly as with the ordinary long bow. It may have been invented by hunters as a killing trap for animals and was certainly used for this purpose and for hunting wild fowl before it became a military weapon. Its chief drawback as a weapon was its slow rate of fire and the great effort needed to cock it when its short bow was stiffened to give long range and good penetrating power. Usually some kind of pulley or crank, using the whole body or legs, was needed to cock the weapon. For this reason, it never became an effective, or even useful, weapon for mounted fighters, who continued to use the reflex bow until the advent of modern firearms in Asia. But with massed infantry forces the crossbow was very effective in combat, especially along city walls, either in offense, by clearing the walls of defenders as a preliminary to storming it, or in defense, for firing down on the assault forces without excessive bodily exposure by the defenders.

In the fourth century B.C., the impact of steppe cavalry armed with bows began to present a critical problem to the Chinese states. This was not easy to meet because of the elimination of grazing animals (in distinction to scavenger animals like fowl, the pig, and the dog) from the intensively organized Chinese agricultural system with its maximizing of human labor on each plot of land. Generally, the solution reached was to make some kind of arrangement with one of the semi-pastoral peoples to serve as auxiliaries to Chinese forces, but this was possible only in the north and west. The first strictly Chinese cavalry corps was in the northern state of Chao in 307 B.C. when the government made a deliberate decision to adopt steppe warfare methods including shifting from the loose Chinese clothing to the steppe dwellers' trousers.

By that date, 300 B.C., China had been reduced to seven states from the twenty-two which had existed in 463. Over the next century or so, these seven were reduced to one. As the struggle intensified, each contestant was being served by a complex armed force of infantry, cavalry, and engineers. The infantry were peasants, armed with spears and crossbows. The cavalry were mounted bowmen. The engineers and supply forces had relatively advanced techniques of rams, assault towers, undermining techniques, and stone throwers (including mangonels which hurled stone balls of about five kilogram).

China had been brought to this high stage of military dominance by organizational advances rather than by weapons technology. These advances in political and military organization operated in an economic and social system of increasing expansion, disintegration, and fluidity. These conditions gave rise to developments very similar to those which arose among the Greeks. The chief obvious difference was that the Greeks never reached political unity from their own actions, probably from the combination of a broken and difficult terrain surrounded by a very navigable sea with a quite different outlook which emphasized loyalty to a microscopic city-state as the ultimate good. In China more universalist political ideas, leading backward through worship of ancestors and the forces of nature to the supremacy of the Asiatic steppe deity "Bright Sky" or "Heaven" was combined with a wide and relatively open terrain crossed by navigable rivers and an expanding net of canals.

Thus the Chinese were able to reach political unity within their own cultural patterns and escaped having it imposed by a semi-alien people, as the Greeks were subject to the Romans.

The general pattern of these power struggles was that the central core of smaller and older Chou states in the middle Yellow River valley was threatened by the more peripheral, larger, less restrained, and more barbarized states on the frontiers of the Chinese cultural area. These more peripheral states could increase their areas and manpower at the expense of their outer more barbaric neighbors and could use this increase in resources to threaten conquest of the alluvial core of Chinese culture. But the peripheral states, including Ch'i in the northeast, Chin in the north, Ch'in in the west, and Ch'u in the south acted to oppose the triumph of any one of them over the core area. Within that core, smaller states like Cheng, Sung, Lu, and Wei developed skilled diplomacy, using balance of power tactics to a degree which was even more sophisticated than European international politics in the period 1500-1800. These diplomatic skills were combined with limited transportation facilities and the defensive strength of walled ramparts to slow up the process by which states were slowly reduced from twenty-two in 464 to one in 221 B.C.

For many years, the core states of Cheng and Sung acted as a kind of keystone in this dynamic state system, calling in the peripheral states against each other to redress any unbalancing of the system which threatened to extinguish additional core states. The early preponderance of Ch'i (seventh century) was replaced by the rise of Chin and Ch'u in north and south, leading to a long struggle between them (640-550 B.C.). In the next century, new states (like Wu and Yueh) came into the struggle, and leagues of states replaced single states as contestants in the conflict. Such leagues, however, since they were themselves of a temporary and unstable nature, simply prolonged this era of unstable conditions since they could prevent conquest of individual states without creating any wider areas of unified political rule to provide more permanent stability.

476

In this period, no one of the peripheral states had a supply system capable of sustaining an offensive in the core area long enough to reduce fortified towns and areas within which additional supplies could be captured. At the same time, the core state thus attacked did not need to eject the invader but merely had to hold out long enough for its allies to come to the rescue. These allies, in turn, had no need to defeat the invader in battle since they could eventually compel his withdrawal by attacking his territory (or the territory of one of his allies) at some distant point. Thus the intrinsic instability of this system of power units continued to perpetuate itself as a system in continuing, but unstable, equilibrium.

The nature of this system was fully recognized at the time and so was the diminishing influence of non-military elements, such as ritual, conventions, social status, economic practices, or personal honor, in the struggle. Any military, administrative, or political innovation which gave a state a momentary advantage was quickly copied by the others. The ultimate consequence was a steady movement within the system toward naked force. The dominance of such force was evident in many ways, not only in the slow reduction in the number of states within the system, but also in the growing size of armies, the increased frequency and longer duration of wars, and the growing ruthlessness of the struggle. The nature of the process became clear in the multi-state battle of Ch'eng p'u in 632 and led to the abortive 14-state disarmament conference of 546 in Sung. A relatively meaningless agreement was signed by eleven states but, when the Sung minister who had been the moving spirit in the conference gave the signed document to his prime minister, the latter tore the paper to pieces and upbraided him for deceiving himself and others about the political realities of the situation. His long harangue ended by saying, "Who can do away with the instruments of war? They have been with us always. Only with their help are the lawless kept in fear and is virtue recognized. Wise men have risen to high position by them and troublemakers removed. The ways which lead to decline or to growth, to preservation or to ruin, to blindness on one side or intelligence on the other, are all traced to these

477

instruments--and you are trying to do away with them--
isn't your scheme a delusion? Can any crime be greater than to lead states astray by such delusions?"

This growing Realpolitik is evident in both
speech and behavior in the period 550-200 B.C. Earlier the great Duke Wen of Chin (636-628) had refused to break his word, even to annex territory
which was available without use of force. He won
great prestige for himself and his state, but the
latter was not one of the survivors in the final
struggle. Other leaders and advisors, such as Yen-
tzu, minister to three rulers of Ch'i in the sixth
century, advocated economic improvement and internal
consolidation rather than foreign conquest. It is
true that victory, in the long run, depended on internal consolidation and, perhaps almost equally, on
a peripheral territorial position, but ultimate
political victory (at least on a short-run basis)
went to Realpolitik.

Even in the sixth century the nature of such
Realpolitik was recognized. In 578 Ch'u and Chin
made an alliance, but within two years Ch'u saw an
opportunity to win advantage by attacking Chin. A
minister of Ch'u asked his prime minister, the
famous Tzu-fan, "Is it not improper to violate
a covenant which we made so recently with Chin?"
To this the leader retorted, "When we can gain the
advantage over our enemies, we must advance without
considering covenants."

As a result of this growing violence, the whole
period from the fifth century to late in the third
century, known as "the period of the warring states,"
was an era of very contradictory influences. Improved agricultural practices, including the spread
of iron tools and the plow, and the growing use of
draft animals, including the ox, the horse, and the
donkey, gave greatly increased production of food
and increased population. These made possible improved waterworks, for flood control, irrigation,
and water transportation which also increased affluence. Such surpluses of food, manpower, and
draft animals, along with the increased production
of swords and crossbows, increased the offensive
power of military systems chiefly by improved mili-

tary logistics. In all these changes the western state of Ch'in had distinct advantages. Partly protected from the other warring states by mountains, it had all its enemies in front of it. The barbarians on its flanks and rear were not yet strong enough to threaten it, yet were strong enough to test its mettle and could provide draft animals in large numbers. The area was well adapted to large economic gains from irrigation and was rich enough to carry this out. Part of Ch'in's wealth came from its position on the chief trade route from China to Turkestan, which gave it access to supplies of movable wealth and of draft animals, and also won support from numerous rich merchants. Moreover, as a peripheral state in the Chinese cultural area, Ch'in overcame the forces of feudal decentralization earlier and more completely than other Chinese states. It has been said that Ch'in was the only Chinese state which never was shaken by domestic disturbance. Unlike most Chinese states, it had no strong noble family except the royal family, made much use of foreign experts from other states, and at an early stage established a system of taxation to replace dues of military service and payments in kind. It early obtained private ownership of land, tenancy and use of hired agricultural labor to replace serf labor, and established severe law codes with group responsibility for criminal activities. Much of this had been established in the ministry of Shang Yang (361-338 B.C.). Equally important in the rise of Ch'in was the fact that its rival neighboring state to the east, Chin (or Tsin) had become overextended in the fifth century B.C. and had split up into three states (Chao, Wei, and Han, from north to south) in 403 B.C.

From this background, Ch'in in the third century was able to combine together a relatively advanced transportation system, a centralized military and administrative system, a productive economy, and a ruthless Realpolitik ideology.

While all this was going on the west, the other Chinese states were busy fighting each other. They continued to ignore Ch'in and to underestimate its capabilities because they regarded it as a barbarian state. As a consequence of these misconceptions,

while Ch'in grew in power in the first two-thirds of
the third century B.C., the other six states continued to fight among themselves. Only in 233 did the
six form an alliance against Ch'in, but even at that
late date, their rivalries against each other were
so ingrained in their outlook that they were unable
to cooperate effectively in action. Accordingly,
over the next dozen years, Shih Huang-ti, ruler of
Ch'in, under the guidance of his clever minister,
Li Ssu (280-208 B.C.), split the other Chinese
states and conquered them piecemeal, joining them
together in the first united Chinese empire in 221.

The unification of China by Shih Huang-ti and
Li Ssu was a triumph for Realpolitik. So also was
the consolidation of the conquered territories
which followed. The victorious ruler was determined
to create an autocratic and totalitarian system dominated by his personal rule. All feudal survivals
were outlawed, and China was divided into thirty-six
provinces under royal agents. The Great Wall of
China was constructed across the northern frontier,
largely by linking together previously existing
walls. South of that barrier, all local fortifications and city walls were ordered destroyed and all
private arms and weapons were ordered collected to
be melted down and cast into huge bells and statues.
To eliminate any independent local leadership,
120,000 wealthy or powerful families were ordered
to move from the newly conquered states to the capital city of Hsien-yang, where copies of their previous homes were built for the feudal lords among
these. To eliminate resistance from the scribes
and intellectuals, all books except those concerned
with agriculture, medicine, drugs, and divination
were ordered to be destroyed or surrendered to the
government. Other books were kept in official versions by the government or were permitted to seventy
chosen intellectuals. This "burning of the books"
was not total nor fully carried out. The decree
promulgated in 213 B.C. was not revoked until 191
B.C., but it ceased to be enforced after the execution of Li Ssu in 208. However, the overthrow of
the Ch'in dynasty in 206 led to the destruction of
the capital in a conflagration which burned for
three months and a major loss of the books and records which the government's attempt to monopolize

information had collected together.

The year following the "burning of the books" (213) was the year of the "burying of the scholars"; Shih Huang-ti had some four hundred intellectuals buried alive, for, as Li Ssu put it, "Those who use the past to oppose the present must be exterminated."

Shih Huang-ti's policy of complete centralization was facilitated by constructing a network of military roads radiating out from the capital. These highways were 300 feet wide and bordered with trees. Until that time, roads in China were simply cart tracks deeply scored in the earth. To ease use of these ruts a decree was issued establishing a uniform gauge for all chariot and cart wheels. This pleased the merchants who had supported the unification, so also did decrees establishing a uniform coinage system of copper and gold, uniform weights and measures, and a uniform written script for the whole empire. The local laws of the previous states were brushed aside and replaced by a single, very severe, imperial code which covered every possible action "like a fishing net through which even the smallest fish cannot escape." Waterworks were extended, both for irrigation and transportation (especially in Szechuan), and hundreds of thousands of coolies were moved around the empire on construction works of all kinds.

This system of absolute personal despotism operating on the basis of uniform rules which ignored individual or local differences, sustained by a political structure resting on a basis of almost undiluted force was largely a creation of the outlook of Li Ssu (280?-208 B.C.) and was achieved by the hyperactivity of Shih Huang-ti.

This first ruler of united China was restless and ignorant, filled with shamanistic superstitions and fears, driven by insatiable ambition and with a psychopathic emotional insecurity which could be satisfied only by constant accumulation of personal power in a regime of growing violence. He lived in constant fear of death in general and of assassination in particular, consulting with all kinds of ideological cranks and charlatans in search of the secret of immortality, moving restlessly about his empire on trips of personal inspection, while sleeping every night in a different bed, a different room, or a different palace for fear of assassination. The chief consequence of this system was a large scale alienation of his people, his army, and his officials which built up secret opposition fully justifying his personal fears. Born in 259, he had come to the throne at age 13 in 246 and died in 210 at age 50. For the first ten years of his reign he was dominated by a rich merchant from Chao, Lu Pu-Wei; for the last twenty-seven years, the chief minister was Li Ssu, a native of Ch'u. Both of these were aliens, both died violent deaths (by forced suicide and public execution), and together they contributed more than Huang-ti himself to the first Chinese empire.

The nature of that Ch'in empire, apart from Huang-ti's personal idiosyncrasies, was the forced imposition upon all China of the distinctive features of the centralized, non-feudal, militarized, and secular system which had grown up in Ch'in and made it quite different from the rest of China. These differences gave Ch'in the ability to conquer China without giving it the ability to continue to govern what it had conquered. In fact, this distinction between the ability to conquer (which may often be based largely on force) and the ability to govern an area as large as China (which requires considerable elements of cooperation and consent) later became a permanent element in all Chinese theories of government, partly as a consequence of the fate of the Ch'in.

From our point of view, it is clear that Ch'in did not have the weapons system to justify its conquest of all of China in 221 B.C. Its success rested on factors which were distinctive to it and to the circumstances of the moment. The chief element in its military success was logistical, namely its ability in a quantitative way to move men and supplies across China rapidly enough, and to sustain this long enough, to force the surrender of fortified resistance points.

Once the conquest was achieved, on this very precarious and temporary basis, an extremely unstable political system appeared. On the one hand, as we have said, it became clear almost at once that the advantages which Ch'in had which allowed it to conquer China were not the advantages it needed to sustain its control over China. But, on the other hand, these advantages allowed Ch'in to control China long enough to change permanently the elements of applied force in the Chinese cultural area. We might examine these in reverse order.

In the final ten years of his rule, Shih Huang-ti changed the Chinese cultural area in ways which left it much more subject to control by a single power. Construction of the Great Wall, elimination of weapons and fortifications within the Great Wall, and improvements of communications and transportation in that same area by both roads and waterways meant that China could be held together in a single power area much more easily than before 221 and without the special advantages which had allowed Ch'in to unify the area. The succeeding Han dynasty could take advantage of this new situation to reunite the Chinese cultural area, after the civil wars of 206-202 had broken it up, once again, into nineteen states. To be sure, the three factors we have mentioned (the Great Wall, elimination of internal weapons and fortifications, and a system of military roads) all weakened under the Han dynasty and especially after A.D. 180, but by that time a number of other factors had entered the situation.

Of these new factors, two were concerned with the use of horses. These had a direct influence on military power and tended, in general, to act in opposite directions. These two were the barbarian development of the stirrup and the earlier Han development of a much more effective method for harnessing horses.

Full nomadism, in which tribes are totally supported by domestic animals and, accordingly, can (and must) move constantly about to new grazing areas, was developed by peoples of the Asiatic steppes about the fourth century B.C. There was a constant tendency for such nomadic peoples to fall backward toward a less specialized way of life, either by establishing commercial relationships with agricultural peoples on the edges of the grasslands or by raiding such agricultural peoples to rob them of their goods produced by a sedentary society but not fitted to a fully nomadic way of life. The great weakness (and great strength) of such a nomadic way of life was that it was harsh and austere, breeding strong peoples who, however, could retain their strength only so long as they were prepared to continue in the harshness and austerity of full nomadism. Any temptation to acquire agricultural food or cumbersome luxuries weakens nomadic systems and reduces both their strength and their autonomy. For more than a thousand years, the Chinese tried to beguile and weaken the nomads on their borders in this way by gradually accustoming them to Chinese goods so that they were willing to provide the Chinese with goods of steppe origin (such as horses, leather, wool, etc.) and become weaker and less free by becoming entangled in the more affluent and sedentary Chinese way of life. Few nomadic peoples had the willpower to preserve their freedom and their nomadic way of life by rejecting such Chinese affluence.

The invention of the stirrup, like the later invention of the horseshoe, was revolutionary because both of these greatly increased the military strength of the steppe nomads and offered them the military possibility of replacing commerce or raiding as means for obtaining civilized goods by all-out conquest of civilized areas. Stirrups greatly increased the military effectiveness of mounted fighters, by providing increased stability and freedom to use both hands on weapons, either the reflex bow or the cavalry lance. The almost simultaneous invention of the firm saddle and of horseshoes greatly magnified this improvement in weaponry. While we have no exact chronological information on the advent of these three innovations, all of them were acquired by the steppe warriors during the Han period (221 B.C.-A.D. 220).

As the military threat of the steppe peoples increased, during the Han period and later, from these innovations, the direct impact of these innovations within China was reduced by a number of con-

484

ditions such as the presence of innumerable water barriers, scarcity of fodder, and the general Chinese reluctance to use either soil resources or peasant manpower for pastoral activities, especially for a military purpose. As a result, China itself, while fully recognizing the use of cavalry in warfare, was never ready to make it a chief weapon nor to sacrifice infantry to obtain it and, thus, had a constant temptation to obtain cavalry by some special arrangements with barbarian horsemen. In this they were like the Romans and very unlike the medieval rulers of western Europe. But in consequence, like the Romans, they ran the danger, after A.D. 100, of introducing barbarian cavalry auxiliaries for military purposes and subsequently discovering that they were unable to make these peoples leave the territory when they wished to be rid of them. This happened in a major way following the end of the Han dynasty in the third century A.D. (the period of the three kingdoms).

If the advent of the stirrup increased barbarian pressure on China, the situation was more than balanced by Chinese improvements in harnessing. In China, as in western Asia and in Europe, harnessing of draft horses was originally very inefficient because the harness was attached to the horse's throat, hampering its breathing whenever it attempted to pull a load of more than 200 pounds (or even less). The final solution to this problem was the invention of the horse collar: this allowed the horse to pull with his shoulders by leaning his weight on a rigid collar so that, in effect, he was moving the vehicle by leaning his weight against the vehicle's resistance (through the collar). A solution to this problem, intermediary between the very ineffective throat harness and the fully effective horse collar, was the relatively efficient breast strap harness which was invented in China before 400 B.C. It, in turn, began to yield to the horse collar in China about A.D. 500, at a time when Europe was still using the throat harness. In Europe, the breast strap, accordingly, was used only briefly and in scattered localities before it was replaced by the horse collar after the European Dark Ages (after A.D. 900).

All of these innovations, as we shall see, had

485

revolutionary consequences in the west, especially
in western Europe, but had relatively moderate influence on China. The chief reasons for this difference were that China had inadequate fodder and
a relatively resilient social system (after about
100 B.C.), while Europe (north of the Alps) had adequate fodder and a very chaotic social system. In
China the chief consequence of these technological
changes was an improvement in horse-drawn transportation which greatly improved military logistics and
thus, by increasing the power of the military offensive, was able to strengthen ability to maintain the
political unity of the Chinese culture area, but
lack of fodder for horses put considerable limits
on this consequence, since it compelled use of other
methods of transportation such as the use of inland
waterways or the use of pack animals, especially
donkeys (which were acquired from the steppe peoples
in this same crucial period of the Han dynasty).
In the same period came the wheelbarrow, probably
adapted from the pack animal and used successfully
in military logistics by Chuko Liang in the third
century A.D., a thousand years before the wheelbarrow reached western Europe.

The overthrow of the Ch'in dynasty was a rejection both of its despotic violence and of its
amorality. This uprising began, as most such movements do, within the system itself, when the death
of Shih Huang-ti precipitated a struggle to control
the succession between the chief minister, Li Ssu,
and the palace chamberlain, the eunuch Chaokao. The
eunuch won this conflict and had Li Ssu executed,
but their struggle opened a civil war which showed
that the Ch'in personal despotism of brutality and
force was not acceptable to the real power elements
in Chinese society. After a civil war (206-202 B.C.)
with large destruction of life and property, a peasant general, Liu Chi, was victorious over his noble
rival and became ruler, the first emperor in the Han
dynasty. The victor made few changes in the Ch'in
system at first, but gradually he began to move toward arrangements which were almost antithetical to
those of Ch'in. This new system, which became the
basis of the new Chinese civilization of A.D. 300-
1950, centered on a bureaucratic structure of scribes,
known in the west as the mandarinate, which combined

an oligarchical control of governmental administration
with an autonomous economic base in local landholdings
and an ideological justification in Confucianism. The
mandarinate, sustained on this tripod of bureaucratic
access to government office, local landlordism, and
Confucian ideology, became the backbone of Chinese
society, the intermediate level in a triple-layered
society in which the upper layer of dynastic kingship
and the lower layer of peasant villages were periodically shattered by violent disturbances (often in interactions with each other), but the intermediate social
structure centered on the scholar-gentry or mandarinate persisted relatively intact (or at least sufficiently intact to reconstitute itself and its position) through the disturbances and vicissitudes of
both dynastic history above and agrarian history below.

From this point of view the history of the former Han dynasty constituted a "thermidorean reaction"
to the "reign of terror" of Shih Huang-ti by linking
back to the developmental process of Sinic history
which had been interrupted in shifting from an evolutionary to a revolutionary historical process in
the fifth century B.C.

That older evolutionary process from the 9th
to the 5th century had been one in which government
was slowly shifting from a basis of nobility, family,
and ritual to a basis of acquired literary expertise,
individualism, and aristocratic ethical conventions.
In the fifth century, this evolutionary process had
been interrupted by the divergence toward a quite
different kind of development resting upon weapons
control and Realpolitik.

This new direction, as in all revolutionary
processes, was marked by an accelerating movement
toward greater violence from fewer hands leading to
greater centralization of governmental decision-making. Such an accelerating spiral of revolutionary
activism brought the governing of the whole Chinese
cultural area into the hands of one man, Shih Huang-
ti, just as the same process on a smaller scale concentrated the power of the French Revolution in the
hands of Robespierre within the Committee of Public
Safety which was acting on behalf of the Convention
in the name of the French people. But, just as in

France in 1794, there was, outside of Robespierre's exercise of power, the whole of French culture and the French people, so in 210 B.C. there was, outside of Shih Huang-ti's exercise of power, the whole of Chinese culture and the Chinese people. In both cases, the thermidorean reaction restored authority to a wider group, closer to the real distribution of power in the culture area concerned. And in both cases, this reaction went back to an earlier period, in an effort to restore a linkage between the contemporary, post-revolutionary developments and the evolutionary processes which had been interrupted when the revolution began. In China this meant an effort by the Han dynasty to go back to the bureaucratic, merit-based, aristocratic and ethical outlook of the scribes.

Such an effort to return to an interrupted evolutionary process is, of course, never completely successful, since the intervening revolutionary era can never be wiped from the scene or from human memory. Especially will this be true when the revolutionary period, as in China, has continued for several centuries. The result is a double one: on one hand, the restoration becomes a kind of synthesis, or at least a compromise, of the two periods (the more remote evolutionary one and the more recent revolutionary one) and, on the other hand, people pretend that the restoration has been more successful than it is in fact, by talking and thinking about the more remote model while they continue, in fact, to act in ways which are closer to the more recent model.

Thus the Han monarch restored some feudal states, but gave them to the members of his own family and, after a futile feudal revolt in 154 B.C., appointed a personal agent in each and, in 127 B.C., replaced primogeniture inheritance by equal division among sons of feudal lords. Under Emperor Wu-ti (140-87 B.C.) the whole empire consisted of 19 feudal kingdoms and 89 provinces (chun, usually translated "commanderies," although they were under civil, not military, governors).

Han also abolished the Draconian law code of Ch'in, establishing capital punishment for murder only and other punishments for robbery and wounding, but ending many other provisions, including joint responsibility and punishment of a criminal's relatives and associates and the use of bodily mutilation as punishment. Eventually a new more rational criminal code was adopted by Han and became, through judicial interpretation, the basis of criminal justice in China down to recent times.

The Ch'in vendetta against ideas and particularly against the Confucians was ended under Han. Literary freedom was reestablished and the proscribed books were restored. A bureaucratic system open to merit was established and fell, very quickly, under Confucian domination. At first, recruitment was based on local recommendations, but in the last century of the former Han, a system of examinations was established. Since these examinations were based on Confucian ideas of literary value and ethical priority and were under Confucian control, with the preparatory teaching largely dominated by Confucians, the whole process, with the bureaucracy resulting from it, soon came under Confucian control.

Han retained and extended over China the Ch'in system of private ownership and sale of land. This, of course, permitted mortgaging of land and purchase of peasant holdings by the landlord group. This gave rise to a persistent tendency toward large estates in China's subsequent history despite frequent efforts to restrain this tendency by restrictions on acquisition of land and efforts to make minimal amounts of land inalienable in peasant hands. The ineffective character of these restraints arose from the fact that the mandarin gentry who were supposed to administer these laws locally were also the most avid monopolizers of lands in each local area. Although they sometimes lost their holdings in the periodic local agrarian uprisings, they were able to retain their administrative offices because China could not be governed without their help, and, from these posts, they were usually able to rebuild their landholdings in the following generation. Similarly mandarin gentry families who were wiped from the central bureaucracy in the course of periodic dynastic upheavals were usually able to restore the family's position from their provincial base in local

489

land ownership and local administrative office. In
fact, this combination of land ownership, office
holding (both central and local), access to literacy
and to the examination system combined with a peren-
nial ideology and strong family feeling, allowed
many mandarin families to retain their privileged
positions (at least in their local provinces) for
a millennium or more and, in some cases, for almost
two thousand years (c. 50 B.C.-A.D. 1950).

The power of the emperor, absolute in theory,
was severely limited in fact. The emperor himself
generally accepted the Confucian ethical restrictions on his actions and sometimes criticized himself for his failure to fulfill these standards. His
dependence on his administrators was so great that he
had great difficulty carrying out any projects (especially in the provinces) of which local bureaucrats
did not approve. He was also subject to great restrictions in his influence over law and justice.
Only the criminal law was subject to governmental
processes and this was under the restraints just
mentioned: general reluctance to change in fact
what already existed, and local control of judicial
processes. In civil disputes the rules were largely
local custom, and the processes were closer to village arbitration than to any generalized system of
judicial decision.

Above all, the emperor's authority was restrained
by the administrative structure of the central government and its relationship with local administration.
Peasants were subject to heavy taxes, often in kind,
and to compulsory labor service (corvee) to the community. The payments in kind and the corvee were used
locally in major part, so the resources of the central
government were usually limited. The same was true of
military service, the third great burden on the peasants. There were two general kinds of armed forces,
the imperial palace guards and the local militia,
both recruited from the peasants by the same process.
But neither of these provided a standing army. In
wartime such an army had to be recruited, during the
war, from the local militia. As a consequence of this,
the emperor had no ministry of war and no permanently
assigned general (beyond the commanders of his palace
guards). In theory, in wartime, he was expected to

act as minister of war himself, appoint generals for the war, and raise men and supplies through local administrative actions, supplemented by the palace supply system. In general, the central government and its ministers were mostly concerned with operations of the palace and the court as an imperial household and with matters of ritual, state sacrifices, and ceremonials.

The system of local government was only remotely under imperial control. Each province and district was under the control of a centrally appointed official who was not a native of the area, but he had to operate entirely through unpaid subordinates from the local gentry in the local bureaucratic structure. As a result, the appointed governor was greatly hampered in doing anything which was not acceptable to the local mandarin establishment and the emperor's powers on the local level were very restricted in fact, however extensive they may have been in theory. As Wolfram Eberhart says, "Chinese emperors--excepting a few individual cases--at least in the first ten centuries of gentry society were not despots." In theory they were absolute, and in fact, under very energetic emperors and under very special conditions, they could exercise very extensive powers, but the nexus of ideological, administrative, social, and technological conditions was such as to restrain and restrict imperial powers.

Not least in this combination of factors which restricted powers on the dynastic level and built up powers on the intermediate, sociological level of the Chinese system was the ideology of the scholar-gentry, "Confucianism." Like all ideologies this one has changed from time to time and from place to place, but it has its established tenets and above all has had a basic outlook and value system.

It would be a mistake to regard Confucianism as the only or even as the dominant, factor in Chinese intellectual life. Like all great civilizations, China has been the locus of competing value systems. In fact, as Wertheimer has shown, all successful communities have several fundamentally inconsistent value systems, a fact which permits a more complete and more rounded development of human potentialities

491

and provides a total culture more able to cope with a variety of external and internal challenges.

In China these competing value systems or "ideologies" were born in the accelerating change and increasing organizational chaos from about 600 B.C. to the unification. The intellectual controversy of this period can be compared, in variety and intensity, with that of the Greeks in the same four centuries. The content of these two intellectual experiences was quite different, especially in their ultimate outcomes, but they were also quite different in their earliest emphases since the Greeks put greater stress on natural science and on metaphysical questions, while the Chinese were more concerned with ethical and social questions.

Over these four centuries, Chinese intellectual controversies tended to aggregate into five or six "schools" or general outlooks. Each "school" was later attributed to the teachings of a "sage" who gathered about him a group of disciples, often under the patronage of some feudal lord or ruler. The five leading schools of this kind are known as Tao Chia (the Taoists), Mo Chia (the Mohists), Ju Chia (the Confucianists), and Fa Chia (the Legalists), with the fifth, Ming Chia (the Logicians) in a somewhat different position. There were, of course, variations of each of these five, and the contemporary accounts of their disputes speak, quite accurately, of "the hundred schools."

We have no need to go into these disputes or to make any lengthy explanations of the meaning of any one of them, except in a general way. Much more important for our purposes are the basic assumptions of all of them and the relationships among them.

All of these schools arose from the intellectual questions raised by the disruption of a relatively organic and static society and its disruptive and accelerating movement toward a more chaotic and atomistic situation. The reactions to this experience, like the reactions to a somewhat similar experience of social dissolution and growing anomie in our own time, might be divided into three types: (a) those who wish to return to their (often idealized) version of the "world they had lost" in the past; (b) those who wish to impose on the existing anomie some external and mechanical arrangement of "law and order" by force; and (c) those who wish to opt out of the chaos, without much attention to either the past or the future, to adopt some kind of existential life in emotionally satisfying, if temporary, relationships with other humans and with nature.

Among the Chinese we might place type (a) reaction, among the Confucians and Mohists, near the center of the ideological spectrum, with (b) the Legalists, on the ideological Right, and (c) the Taoists, on the ideological Left. The fifth school of thinkers, the Logicians, were not only the least significant of the five but they became less significant. In sharp contrast with the situation among the Greeks, where rationalism was always a very significant, even dominant, tendency and where the extreme rationalists (the "exaggerated philosophic realists," such as the Pythagoreans, Platonists, and neo-Platonists), were generally allied with the political Right, in China rationalism was never a significant intellectual tendency, the Logicians were of decreasing importance, and they were distributed widely across the political spectrum from Right to Left.

The reason for the weakness of rationalism as an ideology in China and for the dwindling importance of the Logicians, and even of logic, on the Chinese scene is of vital importance in Chinese intellectual history since it spared China from the extravagances of exaggerated realism, otherworldliness, and ideological fanaticism and, instead, firmly grounded most Chinese schools of thought in this world, using common sense and empirical observation, to work out compromise solutions of conflicting points of view.

Closely related to these common and widespread assumptions of Chinese thinkers were a number of derivative assumptions: (a) that human personality is largely the consequence of training and upbringing and not of inherited traits; (b) that, accordingly, education (informal as well as formal) is of dominant significance and that being "Chinese" is

493

not racial, but a cultural condition to which any people may aspire and, thus (c) social, including ideological, factors are more significant than either force or politics in determining the quality of human life. Because of the weakness of rationalism and logic in Chinese ideological controversy, two things which the Greeks found it almost impossible to handle (motion or change, and the role of human feelings in social life) were taken as given by the Chinese.

These fundamental tendencies in the Chinese outlook were reflected in their basic reactions to the social dynamism of the period 600-200 B.C. In China, as among the Greeks, the central feature of this dynamism was a process by which a relatively organic society of clans and villages based on custom and traditions was disrupted and moved with increasing speed toward a social chaos of atomistic individuals. This process gave rise to numerous controversies of which the chief centered around the nature of human nature and the nature of human communities. All the chief schools of Chinese thought (with a few minor exceptions among the Taoists) agreed that man was by nature potential and could, by training, be bent in any direction. But beyond this was a distinction as to whether this inherited general potentiality of man included a tendency toward goodness or a tendency toward evil. In general, in China the belief that man had an innate tendency toward evil was held on the Right, among the Legalists. This was why they insisted that atomistic individuals must be made to behave in socially acceptable ways by rigid organizational structures, explicit rules, all necessary force, and severe punishments. On the other hand, the belief that men have an inborn tendency to be good was found on the Left in Chinese thought, among the Taoists and (most explicitly) among the left wing of the Confucianists. In general, Confucianist thought, beginning with Confucius himself, saw men as neutrally potential without any innate tendency toward either evil or good, but later members of his school, like the more rationalist Hsun-tzu on the right wing and the more intuitive Mencius on the left wing, regarded human nature as having tendencies toward evil or toward goodness.

These somewhat divergent ideas on human nature among Chinese thinkers interacted with much more significant differences of opinion on the nature of the community. Here there was a variety of opinion across the political spectrum from the Taoists on the Left who saw community as a perfectly natural thing to the Legalists on the Right who assumed that the only social reality was the atomized individual.

The Taoists saw man, society, nature, and the universe as a single, complex, natural entity in which all parts reacted upon all other parts by innumerable and subtle interconnections to create a single, dynamic Oneness beyond the ability of human reason to understand or of the human senses to observe. It could be dealt with only by intuition and ritual in terms of the innate goodness of each individual's feelings (which were "good" just because each was a part of the larger whole). Thus the Taoists were well prepared to be philosophical anarchists who reject all organizational structures and rules of human devising including governments, rulers, and property rights.

At the other extreme from this relatively primitive point of view were the Legalists who looked about them and saw a world of competing atomistic individualists whose selfishness and egocentric emotional impulses seemed a flat contradiction to the Taoist ideas of good, holistic, intuitions. The Legalists accepted the Chinese view that men are capable of being trained but they also insisted that they were evil and selfish, motivated by little more than a desire to enjoy pleasures and avoid pain. Such men were capable of forming a community because they were teachable but there was nothing natural about such a community. It had to be imposed on men by setting up a system of detailed rules to govern almost all human behavior and by insisting on obedience to these rules with a maximum of force and the severest possible punishments. Those who resist would be liquidated; the rest in time would conform to the rules, become largely incapable of conceiving any alternative to these rules, and the community would then continue to function along lines of habits conforming to the rules with relatively little need to use the avail-

495

able force to inflict the necessary punishments. The essential first step toward obtaining such a system was to maximize the powers of the state in the hands of a despot who could then draw up the system of rules applicable to everyone except himself.

The Confucianists' position was on the broad middle ground between the Taoists and the Legalists. To them the community was natural and essential if men were to be men rather than animals. But the forms which the community may take are relatively free because of the educability of individual men. The Confucianists however saw education as something much more than either formal schooling or threats of force from a remote government. To them education was the total experience of any growing person. Such experience takes place in a social context which is both very complex and constantly molding. Thus the chief forces in the community must be social and not political or military. They must be found in the context of the family, the clan, the village, the country, and voluntary associations. In all of these will be found persons who are more experienced, more mature, better informed, more mannerly, and more altruistic. In general, these more developed personalities will be the natural leaders in each group, the father, the elder brother, the village elders, the scholars, the local officials, the ruling officials of the central government. All of these should function within the traditions of their group in the context of that group's position in Chinese society as a functioning entity. Only those who embody the traditions and ideals of their position justify the name of that position: "father," "elder brother," "master," "governor," "king," "emperor." Those who do not justify the names they bear may be replaced, not by violence or sudden overt action but simply by shift of allegiance to someone more worthy of the name. Mencius (c. 382-289 B.C.) and later Tung Chung-shu, Confucian advisor to the Emperor Wu (140-87 B.C.), were much more explicit than Confucius himself on this question of shifts of allegiance. Confucius himself was a moral conservative whose ideas reflected the outlook of an idealized feudal class such as some of the shih had sought before the period of the warring states began. He wanted a hierarchical society based on moderation, respect for conventions and traditional rites as for learning and personal character, acting on an empirical and rather relativistic basis but constantly motivated by efforts at self-improvement and respect for others. The later Confucianists were more explicit about the pressures which could be used to enforce this kind of behavior, at least in government if not in the village and family. To them a failure to fulfill the expectations of a position constituted abdication of that position, an abdication which it would be sensible to recognize by establishing a successor. In the case of an emperor or ruler, these Leftish Confucians inclined toward the Taoist belief that mismanagement at the top would soon be reflected in obvious disturbances on all other levels, both in nature and the universe above as in the village and families below. When such maladjustment becomes evident, all parts of the system will cooperate together, to rectify the balance and, in the case of the emperor, the Mandate of Heaven will pass, perhaps with a certain amount of violent disturbances, to a more worthy person.

The rejection of the personal despotism of the Ch'in dynasty was such a shift of the Mandate of Heaven. At the same time, it was a shift from Legalist ideology to Confucianism, and also a shift from force, rules (fa=law) to social pressures, moral suasion, and accepted social customs (li).

The significance of this Han counterrevolution cannot be overemphasized. It changed China to a totally different kind of society, rooted in Sinic civilization but quite different, and created, in this new Chinese civilization after A.D. 300, a society which was so different from our western civilization as to be almost incomprehensible to us. Where our western civilization grew, in time, to conceive of government in terms of power based on force, wealth, and ideology, China came to see government as a relatively less significant crowning dynastic embellishment over a community which operated in terms of social context, administrative procedures, and ethical values. In such a system, unlike the west, weapons and weapons systems were relatively insignificant, fully capable, perhaps, of changing dynastic arrangements at the top, or of rearranging agrarian arrangements at the bottom but not capable of making any significant permanent changes in the middle levels whose social-administrative-ethical arrangements were almost self-rectifying. In this way Chinese civilization found a kind of stability which reduced weapons and weapons systems to a relatively minor role. In this, despite a very different superficial appearance it was (as a three-layered system) much closer to the later (two-layered) Islamic civilization than to our western civilization.

These successive Chinese civilizations, based on intensive agriculture and water controls, spread outward in all directions, especially southward toward, and then across, the Yangtze River. As it spread southward, its advance was assisted by the gradual acquisition of rice to replace millet and other grains in the agricultural system. Accordingly, this southward advance continued a long time and, in a sense, is still going on, being blocked only by high mountains and forests as in the southwest. The movement of this Chinese system northward was less easy, as it soon encountered hardwood forests in the northeast (toward Manchuria) and increasingly arid grasslands in the northwest, toward Mongolia.

In the latter direction there was no substantial opposition from other human societies until about 400 B.C., when the Hunnish peoples of the steppes, hard-pressed by the Chinese coming from the south and by the Indo-Europeans to the west, adopted a new weapons system and a new economic basis to support it. The new weapons system was the combination of the composite bow with mounted cavalry, while the new economy was nomadic pastoralism. Neither of these was a Hunnish or Mongol innovation, but each arose from an adaptation of techniques previously available on the northern grasslands, integrated together with numerous detailed innovations which culminated, after centuries of development, in the terrifying military striking power of Jenghis Khan (1206-1227).

We have no clear or agreed picture of the details of this development and much of the chronology is still very disputed, but the main outlines are clear enough.

498

In the early part of the first millennium B.C., the demographic and cultural situation on the northern grasslands was very fluid. In the simplest terms there were, from west to east, three kinds of peoples from the linguistic point of view and two from the physical point of view. Linguistically there were Indo-European speakers, who could, perhaps, be called Celts in the widest sense, from central Europe to the Altai Mountains just west of Gobi. East of these were Ural-Altaic speakers to the Manchurian forests and beyond, with Turkish-speaking groups in eastern Turkestan and most of Mongolia and Mongolian speakers in eastern Mongolia and western Manchuria.

In racial terms the physical types of men did not run coterminous with the language divisions, since the Turkic speakers were probably what we would consider white race, while their fellow Ural-Altaic speakers to the east, the Mongols, were of the yellow race. In general, both racial and linguistic groupings were very mixed, especially in what we now consider to be Chinese Turkestan and Mongolia, with both groupings extending much less far to the west than has been true in more recent times. Thus the Huns, speaking Turkic, were where we expect Mongols today and were of white race, while most of the central Asian steppes west of the Huns were occupied by peoples more akin to the Celts than to any of the peoples found in the area in modern times. These Indo-European peoples of the steppes are known to us by a large number of names such as Celts, Cimmerians, Scythians, Sarmatians, Sakas, Tocharians, and the Yueh-Chi of northwest Mongolia. Other peoples, such as the Teutons (Germans and Scandinavians) or Slavs, are later derivatives from the Celts. As we have seen, the earlier historical role of these peoples on the steppes rested on their superior weaponry (the composite bow) and superior mobility (the horse), but these might not have had a major impact on the civilized areas of the Old World had it not been for two other factors, one organizational (clientage) and the other climatic (the alternation of humid and less humid periods in climate history, especially on the more eastern grasslands).

Innovation in both mobility and weaponry was

almost continuous in the grasslands from almost 5000
B.C. until after A.D. 1000, but this is largely concealed from us by the fact that these peoples broke
into the attention of civilized peoples only episodically, as a result of the interactions of population
increase and climate changes. These innovations,
both in mobility and in weapons, seem to have resulted
from the actions of two successive language groups,
the earlier discoveries by Indo-European speakers on
the more western steppes, and the later ones by Al-
taic-speaking peoples on the more eastern grasslands.
The dividing line between the two is just about the
time of Christ, except that the invention of the composite bow was so early and so far north (on the
edge of the forests) that it is probably an Altaic
invention.

We have already mentioned many of the steps in
the increases in equine mobility in the earlier period and have seen that the horse could serve as a
draft animal from 2000 B.C. but could not be used
as a riding animal until just after 1000 B.C. In
the period around 1000-800 B.C., in which the Scythians were driving the Cimmerians off the Pontic
steppes, bareback riding of mares in non-combat activities was replaced by cavalry archers and spearmen. This was achieved by a series of innovations:
experimental gelding of stallions at various ages;
supplementary feeding with grain to increase size;
postponement of the first riding of animals for the
same reason; introduction of the metal bit, the
first known as "3-hole" about 800, and an improved
form known as "2-hole" several centuries later; the
saddle, at first soft, but gradually increasingly
firm, thus giving the rider more stability; the
gradual development, by selective breeding, of a
larger, more "thoroughbred" horse; and finally,
possibly as late as 400 B.C., the introduction of
full pastoral nomadism, which may have been an Indo-
European innovation but spread so rapidly to the Altaic peoples of the eastern steppes that it was
presenting a great danger to the Chinese as early
as the fourth century B.C.

The later improvements in riding equipment,
the stirrups and horseshoes, are clearly Asiatic
in origin, probably Altaic, although there are some

reasons for believing that the former may be Hindu, and both could even be Chinese. The date is just as disputed as the place. Most authorities would uphold a late introduction into Europe, after the "fall of Rome," probably by the Avars in the sixth century. Since the Avars seem to have crossed most of Eurasia, from north of China, in about a century, stirrups are often regarded as an Avar invention of the fifth century after Christ. It is still possible that they may be an eastern steppe invention from before the time of Christ, as we have two reports of stirrups in graves of grassland origin, one reported as found by N. Veselovski in a Siraci grave in the Kuban, east of the Black Sea (1902); the other found by J.H. Rivett-Carnac in a similar steppe warrior grave in the Nagpur district of central India (1879). Both of these are dated about 100 B.C., the approximate date of an apparent stirrup of rope reported by Sir John Marshall as carved on the Second Stupa at Sanchi, India. The dates of the two graves, however, are not firm, and it has even been denied that the Kuban example was ever found, so the question still lies uncertain.

This uncertainty is taken very seriously by those who believe this question is of major importance because they are certain that mounted spearmen cannot use shock tactics without stirrups. The fact, however, remains that mounted spearmen did charge each other, and at full shock, for many centuries before men had stirrups, and in some cases did so in full armor with a heavy pike. They also slashed at each other with sabers from horseback, something which seems impossible to modern cavalrymen who have, apparently, been spoiled by such modern conveniences as stirrups. Paul Vigneron, who has made a thorough study of the role of the horse in classical antiquity, says (1968), "An enormous error has been made. It has been stated that real horse-lancers were unknown in antiquity, that riders practically never made rupture charges, that is to say shock combat. . . ." He attributes this error to Charles Ardant du Picq, famous military theorist, in 1868, and flatly contradicts it, giving many examples of cavalry lancers, on coins, in tomb paintings (one of 300 B.C.), and in texts from Herodotus, Thucydides, Xenophon, Livy, Plutarch, and others, but admits that after the establishment of the solid mass of heavy infantry, cavalry refrained from charging such a formation, while still prepared to charge dispersed infantry or other cavalry. With heavy infantry, ancient cavalry used harassing tactics, hurling javelins or other missiles from short range. Vigneron says that shock tactics were frequently used by cavalry spearmen in single combat as a way to become celebrated, but ceased at the end of the second century B.C. I should like to point out, however, that the custom continued through the classical period, as Procopius tells us of a certain Andreas of Byzantium, who in 530 engaged in single combat before the Persian army by galloping at his opponent in full shock: "The two rushed madly upon each other with their spears, and the weapons, driven against their corselets, were turned aside with great force; the horses, striking their heads together, fell and threw off the riders. The two men, falling close to each other, hurried to rise to their feet. . . . Andreas hit him as he was rising on his knee and, as he fell to the ground, killed him."

Thus the use of mounted spearmen in shock tactics continued against other mounted spearmen and dispersed infantry from about 800 B.C., but could not be used against massed infantry spearmen when these were encountered, as they often were, when cavalry lancers invaded civilized areas. The confusion on this subject has arisen from the belief that the mounted armored spearman was an invention of the early European Middle Ages, when the fact is that he existed from the earliest days of cavalry, but became a dominant weapon only in places and periods where massed infantry spearmen were lacking, as was true of the European Middle Ages (850-1350). As soon as such infantry reappeared, as it did in the fourteenth century in Europe, the cavalry lancer was reduced once again to a harassing role, except against dispersed infantry or other lancers.

This sequence, of course, was much more important in Europe, because of its shock tradition. In Asia, the missile tradition, especially on the grasslands, where infantry of any kind would have been an anomaly for most of history, provided a

quite different sequence. However, even in Asia,
or in the southern grasslands when they joined in
with the historical development of cavalry warfare,
infantry archers were generally superior to cavalry
archers in a fixed battle, since infantry was less
likely to run out of arrows, could often shoot back
arrows which had come at them, could take more careful aim or engage in coordinated firing, and often
could use longer and thus more powerful bows with
greater range. But, of course, there was no need
for cavalry to engage in a fixed battle with infantry archers (or with infantry spearmen, for that
matter), because the greater mobility of cavalry
could be used in harassing tactics to cut any infantry force off from supplies and thus force it to
move from its fixed battle position.

The ability of disciplined infantry to stand
up to cavalry is well shown in another example from
Procopius, in A.D. 531, when Belisarius, defeated
by the Persians, saved the remnants by dismounting
his cavalry, placing them behind shields with their
backs to the river, and fought off the enemy until
night fell. Procopius says, "The two sides were not
evenly matched in strength, for foot soldiers, and
very few of them were fighting against the whole Persian cavalry. Nevertheless, the enemy were not able
either to rout them or in any way to overpower them.
For standing shoulder to shoulder, they kept themselves constantly massed in a small space, and they
formed with their shields a rigid, unyielding barricade, so that they shot at the Persians more conveniently than they were shot at by them." This
was not a unique case, but an illustration of a
general condition, which the Crusaders had to discover much later in their battles against the Saracens. It is still largely unrecognized by historians,
who share the aristocratic prejudices of most cavalrymen that there is a kind of intrinsic superiority
of cavalry over infantry, a totally mistaken idea so
long as infantry stand solidly together.

Mobility on the northern grasslands would have
yielded few military benefits without the parallel
development of missile weapons, culminating in the
Turkish bow as it existed in the eighteenth century
of our era. Such a bow, essentially a cavalry weap-

503

on, the final product of almost 6000 years of accumulated craftsmanship in 1800, was about 40 inches long and shot arrows less than 26 inches long more than 350 yards, with killing range of over 200 yards. Unstrung, it lies coiled like a rattlesnake, in a circle with a layer of horn on the outside and a layer of sinew on the inside. To string the bow this circle must be reversed, so that a strung composite bow has the layer of horn on the belly or inside face nearest the string, with the sinew on the back side farther from the archer. Stringing such a bow requires a practiced coordination of torso and leg muscles (since it is strung by bending over and placing the left foot in a position which ends up between the bow and the string) that only an expert can string it without it twisting over and perhaps shattering.

The great power of the Turkish bow in such a short length comes entirely from the horn and sinew and not from the strip of wood to which these are attached, since this serves only as a framework. The horn resists compression and the sinew resists extension, so that drawing such a bow pulls the sinew around a resisting core of horn. Since the pull of a Turkish bow was about 120 pounds, about twice that of the English longbow, it required a special "draw" and required trained arm and shoulder muscles to keep such a drawn bow steadily on target. Modern sporting and hunting bows of metal or glass are not superior to a Turkish bow in either range or accuracy and generally have a pull of 40 to 70 pounds.

A powerful composite bow requires a special method for holding the bowstring while drawing so that it will not slip from the fingers under the strain and can still be released smoothly. The so-called "primary draw," with which we are all familiar, simply pulls the arrow back with the thumb and index finger of the right hand, as far as the right ear, but this would not be possible with a very strong bow. The so-called "Mediterranean draw," used by all of classical antiquity and now widely used, has the index, middle, and ring fingers over the string, with the arrow held by the index and middle fingers, with no use of the thumb. The Mon-

golian draw, used by most of Asia and now by the Moslems of Africa, uses the right thumb to grasp the
string from the left and locks the index finger over
the thumb to the right of the string, while holding
the nock of the arrow between the thumb and the upper joint of the index finger. Both the Mediterranean
and Mongolian draws require protective devices to
hold the string, the former using a tab of ivory,
bone, or horn on the finger tips, while the latter
uses a thumb ring of ivory with a lip off which the
string is allowed to slip when shooting.

It is worth noting that the European and Asiatic
traditions about archery were always very distinctive,
not only in such techniques as different draws and
the fact that the west shot the arrow to the left
side of the bow, while the Asiatics shot their arrows to the right side, but also from the different
tradition that I have mentioned as European shock
and Asiatic missile. Even when the two had the same
or similar bows, they used them differently. These
differences can be examined in terms of a number of
distinctions, such as between hunting and fighting,
between infantry and cavalry, and between the emphasis placed on the three stages of a battle.

In general, even when Europeans had good composite bows, as Odysseus did or as Charlemagne did,
they tended to use them only for hunting and not in
war. Thus the composite bow tends to fall out of
use, as occurred in the period after Odysseus and
also after Charlemagne. The reason is partly because any composite bow requires so much time and
care that a society will cease to make it when it
falls into economic depression and can no longer
devote such economic resources to an artifact which
is not essential. According to Wallace E. McLeod,
a composite bow took from five to ten years to make,
and, while the meaning of this is not clear, it is
evident that making such a bow was a drain on limited economic resources, especially in any society
where these are diminishing, as is true in a dark age.

In a society where the bow is used in hunting
but not in war, the composite bow is an unnecessary
luxury, since most hunting is done, at least in
wooded areas such as Europe, on foot and not from

505

horseback. A hunter on foot can get as much power as he needs by increasing the length of the bow, but a horseman cannot do this because any bow more than about 50 inches long is too difficult to draw fully by a rider. The length of a hunting bow thus is limited by the length of the arms of the archer, not by his seated position as with a rider's bow. Of course, as a bow gets longer, its arrows also get longer and thus become heavier with a loss of range. In wooded Europe this does not matter so much, since hunters are not likely to see game at any great distance through the cover. But to the grassland archers in the east, range is of supreme importance either in hunting or in war. To increase the range on the grasslands, pastoral peoples made a number of ingenious innovations. They shortened the arrows, even to a length less than the draw of the bow. Sir Ralph Payne-Gallwey found that Turkish arrows 28.5 inches long, weighing 3/4 ounce, averaged 275 yards, while the same arrows cut to 25.5 inches and weighing 1/2 ounce each averaged 360 yards.

To use such short arrows, the Turks used a horn groove several inches long attached to the left thumb, which allowed the arrowhead to be pulled back three inches inside the string, with the arrow guided past the string along the groove. Another late innovation, probably Turkish, was the use of parchment, instead of feathers, to fledge an arrow; this added at least 30 yards to the range. A third innovation was an improved nock which never broke under pressure, as a European nock would in a Turkish bow. There were other improvements, much earlier than the Turks or even the Huns, which we must mention.

Sometime before 500 B.C., the nomads of the eastern grasslands improved the composite bow by adding bone rods or plates to the existing composite bow of sinew and horn. These were added to stiffen the ends of the bow (the "limbs" or "ears") or were added as plates on the grip. Professor Paul E. Klopsteg has shown that such additions store more energy and make it easier to hold (1947). They give the limbs a more whip-like action and deliver power to the arrow more evenly through the full span of the draw. Today, we call the composite bow with bone "ears" a Yrzi bow, while the bow which also has bone plates on the grip is called Qum Darya (the Hunnish bow). But there are many variations of each, depending on how many bone rods and what kinds have been added to the ears or how many sides of the grip have bone laths. These additions may be very old, as the Chinese inscriptions about 1300 B.C. seem to use the symbol for bone, rather than horn, in reference to their composite bow. Certainly, the Chinese knew both types before 200 B.C. The ultimate in such additions to a composite bow may be the Avar bow of about A.D. 560, which had ears bent sharply forward and stiffened with four bone rods each and a grip reinforced with bone plates on three sides.

These improvements in weapons on the steppes not only allowed a sequence of pastoral peoples to push westward along the steppes, but also allowed them to raid into, or even defeat, the more civilized peoples to the south, in China, Rome, Persia, and Byzantium. All four of these were well acquainted with the composite bow, and were quite prepared to adopt new types and even new draws as they became aware of them. Rome adopted both the Median "Great Bow," a crescent bow of considerable length and of Yrzi type, as well as the shorter Yrzi cavalry bow, both of these before A.D. 100. Byzantium adopted these from Rome and later adopted in sequence the Hunnish Qum Darya bow and the Avar bow. The neo-Persians and Byzantium both adopted the Mongolian thumb draw, although Rome, being earlier, used the Mediterranean draw. We know that the Roman military bow was of Yrzi type and was a regular part of Roman military supplies in the second century, because the distinctive bone ear pieces have been found in large numbers in Roman camps, especially in military magazines in Pannonia and in Scotland (at Bar Hill) and are not found in the archaeological remains of the native or provincial peoples. The military camp at Bar Hill was held by the Romans for only a brief period between Antonius Pius and Commodus (that is, at the outside, from A.D. 138 to 192). That the bow and archery were held in high repute at that time appears from the fact that the Emperor Commodus, according to his contemporary Herodian, took great pride in his skill as a bowman and hired Parthian experts to coach him.

The Qum Darya bow had a sunken grip and ears turned forward and became the typical bow of most of east central Asia and China. It gradually lost its sunken grip, both in China and among the Turks (fourteenth century A.D.), spreading from the former to the Huns before they invaded Europe in the fourth century and to most of eastern Europe from the Mongols and the Turks after the thirteenth century.

The Scythians and the Cimmerians seem to have had the same type of long composite bow about 1000 B.C., when the former began to drive the latter off the Pontic steppes into Europe and down into civilized west Asia. The Scythian superiority seems to have rested on their more rapid adoption of cavalry, since the Cimmerians clung to the chariot, especially those who were driven out earlier. As I have said, the Scythians either improvised or passed on from Transcaucasia many of the cultural elements which were ever after associated with steppe warriors: trousers, pointed caps, high boots, a high protein diet of meat, milk, and cheese, rather than the high carbohydrate diet and flowing clothing of the more civilized peoples, with the steppe tactics of mounted archers, moving rapidly, shooting arrows more or less at random, rarely pressing home a charge but seeking to break the opponents' formation by feigned retreats, withdrawing as soon as the enemy retaliated, and much better at cutting off supplies than at shattering an enemy force in a fixed or defended position. They were not yet fully nomadic, had no siege equipment, and had limited numbers as well as limited metals. Nevertheless, they established the patterns which were followed by many subsequent grassland empires: a nomadic peace, a ruling family over client tribes, a royal city where the rulers gradually softened in sedentary luxuries, and the gradual disruption of the system, to be replaced by a similar one.

By 500 B.C. the Indo-European peoples were arrayed in a series of pastoral or semi-pastoral tribes across Eurasia from central Europe, or even from Gaul, to the Altai Mountains. East of the Altai, as K. Jettmar has told us, were the Mongolian racial pastoralists arranged in similar groups of Ural-Altaic-speaking peoples, the Turks, Mongols, and Man-

chus. The Indo-Europeans in 500 B.C. had already
been moving westward for thousands of years. As
a result, the Celts were in occupation in Gaul,
central Europe, and Hungary, with offshoots across
north Germany, into Italy, and even in Iberia. By
500 the Cimmero-Thracians had already been replaced
on the Pontic steppes (between the Pruth River and
the Don) by Scythians, while the Kirghiz, Kazak,
and central Asian steppes (between the Don and the
Altai Mountains) were held by several different
tribes of Sarmatians. In the centuries after 500
B.C., all of these peoples increased in population
and split into more specific tribal groupings.
Among the Sarmatians these later included, roughly
from west to east, Royal Sarmatians, Siraces, Iazyges, Aorsi, Roxolani, Massagetae, and Alans, but
the order of these names is not rigid, since some
eastern tribes destroyed or absorbed their western
neighbors or drove westward themselves through several tribes. After 200 B.C., there was an increasing tendency for groups farther east, especially
Turkic-speaking peoples, to move great distances,
from the Far East into Europe through numerous tribes
of other peoples, scattering them or destroying them
in their passage. This is evident, for example, of
the Huns in A.D. 200-455, the Avars in 403-562, and,
above all, of the Mongols in 1216-1242.

As early as 400 B.C., the Royal Sarmatians
were crossing the Don and pushing the Scythians
westward. At the same time, the Siraces crossed
the Volga, and the Massagetae established their
domination over the eastern Sarmatians. Just before 200 B.C., the Iazyges crossed the Don, followed by the Roxolani after 200. By that time, the
Sarmatian drive westward was being accelerated by
the invention of a new weapons system, the cataphract, which I shall discuss in a moment. As a
result, the Iazyges, Roxolani, and Aorsi in sequence
crossed the Dnieper after 100 B.C., with the Iazyges
advancing up the Danube to Hungary after 78 B.C.,
followed by the Roxolani, who reached the Danube
about A.D. 20 and invaded Roman Dacia in 69. In
the east, meanwhile, the Huns had appeared on the
Altai about 200 B.C. With their Qum Darya bows
the Huns shattered the Sarmatians and drove the
greater part of them westward into Europe. The

Sacians were defeated in eastern Kazakhstan in 178
B.C.; the Massagetae were overcome in central Asia
about 165; the Alans were forced across the Volga
about 60 B.C.; and the Alans, Roxolani, Aorsi,
and Siraces were driven beyond the Volga and the
Don in A.D. 200-350. As a consequence of these
Hunnish victories, extending over six centuries
(200 B.C. to after A.D. 440), the Asiatic steppes
abandoned their brief experiment with shock tactics
and resumed their old missile tradition.

Thus the sequence of weapons changes on the
steppes was (1) the Cimmerian chariot; (2) the Scythian cavalry with composite bows; (3) the early
Sarmatians with Yrzi bows; (4) the later Sarmatians
(chiefly 200 B.C. to A.D. 200) with cataphracts;
and (5) the Huns with Qum Darya bows. This sequence
has already been made clear except for the cataphract,
an aberrant interruption of the long dominance of
missile weapons on the Asiatic grasslands.

The cataphract was the shock weapon <u>par excel-
lence</u>. It appeared in a brief period when metal
armor gained a lead over the development of the composite bow in the competition between missiles and
armor. We have seen that the Assyrians had armored
cavalry, both lancers and archers, from the combination of Transcaucasian metallurgy and steppe cavalry
in the ninth and eighth centuries B.C. This combination reentered the steppes in the years from about
600 to 400 B.C. The armor was gradually improved
as metallurgical skills produced protection of
metal plates sewn onto leather tunics (<u>lorica sege-
mentata</u>), then later scale armor (<u>lorica squameata</u>),
to mail armor of chain links riveted together
(<u>lorica hamata</u>). Each of these types was more expensive than its predecessor but could be obtained
by an increased part of the warriors as the system
became more powerful and thus more affluent.

These developments in armor were for defense
against missiles. Even before 400 B.C., these improvements were having an influence in tactics, by
reducing the duration of the first (missile) stage
in a battle and speeding up the shift to the second
stage of hand-to-hand shock combat with swords or
spears. In 600 B.C., many steppe battles never got

510

to the shock stage, since those getting the worst of
the fight turned and fled. By the fourth century,
the Sarmatians near the lower Volga, wearing scale
armor, were shifting almost immediately to the shock
stage, shooting only a few arrows as they approached.
It had become clear that the heavier the armor and
the faster the charge, the less time there was for
the defense to get in return shots of its own over
the brief interval during which the galloping cataphract was in penetration range (at that time, not
much over one hundred yards, which could be covered
by a galloping horse in about 7 seconds). The success of such a charge was greatly increased if the
cataphracts reached their enemies in a compact mass.
Moreover, steppe archers had always known that they
could shoot more accurately and more rapidly to
their left than to their right (because they drew
the bow with the right hand). Accordingly, when
only part of the warriors could afford heavy armor,
this part attacked the enemy at full gallop in a
close mass from the left, while their poorer associates flooded the enemy with arrows from a safer
distance from the right.

One obvious defense from such an attack by armored riders was to shoot at the unprotected horses.
The offensive response to that was to armor the
horses as well, a step which was taken before 200
B.C. by some Sarmatian peoples, probably the Massagetae in Khorezmia (now Turkmenistan) southwest
of the Aral Sea.

Such an armored horse and rider was a very expensive weapon, but it was so successful that the
Sarmatian tribes which adopted it (the Roxolani,
Siraces, Massagetae, and Alans, but not the original
Royal Sarmatians nor the Iazyges) became the dominant people on the steppes for about three hundred
years and were widely copied, as far east as Korea
and China (to some extent) and as far west as Persia and Rome. About 130 B.C., this new weapon
played a significant role in the destruction of
the Greco-Bactrian kingdom, a survival from Alexander the Great, by raiders from the steppes, and
it was the chief weapon on both sides in the replacement of the Parthian dynasty of Persia by a
new Sassanian dynasty about A.D. 226, although A.D.H.

511

Bivar believes that the Sassanian success against their Aracid overlord may have rested in the fact that the victor had mail armor, while the defeated knights had the older style of scale armor (1972). But the Alan cataphracts failed in an invasion of Roman Asia Minor in A.D. 123 and of Parthia in 133 and, as we shall see, all cataphract invaders were defeated by the Romans.

Despite its limited successes against civilized states, the new weapons system looked good on the steppes and the Sarmatians became ever more deeply committed to it. Probably its great expense contributed to this commitment, for the Sarmatians had so much invested in this weapons system, that they continued to invest even more resources in what was this overly specialized method of warfare, making the spear longer and heavier until it was a pike up to 18 feet long and had to be supported on a hooked bar attached to the horse's neck. This pike (contus Sarmaticus), as well as a very long and heavy sword which the cataphracts sometimes carried, required both hands, so the rider could carry no shield, with the consequence that the armor was made heavier past the point of decreasing returns. By 50 B.C., according to Strabo, if a rider fell from his horse, he could not get up again. It is this growing difficulty in mounting that may have led to the invention of stirrups and which gives rise to the theory, held by Sulimirski and others, that stirrups may have been invented by some Sarmatian tribe, possibly the Siraci, before 100 B.C.

The worst liability of this increasingly heavy armament was that the size and strength of the horse could not keep up with it, so that the animal quickly wearied in battle and, without shoes, sometimes slipped and fell on wet or sloping ground, as Tacitus observed, after Trajan defeated the Roxolani cataphracts in Dacia in A.D. 101. It is worth noting that in more than eight battles with cataphracts from Magnesia in 190 B.C. to the late fourth century after Christ, the Romans were never defeated by them. At Carrhae in 53 B.C., where Surenes, a vassal of the Parthian king, with about 10,000 cavalry, of which about a thousand were cataphracts, destroyed seven legions (about 40,000) led by Crassus, killing

about 20,000 and capturing about 10,000, the real
damage to the Romans was done by the archers and
not by the lancers (although these latter contributed
at least their share of the killing) and was made
possible because the Parthian horse archers were
able to replenish their ammunition from baggage camels loaded with arrows. As R. Ghirshman has pointed
out, the cataphracts were almost as much of a novelty
to the Parthians as to the Romans at Carrhae, since
the royal Parthian forces at that time used only
light cavalry; the army which destroyed the Romans
at Carrhae consisted of the personal dependents of
Surenas's family, who were of Sarmatian origin, settled in Seistan by Mithridates II. Surenas himself
was killed by the Parthian king after his great victory as a threat to the monarchy, but cataphracts
were added to the Parthian weaponry, and seem to have
played a significant role in later Parthian forces.
In the same period, as a consequence of the defeat,
cavalry archers were added in significant numbers
to the Roman army.

The Romans also added some units of cataphracts
to the imperial forces. They are recorded by Josephus
in A.D. 70, are to be seen on Trajan's Column and his
arch at Adamclisi in Dobruja (both after 115), and
are recorded in Ammianus Marcellinus, in the Notitia
Dignitatum, and in Procopius (that is to say from
A.D. 70 to 554). The word cataphract is not used
in Procopius, but armored lancers were still present
in the Byzantine army at the mid-sixth century, although the horses were probably not armored in most
cases. John W. Eadie, who has made a serious investigation of the development of mailed cavalry
lancers in antiquity (1967), feels that the word
"cataphract" should be used for lancers only when
the rider is armored, and the word "clibanarius"
should be used when both horse and rider have armor,
but Ammianus Marcellinus definitely regarded the
terms as equivalent.

Cataphracts, or any cavalry lancers, are intrinsically weak and are useful only against an inexpe-
rienced enemy or in the late stages of a set battle,
after the enemy formation has been broken in the
first stage by other weapons. In the first stage of
a set battle cavalry spearmen can be defeated by

massed infantry with spears, or by adequate missile
weapons either mounted or on foot, or even by light
cavalry with moderately good missile weapons, as we
shall see.

Even before the Sarmatian cataphract had reached
its full development, the Qum Darya bow had demonstrated its ability to defeat it, especially when
used by the Huns. The Huns in 209 B.C. had formed
a fully nomadic confederacy (Hsiung-nu) in the Far
East; this soon conquered and took as client peoples
the Indo-European-speaking Yueh-chih and Wu-san. Expanding westward, the Huns shattered the Sarmatians,
including the cataphracts, taking the Alans in as a
client people, as we have seen. In fact most of the
Sarmatian threat to the west after about 100 B.C.
came from the fact that they could not withstand
their enemies to the east.

Even without the Qum Darya bow and Hunnish tactics, the Sarmatian cataphracts and clibanarii
could be defeated by light cavalry with the proper
tactics, that is by using their superior mobility
against the more limited mobility of the overburdened
cataphract horses. This method was shown to perfection in A.D. 272, when the Emperor Aurelian invaded
Mesopotamia and destroyed Queen Zenobia's clibanarii
at Emesa, ending forever the kingdom of Palmyra. The
lighter cavalry archers used their superior mobility
to repeatedly evade the charges of the heavy knights,
leading them over the desert until the latter's horses
were exhausted, at which point the light horsemen came
up to kill the armored men and horses at point-blank
range. This same tactic was used by the Hephthalite
Huns of Bactria to defeat the Sassanian cataphracts
of Persia in A.D. 484. The tactic was incorporated
into the Byzantine military Strategicon, attributed
to the Emperor Maurice but dated about A.D. 610.

In spite of its intrinsic weakness as a battle
weapon, especially when used alone, the heavily armored knight continued to be used in many areas
and survived to become the principal weapon of western Europe in the medieval period, after A.D. 900.
The elimination of this weapon from the steppes as
early as the time of Christ by Hunnish missile weapons did not in any way end the pastoral threat to

514

civilized societies; it probably made that threat
more dangerous, in the west rather than in the east,
where the Chinese began to adapt to the challenge
from the steppes in the fourth century B.C. if not
earlier. As we have seen the steppe peoples become
a threat to the west just because the Chinese were
so successful in pushing them back.

In both areas, east or west, the real challenge
to civilized states did not come from the intrusion
of new weapons or even from the vigorous energies
of barbarians, so emphasized by some nineteenth century writers, but from organizational decay and
shifts of allegiances within the civilized states.
Civilized societies, just because they are civilized,
with great capacity for capital accumulation, considerable productive capacity, and complex division
of labor, can adopt any threatening barbarian weapons, organizations, or tactics, if they are not already in decay themselves. In both east and west,
the Sinic civilization and the classical civilization were in decay when the challenge of full pastoral nomadism arose before 200 B.C. It is a mark
of the civilized structure of both that they did not
collapse for centuries and, when they did disappear
as distinctive civilizations, it was more from internal collapse than from external challenge.

We have seen that this external challenge in
the Far East was much earlier and more immediate,
because it was right on China's doorstep. It was
met by building the Great Wall, by adopting some
steppe weaponry and tactics, including other nomadic
cultural traits such as fitted clothing, and by many
organizational changes. Without siege weapons,
without permanent political forms, without adequate
infantry with "police" weapons, the nomads were not
capable of taking over China as conquerors, as was
done later by other, more advanced steppe peoples.
The first peoples on the eastern steppes to get full
pastoral nomadism, the Huns or some other Turkic
peoples, were not advanced peoples. It has been
suggested that the Huns got their Qum Darya bow from
the Chinese; as we have hinted, it is possible that
stirrups and horseshoes may be Chinese inventions.
In any case, the Chinese were as capable in this period of putting as much pressure on the nomads as

these barbarians were able to put pressures on the Chinese.

Two ways in which any civilized peoples could put pressures on pastoralists or nomads is to exploit the brittle organizational features of any structure based on clientage or any other personal loyalty and to use access to civilized luxuries to soften up nomad leaders, to tie them down to sedentary bases which will limit nomads' mobility and which can be reached and destroyed by civilized weapons if that becomes necessary, and to instigate rivalries among pastoral clientage and political succession systems.

A nomadic power system remains strong only so long as it does not divert its strength into extraneous activities. This can be assured only so long as the leaders are willing to restrain their desire for luxury goods and concentrate their wishes and resources on necessities. This almost never happens; just as the Scythians and Sarmatians tended to cluster around the Greek and later settlements along the shores of the Black Sea, seeking to exchange their goods of pastoral origin for the softening and often cumbersome luxuries of the Mediterranean, so in the east, the steppe peoples clustered around the edge of Chinese civilization to obtain the luxury goods of China. Not only did such goods soften the ways of life of individual nomads, but they set up rivalries among them, hampered their mobility and their readiness to move, introduced foreign traders and foreign customs, such as the use of money, and generally had a socially disruptive influence.

This was inevitable. The nomad power system was built up as much for the profits of the pax nomadica as for security. The commerce it sought to ensure and to tax was largely a commerce in luxury goods. Having created the system for that purpose, it would be almost impossible to eschew the profits when they came; in fact, any nomad leader who seriously attempted to do this would lose the support of his direct subordinates upon whose loyalty his own position depended. Thus the system was almost self-defeating.

516

There were also more subtle weaknesses; I
shall hint at only one. A nomad leader would have
great difficulty avoiding some feelings of inferiority in close contact with the affluence, complexity,
and style of an advanced civilized people. One way
in which he would frequently seek to assuage that
feeling and to share in the luxuries of the more advanced community would be to share in their women,
to get for himself a wife or concubine from the up-
permost ranks of the civilized society. Such a nomad leader might be able to resist the anti-nomadic
influences of such a woman in his bed, but the
children she produced would be less resistant to
such influences, and the sons of such a union might
well be candidates for the leadership of the tribe
or group as the father grew old or died.

The nomad way of life was a very complex one,
especially in a confederation or large tribal system. It involved much more than herding animals,
practicing or engaging in war, and imposing tolls
on passing merchants. It required expert knowledge
of nature, good judgment in facing complex decisions,
and great diplomatic skills in getting cooperation
from one's fellows in carrying out the decisions
which have been made. Daily life was an elaborate
cycle of movements between summer and winter pastures to find fodder for the varied needs of horses,
cattle, and sheep, alternating these apart or together in accord with the season, the water resources,
and their own interrelations, since sheep can graze
after cattle and cattle after horses, but not the
reverse.

The ability of the Chinese to put pressures
upon a bordering nomad system was related to all
these conditions; it was as much social and cultural as it was military or economic, and must be
examined a bit more.

The areas of Mongolia and Turkestan into which
the Chinese labor-intensive system was moving in the
period 600-200 B.C. was an area of grasslands, scattered woodlands (mostly on small and intermittent
streams), and widely scattered oases stretching
westward toward Turkestan and the Pamirs. It was
an area which could have been used for extensive,
mixed farming, something which was quite acceptable

517

to the Hunnish and Mongol peoples in this period, but which was not acceptable to the overly specialized Chinese economic system of hand tools, few animals, rejection of milk products, water controls, and intensive use of labor. This Chinese system could be applied to the oases but only if the Chinese had political control of the grasslands between the oases. Moreover, the Chinese, as a grain-eating people, had a great need for salt which was plentifully available on the northern steppes but was in very short supply in China itself, especially on the loess and alluvial river beds on which the Chinese system was founded.

For these reasons the Chinese pressed their political and military control of the grasslands, either pushing the steppes people further out on the steppes away from water and the more nutritious grasses or sought to force them into a subordinate, auxiliary position as salt suppliers and animal tenders for the Chinese system. Rather than accept this subordinate position, the steppe peoples abandoned crop cultivation and sedentary living and became completely sustained by their animals in a fully nomadic pastoralism. At the same time, by adopting the technique of mounted warriors armed with the composite bow, they won an offensive military power which made it possible for them to strike back at the Chinese and threaten Chinese communications on the grasslands and their control both of the oases and of the sedentary agricultural enterprise of China itself.

The Chinese response to this steppe challenge was to adopt a cavalry of mounted archers themselves (307 B.C.), but they did this to defend their sedentary agricultural base and not, as the steppe peoples were doing, as part of a new economic base of pastoral nomadism. Accordingly, the Chinese use of this new weapon could not be as effective on the grasslands as the steppe peoples' use of it was, especially as the maintaining and feeding of any large numbers of cavalry horses was a great burden on the Chinese crowded and intensively worked lands. On the other hand, the Chinese system had developed into a complex class system in which very large fractions of agricultural products (especially grain) were taken

518

from the Chinese peasants as taxes and rents to be
stored in walled towns.   Thus it had become, as we
have said, a collection of numerous compartmental-
ized agricultural enterprise units, each nucleated
around a walled town.   These towns were about one
day's travel (say twenty miles) apart and were
walled for protection as much against the Chinese
peasants as against external enemies.   But such
walled towns could not be taken by storm or by siege
by the steppe cavalry and could usually be captured
by them only through Chinese treachery (which was
not uncommon, for reasons we cannot go into).

Thus, while the military striking power of the
nomads was increasing on the grasslands, it was not
improving in Chinese agricultural areas except in
the form of destructive raiding against the rural
Chinese peasantry;   this was annoying but hardly
vital to the survival or functioning of the Chinese
system.

However, in this same period, within China an
age of conflict was raging, in which the various
states into which China had disintegrated under
Eastern Chou (since 771 B.C.) were fighting to conquer each other and restore the political unity of
the Chinese system.   This so-called "period of warring states" (480-221) ended with the triumph of
Ch'in in 230-221 B.C. and the political unification of the Chinese system.

The victory of Ch'in in the Chinese age of conflict resulted from this state's success in changing
its own socio-political system from a feudalized
decentralized system based on personal loyalties
of leaders and the personal obligations of service
in kind into a centralized militarized system.
This new system as applied by Ch'in brought victory
in the struggles with its enemies, and from this
victory was extended to the whole of China.   The
change consisted in part of freeing the Chinese peasantry from obligations to their lords for labor services and payments in kind and the lords' obligations
for feudal military services, imposing on the one the
obligation to work the lands for themselves subject
to payments of rents and taxes, while the fighting nobles were transformed into a more disciplined force

of paid professional soldiers. The efficiency of peasant labor was greatly increased so that output remained the same with a smaller labor force, the extra labor being displaced from the land and put to work by the state on large-scale projects, including waterworks, canals, and above all defensive fortifications. The chief of these latter was the construction of the Great Wall of China built in the period around 214 B.C. by linking together many older walls into a continuous fortification extending from the extreme northwest across northern China to the sea, over 1400 miles with about 25,000 fortified towers. Much of this wall was made by linking together earlier sections of walls which had been made by the "warring states" against each other and against the steppe peoples. Against the latter it was far from a complete success, as the Huns over the next six or seven centuries broke through and ravaged China when they had aggressive leaders, but these raids were no more effective than the Chinese raids against the Huns. Each power, the Chinese and the Huns, had reached the ecological limit of its technological and organizational system along their common frontier, and any success made by one was counteracted and undone by the other, either immediately or in the following generation.

The Great Wall became the boundary between these two systems, making, as Owen Lattimore has insisted, a sharp demarcation where nature had created a zone of gradual transition, and making impossible the use of that broad transitional zone for any system of dry farming or mixed farming, for which it was well suited. Only the almost total destruction of both the traditional Chinese intensive-labor system and the nomadic pastoral system of the steppe peoples at the end of the nineteenth century and in the twentieth century has made it possible to turn that transitional zone of non-ocean-flowing waters toward this third system of "mixed" farming.

While the steppe system would not function within the Great Wall and the Chinese system would not function outside the Great Wall sufficiently well to allow either system to conquer and hold the ecological area of the other, a third ecological

520

area, that of deserts and oases, west of both China and Mongolia, in Turkestan and Zungaria, was not fitted to be held by any unified power system of its own, but at the same time, could not be held indefinitely by either of the other power systems so long as the other was present.

This means that the steppe peoples could hold the oases so long as China did not challenge them there and the Chinese could hold them so long as the steppe peoples did not challenge them there. Thus each of these, in the oases, was attempting to operate outside its own ecological area and could do so, from the lack of power and unity of the oases themselves, so long as the personal attention and energies of the rulers of either were left free by the other to do so.

Three implications of this situation may be mentioned. Neither the steppe system nor the Chinese could rule the oases directly and had to be satisfied with indirect rule in which the oases ruled themselves, simply recognizing either of the others as overlord worthy of allegiance and tribute. Secondly, since the success of either outsider in the oases area did not depend on technological or structural factors, it depended on personal factors, that is the whims, energies, attention, and wills of the rulers in each. And similarly, the success of either intruding power against the other also depended upon personal factors like skill and energy or on luck (such as the overwhelming Chinese victory over the Huns in the battle of the sandstorm in 119 B.C.). The significant role played in Chinese-Hunnish relations by personal intrigue, including the harem intrigue of concubines, is a reflection of the delicate balance of power between the two systems from about 200 B.C. to about A.D. 800, and the inadequacy of both in the oases zone itself.

This third implication involves this oases zone as a distinct entity. The Chinese system could be applied easily to the oases while the steppe system, with the addition of camels to its herds, could adapt to the intervening deserts, but the oases were so similar and each so self-sufficient that only weak economic, military, or logistic bases existed for creating a larger unity of the oases as a whole. And little basis for intellectual unity appeared until the introduction of Islam in the tenth century. The chief exception to this situation occurred about A.D. 25 when the simultaneous internal disruption of both China and the Huns allowed the kingdom of Yarkand in southern Turkestan (Kashgaria) to maintain its independence, but the efforts of this local kingdom to extend its rule over increasingly wide areas of oases resulted in appeals by these oases to the Huns for support. The Huns intervened (after China had refused similar appeals for help) and reestablished the Hunnish overlordship in much of eastern Turkestan and Zungaria by A.D. 65.

The intermittent Chinese-Hunnish struggle continued in the first two centuries of the Christian era, with both becoming weaker, as a consequence of internal decay and disruptions. This weakening process was more rapid among the Huns than in China, with the result that the Hunnish kingdom was split into northern and southern halves by 55 B.C. and the southern portion, seeking help against its northern rival, became a vassal state to China (51 B.C.). This process was undone during the disturbing reign of the socialistic Chinese emperor Wang Mang (A.D. 9-23) but was reestablished once again in permanent form in A.D. 48-50. Forty years later, the southern Huns, as vassals of China, defeated the northern Huns who also became vassals of China. But the growing weakness of both Chinese and Huns left their relative power in continued balance and permitted the rise of other powers outside their respective spheres. The chief of these new powers was an ephemeral alliance of the Sienbi peoples in A.D. 155-180 in the area northeast and east of the Huns. For a considerable period, the growth of these people had forced a movement of the northern Huns from western Manchuria and Outer Mongolia westward into Zungaria, but in the 170s after Christ, these people not only shattered and permanently dispersed the northern Huns but also (177) annihilated a Chinese army sent against them. The southern Hunnish state disintegrated from civil conflicts shortly afterwards (188) and many of its inhabitants took refuge in China, where a direct descendant of the previous Hunnish rulers rose to establish a Chinese imperial dynasty (A.D. 420-479).

The southern Hunnish kingdom ended in A.D. 216, many of its inhabitants fleeing into China, some becoming subjects of other northern tribes led by the Sienbi, and the rest broken up into five local tribal units. The Han empire of China also ended, at almost the same time (A.D. 220) when the last emperor of that dynasty was deposed and China broke up into three major sections. Thus the Han empire of China and the Hunnish empire of the steppes had a remarkable parallel existence, each in two stages with a brief hiatus: the Han 200 B.C. to A.D. 9 and A.D. 25-220; and the Hunnish empire 209 B.C.-51 B.C. and A.D. 13 to 216.

An even more remarkable parallel can be made between the Han empire and the Roman empire. The Huns in China, like the Germans in Europe, were triggered to invade by attacks from other outsiders, the Huns in Europe and the Sienbi in the Far East. The invaders wandered about within the stricken empires, setting up their own kingdoms and even seizing the imperial throne, with constant disputes over sucession and seizure of power by military leaders. In 311 the Huns captured the Chinese imperial city at Loyang and sacked it, just as the Germans sacked Rome in 410 and again in 455. And to complete the parallel, the native Chinese in the Far East were able to retain control of part of the Chinese territory along the Yangtze River and south of it, just as the Romans were able to retain control of the eastern Mediterranean under the Byzantine empire while the west fell under barbarian control. Moreover, in both areas, a new civilization emerged from this period of chaotic mixture, to form the new Chinese civilization in the Far East and the new western civilization in Europe. And, finally, an additional new civilization emerged on the periphery of each destroyed empire, Japan in the Far East and Russia in the west. These two (Japan and Russia) became parallel civilizations to the two new descendant civilizations of the stricken Sinic and classical civilizations (as represented by the Han and Roman empires). Thus, in the period following that covered by this chapter, we had two new civilizations in the west (western civilization and Rus-

523

sian or Orthodox civilization) and two in the Far
East (the new Chinese civilization and Japanese
civilization).

3.   The Roman West and the Germanic Migrations

The Roman empire reached its ecological boundaries in the same centuries, about the time of Christ,
as China did.   From that period under Augustus Caesar
until the culmination of the Dark Ages a thousand
years later, power in the west shifted completely
from the offensive peak of 50 B.C. to the defensive
peak of about A.D. 950.   And in consequence of that
change, political structures in the west also shifted
from the huge political unity of Rome to the almost
complete political decentralization of feudal Europe.

The Roman system was based on infantry forces
tied into a political unity by rowed naval power on
the Mediterranean Sea.   In the last century of its
growth, it pushed inward from the shores of that
sea until it reached ecological boundaries which
the Roman political-military structure could not
penetrate.   Only in one area, Syria, did it find
its way blocked by a civilized social structure,
the neo-Persian empire.   As a result of this obstacle,
the natural east-west corridor across the Syrian Saddle from the Mediterranean Sea to the Euphrates River
was cut by a north-south political barrier along the
fluctuating frontier between Roman and Persian power.
And as a consequence of this, as Freyda Stark has
shown in her Rome on the Euphrates (1967), the most
feasible road between east and west, capable of providing a vital link in the long route between Rome
and China, was hampered and frequently interrupted
so that there was, century after century, search
for alternative routes, either to the south which
tended to look for a water route, through the Arabian, Indian and South China Seas, or to the north
of the highland zone along the steppe corridor and
the oases of its southern edge.   The southern route
dominated by the Persians and the Arabs eventually
led Islamic religious influences across south Asia
from the Red Sea to Indonesia.   The northern route,
dominated by the Ural-Altaic peoples of the steppes,
became "the Silk Road" with its numerous variations.
This also became a route for the spreading of reli-

gious ideas to the Far East, including Buddhism in the earlier period, Nestorian Christianity and Islam in the later period.

With this exception in Syria, the efforts of Roman power to push outward from its base in the Mediterranean Sea were frustrated by natural ecological obstacles rather than by alien social systems. The inability of Rome to find methods of coping with the new ecological conditions were rooted in the Roman social system itself, especially its great waste of manpower and its inability to find innovations in artifacts and technology which could remedy the growing shortage of manpower by more effective use of labor.

The ecological barriers which the Romans met in their efforts to extend the empire beyond the boundaries established by Augustus were very diverse.

The first of these ecological boundaries was between the Mediterranean area with its winter rain, summer drought, and winter growing season and the zone of the prevailing westerlies north of the mountains which had rain in all seasons of the year, with its growing season in summer. The basic distinction here was that the growing season in the south depended on precipitation, while the growing season in the north depended on temperature.

The Romans had no trouble crossing this ecological barrier because the techniques of how to do so had been worked out millennia before the Romans by the Neolithic peoples (about 4000 B.C.). Accordingly, the obstacles to the Roman conquest of Gaul were social rather than natural and were, despite Caesar's self-praise in his Commentaries on the Gallic War, not of major difficulty.

We do not need to be as skeptical as the great historian Ferdinand Lot to recognize that the Roman conquest of Gaul was a relatively easy task. The Gauls were not only divided into numerous, rival kinship groupings, but they were, at Caesar's arrival, shattered into bitterly antagonistic social classes, as the nobles, in process of overthrowing their kings, were simultaneously engaged in a ruthless exploitation of their lower classes. The results were parallel to what might have been expected if Greece had been attacked by an aggressor like Rome in the middle of the Greek social, economic, and political controversies about 650 B.C.

In such a situation it was quite impossible for the Gauls to make any pretense of a united front against Rome. The latter could always find tribal groupings willing to collaborate or even fight against their "fellow" Gauls. Moreover, within each tribal unit, the Romans could find traitors and collaborators on an individual or class basis. In general, the Romans favored the "kings" or the dissident nobles, opposed the nobles as a class, and generally ignored the common people, who were at that time violently resentful of the way they were being exploited by the nobles as these replaced the kings' limited political powers within the Celtic system. One consequence of this is that Caesar's intelligence was always effective, for no plans or movements of the anti-Roman groupings could remain unreported to him. With such information Caesar was in a position to exploit the divisive forces within the Celtic world, to bribe some, or to offer future favors and privileges to others.

There was in Gaul, when Caesar invaded, only one force for unity larger than the tribal groups and personal clientage. This was Druidism, of which we know very little. This was a kind of semi-secret society of religious initiates which maintained personal contacts over much of Gaul, part of Britain, and possibly some districts of central west Germany which were still Celtic. It carried out its policy and judicial decisions by working on the superstitions of the ordinary Celts. Its members were the only educated group in Celtic society, had a form of writing in Greek characters but depended for preservation of its cultural and religious beliefs on memorized folk stories whose mastery was the chief task of its initiates; it settled most inter-tribal disputes and serious crimes within tribes by judicial processes that it conducted periodically. It had a headquarters near Chartres and a single leader in Gaul, who may have been subordinate to a higher leader in Britain, where Gauls went to finish their higher Druidical studies.

The Romans attacked Druidism ruthlessly by infiltration, bribery, and violence, including assassination. It is very likely that many of Caesar's actions were based on this anti-Druid policy, including his ill-prepared and incompetently executed invasion of Britain. The destruction of Druidism followed by the destruction of tribalism left an amorphous Celtic population, a major part of which was enslaved in what E. Badian (1968) called "the most disgraceful act of Roman imperialism."

Apart from his political advantages, Caesar had overwhelming military advantages. The Gauls were poorly armed, on a quantitative as well as a qualitative basis. Only the nobles had weapons in any way comparable to the Romans, and even they lacked defensive equipment (metal helmets, shields, breastplates, etc.) such as the Romans had. Moreover, on a quantitative basis, in terms of logistics, supply, transportation, and such, there was no comparison between the two sides. Many factors, including the much higher level of general literacy on the Roman side, contributed to the latter's ability to conduct a sustained offensive by a large body of men over shifting lines of supply.

Another significant factor in Roman superiority was the far higher level of discipline in the Roman system at all levels. The Gauls debated, while the Roman commander issued orders. The Gauls' decisions were carried out haltingly, or not at all, with much sulking and procrastination by those who had been overruled in the debate which led up to their decision.

The only advantages the Gauls had were in cavalry and in fortifications, but these were not sufficiently important to influence the outcome of the struggle in any significant way. The Gauls' cavalry, consisting of only part of the noble class, was a threat to the Romans because of its mobility and because it could strike successfully at detachments of Roman troops when they were scattered, foraging, making camp, breaking camp, or on route march, but they were not effective against the legions in battle.

527

Thus, in essence, their role against the Romans was of guerrilla nature rather than as a combat arm, and they could be countered well enough by a policy of constant alertness.

The Gallic fortifications were also an obstacle, but a nuisance to the Romans rather than an effective element in the military situation. The nature of these fortifications has been much misunderstood, largely because Caesar called them by the Latin word oppida or "towns." They were not towns in the sense of permanently inhabited centers of substantial numbers of persons nor did they serve any economic functions. They were rather small, generally uninhabited, fortified places to which non-combatants or cattle could be sent for temporary security in a time of danger. Some were inhabited on a purely seasonal basis (in winter). Although the fortifications (consisting of a lattice-work of large logs buried in earth) were relatively effective, they were far inferior to the Roman level. Their effectiveness was rather in the nature of their ability to delay or postpone Roman victory. But in this they were much hampered by the fact that they were used as places of safety for supplies and non-combatants and not exclusively, or even primarily, for military purposes. For this reason the oppida cancelled out the slight advantage of mobility which was provided by the Gallic cavalry, tying down the Celtic combat forces, encumbering these forces with an entangling chaos of non-combatants, dependents, property, and materials which drastically reduced their fighting effectiveness. Thus the last and "greatest" of the Gallish resistance leaders, Vercingetorix, allowed his forces to be tied up in the fortress of Alesia with only thirty days provisions and a very large number of combatants to consume these.

This last point indicates the final weakness of the Gauls: they had no conception of military or political realities, largely because they were in a backward and semi-civilized social system still tangled in an oral and semi-heroic tradition without either the necessary historical experience, social memory (as embodied in a written tradition), nor rational intellectual tradition to untangle these.

528

As a result, they had no way of deciding what were their strengths and weaknesses in comparison with the Roman strengths and weaknesses in order to create a conflict situation which would maximize the influence of their own strengths and the Roman weaknesses. Unfortunately, the influence of Caesar's writings on the history of this period, full as they are of misinformation and disingenuous interpretation and reinforced by the influence of classicists, have made it very difficult for us to see what was the situation.

That situation, it seems to me, both in Gaul and in southern Britain, was such that the Roman conquest was relatively easy except for the pressures on total Roman resources from the needs of other, remote areas such as the Danube or the Levant.

This limitation of the total Roman resources, as established by the inefficiency of the internal Roman socioeconomic system, was what made it impossible for Rome to extend beyond the new ecological boundary which was reached in the extremely broken terrain of northern England and in the dense continental forests of western Germany.

In Britain, as the Roman system moved northward across the midlands, it found a situation not unlike that it had faced successfully in crossing Gaul, except that the cleared and cultivated areas were less extensive and the routes of commerce or travel were less clearly demarcated. The social obstacles were even more primitive and less effective in their resistance than in Gaul. The tribesmen were more undisciplined, more broken up in their allegiances, more lacking in literacy, and in general at a social, economic, and intellectual level lower than the Gauls although higher than the Germans.

This means that agriculture was less developed, hunting was a more significant element in the economic system, commerce and town life were much less developed than among the Gauls. The agricultural system was still largely restricted to the highest upland soils which were tilled with the light scratch plow or with hand tools (hoe or maddock) while the heavier, richer alluvial lowland soils were still largely under forest, but forest less dense than in Germany, especially in the west and in the north of the islands.

Thus, in a sense the British terrain and vegetation should have been better adapted to the Roman technological-organizational patterns were it not for the fact that the terrain rose in altitude and became more broken as the Romans pushed north and west. This increasingly broken character of the terrain, in view of the closeness of the sea, meant that the waters cut into the land more deeply as the Romans reached the western and northern boundaries of England. This created very difficult obstacles to the extension of Roman power which was almost exclusively based on land with no adequate naval arm. Thus, while the Romans did get established in both Wales and Scotland, their grip on these remote areas was precarious and costly to a degree which produced no commensurate increase in security or wealth.

The whole occupation of Britain from the beginning was a waste of Rome's political resources and was a reflection both of the deficiency of Roman ideas on security and the imperialist drives of their social-economic system. The Romans, like the Chinese and the Russians in more recent times, did not feel secure if any organized political system was adjacent to their own frontiers and, accordingly, felt endlessly urged to extend clientage, vassalage, and eventually annexation to any political system which existed on their frontiers. For this reason they had expanded into Gaul to protect the provinces of Cisalpine and Narbonne Gaul and had then expanded into Britain to protect their new territories in Gaul and northwest Europe. Once in Britain, the same urge drove them relentlessly northward and westward to reach the outer seas. But this could not be done, regardless of cost, so long as Rome lacked the sea power to control those outer seas.

In fact, Britain was almost totally conquered in A.D. 74-84 by two Romans who had some conception of sea power. These two were Frontinus who conquered most of Wales (74-77) and Agricola who com-

530

pleted the conquest of north Wales, conquered most of Scotland except the central highlands, and sent his fleet to circumnavigate Scotland. But two serious Roman defeats on the Danube in A.D. 85-86 made it necessary to stop the forward policy in Britain, and it was never resumed. On the contrary, Scotland was largely abandoned in 85-90, and it became a question where and how the line should be drawn across the island south of Scotland.

To most Romans the seas and their inlets were regarded as barriers rather than as ways of communication (as they were to the Vikings later). Accordingly, the Romans tried to control these from the land. Thus, if they were to defend Britain by an east-west line across it, they needed a place where the distance across would be a minimum. In 122-128, under Hadrian, they constructed a wall, about 78 miles long, running from the Tyne to the Solway. More than a dozen years later, when the area south of Hadrian's Wall seemed more pacified and more responsive to the recruiting of local auxiliary forces, the line was pushed 140 miles farther north by the establishment of the fortified wall of Antoninus running 37 miles from the Firth of Forth to the Clyde (A.D. 142). This line was held for about half a century and then abandoned and the defensive frontier withdrawn again to Hadrian's Wall which was reconstructed (about A.D. 195).

From about A.D. 200 onward, the inability of the Romans to control the sea (or rather their effort to control the sea from the land) became increasingly evident. Raids from pirates, especially Saxons, became a growing threat, and the construction of watch towers and forts along the shores, begun about A.D. 280, was not effective, as these could be avoided by a mobile enemy.

The growing mobility of the enemy and the growing static and defensive character of the Roman response, on an empire-wide basis, was what finally ended the effort to control Britain. In A.D. 85 Britain held 4 out of a total of 28 legions for the whole empire. This was reduced to three about A.D. 90, but even at that level, the use of more than a tenth of the total Roman army to hold an area which

contributed so little to the security of the empire
was not a policy of wisdom. Yet Britain was held
to the bitter end. In 367 the garrison there revolted but was subdued, and the Roman forces stayed
on, as late as 442 according to J.B. Bury, or about
409 if we believe other writers. By that time, the
Roman frontiers on the Rhine and Danube had been
torn to tatters, pirate raiders were taking over
the northern seas, and Rome was sacked by the Goths
in 410.

The problem of the defense of Rome in Germany
was quite different from in Britain. In both places
the original Roman intrusion had been led by Julius
Caesar, and in both he withdrew immediately (55-54
B.C.). At that time, the Germans, who had been evolving from the Celts around the Baltic for more than a
millennium, were expanding slowly, pushing the Celts
out of central Europe, and making raids in various
directions. The famous Cimbri and Teutons raided
into Italy and were defeated by Marius in 101 B.C.
Others whom we know as Goths moved southeast after
A.D. 166, according to Gimbutas, reached the Pontic
steppes about A.D. 230, and by A.D. 250 had reached
the Don River, just as the Huns, driving the Sarmatians before them, reached the same river coming
from the east. These Goths began to adopt horse
riding and other customs (but not, apparently, the
composite bow, as such bows used by the Goths were
obtained from the Romans, according to Rausing).
As early as 238, some Goths were beginning to raid
the Roman frontier along the Danube.

Long before this, however, the Romans had personal contact with the Germans along the Rhine where
the steady increase of German population was pushing them westward across the river from before 60
B.C. Having defeated some of these forces during
his campaigns in Gaul, Caesar in 55 B.C. raided
across the Rhine into Germany and spent eighteen
days east of the river. The civil wars in Rome from
49 to 31 B.C. made it impossible to repeat this attempt, although German raids into Gaul continued
during these wars and for the early years of the
Augustine principate. In 16 B.C. a group of tribes
raiding into Gaul defeated the proconsul's army and
escaped back to Germany. Accordingly, Augustus de-

termined to conquer Germany as far as the Elbe and did so with armies commanded by the two brothers, Tiberius and Drusus, in 12 B.C.-A.D. 6, but in A.D. 9 Varus with three legions was surprised by Arminius in the Teotoberg Forest near Osnabruck, and the Roman force was massacred. Tiberius was rushed back to the Rhine with ten legions but made no effort to recover the area east of the river. This was attempted in three indecisive campaigns by Germanicus in A.D. 14-16, but in 17 the attempt to recover central Germany was given up, and the Rhine, with the Romans controlling both banks, became the approximate boundary of the empire in northern Europe.

In Germany and also in central Europe along the Danube, the ecological boundary of the Roman system was reached in deep forests with heavy winter snowfalls. The Romans could invade every summer but they could not remain over the harsh winter, as their troops lacked the clothing, diet, and means of heating their dwellings in such cold weather.

Along the Danube, the Roman policy was more successful than along the Rhine, although the underlying conditions and outcome were similar. Raids and reprisals led to a Roman decision to establish a permanent line along the frontier, close to the river, but in A.D. 101-106 Trajan conquered Dacia north of the river to establish it as a forward defense area. It had to be abandoned under growing barbarian pressures in the third century (270).

The whole Rhine-Danube frontier (including the area known as Raetia joining the two rivers and made into a province under Augustus) was marked by elaborate fixed defenses of palisades, stone walls, and earth ramparts marked by watch towers, parallel roads, and camps for the legions. These were begun generally in the later years of Augustus and put into fairly permanent form by Hadrian. They marked in a formal way the shift from an offensive to a defensive policy in Roman strategy and formed a sharp contrast with the growing mobility of the barbarians. The Roman system was already beyond the limits of its resources by about A.D. 50, although its superiority over the barbarians was so great in regard to equipment, training, discipline, and morale that the

533

structure continued to stand for centuries. But with a total force varying from 25 to 30 legions, about 160,000 men, it was not possible to continue an offensive policy, even with a larger number of auxiliary forces. We do not have any accurate idea of the population of the empire, but it has been estimated at about 50-55 million, of which less than half lived west of the Balkan mountains. An armed force of less than 350,000 from a population this size (less than 0.7 per cent) is no great achievement and would not be, even if the real population of the empire were only half as large as this estimate.

The frontiers in the east were fairly well set at the death of Augustus, along the shores of the Black Sea, across the base of Anatolia, and along the Euphrates River southward. There was constant conflict on the middle section of this line, over where the frontier with Persia would be drawn in Syria and over which would dominate Armenia to the north of Syria.

The weakening of Seleucid power in Persia had allowed Bactria and Parthia to become independent in northeast Iran (248 B.C.). The Parthians, under a dynasty of warrior horsemen, the Arsacids, controlled varying portions of the Persian empire, including Mesopotamia and parts of Syria, until replaced by the more formidable Sassanians more than four centuries later (A.D. 226). These two dynasties in sequence fought Rome for control of Armenia and the Syrian Saddle until the whole Near East was swamped by the Saracens about A.D. 640.

Over this long period, each side suffered disastrous defeats at the hands of the other, without either being able to eliminate the other permanently from the area. Tactically, the Parthian or Sassanian horsemen and the Roman fortified towns cancelled each other out. Thus each had a defensive weapon which the other could not overcome. The Roman fortified towns could not be taken by Parthian cavalry, unsupported by an adequate siege train, while the Roman legions advancing into the hot plains of eastern Syria could not come to decisive grips with the mobile Parthian horsemen and could

be worn down by this cavalry force or cut off in an
unwary moment. Yet neither side would accept a
frontier which recognized this situation, because
each had the Oriental adversion to a frontier with
a great power, and instead felt secure only with barbarous peoples or tributary and client states on
its borders.

The real crux was Armenia, possession of which
would allow either power to outflank the other in
the Syrian Saddle. Control of Armenia made it possible to move southward onto the plains of Mesopotamia by the passes of Mt. Masius or farther southwest to the ford on the Euphrates at Melitene, from
which the Roman province of Syria could be invaded.
Trajan in 114-117 pushed the frontier eastward from
the Euphrates to the Tigris and made Armenia, Mesopotamia, and Arabia into new provinces, but Hadrian
(117-138) had to withdraw the frontier to the Euphrates again. This began an oscillation of Roman-
Persian power in the area which continued century
after century.

South of the area of neo-Persian power Rome
found itself limited by natural ecological boundaries.
Here the limiting conditions were heat and desert
sands which made operations by the legions, in metal
armor and with no adequate animal transportation,
almost impossible. From Syria southward to the
Red Sea, then west across all of Africa to the Atlantic Ocean, the limit of Roman rule was marked by
the grasslands on the northern edge of the deserts.

The camel which had been domesticated about
1200 B.C. did not become known to Caesar until 46
B.C. and could be raised and handled only by the
grasslands peoples. But these peoples could not
be controlled by the Romans and could not be ruled
by the legions. The great prize in the Red Sea area
was the trade in incense from the Hadramaut on the
south coast of Arabia to the consumers in the temples
of Egypt and the Near East. This trade continued in
local hands, such as the Sabaeans, who carried it by
camel overland from the south coast to Yemen and
Hejaz on the west coast, then northward into Nabataean
country in the Negev. The Romans would have liked to
cut out these middlemen and their profits either by

535

the conquest of Arabia or by establishing a sea
route down the Red Sea and through the Arabian Sea.
But the Romans were too much landlubbers to be able
to do the latter. There was never a Roman fleet in
the Red Sea, and the commercial shipping down that
sea was in Egyptian and Levantine hands with a few
Greeks mixed in. It was a difficult and dangerous
voyage, threatened by Semites along the way who attacked with poison arrows. In the end, it proved
more feasible and more profitable for this shipping
to avoid Arabia almost completely and go on to India
directly. Thus in the first couple of centuries of
the Christian era, there was a fair amount of commercial sailing from Egyptian Red Sea ports to India,
but the incense trade remained in Arab hands overland.

One effort was made by Rome to conquer Arabia
itself. In 25 B.C., Augustus ordered the second
prefect of Egypt, M. Aelius Gallus, to conquer
southern Arabia. His invading force wandered about
in the dry grasslands for two years with much suffering from the heat and thirst without any success
in establishing Roman power over the inhabitants.
The attempt was never repeated. The overland trade
remained in Arab hands, and by A.D. 200 the seaborne
trade from the Red Sea to India, much facilitated by
the discovery of the periodicity of the monsoon winds,
fell from Greco-Levantine control to local hands,
mostly Arab in the west and neo-Persian on much of
the Indian Ocean.

Somewhat similar vain efforts were made by the
Romans to cross the Sahara from the northern grasslands to the savannah grasslands south of the desert
and thus to eliminate the Saharan peoples (whom the
Romans called "Garamantes") from the trans-Saharan
trade in gold, ivory, slaves, ostrich feathers, and
salt. In 193 B.C. the proconsul of Africa, L.D.
Balbus, led an expedition southward against the Garamantes and may have reached the savannahs south of
the desert, but the expedition, although hailed as
a great success, changed little. Years later, in
A.D. 70, Valerius Festus, using a new route and
probably using camels, caught the Garamantes by
surprise and defeated them. Apparently this success
did not change the situation much.

Roman efforts to reduce the nomadic peoples of
North Africa to sedentary agriculturalists by changing transhumance pastoralism to irrigation agriculture and to submerge the antipathies of kinship
tribalisms into collegial municipalities was on the
whole successful, but it meant that the whole orientation of life across North Africa was changed. Just as
the Chinese in the Mongolian grasslands sought to
transform an area of ecological transition, in which
life operated on lines perpendicular to the edge of
the desert, into a sharp demarcation, with life operating on lines parallel to the edge of the desert, so
the Romans in Africa made a similar effort. Thus
the life of North Africa, under the Romans, was organized in social zones running roughly east and west
between the sea on the north and the desert on the
south with sharp lines of demarcation between them.
The chief of these lines was the line of forts built
by the Romans just beyond the irrigated zone to fence
off the civilized areas from the grasslands peoples.

This policy in Africa was a great success, due
as much to the work of the Carthaginians as the Romans, which is why the area of greatest prosperity
was around Tunisia. On the whole, across all of
North Africa in the Roman period, the area of sedentary and even irrigated civilization was much more
extensive than it has ever been since. As a result,
water was more available, population was much more
dense, urbanized living was well established, and
there was a great agricultural productivity, so
that large quantities of grain and olive oil flowed
from Africa to Italy. In many areas of North Africa
today, there are more extensive areas of Roman ruins
than there are areas of occupied Arab villages.

The prosperity and growth of Roman Africa was
late, almost entirely in the imperial period, and
continued longer than elsewhere, until after A.D.
250. This may also have been true of Spain a century earlier. But the area between these two, from
Algiers to Casablanca, organized by Rome as the
province of Mauritania, remained a realm of semi-
civilized Berber peoples, and east-west communication was largely restricted to the adjacent sea.

In southwestern Europe the situation was similar to that in northwestern Africa. The Romans held

the whole of the Iberian peninsula, although their
control of the mountainous interior was always much
less complete than in the coastal valleys. This was
a consequence of the inefficiencies of Roman land
transportation. But the area as a whole flourished
under Roman rule and became more flourishing in the
imperial period. As a consequence, much of the
wealth and manpower which Rome had available to
defend its northern and eastern frontiers as these
became increasingly threatened from the northern
grasslands after A.D. 200 came from the provinces
of the south and west in Africa and Iberia. This
is why the survival of a Mediterranean civilization
became impossible when the Germanic invaders conquered Spain and Africa after A.D. 409.

The stabilization of the Roman frontiers from
about the time of Augustus to the disruption of
those frontiers almost 400 years later resulted
in vital changes in the Roman system. These changes
might be attributed to two basic causes, although
obviously many other factors contributed to a very
complex situation.

The shift from offensive dominance to defensive
dominance in the Roman military posture after Augustus
gave rise to two acute economic problems: the supply
of slaves from war captives was cut down and the ability of the Roman system to recapture the gold and
silver which flowed outward from Rome and from Italy
to the provinces and beyond the frontiers was greatly
reduced. The first of these made it necessary to reorganize the large estates of the Roman area from
plantation slavery to a system of tenancy, called
the colonate. And the latter led to acute financial
problems, to growing difficulty in collecting taxes,
to steady devaluation of money, to runaway inflation
of prices (in terms of copper and silver coinage,
rather than gold), and to a steady reduction from
an economy of monetary interchange to transactions
in kind and even to self-sufficiency and a reemphasis
on subsistence agriculture.

At the time of the principate, according to
Pliny, smaller farms operated by their owners for
their own benefit were much more efficient than the
latifundia of central Italy, producing up to five

times as much crop per acre. There can be no doubt
that the latifundia were notoriously inefficient,
whether efficiency is measured in output per unit
area or output per man employed. But the inertia
of a system of entrenched economic and social privilege was so great that there was no economic reason
to change it until the second century A.D. By that
time, and increasingly from then on, the double pressures of shortage of labor and excessive taxes made
it almost impossible to reform the system by any
remedial actions within the Roman political and
social structure.

The remedy for this shortage of slaves (or the
increased cost of slaves) which excluded the use of
slave labor in agriculture was to turn to tenants,
even when this involved turning slaves, as well as
free peasants, city dwellers, ex-soldiers or others
into such tenants (coloni). These coloni originally
owed money rents, but in time these were gradually
replaced, at least in the west, by payments in kind,
shares of the crop, or in the later period, by labor
services on the land the owner retained for himself.
As the labor shortage became worse, especially when
decreasing general population became a problem,
several centuries after slaves became short in supply, there was a tendency for the tenants to become
attached to the land and non-removable, in the
sense that if the land was sold the tenants went
with it, or even when a tenant died his son became
colonus with the same obligations as his father.
Of the many causes contributing to this fastening
of the tenant to the land, one of the most significant was the landlord's argument that he could not
pay the taxes due on all the land if much of it was
uncultivated from shortage of labor.

This pressure of taxes is another most potent
element in the whole situation. As the problems
faced by the state became more numerous and more
acute, following the curtailment of incomes from
war booty and from the looting of the provinces,
it became necessary to increase taxes. The costs
of a standing army are only one of these expenses,
but equally important were the costs of the growing
bureaucratic structure of the imperial system.
Every new problem, a great fire, a crop failure,

539

an epidemic disease, the increased and unruly population of the cities, the effort to unify, at least to some extent, the customs and especially the laws, of the diverse peoples living under the imperial system, the growing demands of urban problems (for food, water, entertainment, public order, etc.) all required some new activity of the state and often some new bureaucratic organization to handle these.

The greatest cost by far was that of a standing army and the need to provide for its loyalty by bribes and payments beyond the recognized costs of pay and maintenance (so-called "donatives"), and, above all, the need to provide lands and pensions for veterans. To obtain these incomes, amounting to two-thirds of the total imperial income, it was necessary to unleash the violence and destruction of the armed forces onto the richer citizens (since the soldiers were no longer capable of taking wealth from the enemy). And since so much money was needed, this violence had to be released against those who had the wealth, the richest citizens, including the senatorial families of Rome itself. Expropriations, confiscations, judicial condemnations, and simple murder destroyed all the old senatorial noble families in the century following Augustus. Naturally these were replaced by new senators and new families. But these, in turn, were destroyed again by the time of Diocletian (285), and the process continued, until the old traditions were wiped away with the families which had embraced them. At the same time, since the new senatorial families were largely recruited from the army generals, and these were largely men of provincial and rural origin who had risen from the ranks, there was almost total loss, not only of the older traditions of public service and self-sacrifice, but there was a similar loss of Roman, Latin, and even Italian traditions, replaced very largely by traditions of Asiatic or barbarian origins.

Much has been written on these two factors and their consequences. Together they led to mountains of legal enactments vainly trying to deal with the problems arising from shortage of labor, inadequate state revenues, proliferating bureaucracy, growing inflation and increasing violence and disorder. Not nearly enough, however, has been written on one as-

540

pect of this problem which is very close to the subject
which we have been pursuing--the role of organized
force in the community.

Before we focus on this very critical issue,
we must have a more adequate picture of some of the
problems of the centuries after the principate.

The traditional belief in the political and
legal genius of the Romans has made it difficult
to recognize that they were very inept in skills
of government. The most vital attribute of any
government is stability or, looking at it from a
more legal point of view, responsibility. As we
have said, both of these require that the subjective
or legal picture of the power situation must reflect,
fairly closely, the actual distribution of power
within the community (as power is understood within
the terms of the cognitive system of that community).

The Roman system was never either stable or
responsible in these terms, either under the republic or during the principate. This situation got
worse under the empire.

In theory and in law the ruler was the imperator,
that is the person on whom the senate conferred the
powers of commander-in-chief by a lex de Imperio.
But the content of this power was variable and ambiguous, and its bestowal by the senate was increasingly meaningless, legalistic rather than legal,
since the senate conferred something it did not
possess itself.

In contrast to this theory was the fact that
after Actium the power of imperator rested in the
hands of the commander of a loyal military force
capable of defeating any other claimants to the
title. So long as claimants did not appear, this
ability would be assumed to rest with the existing
commander-in-chief, but whenever a claimant did
arise, the merits of the conflicting claims could
be settled only on the battlefield. The fact that
the legal disposition of the office, by vote of the
senate, was so remote from this fact served to encourage such dissident claims, as did also the fact
that the increasingly decentralized nature of the

Roman armed forces into local units with local economic bases, local recruiting, and local interests.
To reduce this danger of rival claims to the office,
various legal devices were tried, but all failed.

Originally, some effort was made to establish
a hereditary claim to the position in the family of
Julius Caesar. This never became in any way a hereditary principle. It was based to some extent on the
fact that Caesar was deified and the members of his
family, even by adoption, or through a female connection, were somehow descended from a god. But
much more significant than this tenuous connection
was the fact that the family of the deified Julius
was popular with the armed forces because of their
memory that he, when alive, had been consistently
victorious, had never neglected the interests of
his troops, and had been martyred by persons who
were concerned with other interests than those of
the army. For this reason, there was, until A.D. 68,
the idea that the Imperator should be in the family
of Julius Caesar, but the precarious nature of this
claim can be seen in the fact that, of the five emperors of the Julio-Claudian line after Augustus,
four died violent deaths. The year of the four emperors (A.D. 69) showed that other military units
than the Praetorian Guard could engage in the task
of making, and unmaking, emperors. Three of the four
died violently in that year. The victor and sole
survivor, Vespasian, and his two sons ruled from
A.D. 69-96, but the second son was murdered in 96.
The next five emperors (Nerva, Trajan, Hadrian,
Antoninus Pius, and Marcus Aurelius), known as "the
Antonines" (96-180) were able to rule without significant challenge from either army or senate, supported by the one and accepted by the other, but
the efforts of the last of the five, Marcus Aurelius,
to establish a hereditary system by associating his
son with him in the last few years of his own reign
did not establish a viable precedent, and the son
was murdered in 192.

After that crime, for ninety-two years (192-284),
the empire was racked by civil war, riotous disturbances, plague, acute economic collapse, and increased
enemy pressures on the frontiers. During that 92
years there were 28 emperors of which only two (pos-

sibly a third) died from natural causes, two died from enemy action, and 24 were murdered. The military anarchy associated with this struggle for the throne became so violent at the middle of the third century that it is said that the 46 emperors and would-be emperors died violent deaths in sixteen years. Election by the senate ceased in this period.

In fifteen years, 270-285, there were seven emperors, yet the next emperor, Diocletian, ruled for twenty-one years and then departed from the throne by voluntary retirement. This man, famous as a persecutor of the Christians, may be the most able man who ever held the office of emperor. Certainly he was one of the most energetic and innovative. If it is true that most of his efforts were failures, this was not his fault so much as it was the fault of his successor, known as Constantine the Great.

Diocletian (284-305) tried to establish a mode of succession by cooptation and sought to strengthen loyalty to it by enveloping the emperor and all his acts with the religious sanctity of an Asiatic sacral kingship. The method of succession provided that each emperor, now called "Augustus," would be associated with another "Augustus" as co-emperor, dividing the administration of the empire into two parts (east and west). Each "Augustus" would then pick an assistant, called "Caesar," for his half of the empire, with the understanding that each "Caesar" would be successor to his respective "Augustus."

In this system the political and legal unity of the empire would be retained, but it would be administratively divided under the four co-rulers. The largest division was into four prefectures (Italy, Gaul, Illyrium, and the east) each under a praetorium prefect. Each prefecture in time became divided into dioceses, each under a "vicar" responsible to the emperor rather than to the prefects. Each diocese was subdivided into provinces under "presidents" or "rectors." The continuing process of localism, running parallel to the growth of a centralized despotism at the center, resulted in an increase in the number of provinces from twenty in A.D. 14 to about sixty in 284, raised to 116 under Constantine (d. 337), and this process of division continued.

543

The history of Roman weapons over this period
is very complex. All aspects of defense, including
cognitive patterns, were changing constantly. In
general, the army became more complex, with a greater
variety of arms and more varied relationships among
arms. On the whole there was probably a considerable
decline in quality over two hundred years (A.D. 60-
260), which might be called "the eclipse of the legion," but this was not really serious, since the
Roman forces in that period, despite occasional defeats, did not encounter any enemy of comparable
quality. The only battles between armies of similar
quality were those with other Roman armies in the
civil wars. Of course, as I have indicated, Rome
was still having difficulties with ecological and
social conditions as bases of opposition to Roman
power, as in Scotland, which they could not handle,
and such conditions could make trouble at any time
in Illyria, western Iberia, Raetia, Morocco, even
Brittany, or along the grasslands and deserts of
the south and southeast. But all these difficulties
could have been contained but for the fact that
Rome was overextended and public spirit was decreasingly good, as Ramsay MacMullen has well shown (1966).
As we shall see, these last two weaknesses continued
after 260 until after 500, but from 260 onward there
was a great qualitative improvement in Roman military affairs. Let us look at the period before
260, "the eclipse of the legion."

We have seen that the legion was reorganized
about 200 B.C. into ten cohorts of about 480 men
each (with the first cohort twice as large) with
attached cavalry for each cohort (originally, perhaps 32, but eventually 120), while the legion had
artillery of ballista and catapults. There were
also separate cavalry units (alae), which after 100
B.C. were recruited from client and barbarian peoples. In a similar way, there were units of light
armed skirmishers and missile infantry armed with
javelins, slings, or archery. Until the imperial
period, the amount of artillery, cavalry, or light
forces an army had depended almost entirely on the
desires of the commanding general and his ability
to obtain money to hire these. It is interesting
to see that Caesar in his Gallic Wars uses the word
"legion" for most tactical operations, while in his
later Civil War he uses the word "cohorts" in de-

scribing his operations. In a similar way, he had very limited cavalry, light missile troops, and artillery in the earlier work, but was plentifully supplied with all three of these in the later period. The reason for this change is that he had only limited funds in Gaul, but, from his conquests there, he obtained adequate funds as well as increased access to public monies.

The "eclipse of the legion" was a slow process by which the legion ceased to be a tactical unit and became exclusively an administrative unit, at the same time it was settled at a fixed point in the frontier defense system. The legions were placed on the borders by Augustus and were moved with decreasing frequency. Cohorts were moved about wherever needed, but the administrative center of the legion remained fixed, and there was usually at least one cohort left at headquarters. Local recruiting for the legion around its headquarters, and thus of frontier and semi-barbarized peoples, began under Hadrian (117-138). This led to growing resistance by the cohorts to being moved from their own provinces or regions, at least for extended periods, especially as they became part-time farmers, and increasingly part-time soldiers, with their farms and families in their home district. By the time of the Marcomanni Wars (167-182), the legion had ceased to have any significant tactical function at all, and its soldiers were becoming frontier militia. But the legion continued to exist near the frontier, in most cases for over 200 years at the same place, as an administrative center for the cohorts of infantry or the alae of cavalry.

At some time before 260, and the time varied greatly depending on the area, names began to change and new units began to appear, at first attached to the headquarters site. The older sedentary cohorts and the alae were apparently renamed auxilia (infantry) and cunei equitum (cavalry, or at least mounted infantry), but they were supplemented by new units which were locally recruited but could be moved about the empire (or at least the major regions of the empire) in tactical use for strategic purposes. These were called originally cohortes (infantry) and vexillationes (cavalry) except when

545

they were native peoples using their own weapons and
tactics and receiving orders in their own languages,
who were called numeri. At some time the name vex-
illation shifted from cavalry to infantry (probably
from the fact that they often fought on foot even
when they rode to the battlefield). These vexillationes continued for a long time to be moved about
the empire as needed but attached administratively
to the legion headquarters. In 275, for example,
an expeditionary force sent to crush a revolt in
Egypt had vexillationes from eighteen different
legions.

While this process was going onward on the
lower levels of defense, another process was providing mobile forces. This second process was one by
which the emperor's personal forces became larger
and larger until he could no longer rely on their
personal loyalty and allowed them to become field
forces while he created new personal forces of guards
for his own protection. This process occurred continuously but can be marked by four breaks over four
centuries, each event of a somewhat different kind.
The four are known as the Praetorians, the Comitatenses, the Palatini, and the Scholae, with the last
three mostly in the period after 260. This last
phase is important, for it was in a sense the failure to keep up regional field armies by releasing
personal forces of the emperor which led to the
qualitative decline in the defense forces as a whole
in the period A.D. 60-260.

The Praetorians became attached to the palace
rather than to the emperor personally and were destroyed by Septimus Severus and replaced by Illyrian
legionary cohorts in 193. The former were recruited
from Italy long after Italians had vanished from
other units and thus had a somewhat higher level
of social origin and of literacy. The officers,
especially the centurions, for all other units were
taken from the Praetorians, were constantly
moved about from unit to unit and from region to region long after the units had become sedentary, and
they were regularly moved when promoted through the
many grades of centurions (in theory sixty grades)
or other officers. The units which replaced the
Praetorians and served as the emperor's guard for

most of the third century were designated "legionary cohorts" and did not earn a special name until almost the end of that century when they became known as "companions" (comitatus); when they were released to be used as ordinary field armies under the command of subordinates, they retained the name as Comitatenses. About the same time, the frontier forces became limitanei. An emperor, probably Diocletian (284-305), created a new personal guard, the Palatini, but these were absorbed into the field armies of Comitatenses and replaced by new units of guards, Scholae, by Constantine (c. 312).

As a consequence of this double process by which frontier forces became sedentary and largely evaporated and by which field armies were created at the top but in time also tended to become regional forces, the Roman army, for much of the empire, existed on three levels of frontier, field, and guard forces. As a result of failure to keep the field forces up, culminating in the actions of the Severi (193-217), the field forces settled down on the frontiers in greatly strengthened fortifications, but without adequate manpower and with a sharp decrease in that aggressive spirit which is so necessary even for defensive warfare.

There can be no doubt that Roman defenses were greatly weakened by Septimus Severus (193-211) and his son, Caracalla (211-217). The former won the throne with the support of his Illyrian legions, after three other emperors had been murdered in the same year, over the opposition of the Praetorians. As a result, Septimus was devoted to his frontier legions and granted them every favor, including an initial gift of 5,000 denarii (more than three years' pay) to each man. He disbanded the Praetorians, thus ending the supply of centurions, and opened promotion to rankers. The distinctions between Italy and the provinces and ultimately the distinctions in law between legionary and auxiliary forces became meaningless when Caracalla, in 212, gave Roman citizenship to all subjects (so that all became subject to certain taxes and also eligible to be recruited to legionary cohorts).

Septimus permitted his soldiers to marry while

547

in service and allowed the frontier forces to live
at home, behind the fortifications, with their
families, reporting to their camps and barracks
where they had previously lived only when on duty.
To pay for these families, pay was raised from 1500
to 2000 denarii a year and the soldiers were provided with subsistence farms or encouraged to work
in craft enterprises in their free time or as duty
assignments. When cohorts were moved any distance,
the army provided transport for their families and
possessions, with a great increase in the costs and
effort of military transportation. The soldiers became reluctant to move, married local girls, mostly
barbarians, and became a part-time army. The farms
were reserved for soldiers and became, with the profession, hereditary, but were frequently lost when
no son became a soldier.

The recruitment of the armed forces was a growing problem and steadily got worse. There was growing reluctance of citizens to serve in the whole imperial period. The percentage of Italians in the
army decreased from 65 per cent in A.D. 14-41 to one
per cent in 138-195. It became necessary to lower
standards and to increase duress. Physical standards
were lowered, such as height to 5 feet 7 inches, and
literacy decreased, and by 200 most soldiers were
semi-literate provincials. In the third century,
assessments of recruits, like assessments of taxes,
were imposed on local landlords. Since these could
not find the manpower to till their fields to pay
their taxes, they found only poor quality recruits
or commuted this obligation to a money payment which
could be used by the government to hire barbarians.
Inflation was raising prices at least twice as fast
as soldiers' pay was increasing, so there was little
incentive for citizens with other prospects to seek
a career in military service. Pay was increased
only once in the period A.D. 14-183, when Domitian
(A.D. 82) raised it from 225 denarii a year to 300
(that is, from nine gold pieces to twelve). The
Severi raised it to 750 by 215, but prices went up
faster, population was decreasing, manpower needs
were going up, and the government's income was in
constant deficit after Caracalla. In the third
century, barbarians began to come into the army,
at first in special units (numeri), but later, be-

ginning in Africa, as tribal units called <u>federati</u>,
hired to guard the frontiers.

As a consequence of these and other factors,
it seems likely that Roman arms reached their qualitative nadir about 260, after two centuries of decline. At the same point a severe economic depression, an acute financial crisis, a devastating plague,
which continued for over a dozen years (251-265), and
almost constant civil wars, in which nine emperors
were murdered in thirty-two years (217-249), made it
almost impossible to defend the frontiers. In Britain the Caledonians forced the Romans out of Scotland
and back to Hadrian's Wall, while on the opposite
end of the empire, the Sassanian dynasty replaced
the Parthian Arsacids in Persia and soon overran Syria (256). In between, the Franks crossed the lower
Rhone; the Alemanni invaded southern Gaul and northern Italy from the west end of the Danube, while the
Goths, supported by a fleet from the Black Sea,
crossed the lower Danube seeking to settle in the
Balkans. The bottom was reached when the Emperor
Decius was killed by the Goths (251), and the Emperor Valerian was taken prisoner by the Sassanians
and soon died (259). It was not much consolation
that both of these last events resulted from treachery, rather than from military inadequacies.

The qualitative military recovery of Rome from
this low ebb began with the reforms of Gallienus
(259-268) and the superior military abilities of
his successors, Claudius II "Gothicus," Aurelian,
Tacitus, Probus, and Carus, all five in fifteen
years (268-283). Four of these were murdered and
the fifth died from plague, but in their brief
reigns they pushed back the invaders, abandoning
only Scotland and Dacia.

The military reforms of Gallienus, Diocletian
(284-305) and Constantine the Great (306-337) helped
restore Roman arms to qualitative excellence, but
their quantitative inadequacy remained and became
worse probably for the whole period from after A.D.
through the reign of Justinian (527-565). It was
this quantitative lack and the decline in public
spirit and morale (which continued through the
fourth and fifth centuries) which forced the imperial system to withdraw reluctantly to the east

and abandon the west in the fifth century.

Gallienus built up the mobile field armies, partly by creating new units and partly by permanently drawing units back from the frontier. It seems likely that he also increased the size of the units somewhat, ordinary cohorts ly about 75 men to 555 and the double cohorts to twice that. Many of the new units were cavalry or mounted infantry, and came to be known, in some cases, by the areas where they were recruited, thus Mauri, Dalmatae, Saraceni, Illyriciani. Others were known from their arms, as Sagittarii (archers) or Cataphracti (armored lancers); the cavalry which had been attached to the legions for centuries were detached to form separate units in the field forces, called promoti. We do not believe that all of this was done by Gallienus, but Diocletian and Constantine continued the process. By Diocletian's day, about 300, the units had been doubled and the men in these units increased to 455,266; this figure comes from John Lydus, who was in a position to know. To keep the figure up, service was made hereditary (313). As barbarians were defeated, the captives were placed in colonies all about the empire on the uncultivated lands with the obligation to work these for themselves and provide military service when needed. In this way, peoples were mixed up, with Sarmatian colonies in western Gaul and Franks placed in the east.

The increase in field forces as backup reserves to the frontier forces made it necessary for them to be available on a regional basis. This was the reason Diocletian created a co-emperor, with four areas of responsibility for them and their Caesars. The civil wars of Constantine and his successors in the fourth century destroyed this arrangement as barbarian pressure increased outside and disintegration grew within.

To pay for all this, Diocletian radically reformed the whole fiscal system and coined vast quantities of copper coins. This greatly accelerated the price inflation, so in 301 he issued an edict on prices which fixed in detail prices and wages, with very severe penalties for violations, including the death sentence. As a result, sales decreased, and many goods practically vanished from the markets.

The army and the government were largely protected from the consequences of these errors of economic management by a detailed assessment of wealth for the whole empire and a new system of taxation in kind, especially a tax in grain (annona). Non-agricultural needs of the army and government such as uniforms and armaments were largely provided by state-owned factories whose workers were soldiers, or at least under military discipline. Outside the cities the population was registered for tax purposes, and it became illegal for the peasant to leave his registered domicile, either village or estate.

In reference to this, A.H.M. Jones wrote: "Diocletian made it possible for the state to dispense with the use of money except for minor adjustments and to rely almost entirely on requisitions in kind. . . The new system made it possible for the first time for the Roman empire to have a budget in the modern sense, an annual assessment of governmental requirements, and an annual adjustment of taxes to meet those requirements."

But, he adds, "Lactantius declares that the burden was intolerable: 'the number of recipients [of government money] began to be so much greater than that of the taxpayers that the resources of the cultivators were exhausted by the enormous levies, and the fields were abandoned, and cultivation returned to woodland.'"

In 305 Diocletian and his co-emperor resigned and retired to the country to see how the new system would function. Their respective Caesars took over, becoming Augusti and naming Caesars, and presumptive successors of their own. But the system broke down almost at once and, after nineteen years of civil war, Constantine emerged as victor and sole emperor.

Constantine (311-337) undid most of the work of Diocletian. He created a new guard of picked barbarians, mostly Germans, all mounted and very well paid. In all military units barbarians and especially Germans were raised to the highest ranks. The frontier legions were somewhat reduced and put under the command of duces (dukes), while the field armies were greatly enlarged and put under command

551

of new officers known as Magister Peditum for the
infantry and Magister Equitum for the cavalry. These
mobile forces soon broke up into regional armies,
whose leaders in Gaul and the east, retained the
title of "Magister Militum," while smaller forces
in Thrace, Illyricum, Britain and elsewhere were
each under a comes (count). These, like the frontier legions which had become completely static,
also tended to become localized and to resist orders
to move to different parts of the empire. Recruitment took place anywhere that men could be found,
even outside the frontiers and by the end of the
century, barbarian tribal leaders were being subsidized to keep a specified number of their tribal
followers available to fight for Rome when necessary.
Such fighters, called federati, may have had loyalty
to the chiefs who paid them, but they had no reason
to feel loyal to the Roman state or to its emperor
who were remote abstractions.

Other less obvious changes were weakening the
whole system, especially after 195. As the system
became more elaborate and more bureaucratized, it
may have looked rational and hierarchical in a verbal
description but was very incomplete and had no real
chains of command, so that higher officials could
intervene at any level. Whole areas of what we
should regard as essential public services and public
authorities were lacking. This was especially true
of police and fiscal authorities. Until Augustus
there had been no local police, and any need for public authority on a local basis was provided by the
local landlords; there was nothing similar in the
cities because, there, each potentate had his own
band of associates, clients, and relatives who provided him with a bodyguard. Rudimentary police and
fire brigades appeared, as military organizations,
about 50 B.C. and were formally organized by Augustus.
In time the members of the municipal senates of other
cities (the so-called curiales) organized similar
units where they thought it necessary, but nothing
similar arose in the countryside. As a result, the
rural areas became relatively free areas for runaway
slaves, bandits, tax evaders, draft dodgers, and
others without anything being done unless these dissident persons began to form bands or large groups
when military forces were sent against them. But

552

the lack of ready communication or of any rural police meant that any single individual could not be controlled and could hardly be compelled to do anything. At the same time, it meant that any single individual had little protection against oppression either from outlaws or from local potentates who had a few henchmen to enforce their orders. Accordingly, such local rural potentates, almost all large landowners, could become foci of local despotic rule, of local resistance to public officials, and local protectors of lesser men who needed protection against either outlaws or government agents.

In the later empire, all local government was still municipal government, covering not only an urban area, often quite small, but also its surrounding rural district, often very extensive. In law the inhabitants tended to divide into five levels:

clarissimi: great men who were members of the senate in Rome.

curiales: landlords who were members of the local senate.

vici: free peasants who were enrolled on the village census.

coloni: tenants of various kinds.

servi: slaves.

The curiales were made responsible for all local matters including local government, religion, and eventually all taxes, simply because they had lands which could be seized to enforce payment. This burden became so great that many curiales tried to escape from the burdens in any way possible which would un-list them from the curiale status.

The clarissimi had many privileges and were exempt from local obligations on the theory that they were subject to central obligations, but really simply because being in Rome and being very rich they could get benefits, immunities, and exemptions. But of course, they lived in danger of confiscation or liquidation just because they were rich, available, and known in Rome.

553

As government pressures increased, evasions increased, local dangers and disorders increased, from rural outlaws and eventually from bands of invaders, and the power of the government in the rural areas weakened. At that point, many <u>clarissimi</u> and great <u>curiales</u>, forced to make their estates more self-sufficient from the shift to tenancy and the breakdown of commerce, distant sources of supply, and marketing arrangements, and the instability of prices, began to leave the municipalities to live on their estates which they sought to make into autonomous centers not only in economics but also in defense, in settlement of disputes, and in social life. These estates, with bands of armed retainers, sought to exclude outlaws, tax collectors, recruiting officers, and the <u>curiales</u> seeking to enforce their joint obligations in the local municipality. If this organization of estate power was to any degree successful, local free peasants and tenants sought protection and immunity against outside interference from this local potentate. Such protection could be obtained through the old traditional Roman custom of clientage, even if that involved, to escape the government's opposition to such relationships, becoming a tenant or otherwise legally a subordinate of the local great man.

The crisis of the third century shook the Roman system to its foundations. Population decreased, not only from the disturbances but from great plagues which came from the east and ravaged the west; there was considerable and growing ruralization of life and of population as people began to flee from the city following the uncertain food supply back to its source; nevertheless much land fell out of cultivation from lack of manpower and lack of attention, so that whole districts became semi-deserted. In 400 about a tenth of the land of Campania south of Rome was deserted, but in Africa at least 40 per cent was abandoned by 425. Remedial legislation, which goes back before A.D. 200, was little help, although deserted and abandoned lands were offered to veterans and eventually to anyone who would cultivate them. When the armies took barbarian prisoners in war, they were no longer sold as slaves, but were placed on estates as tenants, so that they and their descendants would be available as recruits for the army.

The manpower shortage, like the growing evasions of public responsibilities, led to torrents of laws which did not help much, since human ingenuity could find ways of evading old regulations faster than the government could devise new rules to plug loopholes. In general, many of these laws sought to legislate the perpetuation of the status quo, forbidding persons to move about, change their occupations, or their legal status. Many activities were made compulsory for those who were in them and then were made hereditary. This included various activities associated with the metalworkers, the food supply of Rome, and the obligations of municipal life and defense: miners, smelters, armorers, millers, bakers, all engaged in shipping grain to Rome, the curiales, the soldiers, tenants, all free peasants, and many others. But evasion was extensive and enforcement increasingly difficult.

The curiales, for example, were made responsible as a group for the taxes of the whole population of their municipality and its environs. They already were responsible for all the municipal functions of the town, including heavy burdens for religion, entertainment, and public welfare, as well as buildings, streets, and water supply. It was assumed that they could recover from the non-curiales and, at any rate, their lands were there, immovable, to serve as security for the town's obligations to the central government. But as population decreased, lands went out of cultivation, and the greatest landlords closed the gates of their estates to all outsiders, defending them with savage dogs and armed retainers, the curiales sought to escape that status, which had once been eagerly sought as an honor. They were forbidden to become clarissimi, to give up their estates, or eventually, even to visit their estates, under penalty of confiscation, lest they stay there and become unreachable.

In this growing frustration and futility of the Roman government, we are dealing with a fundamental truth of all social life, including all organized power systems or organized force: any organization functions effectively only against organizations which operate in terms similar to itself, yet, in the final analysis, every organization functions only when it can influence or control the moment-to-moment lives of concrete individuals. It is, in fact, impossible for any organization to do this except to the extent that the society as a mass of people tacitly accepts and supports, not only the legitimacy of what is being done in any case, but the assumptions behind the organizing principles of the organization itself. Caesar as Imperator in the organized structure of his army and legions cannot be injured by any organized force he is likely to encounter, but Caesar as a man bleeds to death through the hole left by Brutus's dagger like any other man. So too, Diocletian or Constantine, from the pinnacle of his impressive power, issues a decree, but the enforcement of that decree against ingenious individuals, each in his own unique circumstances and scattered individually over countless thousands of square miles of territory, is quite a different matter.

It might be stated as a general rule that any organization functions only with and against those who accept its basic principles of organization and values. So the Roman system functioned only so long as dignitas and the cursus honorum and the death masks and ceremonial robes of the ancestors were the most important things in life. When they ceased to be important and other things, such as personal relationships with one's loved ones or hope of salvation in the hereafter, became more important, then the organized structure based on earlier beliefs worked increasingly ineffectively. And, since any organizational structure requires its members to subordinate their own wills and whims, their own pleasures and material needs, to some less immediate goals, so no organizational structure can continue to function in a society where the people involved in it become increasingly selfish, self-indulgent, materialistic, and atomistically individualistic. In these terms the wonder is not that the Roman system collapsed but that it survived for so long, century after century, when the spiritual values which created it no longer existed.

Once the great mass of the Roman people, and especially the politically active minority, adopted values and general outlooks different from and anti-

556

thetical to the Roman outlook and values, the system was doomed. In this connection we usually think of Christianity as the great contrast to the Roman ideology, but this is to misconceive the whole civilization. Christianity as an organization was in no way incompatible with Romanism as an organized structure. The teachings of Christ were, but these teachings were so very alien and strange that no one took them very seriously and being a Christian soon meant, not belief in Christ's teachings but belief in Christ, a totally different thing. The same thing happened in Islam where Muhammad's teachings were soon ignored, and the requirements of Islam became a few rituals, plus monotheism, and so far as Muhammad was concerned, belief that he was the Prophet of the One God.

The Christians cut down Christ's teachings to a minimum also, insisted only on the belief that Christ was the Son of God and some related beliefs and certain rituals, and then began to engage in violent controversy on minute details of implications of these, very remote from Christ's teachings or attitude. On this basis, there was not much in Christianity which could not be reconciled with the Roman system, and the original enmity between the two came more from the Roman side than from the Christian.

Earlier there were other ideologies and other religions, at least as incompatible with the Roman system as was Christianity. These became a confused mixture of Epicureanism, Platonism, neo-Pythagoreanism, Stoicism, various corruptions of eastern religions, Orphism, astrology, hermeticism, and ancient superstitions and magic. Their injury to the Roman system rested on the fact that they were generally not compatible with the old Roman idea of dignitas, nor its emphasis on the solidarity of the social group and the community, nor its emphasis on this-worldly values, notably the opinion of one's fellows in the same community. The Christians, on the other hand, were quite prepared to accept the Roman system so long as it refrained from attacking them. This latter occurred under Constantine (A.D. 313) who saw the situation clearly. The willingness of the Christians to become part of the Roman system

557

can be seen in the present survival of the Roman
Catholic Church as a copy of the Roman empire, a
system organized in municipalities and provinces
under an absolute ruler who uses the robes, nomenclature, language, and modes of action of the late
Roman empire.

The deterioration in Rome's ability to enforce
its will over its own subjects and to maintain law
and order within its own frontiers was followed,
much more slowly, by a weakening of its ability to
defend those frontiers. The pressure along those
frontiers, especially in the north and east, was endemic for the whole imperial period, but there was
no real danger until the third century because the
barbarians and even the Persians were inferior to
the Romans in weapons, morale, and tactics. As the
frontier forces became increasingly sedentary, they
became increasingly unable to deal with raiders crossing the frontier, especially when they were mounted.
To cope with this situation, the Romans needed mounted infantry who could catch up with the intruders.
Such units were provided, but never in sufficient
numbers. The situation remained in control, however,
until the third century when the barbarians increased
in numbers and boldness just as the Romans were increasingly distracted by civil wars. The growing
population of the Germans combined with manpower
shortages among the Romans to create an explosive
situation.

These problems came to a head in A.D. 251, when
Decius, a local commander on the Danube, left his
post and rushed to Italy to battle a usurper to the
throne, Philip the Arab. Decius fought and killed
Philip, claimed the imperial title for himself, and
hurried back to the Balkans which had been invaded
by Goths and other barbarians through the opening
Decius had left on the frontier. The Goths defeated
and killed Decius, through the betrayal of the governor
of Moesia, who claimed the throne himself but was soon
killed by another pretender. While the Goths ravaged
the Balkans, Alemanni and Franks crossed the Rhine to
plunder Gaul, and the Sassanians captured Syria. The
line of the Rhine and Danube was restored, but Gaul
and Thrace were devastated, and Dacia had to be
abandoned permanently.

The reforms of Diocletian and Constantine sought to remedy this collapse of the third century, but the basic problems remained unsolved while the emergency problems became more acute.

The basic problems were those associated with the great mass of the people, while the emergency problems were those faced by the ruling minority (notably the growing pressures from outside intruders and the growing inability to have orders carried out among the mass of the people or at any considerable distance from the source of the order). Moreover, there could be no real solution to the emergency problems, which everyone saw, unless solutions were found to the chronic fundamental problems which attracted less attention. And basic in the whole situation was a growing gulf between the ruling group, itself dwindling in numbers and increasingly recruited (through military channels) from barbarians, and the great mass of the people increasingly concerned with keeping body and soul together (in terms of food, personal security, and personal emotional frustrations) and the growing thirst for religious solace in the exhausting struggle to keep alive.

The fundamental chronic problems continued to grow: (1) decreasing agricultural output, resulting from poor technology applied to an unfavorable natural environment; (2) heavy taxation and heavy rents which drove poorer lands out of production, even on a subsistence basis; (3) decrease in population, from a rise in death rates and a possible fall in birth rates (from late marriage, abortion, infanticide, and other causes) especially among the peasants; (4) a great increase in the demand for nonproductive manpower, because of the increased army, bureaucracy, and clergy; (5) the impact of inflation, the slow shift from money relationships and obligations to relations in kind (that is the drift from a commercialized to a non-commercialized economy); (6) the inability of the backward ancient technology in land transportation to service a great empire, largely with two-wheeled ox-drawn vehicles; and (7) the way in which the great mass of the population were increasingly excluded from the system, totally disarmed, economically exploited so that their very survival on the lowest level of subsistence was threatened, alienated from it socially, emotionally, and intellectually, so that the shift from Roman rulers to barbarian tribesmen roused little real opposition.

One additional element in this situation, which links the ruling minority and the alienated masses together, was the steady increase in the inequality in distribution of incomes, something which was supported, defended, and intensified by the power structure. This surplus in incomes at the top, used for non-productive purposes, kept the demand for luxury goods high for centuries after the curve of production in necessities had turned downward. The crisis in the production of necessities came in the third century, but the production of, or at least the demand for, luxuries was still as high as ever in A.D. 600. Moreover, during that period of almost four centuries, the growing corruption and violence excluded honest and hardworking people from access to the ruling system or even from the state, including access to justice or to public office. Both of these were increasingly expensive to a degree that honest, hardworking men could not pay. Both justice and public office required higher and higher costs of access (bribery or sale, if you will) from the fact that these two, plus access to the higher levels of the military system, became access to the affluence of the ruling minority and escape from the grinding poverty of the ruled majority.

From this point of view, the question, "Why did Rome fall?" is not difficult, but it is the wrong question. The correct question is, "Why did the eastern part of the empire survive, when the western part fell?"

The answer is that the resources of the empire as a whole were increasingly inadequate to support the whole empire, especially in a period in which problems were growing in intensity. The empire had to reduce its commitments to a level on which it could handle problems of growing intensity with reduced resources. This reduction of commitments could be made most easily by a reduction in size of the area over which there were commitments. The basic commitments were (1) a frontier too long by

far, because it included too many large areas (like
Britain, the Rhineland, and Danubia) which contributed much less in strength than they required in use
of defensive resources; and (2) the internal area,
within these extended frontiers, was far too large
for the government, in the existing low level of
communications and transportation, to control, or
even to respond adequately to rapidly changing conditions or to sudden crises.

The key to both of these was that Rome, by pushing outward from the Mediterranean basin, in which
the empire had begun, had extended itself into areas
which could not be serviced or reached by sea power,
but had to be serviced by land transportation and
land power, at a time when the barbarian mobility
on land was growing and the Roman mobility on land
was decreasing. The solution to this problem was
to retract to the Mediterranean basin, or part of
it, to an area which could be serviced by sea and
would include all areas whose resources substantially
exceeded those needed to defend themselves.

That this was the real problem is clear from
all the evidence, especially the evidence associated with the mobility of defensive forces. Constantine created a central field army within the
empire as a force to sustain the frontier defenses
when these were threatened. But it was clear, within one generation, that this force could not be
moved about quickly enough to respond to threats,
even if they did not occur simultaneously, which
might arise in Britain, in Syria, on the Rhine, in
Dacia, or in Africa or Anatolia. Consequently this
field army had to be broken up, at first into four,
but soon into seven, sections. But these seven
field armies soon became fixed at garrison towns,
became increasingly diverted to maintaining public
order within the empire, and were so expensive and
so favored, that the frontier forces became increasingly incapable of slowing up an intruder long enough
for the nearest field army to come up in time to
stop the intrusion.

This situation is parallel to what happened in
American football, after the forward pass was introduced in 1906. The secondary defense had to with-

561

draw backward from the 7-man line of scrimmage and, by 1920, began to withdraw linemen into the secondary defenses, so that the 7-man defensive line was gradually reduced to six and to five-man lines. By 1930 the Southwest, which emphasized the pass more than the rest of the country, was using four and even three-man defensive lines on expected pass plays, but this opened the way to running plays, developing from fake pass formations, to make sufficient yardage to earn first downs. At that point the rulemakers began to change the rules, including the size of the field, the shape of the ball, and the rules of the game to favor passing plays.

In the late Roman empire there were no rulemakers, but the late Roman emperors were in a position to change the size of the field, the shape of the ball, and how they used their limited manpower. They failed to do so, until forced into it in the third and subsequent centuries.

What they were forced into was the decision to retract the empire to the Mediterranean and to the eastern end of that basin, even if that involved abandoning Rome and Italy. It was a correct decision as is evident from the fact that the eastern empire lasted another thousand years (to 1453).

Accordingly, the answer to the question, "Why did Byzantium survive, while the west fell?" is: "Because the government decided to save the east and sacrifice the west, and the objective conditions sustained the correctness of that decision."

The decision was correct because the east was much more developed, both in agriculture and in manufacturing, was more populated, had more cities, and had a shorter frontier. Most of these advantages came from the fact that the east was older, while much of the west was still semi-frontier communities. In the west, south of the mountains, irrigation was not developed nearly as much as in the east and, of course, the west had nothing to compare to Egypt in agricultural productivity, since the Abyssinian monsoon not only refertilized the Nile valley but allowed a crop to be raised on the same fields each year. The ordinary classical two-field system, used

562

regularly in the west, allowed cultivation no more than every alternate year, made little use of fertilizers, had much less irrigated land, and its best lands were uncultivable, with the existing technology and were accessible only by inefficient land transportation. North of the mountains, in Gaul, Germany, or Britain, where irrigation was unnecessary, the primitive classical scratch plow could not turn the best lands (the alluvial river valleys or bottomlands) but was largely restricted to the higher and lighter upland soils because of lack of any adequate system of animal traction capable of turning heavier soils with a plow.

The east had other advantages. It had a more equitable distribution of both property and incomes, had a stronger tradition of law and order and of loyalty to a monarchical ruler, so that civil wars were less endemic in the east, and the east came much closer to finding some answer to the problem of succession: the method devised by Diocletian for providing a successor by cooptation to a college of rulers and choice by that college, worked somewhat better in the east and made intervention by either the army or the senate less likely. In effect, the designation of a successor by a ruling emperor, which was used in the subsequent Byzantine, Arabic, Ottoman, and Romanov empires, functioned better in the east than in the west.

At least as significant as these basic reasons, dealing with non-military factors, were the military factors, both strategic and tactical. This involves the much better strategic position in the east, especially the defense of Constantinople. From the Bosporus sea power could control and link together the eastern basin of the Mediterranean, including areas of high productivity such as Egypt with areas of large population such as the Levant, Anatolia, and the Balkans. Constantinople, with its great walls, could hardly be taken by direct attack and, so long as it controlled the sea, it could hardly be starved out. Moreover, if it controlled the Straits, it could prevent a besieger from crossing between Europe and Asia. If the enemy came from Europe, the eastern emperors could draw resources from Asia; if the enemy came from

Asia, they could draw on Europe's strength; and, if the enemy came from both Asia and Europe, as sometimes happened, control of the sea allowed the city to draw resources from elsewhere in the Mediterranean, including the islands.

In spite of this emphasis on sea power, Constantinople had, almost by nature, a system of land defenses in depth. If an enemy burst over the Danube, or the Black Sea, coming from Europe, they became dispersed in ravaging Thrace, Macedonia, or the northern Balkans, had to cross the difficult terrain of the Balkans (which tends to disperse any offensive from the north), had to get control of the Straits to besiege the city completely, and finally came up to the impregnable walls of Constantinople. If the enemy came from Africa or Asia, he had to break into Anatolia through some passage in the Taurus Mountains of southwest Anatolia (such as the Cilician Gates), then had to cross the difficult terrain of Cappadocia and all Anatolia, then had to break across the Straits into Europe to reach the walls of Constantinople. As we shall see in the next section, this natural strategic strength of the eastern empire was increased by a conscious policy of defense in depth, a mobile field army, a recognition of the role of sea power, a new ideology based on a fanatical version of Christianity, and a policy of diverting invaders who could not be stopped outright westward into Italy and Gaul or across North Africa.

In the west, Italy could have been defended from Milan using a force across the Po valley and its adjacent plains to destroy an enemy emerging from the Alpine passes, but no naval power could be directed from Rome (or Milan), and any effort to defend the west from Italy would have meant abandoning both the Balkans and Gaul to the Germans who would then cross Spain and invade Africa from Gibraltar, as they did in 429.

In the west, Italy, the Balkans, Gaul, Spain, and Africa were too separated to defend all five from any one of them, and any attempt to do this would inevitably create a situation in which the area of occupation was too large to be held with

the resource base which could be controlled from
any one of the five.

Moreover, when the decision was made to abandon the west in order to save the east, not only was
the resource base in the east greater, and the strategic control from a single center far more hopeful,
but it was unthinkable in the fifth and sixth centuries that any threat could arise from the southern
deserts, so that the greatest area of food resources
in the east, Egypt, seemed remote from all serious
danger and could be protected against the only apparent threat, Persia, so long as Constantinople
could control the Syrian Saddle and the sea lanes
of the eastern Mediterranean. The fact that the only
civilized enemy on any Roman frontier was Persia and
that no one could forsee the totally unexpected rise
of Islam in the seventh century made the decision to
save the east at the cost of the west a sound one in
the fifth century.

We have said that the barbarians along the Rhine
were still fighting on foot, when the Ostrogoths and
Visigoths on the lower Danube had adopted cavalry.
Moreover, the Germans on the lower Rhine, the Franks,
were already federati by 400. It is very likely that
the Rhine could have been held, but the threat across
the Danube was greater and, accordingly, the Rhine
was weakened by withdrawal of forces from Gaul to
strengthen the Danube. Even on the Danube the frontier could have been held, or reestablished, if it
had not been for the Huns who emerged from Asia along
the steppe corridor, north of the Black Sea, shattered
the Ostrogoths and defeated the Visigoths in A.D. 372.
While the Huns turned westward into central Europe,
eventually assembling a great variety of peoples into
a great, semi-nomadic empire centered on the Danube
and Theiss Rivers, the Visigoths sought refuge by
crossing the Danube into the underpopulated northern
Balkans, but were so ill-treated by the Roman administrators that they took to the warpath and eventually annihilated a Roman force, killing the Emperor
Valens, near Adrianople, in 378.

After ravaging the northern Balkans for years,
the Visigoths moved into Italy in 401, sacked Rome
in 410, crossed the Alps and invaded Gaul in 412,

finally moving into Spain in 415, where they defeated the Vandals and Alans on behalf of Rome, before they were settled as federates around Toulouse with two-thirds of the land.

These disturbances in the south weakened the Rhine frontier over which various German tribes, led by the Vandals, poured in 406-407. After sacking Reims, Amiens, and other towns, the Vandals crossed Gaul, entered Spain (409), and, twenty years later, crossed into Africa. There the Vandals ravaged widely, entirely displaced Roman authority, and acquired a fleet in which they crossed the sea to sack Rome (455). This Vandal sea power disrupted control of the Mediterranean, broke up the empire, and by cutting off much of Italy's food supply, forced abandonment of many of its cities.

The Ostrogoths had been shattered and scattered by the Hunnish attack in 372, but a considerable number of them became part of the Funnish empire in Hungary for the next 80 years. In 451-452, under Attila, this motley association of semi-nomadic peoples raided westward again, ravaging Gaul. Defeated by a force of Visigothic and other federati near Troyes in 451, Attila turned south into Italy, where his army, hungry and weakened by plague, was deterred from sacking Rome by a delegation led by Pope Leo. Retreating north into Pannonia Attila died, and his empire broke up into its constituent peoples (453-454).

The Ostrogoths, freed from Hunnish domination in 454, settled in Pannonia as federati, but a generation later, under Theodoric, invaded the Balkans and marched on Constantinople but were diverted into Italy by the eastern Emperor Zeno. In 488 Zeno gave Theodoric a commission, as federatus ally, to expel from Italy the rebel Odovacar who had compelled the last western emperor to resign in 476.

Theodoric killed Odovacar with his own hands, massacred his troops, and set himself up with his Ostrogoths as agent of the eastern emperor, ruling northern Italy from Ravanna (493). He took one-third of the land for his Ostrogoths, using these Germans exclusively in all military posts as agents, through himself, of the eastern emperor. Theodoric admired the Roman system and way of life and kept all of its forms, laws, coinage, taxes, and offices in operation, as much as possible, while seeking to raise the cultural and social level of his own Ostrogoths to the point where these Roman ways could be applied to them also.

Theodoric allied himself, both politically and by marriage, with the Visigoths in Spain, the Franks in northern Gaul, and the Burgundians in southeastern Gaul, annexed southern Gaul to Italy, and acted as regent of the Visigothic kingdom on behalf of its child-king, his grandson. Shortly after his death, in 526, the eastern imperial forces, under Belisarius and Narses, conquered Ostrogothic Italy, Vandal Africa, and southeastern Visigothic Spain (533-554), but all of these were lost in the next century, Africa and Spain to the Saracens, and Italy to the last Germanic invaders of Italy, the Lombards.

The Lombards, who had formed part of Attila's Hunnish empire in the fifth century, fought as allies of the Avars against other Germanic peoples (Ostrogoths, Gepids, etc.), helped Belisarius to reconquer northern Italy and carved out an area around Pavia as a kingdom for themselves, with the popes south of them in Rome and the quiescent Byzantines east of them in control of the Adriatic Sea and Ravenna.

All of these Germanic peoples were either pagans or became Arian Christians (from the influence of the Arian bishop, Ulfilas, 311-381, who translated the Bible into Gothic). As Arians, the Visigoths, Ostrogoths, Lombards, and others were regarded as heretics by the Roman provincials over whom they ruled, and by the clergy of both Rome and Constantinople.

This situation was used to their own advantage by the only orthodox Christian German tribe, the Franks. As a non-Arian Christian, Clovis, king of the Franks, in northeastern Gaul and along the lower Rhine, found support among the Christian Roman provincials and from clergy and bishops everywhere. With this he combined political skills, ruthlessness, and great military success to become the dominant political figure in the west.

With the withdrawal of imperial forces from the Rhine and northern Gaul, Clovis used his position as _federatus_ in that area to seize the Roman administrative system (including the treasury at Soissons) and to administer it in the name of the absent Roman emperor. The provincials generally acquiesced, the pope and bishops approved, the emperor could do nothing, and all other tribes or persons who opposed were crushed and killed.

The Franks did not migrate as a nation, like other Germans, but expanded from their base on the lower Rhine, making skilled use of their triple power: religious orthodoxy, legal and political position in respect to the Roman emperor, and military superiority. By 560 they had control of both sides of the Rhine, most of northern and central Gaul as far as the Garonne and the Loire valley. By that date, classical civilization had ceased to exist, Byzantine civilization was already born in the Near East, and the Franks, without clearly knowing what they were doing, were trying to revive or maintain, to their own benefit, whatever they liked of classical civilization.

The military aspects of this process, both the disappearance of Rome in the west and the ability of the Franks to take over control of the west, have been much misunderstood until recently. The Franks obtained their control of the west, at a time when Byzantium had abandoned that area, by copying Roman weapons, tactics, and military organization as closely as possible. The Franks succeeded in doing this when other, more numerous and more powerful groups of Germans failed because they were, in the earlier period, say the third and fourth centuries, the least qualified to defeat the Romans on any battlefield. The failure of historians to see this, or to understand the military aspects of this crucial period until recently, lies in a total misconception of the military side of the "fall of Rome." This misconception was the belief that the barbarian invaders defeated Roman armies and destroyed the classical way of life by superior weapons and tactics. Nothing

could be further from the truth. Except for the
Huns, who had a special position and are, in some
ways, the key to the whole situation, the barbarian
military threat was pathetic. It can be stated
truthfully and dogmatically that no Germanic people
had weapons, tactics, military organization, or
even military leadership superior in quality to
Roman weapons, tactics, organization, and leadership. The Roman failure was not in these elements,
but in the fact that it was drastically overextended
in a quantitative sense at a time when the external
pressures were maximized and when the Roman system
was undergoing a drastic shift of allegiances.
This shift of allegiances began as a loss of the
outlook and beliefs of classical civilization before the appearance of any consensus on the new outlook and beliefs of Byzantine civilization; this
greatly weakened the Roman defense system, whose
quality was still comparatively high, but whose
quantity was not sufficient to cope successfully
with the challenges triggered by the arrival of
the Huns when the imperial frontiers were far too
long and its territories far too large.

Qualitatively, of course, there were fluctuations in Roman military capacity. This may have
reached a low ebb about 260, but the great challenge to the empire came more than a century later
when a considerable qualitative, and some quantitative, recovery had taken place. At the time of
the Hunnish and Germanic invasions, from 373 to
after 500, the Roman defense still included artillery and a navy, considerably reduced in both
quantity and quality but still far superior to
their enemies who had nothing of the first and very
little of the second; it had massed infantry
armed with missiles, swords, and spears; it had
cavalry, both fully armored and less well protected,
equipped with both archery and shock weapons; and
the Romans still had fortified bases, an effective
supply system, and an outstanding tradition of military skills and knowledge. The Germans had almost
none of these things, although the Huns did have
excellent cavalry with outstanding composite bows.
However, for most of the period of the German threat,
the Huns were not part of this threat but were allied with the Romans, or at least were on the Ro-

man payroll, either as clients or as recipients of tribute payments. These payments were made because the Huns were recognized as a potentially dangerous enemy. But they were also seen by some as a very helpful ally against the Germans, whose military incapacity in comparison with the Huns, although much less wide than their inferiority in comparison with the Romans, was such that the Romans could use the Huns when they saw fit to destroy any German people totally. This was done to the Burgundians by Aetius in 436 and was almost done to the Visigoths three years later, but these were saved at the last moment and raised again by Aetius to a unique position among all the Germans in Gaul (as an independent sovereign entity) in the hope that, having learned a lesson, they would abandon their usual anti-Roman attitude and perhaps be available in the future as a counter-weight against the Huns. This was exactly what happened in 451, when Aetius used the Visigoths as his chief force in the defeat of Attila at Troyes.

In any battle between the Huns and an approximately equal force of Romans, the latter were, on the whole, superior, but the outcome could go either way. But battles between the two were very rare and occurred only when the Romans tried to curtail their patronage to the Huns and were, at the same time, fully occupied elsewhere with other problems. The Huns had no desire to fight or to defeat the Romans, since they recognized that trade with Rome and payments of gold from the imperial government, whether subsidies as allies or tribute extorted by blackmail, were the chief source of the income which was the main purpose of the Hunnish federation and held it together. Attila's position depended on the continued existence of the Roman system as it was, with its trade restrictions on exports (except to the Hunnish chief), its closed frontier (which could retrieve Hunnish runaways, either slaves or traitors), and its ability to gather gold from its own subjects. Accordingly, there were no real battles between Huns and Romans until 443. There were a few raids of dissident Huns into the empire earlier, notably in 395, when they were repulsed by local Roman forces, and in 408, when they entered through a

betrayed border fortress and were bribed to withdraw.
On the other hand, the Huns were allied with the empire as early as 388 and, allied or not, were regarded at all times as potential allies on the rear
of the Germans whom they were pushing into the empire. It must be recognized that the whole situation was not at all the simple challenge which is
portrayed in most history books. No leaders in these
struggles wanted to end them in order to get back to
peaceful constructive living through hard work and
economic production. Whatever the exploited masses
may have felt, the struggles themselves had become
a way of life, the only way of life the leaders
knew and could do, and they had no desire to end
them. Moreover, all parties in these struggles
were themselves divided, and treachery, or semi-
treachery and tacit treachery, was at least as important as skill in battle.

As Ernest Stein, E.A. Thompson, and other
students of this period have pointed out, Romans
were very dissatisfied with their society at that
time. Many of the Roman masses, especially in Spain,
welcomed German rulers because the taxes and other
burdens were much lighter. Other Romans, sometimes
of the upper classes, had renounced Roman society
and gone to live with the Germans or the Huns and,
in some cases, had gone to fight with them, as the
priest, Salvian, tells us in detail. A Roman,
Orestes, whose son Romulus was later to be the
last Roman emperor in the west, was one of Attila's
chief lieutenants. In 449, when Priscus went with
the imperial ambassador to Attila's camp, he found
a once prosperous Greek merchant living there by
choice. The ex-merchant's complaint against Roman
society was the same as Salvian's expressed in that
cleric's book, De Gubernatione Dei, written in the
same decade; both decried the all-pervasive injustice and corruption of Roman society.

The gist of Salvian's plaint was: "Who can
help the poor and oppressed when even Christian
priests do not oppose wicked men. The poor are
oppressed, widows mourn, orphans so crushed, that
many well-born and cultured persons flee to the
enemy to escape death here from public persecution,
seeking Roman humanity among the barbarians because

571

they cannot stand the barbarous inhumanity of the Romans. And, although they differ from these in customs and language, and in the smell of their bodies and rough clothing, yet they would rather put up with a different way of life among barbarians than with raging injustice among the Romans. They do not regret their flight, for they would rather live free under apparent captivity than live as captives under apparent freedom. So that the name of Roman citizen, once esteemed so high and acquired at great cost, is now voluntarily rejected and fled from and considered not only cheap and contemptible, but as abominable and a burden."

Thompson believes that the social divisions in Rome helped to paralyze policy within the government, between the landlords who wished to fight the Huns at the cost of the merchants and lower classes and the commercial class who wished to keep peace with the Huns at the cost of tribute payments which would come, at least partly, from the landlords.

But Attila did not want either peace or war; he wanted intermittent episodes of both, to get tribute, arms, and luxury goods for his ruling groups and lieutenants in time of peace and to get plunder to keep his warriors satisfied in briefer intervals of war.

Similarly, the Roman generals in the west, especially Aetius, did not want to destroy either the Huns or the Germans, since the general's own autonomous power depended on the continued existence of both and the pressure of at least one of them on the Roman government in the east.

Fundamentally the situation during the invasions involved at least four parties, all of them divided and none of them willing to see one of the others destroyed and thus eliminated from the interplay of the four. The four were: the imperial government, largely in the east after 384 (or even after 284); the Roman generals, especially those of barbarian origins in the west, who were more like Chinese warlords of 1920 than military agents of the imperial Roman government; the Germans; and the Huns. It was this reluctance to see any party eliminated which partly explains much of what happened for more than a century after the appearance of the Huns about 371. It explains why Attila tacitly cooperated with Aetius throughout and especially why he made no real effort to destroy Rome by allying with the Vandals of Africa, the Visigoths of Gaul, or the rebellious Gauls (Bagaudae) when the Huns invaded Gaul and Italy from central Europe in 450-452; it also explains why Aetius prevented the allies he had assembled to resist this invasion from destroying the Huns after the latter were defeated in 451, by dismissing the Visigoths and Franks so that Attila could escape. In a similar way, German forces under leaders such as Alaric were allowed to roam about the empire, defeated but never annihilated, and encouraged by Roman governments or generals, east and west, to go toward the other half of the empire.

To understand the events of these years in order to evaluate the role of weapons and the military factor in what was happening, we must keep in mind not only the divided interests and ambivalent aims of the four parties in the chaos, but we must also be aware of the fact that the names we give to the barbarian forces are quite misleading. We call them "tribes," thus implying that they were kinship groups with presumably solid loyalty to members of the "tribes." This is totally erroneous. There may have been kinship groupings, or even tribes, involved in the chaotic struggles of this period, but the terms Huns, Visigoths, Ostrogoths, Vandals, and Franks do not refer to kinship groupings at all. They refer to federations (often very brittle and ephemeral) of peoples held together by clientage and similar mutual relationships, that is by reciprocal benefits along lines of personal loyalty between the leader of the federation and the leaders of the lesser parts of the federation. Each leader probably had a kinship group, at least his own family, in his part, but neither the federation nor its chief parts were based on kinship, nor on any objective or permanent basis of mutual loyalty. The names of the federations reveal nothing about the parts, which could often have quite different languages and customs. Thus Attila's chief lieutenants seem to have been mostly non-Huns including one Roman citizen and his closest personal advisor was a Gepid German.

573

As a result of this situation, "Huns," "Franks," or "Goths" were to be found fighting on both sides of most battles of this period. Thus at Adrianople in 378, there were Goths, and probably Alans and Huns on both sides, and at Troyes in 451, there were Franks, Alans, and probably Huns on both sides. As a consequence of this lack of solid loyalty and the dominant role in individual and group decisions played by momentary self-interest, in many battles and most campaigns, there were betrayals and semi-betrayals on both sides. Frontier fortresses and even fortified cities were captured by barbarians who had neither the knowledge nor the equipment to capture any fortified place; they were taken by betrayal. Such betrayals were even made to the Huns, who were regarded with special repugnance by most Romans, as in the case just mentioned in 408, when the most important border fortress in Moesia was betrayed. When Attila invaded the west in 450, he had just received an appeal for help from Honoria against her brother, the Emperor Valentinian III.

These conditions of precarious loyalty continued through this whole period and were a constant factor in the political structure of providential monarchy which I shall describe in the next section. For example, when Belisarius was besieged in Rome by the Goths in 537, the Roman people caused him more worry than the Goths, and he walled up most of the city gates so they could not be opened from inside the city.

I have said that the Huns were capable of defeating the Romans in an equal fight, but they had no real weapons advantage over the Romans except perhaps in the single arm of cavalry archers and the slight superiority of a Qum Darya bow over a Yrzi bow. They did defeat the Romans in 443 and again in 447 and used these victories to impose tribute payments, but the Romans were able to defeat at least parts of the Huns as they did in the final battle at Sardica in the 460s, just as the Germans defeated the Huns after Attila's death, in a battle on the Nedao River in 454. The battle at Sardica is interesting because Roman infantry defeated the Huns after the Roman cavalry had deserted to the enemy, according to Sidonius Apollinarius (c. 430-480).

While the Huns could defeat Rome in battles, they could never have defeated Rome in a war or have destroyed the Roman state, because the clientage structure which supported Hunnish power was on a level of political organization far inferior to that of Rome even in its worst days. The evidence for this lies in the fact that Attila's organization must fall apart after a couple of defeats (or after his death), because his chief lieutenants could be rewarded or sustained only by victories which would yield booty or tribute which they could pass on to their followers. As soon as such incomes ceased, these subordinates would be compelled to abandon the leader to seek some other system which would yield the incomes needed to retain the allegiance of their own subordinates. Rome, on the other hand, could be strengthened by defeat since this could force it backward to less extensive borders which could be more successfully held intact with the available resources. In fact, the Hunnish system could even be destroyed by a series of victories because it could not stand excessive prosperity which might encourage any lieutenant to go into business for himself, that is to use his greater income and accumulated wealth to dispense with the leader by hiring more lieutenants of his own and making himself top leader. With Rome a series of victories might make it stronger and wealthier. That is why we place the state form of power structure on a higher level than the clientage form, which is itself higher than the kinship form.

As Thompson has shown, Hunnish "society" by 449 was no longer a nomadic society of herders but was "a parasitic community of marauders." Attila himself was an incompetent whose whole success was based on his recognition (not invention) that a larger and more powerful system could be constructed by using clientage links of personal loyalty and reciprocal advantages than by using kinship. As J.B. Bury showed (1928) it was the widespread recognition of this discovery by the Germans that explains why the German "tribes" mentioned in Tacitus (c. 100 A.D.) have such different names from those mentioned in the same areas in the fourth century. Except for this recognition and his insatiable desires, Attila had very little. His military skills were limited, and his diplomacy was nonsensical, even in terms of his own desires. In both of these he was far inferior to another much greater, and much later, nomad ruler, Jenghis Khan.

Attila had one slight weapons advantage, the Qum Darya bow. The Germans had none. They had no weapon, tactics, organization, leadership, nor ideology superior, or even equal, to those of the Romans. In fact, without either a fully nomadic or a fully agricultural base, they lacked the resources either to defend themselves against the Huns or to challenge the Romans. All they could do was to wander about in a semi-starved condition, until they were torn to shreds by the Huns and forced into the empire where they were torn up even more as refugees. They had nothing except numbers and desperation.

Here, once again, we reach a historical myth which has been in the history books for a long time. This error is that the Germans had effective cavalry forces, even "heavy cavalry," earlier than the Romans and that the Germans brought about "the decline of Rome" by using their superior weaponry to inflict irreparable military defeats on the Romans. Specifically, this error centers on the statement, to quote Bury (1928), that at Adrianople in 378 "the legions had the novel experience of being ridden down by the heavy cavalry of the German warriors." As a result, according to Bury, the Romans themselves turned from infantry to heavy cavalry in the following century. This shift was necessary in order to survive, but the time and effort to do this was so great that the Germans were able to destroy the Roman empire in the west, a fact symbolized by the removal of the last emperor in Rome, Romulus Augustulus, by the German general Odoacer in 476.

It must be stated firmly that the sense and implications of that last paragraph, and of many of the nouns in it, is erroneous or misleading. The Germans did, occasionally, defeat Roman armies, usually as a consequence of the incompetence, errors, or betrayals by individual Roman commanders. The Germans also were able, on numerous occasions, to capture Roman cities and towns in spite of the fact that they had no siege trains or artillery, or much understanding of siege techniques until after the sixth century. They could capture towns because urban walls had been constructed after the defeat of Decius in 251 and were in poor repair when the Germans broke into the interior after the defeat of Valens in 378. Moreover, the steady decrease in population, especially urban population, left the defenders with insufficient numbers to man the whole extent of the third century walls and with neither the time nor the resources to build new shorter walls.

These erroneous ideas about the military history of the late Roman empire have been rejected by a number of recent scholars (since about 1930), although no one of these has had a complete idea of the problem. The errors are still entrenched in many history books, especially in the English-speaking world, where the mistakes on this subject of Sir Charles Oman and others (including Bury) are still prevalent. Oman's theories were first persuasively stated in his undergraduate essay, The Art of War in the Middle Ages, 378-1515, written at Oxford, first published in 1885, and still in print and widely read in a somewhat revised form (1953). Bury, who was a very great scholar, had little grasp of military realities and seems to have adopted his general interpretation on too many points from Oman. Other historians of lesser scholarship than Bury seem to share his inability to rid themselves of Oman's facile generalizations even when the facts they know do not support these.

The specific errors to which I refer are these: (1) that the Germans had heavy cavalry in the invasion period and the Romans did not; (2) that the Romans adopted such heavy cavalry as a consequence of the German threat; (3) that Rome still had the legion as a tactical unit in 378; (4) that Rome "fell" because of military defeats caused by its inferior weaponry; and (5) that mounted spearmen, per se, are a more effective weapon than infantry and other arms.

The historian of military matters in any period needs factual information and some understanding of military realities in order to interpret the facts. Bury did not realize that he had neither.

577

He tried to bridge over the gap of the poorly recorded fifth century between Ammianus Marcellinus in the
fourth century (covering 353-378) and Procopius in
the sixth century (covering 527-554). Leaving aside
the errors which Bury made in his bridge, he was
mistaken in his belief that either Ammianus or Procopius was a satisfactory source for information on
military matters. They are almost all we have, but
their accounts of battles, weapons, and tactics are
very deficient. In many cases they describe military actions in such general terms that it is not
possible to be sure if the fighters are on horses
or on foot, nor, in some cases, what weapons they
are using.

There were hundreds of battles in Europe from
A.D. 250 to 950. Of these at least a score were
of major significance. We do not have, and are
never likely to have, a satisfactory description
of a single one of these combats. Such a satisfactory description would include the following
elements: (1) the terrain; (2) the weapons; (3)
the numbers of men engaged and their organization;
(4) the tactics used; and (5) the strategy being
followed. Almost none of the written sources come
from writers who thought in terms of these five
factors or considered it necessary to write of these
even when they were actually present at the battle
and must have observed them. This may be because
most writers of the day were not directly concerned
with how the battle was fought but with the meaning
of its outcome. So long as the classical outlook
remained dominant, the writers were often military
men, from Caesar to Arrian and Procopius, but they
were concerned with questions of how individuals
conducted themselves, with their valor, honor, and
"immortality" (in the classical sense). When their
attention shifted to a broader frame, their interests shifted from the military to the political aspects of the combat. Later, as the medieval outlook
increasingly replaced the classical, writers came
increasingly under religious influences and had
little concern with tactics or weapons, but were
concerned again with the outcome of the battle, but
this time as evidence of divine providence. The
question of how it was won would have been of little interest to the religious who increasingly kept
the written records. The few surviving monumental

records are equally remote from any concern with weapons or tactics and are concerned either with personal honor (in the classical context) or with divine providence (in the medieval context). Pictorial evidence, as I have already pointed out, such as Trajan's Column, the Bayeux tapestry, illuminated manuscripts, and tombstones, is very difficult to understand because of the distortions of artistic conventions or from simple ignorance based on the fact that it is often produced by non-military persons such as artisans, clergy, even women, who have little knowledge or interest in weapons or tactics.

We may find new archaeological evidence, especially from grave goods or from battlefields themselves, but they will not reveal much about tactics, which is our chief lacuna. It must be emphasized that it is very dangerous to attempt to infer tactics from weapons, or even to be sure that an object is a weapon when it is found. The Paleolithic "hand axe" was probably a tool for digging roots originally and may have become a tool for skinning or cutting up meat, but many persons simply assume that it was a weapon. Similarly the bayonet was a defensive weapon of infantry against cavalry when it was invented about 1690; by 1916 it was an offensive weapon against entrenched infantry; in 1944 it was used chiefly for opening containers and most bayonet wounds were accidentally self-inflicted. So we cannot infer that a long curved sword in a grave of 1200 B.C. or of A.D. 650 was a cavalry saber, as is sometimes done.

Many historians who touch on military matters are victims of a pervasive misconception which we might call the "myth of the crucial weapon," that is the belief that possession of one specific weapon assures victory or security. We saw one version of this idea, on a wide scale, in 1946-1950 when many neo-experts were calling the A-bomb the "final" or "ultimate" weapon. It may be true that the introduction of a new weapon can determine the outcome of a battle, but it is most unlikely to determine the outcome of a war. The outcome of a war and the military security of a community depends on a balance of factors, including much more than any single weapon. Every weapon has its weakness which can be exploited by the enemy by using the same weapon or a different one; in the latter case, defense against it requires a different weapon, or at least a different tactic. The idea that the Roman legion, the medieval knight, or the Hunnish archer, or any weapon at all, is "invincible" is nonsense, not only because no weapon is invincible but equally because the important thing about any weapon is not the weapon itself, but the way it is used, and this depends on many other things such as morale or even terrain. Military security depends on weapons mix and flexibility.

If we try to enumerate what is involved in weapons mix, we can hardly do so. In the period we are considering we might say that a satisfactory weapons mix would include four elements: a sturdy mass of infantry; a solid cavalry force; a good shock weapon; and a good missile weapon. If we obtained this by a strong combination of legionary spearmen and cavalry archers, we might win a battle, if we also had good leadership and an adequate knowledge of the enemy and his movements. But since the enemy can usually avoid a battle, this leads to a campaign, which requires supplies and secure bases. But secure bases leads to questions of fortifications and siege trains. Any adequate weapons mix must have all these things, and, in addition, these factors, with other factors, must be used flexibly.

One weakness in much writing about this period of military history is the unconscious assumption that whatever is later must be better (a 19th century idea). Thus if the medieval knight followed the Roman legion, the knight must be a better weapon. This again is nonsense. A later weapon is not necessarily better; it may only be different. Since all these matters are relative, it is inadvisable to make absolute judgments about weapons, but in this case it is probably safe to say that the mounted spearman is so inferior a weapon that the chief weapon below it in merit would be a single infantry spearman. Several infantry spearmen cooperating together would be superior to a mounted lancer, but only if he attacked them, which he does not have to do because he has mobility.

Certainly the Roman experience with armored lancers over several centuries (200 B.C. to A.D. 312) seemed to show that they had little value, and Constantine seems to have ceased to recruit for them after he defeated the cataphracts of Maxentius before Turin in 312. They were revived by Constantius II (337-361) who seems to have taken great pride in them, and they reciprocated by helping to win the battle of Mursa, after which they were a focus of attention in his triumphal entry into Rome in 357. They continued as an arm of the Roman field army, and there were at least eight units of cataphracti in the Notitia Dignitatum of the early fifth century. John W. Eadie, who made an intensive study of the Roman experience with this arm (1967) concluded, "The Roman experiments with mailed cavalry, especially the clibanarium, ended in failure. In their attempt to defy reality, however, the Romans demonstrated once again their willingness to adopt military techniques and tactics--even if these were manifestly impracticable." I can only agree with this conclusion, while pointing out that armored lancers may have had a different use and value in western Europe in the tenth century, with a better horse, more fodder, and a forested terrain.

In discussing matters of this kind, historians concentrate on defeats while often ignoring the reasons for the defeat, drawing conclusions about weapons from the mere fact of the defeat. They ignore the fact that anyone can lose a battle, but it is not true that anyone can win one. A single defeat is often very important and may be fatal to a regime (as it was at Hastings in 1066), but the quality of a weapons system cannot be judged from a single defeat; it can only be judged by a series of victories. Historians ignore this truth and make judgments about the superiority of German heavy cavalry at Adrianople (378), at Tours (732), or at Hastings, when the Germans had no heavy cavalry at the first, although the Romans probably did; neither side had heavy cavalry at Tours; and the heavy cavalry won at Hastings for reasons that had nothing to do with the heavy cavalry.

From what we have seen in this book, it is clear that, in weapons mix and tactical flexibility the Romans in 350-500 had little to learn from the Germans, or even from the Huns. The best the Germans had to offer were unarmored mounted spearmen, with some of their leaders wearing segmented corselets. The Sarmatians, by this date scattered all over Europe and invariably defeated by the Romans whenever they met, were originally armored, and sometimes fully armored, clibanarii. But the Romans had met and defeated such units since 190 B.C., usually with their infantry, and at Strassburg had won the battle with their own infantry after the German infantry had dispersed the Roman cataphracts; they had defeated them with Roman cavalry archers at Immae in 272 and had used such cataphracts themselves successfully at Mursa in 351. The Romans had such cavalry lancers themselves since at least 150 B.C., had them fully armored by A.D. 150, and had cavalry archers before A.D. 100. Arrian, who defeated the Alan invasion of heavy cavalry in A.D. 134, had written a number of treatises on Asiatic military history and on tactics including instructions on how to defeat such enemies. Any consideration of Strassburg in 357 or of Mursa in 351 will show what Roman armies were capable of in the same generation as Adrianople.

The battle of Mursa (September 351) was fought between two contenders to the imperial throne, entirely by mercenaries, and was the bloodiest battle of the fourth century (much worse than Adrianople). Zonaras says that the victor, Constantius, lost 30,000 of his 80,000 troops, while the usurper, Magnentius, lost 24,000 out of 36,000. This was a notable battle in the history of tactics, and this may have had something to do with the heavy casualties. Both cavalry and archers made major contributions on the winning side. The opposing forces were drawn up in a bend of the Drave River, with Constantius' cavalry on his left overlapping Magnentius' right. Armenian archers (infantry) were used by the victor to inflict heavy losses on the enemy, but the decisive blow seems to have been an oblique cavalry charge by cataphracts from the left against the usurper's main force of Gallic legionary cohorts. Thus the victory went to Roman shock cavalry.

Six years later, when Constantius made his

triumphal entry into Rome, Ammianus Marcellinus
admired the emperor's glittering cataphracts (without, apparently, realizing that their totally enclosed plumed helmets, which he describes, were
only parade gear). But that same year, the other
co-emperor, Julianus, won a great victory over the
Alemanni near Strassburg with his infantry after
his cavalry fled from the German foot warriors in
the opening phase of the battle. In this case,
the victory was won by Roman shock infantry.

These two examples make it clear that Roman
quality was fully able to defeat German invaders.
But Roman quantity was not only quite inadequate;
it was misused. For example, in 363 Julian invaded Mesopotamia with 65,000 men supported by more
than 1000 boats transporting supplies on the Euphrates. We can see that adequate manpower was
available for non-essential wars by advance Roman
planning. But when the Germans invaded at some
unexpected point on the frontier, it was often
difficult to assemble the forces needed for defense
in a short time. In the fourth century men and
supplies could be moved about by the Roman government in quantities and at speeds which would not
be matched for a thousand years, at least in Europe.
For example, when Julian was proclaimed Augustus by
his troops in Gaul in 361, Constantius II, the co-
emperor in Antioch, decided to crush Julian and
sent 6 million bushels of grain to bases ahead of
his army as he advanced across Anatolia.

Despite such capacity, the empire was so overextended that the barbarians could break through at
many points, to sack and pillage until some later
date when forces could be gathered to catch up with
them and either eject them over the frontier or
settle them as military colonies on vacant lands
within the empire.

In 372-376 the Huns shattered in turn the Alans
north of the Caucasus, the Ostrogoths north of the
Black Sea, and the Visigoths on the lower Danube.
Fragments of these peoples were taken in as clients
of the Huns, while other fragments fled in different directions, some even attempting to escape into
the empire by crossing the Danube frontier.

A large group of Visigoths was allowed to cross the frontier in 376, but many more flooded in than could possibly be handled by the local Roman forces and violence broke out, with the result that other groups, including Alans, Ostrogoths, and even Huns came over the border without permission. There was confused violence, almost warfare, in the area for two years, but early in 378 the incompetent Emperor Valens continued his plans to make war on Persia that summer, leaving to the co-emperor in Gaul, his nephew Gratian, the task of restoring order on the Danube. Unfortunately, an invasion of Alans across the Rhine in the spring of 378 kept Gratian busy until early summer, when, after a brilliant victory over the Alans, he began to move eastward to the Balkans.

Valens, finding all quiet on the Persian frontier and increasingly alarmed by reports from the Danube, received news of Gratian's delay on the Rhine and returned from Asia to Thrace himself. As he passed through Constantinople, Valens was jeered by the people, just as Gratian's praises began to be sung for his victory in Germany. Gratian, coming to his uncle's aid and already crossing the Balkans, sent a hurried message to Valens not to engage the Visigoths until he arrived with reinforcements. Valens' council of war advised the same, but the senior emperor was determined to show the jeering people and his nephew that he could do the job alone. He left Adrianople on a hot day (9 August) and marched over rough ground, reaching the Gothic wagonlager at the eighth hour (early afternoon) with his men hot, thirsty, and hungry; he attacked the enemy with only part of his infantry, before his left wing cavalry were fully in position and with much of his foot in reserve. We do not know how many men were involved on either side, but Valens had heard that the enemy were no more than 10,000; it has been estimated by modern scholars that he may have had between 30,000 and 40,000 men. The Goths tried to negotiate, as much of their cavalry, including Ostrogoths and Alans and possibly some Huns, were away foraging and had not returned to the camp. But Valens attacked the camp with archers and shield carriers, who were repulsed. Other units joined in, and the fighting became fierce, with the Romans pressing against

the camp and many enemy coming out to meet them.
In the midst of this, the absent cavalry returned
"like a thunderbolt" and hurled themselves on the
Roman left wing forcing this in upon the infantry,
who were already pinned against the camp, so
tightly that they could not draw back their arms
for a blow or draw their swords if they had not
done so. Ammianus Marcellinus' account does not
give any clear idea of the order in which events
happened or where the invaders' cavalry hit first,
or what arms they were using. It is clear that
the mass of Roman infantry were massacred from all
sides and those who could escape from the crush
fled, led apparently by the generals. Only about
a third of the Roman force got away from the field,
including Valens, who was killed in a peasant's
hut during the night.

Clearly such a battle proves nothing about
either weapons or tactics, although it demonstrates
what can happen when a commander is determined to
show his arrogance, jealousy, and incompetence.
The returning cavalry who played a decisive role
in the battle were not Visigoths, but Alans and
Ostrogoths, and they were not heavy cavalry,
that is armored; we do not know what weapons
they carried. However, the battle was lost before
the cavalry returned; they made it into a massacre. Thompson's conclusion, after reviewing
the sources, is, "There is no evidence for the
traditional view that the battle of Adrianople
was a great cavalry victory. Although Ostrogothic
cavalry took a decisive part in the struggle, Adrianople in fact was a victory of Visigothic infantrymen over Roman infantrymen." The situation
was made worse after the battle, for, as soon as
the news was received, the Roman forces in Asia
killed all the Goths in their ranks, while Gratian,
in the Balkans, was enlisting all he could find to
provide an army for the new emperor, Theodosius.
The latter at once defeated a force of Alans who
were invading Pannonia, but before he died, in 395,
the first step toward the abandonment of the west
was taken, when the headquarters for the military
command in Gaul was withdrawn from Treves, northeast of Luxembourg, to Arles in the extreme south
of Gaul, near the mouth of the Rhone. This was

585

before the great German invasion across the Rhine on the last day of 406, the abandonment of Britain in 442, or Attila's invasion of the west in 451.

This withdrawal of the Roman government from the west was not voluntary and may not have been fully realized by those who were doing it. It arose out of tactical decisions made on a day-to-day basis, probably with the intention to return as soon as conditions improved. Moreover, the withdrawal was concealed by the fact that Roman generals (that is barbarians operating under imperial authority, in most cases) continued to operate in Gaul, with forces recruited locally and maintained on local resources. These generals continued trying to expel the invaders, or at least to settle them down in agricultural activities, so that the Gallo-Romans could live and the barbarian manpower could be available for recruits.

The Franks were willing both to settle down as landholders and to provide recruits and generals to the imperial system. By 560 they were the dominant force in the west, and by that time, this position may have been sustained by their military superiority. But their early rise to this position did not rest on any military advantages or on any superior weaponry. Quite the contrary. The great puzzle of the rise of the Franks seems to rest on the fact that they were so very unsuccessful in their military efforts in the third and fourth centuries that they made no real effort to move about seeking plunder, but, as a group, settled in one area and became farmers, while individuals volunteered for service in the Roman armies, where they obtained those skills which could be used by the group in the sixth century.

The one fact which is clear is that the early Franks were not a military success. They had no significant defensive weapons such as helmets, corselets, or shields, which makes them little different from other Germans. Their offensive weapons were a heavy spear and a light throwing axe, the <u>francisca</u>. They had few horses, but seem to have known archery, but, like most Germans, were reluctant to use this in war. In battle, in

586

massed formation, they held off cavalry with their
spears and crippled the horses with their axes.
In combat with infantry they tried to embed the
spear in the enemy's shield, pull down that shield
by dropping the spear and stepping on its heavy
buttend, and then strike at the enemy's neck thus
exposed. In some cases the francisca, the direct
ancestor of the tomahawk, was thrown at the enemy.

Unable to win any victories over the Romans
with these weapons, the Franks enlisted as mercenaries and by the time of the crisis of 378 were in
the highest military commands of the army. They
were defeated again and again by Constantine and
his father, from 293 on, and were recruited in
large numbers by the great emperor. As recruits
they played a significant role in his first victory as emperor in 306, but as a people they were
defeated by him at least four times, with boring
regularity, in intervals between his civil wars.
They formed a substantial part of Magnentius' army
which was beaten at Mursa in 351; just before
that battle, Silvanus, a Frank commanding the
usurper's guard regiment, brought that unit over
to Constantius' side and, within three years, was
Magister Peditum in Gaul. The following year, a
great force of Ripuarian Franks burst over the
Rhine near Cologne, as they did periodically; this
so alarmed Constantius that he made Julianus Caesar
in Gaul. The new Caesar at once defeated the
Ripuarians, drove them back, and made the Salian
Franks federates in 358. From that time, a significant part of the recruits from the west were
Franks, and they rose to high office. In Julian's
invasion of Mesopotamia in 363 both the rear guard
and the right wing on the march were commanded by
Franks. After Adrianople, in 380, two Frankish
generals, Bauton and Arbogaste, who had come from
Gaul with Gratian too late to rescue Valens, imposed peace on the Visigoths. In the same decade,
another Frank, Merobaudes, was commanded of the
household guards (comes domesticorum) and Master
of Soldiers; he raised Valentinian to Augustus in
375 and was twice consul in Rome, in 377 and 383.
Bauton was the chief minister of Valentinian II in
383, and his daughter married the Emperor Arcadius
in 395. Arbogaste held all the high commands, was

involved in the strangling of Valentinian II in 392, and made Eugenius emperor in his place. Thus Frankish generals Bauton, Merobaudes, and Arbogaste were involved in the high levels of Roman politics in the west in the final quarter of the fourth century, and two of these ended as suicides.

Through all of this, the Franks as a "tribe" could not win a battle. Again and again, they (chiefly the Ripuarians) created a disturbance and were punished by Roman forces, increasingly commanded by Franks, as Arbogaste did in 389 and 392. The first victory of Franks over a Roman force was in 388 and hardly counts; as the Ripuarians were chased across the Rhine into deep forest by the Master of Soldiers, Quintinus, they entangled the Romans among fallen trees and attacked them from hiding with poisoned arrows (a hunting weapon, not suited to regular warfare because of its slow action). Quintinus was killed and his force destroyed, but the following year the Franks were defeated and forced to make peace by Arbogaste.

It is possible that the law of Arcadius of 398, which gave one-third of the land to federates in any area assigned to them as a zone of settlement, was issued as a consequence of his barbarian advisors. As interpreted, this law allowed federates, in return for defense service, to settle on a third of the lands of a Gallo-Roman landlord and obtain, as well, a third of his coloni or slaves to work the land. The Franks were such federates, established in 358 by Julianus and renewed several times, notably by Aetius in 446.

When the Emperor Theodosius died in 395, he left his brother-in-law, the Vandal general Stilicho, as protector of his two young sons, Arcadius in Constantinople and Honorius in the west at Milan. At the news, the Visigoths in the Balkans elected as king Alaric, an enemy of Rome, who at once began to plunder and devastate Greece including Athens. Stilicho caught up with Alaric several times and could easily have destroyed him but abstained. In 400 and again in 402, Alaric invaded Italy. Both times Stilicho defeated the Visigoths, but refused to destroy them, with the result that Honorius moved his capital from Milan to Ravenna and withdrew troops from the Rhine to defend Italy. Ravenna was much safer because of its strong defenses and its direct route to the sea for supplies in a siege or escape to the east.

But the Rhine frontier had been left open. On the last day of 406, the Vandals, Sueves, and Alans crossed the Rhine into Gaul. The Frank federates threw themselves in the way and were swept aside, leaving Gaul open to the invaders. In the south, the two halves of the empire became engaged in a bitter controversy, which threatened to break into open war, over which half should control Illyricum, the best recruiting ground in the empire. Stilicho was executed for treason by Honorius in 408. This gave Alaric the opportunity to blackmail the western government, and, when this was resisted, his Visigoths sacked Rome.

From this time on, in a period of complete turmoil, the Franks played no role in history for more than a generation. They supported several usurpers in Gaul, but were defeated by Aetius who was engaged in his ambiguous relationships with the Huns (chiefly 433-454), as Stilicho had been earlier with the Visigoths. In 454, when the Hunnish threat was ended, Aetius was murdered by his Roman employers, and the Salian Franks, under their Merovingian king, seized Cambrai and extended their influence from southern Belgium around Tournai to the Somme River. The great period of Frankish expansion was beginning.

We have no need to follow the rise of the Franks in detail. It rested on a number of factors, which were most evident in the reign of Clovis (481-511). As federates, the Franks could make a claim that they were the legitimate representatives of Roman power in Gaul. This allowed them to take over the Roman fiscal system, public domains, and military colonies. It also allowed them to claim the support of the Gallo-Roman magnates and of the Catholic clergy, a claim which was greatly strengthened when Clovis gave up his pagan religion for Roman Christianity, making the Franks ultimately the only significant barbarian people who were not Arians. Moreover, as I have said, the Franks did not move around as

589

other barbarians and made no effort to maintain themselves as a superior class distinct from the earlier inhabitants. All the peoples of Francia, including Franks and Gallo-Romans, had the same obligations toward the Frankish monarchy, to pay taxes, to support the army, and to be subject to its justice (although subject to different private law). The non-Franks were left in possession of their lands, were allowed to intermarry with the Franks, and were not a subject people. The Franks, or at least Clovis, had a shrewd sense of power politics and of balance of power, playing off one rival against another, destroying surrounding rivals such as the Burgundians and Thuringians by intervening in the rivalries or civil wars between brothers or among members of ruling families.

None of these advantages would have availed much, if the Franks had not been able to win battles and to impose the royal power on the king's subjects. This military capacity seems to have emerged from the Frankish experience in the Roman armed forces and from their efforts to copy the weapons and tactics, but certainly not the organizations, of the Romans. As Bernard S. Bachrach puts it (1972), "It can therefore be concluded that Clovis resuscitated the remains of the imperial military in Gaul and created the Merovingian military."

The chief weapons of the Merovingian period were shock (spears, axes, and swords), both cavalry and infantry, although the cavalry often dismounted to fight. They knew composite bows and javelins, both derived from Rome, but seem to have used few of either. There was a great deal of stone throwing, most frequently in sieges. All rich men, especially kings and officials, but also private persons, had mercenary fighters on their lands, varying in numbers from thousands on royal lands to a small handful on a small estate. There were also standing forces, available for long service, including service in winter or out of the kingdom, mostly from surviving Roman units and from Roman military colonies. These were more adequate in Burgundy than elsewhere. All of these were able to serve because they were supported by lands worked by slaves, coloni, or tenants. Finally,

there were local levies which could be called out
by royal order for limited service within the kingdom. Since these last were self-supporting and
provided their own arms, which varied with their
wealth, they varied greatly in quality. Those of
less wealth and poorer arms were decreasingly likely
to be called for service.

On the whole, this heterogeneous army was not
of good quality in any sense, but it was better than
anything else in western Europe, except the Burgundians, who had been almost exterminated by the Huns
in 436 and then, when Clovis was threatening, allowed him to intervene in a civil war between the
king and his brother (501). The Franks were constantly trying to improve their weapons in mobility,
quality, and quantity. They had no naval forces,
except the remains of some Roman naval colonists on
the northwest coast. These latter were used successfully to destroy a Danish pirate fleet at sea in 515,
but we hear no more of navy until the Carolingians
reached the Mediterranean Sea. The siege train and
artillery were almost totally lacking among the Merovingians, especially the latter, for the former improved greatly later, under the Carolingians. Mobility of men increased under both dynasties, as cavalry
became increasingly available for most fighters, and
transport may have been maintained, by using greater
numbers of carts and animals, but roads became
steadily worse.

The basic Roman territorial organization in
municipalities, districts, and provinces persisted,
chiefly through the ecclesiastical structure, which
was used as the territorial basis for Frankish government. The names of officials, such as count,
duke, and patrician, continued, but meanings shifted,
as both became localized residents. Writing continued to be used, but sparingly, in government,
with persistence of Roman forms. On the whole, we
might say that the Merovingians (c. 454-752) and
the Carolingians (752-887) tried to preserve the
Roman system but they failed, partly because the
material bases for supporting it evaporated, but
equally because the classical outlook was being
replaced by a totally different outlook with different subjective categories and values.

The fundamental military and political realities of the period 250-950 do not rest on changes
in weapons at all, since these were not changed
but simply became more restricted by the disappearance of the more complicated forms. The changing
realities to which I refer rested on shifting relationships, on a holistic basis, of weapons, control
of revenues, patterns of social organization, and
changes of cognitive outlook and values. The non-
military aspects of this holistic picture must be
analyzed in terms of at least six factors: (1) a
prolonged and fluctuating economic depression from
250 to 950; (2) a catastrophic population decrease
from about 250 until after 760; (3) even more
drastic de-urbanization and ruralization of society
in the west from 250 to after 950; (4) a decline
in public spirit in the west from before 150 to
after 1000, marked by increasing localism; by increasing concern for socialization in one's own
local group; by decreasing interest in political
relations with a distant state; and by a growing
concern for personal salvation in the hereafter,
rather than the pursuit of wealth, power, or honor
in this secular world; (5) a steady erosion of
transportation from at least 350 to after 950;
and (6) a fluctuating and decreasing ability to
control and centralize economic surplus from before
400 to after 900.

These tendencies and datings apply only to the
west and not to the east. In the east, the significant events were: (1) the voluntary shift of
the center of the empire to Constantinople for
strategic reasons; (2) the retraction of imperial
political control to the east by the involuntary
abandonment of those areas which could not be controlled with limited resources from Constantinople,
beginning with Dacia in 271; and (3) the total reorganization of the reduced eastern areas to create
a new civilization different from classical civilization. The central element in that new civilization was the adoption of an Asiatic form of political structure which I call providential empire.
This form of political organization, which will be
described in detail in the next section, dominated
the area from the Elbe River to China, from as
early as 200 in civilized areas until after 1900.

592

It was as much the product of the Asiatic grasslands as pastoral nomadism or the cavalry archer with composite bow. Its chief features were an idea of deity and a political theory derived from this. It saw deity as "Heaven," a Being of Willful and arbitrary Omnipotence, and it saw the Ruler as the Vicar of this Omnipotent Will on earth. Its most perfect example was its latest embodiment, the Mongol empire of Jenghis Khan, but it had many earlier and less perfect manifestations, as in the successive dynasties of China, the various Islamic caliphates and empires culminating in the Ottoman sultanate, the Byzantine empire from Heraclitus on, the Sassanid empire of Persia, the Czarist empire of Russia, and the Carolingian empire of the Franks. One distinguishing mark of such an empire is the lack of any constitutional rules of succession to the throne.

In the west with which we are concerned here, there was a climate change after A.D. 200, marked, it would seem, by a retreat of the polar icecap and the polar area of high pressures; this allowed the prevailing westerly winds and rains to move northward so that they passed over the Baltic Sea and Scandinavia, with great growth of forest in all northern Europe, and with greatly reduced rainfall in the Mediterranean, North Africa, and east of the Caspian Sea. In the same period, war and disease resulted in a decrease of population of up to 60 per cent in Europe or in the Roman empire from about 200 to after 800, that is to say over six hundred or more years. Careful studies of the population of the Roman empire seem to indicate that its population fell from about 70 million persons at the time of Christ to about 50 million in 300. The wars, migrations, spread of plagues, and abandonment of much family life, including the spread of chastity for religious reasons and of sexual perversions for other reasons, all contributed to this decrease. This had a very adverse influence on economic production as well as on defense, especially when it was combined, after 200, by a flight from the cities to the rural areas, and a movement of economic activities toward self-sufficiency. One of the chief characteristics of an economic depression is a reduction in roundabout modes of production by a decrease in investment, although not necessarily in savings, along with a reduction in the specialization of production and exchange of products. The links in any chain of activity from the original producer to the final consumer are reduced in number; individuals retreat from very specialized activities to more general ones; the use of exchange and of money decreases. All of these changes are to be found in weapons systems and in defense, where we find a similar tendency to fall back on the simpler, less complex, and more general forms of weapons, tactics, and organizational arrangements, including, for example, the belief that the same man should produce food and fight (peasant militia) or a reduction of defense to a single weapon or only two. We may not notice these military consequences when the depression is brief, as the world depression of 1929-1940, but these effects do appear when such an economic collapse continues for centuries, in a dark age.

The effects of such a change are also important on the non-material aspects of the society, where we find a tendency for people to turn toward a more personal and existential life, with emphasis on day-to-day interpersonal activities, decreasing emphasis on planning for the future in this secular world, and a decrease in abstract thinking and generalizations, but instead, a great emotional and intellectual emphasis on a few symbols and words. Life tends to polarize into almost total absorption in momentary empirical activity, with intellectual life reduced to a few large symbols.

One of the significant aspects of the decline of Rome, which began as far back as 200 B.C. and became an unstoppable slide after A.D. 200, was that the inequitable division of economic product continued, with the result that the production and commerce of luxuries for the ruling groups continued when the ruled groups were already hungry if not starving. This, of course, is one of the reasons for the great shift of allegiances which finished off classical civilization in both the east and the west. Such inequitable division of the national product is necessary for any civilized society, but the incomes of the upper class must be saved and invested, not wasted in non-productive uses, including war and ostentatious display of luxury. The continued collapse of the system through the whole Merovingian and Carolingian periods was based on this failure of productive investment and waste on wars.

In the west the two centuries from the battle of Tertry, which established the Carolingian family as the dominant power in Francia in 687, to the deposition of Charles the Fat in 887, were marked by an effort by that family to establish a providential imperial system in the west such as Byzantium was creating in the east. Failure of this effort in the ninth century led to the European Dark Age of the tenth century, which, like the Greek Dark Age of the tenth century B.C., became the basis of a new, and unique, civilization.

The failure of the Merovingians and the Carolingians to create a permanent providential imperial system in the west was due to their almost total misdirection of resources and economic surplus. While they were rushing about trying to subdue distant peoples, arable lands at the very center of their system were falling out of cultivation, forests were overgrowing the open lands of Gaul, and travel, to say nothing of transportation of goods, was becoming more and more difficult. If we compare personal reports of what Gaul was like in the early principate or even in Caesar's day, we can see this process. Eigil's Life of Sturmi, who died as Abbot of Fulda in 779, tells us of a trip Sturmi made in his younger days from Francia across the Rhine, traveling for days in "a frightful wilderness, seeing nothing but wild beasts, of which there were many, birds and enormous trees," but few humans. Two centuries later the situation was similar at the very center of Charlemagne's kingdom: a monk, Richer, traveling with a knight from Rheims to Chartres on the main route, lost his way in the thick forest; when they reached a bridge, it was so dilapidated that they had to repair it before they could cross, covering one hole with the knight's shield so the horse's hoof would not go through; the two travelers finally reached Chartres, but Richer's horse died of exhaustion on the way. By that date, in the tenth century, the new western civilization had begun to grow, by small investments of local savings in clearing forests, breaking new arable land, and better harnessing of animals for plowing and for travel.

The weapons component in the rise and fall of the Frankish empire operated through the ability to subdue fortified strongholds and to centralize economic surplus. The imported ideology of providential empire made it possible to reverse the military trend and thus the political trend, without, however, reversing the economic and technological trends, and did so by skimming the constantly thinning economic surplus from wider areas. This provided, in the aggregate, a relatively ample accumulation of capital but, in the long run, doomed Europe to a deeper and lengthened depression by devoting that surplus to conquest, ecclesiastical and imperial architecture, a widespread administrative system, with some sponsoring of literary and artistic activities, rather than to advances in agriculture and transportation which could have increased economic production and capital formation in a more limited territory. The consequences of this failure were intensified by the combination in the same system of three other tendencies: (1) the Frankish practice of dividing a patrimony among several sons; (2) the drive of any providential monarchy to universality and world conquest, beginning with the extermination of rivals within one's own family; and (3) the tendency in such a system to seek other-worldly goals, especially personal salvation, to the neglect of more mundane needs. This last tendency emerges often as a way of escape from the violence engendered by the drive to world empire. These and other problems intrinsic in providential imperial systems were solved in ways which need not detain us here. The point is that they were not solved by the Carolingians.

The fact that the Franks regarded the kingship as personal property and divided it equally among the king's sons led to fratricidal warfare seeking to reunite the kingdom, but whenever this was achieved, it was divided again in the next generation. The situation was made worse by the fact that the kings were polygamous and had concubines, which left more claimants to the territory and to the kingship. Charlemagne, for example, had five wives and several concubines, who produced numerous children, although he divided his empire among only three sons. Civil war became endemic, and the kingdom was united only briefly among the Merovingians (in 558-561 and 613-638). The situation was better under the early Carolingians, either because sons died or were killed before their fathers, but after 838 it was divided into three parts.

In the short run, the Carolingian efforts to construct a providential empire on a dwindling economic foundation gave us the "Carolingian revival" and the Carolingian empire, but in the long run, both of these were doomed to failure. The Carolingian armies, in almost yearly campaigns, rushed about Europe from Spain to central Europe, from the Baltic Sea to central Italy. The result was an ephemeral empire within which any opposing force could be defeated and any recalcitrant stronghold could be captured, but these opposition forces did not stay defeated, nor did captured strongholds remain obedient. On the contrary, the same peoples and the same fortresses had to be defeated and recaptured again and again. The Avars were destroyed totally because they, like the Huns, were nomadic peoples, organized on a clientage system which disintegrated when their leaders were killed, but the territories they inhabited did not remain under the Carolingian writ. The Saxons and the Aquitanians were defeated periodically, yet continued to be disobedient. If they remained docile for awhile, the Carolingian agents set over them as rulers ceased to be obedient agents of the monarch and did very much as they wished. The point is that the Carolingians could conquer and capture, but they could not control or govern, because both economic production and economic integration continued to deteriorate through most of the Carolingian period. The constant military campaigns, by ransoms and looting, increased the centralization of economic surplus, but it did not create a centralized social or economic system.

On the whole there was little if any improvement in ability to defeat a mobile enemy in this period, either a pastoral invader on land or an enemy so skilled in boating and seamanship that he could use the waterways of Europe, including those of eastern and northern Europe, and its extended coastline, bays, and seas to strike almost anywhere without warning. In 814 Carolingian Europe was probably no better prepared to cope with these two possible dangers than it had been at the death of Pepin II in 714, except in quantitative terms. This quantity had permitted the Carolingians to stop the Saracen invasion near Tours (732), then to ally with the papacy to crush the Lombards in Italy (754-774), to create an empire from Brittany to Bohemia and from Barcelona and Rome to the Baltic Sea, and to carry the titles "King of the Franks" (752), "King of the Lombards" (774), and "Emperor of the Romans" (800). But the methods which Charlemagne used to preserve order within his empire helped to destroy it in the long run.

Among these methods we may include increasing emphasis on personal obligation to God to obey the ruler, to stay firm with oaths to do this, and to remember the future judgment of God on one's behavior here. Another method was to remunerate the royal agents and the fighting men in the provinces by grants of land whose incomes could support these agents and fighters. But for the last dozen years of Charlemagne's reign, the evidence of disintegration, corruption, and injustice was growing, and the old emperor knew it. As F.L. Ganshof, the greatest authority on this subject says of 814, "It was an empire already far advanced along the road to decomposition." There was no real central government or administration; just one man with a few assistants, in a situation in which nothing was done by routine but only if that one man made an effort to find out what was going on and gave an order to do something about it; but in most cases the order was not carried out, and there was no way that the emperor could know. To quote Ganshof again, "Even a rapid reading of the capitularies reveals all the symptoms of a defective administration. It is clear that the counts and their subordinates were guilty of serious negligence, abuse of power, extortion, usurpations, and the rest, and to such a degree that excesses and irregularities became endemic." Only Charlemagne's energy and personal character kept the system--or

rather lack of system--going, and both of these
were dwindling before death took him in 814.

The emphasis placed by Charlemagne on providential deity and on the individual's personal obligation to God, which he used as an instrument
for better government, could easily have the opposite result. This appeared when Louis the Pious,
the only survivor of the three sons to whom Charles
had bequeathed his realms in 806, became emperor.
Louis was unusual both in his piety and in his
powers of abstract thought which permitted him
to grasp the idea of a state as an organization
of sovereign power and not simply as the patrimony
of a Frankish family, which was as much as most
Franks, including his late father, could grasp.
Accordingly, in the early years of his reign, Louis
made a number of reforms to establish a state, whose
abstract power would be passed on, with its territory undivided, through primogeniture, to an heir
under public law. Beneath this imperial unity,
the empire would be divided into administrative
sections for the chief descendants of the deceased
emperor. We need only say that this difficult scheme
broke down completely in the years 829-843 in squab-
bles and eventually in war among Louis' four sons.
In 843 there was a formal division into three parts,
of which one was a middle kingdom called Lotharingia,
including Italy, Burgundy, and the Rhineland, with
the imperial title. Louis was king of the area east
of the Rhine, while Charles the Bald was ruler of
the area roughly west of the Scheldt and Rhone Rivers.
The struggles of these three and their descendants
reduced the empire to anarchy after 875, as the west
reeled from the double impact of internal disruption
and external invasions.

4.   Defensive Power and Providential Empire, 31
      B.C.-A.D. 1200

The whole period covered by this chapter, and
especially from about A.D. 200 to about A.D. 900,
was a period of weapons confusion. Before 200, in
the west at least, war included substantial use of
infantry forces in collision; after 900, it revolved about the impact of cavalry. But in between
was a period of weapons confusion, in which many

weapons, including missile weapons, played a substantial role. This weapons confusion of 200-900 was similar to that which had existed in 1200-600 B.C., which existed again, especially in Europe, in A.D. 1300-1600, and which has again been evident since 1917.

The confusion of weapons in this period arose from the fact that the great civilized empires of the age, Rome and China, were moving toward increasingly static defense systems when they were suddenly challenged by the increasingly mobile weapons of horse-riding grassland pastoral peoples. The real problem of the periods covered by this chapter and the chapter which follows, running from A.D. 200 to after 1500, was the problem of how to reconcile weapons mobility with a static economic base. This could be found in unstable balance of almost any degree of mixture of the two, from, on the one extreme, a very static weapons system like the medieval castle supported on a static economic base like the self-sufficient medieval manor to, on the other extreme, a very mobile weapons system on a very mobile economic base, like Mongol nomadism. Most systems tried to find a solution somewhere between these two, but any such mixture was usually precarious. We have seen, in the second section of this chapter, how the introduction of many elements of a static character, such as the acquisition of immobile or simply cumbersome forms of property, into full nomadism, by restricting its mobility, made it vulnerable on the security side. In a similar way, but from the opposite extreme, the introduction of any elements of mobility, such as the introduction of Viking boats on the rivers of northwestern Europe, introduced great insecurity into Europe's incipient and static feudal-manorial system.

Most of the weapons systems, with their accompanying politico-social-economic systems, in this period tried to find a solution somewhere between the two extremes by trying to reconcile the static and mobile elements within a single system. The result was a very great degree of instability both within each system and in the interrelationships between systems. Since the two extremes were in the extreme west (western Europe) and the extreme east (Mongolia), the greatest mixture was in the Byzantine empire in the Near East.

While there was such great instability in the systems themselves, such as Byzantium, Sassanid Persia, the Moslem Caliphate, and their attendant lesser systems, there was a considerable degree of stability in the whole constellation of such systems from the Mongolian Far East and China to the Viking Far West and the Holy Roman Empire. This is probably why some of the individual systems survived so long despite their extreme instability. They survived from the stability of the constellation of systems despite the instability of the members.

The static element in this constellation rested on the fact that all vegetation is local and static: plants do not move around. So long as horses feed on grass and men feed on agricultural produce, they are bound by the fact that fodder and food are produced in specific localities. Pastoral nomadism of the Mongolian kind freed itself and gained complete mobility by moving its herds from one locality to another, consuming the grass as they moved, with the cattle following the horses and the sheep following the cattle. The process was completed when these peoples largely gave up food of agricultural origin and obtained food, shelter, and even fuel from their herds, eating meat and milk products and living in wagons and felt tents. This new way of life could continue as long as there were new pastures to move to each day. The success of this new way of life, as reflected in the increase of both men and animals, with the increasing dry spell after A.D. 200, drove these peoples outward in the grasslands migrations with which we are concerned. This new nomadic way of life also possessed a weapons system--cavalry archers--which had a devastating impact on the sedentary societies of the Old World.

This collision of pastoral nomadism and the sedentary agricultural communities served to transform both. On the one side, the sedentary agri-

culturalists, including the Roman empire, had to
defend themselves against the pastoral nomads.
On the other side, pastoral nomads had to discover
how they could exploit the greater productivity of
the sedentary agricultural communities. The unstable and fluctuating interrelationships of these
two, and the solutions they reached, are represented by the transitory providential empires which
we are examining in this chapter. But as we shall
see, there was a basic contradiction in all these
solutions from the fact that providential empires,
by their nature, are universal and therefore must
be aggressive, while the supreme weapon of this
period was the fortified stronghold, an almost completely defensive weapon. The linkage between these
two gave rise to acute problems of control, problems
of how a widespread governmental structure can get
its orders enforced against subordinates who have
possession of supreme defensive weapons like castles.

Let us be very clear what the problems were.
The pastoral nomads and their semi-pastoral cultural ancestors or descendants had mobility; but
such mobility was a weakness in trying to control
or to exploit sedentary agriculturalist communities.
The pastoral hordes not only moved, they had to keep
moving. They could not stop, because their animals
ate up the fodder where they were, and they had to
move on. Thus they could conquer territory, but
faced great problems in organizing it in any stable
system for long-term use of its resources. The
only alternative to such constant movement was to
break up the horde and disperse it widely so that
each animal's grazing area could grow grass as fast
as it was eaten up. Only in western Europe, with
adequate rain in all seasons, was the grass nutritious enough and did it grow fast enough to allow
cavalry warriors to exist in small areas and thus
be able to provide defensive support for each
other. Elsewhere, each warrior had to have a
very large area or had to have some method of
land transport which would make it possible to
draw forage from a large area to a central point
where it could be consumed. In the period with
which we are concerned in this chapter, no such
land transport existed. Moreover, no system of
transport would be likely to be invented which

would make it cheaper to haul fodder to a horse by horsepower than to allow that horse to go to the fodder. Of course, economic costs of this kind are not necessarily important in government.

As a consequence of these factors, any pastoralist exploitation had to be one of wide area control. But this meant both that the land was being exploited extensively rather than intensively (that is, for pasturage rather than for food production) and that the conquering pastoralists were so widely scattered that they were defensively weakened as a group and could escape from any centralized political control as individuals. This defensive weakening, of course, was a weakening of defense against other pastoral systems, since the sedentary agriculturalists themselves were not only peaceful but were without weapons capable of threatening pastoral peoples.

These relationships meant that a combination of agricultural and pastoral elements would be stronger than either alone, and, accordingly, that land areas under both extensive and intensive exploitation had to be included in the same power unit, the one providing the forage for animals and the other providing the food for the people. Also, the pastoral overlords had to find some solution to the relationship between weapons mobility and productive stability. Moreover, such pastoral overlords, in order to retain control over such a variety of land-utilization areas, had to cooperate together within a single political system despite the decentralizing tendencies of local agricultural production and defensive weapons superiority (that is the difficulty for pastoral peoples to capture a fortified stronghold). The inadequacies of transportation and communication technology were such that no single political system could control on a long-term basis a large number of units of combined intensive and extensive areas of land utilization: each unit of combined exploitation sufficient to sustain any power system would have a tendency to break away from any political superior whose base was in some distant combination of units.

As we shall see, the only way to unite any

603

large area of combined units was on an ideological
rather than on a military or political basis, since
areas had to be combined on a purely additive basis
rather than on any organic basis.

These problems were faced by all significant
political units of this period because all were,
in varying degrees, constructed of a ruling superstructure of pastoral traditions over a basic
foundation of peasant traditions. As we shall see,
the central structure in a geographic sense, the
Byzantine empire, was most successful in coping
with these problems, but even it was eventually
submerged by the rising tide of grasslands pastoralism, as were most other large political systems
in the period up to 1500. Even without this pastoralist threat, the inadequacies of transportation
and communications technology made it almost impossible to keep any large political unit intact. Thus
a political dynasty like the Seleucids of Syria
found it almost impossible to control their subordinates in Iran or Africa, while the Muslim Caliph in Mesopotamia would find it equally difficult
to retain control over his legal subordinates in
Arabia, Iran, Egypt, Morocco, or Spain.

This inability to control subordinates, acting alone, would have broken up most political
systems consisting of large areas of land exploitation. But it was not acting alone, for the mobility
of pastoral fighting men was so great and remained
so great that a political system based on such mobility could often retain control of numerous areas,
especially when unity was reinforced by ideological
elements and by economic cooperation and other
kinds of reciprocity. It should be noted, however,
that the greater the mobility of weapons systems
in this period, the greater the geographic extent
over which control could be exercised, but the more
superficial was that control over life in the villages which formed the sedentary basis of the society. The Mongols, who had the greatest mobility
and had the largest empire, had the least influence;
the Arabs who had somewhat less mobility and a smaller empire had greater but still superficial influence, while Sassanian Persia or Byzantium with
less mobility and smaller empires had much more
influence on sedentary agriculture, in neither case,

however, to any degree as much as the non-mobile and localized system of western Europe.

It is very difficult for us to grasp the organizational features of this period because our ideas are rooted in the many misconceptions of the nineteenth century; these form a screen which distorts our vision of the realities of this period. Among these misconceptions are our emphasis on land ownership rather than on land revenues; an excessive attention in the history of military tactics to charging cavalry rather than to fortified castles; a misconception of the role of the castle; and a belief that the purpose of war is to smash the enemy's mobile armed forces as completely as possible and as soon as possible (an idea invented by Napoleon and made into a religion by Clausewitz). The period covered by this chapter had quite different ideas, totally different aims, and, accordingly, different tactics.

In those days, fact was much more important than law, because the law was incomplete and the judicial system was inadequate. Land ownership, to the ruling class, was of little significance, while land revenues were of great importance. Ownership of land meant little for three reasons: (1) the ruling group knew little and cared less about how land was utilized; they had no intention of changing how it was used in any way; (2) this ruling group knew that land without peasants upon it and therefore functioning as a productive enterprise was almost worthless; (3) the gap between the ruling groups and the peasants who operated the lands in agricultural enterprise was gigantic; the peasants were peaceful, while the ruling classes were warlike; the peasant was locked into local immobility with local concerns; while the rulers were obsessed with wider and more mobile interests; and (4) thus, the ruling groups cared only about revenues, not about agricultural operations and even less about land ownership.

We might view the agricultural areas of the whole Old World as supporting an enormous extent of such land revenues gathered into bundles known

as "tenures" in western Europe, as _pronoia_ in Byzantium, and as _iqta_ in Muslim areas including
the Seljuk empire.

The ruling classes were concerned with the
control and use of such tenures. Since these
tenures were simply social organizations, the
revenues in them could be re-bundled into larger
or smaller tenures as desired, but generally these
tenures were very persistent just because the ruling classes, that is "the System," were interested
only in such bundles of revenues.

These revenues, however, did not come in the
form of money. They consisted of food, fodder,
manpower, raw materials (such as wool or hides),
and the products of peasant handicrafts. Thus the
problem of tenures became a problem of how these
could be controlled.

Control means how they could be extracted
from the peasants, where they could be stored
safely, and how they could be transported to
where they would be used. The ability to transport incomes was so limited that distance of
transportation was always minimized by having
the consumer go to the goods rather than taking
the goods to the consumer.

The castle, walled town, or fortified place
was the key to all control of revenues. It was
a multi-purpose artifact: usually a residence,
storage depot, a control center, and the supreme
weapon of the period. Its primary purpose was
control over revenues, not to be a weapon against
an enemy (either external or another member of
the same system). We must recognize that there
was, at that time, and up to about 1800, no rural
police forces. If revenues were to be protected,
the owner had to protect them himself. This was
the chief function of a castle or fortified place.

It also must be clearly recognized that the
castle did not have as its primary function to be
an instrument of frontier defense against an external enemy. Its primary function was aimed at
the peasantry of the tenure. Its military role

606

against other members of a ruling group was as significant against members of the same system as
against those of some other system. In fact, one
of the keys to understanding this period is to
recognize that Saladin's and Richard the Lion-Hearted's common interest in preserving tenures was
stronger than their enmity as representatives of
different systems or as champions of Islam and
Christianity. This was generally true of the Crusader leaders and the Levantine Saracen rulers as
it was of the Byzantine emperors and the Persian
kings or of the emperors and the Saracen or Seljuk
rulers. It was not, as we shall see, true of the
ruling groups of any of these and of the nomadic
Turks or Mongols (because these represented a
totally different kind of system).

I have said that the primary role of a castle
or a stronghold was to control tenures (including
revenues from such tenures). The possessor of the
tenure stored his revenues in his stronghold until
he could come to consume them. He was a greater
or lesser lord depending on the quantity of such
revenues he possessed, because the greater the
revenues he controlled the greater the armed forces
he could command and the more extensive the area
over which his power could be extended.

It must be recognized that nationalism and
ideology in general had nothing to do with this
system. The fact that people in an area had a
common language or common religion was of almost
no significance. The gap between lord and peasant
was almost total. Their traditions, interests,
and aims were so different that it was almost completely irrelevant whether their language, race,
or religion were the same or different, just as,
to a much lesser degree, the interests of lords,
whether they were members of the same system or
of a different system (of the same kind, based
on peasant agriculture), were sufficiently similar
to overcome most divergencies of language, race,
and religion. I say "to a much lesser degree" because those systems which were capped by a providential empire were held together in a single system by an ideological (religious) bond, but this
was significant only for the greatest lords and

607

much less so for the lesser lords. And even the greatest lords found that their interest in preserving the system as a system was generally stronger than their religious or ideological convictions.

Any lord, as he became greater (that is obtained dominion over more extensive tenures), had more and more strongholds (control points over tenures), and could use these to support fighting men. Much of his life was spent in moving about from one stronghold to another to consume the goods stored in each. An ambitious lord thus would seek to increase the number of his strongholds as a measure of the quantity of his tenures and the amount of fighting men he could "control."

I put the word "control" in quotation marks because control of strongholds is the key to the system and the point where mistaken nineteenth century ideas lead us completely astray. The castle was the supreme weapon of this period. More than that it was largely (though not completely) a defensive weapon. The lord could control it only if he was in it (even then his control was never complete because he could always be betrayed or even assassinated).

The aim of all warfare in this period and over the area of peasant agricultural enterprise was to capture strongholds. Field armies engaged in battle only as preliminary to such sieges or to prevent a siege from being successful. This can be understood only in terms of the strategy and tactics of the period.

The strategy was not aimed at "total victory," at destroying the enemy regime or "system," at defeating his field armies in order to "break his will to resist." All of these are modern ideas. In the period with which we are concerned the aims of strategy in any specific campaign were generally very limited, to get control of certain strongholds and thus of the tenures they controlled in order to increase one's own power.

This strategy was based on the relationship

between the two chief weapons, the mobile horseman
and the static castle, representing two quite different ways of life since the former emerged from
the traditions of pastoralism and the castles came
from the traditions of peasant agriculture. The
key to the relationship of these two weapons was
that neither could directly defeat the other. Castles could not prevent a pastoral offensive from
passing through, but they could prevent such an offensive from reaping much benefit from its passage,
such as replenishing its supply of food or controlling local manpower and, most notably, they could
preserve a different system of wealth and use of
resources which would still be on the spot after
the pastoral offensive had passed by. Above all,
if such fortified strong points could not be captured, they put limits on the extent of pastoral-
controlled political systems.

The size of any political system in this
transitional period was, from the military point
of view, a function of its ability to sustain an
offensive and its ability to supply such an offensive over distance. Both of these were hampered
by the deficiencies of land transportation in this
period. Closely related to this was the fact that
any sustained power system could construct fortifications, especially effective walls around towns
or cities, but very few power systems could operate
a siege train and get it delivered to the walls of
such towns and operate it there long enough to
force the town or stronghold to submit to its will.

To capture a fortified place, unless it could
be betrayed, involved taking it by storm or starving it out. The former was unlikely to be successful without elaborate and heavy siege machinery
which few systems possessed, which were possessed
only on the highest levels of power (the level of
emperors or the greatest kings), and which could
be brought up to a besieged stronghold only with
great effort over a long period. Moreover, possession of a siege train required the possession
of adequate supplies of lumber and of specialized
workers, particularly in metalworking and in earth-
moving. Lack of such skilled workers and above
all lack of adequate lumber put severe restrictions

on the besieging activities of grasslands pastoralists. The abilities of the Mongols and Ottoman
Turks to overcome these deficiencies made it possible for these peoples to combine the ultimate in
grasslands pastoral mobility with successful besieging activities and use this combination to destroy the earlier Islamic, Byzantine, Seljuk, Indian, and Chinese empires (after 1200).

Lacking such siege trains most of the empires
before 1200 had to rely on capturing a stronghold
by surprise, betrayal, or starving it out. Surprise
meant arriving at a fortress suddenly enough to
find its manpower insufficient to man the walls
adequately. In such a case, the walls could be
stormed after clearing them of defenders with missile weapons (especially crossbows) or after a period of attrition of the defenders made their manpower even less adequate. To deal with such an
emergency, most fortified places had an inner citadel or "keep" to which the defenders could withdraw when their numbers were reduced below the
point where they could continue to man the outer
walls.

Betrayal of a fortress was very common, especially in view of the lack of ideological loyalty
to which I have referred. The strongest loyalty
was personal loyalty to the leader, often a wasting asset and frequently in conflict with self-
interest. The capture of fortified places by the
early Arab attacks often was made possible by betrayals, or at least inadequate loyalty to the
nominal ruler. Such disloyalty could be encouraged
and generalized if the attacker offered generous
terms. This factor was so significant that it can
be said that many fewer strong places were taken
by storm than by betrayal or various degrees of
voluntary surrender in the period covered by this
chapter.

Starving out a strong place required that the
besieger be able to keep around the fortifications
a stronger force than was trapped within the fortifications. Otherwise, the besiegers would make a
sortie and drive the attackers away. This need for
a larger or stronger force of besiegers was not
easily met, because those within had stores of food,

water, and supplies while those outside had either
to bring these up to the walls or to disperse in
order to find them. In view of the poor technology
of land transport at that time to supply a besieging force on the spot was almost impossible. Accordingly, having used up all the food and fodder
they had brought along or could find in the immediate vicinity of the fortress, the besiegers
had to range more and more widely to obtain supplies from the countryside. This reduced the numbers around the walls so that a sortie became increasingly possible. To guard against this, the
besiegers often constructed a counter-fortress
(Gegenburg) near the gates of the besieged stronghold to which the besiegers could retire if necessary to avoid being destroyed by a sortie before
their ranging foragers could return. Such an unsuccessful sortie would not break the siege because
the sortie-makers could find no supplies near the
walls and had to return inside before the foragers
returned. But without such counter-fortifications,
a besieging force might be destroyed by a sortie,
reducing the total number of besiegers below the
level able to continue the siege.

In this period the primary role of a field
army was not to engage and destroy other field
armies, but to prevent such armies from conducting a successful siege. This was done, not by defeating the enemy in battle but by preventing him
from foraging. This could be done merely by being
near. With an enemy field force nearby, the besieger could not disperse his forces to get supplies.
Where previously the besiegers' military problem
had been to keep a force outside the walls strong
enough so that it could not be driven away (or
defeated) by a sortie, now, with a field force
threatening, his military problem was enlarged:
he had to keep together, ready for combat, a force
strong enough to defeat a sortie and an attack by
a field force simultaneously, or, at least, strong
enough to withstand any attack by the field force.
This need to keep the besieging force concentrated
made foraging impossible and usually made it necessary to break off the siege and withdraw. It was
not the job of the enemy field force to attempt to
destroy the besieger during his withdrawal. The
task of the relieving field force was to relieve
the siege, and it was strategic incompetence to al-

low itself to be distracted from this primary objective. A relieving force which attacked a retreating besieger risked being defeated, in which case the besieger could return to the siege and might carry it to a successful conclusion.

Thus the primary task of a field force was to stay in existence in order to prevent successful sieges by preventing a besieger from dispersing his forces in order to forage. Of course the relieving field force had to forage itself in order to remain in the field. This was not easy unless other fortified supplies were locally available, but, even without these, a relieving force could forage more successfully than a besieging force because it was in "friendly" territory and could range in a wider circumference than the besieger could. In such a case, the latter was in a sense trapped between the sortie force and the relieving force and was threatened with inadequate supplies and ultimately with starvation unless he withdrew.

Two things might be pointed out about this strategy of medieval warfare: (1) it was closer to naval strategy of about 1910 than it was to the strategic ideas of land warfare in 1910 (or even today); and (2) it was a system of defensive superiority rather than an offensive one.

The naval strategy of 1910 was conceived in terms of one supreme weapon (the battleship), but this weapon required protection of a force of destroyers and lesser vessels to prevent attacks upon it. By 1945 the battleship had been replaced by the carrier but the relationship was the same. The purpose of the whole fleet was to continue in being in order to protect the economic base of waterborne world commerce which sustained the system of which the fleet was the defensive arm. In this parallel the medieval stronghold was the naval base; the field force was the protecting fleet; and the system of agrarian-based tenures was the equivalent of the modern system of widespread commerce and industry, which sustained the system and the armed defense which protected it.

The defensive strength of the medieval system

612

rested on the fact that (1) fortifications were
stronger than existing siege methods and (2) land
transport technology was so inefficient that food
and fodder could not be taken to consumers nearly
as effectively as the consumers could be taken to
the food and fodder. But these two rested on the
much more fundamental fact that food, fodder, and
manpower were all produced locally in immobile
enterprise units (in a peasant agriculture system).

Thus we have an immobile supreme weapon (the
fortified stronghold) sustained above an immobile
agricultural enterprise. But in the same context,
we have a very mobile military force, mounted
horsemen in a field army. This army could pass
easily through the system, over the agrarian units,
living off them (briefly) as they passed and between the strongholds which could not defeat the
field army and could, as we have seen, hardly be
defeated by it.

The defensive power of this system was increased by the fact that its activities were seasonal. Agricultural production was an annual
process, with the harvest in the spring (April-
May) south of the highland zone and in the summer
(July-August) north of the highland zone. This
meant that foraging by field armies would be easiest
toward the end of the harvest season (May-June or
August-September). In both areas, campaigning in
the winter was very difficult from wet and mud, extended by winter cold in the north and summer heat
and dust in the south. Thus the field armies interrupted their campaigning activities and returned
to their fortified bases (or "winter" quarters) for
a considerable fraction of the year. This interruption, by breaking off offensive attacks, served
to increase the superiority of the defense.

I have indicated that the greater the size of
a besieging force, if it could not take the stronghold by storm, the more the besieging force was
weakened. This was because the larger the force
of attackers, the more quickly the supplies of fodder and food in the vicinity were used up and the
sooner it would become necessary to break off the
siege and move on. This was particularly true when
the attackers included large numbers of non-combat-

613

ants as would be the case with migrant tribes such
as the Germans after A.D. 300. We often forget
that many of the moving tribes which crisscrossed
the Roman empire after 378 were seeking fodder
and food and were often starving. This was especially true of Attila and the Huns in the period
450-454.

Thus to besiege a town as a sustained operation was far beyond the ability of most power units
of the period we are now discussing. Few political
systems of this period could do this. In fact, the
Romans and Byzantines were almost the only ones
which could; the Moslems could not do so until
they ceased to be Arabic in the Abbasid period
(after 750); the Persians could do so only on a
limited scale and in the Sassanian period and
later periods.

The relationship of an invading field army to
the peasantry is of considerable importance and
brings up the problem of medieval military tactics
in general.

We have indicated that medieval strategy saw
no real merit in battle because it recognized that
the element of luck or chance was present to a
high degree in all such conflicts. Moreover, it
recognized that the morale of the forces was also
a significant factor in success and that this also
was difficult to control. For this reason, a commander generally would not engage in a battle unless his force was much superior in numbers or he
caught his enemy at a disadvantage or by surprise.
Moreover, because of the mobility of forces, it
was very difficult to bring an opponent to battle
if he was unwilling; he simply moved away. Such
an army on the march could be attacked but not very
successfully, except in a piecemeal way, as a harassing tactic. Thus most battles occurred because
both commanders were willing or at least had been
forced into a position where there was no easy alternative. Willingness to engage became much less
frequent in the post-Roman period.

The purpose of battle tactics remained what
it had always been, to break up the enemy's formation so that his forces could be destroyed as in-

dividuals and small groups. The chief influence
of grasslands pastoralism on tactics was a reduction in the use of the shock of massed fighters
as a method for doing this. Throughout antiquity,
from the Greek hoplite, through the Macedonian
phalanx, to the Roman legion, victory had gone to
the side which could maintain the solidarity of
its formation as the enemy hacked away at it. The
chief way of disrupting such a formation was by
shock, hurling one's own intact formation upon
the enemy's formation in an effort to break it
up by force. This tactic continued in the west
until the fifteenth century, with the favored tactic to hurl a mass of heavily armored horsemen
upon the enemy mass, break it up, and force it
to flight.

In the east, the nomadic fighters used "Parthian tactics," that is they tried to entrap the
enemy into disrupting his own formation by trying
to retaliate against attack with missile weapons.
The Turks and often the Saracens used these "Parthian" tactics, riding around the enemy in a whirl
of galloping horses, firing clouds of arrows at
his formation, especially at his horses, pretend-
ing to attack his flanks and rear rather than his
front, forcing him to turn about, making feint
charges on his formation and feint retreats to
entice him into pursuit. In such pursuits these
fighters used the "Parthian shot," firing arrows
backwards as they galloped away, until, when they
had the pursuers strung out behind, they might
turn and overwhelm their pursuers or lead them
all into a previously prepared trap or ambush.
Sometimes this feigned retreat might continue
for days. Sometimes, in such cases, the horsemen
were only a detachment of the main enemy force to
which they led their victims in tantalizing pursuit. In any case, once the enemy formations were
disrupted, these mobile horsemen generally sheathed
their bows, drew their swords, and rode on to their
harassed enemies for the kill.

Western European knights, who were committed
to disruption of enemy formations by impact and
were intellectually and emotionally unable to retreat or even feign retreat because of their exalted
conception of personal honor, were as bewildered by

615

these Parthian tactics when they first met the Turks (at Dorylaeum, during the First Crusade, July 1097) as Crassus had been when he met the Parthians at Carrhae in 53 B.C. Unlike Crassus, who perished with most of his forces, the Crusaders soon found a defense against such tactics. In its full development this new western tactic had several parts: (1) if possible, make a formation with one's flanks on natural obstacles so that the enemy could not ride round the formation; (2) if this was not possible, place a detachment of one's knights at the rear to ward off any Turkish charge there and to keep them off at long arrow range; (3) protect the front and flanks of the formation with massed infantry armed with spears or missile weapons; (4) divide up one's knights into several detachments which could be hurled separately at the galloping enemy to ensure against missing them with a single charge that they might elude; these western charges were to be withheld until the circling enemy horses were tiring; (5) keep one detachment of knights in reserve, with the commander, as a rear guard for the formation and as a final bolt to hurl at the enemy when he began to waver; (6) the charge of the knights could not be kept too long because as the enemy horses were tiring, the knights' horses were being killed by arrows. On the other hand, the enemy would begin to run out of arrows about the time his horses began to tire and if the knights' formation had not been disrupted by that time, the enemy would usually break off. The willingness of the knights to allow him to do this depended on the strategic situation.

The most significant tactical development from this encouter of western impact cavalry with eastern mounted bowmen was the western discovery of the effectiveness of infantry against cavalry attack even when the attacking horsemen were armed with missiles. We know very little about the role of infantry in Europe in the High Middle Ages, since the chroniclers were interested only in the mounted knights (because these were nobles), but we do know that they existed. In the Crusades, however, the western knights discovered at Dorylaeum in 1097 that a compact mass of infantry armed with spears could stand off cavalry and with bows could keep them at such a distance that the enemy arrows had insufficient penetrating power to kill armored knights. Moreover, infantry bowmen did not run out of arrows as quickly as mounted bowmen, since they could shoot back arrows shot at them.

The greatest success of infantry in the Crusades was in August 1192 when Richard the Lion-Hearted was caught in a surprise dawn attack in camp outside Jaffa. He had only ten horsemen and 2000 infantry of whom many were armed with crossbows, more with spears. He put the spearmen kneeling in the front rank close together with the spears held pointing forward and their buttends in the ground. In the second rank he placed the crossbows, stationed with two men and two bows in the intervals between the spears. One crossbowman fired as the other reloaded the second bow, then exchanged bows, keeping up a very rapid rate of fire. The ten knights were posted behind this formation to protect the rear. The Muslims did not dare charge this arrangement.

In all this warfare the peasantry played little role. Their task was simply to provide the wealth which supported it. Since the contending military forces were fighting for control of tenures sustained by operating agricultural enterprises, there was a common interest among the fighters to keep those enterprises functioning and that means to keep them intact, including the peasants. On the other hand, the vital role which foraging played in the whole military system exposed the peasants to the frequent danger of having their own share of the produce "requisitioned" by armed men of either side. When this happened, the enterprise was not destroyed but the peasant operators might well be exposed to want or starvation. Their women were often raped. If they resisted any of this, they might be killed. Thus their lives were very difficult, even dangerous. However, the basic desire by both sides to keep the enterprise functioning was an insurance against total destruction of the farm, the livestock, the tools, and even life itself.

There were, however, certain conditions in which the peasant life was put into total jeopardy

and the ravaging of the countryside might become
general: (1) if the invader wanted slaves, as he
sometimes did, he might totally devastate the
countryside and send the enslaved peasants back
to his own country, (2) if the invader wanted to
bring a defending field force to battle, he might
devastate the countryside to force it to do so in
order to protect the agricultural base of the defender's tenures, (3) if an army or garrison was
starving or dangerously short of manpower, it might
kill all the livestock, consume the seedstocks,
and impress the peasant into garrison or auxiliary
services, and (4) if an invader wanted the land for
himself either because he had a surplus of population himself or he wanted to use the land for some
other system. Of these two, the former (that an
invader might have surplus population and want
land for his own immigrant population) is unlikely.
It occurred only in those cases where people were
migrating, like the Germans coming into the Roman
empire (especially the Angles and Saxons into Britain) or the Northmen and Magyars who settled in
Europe, mostly in the tenth century.

The last possibility is of greater significance. If a fully nomadic pastoral people, like
the Turks and early Mongols from the north or
Bedouin raiders from the south, came in with their
herds to settle, they also would exterminate the
peasants to transform the countryside from a system of peasant agriculture to a system of pastoral nomadism.

These possibilities of immigrant settlers
were not the normal motive or pattern for medieval
warfare. On the contrary, it might be said that
they marked the beginning and the ending of the
medieval period. Certainly they marked the beginning and the ending of the Byzantine system, which
began with the Germanic immigrations of the 4th
and 5th centuries and ended with the Turkish migrations following Manzikert (1071).

The period between these two periods of migratory tribes, say from Adrianople to Manzikert
(378-1071), was dominated on the highest political
levels by a strange type of political organization

which I shall call "providential empire." This was
a political structure whose chief element was ideological, or rather the ideological implications of
a religious outlook. It was this new type of political organization, invented perhaps by Persia but
brought to perfection by the Byzantine emperor, the
Abbasid Caliph, Jenghis Khan, and the Ottoman sultan, which dominated the high politics of the Old
World from the age of Constantine. In order to
understand its nature we must take a glance at
religious history. This need to look at religious
history when the subject with which we are primarily
concerned is the relationship between political organization and weapons history, is of major significance to our subject, since it shows the limitations
of weapons technology in history.

It also shows why this whole period is so unstable. The weapons factor in that instability
has been pointed out as the basic contrast between
cavalry mobility and fortress stability. The fact
that the strong point was superior in this pair
and was purely defensive, combined with the static
nature of agricultural production and income tenures
based on agriculture created an almost overwhelming
tendency toward small, local, private units of political power. Only in Europe and in Europe only
west of the Elbe, or even west of the Rhine, was
this tendency toward localization able to prevail.
Elsewhere it was overborne by the domination of
providential empire. This combination rested on
the ideological implications of religious belief.
But the stability of providential empire itself
was threatened by the fact that the religious belief on which it was based was a halfway point in
the development of religious ideas and was already
obsolete in A.D. 330, when the Greek providential
empire was being constructed by Constantine. Thus
weapons confusion, defensive superiority, the localized nature of agrarian tenures, poor transportation,
communications and general control, and the obsolete
character of the prevalent religious beliefs, all
contributed to move human power organizations toward localism. Yet the ideology of providential
empire was strong enough to override these, at
least episodically, and, as a consequence, this
period, from 300 to about 1600, was the period of

the largest territorial empires in history. But
for these same reasons, and others we must mention,
these large territorial empires were temporary and
ephemeral. This ephemeral and unstable character
of providential empire rested on the fact that the
whole organization was personal, resting on the life,
ability, and health of one individual man who had
been chosen by a providential deity to rule. Such
personal rule is bound to be temporary, ephemeral,
and unstable, for nothing is so erratic as the life,
abilities, and health of any particular individual,
especially an omnipotent ruler.

This new form of government became prevalent
in the period A.D. 300-800 because the religious
developments of the peoples directly concerned,
notably the Romans, the Arabs, the Germans, the
Asiatic peasantry, and the Uralic-speaking peoples (but not educated Greeks or Hebrews) were so
backward. Most of these peoples in A.D. 300, whatever their nominal religious affiliation, were
still on a very primitive level of paganism, and
viewed the world as under the influence of a myriad of conflicting spiritual powers. In this
sense they were about on the level that the Greeks
had been about 900 B.C., or the Hebrews had been
before Moses. In the period A.D. 200-800, these
peoples became aware of monotheistic ideas and
eagerly adopted them, but continued to interpret
this new conception of deity in a very primitive
way, as a personal, anthropomorphic, grandfatherly
god who was omnipotent but not really transcendental,
since he constantly watched what individual men were
doing and constantly intervened in human affairs.
Moreover, this intervention took the form of arbitrary acts of will and did not occur, as the most
advanced Hebrew and Greek thinkers already recognized, by His support of rational unchanging laws
to which He conformed Himself. Thus, while the advanced Greek thinkers were almost too transcendental
(seeing God as not only separate from the world but
as opposed to the materialism of the world yet
under the rules of a rational cosmos), the more
backward neo-monotheists saw the deity as above
the laws, able to do anything including reversal
of all laws, and running the universe by a fickle,
personal, and unpredictable (because incomprehensible)
Will, but not by laws.

620

Under this kind of a religious outlook, public authority (indeed, all authority) was simply a reflection of the temporary whims of the divine will, and all secular rulers were providential rather than <u>constitutional</u>. That is, such rulers were representative of god's will and not of established rules, including <u>rules of succession</u>. In such a system any effort to restrain the monarch's will by public law would be a futile effort to restrain God's will be human enactments. On the other hand, if the monarch did violate God's will, God would take care of the situation, removing the miscreant ruler when He saw fit. In theory, of course, the ruler was expected to follow "rules," but they were the "rules" of ethics as laid down by God and were not necessarily universal, eternal, rational, or comprehensive to us, but (like the Mosaic dietary restrictions on eating milk and flesh together or on not eating things which crawl, especially things that crawl in the sea) were simply <u>orders</u> from God-- to be obeyed and not questioned.

In such a context of outlook, a cruel king was simply God's instrument of reprisal against sinful men. At the same time, political changes, including natural death of the ruler, military coups, revolutions, or defeats in foreign wars, were similar manifestations of God's providence ruling the world and were to be accepted by mortal men. If resisted by such mortals, the outcome would be determined by God's will, for the will of God could neither be questioned nor understood by men.

Thus, in these providential monarchies, political changes were to be suffered through and accepted. A ruler was providential in the sense that he came to power by God's will, continued to rule so long as God willed, and passed from the scene at the time and in the fashion that God willed. All of these events were "Mandates of Heaven," as the Chinese called them and were to be accepted as the will of God--that is <u>Islam</u>. The Crusader's war cry, "God Wills it!" reflects the same outlook.

As we have said, this idea of the nature of deity was a very underdeveloped one. It was on a

level reached by some Hebrew thinkers before 800
B.C. or reached, along a different route, by some
Greek thinkers such as by Xenophanes 500 B.C. And
it was, of course, much more primitive than the belief that "God is Good" or Christ's message that
"God is Love." These providential monotheists saw
God as One and as Omnipotent, but they also saw Him
as despotic and arbitrary. By A.D. 200 some thinkers, without any numerous popular followings, saw
God as Good (that is, under the rules), as totally
transcendental (that is abstract and not personally
involved in the world of space-time), as unchanging
and unmoving (that is guiding the cosmos by His unchanging Reason rather than by his changeable Will),
and as Love (that is, providing men with the freedom, resources, autonomy, and potentiality to grow
in godliness). But these more advanced religious
thinkers, using the ideas of Xenophanes, Aristotle,
Zoroaster, and the later Hebrew prophets, had little real influence on the general outlook of the
period we are examining.

On the other hand, the outlook we have described as prevalent during this period, the idea
of God as a single arbitrary despotic Will, was
held by a large number of persons, perhaps by a
majority in the chief political communities we
are discussing. But, when we say this, we must
recognize that we are saying something which is
really ambiguous, for the statement that something
"was held by a large number of persons" obviously
has two distinct meanings. It may mean "held" as
an explicit, conceptualized, conscious, verbalized ideology, which may be used to rationalize
actions decided on other grounds, or it may be
"held" as a fundamental, neurological structure
of categories and values which may be only partially conscious but which is, nonetheless, one
of the chief elements in personal decision-making
and action. I make use of this distinction by
calling the former "ideology" and the latter "outlook." Outlook is the basis of decision and action, while the ideology is the basis of rationalization and verbalization. This is a distinction
we all make when we say of someone that he is a
"nominal Christian" or a "real Christian."

In the period with which we are concerned

622

there were many "nominal Christians" and "nominal Muslims," both of them "nominal monotheists" but there were few real Christians, Muslims, or monotheists. Nevertheless, these nominal attributions became the chief bases of ideological loyalties and of political groupings. In such political groupings and under the banners of such ideological loyalties, a small minority of persons who were real monotheists, whether Christians or Muslims, worked with an overwhelming majority of nominal Christians or Muslims who were largely motivated by the same superstitions of polytheistic powers, the same drives for wealth, power, and sensual enjoyments as they would have been had they remained polytheistic.

The reason for this excursus on ideology and outlook is that it is essential background to our understanding of the processes of military success and political stability (or instability) in this period 200-1500. We have shown that weapons confusion and resulting organizational ambiguities had the consequence of giving a greater influence to morale in the power nexus. This was especially true in respect to the convinced monotheists who were, whether Christian or Muslim, convinced that they would win immediate admission to paradise if they died fighting against unbelievers. This theme was clearly stated in the speeches which Muslim leaders gave their followers before the early battles won by the advancing tide of Islam. It was constantly reiterated in the speeches and writings of the Christian Roman empire. Indeed, in the latter, several efforts were made, at various times, to establish as a religious rule that those who lost their lives in battle against unbelievers would win the sainthood of martyrdom. The same ideas were found in the pre-battle exhortations of the kings of Sassanian Persia. Among the Seljuk, who came in as nomadic tribesmen but soon became providential monarchs, the ruler was "the Shadow of God on Earth." A Seljuk royal diploma began, "Since God, glory and exhaltation be to Him, by His perfect action has bestowed upon us the lordship of the world and has placed in our control the affairs of the kingdoms of the world and the ordering of the affairs of the peoples of the world, and has caused the

standards of our rule to be signs of His power and
might, may He be honored and glorified. . ."

Another political idea which flowed from the
religious outlook of all these providential empires
was that each had to be universal. We have seen
that their monotheism was not a casual belief but
was a necessary consequence of their obsession
with God's omnipotence. But, if there is only
one God supreme over all men and if the ruler is
His vicar on earth, there can be only one such
vicar and he must rule over all men, in theory at
least. All of these providential empires saw the
situation in a similar fashion: polytheism might
allow polyarchy, but monotheism required a universal empire: one God in Heaven requires one
Emperor on Earth, for the Imperial Power is Divine
Power. This belief is the ultimate ideological
justification for the constant aggressive wars of
all these similar political structures and for the
religious intolerance and compulsory conversion of
many of them. When, for practical political reasons, some of these structures, such as Byzantium
at certain periods, failed to practice intolerance
and forced conversion, they were subject to criticism by their more intensely religious subjects.

This claim to universalism had certain incidental consequences associated with titles and
symbols. For example, the title basileus came
to be regarded as a title of universality after
Heraclitus won it from the Persians in his great
victories of 628. It had the same implications
as the Persian title "King of Kings" or the title
"Vicar of God" used by many rulers including the
popes.

A similar implication of universality was
registered by a ruler's claim to put his image
on gold coinage. It was generally recognized
in the area west of India that the Byzantine emperor had exclusive right to do this. The Sassanian king recognized this by treaty in 562.
This does not mean that other rulers could not
issue gold coins but, if they did so, such coins
had to be struck in the weight and design of the
Byzantine ones, as Persia and other rulers some-

times did. Only when other rulers wished to challenge the Byzantine claim to universal rule did they issue gold coins with their own images. This was done, for example, by the grandson of Clovis, Theodobert (534-548), after an attack on imperial territories in Italy, and by the Saracens after 692. But, generally, even the greatest rulers, like Charlemagne, put their own images only on silver and copper and issued gold coins only rarely and as copies of the Byzantine gold nomismata. When Theodobert violated this in order to defy Justinian, the contemporary historian, Procopius, wrote, "The German kings are using gold from Gaul to mint solidi on which they have stamped, not the head of the Roman emperor, but their own effigy. Yet the king of Persia himself, who has complete freedom with regard to his silver coinage, would not dare to put his image on gold coins: that is a right which is denied to him and to all barbarian kings."

These providential rulers were totalitarian as well as universal in their claims. The monarch was the head of all activities, including the church and the armies, with the latter increasingly more important than the former. About A.D. 400 Synesius said, "The emperor's business is fighting." This idea, rooted in the fact that the origin of the imperial office was to be found in the function of Imperator ("Commander in Chief"), continued in all these providential monarchies. In Byzantium, over centuries of changing coronation symbolism, the most essential part was the acclamation by the troops in the Hebdomon (Byzantium's equivalent to Rome's Campus Martius). Designation by the senate or consecration by the church were less significant, although the church constantly sought to make its part in the process the essential part, even going so far as to concede that the unction made the emperor one of the clergy with most of the rights of the clergy (such as access to the sanctuaries, the Eucharist in both forms, etc.). Of these rights the most important was that the unction made the ruler basileus holding his power directly from God without intermediaries. This meant, among other things, that "The emperor was now acknowledged not only as the supreme court of appeal but as the actual fons iuris, the source of law" (to quote H. St. L.M. Moss).

625

The first coronation of an emperor by the patriarch was that of Leo I in 457, after the soldiers gave him the diadem in the Hebdomon. In 491 the patriarch would not anoint Anastasius until he made a confession of faith in which he accepted the canons of the Council of Chalcedon (which condemned the monophysite doctrine). The patriarch's function in the coronation soon became essential, but choice of an emperor by the church was never established nor claimed.

Originally the title of basileus was used by the king of Persia and not by the Byzantine emperor, but Heraclitus adopted it on the ground that he won it from the Sassanians by his victory over them in 628, and it was reserved exclusively for the emperor after the Sassanian empire ended in 651. This title signified universal domination and, unlike the title of "king" could, in theory, be held only by God's sole vicar on earth. This rule did not apply only to Christians or to members of the Byzantine political system, for the emperor, who enforced the civil law over this system, had equal authority to enforce the Ius Gentium over all civilized men and the Ius naturale over all living creatures. This is why he held the orbis or earthly globe in his right hand and was called "divus" or "master of earth and sea and of all men," "sovereign of life which he may grant or take away since his power extends to all." He was regarded as "co-regent of God" and his bureaucracy was known as the "divini officii." He was chosen directly by God, "from the womb of his mother" to be "co-regent" and "autokrator on earth." All the imperial victories were given to him by God so that no other general (after Belisarius in 534) could celebrate a triumph in the old Roman fashion. In the same way, no other ruler could be "basileus," neither Charlemagne nor the later Holy Roman emperors (the title was used for Charlemagne only once, in 812). The empire was the same as the church, both forming the mystic body of all Christians which would be the celestial empire after the Last Judgment.

Ideas such as these, found (perhaps in a less extreme form) in all the providential empires, were not "just theory." Among ordinary persons

626

ideas such as these, that God is on your side, that
death in battle provides instant admission to Paradise, and that your cause must win out in the long
run, can play a significant role in determining
the outcome of battles between forces with similar
weapons and similar degrees of disorganization. To
be sure, no battles are likely to have all, or
even a majority, of one side made up of such convinced believers. There may be a majority if the
forces are small, united primarily for this purpose,
and clearly operating against the enemies of their
beliefs, but as soon as forces become large or the
system of the community gets well established, the
majority of fighters will not be convinced believers
but will be nominal believers dominated by other
motives.

In the period we are considering and in the
area we are considering, the chief of these other
motives was personal, material gain. It was an
age of professional mercenary soldiers or of raiders and armies seeking plunder. Such fighters
fought about as well as the ideologically impelled
warriors because what they lacked in motivation
was usually made up for by greater experience and
professional knowledge. Such mercenary fighters,
once they got into the battle, fought hard simply
because they wanted to survive to share in the
plunder or to collect their pay. Soldiering was
simply a way of life for them, and once the battle began, it often became a case of kill or be
killed. Accordingly, the battles of this period,
even when the ideological issue was relatively
minor, often were fought to the death with heavy
casualties.

The battle of Mursa was fought entirely by
mercenaries, and there was no reason why the soldiers could not have looked forward to employment
by the victor even if they were on the losing side.
Yet, Ernest Stein calls it the bloodiest battle of
the fourth century.

In combats where the ideological issue was
more significant than at Mursa, the casualties
were often heavy, not from the battle directly,
but because the ideologues often continued to kill

627

the defeated without surrender while fleeing, or even after surrender.

The point of view of mercenary professional soldiers is still rather difficult for us to understand, although it is growing rapidly today. To us, war is an interruption of our normal life and activities and is an unnatural and usually objectionable separation from our families and friends. The mercenary soldiers of the period we are considering would hardly have understood either of these objections. They had no other life, no other "normal" activities and skills, so that soldiering was their way of life. It was the way they lived, and they could imagine no other which they would prefer. Moreover, to a considerable extent, soldiering, to them, did not imply any unnatural separation from their families and the people they knew. These all went along with them, so that the life of the barracks or the camp was shared with family and friends. In the later Roman armies (after 350 or so) the soldier often owned a slave who went along with him to act as his batman.

Under these conditions, a moving army of this period, except in unusual circumstances (such as the raids of the early Moslems, or of the Huns, and of the early German invasions before 350), was an enormous, disorderly horde, covering many miles of route, in which the combatants were outnumbered, at least five-fold, by non-combatants, families, camp followers, and servants, all enclosed in a great mass of baggage, moving animals (for transport, but also as food), wagons, and furniture. In general such a moving army tended to adopt fixed relative positions for the combatants, the so-called "five-part army," with a center, flanked by two wings, preceded by an advance guard and followed by a rear guard. But in most armies of the day, the discipline associated with the Roman armies of the republican period was long past.

This lack of discipline was reflected in all aspects of military life, but was, perhaps, most obviously in the fact that the carefully constructed fortified night camp of the old Roman army was no more. With so many camp followers, it was no longer possible to make a camp with ramparts large enough

to enclose all the non-combatants. But even when
the army was made up almost exclusively of combatants, they could no longer be compelled to fortify the camp at night as the Roman soldiers of
the republic had done. The most that could generally be obtained was that, like the Germans,
they drew up their wagons into a defensive circle.

A similar weakening of discipline was to be
found throughout all military operations. Battle
could no longer be given simply by issuing orders,
as Caesar had done. By A.D. 400 it was generally
necessary to discuss the prospects with the mercenary leaders and to persuade them that the plans
were likely to succeed before they would agree to
move against the enemy. As a result, it was frequent for armies to camp in each other's presence
for days before both commanders could get both
forces to agree to fight. On the other hand, it
sometimes happened that the mercenaries, bored,
frustrated, or eager for booty, insisted upon a
battle which the commander wished to avoid. Similarly, once the engagement began, the commander's
control of the various units was rather tenuous.
Thus, tactics beyond the simplest were impossible.
Various units and arms operated relatively independently, engaging when they saw fit, breaking
off when they had had enough, stopping to loot
before the battle was half over, even, in a few
cases, refusing to join in until they could see
which way the battle was likely to go, at which
point they attacked the loser and pillaged his
baggage, even when this loser was their erstwhile
employer.

The use of Parthian tactics and mercenary
troops under conditions of weak discipline, poor
communications, and shifting loyalties were risky
and often had unexpected consequences. Frequently
a feigned withdrawal could not be stopped or a
pretended attack could not be controlled and was
carried to full shock by warriors thirsting for
plunder. Under such conditions it is not surprising that there were drastic shifts in power, since
victory no longer was a matter of weapons, of organization or of tactics, but was rather a matter
of personalities, of ideological feelings, or of

629

random chance. But at the same time, while victories, even overwhelming ones, could occur to any organized political system or wandering tribe, this could well be reversed in a second battle. Thus, in general, a consistent series of victories sufficient to lead to a total change in political geography was unlikely unless a system had some long sustained advantage or disadvantage which would lead eventually to its total eclipse or to the total defeat of its enemy.

In the period with which we are concerned, such a sustained advantage or disadvantage was more likely to be ideological than technological or organizational, because technological advantages spread sufficiently rapidly (with the possible exception of "Greek fire") to become the common possession of all powers involved in our constellation of power systems, and all power systems in our constellation were almost equally badly organized, so that this element did not provide a long-sustained advantage to any one of them.

If we look at the constellation of power systems we have described in the area west of the Hindu Kush, we shall see that three were successful in maintaining their power over sustained periods. These were the eastern Roman system (in the next section), the Islamic system (in the following section), and possibly the Frankish system (in Chapter 8).

On the other hand, the power systems which were eclipsed or barely survived this chronological period were numerous. Many were tribal or at most semi-civilized power systems, usually monarchies. These included the various Germanic kingdoms of the west, the Slav kingdoms of the Balkans (Bulgarian) and Kiev, the Uralic kingdoms of this same area (Huns and Avars), the Arab kingdoms of South Arabia and of the Syrian Desert (Palmyra, Petra, Lakhmids, and Beni Ghassans), Armenia, the neo-Persian empire, various Caucasic and Afghan kingdoms, the Khazar and Kushan kingdoms of the Caspian area, and the Ephthalite kingdom (White Huns). Moreover, all of these various kingdoms in this period were threatened by mobile enemies on their grassland borders.

We have no need to examine in detail either these kingdoms or their grassland enemies, but these latter included local pressures from Berbers and Moors in North Africa, from Libyans and Nubians in Egypt, and of Semites into Abyssinia. Some of these grassland pastoral pressures still occur (as the Somali pressures on Abyssinia), but most of them, such as those of the Kurds of Iraq or Iran, or those of the Pushtu on Afghanistan or Pakistan, are now being reduced rapidly by transforming their nomadic way of life into a sedentary one.

From this examination, it would seem that the power systems of this period which survived into our next period had some ideological distinction. They were generally monotheistic or (like the Franks and the Abyssinians) monotheistic in a distinctive way. Thus in the west one chief reason for the failure of the Germanic kingdoms to survive was that they were all Arian, except the Franks.

The very nature of providential empire, with its emphasis on the individual ruler as the key to the system and with its religious justification of whatever happens (including successful revolt or assassination), was such as to encourage internal political instability also. We have seen how heavy were the casualties among the rulers of Rome in the west: from 44 B.C. to A.D. 392, of 63 rulers, 5 were killed in battle, 19 died naturally, and 39 were murdered. In east Rome, over 1058 years (395-1453), 39 died naturally, 8 were killed in war, 41 were murdered, and 24 others were deposed. Of the Moslem Caliphs over 300 years (632-932), 2 were deposed, 9 were murdered and 21 died natural deaths. The casualties among the Sassanian Persians or the Abbasid and Turkish sultans were just as high as among the Caliphs.

In addition to the murders of rulers, outbreaks of civil wars were also frequent in the civilized states of this period. This was partially a reflection of the lack of any established constitutional rule of succession (or even of any established constitution) among these states, but it was also a reflection of the pervasive disrespect for human life and of the equally pervasive ideological

631

and moral confusion of the period.

This was a period in which political activity was associated with all kinds of personal outrages, bestialities, cruelties, vindictiveness, betrayals, and sadism. These were accepted as part of a providential world in which everything occurred in accordance with the Will of God, and if this Will was violated, God could rectify the balance, either immediately or in the Hereafter. Thus, untold millions were murdered, tortured, betrayed, exiled, enslaved, mutilated, imprisoned, sexually abused, or driven insane as part of the regular processes of operations of these transitional providential empires in the first millennium or more of the so-called "Christian era."

The Emperor Constantine VI "vented his rage against his five uncles," blinding the eldest and tearing out the tongues of the other four; Constantine himself had his eyes torn out on orders from his mother, the Empress Irene; the Emperor Basil II had the eyes torn out of 15,000 Bulgarian war captives, leaving a single eye to 150 of them to lead the others home; the Caliph Saffah invited all the members of the rival Omayyad family to a banquet of reconciliation, where he massacred some 85 of them in cold blood, before seating his own followers down to the banquet, "while the floor of the hall was still covered with blood-soaked bodies, and the revelries of the living were interrupted by the groans of the dying" (to quote Sir John Glubb); in 531 and again in 629 the Sassanian King of Kings murdered all his brothers and their male offspring to prevent their plotting against his tenure of the throne (in 629 this included 17 brothers); modern historians like Arthur Christiansen refuse to believe the Annals of the Sassanian Kings of Tabari (died in 923), when they tell us that the Sassanian king Hormazd VI (579-589) had 13,600 of his own nobility executed and on one occasion, apparently on a whim, ordered all the state prisoners, amounting to about 36,000, killed. We need not be unduly skeptical of such figures, since even in the last century we have seen the capabilities of a providential monarchical system in the exercise of mass political murder, in Ottoman Turkey, Manchu China, or Russia. In this

632

kind of political organization fratricide and parricide were the frequent (and almost the normal) mode of political action. Such a system operated in a religious and ethical outlook alien to modern minds, but we must recognize that this alien system was widespread and long-protracted, covering a major part of the Old World for almost 1500 years and was, thus, more extensive and of much longer duration than any of the democratic, parliamentary, or constitutional systems which are more familiar to us. Such a system, by its very nature, reduced the influence of both weapons and weapons systems on political arrangements, including political stability.

This greater dominance of the moral factor over either the artifactual (technological) or organizational factors makes it possible for changes of morale to give rise to sudden and dramatic shifts in power, so that a power structure which seems invincible one day may be reduced to a puny and insignificant structure a decade or so later, but may return to a peak of power again within the same generation.

Moreover, in such a transitional situation two other processes may be observed. One of these is the greatly increased historic role of individuals and of random chance ("fate") in determining events, and the other is the process already mentioned: that organized power, and especially organized force in weapons systems, is only effective against those who accept the principle of organization involved in the system itself and may be totally ineffective either against systems organized on a different principle or against individuals with high personal morale who are not part of the established system. Thus a single individual, like Christ or Gandhi, may completely frustrate and eventually disorganize a power system.

In the area with which we are now concerned (roughly from the Adriatic Sea to the Hindu Kush) the power systems which formed the constellation of powers in that area had many similar characteristics. Most of these characteristics were of pastoral origin, such as strongly patriarchal social structures, substantial anarchistic elements

633

(associated in the successful societies with equally strong authoritarian elements), an obsession with war and violence, an exploitative attitude toward women (including polygamy, casual divorce, concubinage, and harems), a tendency to seek wealth through use of force to obtain plunder and booty rather than through hard work in bringing the resources of production together in some productive system, and a continuance of the heroic traditions of grassland tribalism in regard to immortality, extremism, and poetic or bardic traditions.

These pastoral elements were combined with other elements, often Persian, to give fundamentally similar patterns to the power systems of this area in the period. Among these were: a cooptative or selective element in monarchical succession, widespread dependence on soldiers, and a divisive and unstable politico-social system of at least four or five elements, in shifting balance, in a system which involved large-scale confusion of the public and private spheres. These elements generally included: (a) mercenary military leaders; (b) a civilian bureaucratic structure, controlling financial resources and justice; (c) a wealthy feudalized landlord class which tended to usurp control of finance and justice; or (d) a religious or clerical element; and often, (e) a commercial, urban class. Three other aspects of the whole system were: (1) a tendency toward ideological fanaticism, often monotheistic, used to rationalize the aggressive and violent aspects of the system; (2) the use of clientage, or personal loyalty, often hereditary, on a basis of unequal social position as an element in personal power structures; and (3) a tendency for the despotic ruler to create an administrative structure of social outcasts, such as slaves, freedmen, eunuchs, racially distinctive, or heretical persons, in relationships of personal loyalty to himself, as a means for exercising his despotic powers outside the control of the established social groupings, such as the generals, the landlords, or the clergy.

The custom of clientage, used by all influential persons in these power structures (as it was used in the Roman republic from its earliest days) found its strongest ties in the relations which a freedman and his descendants had toward the family of his manumitter. This practice was well established in this period in societies as diverse as Rome, the Mongols, and the Islamic Arabs. On a somewhat different basis, it existed between a military leader and his established followers and is closely related to the Germanic idea of personal loyalty which has been widely discussed under the institution of the "comitatus" (a band of personal followers) often regarded as a precursor of the personal loyalty or fealty of the later medieval vassal to his lord.

In the period with which we are concerned (roughly the millennium 300-1300 A.D.) the growing influence of personal loyalty, like growing rural localism and, to a lesser degree, growing intensity of devotion to a personal, monotheistic God, arose from the turmoil and disruption of existing organizational institutions and behavioral patterns so that increasingly rootless and emotionally frustrated peoples tried to create some elements of permanence in the chaos of their lives by accepting fixed links of loyalty to specific persons, places, and beliefs. Such a development is parallel to the "existential" movement in the European outlook of the 1950s.

The growing confusion of public and private to which I have referred arose from both sides. By that I mean that uncivilized tribes, such as Bedouin Arabs, Germans, and Huns or Turks, who had no real grasp of the concept of public and had lived previously in a world made up entirely of private relationships, in this period began to grasp the idea of public relationships. On the other hand, the established civilized societies, notably Rome and Persia, which earlier had a clear distinction between public and private, began to blur that distinction by a growing tendency to treat public matters as private ones.

This last development is most evident in the growing tendency to regard the public authority (the old Latin imperium) as a possession disposable by testament (or at least by the private wish of the incumbent). The restrictions on such testamentary disposition (that it could not be given to slaves, eunuchs, freedmen, or heretics) were not so much a consequence of the persistence of older ideas of public law or even of archaic kingship, but were based much more on the fact that if these excluded groups of persons did become eligible to hold the imperium, the ruler would have no persons about himself with whom he could feel safe from plots since they would no longer be restrained from plotting by legal ineligibility. This factor, observable in Rome as early as A.D. 50, became one of the dominant elements in the Ottoman empire, but is observable in all large states of this transitional character.

On the other hand, the practice of disposing of the imperium by private testament as if the res publica were a res privata became increasingly evident in the Byzantine, Islamic, Persian, and their successor empires (notably the Mongol, Ottoman, and the Russian) and occurred in these latter as late as the nineteenth century. In fact, one of the clearest examples of this attitude was the fact that Czar Alexander I (who died in 1825) left his throne to his younger son, Nicholas, in a secret will, informing his older son, Constantine, but not telling the beneficiary of his intention.

Despite the murders and violence associated with providential empire in this period, it must be recognized that it was successful, simply in terms of its ability to survive the terrible challenges which rose against it over a period of more than a millennium (from the founding of Constantinople as capital in 330 to its capture by the Ottoman Turks in 1453). We have given some reasons for east Rome's ability to survive the collapse of west Rome in the fifth century, but we must now proceed to a more intensive examination of how east Rome was able to cope with its external and internal threats during some thirty-five generations.

The constellation of power systems with which we are concerned in this period of weapons confusion centered on the states of the Near East: the

636

Hellenistic kingdoms of the successors of Alexander the Great, the neo-Persian empire which replaced these, and the Byzantine empire which succeeded both Rome and the neo-Persians in that area. The area included both civilized and uncivilized communities. The chief axis of this constellation of powers in the first millennium A.D. extended from the Mediterranean Sea to the Indus River. Following the death of Alexander the Great in 323 B.C., most of this area had fallen into the control of the Seleucid dynasty, whose capital city was at Seleucia on the lower Tigris. The pressures on the Seleucid kingdom from the other Hellenistic successor kingdoms and ultimately from Rome made this power seem most insecure in the west (the Mediterranean) and distracted it from what might have been its chief role as a buffer state against the pastoral peoples of the north coming across the Caucasus from south Russia or coming across the Oxus from central Asia. As a result, the northeastern districts of the Seleucid kingdom broke free from Seleucid control in the third century B.C., notably Parthia (southeast of the Caspian Sea) about 260 B.C. and Bactria (northeast of Parthia, between the Oxus and the Hindu Kush). Both of these areas soon fell under the domination of grasslands pastoralists and became the core areas of grassland pastoralists' empires for more than 800 years (until the Islamic conquests, 638-680). For much of this period there were two major powers in this area, one centered in Iran under the Parthian Aracid dynasty (247 B.C.-A.D. 226), and the Sassanians (A.D. 227-641), the other farther east, under the Kushans (c. 50 B.C.-c. A.D. 150, with capital at Peshawar), and the Hephthalites or White Huns (c. 425-c.567). The grasslands area north of these was held by Sarmatian pastoralists, extending from the Danube to Chinese Turkestan, about 300 B.C., but gradually these were replaced over the next few centuries by Germans pushing into south Russia from central Europe and by Hunnish-Mongolian peoples pushing into central Asia and the Kirgis Steppes from the east. This latter movement continued century after century, culminating in the Mongol conquests of Jenghis Khan, Tamerlane, and others in the period 1200-1400.

In the earlier period with which we are concerned now, the Parthians found themselves under
pressure from Rome in the west, from the pastoral
nomads in the north (coming over the Caucasus)
and from the Kushans in the east. Nevertheless,
as the Seleucids crumbled under Roman pressure,
the Parthians took over, and under Mithridates the
Great (124-88 B.C.) ruled an empire extending from
the Euphrates to India. But the nomadic threat
remained: Mithridates' two predecessors had been
killed (in 127 and 124 B.C.) fighting northeastern
nomads, the Kushan-Tochari ("Sacae" to the Greeks).

The Parthians remained very much a nomadic
upper class dominated by a feudal, warrior, nobility
consisting of seven great Pahlavi families and lesser nobles, with their retainers, superimposed over
the mixed Greco-Iranian Seleucid system. Their
power rested on their weapons system adapted from
the Sarmatians. In this the great nobles, riding
especially bred, powerful Nesean horses, with both
horse and rider clad in mail, fought with heavy
spears, while their retainers, with lighter protection, served as horse archers. They made a
commercial treaty with China in 115 B.C. and tried
to keep open a trans-Asian trade route between Syria and the Far East across the steppe oases, but
they were harassed by the grassland nomads and
were greatly hampered by their own internal political system in which the king was constantly
threatened by his feudalized nobles. The kings
sought to form an alliance with the Romans against
the Trans-Caucasia nomads, but the Romans, whom
they first encountered in 92 B.C., treated them
with contempt. In 53 B.C. Crassus tried to conquer the Parthians but was killed with most of
his army at Carrhae in northern Syria. It is said
that 20,000 were killed and 10,000 captured, from
a force of 40,000 Romans in this battle.

The significance of Carrhae which showed the
vulnerability of the legion to horse archers was
lost when the Parthians invaded Syria in 40-38 B.C.,
with their cataphracts but without their horse archers, and suffered a severe defeat. The Roman
civil war, followed by Augustus' peaceful policy
in Asia, covered a period of Parthian domestic

disintegration. Trajan annexed much of Caucasia, Armenia, Assyria and Mesopotamia in A.D. 114-117, but most of these were abandoned by Hadrian in 117. By A.D. 77 the Parthian empire had almost disintegrated from the struggles of its unruly nobles to control the monarchy, and the Parthian capital at Ctesiphon (across the Tigris from Seleucia) was sacked by the Romans three times in the second century (in 115, 165, and 197).

During this period of Parthian decline, the Tochari of Bactria expanded under a Kushan dynasty, crossing the Hindu Kush to conquer much of western India, including all of the Indus valley. They also controlled all of the navigable course of the Oxus and the Caspian passes, extending westward into the deserts of Iran, and cooperated with the Romans to divert all Far Eastern commerce either north or south of Parthian territory. This Kushan empire, which reached its greatest extent, from Benares to the Caspian Sea, about A.D. 90, had its capital at Peshawar in the northwest Punjab. It gradually weakened and was conquered by a new Iranian dynasty, the Sassanians, in their period of greatness, 226-540.

The Sassanians were a native Iranian dynasty from Fars and were much stronger than the Parthians because they had more success in curbing the Iranian nobles and in constructing a more bureaucratic administration under royal control. They had a more effective cavalry than the Parthians because it was under more disciplined control. They did all they could to free the routes of east-west commerce from the Far East to the Mediterranean. To this end they sought in vain to cooperate with Rome which, instead, sought to control the Syrian Saddle and Armenia and to exclude the Persians from political access to the Black Sea at Lazica (ancient Colchis). At the same time, Rome tried to divert the trans-Asia route either north of the Persians by way of the Khazars of south Russia or south of Persian control by way of the Red and Arabian Seas through the hands of the Axumites of Abyssinia and the Himyarites of south Arabia. This effort was largely frustrated by a great efflorescence of Sassanian mercantile sea power on the Indian Ocean after 540.

In their efforts to control the sea trade of the south, the Sassanians expelled the Axumites from Yemen, which they had controlled for 41 years (529-570). About the same time, a Sassanian fleet expelled the Axumites from Ceylon which served as a meeting place between Far Eastern and west Asian traders. Although the neo-Persians probably did not maintain a fighting navy on the Indian Ocean, their merchant shipping dominated its commerce so completely that the vocabulary and nautical nomenclature of that ocean used by Arabs even today is largely Persian (according to Gabriel Ferrand). The Moslems conquered the countries concerned with this trade (Syria, Mesopotamia, Persia, and Egypt) in the seventh century, but actual operation of shipping on the Indian Ocean did not begin to pass into their hands until **several** centuries later.

The Sassanian influence on trade and commerce is reflected in other activities. They continued the old Persian tradition of road building and established a system of transportation and postal service which must have been the best available anywhere. One Sassanian usurper covered 350 miles in two days using the postal service.

The neo-Persian empire served as a great transmitter of culture and technology between east and west. They introduced steel to Damascus from China by way of India and were among the earliest users of metal horseshoes. They greatly facilitated international trade by innovations in foreign exchange methods including the use of bills of exchange.

The constant wars of the Persians with the Romans and east Romans tended to exhaust both sides. The precarious nature of the balance between them is evident from the overwhelming victories they won over each other sometimes in successive years (as in A.D. 296 and 297). Neither side could destroy the other nor could any established use of weapons or tactics be reached. Moreover, in their obsession with their own rivalries on the east-west axis, and with the obvious danger of pastoral intrusions from the north, both east Rome and Persia ignored the possibility of danger coming, in any major way, from the southern grasslands. Yet it was the Arabs invading from the south in the century after 632 which destroyed the Persian system in 641 and came close to doing the same to the Byzantine system over the following century.

5.   Western Asia and the Byzantine State

    a.   Introduction

    We have said that the Roman empire survived in the east as a consequence of a series of decisions to abandon (temporarily) areas of the west which drained defensive strength without an equivalent contribution to defensive resources. At the same time, under the pressure of events, east Rome changed many of its modes of thought and action to provide a stronger system able to survive for almost a millennium after the collapse in the west.

    We have already listed some of the advantages which east Rome had over west Rome, such as the strategic superiority of the east, especially Constantinople over Rome, particularly in regard to the use of sea power for tying a defense community together. To this we added denser population, more cities, many more craftsmen, greater food production, less inequitable distribution of incomes, a stronger tradition of authoritarian government (helpful in a period of mercenary soldiers), a greater proclivity to ideology (often helpful in adversity), and a closer acquaintance with tactical and technological innovations of eastern origin.

    This last point, covering such matters as cavalry, improved methods of animal transportation, better knowledge of missile weapons (such as archery and the sling), and earlier acquaintance with new technology (such as the waterwheel, the horse collar, and the windmill), was something which east Rome shared with its eastern enemies, especially Sassanian Persia and the later Islamic and Turkish threats. Thus it was not something which gave any relative advantage to Byzantium, but it did create a situation in which east Rome as a power system could operate in a constellation of similar power systems sufficient for survival.

As we have seen, all of these power systems were of a new type which we call "providential empire," a form of monarchy quite different from the earlier archaic monarchies and equally different from our modern ideas of monarchy. In essence, we might say that east Rome survived while west Rome vanished because east Rome was able to replace the aristocratic pursuit of honor (which had made classical civilization function) by providential empire (which made east Rome function) after an interval (130 B.C.-A.D. 330) during which both were brought close to destruction by the mad pursuit of power, wealth, and sensual enjoyment among the ruling groups. This does not, of course, mean that the pursuit of power, wealth, and sensuality was absent from Roman society before 130 B.C. (or 400 B.C. among the Greeks) or was absent from east Rome or any of the other providential empires after A.D. 330. But it does mean that the pursuit of these mundane aims was balanced sufficiently by other, less self-centered and more social aims, so that the fabric of society could be maintained in a degree of integrity sufficient to allow the community to survive.

The gradual separation of east Rome and west Rome arose from the fact that the east was able to cope with the challenges which rose against it, while the west was not able to do so and collapsed, leading to the European Dark Ages and the rise of a totally new civilization north of the mountains, our western civilization. As we have seen, the ability of the east to cope with the Germanic challenge rested, to some extent, on its willingness to sacrifice the west. It also rested almost equally on the fact that in order to deal successfully with the series of challenges we have mentioned, the east had to move in directions of reform and change which the west was unable or unwilling to follow. As a consequence of these changes (which built upon previously existent differences), the separation of east and west became permanent. It should be noted that the date usually given for the ending of Rome in the west, A.D. 476, the year in which the general Odoacer forced Romulus Augustulus to resign his _im-_

perium in the west, is of no importance in this process. The real separation took place either earlier, under Constantine (311-337), or later, in the period 525-675.

The vital aspects of this separation were at least six in number:

1. In the west there was a steady development toward static defenses, while the east moved toward mobile defense (including use of sea power to increase mobility).

2. Static defense in the west came to be associated with payments in kind (as begun by Diocletian), especially payment by land grants for the highest military ranks in the west; but in the east such land grants were associated with defense only on the lowest levels, while on all higher levels of military service there was, after 500, a steady movement away from payments in kind (or in land) toward payments in money.

3. Static defense and payments in kind in the west led to localism, while in the east, mobile weaponry and payments in money permitted sustained centralization. A major part of this difference was that techniques of transportation and the operations of a siege train (which are closely linked together) were sustained in the east, but drastically declined in the west. In the west, large cities, like Rome or Naples or Milan (but not Ravenna), could be captured because the urban population was no longer sufficient to man all the walls; but smaller places with walls short enough to be covered by the inhabitants could not be taken. The result was a movement toward smaller (and more rural) fortified sites. Ravenna, of course, could not be taken because so much of its defense perimeter was covered by marshes.

4. Part of this difference between east and west came from the fact that luxury goods traditionally came from the east and continued to do so in the four centuries from the crisis of the third century to the Islamic assault of the seventh century. The result was a continued flow of precious metals to the east, a flow which rested on the ex-

traordinary skills of craftsmen in the east, from
the silk workers of south Asia, the rug weavers
of western Asia, as well as the spices, incense,
and precious stones of southeast and southwest
Asia. The greater inequity in distribution of
incomes in the west helped to contribute to this
flow by sustaining the demand for luxuries in the
west when the ability of the masses of the population to command necessities was already decreasing.
The chief exceptions to this flow of precious metals
toward the east was the flow of coins (originally
Byzantine, later Saracen) toward the Baltic forests
or East Africa for such specialties as furs, amber,
slaves, or ivory. Moreover, this whole tendency
was intensified by the Byzantine control of the sea.
Writing of the period 752-827, A.R. Lewis said,
"Byzantium used her naval power to channel trade
as suited her interests. The result was a series
of economic dislocations; severe economic depression in Spain and Egypt, virtual abandonment of
cities in southern France, northwestern Italy,
Cyprus, and the northern coast of Africa, unimpor-
tance of the old Syrian, Red Sea, and Rhone valley
trade routes, and a new enhancement of the Adriatic-
Po-Rhine and the Varangian routes to the northern
sections of Europe and of the Black Sea-Caspian
and Trebizond-Armenian-Mesopotamian routes to
the East."

  5. One element in this divergence which is
of great importance is that the west was threatened
only by barbarians and was underpopulated, while
the east, which was heavily populated, was threatened
by a civilized state, Sassanian Persia, in the crucial period of transition (212-628). In the west
the advantages of local fortifications in providing
security against barbarian raiders were curtailed
neither by any successful siege tactics nor by sea
power, while the developing situation of local fortifications scattered in a depopulated, non-forti-
fied, countryside continued to encourage barbarian
migration and settlement in the west. Indeed,
what sea power continued to exist in the west fell
into barbarian (chiefly Vandal, and later Scandinavian) control and by making it possible for the
barbarians, using that sea power, to reach North
Africa, cut off the grain and oil supplies of

Italian cities and made the Vandals a direct threat
to the security of these cities, thus encouraging
the twin movements there toward decentralization
and the ruralization of both security and economic
life: that is the lower classes in the western
cities began to follow the upper classes in fleeing from the cities to seek both security and food
in rural areas protected locally by the upper
classes in fortified, rural, residences.

But in the east, sea power was regained by
Roman (that is, Byzantine) hands in this transition period after 518, especially following east
Rome's great naval victory over Islam in 747. This
continued until the North African Muslim counter-
assault of 827, which captured Sicily and Crete
and established an Islamic, but non-Abbasid, control of the central Mediterranean for the next
five generations (827-960).

The long period of Byzantine naval power (say,
518-827) made it possible for Byzantium to inaugu-
rate developments in directions such that the existence of Islamic naval power in 827-960 did not
reverse the earlier developments but accelerated
them. The chief of these developments was decentralization of power and increased localism,
especially in the west.

6. There is another, rather subtle, element
in the divergence between the fates of Rome in the
west and Rome in the east. This rests on the ancient distinction between Greek rationalism and
Latin pragmatism. It can be seen, for example,
in the more sophisticated Greek idea of the nature
of deity as an abstract rational principle of perfect spirituality and the less sophisticated western view of God as a personal and intimate Father-
figure; related to this, it can be seen in the
different emphasis in doctrinal thinking between
the eastern emphasis on theology (that is knowledge of God's nature) and the western emphasis on
ethics (that is on man's behavior toward God and
man). And it can be seen in the eastern taste for
doctrinal disputes and iconoclasm compared to the
Latin taste for images, relics, and local saints.
The political impact of this difference in outlook
appeared in the great shifts in loyalties which be-

came necessary in the period from the third to the sixth centuries because of the collapse of the old loyalties which had sustained the Roman republic and Roman paganism. These older loyalties had been refurbished in the Augustan principate and revived under the Antonines, but collapsed into ruins in the third century. These old loyalties had, at one time, provided the emotional attachments and social solidarity so essential to community life. But, because of the different traditions of east and west, the search for new loyalties and new community emotional expressions took quite opposite directions in the two parts of the Roman empire: in the west they became existential in form, while in the east they became abstractly symbolic.

By "existential emotional satisfactions" I mean those which are provided by moment to moment relationships with other individuals or with nature. Such emotional satisfactions rest on externalized relationships and are reflected in actions in the space-time continuum.

Symbolic emotional relationships, on the other hand, are largely internalized, more likely to be endocrinological than neurological, and are triggered by symbols, often symbols for abstract concepts such as the flag, the Cross, or words like "Marx," "Red," or "fascist."

The fact that emotional expressions in the west became more existential than symbolized increased the movement toward localism and existential everyday activities. But in the east the attachment of emotional experience to symbols not only gave continued meaning and social solidarity to the groups or communities represented by these symbols but also gave rise to considerable amounts of sporadic and pointless violence from the need to externalize in some way the internal chemical metabolic conditions engendered by the endocrine responses to social symbols. It also led to controversy over such verbal and symbolized issues as the monophysite and iconoclastic struggles.

In general terms the eastern empire, for the reasons we have given, was able to get through the challenges of the fifth century which disintegrated the empire in the west. Only in the 12th century did the eastern empire experience what the west had experienced in the fifth century. Although this parallel is real, it is not, of course, exact. The defeat of Byzantium by the Seljuk Turks at the battle of Manzikert in 1071 is similar to the Roman defeat by the Goths at Adrianople in 378. The period following each of these saw similar developments in the respective areas: manpower shortage, depopulation, use of barbarians as mercenary soldiers or as client tribes, the growth of tenancy on large estates, the usurpation by holders of such estates of public power over their tenants, growth of localism and autarchy on such estates, and a turn toward existential emotional satisfactions in a narrowing social contest. Similar changes occurred in Islam under the Abbasid Caliphate after 900.

Over this long period, the greatest threats to the Byzantine power structure came from the barbarians, especially the Huns and Germans, in the fourth and fifth centuries, from the Avars and Sassanian Persians at the beginning of the seventh century, from the Arabs in 634-779, and intermittently thereafter, and from the Bulgars and Slavs from the middle of the seventh century to 1018. The final challenge, by the Seljuk Turks and later the Ottoman Turks from the east and by Venice and the Normans from the west, began about 1050 and eventually destroyed the whole power system as is evident from the sacking of Constantinople in 1204 and its final capture by the Turks in 1453.

The gradual separation of east Rome and west Rome began with the military reforms of Diocletian and Constantine (284-337). These collapsed in the west but in the east became the basis for survival until the Persian and Arab attacks in the 7th century required new reforms. At the same time, Constantine, by his movement of the capital to the east and by his conversion to Christianity, established the basis for providential monarchy within the Roman system. As Norman Baynes expressed it from a somewhat different point of view, "Constan-

tine sitting amongst the Christian bishops at the
ecumenical council of Nicaea is in his own person
the beginning of Europe's Middle Age." I say
"from a somewhat different point of view" because
the expression "Europe's Middle Age" has a totally
different meaning in western Europe from what it
has in the east. In the east, Constantine marks
the discovery of providential monarchy as the organizational principle of the Roman empire (which
had lost its original organizational principle,
the pursuit of honor, and then tried, unsuccessfully, to survive on the basis of a naked struggle
for power and wealth). In the west, Charlemagne
tried to copy the Constantinian solution when he
also sat amongst his bishops at the Council of
Arles, but this western effort to establish providential monarchy west of the Adriatic Sea failed
with the Carolingians, as it failed later in the
west with the Ottonian and Hohenstauffen rulers.
As a consequence of these failures to copy Constantine's system in the west, the Middle Ages
in the west became a period of defensive weaponry,
dispersed power on a non-state basis, and economic
localism totally different from the "medieval"
political systems struggling in the constellation
of powers east of the Adriatic.

Because all the power structures of the east
had the same weapons, with minor exceptions, their
relative force in terms of weapons depended upon
the "weapons mix," that is the balance they made
among weapons and the relative emphasis they put
upon one weapon or another. Thus the relative
power of such power systems depended upon weapons
systems rather than on weapons themselves. In
the case of Byzantium, as we shall see in this
section, the decisive elements in such a system
were social and economic, while in the Islamic
power system (as we shall see in the next section)
the weapons system must be examined in a much
wider framework since the decisive elements there
were ideological and religious (at least at the
beginning).

In the Byzantine system these decisive elements were precisely those which could not be kept
up in western Europe and which therefore explain

why east Rome and west Rome moved in such different directions (after about A.D. 300) that they became different civilizations. This difference emerged from the fact that the east was able to reverse, in the period 300-700, the tendencies which appeared in the Roman empire after about A.D. 200, while the western areas of the empire could not do so, with the result that these disintegrative tendencies continued to develop in the west and reached their logical conclusion about 950. In the east, on the other hand, as a consequence of the reversal of these tendencies of A.D. 200, Byzantium was, by the year 1000, reaching the apex of its power and extent under the Emperor Basil II (976-1025).

The tendencies to which I refer must be obvious by now. They include defensive dominance and localism in both military and economic activities (and thus, inevitably, in political life as well) marked by the supremacy of the castle and the heavily armored knight as weapons, the self-sufficient manor as the predominant element in economic life, the decrease of a market economy and of the use of money, with such incidental consequences as the ruralization of society, large-scale illiteracy, and the reduction of society to a simple two-class system of nobles and serfs.

These tendencies were embodied in law in the reforms of Diocletian throughout the empire, but their implications began to be reversed in the east by the reforms of Constantine. This reversal was continued by the work of Justinian and carried to a solid foundation by the reforms of Athanasius and Heraclitus. It is interesting to note that these three steps were spread over three centuries, with each associated with an emperor who had an extended reign: Constantine in 311-337; Justinian in 527 (really 518)-565; and Heraclitus in 610-641. Naturally the foundations laid by these three over three centuries continued to be built on by their successors over the next three centuries to culminate in the peak of the power and extent of the Byzantine state in 1025.

There were at least three aspects to this reversal: (1) the establishment of a sound system of money and the return from the barter system of rents and taxes established by Diocletian to an economy of monetary markets and exchanges; (2) the reintroduction of elements of mobility and of offensive power into weapons systems; and (3) the return of peasant life from a narrow sphere of weaponless serfdom to a life of free, landowning, peasant soldiers.

Thus, from the simplest point of view, the history of Byzantium could be divided into three stages: (1) the period of transition, 311-610; (2) the period of the themes, 610-1025; and (3) the period of decline. This is almost an over-simplification, as there were other major oscillations of Byzantine power, associated, in most cases, with a factor of weaponry omitted from this triplex: naval power. When the emperors neglected the navy, Byzantine power declined rapidly; when they reconstructed the navy, the state's power revived rapidly. This naval factor will be introduced in this analysis when necessary.

b. The Period of Transition, 311-610

In this period of transition, there were no real innovations in weapons, but there were very great changes in emphasis and in organization which continued throughout Byzantine history. Since the chief threats in this period were the Sassanids, the Huns, and the Avars, all three cavalry archers, the chief shift in emphasis was in this direction, notably in the sixth century. Cavalry became more heavily armored, while infantry, which also became primarily archers, became less armored.

More important than changes in weapons were changes in organization and arrangement, with almost total changes in names. The continuous frontier fortifications were replaced by fortifications in depth, which ultimately, by 900, covered much of the country. This could be regarded as consisting of at least five zones: (1) a screen of client tribes in front of the border itself; these were barbarians bound by treaty to serve the empire with their own military customs under their own leaders; (2) along the frontier itself was the beginnings of a defensive network of military settlements in fortified villages and detached blockhouses linked by a strategic road; (3) behind this was a zone of walled cities used as administrative centers, supply bases, and refuge sanctuaries, with some mobile forces. Since most of the anticipated invaders had no siege trains, it was expected that these cities could hold out until one of the field armies, of which there were ten by the time of Justinian, could come up to drive the enemy away; (4) these field armies formed the fourth zone of defense in this transitional period, but in the following period, this fourth zone was much changed by the spreading inward across the empire of the defensive pattern of the second zone, that is a network of strategic roads guarded by fortified military settlements and scattered blockhouses over much of the interior of the country. In the following period (600-900), this network was organized on a regional basis under a strategos (general), who had administrative and mobile forces and gradually took over the outer zones, of which the second was under the command of a dux (duke) and the third was under the command of a comes (count) whose responsibilities covered several dukes, just as the strategos had charge ultimately of several counts. This ultimate system, fully achieved by 900, was Byzantium's distinctive contribution to military organization and is known as the system of themes, since the military responsibility of the strategos was known as a "theme." In the period before the establishment of the themes, this fourth zone was the area of operations of the emperor's field forces.

The fifth and innermost area of defense was the fortifications of Constantinople itself. In Thrace, under Theodosius II (408-450), the capital was shielded by massive walls, the so-called "Maritime Walls," and a chain, to exclude enemy ships, across the Golden Horn. Almost a century later, in 507-512, Anastasius built a wall about forty miles away from the city running across the peninsula from the Black Sea to the Propontus. A generation later, Justinian built fortifications and ramparts even farther away, in the Chersonese of Thrace and before Nicaea.

To facilitate the movement of the field armies, Anastasius and Justinian, in the sixth century, built up the navy which had decayed to the point that Vandals, Goths, and even Avar Slavs threatened Byzantium on the seas. The possession of a navy, which allowed the field armies to be moved about the empire more rapidly, reduced them in size, something which Justinian rather overdid, sending Belisarius to recapture North Africa from the Vandals with only 15,000 troops in 533 and, when that was successful, sending the same general to recapture Italy from the Ostrogoths with only 10,000 men in 535. Since this force was far from adequate and the navy was not kept up, Belisarius wasted seventeen years on the task, almost fatally handicapped by lack of men, ships, money, and supplies. Eventually, the Franks came in to help, and finally Narses led a force of 15,000 men overland across the Balkans (for lack of ships), and the Ostrogothic kingdom was destroyed. All the chief Mediterranean islands were retaken in this process, and in 554, part of Visigothic Spain was also recovered by Byzantium.

During this period the tactical units became smaller and underwent a complete change of names. The federati came to refer to cavalry units largely recruited from barbarians but now forming a part of the regular army under Roman officers. The comitatenses and limitanei units came to be called numeri and consisted of infantry, mounted infantry, and cavalry. Something new were the bucellarii, mostly cavalry archers, who were the private retainers of generals and other wealthy men. This had long been a Persian custom, and the whole military system became so similar to that of Persia in this period that they were almost interchangeable. Belisarius had seven thousand bucellarii, but few others had as many as a thousand, although many persons had a handful.

There was a high level of skill and flexibility in tactics, especially among the leaders we know best, like Belisarius and Narses, in this transition period. Tactics, strategy, diplomacy, and economic policy were closely interrelated. Economic policy provided a large supply of gold, which could be used as subsidies to the client tribes and allies, but soon came back to purchase Byzantine luxury goods. Sassanian Persia often shared in this largesse, especially when the emperor wanted peace on his eastern frontier. It was the breakdown of this stable situation in the east in the seventh century, from the Byzantine destruction of Persia and the Arab invasions, that made it necessary to extend the themes over the empire. The whole of the armed forces under Justinian amounted to about 150,000, compared to more than 400,000 (for a larger area) under Diocletian and over half a million in the Notitia Dignitatum about 405. There can be little doubt that Justinian needed about twice the forces he had and was still overextended, a situation made much worse by his reconquest of the west.

The themes were not set up at a fixed date but grew gradually from 500 to after 800. The first stage of client tribes backed by military settlements on the frontier was established first in Libya under Anastasius about 500, was extended to all North Africa by Justinian, and began to be applied to the Saracen lines in Asia about the same time. In fact, in Syria its origins go back to Diocletian. The Lombard threat to Italy after 560 led to a similar development there and to the extension of military settlements on much of the peninsula by Maurice about 590. As a consequence of the Arab victory over Byzantine forces at Yarmuk in 636 (see the next section), Constantinus (641-668) settled many of the forces which had been driven out of Egypt, the Levant, and later from North Africa in military settlements in Anatolia, thus formally creating the themes with their strategoi over the remaining Asiatic parts of the empire. The system was not extended to Thrace until the Slav attacks under Constantine IV (668-685) and was probably not extended to the rest of the Balkans until the Bulgar attacks after 750. By 900, there were 31 themes, of which two were naval themes of sailors. In addition, by that date, the emperor had his personal forces of four regiments of land forces and an imperial fleet at Constantinople.

These changes in military organization were

accompanied by changes in tactics, largely drawn from past practices. The Byzantine forces moved toward the strategy which I have called medieval, in which the chief strategic aim was to prevent the capture of strongholds and thus to frustrate sieges by using field forces to prevent foraging. That means that the Byzantine generals did not share the eagerness for a decisive battle as early as possible, which we find in classical antiquity or in western civilization for most of its life. Thus battles were rare, occurring only when one side could not avoid it, or when both sides desire it. In such battles the Byzantine tactics involved the use of relatively small units of about 500 men, distributed on the field so that any enemy penetration or flank movement would expose his forces to one or more violent blows from other Byzantine units. In general, infantry were placed in the center, with cavalry on the wings, but rarely in large solid masses. Instead, they were placed on the field in units, somewhat in the fashion of the old Roman maniples, so that advance would bring that enemy into positions of more intense fire from more than one direction. Wings were rarely placed on line with the center but were frequently detached or at an angle. Reserves were placed on the sides or rear, in a concealed or semi-concealed position, so that new blows could be delivered from new directions and as surprises. To assist in this and to channel the enemy attack, Byzantine tactics made considerable use of both natural and artificial obstacles on the field. For this reason, Byzantine armies remained digging armies after the fall of west Rome, and this characteristic remained for a long time, but decreased after 600.

The Byzantine theory of tactics was in complete opposition to the old Indo-European idea, which had continued much longer among the Indo-Europeans who remained barbarians in the west (Celts, Iberians, Germans, and Sarmatians). The latter believed that the battle must be won with the initial attack and, accordingly, that all their forces should be committed with the maximum violence in the first blow. The Byzantine theory was that victory goes to the side which strikes the last blow, especially if

that final blow comes from an unexpected direction
at forces previously committed which are locked
together and wavering in the balance. As we
shall see, the classical and Indo-European attitudes, with their commitment to shock weapons,
to the maximization of violence at the first blow,
and even to the desire for a decisive battle as
soon as possible, continued to be very influential
during the European Middle Ages until the Crusades
forced Europeans to learn other tactics and to
start thinking, rather than simply acting, in the
military sphere.

One of the great achievements of the eastern
empire in this period was to get free from both
barbarian federati and barbarian generals within
the empire and to begin the effort to draw units
from the peasants of its own territories. As a
result, Byzantium in the fifth century was able
to get free from the problem which continued in
the west, in which barbarian generals like Stilicho
or Odoacer had control of the situation because
they had control of the army. As early as 400,
the Germans in Constantinople were divided up and
massacred. Later, Leo I (457-474) and Zeno (474-
491) used Isaurian mountaineers from southwestern
Anatolia to replace Germans. In 471 the Avar commander of the Gothic forces was murdered at Leo's
instigation. This made it possible for the middle
period of Byzantine history to rely on its own
peasant forces and not on foreign mercenaries,
as both east and west had done earlier, nor upon
exclusively noble warriors as the west did in
this middle period. Later, after 1000, when the
eastern empire began to return once again to the
use of foreign mercenaries, the eastern emperors
began by hiring fighters of remote origin, such
as Swedes, Saxons, and Russians, rather than
those on their own frontiers.

The chief weakness of the eastern empire in
this and subsequent periods was religious intolerance, which inevitably weakened political stability
because of the diverse religious outlook of the
various parts of the empire. In general there were
two stages in this process: (1) the earlier dispute
over the nature of Christ, in which the Latin west
and the Byzantine government accepted the decrees

of the Council of Chalcedon (451) that Christ had two natures (human and divine) in one person, while the opposing monophysites insisted that Christ had only one nature in one person; and (2) the later dispute (after 700) over iconoclasm.

These two disputes would have little relevance to this book were it not for the fact that they weakened and divided the empire. In the monophysite controversy, the dissenting group were largely in the east, in the Levant, Syria, and Egypt. The government was on the orthodox side of the issue and used violence and duress to enforce uniformity and to stamp out what it regarded as a pernicious heresy. The persecution of the monophysites was especially cruel under Justinian (527-565) and Heraclitus (610-641) leaving the inhabitants of the eastern provinces thoroughly alienated just before the Arab invaders struck in 634-643. Since the Arabs had no interest in this controversy and offered religious toleration to those who would pay taxes to them, few persons in the eastern provinces of the empire were willing to fight the Arabs.

The Arab conquest of the monophysite portions of the empire removed that particular religious controversy from the file of current issues. But within seventy years, a new controversy arose over the role of images in the church. Here there were really three points of view of which the Latin church, on the whole, embraced the center position: that holy images should neither be worshipped nor destroyed. The Greek church, unfortunately, tended to embrace, in a generally intolerant way, the two extreme positions: on the one hand the popular position that images could be honored (or in effect, if not in theory, worshipped) and the reformist position that all images should be destroyed as distractions from the recognition of the pure abstract spirituality of God. The government was controlled by extreme iconoclasts in 726-780 and 813-842; it was controlled by fairly extreme iconophils at other times, most notably in 786-802 under the Empress Irene. Since the divisions on this issue were not so clearly established either on a geographical basis nor on the basis of a pro or anti-governmental position, it did not create permanent fissures contributing to durable elements of political instability, but it did greatly weaken the government as a whole and, under Irene, damaged the armed forces by efforts to purge the iconoclasts from the military rolls.

In general terms, we might say that the decline of the Roman empire was fairly steady from the time of Augustus but became precipitous in the third century. Then, under Diocletian and Constantine (284-c.350) there was a substantial recovery which was soon followed by another period of rapid decay (c. 350-475). Anastasius and Justinian reversed this process once again (491-565), but after 565 there was an extended period of decline until about 715 (broken only by a brilliant and exhausting recovery under Heraclitus in 619-629). This oscillating process continued, with considerable recovery in 715-782 (under the Isaurian dynasty) and 856-1025 (the Macedonian dynasty) but declined in the interval between (782-856) and in the long period after 1025. This final decline is marked most spectacularly by the defeat at Manzikert by the Seljuk Turks in 1071, the capture of Constantinople by the Fourth Crusade in 1204, and the final fall of the city to the Ottoman Turks in 1453. This long final period of decline was marked by two major movements, the slow attrition of the resources of the empire, in manpower, financial resources, and area, as the Turks steadily nibbled away the city's supporting territories, and, within those territories, the steady loss of imperial power, in all its aspects, to the great landlords and, in a lesser degree, to the church.

Throughout this whole period, the empire was caught in the squeeze which had faced Augustus in his later years: the wide gap between limited resources and almost unlimited aspirations and the impossibility of closing that gap, even partially, in a system which was essentially too conservative to seek or accept new methods which might achieve more satisfactions with less using up of resources (the old, and vital, dichotomy between extensive and intensive use of resources).

657

This emphasis on extensive expansion is part
of the explanation of the territorial expansions
and contractions of the Byzantine empire, almost
as if it were breathing in and out. Because the
center at Constantinople could not be taken, especially by the semi-civilized and semi-pastoral
peoples (without siege trains), the empire could
usually apply its resources to one area and expand
there by putting the other areas on the shelf for
awhile. Only when two or more areas (usually in
Thrace and Syria) were attacked simultaneously
was the empire really under very heavy pressure
and forced to retract to its main base in Anatolia.

The two other elements in the recovery
achieved in the first period were the establishment of a money economy and the first steps in the
reestablishment of a free peasantry. These were
interrelated.

In the fifth century the peasants were tenants (coloni) reduced almost to serfdom by Diocletian's new taxes, especially the annona, which
was payable in kind and fell only on the rural
peoples. In addition, the rents and services
which the peasant owed the landlord were also
in kind. These obligations had a double result:
they kept the peasant so busy that he became tied
to the land and, they, in addition, kept him so
poor that he could obtain neither weapons nor
skills in the use of weapons. Thus the peasant
was tied to the soil and separated from all direct
concern with security, a matter which was left to
a different social class, the landlords, who, in
turn, became almost entirely concerned with military security and not directly concerned with the
system of economic production. In the west, where
this process continued to develop, the result was
a sharply separated two-class society of serfs and
nobles. But, in Byzantium, this process was reversed by Constantine, Athanasius, and Heraclitus.

Constantine took the final step toward the
reestablishment of a money economy by establishing
the gold solidus at the rate of 72 to the pound of
gold. This coinage remained stable until the eleventh century because the government remained strong
enough to resist any tendencies to depreciate the

currency, and the supply of gold in the east, unlike the west, remained adequate to support such a currency for many centuries.

The revival of urban commercial and artisan activities associated with the revived market economy made it possible for Constantine to tax the cities to balance the very heavy taxes that Diocletian had imposed on the rural population. This urban tax, known as the auri lustralis collatio, was a heavy tax in gold on commercial and craft activities in the cities.

Later the financial and naval reforms of Anastasius (491-518) laid the foundations for the political activities of Justinian (527-565) and the military reforms of Maurice (582-602) and of Heraclitus (610-641). Anastasius stabilized a subsidiary copper coinage, of particular concern to the peasants; he shifted the responsibility for collecting taxes from the curiales to agents of the central government, the vindices, under the four praetorian prefects; he abolished the urban gold tax on trades and crafts; he shifted the rural tax, the annona, from payment in kind to gold; and he obtained the rural produce necessary to the state and the capital city by a system of compulsory state purchasing at fixed prices.

At his death, Anastasius left a surplus of 320,000 pounds of gold in the state treasury. This provided the funds which could be used to hire fighting troops or to bribe enemy neighbors to refrain from attacking. Thus Justinian, in preparation to reconquer the west, signed a treaty "of perpetual peace" with Persia (532) and granted an annual subsidy of 30,000 pieces of gold to the Sassanian king.

Anastasius also began the process of rebuilding the imperial navy which was a second great asset in Justinian's project, especially as the Vandal navy had been in decay since the death of King Gaeseric (A.D. 477) and was down to less than 150 old galleys. With gold and a small naval force, Justinian stirred up a revolt against Vandal rule in Sardinia. When the Vandal king sent his war fleet with 5000 men to Sardinia, Justinian's expeditionary force of 10,000 men in 500 transports escorted by 92 war vessels was able to land in Tunis without opposition. Once North Africa was conquered, the Mediterranean islands fell into Byzantine control without much more than naval demonstrations. As we have already said, the conquest of Ostrogothic Italy took eighteen years because Justinian starved Belisarius of the necessary resources in men, money and ships. In the same year in which the conquest of Italy was achieved (554), Byzantine forces reconquered southeastern Spain from the Visigoths.

These conquests were glorious but neither strategic nor sensible. The reacquired areas provided few resources to balance the additional defense forces necessary to hold them. The major role played by sea power in their reconquest meant that they could be held only from the sea, and that Byzantium lacked the land power to reconquer the hinterland in from the littoral margin. Thus in North Africa the eastern empire could control the coast and the main coastal road running parallel to it, but they could not conquer the Moors, Berbers, and Libyans of the interior nor could they prevent these pastoral peoples from raiding down into the more heavily populated coastal strip. It is worthy of note that when the Arabs entered North Africa in the following century they did so by moving westward along the grasslands inside the coastal road.

Strategically the whole Byzantine involvement in the west and the subsequent efforts, over many years, to hold on to at least some of these recaptured areas, especially Italy, was a major error, because it involved commitment of real power at a distance on the basis of the diplomatic (that is theoretical) neutralization of more immediate dangers nearer home. Of these dangers, the Persians of course, were the chief, since at any moment they could decide that an immediate attack on Anatolia, when the emperor was over-committed in the west, might bring greater advantage to the Sassanians than the annual receipt of 30,000 gold pieces from the emperor. Moreover, the barbarian threats into

Thrace or on the Black Sea were also serious.

This good but overextended defense system was accompanied by a faulty economic policy and a very destructive religious policy. The economic policy was similar to that of western Europe in the 17th century, which we call "mercantilism." That is, economic life and especially commerce were regulated to maximize the amount of gold in the imperial treasury on the grounds that a large gold reserve permitted payment of mercenary soldiers and the use of subsidies and bribes to influence foreign potentates. In this case the Byzantine empire was the only state on the gold standard, maintaining its coinage at full purity, century after century, so that it was not only acceptable to all peoples, but foreign rulers, if they coined gold, did so by copying the Byzantine coinage at full weight and purity. For a considerable period, rulers like the Franks and Visigoths did this, and even the Persian monarch did so on occasion. Other great powers, such as Persia and later the Caliphs, did not coin gold of their own except in rare cases. The Persians as late as 562 signed an agreement to refrain from doing so. The first Arab gold coinage was 692.

Like the European monarchs of the 17th century, the Byzantine emperors controlled trade so that it passed through areas they dominated and was allowed to pass through rival states only in amounts and conditions which would increase Byzantine gold holdings in the long run. Thus the empire sought to establish favorable balances of trade by exporting or channeling luxuries to bring in gold. All trade to the east passed through a few controlled trade portals, a policy which had been practiced by the western empire along the Rhine-Danube frontiers from an early date and was accepted by Persia in a treaty with Rome as early as A.D. 287.

But as part of this program of mercantilist economic warfare, Byzantium continued the mistaken policy of the western empire (since 92 B.C.) of refusing to cooperate with Persia to defend the civilized areas of the known world against pastoral intruders from the northern grasslands, and, instead,

661

did all it could to injure Persia's commercial activities by shunting the profitable Mediterranean-Far Eastern trade either north of Persia through the steppe corridor or south of Persia through the Red and Arabian Seas. To achieve this, Byzantium allied with the Turco-Khazar kingdom of the lower Volga, which had direct connections eastward to China, and with the Abyssinian Christian state of Auxum west of the Red Sea (to bypass both Arabs and Persians to India). These efforts led, as might have been expected, to defensive reprisals by Persia, in the north to attacks on Armenia and the client kingdoms of the Caucasus to cut off the Byzantine-Khazar connection crossing the Black Sea and, in the south, to establish naval control of the Arabian Sea and Indian Ocean and to obtain political dominance in the Red Sea-western Arabian area (the Hejaz).

Neither Byzantium nor Persia could win a decisive victory either in the Caucasus nor in the Red Sea with the result that these two powers fought each other to exhaustion in these two areas (as well as along the more direct Syrian frontier between them). As a result both were weakened in their mutual security areas through which the grassland pastoralists penetrated, the Arabs from the south and various barbarian peoples, culminating with the Turks, in the north.

Of these two threats, the Arabs came earlier and were able to destroy the Persian political structure finally and forever (A.D. 651). Much of the success of the Arab advance rested on the errors of Byzantine religious policy, especially the practice of intense religious intolerance based on abstract, and often obscure, religious distinctions. Here again, Justinian's policies were less than a success. In his later years he became increasingly violent against the monophysites and, by the end of his long reign (527-565) he had alienated a large proportion of the inhabitants of his eastern provinces.

In fact the Justinian defense system broke down before the Arab invasion of 634 and was in a shambles within fifty years of his death. The Lombards, whom Justinian had settled in Noricum

662

and Pannonia (modern Austro-Hungary south and west of the Danube) and used as allies to defeat the Ostrogoths in Italy, allied with the Avars in the year Justinian died (565) and seized much of northern Italy, with Pavia as a capital, within the next few years. The emperors retained Ravenna with difficulty until 751, but then lost it to the Lombards. The pope had already (739) sought an alliance with the Franks against the Lombards and, in 751-774, this papal-Frankish alliance eliminated both Byzantium and the Lombards from northern Italy. In the following century the Saracens drove Byzantium from much of southern Italy and the islands (Sicily taken, 827-902).

Even before Justinian died, major threats arose in the Near East. In 540 the Huns, Bulgars, and Slavs crossed the Danube and by 559 were at the gates of Constantinople; in that same year, the perpetual peace with Persia was disrupted (in its eighth year) with fighting in Mesopotamia and in the north. By 580 the Slavs were settling in Thrace in large numbers, while the Avars destroyed the Danube defenses and besieged Constantinople in 591.

Both Persia and Byzantium were wracked by domestic and dynastic disorders in this period (as they so often were); Justin the emperor went insane in 574 and Maurice (emperor in 582-602) was murdered by mutinous troops from the Danube sector, led by the incompetent Phocas (emperor, 602-610). Phocas was overthrown, in turn, by Heraclitus (610-641).

Persia suffered even worse disasters at the very time that it reached its greatest geographic extent, almost equal to the size it had been under Darius in 500 B.C. About 620 the Sassanian Persian empire stretched from the Indus River to the Aegean Sea and from the Caucasus Mountains to the First Cataract of the Nile. In the 70 years after 550, the Sassanian Persians had conquered the Ephthalite Huns and defeated the Khazars, had conquered much of Arabia including Hejaz and Yemen, had conquered Mesopotamia, Syria, the Levant, Egypt, and most of Asia Minor. By 617 they were

663

a mile from Constantinople but, as usual, could not take it, although the siege dragged on for years.

In this same period the vicissitudes of the Persian dynasty fluctuated between the heights and the depths. The great Persian general Varahan defeated a Turkish invasion in 589 but, insulted by King Hormisdas, he revolted. Hormisdas was deposed and murdered, but his successor, Chosroes II (589-628), was unable to quell the revolt and had to flee to Constantinople for refuge. He was restored to his throne by the Byzantine emperor Maurice; as a result, the murder of Maurice by Phocas in 602 provided an excuse for a Persian attack on Byzantium. Persia, at the peak of its geographical extent, reached Chalcedon, across from Constantinople, in 617 and continued to besiege the city from the Asiatic side, while the Avars from the north crossed the Danube and Thrace to besiege the city from Europe.

Heraclitus (emperor 610-641) wished to move the capital to Carthage but was dissuaded by the city authorities, led by the patriarch, and instead, in 622, took many of the cities' troops by sea to Alexandretta (where southeast Anatolia joins northwest Syria), thus cutting the Persian forces off from their homeland; he invaded northward to the southeast corner of the Black Sea near Trebizond; in 623 he brought additional men and supplies there from Constantinople across the Black Sea, and then, for four years, ravaged eastward across Armenia to the Caspian Sea (623), southward deep into Persia in 624, westward again to the Alexandretta area in 625, then back across Cappadocia to Trebizond, northward through the Caucasus, then south again to Tiflis in 626, then directly south, by Lake Van, into Mesopotamia in 627. There, at Nineveh, the Persian forces, in December 627, caught up with Heraclitus. Already defeated by the walls of Constantinople in 626, the Persians were now destroyed by the Heraclitus field force. They had to withdraw from Egypt, the Levant, and Syria, after the Persian ruler, Chosroes II, was murdered by order of his son (628). The Avars, exhausted by a violent ten-day assault on the walls of Constantinople in the summer of 626, had already withdrawn.

c. The Period of Greatness, 610-1025

These great, if exhausting, victories of Heraclitus were made possible by the reforms, both military and civil, of Maurice and Heraclitus himself.
The military reforms were partly a copying and response to the Avars. These nomads had been driven
out of Mongolia after 550 and fought their way
across Asia to settle in Hungary about 567. According to the Russian archaeologist, S.V. Kiselev,
they brought stirrups to the west for the first
time. They also seem to have brought the Mongolian
thumb-lock draw which permitted use of a more powerful composite bow. Both of these were adopted by
the Byzantine forces but not by Persia, which had
not had contact with the Avars. A Byzantine
treatise on tactics, the Strategicon, often attributed to the Emperor Maurice but more likely
from the time of Heraclitus, reflects the Byzantine
response to the Avar threat. This shows an effort
to use cavalry archers and lancers in sequence and
in mixed units and the use of dispersed units in
the line of battle.

In this period the themes were applied to Anatolia, and there was a great outburst of patriotic
loyalty to the state. The strategos of a theme was
essentially a viceroy, with a proconsul in charge
of civilian administration. At the same time, landholding was reformed to create self-supporting peasants on inalienable grants of land in return for
military service. They were required to appear
when needed, with their arms and a horse, and received a small fixed payment for service. The land
and obligations were heritable. In some cases,
they owed nominal rents to the previous landlord,
and in all cases they owed taxes to the government.
In many depopulated and devastated areas, foreigners
and war captives were placed in military settlements
such as existed already on the remaining frontiers.

This change provided a more numerous army at
much lower cost than the previous army of mercenaries and, for some time, provided higher morale.
But the strategos was the total ruler of his theme,
especially after his proconsul for civilian affairs
was abolished about 860. The general had military

665

autonomy in the theme and, as tax collector, reported, not to the Praetorian prefect, who gradually disappeared, but to the financial secretary (logothete). Thus the strategos had military command, was tax collector for both soldiers and civilians, and had judicial control over the theme. Such powers inevitably led to wealth, which in this period meant landholding. These powers had to be delegated to his inferior officers, who like their soldiers, became hereditary in local families, combining in their hands, landholding, tax collection, and judicial settlement of disputes. These began to buy lands, local estates, farms which were not parts of the military settlements, and eventually to usurp military holdings which became vacant from failure of heirs. Thus, in time, great provincial landholding families emerged again, almost before the central government recognized the fact. In some cases, these families were descended from the dukes and counts of the frontier zones over which the strategos had taken command when the theme was set up. But the bad consequences of the themal system did not emerge for some time, to be measured in generations, rather than in years, and certainly in the seventh century it strengthened the Byzantine state to resist the great challenges of the century. In the earlier period, the shift of taxes from the annona to cash payments, the replacement of the curiales by government agents as tax collectors, had freed the peasants in the east from servile status to freedom.

This is clear from the "Farmers' Law," a Byzantine agrarian code of about 700, found in several copies and thus probably widely used. This shows a free and mobile peasantry, with land held in private ownership, but with the village community as a cooperative group for use of woods, meadows, and wastelands in common, and serving also as a tax unit with all members jointly responsible for a lump sum. This was probably established in this form by the Emperor Justinian II (685-695; 705-711). It marked the end of the Diocletian-Constantine military system and of Diocletian's agrarian and land tax system. The capitatio-iugatio tax system had combined the land tax and the personal tax together, by assum-

666

ing that neither land nor person could pay taxes unless combined together in an enterprise unit. Now by separating the two, Justinian II could subject everyone to the poll tax and could make the village responsible for the land tax. This policy was so resented by the landlords that they overthrew the emperor and cut off his nose (695), but he was able to escape to the Slavs and Bulgars who provided him with an army with which he recaptured his throne in 705.

Justinian's deposition in 695 by a revolt led by the strategos of Greece showed the danger of establishing such a self-sufficient military power within the state. A more vivid example occurred in 716-717, during the great Arab siege of Constantinople, when the strategos of the Anatolian theme, Leo the Isaurian, siezed the throne from the helpless Theodosius III and repulsed the invaders. To avoid this danger, the themes were made smaller. Originally, there were four, three military and one naval, in Anatolia and the islands. The number increased, both by extension and subdivision, until by 900, there were 31 (13 in Europe, 2 in the islands, and 16 in Asia). The civil administrator of the theme, the proconsul, was abolished about 860, and another such official, the theme praetor, was not created until about 1050, so in the intervening period, during the greatest age of Byzantine power, the strategos was almost completely in control of his theme.

The great achievement of Heraclitus had other elements in it beyond the financial and agrarian changes, and the military reorganization. It was also marked by a very great upsurge of patriotic feeling, associated with the idea of Greek Christianity, rather than any nationalist considerations. As part of this, the official language of the government was changed from Latin to Greek and the title of the ruler shifted from "Imperator" to "Basileus." Where "Imperator's" chief connotation was military, that of "Basileus" was religious. Here again, there were elements of weakness as well as of strength.

On the side of strength, the outburst of religious feelings brought the church to the side of the government in a solid alignment so that the final attack on the Persians took the tone of a crusade. The patriarch acted as regent in charge of the government at Constantinople while Heraclitus was absent from the city on campaign for six years, and the church mobilized its wealth to advance loans to the government to finance the wars. But, on the other hand, the effort to win patriotic allegiance by an appeal to Greek Orthodox religion could not expect to be successful in the Aramaic and Coptic areas of the eastern provinces where Nestorian, monophysite, and Coptic Christians were in the majority. Moreover, the effort to define "orthodoxy" in the narrow and rigid fashion of the Greek rationalist tradition made it almost impossible to find a formula for religious belief which could satisfy Anatolia and the European provinces as well as the Levantine and Egyptian areas.

The long Byzantine-Sassanian War of 603-628 left Persia and Heraclitus both exhausted and quite incapable of withstanding the Arab assault which hit both five years later. During that five years, the neo-Persian kingdom had at least five rulers, with additional usurpers, and vanished from history in the face of the Arab attack by 651.

The Byzantine empire could not be destroyed by the Arabs because they could not capture Constantinople and did not have the sustained offensive power needed to wear down the great city's economic base (in manpower, fodder, food, ships, and money) as the Turks finally did in 1300-1453.

But the Arabs did have the offensive power to tear away the eastern provinces of the Byzantine empire. An analysis of this relationship will be found in the next section, but it is of some significance here to point out that the great advantage which the Arabs had over the eastern empire arose from two things: (1) the Arab mobility on deserts and grasslands and (2) the discontent of the Byzantine subject peoples. Both of these were greater in the eastern and southern provinces, from Cilicia around the eastern and southern shores of the Middle Sea to Gibraltar. These were also the areas where Semitic peoples had expanded in earlier times. The principal areas where the Arabs were notably more successful than earlier Semites were in the conquest of Iran, the Arabization of Egypt, and, to a lesser degree, of the rest of North Africa.

In general, the areas Byzantium lost to the Moslems, especially Syria and Egypt, were of great economic importance and their loss from this point of view was very great, but the religious alienation of these areas had been so intense that the economic loss was to some extent counterbalanced by ideological gain from the fact that the amputation of these areas of dissent made it possible for the remaining territories, especially Anatolia and the Balkans, to become the bulwark of orthodoxy as represented by the Orthodox empire. The fact remains, however, that the religious divisions were largely needless and were repeated in the eighth century by the even less justifiable iconoclastic controversy. It seems likely that this kind of ideological warfare over symbols was an emotional necessity of the Near Eastern world.

From the return of Heraclitus to Constantinople after his final victory over Sassanian Persia in 628 to the beginning of Byzantium's final decline to destruction about 1050, east Rome passed through three periods of decline in power and two periods of recovery. The famous sieges of Constantinople naturally occurred in the periods of decreasing power when the enemy was able to advance to the walls of the city, or at least to the shores of the Hellespont and Bosporus (at Chalcedon).

These periods of fluctuating Byzantine power may be dated roughly as follows:

Decline	628-717
Recovery	717-782
Decline	782-856
Recovery	856-1025
Final Decline	1025-1453

The period of decline in 628-717 was marked
by the first Arab siege of 673-678, the Bulgar
attack of 712, which reached the city's walls,
and the second Arab siege of 717-718.

The first Arab attack on Constantinople lasted
five years, mostly in the summer months. By 674
the enemy had a permanent base on the Marmora, but
were unable to starve out the city or to take it
by storm. The final all-out attack in 678 resulted
in a total Arab defeat. Many of their naval forces
were destroyed by "Greek fire" in an amphibious assault from the sea. In the subsequent withdrawal,
most of the Saracen fleet was destroyed in a storm.

Immediately upon the Arab retreat, Byzantium
was faced by a new threat, the rising power of Bulgarians advancing from the north. This culminated
in an unsuccessful attack on the city in 712. Four
years later, the Greeks and Bulgars signed an alliance which lasted for 39 years (716-755). As a
result of this agreement, the Bulgars were allies
during the second Arab siege of Constantinople
(717-718). Once again, the Arabs were frustrated,
and lost most of their ships from storms during
their retreat. We are told that their loss of men
in the expedition amounted to 130,000 out of
150,000 which started the attack.

This Arab defeat marked the beginning of a
period of Byzantine recovery of power under Leo
III, the Isaurian (717-741), and his son, Constantine V (741-775). The recovery reached its
peak about 780 when the Arabs were ejected completely from Anatolia. In the same period, two
victories over the Bulgarians (in 763 and 773)
forced them backward in the Balkans.

These victories took place in a period of
constant internal turmoil from threatened re-
bellions and coups d'etat and from the consequences of the iconoclastic controversy. One of
these consequences was an almost total break
with the papacy, which excommunicated all iconoclasts in 731. This controversy did not weaken
the state nearly as much as the earlier monophysite controversy had done, because one of its
motives was to strengthen the army and to weaken

the clergy; the latter were becoming increasingly independent of the state, especially the monastic orders to which people were flocking by tens of thousands. This period began with the defeat of the second Arab siege in 718 and ended with the almost complete expulsion of the Arabs from Anatolia in 778-780. During this period, Byzantium recovered control of the sea from the Arabs in a great naval battle off Cyprus in 747, thus reversing the consequences of the Arab naval victory at the "battle of the masts" in 655.

Despite the Byzantine recovery in the eighth century this period began to reveal more clearly the chronic problems of political organization which had to be faced by the Byzantine state over the rest of its existence. These were the same problems which the western empire had failed to solve in the third and following centuries. They involved problems of manpower, money, and control. The key to all of them was the need for a sound and prosperous peasantry, sufficiently affluent to have a loyalty to the system, to be able to pay fairly heavy taxes, to arm themselves with the necessary weapons (or to provide the money which would permit the government to arm them), and sufficiently well-organized so that their agricultural enterprises could function while they were absent on their military duties. Among those enterprises some could be sufficiently large and prosperous to provide cavalry and officers to handle peasant soldiers, but not be so large that they monopolized the land in any districts or, by their existence, deprived local peasants of their lands so as to create a substantial number of rural proletariat. The constant tendency for agrarian arrangements to move toward very large estates surrounded by landless rural laborers, tenants, or impoverished peasantry had to be overcome (as it still does) by almost constant governmental attention and actions.

If these preventive actions are not successful, the landlords are able to force most tax burdens onto the peasants, driving them below the level at which they can retain their lands, and transforming them into laborers or tenants, lead-

ing to a reduction in the rural population (manpower) and an attrition of the rural taxation
base (money) intensified by the ability of large
landlords to evade taxes themselves and use their
own local political and social influence to acquire judicial and other powers over the rural
population (control). With these powers, the
growth of very large landed estates becomes almost irresistible and continues to grow from various illegalities including usurpation of government (or imperial) lands as well as of peasant
farms. Moreover, when landlordism reaches this
point, the ability of the central government to
control its own local agents (including its military leaders) is greatly reduced. In time, such
local power centers not only become direct threats
to the stability of the central government but develop or condone growing military incapacity until
finally the point is reached where these local
powers may rebel against the central government
or find it more advantageous to make a collabora-
tive deal with an invader than to fight him.

These problems were never finally solved in
the Byzantine empire, as they were not solved in
China, nor in any state since. They were less
likely to be solved in the period of providential
monarchies, when the agricultural productivity of
labor was so limited, when weapons and other supplies were made by handicrafts rather than by industrial power, and when communications were so
poor that the central government had great difficulty discovering what was going on until after it
had become legitimized by long prescription. But
the problems were recognized at least by the more
able rulers. One of the greatest of these, Romanus
Lecapenus (emperor 920-944), said, "The small
landed proprietor is immensely valuable, since
his existence implies that the state taxes will
be paid and the obligations of military service
observed: both of these things would completely
founder if the number of small proprietors were
diminished."

In view of the stated advantages in having a
prosperous peasantry, we may wonder why any ruler
would allow the land to become monopolized and

the peasantry reduced and impoverished. The reason
is that there were other counter factors encouraging a ruler's acquiescence in this direction. Of
these factors we shall mention only two here.
They involve (1) the problem of administrative
span; and (2) the presumed advantages of mercenary armies.

By administrative span we mean that any government finds it easier to deal with a few subordinates
rather than with many. Today, with modern techniques, a government can deal with millions of
taxpayers or military recruits. But in the period
of providential empires, it was a very difficult
task for any government to deal even with thousands
of citizens as individuals. Why not allow some
local magnate to do it instead?

The impulse to allow this was almost irresistible. But once the local landlord is made responsible
for the taxes and the military service of the local
peasants, the incentive for the central government
to keep aware of local agrarian arrangements in order to protect peasant land tenure becomes very
weak. In most such cases, the central government
would be unlikely to know that peasant lands had
been reduced or usurped until it was almost too
late to reverse the process. In Byzantium many
laws were enacted to protect peasant landholdings
or to reestablish such holdings when they had been
destroyed. Under many of these laws changes in tenure could be reversed up to forty years. In some
cases, the lands of soldiers were made inalienable
in order to protect their tenures (law of 947).

Another motive which sometimes weakened a
government's zeal in protecting peasant land ownership was the belief that mercenary soldiers (recruited from landless peasants) were more skilled
and more reliable than peasant soldiers. They undoubtedly were more skilled, but they were not
more reliable nor so energetic in their loyalty
to the system. The belief of many rulers that
mercenaries had greater personal loyalty to them
(rather than to the system, as was the case with
peasant soldiers) was generally an error, as many
rulers found out too late, because a soldier whose
loyalty depends on pay can always sell his loyalty

to someone else for more money or even for his own life.

This brief discussion has given only a scanty indication of the complexities of the issues involved in reforming the quality of a military system in a providential empire. On the whole, the issues were so complex and so delicately balanced that drastic reforms or even drastic collapses were very rare. Reform when it occurred usually involved little more than minor changes especially changes of persons, with new brooms sweeping somewhat cleaner for a few years. Decline similarly occurred by minor changes and became fatal only when these continued over many generations.

The period of recovery under the Isaurian dynasty (717-780) was based largely on changes of personnel, while the second period of recovery (856-1025) added to this a considerable quantity of administrative reform. For this reason the later recovery was of longer duration.

On the whole, these periods of reform and corruption could be counterbalanced by other factors, such as the simultaneous occurrence of corruption or reform in other, neighboring political systems. When two or more of the neighboring states of the eastern empire reformed enough to increase their pressures on it, the empire was almost necessarily reduced in area, an occurrence which usually led to a new effort at reform and might well encourage corruption within its rivals. This is why I have said that the issues of political stability in this period must be viewed in terms of a constellation of power systems rather than in terms of any single system in itself.

The Byzantine decline of 782-856 was such a rearrangement within the constellation. The Saracens (Harun al-Rachid, 786-809), the Bulgars (Krum, 803-814), and the Franks (Charlemagne, 768-814) were growing in strength and forced the Byzantine power area to retract in the Near East, in the central Mediterranean, in the Balkans, and in Italy. Muslim victories in Asia Minor in 782 and 791 brought their forces to the Bosporus again in 782-783. In 808 a great victory by Harun al-Rachid imposed tribute of 30,000 pounds of gold per annum. Other Saracen forces from Africa and Spain captured Crete and Sicily, sharply reducing Byzantine naval power in the central Mediterranean. The Bulgar advances began with substantial military victories in 791 and 792 and culminated in a great victory by Krum in which the Emperor Nicephorus was killed (811). In Italy and the Adriatic Charlemagne's forces advanced steadily into nominally eastern areas (788-798), but in 812 Charlemagne restored Venice, Istria, and Dalmatia in return for eastern recognition of his title of Emperor of the Franks which he had obtained from the pope in 800.

The next period of Byzantine recovery (856-1025) brought the empire to the peak of its territorial area and cultural achievement. In the themes the local authorities were busily concerned with building up their local wealth and powers and left the central dynasty relatively unchallenged from their full occupation with these more local tasks. As a consequence, the hereditary principle almost became established as a rule of succession at the center, but, at the same time, a kind of feudal system began to grow up locally. The iconoclastic controversy had been settled by a moderately pro-icon compromise at the ecclesiastical council of 843.

This recovery of Byzantine power is usually attributed to the Macedonian dynasty of the regicide Basil I (867-886), but it began in the reign of Basil's victim Michael III (842-867). As early as 856, Byzantine forces recovered all of Asia Minor and much of Syria and were able to cross the Euphrates River. In 864 the Bulgars were overcome, forced to accept Christianity and to give up their alliance with the Franks (who were themselves in political collapse). In the period after 875 a revived Byzantine fleet reestablished its power in the Mediterranean.

By the year 900 this recovery began to reverse its course. The Bulgars under their greatest king, Symeon (893-927), mounted an offensive which brought his forces to the outskirts of Constantinople several times in the years 913-924.

In the Mediterranean, Sicily was lost to the
Arabs completely by 902, while two years later
Saracen pirates captured Thessalonica with 30,000
prisoners.

These temporary reverses were overccme by the
reforming Emperor Romanus I Lecapenus (920-944),
who began another century of Byzantine advance.
Much of the Mediterranean was recovered in a new,
brief period of Byzantine naval power (960-1024).
Cyprus and Crete were retaken in 961-965. The
second Russian attack, under Prince Igor, was
turned back (941-944). The Bulgarians, after
their attacks on Constantinople in 913-924, found
themselves under growing pressure from the Magyars
to the northwest and the Russians to the northeast;
they were defeated by the Greeks, and all their
territory below the Danube was annexed to the empire in 972. The Arabs were ejected from Anatolia,
and Syria, reconquered in 969-971, was also annexed to the empire in 995.

This new surge of Byzantine power, continued
by the Macedonian dynasty, was accompanied by a
series of agrarian edicts which tried to protect
peasant ownership of the land and to ensure that
many of these would have incomes sufficient to
provide cavalry contingents for the imperial forces. It is likely that these reforms were pressed
to avoid repetition of a great famine which occurred
in 927.

These reform edicts were not generally successful because of the difficulty of enforcing them
locally, however skillfully they were formulated
in words in the central administration. Thus they
had to be constantly reissued with a variety of
modifications, from the edict of Romanus I in 922
to the last and most extreme one of Basil II in
996. In general, these laws tried to reverse
forced sales or usurpations of peasant holdings
by the great land monopolizers. They also sought
to counteract peasant poverty which led to this
loss of lands by forcing the landlords to pay collective village taxes and by curtailing the need
for smallholders to submit to the great magnates
for protection because of the remoteness of the

676

central government's agents. Peasants were forbidden to become <u>coloni</u>; all landed estates lacking documents to show ownership of at least 75
years were restored to their previous owners and
all documents showing concessions of public lands
in a more recent period had to be revalidated by
the emperor (Basil II) personally.

This legislation led to much resentment by
the landlord class. The Emperor John Zimisces
(972-976) was poisoned by his chief minister who
feared he might have to disgorge his usurped
landed estates. There were three substantial
revolts by landed feudatories (in 971, 976-979,
and 987-989). These were crushed, but the means
required to do this offered very ominous portents
for the future. In each case, the rebels could
be defeated only by calling upon similar, but rival,
landlords from other areas or by seeking help from
foreign warriors. The revolt of Bardas Phocas in
971 was overcome by Bardas Scleros, fresh from a
victory over the Russians. The revolt of 976,
led by Bardas Scleros, was defeated by Bardas
Phocas using Georgian forces. The third revolt,
led once again by Bardas Phocas, was defeated by
6000 Russian fighters borrowed from the Grand
Prince Vladimir of Kiev.

Another dangerous sign was the growing need
for heavy cavalry in combat. This burden could
be borne by larger landowners rather than smaller
ones. In an effort to increase the number of the
latter, an edict of 969 increased the value of inalienable peasant farms from four gold pounds to
twelve, but this simultaneously increased the difficulties of enforcement, particularly as increasing numbers of peasants were willing to give up
their lands and freedom, along with the burdens
of military service and taxpaying, in return for
submission to a great landlord and protection from
him.

These ominous signs were concealed in the
last years of the reign of Basil II by the fact
that the empire reached the apex of its power
and glory. The annexation of Syria in 995 was
followed by the final crushing of Bulgarian re-

sistance north of the Danube in 1014 and the acquisition of Georgia and Armenia by bequests from the wills of their rulers in the period 1000-1045. These bequests were made for an ominous reason: the Seljuk Turks from the northern grasslands were beginning to press down into the Near East across the highland zone and this seemed a good way to establish a defensive posture for these exposed countries.

At the death of Basil II in 1025, the Byzantine empire stretched from Azerbaijan to southern Italy. Its army was at the peak of its power, largely from the iron discipline and minute supervision of administrative and logistical details by Basil himself. The old enemies of the empire, Arabs, Bulgars, and Russians, had been subdued. The church and its clergy were under imperial control, and Byzantine culture, including art, literature, and education, were the highest they had ever been. The law was codified; the University of Constantinople, which had been founded about 850, became a great center of literature and scholarship. The Slavs, including Russian Prince Vladimir and many of his people, were converted. In politics, for the first time, a system of hereditary monarchy seemed to be established, with five reigns, including several co-rulers, over 161 years, from 867 to 1028.

On the other hand, Basil, who never married, left no heir. Two powerful new enemies were appearing on the horizon, the Turks from the east and the representatives of western civilization, including the Normans and the Italian cities, such as Venice and Genoa, from the west. The Crusades were about to begin. The need for increased cavalry forces was tending toward the kind of social and economic changes which had destroyed the western empire in the fifth century.

The period of decline associated with the later Macedonians (1025-1086) is marked by these foreboding signs of a darker future. As late as 1042 and 1048, the emperor's forces were able to defeat the Normans in the west and the Seljuk Turks in the east, but by 1068-1071 both of these won significant victories over his forces. Loss of

678

control of the sea began in 1042, not this time
to the Saracens, but to new Christian enemies,
the Normans and the Venetians, who moved forward
to dominate the Adriatic and the central Mediterranean in the next two centuries. Not least
foreboding, perhaps, was the series of female
regents and rulers which dominated the period
1028-1056.

     d.   Decline of the Byzantine State, 1025-1453

    The decline of Byzantium from 1025 to its
final disappearance in 1453 was neither constant
nor inevitable. But it is clear, despite a brief
recovery of less than a century's duration under
the Comneni dynasty (1081-1186) that it was not
finding any solutions to the increasingly acute
problems which were rising against it. In 1042
it inflicted a defeat on the Normans and six years
later it defeated the Seljuks. But by 1060 both
were advancing again. Even more threatening was
the alliance of an aggressive papacy, the land-
hungry feudal rulers of western Europe led by the
Normans, and the Italian commercial and naval aggression led by Venice. This triple aggression
from the west advanced against the Byzantine empire after 1060 on many fronts, of which the most
threatening was the Crusades. At the same moment,
the Turkish advance from the east began to break
through the eastern frontiers. Together, these
two ultimately destroyed the eastern empire by
a slow process of attrition. The outcome was not
determined by weapons or by battles except in the
most obvious and superficial way. Moreover, the
struggle was not a conflict of ideologies as has
often been stated. The Emperor Andronicus (in
1183) and his successor Isaac (in 1189) made alliances with Saladin against the Crusaders. Later
emperors made alliances with the Tartars and the
Mongols against their Christian neighbors. Even
the Crusaders, who might have been expected to
have somewhat higher levels of ideological, or
at least religious, loyalties did not hesitate
to betray their fellow Crusaders to the Saracens,
as Raymond de Saint Gilles betrayed Godfrey de
Bouillon before Asqualon in 1099. Similarly any
government, whatever its ideology, was willing

to use mercenary forces from any source against
its own ideological fellows. There were no firm
loyalties, at that time, at least among the ruling groups, on the basis of ideology, religion,
linguistic or cultural groupings, or even family
loyalty. Even mothers murdered or maimed their
sons, as brothers did their brothers. There can
be little doubt that loyalties such as I have
mentioned had influence among ordinary people,
but the upper classes and ruling groups of providential empire had little real use for such loyalties. Their motivations were much more narrow
and egocentric, either self-interest without
scruple or loyalty to a system in which they
were significant members. Thus among the Crusaders,
the great mass may well have been motivated by the
desire to visit Jerusalem on pilgrimage or play a
part in freeing the Holy City from Moslem control
to bring it into Christian hands. But the leaders of the Crusades, the barons, while no less
believing in their religion and in the holiness
of the Holy City, were not motivated by these beliefs. They were committed to a certain social
structure in which they held significant places
and were motivated by a desire to obtain landed
estates and enserfed peasants in the Near East
for themselves as parts of that social structure.

     The real subject of history, in this period
as in most periods, was the changes of systems as
organizational structures. There was a Byzantine
empire apart from the people, including rulers,
who made it up. The subject of history is how
this structural entity, with its persistent yet
changeable patterns of arrangements of people,
artifacts, ideology, and symbols, acted to preserve itself and to extend itself over additional
lands and peoples. The struggles of historical
importance which went on here were not the intrigues and actions of individual men, but the
conflicts and struggles of these organizational
systems (in this case, providential empires) with
each other and with quite different kinds of organizational systems represented by the Normans,
the Venetians, the Turks, and even the papacy.
It also includes the constant changes, which always go on within each structural system, until
each of these either disintegrates and disappears

or is changed, perhaps after centuries, into a new system.

From this point of view, the providential empires whose clashes and changes we are examining in this chapter have little to do with the great mass of the peoples who lived, produced crops or other goods, acquired a cognitive outlook and verbalized ideology, had children, and died. These systems were far above this mass of people and could be changed with only minor changes in the lives of these masses, even when these changes included wholesale changes in ideology or religion. The great strength of western civilization after about 1750, was that it devised a structure which was able to incorporate a large percentage of the mass of the peoples into the system. Today, as with the Roman system about A.D. 250, that percentage is falling rapidly as increasing numbers of the masses become alienated from the system or try to opt out of it.

There is no need to follow this period of decline of the Byzantine system in any detail. Chronologically it falls into the period of the next chapter, associated with the rise of the Turk and of two new civilizations in Russia and the west. But it should be recognized that only the last stages in the decline of the eastern empire (those associated with the period after 1300) had anything to do with changes in weapons. The decline of providential empire in Byzantium and in the Caliphate, like the earlier decline of the neo-Persian, Bulgarian, and other empires, was the consequence, not of weapons changes, but of other factors closely associated with the nature of providential empire itself, including its inability to establish any stable relationship between the mobility of its weapons and the stability of its sedentary agricultural base. The chief factors in this decline were similar to those in the decline of Sassanian Persia, the Abbasid Caliphate, the Seljuks, and later the Ottoman empire (which replaced all of these).

This relationship was based on an unstable balance of three pairs of factors or institutions. These three were: (1) the countryside divided

681

into agricultural enterprises supporting tenures
of bundles of revenues and the urban centers; (2)
the mobile mounted warrior and the static fortified place; and (3) the ruler and his local agents.

The power unit we are discussing was an unstable relationship among these three with each
of the three pairs properly balanced. This unit
was not a nation or a country, and, in most cases,
it was not a state. The Byzantine empire and China
were states; the Sassanian empire (but not the
preceding Parthian empire) was a state; it could
be debated whether the Moslem power unit ever was
a state; if it did rise to that level, this occurred under the Abbasids for a relatively brief
period, but it is notable that the Moslems never
had a word for "state" (meaning an organized structure of public authority with its own rules of
operation and procedures in a system of law). Most
of the other power systems we are concerned with
from the Holy Roman Empire in the west to the Mongolian Great Khanate in the east were not states.

Even when these power structures were states,
they were not "nations" or "countries." They were
not "nations" because the rulers and the inhabitants,
or even the inhabitants apart, did not form a community bound together by common language, culture,
traditions, and interests so that they considered
themselves a single community. No such national
communities existed in modern times until about
1800 (with the exception of England). In earlier
times, and especially under providential empires,
the inhabitants were divided into a multitude of
separate communities.

Nor were these providential monarchical power
structures "countries," that is territorial areas
whose inhabitants regarded themselves as forming
a political unity even when they recognized that
they formed numerous distinct communities. The
fact that the base of any of these power structures
was simply an additive assemblage of similar tenures (or economic enterprises) rather than a more
organic system of social and economic interrelationships makes it impossible to regard any such assemblage as a "country" with a frontier or boundary
with any real functional significance.

682

This last fact (that the bases of these systems were simply additive) is vital, as we shall see, since it permitted any system to be destroyed simply by long sustained subtractive activities at this socioeconomic base. This is what the Turks ultimately did and explains why they succeeded in destroying the three greatest of these power systems (Byzantium, the Moslem empires, and the Seljuks).

We shall return in a moment to this relationship between these power structures and communities of peoples, but now we must review the balance between our three pairs of factors.

The relationship between the rural peasantry and the urban centers is fairly obvious. The latter were a convenience to the former, but the former were a necessity to the latter. The towns provided the countryside with outlets for some of its surpluses and for commercial interchange through which the peasantry could obtain money with which they could pay taxes and rents. They may also have provided them with some craft products (such as iron) although most craft products, at that time, were of rural origin. In theory also, the towns could provide the peasants with defense, but this was more often theoretical than factual. Indeed, in a backward system, such as western Europe was about A.D. 1000, where almost all economic interchange, including "taxes" and "rents" were in kind, the countryside had little or almost no need for towns. But towns, on the other hand, always have a need for rural surroundings as their source of food and the raw materials for fuel and shelter.

Our second pair of elements, concerned with defense, are the mobile warrior and the static castle, each caught in a dichotomy involving the logistic need for dispersal and the security (defensive) need for concentration of manpower resources. The mounted fighter could move across the country between the fortified centers, but he could not stop to consolidate or to organize his conquest on any permanent basis unless he could capture fortified centers to rest, to get access to their stores, and often to find workshops to

683

replenish his equipment. To capture such centers he had to concentrate his forces and reduce his mobility whether he stormed it or besieged it. Yet for supply these forces had to forage over the countryside where they became subject to piecemeal attacks and destruction by any enemy field forces. Thus the attacker was trapped between the logistical need for small dispersed forces and the military need for large concentrated ones.

The same pressures worked on the defenders within the walls. The smaller the number of defenders, the longer their supplies would last in any attempt to starve them out. But the number of defenders had to be large enough to man the walls with replacements or to mount a sortie against the besiegers if the number of these latter were reduced by dispersal in search of food and fodder. But on the whole, a large fortified center, a great city, was weaker in a siege than a smaller place, not only from the extent of its walls which had to be defended, but also because of the difficulty of knowing what was happening along the whole length of the walls and thus the difficulty of moving defenders to the spots where they were most needed, and also from the simple fact that the larger the center, the greater the proportion of non-combatants who consumed supplies without contributing much to defense.

Thus both the attacker and the defender were caught in a pair of difficult alternatives: the one between military manpower and supply based on the differential mobility of these two and the closely related military problem of making a choice between concentration of forces (and supplies) for military operations and dispersal of forces (and supplies) for the purpose of easing the supply problem. Because of these difficult choices, military strategy in this period (and later to the end of the eighteenth century) concentrated on control and interdiction of military supplies and not on the destruction of field forces in battle.

The third of these pairs of elements was the one of most immediate concern to any providential ruler. It was the relationship between him as ruler and his local agents as semi-autonomous powers. What the ruler wanted from his local agents was loyalty, military contingents, and possibly monetary contributions. But, for the reasons we have already indicated (namely that power and the economic and social bases of power were fundamentally local), he found his ability to command these very limited.

All of these relationships are clearly illustrated in the decline of Byzantium and in the rise and fall of the Seljuk empire in the period we have now reached, following 1030.

The Seljuks were a family of Oghuz Turks who were driven from beyond the Jaxartes River by other Kipshak Turks (Cumans) and found refuge in the Islamic empire as mercenary soldiers of various Muslim rulers. The descendants of Seljuk, especially his grandsons, Tughril Bey and Chaghri Bey, conquered the Ghaznavids of eastern Persia (1040) and advanced into western Persia, Iraq (fall of Baghdad, 1055), Georgia, and Armenia (1064). In the next generation Chaghri Bey's son Alp Arslan advanced into Anatolia (victory at Manzikert, 1071) and the Levant (1074).

Alp Arslan, a wise and magnanimous conqueror, had no desire to conquer the Byzantine empire but, as a loyal Muslim, was satisfied to conquer and reunite all the disintegrated territories of the Islamic Caliphate. He found himself in a difficult position, however, from the fact that family ambitions to adopt the providential monarchical system of Near Eastern civilized society with its agricultural base and cosmopolitan imperial superstructure conflicted with the fact that much of his conquests came from the military successes of his totally uncivilized tribal contingents of Turkish pastoralists (the Turkmen). As rapidly as possible, the Seljuks replaced these Turkmen tribal pastoralists, whose economic base was pastoral herds supplemented by plunder, for mercenary forces, whose economic base was money derived from taxation and the incomes of established peasant agriculture. Since this shift could not be made quickly enough and could never be made completely, it was necessary to divert the fanatical attachment of the Turkmen for Islam, pastoralism, and

plunder outward, against the non-Islamic world such
as the Christians of the Caucasus or Anatolia or
against non-Orthodox Muslims like the Fatimids of
Egypt.

This outward pressure of Turkmen holy warriors
sent bands of nomadic Turks roaming throughout Anatolia from about 1060 to the end of that century
(defeats of Turkmen at Nicaea and Dorylaeum in 1097).
A retaliatory expedition by the Byzantine Emperor
Romanus IV Diogenes in 1071 led to a great victory
for Alp Arslan at Manzikert, in which Romanus was
captured.

Alp Arslan won this great victory from the
treason of a number of the emperor's subordinate
officers, especially Andronicus Ducas in command
of the rear guard who abandoned his position and
allowed the Turks to attack the center of the imperial forces from the rear, while he withdrew
from the field. As soon as the defeat was reported
in Constantinople, the traitor's father, Caesar
John Ducas, seized the imperial throne, while the
son completed his treason by killing Romanus on
his release from captivity. The victorious Alp
Arslan was assassinated shortly after his victory
and succeeded by his son Malik Shah, last of the
great Seljuk sultans (1072-1092).

The Turkmen nomadic warrior bands continued
to roam about Anatolia plundering and destroying
the basic peasant agriculture economy in order
to create the wide areas of underpopulated countryside which their nomadic base required. By this
process they revealed how the Near Eastern providential empires could be conquered without capturing the fortified strongholds, that is by the almost total destruction of the peasant agricultural
base which sustained these strongholds. This was
a method, however, which could only be used by a
power system based on a different organizational
pattern. It was not a method which could be used
by any other providential monarchy or by any system with an agricultural base, such as the feudal-
manorial system of western Europe, the profit-seek-
ing commercialism of the Italian cities, papal religious imperialism, or Norman military adventur-
ism. All of these other organizational patterns

were beginning to threaten Byzantium from the west, just at the time that the Turks were beginning to attack it from the east. The two threats from the east and from the west were entirely different in character, because the Turks largely concentrated on occupying the countryside, while the west (including the Crusaders) largely concentrated on capturing walled places. The reason was that the Seljuks were really a mass movement seeking supplies and a place to live. The western attack on the eastern empire was really a non-mass, ruling group operation, not seeking a place to live (which they had at home) or supplies, but seeking control and power. This was as true of the Crusaders or the Normans as it was of the Venetian traders or the papacy. The cities were the centers of power and control, of profits and security, so the west went east in limited numbers seeking these. In a sense, the contrast between Turks and Crusaders in the Near East was similar to the contrast between the Anglo-Saxon and Norman invasions of England. And just as England remained English and did not become French, so Anatolia became Turkish and the Levant remained Arabic, but neither became Latin, French, Italian, or German.

The Ottoman Turks eventually won out over all contenders because they combined both: they occupied the countryside, changing it from Greek to Turkish, and they captured the cities as centers of power and control because they improved transportation, including an elaborate siege train, to a level closer to the mobility of their armed horsemen.

The Turks were able to win not only because they had this double working attack but because the ground had been prepared for them by the Seljuks and the west. The Seljuks occupied the countryside, while the west occupied the towns. The one reduced Byzantine manpower and destroyed its economic basis, while the other usurped its organizational structure, especially fiscal, so that its ability to hire mercenary fighters and other manpower was crippled.

This decline had three stages. From the situation under the Macedonians, in which Byzantium had its own manpower and wealth to provide its own defense, it was reduced in stage two to a condition where it could defend itself only by playing off its enemies, one against the others. This was largely the situation under the Comneni dynasty from 1081 to the sack of Constantinople by the Fourth Crusade in 1204.

The third stage, under the Paleologi dynasty, from the Greek recapture of Constantinople from Latin control in 1261 to the final Ottoman attack in 1453, was largely a period in which an effort was made to provide defense by purchase, but, since the money was constantly insufficient, many tasks were left undone, especially in Asia whence the Ottomans were coming, because of the Paleologue emphasis on the European side.

The extent of the western injury to the Byzantine fiscal situation can be seen by one example. In 1264 Emperor Michael VIII was unable to provide regular pay for his Seljuk mercenaries in his war with the Latin "Franks" so the Seljuks left him and went over to the Franks. This combination defeated Michael in battle immediately. To obtain help, Michael offered Genoa (which had just been beaten at sea by Venice, 1266) a trading site at Galata, a suburb of Constantinople on the Golden Horn, in return for support. Galata, under Genoa's control, flourished and not only supplanted Constantinople itself as a trading center, but the Genoese replaced the Greeks as the naval power on the Black Sea. In reprisal Venice allied with the Golden Horde of the Tartars north of that sea and destroyed Galata, forcing the emperor into a war with Venice. Galata was rebuilt and continued to flourish, so that by 1346 the customs revenues of Galata were about 200,000 hyperpyra a year compared to a bare 30,000 hyperpyra in Constantinople's own customs. This was at a time when the empire was in dire straits, being pressed to death between the Ottoman Turks and Stephen Dusan's Bulgarian empire. To remedy the situation, the emperor lowered tariffs at Constantinople to attract more trade and raise more money for defense. The Genoese retaliated by destroying the Byzantine fleet.

Thus the Byzantine empire was destroyed, slowly strangled to death between Turkish pressure from the east and European pressure from the west. The ultimate victors were the Ottoman Turks because they combined (1) ability to occupy the countryside; (2) ability to capture towns; (3) a flexible and adaptable organization of political power; and (4) a newly revived and fervent vision of orthodox Islam.

When Byzantium finally perished, it was more than a thousand years old and had been, simply from this point of view, a success. This success could be attributed to its ability to combine together diverse elements in a single system better than any other providential monarchy. From the point of view of weaponry and tactics, this is obvious. It not only combined infantry, cavalry, and fortifications together in a better balance, thus reconciling the divergencies of static and mobile elements, but it came closer than any other similar political structure in efforts to remedy the chief technological inadequacy of the period, inability to move supplies effectively. It did this by the use of sea power, but also by the creation, within its military formations, of the best system of logistics of the age. This supply service was combined with what we would regard as an embryo engineering service (undoubtedly a survival from the first great engineering army, that of the Roman republic). According to Oman, each unit of sixteen men in the east Roman army had two carts and a pack animal; one cart carried food, chiefly biscuits, and extra weapons, especially arrows; the other cart carried tools and utensils, such as an ax, a saw, two spades, two pickaxes, and such; the pack horse could carry about a week's provisions for the unit in terrain where the carts could not keep up.

To these essential services, the Byzantine defense forces added other advantages, such as an outstanding siege train, the most sophisticated mechanical artillery of the day (catapult, ballista, and trebuchet), and the most sophisticated understanding of strategy and tactics. This last was embodied in the Strategicon attributed to the Emperor Maurice (about 579) and the Tactica attributed to the Emperor Leo VI the Wise, about 900.

These works were practical and empirical rather
than theoretical, but they continued to be valuable because of the fact that there was so little
weapons innovation in this long period of weapons
confusion. The only significant new weapon, Greek
fire, was Byzantine (c. 675).

Outside the area of weapons systems and military operations, where the Byzantine achievement
can be summed up in the one word "balance," this
system had other advantages.

These also can be summed up in the word "balance" but here we must add the additional word
"advanced." The Byzantine society was the best
balanced organization of advanced practices of
the day except China. It was a society with a
more productive agriculture than any other except
Egypt, China, and (later) western Europe; it had
a more highly developed crafts industry and commerce than any of its competitors except Islam at
the peak of the Abbasid Caliphate. Byzantium above
all kept on an exchange economy and on a money
economy longer and more fully than any of its
rivals. It was more fully civilized, in the sense
that its population was more literate, more urbanized, with a larger percentage engaged in non-
agricultural activities than any rival. And in
these attributes of a fully civilized society with
a fully developed state organization, as in its
military system, it kept a balance of diverse elements better than its rivals were able to do. As
a consequence of this and especially of its ability
to maintain a higher degree of control over local
agents of the central authority and keep these relations longer on a monetary basis, it was able to
ward off disintegration of its authority and of
its ability to respond to external threats.

Its greatest weaknesses were two: (1) its
failure to recognize and retain control of the sea
in terms of both a naval and mercantile marine;
and (2) its inability to retain the loyalty and
ideological support of its agents and subjects.
Part of this second weakness was intrinsic in the
very nature of providential monarchy which, by
making God rather than man responsible for what
happens, tends to destroy individual moral respon-

sibility, but much of this weakness was based on the elements of ideological fanaticism which were parts of its Greek heritage.

Thus Byzantium survived because it was the most effective of the providential empires, a system more effective, perhaps, than any earlier system of human political organization except China, but one which had intrinsic weaknesses. It is worth noting here that these weaknesses were generally overcome in the new, and unique, form of political organization discovered by western civilization in the second millennium of the Christian era.

6.   Islam and the Southern Grasslands Offensive

The birth of Islamic civilization and its expansion to form an empire stretching from the Atlantic Ocean in Morocco and Spain to India and the borders of China is one of the most complex and astounding achievements of human energies. To explain how this came about is no easy task. It is made more difficult by the fact that it is a double task. On the one hand, it is the story of how an organized political structure expanded to cover much of the area of classical civilization and its Byzantine successor, plus all the area of Sassanian Persia, and many other areas extending into the steppes of central Asia, as well as most of Pakistan and Afghanistan and all of Arabia. On the other hand, it is the more complex story of how an organizational power structure which was not really a state changed its organization constantly as it expanded.

Since these changes of organization were continuous from its beginnings at the first religious revelation of Muhammad about A.D. 610 until its total conquest by the Ottoman Turks about 1560, any words we use to divide this almost continuous process into discrete stages will give a false impression of its actual conditions for much of that long period.

It is usual to divide this history into periods in terms of rulers or dynasties. This would give the following:

1. The age of Muhammad, to 632;
2. The first four Orthodox Caliphs, 632 to 661;
3. The Omayyad Caliphate at Damascus, from 661 to 750;
4. The Abbasid Caliphate from 750 to about 1100, chiefly at Baghdad and Samarra;
5. The Seljuk empire, from about 1100 to about 1200;
6. The Mongol threat, 13th century; and
7. The Ottoman conquest and empire, from about 1300 to 1922.

This dynastic periodization could be made more complete and more complex by adding sub-periods, notably stages of decay and political fragmentation, in the late Abbasid, Seljuk, and Ottoman periods (that is, after 900, 1200, and 1650).

However, this dynastic periodization gives us little idea of the changes in organization over this dynastic sequence. The subject which interests us, the role of weapons systems in these changes, is closely associated with organizational changes but only remotely related to dynastic changes.

The organizational changes experienced by Islamic society are those covered by this volume to this point in history. These are: (1) organizations based on blood kinship, real or assumed (tribalism); (2) a religious community; (3) a semi-secular public authority (a state); and, (4) a providential empire. In the course of this sequence, the transitions tended to take place through periods of personal military despotisms.

This sequence, while it does reflect the organizational sequence on a historical basis, is not very helpful because the whole of Islamic society did not move forward simultaneously from one of these stages to the next. On the contrary, whole sectors of the society, on a geographic basis, remained on an earlier stage (or even returned to an earlier stage, as the Arabs generally turned back from the religious community to the multiplicity of kinship groups). This led to such confusion and such conflicts that it could be argued that Islamic civilization never did have a single society but always remained a congeries of diverse communities.

Another alternative chronology, suggested by Vladimir Minorsky, would be simpler in appearance but much more complex in application, since it would have only three periods based on cultural (that is linguistic) distinctions. These would be:

1. Arab tribalism, 622-
2. The Iranian intermezzo, c. 850-
3. The Turkish domination, c. 1000-

This chronology could be made much more elaborate, but again it is not closely related to the main subject of our concern, the relationship between weapons systems and political stability on an organizational basis. From this point of view, I shall use a sequence as follows:

1. Arabic tribalism (before 622);
2. The effort to establish an Islamic religious community, 622-;
3. The failure to integrate the state and the community;
4. The emergence of military despotism over the community;
5. The rise of providential empire;
6. The decay of Islamic civilization.

This sequence reflects the interrelations of two chief factors: religion as the basis for an integrated community and weapons as the chief element in applied force. The two generally worked in opposition to each other: when one was operating to establish a larger or better integrated community, the other was working to make the community smaller or to disrupt it. In a couple of brief intervals, notably in the earlier portions of stages 2 and 5, the two seemed to be working together to provide a larger and better integrated community. The reason for this rather confused interrelationship is what I have called weapons confusion and the equally confused role of religious feeling in any community, capable of integrating it when people agree on religious ideas, but equally capable of totally disrupting it when they chose not to agree. Even when weapons and religion work together to create unity, the result is a system which may seem despotic to some persons, alienating them from it and even leading them to decide that they have a religious obligation to resist it or to break it up.

In Islamic civilization such dissenting groups often had very poor prospects of achieving much on the basis of force or power, or even of obtaining simple local autonomy on any political basis. As a result, they turned their political opposition into religious opposition by creating a heretical sect. The proper tactic for dealing with such opposition is to make orthodoxy wide enough to include all but the most extreme dissent. This was eventually achieved in Islamic society, under the stage we have numbered 5, especially in the Ottoman period. In the earlier periods, when a serious effort was being made to create a unified and integrated society, the heretical sects, such as the Karamathians in Arabia, the Order of the Assassins in their mountain fortress in Persia, and the rival caliphates in Egypt and Spain, were able to maintain their autonomy because the power of weapons held by orthodoxy was not sufficient to overcome the allegiance of religious dissent until orthodoxy could itself assume a form wide enough to include most believers. This wide orthodoxy, in turn, could not be adopted by the political establishment until Islamic religious communities had been created by non-governmental activities below the superficial level on which governments which were almost wholly military were operating.

At this point in our study, this may seem to be a very complex situation, but it will clarify as our examination of the history of Islamic civilization goes on. The significant point, much clearer in this civilization than in some others, is that no society can be stable which is not based on both power and outlook (or, more narrowly, on weapons and religion). Too much reliance on either is disruptive. In this case, the disruptive influences of such excess reliance on either were eventually overcome by the slow growth of a third element, the sociological element of a community in which people were sufficiently secure in sufficiently intimate social relationships to restrain their use of weapons and force and to be

694

tolerant in their religious beliefs within a
broad religious consensus. This is basically
an Asiatic solution of the problem of ideological
intolerance and the equally dangerous, and parallel, problem of excessive reliance on force as an
element in preserving any society's unity.

Any society with a weak sense of social community, as Islam was for centuries and as our
western civilization is now, will find great difficulty in handling the two extreme elements of
force and ideology and will tend to become more
extreme in both until these two extremes totally
disrupt the essential social community without
which men cannot survive. The movement toward
a secular political system such as began in Islam
under the Omayyad caliphate (661-750) or as western civilization has been experiencing it during
the past century, turns any weapons control element into a disruptive force within the society.
In Islam this was very evident because of the
general superiority of defensive weapons and of
local economic bases (up until the creation of
the international commercial economy in the middle Abbasid period). This disruptive influence
of weapons was not only direct, but also indirect, through the disruption of community, of
commerce, tax collecting, and monetary flows,
and through excessive reliance on weapons in an
increasingly secular system. In the period of
our concern here, this led to a movement away
from a money economy and toward an economy in
which taxes, rents, and salaries were made in
kind instead of in money. This decentralized
the system by forcing its operations into closer
and more immediate contact with localized agrarian
enterprises and toward more static weapons (fortified strongholds to hold such supplies in kind).
Such a movement toward localism and military disintegration served to expose the whole system to
growing pastoral raids (bedouins) and to invasion
by more mobile foreign enemies (such as the bedouins, Seljuks, Mongols, and Ottoman Turks).

This sequence begins with the chaotic picture
of what Arab tribalism was like in the seventh
century when Muhammad began to preach a monotheistic religion to the polytheistic pagans of

western Arabia.

Arabia is a relatively complex area and had a relatively complex history before Muhammad. In shape it is like a huge rectangle, running north-west-southeast, with an additional semi-circular area superimposed on its northern boundary (the Syrian Desert). The surface is that of a sloping plateau, higher in the west, near the Red Sea, and sloping down toward the Persian Gulf in the east. Its rainfall is scanty and precarious, since it lies between two systems of precipitation. To the northwest, there is the system of temperate zone cyclonic westerlies which bring rain to the northwest corner of Arabia only in winter; to the southeast is the zone of monsoon rains which reach that corner of Arabia only in summer. In both corners the rain is unreliable and insufficient, with the result that the vegetation is one of grasslands and shrubs rather than trees. The central core of Arabia is permanent desert, known in the south as "the empty quarter" and in the north as the Syrian Desert. Outside these deserts, most of the terrain is grasslands, suitable for pastoral life, but sedentary agriculture is possible only where mountains scrape water from the clouds to create oases or where intermittent rains allow alluvial basin cultivation.

In spite of these handicaps, southern Arabia developed one of the earliest advanced civilizations, with town life, writing, an organized priesthood, and an archaic monarchical government. This civilization was almost contemporary with classical civilization (c. 1200 B.C.-A.D. 500) but collapsed more rapidly and more completely because of the ending of the sub-Atlantic climate period in the third century after Christ. The increased dryness of the period A.D. 200-1300 made it impossible to continue the specialized techniques of alluvial basin agriculture by which the South Arabian civilization was supported.

This South Arabian civilization was associated successively with a number of local monarchies of which the chief were the Mineans (c. 1200-650 B.C.), followed by the Sabaeans (to about 115 B.C.) and the Himyarites (c. 115 B.C.-A.D. 300), all of which

696

were typical archaic monarchies, resting originally on an assumed identity between the deity (as embodied in the forces of fertility and virility) and the priest-king whose health insured the continued functioning of these essential forces.

The total destruction of this South Arabian civilization in the fifth century A.D. was associated in Arab folk memory with the drought resulting from the destruction of a large irrigation dam at Marib (the capital town of the Sabaean monarchy about 60 miles east of Sana). But the real causes of the collapse were much more profound and pushed the whole of Arabia backward to a much earlier type of social organization. For all practical purposes, civilized life ceased among the Arabs. While some Arabs continued to exist on an agricultural level in oases and others continued to live on a commercial level as camel-borne merchants over semi-desert trade routes, the greater part of Arabia was reduced to sheep and camel pastoralism, moving endlessly about on scanty seasonal grasslands.

This crisis, which existed for more than two centuries before Muhammad, gave rise to violent struggles for survival on reduced grasslands, created a general atmosphere of insecurity and mutual distrust, made settled agriculture and distant trade more precarious, ended almost all conception of the state or of public authority, gave rise to almost universal illiteracy among the Arabs of Arabia, and forced the level of political organization backward to the stage of narrow tribalism. The two points of greatest significance for Arabia itself was this last development, while for surrounding areas the chief point of importance was the fourth great outsurge of Semitic peoples from Arabia.

We must look in somewhat greater detail at these two points.

Arabia was the original home and source of the Semite peoples. By "Semite" we refer to a linguistic classification. Racially and physically, the peoples of Arabia were rather mixed, and this racial mixture has been increased fairly steadily over the last 5000 years, chiefly from the introduction of agglutinative-speaking round heads such as the Hurrians after 2000 B.C. and the Mongols and Turks in the period since A.D. 1100. Fundamentally, the peoples of Arabia have been of Mediterranean physical type, that is slender, long-headed, dynamic persons, with dark hair and eyes. There has, however, always been among them a substantial percentage of lighter-eyed persons (gray or even blue), a trait which is probably of Saharan origin in contrast to the generally brown-eyed trait of the basic Mediterranean race.

Linguistically, the Semites speak inflected languages with considerable development of time relationships in the forms of the verb. Such Semite speakers, like their collaterally related Indo-European speakers of the northern grasslands, were generally violent, warlike, patriarchal, polytheistic (sky, nature, and weather worshippers), with no direct cultural descent from the peaceful, matriarchal earth worshippers of the Neolithic garden cultures, except for the South Arabian agriculturalists. These more primitive cultural traits survived among both Semites and Indo-Europeans because the cultural history of both passed from the heroic hunting stage to a semi-pastoral stage without any considerable period of the sedentary gardening cultures between these two stages.

From before 1500 B.C. many Semites were in this pastoral or semi-pastoral stage of social development, living from herds of sheep and donkeys in a cultural condition which is often called "ass nomadism." In the course of the second millennium B.C., both the horse and the camel were added to their herds, the horse in a very limited way shortly after 1800 B.C. and the camel in a more widespread fashion in the centuries before 1000 B.C.

The periods of more extensive rainfall, before 3000 B.C. and in the sub-Atlantic period of the first millennium B.C., gave rise to considerable increases in numbers of the Semites of Arabia, while the drier periods, of the sub-Boreal climate from 3000 to 1000 B.C. and the drier period A.D. 200-1300, forced these increased populations to migrate outward from Arabia, often with violence.

These outward movements of Semites from Arabia went generally in three directions: (1) northeast towards Mesopotamia and the Asiatic highland zone; (2) northwest towards the Levant and the Mediterranean; and (3) westward across the Red Sea toward the Ethiopian highlands. Only in the Islamic period were these three directions supplemented by a fourth, a movement by sea, eastward across southern Asia and southward to east Africa.

The turmoil and violence engendered by these periods of drought tore to shreds more advanced forms of political and social organization, made agriculture uncertain except in isolated spots, made distant commerce more dangerous, reduced town life to very little, and reduced most specialized and literate groups, such as priests, scribes, craftsmen, soldiers, and rulers to almost nothing.

These changes, especially in the centuries before Muhammad, led to the disappearance of all state organization and of the idea of public authority, so that all power became private power (almost personal power), and security could be found only among one's immediate kinfolk or under the protection of a few religious taboos.

Just as political and social organization collapsed in this way, backward to the stage of narrow kinship grouping (the descendants of a known ancestor no more than five or six generations back), so religious development fell backward to that level of primitive belief in which the world consisted of a myriad of spiritual forces in all objects, both animate and inanimate, including rocks, waters, trees, clouds, the forces of nature, and the celestial bodies. The very idea of law or of fixed rules was absent from such a world of conflicting powers, in which man's fate was almost entirely outside his own control except to the degree that he could placate or influence such powers by magic, sacrifices, or verbal blandishments.

Among his fellow men, the individual was equally insecure, able to rely upon little outside his own immediate relatives with no system of law and with

no method of enforcement of security or rights
except through family feuding. In fact, the individual hardly existed as a discrete social entity except for his membership in his family,
which was itself secure only in its membership
in a clan, which was itself protected, even more
precariously, by its membership in a tribe, made
up of the male descendants of a single remembered
ancestor. All of these relationships, even that
of the domestic family, were unreliable and uncertain, because of the anarchistic individualism
of the Arabs and because the only sanction for any
rights or agreements rested on violence. In the
ultimate showdown, what an Arab got in life, about
A.D. 600, depended on the assertion, aggressive-
ness, and violence of his kin group. As Professor Hitti says, "the clan or tribe is a unit by
itself, self-sufficient and absolute, and regards
every other clan or tribe as its legitimate victim
and object of plunder and murder." As a result,
the raid "is raised. . .to the rank of a national
institution. . . . In desert land, where the
fighting mood is a chronic mental condition,
raiding is one of the few manly occupations."
The only other factor of much significance was
the widespread Arab admiration for any talent in
poetry and verbal skills.

These characteristics of Arab life were most
evident among the bedouin, that is the nomadic
pastoral peoples. Among these, smaller and often
isolated clans sought to live less insecure and
more stable lives either by trade or from oasis
agriculture.

The chief avenue of trade in western Arabia
was from the seaports of southwestern Arabia (in
the western Hadramaut and Aden) to the Negev and
the southern Levant. These trade routes passed
across Yemen and Hejaz parallel to the eastern
shore of the Red Sea and its bordering mountains,
chiefly along the line of oases and wells which
existed between these mountains and the deserts
farther east. A similar trade route went up the
Persian Gulf and the Euphrates River east of Arabia.

The general collapse of settled life in
Arabia in the fifth and sixth centuries had adverse

effects on these lines of commerce, greatly intensified by the collapse of the South Arabian civilization and the wars between Byzantium and Persia, which disrupted commerce both on the Euphrates and along the Red Sea. The disruption of traffic across the Syrian Saddle from the Euphrates to the Mediterranean may have made the traffic across the Hejaz more profitable, but it certainly did not make it any easier. On the contrary, it was threatened by increasing bedouin raids and also from the growing competition of Jewish and Christian traders, often Arabs but not for that reason any more acceptable to the pagan, violent, kinship-obsessed majority of Arabs. Many of these "peoples of the Book" (that is, the Bible) came down into the Arabian caravan routes with the advantages of a higher civilized culture, including literacy, a money economy, and a monotheistic religion. Some of them were religious refugees from the intolerance of the Byzantine empire, since the Jews were episodically persecuted, while the Christians were monophysite or Nestorian, systematically persecuted from Constantinople.

About halfway along the caravan route which crossed the Hejaz, from north to south, was Mecca. This was both a caravan entrepot and a religious center, with the former dependent on the latter and the inhabitants totally dependent on both. The area was too rocky for agriculture, so many Meccan families continued to have pastoral interests, especially as their camels were the basis of their caravan movements. But this commerce, which was expanding rapidly about 600, would have been impossible without the religious sanctuary from which war and the violence of family feuds were periodically excluded.

The chief object of veneration at the sanctuary was a black stone meteorite which evoked such superstitious reverence that it brought pilgrims from considerable distances. The residents of Mecca lived from the profits of the caravans and from the business of the pilgrims to the shrine. The cult idol was housed in a cubical building or temple, the kaaba. Custody of this building and the activities associated with it, including care of the pilgrims, was controlled by the tribe Kuraish, descendants of a certain Kusaiy who flourished about A.D. 440, when he took these activities by force from the clan Khuzaa. Kuraish, in turn, was divided into about ten clans, of which the two dominant ones were descendants of Kusaiy's grandson, Hashim, and the latter's nephew, Omayya. The rivalries of these two clans, the Hashimites and the Omayyads, repeatedly have torn apart the Moslem religious community created by the Hashimite Muhammad.

The general collapse of Arabic culture in the fifth and sixth centuries gave rise to such confusion that one consequence was a widespread discontent with the primitive and chaotic religious practices of the area and a thirst for more convincing religions. At the same time, the profits of the Arabic caravan routes and the growing political disorder of the peninsula encouraged intervention by outside powers. The violent struggles of the Byzantine and Persian empires farther north, seeking to exclude one another from the profitable trade from the Middle and Far East into the Mediterranean basin led to intervention in the Red Sea area. In 522 Constantinople persuaded the Negus of Ethiopia to cross the Red Sea and seize Yemen, which he held until the Persians came down and drove the Africans out in 575. The excuse given for this intervention was that a newly converted Jewish ruler in Yemen was attacking local Christian clans. The intervention, as well as the excuse for it, shows the confusion and weakness that prevailed in western Arabia in the century before Muhammad.

Muhammad, "the Messenger of God," provides one of history's best examples of the right man in the right place at the right time. He was an unusual man and a very unusual Arab. As a great, great, great grandson of Kusaiy and a grandson of Abdul Muttalib (c. 497-578), Muhammad had an established place in the community of Mecca. Abdul Muttalib, head of the Kuraish tribe in Mecca, had seven sons. Muhammad's father, Abdullah, the fifth son, died before Muhammad was born, so the infant was placed to be suckled with a tribe outside Mecca. He returned to his mother and grandfather at the age of six, but his mother died within a year (leaving him

702

in care of a slave girl) and his grandfather died the next year, leaving the child to his second son, Muhammad's uncle, Abu Talib, who was not rich.

Muhammad had no notable talents and no economic position until, at age twenty-five, he went on caravan to Syria as agent for a well-to-do widow of 40 years, Khadija, who was also a great, great, great grandchild of Kusaiy, and was thus a fourth cousin of Muhammad. On the latter's successful return from Syria, his employer suggested that they marry. This, the first of Muhammad's eleven marriages, was a great success, from Muhammad's point of view, despite fifteen years difference in age. They had six children of whom two sons died in infancy, while four daughters survived. Khadija gave Muhammad economic support and unwavering personal loyalty, even when he turned increasingly to a life of solitude and meditation.

From this meditation, which sometimes kept Muhammad alone for days in the hills east of Mecca, came Islam. The archangel Gabriel appeared to Muhammad and instructed him to restore the religion of the one true God. This religion had been revealed to Abraham, to Moses, and to Christ but in each case had become corrupt. Now Muhammad, as the last and final messenger of God, was ordered to reestablish it in its correct form.

There can be no doubt that Muhammad was convinced of the divine mission revealed to him by Gabriel and supplemented by an inner voice. But the religious message he brought was a backward version of Judaism.

We have already indicated that the development of men's ideas on the nature of deity passed through numerous stages over two millennia, from about 1500 B.C. to about the time of Muhammad. Of these stages we have mentioned the beliefs that God was: (1) omnipotent; (2) one; (3) transcendental; (4) good; and (5) love. Of these five stages, Allah, the God of Muhammad, had only the first two, a deficient version of the third, and little of the last two. Allah was One God, the Only God, and Muhammad was his last and final prophet. This God was omnipotent, the

703

essence of Will and total Power. Since everything that happened was a consequence of his Will and could just as easily have been otherwise, there were no rules or law, in the cosmos. Everything was totally entangled in the Will of Allah, which was Fate. The mission of man was not to exercise freedom or growth or to develop his potentialities, but to submit totally to God's Will. Such submission was "Islam."

Man had free will and thus was responsible, in the sense that he could submit to God's Will or defy it. But, since the universe was a reflection of God's Will (which was totally free and unhampered), there were no rules or laws independent of God. Accordingly, there were no distinctions of good and evil. God was not under any ethical restraints and the ultimate rule of the universe was still power (even if God's power) and not law. Thus individual growth in personal freedom and responsibility under law was not possible in the Moslem system. Those who submitted to God's Will were rewarded in Paradise; those who violated His Will burned in Hell.

According to Muhammad, God's demands on men were relatively simple: Belief in one God, Allah, and submission to Him and to His Messenger; brief prayers five times a day; fasting in daylight in the month of Ramadan; no use of alcohol; alms to the poor; no more than four wives at a time. Those who obeyed these rules would win eternity in paradise, which was a bedouin's idea of perfection: cool, flowing waters, green trees with luscious fruits, and beautiful virgins, forever young for endless enjoyment. This perfect state was promised immediately to those who died in battle against unbelievers.

Islam, while offering what any bedouin would want in the hereafter and at relatively small cost, nevertheless was an almost total rejection of the bedouin way of life. It rejected enjoyment and power in this world for rewards in the hereafter. It rejected the security and loyalties of the kin group for the solidarity of the community of believers. It rejected the narrow values of the pastoral nomad, challenging their ideal of manliness

with a new concept of holiness, and rejecting the
bedouin need for revenge to wipe away any personal
affront or injury with the new (and, to the bedouin,
effete) idea of forgiveness. Muhammad's emphasis
on moderation and fasting, and his ambivalent, if
not suspicious, attitude toward women and wine,
were an almost complete reversal of bedouin values.
Above all, the Arab emphasis on the basic reality
of personal, face-to-face relationships within the
narrow confines of the blood grouping, was overturned by Muhammad's emphasis on social equality
in the universal unity of Islam.

On this basis, Islam and Muhammad's substitution of a single divine will and power for the myriad of powers and spirits of Arab superstitions
pointed toward a world empire in which the ordinary
Arab would be lost. For this reason, as Islam
moved toward a universal world empire based on providential monarchy, the Arabs, particularly the bedouins, were left behind in a backward localism of only
nominal adherence to Muhammad's teachings.

The Arabs' inability to free themselves from
kinship loyalties and to rise emotionally, con-
ceptually, and socially to a wider sense of community explains why the Arab Near East today is unable to organize an effective community. This inability is reflected in the fact that Arab marriage
is still endogamous within the kinship group. While
other, more advanced, communities generally forbid
marriage with first cousins, the preferred marriage
among the Arabs has traditionally been of this
kind, with father's brother's daughter (what anthro-
poligists call parallel cousin marriage).

This imprisonment of Arab experience, and especially of security and trust, within the narrow kinship group also explains why it became necessary for
Muhammad's Islamic community to become non-Arab if
it were to cover a larger geographic area. It did
this by becoming cosmopolitan imperial, although
the Arab language, by growth and adaptation, was
able to respond to the challenge and became fully
capable of functioning as the linguistic vehicle
of a universal empire and culture. The Arabs, in
other words, were simply left behind by the growing

community which Muhammad started, and they were
left behind from inability to adapt emotionally
to such a larger community.

The new community invented by Muhammad had
at least three characteristics: (1) it was a religious community, that is a community of belief,
not of blood or other allegiance; (2) within that
community all men were brothers and fundamentally
equal in value in the eyes of Allah; and (3) all
authority within that community was in the hands
of Muhammad, as the direct Messenger of God on
earth. A possible fourth point was that Muhammad's
authority was not differentiated so that he was
lawmaker, judge, commander-in-chief, religious
leader, economic expert, and first in social precedence all rolled together into one. This totalitarian jumbling together of all authority into
one gave rise to gigantic organizational problems
when Muhammad died and the community began to move
outward toward a universal system on a non-Arab base.

Muhammad's religious community was not created
by the fact that a certain number of Arabs accepted
his claim that there was but one God and that he
was the Messenger of God. Rather it was created
by the second oath of Aqaba in 622.

Muhammad's teachings were a direct challenge
to the basic kinship loyalty on which Arab society
was based. This challenge did not come from his
insistence on one God, something that many Arabs
were willing to accept, but from his equal insistence that the believers in that one God must
be totally subordinated to himself as Messenger of
that God. This was subversive to the precariously
balanced structure of kinship loyalties on which
Arab society and all personal security in that
society rested. Few could conceive of loyalty to
a larger social grouping as capable of providing
greater personal security, especially when that
larger grouping did not yet exist and when its
absolute leader would be Muhammad. For Muhammad's
personality was almost antithetical to the Arab
idea of manliness. He was neither a fighter nor
aggressive and he taught of a God who was "Lord
of the Weak" when the only attribute of deity

706

which the **average Arab** could understand was power
and strength.

Muhammad's teachings were subversive to Meccan
society, whose position was based on its trade,
which, in turn, was based on its position as a
pagan shrine. The people of Mecca were not bedouins,
although fully familiar with the nomad way of life.
They were a commercial oligarchy, in which the richest and most powerful, working through their clans,
dominated the life of the town with great profit to
themselves. In the growing political disturbances
of Arabia, only the existence of Mecca as a religious center in which all Arabs could meet in peace
allowed the growing profits of the Hejaz trade routes
to be exploited. The merchants of Mecca were losing
their tribal way of life in a growing rich and individualistic way of life, completely opposed to the
bedouin way of life. But as the latter grew weaker,
the Meccan leaders had no way for replacing those
things which tribalism had provided: protection,
support for the weak, poor, unfortunate, and exploited. The tribal way of life in Mecca itself
was being replaced by a selfish and individualist
materialism, with accumulation of money and luxur-
ious living of which the bedouins had never dreamed.
Muhammad's teachings were just as individualistic
as the practices of the rich of Mecca, perhaps more
so. He insisted that the individual would stand
alone at the Last Judgment, without family, weapons, wealth, or high birth, to answer for his sins.
At that time, what would count was how he had
lived during his life on earth. There was, of
course, nothing new in these ideas, except in Arabia; they could be found in Egypt more than 2000
years before Muhammad. But these teachings were
not only new in Arabia; they were essential if
some substitute was to be found for the disrupting
tribal way of life. The leaders of Kuraish did not
see this need for a new political organization. All
they could see was the threat of Muhammad's teachings offered to their economic organization. For
this reason, they determined to be rid of him.

Getting rid of Muhammad was not simple, for
he was still protected by his own clan, the Beni
Hashim. Anyone who injured him would be subject

707

to their tribal vengeance. When Muhammad denounced the idols in the Kaaba as "nothing but names which you and your fathers have given them, on whom God has given no authority" and when he insisted that the ancestors of Kuraish were in hell fire for worshipping these idols, the elders of Kuraish asked Abu Talib, Muhammad's uncle, to withdraw his clan's protection from Muhammad, so that the prophet could be killed. Abu Talib refused, but the strain on tribal loyalties was almost at the breaking point. The leaders of Kuraish decided to establish a boycott of the Beni Hashim, agreeing to have nothing to do with its members, especially no business nor social relationships, including marriage. This ostracism of Beni Hashim lasted for three years and then was lifted because it applied to all members of the clan when only a few were Muslims.

As the danger grew, Muhammad decided to move his followers to the agricultural oasis of Yathrib (later Medina), 210 miles northeast of Mecca. During the pilgrimage of 619, Muhammad converted twelve men of Yathrib to his beliefs. The following year, these twelve came again on pilgrimage and met Muhammad secretly in the valley of Aqaba, four miles east of Mecca. There they took the first oath of Aqaba, swearing to worship only the one true God, to obey His Messenger, and to abstain from theft, adultery, infanticide, and slander. For this they were promised eternal life in paradise.

The situation in Medina was even worse than in Mecca at that time, since the town was divided in a cold civil war. It was a purely agricultural oasis, whose original inhabitants were either Jews or Judaized Arabs. Following the break of the Marib dam, Arabs from the south had settled in the oasis, originally as clients of the established Jewish clans, who continued to hold the best lands. The Arab arrivals soon split into two clans which, by 620, were in open warfare with each other. About that time, they had a battle, in which some of the Jews and some local bedouin Arabs took part on both sides. Peace was restored, but the situation remained precarious. Obviously, there was no

708

solution to this political problem within the Arab tribal system. A number of local people from both Arab clans were looking about for some way to restore security in Medina and were at the same time hearing rumors of monotheism, but were not eager to add more difficulties to the situation by becoming either Jews or Christians. At this point, members of one Arab clan of Medina made contact with Muhammad and decided that he would be an objective arbitrator of Medina's disputes. Muhammad, however, would not go to the town until the invitation came from both Arab clans.

During the pilgrimage of 621, many more believers came to Mecca from Medina, including members of both Arab clans. In the night following the ceremonies, 73 men from Medina met with Muhammad and gave the second pledge of Aqaba. Each of them individually touched Muhammad's hand and swore to receive him and his followers in their town and to protect them there. Twelve of these converts were named as an advisory council, drawn from both clans. In return, the Messenger of God told them: "I am of you and you are of me. I'll war against them who war on you, and I will be at peace with those who are at peace with you."

This agreement created Muhammad's community, the Umma. Once it was established, the Prophet instructed his followers in Mecca, few in number and mostly poor, to go quietly to Medina, where he would join them. These departures could hardly be kept secret, and Muhammad's bitter opponent, Abu Jahal, suggested how Muhammad could be killed without risk of a blood feud with Beni Hashim; he thought that the deed could be done by a representative of each clan in Mecca striking with his dagger at the same moment, since Beni Hashim could not feud on all the clans at once. When news of this plan spread, Muhammad and his most loyal convert, Abu Bekr, fled on camels with a hired guide to Medina. This flight, known as the Hegira, opens the Muslim era (June 622).

The emigrants to Medina, about 75 in number, were without land or money. Since the Medina helpers outnumbered the refugees, Muhammad arranged for each emigrant to be adopted by a helper

709

as a brother. A written charter was drawn up
among nine groups, the eight local clans and
Muhammad's emigrants. This was really a confederation, having the same friends and enemies,
agreeing to settle all disputes peacefully and
to leave critical ones to Muhammad's arbitration.
The inhabitants of Medina did not have to become
Muslims, but all shared in the peace of the city
as equals. Thus the protection and security of
the tribe was replaced by the security and protection of the place, guaranteed by the confederation.
Later, when all the inhabitants of Medina were
converted or expelled or killed, this arrangement
became the religious umma of Muhammad.

The creation of the umma may have provided
security, but it did not provide any economic basis
for the emigrants. This the Messenger sought to
find in odd jobs, alms from the faithful, and banditry. He announced that God, through Gabriel,
commanded the Muslims to fight the unbelievers.
Combining economic advantages with religious zeal,
the Prophet directed his emigrants in bandit attacks on the caravans going south past Medina from
the Levant to Mecca. The first attack, in January
624, was against a great caravan of a thousand
camels, owned by the leaders of Mecca and commanded
by Abu Sufyan. This skilled trader evaded the Muslim ambush of 314 men near Bedr. A Kuraish rescue
force of about 750 men from Mecca intercepted the
Muslim raiders and were badly beaten. Kuraish lost
about 50 killed and 50 more were captured. The captives, including Muhammad's uncle Abbas, who had
accompanied the Prophet at the second oath of Aqaba,
were ransomed. Following the battle, Muhammad had
his followers drive one of the Jewish clans from
Medina and appropriated their property for his
believers.

This great day set the pattern of expansion of
the Muslim community. By raids on caravans, attacks
on Jewish groups, and assassination of opposition
leaders, Muhammad's power was consolidated. From
the booty the Prophet took one-fifth for himself,
to finance his charitable and political activities.
The bedouin tribes were gradually won over, by alternation of attacks and bribery, to sign agreements
of various kinds with Muhammad. Since with the bedou-

ins nothing succeeds like success, the growing strength of the Muslims made such agreements desirable. Soon many bedouins wanted to join this profitable raiding.

The key to these Muslim victories did not rest in weapons, weapons systems, or tactics, for the Arabs did not get the composite bow or such complex weapons as artillery, a siege train, a navy, or stirrups for their horses until after the conquest of Syria. They had the wooden bow, but rarely used it in war. Thus they began their conquests with little more than mobility, combined with swords, spears, daggers, and archery, with some coats of mail for defense. Fighting was generally on foot, in a melee of hand-to-hand fighters. General lack of discipline made any group tactics almost impossible, except, perhaps, in timing the first assault.

The great Muslim advantage was in morale. Before the battle, and often in the course of it, Muhammad promised the fighters that those who were killed would go immediately to paradise. The pagans fought simply to establish superiority, not to annihilate the opposition and had the primitive belief that a battle should be fought only to the point where superiority was indicated for that day. They saw no point in fighting to the death, had no desire to destroy their opponents totally, and had little desire to kill them. To them fighting was an opportunity for booty or ransoms, or simply to obtain a recognition of superiority. It had many of the elements of a game, offered an opportunity to demonstrate one's masculinity, and was carried on with chivalric overtones. On the other hand, the Muslims fought to win, to destroy the enemy totally, and to wipe him permanently from the earth. This difference gave a very great advantage to the Muslims. Moreover, it was soon combined with a moderate policy toward those who surrendered without a fight, thus encouraging surrender when the only alternative seemed to be total destruction. These differences appeared clearly at the battle of Uhud, which the Muslims lost.

Uhud occurred as a result of a Meccan attack on Medina in an effort to reopen the caravan route northward to the Levant (625). The attackers numbered about 3000 men, of which 700 had coats of chain mail, and 200 had horses. Medina sent out a defensive force of about 1000. Just before the battle, the elected chief of Medina abandoned the field with 300 followers, leaving Muhammad with only 700 men, of which about 100 had defensive armor, and none had a horse. The Muslims won the battle but fell to looting before the enemy left the field and were overwhelmed in a counterattack in which the Kuraish riders circled the Muslim position and attacked it from the rear, wounding Muhammad and sending the Muslim remnants fleeing on foot into the surrounding rocks and hills. The Meccans, instead of hunting down the fugitives and sacking Medina, casually plundered the dead and withdrew to Mecca with a parting message from Abu Sufyan, "We'll meet again next year at Bedr."

The failure of the pagan Meccans to push their victory at Uhud to conclusion by destroying the Muslims and by sacking Medina, or their failure even to impose terms on the defeated shows the casual Arab attitude toward warfare. They were satisfied with moral victories. Muhammad was not. He sent an assassin to Mecca in a vain attempt to murder Abu Sufyan and, when that failed, compensated for the defeat at Uhud by having his followers seize all the property of the second Jewish tribe in Medina and force its members to migrate to Syria (625).

Two years later, an overwhelming force from Mecca marched on Medina again. A Persian convert in Medina suggested that the open side of the town be protected by digging a trench along it. This was done, under Muhammad's direction, in six days. The military ignorance of the Arabs is evident from the fact that the attackers were unwilling to cross the open trench and were soon forced to give up the siege and return to Mecca by their own dwindling supplies.

Muhammad used this attack of 627 as an excuse for putting to death all the men of the third and last Jewish tribe of Medina. In this heroic deed 700 Jews were beheaded after they were forced to dig ditches as graves for their own bodies. Later,

Jewish groups in other settlements were despoiled of all their movable property and left on their lands in return for 50 per cent of their crops as annual tribute.

The Muslim feud with Mecca was ended in 629 when Muhammad led the Muslims there on pilgrimage and agreed to accept the kaaba, with its meteorite, as a pilgrimage shrine, in return for the removal of the idols. As the number of Muslims grew, the prospects of Mecca becoming their pilgrimage site won over most of the people of Mecca to accept the arrangements, even when they would not adopt Islam themselves. The Muslims occupied the town, executed four opposition leaders, and forced all the residents to swear loyalty to Muhammad (630). The following year, non-Muslims were excluded from the pilgrimage, but by that time, Muhammad had bought off the surviving opposition leaders by rich gifts paid from the one-fifth of the booty he reserved for himself. The richest gifts went to Abu Sufyan and his sons of the Omayyad clan.

By 632 when Muhammad died, only ten years after the Hegira, much of Arabia was in some kind of political relationship with him, usually consisting of a pact of friendship with tribal leaders in which they agreed to pay nominal tribute and Muhammad reserved the right to settle dangerous disputes. By that time, many Arabs were turning their minds to the idea that cooperation with the Muslims would open the doors of opportunity to great material benefits in this world as well as eternal blessings in the next world.

When Muhammad died in 632, no one knew what to do, because the umma was Muhammad's possession, and no constitution nor rules of succession existed. Tribal leaders who had made agreements with Muhammad considered that these were purely personal agreements which lapsed at the death of either party. At the Prophet's death, Abu Bekr was chosen as caliph (successor) to Muhammad by general agreement and at once set out, by force as necessary, to compel the reestablishment of the bedouin tribes' agreements with Muhammad. This, by a combination of fighting and generous terms, took about a year. But at the end of that year, the fighting did not stop. The whole process continued northward against the soft underbelly of the decaying Persian and Byzantine empires north of Arabia. The Arab raiders, who had been subduing Arabia, could not be reduced to unemployment and idleness; they were simply directed outward, plundering traders and tribesmen, and offering the sword, tribute, or conversion. In some ways, there is a parallel between these methods of Islamic expansion and the methods by which large corporate conglomerates have been built up in recent years. In each case, the victim has been offered a choice, to join the system by becoming part of it through conversion or to be taken over as a subordinate subject to tax. The difference was that Islam's alternative to submission (conversion) was conquest by force, while the conglomerate's alternative to submission (by exchange of securities) was conquest by a battle of proxy votes. In both cases, it is not surprising that many elect to join an expanding system rather than to fight it.

The achievement of Muhammad was very great, but the whole subsequent history of Islamic civilization was marked by his errors and omissions. Most of these rest on his very backward conception of the nature of deity and of the relations between God and men. His God was not fully transcendental since He constantly interfered in the world, and indeed, had to interfere in order to keep it going, for Muhammad had no conception of natural laws. His God was a God of supreme power, but was not transcendental or good. Thus the failure to recognize the nature of law as a process of relationships which function apart from the constant personal intervention of God included the failure to recognize rules of ethics (which included God). This meant that God was not recognized as Good but only as Power. To some extent Muhammad did reach the idea of God as love but only in the rather limited form of compassion. This involved divine recognition of man's weakness and pity toward man for this reason, but did not involve the love of God in the Christian sense which includes God's wish that man should develop his potentialities toward strength.

714

All of these weaknesses in Muhammad's ideas of the nature of deity continued in Islam and left it a permanently flawed society. It left an idea of the nature of man as weak, with limited free will and thus a limited sense of individual personal responsibility (since freedom for man allowed only the acceptance or rejection of the Will of Allah and rejection was punished by God's retaliation in the Last Judgment by inflicting personal suffering on the sinner).

This failure to achieve any idea of law as a relationship higher than will influenced every aspect of Islamic life subsequently. Among other things it prevented any real idea of the rule of law or of a constitution. This lack was made worse by the fact that Muhammad established no rules of government or of succession to his office. His own rule was personal, reinforced by his claims to be the Messenger of divine revelation. This meant that his successors, however chosen, would have to rule personally, without this power, since revelation, according to Muhammad, ended with him. Thus Islam, unlike western civilization, never could achieve the latter's idea that "the truth unfolds in time." In Islam "the Gates of Truth" were closed and, in consequence, a very unfinished community had to be regarded as finished, just as a very unfinished idea of the nature of deity had to be regarded as finished.

This idea of truth as finished was crippling to many aspects of Islamic society (such as science, law, and politics), and became especially crippling in the extreme form it took in Islam with the establishment of the idea that the Koran, as the vehicle of revelation, was not only sufficient, complete, and finished, but was also uncreated (that is had existed with God in all eternity before it was revealed to Muhammad). This had the effect of putting Truth outside the world of space-time (the world of created things), leaving this temporal world the area of evil in an almost Zoroastrian sense. All of these beliefs served to discourage human effort to improve this temporal world or their own behavior in it. This dualistic tendency, which was one of the outstanding characteristics of the whole period covered by this chapter, was also observable

715

in the late classical civilization, in Byzantine civilization, and in western civilization in this period, as well as in Islam.

Thus we have a very flawed heritage left by Muhammad as in Islamic civilization because of three omissions (failure to move from a universe of will or power toward a universe of rules and law; failure to establish rules of government, or at least of succession for the ruler; and insistence that his ideas of deity and human relations with deity were the final truth, thus ending revelation and intellectual growth). But Muhammad also left a positive decision which was more obviously and more directly fatal to the future of his community. This is his decision to support the religious community by raiding, plunder, and war.

The whole future of Islamic civilization was marked by this decision which eventually made it almost impossible to achieve a community, for the two were almost antithetical: that the community be based on religion (that is on persons who trust each other because they have the same God and the same relationship to Him) and the belief that that community can support itself in this world by plundering and enslaving other persons. This cannot be done, simply because the effort to support any community by war creates a military machine which comes to dominate the community on a basis totally different from the religious basis on which it is presumed to rest. In Islam, centuries of confusion were spent in conflict over the vain effort to achieve a government which was simultaneously both military and religious. The very effort to do this gave rise to extremist religious sects who, as microscopic minorities, were determined to get control of the government. Other sects, despairing of this, tried to withdraw into a small segregated community of their own. The Kharijites were an example of the first, while the Assassins (Ismailis) were an example of the second. The final solution of the problem, which grew very slowly in the period 900-1300, was to abandon any effort to combine the umma and the militarized government in the same community. This was equivalent to permitting a government which was little more than a military machine to ride over a community which was a structure of private relationships operated as a community under customary relationships among individuals and groups.

This solution was well adapted to the socio-economic conditions of the period, especially to the autonomous nature and stable structure of economic (especially agrarian) enterprise at that time, but it was not a system which could adapt to modern conditions because the ruling entity, under this Islamic compromise, was a government without being a state; it was in fact a military organization and little else. It was not a state because it did not control and hardly influenced justice, law, education, social life (including family life), economic affairs, or intellectual and religious life. As a largely military machine it did not have, and could hardly expect to obtain, loyalty from its subjects or their active or spontaneous cooperation.

Efforts were made, at various times, to overcome this fissure between government and community, usually by the former displaying great respect and support for the orthodox Islamic community (the ulama and the caliphate). This was done, for example, by the Seljuks and, most successfully, by the Ottoman Turks, but the fundamental problems which had been left by Muhammad were never overcome.

The Arabic expansion after the death of Muhammad was Arab rather than Muslim, since many raiders went along simply to share in the plunder, remaining unconverted (or only nominally converted) to Islam themselves. Indeed, the original expansion was regarded by those who started it as a series of raids rather than a conquest. It became a conquest because so many submitted so easily. Where Islam triumphed from sustained tenacity of purpose and simply because it was a going and growing concern which anyone might agree to join, the enemy crumpled before this pressure because of their own disorganization and low morale.

No superiority of weapons or weapons systems was involved in this conquest, although a tactical factor was of great significance. In this attack, as in the nomadic assaults from the northern grass-

lands, the intruders had the advantage of mobility
in contrast with the fundamentally static organization of the systems they were attacking. In the
Arab invasion this mobile superiority had the additional strength that the Arab monopoly of camel
transport meant that their forces could operate
across more arid lands than the enemy could cross
or could pursue them into. The Arabs moving from
the desert, into a network of trade routes and
cities, could strike by surprise and then withdraw
with their plunder or their wounded farther and
faster than the more highly organized forces of
the defense could achieve. Moreover, the Arab
forces, using these tactics, did not need to retreat; they could continue to advance, living,
like any nomads, from their animals, so long as
they could find sustaining grasses day after day.

The real problem was not the ease with which
the Arabs advanced, but how they were able to
capture cities and thus organize the territories
they covered. Here again, their successes had
little to do with weapons, weapons systems, or
tactics, but resulted from the fact that the political systems they encountered were exhausted at
their centers and were alienated and unwilling to
resist in the peripheries where the Arabs first
entered.

We have indicated that the Fertile Crescent
north of Arabia was a great arch of trade routes,
fertile lands, and cities running from Sinai, north
along the Levant, across the Syrian Saddle, and
down Mesopotamia to the Persian Gulf. Enclosed
by this arch was the Syrian Desert, separated from
the Fertile Crescent by grasslands. When Muhammad
was born about 575, these grasslands were held by
Christian Arab tribes, the Beni Gassan, on the
fringes of the Levant and the Lakhmites along the
Euphrates. The former were subsidized allies of
the Byzantine emperor, while the Lakhmid leaders
were in a similar relationship to Sassanid Persia.
These two satellite tribes engaged for generations
in raids back and forth against each other, across
the grasslands south of the Syrian Saddle. As Persia and Byzantium fought each other to mutual exhaustion in the period 602-628, commerce across the

Syrian Saddle was disrupted, and both satellite tribes used these wars as covers for plundering each other and the agricultural settlements of the Fertile Crescent for whom they were supposed to provide cover against the polytheistic Arabs farther south. In 605 Persia ended the satellite relationship with the Lakhmid dynasty and abolished the dynasty. This created a situation of chronic warfare along the Euphrates and greatly weakened the Persian control of southern Mesopotamia.

Even earlier, Byzantium had weakened its relations with Beni Gassan by trying to crush out the monophysite creed among these tribesmen. In 581 the emperor arrested the ruling prince of Beni Gassan and took him off as a prisoner to Constantinople. When his sons revolted, their resistance was crushed, their subsidy ended, and the dynasty abolished.

In this way, the shields of Christian Arab tribes were completely alienated from the two imperial powers, while Muhammad was still a young man. The situation was not much better deeper within these two empires in the commercial and urban settlements of the Fertile Crescent. In the Levant and Egypt the peoples were cruelly persecuted by Heraclitus (610-641) for their monophysite beliefs, while along the whole Fertile Crescent, especially in Mesopotamia, the traders were alienated by the disturbances of the Byzantine-Persian War. The king of Persia controlled Egypt, the Levant, and much of Asia Minor from 616 to 626, just before his final defeat by Heraclitus in 628. This defeat was so total that Persia disintegrated as an organized state in the next four years. At the same time, Heraclitus, because of the Persian control of his eastern provinces until almost the end of the war, was unable to establish in these recovered areas the new military organization which had prepared the way to victory in the empire's more western districts.

Thus, when the Islamic raiders rode north along the grasslands on either side of the Fertile Crescent in 633, they found only weak resistance. They intruded into areas of disorganized peoples, largely alienated from their former rulers and protected by weak, unreformed, and passive military garrisons. To many of these peoples the alternatives offered by the Muslims seemed a welcome relief from disorder, religious persecution, and uncertainty. There was sporadic resistance from some garrison forces or from some of the more fanatical Byzantine administrators, but most people regarded the Muslim intrusion in a neutral or slightly favorable way. The Arab demands for tribute were modest compared to the previous war taxes of the two great empires, and the basic indifference to religion of the Arabs gave relief from religious persecution. This whole tendency was increased by the fact that the Muslims, while they offered the choice of conversion or tribute, did not insist on conversion, simply because they wanted tribute.

The inability of the Arabs to rise above the narrow and suspicious world of blood kinship was so great, that the original expansion of Islam took the form of moving tribes. These tribes did not mix together but retained their separate identity, quartered in separate camps in the field or in separate districts in cities. Conversion to Islam, for several generations, was not conceivable in terms of joining a religious community (as it had been viewed by Muhammad himself) but was seen in terms of joining an Arab tribe by adopting an Arab clan name. These converts acquired a permanently subordinate position as clients of the Arab tribes into which they were adopted.

Such conversion was intimately associated with a growing system of taxation and finance. The basic idea, going back to Muhammad's original use of raiding as a means of support for his community, was that the believers should be supported by the non-believers. All plunder of war, all lands overrun, were regarded as the possession of the community, with one-fifth going to Muhammad and to his caliph successors and the rest divided among the tribes. As the conquests rolled onward, it was necessary to consolidate the conquests for a more permanent method of exploitation than war plunder. Since the conquerors had no desire to mingle with the conquered, had no administrative rules nor skills or their own, were generally il-

literate, and were not eager to assume any burden
of routine work, they simply allowed the arrangements they conquered to continue, fixing global
sums of tribute and allowing these to be collected
and administered by those who had been doing these
things. Gradually the conquerors had to take a
closer concern with such matters but, for at least
twenty years, conquest was more important than consolidation and booty more significant than taxes.
Until 661 the caliph remained in Medina, far from
the firing line, flooded with his one-fifth of the
plunder and making little real effort to control
what was going on.

The basic decisions on how the conquests should
be consolidated and what should be the relationship
between the conquering Arabs and the overrun systems were made by the second caliph, Omar (634-644).
His decision was that the Arabs be kept totally
segregated from the conquered peoples, as an army
of occupation superimposed over the existing systems. To this end the Arabs were kept in military
camps, organized as tribes, close to the edge of
the grasslands. They were forbidden to acquire
land or to engage in commerce, while the conquered
peoples were forbidden to have weapons. The only
relationship between the Arabs and the conquered
was administrative, chiefly fiscal. And, as Joel
Carmichael put it, "the fiscal theory of the Arab
kingdom rested on this simple concept of mulcting
the unbelievers on behalf of a treasury on which
all Muslim Arabs had a collective claim."

The conquered systems were left intact, as
much as possible, with their own laws, officials,
and customs. Local officials, generally on a
religious basis, continued to administer justice,
while taxes, including the imposed Arab tribute,
continued to be collected by the local officials
who kept their accounts in the same language as
before. Even the coinage continued to be used
and minted with the old images on them: only in
692, more than half a century after the conquest,
did the Arabs begin to mint gold coinage of their
own. Five years later public accounts were ordered to be kept in Arabic, except in northern Iran.

721

The treatment of conquered areas varied greatly from place to place and changed in the course of time, often very rapidly, for lack of established traditions or written rules. In most cases the original treatment of the conquered depended on whether they surrendered on terms or were overwhelmed by force. In the former case, the area covered, usually a city or district, obtained a written agreement regarding terms. Similarly, treatment of individuals depended on whether they accepted Islam or retained their previous beliefs. There was little compulsory conversion, as we have said, but there was, naturally, a steady movement toward the acceptance of Islam, simply because of the social and economic advantages this provided. Because of these advantages, some Arabs tried to establish a rule restricting Islam to Arabs. This, of course, could not be done, and by 800 not only were many non-Arabs in the Near East Muslims, but it was almost impossible to tell an Arab from a non-Arab except on the basis of language (although, to the Arabs, "Arab" did not mean "Arab-speaking" but "descended from an Arab tribe").

Muslims were subject to the tithe (zakah) justified by Muhammad's order to give alms to the poor. Non-Muslims were subject to tribute. In many cases this was set at one dinar and one measure of wheat a year from each person. This was usually assessed as a lump sum on each territory, collected by local officials and handed over to the conquerors. To assure its collection, Omar ordered that there be no interference with local agricultural enterprise and arrangements. About the same time, he forbade any enslavement of Arabs, even prisoners of war.

In time, the tribute on non-Muslims became divided into a poll tax (jizya) and a land tax (kharaj). This created problems, as converts to Islam had to be exempt from both. Efforts were made to prevent the reduction of tribute by conversions, by shifting the land tax from the person to the land itself, regardless of who owned it. At other times, efforts were made to forbid acquisition of kharaj lands by Muslims. All of these things led to an increasingly diverse and complicated situation, in view of the lack of records, the ease of local evasions, and the difficulty in enforcement of general rules, as well as other complications such as the rental of lands, the fact that some areas (such as Egypt and parts of Persia) had no private ownership of land but only ownership of the use of it, and the large areas of land which had come under ownership of the caliph and other Arabs as plunder in the original conquest.

The original rule regarding plunder, established by Muhammad, was that one-fifth went to Muhammad, with the rest divided among the combatants. This was soon changed so that the four-fifths went to the Muslim community. Very great complications arose from the acquisition of enormous booty, including vast estates, which had been held by the defeated rulers and their princes.

As soon as the original impetus of the conquests began to slow up, problems arose: the plunder was reduced, steady collection of tribute became essential, the warriors in the great encampments fell into dangerous boredom and idleness, and they had to be supported since there was little plunder (which previously had been the sole reward for their efforts). Accordingly, Omar established regular payments for all (granted on a tribal basis and distributed within the tribal organization) and pensions for retired fighters as well as for the dependents of soldiers.

Most of these dependents were already in the camps, for, as early as Omar's time, the army was really a collection of tribes moving with all their families, animals, tents, and possessions. As a result, the segregated encampments almost immediately became great cities, and segregation became almost impossible to maintain. Non-tribesmen and non-Muslims crowded around these encampments, attracted by the relatively high incomes the soldiers had, without easy ways to spend it and with no real experience in spending money. Since Muhammad had allowed each believer to have four wives and as many concubines as he could afford and had justified taking captured women as concubines, the camps soon had scores of thousands of non-Arab women and hundreds of thousands of mixed blood children living in them. Moreover, even

723

ordinary soldiers had from one to ten slaves.

As we have said, these camps were laid out in formal fashion with each tribe in its own section. The first such camp was Basra (635), followed by Kufu (also in Iraq), Jabiya (in Syria), Fustat (near Cairo), Kairouan (in Tunisia), and others. These camps rapidly became permanent cities in which the soldiers were almost swallowed up by the Arab and non-Arab camp followers and traders. The Arabs, of course, kept track of their genealogies as Arabs, in their legitimate marriages, but they were increasingly flooded by the mass of mixed peoples of very diverse origins.

The conquest continued to roll until almost 750, although there was a long period of little expansion from about 645 to about 705. The limits of conquest were established by ecological rather than human obstacles, chiefly by mountains and forests. The boundaries of conquest were reached in the period 717-755, and the empire began to fall apart almost at once. The failure to capture Constantinople in 717-718, the check in central France, at Tours, in 732, and the victory over a Chinese force in central Asia in 751, mark the limits of the Arab conquests (although not the limits of the expansion of Islamic civilization).

The conquest of Mesopotamia was relatively easy, as the Persian empire was already in tatters and its southern area had been in revolt for years. The Levant was somewhat more difficult, but was achieved at the second battle of Yarmouk (August 636) when the Arabs stormed the Byzantine defenses at the Deraa Gap with a sandstorm at their backs. Damascus was betrayed by its Christian bishop (probably a monophysite); the Patriarch of Jerusalem surrendered that city on terms. Other walled towns gave up when it became clear that the surrounding countryside was being permanently occupied by swarming tribesmen. Only Caesarea, with a Hellenized population and supplied by the Byzantine fleet, was able to hold out for awhile longer (640).

The Arabs advanced quickly across the plains to the west Asian highlands, but the conquest of

these latter was a slower task. The steady flow
of tribesmen from Arabia with their families,
tents, and flocks of animals made the outcome almost inevitable so long as no effective organized
resistance appeared. The only such resistance to
be found at that time was in Byzantium.

As the Arabs advanced, they acquired tactical
skills and more advanced military organization,
including supply and a siege train, partly by
learning themselves but increasingly by adopting
into their system the knowledge and skills of the
peoples they overran. It is doubtful, however, if
Muslim military strength reached the usual Byzantine level much before Saladin's day (c. 1190).
Even then, no Saracen military force reached the
excellence of the Byzantine military level as it
was, for example, under Basil II (c. 1000), just
before the Seljuks arrived. Right up to the completion of the conquests, about 750, the chief assets of the Arabs were their own sustained high
morale and the disintegration of their opponents.
As Hitti put it, "The Arabian warrior received
higher remuneration than his Persian or Byzantine
rival and was sure of a portion of the booty.
Soldiering was not only the noblest and most pleas-
ing profession in the sight of Allah but also the
most profitable. The strength of the Muslim Arabian army lay neither in the superiority of its
arms nor in the excellence of its organization,
but in its higher morale, to which religion undoubtedly contributed its share; in its powers
of endurance, which the desert breeding fostered;
and its remarkable mobility, due mainly to camel
transport." Of the Arabs' opponents the only
spirited opposition came from the Greeks, from
some of the Berber tribes of North Africa, and
from some Persian forces, especially in the north.
The Arameans, Copts, and most of the North Africans
offered little resistance. In Egypt, a new and
fanatical Byzantine governor and Patriarch of Alexandria, Cyrus, alienated most of the country by his
bloody persecution of the Coptic church in 632-640,
became completely defeatist on the arrival of the
Arabs, and secretly surrendered the country as soon
as he conveniently could (November 641).

The first outburst of the Arabs took only a

dozen years, covering the rule of the first two caliphs, Abu Bakr (632-634) and Omar (634-644). Under the third caliph, Othman (644-656), the expansion slowed up and the whole system went into a profound crisis. For the next sixty years (until 705), there were periodic raids across North Africa toward Morocco and across Anatolia toward Constantinople, while a slow and more secure extension of Islamic power continued across Iran towards the northern grasslands. There was a second wave of expansion early in the eighth century, from 705 to about 738, but by 740 the Islamic system was again in acute crisis.

These crises of Islamic civilization were not, like those of most civilizations, a consequence of the institutionalization of social organizations which had hitherto functioned effectively. The crises of Islam were endemic in the system, as the crises of polarization have been endemic in western civilization.

These Islamic crises were a consequence of the ingrained inability of the Arabs to grow into a higher level of social organization beyond the kinship group. As a result, it was impossible to create a stable organizational structure broad enough to embrace the wide territories and great divergency of peoples which the energies and spirit of the Arabs were able to conquer.

It is very likely that all human beings are so closely related genetically that they have about the same potential capacities, but, if there are inequalities in the natural endowments of the peoples of the world, the Semites, and certainly the Arabs, have the neurological and metabolic equipment, the intellectual agility, the physical stamina, and even the language to rank near the top of any listing of the natural abilities of mankind. Yet despite these great capacities, the whole history of the Arabs, even in the period of their great conquests, has been a tragic failure.

The key to this failure is social and above all emotional. It is a failure to develop social arrangements and emotional responses able to win

726

allegiances and to subordinate self-interest to a
social grouping wider than kinship. This failure
rests upon the speed with which opportunities came
to the Arabs to organize such wider groupings, opportunities which they were unable to use because
they came so fast and came on such a gigantic scale
of size, that the Arabs were unable to grow up emotionally fast enough to consolidate these opportunities into a workable system of wider allegiance.

This failure was, to some extent, caused by
the great metabolic power of the Arabs. They were
like an engine of enormous thrust and horsepower
with a totally inadequate guidance system or controls. Their physical appetites, for example,
especially sexual drive but including all physical
needs and sensualities, were so great that when
the opportunities came, through conquest, to satisfy
these appetites on an enormous scale, many of them
could not resist. On the other hand, their capacities for self-discipline and spirituality were
equally great, and were developed by some of them.
Their capacity for endurance, work, and sustained
application was also great. And finally, their intellectual and rational qualities were of such a
high level, that some became almost totally involved
in theories and abstractions remote from the humdrum
routines of daily living and governing.

The task of combining such diverse and high-
quality attributes into a broader system of allegiances by which the egoistic self-interests and
narrower perspectives of a sufficient number of
the ruling elements could be fused into a common
community was beyond the ability of the Arabs.

I have said that this failure was caused by
lack of time. Let me be more specific. What could
have been done in a longer time, that was not done
in the crucial first century of the Arab expansion
(633-733)?

The egocentricity, self-indulgence, and narrow
emotional focus of the Arabs was (and still is) a
consequence of the sexual attitudes in which Arab
children, especially boys, are trained. In the
Arab family, from the earliest history we know,
the male was taught that he had a natural, inborn

727

superiority and that the most fundamental obligation of all females, beginning with his mother, was to indulge that superiority. Women existed to be used for the males' most egocentric and immediate whims. The female had no value in herself and could achieve value only indirectly to the degree that she could satisfy a male and indulge him in his transitory needs, for food, sex, sensuality, self-esteem. As a result, the Arab male came to seek achievement and security in the abasement of others rather than in the growth of his own personality (or even in acquisition of material artifacts, as in the recent centuries of western civilization). The inadequacy of the emotional life of the Arab woman, both from her function as an instrument (rather than an end in herself) by her husband, has tended to drive these women to find their emotional satisfactions in their relationships with their sons. But these maternal filial interrelationships have not been based on any insistence by the mother that the son grow up, mature, develop in self-reliance and personal responsibility because success in this direction would have meant that he was being encouraged to grow less and less dependent on her. Instead, Arab mothers have tried to keep their sons in emotional dependency on themselves, which meant emotional immaturity in general and a sharp separation between emotional relationships (narrowly restricted within the family and especially with the mother) and sexual relationships (obtained casually outside the family, often with the encouragement of the mother). These patterns tended to become self-perpetuating from generation to generation, especially when the young male was encouraged to divide women into two sharply separated groups, objects of his own sexual gratifications and incubators for his male children, with his mother in neither group as an object of ambivalent emotional attachments. This relationship with the mother was emotionally ambivalent because the male ego, while emotionally dependent on the mother, was, nevertheless, unconsciously resentful of the mother because dependence is a kind of inadequacy and insecurity which the ego had to resent as a primary cause of personal emotional insecurity.

This insecurity sought reassurance and security within the family or the wider blood grouping, but

generally on a kinship basis and a rather narrow
one. This tendency to seek security within the
kin grouping was increased, as we have shown, by
the backward and chaotic conditions of Arab life,
especially in the Arab "dark ages" from the fourth
to the seventh centuries.

These conditions drove the Arabs outward to
conquest, but at the same time made it almost impossible for the Arabs to consolidate these conquests. For, in order to consolidate the wide
territories, diverse peoples, and varied systems
which were conquered, it was necessary for the Arabs
to devise some wider organizational system in which
all of them (but, above all, the major parts of
the ruling groups) could be fused together into
a single community or system of wider allegiance
in which individuals could feel secure as individuals and in voluntary groupings rather than
only in kinship groupings.

Muhammad offered such a wider system, the religious community or umma, but in order to obtain
acceptance of his umma (and of his own leadership
in it) he had to make concessions and compromises
to the prejudices, backward customs, and emotional
inadequacies of the Arabs. These concessions were
doubly needed, it may have seemed to him, from the
fact that so much of his teaching was contrary to
the established values and customs of the Arabs,
especially the bedouins, but also from the fact
that he himself could not get free from many of
the weaknesses of his own society. For example,
he indulged his grandsons to a degree which was
noted at the time, and his concessions to personal
sensuality in his allowance of four wives and innumerable concubines as well as his generally ambivalent attitude toward women and sex show this.

As the Arab conquests rolled along after 633,
it was necessary to consolidate them. This means
something more than simply establishing rules regarding the flows of tribute, regulations about
conquered lands and peoples, and systems of logistics and organizational discipline regarding
the control, recruitment, and retirement of troops.
In fact, a great variety of arrangements of these
more practical matters might have worked about

729

equally well if it had been possible for the Arabs to replace their loyalty to kinship groups with a system of allegiance to a wider group. Such a wider group was already there, Muhammad's umma, and it was, to a great extent, accepted, in words, explicit conceptual schemes, and ideology as the correct vehicle of loyalty and allegiance. But it did not become the vehicle of such loyalty in the neurological and endocrinological arrangements of most Arabs. These less conscious, but more significant, loyalties remained fixed on the older kin groupings. Where these kinship groupings were increasingly shattered and lost, as they were for more and more people, and especially for mercenary soldiers, they were replaced, as the vehicle of the human need for security, not by the religious community nor by a state, but by individual possession of power or of wealth.

Thus, to sum up, the consolidation of the Arab conquests required the creation of a wider organization of allegiance within which individuals could feel secure. This was prevented by the continued persistence of kinship loyalties and, as a result, no consensus of allegiance could be achieved. Instead, the ruling groups were disrupted, many persisting in kinship loyalty, some going on to religious loyalty (often of a very mystical or spiritual kind), a few seeking to establish allegiance on the basis of a secular state as an organized power system, and many seeking to obtain their own individual security on the basis of their own personal power and wealth or their individual emotional relationships in their personal lives.

This drive for community was the great disruptive force of the Islamic world for centuries (from 650 to about 1050). As we have said, its achievement was made very difficult by Muhammad's original decision that his umma would be supported economically by raiding and violence. Political life moved toward an increasingly narrow base of organized violence until finally it was nothing more than military despotism. Somewhat later religion moved along a path of its own to create a religious community that had nothing to do with

730

politics or organized violence or even with political boundaries. Thus, by 1100 the Islamic world had a political establishment and a religious establishment, the latter forming a community but the former little more than a gangster's mob.

In the earlier period (that is, to at least 1000), the chief source of political instability within Islam was the inability to see that a religious community could be formed separate from the political-military establishment. This was the same inability found in all people recently rising from tribalism to abandon their aspirations to continue to live in a totalitarian system. We have seen it in the Greek effort to make the polis as totalitarian as the tribe from which it developed (as described, for example, in the political fantasies of Plato's Republic and Aristotle's Politics). We shall see it again, in the next chapter, in the German effort to make the imperial system a totalitarian organism as the German tribes had been originally (a tendency which still remains a major force in all German political emotions). Now here, in the effort to form an Islamic civilization we see the same desire, to create an Islamic community which would include all aspects of human life from the military-political, through the socioeconomic, to the religious-intellectual.

This aspiration was impossible once Muhammad put the military-political aspect of his umma in the predatory direction of raiding and conquest for the economic support of his still unconstructed religious community. But it took centuries before this impossibility became emotionally acceptable to many Muslims. During these centuries, instability was endemic in the system, not so much by the superficial (and obvious) struggles of power-hungry and materialistic groups to control the developing military-political establishment but from quite different aspirations of spiritual persons to overthrow this political establishment and replace it with a different system better fitted to their religious-intellectual aspirations. These latter efforts were behind the revolts of the "sects," the Kharijites, Shiites, Karmatians, and others.

731

These efforts were drowned in blood, mostly their own but also that of almost anyone who opposed them. Gradually these efforts began to move in a different direction: efforts to take over the military-political establishment were replaced by efforts to find an area of autonomy within which a religious sect could have its own community with its own military-political establishment in its own totalitarian community. This effort is seen, as an example, in the efforts of the Ismaili and others to break free from the established system of Islam to create their own separate system, either on a wide stage like the Fatimid caliphate of Tunisia and Egypt or on a narrow stage like the Order of Assassins.

In the long run both of these efforts (takeover of the establishment or separation from the establishment) were impossible to achieve. But it took centuries of instability and struggles to recognize this. Before that stage was reached, an intermediate stage was necessary. This intermediate stage was developing almost unnoticed while the struggles mentioned in the last paragraph were still going on. This intermediate stage had two aspects. On the one hand, while the military-political establishment and the religious-intellectual forces were continuing their fruitless conflicts, ordinary people (and some very extraordinary ones as well) were going on with their daily living, mostly in the social-economic spheres of existence. There they gradually were creating communities of people who managed to get along together, to establish families, to make a living, to bring up children, and, above all, to trust each other (which is the essence of any community). In a sense, these were the people who opted out of the rat race for power, prestige, and fanatical ideological uniformity in favor of daily living. But in the process of this daily living they created communities.

They were able to do this (to create a community) because of a parallel development. This was the fact that, as the military-political establishment became narrower and narrower in its movement toward a total concentration on organized violence, it abandoned any effort to deal with many matters, such as religion, law, justice, education, social welfare, economic life, marriage, etc. which we would consider to be aspects of state action. In doing this, it not only ceased to be a state, becoming instead merely an exploitative military machine, but it left all these activities to be picked up and taken care of by the growing social-economic community. Only then, in the eleventh century, when that social-economic community was developing rapidly, did the religious intellectuals reach the point where they were willing to join it by abandoning their aspirations to include military-political life within their idea of a community. Before they could do this in great numbers, however, it was necessary for the actual conditions of life of that growing social-economic community (which they were about to join) to adopt a broad and tolerant practice of religious-intellectual life.

This broad practice of religious-intellectual tolerance was achieved in the social-economic community by the late eleventh century. About the same time the military-political establishment, under the Seljuks and the Ayyubids (the House of Saladin) began to adopt a broad, orthodox Sunni approach toward both the religious-intellectual and the social-economic aspects of life. This process, after the incredible disasters of the Mongol invasion in the thirteenth century, culminated in the providential imperial system of the Ottoman Turks, who, more than any other rulers of Islamic history, came close to creating an integrated Islamic society.

None of this future evolution of Islamic civilization was forseen about 650, when the crisis of instability and integration of society began. In fact, at that time, it is doubtful if anyone saw the crisis in terms of the need to create a community or even as a crisis of allegiance. At that time, the crisis appeared simply as a power struggle within the ruling groups.

The great mass of the peoples, peasants, craftsmen, and traders had little to do with this crisis. They were, after centuries of exclusion from military-political life, concerned with such

733

matters only to the degree that they disrupted their daily living. But the crisis came sooner and in a more acute and dangerous form from the efforts Omar had made to segregate the Arab conquerors from the conquered peoples. This segregation called attention to the inequities of the system, even among the conquerors, and created an explosive mixture by its concentration of thousands of bored and discontented Muslims in the army camp cities.

The crisis came to a head under Othman, the third caliph (644-656), because his extreme nepotism provided the spark to explode the growing tensions among the bored and disillusioned troops in the encampments in Iraq.

Omar, the second caliph, kept things together because of the general respect for him as a person, based on his piety and simple personal life and recognition that he was trying to keep in touch with the situation from his remote capital in Medina. He was murdered by a Persian slave but, before he died, he offered the caliphate to Abdul Rahman ibn Auf, an early companion of the Prophet, who refused. Omar then made Abdul Rahman head of a committee of six, all similar companions, to choose a successor. Omar excluded his own son from consideration and stipulated that the committee must announce its decision in three days, unanimously if possible, but, if not unanimously, the minority electors were to be killed. This last provision of the dying octogenarian showed his recognition of the tensions within the Arab community and his determination to prevent the minority from leading any revolt against the majority's choice. It also shows the lack of any rule of law in the system.

There were only two serious candidates, both members of the committee of six and both sons-in-law of Muhammad. One, Ali ibn abi Talib, son of Muhammad's guardian and thus his first cousin, had married the Prophet's favorite daughter, Fatima, and fathered Muhammad's only male descendants, his grandsons, Hasan and Husain. The other candidate, also a son-in-law of the Prophet, was a first cousin once removed of Abu Sufyan, the leader of the anti-Muslim opposition in Mecca in 622-

630. The ominous fact was that the two candidates personified the opposition to Beni Hashim and Beni Omayya in the Kuraish tribe.

When the committee of six could not reach a decision, they authorized Abdul Rahman to make the choice on his own authority. He did so by public announcement on the third day, naming Othman ibn Affan and thus passing over Ali for the caliphate for the third time. As opposition to Othman grew in the next few years, increasing numbers of Arabs, not only the Beni Hashim, "stoutly averred that from the beginning Allah and His Prophet had clearly designated Ali as the only legitimate successor, but that the first three caliphs had cheated him out of his rightful office."

Under the first three caliphs, most significant offices had been reserved to members of the Kuraish tribe. Othman, who was a weakling, yielded to family pressures and made his significant appointments from a narrower group, restricted not just to Beni Omayya but to his own family. For example, he immediately dismissed as governor of Egypt the supremely able Amr ibn al Aasi, who eventually conquered and reconquered that rich country three times, and put in his place his own foster brother, Abdulla ibn abi Sarh, one of the few persons hated by Muhammad and who had been condemned to death by the Prophet in 630.

Such nepotism alienated many groups besides the Beni Hashim and particularly outraged the more idealistic, more spiritual, and increasingly bored soldiers in the seething military encampments so far away from Othman and his cronies in Medina. In the camps, each soldier was expected to do one year of active service in each four years, so that the 40,000 active soldiers at Kufa could keep an army of 10,000 constantly in the field. But this left 30,000 free to intrigue and agitate, under very undisciplined conditions. When the troops at Basra mutinied against their commander and asked to name their own general, Othman removed the object of their discontent but named his twenty-five year old cousin to the place. Othman had already removed, as commander at Kufa, Saad ibn abi Wakkas,

735

the conqueror of Iraq and replaced him with his
own half-brother, Waleed ibn Okba, whose father,
taken prisoner at Bedr, had been executed by the
Prophet's order, while Waleed himself had once
spat in Muhammad's face. Waleed soon had to be
removed for drunkenness and was replaced by another youth of Beni Omayya whose father had been
killed fighting the Muslims at Bedr in 624. This
was narrow nepotism, but it was also stupid since
it could be interpreted as a sustained program to
turn the Prophet's umma over to his personal enemies. Othman defended his appointments with the
statement that God had ordered men to help their
own families, and he even criticized Abu Bekr and
Omar for neglecting their relatives.

In 655 the camps in Iraq and Egypt mutinied
and sent delegations to Medina. There they besieged Othman in his house, without any interference from the leaders of Kuraish, including the
companions of the Prophet and four members of the
committee of six which had chosen Othman. Finally,
a handful of mutineers broke in and killed the
caliph while he sat reading the Koran. Most of
these mutineers were bedouin, but the first blow
at Othman was struck by Muhammad ibn abi Bekr,
son of the first caliph and brother-in-law of
the Prophet. When the mutineers departed,
thousands of slaves roamed through Medina, for
there were no troops in the capital. As soon as
possible, the leaders of the city pledged allegiance to Ali, foster son and son-in-law of Muhammad, who thus finally became caliph (656-661).

Many persons advised Ali to proceed at once
against the murderers of Othman. Instead, he removed many of Othman's chief appointees, including
the governor and commander-in-chief in Syria,
Muawiya ibn abi Sufyan, second cousin of Othman,
who had been named to that post by Omar in 642.
Muawiya refused to give up his post and demanded
that Othman's assassins be punished. Instead, Ali
employed the assassins and mutineers as his chief
agents and advisers. He even made the principal
murderer Muhammad ibn abi Bekr governor of Egypt.
By using the Prophet's grandson (his own son),
Hasan, Ali was able to raise an army from the
mutinous camp at Kufu, while two members of the

committee of six mobilized a rebel army at Basra.
The guilty mutineers, to prevent Ali from handing
them over for trial, were able to precipitate a
battle between the two camps, during the negotiations. Ali won this engagement, known as the battle of the camel because the Prophet's favorite
wife, daughter of Abu Bekr, urged on the anti-Ali
forces from her camel beside the field (656).

By this victory, Ali took control of the Iraq
camps at Basra and Kufu, where he raised forces to
remove Muawiya as commander and governor of Syria.
After many months of fighting and negotiations,
during which Muawiya conquered Egypt from the murderous son of Abu Bakr, the Islamic empire was
divided de facto near the boundary which had previously divided Byzantium from Sassanid Persia.
The two were governed from Kufu and Damascus, in
each of which the religious services called down
Allah's damnation upon the opposite leader.

This crude struggle for power and wealth dis-
gusted many pious Muslims, who felt that the Islamic community should be a religious community of
social equals ruled by the most pious, chosen, in
some unspecified way, by God Himself. This group
began to organize as a separate religious sect,
the first of many in Islam, called Kharijites
(seceders), who varied across the political Left
from moderate reformers to extreme spiritual nihilism
or anarchism. In general, they were opposed to any
political arrangements based on family, wealth,
military conflict, or any basis other than spiritual worth. Early in 661, three of these Kharijites
attempted to assassinate on the same day, Muawiya,
his chief lieutenant, the conqueror of Egypt, Amr
ibn al Aasi, and Ali. Only Ali was killed. The
soldiers at Kufa, Ali's capital, at once proclaimed
Ali's son, Hasan, as caliph, but he soon sold out
to Muawiya for a substantial fortune. In consequence, the Islamic empire was reunited under Muawiya ibn abi Sufyan, the most able of all the
caliphs.

It is notable that when the troops of Iraq
and Egypt were in mutiny against Othman, the soldiers of Syria remained loyal and disciplined.
This was because Muawiya, of the Omayyad clan,

737

was governor and commander in that province, as his elder brother had been before him. Muawiya was a strong ruler and immediately appointed equally strong men to rule as his lieutenants in Basra and Kufa. It is said that Muawiya was the only caliph against whom there was never any rebellion after his accession.

Even before his accession Muawiya had begun to establish a new system in Syria. In general, he abandoned Omar's idea of a segregated Arab army of tribes superimposed over, and isolated from, a conquered people of exploited subjects. He moved his capital from the Syrian encampment at Jabiyah to Damascus, where he was accessible to Syrian and other peoples (personally, he was very free and informal). The orders segregating the soldiers were unenforced. In this way, both Syrians and soldiers began to feel that they were part of a community.

Muawiya made extensive naval and military reforms, which were continued by Abdul Malik (685-705). Muawiya was the first Arab to recognize the role of sea power and, in cooperation with the governor of Egypt, he built a fleet which defeated the Byzantine navy in 655 ("the battle of the masts") and provided transport for military operations against Byzantium after 672. In preparation for his attacks on Constantinople in 673-678, Muawiya encouraged the capture of various Mediterranean islands such as Cyprus, Rhodes, and others. In general, he felt that the Islamic conquests of Syria, Egypt, and North Africa could not be secure so long as Byzantium was unchallenged on the sea.

On land Muawiya began reforms of the Arab armies which revolutionized their organization and tactics. Most of these reforms simply copied Byzantine methods and sought to create a solid and disciplined army quite different from the whirling, hand-to-hand, individualistic fighting of the bedouins. His general attitude was that individual, undisciplined bravery was too precarious and that steadfast discipline and training with immediate obedience to orders was more reliable. His line of battle centered on three lines of infantry with cavalry on the wings. The

infantry had front ranks of pikemen, kneeling on
the ground, covered by their shields, with the
butt ends of their pikes thrust into the earth;
behind this were ranks of swordsmen; and behind
these were ranks of archers. In general the enemy
were permitted to charge first, and, when the force
of their attack had been broken, the Islamic forces
advanced slowly, in formation against them. These
tactics capitalized on the extraordinary endurance
of the Arab forces. Similarly, the cavalry were
restrained so that they held their attack until
ordered, then advanced in a mass at less than a
gallop, refraining from wild pursuit until ordered
to do so and returning as soon as possible to their
wing positions to guard the infantry from flank
attacks.

If Muawiya copied Byzantium in his military
reforms, he appears to have copied Persia in his
general administration. Like his military changes,
his administrative reforms were not completed at
the time of his death in 680, after a reign of
nineteen years (661-680). The direction of these
reforms was toward a more centralized system,
with judges, commandants of police, and treasurers,
as well as governors, appointed to all provinces.
He also established a postal service which served
as well as a central domestic intelligence service.

Muawiya's chief reform was in political organization. It is possible that he was not clear
as to his real aims in his own mind, but the general trend of his reforms was to replace the previous system of Arabic tribal exploitation by a
relatively secular state organized as a dynastic
monarchy in the Omayyad family. This system would
have subordinated all subjects, Arabs and non-
Arabs, Moslems and non-Moslems, to the state. It
failed.

There were several reasons for this failure.
In the first place, the continued domination of
kinship loyalty made the higher loyalty to the
Omayyad dynasty precarious. In the second place,
the Arabs and many others, including the armies
in general, could not conceive of loyalty to an
abstract state; they could conceive of loyalty

to a man or to a religion, but the conception of the state was outside their traditions. As Sir Hamilton Gibb put it, "There is no Arabic word for 'state' as a general concept. Even for Ibn Khaldun, the word dawla often explicitly means and always implies the membership of the ruling family." More succinctly, S.D. Goitein wrote, "The concept of the state is alien to the political glossary of both Islam and Judaism."

In the third place, the Islamic tradition, like that of all pastoral peoples (including those of the northern grasslands) could not accept the idea of personal hereditary possession of authority. They could accept the idea that it be held in a family or clan but could not possibly accept primogeniture as a basis for hereditary rule. Moreover, in Islamic family traditions, as I have indicated, the emotional relationships within the family and the complexity of such a family, in which women were inferior and the polygamous element was dominant, made the chances of rearing up a first-born son with the strength of character to become an acceptable ruler unlikely.

In the fourth place, the Islamic, and especially the Arabic, tradition made it impossible to conceive of any system of authority which was not basically religious. This made the kind of dynastic government attempted by the Omayyads impossible, above all for their family. For the Omayyads were descended from the most persistent enemies of the Prophet. This was a chief basis for the opposition to Othman. Muawiya, like Othman, was of the Beni Omayya (in fact, they were second cousins), and his effort to establish hereditary rule in his family to replace the elective rule of the first four caliphs was a counterrevolutionary effort in terms of the forces which mutinied against Othman. Muawiya was trying to accomplish in public law what Othman had tried to do by personal nepotism. Both were moving against Arab tribalism, something which Muawiya could do from Damascus with a loyal army, but which was impossible for Othman from Medina with no armed forces to protect himself.

Muawiya's personal attitude to politics was

that of a secular ruler. He based his administration mainly on Syrians, who were still mostly Christians, and upon Syro-Arabs who were chiefly South Arabian and not bedouins or Hejaz emigrants. His chief wife, mother of his successor Yazid, was a Christian bedouin. His personal physician was a Christian whom he made financial administrator of the province of Hims, "an unprecedented appointment," according to Hitti. For three generations, the financial administration of Damascus was held by a Christian family, that of Sergius, the Greek holder of the office before the Arab conquest, who plotted with the bishop to betray the city to the Arabs in 635 and kept his job, passing it on to his son and grandson. The grandson, who became St. John Damascene, grew up as the youthful associate of Yazid and another Christian, al Akhtal, who became court poet. In that court, Christianity was freely practiced and strongly defended in a completely tolerant atmosphere. We can imagine what pious Moslems thought of this situation.

This then was the essence of the political achievement of Muawiya, that he freed the Islamic empire from Arab tribalism, but still failed to devise any adequate substitute on which to rear an alternative system of allegiance fit for such a diverse empire.

The consequences of this political achievement were two: (1) that the reform went far enough to sustain a resumption of the conquests and (2) that it did not go far enough to avoid domestic unrest and political instability within the system.

The conquests were resumed briefly under Muawiya himself but were then interrupted again by the outbreak of civil wars in 680. These were settled by 685 and the fundamental reorganizations of Abdul Malik (685-705), continuing the work of Muawiya, made possible the second great period of conquests in 705-745.

Muawiya's conquests were to the east and northeast into Sind and the lower Indus, across Afghanistan (Kabul taken 664), and toward Turkestan, crossing the Oxus to capture Bokhara and

Samarkand, and extending Islamic rule to the Jaxartes. After 705 this eastern expansion was continued into the Punjab and Turkestan to Kashgar,
but the great conquests of the eighth century were
to the west.

The Arab conquest of North Africa was long
drawn out because of the geopolitical conditions.
The Arabs could raid westward along the grasslands
inside the settled coastal strip, but the farther
west they went, the greater their distance from
their eastern base. As soon as something went
wrong or the raid was ended, it was necessary to
fall all the way back, sometimes 1500 miles or more,
to the base at Barka on the Egyptian border (which
had been conquered as early as 643).

To avoid this, an advanced base was established in 670 at Kairouan, 1500 miles west of the
chief Arab encampment in Africa at Fustat. This
new encampment was placed in the desert south of
the grasslands highway used by the Arabs for their
east-west movement and even farther south from the
chief Byzantine base in Africa at Carthage in the
settled coastal strip of the seashore. At the
same time, Kairouan was at the eastern edge of
the mountains of northwest Africa, which constituted
the chief danger zone for the Arabs because these
mountains formed the stronghold of the Berbers.

Thus in North Africa west of Barka, we see
three geographic areas corresponding to three different peoples and cultures which, in turn, cor-
responded to three different power systems. These
were (1) the coastal strip of settled, urbanized,
communities reflecting an ancient tradition of
Phoenician-Roman-Byzantine civilized living; this
was controlled from the sea by naval power; (2)
the parallel grassland strip south of the civilized zone, which could be traversed so easily
by the Arabs, but could be controlled only along
the east-west line so long as the Arabs did not
control the sea (which would allow north-south
intrusion into the coastal strip from the sea);
the deserts south of the grasslands could also
be controlled by the Arabs. But from Kairouan
westward to the Atlantic shores of Morocco was

(3) a great wedge of mountains, widening and rising to the westward and culminating in the Atlas
Mountains; these mountains were a great danger
to the Arabs because they were controlled by the
semi-pastoral Berbers who were quite as warlike
as the Arabs and found security in the mountains
just as the Arabs found it in the grasslands and
deserts.

The control of North Africa from Kairouan
(in eastern Tunisia) westward another 1500 miles
to the ocean thus was a three-cornered affair in
which the Berbers held the balance of power. The
whole area, now known as Tunisia, Algeria, and
Morocco, was then called "Ifriqiya" (that is
"Africa") by the Arabs, but, as this name came
to be applied to the great southern continent
as a whole (replacing "Ethiopia"), the northwest
came to be called "Maghrib" (or Magreb) from the
Arab word for "west."

The Berbers held the balance of power in this
area because they had security in the mountains
(except from each other) and could determine who
would dominate the whole area by shifting their
support from the Arabs to Byzantium and back again.
But the Arabs, by getting control of the sea
(rather than the grasslands), could exclude the
Byzantine power from the whole area and thus subdue the Berbers.

Naval control of this area had been taken by
the Vandals in 439, operating from Carthage, after
the fall of Rome, but was recovered by Byzantium
after Justinian's victory over the Vandals in 533.
At the time of the Arab explosion, Byzantium had
naval bases at Constantinople, Acre (in Syria),
Alexandria, and Carthage, with lesser bases at
Ravenna, Syracuse (in Sicily), and at Ceuta (in
Morocco). The Arabs took Acre, Alexandria (642),
Carthage (698), and Ceuta (710), all from the
land side, as the Japanese took Singapore in 1941.

The long delay in the conquest of North Africa
covering about sixty years from the capture of Barka
in 643 to the fall of Carthage in 698, the defeat
of the Berbers in 700, and the alliance with Count
Julian, the Byzantine governor of Ceuta, in 710,

743

was caused by the Arab neglect of sea power. Even the establishment of Kairouan half way between Cairo and Agadir was of little help because it was deliberately placed far from the sea, on the edge of the desert and mountains, where the Arabs felt secure. Even when the Arabs finally got Carthage, they refused to use it as a naval base, because it was too close to the sea, but built a new naval base (Tunis) some distance from the sea, and connected to it by a lagoon and a canal.

Because of this neglect of sea power, the Arabs could raid westward but could not hold the Magreb so long as the Byzantine navy was still in the area and the Berbers were unbeaten. Accordingly, the raids were largely meaningless, even the greatest of them, that of Okba ibn Nafi in 681-683.

The whole career of Okba is of considerable importance as a symbol of the Arab methods of conquest and especially of the Arab inability to deal with geopolitical realities, especially in Africa.

Okba was the nephew of one of the most able Arabs of the conquest period, Amr ibn al Aasi, who conquered Egypt no less than three times (the first time, in 639-641, with only 4000 men) and was Muawiya's chief lieutenant in his victory over Ali in the struggle for the caliphate. As soon as Egypt was taken in 642, Amr sent Okba up the Nile to conquer the Sudan, but the Nubian bowmen of the Christian kingdom of that area badly defeated the Arabs, excluding them from the area for many centuries. Although Okba subsequently gained great fame for founding Kairouan in 670 and for his spectacular raid across all Africa to Agadir in 681-683, he was really a failure because of the Arab neglect of sea power and his own arrogant underestimation of the Berbers.

There were, in the seventh century, nine raids from Egypt along the North African grassland road to the west. These were motivated by a desire to find the source of the great wealth in gold which the Arabs captured from Gregory, the patrician of Africa, in 647, which they were told came from sales of North African olive oil for gold to the

744

Greeks of Byzantium. But, of course, the oil came from the coastal strip and could be moved only by control of the sea, not by futile rushing back and forth by Arabs along the inland grasslands. In 781 Okba raided, without meeting any opposition, across Algeria and Morocco, to capture Tangier, and then south hundreds of miles to Agadir at the mouth of the Sus River where he rode his horse into the ocean in frustration that he could go no farther. On his return, which he unwisely made through the mountains, he was massacred with all his men near modern Biskra. This attack signaled a general uprising of the Berbers with Byzantine support. A Byzantine naval feint at Barka in Cyrenaica forced the Arabs to evacuate all the Magreb, including Kairouan, and fall back to Barka.

On the death of Muawiya in 680, many areas, especially the Hejaz, refused to accept Yazid. The camp at Kufa invited Ali's surviving son, Husain, grandson of the Prophet, to come from Mecca to be their caliph. He did so with his family and 72 men but was cut off by Yazid's forces in the desert at Kerbela and massacred. Thus the Shiite supporters of Ali obtained a martyr (whom they still revere) and were irreconcilably alienated from the orthodox Sunni caliphate. To the Shiite sects the essence of divinity which existed in Muhammad passed on through the male descendants of Ali and entitles these so-called "imams" to be the rulers of all believers.

A second pretender to Yazid's throne in 680 was Abdulla ibn Zubayr, grandson of the first caliph and nephew of the Prophet's wife Aisha, who presided over the battle of the camel. His father, Zubayr ibn al Awwam, one of the committee of six which made Othman caliph in 644, had perished fighting Ali in the battle of the camel in 656. Now the son, proclaimed caliph in Hejaz, survived the capture of Medina and a long siege of Mecca (in which the Kaaba was burned) by the Syrian forces (683). Turmoil in the north from his own adherents and from the spiritually intoxicated supporters of Shia, as well as the deaths of three Omayyid caliphs in three years (Yazid in 682; Muawiya II in 683; and Merwin I in 685) made it possible for the rebel to hold out until 692, when the forces of Abdul Malik,

745

after a siege of eight months, captured Mecca and
killed ibn Zubayr. This left a single caliph over
a united empire for the first time in twelve years.

During this dozen years, the ruling families
of the Arabs were either wiped out or decided to
withdraw from the high tensions of imperial life
to live off their possessions in Arabia. In the
final battles of the civil wars, the actual fighters were increasingly of non-Arab origin, either
the mixed peoples of the Near East or Persian.
The Arabs themselves in this period divided into
two antipathetic groups, the Kaysites and the Kal-
bites or Yemenites. This largely mythical distinction rested on a belief that many of the Arabs
of Syria were of South Arab origin, while those of
the Hejaz and many of Iraq were of North Arab origin. This hatred of Arab for Arab, combined with
their violent, and mystical, religious rivalries,
fissured the ruling groups of the Islamic empire
and contributed to three simultaneous developments
after 700: (1) the growing Persian and decreasing
Arab influence in the empire; (2) the weakening
of the Omayyad dynasty before the secret plotting
of the Abbasids; and (3) the growing autonomy of
the provinces, especially in the west.

These provinces of the west, which were the
last to be acquired, were the first to be lost to
local rulers, whose subjection to the caliph was
increasingly nominal rather than real.

The first period of Arab sea power, from the
battle of the masts in 655 to the Byzantine naval
victory off Cyprus in 747, was the key to the
completion of the Saracen conquests in the west.
While the Arabs never had complete control of the
sea in this period, they did have sufficient intermittent and local control to stage the two sieges
of Constantinople (673-680 and 717-718), to conquer the Magreb and Spain, and to make frequent
raids on the islands of the Mediterranean, especially Cyprus, Rhodes, Crete, Sardinia, and Sicily
(first raided from Syria in 652 and 669, then increasingly from Carthage after 700).

In 700, with Carthage taken and the Berbers
defeated, Abd al Malik sent a thousand Egyptian

shipbuilders from Egypt to Tunis. In 711 a Berber
freedman, Tarik, with a largely Berber force, using four transports provided by the traitorous
Byzantine governor of Ceuta, crossed the Straits
of Gibraltar into Spain. That country was so
ripped by local hatreds that Tarik, having defeated the Visigothic army and killed its newly
elected king, decided to drive straight for the
capital at Toledo; this he found undefended. The
Gothic kingdom, which had existed in Spain since
466, vanished overnight. Generally, agricultural
enterprise was left intact, worked by the peasants;
lands of Visigoths who resisted or fled were taken
over by the Saracens, while other males were subject
to the poll tax (a gold piece a year from nobles,
half that from commoners), plus a land tax in kind
to support the Saracen forces. On this basis these
forces crossed the Pyrenees in 718, and took control of much of southern and southwestern France.
Their effort, however, to move northward toward
Paris ended in defeat between Tours and Poitiers
in 732. The Saracens continued to hold much of
southern France until the 740s when Berber risings
in the Magreb and Spain, Arab conflicts in Spain,
and Carolingian pressures in France itself forced
them to withdraw from most of France.

During these same years of the early eighth
century, the Islamic expansion to the northeast
continued to Kashgar in Chinese territory whence
an embassy was sent to visit the Emperor of China
in 713.

But in the vital center the expansion was
stopped by the failure to take Constantinople in
717-718. Both of the civilized powers were hampered by religious and sectarian divisions, by
constant domestic violence, threats of civil war,
and assassinations of rulers, but similar as they
looked on the surface, the realities beneath that
surface were quite different.

Byzantium was a much more solid political
structure than the Islamic caliphate. It was a
fully civilized state, freed from any significant
residue of tribalism, with a long tradition of
sophisticated thought on the nature of the state,

public authority, and the nature of law. It was
more compact and much more capable of being held
together in a single power system because it was
not strung out as the Islamic empire was, from
east to west (the directions of lesser resistance
to Arab pastoral mobility), much more capable of
being kept together by sea power, and with a much
clearer tradition of individual loyalty to the
system by all subjects, even the humble tillers
of the soil (who were, for centuries, the backbone
of the Byzantine infantry forces). Moreover, the
Byzantine system was subject to greater and more
sustained challenges from both the Slavs and
various Turkic groups and later from European
pressures.

On the whole, Byzantine difficulties were of
their own making and were three in number: (1)
periodic, and eventually fatal, neglect of sea
power; (2) unnecessary creation of heresy by
their narrow interpretation of orthodoxy; and
(3) failure to maintain a plentiful, loyal, and
prosperous peasantry by allowing landlords to
monopolize the land. Of these the second is dis-
putable, but there can be little argument about
the importance of the first and the third. Both
of these are directly concerned with the defense
forces, the navy and the land army. Failure to
keep them both up may be linked to inability to
sustain high state incomes, especially bullion,
which, in turn, may be linked to trade relationships whose details are not yet sufficiently well
known. The best work on this subject has been done
by Professor A.R. Lewis, formerly of the University
of Texas, later at the University of Massachusetts.

The difficulties of the Islamic empire were
quite different from those of Byzantium. They
were not failures of performance but failures of
materials. The ideological diversity of the empire was not something that could be overcome by
anything that the government itself could have
done, any more than the difficulties of keeping
Spain, and Sind, or Khurosan and Yemen together
in a single political unit were problems which
could be overcome simply by taking thought. Sea
power, from lack of lumber alone, was a much
greater difficulty for Islam than for the Greeks

748

and would, at most, have linked only part of the empire together (the Levant, North Africa, and Spain). Moreover, the problem of financing the empire of Islam, on a cash basis, was greater than that of financing Byzantium, from simple scarcity of precious metals. Also the whole basically pastoral foundation of the Islamic system in contrast with the basically agricultural foundation of the Byzantine system provided Islam with a much more diffused and dispersed basis on which to rear a power structure. The one great economic asset Islam had was the vital commercial linkage across the Syrian Saddle, but this had a number of weaknesses, one of which was that it had been divided, in a cultural sense, for so long as a frontier between Rome and Persia that this tradition of being a barrier could be overcome only with difficulty and, secondly, it was vulnerable to Byzantine attack and often tended to become a frontier itself because of the Byzantine control of the Taurus passes to the north and the threat of Byzantine sea power from the Mediterranean on the west. This weakness became much greater in the Abbasid period (after 750) when the government retired from the Mediterranean into the interior of Asia by shifting the capital to Baghdad.

On the whole, the Omayyad period, which lasted less than a century (661-750), was a period of transition. The effort to make the Islamic system into a dynastic state failed because the human materials available were not yet ready for such a structure (just as today the Arabs are not yet ready for the national state of the nineteenth century). The Abbasid regime (nominally 750-1258) overcame this problem, to some extent by becoming a providential monarchy, a basis for establishing political allegiance which was much more fitted to the available human materials, especially to the intensity of religious feeling and the level on which that feeling operated. But this was still a system in which the allegiance of many could not be obtained simply because so many had different opinions as to the family on which Providence might have placed its favor. But this change did little to overcome the two great problems of the Islamic empire as a power system: (1) how to overcome the realities of logistical problems, of communications and trans-

749

portation, to obvert the forces of local autonomy; and (2) how to keep a single political system when the realities of the relationships between weapons systems, religious allegiance and their economic bases tended so easily to localism.

This inevitable localism of the economic base was also reflected, under the Omayyads, in both military and political arrangements. In theory, in Islam, all power was delegated from above, undiluted by any ideas of individual or natural rights. Just as God had all power in the universe, the caliph, who was God's agent, had all power on earth. But most of this authority was delegated downward to the governors of provinces, who, in turn, delegated some of it downward to the governors of cities, who passed authority down further to cadi (judges), treasurers, and other local officials. Each governor was almost autonomous, consulting with the caliph only on questions of general policy or great importance, spending the money collected in the province on provincial needs (chiefly the army) and sending on to the caliph the surplus, if there was any. Generally there was little surplus, and the chief obligation of a governor to the caliph was to be sure that the latter's name was mentioned in the public prayers on Fridays. The caliph had no central bureaucracy, no imperial army, and not even a fixed capital city. The first Omayyad, Muawiya, was the only one who lived in Damascus. Most of his successors lived in the country, usually on the edge of the desert; several lived in Jordan, and the last Omayyad, Marwin II, lived in Harran.

This limited nature of the central government made it necessary for the caliph to hold a governorship for himself, in order to have any power or funds. The Omayyads, accordingly, held the governorship of Syria, which was the basis of their incomes, armed forces, and power. The fact that the caliph had neither weapons nor tactics superior to his governors and had only the resources of Syria meant that his power over the governors was relatively slight. Various efforts were made to remedy this situation under the Omayyads, such as the caliph appointing some of the subordinates of the provincial governors, including the provincial treasurer or the chief cadi, or naming the governor of a major

750

city, but rarely did the number of posts filled by the caliph within a province amount to more than a half-dozen or so. So long as the governor controlled the provincial armed forces, he was in an excellent position to control the province.

The regular army units were stationed in cities and obtained the same pay in peace as in war, so the soldiers were often reluctant to go to war, unless there were good prospects for plunder. These forces were directly under the governor of the city or his agent. Cities, including garrison towns, had police forces (<u>shurta</u>) which joined the army in wartime. Near the frontiers were forts and garrisons to resist invaders. Finally, each commander, including the caliph, governors of provinces, and governors of cities, had a bodyguard (<u>haras</u>). In the case of the caliph, this was the chief and most reliable force he had, although he also had control over any regular forces based in his province.

When a general war occurred, the frontier garrisons, the provincial forces under the governors, the urban police forces, and all the various bodyguards including the caliph's (which was as large as he could afford), assembled together. Islamic religious doctrine required that the empire must remain at war with all independent non-Muslim rulers, with truces permitted for a maximum of ten years. To carry out this requirement, it was customary to send annual raids from each province (except Arabia, which had lapsed back into the chronic civil wars which had existed before Muhammad) into the bordering non-Muslim areas. This was also a good way to keep the provincial and border garrisons in training and to protect them from boredom. Such raiding flourished best on the Byzantine border in Anatolia and thus rested on the caliph's own province of Syria, but the practice also flourished on the Afghan border to the east and in the Turkish area of Transoxiana.

Such raiding also helped the financial stringency which was especially acute for the caliph. The Omayyads made various efforts to increase their own incomes, as by insisting that the provinces send up regular annual contributions. To increase such

surpluses, some of these caliphs tried to reduce
expenses by curtailing the pensions granted to
all Arabs by Omar. In theory, all incomes were
expected to be spent in this way each year, so
that there would be nothing left at the end of
the year. Muawiya and some of his successors
tried to remedy this by insisting that pensions
and government payments go only for services rendered, but this raised such outrage as an ungodly
act that it was difficult to enforce it, and it
was never successful.

Since the caliph's revenues were so inadequate
from taxes, yet were essential to sustain his power
to rule, efforts were made by several caliphs,
especially Hisham (724-743), to build up their
private incomes from their own private estates.
In Hisham's case, his private income was larger
than his imperial income from the provinces, despite all his efforts to increase taxes and to decrease expenditures in order to increase the provincial surplus due to him.

The decentralized character of the military,
financial, and administrative systems of the empire made it very unstable politically. Many
revolts began with groups of less than a hundred
persons who inflicted a setback to the local police
and thus attracted a larger group which, by seizing a local treasury, could reward its recruits.
Such an uprising could then spread with incredible
rapidity, the rebels marching on local treasuries,
swelling in numbers with each success, until an
army of tens or even scores of thousands was needed
to suppress the insurrection. Boredom, religious
discontent, or economic want were all so widespread
that a few small successes opened the way to money
and a rapid swelling of any revolt. Even when such
a movement could not overthrow the government, it
could persist as large-scale rural banditry for
years. In fact, there is little evidence that overthrowing the government was among the aims of most
revolts against the Abbasids. Only when the uprising was based on religious discontent was this a
significant element in the motivations of insur-
rections, and these remained the most persistent
ones. In any case, the conditions of intrinsic
instability in this governmental system explain

the steady series of Kharijite, Shiite, Yemenite, and generally anarchistic revolts in the later years of the Omayyads.

Such instability was increased by other factors such as the lack of any rules of succession and the neglect by many caliphs of their obligations as rulers because of the distractions of their personal pleasures.

Establishing rules of succession was not possible because of the general aversion to rules as inhibitions on the will of God and of His caliph. This was increased by the general chaos of Islamic family life among the upper classes. As a result, only four of the fourteen Omayyad caliphs were succeeded by their sons. Generally the caliph, before his death, designated his favorite son as successor or, what was worse, named two sons to succeed him in sequence. The first to succeed, however, generally wished to set aside his designated brother in favor of his own sons. This led to constant plotting and frequent civil wars between uncles and nephews.

Another root of instability was the caliph's increased concern with other matters, such as harem intrigue and sensual pleasures. The harem and the use of eunuchs to manage it was probably introduced from Sassanid Persia or Byzantium and was well established by the time of Walid II (743-744). Yazid III (744) was the son of a slave mother; many subsequent caliphs were sons of freed slaves and concubines.

Parallel with this were changes in the caliph's other activities. Muhammad had forbidden the use of wine and had disapproved of music. Both of these became major concerns of the caliphs, supplemented by gambling and hunting. Yazid I (680-682), himself a composer, introduced singing and musical instruments to court, to the horror of his more pious subjects. As Hitti put it, he introduced "wine and song, forever after inseparable in Islam." In reaction against this trend, Omar II (717-720) was a religious fanatic, excluding Christians and Jews from public employment and imposing humiliating restrictions on non-Muslims, such as prohibitions on wearing the turban, requiring special hair-

753

cuts, forbidding Christians to ride horses or to use a saddle on donkeys. But such brief personal reactions could not slow up the general movement of the caliph's court in directions which many Muslims considered ungodly. This feeling in combination with the chronic political instability provided the background for the overthrow of the Omayyads.

The Abbasid revolt against the Omayyads in 750 was quite different from Muawiya's revolt in 661. The latter, even in its effort to establish a secular government, was fundamentally counterrevolutionary. That is why it lasted so briefly. It was an effort to retain control in Arab hands on the basis of blood, at a time when the whole trend of Islamic civilization was striving, with little success, to create a system based on creed rather than on blood. This counterrevolution was challenging the nature of providential monarchy at a time when the Islamic peoples were in a cultural stage which was adapted to no other type of wide political structure. This counterrevolution was possible only because the development of the military-political establishment was so much in advance of the development of the religious-intellectual establishment that the Omayyads were able to use the former to suppress the demands of the latter a century longer.

But the Abbasid revolt of 750 was a real revolution. Like all revolutions, it brought together, in opposition to the existing situation, very diverse forces which had little in common beyond the fact that they were in opposition. Moreover, the plotters were able to combine these elements together by concealing the fact that the revolt was to bring the Abbasids to power rather than the Alids, for whom there was considerable religious support. Once the Abbasids were in office, the support which had brought them to power disintegrated, and they were able to remain in office only by use of the military establishment on a divide-and-rule basis. This became an additional source of disillusionment for those who wished to create an Islamic religious community. The Abbasids remained in office in the caliphate so long (until 1258) only because their

754

power evaporated so completely into the hands of
the military system that it was not worthwhile to
remove them from the caliphate.

The Abbasids came to power by an elaborate
conspiracy which combined the many rivalries which
split Islamic society. The basic rivalries were:
(1) the North Arabs and the South Arabs, or Kaysites and Yemenites;   (2) the Omayyads and the
Hashimites;   (3) the Arabs and non-Arabs or neo-
Muslims;   (4) the Syrians and Iraqis;   (5) the Sur-
nites and Shiites;   and (6) the Semites and the
Iranians. The Kaysites had supported the non-
Omayyad caliph, Abdulla ibn al Zubayr, in the civil
wars of 681-692 and had been beaten by Marwin I
in 684 and in the final battle of Mecca in 685.
Nevertheless, the Kaysites remained influential,
and these two groups became like two informal political parties of the "Ins" and the "Outs." Of
the four sons of Abdul Malik (685-705) who became
caliphs, two were openly inclined to the Kaysites,
while an intervening brother was a Yemenite. This
reflected the influence of their various mothers,
who often prejudiced their sons against their half-
brothers because of harem rivalries with co-wives
or concubines of different tribal origins. The
conquerors of the early Omayyad period in the east
(Hajjaj ibn Yusuf, strong governor of Iraq and Iran;
his cousin, Muhammad ibn Kasim, conqueror of the
Indus valley and Sind; and Kutayba ibn Muslim,
the conqueror of central Asia) were all Kaysites.
For this reason, they and the caliphs of the same
party who supported them, have been deprecated by
most Islamic historians who have generally written
under Abbasid (that is, Yemenite) influence. On
the other hand, these have written approvingly of
the colorless glutton Sulayman (715-717) and of
his cousin, Omar II, to whom Sulayman left the
caliphate in a secret will sealed in an envelope,
thus bypassing his Kaysite brother, Yazid II (720-
724), who succeeded Omar.

These petty rivalries, probably rooted in
harem intrigue and certainly rooted in irrational
factionalism, are of historical significance only
because of the skill with which the Abbasids joined
them together in a loose coalition which held to-

gether long enough to overthrow the Omayyads.

Abbas, the uncle of the Prophet, played an ambiguous role in the events of his own day. He accompanied Muhammad to Aqaba for the second pledge of the faithful from Medina, but generally supported the Kuraish opposition and was captured fighting against the Muslims at the battle of Bedr and had to be ransomed. The great grandson of Abbas, Muhammad ibn Ali, living in obscurity in a remote village in Jordan, and his son, known as Ibrahim the Imam, conducted an underground conspiracy against the Omayyads beginning in 722. Their most successful secret agent, working in Khurasan in northern Iran, was a Persian slave, Abu Muslim. In 747, when civil wars were raging in both Iraq and Iran, chiefly between Kaysites and Yemenites or between the caliph's forces and Karijite anarchists, Abu Muslim raised the black flag of the Abbasids in open revolt in Khurasan and soon controlled the province. The stated aim of the revolt was to restore the caliphate to "the family of the Prophet," the Beni Hashim, which many Shiites took to mean the descendants of Ali. To confuse the issue, rumors were spread that Ali had bequeathed his unique inherited sanctity, the imamate, to the Abbasids; this is why Ibrahim was known as the "Imam." Ibrahim, in turn, bequeathed this mystical spiritual power to his brother, Abdulla, who became the first Abbasid caliph under the name "al Saffah" (the "blood spiller"). In a series of battles in 749-750, Merwin II, the last Omayyad caliph, was totally defeated and all members of his family, save one, exterminated. Later, all those who had helped in the revolution, including Abu Muslim, were murdered by the Abbasids.

The key to the early Abbasid period was the dynasty's fear that someone would conspire to overthrow them, as they had overthrown the Omayyads. No one did, and the dynasty survived through thirty-seven caliphs, until overrun by the Mongols in 1258. But the steps taken by the Abbasids from fear of such an attempt helped to destroy their own real power. Even from the beginning, in 750, the Abbasids held by law an authority which was not a reflection of the real power situation. This, as I have indicated, is of the essence of political

756

instability. They could not be overthrown because no other power center in Islamic society
was more powerful than they were, although the
conflicting powers in that society were, except
for their divisions, far stronger than the Abbasids.

By 750, political allegiance in Islamic society, even within the ruling groups, was so split
and diffused that the Abbasids could barely hold
together a sufficiently widespread bundle of allegiances as to maintain their control over the
empire. This tenuous bundle contained allegiances,
such as the Abbasids and the Shiites, which were
so irreconcilable in their aims that they began
to split apart almost as soon as the Omayyads were
gone. As a result, the Abbasids began to lose
control of the western portions of the empire.
A rapid reduction of these areas of allegiance
to the core of the empire, in Iraq, Iran, and Syria, left the Abbasids with inadequate funds,
while, at the same time, their suspicions of
their own peoples and their reluctance to rely
on them for armed forces pushed them toward the
use of mercenary forces and administrative personnel who would be ineligible to take the caliph-
ate--that is, Turks, heretics, slaves, and eunuchs.
They thus put their personal security and their
future dynastic fate in hands they could not control and could hardly trust. As a consequence, in
the ninth century, the caliphs were reduced to an
almost powerless condition of nominal religious
leadership, and all real power fell into the hands
of Turkish military despots. This destroyed the
power and prosperity of the core area with consequent increase of both the power and the cultural
achievement of the peripheral areas of the empire.
This whole process was completed by 870, that is
in a little over a century from the beginning of
the process under the late Omayyads about 740.

In that brief century and in a relatively small
area in the eastern provinces of the empire, the
Abbasids produced a brilliant cultural achievement.
In fact, beneath the superficial brilliance of economic and cultural life among the Abbasid ruling
groups, they took giant steps toward the creation
of an Islamic community, which was, however, much
more evident in the eastern provinces than in the

empire as a whole. From the beginning, the new dynasty was not accepted in Spain, North Africa, Oman, and Sind, and was given only nominal allegiance in Egypt and Khurasan. The one Omayyad who escaped, abd al Rahman, a grandson of the Caliph Hisham, made his way to Spain, where he reestablished the Omayyad caliphate.

The Abbasids withdrew from the Mediterranean into Asia by shifting their capital from Damascus to a fantastic new place which they built, at enormous cost, at Baghdad on the west bank of the Tigris, where a navigable canal linked the Tigris with the Euphrates. The motives for this move were both political and economic: the Abbasid takeover had been supported by Iraq and Iran against Syrian opposition, and the site chosen was on two trade routes, one up the Tigris from the Persian Gulf and the east, the other running northeast toward central Asia, both being linked to the Syrian Saddle through Baghdad. But this change of site made it almost impossible to control the Mediterranean and the west by sea power.

The greatest achievement of this dynasty was to move toward the creation of an Islamic community centered in Iraq. By shifting from an Arab to a Muslim ruling group and equipping it with a Sassanian administrative system, the Abbasids moved toward a more integrated complex society of commercial, artisan, intellectual, and religious groups which in the ninth century became the basis for a rich cultural and artistic tradition. As we shall see, the government itself did not become a part of this cultural community.

This growing Islamic community was cut off from the military-political structure by the Abbasid fears of a revolt against the dynasty. To avoid this, they established at the core of their defense forces an alien element, a mercenary force of Khurasani Iranians. After 780, these alien mercenaries were increasingly made up of Turkish soldiers, most of whom were slaves. At the same time, the Caliph Mansoor (754-775), who distrusted most Arabs, turned over many administrative positions to his freed slaves who, like most freedmen, remained his clients. He also brought in numerous Turkish

758

slaves for his service. And finally, he handed
over control of the administration to a native
of Balkh, Khalid ibn Barmak, who had supported
Abu Muslim in the original Abbasid revolt in the
north, became chief collector of taxes when the
revolution was successful, and gradually brought
in his sons and grandsons to dominate the government. Their power was as great as that of the
caliph himself, and they lived in almost equal
splendor, using government funds, as they wished,
for their own purposes. One of the grandsons spent
twenty million dirhems building a palace for himself. In 803, after almost twenty years, the whole
family was destroyed by Harun al Rashid, but this
did not end the custom of allowing all-powerful
viziers to take over the government. Such viziers
were generally freed slaves who often came into a
future caliph's life as a kind of tutor-nurse-com-
panion when the prince was still a child.

Harun al Rashid was caliph for 23 years (786-
809) during which the Islamic empire reached its
greatest splendor. But the caliph's position was
destroyed almost totally under the rule of his
three sons and two grandsons, covering the years
809-861. Harun himself contributed substantially
to the deterioration, not only by allowing both
civil and military posts to go to slaves and freedmen, but by dividing the empire itself. In 800 he
made Ibrahim ibn al Aghlab governor of Africa with
complete authority provided he never asked for
troops nor financial support. The Aghlabids became in fact independent monarchs, built up a
Moslem sea power in the central Mediterranean
and conquered Sicily (827-902) and southern Italy.
The Aghlabids were replaced by the Shiite Fatimids
in 909, and this family transferred its capital to
Cairo in 969, thus removing all North Africa from
Baghdad's control.

Harun al Rashid in 802 drew up an agreement,
which was deposited in the Kaaba in Mecca, dividing his empire among his three sons. Ameen was
to be caliph and hold most of the territory, but
Mamoon was to be governor of Iran, and Mutamin was
to be governor of the Jezira (ancient Assyria),
with each of the three free from any interference
from the other two. Everyone of importance in the

government swore oaths to support this arrangement. When Mamoon sent an army against Ameen, the latter's soldiers refused to fight until they were given a large donative. When Arab reinforcements were brought from Syria by Ameen, his Iranian mercenaries fought these in the streets of Baghdad. Nevertheless, the city withstood a siege of a full year before it fell. Ameen was killed, and Mamoon became caliph, but remained in Merv (Turkmenistan) and refused to go to Baghdad for four years. Apparently he was not told by his viceroy that the capital was in chaos and Iraq torn by civil war. In 819 Mamoon returned to his capital, but sent his victorious general, Tahir ibn Husain, to Merv as governor of the whole northeast. There Tahir established a dynasty of his own, the Tahirids (821-873), which gave only nominal suzerainty to the caliph. Back in Baghdad, Mamoon was married to the daughter of his chief minister in a wedding which cost the vizier fifty million dirhems.

Such extravagance could be financed by the profits of Asia's commerce which flowed from the east up the Persian Gulf to Iraq, while other goods flowed north to the Caspian Sea, then through Kazar country and across Russia to the Baltic and Scandinavia. Most of these routes were cut off in the late ninth and the tenth centuries, the Persian Gulf route replaced by the Red Sea route controlled by the Fatimid navy from Egypt, the central Asian routes disrupted by rising disturbances among the Turks, both routes hampered by increasing unrest in China, and the Kazar-Russian route diverted by the Varangians (Swedes) to Constantinople. At the same time, the caliphate found its access to newly mined gold restricted by unrest in Arabia and elsewhere, while new sources of gold in Guinea, West Africa, began to flow across the Sahara to the independent Islamic states of North Africa and Spain.

The financial situation of the Abbasid caliphate was unsound from the beginning, just as its political situation was unsound. In fact, the two interacted on each other to bring about conditions where control of weapons became the key to political control and did so at the cost of total political instability.

From the beginning, the financial situation
of the Abbasids was unsound, because they had lost
control of the peripheral parts of the empire
which were the parts where plunder was still possible. The decrease in the relative importance
of plunder was made worse by the efforts to shift
from an Arab ruling group to a Muslim ruling group,
a necessity if Arab tribalism was to be replaced
by a Muslim umma, but a shift which was financially
impossible because of the system of taxation and
financial privilege which had grown up in the Arab
period. This was made very clear when the pious
Omar II (717-720) tried to make the shift.

Omar tried to establish the Muslims as a
privileged ruling group over non-Muslims by extending the privileges of the Arabs to the neo-Muslims
(that is, those who were converted to Islam later
than the Arabs). At the time, the neo-Muslims,
unlike the older Arab Muslims, continued subject
to their pre-conversion taxes, especially the land
tax, and not merely the tithe which, in theory,
was the only tax Muslims should pay. Omar established that no Muslim should pay any tax except
the tithe and was entitled to a state annuity as
all Arabs were. Thus, at a stroke, the caliph
greatly reduced the state's incomes while greatly
increasing its obligations. He shrugged off this
difficulty with the statement, "God sent His
Prophet to do the work of an apostle, not that
of a tax collector." In compensation, however,
he declared that all lands subject to the land tax
were owned by the Muslim community jointly; he
prohibited sale of such lands to Arabs or Muslims
and declared that if the holders of such lands
converted to Islam, the property reverted to the
community and the occupant could remain in possession only as a rent payer.

These provisions were soon revoked, but Omar's
persecution of non-Muslims greatly increased conversions, also increased the number of clients
naming annuities in the cities and diminished the
state's income.

This income decreased fairly steadily from the
period of the conquests to the Mongol invasion because so much of the earlier income was plunder.

This made constant financial problems, which the caliphs generally ignored. In fact, the caliphs, as public revenues decreased, wasted more and more on their own whims, including innumerable palaces, huge harems, and incredible luxuries.

This decrease in revenues was one of the motives, both with the government and the common soldiers, for the continued conquests, in an effort to keep up the level of incomes from plunder. But it also had another very grave consequence, the movement toward self-financing of government services.

Much of the original plunder consisted of landed properties of defeated princes which became the property of the caliph's government. Most of these were landed estates, with peasants, livestock, buildings, and tools, but many of these were not operating effectively, from lack of some of these accessories or simply from lack of management. The caliph had no way of managing such enterprises, so he began to grant them out to privileged individuals or groups or simply to government officials to be managed in return for the increase in tax yields. In most cases, these rights of possession (not ownership) were disposable by gift, sale, or inheritance (or, at least, became disposable in time). Such a property, or usufruct, was known as a katia.

Parallel with this effort to keep up public revenues by handing out obligations to keep agricultural enterprises functioning was a later development which is often confused with this one.

This second development was an effort to pay for services rendered to the government by allotting sources of public revenues yielding income to remunerate for such services. In a sense tax-yielding property was allotted to such persons with the right to collect the tax for themselves. This is not the same as tax farming (the Roman and Biblical "publicans") in which a businessman bids on a public contract to pay so much to the government for the right to collect the taxes from some district and them tries to wring considerably more from it. The Muslim allotment, called an

762

<u>ikta</u> or grant, was expected to yield to the re-
ceiver only enough to pay him for his services
to the government without any obligation to pass
any of it on to the government (except for his
own taxes).

Such an <u>ikta</u> was not ownership, which, in
theory, continued to rest with the ruler, and
the rights entailed in the grant were not disposable by the holder by sale or bequest because
they were expected to revert to the government
when the grantee's services ended.

It is easy for us to make distinctions be-
tween <u>katia</u> and <u>ikta</u>, but in fact, at the time,
the two seemed similar: someone was getting an
income from a property which was not his own.
In time, especially as governments became weaker,
records were destroyed (or, if verbal, were forgotten), distances became greater, usurpations
became rights, and in general all distinctions
became confused, not only between <u>katia</u> and <u>ikta</u>,
but between these and tax farming, between land
taxes and land rents, between ownership, usufruct,
and possession, and between disposable and revocable grants.

Among all these confusions was one reality:
that incomes which once went to the government
now went to private persons as unearned incomes
from agricultural activities and, by this, to
some degree, these persons became less subject
to the government's authority because of a natural
increase in their economic independence.

These confusions began to appear from the
very beginnings of Islam and were becoming a jungle growth of complex individual cases by 750 when
the Abbasids replaced the Omayyads. The confusions were particularly dangerous from the point
of view of the state's authority when the government's revenues were diverted for military service. This danger appeared in its most extreme
form when the governor of a province was authorized
to collect the taxes of his province and send to
the caliph only the surplus over and above his payments for the provincial government, including the

763

provincial military forces. Even when this fiscal function did not belong to the governor (amir) but was in the hands of a provincial tax collector (amil), the governor's command of all local armed forces made it possible for him to persuade or force the amil to collaborate with him in subverting the power of the central government in that province. In fact, both the governor and the tax collector, if they were separate, probably had personal landed estates in that province and thus had a joint interest both in reducing the interference of the caliph and in making their holdings of wealth and power hereditary.

Once we add to this situation the shift from a drafted army to a mercenary army and then, by an additional step, make that mercenary army a collection of non-Arab, non-Semitic, or even non-Muslim individuals from remote places, such as Berbers, Iranians, Turks, and Kurds, the possibility of a caliph in Damascus or Baghdad enforcing his wishes anywhere became less and less likely.

This is what happened in the Islamic empire in the ninth and tenth centuries. The shift from Omayyad to Abbasid in 750 did not slow this process; it accelerated it.

When the Abbasids siezed power in 750, one of their most brilliant supporters, Ibn al Mukaffa, an erudite Arabist from Basra, who was a recent convert, wrote a guide for the new regime's political behavior (Kitab al Sahaba, c. 754). He advocated placing their chief political support on the religious convictions of their military followers, especially on the Khorasians, whose prowess had won the caliphate for them, to make religion and justice chief activities of the government, and to prevent the military forces from obtaining control of the collection of taxes. We do not know if this program would have worked, for it was not followed. At the beginning a few of the Abbasid caliphs tried to control religion and justice, and kept the offices of amir and amil separated, but by the time of the death of Harun al Rashid (809), the course had been set on opposite lines. By 833 the yield from taxes was so

764

inadequate that military pay was in arrears, and
the military obtained assignment of taxes directly,
with authority to collect it themselves. Soon the
offices of governor, local _amil_, and tax farmer
were combining in one person in return for a promise
that a military contingent would be provided to the
central government in time of war. This made it
possible for these local potentates to assume all
governing power in their provinces, to accumulate
large estates, to confuse in one mass local military, political, and financial powers, and to exclude the central government not only from local
control but even from knowledge of what was going
on. In theory the central ruler's will was supreme,
and everything depended on his whim, but in fact
his influence hardly went beyond the right to have
his name on the coinage and mentioned in the Fri-
day prayers. Above all, the caliph had few public
funds flowing through his control and had no guarantee that the obligated contingent of troops would
be forthcoming in time of need. Indeed, the caliph's loss of control of his own troops and his
own incomes in his capital and even in his own
palace guaranteed that he would have no power to
enforce anything on anybody. The ultimate in weakness was reached when the orthodox caliph found
his government and palace controlled by the hetero-
dox Shiite Buwayhid family (945-1055), who governed
through a Christian vizier (Nasr ibn Harun).

It would be a mistake to attribute this failure of the caliphs to create a Muslim community to
the personal weaknesses or failures of the rulers.
Both failures of the government and the personal
weaknesses of the rulers were intrinsic in the
situation. They rested on the social, emotional,
and intellectual backwardness of the Islamic organization from its origins, on its inability to
conceive of an organizational structure as anything
more than a nexus of personal and, above all, kinship relationships, and its total inability to
achieve an advanced conception of deity, of human
nature, or of nature itself in terms of reciprocal,
autonomous, and mutually interdependable entities
operating in terms of the established rules of the
organizational system itself. So long as God was
envisioned as arbitrary Will, even of Will capable
of compassion and mercy, and man was seen similarly

as a creature of Will helplessly entangled in the deterministic Fate of God's Will, and so long as the only significant value of individual man was his own personal salvation to be won at the Last Judgment by submission to God's Will and to the will of the ruler, it would not be possible to obtain a stable governmental system, a fusion of government and community, or a society based on law and reciprocal rights.

As a consequence of these failures of the society, there was a government and a religion, but there was neither a state nor a church. There was no state because the government, as a war-making machine, did not acquire the chief attributes of sovereignty or of state authority. These attributes, at their narrowest, would include the legislative power, the taxing power, the judicial power, the administrative power to deal with social and economic questions and, in a theocracy, it might well be expected to establish its control of religious life. Under the Omayyads, for a brief period, it may have looked as if the government might obtain these powers and functions and thus become a state. It failed to do so, and the Abbasid caliphate failed even more completely.

To be sure, as a war-making machine, the government had the power to take people's lives and property and to make rules about its own operations. Thus we might recognize that it had the taxing power and certain elements of the police power, but it did not have, except in a very tenuous way, either the legislative power or the judicial power. The reason for this failure was that both law and justice were regarded as religious attributes, and the caliph's government failed to get control of religion. All of this goes back to Muhammad.

Muhammad created no rules because he kept all power of decision in his own hands and made these decisions on a purely ad hoc basis with little of the generality so essential to law. Even when they were called revelations, these decisions were based on whims. This was not Muhammad's fault; the Arab traditions in which he was reared had little capacity for generalization or for abstract conceptual-

ization, which we have as an inheritance from the
Greeks. Thus Muhammad made no rules regarding
succession, consultation, or future decision-making.
Since all revelation ceased with his death and since
his followers insisted that his revelations were
completed and final, there was no room for future
growth, and the materials left by the Prophet were
the materials on which society had to be operated.
These materials were, however, totally inadequate
to provide the basis for a great community-state
of mature personalities. Accordingly, the body of
revelation as contained in the Koran had to be
supplemented, at first with all the traditions
about the Prophet and his chief companions (the
so-called ahl al hadith) and then with the lessons
which could be derived from Muhammad's own way of
acting (his "path" or sunna). Once the Caliph
Othman established the agreed text of the Koran,
the task of gathering the traditions and the sunna
into a canon and drawing the theological and ethical implications from these ceased to be an activity
of the government and became the activity of the
body of learned scholars, the ulama. This group,
almost a social class, were the ultimate authority
on all questions of theology, ethics, law, and the
constitution. Their authority rested entirely on
recognition and acceptance by the mass of Muslims,
and not on any political power or government office.
To be sure, the various governments often tried to
influence such scholars by giving them offices
(such as that of cadi, or judge) or putting them
on government salaries, but this simply served to
reduce their prestige among the people, especially
if it became clear that this connection with the
government was influencing their opinions. Thus,
most such scholars, including those with the
greatest prestige, remained private and independent
students of theology and law. They were supported
by private work and, as time went on, increasingly
by private gifts and pious endowments.

The community of Islam, the umma, grew up
around these independent and private communities
of scholars, at first by the aggregation of social
life around the activities of religion and scholarship and then by the assemblage of commercial and
craft activities along the lines of such social
life. In this way the solid and slowly evolving

767

communities of Islamic civilization came to provide most of the essentials of human life, except, perhaps, political security, outside the sphere of government, as the latter was slowly reduced to largely military activities with only a reduced shell of political functions (consisting of little more than tax collecting, the appointing of governors and chief judges, and some concern with the framework of commerce and trade). The chief consequence of this was that rulers and dynasties might come and go, but the communities of Islam remained, slowly changing by processes of social evolution, which, on the whole, were influenced only indirectly and remotely by political and military disturbances. As D.B. Macdonald wrote, "It is plain that the organization of the ulama was the solid framework of permanent government behind those changing dynasties."

Before we look more closely at the growth of the umma, which was a slow process from the ninth to the twelfth century, we must take a brief look at "those changing dynasties," since the growth of the communities as the framework of stability in Islam could not take place until there was a general consensus that the umma could not be built on any military-political basis, or even on the caliphate.

The caliphate collapsed completely after Harun al Rashid's third son, Mutasim (833-842). He filled the Iraq military forces with Turkish slave soldiers, demanding these as tribute on an annual basis from the peoples of his northeastern frontiers. At his succession there were two divisions in the caliph's armed forces, one Kaysite, the other Yemenite. Mutasim added a third, Turkish, division of 10,000 men. These latter were out of control almost at once, riding madly through the streets of Baghdad, abusing the inhabitants, and generally spreading terror through the city. To prevent this, the caliph built a new garrison city at Samarra, seventy miles up the Tigris, and moved there with his mercenaries in 836.

The suicidal consequences of these changes were not recognized by Mutasim himself, as he was on constant military campaigns, which kept the soldiers busy and out of the city, but his immediate successors found themselves prisoners of their soldiers in the palace. To make matters worse, Mutasim not only used the Turks as soldiers, which had been going on on an individual basis for two generations, but he also raised Turks to high offices of state.

Wathik, son of Mutasim, spent his whole reign (842-847) in Samarra, never visiting the provinces or leading his armies. All public affairs were left to his Persian and Turkish ministers and generals. His successor was his brother, Mutawakkil (847-861) who hated him and was one of the very few intolerant orthodox caliphs. He reenacted the anti-Christian rules of Omar II and amused himself with his harem, leaving the government to a Turkish slave and former palace butler, Bugha as Shurabi. In 861 Bugha had five Turkish soldiers murder the caliph while they were drinking together, and then offered the caliphate to the victim's son, Muntasir (861-862). From that point on, the caliphate was filled with a sequence of puppets, installed and removed (usually by murder) by various cliques of the Turkish soldiers. At one time (946), there were three former caliphs, who had been blinded and thrown out to beg, wandering around the streets of Baghdad.

When Muntasir died mysteriously in six months, the Turkish commanders assembled in Samarra and raised to the throne Mustaeen, a grandson of Mutasim. Real control of the government, however, rested with a junta of three Turkish officers until 865 when a second group of officers raised their own candidate to the caliphate, Mutazz, brother of Muntasir. The two groups of officers fought from Samarra and Baghdad until the latter city was largely destroyed and half depopulated; they then made a deal which killed Mustaeen. Mutazz was similarly killed in 869 and his successor in 870. Thus four caliphs were murdered by their officers in nine years, while the soldiers plundered the treasury of the eight million gold dinars reputed to have been left by Mutasim. This carnage among rulers, it must be recognized, was not a passing phase but was an intrinsic feature of Islamic society. I have just mentioned that three caliphs were blinded and thrown into the streets of Baghdad a century later (940-946) in seven years, and the history of Islamic rulers later into the twentieth century shows a similar pattern.

Such attrition of rulers was not necessary. The Turkish mercenaries soon recognized that they needed the Abbasid system as a functioning enterprise if they were to continue to milk it. As such it had to have certain elements of prosperity and stability or the government as a tax-raising structure would be of little use to them. Accordingly, certain elements of self-restraint appeared among the Turkish mercenaries, so that not only caliphs but Turkish generals and administrators began to function on a more long-term basis. This more careful husbanding of resources was made urgent by the steady decline in tax receipts. It has been estimated that the revenue decreased more than a fifth over a twenty-year period at the turn from the ninth to the tenth century.

This shift from high prosperity to straitened circumstances was more acute in monetary than in real terms (that is, economic activity did not decrease as rapidly as money became increasingly hard to get). This led to the growth of the process of alienation from public revenues in such forms as the ikta and tax farming, but it also speeded up the territorial disintegration of the empire into its provinces and lesser units. As a result, by 950 or so, the area under the control of the vizier of the Abbasid caliph was reduced to little more than Iraq and western Iran.

Some of the caliph's problems in holding the western provinces to his empire rested on the fact that his efforts to crush out political dissent simply drove the dissenters out towards the edges of his realm where they were more able to set themselves up as independent political entities or to detach border provinces. We have seen that this happened as early as 755 when the sole surviving member of the Omayyad dynasty escaped to Spain and set up a kingdom, and later (929) a separate caliphate, at Cordova. In 788 Morocco was lost, when a descendant of the Caliph Ali, Idris ibn Abdullah, set up the Idrisid dynasty. As we have seen, the

Aghlabid dynasty in Tunis became independent in
fact in 800, when Harun al Rashid granted full
powers to the Abbasid governor of Africa. This
government became a great sea power in the central Mediterranean (800-909) by their conquest
of Sicily (827-902) and other islands, until they
were overthrown and replaced by a Shiite religious
leader who established the Fatimid dynasty in Tunis
in 909 and conquered Egypt sixty years later. The
Fatimids also became a considerable sea power, both
from Egypt and from Syria which they controlled intermittently in the tenth and eleventh centuries.
They, like all Islamic governments, had troubles
controlling their army officers and governors and
were overthrown by Saladin in 1169. The dynasty
of Saladin, known as the Ayyubids (1169-1250), was
replaced in Egypt by the Mameluks (1250-1517).

Before Egypt was taken by the Fatimids in 968,
it had been ruled by two successive dynasties of
Turkish generals of the Abbasids. In 868 Ahmed
ibn Tulun, son of a Turkish slave, was sent to
Egypt as governor by the Caliph Muti. At the time,
Egypt was in deep economic depression. The following year, a great slave revolt broke out in southern Mesopotamia and detached that area from Baghdad's control for fifteen years. Since many of
these slaves were African negroes, this event was
known as the "revolt of the Zenj" (Zenj were blacks
as in Zanzibar). This interrupted the Indian Ocean
trade route from the east by way of the Persian
Gulf, forcing it west to the Red Sea route. This
gave the Tulunid dynasty in Egypt the funds to
build the country and to hire mercenary soldiers
which made it possible to conquer the Levant,
which was annexed to Egypt in 878. These possessions
were confirmed by an Egyptian victory over Byzantium
in Syria in 883 and another victory over an Abbasid
army in Palestine in 884. This situation continued
until 905 when the Abbasids combined a military invasion with the assassination of the Tulunid ruler
and recovered both the Levant and Egypt. But the
Baghdad government could not control its conquest,
and the whole area was soon in anarchy. It was
taken over by another Turkish military adventurer,
Muhammad al Ikhsheed, in 935, and was ruled for
the next 34 years by his African negro eunuch
slave, Kafoor. At Kafoor's death in 969, the

771

Fatimids moved in from Tunisia and stayed for two full centuries (969-1169).

This destruction of Abbasid power in the west provided space for many other principalities to rise and fall, notably various Berber rulers in the Magreb and a number of Arab groups in the Mediterranean and in all of Arabia. In most cases, the political power of these entities rested on ability to intercept income from prosperous agricultural enterprises (as in Spain, Sicily, and Egypt) or commercial flows of luxury goods, from the Middle East, the Far East, from northern forests, or from the tropical forests south of the Sahara grasslands. The chief routes for such trade were: (1) across the so-called "Silk Roads" of central Asia; (2) the Indian Ocean route via either the Persian Gulf or the Red Sea; (3) the Russian river routes from the Baltic Sea to the Black Sea, the Caucasus, or the Caspian; and (4) the trans-Siberian caravan routes between the Guinea savannah and North Africa. From these economic sources, flows of valuable goods could be intercepted by organized groups of weapons controllers and taxed to provide money to hire more fighters who could be used to spread their areas of political control.

In this process the Abbasid caliphate, or rather the Turkish mercenaries who controlled it, could not shine very brilliantly. The agricultural resources of Mesopotamia required skilled knowledge of irrigation and constant care to prevent silting up of canals or the salting of fields. Hardly were the Zenj rebels overcome than the Arab tribesmen of Nejd rose in a wild anarchistic uprising of extreme egalitarian violence motivated by the beliefs of the left-wing Ismaili Shiites (891). These Karmatians devastated most of Arabia, captured Mecca and Medina, carrying away the black stone of the Kaaba, and raided northward into Syria and Iraq. Their invasion of Egypt was defeated by the Berber forces of the Fatimids at Cairo in 972. From this point the impetus of the Karmatian attack withdrew, but these groups still dominated much of Arabia into the eleventh century.

Thus the economic bases of Abbasid power in Baghdad, whether agricultural or commercial, were very shaky. The only significant change was the establishment of a formal office of commander-in-chief, the "Amir of Amirs." This title was created by the Caliph Muktadir (908-932) for the eunuch commander of his bodyguard. In 945 this office was taken from the Turks by a Shiite leader of a warlike horde of Dailamis from the Caspian Sea, who simply invaded the caliph's palace and was given the office, but soon took everything else, including the caliph's property and his life. This heretic, Ahmed ibn Buwaih, was the first of eight successive Buwayhids who controlled Baghdad over the years 945-1055. During that time, the members of this family fought violently with each other; often several ruled simultaneously in different provinces, while other provinces were being gobbled up by outside warlords. The Buwayhids granted lands, districts, and even provinces to reward their followers, alternately abusing or ignoring the caliph, who was reduced to little more than the orthodox Sunni religious leader. But in this process Iraq and western Iran ceased to be a significant power unit.

We have seen how the Tahirids became independent from Baghdad, in fact if not in law, in Khorasan, the northeast province of Iran, stretching from southeast of the Caspian Sea to the Oxus River, with its capital at Merv. The Tahirid dynasty lasted only about fifty years (821-873), when it was replaced by two longer-lived dynasties, the Saffarids and the Samanids.

The Saffarid dynasty was unusual in that it sprang from the lower classes. It was founded in 861 when a coppersmith turned bandit seized Seistan and gradually conquered most of modern Iran. The coppersmith, Yakub ibn Layth and his brother, even invaded Iraq, forcing Baghdad to recognize them as governors of Seistan, Sind, Kerman, Fars, and Khorasan. Thus they replaced the Tahirids as far as the Oxus River (873), but, in the area beyond the Oxus, the Tahirids were replaced by the Samanid dynasty (871-999) with a capital at Bokhara.

The Samanids were descended from the old Persian nobility, converted to Islam about 730, and served as governors of Samarkand under the Tahirids. When the Saffarids conquered the Tahirids in 873, they did not cross the Oxus, so the Samanids became autonomous governors of all Transoxiana. In 900 these Samanids crossed the Oxus, captured Merv, and defeated the last Saffarid. From 903 the Samanids, who were enlightened rulers, held control of all the area from India to Iraq and from the Persian Gulf to the Caspian Sea and the Jaxartes River. Their capital at Bokhara became the intellectual center of Islam. Crafts and commerce were both highly developed, and agriculture was improved by careful attention to irrigation. Under Samanid sponsorship, a great library was assembled at Bokhara, and Persian poetry was reborn after two and a half centuries of Arab domination.

The chief historic function of the Samanids was to hold out the Turks who were building up pressures on the northeastern frontier, for, although the Islamic empire was filled with Turks, these had come in as slaves and as individuals and not as conquering tribes. By 950 the Samanid dynasty was in decline and falling under the control of its own Turkish slave soldiers. In 962 one of these Turkish generals, Alptageen, falling out with the dynasty, marched off to the southeast toward India and seized Ghazna, southwest of Kabul, when the ruler there tried to block his passage.

This Ghaznavid dynasty (963-1186) flourished under the descendants of Alptageen's Turkish slave, Sebutigeen, who was elected ruler of Ghazna by the troops on the death of the son of his former owner in 977. Until 999 the Ghaznavids gave a nominal suzerainty to the Samanids, but in that year the Kara Khanid Turks from beyond the Jaxartes captured Bokhara for the second time, starting a lengthy struggle between them and the Ghaznavids over the division of the Samanid territories.

This struggle was a consequence of the growing pressure of the Turkish nomad tribes moving across the Kirgiz steppes from the east. As early as 552 a Turkish empire had embraced the central Asian grasslands, occasionally sending off mi-

774

gratory tribes westward, but generally diverted from moving south or southwest by the Pamir Mountains and the Islamic defense area between the Jaxartes River and the Oxus (both of which flow from the mountains northwest to the Aral Sea).

As the caliphate and its provincial amirs declined after 900, the eastern caliphate was replaced by unstable systems of competing provincial dynasties, each trying to build an all-inclusive empire, not as a matter of choice but simply because the intrinsic instabilities of the systems themselves did not allow the cessation of effort since that was equivalent to surrender and defeat.

These arrangements of competing systems were fed by the steady pressure of new nomadic waves from the grasslands and steppes to the north and east. Following the Samanids, the chief contenders were the Buwayids (945-1055) and the Ghaznavids (962-1040); in the next period the rivals were the Seljuks (1037-1157) and the Kara Khanids (932-1165); in the following period the struggle became more complex, with a chaotic and unstable balance among the Khwarazmshahs (1072-1231), the Ghurids (1153-1206), the Kara Khitay (1137-1211), and others. In each case, there were other contending groups involved in these struggles, with constant splitting of dynasties, shifting alliances, revolting governors, and ephemeral bands of nomadic raiders.

We have no concern with the details of these struggles and shall restrict our attention to only three of these peoples, all nomads of the Asiatic grasslands. These are the Seljuk Turks, the Mongols in the period 1210-1349, and the Ottoman Turks in the period after 1290. Contemporary with these intrusions into Islam from the east was, of course, the intrusion of the Crusades from Europe (1196-1270). These four intrusions were different from the earlier movements of Turks and others into the Muslim world in the period after 800, since the earlier intruders had come largely as individuals, as slaves or, at most, as hired soldiers and not as fighting units. The last of the great slave dynasties were the Mameluks (1250-

1517; their name means "slave") who defeated the
Mongols and stopped their advance in Syria in 1260
and expelled the last of the Crusaders in 1291.
All of these groups and the whole of western Asia
and North Africa were ultimately conquered by the
Ottoman Turks (1290-1922).

The failure of the Abbasids to create a Muslim religious community as a sustaining social organization for their government left aside, as we
have said, many of the chief attributes of a state,
such as law, justice, education, social welfare,
public services, and most economic regulation except the fundamental bases of coinage and commerce.
Many of these activities, centering in religion,
law, and justice, came into private hands and became organized into schools of persons learned in
the law and religion. Eventually there were four
chief schools and a large number of lesser sects
and religious communities. The chief schools of
the sunna, known as the ulama, were generally recruited from the urban bourgeoisie and remained
allied with this class, which had the incomes
(from land or commerce), leisure, literacy, and
close personal contacts in the cities to build
up the associations, income flows, endowments,
and methods of personal recruitment to provide
a continuous existence for these groups. Thus
a religious-social establishment grew up as a congeries of communities apart from the military-
political establishment, regarding the latter as
a necessary evil, but willing to cooperate with
it and to submit to it to the degree needed to
obtain the political security and public order
which would allow the ulama to function. They
gave the government money and obedience, but not
loyalty. Indeed, some rulers, especially the
Ghaznavids, made it perfectly clear that they
did not want loyalty, or any effort by the non-
military establishment to act in politics, even
to the point of rebuking those who tried to resist an enemy invader instead of submitting, with
pious obedience, to all political vicissitudes
including the final defeat of the ruler himself.
Only briefly, in the early period of the Ottoman
empire and possibly in one reign of the Seljuk
empire, was there a short period in which there

might have been fleeting hopes that the government and the ulama might merge into an umma, that is into a single Muslim religious community, but the Islamic traditions of extreme individualism, of divine transcendentalism, and of the futility and transitory nature, if not the basic evilness, of the secular world, made such an achievement impossible. These cognitive assumptions were rooted in the dualism of the late classical period, as manifested in neo-Platonism, Manichaeanism, neo-Pythagoreanism, and even Zoroastrianism, as can be seen in the fact that they are prevalent in the Mediterranean area to this day and have been almost as extreme in Latin Christian Spain, southern Italy, and Sicily, as they were in Orthodox Christian Greece, historic Byzantium, and Czarist Russia. The extreme individualism of Muhammad strengthened these tendencies in Islam by weakening the chief countervailing influence, that of kinship solidarity, while in the west the influence of Christ, as we shall see, helped to overcome this dualistic influence, but the fact remains that the late classical heritage, in this respect, was stronger than either Muhammad or Christ, with the consequence that both Islam and Christianity must be regarded as failures in their influence on social organization or political stability.

This influence of the late classical period (A.D. 300-600) can be seen in a large number of characteristics of the subsequent societies, notably the Islamic and the Byzantine. These include (1) a general absence of corporative autonomous groups recognized as independent, self-governing legal entities, such as municipalities, craft guilds, and professional or occupational associations; (2) the extreme individualism of social attitudes, which is not restrained by such voluntary or customary social entities, but is limited only by the two extreme alternatives of kinship or of a totalitarian government; and (3) a pervasive lack of public spirit and communal feeling based on an assumption, often unstated, that all government is evil, that governors are corrupt, and that all wealth and power is based on robbery, corruption, and force. These attitudes were lacking in classical antiquity until

777

the late Roman period, when they appeared, with
the doctrine of providential empire, from Constantine to Charlemagne. They were generally prevalent
in Asia (only partially in China), but in western
civilization they were largely overcome as the result of the triple influence of the nature of Christ,
the Germanic kinship tradition, and, above all,
the influence of the European Dark Age in which
both state and kinship vanished and were replaced
by the local village community, a church organized on traditional Roman law principles, and a
dispersed feudalized political structure.

Islamic government in the Seljuk, Mongol,
Mameluk, and early Ottoman periods remained in a
condition of pervasive political instability with
few innovations in weapons or weapons systems and
with a continuation of the weapons ambiguity which
is the chief theme of this chapter. From 1200 onward, innovations were beginning to appear, such
as steel, increasing use of infantry and of missile weapons (not necessarily together), gunpowder
and various inflammable materials, paper, print-
ing, positional notation of numbers, the compass
and rudder, improved sails and ships, advances
in gearing and power transfer, the windmill, the
clock, improved harnessing, the wheelbarrow and
other advances in land transportation. Most of
these innovations were of Chinese, or at least
Asiatic, origin; none of them played any significant role in our subject until after 1400,
when the Ottoman Turks and western civilization
began to use them, the former to establish a final
providential empire over the whole of Islamic
civilization, the latter to expand on a worldwide
basis as a new, and revolutionary, kind of society
on a largely new basis.

The Mongols were the culmination of providential empire on the ambiguous basis which is
the theme of this chapter. Their providential
monarchical theory was the most successful and
the final ideological statement of that theory;
their balanced use of the traditional weapons of
this period was the most effective which had ever
been achieved; and, finally, their organization
of these weapons, especially their use of provi-

dential monarchical ideology to achieve the ultimate in fanatical allegiance and discipline was also the best ever achieved within this organizational system. All three, weapons, ideology, and disciplined organization between these two, were fused into a military machine of frightening and ferocious violence.

What has been said here about the Mongols could be said, but to a much lesser degree, about the Seljuk Turks who preceded them and the Ottoman Turks who followed them in the conquest of Islamic civilization. In all three cases ideological conviction in regard to religion and balanced organization in regard to weapons were fundamental to success. Neither the Seljuks nor the early Ottomans came near the Mongol achievement in any of these three elements of success.

As in most successful military conquest, weakness of the opponent was just as significant as strength of the victor. We have already made it clear that the Islamic governmental system was very weak, and very corrupt, after 1100. The same was true to varying degrees of the Byzantine system, the governments of India, and, to a somewhat lesser degree, of the Crusaders, and of late Sung China. Russia, which was conquered by the Mongols in 1237-1240, was simply weak and backward, almost primitive.

The members of the Islamic governmental system on which these four intruders came after 1100 were primarily interested in what I have called bundles of revenues. It would be an error to say, as R.C. Smail says, that they were interested in acquiring lands since their interest in the land was nil--they were interested only in the revenues which came from an organized productive system based on land. They had little interest or concern with the productive system itself, did not understand it, did little to improve it, and, indeed, generally despised it and those who were engaged in it. Moreover, their interest in revenues went beyond revenues from land and was fully aware that there were revenues from commerce, although here also their interest was not concerned with commerce as an economic activity (that is, an economic gain arising from division of labor, specialization of labor, and what today would be called "comparative advantage") but with the fact that commerce could be taxed and thus could become a source of revenues. The third kind of revenues with which the governing systems of this period were concerned were the revenues from war and booty, which included as a chief element the sale of war captives as slaves.

This third kind of revenues had, of course, an intermittent and precarious nature which made them somewhat less appealing to established governments, but, for that very reason made them very appealing to their military subordinates, especially ambitious young mercenary or slave soldiers who could hardly hope to work up in the system to a position commanding large revenues from land and commerce unless they could obtain the initial big step from the booty of a successful campaign. Thus ambitious young soldiers looked forward to the precarious gambles of war and battles, while their seniors, already established in a nexus of revenues from land and trade, were much less enthusiastic about such adventures for themselves, although they welcomed these, in many cases, as a way of diverting the energies of their subordinates away from their own possessions and onto the possessions of someone else. This would, of course, mean that the remuneration of these subordinates could be shifted from a burden on the superior's revenues to the booty of war including the revenues of others.

There is another factor involved here. Established revenues from land and commerce, as I have said, were always local, involving a specific place, but booty was always to be found at a distance. In fact, in the Islamic theory, war on Moslems was forbidden, so that warfare should occur only on the peripheral edges of Islam. Fighting on the edges was thus doubly welcome to the governmental establishments of Islam because it took dangerous military subordinates away from the temptations of local revenues to distant, and thus not threatening, points and, at the same time, relieved the establishment of the burden of paying their fighters.

For this reason, all established Islamic governments sent their soldiers off to a distance, at least for the campaign season (May to October), and, if they had to be paid from the establishment's own revenues, tended to divert the burden to those arising in that distant area where the troopers were stationed. This would, of course, keep the soldiers away from the seat of government even in the winter (October through the harvest in the spring), but this advantage was achieved at a very great cost, for the soldiers, being paid from the revenues of a distant place, were, in fact, in a position to control those revenues as well as the people and the government of that area. Thus, regardless of law or theory, government in fact tended to become local military control, especially at a time when, as Ann Lambton says, governors expected from their subjects nothing beyond taxes and their prayers. From the military point of view, such local control meant control of fortified places, castles or walled towns, which were, as I have said, the focus of all significant military efforts, since they joined together the triple value of control of revenues, control of the local population, and security against other governing systems.

This central reality of the governing establishments of this whole period of more than a thousand years (300-1400) means that these establishments were relatively impervious to the appeals of ideology, religion, family, shared language, class interests, personal loyalty, or even gratitude, or what we would call "national origin." Despite these things, men constantly betrayed each other. Brothers murdered brothers, as nephews murdered uncles, while rulers often murdered, or allowed to be killed, their hard-working viziers or loyal ministers, in order to confiscate their possessions or to escape from their own dependence on them. In the Crusades, the Greeks sabotaged and fought against Latin Christians; the Seljuk amirs constantly fought each other, often in alliance with Christians; Greeks betrayed Greeks to the benefit of Muslims, as Andronicus Ducas betrayed his emperor at the crucial battle of Manzikert in 1071; the Muslim ruler of Syria in 1115 fought with the Crusaders against the amirs from Iraq coming in to expel the Franks, because he knew that the Iraqi

781

generals were a bigger threat to his position than the Christians. Situations of this kind must not be regarded as unusual or as the personal weakness of the men concerned, difficult as it is for us, living in a totally different situation, to understand. These acts were not the weakness of the individual actors; this was the way society was organized in the age of providential empire.

Our difficulty of understanding is equally great in regard to military matters, probably because even military experts today are so narrowly encapsulated in their own contemporary tactical assumptions that they have some trouble comprehending the realities of power in any period. Here again, the mistaken assumptions of the nineteenth century rise as a barrier to block our view, not only of the political and military realities of the Old Regime (before 1789), but, to an even greater degree, they block the political and military realities of the medieval period (before 1400). Medieval governors were not concerned with controlling territories but with controlling revenues; they were not primarily concerned with field armies, but with fortified strongholds (to which field armies were necessary accessories); they were not concerned with annihilating the enemy forces, with "total victory," with defeating one ideology by a different ideology, in warfare or on the field of battle; they cared little about protecting populations and even less about defending frontiers or about changing regimes, as distinct from overthrowing rulers of such regimes; they made no efforts to interrupt passage of enemy forces (but rather hoped to speed it up), made no effort to interrupt his communications, and had no desire to blockade commerce, or to obstruct pilgrims or merchants, since these were parts of income-yielding activities. As I have indicated, neither rulers nor soldiers preferred peace to war, and the idea so prevalent in the twentieth century of the urgency of "bringing the boys back home from the front" was totally lacking in that period and area: not only were rulers reluctant to see their soldiers return but the soldiers themselves had little desire to return to barracks in a capital city or frontier fortress, since their families and most of their possessions were

with them "at the front" (of course, there was no
front since there was no idea of a continuous
barrier of military resistance except in almost
purely agricultural areas like China). Muslim
amirs on campaign may have been glad to get back
"home," that is to the stronghold which controlled
their bundles of revenues, especially in the winter when most Muslim campaigning ceased, just as
those Crusaders who had no desire to seize revenues in the Levant were eager to return to their
strongholds in Europe as soon as was fitting to
the oath they had given to go on crusade.

With the realities of military force, political power, and governing establishments such as
these, it is obvious that political instability
was intrinsic in Islamic society, even if it was
not exposed to invasion by outside enemies: the
constant trend toward localism, local bases, and
local military power which arose from the local
foundations of revenues which supported military
forces made it unlikely that any widespread government could prevent the disintegration of its
power, at first at its peripheries but ultimately
at its center as well. This was what happened to
the caliphate up to 1100 as was evident as early
as 850. But, on the other hand, the extraordinary
mobility of horse-riding fighters meant that it
was relatively easy to conquer wide areas in order to establish the thin veneer of political action which constituted a government in those days.
All that was necessary was a certain element of
ideological agreement to bind together a large
number of unemployed fighters who could invade
and defeat the localized revenue-clinging military establishment which was already in possession
and which could hardly expect loyalty or support
from their own local mercenary forces let alone
from their more distant amirs.

This is what happened with respect to the
four invaders of the Islamic area after 1100.
And, in each case, but with a number of notable
modifications under the later Ottoman Turks (after
1517), the invader rather quickly became a localized governing establishment based on bundles of
revenues, without much cohesive strength (either

783

from ideological glue, or from social solidarity,
or other unifying influence).

That was the situation among the ruling groups
in this middle period of Islamic civilization from
850 to 1100 or later. Among the ruled groups who
were excluded from political and even from military
activities, the situation was somewhat more familiar to a late twentieth century eye because it is
somewhat similar to the conditions which are now
developing in our western civilization, especially
in America. In the Islamic world in the middle period, there was a growing recognition of the impossibility of creating an umma, a community of all
Muslims including the ruling and military groups.
The increasing chaos in these ruling circles, the
disruption of kinship groups or even of kinship
loyalty, and the receding possibility of making
an Islamic umma left the great majority of people
in a condition of acute emotional and spiritual
frustration. The two chief results of this condition were the growth of individual efforts for
mystical religious experience by which persons
could escape from this world of space and time
into some intimate relationship with a transcendental deity and, on the other hand, efforts to
join together with one's close associates in groups
of like-minded persons. These groups were often
based on religious sects, although the motives
which formed them were more social than religious,
that is were based on the need for personal emotional relationships with other people. In such
a group the degree of intimacy and thus the amount
of social and emotional satisfaction provided was,
within limits, in reverse ratio to the size of
the group. Moreover, the solidarity and thus the
intimacy of intra-group feelings depended as much
on being different from outsiders as on shared
outlook with fellow members. These two factors,
of course, are found in all societies and social
groups and are especially strong in periods of
atomized individualism, such as existed in Islamic
society in this middle period. The group satisfied its members' frustrated social and emotional
needs best when the group had little internal formal organization but, instead, was sustained by
relatively spontaneous activities and operated on

a largely face-to-face basis in which members
recognized each other. Its emotionally satisfying qualities were increased by shared religious
beliefs and by sharp opposition between Ins and
Outs, that is between members and non-members.
The satisfying emotional qualities of such a
group would, of course, attract frustrated recruits
from outside, but after a certain point addition of
such recruits reduced the emotional satisfactions
of membership and the group would begin to split
into more satisfying smaller groups. The satisfactions of these fractional parts were increased
by intensification of animosity against the other
factions, with the consequence that such factions
of the same sect or belief hated each other more
than they disliked complete heretics or utter pagans.

This is what happened in Islamic society in
the period 850-1150. This process can be seen in
the history of the Shiites, but it also took place
in other sects including orthodox sunna itself.
The Shiites split and splintered not only on the
question of which family should possess the caliphate but on many other questions, often involving
insignificant differences of opinion regarding
asceticism, the legitimacy of property, the nature of sin and its effects on political and social life, and the degree of divine transcendentalism.

One consequence of these social and emotional
frustrations was that for much of this middle period and over most of the Islamic world, the beliefs of the people, however diverse, tended to
be opposed to the declared beliefs of their rulers.
Thus west of Suez, especially under the Fatimids
who were fanatical Shiites, Sunnite beliefs were
prevalent among the people, while in the east,
where the Baghdad caliph was Sunnite, Shiite and
other sects were proliferating throughout the period. As these two rival caliphs lost control
of their provinces, these became heretical, so
that the eastern caliphate became largely a mosaic
of sects and, as we have seen, the Shiites took
over control of the caliph's own administration
and palace, while the core of his realms, in Iraq,
Arabia, and much of Iran and Syria, broke up into

Shiite amirates. During much of this period the
eastern caliphs were personally religiously in-
different, while the Fatimids in Egypt were aggressively sectarian, not only seeking to conquer
all of Islam but also sending secret agents as
missionaries and assassins far beyond their frontiers to spread religious and political subversion.

This middle period of Islamic civilization
from 850 to 1150 began to end in the 11th century,
when new and more peripheral military groups, led
by the Turks but also including other peoples such
as Berbers and Kurds, adopted orthodox Sunnite
theology and a declared support of the orthodox
caliph in Baghdad. At the same time, the theology
of orthodox Sunni beliefs was broadened to accept
many aspects of earlier heresies, such as personal
mysticism, asceticism, and devotion to poverty
(Sufism). Moreover, this Sunnite orthodoxy, as
it widened the area of acceptable belief, adopted
a declared policy of toleration of non-orthodox
belief so long as this dissent remained in the
religious and social spheres and did not intrude
into politics.

The chief consequence of this rearrangement
of the various aspects of life in the 11th century was that military and political rule over
wider geographic areas became possible under a
broad and tolerant Sunni ruler whose peoples were
organized in more satisfying local groupings which
had nothing or little to do with military or political life except to support these in the hope
that they could provide such small communities
with security and the basic framework of economic
prosperity. This led to a revival of the power
of the Sunni caliph in Baghdad as early as 1000,
with Ghaznavid and later Seljuk support, but the
conditions were not yet ready for political stability in the 12th or even in the 13th century
because, at that time, the military and economic
systems were still so much under the influence of
localism, and local social groupings among the
people were still so unstable with emotional frustrations so high, that any powerful influence,
personal or ideological, could join with an organization of military force to change political
arrangements over wide geographic areas. In the

786

13th century, the pagan Mongols, with such a combination of personal influence, ideological cement, and skilled weaponry conquered most of Asia, ended the Baghdad caliphate, and drove the great mass of the Islamic peoples into local social groupings. This prepared the ground for the ultimate triumph of the Ottoman Turks in the period after 1300. In that later period, great technological changes, especially the advent of gunpowder and artillery, assisted this Ottoman achievement by giving them an advantage over other Islamic power systems.

The Seljuks were a "royal" family of the pastoral Oghuz Turks who moved west from Outer Mongolia, south of Lake Baikal, to the Khirgiz steppe north of the Aral Sea in the middle of the eighth century. Since the establishment of nomadism as a way of life, the eastern grasslands had seen one ephemeral confederacy after another rise, dominate a considerable territory, and fall apart again, flinging off fragments westward towards the Volga and Europe. When the Tiu-kiu confederacy broke up from its internal tensions about 744, the Oghuz and Karluk groups of tribes moved westward onto the trade routes emerging from northern Iran (Khurasan), the Karluk in Turkestan west of Lake Balkhash (where they later formed the chief group in the Karakhanid confederacy, as the Oghuz did in the Seljuk empire).

This whole ecologic area was a precarious balance of three economic activities around the contrast between pastoral grasslands and agricultural oases. These were the agricultural groups resident in the towns of the oases, the nomads roaming the grasslands, and the merchants also resident in the towns but dependent on passage for their goods across the grasslands. There were numerous interrelationships among these three. The oases produced food, craft products, and commercial enterprise, while the nomads produced animals for transport, animal products for food, raw materials for artisans (wool, hides, hair, etc.), and "protection" for caravans. The mutual interdependency of the three is obvious, but any stable and peaceful arrangement of their shared interests led to a growth of population and emotional tensions which could not remain stable through the unpredictable climate fluctuations. The nomads, even when they were peaceful, were like a time bomb, a threat of devastation, not only to the trade routes crossing the grasslands but especially to the gardens, orchards, and irrigation systems of the oases towns.

In the 10th century, the Oghuz, under their military leader, the yabghu, were ranging the trade routes from the delta of the Jaxartes River (Jand) at the northern end of the Aral Sea to the Khazar town in the delta of the Volga River, acting chiefly as the military auxiliaries of the Khazars. The Oghuz were at a very low cultural level, illiterate and still pagan, with increasing population and decreasing prosperity, at least in 922 when a diplomatic mission from Baghdad observed them on the steppe. The declining prosperity was from a variety of causes including the shift of the trans-Russian trade from the Volga to the Dnieper, the decline of Khazar power, and, above all, the monetary and economic crisis which had become acute about 950.

Sometime after this date, Seljuk, a chief lieutenant of the Oghuz yabghu, quarreled with this ruler, ejected his supporters from Jand, became a Muslim, collected a force of ghazis, and began to operate in the complex balance of powers on that Islamic borderland. To the north, the yabghu allied with the Russians against the Khazars. The Seljuks, being anti-yabghu, favored the Khazars, but their interests were to the south in Transoxiana and Khurasan, where the doomed Samanids were at bay between the Karakhanids coming from the northeast and the Ghaznavids coming from the southeast. By 980 the Seljuks were in Khurasan. Twelve years later, when the Karakhanids seized Bokhara, Seljuk's son, Arslan Israil, was allied with the Samanids. Seven years after that (999), the Samanid power was finally destroyed by the Ghaznavids, and their territories were shared between the Ghaznavids and Karakhanids. The Seljuks dispersed and plundered much of Khurasan, while the Ghaznavids devoted their attention increasingly to the other extremity of their empire, raiding into India from their base in Lahore for Hindu slaves and treasure. Several times the Ghaznavid Sultan Mahmud (998-1030) had to return to the northwest to subdue the rampaging Turks in Khurasan and eventually took Arslan Israil back to the Indian border as a prisoner until his death in 1036. Leadership of the Seljuks devolved to the imprisoned leader's two nephews, Tugrul Beg and Cagri Beg, who are the real founders of the empire. As self-proclaimed champions of the neglected Abbasid caliphate (1034), they carved out a territory between the Karakhanids of Transoxiana and the Ghaznavids of Afghanistan, and in 1040, in the decisive battle of Dandarkan near Merv, they eliminated the Ghaznavids from Khurasan and made the Seljuks the chief power system in northern Iran.

This victory shifted the Seljuk family from nomad leaders to territorial rulers and made it necessary for them to ally with the landlord-mercantile-ulama establishments of the north Iranian towns and to devote their energies to protecting the bundles of agrarian and commercial revenues which were the basis of those establishments. This alignment had already been forming between the Seljuk leaders and the Khurasan towns before the victory at Dandarkan, as it had become increasingly clear to the latter that the Ghaznavids were no longer capable of protecting them. To do this the Seljuks had to either control or divert their nomad warriors. Since these could not be controlled, they had to be diverted by being sent off to raid outside the new Seljuk territory--into Armenia in 1049, down into Iraq (where they freed the caliph from the Buwayids, increased his incomes, and obtained exalted titles in return) in 1055-1059, into Anatolia in 1059, and across Syria in 1070. In each area relatives of the Seljuk family were set up as amirs and allowed to establish a local economic base by allying with the local economo-social-religious establishment while diverting their own fighters outward. In many cases these fighters were preceded or accompanied by bands of independent Turkomen who were not part of the Seljuk forces and not subject to Seljuk "control." This was especially true in Anatolia after the great, and

not much desired, victory over the Byzantine
forces at Manzikert in 1071, when the Greek defenses disintegrated and Turks, even in fairly
small bands, could raid, or even settle permanently, over much of Anatolia, even to the
shores of the Aegean and Black Seas.

Behind this fringe of raiders, the central
Seljuk dynasty moved to Baghdad in 1091, where
they set up a government based on Ghaznavid (and
thus on Samanid) precedents. Their chief guide
was Nizam al-Mulk (1018-1092), vizier to the two
greatest Seljuk rulers, Alp Arslan (1063-1072)
and Malik Shah (1072-1092). Nizam al-Mulk, who
was probably the greatest Muslim vizier in history, did all he could to make the Seljuk government an absolutist personal despotism, but the
basic weaknesses of all governments of that day
persisted, and Nizam al-Mulk himself contributed
to them.

Nizam al-Mulk's theory of government was
that the governing system was the personal property
of the ruler. The Seljuks, however, retained many
of their Turkish characteristics and thus were,
in some ways, better rulers. For example, they
felt that religious rules, such as abstention
from alcohol, applied to rulers as well as subjects, and they also believed that rulers should
be under some ethical restraints. Thus they reduced the role of the court executioner, the
sahib-haras, whose job, according to the Caliph
Mamun, was "from morning to night, to cut off
heads, hands, and feet, to beat with rods, and
to throw into prison," and they refused to have
a system of domestic spies and secret police,
in spite of the urging of their vizier. But
they remained uncultured Turks for the first
century of their rule, speaking Turkish, illiterate, and wearing clothing and hair in Turkish style. All of these apply to the last powerful Seljuk ruler, the fifth sultan, Sanjar (1117-
1157). Above all, they continued to regard their
government as a family patrimony, allowing their
relatives almost complete autonomy in their amirates. Their aim, apparently, was to conquer all
the traditional Islamic areas but not to conquer

non-Muslim territories, which is why they did not make any direct effort to exploit their victory over Byzantium in 1071. In this aim they were largely successful and, by 1092, had established at least nominal suzerainty over most of the eastern caliphate, from Syria to Afghanistan, including the fringes of Arabia (Bahrain and the Hejaz), but were unable to reach Egypt, and failed in their effort to capture the chief stronghold of the Assassins. These latter, in retaliation, began to assassinate enemy officials, starting with Nizam al-Mulk in 1092.

This great vizier, in the last year of his life, wrote a guide to political conduct for his sultan, Malik Shah, who was also in the last year of his life. This treatise, Siyasat-namah, was full of historical anecdotes and good advice: to pay soldiers with cash rather than by granting them estates or revenues; to have soldiers of different languages and origins, as the Ghaznavids had Turks and Hindi; to refuse to combine offices in the hands of one person; to prevent peasants from being enserfed by landlords; to be accessible regularly each week to subjects who had grievances; to check personally on all officials, including the vizier. These rules were good ones, but, as I have insisted many times in this chapter, the disintegration of governments in this millennium was the consequence of intrinsic factors and not of the personal behavior of individuals. For example, the victories of the various conquerors, including the Seljuks themselves, rested on their fighting spirit and mobility; both of these qualities were parts of their nomadic way of life and were diminished or even lost, as soon as their government shifted from a nomadic to a sedentary basis. Conquest provided possessions, which transformed a band of hardened raiders, all men, into a sultan's expeditionary force of cumbersome comforts, a harem, baggage and treasures, non-combatants and camp followers, in which the fighters were less hardened, less fanatical in combat, and probably did not amount to more than a quarter of the force. Such an army fought with one hand tied behind its back: its mobility was cut to only a fraction, probably proportional to the percentage of its fighting men; it had to be split to guard the

baggage and non-combatants; its movements could
not be hidden and the element of surprise was
reduced as much as its mobility was. All of this
was simply one aspect of the fact that conquest
per se transformed the leader from a nomad to a
territorial ruler and divorced his interests from
those of his nomad fighters. The real core of all
this problem, mentioned earlier in this chapter,
is that nomads had to keep moving because they
used up the grass and they could not capture
strongholds because they did not have a siege
train, but they could get towns to surrender by
disrupting their commerce (including local trade
in food), an action which townsmen were increasingly willing to do once the town dwellers were
totally separated from military and political matters, as happened in the 10th century. Once the
military-political establishment and the economic-
social-religious establishment became separate entities, the latter became quite willing to shift
from one ruling establishment to another, because
all were equally bad and the real lives of the
people went on, regardless of ruler, in their own
local communities. This shift of "allegiance"
(it was not a shift of loyalty, since no loyalty
was involved) was of little political significance
as allegiance, but it was of great military significance from the fact that it meant that towns
became willing to open their doors, as the towns
of Khurasan opened theirs to the Seljuks, even to
invaders with inadequate siege trains, if they
could obtain some promises that their town communities would not be destroyed and that their
trade could be resumed. Since both of these were
things which most conquerors who wanted to become
territorial rulers also desired, an agreement
could usually be made. The big exception would
be when the invader did not want to become a territorial ruler or, at least, was not aware that
he did, as in the case of the Mongols, or when he
was powerfully motivated by religious or ideological intolerance, as was true of the Crusaders
as well as the Mongols. In such cases, the invader had to have an elaborate siege train, for
the towns would resist to the bitter end, and,
indeed, would resist far longer and more vigorously than their military garrisons, as is evident from several cases in this 11th century, in

which garrisons either surrendered or fought
their passage through the besieging forces, but
the towns continued to resist.

Since this was the real nature of power relationships and political stability in the Seljuk
period, the good advice in Nizam al-Mulk's treatise was not much help. Moreover, it was not in
accord with the Turkish-Mongol traditions, that
the government was a family patrimony in which all
members may share. This, in combination with the
usual absence of any rule of succession in a providential government, made the Seljuk disintegration
as rapid as their rise and, indeed, simultaneous
with it. The rulers of various provinces, as members of the Seljuk family (or even in some cases,
as in Armenia, as commanders on the spot), soon
escaped from central control and, like the sultan
himself, shifted as much of their military forces
as they could afford from tribal warriors to slaves
and mercenaries. The empire, almost at once, had
two parts, a core under the sultan's direct control and a periphery ruled indirectly by his amirs.
Parallel to this, the armed forces available to
the sultan consisted of a core of his own mercenaries and slaves supplemented by the tribal contingents owed by his amirs to whom he had granted
territories and revenues. Both the sultan and
his amirs shifted, as much as their resources
would allow, from tribal to slave contingents,
but, in both cases, they found it impossible to
stop the devolution of power downward to local
bases, the commanders on the spot. As early as
1072, the year after Manzikert, when Alp Arslan,
the second sultan, was killed by a prisoner of
war, he was accompanied by a bodyguard of two
thousand Mameluks.

The Seljuks were aware of these dangers. A
15th century Egyptian historian, al-Makrizi,
wrote that Nizam al-Mulk, in 1087, made military
appanages (ikta) hereditary, and this has been
repeated by most writers (such as Hitti, whose
knowledge of the eastern caliphate is very deficient), but the statement is almost certainly an
error. This did occur, but it was not desired
and was not sought, least of all by Nizam al-Mulk,

especially since he warned against it in the last year of his long life. In other ways, he sought to strengthen the central power. Two of these should be mentioned. The shurta, which we have seen were local militia serving as police forces in towns, were replaced by contingents of the sultan's regular army (shihna). This helped to disarm the townsmen further, a process which was already far advanced except in the more peripheral provinces such as Khurasan. This change may have provided some increase in the sultan's ability to prevent townsmen surrendering to invaders, but this restraint was of little importance, as the innovation was fully in accord with the Ghaznavid idea that townsmen should have nothing to do with politics or weapons and should not resist any invader but make the best deal they could if their nominal ruler could no longer protect them.

A second innovation of the Seljuks was closely associated with Nizam al-Mulk, although he was not by any means its inventor. This was the establishment of madrasas, schools of theological and legal studies, including the advanced levels, usually residential, with ample endowments of revenues to support students, teachers, and the necessary physical accessories of buildings and books. These were intended to be training institutions for religious, judicial, and government officials. Since they were organized on a Sunna basis and tended towards the Hanafite school of orthodoxy, they became a principal force in the subsequent alliance of rulers and Sunnite orthodoxy on a broader basis, such as is found under the later Seljuk and the Ottoman empire.

In the twelfth century, the process of disintegration continued, with the sultan reduced to a weak provincial ruler and the amirs increasingly dominated by their slave atabegs (military tutors and companions) who took over the government from the "legitimate" amirs just as the slave viziers had taken over from the Abbasid caliphs. Nizam al-Mulk had served as atabeg to Alp Arslan before the pupil became sultan and the tutor became vizier in 1063. In the 12th century, however, the process went much further, as the atabegs were slaves, generally attached to their pupils in childhood, who married the heir's mother and took the government almost completely from his control.

This process did not take place in the case of Sanjar, the ruler of Khurasan (1117-1157) and nominal suzerain of the Seljuk family. His whole reign was passed in an unsuccessful struggle against those who were, nominally and intermittently, his own vassals. These were the pagan Kara Khitai confederacy in central Asia, beyond the Jaxartes but often in control of major parts of Transoxiana, and the Khwarizmshahs whose home base was in Jand at the mouth of the Oxus; the third major threat was the Ghurid dynasty (1153-1206), a local family of central Khurasan which took over the remnants of the Ghaznavid empire. These three tormented Khurasan under Sanjar, inflicting an overwhelming defeat from the Kara Khitai in 1141, after which the Khwarizmshah devastated Khurasan. When Sanjar occupied Khorezmia in return, pagan Oghuz from the steppes overran Khurasan and in 1153 defeated Sanjar and held him prisoner with royal honors for three years. After Sanjar's death in 1157, the three rivals continued to fight over Khurasan, until a brief alliance of the Khwarizmshah with some of the Kara Khitai (who were always fighting among themselves) allowed the Khwarizmshah to defeat the Ghurids and force them into tributary status (1207). Three years later, in 1210, the Khwarizmshah attacked the fragmented Kara Khitai from the south, while powerful groups of Naimen and Merkits, fleeing from Jenghis Khan, attacked the Kara Khitai from the east. The Uighur, another of the Kara Khitai eastern vassals, wiser than the others and in a more exposed position, renounced their allegiance to the Kara Khitai and sent a delegation to Mongolia to accept the suzerainty of Jenghis Khan.

As a result of the processes I have described, the Seljuk empire, which had commenced its rise about 1037, was disintegrated by 1157, having fallen apart as it was being conquered. Its chief parts were the Great Seljuks of Persia (1037-1157),

795

the Seljuks of Iraq (1131-1194), the Seljuks of
Syria (1094-1117), and the Seljuks of Rum, who
divided and subdivided Anatolia from after the
battle of Manzikert in 1071 until about 1300.
In this last case, the sixth ruler divided his
territory among eleven sons (1188). These divisive processes allowed the Byzantine government
to survive in the west, permitted the Crusaders
to invade and hold on in the Levant, and allowed
the Khwarizmshahs, who started as Seljuk amirs
in 1072, to build their ramshackle empire in Iran
and Turkestan. In the Nearer East, the collapse
of the Seljuks allowed two new dynasties derived
from a Seljuk atabeg, the Zangids (1127-1174)
and the Ayyubids (the dynasty of Saladin, 1174-
1250), to recapture Jerusalem, to end the Fatimid
dynasty and caliphate, and to return the Levant
and Egypt to orthodox Sunnite observance. All of
these turned the Islamic world toward a new late
Islamic orientation of long-lasting Sunnite dynasties, the Mameluks (1250-1517) and the Ottoman
Turks (c. 1300-1922), but before these could be
established the Islamic east was devastated by a
pagan hurricane, the Mongols.

The shock of the Mongol conquests, (1202-1259)
has so dazzled observers that it is difficult, even
today, to see just what was done. It is now increasingly clear, however, that Jengis Khan (1167-
1227) did not invent any of the devices which made
these conquests possible. He simply brought together tools, organizations, and ideas which had
long existed on the steppes and elsewhere, and
welded them together, with his own genius and severe discipline, into a structure of overwhelming
power. His own contribution was his relentless
will, his extraordinary ability in picking his
subordinates, his eagerness to learn from any
source, his own excellent tactical ability, and
his skill in fusing the elements of his system together. He did not invent any of these elements,
as many historians seem to believe, but he did
bring older elements together, each at its peak,
into a terrifying power structure. Without Temuchin there would have been no Jenghis Khan and no
Mongol empire.

The materials from which Temuchin constructed

his empire go back to the earliest period of the grasslands and can be seen quite clearly in the Shang dynasty of China (1384-1122 B.C.), with its sky god, its great hunts, and its reflex bow. The Mandate of Heaven, which was the basis of Jenghis Khan's ideology, was brought into China from the grasslands by the Chou dynasty (1122-770 B.C.). Full nomadism, which was the basis of the mobility of the Mongol armies and thus of their military power, was established on the Mongolian grasslands in the first millennium B.C. The use of a decimal system for military organization on a relatively non-kinship basis was at least as old as the Khitan conquest of China (Liao dynasty, 907-1125) and had been passed on to Jenghis Khan by Jurchids who used it to overthrow the Khitans and set up the Chin dynasty of northern China and Inner Mongolia (1122-1234). It was these defeated Khitans, fleeing westward from the Jurchids, who set up the Kara Khitai confederacy of Turkestan (1130-1211) on the ruins of the Seljuk collapse. Even the Mongolian practice of a royal burial ground on a sacred mountain was to be found among the Khitan.

Thus at Temuchin's birth in 1167, the materials were available to construct a great military machine. The Mongols were a fully pastoral people, on a kinship basis, living on the grasslands and forest fringes between Lake Baikal and the Gobi Desert. They were culturally backward, with strong woodland and shamanist influences. This cultural backwardness contributed substantially to Mongol military success, since it accustomed them to physical hardships and deprivation and, at the same time, made them willing to learn from other cultures and to adopt any cultural items which might increase their power.

The area in which the Mongols arose has the most rigorous climate of any inhabited area of the globe, with great summer heat, intense winter cold, constant high winds, and inadequate rainfall. Nevertheless, the Mongols devised a way of life adapted to these hardships. Socially they were organized in kinship groups with great emphasis on genealogical information, often spurious, in spite of their constant mobility and polygamous, exogamous family life. This kinship system, however, could not stand prosperity, that is the establishment of any degree of security by a period of peace, or the fluctuations of rainfall which gave rise to periods of plentiful, followed by inadequate, grasses, and thus gave rise to increases of population beyond the average sustaining ability of the ecology. This led to violent warfare, as much within kinship groups and even families as between clans and tribes, tearing these kinship groups to shreds and making it possible to form larger and more desperate groups on the basis of personal loyalty to a leader. This process by which shattered kinship groups reorganized into multi-tribal groups based on personal loyalty (the "comitatus" of the Germans reported by Tacitus) was an old story on the northern grasslands, the most outstanding example being that of the Huns, who triggered the fall of both the Han empire of China and the Roman empire of the west in the third and fourth centuries A.D. The early experiences of Jenghis Khan show the opportunities offered to, and the hardships suffered by, an able individual in such a period of post-prosperity and kin-shattering crisis. Similar periods earlier had made possible the creation of nomadic military structures able to unify the steppes politically and even to conquer China south of the Great Wall on many occasions before Jenghis Khan achieved this feat. In fact the Great Wall had been constructed to prevent this, but had failed to do so several times in the 1450 years between the building of the wall and the Mongol conquest of China in 1234.

As Owen Lattimore pointed out, both the Chinese and the Mongols were locked into organizational patterns which periodically led to crisis and disaster, the Chinese labor-intensive alluvial agricultural system and the Mongolian mobility-centered pastoral system. The former led inevitably to overpopulation, crisis, famine, and political disruption, while the latter led, equally inevitably, to violence, disruption of kinship, supra-kinship political leadership, and nomadic empires. The way out of this cyclical grasslands system required the establishment of some non-nomadic system of security which would allow more sedentary occupation, more

798

intensive economic exploitation of resources
through mixed farming, hay gathering, localized
stock raising, and full exploitation of trading
with China and the wealth of the trans-Asian
caravan routes. After the Mongol collapse, in
the 14th-17th centuries, some steps were made in
this direction through a new social-economic structure based on a non-kinship pattern of Lamanism,
a celibate monastic religious system which restricted population and allowed some elements of
sedentary property control within the mobile pastoral kinship arrangements, but no fully successful patterns were worked out on the grasslands
themselves with the result that outsiders such
as the Manchu of China and the Russians, using
the post-1400 technological revolution I have
mentioned, have been able to dominate the grasslands until the present day. In this sense the
Mongolian conquest is one of the last in the
eastern grasslands, as the Ottoman Turks were
the last in the western grasslands, before the
grasslands had to yield to a superior non-grass-
lands technology. But this last development
took a long time, from after 1400 to about 1880.

Jenghis Khan was locked into the old cyclical pattern of pastoral nomadism, which made such
cyclical nomadic empires both possible and inevitable. The Mongols moved about in established
pasturage sequence, with each group following an
established alternation of fields and herds of
horses, cattle, and sheep, breaking up into smaller contingents and reassembling again, on a seasonal basis and in a high level of personal insecurity. Personal property had to be kept mobile,
and was thus largely in livestock and women, land
was not regarded as property while grazing rights
were and had to be protected by force organized
under "noble" leaders. Food was largely meat and
animal products, from hunting as well as herding,
with mobility insured by innumerable riding horses
and a variety of ox-drawn vehicles. Careful planning and good communications were essential to any
leader. Protection from the elements was obtained
in elaborate, windproof tents and enclosed vehicles, with clothing of furs and varied textiles,
including much use of felt (an Asiatic grassland
invention). Meat and furs were still obtained

from hunting, an activity which culminated in great annual "tribal" hunts in which wild animals over hundreds (and under Jenghis Khan, over thousands) of square miles were driven together into a narrow area and slaughtered. Religion was of the ancient grasslands kind, animistic with strong shamanistic elements, an Asiatic woodland trait, supplemented by grasslands anthropomorphic deities of which the chief was Mongke Tengri ("Everlasting Sky"). This last was the "Heaven" (Tien) of ancient China and the dyess, "Bright Sky" (that is zeus or deus) of the earliest Indo-Europeans. This sky god was the providential deity whose commands motivated the Mongol conquests, just as "Mandates of Heaven" changed dynasties in China. The earth and running water were also sacred to the Mongols, as all three had been to the Seljuks.

The Mongol version of providential empire is most clearly stated in their orders in 1245-1255 to various rulers, including Pope Innocent IV and Saint Louis, King of France, to submit to Mongol rule on the grounds that refusal to do so was equivalent to defiance of the will of Heaven and was punishable by total destruction at the hands of the Great Khan, who was Heaven's representative on earth. The order of Heaven, yasa, was that the earth and everything on it was the property of the Mongol imperial family and that all rulers were bound to submit to their rule. Military action, no matter how cruel, was not illegal but was, on the contrary, an obligation placed on the Mongols by Heaven and was to be regarded as legal punitive action on those who rebel against God. As the fourth Great Khan, Mongke (1251-1259) wrote to Saint Louis, "The commandment of the Eternal Heaven is: in Heaven, only one Eternal God; on earth, only one ruler, Jenghis Khan, the son of Heaven."

At the first great conclave (kuriltai) of Mongol leaders in 1206, where Temujin, having conquered all of Mongolia, proclaimed himself supreme ruler, that is, Jenghis Khan, the new leader announced, "Heaven has given me the empire of the earth from east to west; whoever submits shall be spared, but those who resist shall be destroyed with their wives, children, and dependents."

This intellectual conviction of religious mission provided the cohesive and motivating power which erected the greatest territorial empire in history. The early khans and their followers sincerely believed their theories. The army provided the mechanism for assembling this empire, and the traditions of the Mongols themselves provided the self-disciplined mobility which made these incredible victories possible. All these were fused together by Jenghis Khan in the first decade of the thirteenth century.

Like many great leaders and conquerors, Temujin started life with few advantages, a poor orphan from a shattered family with few animals, in a society where kinship and large herds were the basis of all influence. But Temujin used these handicaps as incentives to develop a relentless drive, active intelligence, native shrewdness, and inspiring personality which won him the loyalty and confidence of other men who were willing to risk their lives, families, and herds to carry out his orders. On this basis, Temujin built up a following which allowed him to surprise and destroy in battle Toghrul Khan, the chief Chinese vassal among the Mongol nomads, who had but recently been Temujin's lord and protector. The victory over the Keraits under Toghrul was followed by a great victory over the Naimans, followed by the almost total destruction of the Tatars. These victories in 1202-1205 made Temujin the most significant leader among the Mongols, brought thousands of his fellow warriors to his standard, and allowed him to overcome all dissent in the country. On this basis he made himself supreme leader in 1206.

During this period, Temujin had reorganized the Mongolian military forces, superimposing a rational, flexible yet centralized, command system over the kinship structure of Mongolian society. Later, in the period 1206-1210, he diversified the weapons system by the addition of a highly organized engineering corps and siege train recruited from the Chinese at first, later from Muslims, and by large numbers of non-Mongols, both

as cavalry and as infantry units for mass assaults
in the opening phases of attack on fortifications
or on enemy field forces in a pitched battle.

The Mongol cavalry were organized in the
decimal system of tens, hundreds, and thousands
up to 10,000 (tumen) in a unit. As far as possible, these units reflected kinship groups and
national origins, but the essence of the system
was opposed to kinship or local considerations.
Each unit was assigned pasturage for its remounts
and much of its manpower on a quota basis. An
imperial guard, originally of a thousand but soon
increased to 10,000, accompanied the ruler; it
was recruited from nobles of all clans and operated
as a kind of military training school from which
commanders and staff officers were assigned to any
unit or task. These men remained under the ruler's
direct control and could be given orders but never
be punished by their immediate superiors in any task.

Universal service, both military or civil, was
imposed on all Mongols; they had to serve without
question, and without pay, wherever assigned.
Weapons remained very much what they had been
for almost a thousand years in Asia, except for
minor changes, but the very best of each item,
especially in engineering techniques, siege tactics, and improved missile weapons, including pyro-
technic devices, were adopted. The chief innovations in military organization were in such relatively accessory matters as intelligence, communications, planning, and logistics; but it
was these accessories, joined to the distinctive
Mongol features of mobility, personal toughness,
and discipline which made the difference. These
all reached such perfection that contemporaries
were astounded to see achievements previously regarded as impossible treated as almost routine by
the Mongols.

The Mongol armies could survive wherever
there was fodder and could move for up to ten
days without stopping for a meal or without
lighting a fire, the men surviving on dried
rations and in a final emergency drinking blood
from their horses, as the Huns had done a thousand years before. Where traditional Mongol no-

madism aspired to at least four horses for each
man, since horses were ridden only every fourth
day, Jenghis Khan's cavalry sometimes had up to
twenty horses for each man. These horses, it is
said, were so trained to voice commands and
against straying that up to thirty would follow
each rider without being tied.

Military operations were carefully planned
and carried out on a gigantic scale such as was
not seen again until Hitler's attack on Russia in
1941. The forces moved rapidly, in widely separated
columns, accompanied by their engineering and siege
trains, converging suddenly on their chosen target.
A military commander today would despair of moving forces of up to fifty or a hundred thousand
on an enemy over two thousand miles away, across
an unknown country, without maps, but the Mongols
did this frequently. Moving so quickly and coming
from several directions, preceded by alarmist reports of enormous numbers moving on widely dispersed lines, the enemy were baffled and gave in
to panic. The chief key to these operations was
good planning and, above all, remarkable communications. Mounted courier services gathered intelligence about terrain and enemy forces for
centralized evaluation, and the moving columns
were coordinated by constant interchange of messages. The speed of their advance was increased
by the fact that the great burden of camp followers and baggage which made up the major part of
Asiatic armies in this period were lacking in
these early Mongol aggressions, as they had been
lacking in the early Arab attacks in the mid-
seventh century.

I cannot resist making a comparison of the
Mongol abilities as just described with the campaign of King Edward III of England against a
force of invading Scots exactly a hundred years
after the death of Jenghis Khan. On July 20, 1327
Edward "lost" both the Scots and his own baggage
train, the former for a period of ten days and
the baggage for twenty days; in both cases the
missing objects were found at the same places
they had been seen last, and Edward over the
intervals had never been farther away from either
than 30 miles.

Mongol tactics owed a good deal to the "Great Hunts" (<u>battue</u>) which had been a part of east Asian grasslands life since before 1200 B.C. (in Shang China). In the Mongol imperial period, these hunts continued as military training maneuvers in the winter season. In these, animals over thousands of square miles were rounded up into a ring of warriors about ten miles in diameter and held until the emperor gave the signal to kill them. Any man who allowed a beast to escape was executed, we are told. As they reached their climax, these <u>battue</u> were not interrupted by night, food, or rest. The hunt of the winter of 1221, when Jenghis Khan was in his fifty-fourth year, lasted four months.

There were four chief parts to these Mongol armies: (1) light cavalry armed with composite bows with over 100 pound pull and an effective range of over 200 yards; (2) heavy cavalry armed with sabers, lances, battle-axes, and even lassos, wearing helmets and cuirasses of leather originally, but later with considerable use of iron helmets and scale armor; (3) engineers, originally Chinese but later Iranian, and finally Egyptian, according to B. Spuler; and (4) large masses of auxiliaries, including defeated peoples and war captives of local origins, who were forced into mass assaults on enemy forces.

The sources speak of Mongol armies of hundreds of thousands or even millions of men and horses and use the same range of figures when dealing with enemy casualties and massacres of captives. It is very difficult to evaluate such numbers. On the whole, while the atrocities inflicted by the Mongols may approach the lower ranges of these numbers, there can be no doubt that the Mongol forces were considerably smaller than the source figures. The period of Mongol conquests from Temujin's installation as supreme ruler (1206) to the disputed election and civil war of 1259-1264 between the surviving brothers following Mongke's death covered only half a century, that is two generations. It was preceded and followed by periods in which Mongols were busy killing each other. On that basis, the population of the Mongols could not have increased in numbers to provide hundreds of thousands of fighters even if we accept that the much larger forces of the later conquest period were mostly non-Mongols for ordinary soldiers and used the Mongols chiefly as officers. The casualties suffered by the Mongols themselves and the deaths they inflicted on their victims limited the size of their forces from either source. On the whole, the total population of Mongolia in modern times has been less than a million, of which the major part have been women and children. Thus it is unlikely that the Mongol combatants in the conquests ever rose much above a hundred thousand in any single campaign. The non-Mongols cannot be estimated; originally very few, they increased in numbers steadily and by 1259 certainly outnumbered the Mongols themselves by a wide margin. When we consider that the Mongols conquered from Korea (1231) to the Adriatic Sea (1241) in this period and sacked Hanoi and Baghdad in the same year (1258), with armies operating simultaneously thousands of miles apart, it is clear that no single army had millions or even a hundred thousand Mongols.

The Mongol military experience is of considerable interest in connection with our subject, since it was, in a sense, a system which was able to overcome previous limitations on geographical extent but was unable to overcome previous limitations on temporal duration. In regard to the former, I have made reference to the difficulties experienced by political systems in crossing natural ecological boundaries. Thus the Romans had been unable to cope with deserts, areas of heavy forest or deep winter snows, just as they had not been able to deal with areas which had to be controlled by non-oared sea power. In the same way, Islamic civilization operated most successfully across grasslands and had great difficulties in establishing and maintaining control of mountainous areas or those subjected to seasons of winter freezing (or summer growing). The difficulty with mountains can be seen in the continuous resistance of the Berbers of the Magreb, but above all in the ability of the schismatic Ismaili, in the Order of the Assassins, in holding out in their mountain fortresses across Iran, Iraq, and Syria in the period 1090-1256. Although the various Muslim rulers of the Near East tried to destroy these strongholds, and did succeed occasionally in capturing one of them, they were not able to eliminate the group. The Mongols, on the contrary, under Hulagu, the grandson of Jenghis Khan, were able to destroy the Assassins completely in a systematic campaign which included a three-year siege of the chief Assassin stronghold at Alamut in the Elburz Mountains south of the Caspian Sea (1253-1256).

The Mongols were able to deal with any ecological situation including tropical forest, as in Indochina, the highly cultivated and urbanized areas of China and the Near East, the mountains of Armenia and the Caucasus, and even the icy snows of "General Winter" in Russia. Their greatest achievement from this point of view was the winter campaign of 1237-1238 which conquered Russia under the conditions of ice and cold which later defeated Napoleon and Hitler in the same area. The famous Russian Prince Alexander Nevsky, who defeated the Swedes and the Teutonic Knights in 1240 and 1242, had to submit to the Mongols, starting their domination of Russia for almost two centuries. In the same campaign which conquered Russia, the Mongols defeated the Poles, Hungarians, Romanians, Serbs, Albanians, and Bulgars, crossing the Balkans to the Adriatic shore but withdrew from most of these areas to attend the kuriltai called after the death of Ogodei, the second Great Khan, in December 1241. Almost equally impressive were the campaigns of the second half of the thirteenth century, when the Mongol leaders were already fighting one another (after 1268). North China (Chin empire) was crushed and annexed in 1234, but South China (Southern Sung empire) was not beaten until 1279. In the interval, the Mongols surrounded the Sung territory on the west, passing south across Szechwan, Kwei-chow, and Yunnan (Nan Chao empire, annexed in 1253) into southeast Asia, where they invaded Burma and Indochina three times between 1257 and 1300. Although they won great victories in that area, sacked Hanoi in 1258, and reduced the whole region to tributary status, they did not annex the various states because of tropical diseases and uncertain food supplies, which made permanent garrisons inadvisable. In the course of these Far Eastern operations, the Mongols found

the one ecological zone they could not handle
with success, the sea. Attacks on Japan in
1274 and again in 1281 and an invasion of Java
in 1292 showed that the Mongol forces could land
on distant shores but could not keep an invasion
army supplied, suffering unbearable losses of
men and ships from storms.

At the death of Kublai Khan (1259-1294), the
suzerainty of the Great Khan over the other Mongol
rulers became only nominal or was ignored. At
that time there were four such governments. The
territories of the Great Khan were from the Altai
Mountains east to the Yellow and South China Seas,
and from Lake Baikal south to Tonkin. West of
this from the Altai Mountains west to the Jaxartes
River, and from Lake Balkash south to the Hindu
Kush Mountains, was the empire of Jaghatai, second
son of Jenghis Khan. In western Asia was the Ilkhan empire of Kublai Khan's brother Hulegu; it
was bounded by the Jaxartes River and central Syria, extending from the Black Sea, the Caucasus,
and the Aral Sea southward to the Persian Gulf.
The fourth division was the empire of the Golden
Horde, controlled by the Kipchak Khans descended
from the oldest of Jenghis Khan's sons, Jochi;
it stretched from the Altai Mountains west to the
borders of Romania and Hungary and north as far
as the sources of the Dnieper and Volga Rivers.
This included the Kirghiz steppes and Russia beyond Moscow, including the Ukraine. It was ruled
from Sarai just east of the lower Volga.

These Mongol khanates lasted relatively briefly,
gradually disintegrating into the hands of their
military subordinates like most governments of
this period. The Yuan dynasty of China lasted
from 1260 to 1368; the Ilkhans from 1256 to 1349;
the Jaghatai khanate from 1266 to 1360; and the
Golden Horde from 1237 to after 1400.

In the east, under Kublai Khan, economic
prosperity was excellent because the Great Khan
adopted the traditional Chinese administration to
encourage both trade and agriculture, but in western Asia, especially Turkestan and Iraq, economic
life never recovered from the Mongol attacks.

807

In Iraq the Mongol rulers could not keep up
the irrigation and desalinization operations needed
for the success of agriculture in that ancient land,
and the trade of the Far East by way of the Indian
Ocean and the Euphrates was diverted overland by
way of the Silk Road to the Black Sea. In Iran
and Turkestan the Ilkhan empire was injured almost as badly as Iraq, since its previous prosperity
had depended as much on its skilled craftsmen and
active city life of places like Bokhara as it had
depended on long distance commerce. But the great
cities of Turkestan and Khurasan had been sacked
and their populations massacred and enslaved.
Most of the cities were slowly rebuilt, but the
population and especially their skills could not
be replaced easily. Some cities, like Ray, were
never rebuilt, and elsewhere the devastation of
the original conquest was still to be seen a
century later. I.P. Petrushevsky of Leningrad,
who has made a specialized study of this subject,
claims that Iran suffered a drastic decline of
prosperity in 1220-1296, with a mild recovery,
especially in agriculture, in 1295-1335 (apparently from a somewhat reformed tax system),
but this was followed by another sharp decline
which included a considerable regression from a
commercial economy to a self-subsistence one and
a very great increase in nomadism, which had never
been prevalent in Iran. As a result, the district
of Herat, which had about 400 settled villages in
the tenth century, had only 167 about 1400, while
the tax yield from 17 Iran districts decreased
from over 100 million dinars before the Mongol
conquest to less than 20 million in 1335-1340.

Much of this decline in prosperity was based
on the exploitative character of the Mongol successor governments, but most governments of the
providential monarchical type were exploitative.
The real damage from the Mongols, which was permanent, came from the original destruction of
artifacts and human capital and the considerable
shift back to extensive nomadism from intensive
craftsmanship, as well as the damage to water
control systems over much of western Asia. At
the beginning of the twentieth century, recovery
from nomadism or semi-nomadism to more sedentary

economic activities was still in process among such peoples as the Iranians, the Kurds, and the Pushtu of Afghanistan.

It is worth noting that a similar destruction of a higher level of agricultural and commercial activity also occurred in much of North Africa, from Egypt west to Morocco, in the eleventh century. The Fatimids had moved from Tunis to Egypt in 969, leaving a Berber dynasty, the Zirids, in charge of Tunisia. When the Zirids renounced Fatimid suzerainty in 1047, the latter unleashed on the west two Bedouin tribes, of Arabic origin and of fanatical beliefs, the Banu Hilat and the Banu Sulaim. These had been harassing the Egyptian frontier for decades. Diverted westward, they devastated North Africa and, as G.E. von Grunebaum put it, "caused an economic catastrophe from which North Africa has not recovered to this day. The Arab as destroyer, responsible for the century-long decline of North Africa, is an image which still dominates the historical picture of Ibn Khaldun (c. 1377) more than 300 years later and the travel reports of the late Middle Ages." This increased nomadism in both Asia and North Africa forms the background for the rise of the Ottoman Turks in these places after 1300.

We may sum up the reasons for Mongol military success in half a dozen points: (1) their hardened Mongolian background of self-disciplined mobility; (2) their conviction of a religious mission; (3) their incredible military discipline; (4) their excellent planning, intelligence, communications, and supply; (5) their readiness to use foreign personnel and foreign methods to remedy their own backwardness, especially in engineering, siege techniques, and administration; and (6) their dispersed advance and rapid concentration for battle, which exaggerated their own numbers, demoralized their opponents, and confused defensive tactics. Three points are worth repeating. At a time when most armies consisted of a fighting contingent smothered in an enormous mass of non-combatants, camp followers, and baggage animals, the Mongol armies were almost completely made up of fighting men (although Jenghis Khan took along his women). Secondly these men were eager to fight, not only from their strong convictions but also because they were unpaid and were rewarded only by sharing in the booty. Yet thirdly, discipline was so high that individual looting was punishable by death, and all plunder was gathered together and divided by the leaders after the battle and pursuit was ended.

The Mongol system was the ultimate in mobile warfare, but it was also the last word in providential empire, almost totally submerging the kinship groups in the higher organizational structure. This can be seen in its cosmopolitanism, which used specialized abilities of any persons in any way that could serve the system, regardless of their language, ethnic origin, or religion, so long as they submitted to the Great Khan. It can also be seen in the Mongol encouragement of Asia-wide commerce and of scholarly activities which were likely to weaken kinship and were incompatible with pastoralism and ethnocentricity.

The providential nature of this empire can be seen in the theory of government on which it was based, namely ownership by the imperial family as a private patrimony freely disposable by the Great Khan. Boris Vladimirtsov saw the Mongol empire in these terms and emphasized that the Mongol clans had little role in the great assemblies, the kuriltai, and that these in turn had little power beyond the ratification of the wishes of the Supreme Ruler, as was done when it accepted Jenghis Khan's choice of his third son as his successor (1229). This choice indicates the lack of any rule of succession, either in public law or in the private law of patrimonial inheritance, so typical of providential empire. Only when the empire became so widespread that it became difficult for the kuriltai to know on whom Heaven's choice had fallen, did this assembly take action on its own in selecting a Great Khan (1259). In this case it was not seeking to become an independent power in the government itself but was puzzled as to where Heaven's mandate pointed. When the great area of the Mongol conquests broke up into separate khanates, as it did following the death of Kublai Khan (1259-1294), who had ruled from Peking, each of the separate

systems was ruled by its leader as a providential
governing system. The processes at work here were
the same as those which weakened and disintegrated
other providential empires like the caliphate,
the Seljuk, and their successors, and which were
operating in the Byzantine empire and in the Norman
empire of Naples and Sicily. The same processes,
as we shall see, operated in the dynasties of
China, in the Ottoman empire, in the Carolingian
empire of Europe, in Czarist Russia, in the Mogul
empire of India (1526-1761), and in the Safavid
dynasty of Persia (1500-1736). In the later examples, after 1400, new factors based on technological and organizational innovations made it
possible to preserve the governmental system over
wide areas for much longer periods. The chief of
these innovations was gunpowder, although it must
be recognized that other influences were also
present, and some of these were also extending
the durability of dynasties before the arrival
of guns. This can be seen in the Mameluk dynasty
of Egypt (1250-1517), which resolutely refused to
use guns and was destroyed by the Ottoman Turks
who accepted them.

(blank page 812, intentionally omitted)

1.   The Roots of Western Civilization, A.D. 600-900

The period covered by the previous chapter was
dominated by power systems framed by weapons on one
side and the ideology of providential deity on the
other side. On the weapons side, we had two systems,
the one associated with a stronghold capable of controlling bundles of revenues, derived either from
the agricultural activities of sedentary peasantry
or from the imposition of tolls upon passing merchants, and, on the other side, the mobile horseman,
whose ability to control bundles of revenue was
limited but whose ability to conquer wide areas was
considerable. The precarious interplay of these
two weapons systems, one largely defensive, the
other almost entirely offensive, and each almost
incapable of defeating the other, would have provided little political stability were it not for
the influence of providential deity, which did act
as a stabilizing influence in one sense, while acting in a very unstable way in a different sense.
The stabilizing influence of providential monarchy
came from the fact that it provided a means by which
a political structure could be extended over very
diverse peoples. In doing this, it provided, like
the archaic monarchy which preceded it, a transitional stage between political systems based on kinship (which must always be limited in scope) and the
more abstract political arrangements based on allegiance to a sovereign state. It also provided a
legitimizing influence for the rule of mobile cavalry
forces over the wide areas which such forces could
conquer. But even as providential monarchy did these
things in a stabilizing direction, it provided considerable elements of instability from the fact
that it saw the deity as a figure of power and will
and not as a figure of goodness and law, and thus,
in a very practical way, it encouraged usurpers to
try to shift "the mandate of heaven" from the ruler
to themselves. Above all, by making events on
earth subject to the deity's will and whim, it
prevented the acceptance of any rule of law and
opened the way to rule by force. Specifically it

discouraged any rules of succession, thus providing
a dispute every time a ruler died. In a lesser
way, the legitimization of force by the ideology of
providential monarchy was an obstacle to the growth
of a more sophisticated idea of the state as a
structure of public power because it saw the ruler's
rights as patrimonial, a procession, rather than as
an abstract authority or as a corporate entity capable of survival by its own organizational qualities,
regardless of men who may come and go, be born, succeed to office, and pass from office by death or
resignation. In fact, the idea of an office as
distinct from the man who may hold it was not something which many of the subjects of providential empire could grasp, any more than they could grasp
the idea of law as distinct from a command. For
these reasons, this complex balance between weapons
and ideology, with the political patterns arising
from the interrelations between them, held mankind,
for more than a thousand years, in what may be regarded as a transitional stage in man's search for
common defense and domestic tranquility.

As we have seen, this transitional stage extended across the Old World landmass, from the
China seas to the Bay of Biscay and the North Sea's
shores. It varied greatly across this distance,
and varied from one place to another throughout this
extent, but, on the whole, its patterns were similar from the northern forests to the southern seas,
except where mountains seriously restricted cavalry
mobility. The key to such exceptional areas was
in the hampering influence of forests and mountains
on the mobility of applied force. For these reasons,
but especially because of the forest, Europe was not
adapted to the control of mobile horsemen nor to the
rule of providential monarchy. As a consequence,
Europe, since A.D. 850, has had a historical experience totally different from that of neighboring
areas, just as, for different reasons, the Far East,
in Chinese civilization, has had a different
experience.

In examining the different historical experience of western civilization, we must understand
the situation in which this experience took place.
The destruction of classical civilization in the
period A.D. 300-600 changed the Mediterranean Sea

from the vertebrate backbone of a civilized society
to a disputed frontier between several civilized
societies. Four new civilizations emerged from
the wreckage of Rome, which was the universal empire of classical civilization. These were: Byzantine civilization, 300-1453; Islamic civilization, from about 600 to after the destruction of
the universal empire; Ottoman Turkey, in 1922;
Slavic civilization, from about 800, still continuing following the destruction of the Tsarist empire in 1917; and western civilization, from
about 500, and still continuing. All four are
offspring of classical civilization, although
Slavic civilization has not had the Mediterranean
Sea as a frontier.

The transformation of the Mediterranean from
the core of a civilization to a disputed area between civilizations has given it a distinctive
character which makes it impossible to attribute
it as a culture area to any civilization. It has
remained since 700 an area with distinctive cultural characteristics of shattered loyalties, so
that I have called it, in previous writings, "the
Pakistani-Peruvian Axis," since its special characteristics are along a line from Sind to Peru.

Although the three civilizations of Byzantium,
Islam, and Russia are distinct cultural entities,
they have all retained the basic characteristics
of providential empire. Western civilization, on
the contrary, has not, except, perhaps, as a dangerous heresy. This is one of the reasons that
western society has continued to grow in wealth
and power, while two of the others have perished
as organized socio-cultural entities, the Byzantine
civilization completely, with some help from western power, although Islamic Turkish power gave the
final blow. Islamic civilization has also been
destroyed, largely by western power, although its
peoples and shattered cultural patterns still lie
as wreckage on the ground. Slavic civilization
still survives, although much of its existence has
been passed under the threat of destruction by
western power, a situation which still continues.
Western civilization, of the four descendants of
classical civilization, also continues as the most
powerful and affluent society in the world today,

although it must be admitted that it shows its age, along with the scars and wounds of its several lives.

The key to the unique experience of western civilization lies in the fact that it was able to shake off, almost completely, its providential monarchical influences and was, thus, forced to find a different form of social structure. This distinctive organizational pattern of western society has been much studied by ourselves and others seeking the key to its strengths and uniqueness, but without any agreement on what these characteristics are. The explanation to be offered in this book will not obtain general agreement, but I feel sure we may begin with agreement that our western civilization began to follow the same road to providential monarchy as our sibling societies, but that, in the dark age of the 9th and 10th centuries, our western society failed in its attempt to organize a providential empire and was embarked upon a different course by the year 1000. At this point in our story, I shall not try to show the direction of that course, but shall restrict our attention to the abortive Carolingian effort to establish a western providential empire, especially in regard to the weapons element in that effort.

The attempt by the Merovingian and Carolingian Franks to establish a providential empire in the West, parallel to the Byzantine empire in the East, began in the late fifth century and collapsed in the late ninth century. On the weapons side, it was an effort to reestablish the Roman imperial military structure under such different ecological, institutional, and ideological conditions that it failed. The military failure consisted of a loss of weapons, and of the organizational framework of these weapons, so that sea power, siege trains, artillery, infantry forces, missile weapons, logistics capability, and most military technology disappeared, leaving the West with little more than two weapons, the armored spearman on horseback and the fortified stronghold. From about 900 to almost 1200, western Europe's military and political affairs operated within the framework of the knight, the castle, and the relationships between these which we call feudalism.

816

In recent years, there has been considerable controversy among historians about these matters, especially about the role of Charles Martel in the advant of the medieval knight and feudalism. In fact, our historical evidence is so scanty that we cannot say with any assurance when any single element in a very complex transformation occurred or who was responsible for it. The attempt to do so will inevitably result in controversy among scholars, especially when they assume that great historical changes occur in revolutionary fashion as a consequence of conscious decisions by specific individuals. That is not the way in which fundamental historical changes occur. On the contrary, significant historical changes generally happen as gradual shifts in relationships among numerous factors without any single key decision by anyone and certainly without any conscious decision by any ruler who saw what he wanted and foresaw the consequences of his decisions.

The development of the knight had little to do with the rise and fall of the Carolingian attempt at providential empire and had only partially emerged when that empire began to fall in 829. On the other hand, the chief weapon of the medieval world, the castle, had a great deal to do with the rise and decline of the Carolingian system. This "rise" was associated with a great improvement in ability to capture fortified strongholds, an improvement associated rather closely with the Carolingian family, while the decrease in this ability in the period from 814 until after 1000 was associated with the collapse of this system and with the long-term economic depression of A.D. 250-950.

The belief that the armored knight was a medieval, or post-classical, invention (say, 300-900) is completely mistaken and is accompanied by other widespread errors: that the knight was an effective weapon or that it was necessary for the West to adopt this weapon in order to defend itself against mobile invaders. These beliefs are untrue. The fully armored mounted lancer had been used as a weapon at least since 200 B.C. (the Sarmatians). Moreover, as I have indicated, such a fighter was not much of a success against

either mounted archers or mobile seaborne raiders
(Vikings), and his attacks could be frustrated by
any solid mass of infantry, especially spearmen,
a fact made clear by the Roman cohorts on many occasions in the past and to be demonstrated to perfection by the Swiss against Burgundian chivalry
in the 14th and 15th centuries later. The chief
weakness of such infantry against mounted lancers
or knights was that the knights could use their
mobility to evade infantry and could be beaten
only if they attacked them, which they did not
need to do. The most effective weapon against
mounted invaders of any kind would have been
mounted archers with composite bows and some
shock weapon such as lance, saber, or mace.

It is, of course, true that the diffusion
into Europe from the East of stirrups, horseshoes,
improved saddles, a stronger horse (destrier), and
even spurs, all contribured to more effective cavalry in this period 700-950, but the interrelations
among these items and the problem of military defense have not been understood by most historians.
These items were acquired in Europe west of the
Elbe only slowly and after about A.D. 600, with
the stirrup probably the first, but even this
was still largely unknown in the Carolingian empire in the 9th century. The earliest picture
we have of a stirrup in the West seems to be on
the Sant' Ambrogio gold altar in Milan (about
840), while the earliest example of an actual
stirrup is from a grave in a Lombard cemetery
near Vicenza, Italy, which could be about 50
years earlier. The fact that these two early
examples are from Italy, rather than from
north of the Alps, may indicate that the stirrup
came west (or at least came to Italy) from the
Levant, where it was known in the 8th century,
rather than from central Europe, where it had
been introduced directly from the Far East by
the Avars about 562. Stirrups were known in
China and Korea in the fifth century.

In any case, the dating of the advent of the
stirrup in the West has been much overemphasized.
It was, in no sense, a cause of the "rise" of the
medieval knight, and it is quite untrue to pretend
that cavalry lancers could not be used until the

arrival of the stirrup, or that, without the stirrup, the early Middle Ages would have adopted some other weapons system than the knight. Above all, it is a total error to believe that the Christian West could not have defended itself against "barbarians" or invaders like the Saracens, Lombards, or Vikings without stirrups. Stirrups always make men more secure on a horse, but they are of little significance between mounted lancers when both men lack them or both have them, since, in the one case, both are equally unstable, while, in the second case, the increase in stability is on both sides and the net result is simply to increase the degree of shock, without providing any advantage to either. It is true that stirrups improve the rider's power in respect to infantry spearmen, but the degree of that increase is much less than one might expect, since the spearman met the lancer's shock by placing the end of his spear against the ground, and can meet any increase in shock by making the infantry spear heavier, into a pike, as the Swiss did in the 14th century.

Thus the real advantage of the acquisition of stirrups was not against other lancers but against infantry. But the stirrup did play a very great role in helping a rider to mount his horse; with stirrups, the knight could step up, rather than having to leap up as he had to do before stirrups. This advantage continued to increase, as the rider's armor became heavier, since this required a larger and stronger horse. Heavier armor and a taller horse made "leaping" onto the horse impossible. It is worthy of note that heavier armor was not the consequence of increased shock from enemy lancers, but, as is usual with armor (but not with helmets), was a response to danger from missiles.

The missiles which threatened medieval knights and led to heavier armor until the end of the Middle Ages did not come from enemy cavalry but from low-born infantry, at first from self bows, later from crossbows, and still later from the earliest firearms. These could be used by people on foot who were not soldiers but still were a real danger to knights. It is worthy of note that three kings of England were killed by missiles before one was killed by shock (in 1485). Similarly, in the second battle of Lincoln (1217), the only known casualty, the Count of Perche, was hit by a crossbow bolt fired from a roof through his open visor.

Here we must introduce into the story of the "rise" of the medieval knight a much neglected factor: the relationship between weapons and the developing class structure. The division of European peoples into separate classes of warriors and peasants made it essential that the fighting class ensure a flow of supplies from the producers to themselves. This need unquestionably played a significant role in any decisions about weapons as the protracted economic depression continued to deepen in the 9th and 10th centuries. Most historians continue to repeat the myth that the knight developed from the need to defend Europe against intruders like the Avars, the Magyars, the Saracens, and the Vikings. All these suggested enemies were fighters with missiles, specifically archery, and a mounted lancer, either with or without stirrups, is not very effective against archery, as the Hundred Years War clearly showed. Against such enemies composite bows would have been much more effective, but these vanished from western Europe in the 9th century, just as the mounted spearman became the predominant weapon of the area. Of course, composite bows are much more expensive than spears and require much more care and practice. This question of cost may well have played a role in the loss of the bow and the emergence of the spear, just as what I have called the European shock tradition may have played a similar role. But there can be no doubt that there was a third factor present: that mounted spearmen could play a role in police control of peasants to compel them to supply food, other produce, and labor to build a fortified residence for the rider, even when the peasant had to live in a hut which lacked floor, windows, or heat. Without such a diversion of incomes from producers to fighters, there would have been no medieval society and might have been no western civilization (at least not in the form in which we know it). But the decision to control peasant resources with the spear and from horseback exposed the knight to danger from arrows from peasant archers under cover (for peasants still retained selfbows, as a result of which there was a struggle throughout the Middle Ages to prevent peasants from using such bows to kill game which the lord wished to reserve for himself). Body armor for knights was a response largely to this danger. An incidental consequence of this situation was the great prejudice against the bow on a class basis on the continent (much less so in England).

Other factors also entered into this situation. A composite bow, the only kind which could be used on horseback, was likely to be injured by the high humidity and frequent rainfall of western Europe, but this would not have been a decisive reason for preferring the spear, since the crossbow, which became common after 1000 as a military weapon, was constructed with a composite bow until this was replaced by a steel bow after 1370. It is worth noting that many efforts were made to outlaw the crossbow in the 12th century, and it generally remained a lower-class weapon, used by mercenary infantry.

One other factor in this choice might be made. Any bow requires the use of two hands and is thus difficult on horseback, while a spear could be used by one hand. Since armor was very expensive and armor capable of stopping missiles was almost unobtainable in the early period (to about 1300), a rider would prefer a spear, which would leave one hand free either for holding a shield or for controlling his horse. It is significant that the use of the shield dwindled as armor became heavier, especially with the shift from chain mail to plate armor after 1300.

Changes in fortifications and in siege techniques were at least as important as changes in other weapons and were reflected in a fluctuating ability to capture strongholds. As we have seen, the Roman ability to do this was high for most of their history, increasing substantially with the development of artillery after 300 B.C. and possibly reaching its peak in the early imperial period, as displayed in the capture of Jerusalem and the siege of Masada. There can be little doubt that Roman artillery began to decline in effectiveness in the 3rd century. Ammianus Marcellinus was very critical of the deficiencies in knowledge of defensive siege tactics of two Gallic legions at Amida in A.D. 359 (xix.5.2). As I have indicated, the barbarians were no real threat to Roman fortifications from this point of view, since they had no equipment nor knowledge of siege techniques, and their efforts in this direction were "laughable," according to Procopius. Their successes in this line came from surprise, treachery, or storming the walls when these were much undermanned, as they often were. Because of the tradition that a town which resisted would be sacked and its population killed or enslaved, the inhabitants of many towns preferred to surrender without resistance after A.D. 400. It mattered less to the inhabitants who their rulers were than the fact that an early surrender could save their lives. This view was widespread in the sixth century.

Even when the barbarians could not take a town, they could not be stopped from wandering about in the countryside, or even from settling there permanently, and thus the urban centers of the West came under their control. The great decrease in urban population between the 3rd century, when many town walls were built, and the fifth century, when the real barbarian threat came, meant that most cities lacked the manpower to man or even to maintain their walls. In the next few centuries, as urban populations continued to decrease, the walls were retracted to enclose a smaller and more easily held perimeter, but in the interval from the 5th to the 10th century, most towns were sacked at least once, and many were captured several times.

We have, of course, no reliable figures on population, but we can say with assurance that it decreased drastically after A.D. 300 and that the population of cities was reduced even more steeply than the total population. M.K. Bennett in The World's Food (1954) has given rough estimates of Europe's total population, decreasing from 67 million in A.D. 200 to 27 million in 700, rising then to 42 million about 1000, then slowly increasing thereafter to 73 million in 1300, down again to 45 million in 1400, followed by a slow recovery to 69 million in 1500, an increase which has continued erratically ever since, except for a substantial dip in the first half of the 17th century. Thus

the population of Europe was at about the same peak
in 200, 1300, and 1500, but fell to less than half
that peak in the 8th century, after the epidemics
of the 740s, and fell again to about 60 per cent of
that peak after the Black Death of the 1340s.
These changes for Europe as a whole were greatly
exceeded by the changes in urban populations,
which must have decreased over 90 per cent in the
period 200 to 800.

The problems of siege warfare which resulted
from these changes can be seen clearly in the
futility of the Ostrogoths, the most advanced
of the Germans, who had been in close touch with
Rome for several centuries, in their year-long
siege of Rome in 537-538, as described by Procopius.
Although Belisarius had only 5000 soldiers to defend 12 miles of walls, his chief danger came from
the unreliable urban population, led by the Pope.
It was on this occasion that Belisarius laughed
at the siege efforts of the Germans, as he watched
them trying to draw a siege tower up to the walls
with oxen: in spite of the growing alarm of his
own men, he allowed them to get quite close and
then killed two of the oxen with three arrows from
his own bow, leaving the towers stranded.

As the invaders settled down and became acquainted with Roman methods and even found Roman-
trained workmen to assist them, their besieging
capacity improved without ever becoming outstanding.
We know little about these matters, in spite of
their importance, just as we know little about the
battles of field armies in the centuries after
A.D. 300, but there is little evidence of much
real improvement in besieging skills in the West
until the late Merovingians and Carolingians in
the 8th and early 9th centuries. Since the quality
of fortifications also declined in this period,
the ability of the Carolingians to capture strongholds increased to the point where they could capture almost any fort they wished.

The ability to capture a fortified stronghold requires missile weapons to clear the defenders
from the walls so that the attackers can get close
enough to storm them or to penetrate them or to
undermine them. Transportation is essential to

bring food and other supplies for the besiegers.
Scaling ladders, towers to bring the attackers
level with the top of the walls, and battering
rams could be constructed on the spot, although
iron parts usually had to be brought with the
supplies. Use of these often required construction of a testudo or mobile roof to protect the
ram or the miners and diggers from attacks from
the walls. Smashing the walls with artillery,
as the Romans had done, required very heavy catapults even to throw stones of 60 pounds. It is
doubtful if any Germanic people, even the Carolingians, had the ability to build catapults of
this size or had the transportation capacity to
get such machines to a distant city in this period (to A.D. 950). The strain on such machines
was so great that essential parts, as Marsden has
shown (1969), had to be made of heavy iron, which
became increasingly difficult to obtain as economic resources, including human skills, continued
to decline, century after century. Lack of defensive body armor and helmets discouraged storming walls unless these were seriously undermanned,
as they often were. The lack of a good missile
weapon in western Europe between the gradual
eclipse of the bow in the Carolingian period
and the introduction of the crossbow after 1000
made it difficult to clear defenders from the
walls as a preliminary to storming.

There was, thus, a fairly steady qualitative
decline in ability to capture strongholds in the
West after 400, a decline which continued for more
than six centuries, but this was, in effect, reversed, or at least counterbalanced, by quantitative factors which combined with a more rapid decline in the quality of fortifications. These
factors interacted with decreasing population and
decline in transportation to produce a complex
interaction whose obvious consequences were a
fluctuation in ability to capture strongholds.
This produced a steady decline in such ability
after 400, a brief recovery of this ability from
about 700 to about 850, and an almost total collapse after 850. As early as 500, the Franks were
trying to copy and recover Roman weapons and military skills. These efforts were only partially
successful, but in view of the lack of such skills

824

among the other Germanic peoples and among the local Gallo-Roman population, the Frankish success was sufficient to allow them to conquer most of the West in the period from just after 500 to just after 800. In the last of these three centuries, the Carolingians reinforced the Merovingian efforts to copy Roman military examples by their own efforts to copy the Byzantine providential imperial model. This ideological weapon provided the final impetus to the creation of the Carolingian empire, but the effort broke down after 829 when Louis the Pious (814-840) was unable to transform the Carolingian system from its Germanic patrimonial basis to the more sophisticated Roman basis of an abstract state. As a consequence of this failure, there was a wholesale turning of the minds of the ruling class toward personal salvation in the Hereafter, leaving others to concentrate on the increasingly difficult problems arising from the continuing economic and social decline. Failure to overcome the erosion of the economic and social foundations of the Carolingian system, in combination with the shifts in values and allegiances on the higher levels of that system, explains why this empire was so ephemeral.

Through four generations the rulers of the Carolingian family (Pepin II, 687-714; Charles Martel, 714-741; Pepin III, 747-768; and Charlemagne, 768-814) were able to build an empire which covered much of Europe west of the Elbe River, including a fringe of Spain south of the Pyrenees, the northern part of Italy, and south-central Europe as far east as Fiume. The Carolingians could do this despite the continued economic and population decline from their ability to skim the dwindling economic surplus from a widening geographic area. This ability did not, apparently, result from any advantage in weapons, nor from any increase in the offensive power of their weaponry, but from the extraordinary personal energy of the members of the Carolingian family, the descendants of Arnulf, Bishop of Metz, who died in 641 and of Pepin I of Landen, Merovingian governor of Austrasia, who died in 639; Pepin II was their grandson. This personal energy had one unusual resource on which to build, the growing piety of the people in Gaul in the face of many natural and social disasters.

Of these two assets, the personal energy of the rulers could not be counted on as a permanent element in society, while increasing piety, in the long run, was a very mixed blessing in view of the dualistic character of the prevailing outlook. This intellectual dualism which, as we have seen, was closely related to the Platonic and Zoroastrian ideas behind many of the assumptions of providential monarchy, assumed that the spiritual world and the secular world, if not opposed to each other, at least were mutually exclusive. And the rapid growth of monasticism shows that many believed that the two were opposed. This meant that growing piety in this form persuaded many persons that the struggle to improve or to control the secular world should be given up by anyone who was truly concerned with the eternal salvation of his immortal soul. This factor did not become dominant until after the death of Charlemagne in 814.

Charlemagne escaped from part of the weakness of patrimonial rule when his brother and co-ruler died in 771; thus he did not have to waste time, energy, and resources in a struggle with a rival. This lesson was ignored by Charles who divided his empire among three of his sons, but the premature deaths of two of these delivered the undivided empire to the survivor, Louis the Pious. Louis, with a much higher level of training in abstract thought, obtained from the theological discussions of the day, tried to leave the undivided imperial sovereign power to his oldest son, Lothair, with the administrative management of the empire shared with three other heirs, but these successors were fighting among themselves even before Louis' death in 840. Thus the abstract idea of sovereign power vanished and the patrimonial idea survived, with its constant struggles to restore the unity of the system, wasting resources, which were increasingly misused, in spite of the fact that they were no longer adequate to support the imperial system when it was divided into several parts. The process of subdivision continued, so that in the next generation, eight grandsons of Louis the Pious ruled as kings of Francia, Aquitaine, Saxony, Bavaria,

Lorraine, Provence, and Italy. The imperial title
was bandied about among these descendants, so that
four of Louis' sons and grandsons held it at various
times, before one of the latter, Charles the Fat,
was deposed in 887 for his lackadaisical defense
against Viking invaders.

Charlemagne, a convinced Christian, was a
fairly typical providential ruler, with his many
wives and concubines, his many children with no
distinctions of legitimacy, quite willing to murder his close relatives, including nephews and at
least one son, if they became obstacles to his
political plans, and with almost limitless ambitions to spread his rule over wider territories.
Like most such rulers, he could win victories
over wider areas than he could sustain control
and had to return, again and again, to crush the
same subjects in rebellion. This was also true
of the other members of his family, especially
his father, Pepin III. The Aquitanians and Saxons
were crushed in battle numerous times, but, in
each case, as soon as the royal forces withdrew,
they began to plot rebellion once again, or the
governors who were left to rule them refused to
obey royal instructions from the distant king.
Many administrative reforms were enacted in these
royal orders, but few were very effectual over the
long run. The ruler had difficulty, in a time of
deepening economic depression, in paying his local
agents in money, so they had to be rewarded either
in lands or by grants of local revenues. Once
royal agents obtained local economic resources,
it became increasingly difficult to obtain whole-
hearted obedience to orders issued from the center.
We have seen this same situation in earlier societies, and it also developed in Islamic society
running parallel to western Europe and likewise
in Byzantine society shortly after these two.
But in Europe it would be bound to go much further because European military operations were
much less mobile than in the Near East or in Asia.
Once local political authority, based on local
military structures, found a base in local economic resources, any central government could insist on obedience only if it was willing and able
to embark on war to enforce its authority. Such
war could be waged by a central authority only by

827

calling on other local military structures for, without a prosperous economic system with adequate commerce and sufficient cash flows, no ruler could maintain any substantial part of his military resources at his central base or with him if he moved around. But to call upon locally-based military resources to crush the autonomy of other locally-based power for the sake of a central authority was futile, for all local controllers of power and force had a common interest in resisting central authority. After 850 coinage was too scarce to support royal agents on salaries, and transportation was too ineffective to pay them in kind from areas not under their local control. The use of temporary inspectors sent out as central agents to the provinces (missi dominici) has often been praised by historians, but it provided no permanent solution to the problem because these missi could be bribed or easily deceived in areas where they had no local knowledge and where the ordinary people were not likely to take them into their confidence so long as the count had all local power while the missi had little power and that only temporary. The missi, in most cases, were already half-persuaded in favor of the count, since they had local interests of their own in a different part of the kingdom. The fact that the central authority increasingly resorted to oaths as the chief guarantee of obedience by local agents is indicative as much of the growing weakness of all centralized controls (including this one) as it is of growing piety.

The Carolingian problem rested on the fact that they could conquer by military action far wider areas than they could govern on a permanent basis. They could do this for the reasons we have mentioned: mobile cavalry could conquer distant sources of revenues, but only castles could control revenues; and only foot soldiers could capture castles. So long as kings could get to all parts of their realms with the infantry, manpower, equipment and supplies to capture castles, they could enforce their orders on the local level. As a realm became larger, its ability to skim off sufficient economic surplus to sustain such an effort increased, but it required a major military effort, and such an effort had to be finished up in the summer campaign season (for even Charlemagne did not campaign in winter), and each season could hold only one such campaign, or at least, a campaign in one direction or province. As the number of such disobedient subordinate local officials increased, and the ability of the ruler to compel obedience gradually dwindled, from reduction of the resources of a divided empire, and from the general reduction of resources from the continued economic and population decline, it is hardly surprising that many rulers came to feel that piety might provide a more rewarding use of resources than a continued effort to maintain a large empire which was apparently not a high priority item in the mind of God Himself.

The sources do not give us any convincing evidence on either the weapons or the tactics of the Carolingians, so we cannot be sure whether they fought on horseback or only rode to battle but dismounted to fight. They probably did not yet have either horseshoes or stirrups, so if they did fight from horseback they probably did it by hurling spears as the Normans still did in the 11th century, but it is likely that most of their fighting was on foot. They clearly were not mounted archers, and it is clear that shock tactics by mounted lancers was increasing.

Of the Carolingian armies, we can be sure that foot soldiers much outnumbered cavalry, that relatively few riders had armor, and that a great variety of weapons were used by the infantry, including archery. The old Germanic obligation for military service from all free men was still in effect. There were many parallels with the situation in Anglo-Saxon England, except that the Franks did not keep up sea power. Land was divided into units known as mansi, similar to the English hides, each able to support an average family. Those who had 4 mansi of land were expected to come to fight wearing a mail tunic; those who had 12 mansi were expected to come on horseback; those who had less than 4 mansi were expected to join with their neighbors so that each four would send up one fighter, with those who did not go cultivating the land of the one who went to support his family. Each foot soldier had to have a lance, a shield, and a sword; later a bow and 12 arrows was required. Cavalry also were to have lance and shield.

There were other fighters who were holding land in
return for military service (vassals), and most
large landholders, including the king, had varying
numbers of mercenary soldiers, similar to Anglo-Saxon
housecarles. These special units were mostly cavalry
who served as knights.

The success of this system in reducing strongholds, as well as the need to return again and
again to the same areas to compel obedience to
the royal orders can be seen in the continuation
of the Fourth Book of the Chronicle of Fredegar,
which covers the events of 657-769 in the kingdom.
Pepin was forced to return repeatedly to crush the
same rebellious local lords. When he replaced
these lords with counts as agents of his own, the
same thing happened. Each count had three tasks:
to levy the military forces of his county when they
were needed; to collect the royal incomes in the
county; and to hold court to hear cases of royal
concern. All of these could be used by the count
to increase his own power, wealth, and lands. He
could call up the local military forces needlessly
and fine those who did not come; he could arrange
beforehand to excuse some who paid a fee to him;
he could influence the settlement of judicial
cases in return for favors; he could divert royal
incomes to his own purposes. Since the count was
supported by a grant of land from the king and it
was difficult to recover such a grant on the count's
death, these lands often became hereditary; in many
cases the office also became hereditary; if the
ruler sent out agents to investigate, they could
be bribed, or they could be misinformed by false
witnesses who had already been bribed or intimidated.
Thus the royal lands became the count's lands, the
royal powers became the count's powers, and the
royal incomes became the count's income, in part,
at least. The count could share parts of his
usurped lands, incomes, and powers with third
parties in return for support against the central
authority. Thus the monarch gradually became submerged among a myriad of local lords who had every
interest in dissipating the central powers, lands,
and incomes among themselves and no interest at all
in centralizing these in the hands of the royal
office where they had previously rested. In this

way, as the economic system wound down, with decreasing commerce and money flows, transportation became more difficult and more expensive; as roads washed away and bridges collapsed, the capturing of strongholds at any distance became less and less likely, the royal power became dispersed, localized, and privatized, until by 950, there was no state, no public authority, and no royal power at all. All power had become local, private, and dispersed in what we now know as feudalism. The European Dark Age had arrived.

2. The Vikings and the Normans, 500-1250

The Scandinavians and the Slavs were the last offshoots of the Indo-European peoples to appear. Both developed as linguistic groups before the Christian era, but neither came on the stage of history until after 500. The Indo-Europeans, as we have seen, had appeared north of the highland zone as the glacial age was ending, probably after crossing the mountains from the Levant as an offshoot of the proto-Semites. On the grasslands of the northern flatlands, the Indo-Europeans flourished and, before 4000 B.C., were sending their growing populations westward into Europe. Caught in a triangle of pressures made up of climate changes, population increases, and the existing level of technological development, they were pushed westward in spurts, which archaeologists designate by names like "Battle-axe peoples," "Corded-ware peoples," and "Urnfield peoples." The historian, who is generally aware only of the last few of these waves of migrants, knows them more frequently by linguistic than archaeological names and speaks of them as proto-Indo-Europeans, Celts, Germans, Scandinavians, and Slavs.

As these waves moved northwestward from the grasslands, they pushed through and over much earlier inhabitants of Europe, from a very different language family, the ancestors of the Finno-Ugrian tongues. By A.D. 500, these older languages were largely wiped away in Europe or were forced into remote enclaves in the Pyrenees, the Caucasus, the northern forests, and the tundra, and the more remote shores of the Baltic Sea and the Gulf of Bothnia. They survive today as Basques, Estonians, Finns,

and Lapps, but in A.D. 500, they were still the chief
inhabitants of what is now the northeastern part of
European Russia. A thousand years earlier, in 500
B.C., the Indo-Europeans in Europe north of the
mountains were largely Celtic, except for the Cim-
mero-Iranians of the steppes, the Iranians south
and east of these, and the proto-Slavs farther north,
running east from the Pripet (Pinsk) Marshes of
eastern Poland. From the Celts, the Teutons were
already emerging in the first millennium B.C., on
either side of the middle Baltic Sea near Denmark.
By A.D. 100, these Teutons had become so numerous
that they began to push outward, most notably the
Goths, who moved from Scandinavia to the shores of
the Black Sea in the century from A.D. 150 to 250.
Those who were left around the Denmark Straits
(Scania) continued to multiply and began to develop
the Scandinavian languages.

By A.D. 200, the climate of the Baltic was de-
teriorating in terms of that area's ability to sustain a large population on a low level of technology and general culture. The retraction of the
polar high-pressure zone was followed northward
by the rainbelt of the zone of temperate cyclonic
storms, drenching Scania with water in a somewhat
warmer temperature, resulting in a great increase
of forest, with curtailing of grazing, hunting,
and grain growing. The inhabitants turned to the
sea to supplement their diets, with a rapid development of ships, increased skills in boat handling and seamanship, in piracy, trade, and movements
of peoples. Thus emerged the peoples we know as
the Vikings.

In the course of less than 500 years (600-1100),
the Vikings and their descendants raided or migrated
as far west as Newfoundland, Greenland, Iceland,
Ireland and the Western Isles, as far east as Finland, central Russia to the Urals and to the Black
Sea, and as far south as England, Francia, Iberia,
and the Mediterranean shores. It is possible that
Scandinavians from the Baltic may have met, or even
fought each other, near Constantinople, one coming
across the Black Sea from Russia, the other coming
across the Mediterranean Sea from the Atlantic.
We know as a fact that the descendants of these
two lines fought for control of southern Italy in

1018 at Cannae, when the Varangian Guard of the Byzantine emperor defeated a force of Normans taking over that area.

In the 11th century, the descendants of the Vikings were rulers (even kings) in Russia, Normandy, England, southern Italy, Sicily, and Syria. By the year 1000, the Vikings formed an iron cap over Europe from west of Dublin, across the Baltic and the Gulf of Finland, and southward beyond Kiev and the Crimea.

In the west the Viking attacks fell into two parts divided by a lull about 930 to 980. The earliest attack may have been a Danish invasion of Gaul in 515. This was defeated by the Merovingian Franks, using the last surviving element of Roman sea power, and should, perhaps, be regarded as a final Roman battle, rather than as a medieval conflict. Similarly, the attack itself should perhaps be regarded as part of the Germanic migrations, rather than as a Viking raid, since the intrusion consisted of immigrants from Frisia, forming an offshoot of the Saxon-Jute-Frisian invasion of Britain which followed the Roman withdrawal about 430.

Viking raids properly understood began about 790 and ended about 1070, although sporadic attacks on England continued until the 12th century. Thus we have two chief periods, the first a time of raids and migrations by heterogeneous bands of Vikings from 790 to about 930; the second a period of attacks by Scandinavian kingdoms from about 980 to 1070. The two were quite different in character and motivation, since the earlier were by private war bands, while the latter were by organized kingdoms aiming at conquest. The distinction rests on the fact that the political and military organization of Scandinavia was undergoing a revolutionary transformation in the period from before 790 to long after 1070.

This transformation was similar to the changes we have seen among other peoples, such as the shift from genos to polis among the Greeks in 900-600 B.C., or the changes from kinship to kingship among the Germans from 50 B.C. to A.D. 600. In Scania this change was from a society of semi-pastoral, self-sufficient kinship groups to a military monarchy based on agriculture and commerce. In many such transformations, the change has been made through a transitional stage of war bands based on clientage and personal loyalties to war leaders and was accompanied by several other changes, such as the introduction of money, increasing economic specialization and exchange of goods, as well as some less tangible changes in which a new religion (or at least, a new religious organization) became associated with the new structure of public authority and state power. In each case, this transformation was also accompanied by an increase in offensive military capacity, either from changes in weapons, or in organization, or both, giving to those who control weapons increased ability to impose their wills upon others as well as on their own peoples.

In the case of the Vikings, we cannot be very definite about the course of these changes, especially about the means through which allegiances were shifted from kinship to loyalty to a war leader and later to a king. We have, of course, considerable information about the conversion of the Scandinavians from paganism to Christianity, but we have much less about the interactions between religion and political allegiance, or about the almost intangible shift from piracy and raiding to commerce and settlement. These changes left little evidence because they chiefly occurred in people's minds, as they decided that one was better than the other, or as they obtained the capital which allowed them to shift from one to the other.

In Scandinavia this transformation was triggered, as it was earlier in Greece, Italy, and among the Germans, by the pressures of growing population upon a limited land surface through a low and ineffective level of artifacts and their organizational patterns in the use of resources. If the utilization of resources had been raised rapidly to a more effective level, the excess of population could have satisfied its needs without any need to migrate or to attack other lands and peoples. Such improved use of resources (chiefly land and manpower) would have been intensive growth rather than forced extensive expansion and could have achieved a higher standard of living for a more dense population through increased specialization and growing interdependency of human activities in the same area. When this does not occur fast enough, the excess population moves outward either by peaceful migration (if that is permitted) or by force. The use of force, however, reacts upon the homeland and moves its political structure upward to a higher level of effectiveness, that is the shift from kinship to kingship or even to statehood.

This shift from kinship to statehood (or at least to military monarchy) took place in Scandinavia more through trade than through religion, as is likely to occur in barbarian areas which are peripheral to higher civilizations. The trade in question emerged from piracy and raiding, in what we might call the raid-trade-conquest sequence. The notable feature of this sequence is the significant role played in it by slaves and coinage in the raiding phase to an increasing concern with exchange of goods in the trading phase.

This shift from raiding to trading led to an increasingly complex society by engendering a growing separation of raiders from traders and of sailors from fighters. At the same time, particularly in the Viking case, it allowed successful raiders to retire with coinage, slaves, and other loot to peasant farming, not necessarily (and, in this case, only rarely) back to the previous homeland, but to any area which had attracted favorable attention in the raiding period. Thus Viking raiders became immigrants and landlords, in Normandy, eastern Ireland, in the eastern Baltic and in Russia, and on many islands of the seas. The consequence of this transformation was that the Scandinavian world, with its far-flung extensions, became a more complex society of trading and exchange among farmers, merchants, craftsmen, and mercenary fighters, living both on farms and in towns under the protection of a royal ruler.

In the Scandinavian transformation, the crucial developments were in shipbuilding and seamanship. This was marked by a change from a shallow draft, beach-hauling rowing boat with neither keel nor mast, before about A.D. 600, toward two distinct types of vessels, both of which were harbor-seeking,

keeled ships capable of being sailed. These two,
just as in the dark age of classical civilization,
were a longer war vessel and a rounder and heavier
merchant vessel, the former continuing to resort
to oars when necessary, long after the merchants
had reconciled themselves to the more patient role
of awaiting a favorable wind. This change in ship
types was accompanied by a shift of commercial settlements from non-harbor centers like Hedeby, Birka,
and Gotland to ports, and by the rise of monarchies
to protect this increased concentration of wealth.

The archaic idea that the ship was a symbol of
the earth-mother goddess, who provided survival in
the Hereafter, as well as food and offspring, and
was thus a proper vehicle to carry the dead to
eternity, a belief which was deeply embedded in
ancient Egyptian funerary customs, also existed
in Scandinavia in the Bronze Age, along with the
parallel idea, derived from the northern grasslands,
that a wheeled vehicle had a somewhat similar meaning and function. As a result, ships were used for
burial of great leaders in the pre-Viking and Viking
periods. An eyewitness account of such a ship
burial, including the sacrifice of a woman and
animals to go with the dead warrior, at a Viking
camp on the Volga River in 922, was recorded by
Ibn Fadhan, in an Arabic manuscript which still
survives. Archaeologists have found the remains
of many such burials, so we have a fair idea of
what Scandinavian ships were like and what they
were capable of doing when they were moved by
vigorous men over the seas, from the Valderhang
and Hjortspring boats before 300 B.C. to the Ros-
kilde vessels of about A.D. 900, a period of about
1200 years.

Until after A.D. these vessels had neither a
keel nor a mast; they had to be paddled and later
rowed, and were, accordingly, restricted in range
and use to rivers, bays, and the less violent
waters of northwestern Europe. These early vessels
were constructed of adze-cut (not sawn) planks until the 11th century. Originally, they were sewn
together, strengthened with wooden dowels later,
and fastened with iron rivets after about 300.
The ribs were inserted only after the hull was

formed into a wooden skin, being inserted frcm the
gunwale downward to the bottom of the hull and
fastened by lashings to cleats made integral with
the strakes (the horizontal boards of the sides).
Rowing replaced paddling about A.D. 200, requiring
some strengthening of the row-hole strake and the
gunwale.

Anton W. Brøgger and Haakon Shetelig, the outstanding authorities on this subject, believe that
these early ships were descended from a northern
skin boat made by inserting a wooden frame into a
hull of skins or hides, such as the Eskimo family
boat, the umiak, or the Irish coracle, which used
to be made of hides but is now made of tarred canvas.
However, it seems clear that the adze-made boat of
wooden strakes with integral cleats strengthened by
inserting ribs after the hull has been sewn together
was distributed all around the shores of the Old
World long before the Vikings. It was already old
when Odysseus made such a boat before 800 B.C. If
it is descended from a skin boat, the connection is
much older and occurred much farther east, since
wooden boats of this type probably came to Scandinavia from the Mediterranean across the Atlantic
from Iberia, brought by Bronze Age megalithic traders about 2000 B.C. The coracle-umiak type of skin
boat was a different tradition which came from the
east across the treeless flatlands of northern Asia.
At any rate, it is quite clear, as Brøgger recognized and as Lancelot Hogben explained long ago,
that there was a great age of seagoing exploration
of the world in the Bronze Age before 1100 B.C.,
but this went into almost total eclipse in the period of sub-Atlantic climate (1000 B.C.-A.D. 200),
with a catastrophic loss of geographic knowledge
and human skills, which have both had to be painfully rediscovered since the fall of classical
civilization. Viking ship construction and exploration was part of that process of post-classical
rediscovery.

The Valderhang boat, whose fragments are in
the Bergen Museum, and the Hjortspring boat, of
which there is a model in the Copenhagen Museum,
were both made before 300 B.C. and represent the
old Bronze Age boat building tradition. By A.D.
500, this tradition was being changed, without

837

being replaced, by the development of the vessel
formed on a keel and built of adze-cut strakes held
together by iron rivets, with the ribs still inserted after the hull was formed. In the 6th century, this keeled, nailed ship was improved by the
addition of a mast and sail. The iron-nailed hull
began about the third century, but the Danish Nydam
ship, built after A.D. 300, still lacked a keel.
The famous Sutton Hoo burial ship found in Suffolk,
England, was built in the early 7th century, but it
had neither mast nor keel and must have come across
the North Sea by rowing.

The Sutton Hoo ship was already obsolete when
it was buried under its mound of earth, for a ship
of about 600, excavated by Shetelig at Kvalsund in
Norway in 1920, has a heavy external keel, like a
sled runner on the bottom plank. It also has the
first attached steering oar, on its starboard
quarter. It may also have had a sail.

The movement toward a keel, made from the
trunk of a single tree, limited the size of Viking ships below about 80 feet in length. The
Gokstad ship, built about 850, had a 58-foot keel,
was 76 feet overall, with a beam of 17 feet, and
with its depth of hull, from keel to gunwale, about
6.5 feet; it had a draft of about 3 feet. This
Gokstad vessel is the Viking "long ship" which
struck terror all over northwestern Europe in the
9th century. It had 16 oar ports on each side
(only 20 inches above the water and 37 inches apart),
a steering oar on the starboard quarter, had a 40-
foot mast set in a great block of wood 12 feet
long, was rowed by 18-foot oars, and weighed about
10 tons when fully loaded. It probably carried
35 to 40 men, but had shield hangers along the hull
outside for only 30 shields, so probably some men
stayed with the ship when the raiders left it.
This hull was still of adze construction, with
integral cleats on its lower strakes. There were
16 strakes on either side, of which 9 below the
waterline were one inch thick, the tenth on the
waterline was 1-3/4 inch thick, and the fourteenth,
containing the oar holes, was 1-1/4 inch thick.
The mast step was cut away on the aft side so that
the mast could be lowered backward. The sail, made

of woolen cloth, was about 700 square feet and hung from a yard about 37 feet wide. The lower corners of the sail could be held out from the hull on poles 26 feet long, whose inner ends fitted into sockets in blocks of wood mounted on the deck on either side of the mast. Each block had two holes for these poles, allowing the sail to be set on either side either forward or aft of its normal crosswise position. Thus the vessel could be sailed before the wind or on a reach on either side.

This Gokstad ship was very seaworthy, largely from the extreme flexibility of the hull, which was clinker built, with the strakes riveted together, caulked with animal hair mixed in tar, and lashed to the ribs, so that the gunwale could move as much as six inches in a seaway. A replica of this vessel, under Captain Magnus Andersen, crossed the Atlantic from Norway to Newfoundland, over stormy seas, in twenty-seven days (30 April-27 May) in 1893 and performed magnificently, especially the steering oar, which Captain Andersen considered superior to any stern-post rudder.

The great advantages of such a ship to Viking raiders were: its seaworthy qualities, which allowed them to strike unexpectedly over great distances; its shallow draft, which allowed it to enter rivers and marshes or to escape over shallows from deeper draft pursuers; its retractable mast which permitted it to be rowed under bridges or trees; and the fact that it could be beached without injury, as it had replaceable, protective wooden pieces on both bow and stern, where the keel would hit the beach in a landing. Its deck planks were removable, and horses could be loaded or unloaded by stepping over the sides in shallow water.

In a word, the Viking ship was perfectly fitted to hit-and-run raiding, seeking loot and slaves, worked by fanatical fighting men if that became necessary, but who avoided fighting if that could be done.

The Viking threat to Europe was similar to that of the grassland horse archer. It can be summed up in the two words: "mobility" and "archery." Although the raiders could bring horses in their ships, as William the Conqueror did in 1066, there was usually no need to do that, as they could land almost anywhere, kill a few people, steal all the horses they needed, then ride about the countryside faster than the news of their arrival could travel, looting and enslaving, and often they could get back to their ships before any defensive force could be mobilized. Unlike the fighters of western continental Europe, they had no prejudice against the use of missile weapons and never fell into the later chivalric prejudice that missile weapons were ungentlemanly or immoral. The Vikings and Normans fought for only one purpose: to win.

The composite bow had been brought to Scandinavia by the Corded Ware culture in the second millennium B.C. but was used for hunting rather than for warfare, and it disappeared in Scandinavia, as it did in the rest of Europe, with the arrival of the Iron Age, which was delayed in the north till about 200 B.C. But the self-bow, up to 77 inches long, continued to be used, usually for hunting, but increasingly in warfare, in the Viking period. The Viking warrior had the usual Teutonic love for shock weapons, especially for the sword and for a formidable two-handed battle-axe, but there was no prejudice against archery, especially in naval combat, either to assist escape or as a preliminary to boarding in offensive actions. The ram was not used in naval action in the north.

This willingness to combine weapons and tactics was the secret of Scandinavian military success in the later period, after 980, when royal armies from the north were trying to conquer England. It is probable that Anglo-Saxon armies and later English armies remained superior to continental armies, at least to the French, and is certainly one of the reasons for the superiority of the Normans over most of their enemies after 1050. Those political units which placed their defensive hopes on weakly disciplined forces of feudal knights on horseback never found a solution to the two great challenges of the dark age (grassland archery and Viking raiding), just as they did not find any solution to the two great challenges of the late Middle Ages (the longbow and the solid mass of infantry pikemen).

The Viking adventure began with the Norwegian settlement of the Orkneys, the Shetlands, Ireland, Iceland, and eventually in Greenland and Newfoundland, the latter settled briefly about 1013. The chief Norwegian bases were in Ireland, with forts established at the mouths of rivers, chiefly at Dublin, Wexford, and Waterford. From these bases and later from bases in Scotland and Norway itself, raids were made on England and Ireland, beginning before 780 and continuing until after 1200.

About 830, as the Carolingian empire began its decline, the Danes began to emerge from the Baltic Sea and turned south to raid the lowlands of England, Francia, Spain, and many places on the Mediterranean shores. Very little of their loot made its way back to Scania, for these raiders, working in small groups of several ships and a few hundred men, had left their homelands for good, in most cases. The Danish attacks were heavy from 835 on, and by 876 they were settling in northeastern England, coming with their loot from raids in western France. In 892 they made a great invasion of England, with horses and possibly as many as 1500 men in 200 ships. Those who could not find a satisfactory residence in England, or perhaps did not have enough loot to finance them, returned to the continent and settled in Normandy in 911. Although our sources for the 10th century are far inferior to those of the 9th century, it would appear that the later Viking ships were larger, with about 60 rowers, rather than 30, and were much more numerous, moving in fleets of scores or more.

Before the Vikings finally settled down, they moved about in war bands which sometimes continued to exist for over ten years, with membership changing freely as each individual judged best. Originally they set up winter camps on islands in river estuaries, as Noirmoutier in the Loire, Sheppy Island in the Thames, and Camargue in the mouth of the Rhone. In some places, especially in the Mediterranean, they hired themselves out as mercenary fighters to some city or local lord.

In England, where their attacks and settlements were heaviest, they had great influence.

Before their arrival, Anglo-Saxon England was
probably the most prosperous part of western Europe.
This prosperity continued despite the Danish attacks. To meet this challenge, it became necessary for the English to develop a more unified government, an adequate army and navy, and a more effective system of taxation. Although these things
were achieved, the Danish pressure was so great
that it was necessary to yield part of northeastern
England to Danish control. English resistance was
led by the kings of Wessex, especially Alfred the
Great (871-899) and his children, Edward and Ethel-
freda (899-924). In 886, Alfred surrendered the
land northeast of the line (Watling Street) from
the River Lea to Bedfordshire to the Danes. This
area, known as the Danelaw from its different customs, was slowly reconquered by establishing lines
of earth and timber forts (burghs), copied from
Danish models, as strong points and operational bases.

The interaction of Anglo-Saxon and Dane created
a much stronger form of monarchy in England and the
north just in the period in which monarchical power
was being destroyed by feudal decentralization on
the continent. A more complex military system
emerged; it consisted of three parts: a paid national militia; a royal guard of mercenary fighters;
and a land-based feudalized cavalry; these were
combined with a navy, fortified strong points under
royal control, and a readiness to use both missile
and shock weapons. Since the king remained the
center of this military system, he remained the
center of the political system also, retaining considerable control of the judicial system, the coinage,
and taxation. An important element in this was the
need to raise money for defense and to pay tribute
imposed by the Danes. This last burden, the Danegeld, was of great significance in England since it
became the basis for a national system of taxation
beyond the personal income of the king's family,
which was all that survived of a central financial
system in France. It should, however, be pointed
out that the idea of a national system of taxation
to provide for "the common defense" did not arise
from the Danegeld, but is a part of this new system
of northern monarchy, since it was to be found among
other northern peoples including the Danes who obviously did not pay Danegeld.

Almost equal in importance to this system for taxation was the continued existence of a three-level system of royal justice in England. This consisted of one hundred courts for local justice, shire courts, and central courts. The national militia was based on the same territorial districts of "hundreds," which were used for taxation and justice.

This system of northern royal government is often ignored by historians or is attributed to some special genius of Alfred the Great or to the English people in general. Alfred is fully worthy of his title of "Great," but the Anglo-Saxon monarchy was the consequence of the reciprocal responses of Anglo-Saxons and Danes to each other and should be regarded as one particular example of a more general class of governmental system which I am calling "northern monarchy." Its influence survived in the north as late as the Vasa dynasty of Sweden (1523-1654), but it began with the Vikings and the Scandinavian monarchies established in the Viking period. Moreover, its roots did not lie only in the Teutonic background of the Scandinavians, but can also be traced to more advanced sources, such as Byzantium and the Moslem caliphates, which were linked back to Scandinavia and England through the Normans and the Varangians and their experiences in Sicily, southern Italy, and Russia.

The fact that the Scandinavian and Norman military systems were both varied and flexible allowed the monarchy to retain, or to develop, some elements of a national system of taxation, justice, and coinage. It also allowed it to retain some of the old Germanic ideas of the general obligation of military service by all free men and the need to consult with these free men on questions of general policy. Thus the idea of a national assembly is closely linked with the national militia and with the need to consult with those who will be affected, in their lives and treasure, by royal decisions and actions. Our modern idea which sees the assembly as an organ of governing which is antithetical to monarchical power and our assumption that a strong monarchy will naturally oppose such an assembly is totally mistaken and is based upon the historical experience of the 17th century; it is not based on the history of the Middle Ages when assemblies

were associated with strong kings, not with weak
ones, because only strong kings could make free
men come to such assemblies and only strong kings
dared to meet with free men. The Anglo-Saxon assembly was known as the Witangemoet. In Iceland
such an assembly, the Allthing, was founded in
930 and still exists today, being the oldest continuous parliamentary body in the world.

The Anglo-Saxon version of the northern monarchy should be regarded as the consequence of a
push-and-shove relationship between the English
and the Danes. This included the Danish attacks;
the response of the royal family of Wessex; the
Danish conquest of England in 1013-1042; the
Anglo-Saxon liberation in 1042-1066; and the
Norman conquest of 1066-1072.

The Anglo-Saxon military response to the Danish attacks has been well described by Professor
C. Warren Hollister of the University of California
and need not detain us here. The core of the system was that Anglo-Saxon England was assessed in
units of economic production of agricultural lands
called "hides," roughly the amount of land to support a family. Each hide paid two shillings when
Danegeld was imposed. Although the obligation of
military service rested on all free men, such
service was unpaid and required only within the
county of residence. But there was also a national army, what Hollister calls "the select
fyrd," which required one fighting man from each
five hides for two months' paid service anywhere,
the pay to be 20 shillings provided by demanding
4 shillings from each hide. In the 11th century,
much of England outside of the Danelaw and the
royal estates was assessed in multiples of 5-hide
units by the requirement that they send up a fixed
number of men when the summons arrived. Thus Oxford and Cambridge were assessed at 100 hides and
owed 20 men, while St. Albans was rated at 10 hides
and owed two men. The payment for service was 4
pence a day, which was the current rate for mercenary foot soldiers.

From this military assessment the monarchy
obtained military service, including infantry,
naval service, ships, and the upkeep and guarding

of bridges and forts. These were known as the trimoda necessitas in Anglo-Saxon law. The navy had been reformed by Alfred in 896 when he ordered construction of ships twice as long as the Danish vessels and with 60 rowers rather than the Danish 30. The ships and their crews were provided by special assessment units called "ship stokes" or "triple-hundreds," of 300 hides scattered about England, even in the interior counties. Each of these units provided both the ship and the men needed to work it.

Similar ship-stokes existed in the three Scandinavian countries. When such a district paid a sum of money instead of actually providing the ship and crew, the payment was called a "ship-scot." A similar system of commutation of service was applied to the select fyrd, from which we get the expression "scot free," meaning to escape this obligation. Later, in English history, the obligation to provide ships and crews was concentrated on various seaports, eventually organized into five fleets stationed at five ports which became responsible for the maintenance of their own fleets, hence called the "Cinque Ports."

In addition to these "national forces" which supplied infantry and a navy, the Anglo-Saxon monarchy had several other branches of its armed forces which chiefly supplied cavalry, although the riders usually fought on foot. These included household troops, which were a standing force of full-time mercenaries supported by the king, and the thegns or "knights," who were landed men rich enough to support themselves and their own thegns as cavalry. These were called to service in time of need. The distinction between these two was originally a sharp one, with the mercenary forces living with the king from his money and provisions (therefore called "house-carles"), while the thegn lived off his own land-holding and served the king only when called. In time, however, the distinction became blurred, since the king increasingly provided lands to support his housecarles and, when these lands were remote from the royal presence, military service by the holders of such lands became occasional rather than continuous, and they became almost undistinguishable from the thegns, except that, in many cases, the king continued to supply the housecarles' arms, so that they had uniform equipment when they assembled to fight.

It would seem that in Scandinavia, this blurring did not come so quickly because the military activities of the Danish kings in the 11th century were offensive rather than defensive and were thus overseas rather than local; accordingly they required a large standing army on continuous service. Archaeologists have now shown us how a large part of this standing army was maintained and, in doing so, have indicated how three successive kings of Denmark were able to create the "first" Danish empire, including Denmark, Norway, and England. These were: Harold Bluetooth, 950-985; Sven Forked Beard, 985-1014; and Cnut the Great, 1014-1035. On Cnut's death, his empire broke up and his Danish successors turned their conquests eastward toward the Baltic shores and Finland which had previously been dominated by the Swedes. In Denmark the archaeologists have found the remains of four great camps for permanent armies built about 1000 by Sven Forked Beard. These are so closely modeled on Roman camps that they seem to have been built in terms of precise Roman measurements. Each camp was a circle divided into quadrants by two crossroads at right angles, and the whole was surrounded by a circular wall of interlaced timbers filled with earth. These ramparts were about 10 feet high, were 40 feet thick at one camp and as much as 60 feet thick at another one. They each had four gates, at the ends of the crossroads, and varied in size from an internal diameter of 131 yards at the smallest camp to just twice that at the largest camp. In two camps the roads were paved with logs. In all camps large barracks were arranged in groups of four buildings, of which the largest were 38 yards long and 8 yards wide. Many of the buildings were workshops, but the residential ones could have accommodated 5000 men, with up to 3000 men and 48 buildings in the largest camp.

These camps may have provided the men for the invasion force of 94 ships which Sven Forked Beard and Olaf Tryggvason brought to England in 994. This and the subsequent invasions which conquered

846

England in 1013 were totally different from the Danish raiders of the earlier period. The ships were larger, with 60 men, and the forces were much larger and under strict discipline, so that they no longer sought plunder. The invaders were now Christians, not pagans, and came to conquer, not to settle or to loot. They were successful, and England became part of the Danish empire in 1013-1035 under Sven and Cnut; it became independent again under Cnut's sons (1035-1042) and under the last Anglo-Saxon king of the Wessex line, Edward the Confessor (1042-1066).

While the Norwegians and the Danes were expanding westward to the Atlantic and Europe in the period after 750, the Swedes had been expanding eastward among the Finns and the Slavs, using similar tactics and with similar aims, as we shall see in the next section. After the death of Cnut in 1035, the Danes also turned their efforts eastward, seeking to control the Baltic against growing competition from the Germanic trading cities of the southern Baltic coastline. In this struggle the Scandinavian peoples became increasingly Germanized and increasingly feudalized, especially the Danes, who faced almost impossible obstacles to their ambitious aims. These obstacles were more technical and economic than military and included such matters as access to money, both coins and bullion, continued changes in ships and shipping, as well as changes in trade routes and goods able to command men's services and allegiance. The growing size of ships as well as the complex changes of sea levels in the Baltic gradually forced trade routes of northern Europe from shallow rivers and bays linked by overland portages to seagoing vessels plying the waters of the Baltic between deep-water harbors. As a result, the older trading posts and towns such as Birka (Bjorko) in Lake Malar, Sweden; Hedeby at the head of the River Schlei in western Denmark; and Hollingsledt on the River Treene in east Denmark were replaced by seaports like Riga, Danzig, Lubeck, and Hamburg, leading west to various North Sea ports such as Bruges in the Netherlands. The significance of this shift, so far as Denmark was concerned, was that goods no longer could go across the neck of the Jutland peninsula but had to be carried by larger vessels through the dangerous waters of the Kattegat and the Skagerrak, which together form the Danish "Sound." The chief aim of Danish power, continued through medieval and much of modern history, was to control passage through these waters so that tolls could be collected. Legal claims to do this were based on the theory that these waters were within Danish territory, a claim which required that the Danes must control the southern end of Sweden just across from Denmark. Thus Danish political efforts were directed for centuries at the passive control of southern Sweden and the active control of the north German coast on both sides of Jutland, especially as far east as possible to eliminate the number of middlemen who would raise prices, decrease the volume of goods, and thus reduce the income from the Sound tolls. The modern history of Sweden begins in 1523, when Gustav Vasa led his country in a break away from the Union of Kalmar, which had intermittently held the three Scandinavian countries together under the Danish crown since 1389.

The interesting point here is that the Viking effort in Scandinavia, as in Russia under the Varangians, and under the Normans in the west and later in the Mediterranean, sought to finance a political structure from tribute imposed on distant commerce and not simply on revenues from peasant-worked lands. Thus this whole Viking tradition was closer to the income-raising traditions of nomad Asia than to the manorial tradition of continental Europe. This is of considerable significance because, just as the nomad tradition was based on mobility on land, so the Viking tradition was based on mobility on water. In the whole period from about 1300 to at least 1950, these two traditions in the English-speaking world have had a powerful influence on the power systems of western civilization: in the late medieval period the late Plantagenet kings of England used sea power to take to France and the continent fighting men who were supported largely by tolls placed on commerce, specifically on the wool exports of England; in the period since 1500 the two most dynamic civilizations of the world, Russia and the West, have continued to reflect these two older traditions of mobility on the land and on the seas, and the Cold War of the period after 1950 was formed by the opposition of these two superpowers, one continental, the other oceanic, standing on either side of what I call the buffer fringe of Eurasia, which runs from central Europe, through the Adriatic Sea, the Balkans, the Aegean and Black Seas, and across southern Asia to Vietnam, China, and the North Pacific. As we shall see, much of the strength of western civilization has rested on its ability to achieve an advanced technology and weaponry in seagoing activities with an advanced technology in agricultural production and in land power.

The basis for much of this technology and its organizational patterns have their roots in Teutonic Scandinavia and came to us through the Vikings and the Normans. We must now take a glance at the heroic sagas of these Normans.

The Norman achievement, as David C. Douglas has shown use (1969), is incredible and took a distinctive form, in Normandy, in England, in Italy, in Syria, and even in early Russia.

In 911 a band of Danish freebooters led by Rolf, after a long career of depredation, chiefly in Ireland, entered the Loire River in western France and fought its way northeast until they were defeated by Charles III, the last real Carolingian ruler in France, in a pitched battle before the walls of Chartres. Rolf was baptized and settled, with his followers, as a vassal of the king, in the archdiocese of Rouen. Rolf died in 931, but his descendants remained dukes of Normandy until 1204 and were also kings of England from William the Conqueror (1066) to 1135 in direct male line.

Although the Normans quickly forgot their pagan religion and their Scandinavian language, spoke French and called themselves "Franki" by the 11th century, they retained many of the Viking traditions, as we shall see. In Normandy their rule was violent and chaotic as they fought endlessly with each other and with close neighbors for power and the wealth which is obtained by power. The second duke was murdered in 942; his son, Richard, was "a pirate chief"; a later duke, Richard II, grandfather of the Conqueror, in 1033 welcomed a party of Viking raiders which had been

849

plundering Brittany, and had his brother, as Arch-
bishop of Rouen, baptize the leaders of this band,
including a certain Olof who returned to the north
to become King of Norway and the patron saint of
Scandinavia. According to Ordericus Vitalis, who
lived among the Normans, "When ruled by a strong
leader, the Normans are most valiant men, exceed-
ing all others in the skill with which they meet
difficulties and strive to conquer every enemy.
But without such a leader, they tear at each other
and destroy themselves."

　　　The Normans found such a leader in William
the Conqueror, illegitimate son of Duke Robert I,
who subdued the Duchy in 1047-1060, then united
all his relatives, his defeated rivals, ambitious
neighbors, and Normans recalled from places as remote as Sicily and southern Italy, to join with him
in the conquest of England in 1066. Many
other Normans as masterful as William had gone to
seek their fortunes with their swords in Italy as
early as 1016. In that year, Pope Benedict VIII
recruited a group of about forty Normans to support
a rebellion against the Byzantine governor of Apulia.
At first these Normans fought for pay, but by 1030
one of these warriors accepted a castle at Aversa,
along with the Duke of Naples' sister and considerable land, for his promise to support a band of
fighters for the duke's service. Soon the news
spread back to Normandy that Italy was a land of
opportunity for energetic if impecunious young
Norman fighters. In 1032 the first of the sons
of Tancred d'Hauteville, a small landlord of Normandy, arrived; by 1056 twelve of Tancred's sons
had arrived. These worked their way up, from
banditry, to mercenary soldiering for Byzantium,
and to the business of fighting for themselves or
for each other. The situation in the area was well
adapted to such self-enterprise, since it was
divided among three religions, three languages,
and three basic laws, each of these with a number
of political units ruled by leaders who lacked the
vital Norman asset of being willing to submit their
individual violence to a masterful leader long
enough to complete the job at hand. There were
Papal and Byzantine territories, three Lombard
duchies, three maritime Italian city-states at
Naples, Amalfi, and Gaeta, and numerous competing

Saracen emirates in Sicily. By violence, looting, and what Professor Douglas calls "repeated betrayals," these Normans added to their territories, wealth, followers, and power. Two sons of Tancred, Robert Guiscard and Roger, were particularly successful. When Pope Leo IX led an attack upon them at Benevento in 1053, they defeated his army at Civitate, north of Foggia. When they destroyed the last Lombard dynasty in 1058, the Pope allied with the Normans, accepted them as vassals, recognizing one as prince of Capua and another as duke of "Apulia and Calabria and future duke of Sicily." The latter island was still under Saracen control. The Pope directed his unruly vassals against Byzantine Bari, which they captured after an amphibious siege of 32 months (August 1068-April 1071). An invasion of Sicily from Messina in 1060 culminated, twelve years later, in a similar amphibious assault on Palermo (1072). Once again, the Pope made an alliance of Italians, Germans, and non-Guiscard Normans against the Guiscard brothers. Although the Pope excommunicated Robert Guiscard three times in six years, 1074-1080, the brothers captured Salerno, and the Pope had to accept them back as his loyal vassals and try to direct their fury outwards, this time against the Byzantine territories of Dalmatia and the Balkans, but, after two years, the Normans were defeated by regular Byzantine military forces at Larissa (1083). Robert Guiscard returned to Italy and found that Rome had been occupied by the German Emperor Henry IV, as part of the struggle between Pope and Emperor over the right to nominate bishops to German sees. With a large force which contained many Saracen mercenaries, Guiscard marched on the Eternal City and entered it without resistance as the emperor withdrew northward. The Norman mercenaries sacked the city (1084). A year later Robert Guiscard died, but his brother Roger continued on to the final conquest of Sicily (1091) and, before his death in 1101, took over southern Italy from Robert's successors. This created in fact, and later in law, the Kingdom of the Two Sicilies (since it included Naples). In the 12th century, this was the richest and most progressive state in Europe, and also the most cosmopolitan, drawing knowledge, crops, and techniques from all peoples, with a prosperous agriculture, active commerce, an ef-

851

fective taxation, a Byzantine-style bureaucratic
administration, and a tolerant and possibly enlightened religious and intellectual life.

The last area of Norman political activity
was in the Crusades, especially the first (1095-
1100). Like most rulers of this period, the Vikings and Normans were patrimonial in their attitude
toward political possessions. The ruler did what
he wished with his crown and territories, often
dividing these among heirs. Thus William the Conqueror left the Duchy of Normandy to his older son,
Robert Curthose, and left the throne of England to
his next surviving son, William Rufus. The next
son, Henry, seized England on the sudden death of
William Rufus in 1100 and conquered Normandy from
his brother Robert at the battle of Tenchbrai six
years later. In Italy the Guiscard family held
similar ideas. When Robert Guiscard died in 1085,
he passed over his older son Mark, called Bohemond
(Behemoth) from his great size at birth, and left
his possessions to a younger half-brother, Roger
Borsa, who was too weak to control these. When the
first Crusaders passed through Italy in 1096, Bohemond determined to go east with them to conquer
a country for himself to rule and, at the same time
(for he was quite sincere) to earn credit in Heaven.
As an outstanding fighter and an impatient individual, he took a prominent role in the early
Crusade battles and successfully claimed the first
substantial conquest, Antioch in 1098. This territory was held by seven successive members of Bohemond's family for 171 years, until it was captured
and ruthlessly sacked by the Mamluks of Egypt under
Baybars in 1268. About the same time (1265),
Charles of Anjou, brother of King Louis IX (Saint
Louis) of France, had taken the Kingdom of Naples,
at the Pope's behest, from the German imperial
family of Hohenstauffen who had taken it from the
last Norman ruler in 1194 and held it until the last
Hohenstauffen in 1268.

Norman dynasties had brief careers, but their
influence was very great. Their lives were largely
concentrated in half a century, from 1050 to 1100,
yet they transformed Europe. In 1050 Scandinavian
influence was still dominant in the northwest, and

the Mediterranean was still balanced among three non-western powers: Byzantium, and the two caliphates of Cairo and Cordova, with southern Italy as the division line. In 1050, the break between the Latin church and the Greek church was not yet final, the Latin church was deep in corruption (from local Roman secular control) at its center and was paralyzed by the control of the bishops and clergy in its branches by local feudal lords. As a result of the events of less than two generations, events in which the Normans played an important role, all this was changed. England was brought into the European continental world and the Scandinavians were pushed back to the Baltic; England and France began to emerge toward Great Power rank in Europe, while Germany, not yet at the peak of its imperial authority, was beginning to weaken. The ecclesiastical break between Rome and Byzantium became final and moved to open enmity, largely as a consequence of Norman aggression and the Pope's willingness to direct that aggression toward Constantinople, a move which culminated in the sack of that city in 1204 by the fourth Crusade. The papacy was reformed and freed from both the German and the local Roman lay control, under the leadership of the monastic movement from Cluny which was applied in Rome (chiefly by placing the election of future Popes in the care of a college of cardinals, created in 1059) in intervals of Norman support of the Popes. The Mediterranean was shifted from its condition of stalemate among non-western states to a new dynamicism of cosmopolitan, innovative influences, associated chiefly with the Kingdom of Sicily, the Italian trading cities, the movement of France to the Mediterranean, and the advance of Aragon into that sea from Iberia.

Many of these changes cannot be attributed directly to Norman influence, but there can be little doubt, as Douglas believes, that the Normans stirred things up in the 11th century enough to give a significant push toward the very great changes of the 12th century.

The most significant question still remains: how were the Normans able to do this? what role did weapons play in their achievements?

I have already shown that the Normans were energetic, impatient, violent, greedy, power-hungry, even anarchic. But they were also masterful and willing to accept a master. When one of their number demonstrated that he knew what he was doing and was determined to do it, others accepted him as leader because they all wanted the effort to succeed. They sought power because they were strong, not as men seek power today because they are weak and insecure. And as strong men eager to get the task done so that all could share in the rewards, they were quite willing to accept as their leader a man who showed that he was a leader, again unlike today, when we accept a man as leader merely because he wants to be leader. Because of these distinctive qualities, the Normans could make the feudal system work more effectively than other men could because they were energetic and ready to lead or to be led.

On the weapons side, the Normans were successful for reasons I have mentioned. They had spirit, morale, and organization. They had no weapons which were not possessed by others. But they applied the three qualities named to the existing weapons in a balanced and flexible way. Their warfare was elementary, even primitive, but it was generally better than the opposition, which was usually disorganized and lopsided. The Normans combined cavalry and infantry, missiles and shock, with water transportation (not really sea power), and sufficient discipline so that their forces did not fight either as a massed horde or as isolated individuals in hand-to-hand combat. They could keep their men in formation and direct them as formations in battle, at a time when most of their enemies could maintain a formation only by standing still. Moreover, the Normans were among the first to see the value of a reserve and to use their various formations as assault and reserve when a battle began. Their discipline continued after the first charge and was usually sufficient to prevent looting until the enemy was completely defeated, or to recall a formation from pursuit so that it could be used as a reserve to make the victory complete.

In a period in which physical strength was important in battle and in which combat, even in formation, pitted individual against individual, the Normans had a physical advantage which should not be overlooked. They were very strong and often very large, like Odo of Bayeux, brother of the Conqueror, who fought with a club at Hastings, or Bohemond of Taranto, who "was so tall in stature that he stood above the tallest," according to Anna Comnena, daughter of the Byzantine Emperor Alexis I.

All of this does not mean that the Normans had the best army in the world. Far from it. In their own day and at their best, they were probably inferior to the Byzantines or to the Saracens, when these were at their best. The Normans had excellent fighters, but they did not have an excellent army because they did not have a state as an organized power capable of sustaining a system of supply, a very large force as an organized entity, uniformity of either weapons or tactics, a siege train, or a navy, or other aspects of a fully developed defense system. Norman battles were generally small affairs, sometimes very small, rarely more than a few hundred knights, with five to ten times as much infantry. We must remember that the Normans were early with their great deeds and they did most of these deeds in the west, which was still so backward in 1100 that it was not yet organized in terms of a state with public authority and public law. In the few areas, such as Sicily, where a state was well advanced, it was still patrimonial, and certainly in the case of Sicily, the structure was as Saracen as it was western. It might be argued that the Scandinavians and Normans achieved a state with public authority in Russia or in England, but one of these was not western and both were no longer Viking or Scandinavian by 1150.

In their battles in the west, the Normans generally came up against either mounted knights (as in France) or popular infantry militia. When both were present, they were rarely used in a coordinated effort together. The Normans did use both in such an effort, and they used both shock and missile weapons. At Civitale Pope Leo had an army of Italians stiffened with a force of German mercenaries. They were faced by three Norman units, with Richard of Aversa on the right against the Italians, Humfrey in the center opposite the Germans, and Robert Guiscard as a reserve on the left. Richard's knights charged the Italians and drove them from the field, while Humfrey attacked the Germans who seem to have formed a shield wall and resisted fiercely, just as the English did thirteen years later at Hastings. The German resistance continued even when Guiscard attacked them from their right. But Richard, calling his knights back from their pursuit of the Italians, threw them against the German flank, and they were overwhelmed. The experience of this battle may have influenced William's tactics at Hastings, as he had on his side a number of fighters from southern Italy, some of whom might have been at Civitale, and the story of that victory was well known in Normandy.

The background of Hastings is well known. Duke William of Normandy claimed the throne of England on the death of Edward the Confessor in 1066, but the throne was taken by Harold Godwinson after election by the Witenagemot. Harald Hardrada, King of Norway, also claimed the throne and found support from Harold Godwinson's exiled brother Tostig. When Duke William gathered an invasion force on the beach near the Somme River, Harold rallied his forces on the English shore, but adverse winds delayed the Norman embarkation for most of September. Suddenly Hardrada and Tostig landed at the mouth of the Humber River in northeast England and were joined by numerous Scandinavian supporters from the Danelaw. Edwin, Earl of Mercia, called up the local forces and the militia of the midland shires but was destroyed by the invaders in a battle outside York on 25 September. Harold marched rapidly from Kent to York in five days, collecting shire levies along the way, and, on 25 September, at Stamford Bridge outside York, the new king won a decisive but costly victory in which Hardrada and Tostig were both killed. Three days later, Duke William landed at Pevensey in Sussex, disembarking about a thousand knights, 6000 other fighters, and a large number of horses from at least 700 ships. Harold rushed south with his horsemen, reaching London on 5 October, where he waited a week for his shire forces, marching on foot to catch up. Few did so, but on 13 October, Harold advanced toward Hastings with what men he had. The following morning he placed about 8000 men, all dismounted, on a ridge crossing the road by which William would have to emerge from the Hastings peninsula to advance to London. By returning south so rapidly, Harold had outrun his own infantry and thus had lost his archery; he had also wearied his horses, so he strengthened his infantry line with a shield wall of dismounted thegns (his household cavalry). For this reason his defensive position, which was a strong one, could not be jeopardized by advancing against the Normans, and he had to allow William to deploy from column to front within 200 yards of the English line, but at a lower level.

William opened the battle with an attack by infantry archers, of which he may have had up to 3000, according to John Beeler. The shield wall withstood the attack, and the supply of arrows dwindled rapidly. A second Norman assault by shock infantry achieved little more and suffered considerable casualties from the housecarles' axes. The invader's left wing (Bretons) broke backward down the hill, exposing William's center (Normans), but the right wing of the shield wall was disorganized when some of the English there pursued the Bretons down the hill. The Norman center, to protect its left flank, also began to withdraw slowly, and William, who had been holding his heavy cavalry for a third assault, had to commit it to the melee which was developing on his left side. In this effort, William was unhorsed, and the rumor began to spread that he had been killed. He quickly mounted another horse and rode into the fray with his helmet pushed back so his face could be seen, to reassure his followers. The center was quickly stabilized, since the English center did not advance and William could take his mounted men from that position to hurl them against the English right which was now in a confused struggle with his own left on his left rear. This done, William now ordered his third assault, this time with mounted knights along the whole English line. After a long and costly struggle, in which there were heavy Norman casualties inflicted by the Saxon housecarles, the Normans broke and began to fall backward down the hill. This was the turning point of the battle, for many of the English took off in pursuit of the retreating Normans, disrupting their shield wall

without achieving a decisive charge. William with
all the knights he could gather swept across the
line of pursuing thegns, cutting them down. This
done, all his forces, archers, infantry, and knights,
returned to attack what was left of the English line.
These formed a bloc around Harold, prepared to fight
to the death; an arrow hit Harold in the eye, just
about the time that both his flanks were attacked
and began to roll up. As dusk fell, after more than
six hours of fighting, a group of Normans hacked
their way through the Saxon housecarles, killing
Harold at the spot where the altar of Battle Abbey
church was built later. The bettered invaders
stayed on the field through the night, buried their
dead the next day, then withdrew to their ships
which they fortified and called for reinforcements
from the continent. Although they probably did not
realize it for several weeks, William's collection
of mercenary adventurers and soldiers of fortune had
won a decisive victory, one of the most important
of the Middle Ages.

A great deal can be inferred about the Normans
and even the Vikings from their military exploits.
The Normans contributed more than any other factor,
except the monastic movement in the church, to
create a politico-military system which could draw
Europe out of its slide into a dark age. The Norman
contribution to other aspects of life, to politics
apart from organization, to economic and social life,
and to spiritual, intellectual, or humane activities
was slight, while their contribution to religion
was both mixed and controversial.

In military matters their contribution rested
not only on their combative proclivities, but also
on their cosmopolitan experiences and their willingness to adopt and to adapt features from any source:
from Scandinavia, continental heavy cavalry, Anglo-
Saxon England and Russia, from the Mediterranean,
Byzantium, and the Saracens. As a result, they
started the process by which Europe began to re-
discover the weapons and tactics which had been
lost by the decline of Rome and the Dark Ages, and
they added new methods in the process. They began
to recreate the three-stage battle, as we can see
from Hastings, which required the proper coordination of missile and shock, of foot and horse, and

of mobility and static defense. The English lost
at Hastings because their shield wall had no mobility
and because Harold lacked complete discipline over
his men, while William, like most Norman leaders,
was able to control the direction of movement and
place of assault even in the confusion of battle.

In addition to these narrowly tactical aspects
of warfare, the Normans began the recovery of auxiliary aspects of battle: sea power, fortifications,
and siege techniques. They were too early in this
recovery process to contribute much to problems of
supply, recruitment, or intelligence. They did,
however, contribute considerably to war finance,
to military propaganda, and to strategy.

It is doubtful that the Normans invented war
finance as it developed in early medieval Europe,
but their instinct for organizing the essentials,
especially in matters concerned with power, played
a considerable role in recognizing the two chief
sources of war finance, from land rents and from
tolls on commerce. These were, of course, old
stories, but in the tenth century incomes to sustain war in Europe had been reduced to the relatively small amounts that could be obtained from
peasants whose productivity was no more than 4 to 1
(the crop was about four times the amount of seed
used). In the same period, as we have seen, the
east, not just in pastoral Asia but in areas with
which the Normans were familiar, such as the Mediterranean and across Russia, income arising from tolls
on commerce were still basic in establishing the
financial support of war. The Normans combined
these in the west, both organized in a rational
way, to finance their exploits as conquerors and
rulers. In regard to land rents, the Normans as
well as other Scandinavians, often established a
pattern which consisted of (a) a detailed written
schedule of incomes from land on an annual basis
and (b) a method of assessment of imposts on a
fractional basis which could be demanded and collected very rapidly and which reduced opposition
just because it seemed impersonal and equitable.
We are all acquainted with the Conqueror's establishment of such a system in the Domesday survey
of 1087 in England. This was to some extent a
special case and was used for granting out fiefs

859

rather than for assessing annual contributions. The latter had existed long before the conquest in Anglo-Saxon England, where it provided an assessment for military service as well as for taxes. A similar system spread to many areas under Viking or Norman rule in the form of cadastres. These existed in England and Russia by the year 1000 and may be of Scandinavian or Byzantine origin. Whatever the source, it is non-feudal and was both admired and spread by the Normans, thus contributing to the development of new military and political forms superior to feudalism.

Political propaganda is also not a Norman invention; in fact, few Normans could match Alfred the Great in this field. But the Normans adopted and spread it; starting and propagating favorable rumors; sponsoring poems and chronicles to make known their exploits; making sure that the prologues to documents and the wording of charters had favorable implications. Bohemond, for example, was very inclined in this direction, which may have had its earliest roots in the ancient Indo-European thirst for immortality.

One last point, which is, perhaps, not so much typical of the Normans as it is of the century in which they were working and which they showed in its most notable form. That is their extraordinary ability to combine ruthlessness and religious conviction. These were among the contributions which the Vikings brought to the birth of Russian civilization in the period of Scandinavian expansion.

3.   Russian Civilization, 750-1690

Every civilization begins with a period of cultural mixture, but no civilization has ever experienced this process in such a drastic form as did the Orthodox civilization of the eastern Slavs. This society, which we know as Russia, resulted from the mating of two parents, a Scandinavian father and a Byzantine mother, the resulting fusion being imposed over the great mass of peoples, chiefly Slavs or Finns, whose chief quality was their resilience. To this day, the resulting civilization shows characteristics of both parents, despite the fact that their characteristics were often not compatible.

860

One striking fact about Russian civilization is
that the characteristics of the two parents have
been so dominant throughout Russian history that
the contributions of the peoples who make up the
population have been relatively insignificant.
These people, originally a mixture of Slavs and
Finns, or rather of Finns smothered and almost ob-
literated by Slavs, have been increasingly mixed
with Turko-Mongoloid peoples with a very strong
seasoning of outside elements such as Germans,
Balts, Jews, Georgians, Greeks, Iranians, and
others. This mixture of peoples has not been
very significant in the history of Russia because
they have not contributed many important characteristics to the Russian historical experience,
which has continued to be a working out of the
Scandinavian-Byzantine legacy in a distinctive
geographical setting. In a sense the Russian people have been the stage on which the action of
Russian history has occurred. Of course, it is
obvious that without the stage there could have
been no action in any positive way; these people
have been potential, long-suffering, devious,
moody, inexhaustible, prolific, pacific, xenophobic,
anarchistic, yet passive, acted upon rather than
acting themselves.

In fact, the geographic environment of Russian
civilization has been a more positive instigator and
participant in the events of Russian history than
the people. For this reason, we must begin with
the geographic setting.

Both geographically and culturally Russia and
Russian history are not parts of Europe or of western civilization; they are too different. Of
course, there has existed, both geographically and
culturally, an area of transition between these
two, and the failure to distinguish them as separate
entities has resulted from the ambiguities of that
transitional area or from concentrating too narrowly
upon it.

Geographically, the line between Europe and
Asia is not the Ural Mountains, which are of little significance as a barrier, but rather is the
line joining the Black Sea and the Baltic Sea at
their closest point, passing by the Carpathian

Mountains and the Pripet (or Pinsk) Marshes along
the way. The Pripet Marshes, east of Warsaw, and
the Carpathian Mountains, 300 miles to the southwest, are barriers to movement westward from Asia,
particularly for armies or mass migrations. Together they provide only three passageways across
the line separating Europe from Asia: (1) a northern passage between the Baltic coast and the marshes
leads to Tannenburg and Berlin by way of the Prussian
plain; (2) a central passage goes from Poltava and
Kiev to Warsaw by way of Lemberg (Lwow) and Przemystl;
and (3) a southern passage between the Carpathian
Mountains and the Balkan highlands follows up the
Danube valley by way of Bucharest to Belgrade,
where it divides into three branches, with the
Sava valley going west to Zagreb, the Drava valley
going northwest to Graz, and the Danube itself continuing north and west to Budapest and Vienna.
This southern passage has not been very accessible
to modern armies because it is pinched almost
closed at the Iron Gates of the Danube where the
Carpathians and the Balkan Mountains converge between Bucharest and Belgrade. The Balkan Mountains
offer a number of north-south passages between the
Danube and the Aegean, notably the Vardar-Morava
valley, but most east-west passages in the Balkans
are very difficult and inconvenient. As a result,
the chief land routes between the Asiatic and the
European flatlands have been along the northern
and central passageways, and certainly these have
been the places where the Germans and Slavs have
fought each other over the last thousand years.

The Carpathian Mountains are shaped like a
fishhook whose barbs, pointing west, are at Belgrade, whose curve encloses Transylvania on its
eastern side and forms the western boundary of Wal-
lachia and Moldavia (the chief provinces of the
Romanians), and whose long shank runs northwest,
forming the northern boundary of Ruthenia, Slovakia,
Moravia, and Bohemia (the four together made up
Czechoslovakia as it was in 1938), with the eye
of the fishhook at Prague in central Bohemia on
the upper Elbe River. It is interesting to note
that Berlin, Prague, and Vienna lie on a straight
line.

862

Strategically, the defense of Imperial Germany against invasion from the east (that is, from Asia, as I am defining it) has been to stand in a position west of the Pripet Marshes until the enemy has committed himself to either the northern or the central passage, allow his head to come west to a sufficient distance, and then to cut off that head, either by driving northward to crush it against the Baltic shore or, by swinging southward, to hammer it against the Carpathian range near Lemberg or Przemystl. This strategy worked to perfection in both passages in World War I, but has been hampered by the fact that a German army waiting behind the Pripet Marshes must hold Warsaw as a base, and Warsaw is not a German city, lying as it is in the Vistula valley which is inhabited by Poles most of the way from Cracow to Danzig.

The geographic extent of the Soviet Union today stretches across all of Asia, north of the highland zone, from the eastern edge of Europe as I have defined it eastward to the Bering Sea and the North Pacific Ocean. This great extent of land may be regarded as consisting of three broad belts running from west to east, each of which is split into two for most of its length, thus providing six parallel zones in all. The central belt is of forest, split into deciduous forest in its southern zone and coniferous forest in its northern zone. South of the forests is the belt of steppe, split into the grassland savannah zone in the north and the desert (or even salt desert) zone to the south. The northern belt is primarily split into two zones of which the northern is tundra, or even permafrost, while the southern zone is scrub of bush and scattered trees, a transitional zone, sometimes called taiga, between the tundra and the coniferous forest zone.

This symmetrical pattern of six zones is distorted by changes in altitude of the land surface, by the Ural Mountains which run north and south across the two belts of forest and tundra at 60 degrees east longitude and by the various Asiatic mountains, from the Yenisei River at 90 degrees east longitude to the Bering Strait at 170 degrees west longitude. From Pripet at 25 degrees east longitude to Bering Strait, Russia covers 165 degrees of longitude, of which the first 65 degrees show our three belts of terrain in excellent symmetry, divided into two parts, so-called "European Russia" from Pripet to the Urals across 35 degrees of longitude and so-called "Siberia," almost equally wide (30 degrees) from the Urals to the Yenisei River.

The most significant boundary between belts is that between the grass steppe and the forest, which separates two ways of life, mobile on the steppes and sedentary in the forest (both decreasingly so since 1600); it is also the dividing line between a surplus of shelter in the forest and a surplus of food on the steppes (and increasingly so since 1600). This boundary between two zones providing different necessities of life inevitably results in interchange between the two, with items of food moving from grasslands to forest and items of shelter moving, in exchange, from forest to grasslands.

Such interchange between steppe and forest goes back to the heroic hunting cultures but has become increasingly significant in modern times, especially as the advance of technology has made it possible to break the grassland sod to cultivation by the introduction of the iron plowshare and modern harnessing (chiefly after 1600 and especially in the Black Earth region of the western steppes), or as fossil fuels have been added to wood for fuel, and as improved transportation (lately based on fossil fuels) has made such zonal exchanges easier.

The forest always provided shelter because it provided wood for fuel and buildings, furs for clothing, logs for fences and fortresses, and thickets or swamps to hide in. Later the forested mountains provided coal, and still later, when the Russian political system extended to the Caucasus Mountains and beyond, a somewhat similar exchange of shelter and food took place between the grain-growing Black Earth regions and the mining and petroleum areas of the Caucasus and the Caspian.

The grasslands, as we have seen, always provided food, at first for hunters or grazing animals, later for pastoral peoples, and still later for fully nomadic herdsmen. But it was not an area for agriculture

since the sod was too thick and resistant to be
cultivated by hoes, and the traction power of early
plows was also insufficient to turn the sod. Only
proper harnessing would permit this: traces, horse
collar, bifurcated reins, and, above all, an iron
plowshare to turn the sod so it would disintegrate.
These innovations became available after A.D. 1000
but they were very expensive (and Russians were
very poor). Moreover, by the time these technological advances arrived, the grasslands had been taken
over by warlike nomads who were quite willing to allow peaceful traders to cross the grass (at a price)
but felt no restraints on doing violence to peasants.
Thus the extension of agriculture to the grasslands
in any significant way required not only a technology but also required a political power able to
establish some kind of law and order for peasant
farmers on the grasslands. The technology was found
in the centuries 1000-1500, but the necessary power
system, the Russian state, did not arrive on the
open grasslands until 1500-1900.

In the meantime, agriculture was restricted to
the oases along the edge of the desert zone, or
within the forests, or close to the towns on the
Black Sea shores and along the Russian rivers west
of the Urals. On the Black Sea shores agriculture
was practiced from about 1000 B.C. because of the
presence of the Scythian power which not only protected the peasants but also forced them to expend
the hand labor necessary to cultivate steppeland
with a primitive technology. The Russian state did
not obtain that region until the 18th century, by
overcoming the Cossacks and Turks who utilized it
in ways not very different from the Scythians.

Within the forests, agriculture was simple
but primitive, with limited production from much
hard work. Trees could be killed by removing a
circle of bark and left to rot, while hoe culture
or use of a wooden plow planted crops among the
roots. As the soil became exhausted, cultivation
could be shifted to a different spot, or the whole
enterprise could be moved. Increasing population
made such movements necessary in any case, so the
Slavs steadily spread eastward and north at the
expense of the Finns who were operating on an even

lower level of agricultural technology, with more
emphasis on hunting and animal tending (including
reindeer and swine). Those who stayed on the older
sites, while their children and brothers sought
new lands elsewhere, gradually adopted a two-field
system which cultivated half the arable land in alternate years (about 1450). The three-field system
did not come until after 1500. Thus, for a long
time, the Russian economy was extensive and did not
provide much economic surplus to pay for specialized
craft products, imported goods, luxuries, or even
government and security. The original Slavic method
for getting security was to hide, and in the forest
there were many places to do this.

Any organized system for combining food, shelter,
and security in the Slavic world would have to be
located near the line dividing the forests and grasslands, with adequate transportation between these,
and with both security and capital accumulation
operating over that transportation system. There
was plenty of east-west mobility on the grasslands,
almost too much of it in fact, but north-south mobility between zones was possible only along the
rivers. Such river transportation was most effective
in winter, when rivers were frozen, but that was the
season when food was not readily available. In summer, with greater effort, the rivers could be traveled
by boat, a method which was originally somewhat
neglected among the Slavs (possibly because the
boat they knew best was the skin-covered coracle).

The rivers of Russia are one of its most remarkable natural features. They are interzonal--
that is, they go generally northward and southward
across zones, chiefly in the forest belt but extending into the tundra in the north and into the grasslands in the south, unless they reach the sea in a
shorter distance. They are quite different in the
two halves of Russia, west and east of the Urals.

East of the Urals, the rivers begin in the
mountains or steppes and flow either northward a
great distance through the forests to the Arctic
Ocean or flow southward a short distance toward the
highland zone mountains where they join with oasis
waters from the mountains to form pools and inland
seas which have no outlets to the oceans but are

reduced by evaporation, leaving salt flats and salt deserts, which are useless for cultivation. The northward movement of the polar icecap and of the westerly rainbelt since about 1880, like the similar movement earlier (A.D. 200-1200), has decreased the rainfall on the grasslands and increased it in the forests, creating great problems in the Soviet era; today the Caspian and Aral Seas and other inland waters have been drying up, while flooding on the tundra has increased.

Flooding on the tundra is something which most of western civilization has been spared, since most western rivers, in Europe and North America, flow from cooler areas to warmer ones, usually from north to south, or at least from higher altitudes to lower ones. Thus most of the rivers we know (except a few less significant ones like the Red River of Minnesota) freeze from the source toward the mouth end, much more important, they thaw in spring from the mouth toward the source. In this way, their released waters can flow to the seas as they thaw. But east of the Urals, three of the greatest rivers on the globe, the Ob (3460 miles long), the Yenisei (2080 miles), and the Lena (2680), thaw downstream from source to mouth, the released waters flooding widely while the mouth on the Arctic is still frozen tight; this situation is made much worse by the fact that the water cannot soak into the ground because of the permafrost barrier less than a foot below the surface. Thus the three belts of Russia's terrain east of the Urals are now changing to three different belts of desert, forest, and bog.

West of the Urals, the rivers have been a blessing, radiating outward like the spokes of a wheel from a hub in the forests north of Smolensk. From that hub waters flow westward by the western Dwina to the Gulf of Riga and the Baltic; southward by the Dnieper to the Black Sea; southeast by the Don River to the Sea of Azov, while waters not far away and accessible by portage across low divides flow southeast by the Volga to the Caspian Sea; northeast by the northern Dwina water goes to the White Sea at Archangel or goes north or northwest, by Lake Ilmen and the Volkov or other streams, to Lake Ladoga and the Gulf of Finland. Since rivers formed lines of communication in early Russia, the strategic center of any early Russian power system should have been near Smolensk, at the transportation hub we have mentioned and north of the line separating the forest from the steppes, but within the forest secure from the dangers on the steppes. As we know, however, the strategic center of the Russian power system since 1450 has been at Moscow, in the deeper forest, on an obscure tributary of the Volga River (2290 miles long), far north of the steppe corridor which brought dangers from the east, aiming such dangers directly at Kiev, the earlier Russian power center, on the Dnieper. Moscow was not only north of Smolensk, but it was much farther to the east and thus more protected from the threat of Europe's more advanced technology. In a word, the center of the Russian power system and thus of the Russian civilization was determined by strategic considerations, not by economic, social, or religious factors, nor by any consideration for the amenities of life. It was at Moscow because that spot was relatively safe from the two great dangers which persistently threatened the growing Russian civilization, steppe nomadism and European technology.

Between these two pressures, acting as a hammer and an anvil, a military and ideological despotism was hammered out in Moscow to create a centralized autocratic system, to the detriment of most countervailing elements, such as democracy, equality, or freedom.

The two threats, from the steppes and from Europe, were hammering on that fusion of Scandinavian and Byzantine traits which gave structure to the relatively amorphous and structureless Finno-Slavic materials living in the huge area of taiga, forest, and steppe.

When the Scandinavians, chiefly Swedes, came into Russia from the Baltic after 730, the Finno-Slavs in the forests were so poor that the chief wealth of the area was in their own bodies, as slaves, or in the furs they could get from the forests and a few other forest products such as honey, wax, and hemp. Furs and slaves were so desired in the Near East that a considerable trade in these had grown up through the southern rivers, chiefly

the Volga. This trade was monopolized by the Khazar
khanate, centered in the area north of the Caucasus
between the Black Sea and the Caspian; this had a
wide-flung fringe of tributary peoples, including
the Magyars west of Azov, on the Pontic steppes,
the Patzinak (Pecheneg) nomads east of the Caspian,
and the so-called Volga Bulgars on the middle Volga
near where the Kama River, coming from the northeast,
joins the Volga, to flow together southward to the
Caspian. West of the Magyars on the lower Danube
were the main group of Bulgars in the area which
still bears their name. The Khazars controlled all
trade coming south on the Volga or Don Rivers en
route to the Near East on either side of the Caspian
and were prepared to block access to the Slavs or
Finns by anyone seeking slaves or forest products.
On the other hand, the Khazars knew that peace was
profitable and were prepared to allow trade to go
through so long as they could collect tribute from
it. For this reason, they blocked the Saracens
from coming over the Caucasus Mountains, while keeping friendly relations with the Byzantine empire to
the southwest and with the Turkish nomads to the
east and southeast. The Volga Bulgars to the north
shared this attitude, acting as a switching place
for goods coming down the Kama from the Urals and
Siberia, or along the upper Volga from the Baltic,
and sending goods south on the Volga to the Caspian
or southwest to the Don and Azov. In general, the
Slavs and Finns played a relatively menial role in
this system of trade and tribute. The Slavs, as
they increased in population, were expanding outward, generally northeast from the Pripet branch
of the Dnieper River through and over the Finns
and elbowing aside the Lithuanians who separated
them from the Baltic and were centered in the valley of the Nieman River between the Vistula River
on the west and the western Dwina River on the
northeast. At the time of which we speak, the
Slavs had not yet moved northwest of the line of
the western Dwina and the upper Volga. The Khazar
khanate kept the steppe corridor blocked against
nomad intrusion from the east, and the most recent
arrivals of Uralic-speaking peoples, the Magyars,
had come into Europe, not by way of the steppe corridor from the Asiatic grasslands but down the Kama
and Volga, reaching the Caucasus area in the fifth
century; from there they had moved westward to the

south Russian steppes in the seventh century, and
eventually moved on, reinforced by a second wave
of Magyars coming by the same route, up the Danube
to the Thiess River plain, the area we now call
Hungary, in the ninth century. In moving from
the Pontic area to Hungary, the Magyars passed
north of the Dacians (Romanians) and Greeks and
stopped when they reached the Germans of the upper
Danube (Austrians). In doing this, they split the
western Slavs into two groups, which later became
the South Slavs (Jugoslavs) and, to the north, the
Czechoslovak Slavs.

The Scandinavians broke into the Khazar trading monopoly in two groups. The first came in
about the middle of the eighth century from the
Gulf of Riga by the western Dwina River, whence
they spread out going down the Donets River and
the Don toward Azov and eastward from the Dwina
to the Bulgars on the middle Volga. In the north,
as early as 700, the Swedes and Danes had bases in
Livonia, Estonia, and Karelia, chiefly seeking furs.
Reaching toward Azov in this way, the Vikings
tended to split the Khazars from their tribute-
paying Magyars, while on the upper Don the Vikings could intercept goods going to the Volga
Bulgars en route to the Khazars and, by imposing
their own tolls, increased prices to the Khazars.
Most of the furs and slaves moving southward were
paid for in Saracen coins and not by return of
commodities. In the north, the Karelian furs moving west across the Baltic were largely paid for by
woolen cloth, but in the trans-Russian trade the
chief commodity moving north to Scandinavia seems
to have been treasure and coins, especially coins
of the Abbasid caliphate in the ninth century and
those of the Samanid dynasty from 890 to about 980,
when Saracen silver ceased to flow. According to
P.H. Sawyer (1971) it was the drying up of this
flow of Saracen silver across Russia to the Baltic
which led to the resumption of Danish raiding on
western Europe following the lull in 930-980.

George Vernadsky (1943) believed that the
Russian Vikings (Varangians) had reached Azov by
the early ninth century, thus dividing the Khazars
from their Magyar tributaries. There is no evidence that the Varangians paid tribute to the Khazars.

Their conduct has been recorded by an 11th century Persian historian based on a 9th century source, "The Rus go out to the Khazars and the Bulgars. They have no cultivated lands and obtain grain from the Slavs."

The Khazars tried to cut the Swedes off from the Slavs and probably succeeded for a time by building a fort on the Don at Sarkel about 838. We know that two Swedes who wished to return home from Azov were unable to return up the rivers and went east with a Byzantine embassy to Louis the Pious in 839, meeting the Carolingian emperor at Ingelheim, Germany, before being sent onward to Sweden (recorded 17 January in Bertinian Annals).

It may have been this episode which brought a second expedition of Vikings to Russia about 855, this time led by a Carolingian feudal lord, the Dane Rurik from Jutland. Rurik and his successors established a new route into Russia, by way of Lake Ladoga, the Volkhov River, Lake Ilmen, the Lovat River, and the Dnieper, defended by three forts along the route, at Novgorod on the Volkhov in the north, at Smolensk on the upper Dnieper in the center, and at Kiev, just above the Dnieper rapids, in the south. These invaders came to exploit the native Slavs by enslavement and tribute, compelling them to provide furs, labor, and food, and selling as slaves any who resisted. As early as 860, these Varangians made an attack on Constantinople, probably with the cooperation of the Swedish group from Azov. Since the Byzantines were under attack by the Saracens at the same time, they were taken by surprise but, after a hard fight, defeated the Rus, who lost most of their 200 boats. Numerous subsequent attacks were also defeated, notably a large assault in which a numerous fleet of Russian boats was destroyed by Greek fire in 941. The aim of the Varangians was to take over the Khazar, Bulgar, Magyar, and even the Byzantine, tributary areas. They overran parts of Anatolia in 941, invading Transcaucasia in 943, attacked Bulgaria in 944, but they were unable to retain control of these areas. They were also unable to prevent sporadic nomad raids from the steppes, at first by Patzinaks (until about 1060) and then by Cumans (Polovtsi). These were eastern nomads who had been content to cooperate with the Khazars for a share of the profits. But Sviatoslav, the most aggressive of the princes of Kiev, destroyed the Khazar empire in 969, opening an era of almost constant nomad raids on Russia which culminated with the Mongols in 1223-1241. In the meantime, the Varangians continued to exploit the areas they could control, alternating military attacks and commercial treaties with their neighbors, including Byzantium. At first, they made one great convoy each year to Constantinople, in June. The Rus prince and his retinue of mercenary fighters would leave Kiev in November to circle for five months through the area they controlled, collecting slaves and tribute. By April they were back in Kiev building boats and organizing a convoy of hundreds of vessels. These were loaded with goods, including hides, sheepskins, hemp, and other goods collected around Kiev. They left in June, had to portage the whole enterprise around the Dnieper rapids (using the slaves) and made their way to the Byzantine capital by following the coast of the Black Sea. They sold most of their boats to the Greeks, bringing back luxury goods, chiefly textiles (including silks), metal products, jewels, and money in the boats they retained. Some years they did not go, but sought to expand their tributary area by war, and, in the tenth century, the trading convoy was replaced by more regular commercial links which did not require the personal attention of the prince. Thus the latter found time to pursue his suicidal military and political activities.

The destructive nature of these activities is clearly seen in the career of Sviatoslav I (962-972), who left his three sons as viceroys in three fortresses at Kiev, Pripet, and Novgorod, while he conquered the lower and middle Volga, Azov, and the Kuban, destroying the Khazar empire and overrunning Danubia. He was defeated and captured by Byzantine forces at Silistria (Romania), but was released, only to be ambushed and killed by Patzinaks on his way back to Kiev. His sons engaged in a fratricidal civil war to succeed him, and many of his conquests were lost almost immediately. This became the basic pattern of Kievan politics: an exploitative commercial enterprise superimposed by alien warriors over relatively passive Slavs; constant wars to expand that enter-

prise; conquering areas which could not be controlled permanently; ignoring the rising threat
of the eastern nomads; using a patrimonial political system which constantly engendered fratricidal civil war for control of the whole enterprise.

Expansion of this enterprise was more successful in the forest zone and thus in the north than
in the grasslands where it could not be held against
the nomads, nor to the southwest, where it was
blocked by the Byzantine civilization and by the
Bulgar empire of Krum, Symeon, and Samuel (808-
1018). In spreading through the forest zone, the
Russian system was blocked on the west by the Poles,
Lithuanians, and eventually by the Germans, so the
only way for any great expansion was to the north
and northeast. In this movement, bases were established at log-built forts which soon became stockaded towns, each under a viceroy of the family of
Rurik. Eventually there were ten such centers.
It was almost impossible for the Grand Prince at
Kiev to retain control of these viceroys, especially as there was no fixed rule of succession.
The civil war after the death of Sviatoslav in 972
was won, through treachery and murder, by his son
Vladimir the Saint (978-1015), and the civil war
which followed Vladimir's death was won, by the
same methods of fratricide, by Jaroslav the Wise
(1019-1054). Jaroslav tried to set up a method of
succession in which various cities were ranked in
order of importance (measured by their incomes)
with the rule of each city going to the members
of the ruler's family in sequence of genealogical
seniority. This means that each city would be held
by all the brothers of one generation before going
down to the oldest nephew in the next generation,
the junior members waiting their turns to be Grand
Prince of Kiev by serving as princes of lesser
cities in ascending order of prestige. Such a
complex system might have functioned if some method
of determining genealogical seniority had been generally accepted and if older brothers had had the
decency to die before their juniors, but each ruler
had so many wives and concubines producing so many
sons, legitimate and illegitimate, with nephews
sometimes older than their uncles, that the system
could not work. Moreover, the merchants in Novgorod
and Kiev sometimes insisted on the right to elect

the ruler they wanted from the descendants of Rurik, without regard to genealogical seniority. There were also factors besides incomes which made cities of differential desirability, so princes were often unwilling to accept the established sequence.

The wars which arose from these problems were fought with mercenary warriors, mostly Varangians and Patzinaks, but the former were so dangerous that a prince endangered his security by having too many of them around. After Vladimir defeated his brothers, he tried to get rid of 6000 of these warriors, by sending them off to help the Byzantine Emperor Basil suppress the revolt of Bardas Phocas, with a covering letter which said of the Varangians, "Do not allow a single one of them to come back here." In return for this support, the emperor gave Vladimir his sister Anna as a wife, but required the prince to become a Christian. Vladimir, who had just been defeated by the Bulgarian Czar Samuel (986), needed Byzantine support. He became a vigorous Christian, forcing conversion of the Slavs, building churches, sponsoring learning, and founding charitable houses. Nevertheless, he had at least seven wives and, according to the chronicles, had 800 concubines. At his death seven sons from five different mothers were viceroys in distant places. The oldest son, at Novgorod, was already in revolt. It took nine years of civil war before this oldest son, Jaroslav, won out (1036), and he did not become undisputed ruler of all Russia for another twelve years of struggles. In this dispute three of Vladimir's sons were killed, two of them refusing to resist because of their total devotion to the Beatitudes of Christ. To avoid such struggles in the future, Jaroslav tried to set up the scheme of succession by genealogical seniority just described. At the same time, he rewarded Novgorod for its support by granting the town a charter which gave it a local assembly with independent powers and also, apparently for the first time, established legal equality between Varangians and Slavs. This system of succession (1054) was similar to one that Louis the Pious had set up in the Carolingian empire in 817, with a supreme ruler at Kiev and the rest of the territory divided administratively among the other sons as viceroys.

874

In Russia the system did not work, claimants refusing to await their turns, conspiring together to set the established sequence aside, then betraying one another, with years of civil wars interrupted by occasional family conferences of reconciliation. By 1139 Russia had broken into a number of city-state principalities, each under a prince descended from Rurik and ruling over a surrounding area of considerable extent. Some of these territories were subdivided in time into inferior city-states as patrimonies for younger princes of the local branch of the family. The whole system became a kind of loose federation, with some parallels to ancient Greece, with all Russians regarded as fellow Hellenes, and non-Russians considered barbarians (excluded by differences of language, religion, and general culture), but the Russians themselves divided into territories dominated by city-states whose rule included varying amounts of monarchical, oligarchic, and democratic elements. An additional cause of disturbance arose from the struggles of these three elements to control each city. Like the Greek <u>polis</u>, Russian democracy was direct participation by members of a legally restricted part of the population who had to get to the meeting of the assembly in order to vote. This was not easy for those who resided outside the walls, as the meeting was called on short notice by the town crier, sometimes on the day of the meeting. These democratic elements were strongest in the north, at Novgorod and Pskov; the monarchical element was most strong in the northeast at Suzdal and Vladimir (and later at Moscow), while the oligarchic element, based on the military, was strongest in the southwest in areas which soon fell under Lithuanian and Polish control (Volynia and Galicia).

This Viking exploitative system was not a state, nor even a public authority, but was a private, patrimonial enterprise much like the Hudson Bay Company. Its chief purpose and activities were commercial, and it was superimposed over a backward and extensive agricultural system which was excluded from the Viking enterprise, except as a provider of food, labor, craft goods, and slaves, which were gathered as tribute and were not obtained in exchange for goods or services. There was ab-

solute ownership of property, including land, which
could be disposed of at will. There was no distinction between public and private, since there
was no public authority, and all power was private
power. The powers of a lord over the residents on
his estate were the same as those of a prince in
his principality. Lacking any rule of succession,
possessions were divided among sons, and all sons
were "princes." The word "udel," meaning "share"
of the patrimony of the family of Rurik, was applied both to the private estate of a prince and
to his principality as a unit of territorial power.
The holder of such a share was expected to arm and
mobilize his residents along with his military retainers, to support or oppose other princes, as
seemed advantageous to his own interests.

As early as 1000, crises appeared from two
chief causes, the patrimonial disputes over succession that I have mentioned and the inability
of the system as a whole to maintain profitable
commercial arrangements southward, either to the
Saracens or to Byzantium. The nomads raiding across
the steppes increased in power in 1000-1250; the
civil wars between princes and the civil disturbance
within cities interrupted trade; and, finally,
the whole pattern of political power and commerce
on the steppes and the Black Sea changed, as the
Baghdad caliphate and Byzantium grew weaker, the
Italians (led by the Normans and the Venetians)
grew stronger, and trade on the Black Sea shifted
from its earlier emphasis on luxury goods of remote origins toward more mundane commodities,
such as wheat, dried fish, and lumber, which were
increasingly carried by western shippers and were
drawn from the Black Sea shores and the Pontic area.
As a consequence of a Byzantine commercial treaty
with Venice, the Italians were able to take over
many shipping tasks and to move into the Euxine as
trade carriers about 1082, before the first Crusade
(1095-1100). In 1069 Kiev was captured by the Poles
and a century later was sacked by the prince of
Vladimir; in 1204 Constantinople was sacked by
the Franco-Norman crusaders on behalf of Venice;
and in 1223 the Mongols defeated a great Russian-
Cuman coalition near Azov. In the north, Novgorod
and its neighbors struggled to participate in the
Baltic trade under growing pressure, both commer-

cial and military, from the Germans. In the center, the chief nucleus of Russian life and power retreated northeast toward Moscow (first mentioned in 1147).

In the period 1054-1237, the Russian system was transformed and moved into a dark age: commerce declined; population shifted from town to rural living and from the south and southwest to the northeast, taking along their slaves to establish large estates in virgin forest; the struggles of contending polity among democratic urban assemblies, military oligarchies, and princely despotisms shifted drastically from popular assemblies toward despotism. Smaller people who had neither power nor slaves had to become dependent on the great ones, as tenants or workers. As commerce decreased, local self-sufficiency increased, money became scarce, and land or military protection were exchanged for services of all kinds. The population was reduced by violence and disease; cities were reduced so that many became little more than forts; the social system was totally changed from the Kievan pattern which had legal equality for all men except slaves and recognized only two legal classes (free and slave) to the Muscovite system of many different legal classes of ranked inequality. The Mongols after 1237 killed or enslaved many thousands, abducting any skilled craftsmen they could find, so that each estate tried to establish its own resident craftsmen as part of the general movement toward local rural self-sufficiency. Only the Republic of Novgorod, safe from Mongol attack and increasingly a part of the Baltic trade area, was spared the general collapse backward to darkness and ignorance. It, instead, became subject to a landed commercial oligarchy somewhat like Venice in its later days.

Jerome Blum estimated that in the Mongol period (1241-c.1490) there were 45 Tatar-Russian wars and innumerable Tatar raids (almost every year), 41 wars with Lithuania, 30 with the Germanic crusading orders, and 44 wars with the Swedes, Bulgars, and others.

In this period there was much land and many princes, but a great scarcity of manpower, especially of skilled personnel (either military or administrative). Landlords welcomed any man as a tenant, offering land for any kind of service, but this did not become a feudal system as in western Europe because the obligations were not reciprocal; the elements of fealty and loyalty were lacking; primogeniture did not appear, and patrimonial ideas persisted, with a continued confusion of public and private despite the spread of Byzantine ideas on state and religion.

For a long time, military servants rewarded with land grants could take their services, with the land and jurisdiction over it, from one prince to another, but after 1250 princes began to make such grants of land conditional, at least to the extent that any transfer of services and loyalty to another lord left the jurisdiction, including justice and taxation, over the land to the grantor. By 1400, such grants were made increasingly on a non-hereditary basis, or at least, on a conditional basis, so that the land was revocable if services were shifted to another lord.

As the idea of a state and of public authority grew, the idea of jurisdiction (including justice, taxation, police, and allegiance) appeared, but it was not attached irretrievably to government over a territory, as with us. It could be granted out separately from the land or could be detached from the land, even on small plots. At the same time that the prince became increasingly concerned to retain the jurisdiction when he granted the land, he began to alienate the jurisdiction, either with the land or separate from it. This led to grants of "immunities," that is the right to exclude the prince's agents, such as judges or tax collectors, from that particular piece of land; this was equivalent to a grant of these rights over the land to the grantee, since the grantor's agents were denied these activities. This was done for a long time before it became explicit or was recorded in writing, mostly as a benefit to the clergy, but later increasingly to laymen, especially to military servants. Sometimes, after 1340, only part of the jurisdiction was granted, the prince retaining the right to judge certain crimes, usually murder, brigandage, and theft.

Since there was an almost total lack of any conception of law or of property as we know these, any prince or grantee of lands from a prince assumed that he was the ultimate owner of all the lands in his patrimony. As a result, peasants living in villages with their families under the jurisdiction of a prince sometimes found that their district had been granted by their lord to a military servant, either with or without jurisdiction (or, in the early days, with the question left unstated and ambiguous). Such peasants, who had hitherto functioned as owners, suddenly found themselves reduced to tenants.

In general this whole matter of landholding, services, jurisdiction, and personal rights in Russia seem very confused to us because our ideas on these are quite different. We make a sharp distinction between public and private, between state and estate, between ownership and use, between freedom and slavery, distinctions which are essentially Roman, since we in the west have replaced our medieval ideas on these matters with basically Roman ones as a consequence of the classical revival in western civilization in the period 1250-1700. In Russia, the situation was quite clear in the Kievan period and was based on possession (rather than title) with all relationships private and with little concern for questions of jurisdiction, service, or allegiance. After the conversion of Vladimir, Byzantine influences came into Russia, chiefly in the sphere of less material culture such as religion, ideology, art, literature, theology, political outlook, and general cognitive arrangements (including two-valued logic and the full impact of the sixth century B.C. revolution), but these Byzantine innovations had little influence, except for a few simple elements of religious rites and doctrines, outside the small group of the ruling class, especially the literate ones.

We are now in a position to see more clearly what Russian civilization obtained from its two parents. The Viking contribution was largely on the side of organization, while the Byzantine was mostly on the side of higher culture. From the Varangians came militarism, love of booty, a belief that a way of life could be made out of war, plunder, and tribute collection (the last not fully distinguished from commerce), an emphasis on private property, and on patrimonial succession to such property, a tendency toward anarchy, violence, and suspicion of general rules and laws.

The Byzantine contribution was both more tangible and more abstract. It included Greek Orthodox Christianity with all that entailed, the alphabet, architecture (especially the use of the dome), literature, and painting, political theory and forms of government (including universal providential empire, with a semi-divine ruler, in a totalitarian, authoritarian, absolutist system), patterns of abstract thought, especially two-valued logic and other elements which tended to create personalities filled with Manichaean guilt and ideological intolerance.

These two parental heritages acted and interacted on each other and impinged on the great mass of the Russian people to make an amalgam which was then pounded into shape between the hammer and the anvil of Asiatic nomadic attacks and European technological pressures to create the Russia which we know today, a Russia which was not really finished until about 1780 and which has been modified superficially rather than essentially since.

The nature of this Russian system must now be evident. It has the classical inability to distinguish between the state and society, with the consequent tendency to see the state as totalitarian, in an almost organic sense, in which the individual has no rights against the whole, with a semi-divine, private-property, patrimonial conception of government with the government above the law (since law is an edict based on will), and with a wide dichotomy between government and people. In fact, government were outsiders, often non-Russian, expansionist and semi-paranoid, while the people were xenophobic, devious, and anarchical.

As might be expected, the chronology of Russian history is very different from that of western Europe. The medieval period was beginning in Russia with the breakdown of the Kievan system after 1054, similar to the medieval beginning in the west

after the Carolingian breakdown two centuries earlier. Serfdom which was finished in England before 1400 did not really get established in Russia
until after 1590 and was not abolished there until
1863. Russian technology was almost all adopted
from outside, mostly from the west and very late,
especially productive technology in agriculture,
transportation, commerce, finance, and manufacturing, so that in 1800 it was still about the level
that western Europe had been in about 1300. If we
divide European history into ancient, medieval and
modern with the divisions say, about 850 and 1450,
we would have to divide Russian history into three
similar periods about 1054 and 1789.

A more detailed history of Russia would require at least seven parts:

1. Ancient Russia, to 878
2. Kievan Russia, 878-1054
3. Disintegration and Incipient Dark Age,
   1054-1237
4. Mongol Russia, 1237-1480
5. Muscovite Russia, 1380-1694
6. Imperial Russia, 1694-1917
7. Soviet Russia, 1917-

Russia took shape in the Mongol and Muscovite
periods, from the first Mongol attack in 1223 to
the advent of Peter the Great in 1694. The development of central Russia as an area of militarized
despotic rule had already begun before the Mongols
appeared. Suzdal was established as a princely
patrimony in 1097 at a meeting of six princes trying to find a compromise of their dynastic disputes.
Their solution was that each prince should hold his
own district for his own descendants. Suzdal was
in territory still largely Finnish, so it was more
militarized, autocratic, and exploitative from the
beginning. Its rulers did everything they could to
encourage colonists, traders, and military servants,
cutting roads through the forest, and offering lands
to wealthy immigrants who came with their slaves
from the Kievan area. The new doctrine of state
power was adopted more rapidly in that area, parallel with grants of lands, free from princely jurisdiction, for military service. Almost at once, the
prince of Suzdal was claiming the role of Grand Prince,

using Cuman mercenaries to seize Kiev in 1149, again in 1151, and again in 1155-1157, but losing it in each case. In 1169, Kiev was sacked by Andrei of Suzdal, who allied with Byzantium and systematically introduced Byzantine absolutism into his territories. He moved his residence from Suzdal to Vladimir, and then to a nearby village to escape from the urban assembly of the city. He was assassinated in 1175, but his son Vsevolod III (1176-1212) adopted the title of Grand Prince. Many warriors came to take service with the rising star of Vladimir.

During this period, pressure from the west was steadily rising also, despite the fact that the Hungarians, Poles, Lithuanians, Germans, Bohemians, and lesser subdivisions of these were fighting each other almost constantly in the area between the Elbe River and the Dnieper. The chief pressures came from the Germans along the northern passage between the Baltic Sea and the Pinsk marshes, and from the Lithuanians and the Poles through the central passage between the marshes and the Carpathians. In both cases, this pressure was based on a higher level of general technology and of military experience, rooted in the more advanced economic organization of the west and on its military experience obtained in the Crusades. The west had a more productive economy based on modern harnessing, the mould-board plow, the three-field fallow-rotation system in agriculture, and a more dense population at a much higher level of skills. The west did not have weapons or military organization superior in quality to that of Russia, but it had a greater knowledge of tactics, with superior engineering skills, and the beginnings of a superior logistics. The economic and social organization of the west had been growing in complexity since at least 970, with beginning division of labor, growth of economic exchange and specialized skills, including a considerable expansion in the use of money in central Europe from the exploitation of the silver mines of Germany and Bohemia. In a word, central Europe was in a period of retraction. Nevertheless, the Russians had at least equality in hand weapons, although lacking skills in siege techniques and fortification. The European threat to Russia until the fifteenth century was similar to the European threat to the Saracens and to the Byzantine empire in the same period. What the nature of that threat was, we shall see in the next section. It consisted of the heavily armed medieval knight with lance and sword, assisted by crossbowmen, and transported by relatively skilled sea power and a very skilled train of engineers.

The western threat to Russia from the Germans across the northern passage was quite different from that from the Poles and Lithuanians across the central passage, chiefly because the Germans as represented by the Teutonic Knights were aiming at colonization, settlement of the soil, and replacement of the Slavs, either by enslavement or genocide, while the Poles were chiefly interested in getting control of what I have called bundles of revenues. The latter required that the Russians be preserved on the ground as part of a functioning agrarian system, with the conquerors simply superimposed above, replacing the Russian ruling class, and these could be replaced again later by the return of Russian rulers. Thus in the central and southern areas of Polotsk, Smolensk, Volynia, Moravia, and the Ukraine, there was a periodic shifting back and forth of Magyars, Poles, and others on a relatively superficial level.

In the north, however, across Pomerania, Brandenburg, Prussia, Livonia, and the vast lands of the Novgorod Republic, the German thrust, led by the Teutonic Knights, was similar to that of Hitler 700 years later: extermination or enslavement of the Slavs, colonization by the Germans and the creation of a different economic and social system. The Teutonic Knights were a military order of religious founded in Jerusalem in 1198 as part of the Crusades. It was intolerant and elitist, restricted to Germans and permitting knighthood only to nobles. In 1291 its headquarters was moved from Acre to Venice, and in 1309 it moved again to Marienburg. Loss of the Holy Land to the Saracens left the Order with no real purpose for its continued existence, but in 1229 it was invited by Duke Conrad of Poland to convert the pagan Prussians by force of arms. A somewhat similar military order of religious, the Livonian Brothers of the Sword, also founded in 1198, had established a similar crusading base at Riga in Livonia. The two orders were merged in 1237.

The missionary activities of the Teutonic
Knights were greatly aided by a battle at Born-
horde in 1227, in which the north German princes
ejected Danish rule from the north German coast,
from east of Holstein to the border of Estonia.

Although the purpose of Conrad's invitation
to the Teutonic Knights had been to conquer and
convert the pagan Prussians, their aims were soon
expanded to other ends: to replace the Slavs and
other non-Germans; to force conversion of both
pagans and Orthodox Christians to Roman Catholicism;
and to bring the whole east Baltic region into a
commercial network of fortified cities linked
with the Hanseatic towns of Baltic Germany. With
strong support from the chief rulers of Germany,
the Teutonic Order moved eastward, crushed resistance, forced conversions, established at least
80 fortified towns (including Thorn, Marienwerder,
Memel, Konigsberg, Brandenburg in 1231-1266),
ejected or killed large numbers of natives, either
originally or in subduing subsequent revolts, and
settled large numbers of Germans in the region.
The grand master of the Order ruled from Marienburg
with no political and few religious restraints,
chiefly from the support of the Papacy. In 1234
the Order gave its lands to the Pope and received
them back as fiefs of the Church with no interference by any other ruler; in 1263 the Pope
modified the rules of the Order to allow it to
engage in commerce and thus to allow it to become
a combined military-commercial corporation with a
religiously sanctioned drive for wealth and power
similar to one of today's international conglomerate
business corporations plus the United States Marines.

The Germanic concern with trade, town life,
guild sociability, and water transportation confined their expansion to the Baltic coast and the
rivers flowing into that sea. But their success
in that area was so great that the Russians were
blocked off from the Baltic Sea until about 1700
and the Baltic Germans remained the dominant group
in the area until they were withdrawn to Germany
proper in Hitler's day (1940).

Thus the Russians were faced by two very different kinds of attacks: the nomads trying to cap-

ture booty and men in the south and southeast and the Europeans trying to annex territory in the west and southwest. The need to cope with these diverse dangers played a considerable role in developing the Russian weapons systems, once the country came under a single ruler. But that was not until after 1500 (Ivan III). Before the country was unified, each region faced its own rather different dangers. Even when unity was reestablished in the fifteenth century by Moscow's conquest of Novgorod (1471-1494) the military system was not unified, even in the same defense sector, since different groups with different military obligations entered a campaign with different contingents and operated against the enemy more or less independently. It would be safe to say that Russia's defense was relatively strong in the Kievan period (to 1054), weakened rapidly as the country was pulverized, politically, economically, and socially, from 1054 to about 1400, then became stronger, with many fluctuations and retreats, until, in the 18th century, it reached a level comparable to that of Europe, but undoubtedly it sagged again from 1815 until the 20th century because of its failure to obtain either the agricultural revolution or the industrial revolution. These changes can be seen in the fact that Lithuania and Poland held the Ukraine as far east as the Don River in the 15th and 16th centuries, Sweden and Poland held the eastern shore of the Baltic until well into the 18th century, while Russia did not get the shores of the Black Sea until late in the 18th century. On the other hand, against non-civilized peoples, Russian weapons were very effective, and the Russian state crossed Siberia to the northern Pacific Ocean by the middle of the 17th century and established its boundary with China on the Amur River of Manchuria in 1689 (Treaty of Nichinsk).

The original Finns and Slavs were neither warlike nor aggressive, and the early Scandinavian intruders found their Viking weapons quite adequate to their tasks. These were chiefly sword and battle-axe, with iron helmet and cuirass. The self-bow, and probably the composite bow, were known, but were used for hunting rather than for war. Similarly, cavalry was known but not used as a combat arm, being a mode of transport rather than of conflict. There was, indeed, little need for combat

in the ninth century, and, when the need arose in
the tenth century, the Viking <u>furor</u> <u>teutonicus</u> carried the day with little need for better weapons
or more skilled tactics.

By the time Kievan Russia reached its peak in
the eleventh century, warfare was much changed. By
that date, the chief political entities were the
various city states whose regular armed forces were
infantry militia armed with swords and archery.
These were accompanied by mercenary cavalry, at
first Varangian or other heavy cavalry, hired by
the city or forming the retinue of the local prince.
By 1000, these mercenary horsemen were usually foreigners, various Baltic fighters in the north, and
Magyars, steppe horsemen, or Polish knights in the
south. Many of the battles between Russian princes
for control of the districts of Galicia, Moldavia,
Volnya, or even Kiev were fought between Magyar
and Cuman cavalry, that is between hired foreign
cavalry archers. The Lithuanian-Polish conquest
of the Ukraine and White Russia in the 14th and
15th centuries was a victory of European heavy
cavalry with its accessories of crossbows, firearms, and a European siege train. In the north,
Pskov and Novgorod continued to use citizen infantry militia, supplemented with various local
or Baltic mercenary cavalry. But in Great Russia,
dominated by Moscow, it was necessary to develop a
different military establishment whose chief arm
was local cavalry archers copied from the steppes,
supplemented with local infantry forces used for
engineering and supply services, and whatever other
mercenary fighters could be obtained. The core
of the Muscovite system was the cavalry archers;
these were quite capable of defeating European
shock cavalry, but were unable to cope with a
European army of post-medieval type or with an
organized army of medieval steppe archers such
as the Mongols.

From this point of view the period 1223-1242,
especially the years 1240-1242, are crucial. In
1223 the first reconnaissance force of the Mongol
army of Genghis Khan under Subutai appeared on the
western steppes. It easily defeated a coalition
of Russian princes and Cuman horsemen near the
Kalka River, but it withdrew to the east again.

886

In 1237-1242, as we have seen, the Mongols re-appeared, and in the depths of winter, inflicted stunning defeats on the Russians, the Poles, and the Hungarians, and established their suzerainty over all Russia except Novgorod territory. This suzerainty was enforced by local garrisons, while the main Tatar horde withdrew to the grasslands of the lower Volga, where they established a capital town at Sarai. This Khanate of the Golden Horde continued as suzerain of Russia, demanding tribute and military contingents, but not inter-fering in the domestic governments of the Russians for 250 years.

Alexander Nevski (1236-1263), Prince of Novgorod and Vladimir, defeated the advancing Swedes on the Neva River in 1240 and the invad-ing Teutonic Knights in 1242 in a fierce battle on the ice of frozen Lake Peipus. In both battles it would appear that the cavalry archers of Rus-sia, however inferior to those of the Mongols, were fully able to hold their own against the cavalry lancers of European medieval forces.

The Mongol period was of decisive importance in the creation of the Muscovite despotism. The pattern was set by Alexander Nevski, who was a determined collaborator with the Mongols, while using their authority to extend his own powers within Russia as much as possible. At his death, he left the village of Moscow as the "share" of his youngest son. Under Ivan I (1325-1341) the ruler of Moscow took the title of Grand Prince, won the role of tribute collector for the Mongols over the other Russian princes, and established the bishop of Moscow as Metropolitan for the whole Russian Orthodox church. Under Dmitri Donski (1359-1389) resistance to the Tatar-Lithuanian alliance began, and the Tatars were defeated by Dmitri at Kulikovo on the Don River in 1380, but Tatar raids, wars, and tribute continued for an-other hundred years. The Mongols sacked Moscow in 1382 and forced Dmitri to join them in a war on Lithuania. Only in 1480, in a battle on the Ugra River, were the Russians able to inflict a significant defeat on the Tatar forces and to re-nounce the Mongol suzerainty and all tribute. This battle is notable for the first use of hand guns by the Muscovite forces (the Tatars were still using mounted archers).

Ravaged by the Tatars for two centuries, devastated by conflagrations which burned much of the city every generation, and swept by intermittent plagues, famines, and civil wars, the prince of Moscow continued his efforts to establish his suzerainty over other Russian princes, to increase his military manpower by grants of lands, to extend the rule of the Muscovite ecclesiastical system, and to free himself from any vestiges of popular or aristocratic control. On the whole, these efforts were successful in superficial appearances, however unsound the resulting power structure may have been in essentials. By the death of Ivan III (1462-1505), the independent oligarchic institutions of Pskov and Novgorod had been destroyed, the Metropolitan at Moscow had declared its religious independence from Byzantium (1442), a law code had been issued for the Muscovite territories (1497), the Tatar yoke and tribute had been removed (1480), the Golden Horde itself had broken up into rival parts, and an alliance of Moscow and the Crimean Khan (the Krim Tatars) had been achieved. Moscow's "authority" had reached the forest boundary of the steppe on the south and was on the fringes of White Russia and the Ukraine in the west, preparing to move westward against the Lithuanians and the Poles. The ability of Russian power to advance forward either south or west depended on its ability to adapt to the different military challenges of these two areas. The third area of expansion, eastward through the forests, was opposed by natural rather than political obstacles until it reached the edge of the Chinese power system on the Amur River about 1650.

That was the way the situation looked about 1505. But the appearance was deceptive. The whole structure was a chaos of contradictions, irrationalities, and exceptions, full of holes and tatters, without established rules or laws, simply a tangle of the consequences of past actions which might never be repeated. The only consistency in the situation was the insatiable drive for personal power by the Grand Prince and his successors, and that was not enough to obtain allegiance or obedience from subjects scattered over such a huge area.

This fundamental chaos was reflected in the military system and was largely rooted in it. The chief aim of the military system was its drive for manpower, with large-scale neglect of tactics, organization and coordination, discipline, drill, or even weapons. Even in regard to manpower, the system was chaotic, confused, and uncontrolled. The chief aim of the rulers was to obtain commitments for service from as large a number of men as possible, that they would appear, with their followers, in time of military need, prepared to fight an enemy. Little effort was ever made to enforce these agreements. As a consequence, fighters or contingents appeared or did not appear as they saw fit; if they appeared, they fought or did not fight; if they fought, they did so as they wished and for their own personal aims, such as booty. Rules were established by the Grand Prince, orders were issued, but rarely enforced, although such regulations were often reissued, sometimes many times, over a century or two. When any efforts were made to enforce these, it was usually by a single irrational act of violence against the recalcitrant, often an act out of all proportion to the importance of the rule or the significance of the episode. The law codes, such as those of 1497, 1550, 1649, and others are suggestive of aims, aspirations, or even methods, but are often misleading in regard to practice, since they were usually unenforced. In fact, in numerous cases, especially in the code of 1497, rules were set, crimes were listed, but no penalties were fixed and no methods of enforcement provided. The emphasis was more on the goals desired than on the means to achieve these goals or on the procedures to be followed, either to find out if the rules were being followed or to enforce compliance. Thus the whole tone and character of these enactments were very different from the rules of public law established in western Europe, especially in English medieval government documents with their considerable emphasis on procedures, information-gathering, and enforcement.

In his efforts to obtain the manpower he needed for his military activities, the Muscovite prince made all kinds of grants, concessions, promises,

and immunities. Rarely were these put in contractual form (which is one reason why Russia
never achieved a feudal system), but vague promises
were often made in return. Large areas were
granted to men with slaves or followers without
any clear understanding by either side as to the
conditions of the transfer. The prince was so
eager to have his lands settled or cultivated
that he feared to lose the possibility by too
rigid specifications of obligations toward himself. As a result, each side did what it could
get away with. Even when grants were made with
specific terms, such as service for life from
the grantee and his descendants, or for a term,
or the basis of the grant (in ownership, for use,
with complete jurisdiction, or with jurisdiction
reduced by enumerated exceptions), these terms
were rarely carried out, and, in most cases,
there is little evidence that any real effort
was made by either party to have them carried
out. Even where the military requirements were
very specific, as in the case of the obligations
of a single fighting man's service for each unit
of land, or later (in the 17th century) one fighting man for each ten peasant families on the land,
these rules, no matter how emphatically, frequently,
or universally they were laid down, lapsed almost
immediately and, as soon as this lapse was recognized, the rules were often reissued, to relapse
once more in a short while.

The reasons for this condition are almost
too complex to be explained here. For one thing,
the relationships of the prince to his servants
were personal and patrimonial, almost a family
relationship, and did not take that impersonal and
abstract form which became the mark of the growth
of public authority in the west. In Russia, like
in any large and unruly family, orders were shouted
and repeated, with occasional sudden blows to emphasize their reiteration, but they were constantly
neglected as to obedience or enforcement by both
sides, until they became a kind of constant nag-
ging which was regarded as the normal tone of life.
All relationships were based on will and not on
rule. In general, the ambitions and aspirations
of the rulers of Russia far outstripped their
means or resources. The former were limitless,

890

almost universal, as in any providential government, while resources were both limited and disorganized. Thus fundamental dualism rested on
the very structure of the Russian cognitive system which expected practice to fall far below the
ideal. This attitude, based on the dregs of
classical rationalism, was accompanied by a pervasive lack of rationality, logic, or firm cognitive categories and an equally extensive lack
of discipline, especially self-discipline, or of
internalized individual rules of personal behavior and value structures. The reasons for
these lacks were twofold: (1) the Russian peoples remained barbarous from the lack of any established or adopted traditions of rationality and
discipline; and (2) the dualistic tradition of
Greek Christianity which Russia tried to adopt,
placed such great emphasis on spirituality of a
level which was recognized as unattainable for
ordinary men (since it required renunciation of
most ordinary living), that what happened in the
ordinary mundane world was not important. This
second point can be seen throughout Russian history, as, for example, in the case of Rasputin,
whose lechery in the physical world was disregarded
because of his assumed spirituality in the higher
sphere or reality.

What began as a lack of disciplined thought
resulted in a prevalence of undisciplined action.
Actions, both public and private, were dominated
by impulse and passion. Violence was prevalent
in family, social, and political life, accompanied
by an explicit verbal commitment to its opposite:
submission, renunciation, spirituality, peace,
poverty, humility, and, in general, the teachings
of Christ in the "Sermon on the Mount." Through
a process of compensation, what was lacking in
action was adopted in thought.

It has been said of the Russian political
system that it was "autocracy tempered by assassination." It would be more correct to say of Russian society as a whole that it was "anarchy restrained by despotism." The two go together, not
just in Russia, where it is evident that the prevalent anarchy must be restrained by external controls.

891

A whole book could be written on the implications of these general conditions for weapons systems and political stability. We cannot write that book here, but must be satisfied with only a sketch.

The Russian military system had no guiding principle or strategic pattern, until these were adopted, along with weapons and other technology, from Europe after the medieval period. The Russian ruler took the men he could get, with the weapons they had, using the tactics they were accustomed to, and he directed these, in undisciplined and almost uncontrollable masses, at the enemies he designated. Although he was a "despot," he made what concessions he needed to get "servants," either military or administrative. To this end, he created, after 1400, three levels of such servants generally known as (1) the upper service classes (two sub-levels); (2) the middle service class; and (3) the lower service class. Of these, the USC were centered about Moscow and in Moscow province; the MSC were largely military and found in the provinces; the LSC might be found anywhere, but were concentrated toward the frontiers and served on the lowest levels both military and administrative. The USC was divided into two sub-levels, of which the top consisted of less than a hundred families, were in personal relations with the ruler, and usually had landed estates of more than a thousand acres worked by at least five hundred peasant families; the lower sub-level of the USC were not in contact with the ruler and his court, had estates farther from Moscow (but still in Moscow province), usually held less than a thousand acres, with from fifty to several hundred peasant families as tenants and workers. The MSC individuals had no particular estate or workers at first (after 1450) but were assigned a certain income from peasant rents, frequently from widely scattered sources over which he had no personal control or even contact. In wartime the MSC fighter received a small salary to supplement his regular income from rents. The LSC had neither estates nor peasants. They often had garden allotments in large public fields to work to help obtain their own food, but they were expected to be self-supporting and were paid government wages only when called to active government service.

About 1635, when this triplex arrangement of serving classes was already breaking down, there were only 41 families in the upper sub-level and 2642 in the lower sub-level of the USC; about the same date, there were about 25,000 of the MSC and a much larger but unknown number of the LSC. The USC served in the central administration, as agents of the central government in provincial administration, and as higher officers (down to battalion and company commanders) in the fighting forces. The MSC, which were first established on lands confiscated during the conquest of Novgorod in the late 15th century, were the backbone of the armed forces, the cavalry archers, for about 150 years (say 1500-1650); they were abolished in 1680. The LSC were used in lesser military roles (which had a great future in 1680) in supply, fortification, and labor units, but increasingly after 1550 as artillerymen, arquebusiers, and government cossacks. They were replaced in the 17th century by more formal units of musketeers, engineers, and artillerymen copied from Europe.

This was not a "standing army," as it reported only on call, was largely self-sustaining, was almost never drilled, was not supplied with arms, had no tactical rules or instruction manuals, and fought more or less as an armed horde. A modern army came only after 1682.

The Muscovite army in action moved like all those of providential monarchies, in five units: van; center; rear; right wing; and left wing. The center was usually called "the Tzar's regiment." It was of higher quality, was organized in units of a hundred men (probably copied from the Mongol decimal system) and was the only unit which had artillery or handguns attached to it.

All units, both foot and horse, had similar tactics, rushing on the enemy in a mass formation with different units in echelon, with a sustained missile assault, chiefly of arrows, followed by a final charge with sabers. There was no maneuvering in formation, and, indeed, there was relatively little formation.

Because the attacks upon Muscovite territories were annual, and Moscow's attacks upon its enemies were also annual, the army assembled in the spring as soon as the grass was sufficient to sustain the horses. This custom was, of course, the old March-field (later Mayfield) of the Carolingians. Because the fighters were self-sustaining, however, they were usually divided into two or more contingents, so that half reported in the spring and the other half in midsummer, allowing each contingent time to tend to its agrarian concerns. In an emergency when both halves were called together, mobilization required a long time and was never completed or full: absenteeism was high, and many who did come lacked the proper equipment, even horses and weapons. The rate of desertion was high, so that the army began to melt away before it was ever fully mobilized. The excuse which was given for these deficiencies was poverty, and this was attributed to lack of peasant labor on arable lands allotted to support fighters. It is, however, useful to recall that similar difficulties were faced by George Washington in assembling and holding his forces in the American Revolution.

Such absenteeism, lack of equipment, and desertions were most prevalent among the MSC cavalry archers, the backbone of the army in the Muscovite period. Originally, as I have said, the MSC was assigned only rents from lands to support them and had no control over the lands or peasants which produced these rents. Like most things in Russia, this began to change almost as soon as it was established, and contacts between the MSC fighter and the sources of his income appeared. After all, the warrior had to live someplace, and there was every reason why he should live as close to his source of income as possible, especially when that source was so small that it was a single holding of land. Moreover, very early, these grants of rents began to be replaced by grants of land as revocable holdings from lords to fighters. Such a grant, called pomest'e (benefice or service tenure) was different from the patrimonial holding (votchina) of a "noble" because the former was in theory a contingent income, while the latter could be inherited or even alienated (if at all possible heirs gave consent). Neither of these has anything similar with landholding in fee simple as we know it, since in theory the prince was the ultimate owner of all land in his territory, and both of these tenures were subject to restraints which are unfamiliar in modern law, just as "fee simple" was alien to Russian law.

By the 18th century, the distinction in law between these two Russian tenures was ended by Empress Anne in 1731, but in fact service tenures had tended to become patrimonial in practice from the beginning. The problem was that most service tenures were too small, with too few peasants, who ran away from smaller holdings because they could find an easier, or at least a more communal, life on large estates, on monastic lands, on the frontiers, or in the eastern forests.

A cavalry archer was expected to have a horse, bow, arrows, a sword, and armor. A horse cost about ten rubles, a damascene sword at least four rubles, and body armor about four rubles in 1556. The armor consisted of a conical helmet, a sleeved jacket of chain mail, and knee plates. Most MSC could not afford a damascene sword, many could not afford armor and wore a quilted cuirass with what metal inserts could be obtained. The horses were really ponies, small, unshod, ridden with high stirrups on a Tatar (later Persian) saddle; they were controlled by very long reins tied to the little finger of the left hand, while a whip was tied to the little finger of the right hand, both hanging freely so as not to hamper use of the bow; spurs were not used.

To afford such equipment, a cavalry archer of the MSC needed at least 12 to 15 peasant families on sufficient land. There was still plenty of land, but a great shortage of peasants, and the MSC had no way to retain these workers or to recover them if they fled.

Ivan IV "the Terrible" (1533-1584) had only about 600 fighting men, but he established 1071 more on 118,200 chetverti of land (157,600 acres) and organized in law a system of six grades of MSC fighters, from the highest with about 468

acres of land and 12 rubles a year to the lowest
with about 133 acres and 5 rubles. At the end of
the century, hereditary estates were subject to a
similar requirement of one equipped cavalryman
from each 400 acres, with pay for any extra men
he might bring along. Many persons sent slaves
in their places or brought along slaves to serve
for pay. A.A. Zimin says that about three-quarters
of the fighters were slaves at that time.

This system began to break down almost at once,
especially in the disorders under Ivan the Terrible's
oprichina (a period of paranoid purges) with its
extensive confiscations among the nobles, mostly
members of the USC, and the subsequent social disruption of all classes in the "Time of Troubles"
(1584-1613). After 1600 Russian society became
more stratified, and access to its various classes
began to close. For example, a decree of 1601 forbade the children of slaves, peasants, or clergy to
join the MSC. Service requirements had to be reduced because of the shortage of men. In the MSC
the requirements were shifted from land area to the
amount of available labor, with one cavalry archer
for each 15 peasant families, but the MSC still
demanded cash payments from the state for any
fighter who was supported by less than 50 peasant
families. The MSC was closed to entry by any outsider in 1619; this rule was frequently reissued,
but was constantly violated, especially on the
steppe frontier, where resident fighters were in
such demand that even runaway slaves or peasants
were accepted as MSC fighters without any serious
questioning about their origins. As the class
closed, the shift of holdings from pomest'e to
votchina also speeded up. The inheritance of
pomest'e lands was established by 1600, protected
by law in 1618 and, within sixty years, 59 per cent
of MSC holdings were hereditary. As we have said,
the two types were merged in 1731.

The supply of peasant labor and the supply
of fighting men remained insufficient for most of
the period covered by this chapter. The lack of
fighters was attributed to the lack of peasants
to support them. Accordingly, efforts to prevent
peasants from moving away from the lands they occupied began. In the Kievan period, anyone could
move freely. This continued for peasants until

896

about 1450 and was not legally ended until 1649,
but in the interval between these two dates frequent restrictions were placed on movements of
peasants. The exact dates and terms of these restrictions are not known and have to be inferred.
About 1450 Basil II forbade peasants to move from
one holding to another except during the two-week
period centered on St. George's Day (26 November)
when the crops were fully harvested, debts could
be paid, and the new agricultural year, under the
two-field system, had not yet begun. This was an
age of devastation and depression (from about 1060
to 1480). A similar period occurred in the late
16th century, say from 1550 to 1620, just when
conquest of the steppes opened possibilities for
peasants to make a better life in that region.
Many ran away or were abducted by great landlords
or monasteries who needed labor. A major part of
the lands about Moscow province fell out of cultivation in the 35 years from Richard Chancellor's
visit in 1553 to Giles Fletcher's visit in 1588.
About 1580, the government suspended the peasant's
right to move on St. George's Day. This was made
permanent about 1592 and was incorporated into the
law code of 1649. Until after 1600, recovery of a
runaway or abducted peasant was a civil matter:
the deprived landlord had to find the absentee
through his own efforts and expense and had to sue
in the courts to get him back when he found him.
After an edict of 1607, running away became a
criminal matter, with government officials required to check on all rural residences and arrest
all who were not legitimate residents of the places
where they were found, to return them to their
places of departure. From this time on until today, spying on individuals and coercion of their
movements have been a regular part of Russian life.

This change enserfed about 75 per cent of Russia's population and forced them into a legal status
which steadily became worse. It was done so that
the MSC could survive without work so that they
could fight the Tzar's enemies, and it was achieved
after centuries of efforts to find a solution to
the problem of obtaining an adequate supply of
mounted archers. But like so many reforms, especially in Russia, it was the wrong decision at the
wrong time: in 1650, the MSC cavalry archer was

already obsolete as a weapons system, and the urgent need, by that date, was for disciplined, mercenary, forces of infantry to serve as musketeers, artillery-men, and engineers, with several new kinds of cavalry, including shock cavalry with lances or sabers and light cavalry with firearms (the pistoleers, made possible by the invention of the wheellock handgun which was invented in Germany about 1520).

The fact that Russia made serfdom permanent in the Code of 1649 in order to preserve the MSC cavalryman and then abolished the MSC as a whole in 1682 was a disaster for Russia and for the world. To create serfdom to ensure service and then to per-mit the beneficiaries to evade all service and to live at leisure from the enslavement of millions of humans, as existed in Russia from 1682 till after 1862 is unforgivable.

This tragedy was made worse by the fact that the serfs created in Russia in the 17th century be-came more slaves than serfs. They were excluded completely from contact with the government or the outside world by the fact that their masters had jurisdiction over them, and they could not get a hearing in an outside court nor appeal to any police for protection of their human rights (not that anyone had human rights in the Russian sys-tem). We usually feel that serfs are tied to the land and, as a result, cannot be taken from their families or villages and, thus, that they at least have some degree of economic, social, and emotional security. This was not true in Rus-sia, where the government made frequent concessions to the landed class just in the years that that class was becoming less and less useful to the government. Thus the government issued decrees which permitted masters to sell their serfs or their serfs' services, so that they could be sent anywhere and compelled to do almost anything. Rather than becoming attached to the land, as serfdom was in western Europe, the serf in Russia became attached to his master personally in a de-grading relationship of bondage which was alien-able from only one side, the master's.

The military history of Russia is quite dif-ferent from that of Europe, which makes it difficult to understand for those who have been brought up in the European historical tradition and regard that tradition as the natural and inevitable sequence of events. If we regard the Kievan period as comparable to the classical period, the long post-Kievan period of decline from 1054 to about 1480 seems to possess many of the features which we saw in the west in the decline of Rome and the dark age. Thus the period A.D. 200-970 in the west is similar to the period 1054-1480 in Russia. We might even see the Mongol period in Russia (1240-1480) as a somewhat dissimilar parallel to the Frankish-Carolingian period in the west from about 508 to 888. This would make Russia's medieval period from 1480, or even 1380, to 1682, and the period of Russian expansion in area, population, literacy, commerce, production, and self-awareness from 1480 to 1550 is comparable to Europe's period of medieval expansion from 970 to 1270, with the crisis in the west of 1270-1440 comparable to the Russian crisis of 1550-1620. The terms which we apply to western history, such as feudalism, manorial system, chivalry, beginnings of commerce and the rise of towns, Renaissance, and Reformation, and many others are quite unfitted to the historical experience of Russia and are totally misleading if applied to it. The European medieval town, for example, was quite different from the Russian town or city, since the former was an autonomous municipal organization, self-governing and existing as a distinct socioeconomic entity, with a distinct bourgeois class performing a valuable economic function in society by exchanging its goods and services for the food and raw materials it drew from the surrounding countryside. The Russian town, particularly after Ivan the Terrible, was a fortress which might serve as a residence for the ruling, landlord, and military classes, but it drew rural goods from the hinterland to its walls on the basis of legal, political, and military claims, as the oriental city has always done.

As we shall see, the medieval military system in the west was essentially static and local, based on mounted, armored, shock forces and the rural fortress. The Russian military system was always based on mobility, by boat in the Kievan period and on the cavalry archer in the Russian medieval period. This archer was not associated with a castle or fortress, as in the west, and such fortresses in the east were associated with a quite different organization and outlook, a princely authority in a wide and pervasive system of patrimonial despotic power. Most princely power in Russia was universal in its claims and actions, reflecting the providential monarchical universalism which, in the west, was reduced to a submerged heretical theory after 888. This theory did not revive in the west until the reemergence of the ideas of classical Greece in the late Middle Ages and Renaissance. Then these reached a peak in the so-called "political theories of obedience" in 1560-1640.

The Russian cavalry archer had nothing to do with such matters, except to serve. He lived marginally, in a dwelling which was undefended and non-military, and his military operations were not expected to take place around his residence, but at a distance. The Russian emphasis on mobility reflected, of course, proximity of the threat of Asiatic nomads and the great size of the Russian territory. This territory expanded from 47 thousand square kilometers in 1300, to 430 thousand in 1462, to 2800 thousand in 1533, and reached 15,280 thousand in 1688, all in theory subject to the will or whim of the Tzar. The ruler had to be able to shift his defense forces from the steppe corridor in the southeast to the west, where a threat from Europe could come, by water over the Baltic or by land from Lithuania, Poland, or Germany.

In Russia the castle was not a weapon against external enemies, during the Russian Middle Ages (before 1680), but was rather a protection against the Russian people. It collapsed relatively easily before invaders from outside, and the protracted sieges which are so familiar in the military history of other countries are not generally found in Russian history in this period, except in Novgorod which is Baltic rather than Russian. After 1680, the fortified castle became a very important part of the Russian military system simply because the Russian military system since that date has been largely a copy of European examples (except for some eastern survivals, such as the Cossacks).

This copying of foreign military patterns is of ancient origin in Russia, going back to the Kievan period and is evident in large-scale use of foreign mercenaries, foreign technicians, and foreign advisors in Russian affairs until at least 1840.

The weaknesses of the MSC cavalry archers, both in numbers and quality, led to an extensive use of foreign mercenaries even in the period in which these archers were regarded as the backbone of the Russian defense forces in 1450-1650. The MSC cavalry archers became increasingly unreliable after 1570 as increasing numbers of them failed to appear on call or appeared without full equipment. Richard Hellie (1971) quotes a case in 1577 in which, in one district, less than 6 per cent who appeared had the required armor.

The real problem which Russia faced in this period was that it was threatened by two quite different weapons systems. In the south, the main threat remained the nomad bowmen of the Mongols or Crimean Tatars, who used hit-and-run tactics in annual raids. Only after 1667 did Russia have real military contact with the Ottoman Turks, who offered a third type of military threat and were already in decay before they had real conflicts with Russia. But in the west, the threat to Russia was of a different character and much more dangerous, although its full technological dimensions did not develop until after 1700, because of the fact that Russia's nearest enemies in the west, Lithuania, Poland, and even Sweden, were in political decline before the full threat of the gunpowder revolution had been reached. These developments in the west involved technical questions of artillery, fortifications, field maneuvers, infantry drill, and firepower.

These two threats to Russia from the south and the west overlapped from 1200 to about 1600, after which the southern threat dwindled away, while the western threat continued to grow, through the rise of Prussia, to its peak in Napoleon's invasion in 1812. But Russia's concentration on the Tatar question continued high even after that danger was dying away, because of Russia's own aggressive designs on the resources of the Ukraine and the lower Volga. Because of this distraction, Russia did not face up to the gunpowder revolution until after 1680, although its rulers were familiar with this problem and attempted to use the innovations from an early date.

The gunpowder revolution, namely firepower from artillery and later from handguns, forced a shift from mass infantry formations, as first used by the Swiss in the 14th century and last used by the Spanish tercio in the battles of Breitenfeld (1631) and Rocroi (1643). Missile weapons (crossbows, longbows, and handguns in the west and the Asiatic bow in the east) had made the western heavy cavalry increasingly obsolete in the 14th century. This western knight was ultimately replaced by several specialized kinds of cavalry, including heavy shock horsemen using sabers rather than spears and used at a later stage in the battle after enemy formations had been broken sufficiently by missiles from infantry. In the west this development was accompanied by a very great development of general logistics, including bases, supply, and a warfare of limited aims and maneuver which reached its peak in the period from about 1690 to 1796.

These changes began in the west in the Hundred Years War (1338-1445), were accelerated in the Italian Wars (1494-1559), and culminated, under Dutch inspiration and Swedish development, in the Thirty Years War (1618-1648). The implications of these changes did not reach Russia until after 1680, partly because of Russia's concern with its southern front and partly because Russia was shielded from the full impact of the western military innovations by the Lithuanians, Poles, and the Teutonic Knights. The Poles, who may have inspired the new cavalry tactics which culminated in Conde and Turenne in the 18th century, neglected the role of castles and fortified bases and were so obsessed with maintaining the privileges of the landlord class that they also neglected the role of pikes as a defense against shock cavalry, and finally even destroyed their own government and abandoned their political independence in order to maintain their class privileges (1772-1795).

902

With these buffers against western military developments, Russia reached the end of the 17th century, in the reign of Peter the Great, without realizing the role of pikes or bayonets, of military forts and siege trains, of the proper response to increasing infantry firepower, or the new techniques of western sea power. This neglect allowed the Poles to occupy west central Russia and to capture Moscow in 1611, while the Swedes captured Novgorod and occupied much of northwestern Russia in the same year. These defeats in the Time of Troubles resulted as much from the organizational collapse of the Russian system after 1556 under Ivan the Terrible as from the inadequacies of Russian weapons or military organization. As a consequence, the whole of western Russia including the Ukraine, White Russia, Livonia, and Novgorod territory west of the city itself were lost again, as they had been in the earlier period of depression, depopulation, and disorder in 1054-1480. Since Moscow in this period of collapse (1550-1620) did not yet have the southern steppes, the country was reduced to the Great Russian area of central Muscovy, with the north from Novgorod city east to the Urals, and the trans-Ural east as far as the moving zone of colonization. Moscow was sacked by the Crimean Tatars in 1571, and these enemies returned to the city's walls again in a devastating invasion in 1591. Ivan himself sacked Novgorod in 1571.

The chief contribution to the recovery from these disasters came from the deterioration of power in Russia's neighbors, especially the Poles and the Tatars, the destruction of Germany in the Thirty Years War, and the deflection of Swedish power southward from the eastern Baltic to western Germany. In this recovery, the only contribution made by weaponry was various attempts to introduce into Russia the advantages in firearms which came out of the Italian Wars of 1494-1559 and some improvements in fortifications to meet the threat of artillery. Organizational advances, such as the adoption of a fully mercenary army paid in money, the development of some rational or effective concepts of strategy and tactics, the establishment of some unified system of training (drill) and discipline, the creation of a system of supply, and other improvements were largely neglected.

Cannon came to Russia about 1380 and handguns just a century later in 1480. The earliest cannon were feeble and ineffective. They could be used from fortifications to keep the enemy at a distance but could not be used to attack fortifications. These early cannon were made of sheet iron, rolled into a pipe and bound with iron hoops. They fired stones using pulp gunpowder, which burned rather than exploded, so that an air space had to be left between the stone and the powder to provide oxygen for combustion. As a result, gas pressure built up slowly, much of it escaped past the stone, and when this missile finally emerged from the barrel, it had a short range and shattered ineffectively on impact with any solid surface, such as a fortification. These weapons could fire only about four times a day, were used in twenty-two conflicts between 1382 and 1470, without any notable consequence, but were used between 1470 and 1520 in some twenty recorded cases, with some influence on the outcome of the engagement in sixteen of these cases (according to Hellie).

Granular powder which burned fast enough to be called an explosion and required no air space between the powder and the ball was introduced in the late 15th century. Iron and lead balls came in about the time that the handgun arrived in the 1480s, probably brought to Russia by the skilled Italian gunmaker, Aristoteles Fioravante, who came in 1475 and introduced cast bronze cannon of about 3.5 inch bore. The first Russian use of artillery in the field is said to have been in 1399, but it was more than a century before the wheeled caisson with trunnions on the cannon came from France and made field artillery practicable.

Only in the sixteenth century did gunpowder begin to play a role in Russian warfare, and it was a much delayed and distorted role. Cannon were of growing significance after 1550, under Ivan the Terrible, when gunners who made and operated their own cannon were being paid two to three rubles a year (at a time when a horse was worth about ten rubles). By 1600 Russia had about 3500 guns but was still dependent on imported ammunition and to some extent on foreign gunners. By that date, guns were effective in siege operations, and fortress construction was adapting to that by shifting to a polygon shape with a relatively low profile on open terrain, thus offering few flat surfaces to the impact of cannonballs and increasing the chances of glancing blows. The first of the new fortresses was built on the Narva River against the Teutonic Order in 1492, but was captured by the Swedes and held by them in 1581-1590 and 1612-1704. A similar fortress was built in the south at Nizhnii Novgorod in 1511, and a gigantic one, using 150 million bricks and 620,000 large facing stones, was constructed at Smolensk in 1595-1602, with walls from 40 to 60 feet high, 12 to 20 feet thick, and four miles around. This was captured by the Poles and held in 1611-1654.

Handguns, chiefly arquebus, which reached Russia about 1480, were muzzle-loaded matchlocks and were so heavy (about 20 pounds) that they had to be supported by a stand under the barrel while being fired; they were about .22 caliber and were so awkward that they could not be fired from horseback, although some arquebusiers were mounted until they reached the battlefield. Units of such fighters were in existence in the first half of the sixteenth century, but they were so expensive, being mercenaries, that they were usually disbanded after each period of service and had to be recruited again from scratch when some new emergency appeared. Like all early handguns, these weapons were of limited range (less than 200 yards), inaccurate, and could achieve only a low rate of fire, perhaps less than twice a minute, with no more than a dozen shots in a battle.

In spite of these weaknesses, in Russia, as in the west, infantry arquebusiers and later musketeers had a great future. In 1550 Ivan the Terrible established a permanent standing force of 3000 such mercenary infantry. This was probably copied from the Turkish Janissaries, and was also adopted by Lithuania and Poland in the next dozen years.

905

This Russian force of infantry musketeers, called streltsy, was organized in companies of a hundred and was the first fully organized force of standing fighting units in Russian history. They were supported by a special new tax which fell almost exclusively on the peasants and on a few townsmen. By 1600 there were about 20,000 streltsy in all Russia, with the major part in Moscow.

The weakness of the streltsy as a missile arm, with limited firepower, very limited mobility (about 10 miles a day), and a limited rate of fire, meant that they could be used successfully only in combination with other arms. In the west such forces were protected against shock cavalry by a mass of infantry pikemen among whom the musketeers could take refuge while reloading. Russia had no pikemen, and their infantry were threatened by missile cavalry, whose bows had more range, accuracy, and rate of fire than the streltsy guns. The Russians could find only feeble remedies for these weaknesses, such as training the streltsy units to fire in platoons so that there would always be available a major part of each unit ready loaded. This was expected to keep the enemy at a distance so that their missiles would be less effective, but since the enemy, being mounted, in most cases, had greater mobility and the streltsy themselves were unarmored, this was not much help. For an emergency most streltsy fighters had auxiliary shock weapons, a broad-bladed axe or a saber or lance, but these were not much help against cavalry archers. Accordingly, it became the practice for the streltsy units to be used only with some kind of protection or cover unless they were accompanied by MSC cavalry archers who could keep the enemy cavalry at a distance while the streltsy were reloading. Thus these infantry musketeers were dependent upon the very weapons system they were supposed to be replacing and were inferior to it in mobility and in rate of fire.

For these reasons it soon became clear that the streltsy were useful chiefly behind fortifications. To provide these in the field, wooden panels about six feet high and of varying width, sometimes mounted on wheels, were taken into battle. This made the streltsy even more awkward and even less effective. They were widely scattered in units along the frontiers, usually associated with local MSC cavalry archers, commanded by MSC officers, and with a base in local fortifications. Their chief function in such warfare was to hold up the advance of the enemy to distract these until the interior defense forces could be mobilized. About 40 per cent of the total streltsy force was in Moscow, and about a quarter of this was mounted, although they fought on foot. In 1600, when the total streltsy force in Russia was about 200 companies of a hundred men each, about eighty companies, of which twenty were mounted, were stationed in Moscow.

The need for cover for the streltsy in combat and the fact that the nomads of the steppes raided on a regular seasonal basis helped to determine the ways by which Moscow conquered the grasslands. In 1480, when the Mongol suzerainty and tribute was renounced, the first line of defense was at the forest edge, only about fifty miles south of Moscow, near the Oka River. Over the next two centuries, a number of barriers were erected as defensive lines running from west to east across the plain. The first was built about 1560, still in the forest, but south of the Oka, by cutting trees about six feet above the ground so that they fell pointing south and close enough together to entangle each other. Where the trees were farther apart, logs were set upright in the ground to block the gaps. A later line farther south and away from the forest consisted of a ditch about twelve feet deep and twelve feet wide with the earth piled up on the northern side. Guardhouses were placed at intervals along these lines, the grass was burned away on the outer side and vines were allowed to grow over the obstacles themselves. MSC colonists in the area were assigned to patrol the steppe beyond the barriers each day from the beginning of April until the snow fell in the autumn, operating in eight shifts which were called upon to go out at regular intervals in 2-man patrols, looking for raiders, their tracks, or the dust raised by moving horsemen, and sending back an alarm to summon up stronger defense forces either of MSC or streltsy from their frontier bases.

The first such defense barrier ran over 600
miles, through Tula. The second one, about 400
miles long, built in the 1560s, became the basis
of the 1571 regulations I have just mentioned,
which emerged from the burning of Moscow by the
Tatars that year. The Tatars burned Moscow again
in 1592 and made their last raid in 1618. By this
last date the line was advancing very rapidly with
peasant colonists occupying the soil north of the
line and being organized as MSC archers as they
settled the land. Other peasants, slaves, criminals,
and adventurers moved beyond the line close on the
heels of the retreating Tatars, whose nomadic ways
they copied, living by hunting and fishing, herding, trading, banditry, and crime, but still forming a buffer between the sown land and the nomad
Tatars. This mixed group, perpetuated by new recruits and by the offspring of any women they could
persuade or abduct, were soon as good riders and
fighters as the Tatars. They came to be known as
Cossacks and eventually became a very numerous
group quite willing to ally with Moscow if they
were paid.

In 1625, when there were about 14,000 troops
in 11 frontier garrisons, a new, and final, barrier began to be constructed, running about 500
miles through Kharkov. It was finished about 1653,
but was no longer needed, as the Tatar threat had
largely abated. In the interval the wheellock ignition came in from Germany, making it possible to
construct a carbine which could be fired from horseback. The streltsy, however, continued to use the
match-lock ignition and became increasingly ineffective. Like the MSC cavalry earlier, the government refused to support these so they could provide
themselves with the necessary weapons, but it did
allow the streltsy to engage in business in the
towns, with the result that they were unwilling
to leave their enterprises to go to war.

Thus the errors with the MSC cavalry were
repeated with the streltsy infantry. As both became less effective in the 17th century, the Tzar
sought a quantitative rather than a qualitative
remedy, increasing the numbers of both until they
reached a peak, the MSC to about 40,000 in 1651,
twice the total which had been in 1600, and the

908

streltsy about 65,000 in 1663. Both were made
hereditary groups, which made them even less effective. The streltsy had been used for police
work against the Russian people from their first
establishment and were used increasingly for this
purpose in the 17th century, but after 1640 they
showed a tendency to support the rioters and rebels.
The use of firearms for police work was another indication of the low level of weapons sophistication
in the Russian government in that period.

The ineffectiveness of the MSC cavalry and
the streltsy musketeers gave rise to efforts to
replace them after 1653, the cavalry archers by
new mounted units (reitary) and the streltsy by
new infantry units (soldaty). At the same time,
large numbers of foreigners were hired, especially
as officers, from the many unemployed warriors released by the ending of the Thirty Years War in
1648. Ordinary soldiers were raised by compulsion
from the Russian peasants, who often ran away to
the steppes or into the Siberian forests. The
soldaty were drilled by foreign officers and were
usually paid only in time of war, but were expected
to support themselves in time of peace. However,
the wars were almost continuous, shifting among the
Swedes, the Poles, and the steppe fighters, with
the Turks coming in after 1667. Casualties were
very heavy, with 19,000 killed in five battles in
1659-1664.

The reitary proved to be no solution to the
cavalry problem, as they were required to equip
themselves with a horse, carbine, two pistols,
sword, helmet, and cuirass. Few could afford
this. Numerous experiments were made with hussars
(cavalry lancers without armor), dragoons (mounted
musketeers who fought on foot), but these dwindled
away in the 1680s.

The expense of all this was very great, as
the Russian forces increased in total numbers,
reaching towards 200,000 at the end of the 17th
century, with 129,000 used against the Turks in
1680. While the Russian enlisted man received
four, or at the most five, rubles a year, foreign
officers were given fortunes; in 1634 the pay

scale for a foreign colonel of cavalry was 400
rubles a year, 250 for an infantry colonel, while
captains obtained 100 in the cavalry and 75 in the
infantry. In the 1680s, more than 80 per cent of
Russia's officers were foreign. The cost of defense tripled in about thirty years (1638-1670),
rising to about a million rubles a year in wartime,
of which three-quarters went for the new formations.
This cost was also about three-quarters of all
government expense. Many expedients were tried
by the Tzar to raise the necessary sums, but there
were large evasions of taxes and losses by corruption or incompetence. Much of the costs were
paid by inflation through debasement of the currency, leading to violent riots in Moscow in 1662.
A tax on salt yielded little when the people refused to buy salt; taxes on crops were evaded by
shifting crops and, when this tax was replaced by
a tax on households, peasant families doubled up
and lived together, so that Peter replaced this
tax by a head tax on all males.

The chief weakness of the Russian military effort in the 17th century was intellectual. Nothing
was thought out; there was no idea of aims,
methods, priorities, planning, or best use of
limited resources. Mass quantity was always preferred to efficient quality. Hordes of unequipped
men were wasted, a practice which still continued
in 1914-1917, because of a reluctance to pay for a
smaller, well-equipped, and well-trained force
capable of applying its weapons in an effective
way. The chief aim after 1653 was to replace
militia forces by standing armies, yet the government still refused to pay these in peacetime, to
pay them adequately in war, or to pay for weapons
or training. One of the keys to this reluctance,
in contrast to the often extravagant expenditures
on foreign officers or on the Tzar's own personal
indulgences, is to be found in the profound disrespect of the ruling groups for the ordinary Russian peasant, his life, or his welfare. This feeling probably deepened as the peasant sank into
serfdom, the number of them increased, and the
growing guilt in the Russian soul had to be suppressed (until the 19th century, when both the
Russian peasant and the Russian soul, to say nothing of guilt, were romanticized).

910

There was no established system of supply for Russian armies at that period, even in time of war. Instead, it was expected that armies, both Russian and their enemies, would live off the country, which, once again, meant off the peasants. There was little effort by the ruling groups to find out about the military revolution which was advancing in the West, inspired by the Dutch, carried out by the Swedes, and culminating in the French, except to hire almost any foreigner who offered his services at outrageous cost. The government did pay to produce a Russian translation of Johann Jakob von Wallhausen's Kriegskunst zu Fuss, the third book ever published in Russia, in 1649, but only 134 copies were sold in ten years out of the 1200 printed. When Peter reached the throne in 1692, Russian military affairs were still at least a century behind the developments in Western Europe. The new Tzar fixed as his chief aim to make up that lag, but his efforts were as chaotic and irrational as those of his predecessors, results being achieved largely from his energy, determination, and ruthlessness. Quantity was still preferred over quality, and violence substituted for skilled management. Nevertheless, the collapse of Sweden, Poland, and Turkey in the 18th century made the Russian military system look good and increased its ability to solve its problems by the quantity rather than the quality of its weapons systems.

4. The European Dark Age and Early Western Civilization, 900-1500

The history of Western weapons systems over the last thousand years can be divided into five successive stages, each associated with a different political system:

	Dates	Weapons	Politics
1.	920-1200	knight & castle	feudalism
2.	1200-1520	mercenary men-at-arms & bowmen	feudal monarchy
3.	1520-1800	mercenary muskets, pikes, artillery	dynastic monarchy
4.	1800-1935	mass army of citizen soldiers	democracy
5.	1935-	army of specialists	managerial bureaucracy

These changes in two aspects of Western civilization were accompanied by parallel changes in other aspects. There were three cycles of alternating periods of economic

911

expansion and economic crisis and changing methods of
economic controls which interacted with the politico-
military arrangements on one side and with the social
arrangements on the other side. The three periods of
economic expansion were approximately 970-1270; 1440-
1580; and 1770-1930, while the alternative periods of
crises were about 1270-1440; 1580-1815; and from
1898 onward.

The dark age following the Carolingian collapse
(830-970) was a period of economic crisis and retraction
of economic enterprise toward a subsistence agricultural
base organized in almost self-sufficient units of enterprise. The phase of medieval expansion (970-1270) was
marked by clearing of wastelands and forest, by population increase and agricultural colonization, by local
investment in economic, political, and military infrastructure (such as watermills, better tools, housing,
improved transportation), increasing specialization in
the production and exchange of goods, expansion of handicrafts and commerce, increased use of money, slow rise in
prices, considerable growth of towns, spreading literacy
and recordkeeping, castle building, improved horses,
increased use of armor, and the appearance of a new middle class between peasants and warriors. In the subsequent period of retraction (1270-1440), population
and prices ceased rising. Economic investment was distorted and smothered by growing warfare, increased class
conflicts, growing superstition and irrationality, and
by intensified ideological and religious controversies.

The period of economic dominance by local customs
(830-970) began to break down and be replaced by conscious local decision-making in the first period of
economic expansion, about 1050, as a result of the modest
improvements in mobility during the period, supplemented
by the gradual replacement of customary personal relationships by agreed monetary relationships. This commutation
of goods and services into money payments penetrated eventually into most aspects of life, economic, political,
military, and even, to some extent, into religious and
social life, freeing both goods and men for alternative
uses. The improvements in mobility of men, goods, and
information over the whole period from 970 to after 1750
did not result in the creation of a single market or a
pricing mechanism wider than could be controlled by the
rather limited political systems. These improvements
were, however, sufficient to allow a gradual widening

and improvement of political controls. These widening controls in the long period 1050-1800 were used to direct or restrict the use of economic resources, at first (11th to 15th centuries) to prevent monopolies from exploiting consumers, but later for diverse other purposes including political and military ones. This whole effort to control economic life, especially commerce but later also handicrafts and money flows, is known as "mercantilism" and is sometimes divided into two successive periods of "municipal mercantilism," from before 1200 to after 1500, and "state mercantilism" from 1500 to almost 1800, a change which reflects the widening power of political units.

After about 1700, in the third stage of European economic expansion, mercantilist control of economic life collapsed completely. The great increases in the mobility of men, goods, and information created wider, and ultimately worldwide, markets which could be controlled more effectively by the mechanisms of the laissez-faire price system than by the more limited range of competing political systems. This period of laissez-faire is closely associated with the 19th century and was being replaced, at the end of that century, by a new system of economic activities in which oligopolistic controls were leading rapidly, in 1890-1930, toward a new era of private and public planning.

We can envision this millennium, 970-1970, in terms of a previous dark age followed by three cycles of prosperity and subsequent depression (or phases of expansion and crisis). Each cycle may be regarded as consisting of three successive periods associated, in sequence, with: (1) commercialization of human life; followed by (2) politicalization of life; and ending with (3) militarization of life. Each period of expansion in Western civilization was marked by the extension of commercial relationships to human activities concerned with land, security, neighbors, or even religion, which had previously been customary, personal, and non-commercialized. As expansion begins to slow up, and the phase of crises commences, investment of resources, including money and men, begins to shift from economic activities to political activities, and important changes are increasingly determined by power decisions rather than by commercial considerations. This is marked by a major shift of human energy and attention from the economic level to the political level. As the crisis deepens, the emphasis of attention and energy continues to shift and the politicalization of life begins to be supplemented by the third aspect of this cycle, the growing militarization of life.

In the European dark age about 970, life had some of the qualities we associate with life in a primitive society. A major part of human relationships were customary, personal, face-to-face activities, and many of the controls of human behavior were internalized within the human endocrine and nervous systems. They were not external social controls (such as price levels, traffic signals, police officers, or legislated rules). The internalized controls were the result of socialization within the family and neighborhood, including religious beliefs and behavior patterns. The slow processes by which custom and fixed patterns were replaced by mobility and the need for choice, after 970, served to weaken and disintegrate the social patterns and social entities (villages and kinship groups). This reduced the almost total social immersion of the individual in largely unchanging patterns of behavior and experience. In such a society, socialization of behavior and ideas became much less complete and less integrated, and external controls of an economic, political, and military nature (in that order) became increasingly part of each individual's life. In Europe as a whole, this process moved fairly steadily for the whole millennium after about 1000 toward individualism. The slow development of the state as a form of centralized, remote, impersonal power after 970 made power and violence more remote and impersonal to many people, with intermittent reversals, until the 20th century. In general, the whole millennium was marked by a movement from social and religious (thus internalized) controls toward political and military (thus externalized) controls.

Europe in 970 was not completely a subsistence economy in which each social entity consumed what it produced. While commerce and exchange sank to a very low ebb in the 10th century, they did not vanish entirely. Europe was not reduced to a one-class society, as a subsistence economy would have to be. In 970 there were at least two classes, peasants and warriors, to say nothing of scattered craft specialists, such as smiths, and even a few traders. There were far too many raiders and military adventurers. Nevertheless, Europe at the end of the 10th century, when the dark

age was ending and the Middle Ages were about to com-
mence, can be regarded for our purposes as a two-class
society of peasants and fighters. In theory at least,
there was an exchange between them in which the peasants
produced food and other economic needs for both classes
and the much smaller number of warriors provided defense
for both. In this exchange the peasants did a much better job than the fighters, who had difficulty providing
security even for themselves. In fact, there was a
good deal of simple exploitation of the peasants by the
warriors. It would be naive to regard the peasants'
contributions to the fighting class as voluntary.

Despite the non-voluntary character of most of the
incomes flows from peasants to fighters, these flows became the chief basis of the economic expansion of the
970-1280 period. The inequitable distribution of incomes within European society provided the capital which
made possible the investment in economic infrastructure
and in agricultural techniques. Many of these changes
were more fundamental, and in some cases earlier, than
the new technology of which Lynn White has written so
eloquently (1962), such as horsecollars, traces, horseshoes, and stirrups.

This diversion of incomes and resources into capital
formation was the foundation of the economic expansion of
the early and high Middle Ages. It provided more food,
more manpower for non-food activities, and demand by the
upper class for luxury goods of remote origins, including, ultimately, Russian furs, and Eastern spices, metals, and textiles. Thus, by 1050, distant trade in
luxury goods, by way of the Baltic and the Mediterranean,
was giving rise to periodic fairs, to increasing circulation of money, to increasing demand for wool, wheat,
beer, and wine within Western Europe itself, and to the
three fundamental aspects of medieval expansion: (1)
the beginnings of commerce; (2) the rise of towns;
and (3) the reappearance and growth of a middle class
of merchants and craftsmen between the two older classes
of peasants and warriors.

All of these changes and the subsequent phases of
crisis and expansion had profound impacts on weapons
systems and political stability. The general long-term
trend was toward greater offensive power over this whole
period. Any temporary resurgences of defensive power
were associated with relatively brief improvements in

ability to defend strongholds which became nuclei of local resistance to more distant power centers. Such increased defensive ability sometimes reflected improvements in defensive weapons or tactics. Much more frequently it reflected the decreased ability of an enemy to sustain an offensive at a distance and especially a decrease in ability to maintain a siege long enough to compel a stronghold to surrender. It was a consequence of logistics rather than of weapons. By "logistics" I mean mobility of men, goods, and information.

In the early Middle Ages, the inability to move supplies to a besieging force rested on the basic fact that human productivity was only marginally above the subsistence level, and, once the economically non-productive upper class of warriors and clergy had taken their share, that margin was gone. In the 10th century north of the mountains, agricultural yields were probably close to twice the amount of seed used, and for oats, so necessary for adequate horsepower, was even less. The figures we have from the Carolingian period examined by George Duby (1968) show that fields were sown very lightly (2.3 bushels per acre), and yields for all grain crops were below twice the seed, that smiths were rare even on the largest estates, and that most farm tools, even plows, were of wood. Duby believes that there was an improvement in the position of the peasant from the 10th to the 13th century, in spite of increased amounts demanded from him as tithes for the clergy and other dues for his secular lord. The improvement, which came from improved yields up to 4 to 1 over the seed, gave each peasant family twice as much food. The better yields apparently came from better tools, especially plows, which helped the clearing of waste and forest and allowed lands, especially the fallow, to be plowed better and more frequently. Much of this improvement was lost to the ordinary peasant by the increase in population, which led to higher prices for grain but lower wages for labor, and heavier demands for dues and fees (especially for required use of the lord's mill, ovens, winepress, forests, fisheries, and other so-called "banalites"). In England, according to M.M. Postan, the lord's dues amounted to about half of the peasant's income in the 13th century when the agricultural fields were decreasing in fertility. When we add to this the coincidence of rising prices and falling wages, as demand for food and supply of labor both increased, we can see that the doubling or even tripling of yields could not keep up with the quadrupling of population in England from less than 1.5 million in 1087 to almost 6 million in 1348 (on the eve of the Black Death). J.Z. Titow (1969) believes that the peasants' condition was getting worse for almost 250 years before the great plague arrived and that the heavy mortality from that disease arose from many decades of increasing malnutrition. This was true of most of Western Europe and is reflected in a decrease in size of the average European peasant.

In about twenty-five years, 1348-1373, the population of Western Europe was cut to about half. Prices began to fall and wages to rise. Agricultural holdings became available to any peasant who wanted one. This threw the hardships of decreasing economic incomes from the peasants (where it had been for so long before the Black Death) to the upper, landlord class and was one of the chief motivations for driving these lords toward wars and aggression as a good means for increasing their incomes. Since the economic development of Europe east of the Rhine and especially east of the Elbe was considerably behind that in the West, these generalizations do not apply to the eastern regions until about a century later.

The increased aggression and warfare associated with the period of crisis after 1270 was made possible by the economic expansion of the preceding phase of expansion and above all by the improvements in logistics of men, goods, and information. In 970 small military forces could be sent only a dozen miles or so (by a peasant-sustained system) and kept there for only a brief period; the man who could do this was usually the lord of a small castle of earth and timber. By 1050 a larger force, led by the lord of a more imposing castle (still of timber and earth) which could dominate a much larger territory, could be sent scores of miles and maintained there for weeks. By 1180 a still greater force which was much more heavily armored could be led a greater distance and kept there for months by a lord who was so great that he lived in a stone castle and could aspire to be called duke, or even king. By 1500 a force of tens of thousands, with many more missile weapons (including cannon) could be led hundreds of miles and kept there for more than a year (by living off the victim territory) by a king who had numerous elaborate stone fortresses in his own territories. This increase in the area over which military force could be applied was more the consequence of changes of organizational patterns, ideological factors, and economic changes than it was of changes in weapons or tactics. The territorial bases which supported these increasingly successful aggressions were larger. The leaders who directed them had greater prestige and were supported by different kinds of loyalty and allegiance, and had obtained different titles to reflect these changes. The leader of 970 might have been little more than a castellan (that is, the castle warden of a nominally greater lord) with no title at all. The leader of 1050 probably would have held at least one castle of his own and might bear the title of count. Leaders of the later and more ambitious aggressions would be almost certainly dukes or kings. Five stages of political organization parallel the sequence of five military stages. Without the political changes, especially the shifts in political allegiance, the changes in weapons systems could not have widened the areas of permanent political control from miles to hundreds of miles.

These shifts in political allegiance were especially significant in the two changes evident in the middle and the end of the period 900-1500. The changes were the shift from feudalism to feudal monarchy about 1200 and the shift from the latter to dynastic monarchy about 1500. In both these cases, as also in the next change about 1800, the shifts of allegiance were downward to lower social and military levels which had not previously participated in political life.

In feudalism and in feudal monarchy allegiance was based on personal loyalty. In the former case it was based on the fealty of a vassal to his immediately superior lord, while in feudal monarchy the fealty was expected from all lords, both vassals-in-chief and sub-vassals, and gradually came to be the loyalty of all fighting men to their leader (a relationship which frequently rested on a contractual agreement). But there was little expectation of loyalty from the less significant peoples of the realm, such as peasants, traders, and craftsmen. Nor was loyalty expected to the country or to the state; the loyalty remained personal to the king. In fact, the monarch was not usually regarded as king of a "country" or of a "state," since "country" referred to one's native district, while "state" was, at that time, an abstraction which few, chiefly lawyers, could grasp. The term "nation" at that time referred to a language group.

The fact that the monarch, in the medieval period, was king of a group of persons and not of a country or, still less, of a state, is evident from his title which was "king of the English," or of "the French," or even "of the Romans" (meaning the Germans), while a somewhat similar form was used for lower ranks, such as "Duke of the Normans" and not, as we would say, "of Normandy."

This "intensification" of the idea of allegiance is of great importance and is closely related to the distribution of weapons within the society, except when the army is purely a mercenary professional one. As armies grow larger and recruit to lower levels in a society, it is necessary to find a basis for allegiance which will appeal to such lower levels. At the same time, such a change allows the ruler to demand support from a larger part of the population of his realm, a change which is reflected in a change in the name of his supporters. These were called "vassals" in the feudal period, "liegemen" or some similar term in the period of feudal monarchy, "subjects" in the period of dynastic monarchy, and "citizens" in the period of national states. I suppose they may be called "comrades" in the ideological state, if it ever comes.

These changes of terms have been gradual and not consciously linked with the extension of expected allegiances; in fact, as it occurred, few people were aware that claims of allegiance were being extended to lower social levels. The use of terms lagged behind the shifts in political expectations. Thus the British today are known as "subjects" and not as "citizens." The Tudors as dynastic monarchs (1485-1603) ruling over "subjects" made demands for allegiance to levels which could be expected to respond only in a national state.

The extensive expansion of allegiance to a wider territory (without any intensification of allegiance) which results from the growth of the offensive power of weapons systems is quite different from the intensification of appeal for allegiance, which does not necessarily widen the area of power, and may, indeed, curtail it. A dynastic monarchy such as the Hapsburg empire broke up into several parts as the change from dynastic monarchy to national state spread. As a dynastic monarchy, the Hapsburg ruler appealed to the allegiance of a small upper class, mostly of Roman Catholic landlords, over a wide area inhabited by Germans, Hungarians, South Slavs, northern Slavs such as Bohemians, Moravians, and Poles, as well as Romanians, and others, many of them peasants and often non-Catholics. Such a state was not able to make the advance to a mass army of citizen soldiers supported by a modern industrialized democratic state without breaking up. In fact, this contradiction between the continually growing offensive power of weapons and the need to mobilize the allegiance of the whole population of the state to sustain such a weapons system was one of the chief problems of the century from 1815 to 1914 and destroyed a number of dynastic despotisms, including the Hapsburg, Hohenzollern, Ottoman, Romanov, and Manchu. The vital point is that increasingly powerful offensive weapons systems have not been sufficient to ensure endless increase in the areas of states without periodic intensification of allegiances as well.

The early medieval society, as it was developing about 970 and as it was patently established about 1100, consisted of two parts, an upper sub-system, feudalism, which was military and political, and a lower sub-system, manorialism, which provided the economic base for feudalism. Feudalism was the sphere of the warriors and provided protection, while the manor was the sphere of peasants and provided food and labor. Each became a separate social class, almost a caste (since marriage between them was objectionable).

Fighting men must have economic sustenance and political decentralization results whenever they obtain this by being provided with bundles of revenue to live on. In Asia, such bundles of revenues came from tolls and tribute on distant commerce. When these were enforced by weapons which emphasized mobility and missiles, the resulting political power might cover a very wide area although it might have a shallow intensity. Such weapons and tribute were not adapted to forested Europe as they had long been to grassland Asia. A major reason was that in Europe horses had to be fed a grain supplement and oats were the least productive grain crop.

In Europe mobility of all kind was reduced after

920

830, weapons moved almost totally from missile to shock of armored horsemen, castles could not usually be taken, and fighting men were sustained by revenues from peasant villages. Almost inevitably in such conditions, power became pulverized to the point where the state vanished, with all political power dispersed into private hands. This process was not total, but almost so, with only scattered traces of other methods for supporting fighting men to be found in the 10th century.

Fundamentally, there are three ways by which fighting men can be supported and thus controlled, plus a fourth method of support which leaves them uncontrolled. The three are: (1) militia; (2) mercenary soldiers; and (3) feudal forces. Militia are members of the community who are part-time fighters. They support themselves by their regular economic activities but are expected to assemble to defend the community when necessary. 'This may vary from the obligation of primitive tribesmen to the conscript armies of 19th century national states, including such different forms as the shire militia of England in the 11th and 16th centuries, the citizen soldiers of ancient Greece or early Rome, or the Boer militia fighting Britain in 1900. Such a militia force assumes that wars will be brief and local, in most cases, perhaps to be settled by a single battle. Militia are not professional fighters, and are supported by their usual occupations, with only moderate support from the community for short periods.

Mercenary soldiers are supported by the political structure for which they fight and are professionals. They may be paid in money or they may be supported as retainers of the military leader who commands them. In the latter case, they may reside with their leader and even eat, dress, and shelter themselves from his stores. The Frankish <u>antrustions</u> and the Anglo-Saxon <u>housecarles</u> were retainers who lived with their leaders. Both existed in the pre-feudal period and were under the control of the leader because of their economic dependence on him. As it became more difficult to bring supplies from distant manors to support these minions at the leader's residence, the obvious alternative was to send the fighter to the supplies since the latter could not easily be brought to the former. It was not recognized at once that a fighter in residence is under control, while a fighter autonomous in his own residence is under control only to the degree his personal loyalty

921

may bind him. Thus the housecarle was transformed into a feudal lord in the dark age.

The only alternative to this loss of control was to keep at least some retainers with the leader, the whole group moving together from one manor to another, moving on to a new one as the annual stores of each were used up in sequence. This was done by most great lords and kings in the Middle Ages. With their chief retainers and servants they adopted an itinerant life in an annual round, using up the supplies stored in each residence in turn, and returning again only after the new crops were harvested a year later. The English monarch still follows this annual round, giving rise to what is known as the social season.

When a leader granted manors to his fighters, he could retain his superiority and control only if he kept a larger force of retainers than could be held by any of his vassals on lands granted out by him to them. Then, if any question of superiority or of obedience to orders arose, he could enforce his will by arriving at the vassal's manor with a larger force. But if the dependent fortified his manor, that larger force might not be convincing. The relationship of superior and inferior could be reversed, with the dependent inside the walls with a small force and supplies sufficient for a lengthy siege and the leader outside the walls with a larger force (even much larger) but with insufficient supplies for more than a few days and no means of transport capable of bringing up supplies soon enough and large enough to sustain a successful siege. The two key factors in this situation were the walls and the supplies. Weapons or tactics independent of those factors had little to do with the question of who obeys whose orders in that spot at that time.

If a dependent warrior, a vassal, fortified his manor and intended to resist his leader, his lord, he would probably not do so without conferring with his fellow vassals of the same lord, his "peers," especially with those in the same district, to determine which side they might support in a dispute between vassal and lord, especially if the lord attempted a siege. Usually fellow vassals had greater incentives to cooperate together in resisting any attack on any one of them and would not cooperate with the lord in crushing any one of them or in supporting him in any effort to increase his demands upon any one of them. Thus all tendencies would have worked toward increasing decentralization of power and control. The whole system would tend to disintegrate further into the basic elements of military power, so long as decreasing mobility and ineffective transport prevailed, as they did in the dark age before 1000.

Naturally, this tendency to dispersal of power operated only within the same system. The situation was quite different when a threat to any portion of that system appeared from some outside enemy. When this occurred to any unit of the system, that endangered warrior could call on his lord for help. It was in the interest of all within the system to cooperate together to defend it as a system, that is for the lord to respond to an appeal for help from his vassal and for all the fellow vassals to respond loyally to a summons from the lord. Thus, as the system developed after 1000, there was a tendency for it to cooperate in the face of any outside threat but to disintegrate into its autonomous units when there was no outside threat.

In the dark age and the earliest medieval generations, the system was not yet fully developed. The chaotic conditions of the period must be imagined. The Vikings, Hungarians, and Saracens, to say nothing of local bandits, were raiding across western Europe for three or four generations before 970. The outsiders were non-Christians, with mobility and missile weapons, raiding against a decreasingly mobile society which was being reduced to almost total reliance on shock weapons. There was a strong incentive for dependent warriors to cooperate with their "peers" in accepting their leader's discipline for the sake of their mutual security, despite the continuing collapse of mobility and military logistics. Once the immediate danger passed by, the long-term trends to disintegration reasserted themselves.

We have thus a number of interacting and countervailing factors in the politico-military life of western Europe for about two centuries after 830. The underlying factors tending to dispersal of power, notably the collapse of logistics, was to some extent counterbalanced by the fact that many manors and supply bases were not yet fortified. By the time these were fortified, and could resist the lord, say about 1030 (at which date timber fortifications were being replaced by stone), the system was coming together into a more complete and unified fabric. The mobile threats to it were either incorporated into it (like the Normans) or had been ejected from the scene (like the Magyars and Saracens). This encouraged resistance of vassals to the demands of their lords and thus increased the disintegrating forces in the society. Just at that point, in the mid-11th century, the replacement of wooden walls by stone ones in forts, improvements in logistics, and some improvements in siege techniques (including the slow return of infantry forces and of missile weapons) raised the stakes in the game of military competition to a higher level on which fewer men (the richer ones) could compete. The cost of continuing to compete in the power struggle, like any poker game with no limit, forced many lords to drop out of the struggle, that is to accept the superiority of a greater lord and yield to his conditions in order not to lose everything. Only those who had the economic resources to compete as principals in the power struggle continued to operate on the brink of warfare (or over that brink, when the events turned that way). The others did not, however, fall to a single level of submission without power, but continued as a power toward their own vassals, so that the system as a whole began to form a hierarchy of military power.

Of the four methods of supporting fighting men, three permit controls of the fighters (militia, mercenaries, and feudal vassals). Any of these can be transformed into the fourth method, which provides fighting men but does not provide any method by which the society can control them. This is what occurs when any body of armed men cease to depend on supplies and turn to living off the country. Any armed force can become self-sustaining, or even rich, from loot and booty, either from the enemy or from "friends." This happened in an elaborate form in Attila's Huns, which was a military system without a society or community to fight for, with the consequence that it fought only for itself. Such an army can become complete and self-sustaining, organized through patronage-clientage relations, as we have seen, and finding its women among the booty of war. The Vikings were similar; the mercenary soldiers in Germany in the late stage of the Thirty Years War moved in this direction; and, in fact, any military system can move in this direction if warfare is prolonged for years in a remote place which is under military occupation. A most elaborate system of this kind appeared in France in the late Hundred Years War, when the English armed forces, still supported by manpower and money from home, became a congeries of private enterprises seeking profit and wealth by looting and plunder (such as ransoms of towns and captives) on the continent. Michael Prestwich (1972) has shown us this, even before the Hundred Years War began, under King Edward I.

At all times in the Middle Ages there were traces of all four of these methods of supporting fighting men, but the preponderance of one or another shifted in time with very great consequences in the whole structure of medieval society, especially in its political organization and stability.

In the pre-feudal period, from the collapse of Rome onward, there were considerable elements of the first and the fourth methods, that is of militia and of booty, and this continued to be true both in the north of Europe (in what I have called northern monarchy), including England, and in southern Europe (especially in the municipalities of the Mediterranean area). But in northwestern Europe, especially in the core of the Carolingian empire between the Rhine and the Loire, the militia element was steadily eclipsed by mercenary warriors (chiefly in the form of retainers or of vassals). During the dark age, these mercenary forces steadily moved from retainers toward vassalage in this part of Europe, with a much slower movement along the same line in England and east of the Rhine. By 1000 this process had moved very far in the core area, but in 1066 in England and even later in Germany both militia and retainers were to be found. In the course of the 12th century, the typical military force was made of vassals. The militia still existed but only in theory, while mercenary soldiers, paid in money, were already beginning to increase in numbers, as a supplement rather than a substitute for vassals. By 1200 the increase in mercenary fighters was accompanied by an increase in infantry and missile weapons, the three growing together, since horsemen could not use the existing missile weapons, either bows or crossbows while mounted (and, indeed, regarded them as immoral), and infantry forces, lacking any independent source of income, had to be paid while on campaign. It was this joint development which made it possible in the 13th century to besiege castles more successfully, as soon as logistics began to improve, and began to drive the less wealthy lords out of the

925

power struggle. But soon the expense of maintaining increasingly large infantry forces on pay during extended campaigns and sieges began to push the costs of war so high that only kings or great dukes who could find some way of taxing a large part of their inhabitants were able to continue the struggle.

To relieve this great financial burden, the fourth method of sustaining soldiers (by booty) began to develop very rapidly by the end of the 13th century and through the 14th century. At the same time, in the period from about 1300 until after 1500, there was a return to maintaining armed retainers (housecarles), giving rise to problems which are sometimes known as "livery and maintenance." In some areas, such as France at the time of Cardinal Richelieu (1624-1642), these problems were still rising and requiring attention from the builders of centralized monarchies. After 1680 mercenary fighters paid in money were the dominant form of army (except for elements of militia in England, which were not ended until the 20th century). By 1790-1800 mercenary fighters were being replaced over most of western Europe by citizen soldiers, a form of militia.

The form of military service known as European feudalism was so variable that any generalization would probably not be true in most specific cases. For that reason, we shall describe it as what Max Weber called "the ideal type." In this type a vassal held a bundle of revenues, usually in the form of land, from his lord. This tenure allowed the vassal the leisure to gain military skills and to perform military service for the lord; at the same time it was a symbol of their personal relationship in which the vassal owed fealty to his lord, and the lord owed protection and justice to his vassal.

During the period of turmoil in the 10th century, each vassal wanted as much protection as he could get and, at the same time, was unable to resist the pressures of a more powerful neighbor to become his vassal. A vassal wanted to be the vassal of a powerful lord, that is one with many other vassals. This tended to bring all these relationships into a single system. It also tended to organize this system into a hierarchy of several levels, because a lord who had numerous vassals could organize them better if he granted out numerous tenures to a few men and let these owe him many

military services. In fact, he had to do this, for the
very practical reason that he had to send messengers
out with summonses when he wanted military service.
Since any lord's ability to keep and feed men was limited,
he kept only a few to summon up a much larger number.

In such a chain the lord at the top, who was owed
obligations by vassals but was not himself the vassal
of anyone, was called a "suzerain." He was a very
important person and might have a number of other designations such as king or bishop or prince, but these were
not feudal terms, although their possession usually had
a significant influence on their possessor's power.
At the lowest end of the chain was a vassal who owed
only one military service to his lord and had no vassals
of his own (although he was lord of a manor). In between the suzerain and the simple knight were the intermediate links who were both lords and vassals: vassal
to their feudal lord above and lord to their vassals below.

In addition to the three titles of status (suzerain,
baron, knight), there were numerous titles of function.
When a suzerain called up his vassals for military service, the assemblage was called the "feudal array." It
was commanded by the suzerain himself, but might be
commanded by a lord designated by the suzerain and known
as the "marchal." The array was divided into contingents
under leaders, under whom they usually assembled on the
way to the array. These were called by the Latin word
for leader and known as "dukes." Lesser leaders were
expected to assemble vassals on a territorial basis
before leading them up to the duke or to the array.
These territories were known as "counties" on the continent and as "shires" in England, and their lords were
"counts" in France ("earls" in England). Originally the
counts had been the local officials of the Carolingian
empire, but, in the confusions of the 10th century, some
had seen their power disintegrate into the hands of their
castellans, while others had been absorbed into neighboring counties to become duchies.

Under the Carolingians the counties on the borders
of Christendom had been larger and their counts had had
greater independence so that they could respond more
quickly to any challenge from their pagan neighbors,
such as the Saracens, pagan Germans, Hungarians, Slavs,
or other dangerous (because non-Christian) peoples.
These border counties were known as "marks" or "marches,"

927

and their counts came to be known as "marquesses" or "marquis" (in Germany "margraves" or "archdukes"). These marks were of great importance as can be seen from the fact that some royal dynasties of Europe came from this background. In central Europe two of these margraves became dominant, the Hapsburgs and the Hohenzollerns, and, as late as 1866, fought for supremacy in that area. Both became imperial families. In England and France the Tudor and Bourbon families had a similar background.

These "functional" feudal titles passed through three periods of development. Originally they were not feudal at all but were royal titles, established before 830 for local administration of public authority. These royal positions became hereditary as the Carolingians became weaker, and their possessors took to themselves fragments of public authority, as the Carolingian state disappeared. The state was replaced by feudalism, but the titles persisted as tokens of functions in the feudal system. By the 14th century, when feudalism was replaced by feudal monarchies, these titles tended to become honorary rather than military. In fact, the feudal system ceased to be military and became a system of social status, which we might call "chivalry." Today in England, the feudal array assembles under the Earl Marshal (the Duke of Norfolk) only at the coronation of the monarch. But the hierarchy of titles still continues on at least six levels: knight; baronet; baron; count; marquess; duke. On the continent, where counties disintegrated into lesser districts, the castellans who came to control these came to be called "viscounts" (on a level between barons and counts), and this title was imported into England in 1440 (McFarlane 1973).

In the feudal system the mutual obligations of lord and vassal were very indefinite at first, but gradually became clarified until, by 1200, it was understood that the lord owed his vassal protection and justice, and the vassal owed his lord aid and counsel (auxilium et concilium). With the aid the lord was able to provide protection; with the counsel he could provide justice to all his vassals.

Although these rights and obligations were established originally to protect the society by ensuring the military service of fiefs, considerable abuses

928

arose from them when the need for such service decreased in the 12th and 13th centuries. Guardians abused rights of wardship, plundering the estate and corrupting (or even murdering) the heir in efforts to get permanent possession of the fief for themselves or their families. Heiresses were kept unmarried, or shunted off into nunneries, or married unsuitably to old men or to young boys, in order to get control of the tenure. These rights and the additional right of escheat (which brought a fief back to the lord when a vassal died without either a will or an heir) allowed the greater lords to accumulate vast holdings in the hands of their families. Sometimes fiefs were forfeited, legally or illegally, for this purpose. As the great lords became less dependent on the military service of their vassals because of the growing use of mercenary fighters, they came to regard their vassals less as fighters and more as sources of income for their own purposes and were increasingly willing to see their vassals' holdings come back into their own hands. In this way, after 1300, the royal family in France created a system of "royal appanages" by which most of the great fiefs were in the possession of members of the royal family. Similarly, the Bourbon family of Bearn in southern France acquired extensive fiefs, even the kingship of Navarre, and were able to replace the Valois dynasty as the royal family of France in 1589, just as the Valois had replaced the Capetians in 1328. In England, the families of Lancaster and York built up such powerful bodies of retainers that they struggled for years to control the royal title (1455-1485) until they were replaced by their cousin Henry Tudor. These conflicts between the great duchies and appanages and the monarchy, at the end of the medieval period, were simply one stage of the process by which the territorial size of political units grew larger after 970, a process marked in England by the ability of the Duke of Normandy to conquer all of England in 1066. In France the King of France was so much weaker than several of his surrounding vassals about 1200 that none of them resented his royal title and gave it all the religious and theoretical deference that it deserved, but by 1300 the king was rapidly extending his political power over them. This process, however, was interrupted by the Hundred Years War of 1338-1453.

Originally there were only two classes in medieval society, the peasants who tilled the soil and the warriors. Clergy existed from the beginning, but they were not really a separate class until after the Cluniac, Gregorian, and other reforms which sought to free the church from control by laymen. Earlier, the Pope, archbishops, bishops, and heads of monastic houses were part of the upper class, living and treated as lords, supported by landed tenures (benefices), and even fighting in battle; the lower clergy, at that time, were hardly distinguishable from the peasants, frequently worked as peasants, and were often illiterate. As late as the 11th century both upper and lower clergy frequently married and had children. But in that century, the reforms changed the church totally, so that clerical marriage and illiteracy almost vanished, and the clergy became a separate social class and an independent power in society.

This growing autonomy of the church and the clergy was achieved by freeing the naming of upper clergy from the control of laymen, an effort which was violently resisted by many lords, including the emperor, since control of nominations involved control of the wealth of benefices and of feudal military service obligations. The chief method for obtaining independence for clerical offices was to have a group of electors (also supported by endowments) who could choose a successor when a church office became vacant. This was most effective in the case of the Pope (the Bishop of Rome) who had a College of Cardinals, named by himself, as his agents and advisors as well as electors of his successor. This was established in 1050 and freed the Papacy almost completely from its previous domination by the great nobles of the city. Similar bodies, usually known as Canons, were to be found playing a similar role in episcopal elections, but these remained, to some extent, under the influence of powerful men whose families had provided properties for benefices.

With the separation of church and feudal power there followed distinct legal and religious systems, all of which permitted Western civilization to evolve along lines which were determined by weapons systems quite differently from other societies. In the West weapons and applied force was simply one of several mechanisms for legitimizing historical changes. We might say that it was the ultimate legitimizing mechanism. It may be that the final outcome of history in the West was determined by weapons about as much as in other civilizations such as classical antiquity,

Byzantine, or Russian civilizations (which are the closest similar cases), but that final outcome was delayed for long periods while other, less ultimate, mechanisms produced other, less final, changes. Moreover, in the West, changes in weapons, once the process started, helped to make change more continuous than in most other civilizations because of steady technological and administrative innovations.

The Normans in the 11th century developed an excellent understanding of weapons and tactics, although still lacking the full development of logistical support, naval activities, and siege techniques (both defensive and offensive). These three subsidiary areas were the chief fields of military developments in the medieval period between the slow introduction of the crossbow, coming from the East in the period before 1000 and the revolutionary changes associated with the introduction of gunpowder, also from the East, and of the Swiss pikemen, both after 1350.

By 1100 the Norman understanding of military tactics emphasized the following:

1. The 3-part battle sequence of (a) missile barrage; (b) shock assault; and (c) cavalry pursuit. For the missile barrage they used crossbows, archery, or javelins hurled overhand from horseback (as at Hastings). For the shock assault, they used swords, battle-axes, lances, or maces, either on foot or on horseback. The shock became increasingly powerful as horses increased in size from better breeding and more adequate diet, armor became heavier and was applied to the horse as well as the rider (chiefly as protection against missiles), and the spreading use of stirrups allowed the rider to use a heavier spear locked under his arm, instead of the overhand thrust of a lighter lance, such as the Normans used as late as the First Crusade.

2. The need for a reserve in battle and the dangers of too headlong pursuit if only part of the enemy fled.

3. Recognition that a solid bloc of infantry could withstand cavalry shock if disciplined and properly trained.

4. Recognition of the importance of logistics in keeping a force in the field long enough to perform its

931

task, either to force a battle or to starve out a fortress.

5. Recognition of the role of the castle, both as a base for combat forces or for control of one's own economic base.

6. Recognition of the role of sea power for supply and for amphibious assault. The development of this side of warfare forms a significant aspect of military developments over the period 950-1600, along with logistical support and siege techniques. Norman ability to transport horses across the sea in the attack on England in 1066 and in the conquest of Sicily in 1072-1091 are early examples of this, while the capture of Constantinople by the Fourth Crusade in 1204 is probably the greatest achievement of amphibious warfare in the medieval period.

7. Recognition of the need for discipline to ensure maximum shock and tactical control in battle. Such discipline was not easy to achieve in feudal warfare so long as the knight had his own private economic base, especially when booty and ransom of prisoners became more important (after 1200). A feudal body of horsemen tended to lack cohesion and to operate as a collection of individual fighters, with mutual rivalry, eager to get to hand-to-hand combat with a worthy enemy. Such a force standing still or moving slowly was very vulnerable to a full charge by a similar enemy force because of the attackers' momentum and it could be protected best by a mass of infantry. The ideal Norman battle plan was to hurl such a bolt of charging cavalry from the protection of a mass of infantry upon a standing force of horsemen already badly harassed by missiles. In such an assault, the infantry acted as a shield and the cavalry as a striking sword emerging from behind the shield.

In strategy the Normans recognized that the chief aim of applied force was to control revenues and that this could be achieved only from a fortress. Thus they were aware that the primary role of a field force was to protect strongholds and was not primarily to defeat other field forces in battle. Later in the course of the 12th century, however, there was an intellectual change, a movement from feudalism to chivalry (marked by the development of tournaments, of a "nobility of birth," and of the practice of ransoming wealthy prisoners

932

of war), which made the battle increasingly the focal
point of war. The thirst for "honor" and for ransoms,
added to the extreme combativeness of the Normans,
developed an excessive eagerness for battle and a
tendency for the Normans to lose their discipline
and cohesion as soon as the battle was over. Like
many modern soldiers they became convinced that "the
battle is the pay-off" (as we were told in World War
II) and, accordingly, often concentrated on winning
the battle rather than winning the war. To some extent, with the Normans this weakness was counterbalanced
by their skills in systematizing the raising of revenues
both from land incomes and from commerce and their skill
in fortifications.

These seven aspects of tactics were solidified
by the Crusades which exposed Europeans to each other
and to the very alien military experience of the Near
East. The process covered just over a century, from
the First Crusade in 1095-1100 to the Fourth Crusade
of 1202-1204. Fighting was endemic in the East between
these crusades and continued episodically for centuries
after the Eighth Crusade of Saint Louis in 1270. There
were constant movements of men and goods between Western
Europe and the Moslem battle fronts in the Near East,
North Africa, and Spain, so that a common experience
of military affairs emerged across the Old World from the
Red Sea to Wales and Scotland. In Europe, in this period, there was only one real innovation in weaponry in
land fighting, the trebuchet, until the 14th century.
However, constant improvements in the details of weapons
and changes in the four auxiliary aspects of military
affairs steadily increased the offensive power of weapons
systems and thus increased the size of political entities
as these passed through the stage we have called feudal
monarchy en route from the earlier stage of feudalism to
the later stage of dynastic monarchy.

Most of the military developments of this period
were concerned with the auxiliary aspects of the subject
rather than with weapons or with tactics, which were set
by 1100. The four aspects which we have mentioned were
in (1) logistics; (2) siege operations; (3) sea power;
and (4) organizational improvements in recruiting,
finance, and discipline. All of these were based on
increased population and expanding economic production.
In England, the only part of Europe where there is a
basis for even rough estimates, J.Z. Titow (1969)

believes that the population at least tripled between
Domesday Book in 1086 and the eve of the Black Death
in 1348, as based on the poll tax returns of 1377;
in figures this would be from about 1.6 million to
almost 5 million.

The chief improvements in logistics were in horse-
drawn vehicles, roads, bridges, and more rational supply of food, fodder, and equipment. By 1350, however,
the population pressure upon a limited supply of land
and with only a relatively static technology was at
the danger point as is evident from the severe incidence
of the Black Death. According to Joseph Needham (1970:
34-37), all improvements in horse-harnessing came from
Central or Eastern Asia. The Roman method of harnessing,
in which the horse was attached to the shafts of the
vehicle by a combined throat-yoke and girth was very
ineffective because it hampered the horse's breathing
and, by forcing it to move with its head held up, made
it impossible for it to throw its weight into the task.
This ancient method continued in Europe until after A.D.
500, when it was replaced by a breast-strap arrangement,
known as "postillion harness." This latter began to be
replaced by the horsecollar, which was known in China
about 500 and reached Europe in the post-Carolingian
dark age. In this third arrangement the horse could
throw its weight against the firm, padded, horsecollar
which was attached to the vehicle through leather traces.
Only after the 14th century were the traces extended so
that the animals could pull in file. With the horsecollar, the shafts no longer pulled the vehicle but
merely changed its direction when the horse pushed
against them. Such turns could be made effectively
only with two-wheeled vehicles (like chariots or farm
carts) which pivoted as a single whole. The modern
four-wheeled vehicle, with smaller front wheels which
can turn under the body of the vehicle on a pivoted
front axle, did not appear until the 15th century and
spread very slowly. The first such pivoted front axle
we know was on a German military wagon which was pushed
from the rear, had an armored front and top, and could
be steered by the men inside by a crossbar on the top
of the front axle pivot which came up through the floor
of the vehicle. Springs in vehicles were known in the
Renaissance but, as late as 1600, even royal vehicles
usually had neither turning axle nor springs. An
adequate vehicle for carrying passengers did not become available until the middle of the 18th century.

Until that time, most military land transport was on pack animals and two-wheeled carts, both of which improved greatly in numbers and effectiveness between 1000 and 1350.

Otherwise, land logistics changed relatively little in the medieval period. Bridges and roads became more numerous and of better quality. The real improvement was in the great increase in numbers of men, animals, and vehicles available for military transportation. However, this increase was not enough to allow any substantial military force (over 5000 men) to operate more than about a hundred miles from its base for more than about a week without living off the country. In fact, so much of military tactics in the whole period up to the 18th century consisted of devastating the enemy's territory and resources, either to starve out the opposition or to bring the enemy forces to battle so that there was little incentive to try to support an army from its own supplies; it was as easy to live off the enemy's resources as to destroy them. In friendly territory the alternatives were simply between paying or not paying for what was seized from the local people. On the whole, one of the great advantages of cavalry over infantry was that the former could live off the country, especially enemy country, while infantry often could not.

The improvement in procurement and transportation of military supplies, such as weapons, other equipment, horses, and, to a lesser extent, fodder was greater than for food. The critical item was ability to move siege equipment, even in unassembled parts, because of the vital role that this played in real success in war. In some aspects of this problem, but not in moving siege engines, the English were the leaders in Western Europe. They were engaged in aggressive warfare more than others, against the Scots, the Welsh, and eventually the French. The English were also the earliest in that region to attempt to supply arms to their forces rather than to insist that fighting men must bring their own weapons. There can be no doubt that reasonable uniformity of weapons was almost a necessity for controlled battle tactics, an effort which seems to have been made earlier by the English than by their continental rivals. This supply effort has been described to us recently by Michael Prestwich (1972) in regard to Edward I (1272-1307) and by H.J. Hewitt (1966) in regard to

935

Edward III (1327-1377).

The English were also relatively early, though not the first, in the development of sea power, both as a combat arm and as a branch of military transportation. They were not the first because sea power never disappeared in the Mediterranean Sea (as Ekkhard Eickhoff 1966, and Helene Ahrweiler 1966, have shown us), and because sea power in the Atlantic, which was quite different from that in the Mediterranean, was not developed by the English but by the peoples of the Low Countries and the Baltic, notably the Frisians, with some help from the Basques.

The development of siege operations is quite as complicated as that of sea power and is, paradoxically, both more and less important. The root of this paradox lies in the fact that developments in fortifications and siege operations were much less closely linked to the growth of offensive power than appears at first glance. For one thing, the reciprocal relationship between improvements in siege techniques and the responding improvements in defensive fortifications were linked so closely to each other that the absolute advance in offensive power was very slow (as is evident from the role that fortifications continued to play even after the 18th century). Moreover, the relationship was not a direct one, as might be expected, but was indirect. Indeed, there were, in fact, no sustained improvements in siege techniques and thus there was no increase in the offensive power of weaponry from this source in the medieval period after about 1200. Instead, the appearance of increased offensive power arose from the fact that the mutually cancelling reciprocity between fortifications and siege techniques raised the costs of both to such a high level so quickly that fewer lords could continue in the competition. The less affluent lords dropped out of the game, as the costs rose, and submitted to the power of their more affluent immediate neighbor.

In the military competition of the Middle Ages, superior affluence was less a consequence of richer natural resources than of greater organizational skills and experience in mobilizing the available resources. In the Hundred Years War, for example, the resources theoretically available to the King of France, in terms of manpower and production of economic goods in 1328

936

were far superior to those available to the King of England, as Edouard Perroy (1951) and Kenneth Fowler (1967) have shown. According to Fowler, in population alone France was about five times larger than England. But the ability of the English monarchy to mobilize its lesser resources into military offensives in the very heart of France was so great over a period of more than a century (1338-1453) that the continued existence of an independent French monarchy was seriously jeopardized at several points in that time.

The developments in European techniques of fortification and siege warfare in the period 950 to 1450, unlike the advances in sea power during the same period, involved little that was new compared to the military peak of Roman power, and achieved no absolute improvements until the full impact of cannon was felt in the 16th century. In the medieval period, both offensive and defensive siege operations were recovering what had been lost or forgotten in the period of the decline of Rome and the European dark age. The skills in fortifying which had been reached in the Near East in the period before 1200 B.C. were not far inferior to those achieved in Europe in the Middle Ages. Those Bronze Age skills had been largely lost in the second dark age about 1000 B.C. and had been slowly rediscovered in the classical Iron Age of the first millennium B.C., culminating in the early Roman empire. The Romans, who had more faith in mobile than in static defense (probably because of their allegiance to a centralized territorial state), placed little emphasis on fortification, but they did devote considerable emphasis, energy, and resources to siege operations. The techniques, weapons, and skills which they acquired in such operations were lost again in A.D. 300-900 in Europe and had to be recovered for the third time in A.D. 950-1450. It is doubtful that Europeans, at the end of the Middle Ages, were superior to the Romans in capturing fortified strong points except in a few details.

The Europeans had missile weapons superior to those of the Romans, especially in the steel crossbow, for clearing defenders from the walls. For smashing such walls, the medieval attackers had a form of artillery not used by the Romans, the trebuchet. This was a mechanism for hurling stones of up to one hundred pounds against fortifications, by using counterweights (rather than by the power of torsion or tension, favored in

937

antiquity). The trebuchet was not weakened by humidity, as torsion artillery like the catapult was, but it required a very heavy beam and framework which could hardly have been handled by the harnessing methods of ancient transportation. Essentially it consisted of a long beam pivoted like a see-saw in a frame, so that a missile attached to its rear end would be ejected forward when a very heavy weight was suddenly dropped on the beam's forward end. This mechanism came from China to the Levant in early Islamic times, but there it had been discharged by men pulling the forward end down suddenly with ropes. It was first used in Europe when the Second Crusade captured Lisbon from the Saracens in 1147 (White, 1962), and used as late as 1480 against the Turks besieging Rhodes. Before the end of the 12th century, it was much improved by replacing the pulling ropes by a falling counterweight, and in this new form spread rapidly from the western Mediterranean to Europe, the Levant, and back to China (about 1272). Its range was limited to about 150 yards unless the missile was held in a sling almost as long as the beam. In the most effective case, a beam 36 feet long, with a counterweight of 10,000 pounds 6 feet from the fulcrum, could hurl 100 pounds about 245 yards using a 15-foot sling attached to the 30-foot missile arm. The counterweight had to be raised by a great expenditure of manpower, pulling or winching down the missile arm so that it could be caught on a trigger and the stone placed in the sling.

In Europe the counterweight trebuchet was probably welcomed as a response to the shift of fortifications from timber to stone in that same 12th century. The chief advantage of the new weapon was that its range was constant if all the missiles weighed the same. This allowed a fortification to be hit in the same place, as if by a hammer, day after day, until it cracked open. We are told that in 1244 a wall of the fortress of Montsegur, a stronghold of the heretical sect of the Cathari in southern France, was broken by hitting the same spot every twenty minutes for weeks with stone balls weighing 88 pounds each. Such an expenditure of shot (about 500 a week with total weight over 44,000 pounds) put a considerable strain on transport, especially if the missiles were made at a great distance. Such a machine was limited by its range which allowed defensive sharpshooters to pick off its operators with crossbows. The latter could kill a man at 300 yards, and, when the bow was made of steel (about 1370), this lethal range was increased to over

400 yards. Of course, if the operators wore armor, the danger was reduced, and armor did increase in weight during the whole medieval period as protection against missiles. Usually, however, artillerymen did not benefit by these improvements because of the cost, especially when so many men were needed as with trebuchets.

The improvements in body armor in the Middle Ages were similar to the changes which we have seen occurring in Central Europe in the Late Bronze Age of the second millennium B.C., and for the same reason, as protection against missiles. In the early Middle Ages, the body was protected by quilted cloth and a leather tunic, and even these were too expensive for the non-feudal infantry forces. By the 13th century, the feudal forces (cavalry) were wearing coats of mail, consisting of small metal links joined together, over a jacket of quilted cloth, and increasingly covered by a loose cloth coat. A steel cap helmet with nose guard and a kite-shaped shield completed the defensive gear of the cavalry about 1200. By that time, the mail tunic went down to the knees and wrists, while the hands were wearing mail mittens with cloth palms. Infantry still relied on quilted cloth and steel caps.

In the 13th century, the metal covering of riders spread with thigh pieces, greaves, and pieces of plate added to the knees, the shoulders, and elsewhere outside the mail coat. At the same time, scale armor was appearing, attached to quilted cloth or to leather. By 1250, large plates were added to the breast, and various kinds of protection were added to the horse, in the same sequence of quilted cloth, then mail, and finally plates, but on a piecemeal basis, with no effort to cover the animal completely. Infantry wore little protection in the 13th century beyond a strong tunic and a steel cap. As the knight's armor grew heavier in this century, the sword also became heavier and longer (up to 38 inches). It also developed from a slashing weapon toward a thrusting blade, or a combined form, to seek openings between the heavier plates. At the same time, there was a revival of older weapons, most of them originally for the foot fighters, but, by 1500, often used by mounted knights. These developments were more notable in the 15th century and included axes, maces, halberts, and billhooks. Some slashing swords developed into falchions, one-sided blades with a very wide and heavy point to provide more shearing action against stronger armor.

The 14th century, the age of the longbow and the steel crossbow in the West and a period of growing threat from missiles, saw more rapid development toward plate armor, increased protection to the horse, and rapid changes in helmets to offer protection against missiles as well as slashing blades. Thus the helmet became more pointed to offer a deflecting surface, had an attached visor, with greater protection on back, sides, and front, so that the head became almost entirely enclosed in an egg-shaped basinet by 1400. The shield was generally abandoned by riders by 1370. All of this made the armor increasingly heavy and more expensive, so that body protection alone increased in weight from over 30 pounds with mail to well over 50 pounds with plate. The power of missile weapons was fully capable of keeping up with this increased protection. The self-bows of Western Europe in the 11th century were about five feet long and generally fired by pulling to the chest while facing the target. This was deadly only for a range below 200 yards and could be adequately protected against by mail armor. The wooden crossbow of the same period had greater penetration but was much slower in repeating fire, and reloading required the bowman's full attention so that he had to take his eyes off the target while reloading and could be hit or run down while doing this. An archer, always looking at the enemy, was in a better position to evade any sudden enemy action and could shoot at least three arrows for each bolt from a crossbow.

The crossbow was originally pulled by hand. By 1200 the composite bow was too stiff to do this, and it was cocked by a hook attached to the belt. The crossbow was placed upright in front of its user, who was down on one knee, where he attached the hook to the bow cord and pulled it by rising to his feet. To keep the front of the bow on the earth while he pulled the cord upward, a stirrup was added to the front end of the crossbow, so that this could be held down with the bowman's left foot as he rose, pulling the cord to the trigger, from his right knee. In the 14th century, when the bow became of steel, the stirrup could be eliminated by pulling the cord to trigger by a winch arrangement, either a so-called goat's foot lever in the East or a windlass in the West. The former allowed the crossbow to be fired from horseback, while the latter still required contact with the ground. Of course, the longbow could not be fired from horseback either; although many archers rode to battle, they dismounted to fight.

The increased complexity of cocking the crossbow increased the advantage which the longbow had over it in speed of repeating fire to about five to one. But, in the long run, the crossbow had at least four considerable advantages over the longbow. Pulling the longbow and holding it while aiming required great strength and skill which could be obtained only by lifetime practice on bows strong enough to provide long range fire. The crossbow was pulled by a mechanical advantage and held on a trigger while being aimed, requiring much less practice and skill. The range of the crossbow, with a draw up to 1200 pounds, was greater and was increased over time, which the longbow could not match. English law in the 16th century required that boys practice with the bow and that after age 24 they must practice at ranges over 220 yards, but two centuries earlier, the crossbow could reach over 400 yards. Against charging armored horsemen, both bows required some kind of barricade for protection, and with that the rate of fire was less significant. In fact, as plate armor became heavier , arrows could not penetrate until the range was so close that the archer had little time to repeat his fire. In fire from fortifications, the crossbow had the advantage that it could be shot without the user exposing himself clearly and at his choice of moment since the cord was held on a trigger. Finally, the materials for a good bow, yew or elm grown in the shade, were not in limitless supply, while the crossbow did not require such scarce materials.

In the 15th century, full plate armor, fitted to the body and including fitted gauntlets and shoes, was available, but the use of armor on horses and on infantry tended to decrease, probably because sieges were more important than battles and speed of movement was valued. Moreover, gun fire by that date was more significant and was much less accurate than earlier missile weapons, so that body armor was decreasingly worth its cost, except to rulers who wore it more for show than for its utility.

In the dark age, in northwestern Europe, extended fortification walls were of timber and earth, effective enough if the earth was packed so tight that the timbers

941

would not burn. Castles at that time were isolated towers, sometimes of stone but usually of timber, occasionally round (especially in Ireland, where they were also of stone), but usually square. These towers were two or three stories high, with no windows and no door on the ground level which was used as a storeroom.

Such towers, known as "donjons," continued to be built throughout the Middle Ages, but became more elaborate as time and wealth permitted. In the 11th century, in northwestern Europe, another type of castle which was easier to build and almost as safe became popular. This was known as the "motte and bailey" castle since it consisted of a mound of earth (motte) surmounted by a timber tower, the whole enclosed in a space (bailey) formed by a ditch and stockade. The bailey provided a safe place for livestock and peasants, while the fort on the motte was a final refuge for the lord and his chief dependents.

The motte and bailey castle was favored by the Normans who took it to England with them when they invaded in 1066, thus introducing the private fortress to a country where most castles had been royal buildings.

In the course of the 12th century, the two types of castles, the donjon and the motte and bailey, became more elaborate and were combined together. The bailey was enclosed by a stone "curtain wall" marked by small towers at intervals and faced by a ditch, while the motte was replaced by a square stone tower partly outside the wall and placed on a mound only when this was a natural hillock, as no artificial mound could support the weight of a stone tower. As prosperity and population grew together in the 12th century, efforts to defend the castle became less passive and devised offensive features aimed directly at the offensive measures which could be brought against it. Fortunately, Western Europe did not have to discover these threats and develop defenses against them from its own experience, since these had all been worked out long before in the Near East, which many European fighters visited as crusaders in the generations after 1097. However, the chief structural influences from the East came to European castles in the 13th century (in England under Edward I, 1272-1307).

These offensive threats to castles were: (1) fire; (2) missiles; (3) scaling the walls; (4) battering

942

through the walls; (5) mining under the walls, so they would fall; (6) starving out the defenders; and (7) treachery from within.

Fire continued as a threat even after fortifications were made of stone, because roofs and dwellings inside the walls were still of wood and could be set on fire by flaming missiles. To prevent this, the stone walls of castles were built higher than the wooden roof and were topped with battlements. Fire, like hand missile weapons, could make any castle uncomfortable but could not capture it unless combined with some other offensive actions, such as storming.

Storming by scaling the walls was generally not possible so long as the defenders were fighting from the battlements, so these had to be cleared of defenders by missiles. Slings and archery generally required too much skill, so were largely replaced by crossbows, in spite of the fact that these, being new, were regarded as inhumane and were forbidden to be used against Christians at the Lateran Council of 1139.

Walls were scaled by grappling hooks, portable ladders, or moveable towers brought up to the walls. Sometimes a drawbridge was flung onto the wall from such a tower, and a few agile men might get across before the bridge could be thrown down by the defenders. There was much hurling of fire and other noxious substances against attackers on ladders and towers and walls were increased in height and modified in construction to provide improved defense against such assaults. Slits in the walls and embrasures on parapets allowed defenders to fire down on their assailants. Towers projecting outside the walls allowed defenders to shoot along the walls against the enemy through slits in the towers near the wall. From the East, in the 13th century, the West learned to defend a gate by a portcullis and machicolations. A portcullis was an iron gate which could be slid down like a modern window to block an entranceway, while machicolations were openings above a gate or a wall in the floor of a stone balcony jutting out from the face of a wall on stone brackets. At the same time, the gate, always a vulnerable point of defense, was protected either by bringing the entrance through a tower or between two smaller towers, often across a drawbridge and through several portcullises. As the gate grew stronger and active defense became stronger, the gates were increased in number from one to several, so that the defenders could emerge in a sally from an inactive gate to drive away the attackers at another gate. About the same time, also from the East, came the practice of having two walls, the outer somewhat lower than the inner and within missile range, so that, if the outer wall was captured, the defenders could shoot down on its top from the higher inner wall. The passageways through these walls and into the castle it-self were not opposite each other, so that an attacker who broke through one would be exposed to flanking fire as he made his way to the next entrance.

Battering the walls to breach them was attempted with battering rams, drills, and picks, as in remote antiquity, or by artillery from a safer distance. Moveable sheds and protective roofs were usually brought up to the walls to protect the attackers from the defenders above. A chief means of defense was to set fire to these devices, so they usually had to be pro-tected by fresh hides or by constant wetting.

Mining under the walls, to gain admittance to the interior or to cause the walls to collapse by destroy-ing the foundations, was a tedious and slow method, especially if the tunnels were dug from a considerable distance to avoid observation of the digging activities. Defense against these efforts by countermining led to conflicts underground, although this was rather rare in the medieval period. In later sieges, such as that of Vienna in 1683, fighting in the tunnels of mines was a major part of the besieging conflict.

Since mines were usually directed at corners of the walls, where a collapse of the foundation would provide a major breach, early defense against this was to have a tower at each corner, which also allowed the walls in both directions to be observed and defended from the tower by missiles. In the 13th century the danger from mining was reduced by building the walls on solid rock or over water, or by surrounding the castle with water in moats. Elaborate artificial bodies of water were sometimes constructed for this purpose, as at Bodiam Castle in Sussex (1383).

All history has shown that even the most elaborate and well-defended fortress can be captured. Castle Gaillard, which embodied all the lessons of European and Near Eastern

944

siege operations, was built by Richard I of England (1196-1200), on the Seine River between Paris and Rouen, at enormous cost but, when it was attacked by Philip Augustus of France in 1203, it was captured in six months. This defeat, which led to the loss of Normandy to France in 1204, was largely due to the failure of King John to make a real effort to relieve the defenders of the castle, but Gaillard also had weaknesses and the French were allowed the time to exploit them. No castle or fortification is impregnable, unless it cannot be reached by any attacker more powerful than the defenders inside it. No fortifications will permit a weaker force to withstand a stronger assailant indefinitely; the walls are there to prolong the defense until a relief force can come up to drive the attackers away. If no relief can come, there is no point in defending the fortress.

After the fall of Castle Gaillard, it was recognized that the chief function of fortifications was to delay defeat until relief arrived. For this reason, there was a tendency for castle design to be modified so as to destroy the attackers piecemeal, thereby reducing the dimensions of the task for the relief force. No longer seeking invulnerability from all sides, castles were built so that the attack had to be made from one approach, and had to achieve success by following in sequence from one point to another, passing through a series of ambushes and killing places where the attackers were exposed to murderous fire from angles and directions which could not be avoided. Such castles are sometimes called "concentric castles" because they often consisted of a series of enclosures, leading the attackers through killing points so that few men would be left to cross the final barrier or to face a relief force. However, experience continued to confirm the proposition: any castle can be taken if a stronger attacking force is granted enough time.

The chief consequence of fortifications and siege operations in the medieval period was to raise the costs of military operations and thus to eliminate from Europe's power struggles all but the richest group of lords. After 1350 these were increasingly collateral branches of the ruling families of the chief regions of Europe. But it is clear that the essential element in ability to continue in the power struggles was not family, nor titles, nor weapons systems, but was the possession of an effective organization for collecting money, either from landed incomes or, far more important, from tolls on commerce.

This ability depended upon the traditions and past experience of the various regions of Europe. There were at least a dozen such regions, but we shall deal with only a few of them. Their differences depended upon the interrelationships among a number of elements in a very complex situation.

There were five chief elements which determined the differences in organization of power in the different regions. These were: (1) the degree to which commerce had collapsed, towns had disappeared, the middle classes had vanished, and society had become ruralized in the dark age; (2) the degree to which the idea of the state and of public authority had been lost, leaving only private power; (3) the degree to which the monarchy in its various forms (archaic, providential, and imperial) had vanished and been replaced by a system of private relationships of personal loyalty such as feudalism; (4) the forms which surviving systems of allegiance took: to kinfolk, to the local community, to religion, or to some form of government; and (5) the degree to which economic recovery had built up a more advanced society of commerce, money exchanges, town life, and literacy.

In general, the first four factors had collapsed most completely in West Francia between the Seine and the Meuse Rivers. They had collapsed least in the eastern Mediterranean, in Byzantium, where all four continued to operate at a high level, reaching a peak in the 9th century, just as the situation in the West was approaching its nadir.

The Papal struggles against the Hohenstauffen imperial ambitions in Italy had far-reaching consequences which pointed away from the medieval period and toward the modern world. This does not mean that new elements were brought into Italy but rather that themes which had been present for a long time became more dominant, leading to major changes in political orientations. In the first place, two new outside powers, France and Spain, intervened in the peninsula as Germany collapsed; these remained until the War of the Spanish Succession (1701-1713), during a new era of European balance of power. Secondly, a new tone was given to politics from increasing emphasis on secular goals, political absolutism, economic imperialism, and dynastic interests, all four of major importance in the post-medieval world, especially in Italy with its precocious economic development. Thirdly, the Papacy, in its urgent need to oppose the Hohenstauffen claims, fell under the influence of France to such a degree that the Papacy moved from Rome to Avignon for seventy years (the Babylonian Captivity of the church, 1308-1378). This led to the Great Schism, in which there were two or more popes simultaneously (1378-1415), and to the Conciliar Movement, which sought to restrict Papal absolutism by broader church controls. These controversies made it impossible to reform the growing corruption in the church, so that the extreme secularism and corruption of the absolutist Renaissance Papacy (1447-1545) became a major factor in precipitating the Protestant Reformation (after 1521) and the Catholic Counter-Reformation (after 1547).

The Hohenstauffen failure arose from their effort to extend the control of an ineffective organizational structure, with inadequate resources available, over areas it could not control. From the economic point of view, as Marc Bloch wrote, it was "the attempt of a still backward state, Germany, to extend its domination to an economically advanced state, Italy."

This was only one of numerous similar political and military failures in the Middle Ages after 1200. Others included the Capetian efforts to eject the Plantagenet rulers from western France in the "First Hundred Years War," 1154-1259, followed by the English efforts to conquer Scotland and France in the "second" Hundred Years War, 1338-1453. Similarly futile were the crusaders' efforts to conquer the Holy Land (1095-1291) and the Venetian efforts to take over much of the Byzantine empire (1202-1261). There were many others in the medieval period and they continued after 1450, beginning with the Valois effort to dominate Italy after 1494 and the Aragonese efforts to create a great Mediterranean empire ruled from Barcelona in 1229-1494. Much of the period 1200-1494 and the next period of Europe's history from 1494 to 1715 was filled with such grandiose and futile efforts for which the organizational structures and resources were both inadequate.

It does no good to win battles, even all the battles, if you cannot win the war; and it does no good to win the war, if you cannot make a peace settlement. No one should ever start a war who does not have a feasible settlement ready.

The problem of winning a battle or a war is to disrupt the enemy's organization so that he can no longer resist. The problem of settlement is more difficult. It involves accurate assessment of the total situation, including intangibles, and requires imagination as to how that total situation can be reorganized so that it is preferable to the prewar situation for both sides. The central problem of any settlement is the problem of controls, that is how men and resources can be controlled to maintain the settlement and not to overturn it. A settlement can be achieved only if two things are true: (1) the postwar controls must be largely internal ones rather than external, that is the defeated must act to maintain the settlement because they want to and not because they are compelled to by external controls like force, bribery, and propaganda; and (2) the settlement must have within itself the ability to evolve in a constructive direction and must not simply be static and unchanging in a situation which is continually changing as all societies are. The use of external controls to enforce a settlement implies that the victor must devote resources to maintain it at least as great as the resources which the defeated have for overturning it. This makes it impossible for any victor to maintain any settlement which is repugnant to the defeated for any length of time because it makes it too expensive. It makes it impossible in the long run because any attempt to enforce a repugnant settlement by external controls using the existing organizational structures available will simply force the defeated system to reorganize its resources in new structural patterns which cannot be controlled by the organizational structures used by the victor to enforce the settlement. Ultimately, the victor would have to assign resources to control the defeated system that were unacceptedly costly. Most victors who have failed to achieve a settlement enforceable by internalized controls give up the effort. That is what happened in the Crusades, in the Hundred Years War, in the Netherlands revolt against Spain, in the American Revolution, in Vietnam, and in many other cases.

It is worth recalling, before we turn back to the Middle Ages, that the wars of the 20th century in Europe (1914, 1939), the Far East (1935, 1941), Korea, and Vietnam were all started by aggressors who had ideas about battles but no ideas at all about feasible settlements, that the aggressors won many battles, but still lost the wars, and that the victors in each war lost the peace.

948

The Crusades were a fiasco. While both crusaders
and Saracens could win a battle or take a fortress if
they picked the time, place, and occasion, neither side
could sustain an offensive to win the war; the only
settlements which entered the minds of the contestants
were, on the one side, to remain in the Holy Land and,
on the other side, to eject the invaders. With respect
to men and resources available, the latter aim was the
easier to achieve. Rivalries among the Moslems of Iraq
were so great, however, that no leader dared take an
army westward into the Levant long enough to expel the
Europeans. That task fell to the Ayyubid dynasty of
Egypt (1169-1250), which was strong enough in its early
days under Saladin (1173-1193) to overcome all but a
few remnants of crusader holdings. Thereafter, the
Ayyubid dynasty was overthrown by its own slave soldiers,
the Mamelukes. Three Crusades from Europe, the Fifth
under a Papal legate, the Sixth led by the Emperor
Frederick II, and the Seventh under Louis IX of France,
were undermanned and poorly organized. For most of the
struggle various Italian cities, including Venice, maintained commercial relations and made commercial treaties
with the Saracens. There were even alliances, both tacit
and explicit, of Christians and Moslems against their
co-religious.

The Hundred Years War between England and France
was another prime example of medieval military fiasco.
The contrast between the two countries was enormous, not
only in men and resources, where France was at least
triple the English level, but also in administrative
organization in which the English may have been three
times as effective as the French. The King-Duke of France
as late as 1100 represented the most nearly complete disappearance of public authority and the state in Western
Europe. The term "Francia" included the Seine drainage
from the Vexin, halfway between Paris and Rouen, in the
northwest to beyond Orleans on the southeast, a territory
consisting of scattered holdings of royal estates (demesne)
and the lands of some of the king's lesser vassals. Around
this were the great vassals, all much stronger than the
king so that he demanded little from them beyond homage.
Until about 1100, the Capetians concentrated on their
own lands. After that, for much of the 12th century,
under Louis VI and Louis VII (1108-1180), peaceful means
were used to extend the royal power. The means included
cooperation with the church and the towns, diplomatic
activities, offers of royal justice to any who wished

to make use of it, establishment of peace and order by
admonition rather than by force. During the whole period from 987 to after 1180, the Capetian dynasty was
relatively moderate, fair, and generally pious, and
most notable for stability. It produced sons as successors for eight consecutive generations (to 1328).

The situation in England was quite different, even
in regard to succession to the throne, where the rules
were not established until 1290 (Powicke 1947). The
real difference between France and England, however,
was that the French monarchy about 1000 was almost
eclipsed by feudal decentralization, while the English
monarchy at the same date was one of the strongest,
with a clear idea of public authority and with few of
the negative elements of feudalism. Decentralization
increased, however, in the next two generations under
Scandinavian attacks and the weakness and pro-Norman
inclinations of Edward the Confessor (1042-1066).

The Anglo-Saxon monarchy in the 11th century still
had a royal army, royal justice, and royal taxation,
the three essentials of government. In addition, it
had written laws, a national assembly (the Witenagemot),
established coinage, and a rudimentary chancery and administrative system. It even had a navy (much weakened
by 1066), with an administrative system to support it.
The Anglo-Saxon navy seems to have been unique, but it
is possible that similar systems existed in Scandinavia
and that all of these were descendants from Carolingian
antecedents of which there are no surviving records.
As it existed in England in the early 11th century, it
was part of the regular military system and consisted
of three parts: (1) mercenary galleys; (2) ship-soke
galleys; and (3) transports.

The mercenary galleys were owned by the king (and
possibly also by a few great lords) and were rowed by
paid oarsmen who also served as fighters. In wartime
they apparently carried extra men for both activities.
These vessels were apparently supported by part of the
Danegeld, a tax of two shillings a hide imposed on the
lands of England for defense purposes when needed.

The ship-soke galleys were part of the select fyrd
and closely associated with it. These vessels were supported and operated by special "triple-hundreds" scattered throughout England, possibly with one in each shire

and, it seems also, in several dioceses supported by the bishops. The ship-soke galleys were manned like the select fyrd in that a paid man was provided from each five hides for 60 days service each year. Thus the ship-soke provided 60 oarsmen and a galley, indicating that these vessels were similar to the 60-oared ships of Alfred the Great.

The transport vessels needed to move troops and supplies and to service the galleys at sea were provided in Anglo-Saxon England by specific seaports which in return were excused from other obligations, including taxes and fyrd service. In time these obligations were concentrated on five ports (Dover, Hastings, Romney, Hythe, and Sandwich) with other ports subordinated to these to share the burden. We do not know how many ships were owed by these Cinq Ports in the early period, but in the Angevin period 57 ships and crews were owed to the king for fifteen days each year; the sailors were paid four pence a day by the ports (Hollister 1962:103-126).

This quite un-feudal Anglo-Saxon government should not be regarded as an innovative or precociously modern system but rather as a late surviving example of Carolingian government, just as Germany was at the same time. It was in decay in 1066, but was, as a government, on a higher level than feudalism, especially feudalism of the Norman variety, which had been imposed on the uncontrolled anarchy of Norman violence by Duke William in less than twenty years (1047-1066). It would be a grave mistake to assume from the outcome of Hastings, as many writers do, that the government of Normandy was a better government than that in England, or even that the Norman military system was better than that of the Anglo-Saxons. The victory at Hastings was accidental, or, if not, was the result of planning which had little to do with the battle itself, but rather was the result of diplomacy which achieved the simultaneous Scandinavian attack in the north and the "control" of the English Channel by the naval forces of William's father-in-law, Count Baldwin V of Flanders, after the English fleet had finished its annual summer patrols. At the time Count Baldwin was under contract to William to provide a force of fighting men for payment of 300 marks a year.

This diplomatic planning was effective because of the criminal neglect of the English defense forces,

951

including the navy, by the pious and pro-Norman King
Edward. This holy man, who had used his navy to help
the Emperor to defeat the Count of Flanders in 1049,
abolished 15 ships of his mercenary navy in 1051 and
ended the collection of Danegeld, used entirely for
defense, in that same year.

The Norman Conquest made two broad changes in
England's position. It superimposed a Norman feudal
military occupation on top of the Anglo-Scandinavian
state, and it radically shifted the balance of power
in northwestern Europe, taking England out of its
Scandinavian power configuration and creating a new
"international" situation in which France, Scotland,
Flanders, and Scandinavia appeared as potential allies
against the new Anglo-Norman regime. This potential
threat, rather than any possible uprising by the subjected English people, was the chief consideration of
the reign of William I after 1080, although he remained
alert to both dangers. In fact, under the Norman kings
and during much of the rest of English medieval history,
the chief threat to the monarch came from unruly vassals.
These brutal and violent men, supported by the peasants
on their extensive lands and operating from their private
castles, often rebelled against the royal power. In
many cases, these risings were accompanied by attacks
from Scotland or from the continent. For the period
1075-1154 the monarchy defended itself by using the
English fyrd, the English navy, and such mercenary and
feudal forces as it could rally to its defense (Beeler 1966).

Specifically, the Norman Conquest brought to England
at least six innovations: (1) the private castle; (2)
the crossbow; (3) the heavy cavalry charge in battle and
the horse to do it; (4) royal ownership of land; (5) a
separate system of ecclesiastical courts and justice;
and (6) most important of all, feudalism, that is a system of military service based on land tenure which included
jurisdiction and political control as well as economic support for the feudal lord.

After the Conquest, the older four-part English
military system remained. This consisted of (a) the
general fyrd, a levy of all able-bodied men called up
in an emergency for local unpaid service; (b) the
select fyrd, to use Professor Hollister's terms (1962:
38-58), in which a smaller force of fighters was assembled
and paid 20 shillings to serve anywhere for two months, on

952

a basis of one man serving from every five hides of land and paid by the holders of those hides; (c) the navy; and (d) whatever mercenary retainers were available to replace the old English housecarles who had been destroyed as a fighting unit at Hastings. It is doubtful if any English warriors fought as heavy cavalry; they rode or walked to the field and fought dismounted. The Normans brought the heavy cavalry charge and probably the destrier war horse to England at this time (Ramsay 1906). However, it is worth noting that the Norman knights fought on foot and did so more frequently after 1066, possibly as a consequence of their difficulty in breaking the English "shield wall" (an obvious misnomer applied to men fighting with slashing swords and battleaxes).

The Conquest also brought to England the private castle and the crossbow. There were in England in 1066 only three or four private castles recently constructed as a consequence of the weak negligence of King Edward. In general, the Anglo-Saxon monarchy considered fortresses to be royal possessions. When William gave out large estates of the newly conquered country to those who had fought with him, he expected that they would fortify a residence of the motte and bailey type to defend themselves and the realm. Professor Beeler, who has made a special study of this subject, believes that the castles were built on the basis of an overall strategic plan, since there were several hundred of them guarding every significant town, road junction, or river crossing (Beeler 1971:99).

These grants of land to the Normans were in exchange for military service, although no specific amounts were set at the time. The grantees were left free as to how they would support their military obligations to the king, that is by subinfeudation, by mercenary fighters, or by domestic retainers. When specific military obligations were set later, most vassals met their needs for fighters by subinfeudation, that is by enfeoffment of subvassals, but the obligations were so moderate that the tenants-in-chief had sufficient land to support many more fighters than they owed to the king. In many cases they enfeoffed about ten percent more than they owed, which gave a cushion of extra men available in case of need. The extra land could be used to support domestic retainers, if the lord could get labor to work it, a problem which became easier as excess population without lands of their own appeared after 1200. The dangers from a lord with

953

retainers in a motte and bailey castle was reduced somewhat, in the early period, because labor was scarcer,
and much of it was not yet enserfed in England, and because the original royal grants of lands were not made
in concentrated blocks but were scattered about England.
The grants were taken, in many cases, from already functioning manorial holdings, so that the new lords' lands
were intermingled with those of peasants and other lords
and churches. The rallying of the freemen peasants to
the monarchy in the magnates' revolts after 1075 rested
on their fears that too strong lords, freed of royal
control, would enserf them all immediately. In time,
most of them were enserfed (by 1200), but, as usual in
England, it was done by legal processes, including
legal chicanery.

As a result of the Conquest, William became the
owner of all lands in England by right of conquest.
This shifted the basic idea of landholding from ownership to tenure. All land was held, mediately or immediately, of the Crown. Thus when Sir Thomas Littleton,
about 1470, wanted to write an outline of the English
land laws for his son, he called it Tenures. This
meant that the lands which the Conqueror did not hand
out as fiefs were not owned by the people who had been
living on them as owners, but were held by them as
tenures of the monarch, not, it is true, as rent payers
but by obligations as subjects to give taxes and military
service when asked for these. In this way, the idea of
kingship which William had not possessed in Normandy,
where he was only duke and feudal superior (not suzerain),
was added to the feudal lordship which he created in
England by all the rights of the old English kingship.
Unfortunately, the Normans were still lacking in ability
for abstract thinking, as was most of Europe in the 11th
century, and could not distinguish the man from the office,
nor public from private, so that the patrimonial idea of
the ruler was not really replaced by addition of the royal
title, but was strengthened. This can be seen in the disposition which William made of his properties at his death,
which we shall consider in a moment.

The idea that the king was owner of the land was
particularly strongly held in regard to lands on which
there were no residents, that is no tenures intervening
between king and the land itself. This was true of the
forests, the highways, waterways, and the towns which had
not been granted out to vassals or churches. These were

954

subject to relatively arbitrary royal power and, at the same time, to the royal peace which gave them a distinctive status and law. In general, England about 1100 was at a point that the Carolingian state had been about 830, except that the balance between the patrimonial idea of the monarchy and the idea of the state as a public authority was moving in the opposite direction, from statist to patrimonial in 830 (despite the efforts of Alcuin and Louis the Pious) and from patrimonial to statist in 1100. From this point of view, the introduction of feudalism into England by the Normans was a retrograde step, whose evil effects remained long after feudalism as a system of unpaid, self-supporting military service had passed (by 1200).

Fully as important as the innovations which the Normans brought to England were the institutions which they preserved. England as a unique state came out of the mixture (not fusion) of these two contributions. They retained the fyrd and its associated mechanisms for recruitment and payment of troops: the system of national taxation (geld) and upkeep of the royal establishment (feorm, which they called in French prises); the obligation for maintenance of bridges, strongholds, and town walls; borough rights and minting rights; and the system of royal justice in shires and hundreds. The geld, which H.R. Loyn (1962) calls "the first regular and permanent landtax known to the West in the Middle Ages," was very important, but the system of royal justice was almost as important, providing large incomes to the holder of a court and allowing the king, in the future, to establish an extended system of courts and judges which served to build up the Common Law from judicial decisions. From the existence of this judicial structure the monarch was able to issue formal rules, called Assizes or Constitutions on many subjects of public concern which might become matters of litigation in his courts.

An early indication that the Norman monarchy in England had no intention of becoming merely an archaic king or of remaining simply a feudal suzerain appeared in 1086 with a double project. The king demanded an oath of allegiance at Salisbury not far from his vassals but from his vassals' vassals. In the same year he set in motion a kind of census of all England to find out what rights he had on every piece of land. The results, known as Domesday Book, gives the status of people, animals, and rights as they existed in the time of King

Edward and as they were in 1086. Such an achievement
would have been impossible for any other monarch in
Europe at that time.

The Norman government remained a military occupation
for three reigns (William and his two sons, William Rufus
in 1087-1100 and Henry I in 1100-1135) and remained an
alien domination for more than three centuries. The
ruling class continued to speak French until about 1400,
used Latin or French as the languages of government until
about 1500 or later, and used a dialect known as Anglo-
Norman legal French as the language of law and the courts
until the 17th century. For about a century after the
Conquest there were legal distinctions between French
and English, in order to protect the one and to control
the other. At that time, as today, catching up with
criminals who had no property, fixed jobs, or "last
known address" was not easy. To create joint responsibility
and prevent concealment of criminals by their relatives
and friends, the Anglo-Saxons had required that all non-
landed persons be joined into groups of ten called "tith-
ings," who were jointly responsible for each member of the
group until they turned the wanted person over to the
authorities on legal demand. Periodically, the agents
of government reviewed these groups of ten (called "view
of frankpledge") to make sure they were complete and to
fill vacancies by death with new members by cooptation.
Under the Normans, this was used to control the English
in the name of public order, and the tithing was made
responsible for the deeds, fines, and punishments of any
member. The view of frankpledge often fell into private
hands in the Norman period and could be used for abuse
or to force payment of arbitrary fines for venial acts
or omissions.

More of an innovation was the murdrum, a fine of 46
marks assessed against any hundred where a body was
found killed unless it could be proven to be that of an
Englishman, in which case the fine was forgiven and the
case left to the regular criminal law.

All feudal inheritance was partible and was usually
divided among sons, often with the oldest getting what
the father had inherited from his father, including his
highest honors, and a second son getting what the father
acquired in his own life by conquest, marriage, or purchase. If there were several daughters, the inheritance
was divided, except that honors were non-partible and

either lapsed or went to the eldest if she had sufficient property to support them.

These feudal rules produced frequent power struggles. William the Conqueror left England to his second son, William Rufus, because he had acquired it himself, while his oldest son, Robert Curthose, obtained Normandy. The third son, Henry, was left money in order to avoid partition of either realm. A daughter, Adele, was married to Stephen, Count of Blois. When Rufus was mysteriously killed by an arrow in the New Forest in 1100, Henry seized his brother's crown. Six years later, Henry intervened in the feudal anarchy which had prevailed in Normandy since 1087 and, fighting on foot, defeated Duke Robert, put him into prison for the rest of his days (David 1920), and took the duchy for himself and to the great benefit of the fief. This reunion of Normandy with England alarmed King Louis VI of France, who invaded Normandy in 1119, but was defeated by Henry at Bremule. On the return voyage to England the following year, Henry's heir and many young nobles were drowned in the wreck of the White Ship, leaving Henry's daughter, Matilda, wife of the Emperor Henry VI, as sole heiress. When the Emperor died in 1125, King Henry married his daughter to Geoffrey Plantagenet, Count of Anjou, Touraine, and Maine, to protect the inheritance. On King Henry's death in 1135, however, the younger Stephen of Blois, son of Henry's sister Adele, seized the crown of England, opening almost twenty years of dynastic wars, which were used by many of the feudal magnates of England to make a civil war in which they could usurp lands and franchises at the expense of the people and the monarchy. By a compromise in 1153, it was agreed that Stephen could remain as king until his death, when the crown would go to the twenty-year-old son of the Empress Matilda, Henry Plantagenet.

The English weapons and tactics of this confused period, now more nearly made clear by the work of two American professors, Charles Warren Hollister (1962, 1965) and John Beeler (1966, 1971), were modifications of the Anglo-Norman tactics and recruitment. The tactics were to allow the enemy to hurl himself on a wall of archers and dismounted knights until he was worn down, then to disperse him with the charge of a reserve of mounted knights. Certain secondary tactical rules emerged from this period. One was not to disrupt one's own solid formation by taking the offensive with dismounted men until after the enemy had worn himself down. A second

957

was that an infantry wall could not be protected on its
flanks by mounted men because these could be shattered
by an attack by charging horsemen who hit them while
avoiding as much as possible the archers in the defensive
wall. This meant that any mounted group being held for
the second (shock) stage of a battle had to be kept, for
their own protection, behind the infantry wall until the
enemy offensive had lost its cohesion and momentum. The
first was generally followed by English and British
forces for the next eight centuries and was advocated
by Liddell Hart in his Defense of Britain in 1939. This
fundamental rule, to allow the enemy to adopt the tactical offensive against a standing mass of English, carried England from victory to victory all the way from
Henry I to Waterloo. At both Tenchbrai and Bremule,
the king and his knights were in the "shield wall" with
archers and were attacked by mounted knights, which they
withstood successfully. At Tenchbrai, the weary enemy
were then destroyed by a flank attack from a cavalry
reserve hidden off their left flank, while at Bremule,
it would seem, they were dispersed by a mass infantry
charge. In a small engagement at Bourg Theroulde,
Normandy, in 1124, a band of plundering Norman rebels
was intercepted by a Norman castellan, who had 300 mercenary horse and 40 mounted archers. The cavalry were
dismounted and formed as a wall of spearmen straight
across the road, with the archers, also dismounted, in
a mass just before their left front. The rebel count
charged straight at the spearmen with 40 mounted knights,
but many of their horses were killed by the arrows coming
from their unshielded right side. After a second similar
charge met a similar reception, the castellan advanced
with his spearmen to finish the rebels (Beeler 1971:47-49).

Two battles of Stephen of Blois show aspects of the
basic tactics. At the Battle of the Standard (Northallerton) in 1138, King Stephen dismounted his knights in a
mass as a second line, with the shire levies on their
flanks and rear, and a front line of archers and dismounted knights across the whole width of the front.
The Scots, refusing to obey their king David, formed
in five detached blocks, the Clansmen of Galloway in
a large mass at center front with two detached wings
of mixed arms, with King David holding a dismounted
reserve behind the Galwegians and his son, Henry, with
a group of mounted knights in front of the clans on the
right wing. The Galwegians, without armor, made a number of violent charges on the English mass, with great

losses. To relieve them, Prince Henry galloped at the left of the English line and broke through to the rear, where he headed for the English horses tethered some distance to the rear. By the time Henry's force was ready to return to the engagement, it was almost over, the Galwegians destroyed, the clansmen on the Scottish wings dispersed after a single charge, and King David's reserve, committed too late, soon ran to their horses and left the field. There was no real pursuit, and the royal army soon dispersed also. The defeat was largely attributable to the lack of discipline of the Scots and the total lack of coordination among their five units.

The first battle of Lincoln, at which King Stephen was captured by two rebellious earls, has much more to teach. The king was besieging Lincoln castle which the earls had previously captured by a ruse. The earls mobilized a relief force and marched it 150 miles to Lincoln, forcing the king to draw up in battle to face them. This time the royal formation was in three units, a large block of infantry and dismounted knights under the king in the center, with two detached wings of feudal cavalry. The rebels were in similar formation. Each army's left wing charged at the force opposite it, the royal right wing fleeing the field under the attack, while the royal left wing crashed into its opponent but was soon attacked on its right by the infantry of the rebel center, which was still unengaged by the royal center. The royalist left soon fled, leaving its center, with the king, under a converging assault from all the rebel forces. The king remained like Harold at Hastings, fighting a hopeless immobile struggle, his battleaxe in his hand, until he was knocked down by a stone and over-whelmed. Here, as at Northallerton, there was lack of coordination on the defeated side, but two other lessons may be drawn: cavalry wings may be wiped away if they are hit by charging horsemen while they are standing still; and the rule of tactical defense must be abandoned when part of your forces needs help on another part of the field (Beeler 1966:110-119).

The English military experience of this period was enriched by lessons from the Crusades, of which one of the chief was that a column could continue to march under attack, as the crusaders did successfully to Busra in 1147 and successfully to Hattin in 1187 (Smail 1956: 156-197). Of course, this was an action which could be done more successfully against Saracens, who did not charge until the enemy was almost finished by missiles, than could be done against Europeans who tended to shift from missiles to shock as soon as possible.

The chronology of the kings of England and France can easily be stated, but the sequence of real trends is far from obvious. In general, in the medieval period, unlike today, men and personal relationships among men were more significant than offices or institutions; a strong king encouraged stability, while a weak one permitted disorder. Beyond this, however, there appear to be alternating periods of confusion and consolidation, which were dependent more on patterns of customary behavior than on personalities. In England between the Conquest in 1066 and the Tudor revolt in 1485, there are, perhaps, four periods of such confusion and consolidation, as follows:

Consolidation	Confusion
1066-1135 (William I-II, Henry I)	1135-1154 (Stephen)
1154-1194 (Henry II, early Richard)	1194-1272 (late Richard, John, Henry III)
1272-1294 (most of Edward I)	1294-1330 (late Edward I, Edward II)
1330-1369 (much of Edward III)	1369-1485 (end Edward III, Richard II, Henry IV, V, VI, Edward IV, V, Richard III)

In general, periods of consolidation were those in which resources were being used for relatively constructive purposes to satisfy human needs, while periods of confusion were those in which resources were being used for relatively destructive purposes, to satisfy human desires (often irrational) apart from real needs. Moreover, periods of consolidation were marked by a higher degree of cooperation among monarch, magnates, and people, while in periods of confusion there was a high level of competition or conflict between classes, and resources were used for conflict, class struggles, and violence. In most cases, the periods of confusion were marked by excessive royal demands which led to resistance by the magnates, as under John, Henry III, Edward I and II. Cooperation between monarchy and people, even against the opposition of the magnates, as in 1066-1135, was more important than cooperation between the monarchy and the magnates, as in the whole period after 1330. Indeed, in any assessment of the use of resources in relation to the satisfaction of human needs for the society as a whole, it would appear that the four periods of consolidation were successively less productive, while the four periods of confusion were successively more destructive. The turning point in this, as in the general pattern of economic development, was about 1270, when the medieval age of expansion turned into the late medieval age of conflict.

On this rather general sequence of political patterns, we might impose a more specific sequence of military patterns. Here, again, as in all our efforts at periodization, we must remember that change is constant and that no abrupt demarcations exist between periods.

English military history could be divided into at least five periods in the Middle Ages, thus:

A. National, monarchical forces, to 1066.
B. A combination of feudal forces and national militia, 1066-1181.
C. A transitional period of service based on wealth, 1181-1287.
D. Service based on private enterprise under contracts, leading to neo-feudalism, 1287-1377.
E. Neo-feudalism, 1377-1485.

The fundamental problems of the whole sequence were: (1) the creation of a reservoir of fighting men, with training and arms; (2) the raising of troops from that reservoir; (3) the transportation and supplying of these troops; and (4) financing all these activities.

In general over this whole period, there was a shift from allegiance to compulsion in maintaining the reservoir and from allegiance to contract in raising men from it, partly because of parliamentary objections to compulsory levies. Over the same period, as a result of the eventual failure of compulsion in maintaining the reservoir and the shifting of costs from the individual or from local units to the central government, the latter accepted the obligation to provide equipment but evaded the burden of payment for service, as much as possible, by commercializing war so that it became private contractual enterprise financed by the profits of war itself. These private enterprises for war, largely controlled by the king and his relatives, bogged down in the morass of the endless war with France and became a threat to the royal power itself in the

final years of Edward III, giving rise to a decentralization of political power known as "bastard feudalism"
or "neo-feudalism." The extermination of the Plantagenet
family and the curtailment of neo-feudalism after 1485
resulted in the next stage, Tudor despotism, in 1485-1603.

The change from stage B to stage C began with the
Assize of Arms of 1181, issued by Henry II in an effort
to establish all military service in a single hierarchy
of graded obligations without regard to feudal or tenurial
obligations. It was a very tentative first step, since it
ignored changes in weapons and tactics of which he was
well aware, and it did not apply to non-free men (villeins).
By its provisions all free men in England were divided into
three classes on the basis of their possession of incomes
of 16 or 10 marks (a mark was equal to 160 pence or two-
thirds of a pound). The poorest group, below 10 marks,
were required to have a quilted jacket, an iron cap, and
a lance; the middle group, 10 to 16 marks, were to have
a mail shirt, iron cap, and lance; the richest group,
at least 16 marks, and all knights had to have heavy
mail armor, a helmet, shield, and lance. All these groups
were to take an oath of loyalty to the king and to certify
that they had the required arms by presenting them before
sworn inquests (juries) empaneled by the itinerant justices. Acts similar to this had already been enacted in
Henry's continental lands and were soon copied by France
and Flanders.

Notable omissions from this Assize of Arms were
any mention of horses or archery, which were the chief
elements of English weaponry in the 13th century. Henry
was fully aware of these, as he had already created
mounted archers, who may have used their bows (not longbows) from the saddle, in 1172 when he established his
feudal suzerainty in Ireland (Powicke 1962:54). Henry
was well aware of the value of infantry and was fully
prepared to pay for it. He did not use mercenary knights
in England after the revolt of 1173, but he was the
largest user of paid infantry before the Hundred Years
War, which is what we would expect from one who placed
such emphasis on siege operations. Payment to the shire
militia for service outside their own county did not
begin until 1193.

The period of confusion from 1194 to 1272 began
with heavy financial exactions for Richard's exploits
on the Third Crusade (1189-1192) and to pay for his ransom

on his way home (1194). Demands increased under John (1199-1216) and under Henry III (1216-1272), along with convincing evidence of the lack of royal competence in using these resources and constant efforts to make wars on the continent, where the magnates had no significant ambitions after the loss of Normandy by John in 1204. Neither John nor his successor had much respect for customary restraints on royal demands, which led to baronial revolts against both kings. These revolts led to the Magna Carta (1215), to numerous re-issues and modifications of this document, to inconclusive wars with France, and finally to outright civil war (1258-1265), when the barons, led by Simon de Montfort, tried to reduce alien and papal influences on the king and the country. To do this, the barons, under the Provisions of Oxford (1258), set up a permanent Council of Fifteen barons and officials to supervise and, if needed, to veto royal actions. This drastic constitutional change was precipitated by Henry III's promise to the Pope to pay the papal treasury 135,541 marks and to send no less than 8500 soldiers to Sicily in 1259 to overthrow the Hohenstauffen ruler and replace him as king with Henry's son, Edmund. Although Henry and his heir, Prince Edward, took an oath to support the Provisions of Oxford, the Pope released him from this obligation and it was violated, leading to two years of civil war. In a battle at Lewes, Simon defeated the royalists and captured Henry and Prince Edward. Both again agreed to support the Provisions, but Edward soon escaped to the West where he rallied royalist supporters, caught Simon's forces near Eversham and defeated them, killing their leader.

Edward I (1272-1307) marked a new period of consolidation, which continued the process by which military service was transformed from allegiance to a pecuniary basis. Regarded by some historians as England's greatest king, and sometimes called "the English Justinian" because of his continued development of the Common Law and the English judicial system and frequently praised for his use of Parliament to grant consent to his projects, Edward nonetheless originated many of the evils which marked English history in the last two centuries of the Middle Ages. He was a compulsive warrior, overruling all opposition with force and legalisms, arranging justice, finance, and administration to allow this, and tried to monopolize private landed wealth in England in the hands of his own family. By force, duress, legal chicanery, tricky marriage settlements, and judicial

963

corruption, he fleeced eight comital families, including some of the oldest and richest, murdering the earldoms, as K.B. McFarlane expressed it (1973:251), or concentrating them in the hands of his own family and descendants.

From this policy of building up the landholding of his family came the system of royal appanages which made war a private enterprise for royal princes in the late 14th century and encouraged neo-feudal anarchy in the late 15th century. The policy, like the development of the law and of parliament, was intended to feed Edward's insatiable lust for war. It led, as might have been anticipated, to a "baronial reaction" in 1294-1330, which was compromised in 1330 by an agreement between Edward III and his greater barons to exploit the profits of war together.

The assizes, writs, and judicial decisions which established war as a system of enterprise for private profit do not form a logical progression but rather operate as a series of starts and stops, of false starts and reversals. The final result was to create a system in which war was waged by contract using a hierarchy of military obligations on several levels. The three kinds of service (mercenary, militia, and feudal) continued, but the whole process became increasingly expensive not only from the general price inflation of the period but from the demand for the resources of war based on the growing obsession of the ruling classes with warlike activities. In fact, the demand was so great that it was hardly interrupted by the Black Death, which reduced the population of Western Europe by about 40 per cent in the 14th century, by increased incidence of famine among the lower classes, as in 1315-1317, or by the drop in the prices of necessities in the late 14th and early 15th centuries.

This inflation is reflected in the costs of war by the growth in the wages of fighting men of the heavy armed class (Hollister 1962). In the Anglo-Saxon period the thegns were available for 2 pence a day, which rose to 4d by 1066. Thus a fighter would serve his required 60 days for a pound (240 pence). Under Henry I the price reached 6d per day, with service still at 60 days, which was reduced to 40 days under Stephen. About 1159 the price was 8d per day for 40 days or 2 marks. At that point a distinction began to appear as the meaning of the word "knight" changed, so that mounted men-at-arms

964

who had not been formally "dubbed" into the class of knights became available at half the price of a "belted knight." At the same time, scutage, which reflected the payment cost of a substitute fighter, was charged, under Henry II, at the rate for men-at-arms even for knights' service. Such scutage was collected eight times from 1162 to 1196 at one mark, or 4d a day for 40 days, although payment for the services of a belted knight rose steadily to a shilling (12d) a day by 1180 and to two shillings after 1190. King John tried to close the gap between what he could collect as scutage and what he had to pay for service by raising scutage to 40 shillings in 1215, an effort which helped to trigger the baronial revolt leading to Magna Carta. This scutage of a shilling a day was figured at the price for men-at-arms, not for knights. By 1200 scutage was simply a tax, "an anachronism. But it was an a-nachronism only because the unpaid service of feudal knights had itself become an anachronism" (Hollister 1965:215). Only three of eleven scutages imposed in 1218-1245 were at 40 shillings, but all eight imposed in the sixty years 1246-1306 were at 40 shillings. By that time, the costs of trying to collect scutage were so high and the collections so meager that it was given up as a way to raise money for war.

Another way to meet these costs was to push them onto the local recruitment districts, the hundreds, which owed service as militia. In the 11th century the select fyrd had called one fighter from each five hides, paying him 4 shillings from each hide for 60 days service. Apparently, he was given 10 shillings on call-up and the other 10 shillings on his return, for William Rufus called the select fyrd to assemble at Hastings for service in Normandy in 1094 and, when they had gathered, took the 10 shillings from each man and sent him home again.

Controversy for payment for the militia service filled much of the 12th and 13th centuries with demands from the shires that service be on the royal payroll outside each man's home county, while the king often tried to force pay onto the hundred or vill, at least up to the final mobilization point or even to the port of embarkation for service overseas. At the same time, the king generally insisted that clearly defensive ser-vice, such as in the border shires against the Scots, in the Welsh Marches, or in "the Maritime Lands" (within

965

6 leagues of the sea) should be paid at the local districts. By 1300, it was getting settled that royal pay began when a militia man left his own shire. But by that time, the militia was generally used only for domestic defense service or for police work (called "hue and cry"). The same militia obligation, however, was used as the basis for selective service for aggressive wars abroad.

During this whole period there were successive enactments of Assizes of Arms, to specify national obligations for service equipment. In 1230 the non-free were included, largely for "hue and cry," and the lowest freeholders were separated into two classes, at ₤1, with only an axe or lance and at ₤2 with an iron cap and a gambeson as well. The Assize of 1242, according to Michael Powicke (1962:86), was "truly revolutionary." It divided free men above the two classes just mentioned into three classes: 40 shilling freeholders as archers; men-at-arms with ₤15 rent or 60 marks in goods; and ₤25 knights. There were subsequent modifications of these, but under Edward I the two vital categories of ₤20 "knights" and ₤2 "archers" were clearly established. Somewhat later, the two intermediate classes of ₤5 mounted archers and ₤10 hobelars (mounted infantry with lances) became distinct. These were important, as men on foot could not forage and required supply trains which slowed operations (Warren 1973:231-7).

Until 1253 all these requirements assumed that military service could be imposed only on those who could provide their own weapons. In that year, for the first time, it was ordered that vills should provide "light arms," which included archery, if necessary. This did become necessary in 1264, when a selective service system began to develop. Royal writs that year to the sheriffs of various shires ordered them to pick out the best four, six, or eight men, depending on the population of the vill, armed with lances, bows, axes, swords, and crossbows, and to provide for their upkeep for forty days from the rest of the villagers; the recruits were then to be assembled in groups of tens and hundreds under special commanders.

The last significant Assize of Arms was the Statute of Winchester (1285), which was not repealed until James I, although it was much twisted and distorted in the interval. It set up seven classes for all males aged

15 to 60, of which the upper five were designated by incomes as £15, £10, £5, £2, and less than £2 from land and the lowest two classes were above and below 20 marks in chattels, with review by commissioners every two years of men and their weapons. By that time the longbow was already spreading over England, apparently from south Wales, although it was not distinguished in the documents. By 1340 selective service recruits were provided with cutting weapons locally and with bows and a sheaf of 24 arrows at the port of embarkation (Hewitt 1966).

In 1287 the task of selecting men was shifted from the sheriffs to special commissioners in each shire. Later these were given arrayers to help them, the chosen men being organized in units to march up to the place where they joined the royal forces. After 1340 they were usually expected to support themselves until they left their home shires, to be supported by that shire from its boundary to the port of embarkation, where they were equipped as needed and given an advance of royal pay before setting out for enemy shores.

The changes in weapons and tactics which are usually attributed to the period from Edward I to Edward III (1272-1338) had been in preparation for a long time. The only real change was the longbow and the beginnings of a significant shift in the aims of a battle from killing to capturing the enemy. The origins of the longbow are usually found in south Wales during Edward I's Welsh Wars of 1276-1284. But it involved nothing new and, like siege tactics, was a revival of skills and knowledge which had been lost in the dark age. It could not compare, in cost or skills of manufacture and use, with the contemporary composite bow of grassland Asia. But in Europe it was devastating. And it could not be copied easily by England's enemies, not only because of the prejudice against "lower class" weapons, but also because of the skills needed to make and use it.

The longbow was a selfbow made of the proper wood (elm grown in the shade or yew) and cut so that its back was sapwood, which resists stretching, and its belly was heartwood, which resists compression. This required considerable time and skill. So did its use. These bows were usually about the height of the user, with circumference at the grip over four inches, using arrows about 35 inches long, with steel points and pulled back to the head (Edwards and Heath 1962:53-54). This bow came into use very slowly as people gained skills to make and to use it, and it was replaced by firearms after 1500 as people became unwilling to practice its use. It could not be adopted by England's enemies, because no other country was willing or able to make its people practice its use from boyhood. It was really a popular, not a royal weapon, quite unlike the Asiatic complex bow which had been a royal weapon for thousands of years, as we have seen. The kings of England adopted it because it was available among the English people, but they could not compel its use, as the Tudors discovered when they tried to maintain it over popular indifference in the 16th century.

The tactics which won battles for the English in the Hundred Years War were already known to the Normans about two centuries earlier. The addition of the longbow under Edward I merely made those tactics more effective against any enemy who was willing to make a headlong attack on the English battleline. The French were as committed to the reckless charge as the Scots, but for different reasons, but the painful consequences of doing this against the English battle tactics were experienced by the Scots a generation before the French met up with it. It could be said that the Scots in 1296-1335 provided the tactical training which made it so difficult for the French to defeat the English after 1337.

The Scots had many handicaps. They were still a largely tribal society in which a Norman-style feudal arrangement had been inserted between the clans and the tribal king at the top. Allegiances were confused and precarious. Weaponry was equally confused. Lacking the longbow, some Scots had selfbows, but the traditional Scottish infantry weapon was the pike (schiltron), an effective defensive weapon against mounted knights if the pikes could be held in a solid mass, but very vulnerable to missile attacks. The Scottish claymore, a large two-edged sword, was too expensive for the impoverished Scots and was an upper class weapon used for individual fighting. The strength of the schiltron was lost to the Scots because of their extreme offensive and individualistic spirit. They still envisioned warfare in terms reminiscent of the ancient Indo-European warriors, that is as a wild

rush of howling individuals against the enemy, expect-
ing to sweep him from the field in a single mad assault.
Thus the Scots used pikemen as offensive individual
fighters, not as a solid well-disciplined defensive
mass. For centuries, the Scots, like most Celts and
like the Gauls fighting Caesar, lacked discipline and
cohesion. This lack of organized discipline and their
excessive offensive spirit was exactly what insured
defeat when it came against English tactics which were
fitted to obtain maximum success with such an enemy.

The Scots were also deficient in most auxiliary
services. They had little experience or skills in
castle building or siege techniques, largely ignored
sea power (although usually allied with France after
1295), had no organized supply services, and were
lacking in any effective financial organization which
might have allowed greater use of foreign mercenary
troops. Most financial contributions were voluntary
or customary, not based on the exercise of public
authority.

These weaknesses simply reflected the fact that
Scotland's society was still at an earlier phase of
historical development, unable to make the transition
from kinship loyalty to statehood (probably from lack
of either the time or the religious transition which
appear to have been necessary for this change in other
cases). In consequence they could not handle the Norman intrusion into Lowland Scotland, while the Normans
and their successor kings of England could not handle
Highland Scotland until the 18th century, a parallel
to the Roman experience there many centuries earlier.
The Scots could strike back at the English by raids
southward into English-held lowlands, passing between
castles which they could not usually capture, from
lack of supplies rather than from lack of will or skill.
These Scottish raids achieved nothing significant, except to engender English hatred, which led to English
atrocities and Scottish counter-atrocities. When the
English invaded Scotland, the usual Scottish strategy
was to raid behind them southward to draw the English
invaders back into England to protect the English people and their homes from the devastation of the Scottish
raiders. This rarely worked, because the English rulers
were not deterred by the sufferings of the peoples of
the northern English shires, partly from lack of imagination and partly because the gap between rulers and

ruled in England remained considerable. This failure made it necessary for the Scots to either allow the English invasion to go on or to fight the English invaders, using the inadequate tactics I have described.

The futilities of the Scottish wars of 1294-1337 were followed by the futilities of the French wars in 1337-1453. The reason for the shift was that glory, profit, and status could be obtained in France in greater amounts than in Scotland. And the late Middle Ages was clearly a period in which the ruling classes of Western civilization had a great thirst for glory, profit, and status. The reasons for this are very complex and have not been explained adequately by social scientists or historians. This failure by students of human experience to explain in any adequate fashion the processes of human experiences arises from the fact that the students are themselves part of the processes they wish to explain and lack both the perspective and objectivity to discover adequate explanations. We, in the 20th century, are living in a situation similar to that of the 14th century. In both cases, the rationalizations used to justify and to explain aggressions, wars, violence, and greed were simply explicit rational justifications for deeds which were really rooted in social alienation, emotional frustration, and boredom.

In the early Middle Ages, when life was hard and insecure, emotional satisfactions came, as they always must, from moment-to-moment (existential) events, as unique, direct experiences. During the age of expansion, relationships shifted from customary ones to optional ones, as the social context of each individual dissolved and he was gradually freed from the all-embracing matrix, satisfying but sometimes suffocating, of village, family, and parish. Much of this dissolution arose from the commercialization of relationships which had previously been fixed by kinship, localism, and religious belief. Human energies which had previously been spread widely in a narrow locality but on a diverse range of experience, were increasingly concentrated, through division of labor and exchange, on a few activities based on chosen relationships created by individual decisions. Such concentration of energies on specialized activities helped to increase satisfactions on these aims, mostly materialistic and quantitative ones, but with frustration of other qualitative human needs, mostly emotional and spiritual.

970

This resulted in growing misplacement of satisfactions, so that inadequate social, emotional, spiritual, or even intellectual satisfactions were compensated for by excessive, quantitative achievement of satisfactions in wealth and power. Decreased satisfaction of the need for love was replaced by increased emphasis on material acquisition; later, a decreased satisfaction of spiritual needs was replaced by more insatiable drives for power. But such misplacement of satisfactions, from higher levels to lower ones and from qualitative ones to quantitative ones, led to increased emotional insecurity, especially when emotional needs no longer found satisfactions in fixed internalized personal relationships but instead sought such satisfactions in chosen externalized impersonal relationships. This increased emotional insecurity at the same time that frustration and boredom were growing, the combination leading to hyperactivity in many persons and to neurotic passivity in others. The former became the great achievers, the ones who amassed more wealth and power and thus left more records of their lives and became historical persons known to us. These characteristics were passed on by emulation, within families, from generation to generation; if they were not passed on because children rejected their parents' patterns of living, those families sank down into the mass of people who leave little historical evidence and were replaced in history by other activists.

The major source of frustration and concentration of energies was in family life. Ordinary people, living routine lives in the midst of established relationships, found their wives and husbands and sexual satisfactions, and thus created families and bred children, by proximity and casual opportunities. They lived in a nexus of personal relationships. But among the upper classes, as tenures and rules for the inheritance of tenures became established in the 11th and 12th centuries, marriages were arranged as a means of controlling tenures, as bundles of revenues. Henry II married Eleanor of Aquitaine, not because he was attracted to her as a personality or even as a sexual partner but because he wanted her as a bundle of revenues, that is, as the heiress of Aquitaine.

A heiress was a bundle of revenues and was treated as such in the later Middle Ages. Whoever had legal control of her right to marry could sell her to the highest bidder. To be sure, the law required that she could not be "disparaged" in marriage, but this was simply to keep the tenure and its revenues within the ruling groups. As McFarlane said (1973), only a rich widow could marry freely whom she wished and take her tenures with her. The right to designate whom a heiress must marry could be sold to someone who did not wish to marry her but hoped to resell her at a profit, like an option on the stock exchange. In the period of the Hundred Years War, when this neurotic situation reached a peak, heiresses were sold for Ь4000 and more.

The psychological consequences of all this included an insatiable thirst for intense experience, for violence, money, power, and excitement, and a similar thirst for status, rank, luxury, and the ostentatious external display of these. As a result of all this, means became ends, instrumentalities like law, war, and government became institutionalized, categories became rigid, classes became more exclusive, and higher, artificial levels of status were created to satisfy these urges and the increasingly bitter struggle for higher status on all levels of the ruling classes. Like the struggles for wealth and power among the ruling groups of our Western society in this 20th century, the thirst for these things cannot be satisfied, since it is a symptom of neurosis. Where one earldom had been the apex of aspiration in the 12th century, Edmund Crouchback had three in the 13th century and was not satisfied, nor was his son Henry satisfied with five in the 14th century, and the latter's great grandson, also Henry, held six earldoms and two dukedoms when he seized the throne from Richard II in 1399. To meet the escalating demand for more status, new honors were created and distributed, without in any way assuaging the thirst for more: dukedoms in 1337; marquessates in 1385; baronies by letters patent in 1387; viscounties in 1440.

The situation was almost equally hysterical on the lower levels of hyperactivity. Knighting became formal and legal. In fact, the growing passion for formal evidence of status can be seen in the changing meanings of this word "knight." Originally, the word "knight" meant fighter or soldier, although by the 11th century it was assumed that a fighter would be equipped as a shock cavalryman. By the end of that century, it was coming to refer to a position in the feudal system, to one who held a knight's fee and owed heavy cavalry service to his lord. In the 12th century, it came increasingly to mean one who had been "dubbed" knight in a formal ceremony, that is, had been belted with a sword and kissed as an equal by a great lord. In that same century in England, Henry II placed great administrative burdens on the knights in their shires, with the result that in the 13th century, there was a reluctance to take formal knighthood. The monarch began to order periodic local inquests to find those who had adequate incomes to support knighthood (£20 a year) to force them into knighthood under penalty of a fine. The first general order of this kind was in 1224.

But 150 years later, at the death of Edward III in 1377, the passion for knighthood had become what Michael Powicke called "one of the most striking follies of the day" (1962:71-81, 179). To place some restraints on this, the sumptuary laws of 1363 required that one must have £200 a year from land or £1000 a year from trade to become a belted knight. By the end of that 14th century, belted knights were so involved in the war that there were too few knights left in the shires to carry on the king's work that had been forced upon them, without pay, since Henry II. These duties included work on juries, inquests, commissions, attendance at Parliament, and eventually service as justices of the peace. To remedy the shortage without lowering the scarce value of belted knighthood, these duties were forced upon the local squires by defining all 40 shilling freeholders as "knights of the shire" in 1445.

Closely related to this process in the period 1150-1350 was the shift of knighthood from a military and political status to a social status, just as feudalism was changed into chivalry, with tournaments, romantic love, and ostentatious display of luxury replacing actual military operations. At the same time, people who lacked the proper social status had to be restrained from any display of status, or even affluence, by sumptuary laws.

The mad struggle for status based on lands and titles was a chief force in the rapid development of chivalry, war, sumptuary legislation, law, and justice in the 14th and 15th centuries, as the rules of tenure and landholding were modified and manipulated in a multifold struggle among monarch, great magnates, lesser lords, knights, and smaller tenants to control and divert incomes from lands. Such incomes were essential to bodily survival for the peasantry and for the working class persons in trades and commerce. The neurotic drives of the upper classes to increase their incomes to satisfy their drives were adverse to the physical survival of many peasants, as population increased beyond the ability of the available lands, worked under the existing technology, to yield food and other needs for survival. As early as the end of the 13th century, the death rate among the lower classes was beginning to rise from increasing malnutrition and resulting inability to resist disease. By the second decade of the 14th century, famine struck, especially in the years of adverse weather and very poor crops in 1315-1317. These difficulties continued, leaving little historical evidence, until the enormous disaster of the Black Death in the second half of the 14th century reduced the population by about 40 per cent, simultaneously reducing the pressure of the population on the land and by reducing the supply of labor raised its price to a point at which the working classes were able to increase their relative share of the economic product for the first time in many generations.

This rapid reversal of economic class relationships by which a sudden scarcity of labor allowed workers to obtain higher wages in a period in which many necessities were subject to falling prices could not be handled in any rational way by the governing classes. Their efforts to reduce wages or to force peasants back into the older manorial obligations of unpaid service on the lords' demesnes were, on the whole, ineffective, although they led to great controversies and peasant revolts in many parts of Europe. The neurotic upper class drives for increased incomes could not be satisfied, especially when the king and the magnates struggled to compete with each other for greater shares of the total, as happened in England in 1294-1330. After 1330 these two interests realized the futility of fighting each other for shares in a limited pie and reached a modus operandi by which they could increase their incomes, lands, status, and glory by foreign wars. The history of this problem is of great significance and is part of the context of the Hundred Years War.

974

The monarchy and all the magnates, in spite of their apparent wealth in land tenures, were usually strapped for free incomes and were, in fact, buried in obligations and pestered with needs for which free incomes were not available. To meet such immediate needs, these people borrowed constantly and sometimes enormously, assigning to the lenders, frequently Italian or other foreign bankers, claims on incomes expected to become free in the future, with other, smaller incomes assigned temporarily to provide interest payments until repayment. Borrowing was made against incomes, not against properties, as we do with collateral or mortgages. There was such an emotional attachment to property that alienation was considered objectionable or was, in many cases, illegal, so that properties could not be used as security for loans any more than they could be sold to avoid loans.

In this way, "rich" magnates, loaded down with great properties, were also loaded down with debts and had little free money, although they had the enjoyment of great properties and services represented by these properties and honors. Moreover, the possession of such honors and properties entitled their possessors to be treated with deference and respect by lesser peoples and entitled them to be consulted and to participate in the important political decisions of the day. Just as in the 20th century, business executives and corporation billionaires are treated with deference and respect, are consulted on political decisions remote from their expertise, are often buried in debts, and are constantly subsidized by governments, while their corporations, especially very large ones like Boeing, Penn Central, Rolls Royce, Litton, Pan Am or Chrysler, expect to be bailed out by governments when their debts become overwhelming.

In the 14th century, as in the 20th, the magnates were not only trapped in their misperceptions of reality, but part of that misperception included the "growth syndrome." By this I mean that the only solution they could envision for their problems, both financial and emotional, was to get bigger, to grow, to take over more properties, control more incomes, and create more debts.

In the late Middle Ages there were three chief ways to obtain growth or the resources to finance growth.

These were (1) to take over more tenures, if need be
in foreign lands and, if necessary, by force; (2)
to tap the financial resources of taxation; and (3)
to control, and thus tax, flows of goods in commerce.

The Hundred Years War was an attempt by the English
magnates, led by the royal family, to take over the tenures of France with their incomes, status, and titles.
While the use of force destroyed lives and limbs, shattered families, both noble and peasant, burned homes,
barns, and churches, and destroyed crops and livestock,
it did not destroy tenures, just as the almost total
destruction of the buildings and artifacts of the
industrial areas of Germany and Japan in World War II
did not destroy the corporate structures behind those
buildings. Control of those corporate structures
often returned, when the war ended, to the same people
or their descendants, who had used their corporate
control to work for war before it began, just as happened in France after 1453.

In the Hundred Years War French tenures, or at
least the incomes of these, were taken over by the conquerors, not, be it noted, to the credit of the English
state as a public entity, but to the credit of private
purses of the military leaders and their chief lieutenants, including the reigning king and his relatives.
In addition, in those parts of France which were annexed or under extended military occupation, the victors were able to tax the inhabitants, since control
of the higher tenures also gave control or power over
the local government. Moreover, by blackmail, ransoms,
and other kinds of duress, each side, to some degree,
was able to obtain access to the wealth, taxes, or incomes of the other side to their own profit. The most
astounding example of this is that the ransom of King
John of France, who was captured at Poitiers in 1356,
did not go to the state or to the patrimony of the
English monarchy or to any public purpose, but was
pocketed by Edward III personally. The ransom, amounting to 3 million gold ecus (£500,000), was to be paid
in installments over several years, with various hostages
and tenures held as guarantees until payment was finished (it never was). Edward not only took the payments as his own, but when one early payment was credited
to the Exchequer he rebuked that agency with a warning
not to repeat that error.

McFarlane (1973:37) gives us another less well-known example. In 1412 the Duke of Clarence, in an insignificant raid, was persuaded by the French to leave by an offer of ₺35,000 sterling to be shared among the retinues concerned. The French handed over seven persons as hostages, including the 7-year-old John, Count of Angouleme, whose brother, the Duke of Orleans, arranged the deal and assumed the burden of paying. Of the sum ₺19,000 was paid by 1417, but the Duke of Orleans was captured himself at Agincourt in 1415 and the family estates were overrun by the English who confiscated their revenues without any credit to the ransom due. When the Duke was finally ransomed in 1440, it took him five years longer to pay off his brother's ransom, the total for both reaching ₺75,000, while the two brothers together had spent the best years of their lives in captivity, the one 25 years and the other 33.

In addition to ransoms, in this same period, the occupied territories of Western Europe paid heavy taxes which were used to pay for the men of the occupying forces of all ranks, plus large pensions to the high officers, and control of the incomes from tenures to those who had influence to obtain these. In sixteen years, 1419-1435, Normandy paid at least ₺560,000 in taxes in this way.

It is obvious that the English Exchequer, which means the English people, provided the money to finance the military effort in Europe. Since the profits from this "adventure" did not return to the English taxpayer nor to the English state, this really means that the English taxpayers, chiefly peasants and some townsfolk, were paying for a business whose losses were sustained by the public while all profits were going to the executives (McFarlane and M.M. Postan, 1964). To prevent the ordinary English peasant from realizing any increase in wages, the Parliament, representing the upper classes, enacted the Statute of Labourers in 1351, setting a maximum wage of ten shillings a year for a skilled agricultural worker (a plowman) at a time when knights (who were represented in Parliament) were getting two shillings a day in the king's army.

The third, and by far the most important, way for

the monarchy to obtain money was from tolls on commerce. This method raised funds for thousands of years in Asia, financing mobile armies over great distances and supplemented by incomes from peasant agriculture where adequate water allowed this activity. In Europe the relationship was reversed, since the growth of commerce and tolls came late to an area where localized armed forces were already being supported by the meager incomes to be derived from a peasant agriculture close to the subsistence level. Any effective system of tolls must be able to compensate by reducing the expenses (or losses) entailed in moving goods and must control the territory over which the goods pass, so that too many tolls may not be imposed on the goods as they pass; if this happens, the accumulation of tolls will wipe out the price difference between the source and final destination of the goods and they will cease to pass. This is why the grassland pastoralists of Asia tried to create the pax nomadica across the steppes. Of course, luxury goods which are so exotic that they cannot be produced locally even at a much higher price or for which no suitable substitute can be found, such as silk from China or pepper from southeast Asia, will continue to pass through many tolls, resulting in much reduced volume at much higher prices.

In medieval Europe, power was so localized that it was difficult to control lines of commerce for any significant distance, and goods passed through numerous areas of different power controls. This meant that substantial tolls could be imposed only as power areas became wider in the late medieval period.

The second phase of mercantilist economic policy, which I have called "the policy of the staple," was aimed at using political power to make trade pass through certain points or markets where it could be taxed conveniently. Thus the English policy of the Staple refers to the legal requirement that wool produced in England for export must be shipped to a single selling point, stored there and taxed, before it could be sold to foreign buyers. Such a staple market could be in England or abroad, as at Calais, Bruges, or somewhere else. Part of the advantage of such a foreign staple was that it allowed the king to avoid the problem of shipping money or of exchanging money to pay for his exploits abroad, since he could make payments on the continent by drawing on the proceeds

978

of the sales of wool at the Staple. This is why the
Staple was put at Calais when military operations out
of Normandy required heavy payments of troops there.

Such efforts to use commerce to raise money or
to transfer wealth to the continent in order to pay
for a war had results which were not expected by the
ruling groups in England. Thus the export of raw
wool to the textile artisans of Flanders was taxed
and manipulated for political purposes and was even
cut off on occasions so that the resulting economic
misery of the workers could be used to force the ruling groups in Flanders to cooperate with the ruling
groups in England in making war on France. But these
efforts acted like a protective tariff on the manufacture of woolen cloth in England: the raw wool remained within the country, wool prices there were
lowered, and the manufacture of cloth increased. Soon
the export trade shifted from raw wool to woolen cloth,
which increased from very little in 1350 to about
50,000 pieces at the end of the century (Power 1941;
Carus-Wilson 1967:239-264).

The trade of wine from southwestern France was a
powerful motivation for the English ruling groups to
persist in holding Gascony, not only because they drank
wine (while ordinary Englishmen drank beer or ale), but
because the export taxes on wine through Bordeaux were
a major income to be used to finance the activities of
these ruling groups in both war and peace. The outcome,
however, became a vicious, and destructive, circle.
Control of Gascony provided wine and incomes, but such
control could be maintained only by war which quickly
destroyed much of the trade and most of the incomes.
Margery K. James (1971) shows how the Hundred Years
War injured the wine trade, the tolls, and the incomes
from these, and eventually destroyed the vineyards
themselves. But by 1500 Gascony and its vineyards
were part of France, so that the fiscal advantages
of the trade went to the French and not to the English,
who had to pay at least double the prices of the early
15th century, and the wine was now arriving in non-English
ships, chiefly Breton.

In this process by which the wine trade from Bordeaux was destroyed, concern for the wine-drinking upper
classes imposed a fiscal burden on the beer-drinking
lower classes. In the earlier period, when the wine

came in English ships, transportation costs were reasonable, but the Hundred Years War made the combined costs of transport and security almost prohibitive. Piracy and enemy attacks were almost constant, so that voyage in convoys became necessary with greatly increased costs. In convoy, ships moved only half loaded, with double or even triple crews, armed to withstand attack. To cover these expenses, the monarchy gave a subsidy to wine importers. This began at one-half pence a ton in 1340, but rose to a shilling in 1350, to 2 shillings in 1360, and to three in 1396. These costs were paid from taxes which the ruling groups in Parliament imposed on the disenfranchised masses of Englishmen.

These ruling groups, with their emotions, ideas, and assumptions frozen into unproductive patterns, were not able to adapt to complex changes in incomes and money flows after 1300 in any realistic way. They merely increased their use of violence, at first against foreign enemies and after 1453 against each other. By 1485 the people and the magnates were exhausted from these struggles, and both were submissive to the tyranny of the Tudors for more than a century (1485-1603).

Similar difficulties were to be found all over Europe with different contents from one area to another but similar forms everywhere. The role played by wool and wine in the Narrow seas and the Bay of Biscay was played by herrings, salt, grain, and other commodities in the North Sea and the Baltic, with the Dutch, the Hanse, and other groups struggling in that area, as France and England struggled in the West, while, in the Mediterranean, Venice, Genoa, Aragon, and other states fought to control quite different commodities (Wallerstein 1974; Lane 1973; McNeill 1974; Inalcik 1973). Beneath the level of commercial rivalries were the fundamental problems of agrarian life resting on the interactions of population growth, limited agricultural lands, an arrested agricultural technology in the period 1300-1500, and the demands of an alien, upper-class system of weaponry from which the peasants were largely excluded so long as they continued to be peasants (Fourquin 1969).

The Hundred Years War was part of this chaos. A fundamental crisis arose as the first age of expansion of Western civilization (970-1270) passed into an age of conflict (1270-1440) before our civilization entered into its second age of expansion (1440-1590). Like most ages of conflict, this one was marked by a decreasing rate of satisfaction of human needs in proportion to the resources being used, a decrease in the geographic area of the civilization, growing class conflicts and imperialist wars, a decline in the rate of population growth, and increased irrationalism and ideological controversy (Quigley 1961; Fourquin 1969).

The real causes of the Hundred Years War are to be found in the irrational activism of the large groups of persons who felt increasingly frustrated in their higher human needs (religious, intellectual, social), with growing misplacement of their desires toward material and externalized satisfactions, including power, status, honors, material possessions, pageantry, ideological symbols, and the thrills of hyperactivism.

As in all ages of conflict, the rulers of Western civilization found excuses and rationalizations for their violence and were able to express these in ideological cliches which justified their actions to themselves. These contemporary rationalizations for wars should not be regarded as the actual causes of the wars.

There were, in terms of 14th century values, three chief justifications for the Hundred Years War: (a) disputes over feudal relations between Valois and Plantagenet; (b) the claim of Edward III to the Crown of France; and (c) the belief that the war was a defensive response to the aggressions of the other side.

The feudal disputes went back to 1154 or even to 1066, when the Duke of Normandy, a vassal of the king of France, became king of England. These arguments centered on the legal relationship between the rulers of England and France over the fiefs which the Norman and Plantagenet kings held as vassals of the Capetian and Valois kings. The rulers of France had been so weak before 1200 that they made few demands on their more powerful vassals for the usual feudal obligations of military service and attendance at the French feudal court. In some cases the French king did not even insist on the symbolic acts of homage, or, if he did, was satisfied with simple homage (which promised loyalty) rather than liege homage (which promised loyalty above any other feudal tie). Whether this French inability to enforce performance, over several centuries after 987, meant that these rights were nullified could not be settled in any legal way acceptable to both sides. The extreme view on the French side was that the Duke of Aquitaine owed liege fealty. Since Edward III had given homage to Philip VI in Amiens cathedral in June 1229 (Perroy 1951), it was hardly fitting that he should claim subsequently that he held Aquitaine as a free allod. The specific issue in dispute was: did the king of France have the right to summon his vassal, the Duke of Aquitaine, to appear at his feudal court in France in connection with disputes between the duke and his lesser vassals in Aquitaine? It could hardly be expected that the duke, who was also king of England, would answer a summons to appear in Paris to be questioned, or even to be tried, for his behavior as a vassal to the French king for the fiefs he held in France. The sensible thing on both sides would have been to recognize that such a confrontation was good for neither party and instead to accept that, under feudal custom, a right which has never been exercised, and, in fact, could not be enforced, does not exist as a legal right. But the French king could hardly be expected to admit that the king of England was, in fact, suzerain over the great territories he held in France, any more than the king of England could be expected to go as a suitor to the Valois feudal court. When the duke refused, as he always did, the king of France felt justified in confiscating the tenures under feudal law. Philip VI did this, for the third time in forty years, on May 24, 1337, and this purely legal action is usually taken as the beginning of the Hundred Years War.

The second traditional cause of the war was the claim of Edward III to the throne of France through his mother, Isabelle, sister of the last three Capetian kings (1314-1328). This claim has little merit. Monarchy was not a feudal tenure and had no need to follow the customary feudal rules of succession. The English monarchy did not. In 1290 Edward I, through his testament accepted by the members of his family, had established that the crown of England would be non-partible to a female heir. The French monarchy had an equal right to establish its rules of succession, as it did 27 years later, in 1317, when an Assembly of Notables which included representatives of all significant social groups issued a general rule against succession by females.

A third argument to justify Edward III's aggressions against France in 1337-1340 is based on the claim that Philip VI was, at that time, planning an attack on England in alliance with Scotland. The chief evidence to support this includes: (1) that Philip moved his galleys from the Mediterranean to the English Channel in 1336 when the Pope cancelled a projected crusade (Atiya 1968:111-13); and (2) that, when the English sacked Caen in 1346, they found plans issued in 1339 for a French attack on England to support Scotland in its struggles with Edward (Fowler 1971:6-8). Edward's aggressive designs against Scotland were obvious at all times. Since France had an alliance with Scotland from 1295 (although it had done little to support its ally), it might be expected that Philip VI would move his ships in 1336 or make plans to support Scotland in 1339, after Edward's intentions to crush the northern kingdom became clear in 1332 and his intention to shift his aggressions from Scotland to France became overt in 1336 by his embargo on wool exports in August and his request for a war subsidy from Parliament in September (Perroy 1951:86-94).

The truth is that all the ruling groups of Western Europe by 1330 were motivated by emotional and social pressures of which they were not fully aware, seeking through violence and political expansion to compensate for the chaos of emotional frustrations, decreasing prosperity, overpopulation, falling standards of living for the masses, and their own financial irresponsibilities and unbearable personal debts. This was as true of Scotland, France, and Iberia, as it was of England. The French monarch was expanding eastward, against the decaying Empire, or southward to the Mediterranean or even against Italy all through the Hundred Years War, even when it was reeling backward from the English aggressions in the West. The French king, who already had claims over more lands than he could control, was not so eager for military attacks on new territories, but he was determined, throughout this period and later, to extend and strengthen his control over his existing vassals and their fiefs and to complete what we would regard as the territorial unity, although not necessarily the administrative unity, of France.

Because of the irrational roots of this conflict, the ambitions of both sides far exceeded their resources. As Edouard Perroy put it, "the enormous disproportion

between the weakness of means and the boldness of
enterprises. . .easily explains the inordinate length
of the conflict" (1951:124). As a result, all military
and naval activity was intermittent: "There was an ebb
and flow in both military and naval activity, which was
largely determined by the availability of cash" (Sherborne 1967:170). When money was available, an expedition
or raid was launched, but it rarely achieved anything
significant before money ran out or the campaign season
ended. Money was raised by taxation, by borrowing until
both rulers were bankrupt, by devaluations of the currency, and by ransoms, booty, and plunder taken from
the enemy (mostly from the French). By the end of the
second year of the war, in December 1339, Edward was so
deeply in debt that he had to leave his pregnant wife,
his children, several of his chief captains, the royal
jewels, and a newly made crown as security for his
debts to the Flemish bankers in order to obtain the
bankers' permission for him to return to England for
four months to ask Parliament for more money (Perroy
1951:102-106; Fowler 1969:35-37). In other words,
the king who hoped to conquer France was the prisoner
of a handful of unarmed bankers in Flanders.

The war between the English and the French began
in May 1337 and is usually considered to have ended
in 1453, but there was no peace treaty and sporadic
fighting continued for many years. It has been suggested that the war did not end legally until the
Treaty of Etaples in 1492 (Fowler 1971:2). Most
chronologies of the war are based on the reigns of kings:

England	France
Edward III, 1327-1377	Philip VI, 1328-1350
Richard II, 1377-1399	John II, 1350-1364
Henry IV, 1399-1413	Charles V, 1364-1380
Henry V, 1413-1422	Charles VI, 1380-1422
Henry VI, 1422-1461	Charles VII, 1422-1461

These reigns, however, do not establish any meaningful
sequence in the war itself. For that, the war might
be viewed as consisting of four stages, thus:

The Edwardian War, 1337-1369
The Long Stalemate, 1369-1415
The Henrician War, 1415-1429
The French Resurgence, 1429-1453

The war as a whole cannot be understood in the terms in which military history is usually discussed. The battle is not "the payoff" because there is an essential difference between (a) winning battles; (b) winning the war; and (c) winning the peace. There is a fundamental difference between conflicts of applied force between two organized armies and the ability to control the behavior of individuals outside any organized military structure. The control of individual behavior necessary to "win the peace" requires that controls cannot remain external but must be internalized within individuals so that their behavior will reflect a victorious peace (rather than only a victorious war, or still less a victorious battle).

In the Hundred Years War there were, at most, 21 significant battles. The French won the last three: Patay in June 1429; Formigny in April 1450; and Castillon in July 1452. The one French victory before 1429 was at Cocherel, near Mantes, in 1364. The English won 17 great victories over 90 years but could not win the war. In addition, the English won four of the five significant naval engagements, two under Edward III's direct command (Sluys in 1340, and off Wichelsea in 1350) and two in the time of Henry V (Richmond 1964, 1967). The lone naval defeat was at La Rochelle in 1372 (Sherborne 1969). The outcome of the war was determined by something else, namely the ability to control local fortified strongholds, either walled towns or castles, and thus to dominate the day-to-day behavior of individuals living in the district. Such domination and control was very remote from battles. In fact, even after the great English victories at Poitiers (1356) or Agincourt (1415), the victorious English army could not control the behavior of the residents of either Poitiers or Agincourt. The reason was that the armies could not stay on the spot more than a day or two. In fact, at Poitiers, the English army had no food or fodder the day before the battle; afterwards, after they withdrew in fear of another French attack, to the security and supplies of Bordeaux 175 miles away, they used the food captured from the defeated French army (Hewitt 1958).

During the Hundred Years War there was little control of the seas and not much more control of the land. Armed forces were so dependent on fortified bases that they could operate only briefly away from them. Moreover, at that time, there was no general loyalty to the ruler or to the nation, at least among the troops.

985

Loyalty was to the paymaster so long as payment was forthcoming, but neither ruler was in a position to pay all his soldiers all the time, nor to pay enough soldiers to control all, or even most, of the lands over which he was trying to establish his suzerainty. Moreover, throughout those disputed territories there were local lords in fortified strongholds, with their own armed forces, and these, in many cases, had as their primary ambition the wish to be free of the control of both warring kings. This was true of most of Flanders, its towns and its noble lords; it was true of Brittany and most of Normandy, of Burgundy and much of eastern and southern France, and of large areas of the chief disputed territory, the duchy of Aquitaine. To be sure, in all these areas, if any town or noble lord was forced to choose between the king of France or the king of England as his suzerain, he would have a preference (usually the one who was farther away or busier somewhere else), but that preference never indicated a firm allegiance and was subject to change at any time and with little notice. Any narrative of the Hundred Years War is full of the details of diplomatic intrigue, alliances, betrayals, reconciliations, involving the great nobles and many lesser persons as they changed sides, not once but many times, during the war.

What was true of persons was also true of places. Strongholds also shifted sides, not always or even usually, by siege and capture, but, in most cases, simply by accepting a temporarily preferable change. Calais, captured by the English in 1347 and held until 1558, was very unusual. Most of its French population were driven out when it was first captured and were replaced by colonists from England. Also as the essential English landing point and base in enemy territory, it was well paid to remain loyal. The garrison at Calais cost about ₤14,400 a year under Edward III; this was about 40% of a parliamentary annual grant (known as a subsidy). At that price, Edward could not afford many such bases. Somewhat similar was the situation at Bordeaux, where most of the population were bribed to remain loyal by economic concessions which made the city an economic liability, rather than an economic asset, to the English.

More typical than Calais or Bordeaux were the strongholds which dominated the countryside. Some

of these changed hands, usually without fighting, a
dozen times during the war. La Reole, the fortress
of the central Garonne, changed hands 16 times during
the 300 years that Aquitaine was in English hands
(Burne 1955:131). Allegiance shifted, on the average,
about every twenty years, more than once every generation.

In the Hundred Years War the stated English war
aims were impossible to achieve -- impossible because
the English could not continuously control the countryside (that is, local resources), and because their
political and military control, accordingly, was subject to steady erosion, without overt conflict, even
during truces.

"Local resources" here means real resources, of
food, manpower, time, human experience, and know-how.
Financial resources are less essential, because they
are effective only where money is valued more highly
than real satisfactions, and they will not be effective where people are more strongly committed to
real satisfactions. The Hundred Years War was a period when money was highly esteemed by the ruling
groups in Europe; the only things which were more
highly esteemed were power, honorable status, and
escape from boredom through irrational activism.
These desires could be most easily obtained through
money. Therefore real local resources could generally
be obtained by money, which was not a localized resource.
If the English king had been able to send adequate funds
to those who controlled local strongholds all over the
territories he wanted, he could almost certainly have
controlled sufficient local resources on each spot to
control that area. His central financial resources,
however, were adequate only to pay for a few strongholds, but, since these central monies fluctuated widely
from year to year, control of strongholds also fluctuated
widely, expanding in periods of active campaigning and
collapsing again to the few "essential" ones in the much
longer periods of military inactivity. This was true in
all areas at that time. Speaking of the English experience in Scotland, where Edward III received about Ƀ2000
a year in income and spent Ƀ10,000 a year to hold four
fortresses, James Campbell wrote (1965:186), "Large
areas and a wide allegiance could be won by the use
of big armies, but were lost when they left. As the
French had found in Flanders, and Edward was again to
find in France, the relation between the income of a

987

king and the pay of a soldier was not such as to permit the permanent occupation of a country in the face of widespread resistance from its inhabitants."

This erosion of the central (or alien) control of strongholds during truces and quiet periods is a basic fact of military life which is often ignored by more powerful and aggressive powers. It is also evident in the failure of the crusaders to hold onto Palestine, in the revolt of the Netherlands against Spain in 1559-1648, in the American Revolution of 1775-1781, and in the American intervention in Vietnam in 1954-1975. In the Hundred Years War the decision-makers were distracted into such heady and wasteful activities as winning battles, acquiring status, escaping boredom in tournaments and other "spectator sports," or diverting central resources into their own pockets by seeking booty, ransoms, and cash payments. The numerous English raids ("chevauchees") across France were seeking these superficial goals. Edward besieged Calais successfully in 1346-1347 only because he had to get a secure base on the continent near England as a jumping-off point for subsequent raids. He had Bordeaux as a base in the south, but could not use it regularly because of delays in mobilization in England, uncertain weather, and enemy naval action on the long voyage of more than 10 days to get there. Moreover, since his chief "central resource" was English wool, which was most negotiable in the Low Countries and could be taken there by the relatively safe one-day voyage to Calais, this port had special value.

The most famous battles, at Crecy, Poitiers, and Agincourt, were large-scale set battles under the highest commanders on either side. Such battles, although spectacular, contributed little to the outcome of the war because they contributed little to the control of local resources. Much more important were the failures of English sieges such as Rennes (October 1356-July 1357) or Edward's failure to take Reims (December 4, 1359-January 11, 1360) where he hoped to be coronated.

Confusion of ends and means, of instruments and institutions, of stated aims and real motivations, is an outstanding characteristic of any age of conflict. Any age of conflict or general crisis is an age of rationalization.

Closely related to all this is the fact that the remoteness of central control from local resources left a gap in which intermediate levels of control could operate. If kings could not control the merchants and artisans of Flanders or the peasants of Normandy and Brittany, perhaps the local leaders of these areas could control these lower levels for them. Of course, any king's control of any intermediate leaders was as precarious as was that intermediate leader's control of local resources in his own territory. This led to conflicts between claimants to local leadership, often on several levels: between Bruce or Douglas and Baliol in Scotland; between Louis de Nevers and Artevelde in Flanders; between Charles de Blois and John of Montfort or Charles of Navarre in Brittany; between Pedro I and Enrique of Trastamara in Castile; between major claimants in major provinces and, below these, between lesser claimants at subordinate levels. It was easy to find a basis to dispute any succession in feudal law, and the great disputes between kings over the crown of France encouraged lesser disputes all down the line to the local resources which sustained the whole structure. Lords whose claims would have attracted little attention in time of peace were able to obtain support from embattled kings in return for mobilizing resources on a more local level for these kings. Thus in eastern Aquitaine the families of Foix and Armagnac, which had been fighting each other since long before Edward III or Philip VI, joined their local private war into the larger "public" war, always keeping on opposite sides, so that when one was bribed to switch allegiance the other also had to change sides, as these two frequently did. It is a good example of the irrational grounds of decision-making on the highest level of conflict, that there was no cost analysis of the gains to be obtained by higher level intervention into lower level disputes. For example, such interventions were usually justified on the grounds that alliances with contenders on lower levels would bring control of additional local resources to the side of the upper level intervener. This, in fact, was the contrary of the truth, which was that lower-level disputants sought upper-level alliances just because they lacked control of local resources sufficient to win their local dispute. As a result, each such intervention became an additional drain on central upper-level resources. The Scottish side show drained English resources and the Castilian side show finally broke and destroyed the Black Prince's

989

resources and depleted the English royal resources to the point that the Black Prince's son did not have sufficient resources to hold onto the English throne against the greater resources of the family of John of Gaunt, who was paid to give up his claim to Castile. In fact, it would appear that cost analysis of any feudal claim shows that the only economic value in such a claim was that it might be given up for pay from the other claimant. The fact that the decision-makers of the Hundred Years War did not see these truths and continued to seek support by extensive growth of the struggle, rather than by intensive use of their central resources for investment in more productive and satisfying activities in England, is one of the most revealing bits of evidence that that period was, indeed, an age of general crisis, just as similar kinds of thinking (even supported by sophisticated cost analysis) reveals the same situation in the Spanish attacks on the Netherlands and England in the late 16th century.

The conflict of Valois and Plantagenet not only encouraged lesser disputes to emerge and join with the greater one, but the war also created, sponsored, and enlarged disputes on the highest levels. Even the Papacy joined in, so that from 1378 to 1423 there were always at least two popes (the Great Schism), the chief distinction between them being that one was favored by the Valois while the other was favored by the Plantagenets. In a similar way, the war led to disputes over the thrones of England, France, Castile, Aragon, Portugal, and elsewhere. In England Richard II, favoring peace and with few resources, was replaced by the more aggressive Lancastrian dynasty (1399-1461), leading to the exhaustion of the latter's resources in the futile struggle in France and, eventually, to civil war in England, when the depleted resources of the Lancastrians were challenged, in turn, by the richer Yorkist family from another son of Edward III (Wars of the Roses, 1455-1485). In France the dynasty was not replaced but rivalries seeking to control the monarchy and the king reached the level of civil war with the king's cousins, chiefly the dukes of Burgundy, who favored the English and disliked the war (for tactical reasons), and the Duke of Orleans, with his Armagnac relatives, who disliked the English and favored the war (also for tactical reasons). The Duke of Orleans was assassinated in 1407 and the Duke of Burgundy was similarly killed in the presence of the Dauphin Charles in 1419, leading to the English-Burgundian alliance of 1420-1435.

In general it must be recognized that this was never a war of two sides. It was always a pluralistic struggle among temporary coalitions of powers, major and minor, constantly shifting, each power seeking to establish a hierarchical structure of political relationships rooted in local resources and stretching upward as high as ambition could reach. Above all, it must be recognized that there were no significant nationalistic elements in the chief contending parties. Robert of Artois, cousin and brother-in-law of the king of France, was an active supporter of Edward III in the early years of the war, even leading an invasion of Brittany in 1342. Geoffrey of Harcourt, one of the largest landlords of Normandy, fought vigorously for the English, was chief guide to Edward on the Crecy campaign, and brought 100 men-at-arms to the Duke of Lancaster's campaign ten years later. At a lower social level, the French king was captured at Poitiers by Denis de Morbek, a French knight fighting with the Black Prince. Except for the three "big" battles, a major part of the fighting forces on the English side were not English and on the French side many were not French (Perroy 1951:154-6). Even without nationalism, the terms "English" and "French" are misleading, as the leaders on the "English" side spoke French and most of their official documents are in a French dialect. Some of the chief "English" captains were not English by birth or language, including the loyal Sir Walter Manny of Hainault, and the Captal de Buch, a Gascon, who led the decisive flank attack at Poitiers.

During the truces or periods of little fighting, whole contingents went off to fight in other territories, in Brittany, Germany, Spain, Morocco, or the Balkans, where erstwhile companions in arms fought against each other for different paymasters. In 1367, for example, at the battle of Najera in Spain, nominally a conflict between two claimants to the crown of Castile, the notorious Black Prince had units which had previously fought with Dugueslin against him, while Dugueslin, on the losing side, had a considerable contingent of the subjects of Edward III led by Sir Hugh Cavaley, a liegeman of the Black Prince from his County Palatine of Chester. Dugueslin, who had been captured at Auray in Brittany in 1364 and ransomed, was ransomed again after Najera, and returned to France to lead the French forces as Constable in 1370. The problems involved in such shifts of allegiance have been explained, not completely convincingly, by modern legal scholars (Keen 1965; Bellamy 1970). The Hundred Years War was far different, both in organization and outlook, from any war we have known in recent generations. It has, however, many parallels with modern professional spectator sports, where a player, sold to a rival team, is expected to do very well in his first appearance on the field against his old teammates, with no sense of loyalty to anything but his paymaster. War in the 20th century is now moving toward a similar expression of values.

The threat to the position of the English king from the Lancastrian members of his own family, which increased in the 14th and 15th centuries, coincident with the Hundred Years War, was a consequence of three developments which are symptoms of the malaise of the age. First the efforts of a king to monopolize the land tenures of his realm by getting control of the greatest lordships in order to grant these out to his younger brothers, in the mistaken idea that they would be loyal through family feeling. The second was the use of armed private retainers supported from the incomes from large estates. This does not refer to temporary retinues of military expeditions abroad, but to long-term or lifetime retainers who lived with a great lord as housecarles in his private army. The third factor was the steady growth in personal insecurity and greed for power which made the century after 1380 a paranoid nightmare in much of Europe.

This insecurity was intensified by the economic and social crisis which began with the Black Death or even earlier in the years of the age of conflict of 1270-1440, especially after 1349. In the 14th century, the population of Europe was reduced by malnutrition and disease, intensified by wars, more than 30 per cent. In England this may have been 45 per cent, without much local war, because England was overpopulated in 1300. This reduction in population led to a rise in wages, increased per capita productivity in agriculture (by retracting workers from the marginal and less fertile lands onto the more productive ones), decreased the prices of some agricultural goods, but increased the prices of most craft products. The result was to benefit peasants and other workers' real incomes and to injure many lesser landlords. Class conflicts were greatly intensified when the landed group tried to use statutes to prevent increases in wages (1351), or to restore lapsed peasant obligations to perform unpaid work on the land, or to restrict peasant mobility, in status or locality. Laborers were forbidden to leave their places of work, they were compelled to accept work when it was offered, employers were forbidden to offer wages greater than those paid three years before, alms to able-bodied unemployed were forbidden, and the prices charged by butchers, bakers, or fishmongers were fixed (Ziegler 1969; Bowsky, ed., 1971).

Efforts such as these aiming to force the costs of economic change onto the lower classes led to "peasant revolts" and urban uprisings all over Western Europe, each triggered by some different specific cause, but all emerging from the same general crisis. One general result was that serfdom was weakened, with labor mobility and lower class standards of living improving, in Western Europe, while serfdom was intensified and peasant living standards lowered in Eastern Europe.

The Black Death continued to ravage Europe at intervals until the 17th century and produced at least half a dozen epidemics during the Hundred Years War. Philip Ziegler wrote (p. 239), "The pattern of several centuries was breaking up; not only the pattern of society but the set of men's minds as well." The changes in men's minds seem to have moved in three directions: (1) the majority of the ruling classes became more insecure, increasingly greedy, and more prone to violence; (2) a small minority of the whole population, mostly motivated by what they regarded as religious feelings, were determined to reform or even to destroy the existing society, on the grounds that it was evil, or at least unjust; and (3) a group whose size cannot be guessed, but who seem to have come from all social levels, decided not to reform, attack, nor defend the existing social system, but to find refuge from it in some community of their own where their daily living would be passed in continuous contact with like-minded persons. This last group of "opt-outs" had little influence on history, since, unlike the early Christians, they did not become numerous enough to influence the main trend of the situation. These three responses, which occur in every age of conflict or general crisis, could not overcome the momentum of the majority of Europe's population of that period, who, like the Greeks in the 4th century B.C. or the Muslims of the 11th century, continued their activities in their usual patterns.

In England the effort to monopolize the land in the royal family became a systematic policy under Edward I and was continued by Edward III. The concentration of wealth in families with competing claims to the throne produced civil wars. Edward II had twelve children, of whom five sons and four daughters survived infancy. The third son, John of Gaunt, married three times, first to the only child of the Duke of Lancaster, who was the richest lord in England. His son, Henry of Bolingbroke, far richer than his cousin, King Richard II, overthrew Richard and murdered him, as soon as John of Gaunt died in 1399. This created the Lancastrian dynasty of Henry IV, Henry V, and Henry VI (1399-1461), but being king was so costly that by 1460, Richard of York, descended from Edward III's son Edmund, was richer than the Lancastrian king. With the fighting men obtainable with this capital the Yorkist dynasty became kings for three brief reigns (1461-1485). The use of money and the influence obtained by money made it possible to appoint and bribe judges and juries, to elect members of Parliament, and to mobilize retinues of armed men. The key to much of this was control of the sheriffs, who were the royal agents in the shires. At first, legal processes were used to obtain what one wished by corrupting the law; then political power was used by corrupting Parliament and the royal administration; but that required control of the kingship, so finally the struggle became military in the Wars of the Roses, 1455-1485, which largely extinguished the Plantagenets and their allies, leading to a new dynasty, the Tudors, who came to the throne in 1485 by invading from France with French money and soldiers.

A similar effort to monopolize land in the royal family led to a parallel development in France, known as appanages. There was no real effort to replace the Valois dynasty until 1585-1589, partly because the political development of France was considerably behind that of England, and the country was too disunified to be controlled by any dynasty which lacked the religious mystique associated with the descendants of Hugh Capet and St. Louis. But attempts to dominate the kings, especially under a weak, incapable, or minor

994

ruler, using the influence and military power obtainable by a member of the royal family whose income was comparable to that of the king, did occur in this period, just as in England. In France the chief threat to the monarchy came from the dukes of Burgundy, whose resources were assembled when Charles V, in 1364, had his younger brother, Philip the Bold, marry Margaret, heiress of the Count of Flanders and widow, as well as heiress, of the Duke of Burgundy. Charles did this to prevent Margaret from marrying Edward III's fourth son, Edmund, but success in blocking the increase in Plantagenet's strength in the west created an almost equally great threat in the east and north. Philip the Bold was the first of four ambitious dukes of Burgundy whose threats to the Valois dynasty of France were based on their possession of the richest regions of Europe, encircling France on the east and north from Switzerland to Antwerp and beyond, where they threatened to link up with the English possessions in Normandy. In the latter part of the Hundred Years War, these dukes of Burgundy tried to dominate the French kings and the royal administration, even allying on occasion with the English. The threat to France was ended only briefly in 1477, when the fourth duke, Charles the Bold, was killed in a reckless attack on the Swiss pikemen at Nancy. Within half a century, the menace to France emerged again, in a more threatening form, because the fourth duke's only child, Mary, had married the Emperor Maximilian of Habsburg, and the son of this marriage, Philip the Handsome, married the heiress of Ferdinand and Isabella of Spain, thus almost surrounding France with the possessions of a single dynasty and ruler by 1519. Moreover, these possessions included the most advanced urban and commercialized areas of Europe and the richest mining regions of both Europe and America.

After the death of Charles V in 1380, there were 35 years of internal bickering, in England chiefly over taxation, and in France over rival efforts to control the government. In France by that time, taxation by the monarchy was fairly well established, even without consent, in a clear emergency, but in England what was needed was not consent but a grant of money, a somewhat different matter, since a grant was for a fixed amount of money for a single occasion. Except when Parliament was moved by enthusiasm for some glorious achievement of the royal family or by fear of some foreign enemy, it was generally opposed to substantial grants. It was

995

recognized that the king could not "live off his own" incomes, but there was a general feeling that grants of money for military expenditures should cover defense of England itself against foreign enemies. This reluctance to tax grew stronger after 1369 in England, reaching a peak in the reign of Richard II. In 1381 a Parliament dominated by John of Gaunt triggered the Peasants' Revolt of that year. This increased the parliamentary opposition to grants of money (Dobson 1970). Three of the next four Parliaments in 1381-1383 gave nothing, while the fourth, in October 1382, gave only a half subsidy. As a result, the government's efforts to carry on the war increased the king's debts to ₤120,000 by 1386 and to at least twice that by 1388 (Palmer 1972:134-136). This was a period in which a French invasion of England was in preparation, with a force of 30,000 men in about 250 ships. The invasion was cancelled November 15, 1386 (Palmer 67-87).

During this critical period, the French monarchy had about 3 million francs a year, equivalent to ₤500,000, at least ten times what the English king had available in most years. In France this amount was collected, after 1382, with no need for consent, with the direct tax imposed in some places several times a year. To be sure, French expenses were greater than the English, simply because it was a larger and less centralized country, with very large amounts of income wasted and lost without contributing much to defense.

The real problem was not so much inadequate financial resources as it was insatiable desires and large-scale waste of the resources available. Enormous sums were wasted on needless expenditures for self-indulgence and ostentatious display. The Parliament and various reformers, often religious, railed against the waste. A large expedition to France could be mounted for a single parliamentary subsidy, say ₤34,000. The largest expedition between 1360 and 1415, that of the Duke of Lancaster in 1373, cost ₤31,000 (McFarlane 1965:24-25). But consider this: a brief raid by Sir Walter Manney in 1340 captured a few prisoners, for whom King Edward gave him ₤8,000; the king also bought the Count of Eu, taken at Caen in 1346, from Sir Thomas Holland for 20,000 marks (₤6,666); he gave John Coupland, who captured David Bruce in 1347, an estate producing income of ₤10,000; he bought a quarter-interest in a captive French bishop, taken at Poitiers, for ₤1,000 and, at the same time, bought three other prisoners from the

Black Prince for ₺20,000; he gave ₺5,000 for Charles de Blois in 1348. Possibly such payments could be justified in terms of that day, but it is impossible to justify such expenditures in terms of winning a war, toward which they contributed nothing. Even greater sums were paid simply for entertainment. On his last invasion of the continent in 1359, Edward took along 30 mounted falconers with hawks, 120 hounds with an equal number of greyhounds, using these for weeks of hunting while his army waited, collecting its daily wages. A futile embassy to the Papal Court took along 100 tuns of wine, astonished the city with its lavish entertaining for about two months, and spent ₺5,648 doing this. At every possible break in the war, the court organized expensive tournaments which continued for days or weeks, with the participants wearing expensive clothing provided by King Edward. This reached a peak in his grandiose plan to reestablish the Round Table of King Arthur (1344), from which came the Order of the Garter (Fowler 1969:103-10).

Even in the war itself, much of the royal incomes were wasted. Large sums were used to buy alliances and loyalties which were completely undependable and produced nothing. In Gascony, which had been an English possession for centuries, no loyalty or military effort was expected from the native peoples unless it was paid for, so all the royal incomes in the area were granted away to buy these. Constantly increasing sums were needed from England to provide military defense of the province. As a result, the larger the royal possessions on the continent became, the less they brought to the king's incomes and the greater the need for funds from England. Possibly it could have been different, but the society was frozen into these deficit and spendthrift patterns. When Lancaster reconquered Aquitaine in 1345-47, he gave away, in annuities, pensions, estates, and public incomes, more than the total incomes recovered from the French, including large exemptions from taxes on wines shipped along the Garonne River or through Bordeaux, or he granted away the collection of these taxes to private persons, so that the reconquest simply added a large financial liability to the king's overburdened budget.

The same situation existed in all the overseas territories and, since there were few funds available from England to pay for the defense of these areas, the garrisons needed to control these were expected to support themselves by collecting taxes locally. This had a triple result: (1) the local people were plundered; (2) the garrison, with an autonomous economic base, ceased to be responsive to English control; and (3) the local areas were depleted as economic supports for either royal authority. A similar situation occurred in times of truce when mercenary forces refused to disband after their pay ceased and lived off the country.

Most military histories of this war emphasize that the English surprised the French with a new weapon, the longbow, and with an innovative tactic, the solid line of dismounted men-at-arms between wings of massed bowmen. Neither of these was new, as we have seen. The French weakness was that they were obsessed with the obsolete tactics of a charging mass of knights on horseback. The longbow was in use since at least the 12th century, and the English tactics were firmly rooted in Anglo-Norman traditions of the Third Crusade, and, by 1340, were probably on a lower level than under Richard I (1190). There was no excuse for the French inability to deal with the English, for they had had enough experience to know that mounted knights were of little use in capturing strongholds and were of limited use in set battles against massed infantry spearmen or against missile-armed foot behind field obstacles, such as hedges, walls, or fences. As recently as 1302, French knights had been beaten by Flemish infantry at Courtrai. That defeat was not taken as a lesson, but as a disgrace, and this emotion was wiped out, for French nobles, by the subsequent defeat and massacre of urban infantry forces at Cassel in 1328 and at Roosebeke in 1382. The key to this reversal was that infantry with pikes could withstand attack by mounted knights if the foot stood in a mass so close that there are no openings for their enemy to penetrate past the points of the weapons and especially if they could break the cavalry shock by obstacles in the field. This was something which the Romans knew well. At Cassel and Roosebeke the Flemings did not stand in a firm mass, but, by shifting their positions, broke up their solid formations (Lot and Fawtier 1958:II:526-27). It must be recognized that Courtrai was not a unique case: at Bannockburn in 1314 the English were badly beaten when their armored cavalry under the Earl of Gloucester hurled themselves on massed Scottish pikemen; and at Mortgarten in 1315, Habsburg heavy cavalry were destroyed attacking massed Swiss pikes and halberts.

The French were obsessed with charging heavy cavalry, with offensive spirit, and with the superiority of noble blood to the point that they refused to even think about military tactics. They were destroyed by these at Crecy in 1345, but fifty years later, they were destroyed in the same way, fighting the Turks at Nicopolis in Bulgaria in 1396, while Charles the Bold lost everything, including his life, by leading his knights in a similar headlong charge on massed Swiss pikes at Nancy in 1477.

In the Hundred Years War, weapons and tactics remained frozen for 75 years, from before Crecy until after Agincourt. The only significant change on the French side was the decision after Crecy to attack on foot rather than mounted, because their horses became uncontrollable from the English arrows. The only other change, also on the French side, was a growing reluctance, after Poitiers, to engage in battles at all. From the point of view of tactics, Agincourt was almost identical to Crecy. But in 1417 a new emphasis on siege warfare began to grow on the English side from Henry V's realization that Agincourt had brought him no real help in winning the war. About a decade later, the French began to develop a wholly new tactic, based on sieges and gunpowder, which formed one aspect of the new age of expansion in Western civilization.

The tactics which produced English victories until 1429 had intrinsic weaknesses which the French ignored. The tactics required that the English adopt the tactical defensive, taking a chosen position on which to form a line of dismounted men-at-arms, usually on a ridge or higher ground, with infantry archers in wedges on the flanks, which were also protected by natural obstacles, if possible. The horses and baggage were placed to the rear, shielded, like the flanks, by woods if possible. It was desirable to have some natural or artificial obstacles across the front of the line, so that these, along with the rise in the ground level, could slow up the enemy charge, allowing the archers more time to shoot before the enemy reached the line of waiting men. The archers generally fired at the horses, if the enemy were mounted; otherwise, they aimed at the enemies' faces.

These English tactics, like those of the Swiss which were developed in this same period, were most effective against the individualistic heroics of chivalric warfare as practiced in the old Carolingian heartland between the Loire and the Rhine. But these tactics had weaknesses: (1) they required that the leaders find a good place to draw up their forces, which was possible only because the French allowed sufficient time to find a suitable position fitted to the number of men at hand; (2) the French had to attack; otherwise, as in 1338-1342 and after 1369, there would be no battle; (3) the archers had only a limited number of arrows (at most 48 each, but usually less) and could exhaust their supply unless they were allowed time to replenish their quivers between attacks; (4) when the enemy had sufficient numbers and supplies, as the French usually did, the English could have been held in their battle formation without attack until they were weakened by lack of water and food or were compelled to fight their way out under every disadvantage; and (5) the archers could be destroyed from a safer distance by longer range missile weapons. Such weapons were available to the French in the crossbow which had longer range, greater accuracy, much greater impact, but, of course, a slower rate of fire (which was of no consequence in the Hundred Years War where the English were standing immobile and all the haste was on the part of the French).

Another weakness of the English tactics was (6) that men-at-arms on foot, with their horses hundreds of yards to the rear, could not mount to pursue a defeated enemy. This, on the whole, was not much of a drawback, for history has shown the great dangers from a premature pursuit, and in the Hundred Years War, the French often continued to throw themselves on the English battleline until they were defeated so thoroughly as to make any hot pursuit unnecessary. The English remedy to this weakness was to keep part of their reserve division on horseback, as the Black Prince did at Poitiers.

The French tactics were in the Hundred Years War inferior to those of Philip Augustus who had recovered Normandy from King John in 1204 and had defeated a great continental coalition, including the Emperor, at Bouvines in 1214. By 1340, in France, and on the continent in general, the warmaking class attributed their superior social position and privileges to their noble birth rather than to competence in arms or in anything else. They refused to study military tactics in rational terms

1000

until about 1420. As nobles, secure in their pedigrees and with an autonomous economic base, it was difficult to discipline them to act together, even when operating as units of heavy cavalry. Each French knight was convinced that the gallant thing to do was to demonstrate his individual courage by charging at the enemy as soon as possible. They no longer saw any merit in hitting the enemy in a solid mass but sought to break up the battle into a collection of individual conflicts. Individual display of offensive spirit was the way to honor. They rejected missile weapons as fit only for cowardly, lower-class, persons and ineffective against noble class courage. Unlike England, where the lower classes had been encouraged to have weapons and to be trained in their use, in France the possession of weapons by the non-noble was discouraged until after Philip VI. The pride which Richard I of England took in his skill with a crossbow or which a Roman emperor or a Turkish sultan took in his skill with a composite bow was unthinkably vulgar to the French nobles of the 14th century in most cases. Thus there was no domestic supply of skilled bowmen in France, and these had to be hired from other countries, chiefly from Genoa. But these foreign mercenaries were not consulted on tactics and were abused and ill-treated by their French employers until late in the war. Instead of being used in mass firing to wear down the English archers, which could have been done so long as the latter retained their fixed positions on the flanks of the English men-at-arms, the French insisted that the crossbowmen advance at once on the English position, thus bringing them in range of the more rapidly firing longbows. When the crossbowmen flinched at this misuse of their special role, the French nobles rode them down in their own impetuous charge, as at Crecy, or disrupted and even killed them by riding over them as at Poitiers or at Agincourt. The range of a steel crossbow about 1350 was at least 80 yards longer than the longbow, it was intrinsically more accurate, with greater impact because of its heavier missile, and its flat trajectory dropped less than 5 inches over the first 50 yards of its flight. Sustained attack by such a weapon before any charge by the French knights could have inflicted considerable damage on the English, despite its relatively slower rate of fire.

But such a tactic would have taken time, and time was one thing that the French lords were not prepared

to give their social inferiors. This is clear from
the French battle formation. Where the English formed
a line of battle across the field, with an interlocking
arrangement between missiles and shock, the French saw
the battle as a series of waves of shock attacks. At
Crecy they put the crossbowmen in front of their line
of men-at-arms and then rode them down in the nobles'
eagerness to get to hand-to-hand conflict with the
English knights. At Poitiers and Agincourt, although
the French divisions were dismounted, they placed in
front of these two smaller detachments of mounted knights
to ride down the English archers so that their main divisions could get in contact with their English equivalents
without interference by lower-class missiles. In both
battles the actions of the crossbows on the French side
were ignored by the combatants, by the contemporary
chroniclers, and by modern historians, as they were
brushed aside in the premature charge of the French
men-at-arms.

The contrast between the French and English formations at Agincourt are revealing. Unlike the two earlier "big battles," the field itself was almost flat,
a freshly plowed wheatfield drenched with rain and was
almost square, bounded on the sides by trees and on the
ends by the two armies. However, the lines of trees
converged toward the English position, from about 1200
feet wide on the French line and about 950 feet apart
on the English line. King Henry, with less than 6000
men, of which 5000 were archers, used all his men in a
single line across the field, with no reserve and very
little baggage guard. His men-at-arms were at three
positions of about 300 men each across the line, with
clumps of about 1000 archers between each line of men-at-arms
and two great masses of over a thousand archers on each
end of the front. The French were in ranks to attack
in waves, with three successive divisions, each larger
than the whole English force, and, in front of these,
the two detachments of mounted knights, each perhaps
with 600 men (thus about twice the size of the similar
detachments at Poitiers), with all the missile weapons,
including crossbows, some archers, and some guns, between the first and the second French divisions.
They were, apparently, excluded from action by the
second division crowding forward through their position
to join the first division in the shock action.

There were far too many Frenchmen for the size of

the field, and as they advanced they were forced together
by the converging of the field, by their eagerness to
get at the English men-at-arms who were nearer the middle, and by their natural inclination to turn away from
the arrows from the flanks. Before they reached the
English line, they were too crowded to strike a blow.
The field was so muddy that those who fell, whether from
slipping or arrow wounds, brought down others who fell
over them, and the ones at the bottom soon suffocated
or were crushed by the weight of the plate armor above.
Soon there was a wall of bodies before the English line,
at which the archers gave up the use of their bows and
leaped forward to use their swords on the entangled
enemy knights. Henry's victorious forces had no supplies.
He made for Calais immediately. The port was reached in
four days, only to find that the supplies ordered from
England had not arrived and that there were few ships
to take the army back to England.

The real military innovations of the Hundred Years
War were in organization: in recruitment, equipment,
and transportation. At first most of these were on
the English side, which was to be expected, since they
were the aggressors, had to assemble forces for long
periods of service, and to take these, with equipment
and supplies, across the sea.

The armies of the war were not large, below 10,000
on the English side; usually much larger, but poorly
coordinated, on the French side. Recruitment had shifted
from feudal status to royal obligation before 1338, in
England more than in France, and was moving rapidly toward mercenary service as early as the 12th century in
England. This general sequence--from feudal to royal
obligation to mercenary forces--continued during the
war, but service in the English forces went an additional step which almost completed a circle, back to
a neo-feudal system known as indentured retinues.

In England, as we have seen, service based on
obligation to fight for the king had two levels: (1)
the obligation for service as men-at-arms and other
functions based on levels of income; and (2) the
national obligation for service as infantry which
rested on all able-bodied men. Neither of these, however, could be used for service overseas in offensive
wars, and there was some doubt if infantry obligation
could be used outside of a man's home shire. Both,

accordingly, became paid activities, and there was no
disagreement that service of both kinds would be paid
in the Hundred Years War. Only one attempt was made
in England to summon the old feudal array; that was
in 1385 and was done only to justify collection of
scutage in a year of acute financial stringency, but
it was not a success (Lewis 1958). Feudal service did
continue in France until 1415, since there the war was
defensive and the obligation was still in effect, but
feudal forces were so unreliable and so lacking in
discipline that they were replaced almost completely
by mercenary forces after the disaster at Poitiers
in 1356.

The use of mercenary forces in France continued
to grow with the growth of the royal power of taxation
in the 14th century, but in England parliamentary resistance to taxation resulted in the growth of indentures.
This was to introduce private enterprise into warmaking,
with contractors providing armed retinues on land and
privateers at sea. As a result, the raising of land
armies by commissions of array and of naval forces
through impressment of private ships and the Cinq Ports
decreased, both being replaced gradually by what was
essentially contractual and sub-contractual arrangements
between the monarch and private persons who were usually
great landed magnates or members of the royal family.

An indenture was a contract between the king, or
a great lord, and a "captain" in which the former agreed
to pay a certain sum of money to the latter for an agreed
number of fighters by categories, for a specified period
in a designated campaign. This was different from an
ordinary mercenary agreement only in that it covered a
number of unnamed fighters in addition to the captain
himself. In England the king agreed to pay to the
captain the fighters' wages, with a "regard" (bonus),
to provide compensation for horses lost on the enterprise, and to allow the retinue to share in "the advantages of war" which meant the ransoming of captives
taken, the loot from towns captured, and other benefits.
All these arrangements when not specified in the indenture were regulated by custom.

An indenture might cover any number of men from
a few to many hundreds. It specified what kinds they
must be, and usually paid part of their wages in advance.
For men-at-arms payment was up to half the year's wages

1004

in advance, while for archers it was usually 21, 30, or more days in advance. Both kinds of fighters were subdivided into pay categories with the number of each specified in the agreement. The chief categories of men-at-arms were bannerets, knights, and squires; the archers were usually divided into mounted and foot. The pay scale about the middle of the war was usually 2 shillings a day for a knight, 1 shilling for a squire, 6 pence for a mounted archer, 3d for a foot archer. As the war went on foot archers were largely eliminated because they could not keep up on raids but especially because they could not range widely enough en route to live off the country. A raid of thousands of men moving 10 to 15 miles a day exhausted the food and fodder in a swath at least a dozen miles wide, and men on foot could not obtain sufficient food because they could not range widely enough to take what they needed from widely scattered farms.

The low productivity of the medieval economy required a large territory to support an expedition overseas. Preparations had to begin a year ahead, but usually did not. In England, months before embarkation, the king issued orders controlling resources. Indentures were drawn up, and the captains scattered to their home counties to recruit, often with royal warrants and the king's wage advances to help the processes. Usually the king issued orders forbidding anyone to go overseas without his permission, to export grain, to raise prices on essential supplies, or to hoard these; port authorities were ordered to "arrest" ships and to "impress" seamen to take the expedition to the continent. Sheriffs of various counties were instructed to establish commissions of array for archers and to gather weapons, food, fodder, horses, or other needs at the designated ports of embarkation before a specified date. When the king himself participated in the enterprise, which he did with his own retinue, the royal authority and administration, including sheriffs and municipal authorities, were used more extensively and directly than for campaigns without a royal contingent. But every expedition was under an overall commander or a combined leadership, and thus usually could obtain delegated royal authority to use the local royal administrators and royal funds for designated purposes.

Retinues were sent off from their counties in groups, men-at-arms usually on their own responsibility with pay in advance, archers usually in groups under one of their number who received double pay as their leader. Each archer received pay in advance for the number of days needed to reach the port of embarkation at about 13 miles per day. Many of these were criminals or accused felons whose trials were suspended until their return. In the 1350s retinues began to be provided with distinctive uniforms. Horses were sent as they could be obtained, each horse in charge of a groom. Wagons and carts were loaded with supplies and sent to the port. In some cases they were placed aboard ship loaded, with their draft going along. Fodder and food, as well as equipment and weapons, were sent to the port, the bows in bundles of dozens, the arrows in sheaves of two dozen, and bowstrings in bundles of 12 dozen. In 1355 the bows cost about 18 pence each, the same price as a sheaf of 24 arrows. Thus a bow and a sheaf of arrows could be obtained for less than a week's pay for the archer. Dozens of gangways (called "bridges") were prepared for loading the horses on the ships, as well as large numbers of wooden panels ("hurdles") to separate the horses, each with its groom, within the ship.

The acute weakness of almost every expedition was in shipping. Hundreds of ships with crews of thousands were needed for even a modest expedition of a few thousand fighters. J.W. Sherborne, who has made a special study of this topic and of the naval side of the war, believes that the crews were about as large as the army being transported. In 1372 Edward III had an army of 6000 being moved by at least 175 ships with a minimum of 5000 sailors. The expedition to Calais in 1369 required more than 5000 sailors working 250 ships, half of which were below 50 tons each. The army to Brittany in 1375 required at least 3250 sailors on 180 ships. An expeditionary force of about 4000 men in 1378 required more than 3600 sailors on about a hundred vessels. Since the English government owned almost no ships, even in its period of most active naval effort (under Henry V), it had to obtain its transports by commandeering private vessels. This was usually done by ordering seizure of all ships of a specified size which entered the chief English ports for weeks or months before the date of embarkation. Until 1380 no payment was made for such impressed vessels, and after that date payment was intermittent as an act of grace, usually at 2 shillings per ton of carrying capacity for each three-month period. The crews were also impressed and were paid 2 pence a day, but often payment did not begin until months after they were seized. In 1372 it was 105 days before payment began. Naturally vessels and crews tried to evade such service by avoiding ports where impressment was going on, with the result that it usually took months to obtain the shipping needed to transport an expeditionary force. During this period of delay, the army was collecting pay and using up rations which had to be replaced and, when the force finally could get away, its manpower, morale, and supplies were always lower and the best part of the campaign season, in most cases the major part of it, had been lost.

The majority of the planned English expeditions to France ended in futility; in some cases they were unable to get away at all, or got away so late that their strength was depleted and little could be achieved. The chief cause of such delays was the inadequate supply of shipping, a problem which could have been overcome, with great savings in money and resources, simply by offering adequate payment for the use of ships and crews on a contract basis with firm dates fixed for departure. But since everyone knew that departure dates were meaningless under the existing system of sea transportation, no one made any real effort to get to the port of embarkation on the date set or for weeks afterwards. Those soldiers who arrived on time hung around the port collecting pay without action. Ships for the Black Prince's expedition of 1355 were to be collected by June 11, and some were being held a month before that. Sailing date was projected for mid-July, and most of the retinues were at Plymouth by that date. The Prince left London on July 12 and reached Plymouth on the 26th, but the expedition did not sail until September 9 from lack of ships. During the eight week delay, much of the food and the Prince's ready cash was used up, requiring frantic efforts to replenish these, while still waiting for ships to come within reach of the impressment officers. One item of the Prince's expenses during this delay was ₤1,087 for victuals from Devon, Somerset, and Dorset to replenish dwindling supplies (Hewitt 1958:25-26, 33-38). As has already been mentioned, expeditions which departed after August were often scattered or destroyed by storms at sea.

Failure to solve the shipping problem was one cause of the general futility of the English attacks, but the deeper underlying cause was that the war was not fought on rational lines to obtain an achievable purpose. It was fought because the ruling groups of the day could not conceive of any different way of life and remain part of the ruling groups. The real nature of the war can be seen from the way the Black Prince engaged in it. When he began his first expedition in 1355, at age 25, he was already deeply, even hopelessly, in debt. Whatever may have been the purpose of his expedition, his resources both in men and money were completely inadequate. As I have said, he planned to sail from Plymouth in mid-July but did not get away until eight weeks later. During the delay, he did not use his financial resources to get shipping but went deeper into debt, using up his remaining money and resources on entertainment and expensive gifts to his friends, or even to persons whom he encountered in a casual way. This was the irresponsible fashion in which his whole life was passed, and seemed acceptable to him because it was acceptable to all his close associates. They knew no other way. They were always in debt, from the beginning of their active lives until death; no matter what financial windfall came along, these men gave it away and dissipated it with no regard to past debts or to future goals. Financial irresponsibility was one of the essential characteristics of chivalry.

Even if the English had been able to organize an expedition, including shipping, and get it to France in early summer, in May, or at least June, they had no strategic concept, and there probably were none which could have achieved their stated goals, either of gaining the crown of France or getting sovereignty over their territories on the continent.

Power in Europe in the 14th and 15th centuries was still local power, that is, control of local resources of men and supplies. No king could control local power unless he could control the local lords who held castles in the area. Power in any area could not be transferred unless the castles which controlled it could be transferred. The English expeditions to the continent before 1417 made few efforts to take fortified places, and took no siege equipment with them when they left England. Even in 1415, Henry V took none; although he ordered some from Bordeaux, he cancelled that order. A siege took too long and required differently trained soldiers, with few roles for the heroes of chivalry. Most expeditions were so small that they were not willing to suffer the losses entailed in successful storming of a resolutely defended fortified place.

Even if a fortress could be taken, its capture brought more problems than benefits, after the immediate looting was finished. It could be held only by leaving a garrison of men who could not be spared from the expedition, and such a garrison would involve continuous expenses in the future, even when much of the costs could be forced onto the neighboring territory. Garrisons which were locally supported could no longer be forced to obey their nominal superiors; they became autonomous local powers. Moreover, such support required continuous pressure on the local population, with threats of burnings and violence which, once exercised, destroyed some of the local capacity to support the garrison. Thus any garrison suffered slow attrition and could be held only with steady infusions of men and money from England. These conditions made the whole effort counterproductive, since England's financial resources were always inadequate. The French, on the other hand, with more financial resources and the capacity to exercise constant pressures on the fortress from the countryside (including the influence of French girls who often married men in the occupation garrisons), could eventually recover control of fortified places, especially towns, without a fight. In some cases the garrison simply accepted a bribe to surrender, as Saint-Saveur did for ₤9,000 in 1375 or Corbussin did for 14,000 ecus in 1404 (Vale 1976:50).

For these reasons even a major and "successful" expedition, which usually required a winter campaign (as in 1346-47, 1355-56, or 1416-19), left no permanent change in the relative balance of Anglo-French power within France. In a few years the captured places were lost from English control, which gradually fell back to the few strong points which could be held continuously by men and resources from England. The chief of these were Bordeaux, Calais, and Bayonne.

With conditions such as these, including limited manpower, money, and time, no siege train and little permanent gain from capturing fortresses, the English war on France was reduced to intermittent raids based on no strategic plan except the opportunity for the participants to indulge their taste for vandalism, violence, and loot. No battle could be expected unless the French wanted one, and after Crecy and Poitiers they were not eager for battle with an enemy who fought in an unchivalric way with which they could not cope. Accordingly, the English were free to plunder, burn, rape, and destroy without restraints, except those of inadequate finance. The war never paid for itself. Money was the ultimate reality, as in most ages of conflict. All human relationships were commercialized, at least among the ruling groups of England.

In France, at the outbreak of the war, there were restraints on commercialization, for the decaying husks of an earlier situation still enveloped some of the ruling class. The king was expected "to live off his own," that is from his manorial and feudal incomes, which were inadequate for any serious war. Accordingly, from the beginning, the French kings had to improvise means for obtaining resources, using the dim remnants of the old Carolingian ideas of kingship and the newly recovered ideas of public authority, as taught by lawyers trained in the Roman law. Both of these implied a larger and different political community from any known to medieval feudal or manorial customs and envisioned the king as the head of that larger polity. As such the monarch had numerous powers, most of which were suffering from long disuse. These included the right to call on the nation for military service and economic resources in time of crisis, to regulate commerce to protect consumers, to coin money, and to protect those such as clergy, women, children, and traders who could not protect themselves. This included calling out the manpower of the realm (the arriere-ban) for defense and collecting taxes for defense purposes. The respect for private property was much more pervasive in France than in England, but this did not focus on the need for consent to taxation. Everyone admitted that taxes were inevitable in an emergency, but rather there was emphasis on establishing that there really was an emergency and not merely a false alarm. Thus, where England emphasized consent to taxation and procedural restraints on government actions, in this, as in other fields, France in the Old Regime emphasized consultation to establish the facts of the situation, a distinction which also appears in the differences between the Common Law of England and the French tendency toward inquisitorial procedures to determine the facts of any judicial case. Where the English Parliament was a "consenting" or "granting" body, the French Estates General was a "consulting" body. Once the assembly of the realm had been consulted and the reality of the emergency firmly established, local assemblies were often called upon to advise on the specific ways in which the necessary taxes could

1010

be raised in its own locality (Henneman 1971:322-328; Wolfe 1972).

This distinction is the basis upon which the French monarchs obtained some part of the taxing power and the means to defeat the English after a century of war. The big difference was that the English Parliament consented to a tax for a single year, giving a subsidy of part of one, while in France, once the Estates General had accepted that the emergency was real, the collection of funds continued until it could be established that the emergency was finished. As we all know in the 20th century, emergencies are not easy to terminate, and in late medieval France, even when a term of years (often five or seven) had been fixed in the original authorization, it was clear enough at the end of that period that the emergency still continued. With the channels of public opinion such as the pulpit or royal proclamations controlled by the government, the termination of an emergency was difficult, and the royal agent could continue to collect taxes in one locality by their reports of acute emergency conditions in some other locality.

The military reforms of 1439-1445 in France, according to Ferdinand Lot, were not intended to give France a standing army and did this inadevertently (Lot and Fawtier 1958:II:523-31). They were intended to get rid of the unemployed soldiers who were plundering the country after the truce of 1444. The ordinances did three things: (1) prohibited private armies of the nobility; (2) prohibited nobles from imposing tailles on their peasants; and (3) recruited the best of the routiers into a permanent royal army to be used to get rid of the others. This new force was intended to reestablish public order in France rather than to defend the country against the English. Known as gens d'armes this force consisted of 2000 "lances," each of six mounted men, in 20 companies of 100 lances or 600 men each, with each company stationed in a specific garrison, each lance obtaining 30 livres a month in pay. The expense required a new taille of 720,000 a year. Each lance was treated as a unit and consisted of a heavily armed cavalryman, a page, a varlet, and three archers. This required six horses and provided only four combatants and a single armored horseman. Thus the whole force provided 2000 heavy cavalry and 6000 mounted infantry. The page and the servant were to guard the horses during combat.

1011

In addition to these "Compagnies d'ordonnance" the reform tried to establish a supply of missile infantry. Each group of 50 hearths or households was to support a "franc archer" who lived at home in peacetime but was required to practice archery every Sunday, be inspected by a royal agent once a month, and to assemble together in military formation for review several times a year. For this the franc archer was paid four livres a month and was exempt from the taille (thus franc).

As military reforms these innovations were of little importance. The franc archers were never of much value. In battle they fled from the field in 1465 and again in 1479, while in 1472 against Charles the Bold of Burgundy, they surrendered immediately. They were replaced by a long-term contract with the Swiss for a force of mercenary pikemen in 1474 (Union of Constance).

The compagnies d'ordonnance remained part of the royal forces much longer, but they were generally kept undermanned to save pay, and the role of lances to provide heavy cavalry was increasingly obsolete. The real value of the reform was that the king now had a permanent tax of 720,000 livres a year to add to the old taille worth about 400,000 livres a year, plus whatever could be raised by the aides. No total financial accounts have survived, but it is quite clear that by the last years of the Hundred Years War, the French monarchy had close to 2 million livres each year from taxes. Charles VII's secretary, Phillipe de Comminges, said that the king had 1,800,000 livres a year, but the total steadily increased, especially under Louis XI (1461-1483) who also curtailed all personal extravagance and steadily increased tax collections until he could be assured of more than 4 million livres each year.

It is not possible to make any firm statement about the comparative financial resources of the two sides in the Hundred Years War. Little distinction was made between personal incomes and official or public ones, at least in England. All lords made free use of their own incomes in the war and equally freely helped themselves to what we would consider public money as it flowed by. All important lords or kings had incomes from forced loans, "free gifts," unpaid labor, adulterations of coinage, price fluctuations, ransoms, tolls, and many sources which would not appear in any history of taxes. Many incomes were assigned directly from their source to pay for some purpose and would not appear again in the accounts until they were reassigned, sometimes decades or even generations later. This continued and became worse in France until the French Revolution. However, if we look only at the tax revenues, the French king had larger incomes for war than the King of England, at least after 1360, although it was not used as effectively. A French sou was worth about a third of an English shilling, but it obtained even less in terms of fighting men. The parliamentary subsidy, about Ŀ34,000 in 1380 would be equal to 130,000 French livres, but obtained much less in men-at-arms. The French used unpaid feudal forces as late as 1415, but these were a liability not an asset. At Agincourt the Duke of Brabant arrived just after the final French charge but did nothing (Keegan 1976:79-116). The Duke of Orleans left the field at Crecy without striking a blow. No monetary values can be put on military service of this character.

There are no figures which would allow an estimate of how much money in taxes the King of France spent during the Hundred Years War. This has been done for England by K.B. McFarlane (1962) who says that over 117 years from September 1336 to March 1453 the Parliament granted the king about Ŀ2,250,000, while the English clergy granted about a million pounds more. Indirect taxes, chiefly on wool exports, yielded about 5 million pounds. Much larger sums were extorted from occupied French territories or from plunder or ransoms. There are no overall figures, but a few items will indicate their possible scale. In 16 years, 1419-1435, Normandy yielded about Ŀ625,000, that is more than a quarter the amount granted by the English Parliament over 117 years. Other enormous extortions included the Ŀ172,600 to John of Gaunt for giving up his claim on the throne of Castile and about 1.7 million gold ecus on the ransom of King John, still being paid forty years after his death (Broome 1926). The value of these sums can hardly be appreciated by us because the purchasing power of money was so much greater then. We might get some idea if we recall that an Englishman with an income of Ŀ2 a year (40 shillings) was considered affluent enough to qualify as a member of Parliament at his own expense, while a man with 20 pounds a year was so wealthy that he was required to be a knight ready to perform many unpaid services to the government. On this basis the impact of taxes on the English in the war of 1338-1453 was comparable to that of the war of 1914-1918 but continued thirty times as long.

The full effects of the improved financial condition
of the French monarchy did not appear until the very end
of the war, although the real turning point in the war
itself was in the 1360s. England could not enforce the
Treaty of Bretigny (1361) and was getting weaker while
France was being pounded by misery into a stronger polity.
But peace would not be gained until it was made obvious
to the English that they could not win the war. This
may have been clear to Richard II and a few others before
1400, but Richard's efforts to make peace were frustrated
and he was eliminated three years after he obtained a
twenty-eight year truce in 1396. After 1400 the weakness
of France, torn by dissension between Burgundians and
Orleanists (Armagnacs), encouraged a renewal of English
aggressions. For the next generation, English military
efforts were enveloped in devious diplomatic maneuvers
aimed at exploiting this French dissension. Henry V
(1413-22), determined to win, still had no grasp of the
real strategic situation. At first he followed the mistaken path which had failed to work for Edward III,
primitive raiding in France in the hope that victory
in war could be achieved through victory in battle.
It did not work. Agincourt was as "decisive" as any
Edwardian victory and just as unhelpful to the king's
war aims.

By 1417 it was clear that Agincourt was unproductive,
and Henry V went to France again. He did not return to
England for three and one-half years (August 1, 1417 to
February 1, 1421). In that period he embarked upon the
new road which insured ultimate English defeat. This
was an effort to conquer France district by district by
capturing fortified places and leaving garrisons behind
to hold them. This appeared to be the only way to win
the war, but it was a task far beyond England's resources.
Each additional district brought under England's nominal
"control" failed to bring control of the local resources
needed to hold down that district. On the contrary, each
newly conquered district had to drain resources from
districts conquered earlier (such as Normandy) and ultimately had to appeal to England itself for the necessary men and funds. It is not clear that Henry knew what
he was doing, or even that he was conscious that he had
adopted a new road. He was a strong-willed and energetic
man with a religious conviction in the righteousness of
his own views, including his God-given right to the crown
of England (which his father had usurped), to the throne
of France, and to his personal ownership of Normandy (which

had not been controlled by any English king for more than two centuries).

Among the men of his day, most of them weak, indecisive, and corrupt, his personal courage and convictions made him appear like a superman, or as they believed at the time and for a long time later, as "a true king." But in truth he improvised from week to week without any clear idea of what he was doing. He was led into his new method of warfare partly by a determination to do something and partly by the complexities of the diplomatic situation. In the last analysis he had the basic weakness of Napoleon or Hitler--he was insatiable.

By embarking on his new strategy of subduing strongholds, Henry opened the door to ending the war. The failure of his strategy revealed that the English aims in the conflict were impossible to achieve. There were thousands of strongholds, each of which had to be conquered and garrisoned, and few of which could be supported by the resources which could be extracted from its surrounding district. To do this, Henry and his successors had to draw upon the garrisons of districts which were already controlled, especially when his besieging forces were challenged by a French field army, however small, which could cut off the resources of the English besieging army and force it to call up the reserves from garrisons somewhere else.

The French did not need any coherent strategy; all they had to do was to threaten an English besieging force wherever it was or threaten to besiege an undermanned English fortress wherever it was. Anywhere they threatened they used up limited English resources. And, as always, even overwhelming English victories in pitched battles, like Valmont (March 1416) or Verneuil (August 1424) did not help in any way, except to prolong the agony. Verneuil was as great an English victory as Agincourt, with 7,262 enemy killed (mostly Scots fighting for France), but it did not increase English control over local resources or win "the minds and the hearts" of the French people. But the English had no coherent plan and their human resources were stretched far too thin to carry out the new method of conquest.

The Treaty of Troyes (1420) looked like an English triumph; it was really a death sentence. It provided

that the mentally incompetent King Charles VI and his
wife Isobelle would remain rulers of France while Charles
lived, but that Henry would be regent and accepted as
their heir and son-in-law. The Dauphin Charles was
disowned. Three aspects of the settlement are important:
(1) the settlement could not work if the Dauphin did not
accept it, and he did not, especially when Joan of Arc
in 1428-30 convinced him that he was the true king of
France. He was consecrated in that office at Rheims
(July 1429); (2) the Duke of Burgundy, a party to the
settlement as an ally of Henry, was secretly determined
to frustrate Henry's plans, and to secure the French
throne for himself; and (3) one clause of the treaty,
which Henry took very seriously, allowed Henry to recapture all the strongholds and areas controlled by the
Dauphin. Normandy had been conquered before the Treaty
of Troyes, ending with a six month siege of Rouen (July
30, 1418 to January 19, 1419). Troyes was signed in
April-May 1420. Henry and Catherine of France were
married on June 2 and at once started off on what E.F.
Jacob called, "an indefinite war of sieges and operations
against fortified islands of territory. . . ." After a
four month siege of Melun, Henry spent half a year in
England where he collected ₺38,000 in loans and 4,000
men and returned to his task in France. The siege of
Meaux required six months, over a cold winter during
which Henry contracted dysentery which killed him ten
weeks later (August 1422). He left a son, Henry VI,
nine months old, in the care of his two surviving brothers
and the Beaufort descendants of his grandfather, John of
Gaunt. The son survived as a weakling king, who was
overthrown and replaced by the Yorkist, Edward IV, in 1461.

The intrigue and constant bickering in court circles
in England plus the fact that the public life of the
country was almost wholly corrupt made it impossible
to sustain Henry V's projects in France, although his
brother, the Duke of Bedford, continued the task with
a little help from the Burgundians. In 1436 the Burgundians abandoned the English alliance without notice
and made peace with Charles VII. On hearing the news,
the Duke of Bedford, already sick in bed, "turned his
face to the wall and died." Paris, which had been occupied by the Burgundians since 1418, opened its gates to
Charles VII at once. But the war continued for seventeen
years more.

Over that seventeen years France began a great revival

which continued for almost a century. The military aspect of this revival is of great importance, but it must be recognized that the military aspect would not have been possible without other aspects which made the military situation one that could be handled successfully. One factor was the ability of the French king to obtain money for men and supplies. Closely related to this was the fact that the French people, torn by the English, harassed by bands of mercenary soldiers, and never defended successfully by their local lords, had decided by 1435 that they must look for protection to the king and that such protection must be paid for. The French nobles did not accept this point of view and continued to resist this increase in the royal power until Charles VIII in 1492-94 ended the struggle between king and lords. He did this just as Edward III had done in England in 1327-1337, by joining the rival groups together into a joint enterprise to attack and plunder a neighbor, in the French case, Italy. And just as the English, defeated in France in 1453, returned home to fight with each other in the Wars of the Roses of 1455-1485, so the French defeated in Italy in 1559 returned home to fight with each other in the so-called French religious conflicts of 1572-1589. The subsequent quiescence in new dynasties in England under Henry VII (Tudor, 1485-1509) and in France under Henry IV (Bourbon, 1589-1610), led toward the "absolutism" of Henry VIII and of Louis XIV, which was based, fundamentally, on the fact that the king in both countries had a monopoly on guns capable of smashing down the castle walls of the great lords.

But guns played very little role in the outcome of the Hundred Years War. It is true that the French after 1485 had guns fully able to smash down the walls of medieval-type fortresses and that these guns were operating under the very capable supervision of Jean Bureau. But the possession of such guns does not explain the French success in capturing strongholds held by the English occupation forces, any more than guns, on either side, explain the French ability to defeat the English in battles after 1428. French siege cannon did speed up the rate at which fortresses were taken from the English and thus did speed up the ending of the war. But these strongholds, undermanned with no adequate field armies to interrupt the French sieges, would have been captured by the French in any case, sooner or later. The same is true of the battles. Even in those battles where guns were used, it does not seem that cannon influenced the outcome of any battle until the final one at Castillon in July 1453.

From the triple alliance of England, Burgundy and Brittany made in April 1423, following the death of Henry V, to the end of the war thirty years later, there were six battles of which the English won the first three and the French won the last three. Cravant in July 1423 and Verneuil in August 1424 followed the Agincourt pattern and produced similar results. But the tactical patterns were beginning to change. At Bauge in 1421 the Duke of Clarence, Henry V's brother, got himself killed by galloping with a small force of his chief leaders, but without his full force or any archers, on a village held by French and Scots. This signified nothing. At the siege of Orleans (October 1428-May 1429), the English were so few that they could not completely blockade the city and had to fortify themselves against both the besieged and the surrounding French forces of the Dauphin in an incomplete circle of blockhouses. Under the inspiration of Joan of Arc, the Dauphin's forces were able to capture the chief of these blockhouses, forcing an English withdrawal. In hot pursuit the French overwhelmed the chief English force at Patay (June 1429) before they could get into their usual battle position. Jean Bureau's guns helped recover numerous strongholds before the next battle, at Formigny in April 1450. There the last significant English army in France, about 3800 men, was defeated.

Formigny ended the Hundred Years War. The French conquered all Normandy by August 1450 and all Gascony by August 1451. However, Bordeaux revolted against the French and was reoccupied by the English in October 1452. It was this occupation force under John Tallot, Earl of Shrewsbury (now over 70 years old), which was destroyed at Castillon in July 1453 and ended all English resistance in France except Calais. The Hundred Years War in France was over, and the Wars of the Roses in England were about to begin.

BIBLIOGRAPHY

Ahrweiler, Hbel'ene. Byzance et la mer, la marine de
    suerre, la politique et les institutions maritimes
    de Byzance aux VIIe-XVe siecles. Paris: Presses
    Universitaires de France, 1966.

Ardrey, Robert. African Genesis. New York: Atheneum,
    1961.

Atiya, Aziz Suryal. The Crusade in the Later Middle
    Ages. London: Methuen, 1938; New York: Kraus
    Reprint Corp., 1965.

Beeler, John. Warfare in England 1066-1189. Ithaca,
    N.Y.: Cornell University Press, 1966.

_____. Warfare in England 1066-1189. Ithaca,
    N.Y.: Cornell University Press, 1971.

_____. Warfare in Feudal Europe, 730-1200.
    Ithaca, N.Y.: Cornell University Press, 1971.

Bellamy, J.G. The Law of Treason in England in the
    Late Middle Ages. Cambridge: University Press, 1970.

Bennet, Merrill Kelley. The World's Food; A Study of
    the Interrelations of World Populations, National
    Diets and Food Potentials. New York: Harper, 1954.

Bloch, Marc Leopold Benjamin. Les Rois Thaumaturges.
    Paris: A. Colin, 1961.

Bowsky, William M., ed. The Black Death, A Turning
    Point in History. New York: Holt, Rinehart &
    Winston, 1971.

Brogger, Anton Wilhelm, and Haakon Shetelig. The Viking
    Ships, Their Ancestry and Evolution. Oslo:
    Dreyer, 1951.

Burne, Alfred Higgins. The Agincourt War, A Military
    History of the Hundred Years War from 1369 to 1453.
    Fairlawn, N.J.: Essential Books, 1956.

_____. The Crecy War, A Military
    History of the Hundred Years War from 1337 to

the Peace of Bretigny, 1360. London: Eyre and Spottiswoode, 1955.

Carus-Wilson, Eleanora Mary. Medieval Merchant Ventures: Collected Studies. London: Methuen, 1967.

Casson, Lionel. Ships and Seamanship in the Ancient World. Princeton: University Press, 1971.

Chaudhuri, Nirad C. The Continent of Circe: Being an Essay on the Peoples of India. New York: Oxford University Press, 1965.

David, Charles Wendell. Robert Curthose, Duke of Normandy. Cambridge: Harvard University Press, 1920.

Delbruck, Hans. History of the Art of War Within the Framework of Political History. Westport, Conn.: Greenwood Press, 1975.

Dobson, Richard Barrie. The Peasant's Revolt of 1381. New York: St. Martin's Press, 1970.

Dobzhansky, Theodosius Grigorievich. Genetics and the Origin of Species. New York: Columbia University Press, 1951.

Duby, Georges. Early Growth of the European Economy. Ithaca, N.Y.: Cornell University Press, 1974.

Edwards, Charles Bertram, and Ernest Gerald Heath. In Pursuit of Archery. London: N. Kaye, 1962.

Eickhoff, Ekkehard. Seekries und Seepolitik Zwischen Islam und Abendland. Berlin: De Gruyter, 1966.

Fourquin, Guy. Histoire Economique de l'Occident Medieval. Paris: A. Colin, 1969.

Fowler, Kenneth. The Hundred Years War. London: Macmillan, 1971.

Fowler, Kenneth Alan. The King's Lieutenant: Henry of Grosmont, First Duke of Lancaster, 1310-1361. New York: Barnes & Noble, 1969.

Golding, William Gerald. _Lord of the Flies_. New York: Coward-McCann, 1955.

Henneman, John Bell. _Royal Taxation in Fourteenth Century France: The Development of War Financing, 1322-1356_. Princeton: University Press, 1971.

Hewitt, Herbert James. _The Black Prince's Expedition of 1355-1357_. Manchester: University Press, 1958.

——————————. _The Organization of War Under Edward III 1338-1362_. New York: Barnes & Noble, 1966.

Hill, Herbert. _The Roman Middle Class in the Republican Period_. Oxford: Blackwell, 1952.

Hollister, Charles Warren. _Anglo-Saxon Military Institutions on the Eve of the Roman Conquest_. Oxford: Clarendon Press, 1962.

——————————. _The Military Organization of Norman England_. Oxford: Clarendon Press, 1965.

Hooker, Richard. _Of the Laws of Ecclesiastical Polity_. New York: E.P. Dutton & Co., 1954.

Huizinga, Johan. _The Waning of the Middle Ages_. London: E. Arnold & Co., 1924.

——————————. _Men and Ideas, the Middle Ages, the Renaissance. Essays_. Translated by James S. Holmes and Hans van Macke. New York: Meridian Books, 1959.

Inalcik, Halil. _The Ottoman Empire: the Classical Age 1300-1600_. Translated by Norman Itzkowitz and Colin Imber. New York: Praeger Publishers, 1973.

James, Margery Kirkbride. _Studies in the Medieval Wine Trade_. Edited by Elspeth M. Veale with an Introduction by E.M. Carus-Wilson. Oxford: Clarendon Press, 1971.

Keegan, John. _The Face of Battle_. New York: The Viking Press, 1976.

Keen, Maurice Hugh. *The Laws of War in the Late Middle Ages.* London: Routledge & K. Paul, 1965.

Lane, Fredric. *Venice: A Maritime Republic.* Baltimore: Johns Hopkins University Press, 1973.

Lethbridge, T.C. *A History of Technology. The Mediterranean Civilization and the Middle Ages.* Oxford: Clarendon Press, 1954.

Lewis, Gwynne. *Life in Revolutionary France.* New York: Putnam, 1972.

Lewis, Archibald Ross. *The Northern Seas: Shipping and Commerce in Northern Europe A.D. 300-1100.* Princeton: University Press, 1958.

Lewis, Peter Shervey. *The Recovery of France in the Fifteenth Century.* Edited by P.S. Lewis, translated by G.F. Martin. New York: Harper & Row, 1972.

Liddell Hart, Basil Henry. *The Defense of Britain.* New York: Random House, 1939.

Lorenz, Konrad. *On Aggression.* Translated by Marjorie Kerr Wilson. New York: Harcourt, 1966.

Lot, Ferdinand. *L'Art Militaire et les Armees au Moyen Age en Europe et Dans le Proche Orient.* Paris: Payot, 1946.

Lot, Ferdinand, and Robert Fawtier. *Histoire des Institutions Francaises au Moyen Age.* Paris: Presses Universitaires de France, Vol. 3, 1958.

Loyn, Henry Royston. *Anglo-Saxon England and the Norman Conquest.* New York: St. Martin's Press, 1963.

Luttrell, Anthony. "The Crusade in the Fourteenth Century," in *Europe in the Late Middle Ages.* Edited by J.R. Hale, J.R.L. Highfield, and B. Swalley. Evanston, Ill.: Northwestern University Press, 1965.

McFarlane, Kenneth Bruce. *The Nobility of Later Medieval England.* Oxford: Clarendon Press, 1973.

1022

McFarlane, Kenneth Bruce. The War of Roses. The British Academy, 1965.

McNeil, William H. Venice, the Hinge of Europe, 1081-1797. Chicago: University of Chicago Press, 1974.

_____. The Shape of European History. Oxford: University Press, 1974.

Marsden, Eric William. Greek and Roman Artillery: Historical Development. Oxford: Clarendon Press, 1968.

Morrison, John Sinclair and R.T. Williams. Greek Oared Ships 900-322 B.C. London: Cambridge University Press, 1968.

Needham, Joseph. Clerks and Craftsmen in China and the West: Lectures and Addresses on the History of Science and Technology. Cambridge: University Press, 1970.

Nicholson, Ranald. Edward III and the Scots 1327-1335. London: Oxford University Press, 1965.

Palmer, J.J.N. "Prets a la Couronne (1385)," Bibliotheque de L'Ecole des Chartres, Vol. CXXVI (1968), pp. 419-425.

_____. England, France, and Christendom, 1377-1399. Durham: University of North Carolina Press, 1972.

Perroy, Edouard. The Hundred Years Wars. London: Eyre & Spottiswoode, 1951.

Postan, M.M. Medieval Trade and Finance. Cambridge: University Press, 1973.

Power, Eileen. The Wool Trade in English Medieval History. New York: Oxford University Press, 1941.

Powicke, Frederick Maurice. King Henry III and the Lord Edward; the Community of the Realm in the Thirteenth Century. Oxford: Clarendon Press, 1947.

Powicke, Michael Rhys. Military Obligation in Medieval

England: A Study in Liberty and Duty. Oxford: Clarendon Press, 1962.

Prestwich, Michael. War, Politics, and Finance Under Edward I. Totowa, N.J.: Rowman & Littlefield, 1972.

Quigley, Carroll. The Evolution of Civilizations; an Introduction to Historical Analysis. New York: Macmillan, 1961.

Ramsay, Sir James Henry. The Scholar's History of England. Oxford: Clarendon Press, 1892-1913.

Runciman, Steven. The Sicilian Vespers: a History of the Mediterranean World in the Later Thirteenth Century. Baltimore: Penguin, 1960.

Russell, P.E. English Intervention in Spain and Portugal in the Time of Edward IV and Richard II. Oxford: Clarendon Press, 1955.

Setton, Kenneth Meyer, ed. A History of the Crusaders. Madison, Wisc.: University of Wisconsin Press, 1969.

Sherborne, J.W. The Battle of La Rochelle and the War at Sea 1372-1375. Bibliotheque d'Humanisme et Renaissance. Vol. XVII, May 1969.

Singer, Charles Joseph, ed. A History of Technology. Oxford: Clarendon Press, 1954.

Smail, R.C. Crusading Warfare, 1097-1193. Cambridge: University Press, 1956.

Taylor, Lily Ross. The Divinity of the Roman Emperor. Middletown, Conn.: American Philological Assoc., 1931.

_____. Roman Voting Assemblies from the Hannibalic War to the Dictatorship of Caesar. University of Michigan Press, 1966.

Titow, J.Z. English Rural Society 1200-1350. New York: Barnes & Noble, 1969.

Tobias, Philip V. The Brain in Hominid Evolution. New York: Columbia University Press, 1971.

Vale, Malcolm Graham. *Piety, Charity, and Literacy Among the Yorkshire Gentry 1370-1480*. St. Anthony's Press, 1976.

Van Cleve, Thomas Curtis. *The Emperor Frederick II of Hohenstaufen*. Oxford: Clarendon Press, 1972.

Wallerstein, Immanuel Maurice. *The Modern World System: Capitalist Agriculture and the Origins of the European World Economy in the Sixteenth Century*. New York: Academic Press, 1974.

Warren, Wilfred Lewis. *Henry II*. Berkeley: University of California Press, 1973.

Warner, Philip. *The Medieval Castle: Life in a Fortress in Peace and War*. London: Barlier, 1971.

White, Lynn. *Medieval Technology and Social Change*. Oxford: Clarendon Press, 1962.

Wittfogel, Karl August. *Oriental Despotism*. New Haven: Yale University Press, 1957.

Wolfe, Martin. *The Fiscal System of Renaissance France*. New Haven: Yale University Press, 1972.

Ziegler, Philip. *The Black Death; A Turning Point in History*. Edited by William M. Bowsky. New York: Holt, Rinehart & Winston, 1974.

(blank page 1026, intentionally omitted)

THE STRUCTURE OF REVOLUTIONS:
WITH APPLICATION TO THE FRENCH REVOLUTION
By
Carroll Quigley

Excerpts from Manuscript

Political stability is present in civilizations only when the distribution of political participation and political rights in the polities reflects the potential distribution of weapons in the society. When the distribution of weapons is wider than the polity of "active" citizens, the latter must be widened to obtain stability; when the distribution of effective weapons is much narrower than the polity, the polity should be narrowed, in perception if not in law or there will be danger of coups de'etat in which the possessors of weapons will change the personnel of the governments as established by the legal polity. Changes in the dimensions of the polity (a legal or constitutional issue) may be achieved by political reforms or by revolution (reformist to make the polity wider, fascist to make it narrower).

The actual or potential distribution of weapons in a society depends upon the kinds of weapons available, especially on their costs and the amount of training needed for their effective use. When both of these qualities are large I call such weapons "specialist"; when both are relatively small, I call them "amateur." In general, specialist weapons are associated with narrower polities, while amateur weapons go with a wider polity. Revolutionary situations arise when changes in the dimensions of polities lag behind changes in weapons and ideas. In the evolution of most civilizations, Stages II (gestation) and V (empire) are associated with specialist weapons and a limited polity, while Stage III (expansion) is associated with a wider, even democratic, polity, reflecting the wider distribution of amateur weapons. Accordingly, the revolutions, if any, as the civilization passes from Stage II (gestation) to Stage III (expansion) are progressive or reformist, while the revolutions or changes through Stages III, IV (conflict) and V (empire) are reactionary or fascist. The sequence of polities among the ancient Greeks from 1200 B.C. were: Kings -- Nobles -- Tyrants -- Democracy -- Oligarchy -- military despotism (with the Roman sequence about two centuries behind the Greeks). The same sequence,

1027

at about the same time, was occurring in the earliest
Far Eastern civilizations, from Shang to Han (1500 B.C.
to A.D. 420) with the fall of the Han empire almost
contemporary to the fall of Rome (after A.D. 400).

The overall changes in Western civilization (with
three major oscillations from 1100 to 1880) were
from specialist to amateur weapons, accompanied by a
widening of polities from relatively few participants
to relatively many, from Charlemagne to 19th century
democracy. Thus in England the Tudor polity of 1580
was widened to the landlord polity of 1760 through the
17th century revolutions which showed that the landed
class could mobilize more weapons power than the royal
forces could (Ellis 1974:10-41); but the landlord polity
of 1760 was widened to the more democratic polity of
1868 by reforms rather than by revolution because the
organized force of the landlord class on the military
level (shown at Peterloo in 1819) recognized that the
potential power of the non-landed groups on all levels
was stronger.

The French revolution of 1789 clearly occurred
in a period in which weapons, especially firearms,
were becoming cheaper and easier to use, a process
which continued for another century or more. Even
in 1789 distribution and availability of firearms were
wider than those possessed by the government or of the
polity headed by King Louis XIV. This fact was made
manifest in the revolution, to the king by 1792 and to
the interventionist monarchies of Europe by 1796 and
later. This was like the revelation of truth which
the English king received in England in 1644-49 and
in America in 1776-81. In all three cases the newly
revealed facts of power were subsequently embodied in
reconstructed polities in a new consensus of law and
legitimacy.

There are other qualitative differences among weapons such as those which are dominantly offensive and
those which are dominantly defensive, the one associated
with periods of territorial expansion of polities, and
the latter associated with periods of territorial stability or retraction and splitting of polities. Here
again we can associate these two aspects or levels
with the stages of civilizations, with offensive
weaponry and growing size of polities in Stages
II and III and defensive weaponry with stabilization of territorial areas of polities in Stage IV,
followed by increasing defensive power and

growth of localized power from Stage V to Stage VI (decay of empire).

Equally significant is a third quality of weaponry, the shifting emphasis between missile weapons and shock weapons, the former good for shattering military formations but the latter far superior in obtaining obedience from individuals. For this reason a "model" battle has three stages of missiles-- shock-- pursuit. The contrast between missiles and shock is the same as that between "killing" weapons and "police" weapons; any effective polity must have both, the one for common defense and the other for domestic tranquility, but using both in either area. However, the evolution of any civilization from noble fighters through citizen soldiers to professional mercenaries, as it passes from Stage II to V, is usually marked by a shift of emphasis from too much shock to too much missiles, that is from police weapons to killing weapons. This allows empires to be built out of victories over alien military formations but provides wide areas of less satisfied subjects who cannot be controlled adequately with killing weapons (these cannot handle passive resistance or civil disobedience). At the same time, the shift within the civilization from internal controls to external controls gives rise to increasing episodes of individual crimes and violence which require shock weapons and cannot be handled with missile weapons. But an imperial system or polity built on missiles cannot go back to control of individual behavior by shock weapons, because of the rising costs of defense and the enormous costs of trying to control increasingly dissatisfied externalized persons. Rising levels of dispersed resistance, including guerrilla operations, and tax resistance, bring on a crisis which usually includes price inflation in acute cases. France was in such a crisis in 1789, fortunately in a reformist crisis and not a fascist crisis because of the weapons aspects.

Many historians have asked this question (Rude 1964: 65-82): "Why was there a full-scale revolution in France in 1789--and not elsewhere?" Most of Europe was in a revolutionary condition, more or less, in 1788, but the revolution came to France because the French polity was more obsolete than the others in terms of the development of the other levels, and, accordingly, the morphological strains and discords were greater in France. Political scientists have recognized that revolutions are outbursts

against obsolete or obsolescent polities, although some
historians still believe that the revolution came to
France because it was so "advanced." But George S. Pettee
stated the correct view in the same year as Brinton's
Anatomy of Revolution, in a book called The Process of
Revolution (1938:8); he stated it again, even more
emphatically, in 1966 (Friedrich 1967:12), when he wrote,
"The French Revolution was an explosive release of energy,
in a country growing in all its powers, destroying a system of authority that had failed to grow in capacity to
function as a state." The problem is, why did the French
polity fail to grow along with the other aspects of French
life, instead of becoming an obstacle to expansion. To
answer this question we must go back to the origins of
the French monarchy, since this determined its essential
nature for more than 800 years (987-1792), as what Paul
Schrecker calls "a generative principle" (Schrecker 1948:
24-27, 204-218; Friedrich 37-52).

The duke of the Isle de France, Hugh Capet, was allowed to take the vacant Carolingian throne in 987 by
the feudal lords of West Francia. "King" was essentially
a religious title and was not a feudal title or office.
The more powerful feudal lords of West Francia, such as
the Duke of Normandy, the Counts of Flanders and of Anjou,
recognized the duke of France both as feudal suzerain and
as king because he was so weak that he could not demand
nor enforce military service nor judicial service at
his curia (Lot 1958; Shennan 1969:13-16). The title
of king, as a religious title, was obtained by a religious ceremony, consecration with holy oil in an archepiscopal cathedral, and its chief political aspect was
the obligation to seek justice on earth with God's blessing. To the vassals that really meant that the Capetians
should provide ethical and moral support for their individual political rights. Louis XVI still felt this.

This remained the central core of the Capetian kingship to 1789 even when violated by kings such as Louis
XI, Francis I, or Louis XIV. Its ideal was Saint Louis,
and its popular acceptance is evident in Joan of Arc's
insistence that Charles VII must be crowned at Reims
as soon as possible. It dominated Charles's rule after
Joan's death. Even when kings violated legal rights,
they did so surrounded by lawyers and justified their
violent actions by lengthy legal arguments (Peuges).
This is the background behind Russell Major's insistence
that the kings of Renaissance France were never absolute

and normally acted within a network of legal restraints
(Major 1960; Slavin 1964:77-84). There is considerable
truth in Claude de Seyssel's version of the French monarchy in 1513, yet Francis I's monarchy was legally
stronger than that of Louis XV's or Louis XVI's; while
Louis XIV, both in foreign and domestic policies, was
legally a political criminal. There is no space here
to argue the issue of French "absolutism" in the Old
Regime, confused as it has been by failures to define
terms or to distinguish illegal actions from legal ones.
But two aspects of this subject may be stated: (1) the
medieval idea of property rights persisted in France
longer than anywhere else in Western Europe; and (2)
the later kings, including Louis XIV and especially his
two ancestors, were unable to do many things they wished
because of legal restraints on their actions, especially
restraints based on property rights of medieval character
but of post-medieval origins.

The word "property" includes two different kinds
of property which can be distinguished correctly only
if we use two Latin words: (1) dominia, meaning "rights,"
to cover the medieval idea of property; and (2) proprietas,
meaning property in the Roman and modern sense. These
two are not only different, they are logically antithetical.

Dominia refers to specific rights in an object, or,
more accurately, rights to perform specific actions under
specific conditions in respect to objects and persons.
Proprietas refers to the general and unspecified rights
in an object or person apart from any dominium which may
exist in respect to that same entity. Added together
dominium and proprietas include all possible rights or
actions which can be performed in respect to any object
or person. In its narrowest range, proprietas might
include nothing more than what we today would mean by
"title" to the object. This does not, in itself, include any right to do anything to an object except the
right to dispose of that title to someone else. Thus, if
a man has title to an automobile, which is not registered and his license to drive has been revoked, the
only thing he can do with the car is to sell it. The
king of France, however, had only dominia in most objects or persons, lacking proprietas or titles. Moreover, one of the fundamental laws of the monarchy prohibited any alienation of the royal dominia. For this
reason the monarchy had almost no financial credit, because rights which were inalienable could not be put up
as collateral for loans.

1031

As "suzerain," the monarchy had dominia which did not differ in kind, although much more numerous in amount, than those of any other member of the French polity. But as "king," the monarchy was unique in the French polity. This uniqueness originally was almost entirely religious in nature; that is why the king insisted on his "Divine Right" rather than on his feudal suzerainty. As suzerain, his military dominia included the right to call on specific individuals for specific military service under specific conditions. As king, he had, from Carolingian precedent, the right to call on all the inhabitants of France for defensive military service in an acute emergency (the arriere-ban), but little use was made of this until the king as suzerain had accumulated so many dominia of rival feudal lords and vassals that he had enough power to enforce this claim. Then he used it, in the Hundred Years War, not to assemble a fighting force of national militia but as a method for raising money to hire fighters who were neither feudal nor national, but were a royal army (Lot 1958:501-535). From 1355 to 1789 this divided the king's incomes into two distinct kinds with two different administrations: (1) ordinary, that is, seigneurial and feudal; and (2) extraordinary, that is, royal. Because Necker still made this distinction in 1781, he has been unjustly criticized by subsequent historians who often ignore it. The idea of dominia was applied to both kinds of income, so both became specific customary payments, and efforts by the monarchy to increase public revenues were entangled in smothering controversies about customary limits on financial obligations. The king's supporters, especially the royal lawyers, sustained his efforts by arguments from Roman law and proprietas, rather than on customary law and dominia. But the monarchy never got free from the legal restraints, and, since the kings usually accepted the existence of the legality of the restraints and only disputed applications to specific cases, they usually backed down if controversy continued long enough (except in one significant case, the Concordat of 1516, which most clergy and lawyers still considered illegal up to the Revolution). The existence of these restraints of law explains why the government was bankrupt in 1789.

The true architect of the Old Regime was Charles VII. Charles codified the customary relations of church and state in the Pragmatic Sanction (1438); created the royal artillery which drove out the English and subjected the great vassals; established the permanent royal army; above all he ordered the codification of the customs of each district. This decree, reissued three times by 1505, was carried out by 1580 (Chenon 1929). It left France divided into 365 different laws largely based on dominia. Supported by the kings and interpreted by the courts, this legal structure left the government in semi-paralysis long before 1789. When the king lost control of the courts because the judges obtained dominia over their seats and could not be removed unless they were paid their value, the government was locked in on one side. When the judges then insisted that there could be no changes in taxation without consent, the government was locked in on the other side, and the road to revolution was set. And note that this was not an "Atlantic Revolution."

By the 18th century in France, any activity which brought the actor an income for a generation or so became a dominium which could be taken away only with his consent or by payment of compensation equal to the income capitalized. This was, of course, never stated as a rule of law by French courts in the Old Regime because court decisions were not enunciated as general rules, and there was little need to say what everyone knew. But it was applied in those decisions where the threatened holder could get his case in court and to a decision. We have a weak version of this principle of prescription in the Common Law even today, but it does not apply against the state. In France the king could not abolish the guilds in 1776 unless he could find some way to pay off their large debts, as Turgot discovered (Dakin).

The territorial "unification" of France had been achieved by royal acquisition of the dominia of the preceding lords, leaving all lesser dominia undisturbed. In most cases this was guaranteed by formal royal promises. Thus territorial "unity" did not mean legal, judicial, fiscal, or economic unity; it meant a kingdom of organized and legal chaos, with hundreds of different laws, jurisdictions, practices, measurements, and monetary units. Almost every commodity had different units, which also differed from place to place. Thousands of restraints on commerce, including local tolls, were held as dominia, many by private persons. This made transport costs so high that French goods could not compete in foreign markets in many cases, or even with foreign goods in some cases in more distant provinces of France. When

Colbert tried to abolish internal tolls in 1664, he obtained consent in only half the provinces, and almost continuous efforts over the next 125 years achieved little more, for without consent or compensation the tolls could not be abolished, even by Louis XIV (Bosher 1964). The monarchy's credit was so weak that it had to use the credit of more credit-worthy entities like the cities, provinces, or the church. Royal incomes, actual or potential, were then allotted to pay interest on these. In 1561 the clergy of France agreed to pay interest on bonds issued by the Hotel de Ville of Paris for seven years, and in return won recognition of tax exemption and other concessions which after 1580 made the Gallican church a corporation with more of the attributes of sovereignty than the monarchy; it was, by 1750, better organized, with a responsible paid bureaucracy, assured incomes, and a rational budget which revealed its total financial position on a quarterly basis (LePointe 1923; Clergé de France 1716-71).

Everyone in the Old Regime knew that taxes were chaotic and unfair, but there was no legal way to obtain reforms. Numerous efforts were made to replace the taille obligations by a graduated taille tarifee, but they all collapsed against the opposition of the judges which went so far as to forbid any subject from answering questions about his income under threat of punishment for contempt (Marion 1927:passim). The monarch could discipline judges by exile to remote villages, but this crippled judicial processes with rising public discontent. When he tried to replace them completely by a new judicial system with paid judges under royal control, as in 1771-74, the effort had to be cancelled because he could not raise funds for compensation to the removed judges (Glasson 1901).

Lack of money was so acute that the monarchy rarely could afford paid agents and had to carry on its activities, especially financial, through private entrepreneurs who paid the king to do his business and then used this to make large profits for themselves. They then used these profits as loans to the king at high interest rates (Bosher 1970).

It is a mistake to call a system like this "absolute." In fact, the state was not even sovereign, since it lacked most of the basic elements of sovereignty. There are eight of these elements, roughly in the order in which most European states acquired them:

1. Defense of the polity against outsiders;
2. Judicial (settling disputes within the polity);
3. Administrative (discretionary actions for the public good);
4. Executive (enforcement of laws and judicial decisions);
5. Legislative (making laws);
6. Taxation (mobilizing resources for public purposes);
7. Incorporating (creating legal entities within the polity);
8. Monetary (creation and control of money and credit).

In law the French monarchy had much of the first four of these by the late Middle Ages, but gradually it lost control of the judiciary through the growth of private ownership of judicial seats, whose occupants enforced only laws they had registered freely and insisted on the inviolability of dominia except with consent or compensation. Thus France, unlike other European states, did not obtain a sovereign state with all eight aspects of sovereignty.

Full sovereignty was obtained in the French revolution, but it was embodied in the nation, not in the monarchy. This established the "generative principle" of a new polity which replaced the old generative principle created in 987 but bankrupt by 1789 (Schrecker 1948:216-218). The speed of this shift can be seen in two documents barely five years apart. On May 3, 1788 an arret of the Parliament "declare que la France est une monarchie gouvernee par le roi suivant les lois; que de ces lois plusieurs, qui sont fondamentales, embrassement et consacrent. . .les coutumes et les capitulations des provinces" (Cauviere 1910:61). On August 18, 1792, a decree began, "L'Assemblee Nationale considerant qu'un Etat vraiment libre ne doit souffrir dans son sein aucune corporation pas meme celles qui vouee a l'enseignment public ont bien merite de la patrie. . . ." Thus by 1792, the French revolutionary government had already achieved the eighth aspect of sovereignty, which the new American government had been deprived of through the "Atlantic Revolution" three years before.

Like most historical controversies, the dispute over the 18th century revolution (Amann 1963; Godechot 1965) thrives on the undefined terms of the debaters. There was a French revolution; there was also an Atlantic revolution. They had little in common beyond the fact that they were both revolutions, and the Atlantic revolution emphasized what were belated and incidental features of the French revolution. Neither was a "Democratic Revolution." The Atlantic revolution of the 18th century was a "Liberal Revolution," that is it placed restraints on the power of a state which was already sovereign, using various constitutional techniques such as restricted suffrage, federalism, separation of powers, and the right of an independent costly judiciary to enforce procedural restraints on state actions. It was a Lockean "revolution of possessive individualism" (Macpherson 1962) which refers to a state of atomized individuals with a sacred right to private property as proprietas guaranteed by constitutional restraints. Some of the elements of the Atlantic revolution were in the French revolution, such as (1) atomization of communities into individuals; (2) the sanctity of proprietas by the destruction of dominia; and (3) separation of powers. But in the French revolution those which were restrictions on state actions, and thus essential to the Atlantic revolution, such as separation of powers, were largely ignored. The French revolution concentrated on earlier aspects of the development of public authority: (1) achievement of full sovereignty; (2) the shift of state power from a Divine Right monarch to the nation; and (3) the transformation of the polity from a hierarchy of subjects and communities to a mass of legally equal atomized citizens.

Sovereignty was achieved in England before 1500 and was exercised by "King in Parliament"; it was shifted to parliamentary control in the 17th century revolutions. In Central Europe sovereignty was achieved by the late 16th century through the Protestant revolution and the reception of the Roman law; in western Germany it was embodied in princes, but farther southeast, where princes remained Catholic and often were unable to obtain hereditary succession (Poland, Lithuania, Transylvania, Hungary, Bohemia, and the Holy Roman Empire), sovereignty was often embodied in diets of nobles or estates. In France, the most backward polity in Europe, full sovereignty came with the revolution, and enlightened despotism came only with Napoleon. The final defeat of the efforts of the French monarch to achieve sovereignty came with Colbert's inability to turn Louis

1036

XIV into an enlightened despot, as in his failure to
abolish internal tolls. When sovereignty did come to
France, its advent was so late and so violent that it
became totalitarian, seeking to destroy all legal entities other than natural persons, to control intellectual
life, and giving little beyond verbal expression to the
liberal aspects of the 18th century revolution, which
were the core of the Atlantic revolution. These liberal
aspects appeared in France chiefly as a division of citizens into "active" and "passive" to block any effort to
use sovereignty to establish economic equality.

No democratic revolution was possible until after
a liberal revolution had been achieved, because the
distribution of weapons was not wide enough to allow
the masses to push the rule of equality beyond the political level into the economic level. When the Enrages
and Hebertists tried to do this in France, they were
crushed in 1793-4. In America and France democracy was
generally delayed until after 1800, by which time the
Liberal Revolution had made the polity safe for private
property by a variety of restraints on popular sovereignty.
In France economic democracy was suppressed by gunfire
in 1848 and 1871, while in England democracy was delayed
(1867, 1884, 1911, etc.) so long that liberal restraints
were internalized as "social deference," and more obvious
restraints, like separation of powers or federalism,
were not needed. The whole drive of that generation
in the English-speaking world was to achieve a "Liberal
Revolution" which would limit and divide sovereignty before the spread of amateur weaponry could deliver control
of the state into the hands of mass armies of citizen
soldiers.

References

Amann, P., ed. 1963. The Eighteenth-Century Revolution:
    French or Western? Boston: Heath.
Bosher, J.F. 1970. French Finances, 1770-1795: From
    Business to Bureaucracy. Cambridge: University Press.
Cauviere, H. 1910. L'Idee de Codification en France
    Avant la Redaction du Code Civile. Paris.
Chenon, E. 1929. Histoire General du Droit Francais
    Public et Prive. Paris.
Clerge de France. Actes et Memoires. 17 vols. Paris.
Dakin, D. 1939. Turgot and the Ancien Regime in France.
    Methuen.
Ellis, J. 1974. Armies in Revolution. Oxford University
    Press.

Friedrich, C.J. 1967. Revolution: Nomos VIII. Atherton.
Glasson, E. 1901. Le Parlement de Paris: Son Role
    Politique. 2 vols. Paris.
Godechot, J. 1965. France and the Atlantic Revolution of
    the 18th Century. Free Press.
LePointe, G. 1923. L'Organisation et la Politique Finan-
    ciere du Clerge de France. Paris.
Lot, F. and R. Fawtier. 1958. Histoire des Institutions
    Francaises au Moyen Age. Vol. II. Paris.
MacPherson, C.B. 1962. The Political Theory of Possessive
    Individualism: Hobbes to Locke.
Major, J.R. 1960. Representative Institutions in Renais-
    sance France, 1421-1559. University of Wisconsin
    Press.
Marion, M. 1927. Histoire Financiere de la France depuis
    1715. Vol. I.
Palmer, R.R. 1959. The Age of the Democratic Revolution.
    Princeton University Press.
Pettee, G.S. 1938. The Process of Revolution. Harpers.
    Reprinted 1971.
Quigley, C. 1961. Evolution of Civilizations. Macmillan.
_____. 1971, 1973. "Assumption and Inference on
    Human Origins," Current Anthropology, 12 (1971), 519-540;
    14 (1973), 495-502.
_____. 1973. "Can Man Survive at a High Standard of
    Living?" Paper read at plenary session, Annual Meeting
    of Association of American Geographers, Atlanta, Georgia,
    April 16, 1973.
Rude, G. 1964. Revolutionary Europe, 1783-1815. Collins.
Schrecker, P. 1948. Work and History: An Essay on the
    Structure of Civilization. Princeton University Press.
_____. 1967. "Revolution as a Problem in the
    Philosophy of History," in Friedrich 1967:34-52.
Scott, S.F. 1975. "Problems of Law and Order During 1790,
    the 'peaceful' year of the French Revolution," American
    Historical Review 80 (October 1975), 859-888.
Shennan, J.H. 1969. Government and Society in France,
    1461-1661. Allen & Unwin.
Slavin, A.J. 1964. The New Monarchies and Representative
    Assemblies: Medieval Constitutionalism or Modern
    Absolutism? Heath.

Another. . . .[myth that we have tried] to believe
in the last 150 years--and the idea is now dying in front
of us--is. . . .that the nation. . . .[should] be both a
state and a community. This is the great ideological
innovation of the French revolution, you see. The nation
[as a state] can be the repository of sovereignty. But
suppose weapons systems in a society are such that it is
possible for a government to impose its will over an area
a thousand miles across. And suppose that in that thou-
sand-mile area there are a number of nations, such as the
Bretons, the Catalonians, the Welsh, the Lithuanians.
These are as much nations as the ones that somehow or
other became the embodiments of sovereignty in the 19th
century. Why did the English, the French, the Castili-
ans, ..., and others become the repositories of sovereignty as nations? . . . . They did so because, at
that time, weapons systems made it possible to compel
obedience over areas which were [large enough to include]
. . . .these national groups. As a result, they were
able to crush out other. . . .[national groups], such as
the Scots, the Welsh, the Irish, the Catalonians--who
had a much longer and more cultured history than the
Castilians--the Provencals, and many others. . . .Now
what's happening? They all want autonomy. . . .

     . . . .The individual cannot be made the basic unit
of society [on a self-interest atomistic basis], as we
have tried to do, or of the state, since the internaliza-
tion of controls must be the preponderant influence in
any stable society. Even in a society in which it appears that all power is in the hands of the government--
Soviet Russia, let's say--at least eighty per cent of
all human behavior is regulated by internalized controls
socialized in the people by the way they were treated
from the moment they were born. . . .

     Also related to the problem of internalized controls
is the shift of weapons in our society. . . .The shift
of weapons in any civilization and, above all, in our
civilization, from shock weapons to missile weapons has
a dominant influence on the ability to control individuals: individuals cannot be controlled by missile weapons.

1039

The essential difference between a shock weapon and a missile weapon is this: a missile weapon is either fired or it isn't fired. It cannot be half fired. Once you let it go, it's out of your control. It is a killing weapon. But a shock weapon--a billy club or a bayonet--can be used to any degree you wish. . .

In our society, individual behavior can no longer be controlled by any system of weaponry we have. In fact, we do not have enough people, even if we equip them with shock weapons, to control the behavior of that part of the population which does not have internalized controls. One reason for that, of course, is that the twenty per cent who do not have internalized controls are concentrated in certain areas. I won't go into the subject of controls. It opens up the whole field of guerrilla resistance, terrorism, and everything else; these cannot be controlled by any system or organized structure of force that exists, at least on a basis of missile weaponry. And, as I said, it would take too many people on the basis of shock weaponry. We have now done what the Romans did when they started to commit suicide: we have shifted from an army of citizen soldiers to an army of mercenaries, and those mercenaries are being recruited in our society, as they were in Roman society, from the twenty per cent of the population which does not have the internalized controls of the civilization.

The appearance of stability from 1840 to about 1900 was superficial, temporary and destructive in the long run, because, as I've said, you must have communities, and communities and societies must rest upon cooperation and not on competition. . . .

BOOKS AND ARTICLES BY CARROLL QUIGLEY

Books

The Evolution of Civilizations. New York: Macmillan, 1961; Indianapolis: Liberty Press, 1979.

La Evolucion de las Civilizaciones. Mexico City: Hermes, 1963.

A Evolucao das Civilizacoes. Rio de Janeiro: Editora Fundo de Cultura, 1963.
See the reviews of the English edition in the American Historical Review 67 (July 1962):987; Christian Science Monitor, January 8, 1962; Kirkus Review, September 1, 1961, p. 838; Library Journal, November 1, 1961, p. 3788; School and Society, October 6, 1962, p. 321; and Social Education 26 (April 1962):219.

Tragedy and Hope: The World in Our Time. New York: Macmillan, 1965.

The World Since 1939. New York: Collier Books, 1968.
A reprint of the last half of Tragedy and Hope. Among the reviews are: American Historical Review 72 (October 1966):123; Annals of the American Academy 368 (November 1966):244; Best Sellers, February 15, 1966, p. 434; Book Week, January 16, 1966; Choice 3 (June 1966):348; Library Journal, August 1965, p. 3284; New York Times Book Review, January 23, 1966, and Quigley's reply to same, with the reviewer's rejoinder, in the February 20, 1966 issue; Saturday Review, February 12, 1966, p. 34; and Virginia Quarterly Review 42 (Spring 1966):301.

The Anglo-American Establishment. New York: Books-in-Focus, 1982.

Articles

"Falsification of a Source in Risorgimento History." Journal of Modern History 20 (September 1948): 223-26.

"The Origin and Diffusion of Oculi." _American Neptune_,
    July 1955; and rejoinder in _ibid_., January 1958.

"Aboriginal Fish Poisons and the Diffusion Problem."
    American Anthropologist 58 (June 1956):508-25.

"Comparative Cultural Developments." _The Community
    Development Review_ (December 1957).

"French West Africa." _Current History_ 34 (February
    1958):91-98.

"Education in Overseas France." _Current History_ 35
    (August 1958):102-11.

"The French Community and Western Security." _Current
    History_ 39 (August 1960):101-7.

"French Tropical Africa: Today and Tomorrow." _Current
    History_ 40 (February 1961):77-87.

"Belgium"; "France"; "Italy"; "North Atlantic Treaty
    Organization"; and "Netherlands." In Funk & Wag-
    nalls, _New International Yearbook_. New York:
    Funk & Wagnalls, 1961, 1963.

"The Round Table Groups in Canada, 1908-1938." _The
    Canadian Historical Review_ 43 (September 1962):
    204-24.

"The Brazzaville Twelve." _Current History_ 43 (December
    1962):346-53.

"Weapons Control as Seen from Abroad." _Current History_
    46 (June 1964).

"The Creative Writer Today." _Catholic World_ 206
    (December 1967):111-17.

"France and the United States in World Politics."
    Current History 54 (March 1968):151-59.

"Needed: A Revolution in Thinking." _National Education
    Association Journal_ 57 (May 1968):8-10.

"Lord Balfour's Personal Position on the Balfour Declara-
    tion (ed.). _Middle East Journal_ 22 (Summer 1968):
    340-45.

"Major Problems of Foreign Policy." Current History
    55 (October 1968):199-206.

"Our Ecological Crisis." Current History 59 (July
    1970):1-12.

"Youth's Heroes Have No Halos." Today's Education
    36 (April 1971):46-48.

"Assumption and Inference on Human Origins." Current
    Anthropology 12 (October-December 1971):519-40;
    and discussion in ibid. 14 (October 1973):499-502.

"General Crises in Civilizations." American Association
    for the Advancement of Science news release, 1972.

"Cognitive Factors in the Evolution of Civilizations."
    Main Currents in Modern Thought 29 (November-
    December 1972):69-75.

"The Search for a Solution to the World Crisis."
    Futurist 9 (March 1975):38-41.

"America's Future in Energy." Current History 69
    (July 1975):1-5.

"Public Authority and the State in the Western Tradi-
    tion: A Thousand Years of Growth, 976-1976."
    The Oscar Iden Lectures. Washington: School
    of Foreign Service, Georgetown University, 1977.

Reprint Edition: 2013 by Dauphin Publications Inc.
ISBN: 978-1-939438-08-9

www.ingramcontent.com/pod-product-compliance
Lightning Source LLC
Chambersburg PA
CBHW060318100426
42812CB00003B/820